Aaron Koplin

# THEORIES OF SOCIETY

VOLUME I

*Edited by*

TALCOTT PARSONS

EDWARD SHILS

KASPAR D. NAEGELE

JESSE R. PITTS

Fp

# THEORIES OF SOCIETY

*Foundations of Modern Sociological Theory*

VOLUME I

*The Free Press of Glencoe, Inc.*

A DIVISION OF THE CROWELL-COLLIER PUBLISHING COMPANY

PRINTED IN THE UNITED STATES OF AMERICA



For information, address:
THE FREE PRESS OF GLENCOE, INC.
A DIVISION OF THE CROWELL-COLLIER PUBLISHING COMPANY
640 Fifth Avenue, New York 19

Library of Congress Catalog Card Number: 61-9171

DESIGNED BY SIDNEY SOLOMON

# CONTENTS—AN OVERVIEW

## *Volume I*



## *Volume II*

# CONTENTS

## Volume I

## C. *The Modes of the Institutionalization of Action*



# Part Two DIFFERENTIATION AND VARIATION IN SOCIAL STRUCTURES



## A. *Ascriptive Solidarities*

# Volume II

## Part Three PERSONALITY AND THE SOCIAL SYSTEM



### A. *The Definition of the Situation and the Internalization of Objects*



### B. *The Elements of Learned Motivation*



### C. *Processes of Socialization*

I. SYMBOLISM AND COMMUNICATION



II. PATTERNS OF CULTURE



## B. *Value and Belief Patterns*



I. KNOWLEDGE AND RATIONALITY



II. RELIGION AND MAGIC



## C. *Expressive Symbolism*

## Part Five SOCIAL CHANGE



### A. *Factors of Change*



### B. *Processes of Stabilization and Change*



### C. *Patterns of Change and Development*

# EPILOGUE

# List of Selections by Author

# Preface

> "But I believe in Natural Selection, not because I can prove in any single case that it has changed one species into another, but because it groups and explains well (as it seems to me) a host of facts in classification, embryology, morphology, rudimentary organs, geological succession and distribution."
>
> CHARLES DARWIN, 1861

THUS IN A LETTER, ADDRESSED to an unidentified critic of the *Origin of Species,* Charles Darwin,[1] just a century ago, struck a keynote for the appraisal of his central concept of Natural Selection. This interpretation of the significance of his theory—that "it groups and explains well a host of facts"—can, we believe, be adapted to the contents of these volumes.

The selections we have brought together document what we believe to constitute a major revolution in scholarly and professional thinking about the nature and determinants of human conduct in society. It is a revolution that may well turn out to be as crucial as was the crystallization of the biological theory of evolution a century ago. Like the theory of evolution it was centered in one scientific discipline, but its repercussions have begun to ramify through a major part of the whole intellectual world. Most important, however, like the theory of evolution, the critical contribution has not been the "discovery" of highly specific explanations of highly specific phenomena, comparable to the change of one species into another. There has been a great deal of advance in our knowledge of many social and behavioral phenomena on these more specific levels, during the generation with which our selections deal and even more subsequently, as the Epilogue makes clear. The most important event, however, has been a new kind of *ordering* of our knowledge, of the sort Darwin refers to when he speaks of the principle of natural selection as "grouping and explaining well a host of facts."

In our case the relevant "host of facts" is not in the fields of embryology, morphology, and the like, but of political, economic, religious, social and legal history, of economic and political theory and various branches of philosophy, psychology, anthropology and sociology itself. The intellectual movement we document established the central framework within which sociology as a discipline has found a strategic place in the family of academic disciplines. This framework we have become accustomed to calling the "theory of action."

There is no single principle, organizing the "host of facts," as striking as that of natural selection. We believe, however, that analyses of the *patterning* of the phenomena of social interaction, of their *coherence* as social systems, and of the *establishment* of these systems through the internalization of normative culture within the personality of the individual, together constitute a mode of "grouping and explaining" social facts. This is the main theoretical basis of the new perspective previously mentioned. We have therefore treated interaction and institutionalization as our two central ideas, devoting two main sections of Part One to the principal originators of these ideas, along with a section on the main historical antecedents of this intellectual development.

Our conviction of the importance of this new ordering of facts and perspectives has informed our selection among the multitudinous writings that might be considered relevant to a collection of Readings on *Theories of Society,* as well as the way

---

1. This letter is in the British Museum manuscript collection, Additional Ms 37725, ff. 6–9.

in which we have put these selections together and the interpretive discussions we ourselves have contributed by way of introduction and epilogue.

In this light we have followed the implications of two further convictions. First the generation from about 1890 to 1935, in both Europe and America, produced a major turning point in thought about man in society and culture.[2] Out of this the discipline of sociology as it has now taken shape was born. Secondly, despite the immense variety of works and interests feeding into it, this new set of ideas constitutes in the most fundamental sense a unified movement, one that makes obsolete the older conception of an unending diversity of discrete, competing "schools" of thought. Very important antecedents of this movement occurred in the period preceding it. Classical economic theory—in our opinion, the first clearly articulated theoretical system in the study of society—was mainly articulated early in the nineteenth century. Political theory had a long tradition, and the work of many historians, particularly in legal and institutional fields, contained crucially important theoretical elements whose significance should not be underestimated.

This generation, however, saw the establishment of a number of new lines of work on the borders of sociology. One was the systematic study of non-Western societies—both the anthropological studies of non-literate societies, and the beginnings of much more substantial study of Oriental and Middle Eastern civilizations, by historians, linguists, archaeologists, students of comparative religion, and others. During the same period, systematic experimental psychology developed, bringing animal and, in some respects, human behavior within the scope of the laboratory. In the background lay the biological sciences' rise to prominence in the latter half of the nineteenth century, tremendously stimulated by the Darwinian synthesis. Finally, this period witnessed the beginnings of a type of study of segments of Western societies that departed from the established documentary methods of the historian. It was clearly, over a wide area, a generation of active advance.

As sociologists, we are primarily concerned with human societies, or, more generally, in a theoretical sense, with social systems. With the immense acceleration, in our period, of the accumulation of descriptive knowledge through interviewing and observation, and of knowledge and practice in methods of obtaining and verifying such data, a new form of generalized interpretation of known facts, and hence of ideas which could guide the search for new facts, has also been attained.

This movement has cut across the bounds of discipline and nation. At the central core of the theory of social systems, Pareto performed a special feat of synthesis relating economic, political, and "institutional, non-rational" components. Durkheim pursued the analysis of these problems more deeply. Max Weber carried the comparative analysis of the differences among societies and the interrelations of their constituent spheres to an entirely new level of sophistication. Finally, in the study of the individual's motivation, Freud, though his sociology was much weaker, provided an unprecedented perspective on the articulation of human personality within the system of social interaction. A more "collegial" than individual movement in the United States—involving particularly C. H. Cooley, G. H. Mead, and W. I. Thomas—mediated, in the name of "social psychology," between the more strictly sociological and the more psychological positions.

Selected on the basis of a particular interest, these are the barest highlights of a very complicated pattern of intellectual development. This interest defines the objective of this collection, drawn from the sources which lead to and constitute contemporary sociological theory. The contemporary student of human society will, unless he has devoted prolonged study to this phase of intellectual history, have considerable difficulty in orienting himself to the complex background from which his field of specialized concern has grown. No general history—certainly none which could claim to be complete and definitive—has been written in this field; to attempt to do so would probably be premature. The relevant literature is enormous, and the problems of its interpretation formidable.

However, the student need not be left entirely without guidance. From the very extensive literature, we have brought together a set of selections, with historical and analytical commentaries, that, though filling two large volumes, still comprise only a tiny fraction of the possibly relevant material. We do not consider the reading of these selections, particularly the large proportion presented in translation, as an adequate substitute for reading both the original works of which they are parts, and many other works not represented at all. For certain limited purposes reading the selections may be considered adequate; certainly it is better than no direct acquaintance with the primary sources. But we hope that our anthology will be treated more as an introduction and a guide to the literature—a guide which

2. The most comprehensive single treatment of the European phase of this movement, from the point of view of general intellectual history rather than of sociology, is H. Stuart Hughes, *Consciousness and Society* (New York: Alfred A. Knopf, 1958). For an interpretation stressing schools, cf. P. A. Sorokin, *Contemporary Sociological Theory* (New York: Harper & Brothers, 1928).

will help students to acquaint themselves with it much more fully.

The literature as a whole is too extensive for any individual—particularly one with more specialized interests—to investigate thoroughly. Different people will approach it with different special interests. We hope that bringing the different writers together in the way we have will provide common starting points for a variety of these more specialized excursions; thus someone interested in the relation of personality development to kinship structure would not study many of the same sections as the person interested in the relations between major religious movements and the larger societies within which they occurred.

By the nature of this enterprise, the editors must exercise a very drastic selectivity. They are hence subject to a whole range of possible objections to the policies followed in their selection and organization—no policies could satisfy all critics on this score. The best we can do is to make our own criteria as explicit as possible.

First, within the assumptions stated above, our primary concern has been with the more generalized framework for the theoretical analysis of social systems. We feel that a larger proportion of explicit contributions to this theme have been made at the more "macrosocial" levels dealing with total societies or bearing on their analysis. Hence, though maintaining that general theory in this field is applicable at all levels in the macroscopic-microscopic range, from the total society to the small experimental group, we have tended to select according to our more macroscopic interest. Furthermore, our interest in general theory has led to a certain favoring of writers and passages stressing this analytical level, rather than accumulations of highly detailed fact.

We feel, as we have said, that the major trends in the theory of social systems have been convergent rather than divergent, that the contributions which enrich a common conceptual scheme outweigh those which delineate the positions of divergent schools. For those who, however, tend to stress the divergence, we hope we have included a sufficient variety of points of view so that we are not guilty of a narrow parochialism in selecting only the writings which fit our own predilections, and omitting those which might be construed as incompatible with or inconvenient to our own point of view. In this respect, it is important to note that, though we continue to share the common convictions with which we began, the editors are not in fully detailed agreement among themselves; certain compromises have been necessary. In the introductory materials and commentaries, each author has naturally tended to stress his own interests and evaluations. The fact that all matter written by the editors is the responsibility of each individual editor testifies to the limitations on editorial consensus, far-reaching though the consensus is.

A second very important consideration in our policy of selection is that we have attempted to balance concentration on our interest in the social system as such with comprehensiveness in the inclusion of more concrete analysis. Some sociologists may feel that we have gone too far in the extent to which we have included materials ordinarily classified in psychology, anthropology, history, economics, political science, law, and the humanistic disciplines. Our basic justification for this is our belief that the theory of social systems is a product of the complex intellectual currents of the modern age. We can speak of a central core of theorists whose primary concern has been with social systems as such. However, the most fruitful efforts to understand society have never been a monopoly of professional sociologists; and in the period concerned, none of the greatest figures limited his attention to this discipline. Thus Durkheim was trained in philosophy and jurisprudence, Weber in jurisprudence and economics, Cooley in economics, and Mead in philosophy. We feel that if we confined our materials to "sociology" in a narrow sense we would, considering the intellectual history of the period, be excessively and injuriously parochial.

Within this catholic policy of judgments of relevance, however, certain standards in our decisions may well be controversial. Clearly, we have not included everything bearing on the topic of "human social behavior"; within this immense field, we have had to be highly selective.

Three beliefs have provided the main criteria of selection. First, we have conceived the development of theory as in part a process of the differentiation of a cognitive interest. Hence, we have, in Part One, discussed and illustrated certain fundamental problems in terms which are relatively independent of the differentiations which in our own times have come to constitute domains of particular disciplines. Second, we have attempted to treat the social system as an "open" system interacting with others on its "boundaries." We have, therefore, related social systems to the psychological and biological individual, and also to the culture, as major axes of the organization of our materials. We do not conceive biology and psychology, or the theory of culture, to be, as such, parts of the theory of social systems. We do, however, think that the *relations* of these spheres or systems to the social are crucial, and these relations must be systematically analyzed, not considered in an arbitrary *ad hoc* fashion. Finally, within our general interest in the *social system,* we have attempted to emphasize systematically the study of the *institutional* aspect. In other words, we have attempted to recognize a systemic set of relations to the concerns of the two adjacent disciplines of economics and political science, but to avoid any suggestion that they ought simply to be incorporated into sociology. It is, for example, no more possible to treat problems of social morphology in the economic sphere without reference to materials ordinarily allocated to economics, than to deal with the motivation of social behavior without using psychological materials. Our major criteria have been the same in all three of these cases.

We might have chosen to allow the selections to "speak for themselves"; limiting introductory materials to the bare essentials of editorial identification. This, however, would have imposed a heavy burden on readers not already familiar with the literature from which the selections are drawn, and hence made the selections less valuable to them. We also feel that we would have been missing an important opportunity. One of the most effective ways of estimating the state of theoretical analysis in sociology is to attempt to show, in considerable detail, the continuity between current ideas and problems and the most important contributions of our forebears. We have been particularly concerned with showing the continuity of contemporary views with those in the relatively recent past which, however, are far enough past to permit a certain perspective on the nature and importance of their work. The introductory material and the epilogue are designed to contribute to the understanding of this continuity, and thereby to help define a perspective for better evaluating the work of the many authors represented in the selections.

The editors' material falls into four main categories. The General Introduction has two parts. The first, by Kaspar Naegele, is an essay on the scope of theory in the social science field, and some of the problems involved in the construction of theory. The second, by Talcott Parsons, is an essay on the theory of social systems in what he conceived at the time of writing to be its current state. It is deliberately couched on the plane of the conceptual scheme rather than attempting to formulate empirical generalizations. It is intended as a review of general theoretical problems and some of the more specific problems which contemporary sociology must face, whether or not individual sociologists find the directions indicated for their solution congenial.

A second type of editorial material consists in the Introductions to four of the five main parts of the Reader, i.e., all except Part One. These attempt to review the theoretical problems underlying our selection and classification of materials in more detail for the particular area than was possible in the General Introduction. In each case, we have directly used and stated our own conceptions of the present state of knowledge in some of the most important aspects of the particular field. We have tried to link present problems with the principal themes represented in the selections themselves. We have not, however, in these Introductions, attempted to comment in detail on the selections or on literature we have not included.

This task, so far as we have attempted it at all, has been reserved for the much briefer Editorial Forewords to the sections within each part. These contain very brief statements of the relevance of the selections themselves to the plan of these volumes and their setting in the development of the problem under consideration. Sometimes brief comments on other literature are included.

Part One has been treated as a special case, because of the diversity of the materials included in its three divisions. All are fundamental prolegomena to the theory of social systems, the first in terms of its historical background, the other two in the critical substantive fields of the analysis of social interaction as such and the problem of the foundations of the motivational commitments involved in institutionalization. We have, therefore, not provided a general introduction to Part One as a whole, but have included considerably fuller Editorial Forewords to each Section than is the case with Sections of the other Parts. The Forewords to Sections in Part One contain both a good deal of our own independent theoretical analysis and specific references to the selections and their places in the development of theory.

The fourth element of editorial material is the Epilogue, written by Edward Shils. This essentially treats, in more connected fashion than in the more scattered Introductions, the major themes in the development of sociological theory since the generation primarily represented in the selections, and their general cultural significance. It is one man's point of view, a comprehensive commentary on the problems presented by the selections themselves and by the other introductory materials.

We have also included a Bibliography. This comprises all the principal works of the writers represented in the list of selections that were published in book form. The complete Index for both volumes will be found at the end of each volume. It is confined to proper names, since a full subject index would present a formidable task and seems unnecessary in the light of the detailed table of contents.

Perhaps a word about the history of the project and the division of labor between the editors is in order. The original plan for these volumes was developed in 1952, at the suggestion of Jeremiah Kaplan of The Free Press, by Talcott Parsons and Edward Shils, who also worked out the first tentative list of selections. The list has, however, been revised many times. Because of the pressure of other commitments, progress was slow; the combination of Shils's prospective absence from the country for a year and realization of the magnitude of the task led to the addition, in 1954, of Kaspar Naegele and Jesse Pitts to the "editorial committee." Since then the work on the selections has been carried on by Parsons, Naegele, and Pitts.

Any enterprise of the present magnitude owes debts to many different people and agencies, indeed too many to be acknowledged. It has not as such received direct financial support from any source except The Free Press of Glencoe, but it should be acknowledged that three of the editors did important parts of their work on it during the periods that they were Fellows of the Center for Advanced Study in the Behavioral Sciences. We also severally have used funds from various sources which were either entirely free or where their purposes overlapped so much with this one that the two uses could not be disentangled. A number of people gave important advice, both on the general policy governing selections, and on particular problems in this field. Among these it seems appropriate to mention particularly Robert K. Merton of Columbia University, Francis X. Sutton of the Ford Foundation, Nicholas Grauer of the University of Copenhagen, Robert N. Bellah, Winston R. White, and Daniel J. Levinson of Harvard University, Claude Levi-Strauss of the College de France, Elliott Mishler of the Massachusetts Mental Health Center, and Bertram D. Cohen of Wayne State University and the Lafayette Clinic. Advice in these respects concerning selections has shaded into criticism of drafts of our introductions and editorial forewords. Dr. Anne Parsons of McLean Hospital and Dr. Mark Field of Harvard University gave valuable advice regarding some of the French translations. Finally there has of course been an immense amount of processing of manuscript material. Among the most important contributions here have been those of two successive secretaries of the senior editor, Mrs. Carolyn Cooper and Mrs. Sarah E. Hampson.

*Talcott Parsons*
*Edward Shils*
*Kaspar D. Naegele*
*Jesse R. Pitts*

*April, 1961*

# GENERAL INTRODUCTION

# I. *Some Observations on the Scope of Sociological Analysis*

BY KASPAR D. NAEGELE

THE STUDY OF SOCIETY AS A cumulative and, therefore, scientific, enterprise, is under way. We may bemoan the fact or enjoy it. We may argue about how society can be studied and how its study should be divided among old and new intellectual disciplines. Yet we can no longer deny the possibility of reliable discoveries concerning life in society. Instead we can ask: How is society possible? How does it persist? Or we can ask a myriad of questions about intended or unintended events. We can probe into the ways people vote or slide down some social scale. We can try to unravel any order that may lie behind their decisions to buy or not to buy, to join an army or some club, to emigrate or to stay. We can see what happens when large organizations or small groups change their size, when new weapons in military spheres become noticed in the diplomatic spheres, or when several people want to talk at the same time.

As adults we cannot escape—unless we take deliberate measures to do so—some reflection about all this. We cannot live without society. Yet to participate in society is to take cognizance of other people. Such cognizance includes some anticipation, some inner rehearsal of part of the future. By the same token, as members of society and of the many circles that help constitute it, we also rehearse the past. We "go over again" what happened. Indeed, the greatest, if not the best part of our conversations, in North American society at least, probably consists of various kinds of selections from some immediate or more distant past. In that respect, the endless telephone conversations of certain adolescents, nourished on the slim morsels of what "he said to her and she to him," are just a caricature of the chronic properties of social arrangements.

This book is devoted to the study of the properties of social arrangements. It proceeds from recognizing that social arrangements have always been subject to observation and comment, but that their systematic study is rather young.

On the one hand, the world is full of writings or other symbolic accomplishments, like music and sculpture, that are to some extent direct commentaries on the social world itself. After all, that world—as this Reader documents—contains the necessary (though not sufficient) characteristic of being constituted by an endless process of mutual observation, reflection, confirmation, and transformation of the thoughts and apprehensions of men. On the other hand, cumulative and confirmed knowledge regarding it is scarce. This fact, if properly interpreted, is as much a lack as a source of further enlightenment. It reminds us that social orders are "open" systems. To be sure, they have their determinacy. They are intelligible. Yet they are not organisms, and they are certainly not machines. Still, they have a status as systems—both in the vivid personal sense of the discovered connectedness of the apparently disparate facts of immediate experience, and in the more abstract sense of allowing the growth of a consensus of related terms with which to study "the social."

The "openness" of social systems is ambiguous, the more so since any specific example, be it a tribe or a nation, a political party or the Daughters of the Nile, seems anything but "open," especially if it no longer exists. One must be careful, too, not to confuse our ignorance with openness. At the moment we cannot fully predict how a social gathering will go or what the social structure of Western Germany will be like in 1984. Such inability has several sources, including the fact that all concrete social arrangements are complicated. Each of them is a mixture of constraint on its participants to act in certain ways or to engender, between them, certain results, and of rights and opportunities to improvise or find some ways of their own. The balance shifts. From the perspective of some systems, with their cherished balances, others seem primarily coercive and hence "closed." Besides, the "same" system is not equally open to its constituent members. Furthermore, belief and fact diverge. A man may have more freedom than he thinks—or less. Moreover, the very terms by which we seek to translate our varied experience with the constraint and scope of the social arrangements around (and within) us into communicable, if not testable, accounts, are themselves subject to controversy. Freedom, necessity, determination, order, choice among alternatives—these are among the bedevilled terms and issues which are alike part of the drama of society itself, of the disagreements and agreements that bind and divide groups, and, sooner or later, of the thought necessary to study society, even in the name of science.

These thoughts may appear both too obvious and too aimless; certainly they have every appearance of being a start in the middle. This corresponds with the persistent intention of these volumes: they are concerned with presenting a background from which can grow that part of the systematic study of society that falls within the shifting borders of sociology. Once it has formally begun this is an endless enterprise, provided of course political and social events at least permit the continuity of this undertaking. We are concerned with the proper cultivation of this continuity. We wish to document the growth of sociology considered under the aspects of the major ideas and questions, and their relations, through which sociology is now continuously—though not evenly—being created as a discipline of inquiry, and hence as a field of knowledge.

Growth must have sources and resources. These are not of one piece. In a science, they include the craft and techniques of research. The division of labor among books and readers (and limitations of length) rules out here any consideration of techniques as devices for finding answers to questions or selecting the relevant meaning from gathered facts. We are confining ourselves to that range of ideas, proposals, and controversies without which sociology would be impossible. We hope thereby to help in the strenuous effort of enlarging the range of possible and viable ideas required for sociological analysis. We have no illusion that this is "merely" a matter of the addition of ideas. Sociology depends for its identity on its *difference* from literature, philosophy, and theology. But we are certain, as, logically, any scientific inquirer must be, that this does not mean that sociology can leave unattended the task of clarifying the ideas, and their relations, that constitute its questions. Facts, after all, are like the moon: they derive their light, and hence their import, from an external source. They do not speak for themselves; they merely reply as part of an exchange of question and answer. This exchange, in turn, requires some pattern of ideas to begin. Once having started, the pattern must change. It is also likely to give rise to rival patterns and to become specialized "within" itself. Besides, "difference" does not exclude links; literature, philosophy, and theology are also necessary for the study of society.

This part of the Introduction is confined to some observations on the growth of the patterns of questions and answers that are sociology. It is not possible to forget the present and to present, even roughly or through personal observation, a succession of the strategic ideas and discoveries that preceded what surrounds us now in the name of sociology. We must start with some notion of the minimal characteristics of sociological analysis; we can then turn to some considerations on the timing of its birth, continue with questions about alternative directions in sociology's development, and end with some restatement of available images for the study of society. This is a deliberately limited undertaking. There would have been other alternatives. These were ruled out either by lack of sufficient knowledge on the authors' part or by the nature of this enterprise.

This is not the first effort of its kind. There are histories of sociology, and this is not an attempt to provide another one—even one confined to sociological theory. Nor are we interested in providing a museum for all sociologically relevant proposals that have ever found their way into print. We sought, instead, to provide a convenient reminder of distinctions and proposals necessary for the adequate pursuit of sociology. We believe that such a pursuit involves commitment to *some* pattern of thought; we could only follow the one that held most meaning and promise for us. Such a commitment includes the hope of the continuous revision and improvement of the pattern. There are other patterns which differ from ours, more in part than as a whole, and certainly there are other vocabularies. It is never really easy to know how to evaluate the difference between them. Indeed, there are a number of other collected readings in sociological theory. We cannot judge whether we have accomplished our end: to make strategic selections written before the mid-nineteen-thirties (with some very few exceptions) and after 1600; and to present these with the help of an arrangement of headings and subheadings testifying to our concept of the strategic issues within the discipline of sociology. At the same time, we hope to have presented enough of the data, or of reminders of further data that can be read "in the original," so that others, now and later, can come to different perspectives—and are, in fact, goaded on to seek new perspectives.

But what are "our conceptions of the strategic issues"?

## *Some Essential Sociological Notions*

Strategy concerns the link between positions of departure and positions of arrival. Sociology, like any human enterprise (and the many acts composing any enterprise), is suspended between several notions at once.

It confronts the world (within and without) in order to make discoveries. (The uses of sociology cannot concern us here. Even the most avid "applied" sociologist must discover a link between knowledge, a given situation, and some desired state of change or persistence. Nor can we delay now to debate the validity of the famous proposition that nothing is so practical as a good theory.) Discoveries, however, are not made about the world "as a whole." The world, after all, is full of a number of things. Even its fullness is an impression that reminds us of the discrepancy between what we can say (or feel) and all of what might be said (or felt). Sociology, then, involves a characteristic image, or alternative set of images, concerning one part of the larger order of "the world," that can be increasingly known. Simply put, this is the social order. The other part of this General Introduction is in fact a detailed explication and differentiation of that view of the social order which seems to us, as editors, to be most consistent with the incontrovertible formulations of the past and the gathering volume of the present sociological findings. Similarly, sociology involves a logical as well as a concrete sense of the *difference* (and link) between the actual and the possible within the social order. This difference becomes important to the degree to which one remains alive to the "created," as distinct from the "given and unalterable," aspects of social arrangements and their relativity. As a scientific enterprise, sociology is finally concerned with the discovery of proposals that define or explain regularities characterizing the mutual relations, and the products to which they give rise, among human beings.

This may all seem rather abstract, particularly in view of the fact that sociology is an empirical inquiry, and as such involves a view of the coherence of events. For anyone seeking to be a sociologist, it proceeds through the elaboration of an initially more or less simple (or too grand) sense of orderliness. As a discipline, since its birth, it has had to proceed by fighting alike against oversimple and early grand schemes, and against the claim that the events it seeks to explain are too complicated—or, at least, that their complexity requires primarily the gifts and skills of historians, theologians, philosophers, and artists.

A sociologist must construct his rebuttal in part from the work of those who would question the necessity or the possibility of his existence. Good sociology is inevitably haunted by the labyrinthine immensity of human affairs; it is also always within reach of a governing assumption—without which science itself would be impossible—that this immensity exhibits intelligible and communicable regularities, and that these, at least for the time being, are of several kinds.

## *Some Features of Social Orders*

This *severalness* repeatedly accompanies the study of society. There are various reasons for this, whose examination can provide a reminder of the growing scope of sociological theory, both in range and in depth. Such a reminder will move us closer to answering the questions: What distinctions and proposals help constitute sociological theory; and how, if at all, do these differ from the ideas about society that men must hold in order to live in it?

Social coherence is one possible form of coherence. Music, logic, atoms, and living organisms are other forms. The single form of social coherence—marked by the structure of reciprocal expectations, acts, and their intended and unintended consequences—is, as we all know, magnificently rich and inclusive. Our knowledge of it, studied or experienced, is varied. Such variation is part of the very social phenomena we seek to know. These phenomena, as a rule, combine obviousness with hiddenness. They are all about us. Yet it is the mark of complex societies—and it is in these that sociologists are born and shaped, even if they do not necessarily confine their studies to them—that they are constituted by reservoirs of "anonymous" other persons, whom one has various accidental and deliberate opportunities of meeting "for the first time." For all its dependence on routine and familiarity, society engenders an interminable succession of situations and "other people" who become associated with secrecy or the not-yet-known. These add one kind of severalness to the structure of social life: the severalness of what we have comprehended and what we have yet to unravel as presented by the immediate or distant presence of others. Sociology thus finds its puzzles along a huge line of occasions. Two men loading a haycart, saying nothing; some children in winter, skating on a tennis court; a black market or a grey one; mothers sitting on a bench; a panic and a dance; a slum, Mayfair, or Fire Island —all these are samples of social cohesion. Similarly, the rise of Social Credit as a political movement in Canada, the expulsion of Tito from the Cominform, fluctuations in the birth rate and in longevity, or the shifts in emphasis within the dogma of the Roman Catholic Church—all are samples of society considered as a succession of arrangements. It belongs to the office of sociology, as we would prefer to conceive it, to comprehend within its distinctions the whole range of possible social arrangements, and to be alive to human society as such. A sociology that cannot naturally and logically take into account the alternate modes of social stratification of Russia, India, the United States, and Peru, for instance, or the differences imposed on social reciprocity by differences in age and sex, is, of course, provincial and inappropriately narrow. Yet as a discipline, sociology cannot escape an appropriate narrowness—appropriate to the extent that it is preceded by some general commitment concerning the systematic study of human arrangements.

The growth of sociological theory seems to have proceeded from such commitments, while also helping to create them. These commitments are surrounded by debate. Part of this debate binds and fills the materials of this Reader. Parts of the debate concerning the "proper study of mankind" have been omitted, as settled. We know now that "theory" and "research" are, not alternatives for a scientific discipline, but different sides of one coin. We also know that, in any particular man's active work, there are choices to be made. Some people prefer to spend their life in an enduring effort to build a series of specific studies or to elaborate a set of techniques. Others prefer the equally hard work of formulating patterns of propositions that can do justice to a growing accumulation of established information, and transcend this information for the sake of its greater illumination and its continued growth. Yet the division of labor within a field cannot be taken as a logical description of alternative directions for the field as such. A division of labor combines individual differences, or differences of "position," within a single direction of effort. In sociology, the effort has gone in the direction of formulations concerning social relations, concerning the arrangement of social relations into various kinds of groupings or aggregations, and concerning the directions and conditions of development that can be found within single, or some range of associated, social arrangements. Talcott Parsons has proposed in much more detail, in the following section, a way of ordering, on different levels, our sense of the structure of society.

## *The Unity and Diversity of Sociology*

The inspection of the titles of the three hundred papers that are usually read at an annual meeting of the American Sociological Society, for instance, or of the hundreds of courses that are annually taught in the name of sociology at institutions of higher learning throughout the world, seems to belie this formal claim of unity and replace it with a sense of bewildering confusion. The apparently assured and single-minded inclusiveness of a Max Weber or a Durkheim, a Vilfredo Pareto or a Sigmund Freud, then looms reassuringly large as a refuge. Yet fleeing to them, to avoid the confusion of tongues that lets many people studying the same subject talk past each other, would be to misunderstand their work. We now have a Catholic and a non-Catholic sociology; the "jargons" current at Chicago, Columbia, Harvard, Michigan, Frankfurt, and in many other places; the fads of interest and the resurrections of older lines; the undigestible output of non-cumulative efforts; and the vague sense of a persistent discrepancy between what we do and what we feel to be the strategic issues. Yet this state of affairs is like society itself. There, too, people speak past and with each other, do one thing and mean another, find themselves at loggerheads with their own awareness of their ideals. Experience, and its accompanying multiplication of common sense and common error, then cease to be sufficient, though experience always remains necessary.

It is virtually impossible to keep these contradictions—between consensus and divergence, between the necessity of traditional experience and the insufficiency of it—appropriately in mind simultaneously. Each of the two introductory essays, with its respective emphasis, tends to stress one of the two sides. They should, then, be read as a whole. The present essay emphasizes the *variety* of views through which people studying the "same" phenomena have gone about their work. Similarly, it stresses the "experiential" component in the categories and questions constituting sociology. The following essay is more systematic. It differentiates a comprehensive point of view and proposes patterns of categories—such as values, norms, collectivities, and roles. It is concerned with matters of clarity and consistency.

## *The Realms of Society*

Sociology is concerned with coherence of some meaning, to both its direct participants and its observers, that provides it with yet another kind of "severalness." First, a realm of meaning involves some exclusion and some unevenness. Even the simplest social encounters, like shaking someone's hand, involve the use of a mode of communication, of acknowledgment by another. Yet communication can assume many modes, of which language is only one; their advantages and possibilities differ. Still, any one social occasion, though its character would differ as the mode of talk within it varies, can, in theory, proceed in one of several languages. It cannot proceed at all in the absence of any language. *Language* includes the gestures of the deaf and dumb, the looks of the married, or the salutes of some military occasion. Social occasions, then, in including a mode of communication, also exclude many others.

As occasions, they also represent articulate or vague notions of importance. To eat now is to give up something else for this time; to talk of the weather is not to talk of politics. The actual both excludes many other possible events and comes to represent some sense of inequality of all possibilities. In other words, social coherence always has an economic dimension: it requires decisions of allocation and associated conceptions of relative importance. The social world is always uneven; it always has some features that between and within themselves appear under the aspects of "more or less." In this sense, society is a comparative phenomenon: it always contains some who are "older," luckier, shorter, livelier, or healthier than others.

Meaning, then, differentiates the world. It produces the severalness of question and answer. Relative to social arrangements, questions confront what is so both with speculations about what else could be—thereby reminding us of the created quality of social affairs—and with considerations of appropriateness. The social, after all, always contains evaluation. It implies various kinds of agreements about the ways of responding to the apparent imperatives of being alive and of managing the issues that such response successively engenders. Evaluation is a form of confrontation; it implies some matching of standards to what was, in fact, done. Often it involves balancing standards amongst themselves. Sociology must comprehend a host of confrontations, occurring within and between people. Confrontations within ourselves are an aspect of the differentiation of society itself. Part of our inner conversations reflect our simultaneous involvement in a variety of different spheres demanding from us a severalness of efforts, at times even of standards of work.

Sociology has come to refer to this phenomenon as a conflict of and in roles. Through roles, we participate as persons in social arrangements. For its members, a society engenders a succession and pattern of roles in accordance with its division of labor and of the spheres by which it seeks to keep going. A multiplicity of undertakings are carried on with the help of more or less large populations. The constituent individuals are all suspended between birth and death, but confront the society with the fact that they stand at different positions within this cycle. The spheres are easier to recognize than to analyze.

Any sociology that we have has been created by people whose experience has been confronted and constituted by the fact that, in our society, there are recognizable separations of several kinds. We cohere, for different purposes, into circles of mutual exclusion. Families and kinship are one form and principle of such coherence and exclusion. Friendship, involving different principles of exclusion, is another example. We are also irrevocably part of a process of aging robbed of its continuity by the social divisions of generational differences. These are joined by the radical and inescapable confrontations of the *two* sexes. We know now that this is not just a biological matter. Societies vary sharply in their notions of maleness and femaleness, and of the appropriate relations between them.

These divisions, furthermore, are associated with the distinctions between "realms." Religion, the economy, the polity, work, family, the educational system, the legal system, or the armed forces—these stand for divergent realms of endeavor, each carried forward by its own complement of institutions. Even a child knows that a church and a department store, a doctor's office and a wading pool, a home and a hotel, stand for characteristically different courses of conduct. Sociology has grown up in societies whose very growth is measured precisely by the proliferation of spheres. To a degree, one particular conflict between (or within) societies—engaging the ideological and military resources and loyalties of people, sometimes to the point of death—has become a great issue: how separate should these spheres be? What walls of independence or of privacy should be allowed to whom?

The growth of society, and of sociology, involves proliferation (or differentiation, as we have called it elsewhere in this Introduction). Yet to speak of a society, or of a discipline whose object is its study, is to acknowledge that proliferation is reciprocally related to coherence. Sociology thrives on the simple insight that separation of *I* and *You,* of the economy and the polity, of the church and the state, involves a coherence—in the form of inclusive agreements—that links what is separated.

Ultimately, the very aloneness of the self is thus a social phenomenon. Only because we become human in the company of others, and have to become human to be in their company, are we able to evolve the sense of being different from them. The common sense, in our society, of the strains between individuals and society, thus becomes an experienced confrontation which sociology must take seriously but not literally. In constituting society, the wish to oppose what appears as constraint contributes as much as the wish to carry out outer or inner dictates. It is socially important, however, that what is sociologically co-relative is presented by variously committed groups as an ideological antithesis. The phenomena which sociological theory must unravel include, in other words, the beliefs and moral commitments of people.

The presence of sociology among people creates a further discrepancy. Beliefs and commitments guide their holders in making decisions or justifying decisions made. To a sociological theorist, they appear as constituent facts within the structure and function of social arrangements. As such they are necessary, but not sufficient, for a valid account of what is to be explained. A theorist sees society as transcending the intentions and beliefs of people without being independent of them. He sees it as a deposited order that cannot be comprehended only by knowledge of its constituent members taken singly; nor can it be comprehended as a self-contained system of impersonal forces. Its comprehension constitutes a divergence from the common sense of any circle of society. The divergence itself varies, since the differences among circles and societies lie partially in the variation governing ways of regarding human affairs and assigning importance to the elements that are known or believed to constitute them.

Sociological theory, then, studies the divergence and coherence that make social arrangements. It is driven on by the confrontations of an I and a You and between a We and a They, as well as by the emergent divergences between people's intentions and the issues arising from the arrangements they make to implement these intentions. As part of knowledge, the theory and practice of sociology help differentiate knowledge itself. Moreover, sociology augments—in varying degrees of reliability—our chances to make deliberate changes within social arrangements themselves. The following essay, however, proposes a four-fold set of requirements defining the generic issues that arise for and within the arrangements by which people live with or against one another. A technical exposition of this "functional paradigm" is contained in that essay, the second section of the General Introduction.

## *Requirements of Social Systems*

We might anticipate it briefly here. Concrete social arrangements can be conceived as composed of several elements at once, as we know from simply examining our experience. There are various ways of labeling these elements. We can, as the introductory material of this Reader proposes, speak about roles, collectivities, norms, and values. That is, we can distinguish between the particular ways in which people expect one another to co-operate with each other in some enterprise that one or another has instituted. We can seek the ways in which they conceive of their mutual relation during the time it lasts. We can ask, then, to what extent they think of their encounter as something to be repeated or as a chance affair not likely to recur. We can ask about the kinds of expectations by which each feels surrounded, in the other's presence, with regard to the mode of interaction that is to take place. We can ask about those more basic and more general moral commitments that would make this occasion a particular one, spatially and temporally located. We can also dissect the order that two or more people in each other's presence, or in some less surveyable and larger collectivity, seem to sustain, by starting, not with individual experience as this proceeds within the course of interaction, but with the question: What at the least are the domains to which some attention must be paid if a smaller or larger number of people wish to maintain the possibility of being part of a social order that can in some measure be taken for granted? This is a most cumbersome question, making many assumptions.

The second introductory essay argues that one should remember at least four issues as necessary to the persistence of social arrangements. As issues, they are both matters demanding attention and matters which, as such, help comprise the very arrangements that constitute, in turn, a solution for them. One such issue concerns the mode of coherence among the members of a going arrangement. Social arrangements always involve the integration of the separate actions of its constituent actors. They must somehow solve the problems of coherence and of attachment. In addition to settling the mutual relation among its constituent actors, a social arrangement, since it does take place in time and space, is therefore faced with establishing relations to a surrounding world. These relations settle the problems of adaptation. The terminology is incidental. Adaptation and coherence arise, in turn, with respect to two further matters. Whether they be tangible or not, social arrangements are invested with purposes. People have wants. These may simply involve the company of others; they may take the form of wishing not so much to get as to give, or to express themselves. Besides, the wants with which people begin, or are forced into, social arrangement become compounded by the interaction among wants facilitated by the company in question. Yet in any case, social arrangements proceed under the aspect of some accomplishment. This involves the pursuit of goals.

This, then, is the third domain demanding attention. Goals, coherence, and adaptation, moreover, are pursued within the confines of shared moral commitments and private motives. Commitments and motives posit the patterns which make sense of the world and confront us with alternatives whose solution must constitute our aliveness. In the next essay, this domain will be called the issue of pattern-maintenance.

To repeat: the terminology can well be replaced. Yet by considering social arrangements this way, we can compare them. We can see them as more than unique constellations. We can make sense of the inner struggles and patterns of change characterizing them.

## THE PERSONAL AND THE IMPERSONAL

### *The Form of Sociological Questions*

Question-and-answer involves a set of distinctions and ideas, which may be ordered chronologically. For the individual, we can remember the sequence of questions which appear to accompany (and so help constitute) growth and development. We know that a child has many whys and whats: manners, stars, names, things. By convention and logic, we have come to consider that which we confront, through the questions we can ask of it, as lying in different realms—e.g., the realms of the organic and the inorganic, the mechanical and the logical, the psychological and the meaningless. Though we may be annoyed by the distinctions, we cannot go *against* the fact that doing a Virginia reel or repairing a carburetor, spraying roses against insects, sorting mail, or flying in formation are occasions bringing into prominence different sorts of relations among things, bodies, and people. The picture is not, to the wall, what it is to the viewer—unless he wants it so. This particular set of discrepancies we have tentatively, yet stubbornly, let settle into realms of knowledge. These realms share many properties, and their distinctions lie only partially in *what* they confront and, in much larger part, in *how* they do so. In a measure, physics and zoology are the same thing: we distinguish them by the questions they ask. The sequence of the child's questions does not occur in a vacuum. There are shared traditions to which he must order his questions, as he learns to accept answers that others give him. Indeed, questions presuppose previous answers. This is not the place to explore the significance of the fact that we can ask questions or inquire how it is possible to ask them at all. The chronological sequence of the child's question is not only pulled apart—and in different ways, in different circles and cultures—by an inescapable pattern of grouped distinctions; this pattern itself is subject to change. Physics preceded sociology. Knowledge, that is, has a history. It also is divisible into different forms. To know about the functioning of a person's heart and to know that same person's name or his sense of humor imply different kinds of knowledge. For logic and convenience, we have grouped these kinds of knowing into major classes, of which science is one and philosophy another. There are more than these. Their difference does not deny their mutual dependence. Nor will the matter rest there. Science can be further divided, into either its pure and applied forms, or its natural and social ones. The old quarrels and questions necessarily connected with such a classification need not concern us just yet. To be sure, one cannot go far in pursuing an effort at an orderly unravelling of one or the other puzzle in the ordering of human affairs without also having to ask, for instance: In what lies the difference between the "social" and the "natural"? Between the social and the natural sciences? In what lies the difference between literature and social science?

We shall have to compose some answers to these questions in these introductory essays and in our various Introductions, knowing full well that a later generation will raise the same issues again and, perhaps, come to different conclusions. In this instance, as in many others, discovery and presupposition go hand in hand. One must create some sociology before one can know what it is; and one must know, at least, what it might be, before one can help create it.

My claim has been that sociology must be characterized through an account of the questions it asks and the answers it accepts. Weber and Dickens both asked how one might give an account of a phenomenon called "bureaucracy." In one case, the answer takes the form of propositions that can be revised; in the other, the form of declarations that are accepted as fiction.

Revisable propositions must be clear—i.e., one must be able to consider them apart from their author. Yet their history is not irrelevant. One must be able to ask: How do you know, and how can I come to know this too? In sociology, as one form of confronting the world through science, the emphasis, as in the rest of science, is on the world, not on the observer. The concern is not with quoting one's self correctly—though this may be a necessary beginning—but with formulating claims by routes that others can travel and with traveling to places that others can show not to have been terminal. Such intentions lead to a familiar combination of slightly contradictory qualities that together constitute any and all science: propositions that can be disproved and shared, that are impersonal and public, that involve matters of fact and training in ways of establishing these facts.

## *The Substance of Sociological Questions*

Such, in outline, is the form of at least the answers that questions in sociology must take. But what of their content? Any field of disciplined inquiry involves a provisional image of an order within a wider order that can be made to yield some regularities demonstrably more than personal impressions. In the case of sociology, the order "lies in between." Yet it also lies near at hand. These circumstances have helped to delay its cumulative apprehension. In the West, we manage what confronts us with the help of a number of ideas that seem to sort matters out. "Nature" is one of the most prominent of these; it is a collected and growing set of questions and answers, and the assumption that there is an impersonal givenness. Thus we can give accounts of it omitting some of the qualities that those who give the accounts claim for themselves—we can account for it without having to deal with the issues of choice, intention, or meaning. This, of course, we have to learn. The distinction between the personal and the impersonal is an achievement with an individual and a collective history. We tend, further, to see the natural universe as varyingly distant from the personal realm from which we view and move toward it. We tend to distinguish between inorganic and organic matters, between what is alive, what is dead, and what knows no life or death at all.

The personal moves into view as we succeed in distinguishing it from that which it is not. It is a most rewarding enterprise to see precisely how different categories of people, different cultures, or different members of the successive stages in the history of some society, have in fact thought about the world and thereby fashioned their own. Such an enterprise is possible only if one is willing to assume that some ideas are hospitable enough both to represent a consensus among different investigators, and to allow us to characterize the differences among ways of thinking without distorting these differences through the limitations which are part of any and all ideas. The see-saw between the personal and the impersonal is not a governing distinction among all adults; but it is one mode of dividing the world which has deeply affected the development of sociology.

The discrepancy between the personal and the impersonal is ambiguous. We can use it to distinguish ourselves from that which is not human, does not have a self. (Unfortunately, the word "distinguish" is also ambiguous. For some, it carries an implication of superiority—a connotation excluded here.) We can also use it to distinguish different kinds of relations among persons. This is endlessly cumulative, for we cannot escape reading into the world, as we see and build it, what is true of ourselves; and not reading into ourselves what we deem to be true about the impersonal surroundings helping to provide the contrasts by which we come to know what we are through determining what we are not. Yet the discrepancy is not enough for a conception of a social, as distinct from a personal or a natural, order. Society lies between individuals, and between the personal and the impersonal in the first sense of that distinction. As an expression referring to the unceasing exchange of events between people as members of different groupings, it stands for a way of apprehending the world that seems not to be equally distant from or close to rival *moral* perspectives. When we construct a triangle, in our sense of order, we see that, in addition to the nexus of personal happenings or of natural events, it is promising to conceive as well of a nexus of social exchanges and results. Then we find that we must combine a view of social orders, as involving moral calculations (and the guide lines by which these are performed), with the object of being free, in our questions, to distinguish between "what is" and "what ought to be."

If our own moral universe includes, among its prominent commitments or displeasures, potent notions of "individualism" or "freedom," then the intellectual claim that events in the world can be ordered to *several* comprehensible realms (which here we have provisionally called personal, impersonal, and social) always has its own moral consequences. These affect the search for a discovery of the regularities of the social order. Still, in human affairs, including building science through discovery and invention, it seems possible to imagine a resolution while we are still dogged by many logical and technical difficulties. From these considerations, it follows that, in the investigations of social affairs, one is always liable to some temptations.

One must necessarily begin within the realm of personal matters and see society as an elaboration of the different kinds of relations that people develop toward others. This yields the notion that we are dealing with an order involving me or you, *wanting* something concerning you or me. This can produce a whole set of questions about the ways social relations are constructed and the ways they differ from other sorts of relations, e.g., those of logic or mechanics. What is the difference between the way I am bound to another who has done me a favor, and the way rope is bound to a bushel of wheat?

But society is more than a multiplication of personal relations. The first temptation, in fashioning a guiding image helping to define a social order and its field of study, lies in *not going beyond a proper starting point*. The temptation not to see society beyond social relations is the stronger because the realm of social relations seems so very rich. This realm comprises individuals addressing one another—directly, within each other's hearing, sight, or full presence; or indirectly, through mediators, like, e.g., real estate salesmen and marriage brokers. Social relations are, of course, not confined to straight lines, triangles, or small circles. They are, as it were, not confined to themselves; they appear as webs.

The best example of this is kinship. But kinship is also a special case, growing by two processes alone: marriage and birth. It belongs to those social arrangements which combine a maximum of continuity with a minimum of legal formality. In contrast, many social arrangements proceed within the confines of different kinds of corporate groups. This fact has led to considering social organizations, factories, hospitals, schools, government offices. But neither the web of kinship nor the web of corporate organizations, jointly composed of formal and informal arrangements, exhausts the structure of society. The second temptation then, is to shy away from the multiplicity of comparable yet different arrangements and thus to confine one's self either to the inwardly understandable web of social relations or to explanations referring to social forces.

The image of social forces contains an important clue. It refers in one respect to the experience each of us has had of being surrounded by arrangements—of law, religion, economics, education, or whatever they be—that have preceded us and whose tradition will outlive us. To feel surrounded is one aspect of the fact that society usually contains more people and more patterns than any one person, who is nevertheless a member of the society, can come to know. The society's structure, in addition to involving a division of labor, involves the unequal distribution of power and privilege. Organization and social relations thus fall within the variety of identifiable domains. Conventionally we distinguish between the economic, the religious, the political, the educational, and perhaps the social realms. This will be further discussed in the Introduction to the last two sections of Part One; and the differentiation of these realms is discussed in considerable detail in the Introduction to Part Two. In the case of any one society, the assessment of the actual balance of continuity and dissociation among these domains is one of the most delicate tasks for sociological analysis. As domains, they meet in different ways among circles that differ by virtue of the style of life that they share with one another.

The groups and corporate organizations distributed among the domains of society, and yielding styles of life that help deposit strata among the population of a society, still do not exhaust the major dimensions of a social order. This coherence involves a central value-system—a notion far more fully developed in the essays written by Talcott Parsons and Edward Shils. Central values help constitute such ideas as "individuality," "privacy," "sovereignty," "responsibility," or "rights." At some point, society involves its members in ultimate considerations, even if societies differ in the chances they hold out for different sectors of their populations to challenge, accept, or change these ultimate considerations. Their change, of course, is not a self-contained matter.

We do make distinctions between what people believe and what people do, between ideals and conditions. Often these are not happy distinctions, for people's acts involve beliefs, even though these beliefs may differ from the ones that the people assert. The discrepancy between ideal and practice is less a matter of the attenuation of ideals, more a matter of the fact that, in practice, people act under the aspect of what then become competing considerations. Moreover, as persons with shared ultimate commitments, they are often—especially in the market place—in the presence of what appear as impersonal forces. Social orders, as the history of economics as a discipline illustrates, can profitably be considered through the perspective of measurable regularities that would represent the social order, in turn, as a relatively determinate pattern of variables.

Economics, as later sections of this book will demonstrate, provides, perhaps more than any other sister discipline of sociology, valuable and clear models for the steady study of social arrangements. It comes closest to precision about strategic matters. But sociology's core concerns are considered peripheral in economics. In a measure, sociology grew by opposition to economics. Logically, of course, the two disciplines are complementary; but the conditions of growth of human enterprises are not only a matter of logic. In any case, the sociological study of society, while being one of several disciplines studying human arrangements, their conditions, and their products, seems logically to involve an extended awareness of impersonal and personal patterns and of ultimate commitment.

Slowly, fragmentarily, and from various sources, we have been combining views to bring a social order into view. As one cumulative attempt to study this order, sociology must approach its task on several planes. The order it studies lies not only "in between" the felt coherence of things personal, or the organization of processes called biological, or the clearly impersonal nexus of the physical universe; it also has a severalness of its own. The social implies a recognition of reciprocity sustained by people who are themselves aware of at least part of the reciprocity by which they interrelate. This provides a focus, the focus of *social action.* The next essay develops the central importance, as we see it, of this idea and its particular use for seeing a common theme in much diverse work carried out in the name of the social sciences, and sociology in particular.

*Social action* stands for creating or enacting a course of self-engagement in the world, a course that has a reference, in the agent's calculation, to others considered as likewise capable of being authors of acts toward one's self or others. Several circles can be drawn around this focus.

## People Face to Face

Some sociologists have concentrated on the realm of immediate encounters, trying to learn how the meetings of people run the courses they do. They want to discover regularities among the happenings between people in each other's presence. Who, they ask, talks to whom, and how much? Or, what are the ways by which conversations are begun, deflected, or ended? What are the differences between a cocktail party and a committee meeting? To use a classical expression: How do people come to define different situations differently? Or, to put it yet another way, what can we isolate as the recurring elements together composing social situations, which, by variation in their combination, also allow us to characterize the differences among such situations?

Let us take the case of a man chasing a 'bus that is about to pull away from its stop; there are other people about, watching. At first, it seems most convenient to think of this example in theatrical terms—as a scene involving actors, audience, time, and stage. But who are the actors? The busdriver and his potential, though late, passenger? One might begin with these. Yet each is surrounded by further actors. There are the passengers already in the bus, and the onlookers on the street. Some are near the situation; yet not all are *in* it, for only some have noticed that someone is still trying to board the 'bus. Time can change this, through an onlooker's drawing the driver's attention to the man. Thereby, the distributed passengers on the bus can become a mutually aware grouping watching "their" driver and someone who might join them. The situation is now enhanced, for it allows alternatives. The driver may ignore the man and drive on. The latecomer may see this and give up; or he may run faster, hoping still to be able to knock on the window. The people outside may look to see what will happen, or look away to save embarrassment. The driver, within himself, may balance notions of anger, kindliness, sticking to a schedule. He looks, and responds to what he observes—a man rather than a woman, a young person rather than an old one. His passengers may say things to each other while he drives off. One can see this as the end; it is certainly *an* end. A wish has been thwarted. A man, slightly breathless, has been left behind. Others may surround him and, by watching, help re-define his experience as defeat—showing him as a bad calculator or a bad runner, as a symbol of the little man defeated by impersonal timetables, or as a muddleheaded man who misunderstands the logic of transportation systems. On the other hand, if the driver stops, a different logic may unfold. The driver can put someone in his debt, since he has the right to drive on. The latecomer is now a passenger; while he has left the onlookers on the street behind, he now may be looked over by fellow travelers. He is likely to round out his success not only by a "thank you," but also by referring to the defeat of defeat with the expression, "Just made it." This acknowledges the contingency which hovers about the co-ordination of human affairs.

Some readers may feel that all this is much ado about nothing, another painful elaboration of the obvious—or, at best, the trivial. That might be a useful critique, if it led to a clear distinction between the trivial and the significant in social affairs. Meanwhile, even this admittedly slight example is demonstrably a sample of social reality and is, therefore, one combination of recurrent elements. Our description has been haphazard and personal, but it has indicated some possibilities that social situations have beginnings and ends, that they unfold in time, and that, as such, they have "boundaries." Consequently, the course of social action creates distinctions between *insiders* and *outsiders*. *Participation* can assume different forms; it is, moreover, given through viewing others under some *selected aspect,* as passengers, drivers, onlookers, fellow passengers. That is, others must become *defined;* so must one's self, in *distinction* from them and in *similarity* to them. Actors and onlookers then come to sustain a *division of labor,* which implies some *agreement* on *ends* and *means,* some notion of *appropriateness.* Appropriateness is the recognition of possibility, of alternatives. We often refer to this by denying it. We talk about things "one just doesn't do." To the listener, this may be a reminder of all that one could do. One does not play hide-and-seek in church or treat *Macbeth* as a comedy; one does not laugh at the man as the 'bus drives off without him. Social situations, then, involve *judgments* and *sanctions.* Or, again, they involve *expectations* and *consequences.* This incomplete sample of communicable ideas suggests lines for a dissection and view of the social order as an order that has to be carried on.

## *The Larger Social Order*

One can—and usually must—*start* with social situations as one thinks about the character of the social order and the possibility of studying it. Inevitably, one cannot end there; social situations are only samples of social reality. Their analysis necessitates previous ideas concerning the coherence and differentiation of this order and the processes whereby it is carried on. These volumes suggest one way that, especially during the last seventy-five years, sociological theories, in dissecting this order, can themselves be distributed about a sequence of questions. This sequence—and we must repeat that it is one of a *series* of possible sequences—is itself the collective product, as it were, of the growth of sociological theory, whose nature will concern us presently. For the present, we should continue the attempt to characterize its product. In ten years, this characterization may well be markedly out of date; one of the intentions of this Reader is that this should become the case.

Just as social situations, as the specific occasions for the enactment of social arrangements, are the place to "catch" society, so social acts and the give-and-take of interaction are the stuff of which society is made. The growth of sociological analysis has involved dissecting a given sequence of social acts, as well as comparing large-scale societies. This has led to attempts to distinguish the component spheres of societies. These "opposite" directions of growth are, of course, complementary; they yield a series of planes on which sociological questions are asked. In turn, the existence of such planes raises the question of their links.

There are times when the study of the coherence of men's arrangements seems to have no coherence itself. Sociological theory has analyzed immediate and intimate encounters, like meals and confessions; it has also become concerned with the mass. It might profitably ask, for instance, what social arrangements are necessary for the distribution of urban populations on public beaches on a hot summer weekend afternoon. A thorough answer would reveal much of history and society. This lively phenomenon—combining nature and commerce, leisure and potential danger, the sun-tan cult, the art of swimming, and the enjoyment of sundry pleasures—presupposes notions of private and public property, attitudes about the body, and distinctions of work and play. Concern with the mass can also comprehend an analysis of the distributed audience of a radio program or the gathered collection of a cathedral service. Behind the temporary convergence and dispersal of large and small groupings one can look for persistent structures: the bureaucracies of industry, government, and churches; the formal and informal patterns of procedure in hospitals, universities, and libraries. Then there are the orders of quantitative emergent fact: the rates of population increase and decline; the rates of incidence and prevalence of some countable attribute, like admission to a mental hospital, suicide, marriage, or divorce; or the direction and volume of a choice, like a vote or a car purchase. Sociological theorizing has gone farther: it has become concerned with a wide range of migrations—people moving from the country to the city, from one nation to another, from one religious or political persuasion to another, from one age to another, from one status to another. Such movement has several related aspects calling for distinction and for mutual ordering.

One can examine this ordering in terms of sheer quantity. Rates of migration and mobility, ratios of mobile and sedentary numbers in given congregations of people (be these cities, regions, or nations), or shifts in such rates—including the magnitudes of upward and downward social mobility characterizing comparable social structures—all these are significant in the comprehension of social systems. They become measurable, outward signs of inward and invisible facts. Concern with them is part of the inevitable attempt to make the society manageable, to bring it into steady view. Yet these magnitudes also remove society: they remind one of it as something that lies behind the intellectually comprehended figures of consumption, travel, births, deaths, or years of schooling completed. By the same token, they make society something lying beyond the experienced pattern of social connection that even the richest individual life brings into apprehended clarity, on subsequent reflection, to any of us.

In this connection, another theme of questioning (and charting of fact) has helped constitute the scope of sociology. The social "takes place"—in time and space. As an alive phenomenon—constituted by the succession of encounters, and their products, of persons in their capacity as members of a variety of groupings—any social arrangement has, in fact, a "boundary." (This idea is stated much more systematically in the second part of this Introduction.) A birthday party or a national election, a village or a concert, an army or a university, are diverse examples of social arrangements, all of which have beginnings and ends: they occur in time. One may realistically ask how long they last, when they began, or why they ended. In a sense, social arrangements, like melodies, are disclosed only over time; but usually they lack a directly apprehensible "thereness." Social arrangements are carried on and along by real individuals. Most of the time, in complex societies, they are carried on indoors: they occur inside walls that form patterns between and among themselves. The study of these patterns, ecology, is another dimension of sociological questioning, concerned with the ways in which people settle, stay, or move again, thereby building housing for many purposes. The arrangement of such housing into distinguishable kinds of aggregations—e.g., cities or villages, towns or hamlets, camps or air bases—can be observed and then comprehended as the places where social relations and institutions are begun or carried on, and as visible expressions of these invisible structures. Sociologists, and others, have studied cities, created a distinction between rural and urban sociology, and concerned themselves with a variety of smaller and larger communities. Such explorations are one form of the more general attempt to give even social subject matter some concrete place in which one can see it—to make it tangible, and yet to observe a segment of it large enough to seem to make some difference when one considers the wider realities of national societies. These have their territorial possession and limits; yet, until recently, they seemed to elude clear thought and precise, systematically gathered, documentation.

Face-to-face encounters have ramifications beyond themselves. They also come from elsewhere. We come to them with expectations and carry these, confirmed or revised, away again. A sociology consistent with itself can, therefore, never be only a study of social situations. As it moves away from the latter (though it never really completely leaves them behind), its tasks divide on several planes. It becomes concerned with sorting out the kinds of possible social associations. For example, think of a beach or a ski hill: each places private groupings in public places; each reminds us of distinctions between families, crowds, queues; the sand and the snow become appropriated.

The range of sociological theory has become wide, the planes of sociological inquiry have been multiplied. One way or another we have distinguished at least six planes on which the structure of social arrangements may be dissected. Some scholars work on immediate encounters, or groupings of persons in each other's presence. Some, though not too many, deal with public gatherings, especially when these involve ritual transactions—e.g., a coronation or a parade. Other scholars are concerned with various collective audiences—in a cathedral, or of radio or TV shows. Others analyze the persistent systems, such as science considered as a social enterprise, the civil service, or different political systems; or, more social-psychologically, the specific roles of businessmen, lawyers, teachers, doctors, waitresses—their structure and their context. Still others study emergent facts, ecological distributions, rates of birth and death, the diverse consequences of specific social arrangements, and the conditions for further ones. Finally, some concern themselves with the ultimate grounds embodied in central values, in elites, and in the occasions recognized as great accomplishments.

## MODES OF WORK[1]

The concern of this Introduction, as of the Reader itself, is always the further creation of better theory and research upon social phenomena. We know that men's actions and what they say are not the same. This is not just a matter of hypocrisy; in fact, hypocrisy is likely to play a small part in it. It is due to the coincidence of several stubborn and difficult facts.

A course of social action—taking a child for a swim in a lake; buying a watermelon; or walking

1. The bulk of the ideas in this section have been previously stated, in slightly different form, in my article: "Attachment and Alienation: Complementary Aspects of the Work of Durkheim and Simmel," *American Journal of Sociology*, LXIII, No. 6 (May, 1958).

down the gangway of an airplane, saying good-bye to the stewardess and looking for anyone who might have come to meet one—is too big for one participant to survey fully. What he surveys, knows, or experiences, furthermore, is greater than he can "say"—even if we include in that word the language of his body, his expressions, his hands. What he observes "at once," he must say in sequence. Besides, what is said, in the form of findings or related distinctions with which we are concerned in these volumes, must take a written, printed form.

Usually, a struggle intervenes between inner thoughts and written formulations. The latter, especially in science, must be expressed in such a way that they may be understood by others—in other words, the form of expression must transcend the purely personal. (Gertrude Stein, e.g., does not write science.) Scientific works are written under the additional constraint imposed by the logic of clarity or proof; they are concerned with confirming or disproving proposed regularities. Definite traditions and forms have developed for the steps of positive and negative confirmation. The ability to frame one's reasoning within these forms is a requisite for scientific writing. Yet the step by which one initially made one's discoveries may well have been quite different. In science, process and product almost necessarily diverge. Printed matter, moreover, has a kind of finality about it; once published, it is there to be read.

Nevertheless, reading almost requires reversing the process of writing. The concrete and meandering chain of reasoning connecting hunches or hypotheses with assembled data and subsequent interpretations is not, as a rule, fully stated by any scientific author. It cannot be fully stated. In addition, science involves abstraction. It must regard experience or contrived reality under the aspect of selecting distinctions. These become a part of a triangle constituted by those who produce science, the stream of products that they create together, and the persistence of the reality about which science—in the company of other forms of knowledge or assertion, like art or theology—has something, though not everything, to say.

The struggle of question and answer underlying any one of the excerpts in this Reader cannot easily be deciphered through merely reading it. For each author, this struggle takes its own characteristic form, which others are able to discern only reasonably accurately through considering his work as a whole. This is one of the many limitations, even dangers, of a venture like this. Only the original works, in their chronological sequence and in entirety, disclose an author—be he scientist or novelist—as a person at work. From one point of view, such a picture is dispensable. Science, as a cumulative product, consists in work done: it consists in questions, methods for answering them, findings, interpretations, and continuous revision of these interpretations. How Adam Smith came to formulate his thoughts on the division of labor, or how Machiavelli arrived at his observations on the management of power, is irrelevant. Having been stated, their thoughts can now be examined, used for research, dismissed as outside the present scope of social scientific inquiry or theory, and the like.

Yet a systematic exploration of the social order is an accomplishment. It must be created; and the previous struggle of others can be a guide or a consolation. Examination of the patterns and conditions of creativity of the sociological theorists who preceded us can be instructive in several respects. The printed and irrevocable proposals—like those gathered in these volumes as examples of the resources available to any student of society—are fragments in more than one way. Each is part of larger works and of the completed work of one individual (usually, in this field, a man). Such completed work exhibits its own patterns, whether or not these are known to the author when he finally ends his efforts. Some men may be more productive if they do not think too much about the inner pattern of their productivity. Others are likely to learn useful things from observing how a Weber, a George Herbert Mead, or a Durkheim poses questions, and either moves from one area of questions to another or, staying within some sphere—as Piaget does—deepens or varies his concern. For example, one might—in a necessarily condensed manner—think of Durkheim and Simmel as representing contrasting, though complementary, modes of work.

At this distance, Durkheim's work seems well contained in a few themes; its distinct foci and boundaries give it a completeness. They also invite us, quite appropriately, to use his work as a model. The logic that arranged and interpreted the facts of suicide will serve equally well with the puzzles of alcoholism or cross-cousin marriage. In all three cases, we must distinguish between rates and individual histories; we need to search for types among a determinate, and hence apparently uniform, category of events; we need a commitment to explanations seeking to exploit the constituent elements of social relations and their organization as causes for the unequal distribution of phenomena—a distribution that is not solely a matter of meaningless nature.

The themes combine rejection and acceptance. Part of the assertion that the social is something *sui generis* consists of withdrawing from the image of a single, ultimate order—individual or physical—that alone is real and is thus the only context of all explanations. Instead, Durkheim dignifies society as a moral phenomenon standing stubbornly beside nature; that must be understood in its impersonal "thereness," much as though it were a collection of related things; and that must also be perceived for what it is and what it is not—a coherence of representations coercing individuals by virtue of their ability to fuse what is obligatory with what is desirable, a fusion analogous to the double face of the sacred. Sacred implies distance and the forbidden. Yet it stands for sought-after qualities, for an appropriation that traverses distance. Durkheim remains with his concern with society. He moves through a progression of empirical concerns: the coherence and differentiation of society; the supports and burdens that different kinds of social orders provide their numbers; the ways ultimate commitments and modes of thought are constituted in enduring demands, mediated and expressed through rituals which outlast individuals while, in principle, requiring them. The progression from *The Division of Labor,* via *Suicide,* to *The Elementary Forms of the Religious Life* will probably long remain a double model: as a fruitful trinity of researches into phenomena that one must apprehend as part of the very core of any and all social phenomena; and as an inspired continuity that is cumulative.

But his work comprises far more. There are the recurrent methodological examinations and revisions, initially driven on by the wish to keep sociology a positive science, by recognizing that social facts are moral, and by the ambiguous insistence that social facts be treated as things. In one of these works, a discussion of pragmatism,[2] his persistent concern with the relative difference and connection between ideas and acts is set out, as if under a microscope, in a condensed but decisive dissection of the forms and conditions of certainty.

Further, there are the discussions of socialism, individualism, and the position of intellectuals; of the place of elites in a democracy; of the character of the German mentality and the significance of World War I—pre-political diagnoses that do not keep Durkheim from a continuous reconsideration of the "spirit of discipline," which is "the essential condition of all common life."[3]

No wonder that the related structures of morality and education become at once the labels of his academic chair and, in various forms, the titles of several of his collected series of lectures. In one of these collections, the diverse and complementary bonds dividing and binding the several spheres of economic activity, political coherence, professional service, and familial life are characterized as much for their own sake as to demonstrate that the social is indeed the moral, while society cannot do without crime.[4] Crime and punishment, the normal and the pathological—these are never far from Durkheim's attention; they provide a circle of facts, in quantitative or statutory form, that he likes to use or explain.

Yet he also turns from homicides and suicides, from the formative categories of thought, or from the dominant modes of large-scale social coherence and their historic succession, to the more immediate sphere of the family, the origins of marriage, and the prohibition of incest. He discusses moral education and education and sociology. Very deliberately, he writes accounts of a few predecessors. He finds in Montesquieu two ideas necessary to social science: the lawfulness of society and the existence of discoverable types of society. To formulate such types is to look for generic characteristics of social structure and their alternative combinations. Durkheim is also explicitly interested in Saint-Simon, Comte, Rousseau, and Schaeffle. But it is to the twin issues of anomie and education that he returns again and again. "What," one might paraphrase his insistent query, "are the conditions under which a complex contemporary society can avoid loss of direction or meaning? How adequate, given our growing knowledge of society, are such solutions as the variant forms of socialism? Is it not true that the coherence necessary for a large society requires a deliberate and specialized division of labor, in which people balance a sense of the collectivity with a concentration on their own efforts?" Durkheim sees education as the agency by which society re-creates itself, an agency at once diverse and uniform. In North America during the last decade or so, education has received astonishingly little attention from sociologists; while right now it is singled out as the cause of Western society's failure to remain unequivocally pre-eminent in physical science and technology.

Neither Durkheim nor Simmel completed his work. Yet each left a distinct "whole," as well as a distinct style of question and answer.

Simmel seems almost the opposite of Durkheim—but then, as the French say, extremes meet. His writings are profuse. Happily, to revive attention in his work, in Germany, during his anniversary year of 1958, a selection of his writings—especially of earlier or less accessible pieces—has been pub-

2. E. Durkheim, *Pragmatisme et sociologie* (Paris: Librairie philosophique, 1955), pp. 199–202.

3. Durkheim, *The Rules of Sociological Method* (Chicago: University of Chicago Press, 1938), p. 124.

4. *Leçons de sociologie: physique des moeurs et du droit* (Paris: Presses universitaires de France, 1950).

lished, under the appropriate title, *Bridge and Door*.[5]

This collection is a partially representative sample of the range of specific topics that Simmel discussed: fate, life, and death as the co-ordinates of "experience"; the characters of history and of culture; religion as a mode of coherence of the self, and not primarily as a matter of specific beliefs; landscapes and faces as types of unity confronting a beholder; the moral alternatives proposed by Kant and Nietzsche; the different ways in which a man's work and his life can be connected, as exemplified by Goethe and Rodin. The collection also contains some lesser-known sociological pieces on individualism, on meals (their regularity, sequence, and style, their double meaning), on the role of certain aesthetic categories in social arrangements and in ideologies. With extraordinary ease, Simmel begins with any one of a multitude of obvious events or ideas, and ends by using them as appropriate illustrations of his basic theme.

Simmel's work is so diverse that one could easily be tempted to list at least the major issues with which he is concerned. Yet lists give the impression of being linear; and Simmel's writings do not form a single line of analyses successively emerging from each other. Rather, his work is connected but uncumulative. In the best sense, it is the work of an artist seeking to work the way he saw his model, Goethe, live: re-creating, through the paradoxical use of terms, the experienced relations and activities of our selves and of the varieties of confrontations through which we live. Simmel's work includes several spheres, but it does not fall into disciplines.

It is vain to classify him as primarily a philosopher or a sociologist. It is necessary to see his sociological analyses as an accompaniment to *all* his work: they are not confined to what he himself might have labeled sociology, any more than his work itself is confined to any one discipline. The very range of his reflection is an instructive accomplishment. He wrote about the character of knowledge; but he also discussed the nature of understanding others and historic events, as well as the processes which constitute our apprehension of the other when we see him "first." This last question is pursued in a study of Rembrandt. Simmel focused his thought on the work of a series of men—Dante, Goethe, Michelangelo, Moltke, Nietzsche, Schopenhauer, Kant, George. He considers each man, not as a person, but as the creator or exemplar of one or another alternative solution to a problem of life.

There are the recurrent essays on aesthetic matters: on ruins, mountains, landscapes, bridges, doors, vessels, and their handles. These become, in fact, the occasion for further juxtapositions of opposites: ruins allow one to experience as the work of nature what originally must have been the work of men; handles serve as links between an environment and what is nevertheless a self-contained object placed and seen within it. One can turn from this with mild amusement or annoyed indifference, feel tempted to dismiss it as a play on words, as utterly irrelevant to the serious study of social matters. But in Simmel's view, "the play's the thing": the serious is often best caught in its translated forms—in caricature, in small talk, in the unique event. His essay on adventures displays a parade of complementary notions concerning routine and disruption, accident and fate, periphery and center, repetition and irrevocability, beginning and end—all of which help constitute social situations. Simmel's explicit sociological scope is now known: like Durkheim, he sees in numbers a strategic starting point for accounting for certain differences between social arrangements and for the direction that change can take.

Durkheim fruitfully (yet questionably) proposes links among the complexity of social arrangements, moral density, and an increase in the numbers whose affairs must be co-ordinated; Simmel remains, in the main, among knowable groups of different size. True to his wish to explore an attitude; to ending anywhere, yet always beginning from the same place; to being concerned far more with the *terminus a quo* than with the *terminus ad quem*—Simmel took up other themes: poverty, intersecting group memberships, conflict, secrecy, strangers and nobility, gratitude, competition and exclusion, the social functions of eyes and ears.

Cutting across these studies are several contributions to a sociology of women, beginning with an essay on female psychology (written in 1890) and including considerations of the feminist movement, the relations of women to militarism, and three long pieces on coquetry, "feminine culture," and the reciprocities of male and female. Here Simmel again seeks to formulate facts through stating contradictions: male and female are merely an example of what we might now call the reciprocal differentiation of roles. As such, they imply one another. As a category, each also stands alone: the male represents our image of some coherent, impersonal, or demanding reality; the female represents aliveness that has not yet been complicated by an elaborate self-consciousness. Such formulations are no longer

5. Georg Simmel (Michael Landmann and Margaret Susman, eds.), *Bruecke und Tuer* (Stuttgart: K. F. Koehler, 1957).

likely to attract attention and research; but we can convert them into an approach to the study of types of moral commitment. We seem to balance a sense of the *reciprocity* of our contributions or standards with a belief in their ultimate "so-ness." Perhaps, as adults, we combine two moralities. In different ways, Durkheim and Simmel formulated the respective character of these moralities; while Piaget creates experiments to present them to us as stages in the life cycle.[6]

Par excellence, Simmel is a sociologist of intimacy. Closeness and anonymity, faithfulness and the faithlessness of fashion, private correspondence and adornment—these always concern him. Wider society, as the more impersonal middle between specific selves and general ideas, is included in his dissection more as background than as foreground. However, general ideas, especially in the form of governing webs of attitudes, also attract him—particularly the normative constellations, like optimism and pessimism and love. Ultimately, he is moved and caught by the spectacle of a cumulative conflict between ourselves and the products of our selves. To be humanly alive is to create objects as part of a labor that divides the self into subject and object. Objects can and do grow in number; they outgrow us. To live, we must create the things that, by the oppressive embarrassment of alien riches, destroy us. Durkheim's anomie here finds a complementary notion: *omnia habentes, nihil possidentes.* It should be possible to translate this—into research—and to ask how people see the discrepancies between what they know and what they do not know, what they have and what they do not have. When are their relative deprivations less important than their sense of not having enough inner room for all that is in their grasp?

Simmel collected neither facts nor figures. He sought to represent, through ideas, what he defined as transcending them. This forced him into the device of paradox. He may have been hypnotized by his own penchant.

He constantly represents life as a stream of events which come to confront their authors. Together, events and authors are part of something else. This "something else" and something further compose life. All this involves the facts of distance and exclusion. Life, like individuals and social arrangements, always goes farther (while it lasts) but also involves limits. These limits can be crossed. It is precisely the acts of crossing, of going farther, of leaving something behind, that constitute the very character of aliveness.

By the same logic, boundaries—the divisions between inside and outside, here and there, now and then, I and You, We and They—constitute part of the recurrent structure that the sociologist has appointed himself to explain. Ultimately, it is the discrepancy between what one can say and what one experiences that is the poignant puzzle for Simmel. He holds fast to a solution which would make the discrepancy itself both a gap and a bridge between "life" and the forms or the products of it.

One book contains the theme on which his many books are variations: *Lebensanschauung: Vier metaphysische Kapitel* (1918). We can go back to this source and rework it into a tentative scheme for seeing how people actually see themselves related to others: what do they mean by being "part of something," or "surrounded," or "on the edge"? Or we can ignore this and begin in the middle: for instance, we can concentrate on any one of a series of fragmentary observations on the properties of human groups or on the shifts when one social constellation gives way to another. Or we can extend some of the inquiries he began on topics like consolation or gratitude, secrecy or multiple group membership. In any case, we are bound to fail if we take him seriously by taking him literally.

Formal sociology is dead. It confounds description and explanation. Simmel used many reciprocal distinctions to bring to mind our immediate and receding surroundings, in order that, eventually, their structure could be explained. Formal sociology simply distributes such distinctions over haphazardly apprehended facts. I shall return to this point later. Three lessons, however, seem to lie between the attempt to reformulate his philosophy of life and the immediate use of selected proposals.[7] He seems to urge us to look for the "duplicity" in social arrangements, to determine the boundaries making relations social, and to distinguish varieties of distance through which human acts can be sorted out.[8]

Admittedly, in the end, Simmel wishes to stay with the self—at least, he never wants to leave it for long. But his intentions need not imprison his contributions. A meal, the settlement of a quarrel, a conversation—in Simmel's perspective, these samples of social arrangements exhibit a "severalness" of divergent characteristics which nevertheless cohere. Forgiveness after a quarrel, for instance, can reconstitute a former solidarity on a

6. Jean Piaget, *The Moral Judgement of the Child* (London: Kegan Paul, Trench, Trubner, 1932).

7. Besides the work of Theodore M. Mills, see, in particular, Robert K. Merton's provisional list of group-properties which is, *inter alia,* explicitly indebted to Simmel: "Continuities in the Theory of Reference Groups and Social Structure," in *Social Theory and Social Structure,* (Glencoe, Ill.: Free Press, 1957), pp. 310–26.

8. For a parallel formulation of Simmel's basic procedure, see the circumspect doctoral dissertation by D. Levine on a comparison of Parsons and Simmel (University of Chicago, 1957; unpublished).

higher level—while exhibiting the reciprocities of acknowledging and "forgetting" injuries, of deliberate self-humiliation that runs the risk of rejection while seeking the reward of acceptance, and of a consensus on what is appropriate behavior after a violation of expectations. Simmel directs us to move social reality into focus with the help of a series of co-ordinates constituting a set of mutually contrary ideas. He moreover suggests that all social arrangements are in the first instance sustained, remembered, or rehearsed by selves, who thereby form social relations that can never fully include their parties. Even in excluding us, society has a place for us all. Yet social relations have boundaries; they are as much defined by what they are as by what they are not. Distance and proximity are, at the same time, names for distinguishing between others—related or not—and simultaneous attributes of all social relations. In addition, distance, being variable, stands for alternative possibilities of seeing the same phenomenon close at hand or far away. Sociology itself is a form of distance vis-à-vis the stream of recurrent confrontations of individuals in varying combinations of numbers.

The foregoing are, at best, reminders of the range and direction of the accomplishments of Simmel and Durkheim. A complementary and equally fragmentary comparison might still give the previous sections some coherence and lead to the last questions: What properties of social relations does each man bring to our attention? how differently must the single word "continuity" be applied to this double stream of proposals? and how incomplete would our view of society be if we used only Durkheim and Simmel as our guides?

For clarity and brevity, though at the cost of accuracy, either Durkheim or Simmel might be described as exhibiting what the other is without. Their similarities may then become plain. Durkheim confronts gathered facts, including numerical regularities. He is concerned with method. He has an end in view and wishes to reach it through the answers to successive questions. He moves from answer to question, from the signs of unhappiness to its distribution, from the apparent sameness of a phenomenon to its typical variant forms, from the apparent associations of specific ideas to some "eternal" attitudes. Often he seeks to establish his own position by the successive elimination of rival alternatives. His is a succession of analyses of the generic features of a few strategic elements of society: work, attachment to one's self and to others, religion, education, patterns of injunctions. He pays explicit attention to the succession of shifts within these. He is also concerned with the fact that society moves into the future by educating all its young but dispersing them to different places. He remembers always that society is in transition, although phases—like his own era—he recognizes as "in-between times," jointly characterized by "moral mediocrity" and the possibilities of dispersing coherent images that can be shared. Yet he is not prepared to see the whole process as tragic. Discipline, a sense of the whole, occupational groupings, and meaningful occasions for remembering and so continuing the collective agreements that can distribute solemnity and direction—these seem almost sufficient resources for continuity.

In a series of cumulative monographs, Durkheim economically incloses a sequence of questions leading to the progressive differentiation of the primal concept of social relations as constituting phenomena in their own right. He, too, sees the severalness of person and social pattern; and he speaks about the non-contractual elements *in* contract, the impersonal elements *in* personality, the duality *of* the individual. Yet the methodological device of considering the social as a "thing" facilitates or expresses the substantive view of the social as in serious respects impersonal, as that which (eventually) confronts (and contains) the immediate self. This view leads Durkheim to write about solemnity. In Simmel's hands, when he writes on the inclined plane of tragedy, the "same" confrontation becomes a matter of alienation, of the strange, of proximity and distance—a theme which Durkheim also uses, to describe our encounters with taboos and with the sacred. Simmel, in heuristic contrast, *discloses* a very full world of transitory occasions representing the chronic duality of the self, which thus becomes a pre-eminently social condition and accomplishment. Potentially dramatic or apparently ordinary occasions and a huge panoply of confrontations with the specific accomplishments or completed lives of others, with the contrary features of lifeless objects in space and the meaningful but puzzling coherence of faces and landscapes, styles and money—all are considered, in unceasing succession, and analyzed alike. Subsequent analyses do not grow from previous ones. But all of them seek to catch the flow of temporal exchange between people. Simmel tells us what he sees. While he represents it, it is alive. He stays within the structure of vivid experience and at the same time enlarges it. But he never enlarges it to the point where he arrives at a concept of the social system.

Simmel states his claims via *contrary* notions that claim equal relevance to the *one* phenomenon under discussion. In this way, he manages to isolate and attract facts with one idea, and then attract them away again to another idea. This is more than a literary accomplishment. It proceeds expressly with the help of clear abstractions. Experience is translated into many proposals, each open to examination and revision. Yet this involves style rather than method. It cannot be directly continued. Ironically, for all its aliveness, it completely bypasses the strategic fact that society includes children. Otherwise, Simmel, perhaps more than anyone else, forces upon us the wealth of the surrounding world, the strangeness of the familiar. Now *we* must choose, but now we also *can* choose.

Still, they diverge in their roles as forefathers. Durkheim can be followed as a predecessor: rates, index formation, types of social acts and of social relations, the search for the functions of social patterns—all these persist as direct puzzles or resources. Simmel wants no immediate descendants; he expects only to provide resources that others can use for their own purposes. He does not expect his successors and debtors to remember him as the source of the ideas that, in fact, he originated.[9] One can confront certain of his specific propositions with further or actual facts, as Mills and Hawthorn have done[10] with promising results; or one can, like Merton, collect Simmel's suggestions as part of the continuing effort to set forth a coherent identification of the generic features of social groups. Similarly, Simmel's ideas could be much further exploited in the direction of a sociology of work. After all, the serious gap between producer and product and the playful coherence between host and guest are among Simmel's characteristic themes.

His thoughts, more than anyone else's, lead to the question: What is the significance of the difference between what we study and what we do not study within the boundaries of social phenomena? He had the courage to start with the visible, and the imagination to end nowhere. If we could, step by step, go to the limits of his work, we would, I think, find in it more resources than its "content" alone can yield. But this takes time.

Simmel and Durkheim are complementary within the gathering enterprise of sociology; they also converge. Both see social relations as involving a confrontation of several dimensions. To Durkheim, the emphasis is on the character of commitment; to Simmel, on involvement. The first, as we know, speaks of constraint as the combination of duty and desire. The second sees social relations as typical balances of distance and proximity. Durkheim analyzes sanctions which define and greet offenders, who, through their offense, create gaps between the actual and the ideal. Simmel traces the functions of gratitude and faithfulness, since he sees, in these two enjoined dispositions, resources for continued coherence among persons. Both, then, are concerned with the conditions necessary if people are to act attached. Both distinguish varieties of attachment. Both are prepared to admit some generic features of attachment.

Simmel and Durkheim seem to come back to four reciprocal themes: coherence, differentiation, alienation, and involvement. These may, in turn, be considered as two pairs of opposites. Social relations are constituted in some mutual regulation that can be experienced simultaneously as both impersonal and relevant demands. They involve an agreement, and also a temporal succession of exchanges. They involve the taking and giving of turns, the creation of parties to the agreement. They raise the matter of commitment to the future and to the memory of the past. Even where nothing tangible is produced—as in friendship—the previous coherence and differentiation constitute something left behind, something raising the matter of appropriation and alienation. Given the impersonal component to all personal matters, any one person may in principle select "how much" or how seriously he "puts himself" into the very succession of events constituting his life, while always remaining less than the whole of it.

Both Simmel and Durkheim direct their discoveries toward the serious life and the serious in life. Simmel, unlike Durkheim, considers in some detail the realm between the ordinary and the solemn, or between the actual and the ideal. He analyzes coquetry, sociability, and acting. These can hold up mirrors to the "real" or the "serious." They enact the distinctions and discrepancies between such contrasts as trivial and important, actual and possible; as "play-forms" of society, they help reveal the nature of the dumb and considered calculations, private or shared, that help constitute social arrangements. Social arrangements necessarily both involve and deflect images of relative importance. In that way they yield economies of exchange in emotions, goods, or ideas. The large-scale coherence of such economies does not explicitly concern Simmel. Instead, he writes often about our chances of ordering events to a notion of periphery or core. Questioningly, he comes to the conclusion that "deeper" people can survive only through maintaining a measure of superficiality. Ultimately, what-

9. See both the Introduction to *Philosophische Kultur* (Potsdam: Gustav Kirpenheuer Verlag, 1923), and the introductory quotation in *Fragmente und Aufsatze* (Munich: Drei Masken Verlag, 1923).

10. For one example of Mills's work, see his essay "Some Hypotheses on Small Groups from Simmel," *American Journal of Sociology*, LXIII, 642–50. H. B. Hawthorn has examined some aspects of the proposals on secrecy in "A Test of Simmel on the Secret Society: The Doukhobors of British Columbia," *American Journal of Sociology*, LXII, 1–7.

ever their logical compatibility, the several lines of moral assessment by which we constitute ourselves in society must clash insanely in any member of society who really thinks these matters through. Here Simmel meets Weber, who is said to have responded, when asked why he studied sociology, "To see how much I can stand!" By contrast, Durkheim is concerned with the aliveness of the resources to which collectivities can remain committed. Where Simmel sees conflict and alienation, Durkheim sees emptiness and the uncommitted pursuit of rituals as the inclusive, disruptive forces given with the very constitution of society itself.

Neither Simmel nor Durkheim, however, is adequate, alone or with the other, as a guide to attempting to isolate the major features of societies. They do not communicate a vivid sense of the large and rivalrous political units that claim men's lives and loyalties. Neither Durkheim nor Simmel asks about the ways in which national boundaries create political and other differences, while at the same time being cut across by strategic similarities—especially in the sphere of occupational ranking and the judgments of importance that such ranking can imply. Admittedly, even the relative political indifference of Simmel does not make his work irrelevant to those who wish to examine those commitments and structures involving the co-ordination and representation of men in their capacity as members of civil society or as voters, legislators, and government officials. Of the two, Simmel is primarily the apolitical thinker. Durkheim, after all, concerned himself with elites and with socialism.

As two major creators of sociology, Simmel and Durkheim complement each other. One lays before us a range of phenomena with which we can now compare the actual range of issues that have become included in our efforts. His distinctions must still be translated into the language of research; but his scope, where it exceeds ours, can be used for an assessment of our intellectual patterns of inclusion and exclusion. Admittedly, we may have to subordinate his intent to state, on the plane of ideas, the great flux of inner and outer occurrences to our wish to explain only some of them—yet how should we choose best? By contrast, the other presents an economy of continuous questions rather than a discontinuity of phenomena shown to have a constant structure. He produced a monograph that is a model of procedure. Simmel, for all his wish to write about life, cannot show us how to proceed—perhaps, precisely because he himself succeeded so persistently. But he can tell us clearly how much there is about which to ask. Between them, Durkheim and Simmel represent at least two sides of the study of social relations: the effort to bring social reality into a perspective that can be shared; and the effort to select a sufficiently clear question, whose answer will explain some strategic regularity.

Weber, Mead, Freud, or Pareto would not fit this oversimple pattern. Indeed, the contrast just discussed in no way exhausts comparisons between pioneers. We should now attempt, at even greater length, similar descriptions for Pareto or Mead, Freud or Weber. A huge literature, of course, has accumulated about Freud, including Ernest Jones's impressive three-volume biography. The biography, as its title suggests, deals with both Freud's life and his work, and suggests very clearly the ways that a style of life and a mode of work are—as they always are—mutually related. The growth of sociological thought is not merely a matter of the history of ideas. It is an aspect of the inner struggle of variously gifted people confronting themselves with old and new puzzles. Freud translated, into economic and elegant language, a clear and invading view of the character and cure of men and women; Max Weber, his contemporary, wrestled with an ancient trinity—the issues of economics, politics, and religion.

Weber, of all the sociologists represented in these two volumes, probably took most seriously Aristotle's formulation of man as a political animal. Weber was born in 1864; he died in 1920. Biographies of him have been written by his wife, Karl Jaspers, and Gerth and Mills, among others. These biographies, together with his work, show what he was: one of the last universal scholars, as well as a man much engaged in public life—while often also consumed by an illness that affected his capacity to read, write, or talk, frequently for considerable periods of time. His formal academic career began with the study of law, but it soon included economics and economic history. Toward the end of his career, in April, 1918, he lectured on what today might be called the sociology of religion. His work seems like a succession of huge, rich, dense fragments, unwaveringly reaching the heart of a circle of topics that today are distributed among many kinds of experts. Besides a general economic history, he wrote a series of studies of the political economy in the Middle Ages, in eastern Germany, and in antiquity. For instance, in 1896 he published an essay on the social causes of the decline of classical culture, in which he analyzes the decline of an urban culture surrounded by a rising rural and feudal culture. He shows this to be related to the decline of slavery, the rise of kinship, and private property, within the mass of the otherwise underprivileged. The imagery alone of this essay justifies consulting it in the original; but it is one essay among many within the domain of social economic history and within that wider domain of social change about which Weber wrote. Characteristically, he wrote essays, not books. A series of his essays deal with methodological issues: the notion of understanding, the use of ideal types, the sense in which there can be a systematic study of both the structure and history of society that goes beyond economics and history.

For our purposes, two sequences of essays stand out. One, which in English one might call "Economy and Society," is at once an explication of various fundamental sociological categories and a set of observations on the generic properties of the strategic constituent phenomena of complicated societies. In this connection Weber proposes his famous analysis of authority and of bureaucracy. He writes about forms of social stratification and of ethnic association, about the market-place as well as about the city. The series includes lengthy analyses of the domains of law and of religion. It ends with an essay on music—which, had Weber lived longer, would presumably have been the first in another series of essays devoted to the social relations of art.

Even his most well known series, the essays on religious systems, is in fact incomplete. He was to have filled the gap between the end of the essay on ancient Judaism and the beginning of the essay on Luther and Calvin with a corresponding analysis of the early Christian church. If Weber did have one central intellectual concern, it was with the relations between the major domains within society, seen under the aspect of their change. This involved a concern with the alternative forms of economic life in relation to the alternative forms of moral commitment that have so far provided the structure of history, particularly in the West. He knew how to stay close to important distinctions. If he asked about the conditions necessary for the rise of capitalism, he also assumed that these prerequisites would not be necessary for its maintenance. Concerned with the motives of men, he also was aware that the actions which they impelled would produce unintended consequences. Deeply concerned with the possibilities of freedom within men's actions, he was also concerned with freeing himself from illusions about the conditionality of human actions and the relativity of the moral commitments guiding them. If he saw in the progressive rationalization—facilitated by the engine of bureaucracy—at least one consuming trend in the history of the West, he was not blind to the non- and irrational elements that also guide men.

He was concerned with education and the alternative educational ideals exhibited by the cultures of Greece, of China, of England, and of the contemporary industrialized West. He also saw that educational ideals and practices are discussed and implemented within a going society, whose course of change is always affected by the intended and unintended economic and associated social arrangements that give it shape.

In reading Weber, one can see him in many ways. He may be seen as a man struggling alike against the vague, even irresponsible, claims of the German idealistic and intuitionist tradition of his time, and against the too narrow perspective of a classical Marxian analysis. Or one can read him as a man truly imprisoned by a productive inner treadmill that seeks to declare the anatomy of capitalism and of the inward alternative meanings of Hindu or Confucian or Hebraic or Puritan thought. At the same time, he was engaged in politics; he went to Versailles in 1918; he engaged in political polemics. It is not surprising that the center of gravity of his explicit categorial system is action, and the ways of relating ends and means that are in fact open to the individual. If his work does not include an attempt at a systematic view of human character, Weber's particular greatness appears in its most distilled form in the chapter on the sociology of religion that forms part of his two-volume work on the economy and society. In the twelve sections of this chapter, he reduces the idiosyncratic profusion of a large range of history, and uses types and distinctions that make the systematic study of society feasible.

In the section on estates, classes, and religion, the mutual relations between styles of life, economic position, and forms of religious commitment are masterfully discussed. He shows, for example, how, within the circles of privileged groups, an idea of dignity is consonant with a certain antipathy to salvation religions; while less privileged people are inclined to complement their present deprivation by a concern with future amelioration. In Weber's view, the privileged man receives confirmation of his dignity from the state of things already surrounding him; by contrast, the under-privileged nourishes his sense of dignity on notions of "calling," "function," and "mission." In their intention, these concepts are transcendent.

But out of context, this description is too simple, and unfair to Weber. Yet the full context of Weber's writings is still available in English only unevenly, in a variety of different translations.[11]

Considering Weber, then, makes the previous contrast between Durkheim and Simmel become a more complicated triangle. Durkheim wanted to formulate relatively precise proposals concerning the relations between the structure of social rela-

11. This was written before the appearance of Reinhard Bendix's most helpful *Max Weber: An Intellectual Portrait* (New York: Doubleday, 1960).

tions and identifiable, preferably measurable, specific patterns of events; Weber stated a far-flung and wild profusion of connections between the understandable orientation of different circles in any one society and the characteristic features of the economic, legal, educational, and class characteristics of the same society. Simmel was continuously concerned with the structure of *relations* of two or more people and the paradoxical formulations necessary for their essential characterization; Weber seems more concerned with the conditions of individual action and their intended or unintended consequences, when these are observed within the context of variously distributed styles of life and forms of power. What Simmel enjoys as paradox, Weber suffers as antinomy. Weber confronts us with the conflict between traditional and rational consideration, between an ethic of intention and an ethic of responsibility, between the educational ideal of a specialized and technical expert and that of a cultivated gentleman. More than Simmel and Durkheim, Weber is a pessimist—but a pessimist who is also a stoic. He is free from self-pity.

The study of the perspective necessary for the analysis of society is not the same as the study of the personalities of those who helped create these perspectives. Yet it is equally certain that the theories proposed or the problems selected for analysis presuppose certain combinations of human qualities. In other words, people who are alienated or self-pitying, or resentful about the strivings and circumstances of others whom they wish to understand, are likely to propose different formulations from those proposed by others who are stoic, compassionate, or morally incensed. It is vitally important not to confuse a knowledge of the origins of a view with an assessment of its claim. Jealousy can generate insights which are no less valid for being the fruits of jealousy. Yet certain insights may grow only on the grounds of qualities like courage, compassion, or commitment. This problem must be left unsolved, though the study of society continually poses it.

The readers of this Reader should form their own image of the progression and coherence in the work of the above men and others. There is, after all, more than one way of regarding the direction and whole of their work.

## ON THE TIMING OF THE BIRTH OF SOCIOLOGY

Only living creatures are born in a single act of parturition; a scientific discipline, like sociology, has no clear single beginning. Inherently, it has no end. Still, before the nineteenth century, there was no sociology—at least, none in the sense in which this Reader and these Introductions use the term. Yet, since Comte first coined the expression "sociology," the sociological developments that have occurred would have been impossible without ideas, distinctions, and procedures that had taken many centuries to become settled possessions of the intellectuals, particularly in the Occident.

*Sociology* is a bastard term: it has a Latin beginning, a Greek ending, and many intervening and variable meanings. Comte conceived it as a positive science—as part of the great effort to master life and the world through the impersonal accomplishments of a human reason that had freed itself of what, in retrospect, would then become recognized as the less reliable and less true claims of religion or philosophy. He conceived it as a discipline yielding laws and providing statements of interpreted fact that had the authority of the formulations of physical science. He saw sociology as providing, eventually, means of predicting and of having power over social events. His explicit hopes, and the appropriateness and possibility of their implementation, have led to much argument. We are still debating the precise range of variation of ideas and procedures that the single expression "science" can accommodate, or the exact boundaries that separate it from other forms of knowledge, like literature. There is no simple consensus, either, on the minimal conditions that a discipline must meet before it may appropriately be called a science, or on the actual differences between the social, biological, and physical sciences. The logic of these matters is compounded by considerations of power and honor.

Scientific disciplines are not valued equally within a society. Their fortunes are uneven, and they are subject, among other forces, to destruction by unfavorable political climates. The history of sociology in Germany during the last sixty years fully illustrates this. Still, Comte asserted the systematic intelligibility of social phenomena—and gave this understanding a name that implied methods. These methods were to make the understanding a great scientific enterprise, which in turn would benefit a mankind growing reasonable through practicing the methods and benefiting from their results. The vision has been scattered—in various ways, the component elements of Comte's conceptions have become distributed over the work of his successors. The dependence of science, itself an organized and social pattern of efforts, on institutions, climates of opinion, and specially motivated and trained people, has become established beyond question. The controversy about the actual difference between social and natural science continues. Still, social phenomena—for all their intelligibility and their frequent, almost impersonal, yet constraining "there-ness"—have become irrevocably defined to include a recognition of the fact that they are sustained among persons; they involve previous notions of appropriateness and depend on some emotional involvement of variously placed participants. At some point, it is necessary to ask, in explaining a social phenomenon, with what meaning one or more persons began or continued a sequence of events. Such events are perceived as forming (or coming from) a pattern of regularities that no one person, or plurality of persons, intended. Wars, birth rates, cities, the uneven participation of a few people in a small gathering, the role conflicts of foremen, the volume of suicide and divorce, the class structure of a community—no one intends these, no one can, alone and directly, bring them about. Yet they presuppose persons, or persons intending to form others into persons, who can ask questions or keep quiet, expect others and themselves to do certain things and not do certain other things, draw lines between what makes (common) sense and what does not. Comte clearly argued that such lines are unreliable. Society involves people's ideas concerning it. Yet these ideas may, through being incomplete or mistaken, be quite erroneous. Our economy is apprehended, by a majority, with a mixture of ignorance and distortion; the extent of this mixture might be discovered by research.

Comte and Spencer, without so expressing it, intended to found a discipline that would confront the varied and subjective experience those who in fact constitute society have of it, with a body of reliable (i.e., objective) knowledge concerning the social order. We know that such knowledge must proceed with reference to the subjective experiences of people. The very order of these experiences, and their divergencies from facts collected by a differently placed observer, constitute, at least, in part, that which is to be explained. The vision of Comte and Spencer also included the desire to see the historical and geographic expanse of society, and its fragmentary appearance to individuals, as a valid whole. They were content to realize such desires through the help of ideas from biology and physics. History has demonstrated that the use of such analogies is both inevitable and precarious. Societies are not organisms; yet the idea of function implied in the biological usage of the term *organism* is a useful device for declaring the natural connection, often hidden, between a variety of recurrent events.

Unlike the growth of organisms, the growth of sociology as a field has occurred through its becoming smaller in its reach. Having become concerned with "making findings," it is no longer free from arranging social reality into technically manageable pieces or areas. This has led to a process of inner differentiation. Recently, it has posed problems of the coherence of such efforts. I shall return to these matters in another section of this set of observations on the development of sociological analysis.

To the question, "What explanation is available for the timing of the birth of sociology?" we can give no single or definite answer. We know that the thought of children has its timetable. One of the most productively single-minded and devoted students of the individual history of the categories and logic of adult thinking, Jean Piaget, has persuasively demonstrated the shifts by which we arrive, so far as we do, at the ability to think logically. It is probable that there are some parallels between individual and social development. In biology, this parallel is expressed in the famous dictum: ontogeny recapitulates phylogeny. Yet this mode of thought, unless great caution is exercised, is likely to repeat the errors of Comte and Spencer. The relation between groups and individuals is, after all, different from the relations between individuals and their species or phyla. Besides, the social sciences, as late arrivals, do not represent a mode of knowing and explaining that is "higher" or "more adult"—whatever these ambiguous yet inescapable terms may mean—than the forms of knowledge, be they physics, mathematics, or chemistry, that preceded them. At times, however, people seem inclined to see, in the precision and determinateness of the physical sciences, an unambiguous model for the straggling, late arrival of the social sciences. We cannot stop to wonder now whether many sociologists, with notable exceptions, have, at least until quite recently, had little working acquaintance with the inner struggles of physical science, historically and individually—whether they have exaggerated their precision and neatness, and have then applied models to their own work that are valid for no scientific work.

In reaction against this, some have suggested that social science is, after all, an art. In these terms, the debate seems fast becoming a matter of past misunderstandings and ambiguities. The genuine elements of the debate, as well as the fruitfulness of its very errors, must concern us presently; here, let it suffice to suggest that any explanation of the historic sequence of scientific disciplines must first free itself from those conceptions of a hierarchy (as distinct from a sequence) of the sciences that inspired Comte. This error may have been (psychologically, if not logically) necessary for his conception of sociology. Retrospectively, "correct" as well as "incorrect" ideas are fruitful in the arduous process of accumulating valid proposals about the character of social phenomena.

Our question about the birth of sociology has become complicated. Why was it founded at Comte's time? We also want to know why the sequence of scientific disciplines has taken the form it has. This leads to the question: Under what conditions, if any, could the history of science have been very different? Could Newton and Adam Smith have done their work in reverse chronological order? We shall be concerned with answers to these and other implied questions, to the extent to which they ultimately help define and reveal the structure and history of social arrangements. We shall assume that deliberately gathered knowledge grows only under some social conditions, that a line of intellectual effort continues to pose new tasks, and that science yields many consequences for social arrangements. The last may take the more obvious and massive forms of technology or of the practices of various professions, like medicine. They can occur as conflicts between various circles within a society or within persons. The history of sociology has included a part in the ostensible conflict between religion and science. One might even suggest that the development of the social sciences itself is an aspect of the rationalization and disenchantment of the world—to employ terms which some, notably Max Weber, have used to characterize broad historic tendencies and directions of the drift of social change by which we come to recognize some of the differences between the present and the past.

The social consequences of the sciences are huge and subtle. They include the creation of special institutional forms for the recruitment and training of people capable of sustaining scientific work. They also include the necessity for formal and informal arrangements whereby the continuous dialogue between common sense and divergent discovery may be absorbed by a society, both through a continuous and almost imperceptible process of revising ideas, and through concentrated crises. The debate about evolution and the resultant Scopes trial in the United States, the discussion of the Dead Sea Scrolls, book burning, or the commemoration of men defined as great—e.g., Freud, Durkheim, Simmel, Darwin—are illustrations of such crises or turning points. But they are not sufficient to account for the difference between, e.g., a Detroit automobile worker's conception of nature and society in the 1950's and the conceptions of a Greek slave, an Old Testament Israelite shepherd, a medieval tinsmith in Paris, and a nineteenth-century wall painter in Germany.

This drift is borne along by events within and outside it. By Comte's time, it had accomplished some remarkable combinations of qualities. Physics and chemistry were established. A growing technology and a growing romanticism helped shape the nineteenth century. Biology was about to extend radically our knowledge of organisms as a type of order, by stating regularities concerning the historical succession of organisms. In turn, this involves the *relations* among organisms and between them and the environment. The nineteenth century included the fast-growing establishment of industry and of technology in general, expressing both mastery—and potentially more leisure for more people—and some kind of victimization. Machines can be experienced as the source of boredom and as alien tools.

Marx had much to say on this score. He indicated the processes which he felt divided society increasingly into exploiters and exploited. He linked social diagnosis with political ideology, just as theology had earlier been linked with a view of man. But there was far more than that: the pessimism of Malthus; the Darwinian definition of existence as involving a struggle; the prudery of the Victorians; the increasing ugliness in the growing cities; Nietzsche's call for a certain inner honesty and strength; the discovery—through better communication—of the variedness and consequent relativity of beliefs and moral commitments; the contradictory clamor of romanticism and technological advance, socialist counter-ideologies and rising entrepreneurs; nationalist developments (particularly in Germany, Italy, and France); and, at the end of the century, the discovery through systematic thought, that a "true" image of man must allow far more room for his "irrationality."

In retrospect, it would seem that sociology could have developed only when a certain kind of puzzlement (and even practical urgency) coincided with a faith in inquiry and a disbelief in both "revealed" truths concerning the immediate character of man and his arrangements, and in "rational speculation." The relatively late development of the social sciences in the history of science—if one may put it that way—can be attributed in part to the character of society itself. Only after its complexity becomes compounded by industrialization and its many associated features do conditions arise requiring or facilitating the deliberate and impersonal analysis of personal and social phenomena. This assertion does not imply that the study of society is only as old as the term *sociology*—that would be a silly error. Everything has many forerunners. Here, we are concerned only with the relatively systematic study of social phenomena, carried on within established institutions of the society under examination.

Sociology requires a variety of dissociations. It thrives on the distinction between normative and existential propositions. It must distinguish, almost ruthlessly, a concern with "what is" from a concern with "what ought to be," while also remembering that the relative "openness" of the social order always makes it relevant to ask the further, yet equally distinct, question: What can be? It must retain a keen sense of these distinctions, precisely because many of its facts are, in fact, constituted by the moral judgments of persons in their capacities as members, representatives, or detractors of the multitude of separate and overlapping social arrangements comprising a society.

Yet social arrangements themselves involve judgments and commitments of importance and of appropriateness, as well as various bodies of knowledge or opinion concerning the nature of things—including people. In reality, these judgments are intermingled. Grammatically, they are often confused. The "self-evident truth" that men are born equal is really a moral decision, to see, running across men's uniqueness and their difference, an equal right to certain kinds of opportunity. Only as moral judgments within the same sphere of decision become subject to varied controversy can a previous fusion of moral commitments, opinions about the world, and participation in society be dissolved. It is only when such dissolution affects a number of people and challenges them to share a like interest in its examination that a discipline like sociology can gain momentum. Once begun, such an examination necessarily means questioning any and all social facts. Yet societies involve a measure of secrecy and sacredness, as part of the potent notions of privacy and security; secrecy also inheres in the use of power. Ironically enough, sociology began to flourish just when *private* capitalist enterprise gained great momentum and extended earlier traditions of individualism. Sociology owes much of its impetus in this connection to Durkheim, who demonstrated cogently that individualism itself is a form of social arrangement, and that the disparate goals of lonely strivers after wealth, salvation, happiness, or amusement are possible only as the other side of a consensus that demands and allows this very disparateness.

While Comte and Spencer were, in a sense, the founders of sociology, one might also refer to them as protosociologists and consider that sociology really originated with Durkheim and Weber. Durkheim is the first to make the social order deliberately problematic and, as such, an object of disinterested inquiry. This involves a radical break with the past; but, once this break has been made, sociologists' efforts can be shown, as in this Reader, to exhibit important continuities with the past. Ultimately, the questions that sociologists ask today are continuations of the questions that Hobbes asked.

It has been the theme of this essay, though, that the growth of sociology involves, as a necessary, not as a sufficient, condition, an accomplishment of dissociation. This must proceed on at least two planes. The human order, with its gravitation toward questions of meaning and of value, must be distinguished from the non-human order. Within the human order, the distinction between personal and impersonal patterns must be clear. Distinctions, of course, do not deny continuities; properly used, they warn against reductionism. When reductionism is avoided, one is free to see parallels in, e.g., biological and social evolution, and continuities between the organic realm and the motives of human personalities.

Perhaps, again, the dissociation of society into ostensibly independent actors and seekers is a precondition for the search for the anatomy of society. This search, to return to the previous point, can logically have no end. It cannot exclude the secret or the sacred—both of which are necessary features of *all* societies, as subsequent thought and research has now clearly shown. Sociology cannot proceed, therefore, until a radical measure of intellectual freedom is safe. This freedom is continuous with the freedom requisite for the physical sciences, but presents its own additional complications. The social sciences benefited from the struggles that had to be fought, against a variety of vested interests, so that the theories of Newton or Galileo, the dissection of the body, and the teaching of evolution could be sufficiently accepted as legitimate resources in the further development of valid knowledge.

The only writer prominent in these two volumes whose thought involved him in serious and continuing conflict with significant parts of his social environment was Freud. If a dramatic struggle with an opposing world is a necessary mark for greatness of intellect, sociology has not produced many great men so far. In any case, sociology depends on the freedom to see the constraining and liberating qualities of social arrangements, while looking beyond their "heaviness" and treating any one group or institution as though it could also be otherwise.

In that sense, sociology is a curious mixture of a most sober and secular effort to state the processes through which society achieves its order, and standing beyond that order with a perspective that is logically akin to utopianism but does not seek after perfection. The growth of sociology requires distance; it demands participants who observe. It calls for small- and large-scale "accounting" of the measurable facts, just as economics depends for its growth on the availability of a variety of statistics concerning production, consumption, gross national products, etc. The nineteenth century saw the large-scale development of keeping national accounts of economic, demographic, and medical facts. The arrangement of such facts into rates further symbolizes the non-personal elements in personal affairs.

Many additional considerations must be brought into mutual relation and focus for a proper explanation of the timing of the rise of sociology. A child must learn that the world contains more than human motives; the history of science proceeded almost in the reverse direction.

## CONCLUSION

During its hundred years or so of formal existence, sociological questioning has clarified its focus and widened its concern. Ultimately, the widely distributed efforts at comprehending birth rates and triangles, voting and trade unions, professional activities and the pursuit of leisure, circle about the chronic questions: What are the persistent properties of social relations and the arrangements they imply? What range of combinations do and can social relations assume, and how do these combinations come about, change, or cease? As argued above, these questions lead to efforts on more than one plane within the boundary of the social. Today, inevitably, they also lead to attempts to realign, into productive combinations, the social and cognate concerns with the psychological or the cultural components of life in society. Their proper distinction and combination, leading to a productive division of labor and coherence of effort, is a matter of continuous experiment and revision.

Such experiment and revision can take the form of concerted efforts, in a given and circumscribed area of empirical research, by people trained in different disciplines. Issues of culture and personality, mental illness, national character, the structure of small groups, etc., have become occasions for collaboration among anthropologists, social and clinical psychologists, sociologists, and psychiatrists. At present, sociology is also re-establishing a solid interest in phenomena traditionally labeled as "political" or "economic" and, as such, "reserved" for political scientists or economists.

Co-operation among sociologists committed to seemingly very different theoretical perspectives has been far less frequent. Yet these volumes are likely to be read by a generation of younger sociologists who are taught, if not involved in, a *convergence* of theoretical positions. This convergence—for which there already exist diverse formulations—is accompanied by the growth of inner differentiation. Such growth involves various fashions and fads. It also leads to the founding of special, more or less formal, groupings devoted to a specific line of inquiry, such as research on public opinion, on medical institutions, on social problems, or on industrial organization.

The multitude of sociological endeavors that go on today bear a relation to the past. They also yield an emergent coherence, discussed by Edward Shils at the end of this Reader.

The past, from which we have selected, has here been ordered into an arrangement that is only one of several possible arrangements of these materials. It is, however, not an arbitrary arrangement. The general rationale behind it is discussed in the other introductory essay. These selections illustrate the several planes of sociological analysis. In one way, as stated, the most persistent concern has been with the generic properties of social relations themselves, about which one may well ask: What kind of an order is the social order? Various answers are represented in this Reader. Malthus and Marx, Hobbes and Machiavelli, Weber and Freud would, if they could discuss it together, weave quite an argument. Their logical differences would first be obscured by their different preferences for a starting point and for the respective features of social reality which each prefers to dissect. Their differences might be ordered with reference to a few further questions.

Eventually, they would have to contrast the social form of coherence to other forms of coherence, like those of nature, music, mathematics, or an individual. Various alternatives seem open. Society can be conceived as an entirely natural phenomenon, thus preventing it from escaping systematic inquiry and becoming an ideal or mystic, or even partly supernatural, phenomenon. One can insist that the "natural" is a relatively narrower category and that the "non-natural" comprises a variety of orders, some admitting of scientific exploration. One can leave ultimate questions of reality open, but insist on some provisional distinctions—such as the differences between mechanical, organic, and psychological processes—which in turn stand for the assumption that there is coherence in a working electric range and a bridge party, in a jumping frog and in a man's contemplation during a Quaker meeting. They are coherences that are *similar* and *different.* Their similarity consists in their being, at least in principle, equally open to scientific research; their difference consists in the fact that the distinctions necessary to explain their occurrence or operation would be seriously different.

The constitution of social coherence, in its contrasts or similarity to other coherences, including nature, is a basic theme with sociological theorists. This has been accompanied by three additional themes: Section C of Part One of the Reader introduces one of these, just as the first two sections of Part One introduce the theme of the constitution of social relations. Section C raises the questions: What kinds or forms of social coherence is it necessary or useful to distinguish? What sorts of social relations—and with the help of the combination of what recurrent variables—must be analytically separated? What types of society is it necessary to recognize?

To a degree, this is the theme of classification. Classification is not sufficient for scientific development; but it is assuredly necessary—logically as well as historically. The history of biology bears out this contention most unequivocally.

The growth of sociological theory has, then, included a persistent concern with alternative ways of defining the major elements of social relations—alternatively labeling them actions, norms, ends, means, roles, expectations, and so forth—and then finding ways of distinguishing kinds of them. Such effort has reached up and down; it has included attempts to formulate, e.g., types of society, types of authority, types of groups, types of kinship systems.

A third theme has been to distinguish more inclusive coherences, like communities or national societies, and to propose a steady way for designating their component "spheres." Part Two of the Reader takes up this theme. Together, these themes provide a framework for finding and stating regularities that then need explanation. They confront common sense with the possibilities of seeing connections where our experience might show none; and of proposing distinctions in areas where, impelled by the economy of having to act, we must as acting members of society, "lump things together" in order not to be paralyzed by a sense of complexity.

A further theme, then, has been to state the processes by which social arrangements cohere, endure, change, begin, or end. Less, perhaps, is said directly about this in this Reader than is said about the other themes. Nevertheless, the last three parts contain some relevant material. Theoretical developments that have taken place since our self-imposed time limits have made substantial contributions to this theme of the dynamic of social arrangements.

Two additional themes may now be identified. One concerns the link—and, therefore, the distinction—between social coherences (in the form of formal organizations or purely voluntaristic relations, like those of friendship) and personality, on the one hand, or culture, on the other. Or, more broadly: in what sense is the social a reality *sui generis?* What kind of autonomy does this imply? What kinds of dependence do social arrangements sustain to different kinds of other orders, be these systems of expression and meaning (like language), personalities, or various kinds of non-social conditions, like numbers of people, spatial possibilities, states of organic functioning?

The other theme is related to a matter of method. Lack of space prevented us from discussing the craft of research and developments of specific techniques as integral elements of the development of sociological theory. Yet the Reader as a whole is, in fact, a declaration of sociological questioning. Questions imply a method and demand techniques. Sociology, as a discipline—and, hence, a method—of inquiry deals with the facts of which history is made. In the name of experimentation, it can also create small passages of history. Yet it differs from history as a discipline. It is concerned with regularities. They can be studied only in time and place, but their formulation seeks to be more generally valid and to be applicable to the future. The twin face of sociology—its inevitable link to history, albeit often immediate history, and to the analytic enterprise of discovering regularities indifferent to the uniqueness of events—is best prevented from becoming a caricature by a deliberately comparative perspective.

Comparison can take several forms and proceed on several planes. Much of Max Weber's work has been included in this Reader. On the planes of world religions, national societies, and the interdependence of the spheres of the economy, the polity, and normative orientations, he has used historic comparison. Comparison is possible only when one combines a vivid sense of the variedness of social relations and the relativity of cultural facts with a steady sense of the recurrent features of social arrangements. It remains a difficult task to formulate these features in such a way that one is not unduly influenced by one rather than another pattern of culture and society. Much social reality is sufficiently "soft" that one can read into it interpretations which cannot be clearly corrected. Interpretations of social facts, moreover, become themselves the grounds for additional facts. Their occurrence is no proof of the correctness of one's original claims. Comparison—beyond the point where it inheres in the use of logical reasoning and proof as such—seems to mark the best sociological writing.

In this way, the simplicity and elusiveness of society moves properly into view. Much sociological writing seems suspended between two images. One of these conceives of society as the arrangements of sleepwalkers; and the other, as a play involving both actors and audience, a stage and a realm behind the scene. Obviously, both images are appropriate, and both are incomplete. Nor can sociologists seek after completeness: completeness is the privilege of art. Social action goes far beyond sleepwalking and play-acting. Rational planning and ritual, the deliberate creation of new communities and the destruction of old prerogatives, the serious life—all these are social facts. The excerpts assembled here will surely help in the progressive understanding and explanation of the characteristic ways in which social relations combine simplicity with complexity and unconscious resources with self-awareness.

# II. *An Outline of the Social System*

## BY TALCOTT PARSONS

THIS SECOND PART OF THE GENeral Introduction is designed to present an outline of the main conceptual resources of current sociological theory. It is necessarily incomplete in at least two ways. First, it is inevitably a personal statement, using components and the ways of organizing them that seem most strategic to the author. Any discerning reader will recognize that these materials come from many sources. But this is not meant to be a scholarly essay in the history of theory, attempting to document the immense diversity of sources and influences. It is, on the contrary, guided by a conviction of the enormous significance of the element of system in the theory of any scientific discipline. Because of this, great attention had to be given to the systematic fit of the different theoretical components, regarding both their selection and their empirical significance. At the present stage of theoretical development, any such systematic attempt must be tentative. Major changes are to be expected, as have indeed occurred within the course even of its relatively mature development.

Second, this outline is incomplete because, long as it is for an introduction, it is a mere fragment of what would be required to make the best possible case for systematic theory by outlining an adequate systematic theory; this would clearly require a major treatise.[1] Thus, the present essay is deficient in conceptual precision. It includes only a very fragmentary statement of the logical, methodological, and empirical grounds for selecting such concepts. Furthermore, the development it presents is incomplete, and the application to empirical materials is merely illustrative.

The principal gain, however, bought at the cost of these and doubtless other deficiencies, is the attempt to cover all the main problems that a systematic theory must face.

This attempt has been based on the conviction that there are two essential reference points for this type of systematic analysis: a classification of the functional requirements of a system and the arrangement of these with reference to processes of control in the cybernetic sense. More specifically, the theory of social systems belongs within the more general class of conceptual schemes seen in the frame of reference of *action*. Within that framework, the boundaries of social systems have been defined in terms of their relations, first to each other, then to the behavioral organism, to the personality of the individual, and to cultural systems. The relation to the physical environment is mediated through these others, and hence is not direct. Seen in this context, a social system is always "open," engaged in processes of interchange with environing systems.

It will further be held that most empirically significant sociological theory must be concerned with complex systems, that is, systems composed of many subsystems. Hence the primary empirical type-reference has been to the society, which, in the nature of the case, is highly complex.

The basic functional classification underlying the whole scheme involves the discrimination of four primary categories: pattern-maintenance, integration, goal-attainment, and adaptation, placed in that order in the series of control-relations. But, on another axis, it has been necessary to discriminate the structural components of such systems. These will always constitute patterns of institutionalized normative culture, differentiated both functionally and by levels of specification and of segmentation of units of the system. The structural classification is organized about the concepts of system values, institutionalized norms, collectivities, and roles.

It will also be necessary to categorize and classify

1. From the author's point of view this would take the form of a rather far-reaching revision of his earlier book, *The Social System* (1951). To be reasonably adequate, the result would have to be a longer book than that one was (about 550 pages).

the resources involved in the interchange processes, not only between a society and its environing systems, but between subsystems within the society. From these, finally, must be distinguished the regulatory mechanisms, like money, which are involved in dynamic process.

More generally, a fundamental distinction will be made between the morphological analysis of the structure of systems and the "dynamic" analysis of process. Neither has special priority over the other except that, at a particular level, stable structural reference points are necessary for determining generalizations about process. Furthermore, with respect to process, it is necessary to distinguish the "equilibrium" level of analysis, which assumes structure to be given, from the "structural change" level, which attempts to explain such processes of change. In the empirical analysis of complex systems, however, it is almost always necessary to assume some structural elements to be given while analyzing processes of change in others, particularly changes in the structure of subsystems of the more extensive system.

These seem to be the minimum of theoretical problems and components which must be taken into account in any sociological theory that lays claim to systematic generality. We think that all of them grow out of the work of the authors of the selections which follow. Considerable variations from their proposals here put forward would probably result if other contemporary theorists attempted such a task. But we think they would be primarily variations of emphasis, rather than departures from the basic theoretical structure with which we are concerned. Whether or not this is true, only critical reaction to this and other attempts, and to theoretical analysis of empirical data, can tell. Such reaction will be one of the most important tests of how far sociology can be said to be on the way to consolidation as a genuine theoretically codified field of science.

It may also help the reader's orientation to this introductory material if something is said about the stages by which it has developed in the author's own work. The most important sources are: for the central conception of the social system and the bases of its integration, the work of Durkheim; for the comparative analysis of social structure and for the analysis of the borderline between social systems and culture, that of Max Weber; and for the articulation between social systems and personality, that of Freud. The first main stage of thinking was documented, in terms of critical analysis of the work of several other theorists, in *The Structure of Social Action* (1937). A new phase of theoretical integration, particularly involving systematization of the general frame of reference of action and the articulation of social systems with those of culture and of personality, was documented in the two publications, *Toward a General Theory of Action*, in collaboration with Shils and others, and *The Social System* (both 1951). The scheme was further systematized and extended, particularly by consolidating the "pattern variables" into the scheme of the four fundamental functional problems of all systems of action, in *Working Papers in the Theory of Action*, with Bales and Shils (1953). The articulation between social systems and personality, with special reference to the process of socialization, was further explored in *Family, Socialization and Interaction Process*, with Bales and others (1955); finally, the present phase of the analysis of input-output relations and of the relations between a total social system and its subsystems was further developed in *Economy and Society*, with Smelser (1956).

## *Some Areas of Current Theoretical Consensus*

Part I of this General Introduction has rightly stressed the indefiniteness of the boundaries of sociology and the ways in which these have tended to shift. The diversity of points of view from which important questions have been and may be asked, and of the frames of reference in which answers may be obtained, has also been discussed.

However, we believe that there is a substantial element of cumulative continuity, which becomes the more clearly visible when seen in temporal perspective. This element of continuity can be observed at different levels. In certain very general terms, something approaching consensus can be claimed among those who may be considered professionally competent. But, as the content of theory becomes more particularized, agreement tends to give way to a war of conflicting schools. Even here, however, the question of just how deep these differences are is a relevant one. It is our conviction that much explicit disagreement conceals implicit consensus.[2]

2. In my own case, this conviction was firmly established as a result of the work done in connection with *The Structure of Social Action*, referred to above. That study dealt primarily with four major figures in the theory of social systems of the generation from approximately 1890–1915: Alfred Marshall, Vilfredo Pareto, Emile Durkheim, and Max Weber. Judging by the secondary literature available at the time, they should be considered as diverse in points of view as any four thinkers one could have picked. It was possible, however, to demonstrate that their major conceptual schemes converged in terms of a common frame of reference and, at certain levels, a common substantive theoretical system. This common scheme was not confined to the work of these four men; with important further developments, it has been just as central to subsequent work.

Probably the greatest consensus exists regarding the applicability to our discipline of the general canons of scientific method. The battle about whether science is possible in the field of human social behavior may be said to be over in its main phase, however much may remain to be settled on many of the subtler points, particularly the borderline problems.

This agreement clearly includes the role of theory in science and the nature of the conceptual schemes which scientific theory employs; most scholars would accept the basic methodological premises formulated in the work of such writers as A. N. Whitehead, L. J. Henderson, and James B. Conant. Despite differences of emphasis and preference for personal types of work, the old battle of theory *versus* empiricism may be considered to be over. The same may be said regarding the merits of nomothetic *versus* ideographic modes of conceptualization. Logically, the situation seems to be entirely parallel to that of heredity and environment in the biological sciences, where the formulation in terms of "versus" is now largely obsolete. Since this Reader is concerned with the development of theory, consensus on this point is vital.

With regard to theory itself as a vital component of organized scientific knowledge, and to theoretical formulations as crucial tools of investigation, two somewhat more specific points may also be claimed as fundamental and generally accepted. The first of these is the role of analytical abstraction in all the more general theoretical schemes of science. Theoretical schemes are made up of concepts and logically interrelated propositions. To be capable of logical manipulation, such schemes must always be relatively simple and cannot possibly embrace everything empirically knowable about the concrete phenomena at hand. They must select, i.e., abstract, according to their own criteria of relevance to theoretical problems.

Finally, the concept of system is also vital to science. Besides empirical validity and conceptual precision, there are two other essential criteria of the scientific usefulness of sets of theoretical propositions, namely, their level of generality with reference to empirical phenomena and their logical integration with each other. The concept of system is essentially nothing but an application of the criterion of logical integration of generalized propositions. That is, theoretical propositions are scientifically useful in so far as they are general and are related in such ways that data accounted for by one proposition may, by logical inference, be shown to have implications for data that should fit into other propositions in the set. The difference between description and theoretical explanation is precisely that between the isolation of particular propositions and their integration with each other in such ways that logical inference is possible.

Logical integration, or systematization, is in this sense a matter of degree. The ideal, however, is a system of propositions so related that their logical *inter*dependence is complete, so that all the propositions in the system can be rigorously derived from a set of primary postulates and definitions. Few schemes of scientific theory have approached this goal, but it remains the ideal and provides essential critical canons. We do not claim, of course, that the scheme presented here possesses anything approaching complete logical integration.

Systematization of theory clearly implies the concept of *empirical* system as its counterpart; this follows from the point made about analytical abstraction. If theory is to be empirically relevant, it must present demonstrably verifiable patterns of interdependence among empirical phenomena. In order to do this, however, it must delineate and classify phenomena according to criteria of relevance and importance. An empirical system, then, is a body of presumptively interdependent phenomena to which a given abstract analytical scheme is presumptively relevant. It is impossible to study everything at once empirically. An empirical system is a theoretically defined field of relevant phenomena, with reference to which certain problem-statements have been abstracted.

So far, the points of agreement have concerned matters common to all the empirical sciences. Approaching our own field more closely, another crucial point should be made, namely, that the study of human social behavior necessarily involves a frame of reference here called "action." The term itself is not important. But the content it refers to is highly so. Essentially, it means a type of theoretical scheme incompatible with the form of "reductionism" characteristic of a great deal of our earlier scientific tradition. Action treats behavior as "goal-directed," as "adaptive," as "motivated," and as guided by symbolic processes. The concept of culture as developed in anthropology is crucial here. Another way of putting the matter is that neither the theory of mechanics in the older sense nor that of nineteenth-century physiology would be adequate if simply "applied" to the behavioral field.

A major focus of this problem was the "behaviorist" controversy of the 1920's. The behaviorist position was a major example of reductionism and tended to deny the scientific legitimacy of all "subjective" categories, of all concepts of "meaning." As in the battles over the status of science itself and over empiricism in this area, it can be said that the fight is over. Sociological theory today is clearly couched in terms of motives, goals, symbols, meanings, means and ends, and the like.

In short, I have suggested that general agreement exists regarding the relevance of the classical canons of scientific method; the significance of analytical theory within this method; the necessity of analytical abstraction for theory; the concept of system; and, finally, the "action" frame of reference. For purposes of defining the subject matter of sociology, one more point of agreement can be presumed, namely, that the empirical systems with which sociology is concerned involve the *interaction* of pluralities of human[3] individuals. Clearly, the study of the analytically isolated "individual" is not a problem for sociology. In this empirical sense, the concern with "social systems" is one of the hallmarks of sociological interest. But when we remember that a theoretical scheme is based on analytical abstraction, merely pointing to an empirical field is not enough. In order to achieve any high level of theoretical specificity, it is necessary to take positions on a series of other general issues where consensus, even in the sense so far taken for granted, cannot yet be presumed.

It is at this point that the positions held by the editors must be considered. We have had to follow specific policies of selection from a literature far too large to be included through more than a small sample, and we have had to organize the selected material in a relatively definite and coherent way. We do not think that the present level of *explicit* consensus in the field of sociology is high enough to provide an automatic rationale for the policies of selection and organization which must be adopted in order to produce an intelligibly coherent anthology. We have, therefore, frankly and explicitly brought to bear our own views of the most useful and important organization of problems and concepts in the field.

## *The Concept of Social System*

The function of this part of the General Introduction is to present an outline of our concept of social system, in order to make explicit the main considerations that have guided our policies of selection and organization.

Let us start with the issue just mentioned, that of the delineation of the place of social systems within the frame of reference of action. One aspect of the issue, that of the distinction between the *analytically* defined "individual"[4] and the systems generated by the process of social interaction, can be taken for granted. But this is not enough for our purposes, primarily because it fails to make another analytically crucial distinction, namely, that between social systems and cultural systems. In the case of the individual-social distinction, the distinction itself is scarcely in question; the difficulties center about its analytical character and the ways of drawing the analytical lines. In the case of the social system-culture distinction, the clear need for such a distinction has only gradually been emerging in sociology and anthropology.[5]

*Social and Cultural Systems.* In the most important tradition of thought for the English-speaking countries, that growing out of utilitarianism and Darwinian biology, an independent position for the social sciences depended on the delineation of a field of interest which could not simply be subsumed under the rubric of general biology. It was, above all, the rubric of "social heredity" in Spencer's sense, of "culture" in Tylor's sense, which became the main focus of this delineation. Regarded in general biological terms, this field fell clearly in the realm of "environmental" rather than hereditary influence. The category of social interaction played a secondary role at this stage, although it was clearly implicit in Spencer's emphasis on social differentiation.

The common background of modern sociology and anthropology has emphasized a socio-cultural sphere. This sphere had the properties of creating and maintaining a patterned cultural tradition, shared in various ways between the members of living societies and transmitted from generation to generation through learning processes and not through biological inheritance. At the same time, it involved organized systems of structured or "institutionalized" interaction between large numbers of individuals.

In the United States, anthropologists have tended to emphasize the cultural aspect of this complex; sociologists, the interactive aspect. It seems to us important that the two, however empirically inter-

3. In the most general sense, sociology should be relevant to all living organisms in so far as they interact, but for present purposes it is not necessary to go beyond the human case.

4. The relevance of the term "analytical" is vital in this connection. All concrete behavior is the behavior of individuals, and no theory of interaction can avoid dealing with *components* of the behavior of individuals. But this is very different from what was referred to above as the "analytically isolated" individual. Some versions of empiricist methodology in psychology have tended to erase this vital distinction by treating psychology not as concerned with the analytically defined individual, or a subsystem of him, but as the "science of behavior." Such a conception clearly makes sociology one type of "applied psychology."

5. Cf. A. L. Kroeber and Talcott Parsons, "The Concepts of Culture and of Social System," *American Sociological Review*, October, 1958.

dependent they may be, should be kept analytically distinct. The social-system focus is on the conditions involved in the interaction of actual human individuals who constitute concrete collectivities with determinate membership. The cultural-system focus, on the other hand, is on "patterns" of meaning, e.g., of values, of norms, of organized knowledge and beliefs, of expressive "form." The basic concept for the integration and interpenetration of the two is *institutionalization,* which will be a subject of much attention in subsequent introductory discussions.

Thus, an essential part of our policy is to distinguish social systems from cultural systems and to treat the former as the primary focus of the analytical concerns of sociological theory. However, the relationships between the two are so intimate that we devote an entire part of our Reader (Part Four) to materials emphasizing and analyzing these relations—including, of course, many selections from the work of authors who themselves did not emphasize the distinction or who in many cases were not even aware of it.

As noted, insistence on an analytically independent socio-cultural realm was a major feature of the intellectual history most relevant to the background of contemporary sociological theory. Essential as this was, its proponents overshot the mark by tending to deny the relevance of social interaction to the subhuman levels of the biological world, as well as the relevance of the subhuman prototypes of human culture. But once the fundamental analytical lines have been established, it becomes easier to attempt to restore this type of balance, and we shall attempt to do so at relevant places in our more detailed introductory materials. The clearest single trend since then has been an increasing insistence on the importance of "motivated" social interaction throughout the biological evolutionary scale, especially in its higher reaches.

*Social Systems and "the Individual."* Another set of problems has emerged parallel to the basic distinction between the socio-cultural and the "individual" realms. Just as social and cultural systems were not clearly differentiated, the behavior of the "organism" has tended even more predominantly to be treated as a unitary object of scientific analysis by psychologists. At the same time, the problem of the role of learning has been at the center of psychological preoccupation. Correspondingly, there has recently appeared an analytical distinction parallel to that between social and cultural systems, one that discriminates between the "organism" taken as an analytical category, centering on its genetically given constitution so far as this is relevant to the analysis of behavior and, on the other hand, the "personality," the system constituted by the learned components of the *organization* of his behavior.[6]

In organizing our material in the Reader we have not taken explicit account of this distinction, but have put together, in Part Three, all the main materials bearing on the determinants of social behavior relevant to the analytically isolated "individual" and his interdependence with social systems. When we consider these materials in more detail in the introductions to that Part and to its subsections, we will keep this distinction in mind.

*Society, Economy, and Polity.* Quite clearly, the considerations regarding the principal areas of knowledge located on the boundaries of the theory of social systems concern the broad problem of defining the "jurisdictions" of the disciplines within the behavioral or action area. We do not propose to discuss this problem in detail here. There is, however, another set of problems internal to the social system which should be mentioned before proceeding, problems concerning the place of the subject matters of economics and political science. Clearly, both are disciplines dealing with phases of the functioning of large-scale and differentiated social systems.

Some consider the scope of sociology, in a relatively encyclopedic sense, to include all phases of the structure and functioning of social systems. By this definition, economics and political science would be branches of sociology. This is not, however, our conception. In very general terms, the kind of problem of boundaries which arises between social systems and other types of action systems arises again *within* the social system, becoming more salient as such systems become more highly differentiated. Our view is that the economy and the polity should be treated as functional subsystems within a society. The primary concern of sociology is not with the functioning of these subsystems, but with the other two primary functional subsystems: those concerned with the functions of integration and of "pattern-maintenance." Between the latter, on the one hand, and the economy and polity, on the other, there exists the same order of interdependence and interpenetration that exists between social systems as a whole and cultural and psychological (especially personality) systems.

The economic and political categories occupy prominent places in the organization of the selec-

6. This distinction between (analytically defined) organism and personality was not included in the general analysis of systems of action put forward by Parsons and Shils in *Toward a General Theory of Action* (1951). Emphasis on its importance is a matter of subsequent development. It has been most fully stated in Parsons' "An Approach to Psychological Theory in Terms of the Theory of Action," in Sigmund Koch (ed.), *Psychology: A Study of a Science,* Vol. III (New York: McGraw-Hill, 1959).

tions of Part Two. In dealing with them, however, our main concern will be with institutional structure rather than with the types of functional interconnection most important to the economist and the political scientist. We will select the aspects of economies and polities that are most directly relevant to sociological interest. The rationale of this selective procedure will be more fully explained in two places: later in the present General Introduction and in the Introduction to Part Two.

This rationale will become more evident as we proceed. Though it is true that, historically, the fields of economic and of political theory were defined before that of sociology, it does not follow that the conception of sociology with which we are here working is a residual one. In the first place, in connection with the problem of societal structure, we will deal with the hierarchy of the relations of control in a social system; we will argue that the economic and the political constitute two distinct and relatively well defined levels, the two lowest in the hierarchy from the technical viewpoint of social-system analysis.[7] The other two levels, those dealing with the functions of integration and of pattern-maintenance, are not systematically dealt with in either of the other two disciplines, nor are they, as functions in the social system, merely aspects of culture.

The second reason that sociology is not a residual science is a consequence of the first. The problems of social integration and of pattern-maintenance stand in a different relation to the motivation of the individual than do adaptation and goal-attainment. The latter two are concerned primarily with the mechanisms of "rational" orientation to the conditions of action, a conception most highly developed in economic theory. The former two, on the other hand, have to do with "nonrational" factors, that is, those involved in the operation of *internalized* values and norms. This process, as will be partly developed in this essay, and more extensively in later introductory materials (Introductions to Part One, Section C; to Part Three; and to Part Four), is the essential basis of the phenomenon of *institutionalization* as seen from the point of view of the relation of the individual to his society.

*The Organization of Selections in the Reader.* It should now be clear that Parts Three and Four are designed to deal with the two fundamental areas of "boundary" problems of social systems: those relating to the individual as a system, and those relating to the cultural system. The main treatment of the social system, in a more strictly autonomous sense, will be found not only in the introductory materials of Part One but also in Parts Two and Five. These two Parts are broadly distinguished as follows: Part Two deals with the delineation of the structure of social systems, including the institutionalized mechanisms that regulate the processes within the structure; Part Five concentrates upon the problems connected with the structural changes of social systems, the processes by which a given system is transformed into one of a different character, whether it be through structural differentiation or through an alteration of type in a more fundamental sense.

Part One is composed of selections introductory to the main body of the Reader in three different respects. First, as explained in the Preface and elaborated in the preceding section of this General Introduction, we conceive the generation spanning the nineteenth and twentieth centuries as the one which established the main lines of sociological theory today. Before that time, the sociological element was much more diffused in a general tradition which had strong affiliations with the philosophy of history and with a general theory of behavior of the type exemplified by utilitarianism. Section A of Part One is devoted to selections from the literature *preceding* the decisive crystallizing phase of the newer sociological thinking. In this Section, as will be explained more fully in the Foreword devoted specifically to it, we have attempted to present selections embodying the most important conceptual materials utilized by later theorists.

The other two sections of Part One concern the two aspects of what we conceive to be the most central conceptual components underlying the development of a more technical analysis of social systems as such: systems of interaction between individuals. The first of these (Section B) concerns the ways in which the aspects of behavior directly involved in interaction are focused relative to more diffuse conceptions of the general behavior of individuals. These are the conceptual materials that have led to the basic structural concepts of role and collectivity; the two concepts will be more fully explained presently and illustrated in far more detail in the selections in Part Two.

Section C of Part One, finally, concerns the basic phenomenon of "institutionalization." This consists essentially in the integration of cultural-pattern elements at the levels of values and norms with elements of the motivational systems of individuals in such ways as to define and support structured systems of social interaction. The selections here are meant to illustrate some of the most general types

7. This view has been most fully developed in *Economy and Society*. With respect to the polity it is somewhat further spelled out in "'Voting' and the Equilibrium of the American Political System," in E. Burdick and A. J. Brodbeck (eds.), *American Voting Behavior* (Glencoe, Ill.: The Free Press, 1959), especially in the Technical Note.

of insight and analysis underlying the more detailed developments illustrated in the later Parts of the work. The rationale of the selection and organization with respect to all three of these introductory themes will be discussed more fully in the relevant introductions.

## *A Paradigm for the Analysis of Social Systems*

Let us now turn to a more detailed discussion of our conception of a social system. First, the concept of interpenetration implies that, however important *logical* closure may be as a theoretical ideal, *empirically* social systems are conceived as *open* systems, engaged in complicated processes of interchange with environing systems. The environing systems include, in this case, cultural and personality systems, the behavioral and other subsystems of the organism, and, through the organism, the physical environment. The same logic applies internally to social systems, conceived as differentiated and segmented into a plurality of subsystems, each of which must be treated analytically as an open system interchanging with environing subsystems of the larger system.

The concept of an open system interchanging with environing systems also implies *boundaries* and their maintenance. When a set of interdependent phenomena shows sufficiently definite patterning and stability over time, then we can say that it has a "structure" and that it is fruitful to treat it as a "system." A boundary means simply that a theoretically and empirically significant difference between structures and processes internal to the system and those external to it exists and tends to be maintained. In so far as boundaries in this sense do not exist, it is not possible to identify a set of interdependent phenomena as a system; it is merged in some other, more extensive system. It is thus important to distinguish a set of phenomena not meant to constitute a system in the theoretically relevant sense—e.g., a certain type of statistical sample of a population—from a true system.

*Structural and Functional Modes of Analysis.* Besides identifying a system in terms of its patterns and boundaries, a social system can and should be analyzed in terms of three logically independent—i.e., cross-cutting—but also interdependent, bases or axes of variability, or as they may be called, bases of selective abstraction.

The first of these is best defined in relation to the distinction between "structural" and "functional" references for analysis. However relative these two concepts may be, the distinction between them is highly important. The concept of structure focuses on those elements of the patterning of the system which may be regarded as independent of the lower-amplitude and shorter time-range fluctuations in the relation of the system to its external situation. It thus designates the features of the system which can, in certain strategic respects, be treated as constants over certain ranges of variation in the behavior of other significant elements of the theoretical problem.

Thus, in a broad sense, the American Constitution has remained a stable reference point over a period of more than a century and a half. During this time, of course, the structure of American society has changed very greatly in certain respects; there have been changes in legal terms, through legislation, through legal interpretations, and through more informal processes. But the federal state, the division between legislative and executive branches of government, the independent judiciary, the separation of church and state, the basic rights of personal liberty, of assembly, and of property, and a variety of other features have for most purposes remained constant.

The functional reference, on the other hand, diverges from the structural in the "dynamic" direction. Its primary theoretical significance is integrative; functional considerations relate to the problem of *mediation* between two fundamental sets of exigencies: those imposed by the relative constancy or "givenness" of a structure, and those imposed by the givenness of the environing situation external to the system. Since only in a theoretically limiting case can these two be assumed to stand in a constant relation to each other, there will necessarily exist a system of dynamic processes and mechanisms.

Concepts like "structure" and "function" can be considered as either concrete or analytical. Our present concern is with their analytical meaning; we wish to state in a preliminary way a fundamental proposition about the structure of social systems that will be enlarged upon later—namely, that their structure as treated within the frame of reference of action *consists* in institutionalized patterns of normative culture. It consists in components of the organisms or personalities of the participating individuals only so far as these "interpenetrate" with the social and cultural systems, i.e., are "internalized" in the personality and organism of the individual. I shall presently discuss the problem of classifying the elements of normative culture that enter into the structure of social systems.

The functional categories of social systems concern, then, those features in terms of which systematically ordered modes of adjustment operate in the changing relations between a given set of patterns of institutionally established structure in the system and a given set of properties of the relevant environing systems. Historically, the most common model on which this relationship has been based is that of the behaving organism, as used in psychological thinking. From this point of view, the functional problem is that of analyzing the mechanisms which make orderly response to environmental conditions possible. When using this model in analyzing social systems, however, we treat not only the environment but the structure of the system as problematical and subject to change, in a sense which goes farther than the traditional behavior psychologist has been accustomed to go.[8]

In interpreting this position, one should remember that the immediately environing systems of a social system are not those of the physical environment. They are, rather, the other primary subsystems of the general system of action—i.e., the personalities of its individual members, the behaviorally organized aspects of the organisms underlying those personalities, and the relevant cultural systems in so far as they are not fully institutionalized in the social system but involve components other than "normative patterns of culture" that are institutionalized.[9]

*"Dynamic" Modes of Analysis.* The importance of the second basis or axis of empirical variability, and hence of theoretical problem formulation, follows directly. A fundamental distinction must be made between two orders of "dynamic" problems relative to a given system. The first of these concerns the processes which go on under the assumption that the structural patterns of institutionalized culture are given, i.e., are assumed to remain constant. This is the area of problems of *equilibrium* as that concept has been used by Pareto, Henderson, and others, and of homeostasis as used by Cannon. The significance of such problems is directly connected with both the concept of system and the ways in which we have defined the relation between structure and function.

The concept of equilibrium is a fundamental reference point for analyzing the processes by which a system either comes to terms with the exigencies imposed by a *changing* environment, without essential change in its own structure, or fails to come to terms and undergoes other processes, such as structural change, dissolution as a boundary-maintaining system (analogous to biological death for the organism), or the consolidation of some impairment leading to the establishment of secondary structures of a "pathological" character. Theoretically, the concept of equilibrium has a normative reference in only one sense. Since the structure of social systems consists in institutionalized normative culture, the "maintenance" of these normative patterns is a basic reference point for analyzing the equilibrium of the system. However, whether this maintenance actually occurs or not, and in what measure, is entirely an empirical question. Furthermore, "disequilibrium" may lead to structural change which, from a higher-order normative point of view, is desirable.

The second set of dynamic problems concerns processes involving change in the structure of the system itself. This involves, above all, problems of interchange with the cultural system, however much these may in turn depend upon the internal state of the social system and its relations to other environing systems. Leaving distinctions within the category of internal adjustive processes aside for the moment, one can say that, with respect to its external interchanges, problems of equilibrium for the social system involve primarily its relations to its individual members as personalities and organisms, and, through these, to the physical environment. Problems of structural change, on the other hand, primarily involve its relations to the cultural systems affecting its patterns of institutionalized normative culture.

However fundamental the distinction between dynamic problems which do and do not involve structural change may be, the great importance of an intermediate or mixed case should be emphasized. This is the problem of change involving the structure of subsystems of the social system, but not the over-all structural pattern. The most important case in this category is that of processes of structural differentiation. Structural differentiation involves genuine *reorganization* of the system and, therefore, fundamental structural change of various subsystems and their relations to each other. Its analysis therefore presents problems of structural change for the relevant subsystems, but not in the same sense for the system as a whole. The problems involved concern the organization of the structural components of social systems, particularly the hierarchical order in which they are placed. Further discussion will have to await clarification of these problems.

*The Hierarchy of Relations of Control.* The third of the three essential axes of theoretical analysis may be defined as concerning a hierarchy of relations of control. The development of theory in the

8. In addition, of course, our analysis is couched explicitly in terms of action and not of the type of physiology which has so preoccupied many behavior psychologists.

9. It is too technical an issue to discuss here, but we would take the position that a social system in the *analytical* sense has *no* immediate and direct input-output interchange with the physical environment; all such interchange, which is of crucial importance empirically, is mediated through the "behavioral organism."

past generation in both the biological and the behavioral sciences has revealed the primary source of the difficulty underlying the prominent reductionism of so much earlier thought. This was the reductionist tendency to ignore the importance of the ways in which the organization of living systems involved structures and mechanisms that operated as agencies of control—in the cybernetic sense of control—of their metabolic and behavioral processes. The concept of the "behavioral organism" put forward above is that of a cybernetic system located mainly in the central nervous system, which operates through several intermediary mechanisms to control the metabolic processes of the organism and the behavioral use of its physical facilities, such as the motions of limbs.

The basic subsystems of the general system of action constitute a hierarchical series of such agencies of control of the behavior of individuals or organisms. The behavioral organism is the point of articulation of the system of action with the anatomical-physiological features of the physical organism and is its point of contact with the physical environment. The personality system is, in turn, a system of control over the behavioral organism; the social system, over the personalities of its participating members; and the cultural system, a system of control relative to social systems.

It may help if we illustrate the nature of this type of heirarchical relationship by discussing the sense in which the social system "controls" the personality. There are two main empirical points at which this control operates, though the principles involved are the same in both cases. First, the situation in which any given individual acts is, far more than any other set of factors, composed of *other* individuals, not discretely but in ordered sets of relationship to the individual in point. Hence, as the source of his principal facilities of action and of his principal rewards and deprivations, the concrete social system exercises a powerful control over the action of any concrete, adult individual. However, the *patterning* of the motivational system in terms of which he faces this situation also depends upon the social system, because his own personality *structure* has been shaped through the internalization of systems of social objects and of the patterns of institutionalized culture. This point, it should be made clear, is independent of the sense in which individuals are concretely autonomous or creative rather than "passive" or "conforming," for individuality and creativity are, to a considerable extent, phenomena of the institutionalization of expectations. The social system which controls the personality is here conceived analytically, not concretely. This problem will be further discussed in the Introduction to Part Three.

*Control Relations within the Social System.* The same basic principle of cybernetic hierarchy that applies to the relations between general subsystems of action applies again *within* each of them, notably to social systems, which is of primary concern here. The principle of the order of cybernetic priority, combined with primacy of relevance to the different boundary-interchange exigencies of the system, will be used as the fundamental basis for classifying the components of social systems. The relevance of this hierarchy applies, of course, to all the components distinguished according to the first of our three ranges of variation, to structures, functions, mechanisms, and categories of input and output.

The most strategic starting point for explaining this basic set of classifications is the category of functions, the link between the structural and the dynamic aspects of the system. I have suggested that it is possible to reduce the essential functional imperatives of any system of action, and hence of any social system, to four, which I have called pattern-maintenance, integration, goal-attainment, and adaptation. These are listed in order of significance from the point of view of cybernetic control of action processes in the system type under consideration.

*The Function of Pattern-Maintenance.* The function of pattern-maintenance refers to the imperative of maintaining the stability of the patterns of institutionalized culture defining the structure of the system. There are two distinct aspects of this functional imperative. The first concerns the character of the normative pattern itself; the second concerns its state of "institutionalization." From the point of view of the individual participant in a social system, this may be called his motivational *commitment* to act in accordance with certain normative patterns; this, as we shall see, involves their "internalization" in the structure of his personality.

Accordingly, the focus of pattern-maintenance lies in the structural category of *values,* which will be discussed presently. In this connection, the essential function is maintenance, at the cultural level, of the stability of institutionalized values through the processes which articulate values with the belief system, namely, religious beliefs, ideology, and the like. Values, of course, are subject to change, but whether the empirical tendency be toward stability or not, the potentialities of disruption from this source are very great, and it is essential to look for mechanisms that tend to protect such order—even if it is orderliness in the process of change.

The second aspect of this control function concerns the motivational commitment of the individual—elsewhere called "tension-management." A very central problem is that of the mechanisms of socialization of the individual, i.e., of the processes by which the values of the society are internalized in his personality. But even when values have become internalized, the commitments involved are subject to different kinds of strain. Much insight has recently been gained about the ways in which such mechanisms as ritual, various types of expressive symbolism, the arts, and indeed recreation, operate in this connection. Durkheim's analysis of the functions of religious ritual may be said to constitute the main point of departure here.

Pattern-maintenance in this sense plays a part in the theory of social systems, as of other systems of action, comparable to that of the concept of inertia in mechanics. It serves as the most fundamental reference point to which the analysis of other, more variable factors can be related. Properly conceived and used, it does not imply the empirical predominance of stability over change. However, when we say that, because of this set of functional exigencies, social systems show a *tendency* to maintain their structural patterns, we say essentially two things. First, we provide a reference point for the orderly analysis of a whole range of problems of variation which can be treated as arising from sources *other* than processes of structural change in the system, including, in the latter concept, its dissolution. Second, we make it clear that when we do analyze structural change we are dealing with a different kind of theoretical problem than that involved in equilibration. Hence, there is a direct relation between the function of pattern-maintenance —as distinguished from the other three functional imperatives—and the distinction between problems of equilibrium analysis, on the one hand, and the analysis of structural change on the other. The distinction between these two types of problems comes to focus at this point in the paradigm.

*The Function of Goal-Attainment.* For purposes of exposition it seems best to abandon the order of control set forth above and to concentrate next upon the function of goal-attainment and its relation to adaptation. In contrast to the constancy of institutionalized cultural patterns, we have emphasized the variability of a system's relation to its situation. The functions of goal-attainment and adaptation concern the structures, mechanisms, and processes involved in this relation.

We have compared pattern-maintenance with inertia as used in the theory of mechanics. Goal-attainment then becomes a "problem" in so far as there arises some discrepancy between the inertial tendencies of the system and its "needs" resulting from interchange with the situation. Such needs necessarily arise because the internal system and the environing ones cannot be expected to follow immediately the changing patterns of process.[10] A goal is therefore defined in terms of equilibrium. It is a directional change that tends to reduce the discrepancy between the needs of the system, with respect to input-output interchange, and the conditions in the environing systems that bear upon the "fulfilment" of such needs. Goal-attainment or goal-orientation is thus, by contrast with pattern-maintenance, essentially tied to a specific situation.

A social system with only one goal, defined in relation to a generically crucial situational problem, is conceivable. Most often, however, the situation is complex, with many goals and problems. In such a case two further considerations must be taken into account. First, to protect the integrity of the system, the several goals must be arranged in some scale of relative urgency, a scale sufficiently flexible to allow for variations in the situation. For any complex system, therefore, it is necessary to speak of a system of goals rather than of a single unitary goal, a system, however, which must have some balance between integration as a system and flexible adjustment to changing pressures.

For the social system as such, the focus of its goal-orientation lies in its relation as a system to the personalities of the participating individuals. It concerns, therefore, not commitment to the values of the society, but motivation to contribute what is necessary for the functioning of the system; these "contributions" vary according to particular exigencies. For example, considering American society, one may suggest that, given the main system of values, there has been in the cold-war period a major problem of motivating large sectors of the population to the level of national effort required to sustain a position of world leadership in a very unstable and rapidly changing situation. I would interpret much of the sense of frustration expressed in isolationism and McCarthyism as manifestations of the strains resulting from this problem.[11]

*The Function of Adaptation.* The second consequence of plurality of goals, however, concerns the difference between the functions of goal-attain-

10. When we speak of the *pattern* of the system tending to remain constant, we mean this in an analytical sense. The outputs to environing systems need not remain constant in the same sense, and their variations may disturb the relationship to the environing system. Thus scientific investigation may be stably institutionalized in a structural sense but result in a continuing output of new knowledge, which is a dynamic factor in the system's interchanges with its situation.

11. Cf. the paper, Parsons, "McCarthyism and American Social Tension," *Yale Review*, Winter, 1955. Reprinted as Chap. 7, *Structure and Process in Modern Societies.*

ment and adaptation. When there is only one goal, the problem of evaluating the usefulness of facilities is narrowed down to their relevance to attaining this particular goal. With a plurality of goals, however, the problem of "cost" arises. That is, the same scarce facilities will have *alternative* uses within the system of goals, and hence their use for one purpose means sacrificing the gains that would have been derived from their use for another. It is on this basis that an analytical distinction must be made between the function of effective goal-attainment and that of providing disposable facilities independent of their relevance to any particular goal. The adaptive function is defined as the provision of such facilities.

Just as there is a pluralism of lower-order, more concrete goals, there is also a pluralism of relatively concrete facilities. Hence there is a parallel problem of the organization of such facilities in a system. The primary criterion is the provision of flexibility, so far as this is compatible with effectiveness; for the system, this means a maximum of generalized disposability in the processes of allocation between alternative uses. Within the complex type of social system, this disposability of facilities crystallizes about the institutionalization of money and markets. More generally, at the macroscopic social-system level, the function of goal-attainment is the focus of the political organization of societies, while that of adaptation is the focus of economic organization.[12]

The most important kinds of facilities involve control of physical objects, access to the services of human agents and certain cultural elements. For their mechanisms of control to be at all highly generalized, particular units of such resources must be "alienable," i.e., not bound to specific uses through ascription. The market system is thus a primary focus of the society's organization for adaptation. Comparable features operate in less differentiated societies, and in more differentiated subsystems where markets do not penetrate, such as the family.[13]

Within a given system, goal-attainment is a more important control than adaptation. Facilities subserve the attainment of goals, not vice versa—though of course the provision or "production" of facilities may itself be a goal, with a place within the more general system of goals. There are, however, complications in the implications of this statement.

*The Function of Integration.* The last of the four functional imperatives of a system of action—in our case, a social system—is that of integration. In the control hierarchy, this stands between the functions of pattern-maintenance and goal-attainment. Our recognition of the significance of integration implies that all systems, except for a limiting case, are differentiated and segmented into relatively independent units, i.e., must be treated as boundary-maintaining systems within an environment of other systems, which in this case are other subsystems of the same, more inclusive system. The functional problem of integration concerns the mutual adjustments of these "units" or subsystems from the point of view of their "contributions" to the effective functioning of the system as a whole. This, in turn, concerns their relation to the pattern-maintenance problem, as well as to the external situation through processes of goal-attainment and adaptation.

In a highly differentiated society, the primary focus of the integrative function is found in its system of legal norms and the agencies associated with its management, notably the courts and the legal profession. Legal norms at this level, rather than that of a supreme constitution, govern the *allocation* of rights and obligations, of facilities and rewards, between different units of the complex system; such norms facilitate internal adjustments compatible with the stability of the value system or its orderly change, as well as with adaptation to the shifting demands of the external situation. The institutionalization of money and power are primarily integrative phenomena, like other mechanisms of social control in the narrower sense. These problems will be further discussed in later sections of this essay.

For any given type of system—here, the social—the integrative function is the focus of its most distinctive properties and processes. We contend,

12. It should be noted that the above formulation of the function of adaptation carefully avoids any implication that "passive" adjustment is the keynote of adaptation. Adaptation is relative to the values and goals of the system. "Good adaptation" may consist either in passive acceptance of conditions with a minimization of risk or in active mastery of conditions. The inclusion of active mastery in the concept of adaptation is one of the most important tendencies of recent developments in biological theory. An important relation between the two functional categories of goal-attainment and adaptation and the old categories of ends and means should be noted. The basic discrimination of ends and means may be said to be the special case, for the personality system, of the more general discrimination of the functions of goal-attainment and adaptation. In attempting to squeeze analysis of social behavior into this framework, utilitarian theory was guilty both of narrowing it to the personality case (above all, denying the independent analytical significance of social systems) and of overlooking the independent significance of the functions of pattern-maintenance and of integration of social systems themselves.

13. The importance of adaptive flexibility for the functioning of families as systems is well illustrated in the study of Robert Angell, *The Family Encounters the Depression* (New York: Chas. Scribner's Sons, 1936).

therefore, that the problems focusing about the integrative functions of social systems constitute the central core of the concerns of sociological theory. This point of view will guide our analyses in subsequent introductory discussions and will receive strong emphasis in selections presented at various points in the Reader. Until a broad structural outline of the social system has been presented, it seems best to defer further discussion of the ways in which the integrative function meshes more specifically with the others.

## II. CATEGORIES OF SOCIAL STRUCTURE

Historically, the theoretical preoccupations of sociological theory have emerged from two main points of reference. One concerns the relations of social systems and culture and focuses on the problem of values and norms in the social system. The second concerns the individual as organism and personality and focuses on the individual's participation in social interaction. Generally, neither of these reference points may be considered more important than the other. However, since the foregoing discussion of functional imperatives has started with pattern-maintenance, which chiefly concerns the institutionalization of normative culture, it may help to balance the picture if we begin our detailed discussion of structure at the other end, with the problem of the interaction of individuals.

### *Social Interaction and Roles*

For sociology, the essential concept here is that of *role*. I should like to treat this concept as the "bottom" term of a series of structural categories, of which the other terms, in ascending order, are *collectivity, norm,* and *value*. (It is interesting, and I think significant, that systematic introduction of the concept of role has been, perhaps, the most distinctively American contribution to the structural aspects of sociological theory.)

The essential starting point is the conception of two (or more) individuals interacting in such a way as to constitute an interdependent system. As personalities, each individual may be considered a system with its own values, goals, etc., facing the others as part of an "environment" that provides certain opportunities for goal-attainment as well as certain limitations and sources of frustration. Though interdependence can be taken into account at this level, this is not equivalent to treating the process of interaction as a social system. True, the action of alter is an essential part of the conditions bearing on the attainment of ego's goals, but the vital sociological question concerns the nature and degree of the integration of the *system* of interaction as a social system. Here the question arises of the conditions under which the interaction process can be treated as stable—in the sense, at least, that it does not prove to be so mutually frustrating that dissolution of the system (i.e., for the individual, "leaving the field") seems more likely than its continuation.

The problem of stability introduces considerations of temporal continuity, which immediately brings us to the relevance of normative orientation. It can be shown that, within the action frame of reference, stable interaction implies that acts acquire "meanings" which are interpreted with reference to a common set of normative conceptions. The particularity of specific acts is transcended in terms of the generalization of the normative common culture as well as in the normative component of the expectations that get built into the guiding mechanisms of the process. This means that the response of Alter to an act of Ego may be interpreted as a sanction expressing an evaluation of the past act and serving as a guide to desirable future behavior.

The essentials of the interaction situation can be illustrated by any two-player game, such as chess. Each player is presumed to have some motivation to participate in the game, including a "desire to win." Hence, he has a goal, and, relative to this, some conception of effective "strategies." He may plan an opening gambit but he cannot carry advance planning too far, because the situation is not stable: it is contingent on the moves made both by himself and by his opponent as the game proceeds. The basic facilities at his command consist of his knowledge of the opportunities implicit in the changing situation; his command of these opportunities means performance of the adaptive function. Hence, at the goal-attainment and adaptive levels, goals are defined and facilities are provided, but *specific acts are not prescribed*. The facilities are generalized, and their allocation between the players depends upon each player's capacities to take advantage of opportunities.

In turn, the meaningfulness of the goals and the stability of the generalized pattern of facilities depend on the existence of a well defined set of rules, which forms the center of the integration of the system. The roles, in this case, are not differentiated on a permanent basis; rather, the rules define the consequences of any given move by one player for the situation in which the other must make his next choice. Without such rules the interactive process could not be stable, and the system of adaptive facilities would break down; neither player would know what was expected of him or what the consequences of a given set of moves would be. Finally, the differentiated and contingent rules must be grounded in a set of values which define the nature of a "good game" of this sort, including the value of equality of opportunity for both contestants and the meaningfulness of the goal of "winning."

A stable system of interaction, therefore, orients its participants in terms of mutual expectations, which have the dual significance of expressing normative evaluations and stating contingent predictions of overt behavior. This mutuality of expectations implies that the *evaluative* meanings of acts are shared by the interacting units in two ways: what a member does can be categorized in terms meaningful to both; also, they share criteria of behavior, so that there are common standards of evaluation for particular acts.

We can say that even such an elementary two-member system of social interaction has most of the structural essentials of a social system. The essential property is mutuality of orientation, defined in terms of shared patterns of normative culture. Such normative patterns are *values;* the normatively regulated complex of behavior of one of the participants is a *role;* and the system composed by the interaction of the two participants, so far as it shares a common normative culture and is distinguishable from others by the participation of these two and not others, is a *collectivity*.

One further condition, not present in our chess game example, is necessary in order to complete the roster of structural components, namely, differentiation between the roles of the participants. This is to say that, in most social systems, participants do not *do* the same things; their performances may be conceived as *complementary* contributions to the "functioning" of the interaction system. When there are two or more structurally distinct units which perform essentially *the same* function in the system (e.g., nuclear families in a community) we will speak of segmentation as distinguished from differentiation. When differentiation of roles is present, it becomes necessary to distinguish between two components of the normative culture of the system: that of values, which are shared by the members over and above their particular roles, and that of role-expectations, which are differentiated by role and therefore define rights and obligations applicable to one role but not to the other. I propose to use the term *values* for the shared normative component, and the term (differentiated) *norm* for the component that is specific to a given role or, in more complex systems, to other empirical units of the system, i.e., various collectivities such as families, churches, business firms, governmental agencies, universities.

Where roles are differentiated, the sharing of values becomes an essential condition of integration of the system. Only on this assumption can the reactions of Alter to Ego's performances have the character of sanctions regulating Ego's action in the interests of the system. However, it should be clear that for Alter to be in a position to evaluate Ego's acts, the acts need not be such that Alter is, by virtue of his role, expected to perform. Thus, in marriage, one of the most important diadic relationships in all societies, the roles of the partners are differentiated by sex. The mutual evaluation of performance is an essential regulatory mechanism, but to be in a position to evaluate the partner's performance is not to assume his role.

*The Concepts of Role and Collectivity.* A role may now be defined as the structured, i.e., normatively regulated, participation of a person in a concrete process of social interaction with specified, concrete role-partners. The system of such interaction of a plurality of role-performers is, so far as it is normatively regulated in terms of common values and of norms sanctioned by these common values, a collectivity. Performing a role within a collectivity defines the category of *membership,* i.e., the assumption of obligations of performance in that concrete interaction system. Obligations correlatively imply rights.

Since the normal individual participates in many collectivities, it is a commonplace, though a crucial one, that only in a limiting case does a single role constitute the entire interactive behavior of a concrete individual. The role is rather a *sector* in his behavioral system, and hence of his personality. For most purposes, therefore, it is not the individual, or the person as such, that is a unit of social systems, but rather his role-participation at the boundary directly affecting his personality. It is largely when interpreted as this particular boundary-concept that the concept of role has an important theoretical significance for sociology.

So long as we restrict our illustrations to the diadic interaction system it may seem that the distinction of four analytical structural components—role, collectivity, norm, and value—is overelaborate. At this level it is still possible to identify values and the collectivity, norms and the role. In more complex social systems, however, there is not just one collectivity but many; and a differentiated norm does not define expectations for just one role but for a class of roles (and also for classes of collectivities). The social systems with which the sociologist normally deals are complex networks of many different types or categories of roles and collectivities on many different levels of organization. It therefore becomes essential to conceptualize values and norms independently of any particular collectivity or role.

## *Values and Norms*

We now turn from the analysis of interaction to that of the more explicitly normative content of the structure of social systems, within which values and norms have been distinguished. We have already suggested that such values and norms must be involved in any stable process of interaction, however simple. In the attempt to analyze the structure of complex societies, however, the analytically distinct significance of these components becomes much more salient. The following sections will therefore be devoted to a more explicit analysis of them and of their relations to the segmentation of social structure, to the various levels of values and norms, and to the patterns of differentiation of structure, always taking account both of the problems of function and of the system's relation to its situation.

Throughout this analysis, our major concern will be to make clear the basic functional paradigm we have presented for the intricate relations involved in a complex society segmented and differentiated into many subsystems. A paramount underlying question will be, how is the integration of a system with a large population and high differentiation possible? Or, more theoretically, what kinds of statements have to be made, what concepts formulated, and what discriminations worked out in order to do justice to these empirical intricacies?

The concepts of universalism and particularism will be helpful in this connection. In any given system, the concepts of role and collectivity are particularistic. Though, of course, we must talk about classes and types of roles, a role is always the role of a particular concrete individual. Similarly, a collectivity always has a concrete membership of specific interacting role-incumbents. A norm, however, is always universalistically defined within the universe of its relevance, whether it be a universe of acts, of roles, or of collectivities. To be sure, the definition of a relevant universe involves a particularistic reference of a higher order; thus, a norm may apply only to citizens or residents of the United States, but it may cut across all concrete collectivity-membership differences within that universe. Values are also universalistically defined in terms of relevance. When a particular *type* of society is evaluated as good, the judgment is inherently applicable to more than one specific society.

The universalistic aspect of values implies that, at the relevant level of reference, they are neither situation-specific nor function-specific. In this connection, it should be remembered that the most crucial aspects of the situation of a social system consist in the personalities and the patterns of culture with which the system is in contact. When values are said not to be situation-specific, it is implied that their normative validity is not a function of the particular categories of personalities available for membership, nor, for example, of the particular levels of technological knowledge available for implementing these values. When situation-specificity is introduced, we speak analytically not of values, but of goals.

Similarly, values are independent of the internal differentiation of the systems in which they are institutionalized; they are relevant on a level of generality which "transcends" functional differentiation. The keynote of differentiation, however, is functional. Hence, norms, which by the above definition are differentiated with reference to function, must be function-specific. They are "legitimized" by values, but operate at a lower level of generality with respect to expected concrete collective and role performance. With respect to concrete roles in concrete collectivities, however, most norms are still not situation-specific—especially since they do not specify the particular roles but are generally formulated in classes and types of roles, and hence of persons and collectivities.

The relativity of the universalistic-particularistic distinction must again be emphasized. In general, the principle is that the universe relevant to the universalistic elements of normative culture is defined by the role and collectivity structure at the next higher level of system organization. It thus refers to a hierarchy of system-subsystem organization. The top of this hierarchy is the concept of society, which is the highest-order concrete system of interaction treated as theoretically relevant for the analytical purposes of sociology (including the possibility of an emergent "world society").

In line with the conception of the structure of social systems as consisting in the normative culture institutionalized in the system, we have so far presented a classification of its components organized with reference to the hierarchical order of the organization of the system. Structurally speaking, then, the role component is the normative component which governs the participation of individual persons in given collectivities. The collectivity component is the normative culture which defines the values, norms, goal-orientations, and ordering of roles for a concrete system of interaction of specifiable persons; the component of norms is the set of universalistic rules or norms which define expectations for the performance of classes of differentiated units within the system—collectivities, or roles, as the case may be; and values are the normative patterns defining, in universalistic terms, the pattern of desirable orientation for the system as a whole, independent of the specification of situation or of differentiated function within the system.

It should be made clear that roles are governed or controlled by the normative exigencies of the functioning of the collectivities within which they operate, if the collectivity itself is to be defined as a system. Therefore, in so far as a more inclusive social system comprises many collectivities as subsystems, the behavior of these collectivities is controlled by the institutionalized norms that specify how each type of collectivity must and may behave according to its place within the system. Finally, norms themselves are legitimized, and therefore, in a normative sense, controlled, by the values institutionalized in the society. Subject to exigencies of situation and function, values define the direction of orientation that is desirable for the system as a whole.

## *The Structure of Complex Systems*

Having outlined these essential structural components of a social system and their rank in the general hierarchy of control, we can now outline their main pattern of organization so as to constitute a relatively complex system. What is here presented is necessarily a schematic "ideal type," one that pretends merely to define and distinguish rather broad structural categories; we cannot take into account the immense richness of various concrete social structures. Something more concrete will be found in the Introduction to Part Two.

The main guiding line of the analysis is the concept that a complex social system consists of a network of interdependent and interpenetrating subsystems, each of which, seen at the appropriate level of reference, is a social system in its own right, subject to all the functional exigencies of any such system relative to *its* institutionalized culture and situation and possessing all the essential structural components, organized on the appropriate levels of differentiation and specification.

*The Concept of a Society.* The starting point must be the concept of a *society*, defined as a collectivity, i.e., a system of concrete interacting human individuals, which is the primary bearer of a distinctive institutionalized culture and which cannot be said to be a differentiated subsystem of a higher-order collectivity oriented to most of the functional exigencies of a social system. It will be noted that this conception is stated in terms that leave the question of the "openness" of a society in various directions to be treated empirically. At the social-system level, however, rather than the cultural,[14] the main criterion is *relative* self-sufficiency.

To approach the structural analysis of the subsystem organization of a society, we must refer to the appropriate functional exigencies of both the societal system itself and its various subsystems. The primary, over-all principle is that of differentiation in relation to functional exigency; this is the master concept for the analysis of social structure. By itself, however, it is not adequate; it must be supplemented by the two principles of specification and segmentation. The first refers primarily to the institutionalized culture components of the structure, the second to the exigencies confronting the concrete behaving units, i.e., to collectivities and roles. It seems preferable to discuss the latter first.

We have noted that, in *one* (but only one) of its aspects, a society is a *single* collectivity with a specifiable, though naturally changing, membership of individuals. This fact is related to three fundamental imperatives. First, there must be, to some degree and on some level, a unitary system of institutionalized values, in this aspect a common culture. In so far as maintenance of a common value system requires the kinds of functions collectivities must perform, the society will have to constitute a single collectivity—what Durkheim called a "moral community." Second, however, since the system is differentiated, the implementation of these values for different units requires a relatively *consistent* system of norms that receive a unitary formulation and interpretation. In highly differentiated societies this system of norms takes the form of an integrated legal system administered by courts. The need for coordinated dealing with the external situation is also relevant, as will be brought out presently.

*The Segmentation of Social Units.* But if, for one set of reasons, a society must be a single collectivity, other reasons prevent its being only that. These reasons can be summed up in the generalized principles economists refer to as determining the "economies of scale." Beyond certain points, that is to say, "costs" increase as the size of the unit of organization increases, though what the points are varies

14. By this criterion a system such as the Catholic Church is not a society. It clearly transcends and interpenetrates with a number of different societies in which its values are more or less fully institutionalized and its subunits are constituent collectivities. But the Church, primarily a *culturally* oriented social system, is not itself capable of meeting very many of the functional exigencies of a society, especially the political and economic needs. Similarly, even a "world government," should anything approaching that conception come into being, need not itself constitute a "world-society," though its effectiveness would imply a level of normative integration which would make the degree of separateness we have traditionally attributed to "national societies" problematical.

greatly according to the specific factors involved. Thus, under modern industrial conditions the manufacture of such commodities as automobiles takes place in very large units indeed, whereas there seem to be important reasons which inhibit entrusting the early socialization of children primarily to units with membership much larger than the nuclear family.

Perhaps the most fundamental determinant underlying the segmentation of social systems is the indispensability of the human individual as an agency of performance. But there are essential limits, not only to what a given individual can do, but to the effectiveness with which individuals can co-operate. The problems of communication and other aspects of integration may thus multiply as a result of an increasing scale of organization; in certain respects, therefore, subcollectivities may acquire a distinctive organization, including a special integration or solidarity relative to the larger systems of which they are parts.

By the concept *segmentation* I refer, in discussing the formation of collectivities, to the development of subcollectivities, within a larger collectivity system, in which some of the members of the larger system participate more intimately than in others. In this sense, segmentation is a factor independent of the differentiation of function between the subcollectivities. Thus a large-scale society may comprise millions of nuclear families, all of which perform essentially similar functions in the socialization of children; here the structure is highly segmented but not highly differentiated.

The necessity of segmentation derives largely from the problems of integration resulting from the other exigencies to which units of the system are subject. At the same time, however, it gives rise to new problems of integration: the more units there are, the less likely they will be just "naturally" to coordinate their activities in ways compatible with the smooth functioning of the system as a whole. This tends, in more complex systems, to give rise to special mechanisms of integration, which will have to be discussed in due course.

*The Specification of Normative Culture.* As already noted, there is an important relation between the hierarchy of control and the levels of generality of the components of normative culture. Thus, values were defined as standing at the highest level of generality of "conceptions of the desirable," i.e., without specification of function or situation. In comparison to values, therefore, norms are differentiated on the basis of specification of function of the units or subunits to which they apply. Subcollectivities, in turn, involve further specification on the basis of situation. This is to say that, given its function(s), a collectivity is identified in terms of specified memberships of concrete individuals acting in concrete situations. When the collectivity is treated as a differentiated system, there must be further specifications applicable to the roles of the participating members.

There is, therefore, a hierarchy of generality of the patterns of normative culture institutionalized in a social system, one that corresponds to the general hierarchical relations of its structural components. Each subunit of the society, as collectivity, will have its own institutionalized values, which should be conceived as specifications, at the appropriate level, of the more general values of the society. To cope with its own internal differentiation of function, then, each subunit will have a set of differentiated norms, which should be regarded as specifications both of the subcollectivity values and of the more general norms applicable both to it and to other types of subcollectivity. The principle of specification restricts the generality of the pattern of culture by introducing qualifications arising from specialization of function, on the one hand, and from specificity of situation, on the other.

The last of the three principles of organization of complex systems, functional differentiation, has already been discussed in general terms. In accord with this principle, structured units acquire specialized significance in the functioning of the system. The general scheme of functional categories that we have presented is very simple, being limited to four categories. In using it, however, one must do justice to the empirical complexity of the situation by taking acount of the many steps in segmentation and specification, and hence of the compounding of the patterns of differentiation by their repetition for subsystems at each level of segmentation.

Since our general approach has been in terms of the hierarchy of control observed in descending order, a brief account should now be given of the "anchorage" of social systems at the base. This anchorage is in the personalities and behavioral organisms of the individual members and, *through* these, in the lower-order subsystems of the organism and in the physical environment. Concretely, all social interaction is bound to the physical task performance of individuals in a physical environment; it is bound to spatial location in the physical sense. Following the usage of ecologically oriented theory, I have elsewhere referred to this spatial location as the "community" aspect of social structure.[15] It can be broken down most conveniently into four com-

15. Cf. Parsons, "The Principal Structures of Community" in C. J. Friedrich, Ed., *Community,* Nomos, Vol. II, Liberal Arts Press, 1959, and in Parsons, *Structure and Process in Modern Societies,* Free Press, 1959, Chap. 8.

plexes: (1) residential location and the crystallization of social structure around that focus; (2) functional task-performance through occupation, and the attendant locational problems; (3) jurisdictional application of normative order through the specification of categories of persons, and the relevance of this to the spatial locations of their interests and activities; and (4) the physical exigencies of communication and of the movements of persons and commodities. More generally, the category of technology—not only what is usually called "physical production," but all task-performance involving the physical organism in relation to its physical environment—belongs in this area of borderline problems. Technology relates to physical exigencies, but it is also based on *cultural* resources in their significance as facilities for social action. Empirical knowledge of the physical world is an instance of such a cultural resource.

*The Integration of Societies as Collectivities.* Let us now approach the problem of outlining the structure of a complex society as a social system. As we have said, three different exigencies underlie the fact that a society can always be regarded as a single collectivity, namely, the maintenance of its patterns of institutionalized culture at the value level, the integration of its system of differentiated norms, and the co-ordinated handling of external situations.

The prevalence of fundamental patterns of value and the general commitment of units to common values are so crucial that the problem of the relation of the over-all collectivity to values is a universal one. At the other end, however, the problems of jurisdiction and enforcement with reference to normative order are equally crucial; the over-all collectivity structure cannot be divorced from political organization, oriented to maintaining commitments to this order and to the jurisdictional functions associated with it, in relation both to its own population and to other societies. This means that the boundaries of a society tend to coincide with the territorial jurisdiction of the highest-order units of political organization.

The primary area in which the problems of value-commitment are played out is that of religion; for most societies, the paramount over-all collectivity has been at the same time a religious collectivity and a political collectivity, both a "church" and a "state." Law, we may say, has tended to stand in the middle, to be legitimized by religion and enforced by political authority; often the function of interpreting it has been a serious bone of contention.

However, the formula of religio-political-legal unity is not, by itself, adequate as a universal generalization. In the first place, within the over-all collectivity these functions have tended to be differentiated with respect to personnel and subcollectivities. But, in a more radical sense, in the Western world since the Christian era there has been a process of fundamental differentiation of church and state. In interpreting the sociological implications of this, one must consider this process in terms of the relation between social and cultural systems. Even before its Protestant phase, Western Christianity was characterized by a special type of religious "individualism." In the present context, this means that, except on the most general level of over-all societal membership, the individual's religious and social status did not necessarily coincide. The church was an organization of the religious interests and orientations of the population conceived as independent of (but not unrelated to) their secular or temporal orientations, especially at the level of societal value-commitment. It was a "Christian society," but one in which the function of religion was more specialized than in other pre- and non-Christian types.

This I interpret to mean that, in societal as distinguished from cultural terms, the "moral community" aspect shifted from religious organization as such to the area of interpenetration between the religious and the secular. The paramount societal collectivity became the "state," administered by laymen—or when administered, in fact, by priests, not in their special clerical capacity. This differentiation was never fully carried out in medieval Europe—for instance, it was impossible to divest bishops of secular functions that went beyond the administration of ecclesiastical affairs—but it was, nevertheless, the main pattern.

Since the Reformation, this process has gone farther, particularly where the principle of the separation, as distinguished from the differentiation, of church and state has prevailed. As in the United States today, the values are still clearly anchored in theistic religion ("In God We Trust"), but on the level of collectivity organization the "moral community" is clearly the "politically organized community." What has happened, essentially, is that any agency whose orientation is primarily cultural rather than societal has been deprived of legitimate authority to prescribe values and enforce norms for the society; in this sense the society has become "secularized." The religious anchorage of the values is still there, but religion is pluralistically and "privately" organized. Formally, the values are embodied in the Constitution and in the official interpretations of it, above all by judicial and legislative agencies.

The universal association of the over-all collectivity structure with political organization is based on another set of imperatives, involving the special significance of physical force as a sanction. The central point here is that, while there are many limitations on the efficacy of this sanction, control of sufficiently superior socially organized force is almost always a completely effective preventive of any undesired action. Therefore, without the control that includes "neutralization" of organized force, which is inherently territorial in its reference, the guarantee of the binding power of a normative order is not possible.

I conceive of political organization as functionally organized about the attainment of *collective* goals, i.e., the attainment or maintenance of states of interaction between the system and its environing situation that are relatively desirable from the point of view of the system. The maintenance of security against the adverse use of force is a crucial collective goal for every society. Considerations such as these underly the general tendency of the over-all collectivity to develop an effective monopoly of the internal organization of force through police and military agencies. Such statements are not meant to imply that the control of force is the paramount function of political organization. Force is not the only function that is primarily negative, i.e., "protective" in significance, and, in general, government is a central agency of positive societal goal-attainment. But force is so strategically significant that its control is an indispensable function, a necessary, but not sufficient, condition of social order. Accordingly, in a well-integrated society, most sub-collectivities except those specifically concerned with force are almost totally deprived of it.

Because of the problems involved in the use and control of force, the political organization must always be integrated with the legal system, which is concerned with administering the highest order of norms regulating the behavior of units within the society. No society can afford to permit any other normative order to take precedence over that sanctioned by "politically organized society." Indeed, the promulgation of any such alternative order is a revolutionary act, and the agencies responsible for it must assume the responsibility of political organization.

In this context it is of great significance that in a few societies, notably in the modern West, the organization of the legal system has attained a significant degree of independence in the judicial and, to some extent, in the legislative departments. There are two main aspects of this independent collectivity structure: the judiciary, with certain types of insulation from the pressures of "politics"; second, very notable, the development of a legal profession whose members occupy an interstitial status, partly through membership in the bar, functioning as "officers of the court," and partly by dealing privately with clients—indeed, protected from even governmental intervention by such institutions as privileged communication.

Summing up, we may say that the highest over-all collectivity in even a modern society is, to an important degree, necessarily "multifunctional," or functionally "diffuse." At the same time, under certain circumstances the diffuseness characteristic of the more "monolithic" religio-political structures—even of such high development as classical China or late Republican Rome—has tended to differentiate further. The most notable of these differentiations have been the "secularization" of political organization, which has gone through many stages and modes, and the institutionalization of a relatively independent legal function.[16]

The problem of the kind and degree of differentiation likely to occur at this highest level of societal collectivity organization may be described as a function of four primary sets of factors, all variable over considerable ranges. These are: (1) the *type* of societal values which are more or less fully institutionalized in the society (classified in terms of modes of categorizations of the society, at the highest level of generality, as an evaluated object—the appropriate categories seem to be pattern variables); (2) the degree and mode of their institutionalization, including its "security" relative particularly to the religious and cultural foundations of value-commitments in the society (long-range institutionalization of new values implies a relatively low level of such security); (3) the kind and level of structural differentiation of the society, with special reference to the severity and kinds of integrative problems they impose on the society; and (4) the kinds of situational exigencies to which the system is exposed.

## *Modes of Differentiation within Societies*

*Kinship and the Articulation with Personality.* The question of the kind and level of functional

16. It may be noted that allowing the institutionalized values to be determined through agencies not fully controlled by the paramount political collectivity involves a certain risk to it. The relatively full institutionalization of anything like the separation of church and state is therefore probably an index of the completeness of institutionalization of values. Modern totalitarian regimes are partly understandable in terms of the insecurity of this institutionalization. Therefore totalitarian parties are functionally equivalent to "churches," though they may put their value focus at a nontranscendental level, which is, e.g., allegedly "economic," which attempts to establish the kind of relation to government typical of a less differentiated state of the paramount collectivity than has existed in the modern West.

diffuseness characterizing some social structures arises at an additional and particularly important point, besides that of the society as "moral community." This is the point of primary articulation with the personalities of the constituent members. Any system sociologically treated as a society is likely to include many such members—at least a thousand, and in many cases tens if not hundreds of millions. Because of the types of exigencies noted above, in this context societies tend to be relatively highly segmented. The types of units into which the segmentation occurs are, in the first instance, those known as "kinship units." *Kinship* is essentially the point of articulation, i.e., interpenetration, between the structure of social systems and the relations involved in the biological process of reproduction. Biologically, there are three crucial structural components: (1) the differentiation of human populations into two sex groups, each with different functions in the reproductive process, but both essential to it; (2) the sharp human differentiation between the mature and the immature organism, involving a relatively long period of gestation and then a prolonged period of relative "helplessness" which, though progressively decreasing, makes impossible the order of independence characteristic of the young of many other species; and (3) the fact that the sexual union of two specific individuals of opposite sex is necessary to, and likely to result in, pregnancy and reproduction. Thus, biologically all human populations are differentiated by sex and by generation, and are particularistically related to two ancestral lines through biological descent—the filial generation as the offspring of two specific biological parents and, through them, the descendants of remoter ancestors; the parental, through their common relation by parenthood to their offspring and to more remote descendants. The relation between sexual union and reproduction means that the former is never divested of an underlying relation to potential parenthood.

In social structure there are many variations, but a constant and fundamental point of reference is the nuclear family, the collectivity constituted by a conjugal pair and their biological offspring. In every known society, there is institutionalization of some continuing sexual relationship in relation to reproduction, and of some continuing responsibility for such offspring on the part (often backed up by wider groups) of at least one of the parents, though generally of both. Generally the nuclear family is, during the period of the children's dependency, at least included in the primary unit of residence—it is often, particularly in modern industrial societies, primarily constitutive of it.

Within this setting, the problem of functional diffuseness rests first on the fact that every human individual starts life as a helpless infant, whose development depends almost completely on his relations to the particular, very small circle of adults responsible for his physical care and his socialization. Biological parenthood is not essential to this crucial relation; but, particularly with respect to the mother, the cases where this does not play a strategic role are minor variations and do not anywhere constitute a major structural type.

A generally significant crucial fact is that the types of social structure which, in an evolutionary sense, can be clearly categorized as "primitive" display a special prominence of kinship as a basis of the categorization of memberships and eligibilities in important collectivities. There is also an important group of societies where no important collectivity exists that is independent of kinship, however complex the internal ramifications of the kinship system may be.

Kinship structures as such are clearly subject to important processes of functional differentiation. Economic and political functions are very widely institutionalized in kinship units, though these functions generally, in extension of membership and in time span, transcend the nuclear family. On the higher societal levels, however, integrative functions present a major obstacle to such institutionalization, because of the inherent particularism of kinship references. Hence, at certain stages in the structural development of societies, particularism on kinship bases presents one of the major obstacles to higher-level integration. At the primary levels of the function of socialization, pattern-maintenance is everywhere very closely bound to kinship units. But in terms of the imperative of societal value-stabilization, i.e., a higher level of pattern-maintenance, this necessarily centers at a low level in the specification series. Precisely because segmentation is so important in the kinship sphere, dependence solely on kinship units for pattern-maintenance is precarious. These statements should not, of course, imply that the connection cannot be maintained through differentiation in the statuses of different kinship units. The differentiation of royal and aristocratic kinship lineages from the "common" people is one mechanism by which, within certain limits, pattern-maintenance and integrative functions can be performed without sacrificing the kinship basis of organization.

In this sense, every structural unit carries some share in meeting every functional imperative of the society as a whole. But the effectiveness of allocating such responsibilities among highly segmented units tends to decrease as the functions go from a lower to a higher position in the hierarchy of control. There is, to be sure, a very important countervailing consideration concerning the firmness of institutionalization; as noted above, under certain circumstances a very important part of the pattern-maintenance function may be highly decentralized. Since kinship units, however, are by nature highly segmented beyond the performance of pattern-maintenance functions for their constituent personalities and integrative functions within the units themselves, the other least problematical function for these units is the economic. Indeed, it is striking in comparative sociology that only in the relatively very recent types of modern industrial societies (with minor exceptions, like slave-plantation economies) has more than a small fraction of the function of economic production become emancipated from diffuse "embeddedness" in kinship structures. This development has been closely associated with the fact that in all except truly primitive pre-industrial societies, the major portion of productivity has come from agriculture. Despite important variations, there are certain common structural features of peasant societies where most of the population have been organized as kinship units, living from agricultural production in a subsystem operated predominantly by members of the kinship group working by virtue of their ascribed status in the unit. In such cases, the ascribed pattern has in general extended to institutionalization of generational succession in property-holding and productive function. In an important sense, the family firm, in the earlier stages of industrialism and before, has in nonagricultural fields extended the same basic organizational pattern; but except on a very small scale, this embeddedness has been confined to the higher "managerial" functions, and non-kin have worked in operative capacities. However, various types of patriarchal collectivities have assimilated non-kin employees in patterns of relationship similar to those of kinship. Again, economic function within this structural framework must be performed at a relatively low level of differentiation. It is closely connected with a rather elementary phase of the economic division of labor and the corresponding extensiveness of markets.

Any collectivity is also, functionally considered, a political unit of the society. A unit like the nuclear family is, however, so small that only by virtue of very special status can it perform important political functions at any but a low level of specification. This applies even to lineages, though, since they can institutionalize generational succession, they can be much more important than nuclear families—and, as in the case of royal families, they have been the paramount agencies of society-wide political responsibility. The kinship principle has then been extended to the political role of a complex of aristocratic lineages which stand in varying relations to royalty.

There are, however, severe functional difficulties in the institutionalization of nearly "pure" government by privileged kinship units. It has been most stable in certain small-scale societies, like the city-states of antiquity or the semi-independent city-states of late medieval and early modern Europe—where, incidentally, monarchy has been the exception rather than the rule.

It seems, after the above analysis, that integrative functions tend to become structurally differentiated near the top of the societal system of organization, most conspicuously in the case of the judiciary element of the legal system. Almost always a private legal profession has developed later, and is more exceptional.

## *The Differentiation of Political Structures*

Because of the connection of paramount societal collectivity organization and political function outlined, the functional differentiation of political from other structures also tends to come near the top of the societal hierarchy. There are two preliminary steps. The first is the differentiation of kinship units carrying high political responsibility (and enjoying corresponding privileges)—royal and aristocratic lineages—from the common kinship units. The second is the differentiation of the political from the pattern-maintenance and integrative functions of such high-level units. Because of the imperatives discussed above, this occurs slowly and is never complete at the top; though, of course, as in most modern societies now, all these functions may be taken from the kinship units as such.

Lower down, however, an important process of differentiation involves the political function. The focal initial problem here concerns the restrictions on the mobility of resources imposed by the ascriptive aspect of kinship. One crucial process is the development of some kind of "bureaucracy." For understandable reasons, there are serious obstacles to the relinquishment of control, by the functionally diffuse "highest authorities," of the classical functions of government, in the "top policy-making" and later the legislative fields. It is thus in the "administrative" area of political function—the implementation of decisions through "technical" procedures—that this process of differentiation tends to center. Enfranchisement of political support is generally more difficult to institutionalize but sometimes has happened—e.g., in Greek democracy.

From this point of view, within certain limits, the primacy of the "policy decisions" must be taken as given. Within these limits, the crucial considerations are, first, the disposability of human and material resources, and, second, their quality relative to the need. In the latter context, the competence of personnel is salient. Clearly, kinship ascription imposes frustrating limits in both respects. Though the deficiency may be partly compensated through training ascribed personnel, there is no guarantee that the person ascribed for a function by kinship status is the most competent available; in any case, the very diffuseness of kinship relations severely limits disposability.

In this connection, one must consider the relativity of the functional categories being used here. Of course, the functions of a bureaucratic organization may, from a more general point of view, fall in any category. In particular, early bureaucracies very frequently have subserved "economic" functions for the society. A prominent example is the water-control function in river-valley civilizations, emphasized by Weber and Wittvogel. The essential points, however, are rather that the focus of collective responsibility for the bureaucratic organization is the "top control" of the over-all societal collectivity and that the process of differentiation proceeds from this focal point. This is the primary criterion of its subserving a political function, in that it subserves goals defined as essential to the society as a system (through the eyes, of course, of its "ruling groups"), and not to its subunits in their "private" capacities.

A parallel process of development may occur where a subunit of the society, originally organized on the basis of kinship, undergoes structural differentiation in the political functions relative to the more diffuse matrix of kinship. Perhaps the most familiar example is the evolution of the family firm into a bureaucratic organization. Similar phenomena may, however, be found in the military field and many others.

In this sense, we may say that there are two essential structural features of bureaucracy. The character of the organization unit, seen in relation to its environment, has the primary characteristic of "functional specificity" and thus of the relative emancipation of its subunits from structural amalgamation with structures subserving other functions. For the individual member units, on the other hand, the essential point is the definition of their roles in terms of occupation.

Functional specificity for the collectivity implies the collectivity's relative independence from structural involvements or "fusions" with structural units subserving other functions. As Weber made so clear, however, there must be a "non bureaucratic" element in control of such a collectivity, giving it its primary functional orientations—indeed, there may be several layers of such non bureaucratic control. Also, in so far as its functions are specialized within the larger system, such an organization will, in addition to its internal arrangements, have to be relatively specifically organized in two fundamental respects. First, its own members will not be the primary "consumers" of its output, whether this output be governmental administrative services, economic production, education, or even the "cure of souls." There will, then, have to be some form of institutionalization of the terms on which the outputs are made available to or, in some cases, compulsorily imposed[17] upon, these "consumers." One particularly important line of differentiation here is that between organizations which do and which do not take their beneficiaries into some type of membership status. The ordinary business firm is of the kind which does not; a physical commodity, once sold, usually does not imply a continuing relation of solidarity between seller and purchaser. In such fields as education, however, the process of "selling," of disposal, cannot be completed in a single quick transaction, but implies both a long continuing relation between teacher and student, and a process of interaction impossible without common collectivity membership. Pupils or students are, thus, members of their school or college in a sense in which customers are not members of the firm from which they purchase.

The third basic set of relations of a functionally specific collectivity to its environment concern the processes of procurement of the resources necessary for the performance of its functions. These can be classified under two general headings, namely, physical facilities, including work premises, and human services. The terms of acquisition, utilization, and disposal of the former are institutionalized as property; those of the latter, as occupation. There is a fundamental asymmetry in the relations between these two essential categories of resources, in that physical facilities can be definitively separated from the agents of their production,[18] whereas human services are inseparable from the organism and personality of the individual agent—they require either his physical presence at a work location or control over his activities in some other location; and, most important, utilization of the individual's services is conditioned by his adjustment between

17. For example, the services of tax-collecting agencies are often unwelcome to their "consumers," the taxpayers, but are just as institutionally regulated as are the relations of sellers and buyers in an ordinary commercial market.

18. Land is a special limiting case, both because of its nonproductibility and because the location of a given area is irrevocably fixed.

the expectations in his work role and the other roles in which he is involved.

Given that all human personalities are anchored in the nexus of kinship, the most crucial of these role-adjustment problems is the one between the occupational and kinship roles of the same person. As noted, one very common case is the simple fusion of the two—the "work" a person does is performed in his kinship role as such. At the opposite extreme is full "chattel" slavery, where maximum disposability over services is obtained through complete denial of institutional legitimacy to any kinship roles at all—clearly, an exceptional and inherently unstable arrangement. The most important additional type is the modern one of occupational role characterized by structural segregation of work roles from kinship, but with the concomitant expectation that most normal workers will have kinship roles as well—though some, like celibate priesthoods and religious orders, are similar to slavery in denying kinship roles. The most important features of the modern occupational role are structural separation of the household and kinship group from control over work performance, and control of both performance and rewards by the functionally specific organization. This generally implies the separation of physical premises of work from the household, and separation of property rights in physical facilities and sources of remuneration from the personal property of the role-incumbent. It is important that these criteria have applied to a very small proportion of adult human beings, except in the modern industrial type of society.

The above discussion began with the problem of the structural differentiation of political function from the diffuse matrix involving pattern-maintenance and integrative functions. It also started with the over-all societal level of collectivity structure, i.e., the paramount collectivity which institutionalizes the underlying moral community. By logical progression, however, we arrived at the problem of structure and status in the society of specific-function collectivities generally. When we discussed the regulation of their "disposal" functions and their access to disposable resources, we inevitably touched on what is usually called the economic organization of a society. It is now necessary to discuss the latter somewhat more fully and to relate it to political organization.

*The Structural Differentiation of the Economy from Other Subsystems.* Political function is particularly intimately related to the collectivity component of social structure. It is essentially the facilitation of attaining collective goals and centers on the decisions about such goals and the mobilization of societal resources relative to them, especially the integration of the relevant collectivities for these goals. Political function is, as noted, fundamental to the society as a whole. But analytically, the same considerations apply to all the society's subcollectivity units. It follows that what has been called the specific-function collectivity is defined precisely as a collectivity for which, in its *internal* organization, political function, i.e., effectiveness, has primacy over other functions. For subcollectivities, however, the goals are not in this structural sense set "internally," though they may or may not be set autonomously, and in reference to the more inclusive system their goal may or may not be political. Thus the function of a business firm is primarily economic; its goal is "production," but its internal organization must be analyzed first in political terms. The category *political* is, however, here conceived as analytical; hence, the relation between the political and the other aspects of the subsystem will be different in different types of specific-function collectivities. The respective organizations of a government administrative agency, of a university, and of a business firm naturally differ greatly. In spite of these variations, the relative prominence of specific-function collectivities in the structure of the society is the most important single index of the differentiation of the political from other structures. Societies differ, however, both in the degree of this differentiation and in its incidence. Compared to some European societies, American society, at least until recently, has had substantially less development of bureaucracy in government and more of it in the field of economic production.

Later, we will discuss specific mechanisms by which political function is differentially institutionalized. The most important categories may be defined as leadership, authority, and power.

Economic function, as distinguished from the political, involves the production and allocation of disposable resources. *Economic* function is exercised only when important available resources are means to alternative ends, and at some stage are not committed to a specific use. Analysis of small groups shows that this is always and necessarily true of social interaction. Thus approval as a sanction cannot effectively regulate action if it is committed in advance to one predicted act of one group member without reference to the availability of more highly valued alternatives. This would be equivalent to awarding prizes for success in a contest, without holding any competition.

In society, however, such units are structured as roles and collectivities, as exchangeable physical facilities, and in certain other categories—e.g., "packages" of communicable symbolic meaning.

Traditionally one main criterion of the value of economic resources is relative scarcity. The other most important one is general utility for different functions. Some physical commodities are extremely limited in adaptability, while others have considerable range. For example, land, its utility limited only by type of soil and climate, can be used for growing a wide variety of things. Another example is the automobile, a highly generalized facility of "private" transportation, whose usefulness, however, is entirely dependent on the system of roads.

The possibilities of generalizing about physical commodities and human services as resources are, however, inherently limited. The utilization of scarce resources is dependent on the institutionalization of mechanisms which, independent of possession of or advance commitment to any specific commodities, services, information, etc., make it possible to gain access to wide ranges of different facilities as need for them develops. In known societies, there are in particular two highly generalized mechanisms of this type, namely political power and money; the latter, of course, has primacy of economic function.

Both political power and money require the institutionalization of the disposability of facilities. Negatively, this means eliminating or drastically weakening the ascriptive rights to such facilities, which are always prominent in the more undifferentiated social structures. Positively, it involves institutionalizing adequate rights of control and disposal, in the form of rights of contract, property, and occupational use of human services. The prominence of ascription makes the right of disposal or "alienation" particularly important; especially with regard to human services, relative clarity of rights of control within the limits of occupational commitment are important. The modern institution of property, as applied to physical commodities rather than money, ties together various components which, in European feudal law, were distributed between different units all having rights in the same "thing"—land being of course, the most important single example. Property rights have become much more clearly differentiated from various other contractual rights, notably those involving services, and from political jurisdiction over land and over persons' acts on land. There are limits on the property owner's freedom; but modern ownership is an essential condition of generalized disposability of physical commodity resources, independent of political power. The same applies, of course, to the institutionalization of occupational roles including freedom to contract for services through employment.

Money is not a commodity, but is a very special mode of the institutionalization of expectations and commitments through communication. It is a generalized type of cybernetic mechanism which makes it possible for the unit to mobilize, subject to normative regulation, whatever resources it needs or wishes, within the limits of its "means," expressed in monetary terms. Money, in the social system in which it operates, depends on a balancing system of reciprocities, developing out of the kinds of more diffuse reciprocities which certain anthropologists like Malinowski and Lévy-Strauss have analyzed. Inflation and deflation are symptoms that this reciprocal system is somehow out of balance.

We noted that the usefulness of the automobile is dependent on a system of roads and, it may be added, on the implementation of adequate rules of traffic control. The usefulness of money as a much more generalized facility is dependent on a system of markets and adequate rules governing the continual flow of transactions through markets. A market is a defined social system in which there are institutionalized expectations of willingness to exchange disposable facilities for money and vice versa under a set of rules for settling terms and for the rights and obligations assumed and relinquished in the process. Generally, markets become more significant as access to them is not particularistically restricted, especially on an ascribed basis.[19] The institutions of contract and property, and the monetary mechanism itself, are the bases of the market as a system; and the basis of "labor market," the institution of occupational employment.

*Money and Power.* The concept of political power has been highly controversial in sociological literature, and there is not the consensus about it that there is among economists about money. I would, however, like to suggest a concept which builds directly on the parallel with money as a generalized mechanism for controlling the allocation of resources. The political function has been defined as that of facilitating the effective attainment of a collectivity's goals. Goal-attainment has been specifically related to the processes of change in the interrelations between a system and its environing situation. For those exercising political responsibility, this inevitably involves important elements of uncertainty. Effectiveness, therefore, necessitates the capacity to make decisions and to commit resources, *independently of specific conditions prescribed in advance* by ascription or by some kind of prior agreement or contract.

19. Very specialized markets where access is limited to special groups of "professionals," like the New York Stock Exchange, are not really exceptions to this generalization.

We may define power (in the analytical, political sense) as generalized capacity, independent of prior commitments on the relevant level of specification, to influence the allocation of resources for the goals of a collectivity through invoking the institutionalized obligations (i.e., loyalties) of member units, utilizing such sanctions as are legitimized through these obligations and institutionalized roles involved in the power system. Power should be conceived as a circulating medium and, for any unit, as a scarce resource. Power is unequally distributed in a society, a disproportionate share being held by units carrying political responsibility—just as a disproportionate share of the wealth of an economically developed society is controlled by the units specializing in economic production.[20] Like economic firms, units specializing in political function are dependent on the return of the power they have "spent" or "invested" through their decisions about the allocation of resources. This return, analogous to that from consumers' spending, takes the form of the constituency's satisfaction or dissatisfaction with these decisions, and it thus directly affects the leadership's capacity to make further commitments. The mechanisms of power are not nearly so sharply structured as is the monetary mechanism, though, in democratic societies and in various types of association within them, the vote has functions as a unit which are partly analogous to those of the monetary unit. It does not, however, cover anything like the proportion of the whole range of power phenomena that the monetary unit does.

There is a parallel between political enfranchisement, as the capacity to exercise political power independently of ascribed definitions of obligation or those imposed from above, and the development of consumers' markets where the consumer may select from the offerings available and have their preferences exercise a crucial influence on the process of production itself.

Just as money depends on the institutionalization of contract, property, and occupation, flexible political action is made possible by the institutionalization of power. The institutionalization of leadership is parallel to that of contract in the economic field. It is essentially the institutionalization of the right to make decisions committing the collectivity as a whole and thereby imposing obligations on its member units in their various capacities.

*Authority,* like *power,* is another highly ambiguous term. It designates the political institution which is parallel to property in economics. It is the complex of institutionalized rights over the contributory actions (in economic terminology, "services") of member units of a collectivity. That is, authority institutionalizes rights to make decisions binding in specific respects on the relevant categories of member units, e.g., paying taxes or having to enter military service. Authority comprises the general rules which govern the making of specific binding decisions. Power, on the other hand, is a mechanism regulating the process of making actual commitments. Specific rights of authority can be relinquished, just as specific rights of ownership can be. But "authority" is a non-circulating medium in the same sense that property is. It is the institutional matrix of the functioning of power.[21]

## *Some Limits of Political and Economic Specialization*

As used here, political and economic categories are generalized functional categories that permeate the *entire* structure of the social system. Structures with either political or economic primacy are found at all four levels of institutionalized normative culture and interpenetrate in different ways. Thus, fully differentiated occupational role-performance is a role-category with relative economic primacy, no matter in what functional context it is eventually utilized, and the same is true regarding the command of other facilities, e.g., through ownership of physical commodities. This follows from the fact that the criterion of economic function is that it concerns a resource disposable through market channels. Hence, this resource, the "labor" of eco-

20. In both connections it is important not to confuse inequality, as applied to "consuming" units alone, with that for the society as a whole. Even a socialist society imposing absolute equality of income on all household units would give effective control of most of the economic resources of the society to its socialized agencies of production. Similarly, in a "perfect" democracy, all adult citizens might have equal power to influence the selection of leadership and certain highly generalized orientations of government. But, in the *operative* functioning of collective action, control of power would have to be relatively concentrated in organizations and leadership roles carrying special responsibility for political function. Otherwise, there would be no differentiated political function in the society.

21. These considerations show how voting is quite literally an exercise of power, resting on the institutionalization of the authority of the electorate. That is, after each voter has registered his own decision at the polls, the aggregate result of these many individual decisions is institutionally *binding* on the collectivity as a whole. This is most dramatic when an election turns out an incumbent administration. The incumbents are obligated to vacate their offices and permit the opposition to come in. In the light of the facilities of power commanded by a government, it is clear that this involves a very drastic renunciation, particularly when the incumbents are, as is often the case, convinced that the opposition are little short of scoundrels. The great difficulty with which this pattern has come to be institutionalized is understandable.

nomic theory, is economically differentiated if a developed labor market exists. Inevitably, however, there are various constraints in the structure of labor markets caused by the interpenetration of the economic and various non-economic factors. Even in the types of labor of maximum disposability—e.g., "operative" duties at relatively low levels of organizational responsibility or technical competence—there are basic limits imposed by the incumbent's membership in kinship and other non-economic collectivities. The kin case is, in a highly differentiated society, one of the impinging of pattern-maintenance functions on the economic. As we have seen, the same kinds of limits do not apply to physical commodities. Similarly, the executive role in specific-function collectivities, even in business firms, has special features, because the political component of the role is so prominent within the collectivity. This fact causes much of the persistent recruitment for such roles through channels other than a labor market—e.g., in the family firm—even when management has become almost fully "professionalized," certain constraints remain. One constraint is the "particularizing" of selection for employment—from outside the organization or by promotion. No system of selection entirely by competitive examination for particular posts has been successfully institutionalized, apparently because of the functional diffuseness of the role and the importance of relations between people at the top of an organization. In one sense, the selection of leadership of the nuclear family through marriage, through the "irrational" mechanism of romantic love rather than through rational assessment of suitability for parental roles, is parallel. Both top management and families are small groups whose members must associate very intimately with each other over long periods.

Another constraint on the labor market is employment for professional roles. Here the primary organizational goals belong to either integrative or pattern-maintenance functions. Two prominent structural deviations from the normal commercial market in this field are the "sliding scale" and tenure. They are associated with institutions, like privileged communication and academic freedom, that insulate the role-incumbent from some of the pressures from laymen that might impede the performance of complicated and delicate functions.

The differentiation of economic and political functions from each other and from the other two is found operating at the collectivity level. In the first place, at the entire society's functional level, there is differentiation of collectivities with primacy of one function or another. In the economic category, the business firm is a clear case; with it goes monetary success, i.e., the monetary cost-earnings balance, as the primary criterion—whether or not it is linked with profit actually going to the organization's internal "proprietary" elements. The cost accounting of socialized enterprise is just as subject to this criterion as the profitability of private enterprise. In politics the clearest case, because of the element of inevitable functional diffuseness discussed above, is the administrative agency of government. The exclusiveness with which criteria of effectiveness govern the evaluation of collective performance is the main symptom of the degree of differentiation of political function. In other words, the amount of power generated by a collective unit—the power output relative to the cost of its acquisition, stated in terms of the loss or impairment of loyalties incurred in the process—is the main criterion of effectiveness. Whereas some collectivities in a differentiated society have political primacy in this sense, in all specific-function collectivities a political component centers in what we have called "management" or "administration." In all large-scale organizations, these functions become differentiated from the operative ones.

Just as constraints on the commercial or competitive structure of markets are imposed by impinging non-economic factors, so in many collectivities there are constraints on the political primacy of their organization and orientation to situations. In the business firm, the standard of monetary success incorporates one set of such criteria. In one direction, it limits devotion to "technical" perfection by applying criteria of monetary profit—a fact the importance of which technocrats cannot see—while also limiting the relevance and legitimacy of pursuing political power. In both directions, the limitations take the form of institutionalized mechanisms of control which establish rank orders of considerations which are legitimately taken into account in decision-making.

Another example of the interpenetration of politics and economics is the universality with which, in societies with a highly developed monetary economy, command of adequate monetary funds becomes an indispensable condition of effective operation—especially as the mechanism for mobilizing both physical facilities and necessary human services. The differences between types of functionally specific collectivities lie in the importance of the criterion of monetary success—whether all monetary costs are expected eventually to be balanced by proceeds derived from operation, or it is legitimate for the organization to incur deficits which must be made up by special measures like taxation or soliciting contributions. It is significant that, in the modern liberal type of society, the criterion of monetary independence applies above all to two classes of collectivities, business firms and households.

The leadership and authority-power structure of the modern university provide examples of the limitations on internal political primacy parallel to economic ones in non-business collectivities. The most important operative personnel are highly qualified technical specialists working in many different fields; the tightness of control by top management typical of firms engaged in physical production is impossible. That is, internal to the organization, power is much more decentralized in its distribution than it is in the business organization. The institution of tenure is important both as a modification of the structure of the labor market and as a limitation on administrative power within the organizations.

*Functional Differentiation of Norms and Values.* The same basic order of functional differentiation we have been analyzing occurs at the level of differentiated norms. At the societal level, the legal institutional complex of contact, property, and occupational roles is primarily of economic significance. This complex includes the institutional norms governing money and its uses, involved in all three. Money is integrally involved in the institution of contract, because a large proportion of contracts involve monetary considerations, and because it is an institutionalized symbol—the paramount sanction of "restitutive law," as Durkheim called it. Money also is the apex of the property system; the monetary evaluation of other objects and the convertibility of "real" assets into money are vital features of any modern property system. The controversies about units of account in socialist economies show that money can be abolished only by inventing its functional equivalent; indeed, no socialist economy has seriously attempted to abolish it, however much its market system may differ from free-enterprise. Money is absent only in a primitive *Naturalwirtschaft*. Such a society has not reached a high level of differentiating economic function. Finally, money is involved with the institutionalization of occupation, by virtue of the institutionalization of the legitimacy of monetary remuneration for occupational performances.

Basic economic institutions are embodied in the formal legal system, as are the expected variations between contexts where they are involved, with or without primacy of economic function. Thus the directors of a business corporation are legally obliged, on penalty of liquidation, to operate to maintain financial solvency; governmental units are legally authorized to impose taxes to maintain their functions; and voluntary contributors to religious, charitable, and educational collectivities are legally privileged to deduct such contributions from taxable income.

Similar considerations apply to the normative system governing political functions, in governmental and other contexts. One example is the governmental constitution of the society, prescribing the norms defining the procedures for selecting governmental leadership, the nature and limits of their authority when in office, and the modes in which they may legitimately exercise power. The law involves a complex set of prescriptions for the norms governing leadership, authority, and power in private collectivities, including the definition of variations permissible by virtue of differences in their functions. An important example of this in American law is the doctrine of "public interest." Essentially, this draws a line between two broad categories of activities and, hence, between the collectivities carrying them on. In one case, their actions are their "private" concern, and the law is conceived as regulatory in the negative sense. Rules keeping the activities within bounds preventing them from injuring other parties or otherwise violating societal values and norms must be observed. If, on the other hand, an activity is affected with a public interest, those performing it both enjoy privileges—e.g., franchises to use rights of way—and assume obligations, like regulation of rates charged to the public, not otherwise applicable. Essentially, activities which affect the public interest are defined as involving a larger component of social political responsibility than those that do not. The obligations deriving from this responsibility must be fulfilled; those who undertake them will be given the special privileges, exemptions, and facilities necessary for their fulfilment. Under the law, whether it be formally written or not, every private collectivity has its "constitution" or set of norms governing the political functions necessary for its effective operation.

The type of differentiation under discussion also applies to values. Values cannot control action by mere "emanation." Their institutionalization involves their specification through a series of levels of function and situation. The values of a primary functional subsystem, of a society, like the economy or the polity, constitute the *first* level of specification relative to the general societal values. This specification, it is clear, is by function. For example, the concept of economic rationality has usually been interpreted as a psychological generalization. It also has a definitely normative aspect; and at the highest normative level it is the focus of the value system of the economy as a functional subsystem of the society.

No society can accept economic rationality as its most general societal value-orientation, though it can place the economic highest among its functional priorities. Empirically, economic rationality must be evaluated according to its place and limits in relation to the higher-level societal values, to the system's level of structural differentiation, and to the situation of the society. In so far, however, as units of the society at all three of the levels below that of values becomes structurally differentiated in terms of primacy of economic function, the hallmark of this differentiation is that, relative to *their* functions and situations within the system, units are governed by this economic standard. Thus, though collectivities need not be specifically oriented to economic function, there may still be, in the fields of contract, money, property, and occupation, complexes of institutional norms which are highly emancipated from non-economic considerations. For example, the institutionalization of land ownership makes land far more disposable as an economic resource than it would be, for instance, where rights of alienation were not institutionalized.

Similar considerations apply at the collectivity level. Economic values and norms apply in some degree to all collectivities in certain aspects of their functioning, whether this involves economic primacy or not; thus even a church, whose central function is far removed from economic primacy, must exercise some degree of financial prudence—i.e., subscribe, within a limited sphere, to economic values. It is, however, the institutionalization of the criterion of monetary success as the paramount measure of function which is the hallmark of a collectivity's economic primacy. This, however, is a functional value; and its implications are always subject to qualification in terms of institutional variability at higher levels and situational variability at lower ones. Thus a firm producing dangerous drugs or firearms is regulated to protect incompetent and innocent parties from misusing these products; such protection of third parties is one fundamental focus of the *institution* of contract. Correspondingly, a retail food firm will adapt to the whims (perhaps, "convenience") of its customers as the producer of power plants for large, fast ships will not, because of the overwhelming importance of technical standards of effective performance in the latter case. The classical economists were not wholly unrealistic in speaking of money as a measure of value. Even given the higher-level societal values and still higher-level cultural values, that of economic rationality is authentic and genuine.[22]

22. For the sociologist, the criterion of a "genuine" value cannot be its "absoluteness." In social and cultural systems, as we analyze them, there must be hierarchies of values, each of which must take a relative place. The system governed by a single, unitary, absolute value is the limiting case which is literally "out of this world."

The same considerations apply to occupational roles. Some of these roles are mainly economic in function. Marginal productivity is a primary standard of whether the service should be employed—which can roughly be equated, under economically ideal conditions, with that service's contribution to the monetary success of the organization employing it. Such roles institutionalize economic rationality as their primary value. In other roles, such as most professional ones, it is a subsidiary value. In choosing between employments, the professional, other things equal, legitimately prefers the financially more remunerative job; and the employing organization offers more to those who, from its point of view, are more desirable personnel. But it does not follow on either side that the greatest financial return or financial contribution is the first criterion of desirability for the collectivity.

What is true of economic rationality as a differentiated functional value-system is also true for the other functions. In the polity the value-system centers on collective or organizational effectiveness for the societal collectivity itself or for any legitimate goals of subcollectivities. Such effectiveness (or power, in a larger, e.g., "international" system) may be the paramount functional value of a whole society, though it as such cannot be a societal value-pattern—that would necessitate some higher basis for the legitimate pursuit of power. The range within which greater power is valued will, as in economics, depend on the societal value-system and on considerations of the society's structural differentiation and situation. Similarly, some subcollectivities will be guided within the system by values of political primacy, while in others this component is subordinated. Thus, while a governmental administrative bureau may be evaluated primarily in political terms, a university or a family cannot be. Values of political function will be institutionalized at each of the society's levels of structural hierarchy.

Specialized values for the integrative system are oriented, *within* the societal value system, to maximum internal harmony and mutual complementing among the units of the system. Such integrative values are expressed in various contexts. There is the general ethical one of doing one's duty to others; there is the political one, stressing the importance of collective loyalty and individual self-sacrifice; there is the legal interest in the equitable settlement of conflicts; and there is the medical concern for the patient's welfare. These different levels of expression share the explicit repudiation of the relevance of *unit*-effectiveness, or power, or of economic success as such, as valid criteria.

### *Differentiation between Pattern-Maintenance and Integrative Function*

We have discussed at length both the relations between economic and political function, and social structure at all four levels, because in social science traditions these seem to have been more adequately analyzed and are better known. The same basic principles of the relations between structure and function, between segmentation, specification, and differentiation, apply to the pattern-maintenance and the integrative functions, to the relations of the relevant structures to each other and to the economic and political. We shall here confine the discussion to a very brief outline of the principal components of structural content involved in these other two functions.

There are two important considerations. First, societies will differ in so far as structures with clear primacy of these functions have come to be differentiated from those whose functions are more diffuse. Second, relevant structures will be located at different levels on the scales of segmentation and specification, and may thus not be directly comparable with each other.

Within the framework suggested by the distinction between the theoretical problems involved in equilibrium analysis and in analysis of structural change of social systems, the concept of *pattern-maintenance* as a functional category is not meant to have empirically static connotations. Analytically, specialization in both maintenance and change of values should be placed in this category.

Religion is one of the areas of concern which belong most directly here. Religious values as such should be located in the cultural and not in the social system. Societal values stand at a lower level in the general specification scale of value-patterns than do religious ones. But in some sense, all societal values are here conceived analytically as religiously grounded. However, the structural implications of this may vary greatly, as a function of the nature of both the religion and the social system.

It has been pointed out that sometimes the overall societal collectivity is also a religious collectivity —to quote Durkheim, a "moral community usually called a church."[23] Often, however, this is not the case—as in Western Christianity generally and, more particularly, in recent denominational pluralism as institutionalized in the United States. There are an indefinite plurality of churches, each of which is a voluntary association. The state is no longer a religious collectivity, and there is no established church which claims or is allowed to claim universal religious jurisdiction over the whole society. However, values derived from common religious orientations are still institutionalized. Moreover, an important part of the normative system of the society comprises rules governing behavior in this sphere—for example, the Constitutional provisions for the separation of church and state, and the institutionalization of religious freedom and tolerance. Thus pluralism—at the collectivity level of structure, and, even more, the role level, where every individual can within certain limits adhere to his own beliefs and practices—does not imply that there is *no* institutionalization of religious orientations at the norm and the value levels. This idea is a very common misinterpretation of the sense in which such a society as the American is described as "secularized."

As institutionalization of religious orientation has become a more specialized and differentiated function, it has been allocated to more diverse subcollectivities at lower levels in the social structure's scale of segmentation and specification than was the older type of universal church. But this process has coincided with the development of *higher* levels of generality in the religious requirements of normal societal membership. For example, the societal "common denominator" is considerably more general than was that of medieval Catholicism. It has, as it were, been proved that such a narrow and detailed religious consensus is not a necessary condition of stable value-consensus at the societal level.

A second primary component of the pattern-maintenance function is that usually called "socialization." Whereas the primary focus of religion is in the cultural system, that of socialization is in the personality system. The underlying conditions are the relative shortness of the individual's life-span in comparison to the duration of societies, and the resulting functional imperative for the society to assimilate a continuing stream of new members, primarily through birth and biological maturation. Within this framework, the most important imperatives are anchoring the process of socialization in the genetic sequence of the development of personality, essentially through successively internalizing increasingly complex and differentiated systems of social objects, and the corresponding internalization of increasingly generalized patterns of culture.

Universally, at least one kinship unit, always with the nuclear family's prominent participation, is the primary collective agent of early socialization; in most non-literate societies, the function remains embedded in diffuse kinship structures. In modern

23. E. Durkheim, *Elementary Forms of the Religious Life.* Introduction. London: Allen & Unwin, Ltd., 1926.

industrial societies, however, the nuclear family has become a far more differentiated, though still highly segmented, unit, adapted to the functions of socialization and "tension-management." In the process, its connections with the extended kinship nexus have been greatly attenuated; it has become structurally "isolated"; and most of the other functions of older kinship structures have passed to non-kinship units, notably those of economic production. Because, in this situation, its primary functions concern early, pre-school socialization, the family operates at very low levels of generality in the scale of specification of the value-patterns which are internalized in the process.

All more highly differentiated societies have developed non-kinship structures centering about the functions of formal education in which the higher-level patterns of normative culture and systems of objects are internalized in the personality. In a few societies, there have finally developed institutions of higher education in which a highly important fusion for sub-functions of pattern-maintenance occurs: the combination of the highest levels of training with, through scholarship and research, the functions of codifying and developing important parts of the cultural tradition itself.

This concern with the cultural tradition operates in the aspects having to do with value patterns, and in fields of existential belief systems—non-empirical, as in religious and philosophy, and empirical, as in science, technology, and ideology—and expressive symbolization, as in the arts. It constitutes another basic focus of the society's pattern-maintenance systems, which tends to become closely associated with the higher ranges of the socialization system. Expressive symbolization, which reaches its highest levels of "universal" significance in the sophisticated fine arts, including literature, at lower levels of specification involves the modes of taste constituting the framework within which expressive, i.e., otherwise non-functional, activities—including what is ordinarily called recreation—are carried out.

As these functions become less imbedded in functionally diffuse structures, the same basic imperatives outlined for structures with economic or political functional primacy apply. A school system, like a church or a government bureau, must have institutionalized leadership and patterns of authority; it must have access to mobile resources; and it must regulate the relations of its services to its consumers. This is true of a theatrical enterprise or an art institute, either requiring the appropriately specified values, norms legitimized by these values, collectivity organization, and institutionalization of different role types. In spite of the non-economic or non-political primacy of their functions, they cannot escape involvement in the functional imperatives in these areas—everywhere the conditions of successful institutionalization of any function.

*Structures with Integrative Primacy*. It has been suggested that the focus of the integrative subsystem is the legal system; in a modern Western type of society, particularly in the functioning of the appellate courts, and their relation to the more generalized aspects of legislation (much actual legislation is, considered functionally, more concerned with policy decisions than with establishing generalized norms). The establishment of a norm is not alone functionally adequate. The courts are concerned with fundamental problems: interpretation; determination of jurisdictional problems, i.e., in what circumstances a norm applies and to whom; and problems of sanctions or enforcement, i.e., determining the consequences to the actor of compliance or non-compliance. The central judicial function is interpretation, of which these other two are subcategories.

Norms, however, must be defined and interpreted, and also implemented. (We are not here concerned primarily with the executive function of enforcement, which is goal-attainment rather than integration.)

The first imperative of a system of norms is its internal consistency. This is a primary focus of the function of interpretation and, in highly differentiated systems, is primarily a judicial function, though sometimes codes are prepared and legislatively enacted. Second, however, there is the specification of the application of higher-order norms to levels where they can guide the action of the society's lower-level structural units by defining the situation for them. This particularly involves the collectivity and role levels of structure, and hence the institutionalization of the basic patterns governing these in political and economic respects.

Another major functional problem of a normative system concerns the adjustments occurring because a social system is always involved in processes of interchange with a changing environment—indeed, always is subject to endogenous sources of change as well. These naturally have repercussions on units' interrelationships, whose significance for the integration of the system is focussed in the bearing of these relations on the content of the system of norms, and on the degrees and motivation of conformity with norms.

There seem to be three basic types of processes of adjustment. One concerns keeping the regulatory norms at a sufficiently high level of generality so that much of the adjustment can be left to the spontaneous, i.e., unprescribed, action of the units themselves. A system of norms is analogous to a language, in that its rules as such do not "say" anything concrete, but provide a framework within which very many different things can be said and understood according to the occasion for saying them. In certain respects—not exclusively the economic sense—it is legitimate to refer to this as the area within which self-interest is permitted to operate. This "unit-individualism"—*unit* rather than *personal,* for much of it concerns collectivities—is not emancipation from all control through institutionalized norms. Rather, as Durkheim so clearly brought out, high levels of "responsible freedom" can be attained only through positive institutionalization, through systems of norms and sanctions imposing the *obligation* of accepting responsibility and utilizing freedom over wide areas. It may thus be referred to as "institutionalized individualism."

The second basic process of integrative adjustment is altering the content of normative patterns. The great integrative problem is to make such adjustments meet the varying functional needs without threatening the stability of the higher-level system of norms. The dangers of a system of norms are rigidity, or such flexibility that either adequate definition of the situation is lost or that what there is is functionally inappropriate. This operates at the higher levels through legislative, judicial, and administrative rulings and decisions, and, at lower and private collectivities, through functionally cognate mechanisms.

The third type of process operates, short of major structural change itself, in the areas where the other two are inadequate. The essential common feature of the first two is the expectation that the acting unit whose activities are to be controlled will, properly situated through definition of norms and sanctions, act as desired—operating through the situation, without attempting to change the internal structure of the unit, be it person-in-role or collectivity. The processes of social control, in the narrower sociological sense, operate upon the "internal" system of the unit; in the case of the individual-in-role, on his motivations or sentiments. They not only facilitate or hinder his getting what he wants, but they redefine what he wants. Behavior subject to control can be technically termed deviant only when seen this way.

A complex society has institutionalized a variety of processes of social control. We shall not attempt to list or classify them here. But certain aspects of religious ritual certainly fit—those particularly concerned with reinforcing value-commitment when deviance develops or threatens. For the over-all societal collectivity and the definition of its goals, certain aspects of political ideology and its involvement in the definitions of political orientation have this type of significance. In implementing norms in relational systems, particularly those involving contract in the sociological sense, the private practice of law in the system of courts is such a mechanism of social control. Finally, when concern is focused on the individual's capacity for role-performance, the motivated aspect of illness and its therapy, i.e., in psychosomatic and mental illness, have a similar significance.

*Stratification.* A final aspect of social structure of primarily integrative significance is social stratification. That is, the ordering of units of the system in a scale of relative prestige which, to function in a positively integrative way, must be a genuine expression of the institutionalized system of values. In other words, prestige reflects functional contribution to the society's welfare. Perhaps the most important and necessary functional focus of positive institutionalization of stratification is the tendency of societal differentiation to lead to bases of polarization of conflicting interests. The two most obvious bases of polarization are political power and wealth, i.e., command of more or less generalized facilities. Here, the focus of institutionalized stratification is *legitimizing* differential power and wealth, and, more generally, access to valued objects and statuses.

"Social class" is the most common basis of stratification. This term includes the differential prestige-evaluation of various categories of *kinship* units, differentiated by their members' functions in the social system, by access to power and wealth, and by "styles of life," (i.e., patterns of expressive symbolism associated with their standards of living). Kinship is involved because the solidarity of the kinship unit, including as it does both sexes and all ages, is at some level a central functional imperative of every society, even though many partial social systems can operate without it. Therefore, certain differential advantages, like better living conditions and the younger generation's access to opportunity, must be shared by all members of the unit, regardless of the extent to which they have been "earned" by the individual. Thus the wife and children of a successful man will share the rewards of his performance whether or not they have contributed very much to it—the question of their contribution is irrelevant to the family's status as a unit. Though class mobility is possible in varying degrees, no society has over a long period operated without *any* differentiation in class status. Empirically, the extent to which such class differentiation involves class conflict is highly variable. The major function of the institutionalization of class status is to minimize class conflict; but often it is not very successful.

It is unnecessary to assume that there should always be a single unequivocal prestige-ranking scale of kinship units. As we will argue in the Introduction to Part Two, a highly generalized prestige and power differential between two principal classes is a common feature of early civilizations. In later, more highly differentiated societies, however, the multiplicity of groups with widely varying functional significance, and the corresponding differentiation of reward patterns, mean that only on a very broad and general basis is it possible to speak of a single scale; over considerable ranges, the "upper" groups in different functional categories are not directly comparable. In contemporary society, e.g., it is difficult to compare the prestiges held by leading business men, physicians, scientists, and politicians respectively. Money income is far from an exact measure. There is, however, no question that few families in the United States with incomes under five thousand dollars (at the principal income earner's full career maturity) could be described as in the higher prestige groups.

All these integrative functions are performed in structural settings which must be analyzed in the same general terms applied to the other three functional subsystems. They involve their subvalues at the requisite levels of specification, their own norms, collectivities specialized in this direction, and roles (except stratification, which cannot be specialized on a collectivity or role basis). They must meet their own economic, political, and pattern-maintenance prerequisites, etc. A wide range of structural variation in all these respects exist.

## III. THE DYNAMICS OF SOCIAL EQUILIBRIUM

The foregoing discussion may serve as transition to the consideration of analyzing the dynamic processes and mechanisms of social systems, first, with reference to the problem of equilibrium within a given structural framework. Technical conceptualization in this field has developed more slowly than in structural morphology or in functional categorization. Since, therefore, it is less prominent in the literature of the period covered by these volumes, this Introduction will treat these problems less fully than others. It is, however, essential to give it some place, if only on the agenda of unfinished business of sociological theory—though more than that can be done.

The analysis of dynamic process at the equilibration level must center around two categories of the system's components. The first are the *resources* which, starting from outside the system, go through various phases as they pass through the system, and at certain points are utilized in system functioning, i.e., consumed, some "products" then being finally put out to other systems. The process can be conceived as one combining various resources to produce a new phase, and then recombining the results with still other factors to produce still other phases. The second category of component comprises the types of mechanisms which mediate these processes of generation and utilization of resources and regulate their rates of flow, direction of use, etc. Money and power, as discussed, are the prototypes of these mechanisms.

*Societal Resources: Categories of Input and Output.*[24] First, something about the resource problem. Fortunately for sociology, our sister-discipline, economics, has developed and refined a theoretical model of this process of factor-combination that is capable of generalization. This is the theory concerning the combination of the factors of production to produce commodities and shares of income. In the version important for our purposes, there are four factors of production, namely, land, labor, capital, and organization.

The factors of production occupy an intermediate place in the combinatorial flow, through the social system, from socially ultimate resources to socially ultimate outputs. They are the input-categories into the economy as one of the four primary functional subsystems of the society. There should, therefore, be cognate input-categories for each of the other three primary subsystems. It should also be possible to use the same pattern of classification and analysis at other levels, especially for the societal system as a whole and for units at lower levels of specification than the primary functional subsystem.

Let us attempt to outline this for the society as a system. None of the socially ultimate inputs consists in either actual physical objects or the physical behavior of organisms, nor can any of the ultimate outputs be placed in these categories. The social system is one of controlling behavior and the physical environment through behavior. Its ultimate resources are the factors in the system's capacity to attain such control, and ultimate outputs for aspects of the actual attainment and/or exercise of that capacity, including improvements in previous capacity. Where physical objects and physical behav-

24. For convenient reference, a schematic tabulation of the categories to be discussed in this section is included in the accompanying table.

*Schematic Tabulation of Societal Inputs and Outputs*

| *Primary Social Subsystem* | *Input and Source* | *Output and Destination* |
|---|---|---|
| Pattern-Maintenance | *Given* structure as institutionalized patterns of normative culture<br>(no external source) | Maintenance of structure and specification of values<br>(no external destination) |
| Integration | Plasticity<br>(from behavioral organism) | Patterns for purposive response<br>(to behavioral organism) |
| Goal-Attainment | Capacity for socialized motivational commitments<br>(from personality) | Goal-gratification<br>(to personality) |
| Adaptation | Codes for organization of information<br>(from cultural system) | Validation of standards of competence<br>(to cultural system) |

ior are involved, as they always are, the rights or ways to control these entities, not the entities themselves, are the object of sociological analysis. Thus, in an economic exchange involving a physical commodity, what changes hands is not the commodity but property rights *in* the commodity. Analytically, physical transfer of possession is a "technological" process and not a social system process.

The ultimate resources of a society (and of other social systems on the appropriate level of specification) should comprise the ultimate outputs of the other subsystems of the general system of action as these impinge on the social system itself. It is critical, in the economic theory of the factors of production, that land is a special case relative to the other three. It has two special properties—it is neither consumed in the production process, nor produced; and in consequence, its total quantity in the system is not a function of its price, though, through the market mechanism, particular units of land may be allocated to particular uses and users. For the economy to function, land as a physical resource must be included in this category; so also must the institutionalized structure of the society, so far as this is treated as given for purposes of economic analysis and so far as it is differentially utilized in productive processes.

In the society as a system, the analogue of land is the institutionalized normative culture, i.e., the social structure, which for the system reference and time period under consideration is treated as given. At the highest normative level, this consists in the system's values. Treating values as analogous to the quantity of land thus becomes another way of stating the general methodological postulate enunciated earlier: there is a set of theoretical problems concerning the dynamics of equilibrium analysis which should be distinguished from problems involved in the analysis of structural change. So far as analysis is confined to the equilibrium level, institutionalized normative culture is not consumed in the process but is assumed to remain given and stable. The ways these structural components are utilized in social process, however, are variable as a function of the operation of the same mechanisms affecting the utilization of the other resources.

What are these other resources? According to the logic of our paradigm, there should be three: inputs respectively from the personality, the behavioral organism, and the cultural system. Another interesting point is that the situation of the social system, i.e., its goal-attainment and adaptive boundaries taken together, comprises the personality and cultural systems,[25] which fall into these two categories respectively; whereas the integrative boundary, with certain special features, is, rather surprisingly, related to the behavioral organism.

Tentatively, we suggest that the category of pri-

---

25. It is not possible here to amplify this statement. The reader interested in following it may refer to Parsons and Smelser, *Economy and Society*, Free Press, 1956, especially Chapter II. In that publication, however, the analysis was not applied to the action system as a whole in terms of the interchanges of its four primary subsystems, but only to the primary subsystems of a society.

mary input from the personality system may be called "capacity to socialize motivational commitments," extending ultimately to role-performance. The input from the cultural system may be called codified "information," in that it provides the cultural basis of empirical societal problem-solution. When this input is specified and made relevant to motivational, evaluative, and integrative references in the system, it becomes utilizable knowledge. Knowledge, on the societal level, is the basic facility-category. Finally, the basic input from the organism is that plasticity which, through appropriate learning processes, can be built into patterns of purposive response. These, in turn, can be utilized in integrated social interaction. The patterning of the responses in systems, not the discrete units of response, is of crucial significance in this connection.[26]

What, then, are the ouput categories analogous to the income shares of economic theory? Generally, the output corresponding to the input of institutionalized normative culture is the *maintenance* of that structure intact. Only within limitations would an important process in a complex system operate for long without involving structural change at some lower levels of specification, segmentation, and differentiation in the system. In this case, the essential pattern-maintenance output is the *specification* of the higher-order value-system to the appropriate levels for the functional and situational exigencies of the subsystems involved in the secondary processes of structural change.

In interpreting the meaning of the other three output categories, one must remember that the locus of all the other three subsystems is in individual persons—except for the embodiment of culture in inanimate physical objects, notably written documents. Therefore, in one sense all three of these are of psychological significance.

The primary output to the personality system, analytically speaking, is goal-gratification (and, of course, its negative, deprivation). For the equilibrium of the personality as a system, this is the establishment of a stable relation to a structurally significant situational object or system of objects. Role-partners participate in social structure on an interactive basis through action in a role; the relevant object is social, a role-partner or a collectivity. This output thus matches the input of capacity for socialized motivational commitments. One might say that the promise of gratification is the ultimate reward for accepting the disciplines of socialization.

The ouput to the cultural system that matches the input of information is the validation, by competent performance, of the cultural standard of competence. This is essentially the institutionalization of instrumentally significant culture (as distinguished from normative and expressive). This institutionalization in turn comprises operative units of the society—ultimately, individual persons in roles—hence its specification to the functions, situations, and tasks required by social system operation. This suggests that such institutionalization and specification, which are factors in restructuring the cultural tradition, are products, i.e., ouputs, of the social system. The process is that of adapting knowledge to social uses, and validating it by effective use.

The output to the behavioral organism that corresponds to the input of purposive response is the patterning of responses at the level of behavior, as distinguished from personality psychology. At least one of the meanings of pleasure is associated with this as a reward.[27] For the population, a primary function of the social system is to create optimum situations for patterned regulation of behavioral processes, through mechanisms like pleasure. This includes both giving pleasure and imposing the necessary controls on it, since evidence indicates that the pleasure mechanism, like money, easily gets out of hand. As regulator, it also requires regulation.[28]

*Resource-Processing within the System.* Let us proceed to a brief outline of the dynamics of "resource-processing" within the social system; that is, of what happens between ultimate input and ultimate output. The process may be divided into three major phases: (1) the generation of utilizable factors or internal resources; (2) the allocation of these resources; and (3) their utilization. The first and third may be subdivided. At each phase and significant subphase there is a combination of the categories of resources emerging from the preceding phase, resulting in a set of modifications preparing them for the next phase.

*An Example: The Socialization of Motivational*

26. This suggestion, which may seem strange to many readers, is not arbitrary. It has grown largely from discussions with Dr. James Olds about the application in the theory of action of his findings about the pleasure mechanism in regulating behavior, including this mechanism's base in the anatomical structure of the brain.

27. These suggestions—above all, that pleasure, as a generalized mechanism of control of behavior, not the specific input necessary for metabolic equilibrium (e.g., food), is the focus of the phenomena and significance of reward—are based primarily on the work of Dr. Olds. See Olds, "Self-Stimulation of the Brain," *Science,* Feb. 14, 1958.

28. I might remark, parenthetically, that the analytical distinction between goal gratification and pleasure or, more generally, reward, is a fundamental one which much psychology has tended to ignore. It underlies, in my opinion, the major axis of Freud's theory, the distinction between the "pleasure principle" and the "reality principle." See Parsons, "Social Structure and the Development of Personality," *Psychiatry,* November, 1958.

*Capacity*. Motivation as a resource provides a good illustration, as a fairly well analyzed case. At the societal level, motivation originates as an input from the personality system. The major phase of generation may be divided into three principal subphases. The first is the one known to psychoanalytic theory as the oral phase. In this, through identification with the primary agent of care (usually the mother), the individual builds up a system of "socialized" motivation whereby his maintaining the attachment to this agent becomes the paramount goal of the emerging personality system.

The next phase extends from the resolution of the oral attachment to that of the Oedipus complex. Then differentiation of the original internalized oral-maternal object occurs, yielding a personality system consisting of four primary motivational subsystems or need-dispositions—adequacy, security, conformity, and nurturance.[29] The balance among these differs in different personalities; in particular, one major factor of differential balance is established through sex-role identification, whose foundations are laid in this period. But the relevance of this broad structural pattern may be treated as a constant.

These processes of differentiation, and hence increasing capacity to cope with motivational problems, are clearly not a function simply of the unaided maturation of motivational capacity; the socialization of this capacity is dependent on the combination of original capacity with three other components, at the proper levels of specification. The first component is one of value-pattern internalized, by the time of the Oedipal resolution, to form the primary basis of the super-ego. The second is a component of socialized information which becomes the basis of the child's early cognitive development. The third is a component of properly measured and specified pleasure-rewards, to which the organism responds and which is especially important to motor skills. In relevance to socialization, the primary type, at least, are the rewards associated with pre-Oedipal eroticism, which Freud has made famous. The strength and, possibly, certain other qualitative variations of original motivation, and variations in corresponding inputs of value-pattern, of information, and of the pleasure-reward deprivation balance, explain variations in outcome for the post-Oedipal personality structure.

Even apart from variations in maturational quantitative factors, the motivational capacity of the immediately post-Oedipal child is not yet utilizable for role-performance in complex social systems, because it is too undifferentiated to perform the multiple roles required of the adult. The primary differentiation leading up to this order of capacity for multiple role-commitments occurs in the latent and adolescent periods. There are further inputs, from other subsystems, into the "socialization" subsystem of the society—value-components, information, and pleasure-rewards—but at *different* levels of specification and qualitative differentiation from the pre-Oedipal phases. It is striking that, in our type of society, the informational input is predominantly at the higher levels of generality required by a *literate* culture.

A personality structure results which, with varying emphases in each of the primary role categories, should be capable of playing *differentiated* roles simultaneously: in a family, procreation through marriage and parenthood; in a functionally specialized collectivity, through occupation; in a setting of community responsibility (especially in political terms); and in a setting concerned with the value-stability of the system, especially through religion.

The other three types of input undergo corresponding kinds of "processing." For values, the point of input is the value system's highest socially relevant level of generality; for information, it is the *culturally codified* body of knowledge available in the society; for the purposive response factor, it is the "plastic potentiality" of the constituent organisms. These four factors have an obverse relationship in the societal scale of specification. The value-pattern and the informational components are introduced at the highest level of generality so far as their relevance to social system function is concerned, whereas the motivational and purposive response components are the most specific in terms of social system function. In one sense, concerned with the system-reference of their sources, these factors also are introduced in highly generalized form, and must be redefined on the appropriate levels for their use in the social system. Thus only collectivity- and role-level values are operatively realizable, and only role-level information is "practical." Correspondingly, only role-level motivation is functional to the social system. The old question, "What use is a baby?" is relevant.

*The Allocation of Resources to Operative Units.* In temporal sequence, the generation of internal resources must precede their allocation. Allocation

29. These views are derived from Freud and H. A. Murray. My own treatment is stated most fully in *Family, Socialization and Interaction Process,* Free Press, 1955, Chapter II, and, with some modification and extension, in "Social Structure and the Development of Personality," *Psychiatry,* Nov., 1958. Though important empirical qualifications need to be made for variations in the social structures of different societies, the relevance of the general paradigm of three major phases, marked by the oral, Oedipal, and adolescent patterns is a constant which transcends cultural relativity.

is made to *operative units* of the system, to which resources are committed for use.

Economics again provides us with a prototype of the allocating mechanism, namely, the market. The output of the generation phase which the economist calls labor as a "factor of production" may be defined as capacity for functional performance in occupational roles. It is the product of the socialization process, in "developed" societies focusing, in its terminal phase, at the point of the individual's emergence from formal education. An important current concept of the supply of potential occupational services is that of the *labor force*. The economist treats this concept of supply as relevant; and it is parallel to the concept of "effective demand." Many persons with skills and other usable capacities are not in the labor force, because they are not accessible to offers of employment—perhaps the largest group comprises housewives. A member of the labor force is either employed or seeking employment—presumably with real chance of success.

The labor market is the mechanism by which employing organizations and persons seeking employment are brought together. At the market level, the primary directly operating factor is comparative monetary remuneration. The operation of the market mechanism makes possible a relatively "functional" allocation, without the need of centralized administrative decision.

It follows from the above account of the generation process of occupational capacity that not an undifferentiated stream, but a highly differentiated set of substreams, are fed into the labor market. There is not one completely integrated labor market, but many, partially integrated with each other. There are two main bases of differentiating these from each other. The first concerns level of capacity, from unskilled labor to the high qualifications required for specialized functions or responsibilities. The second concerns qualitative role—once one is committed to medicine or science, he is unlikely to seek a role in governmental administration. Above all, qualitative differentiation concerns different types of combination, in the phase of the socialization process called "training," of more generalized performance capacity with other factors contributing to trained capacity—functional values, information, and types of reward in the behavioral sense.[30]

The closest possible approach to the economist's "perfect market," where labor is the resource involved, is in the field of low-level relatively undifferentiated capacities, where the interchangeability of units is prominent. As capacities become more rare and more differentiated, other factors intervene to "skew" the classical market pattern—e.g., the market for professional services is substantially different from the competitive model.

Where societies are highly enough differentiated politically there are allocative processes, governed by the power mechanism, that are analogous to markets. Leadership capacity is the resource allocated through this type of channel—including the organizational patterning which makes it effective, if this is not ascriptively fixed. One of the best analyzed cases of leadership capacity is that of organization as a factor of production, which as a mobile resource has in particular been analyzed as "entrepreneurship" in Schumpeter's sense, or "organizational responsibility" in the sense Barnard employs.[31]

In executive roles in specific-function collectivities, personalized leadership capacity is acquired through a special type of labor market. In this connection, components of this internal resource are fused with the performance-capacity resource. In other connections, this is not the case. For example, in the allocation of political leadership through the electoral process, voting is an exercise of power through the agency of which those to assume actual operative responsibility are selected from a pool of aspirants to leadership. In the American governmental system, e.g., this operates both in the executive and the legislative branches, and at the federal, state, and local levels. Comparable processes operate in countless democratic associations.

In modern totalitarian regimes (and in some subassociations in democratic societies), effective enfranchisement is made impossible by the one-party system. Nevertheless, that party is ceaselessly concerned with legitimizing, through propaganda and agitation, its selection for leadership in the eyes of the public and, as recently in Hungary, when its claims are not validated a major crisis may develop.

The essential point is that leadership capacity is generated within the society, through the socialization of individuals and through the development of mobile and adaptable potentialities of organization. Then, where this resource is not ascribed to a particular use, there must be some mechanism for allocating it to operative units which can utilize it.

There are comparable processes of allocating the

30. Markets in the present sense appear only on certain levels of the general differentiation of social structure. On less differentiated levels, the functional equivalents of these allocative processes are embedded in functionally diffuse structures. The utilization of the resources is likely to be much less fluid, much more strictly ascribed to particular collective units.

31. Chester I. Barnard, *The Functions of the Executive,* Harvard University Press, Cambridge, Mass., 1938. J. A. Schumpeter, *The Theory of Economic Development.*

other categories of internal societal resource, one deriving from the value-system through processes of specification, and the other deriving from the integrative exigencies of the system: these are ultimately concerned with the relation of purposive response and reward. The former concerns allocating legitimation to new and altered collectivity structures and functions—an important process in a rapidly developing society. The latter concerns the social-control function, discussed above, and the problem of institutional commitment to conformity with generalized norms. This latter is "motivational," but it operates at a variety of levels. There is in this, as in the other cases, a variety of processes analogous to those of the market.

*The Utilization of Resources.* The stage in the natural history of a resource-unit that follows its allocation is utilization. Like generation, this may be subdivided into three phases. First, the usual immediate recipient of a resource-unit through societal allocation is a collectivity. Independent occupational roles, like those of the private professional practitioner or the independent artisan, should be treated as limiting cases, constituting the one-man collectivity. This becomes more significant as resources become more mobile and larger proportions of them are utilized in specific-function processes. Then there is a fundamental structural difference between the field of the allocative process, e.g., a market, and the agency of utilization, e.g., a firm. From one point of view, the difference is one of degree of stringency of control. In the allocative process, the utilization unit is in the position of bidding for resources which other units also want. Once allocated, however, the resource-unit is controlled by its recipient—sometimes to the point of complete consumption. Such complete consumption occurs most obviously with physical commodities—which are not, as such, units of social-system resource, but are facilities controlled in the interest of social-system process.

Utilization is essentially a process of successively more particularized decision-making; action-opportunities, facilities, and responsibilities are allocated more specifically at each step. The most broadly defined stages are the allocation to the collectivity, to the role, and to the task. The function of the collectivity is to define what is to be done; that of allocation to role, to define who is to do it; and that of the task level, how it is to be done.

As in the generation of resources, in the process of utilization, each step (including the substeps within it) involves combining the resource-units in question with other units. The organization employs labor units through the labor market. It supplies an organizational framework within which these units can function effectively.[32] It supplies facilities essential for this, such as physical facilities whose procurement was beyond the worker's control—e.g., office, laboratory, and library—though some of these may be determined by negotiation. The organization may supply funds which, within certain rules, he may use to procure equipment and employ service.

There is, in the operation of the social system, a *terminus ad quem* of the process, i.e., the ultimate accomplishment of tasks. This may be defined as the point at which no further commitment of societal resources is required as "reasonable" in that *particular* task-context. For example, maintaining an elderly person is an institutionalized social obligation. On his death, however, the obligation of maintenance is terminated and the tasks of relatives, health-care personnel, etc., involved are completed, except for the functions of funeral observance, settlement of a possible estate, etc.[33] The resources previously committed to this task are, if still unconsumed, freed for another.

The specific content of the economic paradigm used in this discussion as an analytical model cannot be generalized to apply to all essential social processes, but its *logical structure* can be so generalized. Differences arise from two sources. One is the level of specification of resources in their progress through the system; the most direct relevance of the economic paradigm is at the market level of most general allocation. The second is the qualitative differentiation of types of resources. The only resources which fit the economic paradigm very closely are monetary funds and instruments.[34] Finely divisible, not very perishable, and highly standardized commodities come next. Any form of labor service is a rather bad third; and organization as a factor is probably much farther away from the paradigm of the perfect market.

Value specification (legitimation), institutionalized permissiveness in processes of social control, and the like, cannot be bought, though in a sense they must be paid for. The solution of this apparent paradox lies in the independent yet interpenetrating subsystems of a social system in both dynamic and structural respects. Thus the decision to employ a

32. One example is the framework establishing the main relation to students of the college or university teacher. In a modern society, it would be difficult for the sociologist, for example, just to "hang out his shingle" and hope to attract (and make a living from) competent students and, in turn, to give them prospects of acceptable future employment as professionals.

33. Of course, this does not mean that the fact that the particular person has lived and died has no further social consequences.

34. See Parsons and Smelser, *op. cit.*, pp. 156 ff.

particular professional service involves employer and employee in a special kind of market which involves monetary transactions, among other things. But rights and obligations of privileged communication may be concomitants of the established relationship, and may not then be contracted away or waived—as, e.g., in the relationship between attorney and client. This is precisely what Durkheim meant by one of the "non-contractual elements of contract."[35] Within this sphere, the relationship is protected from both monetary and political intervention; the non-economic resource of permissiveness is utilized to solve the client's problems. A kind of contractual freedom exists: the client may choose what confidential information he reveals to his attorney; and the latter may choose how he reacts to these disclosures or to what he suspects the client of withholding. Hence the interchange, though structurally *analogous* to a market, is, in content and in functional signficance in the system, fundamentally different from *any* market.

## *Mechanisms Controlling Resource-Processing*

For present purposes, this account of the processing of resources through the system will have to suffice, supplemented only by a brief discussion of the mechanisms most immediately controlling these processes. A somewhat fuller picture of the nature of dynamic process can be presented only by discussing the processes of resource-flow in relation to the controlling mechanisms.

*Money.* Again, the best-analyzed control mechanism is economic, namely, money. It has been noted that money is not a commodity, but is essentially a specialized mode of communication mediating in the circulation of expectations and binding commitments of certain types. As such, money has the characteristic two-level structure found in all languages; a system of categorizing meaning, and of operative utterances. In the language of the classical economists, money is simultaneously both a measure of value and a medium of exchange. In the former sense it provides the criteria of *economic* valuation by specification of the general value pattern to the level of economic function. It is the *economic* common denominator of many commodities and services considered as both products and factors of production; thus it serves further as a standard for economically rational allocation of resources. In this capacity, however, the use of monetary standards does not imply that anything changes hands.

When money functions as a real medium of exchange, however—when real dollars and not units of account are involved—the spending unit is relinquishing, the receiving unit acquiring, something of value. But that something cannot be technologically utilized or consumed; it can be used only to *control* the allocating of what economists call "real" resources and products. The significant point is that possessing money involves a power or capacity to get things done, while *avoiding* specific commitments at the moment—i.e., about specific channels of expenditure in terms of object or of source of supply, about time of purchase, and about price. The combination of effectiveness (purchasing power) and freedom from commitment makes money such an important mechanism. Spending money is like speaking: the utterance, once made, has consequences; but the speaker who commands a language and has certain knowledge he can formulate in its terms retains his freedom to say what he likes until he is committed through acts of utterance.

As a medium of exchange, money can function in either of two generalized ways, namely, as a facility, or as a reward. As a facility, it is the generalized capacity to command more specific facilities; as a reward, it is a generalized measure of the value of a performance or of a variety of performances, and also the transmitting of something of value.[36]

Involving money, the paradigm of supply and demand, as a specification of the nature of market process, is important to all social system process. As the paradigm is used by economists, supply functions are always stated in terms of "real" assets, e.g., commodities, services, products, or factors of production; whereas demand functions are stated in monetary terms. This may validly be identified with the performance-sanction paradigm of the general analysis of action, in that supply-demand is a case of performance-sanction. The monetary mechanism, as a mechanism of control, stands higher on the generalization-specification scale than does the resource which it controls; this is generally true of the performance-sanction relationship.

Money is only one of several analogous mechanisms controlling resource combination and allocation in social systems; but the logical paradigm outlined for its case should be applicable to the others —e.g., to political power.

*"Real Commitments."* Economists have gener-

35. *Division of Labor in Society,* Free Press, Book I, Chap. VII.

36. Olds's work indicates that, in behavioral psychology, the relation of goal-gratification to pleasure is theoretically parallel to the relation between acquiring possession of a physical commodity and money. Pleasure and money, not food and commodities, are the primary reward categories.

ally spoken as if market trade were in physical commodities and services. This concept is elliptical; it does not refer to the factor of *rights of disposal* over goods and services that constitutes another mechanism of control over resources standing lower in the control and specification scale than money. The economist's "real" resources and income must not be directly identified with this level. In the case of services, the employment contract establishes certain mutual rights and obligations between employer (typically, an organization) and employee (typically, an individual assuming a role). But a series of decisions of specification must be made before ultimate utilization of the labor resource as a factor in production. Per se, the act of employment excludes units other than the employing one from encroaching on the rights of the employing unit; it also defines both the obligations assumed by the employee within the organization, and the obligations assumed by the employing organization for remuneration, type of work expected, times, etc.

Operative work is performed in a technical subsystem of the employing organization. Employment is neither the process of work nor specific commitment to it; it is crossing the boundary into membership in the employing organization. Particular steps may be compressed, but each must be analytically recognized. For physical facilities, the analogy to employment is the acquisition of property rights.

The institutions of occupation and property are thus structurally analogous to money. At the institutional level they are generalized norms governing the allocation and utilization of resources. But as "jobs" and possessive rights over physical objects, their character is analogous to that of money as a medium of exchange. Rights to jobs and to commodities thus change hands, just as money changes hands. A job commits its incumbent to a series of performances which are still relatively unspecified.

Moreover, markets and money are impossible while the allocation of economically significant resources is sufficiently embedded in ascriptive systems of rights and obligations. These structures' diffuseness is associated with the dispersal of property-rights and work-obligations. Their combination into ownership and occupation is the prerequisite of the resource-mobility necessary for extensive control of allocation through markets. This is a complex hierarchy. Money can control only certain steps in the process—i.e., the allocation of resources to units, but not their effective utilization within units.

The mechanism most closely analogous to money is the utilization of real commitments. These commitments operate by manipulating both property rights over physical possessions and occupational rights over employed persons in their organizational roles. In the latter case, the authority of the organization's management or administration over its personnel is analogous to property rights over physical objects. It is an institutionalized mechanism which, given the commitment to employment, enables management to make realistic further decisions of specification about utilizing the resource. At the time of commitment to employment, the content of these specifications need not be known by or agreed to by either party. Therefore, the same fundamental freedom from detailed advance commitments operates in the case of organizational authority as in that of property. Authority is thus a generalized medium underlying power in the same sense that property underlies money.

In economic parlance, these capacities for utilization, of which property and occupational role are prototypes, may be called real commitments, in the economist's sense of "real" as contrasted with monetary. The allocation of real commitments in this sense is controlled by the monetary mechanism, while these commitments constitute mechanisms governing the processes of further specification of the utilization of resources. At least one intermediate step is necessary to solve the problem of how specification of the physical operations of the behavioral process is brought about.

*Power.* Let us now consider the step above money in the hierarchy of mechanisms of control. This brings us back to the problem of power, whose most important points we will discuss in terms of their relevance to the present context. We may begin with the fact that in complex societies, structurally, there is a gap between the functional imperatives of co-ordinating collectivities relative to their collective goals and the structurally institutionalized obligation of units at the requisite levels of specification. This gap is comparable to the one created by the division of labor between markets for products and markets for labor services. If ascriptive obligations do not close the gap, then particularized "deals" may occur, between units with leadership responsibilities and units on whose co-operation they must depend, about the terms of this co-operation—these deals are analogous to economic barter. But flexible orientation to changing situations on this basis is extremely limited. Higher flexibility, and hence effectiveness, depends on the institutionalization of a generalized mechanism for structuring and legitimating expectations on both sides without too definite advance specification of detailed rights and obligations. In the analytically defined political field, such a mechanism is power. For the leadership function, it is the legitimized capacity to claim loyal co-operation, within institutionalized limits, *without prior specification of the content of the expected performances.* In the political field this takes the form of the rights to make binding decisions—rights which are institutionalized as leadership, authority, and regulation at the appropriate levels of specification.

For "followership," analytically considered, essentially the same considerations apply. Negatively, the institutionalization of power protects status positions against interference and, if interference is threatened, acts against the threat in such a way that those in authority must listen. One example is the institutionalization of civil rights, with access to the courts, to legislators, and to executive officials. Positively, it is the institutionalization of expectations that, within limits, the public's demands will be given a serious hearing—e.g., most formally in the electoral process.

A "power system" in this sense, as in the case of a market, is a mechanism for adjusting inevitably conflicting interests over considerable areas, where the power held on each side must be considered by the other, and where relatively stable "rules of the game" hold conflicts within bounds. The units involved may be identified with those many political scientists call "interest groups." From one point of view, the outcome is always some sort of "compromise." This situation is parallel to the market, where the seller by definition has a monetary interest in a higher price and the buyer in a lower one, so that an agreed price is a compromise (except at a limiting extreme).

The measure of value in the case of power is the concept of the public interest. Interest groups, including governmental incumbents, are never content to operate in terms of "naked power," but always attempt to legitimize their claims in terms of the public interest. However imperfect the integration achieved may be, this concept's weight is far from negligible in a moderately stable political system. At the level of medium, there is no institutionalized unit which is generally comparable to the monetary unit, though in one crucial sector of the power system the vote is a very precisely defined unit. The vote is the followership's instrument of the exchange process of power, though it does not stand alone; there are a variety of other means to exert political influence. Leadership must earn votes by establishing, among groups of voters, the expectation that in future contingencies the leaders will act in ways relatively acceptable to the group in question—but *not* in terms of specified commitments. This would reduce the system to political barter; an economic equivalent of frequent occurrence is the employer's specific contractual provision of family living quarters to employees.

Political power stands higher in the hierarchy of societal control mechanisms than money. They are interrelated, in that money funds can be a means of acquiring political power, while the holder of political power is in a favored position for acquiring money. But these relationships should not obscure the fundamental hierarchical order, as is shown by, e.g., the governmental control of the monetary *system* as a system—a control necessary because in a differentiated, yet integrated, society there can be only one paramount collectivity and system of legal norms. Another indication of their hierarchal discreteness is the fact that the functioning of a market system depends on basic normative conditions controlled more by a governmental system than by the various "private" interest groups involved in market transactions.

*Integrative Communication.* To complete the picture, a suggestion may be made about still another class of mechanisms, these at the top of the hierarchy of control. This class is integrative communication, and is related to the functions of social control in the narrow technical sense discussed above in a structural-functional connection. The operational focus of this type of mechanism is the motivational commitment of units of the system to the fulfilment of institutionalized expectations.

The hierarchy thus far reviewed may be summarized as follows: real commitments form the institutionalized basis for regulating the processes of fulfilling the contractual obligations assumed by units in the social system. They define generalized expectations within which, through authority (in the operative subsystem, not at the societal level), negotiation, etc., the specification of performance obligations, its rewards, etc., can be worked out. In the major allocative contexts, the operative collective unit typically acquires only the real commitments to the use of its essential resources, leaving further specification to be made as new situations develop.

The proximate mechanism of allocating real commitments is the monetary mechanism—qualified, as necessary when one generalizes sociologically about market processes. Operative control of the uses to which these commitments are to be put is not relevant to the monetary mechanism; their contractual availability for use, and the generalized conditions on which this works out—particularly in competition with other utilising units—are relevant to the monetary mechanism. We must still consider both the legitimation of the goals of operating units at the requisite level of specification, and a variety of questions about structuring the situation in which they may operate. The function of the political process is one fundamental level of this specification of goals and conditions. By structural fusion, political authority may, in certain fields, undertake specific allocation below the monetary level, or operation, or both. For example, this is universally the case for the functions of military defense; in a socialist society, it comprises a much broader field.

In all three of these types of process, the "interests" of the units in question can be taken for granted; given the situation, including normative prescriptions and the sanctions attached to them, units know what they want and can be expected to act in accord with their interests. At a still higher level of the problem of control, this assumption is suspended and the question arises of mechanisms for bringing the individual or collective unit to accept the institutionalized definition of the situation.[37] It is probable that applying direct negative sanction will reinforce deviant tendencies; if conformity is to be motivated one must go behind rational mechanisms and modify the underlying structure determining the unit's orientation. One typical case is the mechanism of therapy operating with reference to the motivated components of illness, when the object is the individual's personality. In other cases, however, the object may be a collectivity, like a delinquent gang; and, in others, a relational system not formally organized as a collectivity—as in the practice of civil law, where the typical system is defined as comprising two opposed parties, their attorneys, and the normative system represented through a court; whether or not there is actual resort to court, the presence of the courts is of fundamental significance. Some aspects of the functioning of partisan politics, of religious ritual, and of other phenomena also belong in this category.

The mechanisms of control in such cases must operate in situations insulated from the pressures of normal sanction systems. One such institution is privileged communication. Another example is found in religious ritual, where the situation is defined as exceptional—e.g., the treatment of bereaved persons, set apart as sacred. Permissiveness provides an opportunity for giving an order of support to which the unit would not otherwise be entitled, i.e., in spite of attitudes or conduct which otherwise would be "punished" with negative sanctions. Within this protected sphere, a special process of conditional sanctioning of behavior can operate until a pattern consistent with the general institutional expectations is so strongly established that the special permissiveness and support are unnecessary.

This set of mechanisms has the same formal structure as the others which have been reviewed. So far as the mechanisms operate effectively, permissiveness and support do not imply abandonment of the institutionalized expectations; they are justified by special circumstances making it difficult or impossible for the unit to fulfil those expectations—e.g., because an individual is sick, or a pair of conflicting units cannot know their legal obligations until these have been worked out with their attorneys or through court decision. Thus, the measure of value is very much involved. Facilities, in the form of information, e.g., as interpretations, and rewards, e.g., evaluative sanctions, especially approval, definitely circulate. Moreover, these are scarce media; any good psychiatrist or appellate judge knows that interpretations must not be too lavishly offered. "Just "thinking out loud" without carefully considering the impact of what is said on the patient or on the pool of potential litigants would not be good therapy or jurisprudence.

This set of mechanisms ranks first in the hierarchy. Resort is made to them only when others have failed to operate; indeed, such failure is a direct criterion of the need for them. Thus the disability aspect of illness is the primary criterion of the need for therapeutic help. Furthermore, on theoretical grounds this category of mechanisms is at the top of the whole hierarchical series—going farther brings one to the problem of structural change as such, which has been defined as a different order of problem. It lifts the restriction that the structure of the system, i.e., the institutionalized normative culture, must be treated as given.

*Summary of the Equilibrating Process.* The equilibrium processes of a social system are intermeshing processes involving two sets of changeable factors, each defined in terms of the system's structure. The first set comprises the categories of resources which, at each stage of being processed through the system, are combined with the appropriate complementary resources. The progress of each resource through the system is a process of specification through decision-making about disposition through allocation and about proportions of combination. The second set of changeable factors comprises the mechanisms just discussed. Resources are differentiated from mechanisms in that resources, from the point of view of the system, are, at any given stage, consumed (with the exception of structure, e.g., land); whereas mechanisms, as media of con-

37. In cases falling under the present heading, deviant attitudes toward institutionalized expectations are ambivalent. That is, the problem of institutionalizing *new* expectations must be treated as analytically distinct from that of implementing expectations already institutionalized. See *The Social System,* Parsons, Free Press, 1951, Chapter VII.

trol, are, from the point of view of the *unit,* spent and acquired, while, from that of the *system,* they circulate from one unit to another but are not consumed. For instance, money cannot be consumed, but only transferred from one possessor to another. We have described how the same is true of real commitments, of power, and of integrative communication. The component of structure in which these changeables are based is neither consumed nor circulated.

The general significance of the hierarchical interrelations of these components indicates that the social system as a whole and its internal processes should, in regard to behavior, be considered as a complex set of cybernetic controlling mechanisms —not just one governor, but a complex series of them. In this broad sense, the problem of the dynamics of social systems is not so much a problem of the transformation of energy as of the processing of information.

The analysis of these processes is now in an elementary stage. Some fundamental definitions and classifications are now being formulated, as are some important sequences, such as specification of the broad combinations needed at each stage, and the broad quantitative differences made by grossly different proportions. Furthermore, in an interdependent system, every long sequence of process-stage, to be accurately analyzed, must specifically account for the effect of repercussions through the rest of the system and for the resulting feedback on the original points for analysis.

For all aspects of this problem, important points of reference—e.g., the combination processes of economic theory and their relation to the monetary mechanism; the socialization process in relation to social structure; certain salient aspects of power systems; recent work on decision-making in collectivities; and knowledge of therapeutics. But these are still fragments, at best partially woven into the fabric of a genuinely systematic analysis. The concept of system itself is the most important guide to developing such analysis.

The problem of systematizing the morphology of living—i.e., biological, psychological, social, and cultural—systems is intrinsically easier to solve than that of their dynamics in the present sense. This is the reason that the first major section of this essay is longer than the second and that, in the following selections, there is more documentation in the field of structural analysis than in analysis of dynamic process. Dynamic analysis must, in our theoretical scheme, be referred to morphological premises, or else be subject to complete loss of orientation. The statement that everything empirical is subject to change may be metaphysically correct; but this is often translated into the scientifically untenable doctrine condemning as invalid a heuristic assumption that any reference point is structurally given, on the grounds that such an assumption would commit the investigator to deny the fluidity of ultimate reality. Science is not a photographic reproduction of reality, but is a highly selective mode of organizing man's orientation to reality—however philosophers define the latter. The scientifically specific component of this organization depends on ability to establish reference-points structurally stable enough to justify the *simplification* of dynamic problems prerequisite to logically manageable analysis. Empirically, these reference-points are relative and may be expected to change as the science develops. The categorical assertion that any assumptions about structure are scientifically inadmissible, because in the last analysis everything is in flux, denies the legitimacy of science. In any science, and in sociology in particular, the concept of change is meaningful only in terms of a definable *something,* i.e., something which can be described in structural terms.

## IV. THE PROBLEM OF STRUCTURAL CHANGE

According to the program laid out above, the last major problem area is the analysis of processes of structural change in social systems. The process of structural change may be considered the obverse of equilibrating process; the distinction is made in terms of boundary-maintenance. Boundary implies both that there is a difference of state between phenomena internal and external to the system; and that the type of process tending to maintain that difference of state is different from the type tending to break it down. In applying this concept to social systems, one must remember that their essential boundaries are those vis-à-vis personalities, organisms, and cultural systems, and not those directly vis-à-vis the physical environment.

A boundary is thus conceived as a kind of watershed. The control resources of the system are adequate for its maintenance up to a well-defined set of points in one direction: beyond that set of points, there is a tendency for a *cumulative* process of change to begin, producing states progressively farther from the institutionalized patterns. The metaphor of the watershed, however, fails to demonstrate the complexity of the series of control levels and, hence, of the boundaries of subsystems within larger systems. The mechanisms discussed earlier are involved in the dynamic aspects of such a hierarchical series of subboundaries; if a subboundary is broken, resources within the larger system counteract the implicit tendency to structural change. This is most dramatically shown in the capacity of social control mechanisms, in a narrow sense, to reverse cumulative processes of deviance. The conception of the nature of the difference between processes of equilibration and processes of structural change seems inherent in the conception of a social system as a cybernetic system of control over behavior.

As observed, structural change in subsystems is an inevitable part of equilibrating process in larger systems. The individual's life-span is so short that concrete role-units in any social system of societal scope must, through socialization, continually undergo structural change. Closely bound to this is a low-order collectivity like the nuclear family. Though the institutional norms defining "the family" in a society or a social sector may remain stable over long periods, *the family* is never a collectivity; and real families are continually being established by marriages, passing through the "family cycle," and, eventually, disappearing, with the parents' death and the children's dispersion. Similar considerations apply to other types of societal subsystems.

Within this frame of reference, the problem of structural change can be considered under three headings, as follows: (1) the sources of tendencies toward change; (2) the impact of these tendencies on the affected structural components, and the possible consequences; and (3) possible generalizations about trends and patterns of change.

## *The Sources of Structural Change*

The potential sources of structural change are exogenous and endogenous—usually in combination. The foregoing discussion has stressed the instability of the relations between any system of action and its situation, because this is important for defining the concepts of goal and the political function. We were emphasizing *relation,* and a relation's internal sources of instability may derive from external tendencies to change.

*Exogenous Sources of Change.* The exogenous sources of social structural change consist in endogenous tendencies to change in the organisms, personalities, and cultural systems articulated with the social systems in question. Among such sources are those operating through genetic changes in the constituent human organisms and changes in the distribution of genetic components within populations, which have an impact on behavior as it affects social role-performance, including the social system's capacities for socialization. Changes in the physical environment are mediated most directly either through the organism—e.g., through perception—or through appropriate aspects of the cultural system—e.g., technological knowledge.

One particularly important source of exogenous change is a change originating in other social systems. For the politically organized society, the most important are other politically organized societies. To consider change in this context, it is essential to treat the society of reference as a unit in a more inclusive social system. Even when the system's level of integration is relatively low and chronic conflicts between its subunits continually threaten to break into war, *some* element of more or less institutionalized order always governs their interrelations—otherwise, a concept like "diplomacy" would be meaningless. Of course, exogenous cultural borrowing and diffusion are mediated through interrelations among societies.

*Endogenous Sources: "Strains."* The most general, commonly used term for an endogenous tendency to change is "strain." *Strain* here refers to a condition in the *relation* between two or more structured units (i.e., subsystems of the system) that constitutes a tendency or pressure toward changing that relation to one incompatible with the equilibrium of the relevant part of the system. If the strain becomes great enough, the mechanisms of control will not be able to maintain that conformity to relevant normative expectations necessary to avoid the breakdown of the structure. A strain is a tendency to disequilibrium in the input-output balance between two or more units of the system.

Strains can be relieved in various ways. For the system's stability, the ideal way is resolution—i.e., restoring full conformity with normative expectations, as in complete recovery from motivated illness. A second relieving mechanism is arrestation or isolation—full conformity is not restored, but some accommodation is made by which less than normal performance by the deficient units is accepted, and other units carry the resulting burden. However, it may be extremely difficult to detect a unit's failure to attain full potentiality, as in the case of handicap contrasted with illness. Completely eliminating the unit from social function is the limiting case here.

Strain may also be relieved by change in the structure itself. Since we have emphasized strain in the *relations* of units (instability internal to the unit itself would be analyzed at the next lower level of system reference), structural change must be defined as alteration in the normative culture defining the expectations governing that relation—thus, at the systemic level, comprising all units standing in strained relations. The total empirical process may also involve change in the structure of typical units; but the essential reference is to *relational pattern.* For example, chronic instability in a typical kind of market might lead to a change in the norms governing that market; but if bargaining units change their tactics in the direction of conforming with the old norms, this would not constitute *structural* change of *this* system. In line with the general concepts of inertia and of the hierarchy of controls, we may say that endogenous change occurs only when the lower-order mechanisms of control fail to contain the factors of strain.

*Factors in Change.* In introducing our discussion of the factors in structural change, we must establish the essential point that the conception of a system of interdependent variables, on the one hand, and of units or parts, on the other, by its nature implies that there is no necessary order of teleological significance in the sources of change. This applies particularly to such old controversies as economic or interest explanations *versus* explanations in terms of ideas or values. This problem is logically parallel to the problem of the relations between heredity and environment. Of a set of "factors," *any or all may be sources of change,* whose nature will depend on the ways an initial impetus is propagated through the system by the types of dynamic process analyzed under subhead III, above.

To avoid implying a formless eclecticism we must add two other points. First, careful theoretical identifications must be made of the nature of the factors to which an impetus to structural change is imputed. Many factors prominent in the history of social thought are, according to the theory of social systems, exogenous—including factors of geographical environment and biological heredity, and outstanding personalities, as "great men," who are never conceived of simply as products of their societies. This category of exogenous factors also includes cultural explanations, as those in terms of religious ideas. Furthermore, these different exogenous sources are not alike in the nature of their impact on the social system.

Among these exogenous sources of change is the size of the population of any social system. Perhaps the most important relevant discussion of this was Durkheim's, in the *Division of Labor,* where he speaks of the relations between "material" and "dynamic" density. Populations are partially resultants of the processes of social systems, but their size is in turn a determinant.[38]

The second, related point concerns the implications of the hierarchy of control in social systems. It may be difficult to define magnitude of impact; however, given approximate equality of magnitude, the probability of producing structural change is greater in proportion to the position in the order of control at which the impact of its principal disturbing influence occurs. This principle is based on the assumption that stable systems have mechanisms which can absorb considerable internal strains, and thus endogenous or exogenous variabilities impinging at lower levels in the hierarchy of control may be neutralized before extending structural changes to higher levels. It follows that the crucial focus of the problem of change lies in the stability of the value system.

The analytical problems in this area are by no means simple. Difficulties arise because of the complex ways in which societies are composed of interpenetrating subsystems, and because of the ways in which the exogenous factors impinge somehow on every role, collectivity norm, and subvalue. Thus the collectivity component of social structure has been placed, in general analytical terms, only third in the general control hierarchy. Yet every society must be organized as a whole on the collectivity level, integrating goal-attainment, integrative, and pattern-maintenance functions. Hence an important change in the leadership composition of the over-all societal collectivity *may* have a far greater impact on the norms and values of the society generally than would a value change in lower-order subsystems. Hence a naïve use of the formula, the higher in the control hierarchy the greater the impact, is not recommended.

## *The Impact of the Forces of Change*

Our approach to the problem of impact has already been foreshadowed. Disturbance may result from deficient or excessive input at a given point in the system. The generalization about the disturbing effects of excess is a direct corollary of the concept of equilibrium; it seems contrary often to common sense, but it has been clearly validated for many cases in social interaction. One of the best known cases is the Keynesian point about the relation between oversaving and unemployment; another is Durkheim's generalization about the positive relation between increasing economic prosperity and rates of suicide; a third would be the pathogenic effect of maternal overprotection on a developing child. The point is crucial for present purposes, because, in any important boundary relation of a society, the stability of both systems is a function of a *balancing* of rates of input and output

38. We have recently been reminded by Schnore of the importance of this aspect of Durkheim's analysis. See Leo Schnore, "Social Morphology and Human Ecology," *American Journal of Sociology,* May, 1958, pp. 620–34.

which go *both* ways. This consideration also clearly applies to both exogenous and endogenous sources of change.

Impact will vary as a function of at least five ranges of variation in the nature of the impinging process, as described below: (1) the magnitude of the disturbance—not an absolute quantity, but magnitude of *change* from previous customary input-output rates, which have become accommodated to the system's conditions of equilibrium. (2) The proportion of units in the system at the relevant levels that are affected. (3) The strategic character of the unit's functional contribution to the system —e.g., the sudden death of 50 per cent of the unskilled workers would not have the same impact as the death of 50 per cent of the highest 10 per cent of political leaders. (4) The incidence of the disturbance on analytically distinguishable components of the system's structure. Given the strategic significance of a structural unit, roles are most readily replaceable or reparable, subcollectivities less so, norms even less so, and value-commitments least. The reverse order holds for exposure to the impact of change; the conditions of individuals' role-performances are most exposed and therefore most likely to "give," whereas value-commitments are least exposed because they are neither function- nor situation-specific. Finally, (5) there is the degree of resistance by the relevant parts of the system to the impact of forces of change—i.e., the level of effectiveness of the mechanisms of control. A relatively large disturbance may not lead to major change in a very stable system; a much smaller disturbance may lead to drastic change in an unstable system. Stability is variable both quantitatively and qualitatively.

Empirically, forces making for change seldom operate neatly according to discrete analytical categories; their impact is diffused. Thus the Cold War's impact on American society operates primarily on two levels. One is by its effect on national security—primarily a political problem. Since the United States can no longer rely on a stable European power system for its security, as it did through the nineteenth century, the Cold War is the immediate cause for maintaining a large military establishment and attempting to foster the rapid development of military technology—with all the repercussions that this essentially new peacetime situation has throughout the society. The Cold War also has an important impact at the level of commitments to values and the most generalized level of norms. Without this "challenge of communism"—not just the challenge of a strong military power, but a challenge to the *legitimacy* of the "American way"—the current situation would be far less disturbing.

These two components are empirically associated. But they are analytically distinguishable, and their proportionate importance may vary, in the same case over time as well as in different cases. A comparably serious military threat to national security, unaccompanied by the ideological factor, would be much less disturbing at present to the United States, because internal changes in American society have produced factors of instability at integrative levels that were not previously so acute. Our problem in really accepting our universalistic values, for example, is clearly shown in the present segregation-desegregation issue. A major development of societal political responsibility, as a function of both internal development and changed international position, is necessary. Without special sensitivities to the symbolic reverberations of "communism"—independent of "realistic" dangers—a phenomenon like McCarthyism would be incomprehensible.

Analytical discrimination of factors within the framework of empirical variation makes more precision about matters of impact possible. Thus technological processes concerning the physical environment have quite a different significance from problems of the motivational commitments of individuals and collective subunits to functional performance in the system. For example, in America there has allegedly been a major shift recently in this respect—in Riesman's terms, from "inner-directed" to "other-directed"; in Kluckhohn's, a "decline of the Protestant Ethic."[39] Both interpretations suggest a retreat from occupational contributions into the sphere of private preoccupations. Though discussions of such problems are often couched in the terminology of values, this problem belongs more at the level of motivation to functional contribution. Whether or not a change in the societal value-system underlies this at a higher level of control is an analytically distinguishable part of the empirical problems.[40]

By present definition, a change in the structure of a social system is a change in its normative culture. At the most general level, it is a change in the paramount value system. From this level through the

39. See David Riesman, *The Lonely Crowd;* Clyde Kluckhohn, "Have There Been Discernible Shifts in American Values during the Past Generation?" in Elting Morrison (ed.), *The American Style* (New York: Harper, 1958) pp. 145–217.

40. I have attempted to deal more fully with this problem in "The Link between Character and Society" (with Winston White), in Lipset and Lowenthal (eds.), *Culture and Social Character: The Work of David Riesman Reviewed* (Glencoe: The Free Press, 1961).

series of differentiation, segmentation, and specification, it involves changes in the normative culture of subsystems, of progressively lower order, that are increasingly specific with reference to function in the larger system and to situation. Through specification we arrive eventually at the *role* level and, with this, at the psychological motivation of the individual. It is my thesis that *any* major disturbance will occasion widespread disturbances in individuals' motivations at the role level, and under the requisite conditions will lead to structural changes at least there. But it does not follow either from the presence of widespread symptoms of disturbance, or from important structural changes in such motivational patterning, that the structure of the system at all levels—especially in the paramount value system—has changed.

In considering the general problem of impact, we must remember that every structurally distinguished subsystem of a society is both complex and never fully integrated. Moreover, the structural components are interlarded in all the different subsystems; yet even minimal integration requires some measure of consistency between values and norms both at the higher and lower levels of specification and across the lines of functional differentiation. Such considerations help account for the facts that many processes of change occur simultaneously at several levels, and that influences are propagated through the levels of control in the system from one to another.

An important example is presented by underdeveloped societies at the present time. If we take economic development, in the sense of industrialization, as the focal content of the process, the two primary foci of the impact of inputs are political and cultural, in the value-sense; they are not, in the usual analytical sense, economic. Both focus primarily on the relations of underdeveloped societies to economically advanced societies.

The great stirring which has been going on focuses first on national independence and power, as evidenced by the acute sensitivity to the negative symbol of "imperialism." This political preoccupation's effect then seems to be propagated in two directions: to economic development as *instrumental* to political power (and as a symbol of collective achievement); and to the *functional* value-systems associated with political power and economic productivity. The highest-level values will still be carefully *contrasted* with those of the societies serving as models of political and economic development. Another important symbolic expression of this is the common imputation of materialism to Western societies, whereas it is alleged that India, for example, can somehow have all the advantages of high industrialization without being infected with the materialistic values of the Western world. Further—contrary to the explicit content of Marxian ideology—it is often alleged that communism, because collectivistic, is less materialistic than so-called "capitalism," though communist societies have been marked by a far more exclusive dedication to economic development than *any* capitalistic society. The essential point here is the tendency to maintain the highest-level values while permitting major changes in the next level of value-specification, i.e., that of the primary functional subsystem.[41]

It is difficult to see how, in the longer run, this can fail to engender major strains; however, there is a twofold proximate ideological defense, namely, the instrumental character of political and economic development, and the bridging of the implicit conflict by symbols like "socialism." The important point analytically is that, without at least two different orders of input beyond normal levels, impetus for major change is unlikely to occur. One order is the *real* political inferiority, symbolized as "colonial dependency," of the disturbed society. The other is the existence, in the social environment, of a *model* of instrumentally appropriate reorganization, whose partial functional values can be adopted, initially allegedly without disturbing the highest-level values of the system.[42]

## *Types of Process of Structural Change*

Finally, we must attempt to determine whether any important generalizations can be made about the types of process of change found at the structural level. The phenomena of the institutionalization of normative culture imply internalization in the personality structures of constituent personalities, which in turn implies that institutionalization is embedded in the non-rational layers of motivational organization. It is not accessible to change simply through the presentation, to an actor, of rational advantages in the external definition of the situation.

In social structure, the relation of normative culture to personality is expressed by the fundamental

41. Further analysis of these problems is contained in the paper "Some Reflections on the Sociological Framework of Economic Development," *Structure and Process in Modern Societies* (Glencoe, Ill.: Free Press, 1959), Chapter III.

42. Naturally in the total picture, specifically economic factors of production are also necessary inputs, from other societies or from other "systems" operating in the territory of the society, like motivation, capital, etc. But because of the relation to the hierarchical structure of social systems, the inputs of political urgency and functional value-commitment are far more critical in what Rostow calls the "take-off" phenomenon than is the availability of adequate factors of production in the strictly economic sense.

distinction between two types of integrative mechanism in the social system—those allocative mechanisms, operating through media like money and power, that affect the balance of advantages and disadvantages in the situation of an acting unit; and those which, like integrative communication, operate through affecting the motivational state of the unit, concerning the definition of what he wants and not how he can get it.

Only when strain impinges on and involves this level of the system of behavioral control can structural change in the present sense become possible. Once it has occurred, the question is whether the impetus to change goes "over the watershed" or, under the countervailing impact of the mechanisms of social control, falls back again.

In either case, strain at this level is manifested by a series of symptoms of disturbance showing the psychological marks of irrationality. These will be organized along the major axes of hope and fear, of "wishful thinking" and "anxiety" showing unrealistic trends in *both* respects. Psychologically, this goes back to the ambivalent structure of motivation to deviance already mentioned.

The directions of this positive-negative polarization are defined in terms of the structural possibilities of deviance.[43] The most important variables are the polarizations between activity and passivity, between compulsive alienation and compulsive conformity, that yield the types of rebelliousness, withdrawal, "ritualism," and compulsive performance. In other words, there will be fantasies of utopian ideal future states, of idealized past states, of security in a status quo from which sources of disturbance could conveniently be banished, and of eliminating sources of disturbance directly within the framework of the old structure. There will be corresponding foci of anxiety.

These motivational components are common to all symptoms of disturbance in the institutionalization of social structures. The symbols to which they become attached will depend on the appropriate system references and situations. At the societal level, it is not difficult to detect the utopian element in "communism," in the sense of an alleged actual type of society; or, on the other side, a complete "free enterprise" system. The socially regressive idealization of an unrealistically conceived past appears in such symbols as the simple, unspoiled "Americanism" of the McCarthyites, or in the *Volksgemeinschaft* of German Romantics (particularly in its most extreme version, Naziism). Such symbols as "imperialism," "capitalism," and "communism" are foci of irrational anxiety and aggression.

Another symbolic content is found where the focus of disturbance is a different order of social system. "Authoritarianism" and "conformity" are good examples of anxiety-laden symbols widely current in our society. Some of the irrational symbols in this context have functions in social systems analogous to those of the personality's mechanisms of defense. The equivalents of displacement and projection are found in the imputation of the sources of disturbance to exogenous systems—particularly similar systems—when much of the motivation really arises from internal strain. Indeed, displacement and/or projection on *personalities* of the products of strain in social systems cause much of the attributing of ill-will to, e.g., "ruling circles."

Symptoms of disturbance, with the kind of structure just sketched, are common to processes which do and do not result in structural change. Whether or not the change occurs depends on the *balance* between the strength of the disturbing forces and the kinds of reception they meet—i.e., the balance between acts motivated by response to disturbance and the sanctions that they stimulate in both endogenous and exogenous agencies. This statement is not a tautology if these conceptions are given content through definition of the nature of the performances and sanctions, and of the strategic significance of content for the equilibrium of the system.

Structural change is possible only when a certain level of strain on institutionalized structure is reached. Such strain may be propagated from technological, economic, and political levels; but the fact that a system is faced with severe problems on those levels is never *by itself* a sufficient explanation of structural change. It is necessary to trace the repercussions of these strains on the higher levels of the control system.

Even when the institutional level is reached, severity of strain is never alone an adequate explanation of change. Structural change is only one possible outcome of strain. Other results are the resolution of the strain, through mechanisms of control, that leaves the old structure intact; and the isolation of disturbing forces, at the cost of some impairment of the system's functioning—and, of course, radical dissolution of the system.

Besides the generalized strength-weakness balance of the disturbances and controls respectively, the most important factors favoring structural change are the following: (1) Adequate mechanisms for overcoming the inevitable resistances of institutionalized structural patterns (vested interests) to abandonment. Overwhelming force or polit-

43. See Merton, "Social Structure and Anomie," *Social Theory and Social Structure,* revised and extended edition, Free Press, 1957; and Parsons, *The Social System,* Free Press, 1951, Chap. VII.

ical coercion may impose very severe strains, but, in the absence of such mechanisms, they lead only to active or passive resistance, even though the resistance is realistically hopeless.[44] Endogenously, the balance between positive and negative components in the symptoms of disturbance is the primary factor. For example, if the negative side outweighs the positive, anxiety and aggression will block new institutionalization. (2) Among the positive reactions, there must be combinations with adequate constructive possibilities. The component of alienation must be strong enough to motivate detachment from the older patterns, but not so closely connected with other negative components that it motivates only destructive behavior. On the other hand, too great passivity would motivate only withdrawal. (3) A model, from exogenous sources or endogenously produced, of the pattern to be newly institutionalized is necessary. In socializing the child, the parents, older peers, teachers, and others serve as "role-models" whose personalities and actions embody the patterns of value and norms which the child is expected to internalize; without such adequate models, the internalization would be impossible. (4) The pattern of sanctions evoked by behavior in the transitional phases must selectively reward action conforming with the new model (and must not reward action in terms of the old pattern), and must be sufficiently consistent over a period to bring about the coinciding of the values of units and their self-interest that is the hallmark of institutionalization.

The socialization of the child actually constitutes a process of structural change in one set of structural components of social systems, namely, the role-patterns of the individual—indeed, much of the foregoing paradigm has been derived from this source.[45] These considerations may then be extended to the next level: the corollary of the proposition that the child internalizes new roles in the process of socialization is that the social systems in which this process occurs, e.g., the mother-child system and the nuclear family, must undergo processes of structural change. Thus, the nuclear family with one infant is, structurally speaking, not the same system as that with two adolescent children and one latency-period child, though in another perspective it may still be the same family.

For a more general sociological analysis, however, it may be better to illustrate by two types of process of structural change close to the societal level, in one of which the "model" is predominantly endogenous to the system, in the other, exogenous. The first is the case usually referred to as "structural differentiation" affecting the level of primary functional subsystems; the second, the case involving change in the value-system at the societal level.

*The Differentiation of Occupational from Kinship Roles.* In the above discussion, reference has often been made to the relative "functional diffuseness" of many social structures. The process of functional differentiation is one of the fundamental types of social change, and has evolutionary aspects and implications. In its bearing on the type of system, it involves more than increasing complexity—e.g., the fact that flexible disposability of resources depends on such differentiation. This dependence requires higher-order mechanisms of integration, substituting the more specialized processes of control associated with markets, power systems, etc., for control through embeddedness in diffuse structures.

Perhaps the best example is the differentiation of occupational roles, in the ideal sense already discussed, from embeddedness in kinship structures which have enjoyed ascribed claims to the functional equivalents of such services. On the role-structure level, the change means that what has been one role of an individual in a single kinship collectivity (which may, however, be internally differentiated) becomes differentiated into two roles in two distinct collectivities, the kinship group and the employing organization.[46]

The first prerequisite of change is disengagement from the preceding pattern.[47] In other words, some order of relative deprivation becomes attached to following the old way. The impingement of the deprivation is on the individual and on the kinship collectivity. The impingement may take such forms as deterioration of previously assumed market conditions, or of the availability of new opportunities which cannot be utilized within the old structural framework. Such severe and prolonged relative deprivation would eventually give rise to symptoms of disturbance of the sort discussed.

44. In certain respects, the Hungarian crisis of 1956 seems to fit this pattern, so far as institutionalization of the new patterns of Stalinist communism is concerned. The social system equivalents of the therapeutic mechanisms centering on permissiveness and support seem particularly crucial in this connection.

45. This assumption is based largely on Freud's work. See Parsons and Olds, Chapter IV of Parsons and Bales, *Family, Socialization and Interaction Process,* Free Press, 1955 and Parsons, "Social Structure and the Development of Personality: Freud's Contribution to the Integration of Psychology and Sociology," *Psychiatry,* November, 1958.

46. The operation of this process at the "working class" level has, to my knowledge been most thoroughly analyzed in Neil J. Smelser, *Social Change or the Industrial Revolution,* U. of Chicago Press, 1959.

47. The general paradigm of the process of differentiation somewhat elliptically followed here was set forth in Parsons and Smelser, *Economy and Society,* Free Press, 1956, Chap. V, and much more extensively developed and applied in Smelser, *op. cit.*

In order to prevent the overwhelming consolidation of the negative components of the reactions to disturbance, there must be an adequate range of institutionalized permissiveness and support, in addition to the imposition of deprivations for following the old pattern. There should not be too great immediate pressure for abandoning the old ways precipitately and totally. In the Industrial Revolution in England, this institutionalized permissiveness, as Smelser shows, comprised considerable remaining realistic opportunity in the old domestic pattern of industrial organization, compromise organizational patterns whereby whole families were hired by the cotton mills as units, and considerable "romantic" ideological support for the value of the old ways.

A positive model for the new patterning of work contribution must be demonstrated, first on the immediately relevant organizational level—e.g., factories are organized and jobs made available which offer advantages, i.e., various components of reward, including but not confined to money wages, to the worker and his household. But one crucial problem concerns the ways in which this new model can be made legitimate in terms of the relevant values.

As Smelser shows, it was very important in the British case that the structural changes in the role-organization of the labor force of the late eighteenth century were preceded, and for some time accompanied, by a marked revival, in precisely the geographical section and population groups involved, of the Puritan religion. According to the famous Weber hypothesis, Puritanism has legitimized both profit-making and more broadly effective contribution to instrumental function in society. More immediately, the main justification of the factory system was its greater productive effectiveness. In the typical working-class household, there was promise of both realistic opportunity to organize work in a new way, and legitimation of that way in terms of a firmly institutionalized religious tradition. A steady pattern of sanctions operated to reinforce the change, whose most tangible aspect was the steady increase of real wages, largely derived from the productivity of the new industry.[48]

48. A tragic case of the misfiring of such a process of change, illustrating the importance of the balance of these factors, was the case of the hand-loom weavers. The original impetus for greatly increased productivity came in spinning. The resulting greatly increased supply of yarn put pressure on the weaving branch. But in the absence of usable inventions—which came later—and of other aspects of reorganization in this field, the main result was an enormous quantitative expansion of the weaving trade on the *old* basis of social structure. When the power loom took over, the unrestructured weaving trade was left high and dry. It is not surprising that this group was the main center of disturbance in North England in that period. Smelser, *op. cit.*, treats this case in some detail.

The outcome of the process was the incorporation of a very large new group of the working-class labor force into the factory system, in fully differentiated occupational roles, with the concomitant loss of most of the function of family economic production. Working in factory premises, for an individual wage and under factory rather than kinship discipline, was a main structural feature of the outcome. Smelser makes it clear that this was not a simple matter of attracting workers by better wages than could be offered elsewhere—it was only possible through a major restructuring of the institutional structure of the working-class kinship system.

For the larger system, the part played by the *endogenous* sources of the model components of the process was particularly important. It is not necessary to question the common belief that the immediate impetus came from mechanical inventions. Implementing this impetus at levels bearing on the structure of occupational roles, however, was mainly the work of entrepreneurs—some of whom, like Arkwright, were also the inventors. But the legitimation of the new opportunities could be derived by *specification,* in the light of the new opportunities, of an already firmly institutionalized value-system. The essential point is that enhanced economic productivity was defined as good, in a way justifying the major disturbances of institutional structures at lower levels necessary for taking advantage of the greater opportunities. The legitimation of profit-making is only part of a larger complex, whose focus is on the valuation of productivity.

The distinction between the process of structural differentiation and that involving the value-system of a society is relative. In complex societies, processes of differentiation are continually going on at relatively low levels of specification and high levels of structural segmentation. The differentiation of occupational roles from embeddedness in kinship should, however, be placed among the very important processes having repercussions in the society extending far beyond their immediate locations. It is clearly a function of great extension in the division of labor and, consequently, in the extent of markets. It makes salient a whole series of new problems with respect to the institution of contract and the conditions of employment—including the beginnings of large-scale union organization and collective bargaining, and various other questions about the status of the working classes. When a process occurs of the magnitude of the rise of the cotton textile industry until about 1840—*magnitude* not only absolutely but in terms of its place in the total economy of Great Britain—it constitutes a major change in the structure of the society. It is not surprising that the disturbances associated with it included much agitation in national politics and noticeable "effervescence" in religion. At the same time, the change did not involve introducing a new value system at the national level—i.e., the fundamentals of Puritan orientation and its place in British national values had been settled in the sixteenth and seventeenth centuries.

*Change in the Societal Value System.* At the highest normative level, two main types of structural change may be distinguished. The first, already described, is the one where the principal model component comes from outside the society. This has been true of the contemporary underdeveloped areas, as outlined. To some degree, it was true of all the post-British cases of industrialization, including the American.

The American case went farthest in accepting the British model of free enterprise, though with some important qualifications. This can be attributed first to the fact that the value system deriving mainly from the ethic of ascetic Protestantism had been strongly institutionalized in this country by the early nineteenth century; furthermore, the basic structural position of religion had been settled by the adoption of the Constitutional separation of church and state that paved the way for denominational pluralism. The British model, therefore, posed no serious problem of value-orientation; the American case was considerably closer to a pure culture of the ascetic branch of Protestantism most involved in industrialization than was the British. The problem in our case was primarily the process of structural differentiation. Many religious movements, especially revivalist ones, played an important part on the fringes of the spread of industrialization. These have been essentially similar to Methodism in the north of England in the later eighteenth century.

This is probably one of the major causes of the relatively small role of political agency in the American case, though political agency played a greater part in such fields as the subsidizing of railway-building in America than in Britain. Essentially, there was no very serious problem of gaining general acceptance of the functional values necessary for industrialization, as there was in underdeveloped areas or even in most Continental European countries. It is probably not entirely fortuitous that both Japan and the Soviet Union, although very different, became industrialized under very heavy governmental pressure; in both cases, the ideological justification of the requisite value-commitments played a particularly important part. In Japan, the nationalistic connotations of aspects of the Shinto religious tradition were particularly important.[49] In the Soviet case, the revolutionary force of the Communist movement was grafted onto a Russian social structure that had always emphasized the priority of the state over private interests—far more strongly than in most Western countries. The Party functioned as the primary agency of ideological indoctrination which, under the utopian conception of communism, has inculcated the values necessary for high commitment to economic productivity—values which seem to have been relatively weak in pre-Revolutionary Russia.

The combination of practical urgency and the absence of the functional-level value commitment constitutes a major reason that, for the underdeveloped countries, governmental agency and the importance of the ideological symbol of "socialism" play such an important role in industrialization. Even the rigid authoritarianism of Communist organizational practices occasions far less resistance in these circumstances, since there is both the factor of urgency, to an extent which we do not feel, and, perhaps even more important, the necessity of counterbalancing, in the inevitable ambivalent structure, the profound resistance to value change.[50]

The second main type of societal value-change is that occurring when the cultural model cannot be supplied from a socially exogenous source, but must, so far as the social system reference is concerned, be evolved from within the society. This is the situation to which Max Weber's famous category of charismatic innovation applies. The focus of the change must be in the cultural system's religious aspects. It must concern alterations in the definition of the meaning of the life of the individual in society and of the character of the society itself.

In the process of development, a cultural change which could change values at a societal level would arise, through some complex process involving the interaction and interdependence of social and cultural systems. Considerations such as those reviewed by Weber in the selection on classes, status groups and religion (see end of Section B in

49. On the political primacy of Japanese society and its role in industrialization, as well as its relation to the religious background, see R. N. Bellah, *Tokugawa Religion* (Glencoe, Ill.: Free Press, 1957).

50. The most conspicuous example of a failure to overcome this resistance, very probably because of the failure to provide the necessary permissiveness and support to ease the process of relinquishment of old values, is probably the case of the Russian peasantry. Agriculture is clearly the main sore spot of Soviet productivity, and this seems to go back to the violently coercive procedures adopted in the collectivization program. See Bauer, Inkeles, and Kluckhohn, *How the Soviet System Works,* Harvard Press, 1957.

Part Four) would be highly relevant in so far as they concern society. The whole system of action, and the action-exogenous environment impinging upon it, is also relevant to this problem. The special role of the charismatic personality may involve problems specific to personality theory and not reducible either to sociological or cultural terms.

The obverse is the process of institutionalizing new religious values. The first question arising concerns the specification of the values from the cultural to the social system level, that is, defining of the implications of the cultural premises for the *kind of society* considered desirable. The second basic problem concerns the processes by which, once such a set of societal values is available, the strategically most important elements in the population may be motivationally committed to them. In other words, these elements must be socialized in the new definition of the situation if they are to exert the leverage necessary for extending the institutionalization of the values to all the important levels of specification and areas of differentiated function in the society.

A few points may be mentioned that are pertinent. The bearers of the new values must somehow become established in such a way that they cannot be reabsorbed in the older system. Religious or semireligious movements, churches, etc., must be structurally independent of the paramount politically organized collectivity. Once consolidated, however, the institutionalization of new values in the secular society is possible only when these bearers can acquire a fundamental influence over the leadership elements of the paramount political system, through conversion of these elements, through infiltration, or through revolution. In early medieval Europe, the Church was the main locus of the values which later underlay the activism of modern Western society. The religious orders were the main locus of the values' growth and consolidation. If the Church and its orders had merely been a part of the political organization, this would not have occurred. In the great period from Gregory VII to Innocent III, the Church was able to impose much more of its values on a reluctant political laity than it otherwise could have. This did not happen without a good deal of direct interpenetration of political and religious leadership; but the basic principle of differentiation of church and state, though under considerable strain, was not abandoned.

A variety of other considerations about this process could be discussed, but perhaps these are enough to show the general nature of the process of change involved in the institutionalization of new values at the societal level.

## V. CONCLUSION

Although it may seem long, relative to the task the above outline is obviously just a sketch, and a very tentative one. It is a statement of what seems to *one* particular author at *one* particular time to be the most useful way of organizing his view of the complex problems and materials which must somehow enter into the analysis of social systems. We have emphasized, throughout the introductory materials of this Anthology, that in our opinion sociology, as a theoretical as well as an empirical science, is in an early stage of development. We hold, therefore, that *any* statement made in our generation, even in outline, is in the nature of the case destined to be superseded, and relatively quickly. Any other view would contradict the established fact that science is an *inherently* evolving thing; if it should stop developing and become fixated on any particular set of "doctrines," it would *ipso facto* cease to be science.

This is the statement of our fundamental conviction. It does not imply, as is sometimes suggested, that, in the theory of sociology as in other sciences, there is an indefinite plurality of equally legitimate positions on all questions, an eclecticism which is the counterpart, for the sociology of science, of radical cultural relativism in a broader context. Such an implication would directly contradict our equally fundamental conviction that there has been a definite emerging structure of problems in our field, and a cumulative development of analytical thinking relative to them.

We have conscientiously tried to avoid the Scylla of dogmatism in presenting a theoretical view which is inevitably selective and incomplete, but is the best *we* can do at this time. We think it equally necessary to avoid the Charybdis of that formless eclecticism, common at least by implication in contemporary discussions, according to which in our field "anything goes," or "you pays your money and you takes your choice"; according to which there are alleged to be *no* serious professional criteria of theoretical excellence on any generalized level.[51]

51. It is perhaps pertinent to note (January, 1961) that this Introduction was written in the late summer and early fall of 1958. Sufficient developments have taken place in the interim so that had it been written two years later, it would have been somewhat different and we hope better. It was not, however, possible to undertake extensive revisions at that time. For the interested reader there are two places where some of the pertinent further theoretical developments are available, namely "Pattern Variables Revisited: A Response to Professor Dubin," *American Sociological Review,* August, 1960; and "The Point of View of the Author," the final chapter in Max Black (ed.), *The Social Theories of Talcott Parsons,* New York, Prentice-Hall, 1961.

# PART ONE

## *Historical and Analytical Foundations*

# *Section A*

# The Interpretation of Action in the History of Social Thought

EDITORIAL FOREWORD

# The General Interpretation of Action

*by Talcott Parsons*

SOCIOLOGICAL THEORY, AS WE understand it, has evolved, through a series of steps, from a more general matrix of thought about human action in society. In our opinion, the most decisive steps made, in the Western world, toward a differentiated conceptual scheme were taken by the 1890–1935 generation of writers. Selections from their writings compose the major part of this Reader. Prior to that period, however, a long series of writings had already dealt, in a variety of different ways and contexts, with the principal parts of the field, and had stated a considerable proportion of the conceptual components which have figured in the later work. These earlier writings were the main sources of the statements of problems from which the later authors evolved their own altered and refined statements, through a process of taking over elements from their predecessors and modifying and changing the conceptual structure they inherited.

The volume of early writings relevant here is, in proportion to the space available for them in the Reader, very large—far larger than is true for other areas represented in the Reader. Hence, in this area, the Reader can serve least as a substitute, either for reading the original works represented or others, or for reading the extensive secondary analyses done by historians of ideas. In this section, we can at most present a few samples representing the important currents of thought antecedent to our main period of concern. The object of the present Foreword is to present a rationale of this selection by outlining what we consider these main trends to be and which of their components have been important in later theoretical constructions. The first problem in making such selections is how far back in the historical sequence to go. It is generally agreed that the primary roots of Western culture are in the Hebraic religious tradition and in Greek philosophy: hence one might include selections from the Old Testament and from the Greek philosophers. However, we are not historians; our concern is with the more immediate background of the structure of thought underlying contemporary thinking in our field. Our concern, therefore, should be temporally limited to the first appearance of frankly secular general thinking about human conduct in society in "modern" Western thought; and Machiavelli seems to be the first major figure who fits this criterion.

There were many predominantly secular writers in later antiquity; but within Christian Western Europe this phenomenon did not emerge again until the late Renaissance. Both in the Middle Ages and during the Reformation, most of the writing attempting general analysis of social phenomena consisted in statements and defenses of religious positions. In the sixteenth century, Machiavelli stands almost alone in lacking direct concern for the bearing of what he says on the problem of the moral justification of the conduct he describes. This is one principal reason for placing a selection from his writings first.

There is also a second reason for placing him first. The bearing of "normative" considerations on our problems has a complex—at least double—incidence. The primary significance of the secularization of social thought—of which Machiavelli is the first outstanding example—is that the capacity somehow to stand "above the battle" is an essential prerequisite for attaining a scientific attitude toward the phenomena studied. These phenomena are, on a generalized level, always close to the concerns of religion; and commitment to a specific religous position makes it very difficult to be an affectively neutral analyst of the phenomena in which such positions are implicated. Probably, the presence, in the intellectual milieu, of a plurality of religious positions differing fundamentally from each other—a condition first fulfilled in Europe during the Reformation—was one factor in the possibility of taking a secular point of view bound to none of these positions. There is another sense in which the normative is a crucial category for all social science of the kind concerning us. The observer must be able to achieve a certain "distance," to be uncommitted, in the immediate action sense, to a set of specific normative components; he must also be able to appreciate and analyze the normative components functioning as determinants of the actions of the individuals and groups which are objects of his study. This is the second reason for the selection we have made from Machiavelli's works as well as for selecting his work as contrasted with Luther's, Calvin's, or a Jesuit writer's. Machiavelli is best known for *The Prince,* an extremely pragmatic handbook of measures recommended for acquiring and retaining political power. Considerations of the normative sentiments and commitments of the people with whom the prince must deal are mentioned there. However, Machiavelli's acute awareness of these factors' importance in determining the social process is more clear in the selection we have chosen, where he is more concerned with reflection on the historical record than with action in an immediate situation. Machiavelli began directing attention to the problems, not of the moral rightness or wrongness of a particular religious position, but of the more generalized empirical importance of religious commitments and the sentiments associated with them—which might vary over a considerable range; first, in determining how people will act, and, more theoretically, in the possibility of their action's constituting a stable social organization.

Machiavelli thus exhibits, extraordinarily early, the combination of the attitude of scientific objectivity, of ability to see human action as an external phenomenon, and of awareness of the importance of the normative considerations which are critical *from the actor's point of view.* He was able to state many observations and insights worthy of attention today.

The considerably fuller flow of what would now be termed secular general social thought did not begin until the seventeenth century. When it had become established, sociologically the most relevant polarization there was was that between "individualistic" and "collectivistic" references. However, this is a complex matter; a number of important discriminations must be made between various nuances of the problem.

Regarded historically, the individualistic strain in Christianity—the concern, on the religious level, with the fate of the individual soul—has underlain the problem of individualism in Western thought. Within the medieval tradition, however, it could be insulated from the problems of society, since all the individual's earthly relations to religion had to be mediated through the Church, as an organized collectivity which was held to be the sole trustee of his religious interests. With the Reformation, the significance of the church was fundamentally altered, for Protestants; and the individual, in his ultimate religious concern, was, as it were, immediately juxtaposed with the problems of society in both its religious and its secular aspects.

The very word "Protestant" indicates that, from a normative point of view, defending the individual's rights and freedoms against the claims of ecclesiastical and then also of political authority constituted a major focus of general, i.e., at least potentially theoretical, concern. It is not too large a step from defending the rights of an acting unit to asserting the substantive importance of that unit in the empirical determination of the course of events. There is, therefore, a relatively clear and direct line of descent from the individualistic religious implications of Protestantism, differently structured in its different branches, for the individual's role in society on this earth, to the type of generalization about action in society that claims that, in the last analysis, the actions and decisions of individuals determine social structure and process.

Opposed to this is the one major source of more "collectivistic" social theories that is relatively directly descended from the Catholic viewpoint, which sees a collectively organized church, and the other collectivities of a society infused with the collective Christian spirit, interposed between the essential individual and the system of interactive rights and obligations in which he is involved.

However correct this differentiation may be as the broadest generalization, there are various complications. Substantive or analytical individualism may raise, in an acute form, the "problem of order"—namely, of the conditions making a stable society possible—and one possible solution is to emphasize the importance of restraints on the freedom of individuals as a condition of such order. By this path, especially favored by Hobbes, analytical individualism may lead into normative collectivism. On the other hand, in both Protestant-inspired and secularized branches of Western social thought the church, as the main focus of collective trusteeship over the individual, may be replaced by secular collectivities—notably the paramount political organization, the state, but, under certain circumstances, others, such as "class" or "party"; a variety of possible collectivistic emphases may be derived from this source. It need not be a collectivity as such; certain elements of cultural tradition, like science, may form the primary points of reference. Finally, these two broad traditions may cross in various ways. Just as Hobbes, working from an analytically individualistic base, arrived at a normative collectivism, so Hegel, from a normatively individualistic base, a particular concept of "freedom," arrived at an analytical collectivism, asserting the predominance of the state over the individual.

As social scientists, we must find our primary points of reference in the analytical rather than the normative aspects of the individualism-collectivism axis. But the subtle relations outlined above between substantive and normative considerations make it impossible to ignore either side.

Within this frame of reference, the most important single tradition of thought lying in the background of our primary concern is that of analytical individualism; but the others are also crucially important. Modern sociological theory may be described as a result of a special type of "marriage" between the individualistic and the collectivistic strands. In terms of historical genesis, it is not understandable as one or the other. However, the individualistic strand is especially important in the attempts to formulate *scientifically* the determinants of social behavior. This importance provides the main justification for representing this tradition more than the collectivistic one in our selections.

Significantly, Hobbes, the first major "sociological" landmark after Machiavelli, was the first to pose cogently the problem of order deriving from his version of analytical individualism. Hobbes considered the "passions" of the individual to be the ultimate determinants of his action, and he specifically denied that there could be any "common measure" between the passions of different individuals. Perhaps more clearly than any subsequent writer, Hobbes stated the utilitarian postulate of the independence of any one individual's ends from those of any other. (Hobbes, though he did not carry the point so far as later writers did, implied that the individual himself was motivated by a "bundle" of more or less random wants.) Hobbes was principally concerned with the implications of this independence of one individual's passions from those of another. By adding the postulate of "equality of hope," and through the fundamental insight that other individuals are important as obstacles or aids to one individual in his gaining the ends dictated by his passions, Hobbes came to his famous proposition: each individual's unregulated attempts to gain his ends would, through individuals' mutual attempts to "subdue or destroy one another," result in the war of all against all. This is because, in such a situation, the most effective means of gaining any end through social interaction are force and fraud.

Hobbes's only solution of the resulting problem of order was for each individual to surrender his "natural rights" to use force and fraud to a sovereign who would forcibly constrain everyone to observe minimum rules, so that security would be achieved. From a sociological point of view, Hobbes's type of social contact was most unsatisfactory. Yet he posed the problem of order with a clarity which has never been surpassed, enabling it to enter directly into, e.g., the formulation of what was the major point of reference for Durkheim's quite different solution.

With Locke, the individualistic tradition changed in a way which can conveniently be described in terms of Locke's difference from Hobbes in the treatment of normative problems. Locke, through the implicit postulate which Halevy[1] has called the "natural identity of interests," simply pushed aside the problem of order as Hobbes posed it. Locke assumed that natural rights would be reciprocally respected, except by a minority of "bad men"; and that, on this basis of natural harmony, men could strive to improve their positions, to "appropriate the gifts of nature," and, rather than endeavoring to "subdue or destroy one another," to exchange goods and services to mutual advantage. Locke contributed almost nothing to analysis of the conditions under which such a harmony of interests would hold; he merely assumed that it would occur in the state of nature. But with respect to some societies and to some of their features, he was more nearly empirically correct than Hobbes. In fact, order does exist; and it is not merely a function of the coercive authority of a sovereign. Since he was empirically correct about this, Locke could analyze some of the things men did within the spheres of security and freedom thus enjoyed.

Hobbes is the theorist of the individualistic tradition who, through his formulation of problem of order, focused attention on the political aspects of the problem of institutional order in a society. He was interested in the control of force and fraud

1. Halevy, *Growth of Philosophical Radicalism,* Macmillan Co., N.Y., 1928. This is by far the best guide to the history of utilitarian thought.

and the problem of the functions of authority; but he was more concerned with the negative side—with the ways political organization could prevent degeneration into the war of all against all, rather than with the ways it could serve as an instrument implementing positive values and collective goals. Within the same tradition, Locke was the theorist of the economic aspects—of how, within an assumed natural order, the mutual advantages of association could be attained, especially through exchange and, eventually, the division of labor.

Locke is, if not the founder, at least the spiritual father of modern economics, which is both an essential constitutive part of the theory of social systems and a continual point of reference for the sociological part of the theory. Locke may be regarded as the principal discoverer of the possibility of mutual advantage in exchange and of the modern conceptions of property, prerequisite to such advantage. Above all, however unsatisfactorily he formulated it, he originated the concept of property as founded in the functional necessities of individualistic production as a societal function. In our selections, we have followed this theme one step farther by introducing Adam Smith's account of the advantages to be gained, not merely from exchanging independently held possessions, but also from introducing the division of labor into the process of production itself. These fundamentals, plus the understanding of the positive functions of capital—in which Smith was far more advanced than Locke—laid the main conceptual foundations of the classical economics.

From Locke through Smith and the later economists, the tradition has been to consider the individual, actuated by his own "self-interest," as exchanging with other individuals and thereby bringing about outcomes which redounded to the social advantage. Even in the use of capital, the relation between "capitalist" and "laborer" was considered mainly as an exchange relationship, one of capitalists "making advances to labor" to cover the time-interval before the products of labor could become consumable.

Hobbes initiated consideration of the senses in which an aggregate of discrete individuals could be combined into what we would now call a collectivity—an organized social system in which relations of leadership and authority figure prominently. Hobbes was concerned most with the absolute authority of the sovereign necessitated by the extreme precariousness of even a minimum of order. But the general theme was open to many other variations. One was the translation of Hobbes's concept of the central authority of a real political sovereign into a theory of legal sovereignty, as carried out by the jurist Austin. The most important part of Austin's theory is the conception of the normative integration of a legal system, one in which there could not be a plurality of independent decision-making units, each equally authorized to claim ultimate authoritativeness for its decisions. A second variation concerned the problem of participation in the process of collective decision-making itself. Here Bentham, one of the great forerunners of political democracy, is preeminent; but in our selections, this variation is represented by John Stuart Mill. The postulate, that each individual should be considered equal to every other, characterizing this trend of political utilitarianism, raised questions about social stratification, levels of competence and responsibility, etc., which were embarrassing in that tradition; but within it, no important solutions were contributed.

Generally speaking, the axis on which the statement of problems turned stretched from the Hobbesian pole, where authority was absolute and the sovereign's word not to be questioned, to the democratic pole, where each individual should have an equal voice. Both poles, and their many variants and compromises, implied a set of questions about whether (and how) the analytical individualism of the utilitarians constituted an adequate frame of reference for explaining either the tolerability of such authority as existed, or the elements of responsibility and the like in more egalitarian and democratic arrangements. Contemporaneous traditions of thought like those associated with Rousseau and Hegel would eventually formulate elements essential in this area of problems.

In so far as authority—along the whole range, but particularly toward the democratic pole—was not based on coercion, a crucial problem was that of the basis of consensus: of the coming together of ends, sentiments, values, or "wills" that could motivate acceptance of authority and the definition of collective as discriminated from individual interests and goals. Mill's formula of social utilitarianism may be regarded as the final attempt to deal with this problem within the classic utilitarian tradition.

By a subtle shift, a plausible formula was evolved solving this problem with a minimum of change in the conceptual framework. This was to assume that the variability of the wants or interests of individuals did not matter; but that, because of the uniformities of "human nature" and/or of the conditions in which people were placed, the individualistic competitive element would be eliminated, and social action would then consist mostly of "spontaneous co-operation." Deviations from this model could be explained by some specific obstacles to its realization, the most important of which would be ignorance. The general rationalist utopian strain of much thought of the French Enlightenment tended in this direction; in England, its principal spokesman was William Godwin.

Godwin's espousal of this position provided the principal stimulus to Malthus. For our present purposes, it is relevant that Malthus emphasized the importance of the biological urge—though this early version of such thinking apparently had an influence on Darwin. It is more centrally relevant that Malthus' views on the reproductive urge questioned Locke's version of spontaneous order as well as Godwin's. Malthus raised the Hobbesian problem again. In coping with this, Malthus gave new emphasis to three major themes which had been, in the utilitarian tradition, much less prominent, but that figure importantly in later development. The first theme took a long time to come to fruition; it was concern with the family as an institutionalized social organization—a concern which, to the modern sociologist, was conspicuously absent from the early traditions of thought. Malthus saw the family both as facilitating reproduction and, through enforcing parents' economic responsibility for offspring, as the principal mechanism of controlling the excesses of reproduction. At the same time, the pressure of population would put a high premium on efficient economic production, which would necessitate that production be carried on predominantly in organized units—where the capitalist was both a supporter of labor and an organizer of the productive process, and hence the "boss" exercising authority over his workers. The firm then became a small political organization in which the authority problem, with emphasis on its severe Hobbesian form, had a prominent place. Moreover, the fact that capitalist-employers and workers were of different status, both within the firm as an organization and in their incomes and styles of life, meant that this organizational differentiation became the basis of a "division of society into classes." Thus Malthus emphasized strongly two crucial structural components of an economy with advanced division of labor, managerial authority, and class differentiation—far more strongly than they were emphasized in the economic tradition of Locke, or in the political tradition of Bentham and Mill. The relevance of these themes to the later Marxian concept of the capitalistic economy is clear. Malthus' conception may be said, in these respects, to have resulted from a special synthesis of Hobbes's and Locke's versions of the utilitarian tradition—the organized business firm was pictured as operating under a Hobbesian absolute sovereignty, whose acceptance by workers was motivated, not directly by the fear of force, but by the fear of starvation.

An important feature of early nineteenth-century utilitarian thought that contrasted with its previous phases was the attention given to levels of organization between the individual and the highest-order secular collectivity, the state. The emphasis on the fact that economic production and hence much exchange were not carried on by isolated individuals, but by some kind of organized collective units, was a relatively new one. This made the basis of their organization a problem.

We must mention two additional important ingredients which came into the field of sociological concern from the individualistic tradition; both figured prominently only after the middle of the nineteenth century. The first is the concept of treating the biological nature of the individual as a crucial set of independent factors which could not be modified by environmental influences. The second is the conception that societies undergo essential processes of change rather than remaining static. Darwin and Spencer are particularly important in this connection.

In connection with the biological nature of the individual, Malthus had already forceably introduced the instinctive basis of the reproductive urge as a major determinant of human societies, one whose control was difficult and could be achieved not by will power alone, but necessitated institutionalized situations making it overwhelmingly to individuals' interest to control it. Darwinism, by greatly generalizing biological thought relative to its previous levels, gave a general foundation to a type of theory supporting a more radical analytical individualism than that of the utilitarian tradition. In certain respects, even more broadly than Malthus, Darwin tipped balances in the Hobbesian direction, treating the competitive aspects of human relations as a special case of natural selection. It thereby checked the tendency to shift to a theory of spontaneous co-operation of the sort emphasized by Godwin. The peculiar balance between competition and order seen by Locke and the economists was theoretically precarious. Darwinism, by associating competition with natural selection, strengthened the competitive side of the dilemma—at the cost of undermining the normative element which had accounted for order through Locke's postulate of the identity of interests.

If competition was to be real, then the individual had to be motivated to enter into the competition, to be exposed to the forces of natural selection.

Since in utilitarian terms, it was difficult to see how this exposure could be in the individual's interest, he had to be endowed with inborn "propensities," like the reproductive urge, that would propel him into the fray. This shift would close the gap left yawning in utilitarian theory, which simply assumed that men had a variety of ends or goals as individuals, but did not locate their origin, nor give any clue as to their relative urgency that would enable an estimate to be made of the costs actors would be willing to pay to achieve them. This theoretical closure was, however, attained at the expense of certain degrees of theoretical freedom for development in the direction of special interest here. In other words, if the primary determinants of action are held to be (a) the inborn propensities or instincts of the individual, and (b) the struggle for survival dominated by the principle of natural selection, then there is no room for the normative factors which had been built into Locke's position by the route of implicit assumption, but which had never been given a satisfactory systematic status within it. This is, by and large, the path taken both by instinct theory in psychology and by "social Darwinism" in the latter part of the nineteenth century. It is an important reference point, both for a good deal of the psychological theory to be presented in Part Three, and in much of the discussion of social change to be represented in Part Five.

This is reductionism of social action to an essentially biological process—*biological* in terms of the biological theory dominant at the time.[2] Since then, it has become much more clear that the unit of the selective process is only partially the individual organism; various social aggregates of organisms—notably the species, but also subgroups within it—figure in this respect. Thus the social dimension whereby individual organisms are often, by behavioral mechanisms, sacrificed to the interests of larger systems, has become increasingly built into biological theory itself. Second, the concepts of adaptation and of natural selection have been greatly altered in emphasis. The older emphasis was on the passive aspect of adaptation: the environment presented certain inexorable conditions which had to be met, "or else." Since Darwin did not have the modern theory of genetics at his command, he had no principles of developing organization of biological systems on the genetic side; he tended to postulate a continual set of random variations that were the logical counterparts of the utilitarians' random ends. The more recent trend of biological theory is to emphasize the evolution of progressively higher levels of organization which must be passively adapted to the exigencies of the environment, but which also achieve that adaptation by mechanisms enabling them to cope actively with the environment, rather than merely "submitting" to it. Locomotion is a primary example of evolutionary development; but even more important is the development of intelligence—capacity to react to changing environmental situations without being bound by rigid predetermined patterns of behavior. Natural selection, then, favors not only passively adapted organic types, but types with higher levels of organization—especially those possessing mechanisms enabling them to adopt varying and versatile behavior in reaction to varying environmental conditions. On the whole, however, this important shift in biological thinking, particularly as it became known to social scientists and influenced their theories, occurred only after a corresponding main trend within the social sciences themselves. The major early influence of biology was in the reductionist direction.

If not the prime source, biological theory was at least a major reference point for another critical idea which figured very prominently in the second half of the nineteenth century in the social field, namely, the idea of evolution. The utilitarian tradition, from Hobbes through Locke and later, was concerned less with problems of the change of societies over time, and more with the invariant conditions underlying the problem of social order and of gaining individuals' ends through economic production and exchange, and, peripherally, through political association. Conceptions of evolution had, however, already appeared, notably in the French Enlightenment in the case of Condorcet, who set a model which was important for Saint-Simon and Comte. They also appeared in the early nineteenth century in German Idealism, especially in Hegel's work, which will be briefly discussed presently. There were also overtones of evolution in writers like Malthus and Ricardo. The emergence of the Darwinian theory immediately focused primary attention on this area. We represent this mode of thinking by a selection from the writings of Herbert Spencer, because Spencer was the most prominent evolutionist in the social field, and also because he incorporated the idea with a minimum of modification of the older utilitarian framework. Spencer was not, strictly speaking, a Darwinian. He had worked with the idea of evolution before the publication of the *Origin of Species;* and he never abandoned the belief in the inheritance of acquired characters. In a sense, he never faced the

2. See T. H. Huxley's famous essay, "Evolution and Ethics," N.Y., D. Appleton and Co., 1905, which put natural selection and *all* normative considerations in radical conflict with each other.

problem of reduction that came to a head in later discussion of the relations between social science and biology.

Spencer did present an ingenious combination of components drawn from rationalism and from the Hobbesian and Lockean versions of utilitarianism. An important contribution by Spencer (as in the works of the founder of modern anthropology, E. B. Tylor) was focusing attention on the phenomena of religion, which had been grossly neglected in the traditions of thought we have been reviewing. In part, this attention reflected greater awareness of the customs of non-literate peoples, among whom religious phenomena figured very prominently. This prominence made it plausible for Spencer to see religious beliefs as derived from the relative ignorance of man in the early stages of his social and cultural development. The most clear example was the derivation of the idea of the soul from the experience of dreams. However much Spencer's ideas in this area have had to be modified, he—like Comte, in a different tradition—was among the first to bring a crucially important subject matter back as a focus of attention.

By relating religion to ignorance, Spencer relegated it, as a genuinely important social phenomenon, to the early phases of social evolution. He blended Hobbes and Locke in relation to two later phases, in his concepts of "militant" and "industrial" societies. He was thus able to conceive a formula which, instead of presenting two rigid, mutually exclusive alternatives, allowed both to be right in a sense, as formulating two different special cases derived from the application of the same principles to different conditions. In spite of the ingenuity of this solution, the basic problem of order which Hobbes had raised remained unsolved.

It was also within the evolution framework, with a comparative reference as well, that the concept of traditionalism and its relation to ascriptive immobility of resources entered modern sociological thinking. A selection from the *Ancient Law* of Sir Henry Sumner Maine represents this important conception. Intimate knowledge of a non-European society (in this case, India) as well as of Western legal history played a dominant part in Maine's thinking. His developmental formula of the process of shift from status (to which the modern sociologist would be inclined to add the adjective "ascribed"), to "contract," where rights and obligations could be voluntarily assumed, was a landmark in the analysis of social structures. It influenced much subsequent thinking, including Durkheim's. Another important version of very similar ideas was presented by Walter Bagehot in *Physics and Politics*. This was the concept of the "cake of custom," which held social action in a rigid framework but, with development of such things as markets, tended to be broken up, giving the individual far more freedom.

After enjoying a tremendous vogue in both sociology and anthropology, the conception of social evolution underwent a dramatic eclipse shortly after the turn of the twentieth century. This eclipse was associated with the movement of theoretical thinking which is the primary concern of this Reader. One factor was the sheer accumulation of empirical knowledge that made many of the early generalizations, particularly so far as they involved a simple "unilineal" conception of the process, untenable. On another level, however, the new emphases, particularly on the normative components of culture and the structure of societies, simply did not fit with the ways in which the conception had been formulated, either in Spencer's modified but not basically changed utilitarian terms, or in Comte's special version of French rationalism, or in the Hegelian dialectic. The problem was not solved by these difficulties; and a very interesting symptom of a current shift to a new level of social science theory is a revival of interest in the problem of evolution.

Let us now turn to what is, in an analytical sense, the "collectivistic" side of the main traditions of modern social thought. There are two primary branches of this, going back to common roots in European intellectual history; they can be broadly distinguished as those of French rationalism and of German Idealism. In the former tradition, the most important people are Rousseau and Comte; in the latter, for our purposes, Hegel and, in one aspect of his thinking, Marx—though others like Dilthey and even Sombart, might be mentioned.

It might be questionable to classify Rousseau as a rationalist, since in many ways he was the fountainhead of Romanticism and similar movements. However, Rousseau, though on the whole he shared Locke's conception of the state of nature as one in which each individual had the right to pursue his interests in his own way, treated the problem of unifying such discrete individuals to form a political collectivity as a much more positive problem than did the economically oriented individualists in the utilitarian tradition. Rousseau broke through the Hobbes-Locke dilemma, postulating a factor very different from those they had considered, the famous *general will*. Its difference is made clear by Rousseau's insistence on the distinction between *volonté générale* and *volonté des tous*. *Volonté générale* is generated by a Hobbesian social contract to surrender control of natural rights to an absolute sovereign. The difference is also related to the fact that Rousseau's political theory was formulated in the interest of democracy—not, as in Hobbes's case, of monarchy.

Rousseau and his followers found insuperable difficulties in defining an acceptable relationship between his postulated general will and any concrete political institutions which could effect it without risking uncontrolled dictatorship by a self-appointed minority or a tyranny of the majority. The difficulties arose from the fact that Rousseau, like his utilitarian predecessors, did not consider a basis in societal values and institutionalized norms somehow independent of and underlying the state; he tried to elevate political theory into a general theory of social systems. At the same time, he did contend that there was a factor of the integration of the system that was not reducible to terms of the discrete individual rationally following his self-interest or his "passions," nor a matter of inborn instincts. It was an analytically independent set of factors which (to use Durkheim's term) must be postulated to account for solidarity.

In the French tradition of social thought, Rousseau's new note blended with one derived from the conservative thought of writers like De Bonald and de Maistre, who tended to challenge the tradition of the Revolution and to defend the record of the Old Regime. In this period, the most significant figure for the development of sociology—particularly for Durkheim's work—was Auguste Comte. In Comte's theory, the concept corresponding to, and certainly at least partially derived from, Rousseau's general will is that of *consensus* as the essential basis of the cohesion or integration of a society. Comte said very little about the ways in which a basis of consensus, once established, could be understood to be implicated in the complex differentiated subsystems of a society—how, in other words, a consensus which must, by the terms of his statement, be conceived at a very high level of generality, could effectively control the varieties of behavior of many different types of collective and individual units of a social structure in many different and varying situations. Serious progress toward solving these problems was not made until Durkheim's generation.

Comte undoubtedly was a certain type of rationalist, in that he conceived the consensus in terms of ideas or common cognitive orientations. (This focus on ideas was the basis of his famous law of the three stages, which will be discussed later, in relation to the problems of social change.) In making science the essential basis of consensus in his final positive stage, Comte approached the position of Godwin and other utopian rationalists. The basis of a possible difference from this utopian position lies in the special sense in which society is simultaneously both an object of scientific study and a creation of the processes of human action. This theme is prominent in Comte, for whom sociology was both the science of society as an existing object, and the primary guide to building a different and better society. The structure of problems—including the very formidable difficulties Comte's positivism involved—leads directly into the later work of Durkheim. Comte's version of evolutionary theory, built directly on the predominance of ideas as a factor, was not immediately so fruitful for a theory of social change as was that of Marx, since Comte's did not even begin to present an acceptable account of the mechanisms by which the influence of ideas could operate. However, the pattern of the stages, from theological through metaphysical to positive, shows a process of "rationalization" affiliated with various contemporary and subsequent trends of thought, including Max Weber's.

From the present point of view, Comte's most important contribution was his injection, into a strategic point of the stream of sociological thinking, of the collectivistic element with respect to the problem of integration. Though Comte's accounts of the basis of integration and of its working within the society are not acceptable to the modern sociologist, he posed a problem which had proved essentially insoluble within the utilitarian tradition. In the history of ideas, posing a problem fruitfully is almost as important a contribution as its positive solution.

For the future development of sociology, Comte provided, more directly than Rousseau, a fruitful antithesis to the individualistic utilitarian tradition of thought. That it was a genuine antithesis is vividly shown in the relations between Comte and John Stuart Mill, which ended in a break in their personal friendship.[3] The problem of synthesizing these apparently antithetical elements in one very important way set the stage for the new phase of the development of sociology.

The second most important source of the collectivistic trend is German Idealism. This was greatly influenced by Rousseau, as well as by other sources which need not be discussed here. The relevant version of the idealistic movement is Hegel's—not least because of Hegel's influence on Marx. Relevant to our present interest, there are

3. See John Stuart Mill, *Auguste Comte and Positivism*, London: Kegan Paul, Trench Treubner & Co., Ltd., 4th ed., 1891.

three essential components in Hegel's thought. The first is the concept of the primacy of the "ideal" component (*Geist* is the almost untranslatable German term), or, as we would now be inclined to say, the component of cultural orientation. The second is the evolutionary conception—culture is not static, but is involved in an inherent "dynamism" of development from an initial to a terminal stage. The third is a conception of the nature of this process, which Hegel called "dialectic" in the famous formula that a thesis gives rise to its antithesis and then, when both are present, a synthesis can be formed.

Consideration of Comte's theories has shown that there is a natural line of reasoning from Rousseau's concept that consensus consists in some kind of unification of "wills" to the concept of a basis in common cultural orientations, in ideas or values. Comte's thinking went in this direction, ending with the concept of science as this basis, and sociology functioning, in this respect, as the queen of the sciences. In general, at the time of Hegel and Comte, clear discrimination between the normative and the existential aspects of systems of ideas was not easy to make; neither in Comte nor in Hegel does this distinction, so essential later to Max Weber, figure at all prominently.

This central problem is closely connected with the one mentioned in connection with Rousseau and Comte, namely, that of an intelligent account of the processes and mechanisms by which ideas, existential or normative, in fact influence the processes of action. Theories which have approached the philosophical idealistic pole have continually been forced into postulating a mysterious process of emanation which, like Locke's identity of interest, becomes a name for a problem rather than a solution of it. This is the case with the Hegelian version of idealism in relation to society. Nevertheless, however unsatisfactory the account of *how* common cultural orientations can become crucial determinants of social action is, sharp focusing of attention on the fact that they *are* centrally involved in the structure of societies can be a factor of the first importance in leading thought toward a solution.

The second virtue of the Hegelian tradition as a forerunner of the theoretical development in which we are interested is that it did not confine itself to asserting the importance of the cultural factor—in two different contexts, it introduced conceptual differentiation into its concept of the role of culture. The first context was the evolutionary, in which the recent stage of development of the *Weltgeist* was considered the culmination of a process of dialectical development from a primitive beginning. Condorcet had treated the evolutionary process as a very simple continuous process of the growth of "reason." Comte elaborated this by a concept of well-marked stages involving an element of qualitative difference from one another. The Hegelian concept, presented a little earlier than Comte's, added the dialectical principle of interconnection between the stages that raised, on a certain level, the question of the mechanisms of the transition from one stage to the next. Another noteworthy feature of Hegel's philosophy of history is that he began to pay serious attention to the significance of the development of civilizations in areas of the world other than the West.

The second context in which Hegel differentiated the application of his ideas was with reference to the structure of society contemporary to him. This aspect is especially emphasized in the selection from his *Philosophy of Law* below. Here he distinguished the levels of "incorporation" of the *Geist* in society—the state as the highest, the "bourgeois society" as next in line, and the common people (which, in his time, meant primarily the peasantry) as the lowest. This was a step toward a more differentiated treatment of the relation of culture to society than had, from a collectivistic starting point, been prominent either in Rousseau or in Comte. The concept of bourgeois society was a recognition of the possible soundness in the utilitarian conception of a market-oriented system of relationships; it was used as a point of reference for Marx's theory of class conflict. It represents a genuine convergence between idealist-collectivistic and utilitarian-individualistic patterns of thought—again, however unsatisfactory to the modern sociologist Hegel's specific formulations may be. It helped set the stage for a more scientific treatment of the problem of emanation—of the ways, given the existence of cultural ideas and ideals, these could be conceived as related to the other components of systems of social action.

The Hegelian pattern of idealistic evolutionism provided an important reference point for three subsequent developments, all sharing, in certain respects, its cultural-collectivistic orientation. These were German idealistic "historicism," Marxism, and the type of analysis of the involvement of ideas in action of which Max Weber was the most eminent exponent. The third is central to the material included in this Reader, but the other two should be discussed briefly for background.

One important consequence of the Hegelian method was the breaking of the evolutionary sequence into what were, to some extent, qualitatively distinct phases of the *Weltgeist's* development. It was natural for some, skeptical of the dialectic's sweeping generalizations, simply to cease worrying about the connections and to attempt to portray a cultural epoch in terms of its unique and independent *Geist*.[4] This tendency fitted well with the general emphasis on uniqueness and historical particularity that was prominent in the nineteenth century, particularly in Germany; it also fitted with the general idealistic tendency to see the key to understanding in the spirit or particular themes of a culture. This type of thinking permeated a whole range of historically oriented fields, concerning the arts, jurisprudence, and economics.

In German philosophy and methodology of science, it was associated with the Kantian dualism between the worlds of nature and of *Geist* or *Kultur*. The most important tenet was that, whereas nature was subject to understanding in terms of systems of generalized analytical concepts, culture could be "depicted" and "appreciated" only in terms of its specific uniqueness of configuration. Toward the end of the century, a moderate version of this view was presented by Windelband and Rickert, a more radical one by Dilthey. In something approaching sociology, perhaps its best-known exponents are Sombart and Spengler.

This approach is fundamentally at variance with the aims of generalized theory central to this Reader. It either eliminates generalized theory completely from the field of the social sciences, or it establishes an unbridgeable duality between the naturalistic and the cultural components. For this reason, Max Weber's fundamental critique of the methodology of *Historismus* is so important a reference point in relation to the question of the status of normative components in social action. Weber did not carry his position through to a logical conclusion; but his break with the tradition of historical uniqueness was a major turning-point.

The views Weber criticized have continued to be influential in many connections, as represented in this Reader in the work of Weber's brother Alfred and in that of a number of anthropologists particularly concerned with the configurational aspects of culture. These writers have made important contributions to a variety of more specific problems, but their methodological position cannot be considered to be in the primary line of development of social science theory as such.

In one sense, the use to which Marx put Hegel's ideas is diametrically opposed to that of the historical schools. Rather than accepting literally Marx's own statement that he "set Hegel on his head," we would be more accurate in saying that Hegelian idealism, like utilitarianism, was an inherently unstable conceptual scheme, and that it tended to break down in two antithetical directions, whose opposition, in the absence of a synthesis, was irreconcilable. In utilitarianism, the central point of reference was "economic." One half of the dichotomy was biological—instinctivism and social Darwinism—while the other was Hobbesian concept of a coercively unified collectivity-system where action was motivated by the "rational" hopes and fears of men. In the Hegelian case, one part of the duality was "pure" idealism, tending to taper into historicist emanationism of the Spenglerian variety. The other part was best represented by Marxism, which should be considered in a special sense as one particular variety of utilitarianism, with certain infusions from its idealistic antecedents.

Marx's central concept of human social action is inherited from Locke and the classical economists; it is that of individuals rationally pursuing their self-interest, in a system of the division of labor, through relations of exchange. In his more technical economic theory, Marx built directly on Ricardo, incorporating many of the now obsolete —if not erroneous—elements of Ricardian theory. At the same time, in his work there appear—far more accentuated than in the liberal and classical traditions—the two fundamental structural elements of a "capitalist" economy that had already appeared in Malthus, namely, the authority-structure of the productive unit, and the "division of society into classes."

In his sociological theory, Marx added two further essential components, both somehow derived from the Hegelian tradition. One of these was the conception of a dialectically structured evolutionary process, in the course of which there were well-marked, qualitatively different stages, and a "dynamic" built on the thesis-antithesis model of a conflict between two opposing elements. Here, however, what evolved was not a *Geist* but an empirical social system, a system of the "relations of production"; and the conflict was not a logical one, a contradiction, in the Hegelian sense; it was a conflict of the interests—in the last analysis, the economic and power interests—of social groups, the classes involved in the productive process.[5]

It is most important to note that utilitarian

4. Thus substituting the particular *Zeitgeist* for a phase of the more comprehensive *Weltgeist*.

5. It is, however, significant that Marxist language today speaks of "contradictions" as if there were no essential difference between logical incompatibility of ideas and conflicts of economic or social interests.

theory was, in a psychological sense, not "deterministic," rather "voluntaristic"; and this is true of Marxism. There were, however, essential deterministic elements in the *system* of social relations involved in the interlocking interests of many men. For the system of capitalism, Marx elevated these deterministic elements to a far higher degree of inevitability than his predecessors had. Within the general scheme of rational goal-oriented action, the effect of this was to emphasize the situational as opposed to the volitional element. Men acted as they did because, in the situation in which they were placed in the particular set of relations of production, they could not act otherwise: for the worker, the alternative to accepting capitalistic employment, and thus being exploited, was starvation; for the employer, the alternative to employing was, through the mechanism of competition, elimination from business, presumably reduction to the status of worker.

In the discussion of Comte, attention has been directed to the possibility of changing the whole basis of such a situation by concerted action. The environment of the individual is composed of the actions of others. Hence if interests can be structured in a given direction, the constraints of a particular set of the relations of production can be overcome. Then it is possible for an impetus toward change to become what Merton has called a "self-fulfilling prophecy." This possibility is inherent in any form of collectivist theory—including the idealistic branch, so long as it is not a pure form of "emanationism"; if it is, nothing like a mechanism of change is felt to be necessary. Marxism cannot be classified here, but it was caught in this aspect of its theoretical structure, in a dilemma of considerable interest in the present context.

The great shift is defined as the "leap into freedom," the *Sprung in die Frieheit*. The first inquiry is how this is to take place, and here, in turn, it is a question of how far the change is the consequence of the unplanned evolution of the forces of production, and how far it is to be furthered by a voluntaristic movement bringing about the revolution and engineering the transition. Here Marx was, as Schumpeter said, both a sociologist and a revolutionist. As revolutionist, he was committed to foster the possibility of aiding the forces of production and the "contradictions"—this has become the dominant note of recent Marxist thought. The emphasis has, particularly through Lenin's influence, become placed on maximally effective *organization* for revolutionary, i.e., political, action. Hence the conception of the centrally led and controlled party, introducing the dictatorship of the "proletariat"—in effect, of the leadership of the party.[6]

What happens, then, is that for the unplanned constraint of the capitalistic system, operating through the mechanisms of competition, are substituted the planned and coercively enforced constraint of the party, and the "building of socialism" under stringently dictatorial party control. The result is a very Hobbesian version of absolute sovereignty, serving, not a negative concept of security (except, of course—and a far from negligible exception—so far as the revolution is felt to be threatened), but a positive programming for building a new society. The new society is purported to be the most free in history, but the process of achieving it involves a drastic minimization of freedom. Hence the problem of when and under what circumstances the famous "withering away" of the state is to occur becomes cardinal for Marxism.

The other side of the dilemma lies in the extent to which Marx took over the elements of utopian rationalism, largely from the French Enlightenment. His statements about the state of communism itself are notably vague, but on the whole they are far more Godwinian than anything else. They seem to hold that only the special constraints of capitalism have been obstacles to spontaneous order and happiness for all; once these have been eliminated, there will be universal freedom without political coercion or institutions in any form. From the above discussion, it seems clear that Marx did not solve the Hobbesian problems of order, any more than did the utilitarians. In "setting Hegel on his head," he threw away the normative component which might have been built into a solution; and by projecting the problem into the vague future state of "communism," he in effect "swept it under the rug." For the intermediate period, however, he provided, through the concept of the dictatorship of the proletariat, a rationalization for a truly Hobbesian version of order through coercion.

However, this is not quite the whole story. The Communist parties have recognized that "educating" their followers through propaganda and "agitation" is a necessary factor in success. It could not rest on coercive measures alone. Essentially, this education has been directed to inculcating belief in the Marxist-Leninist system as an eschatological system, a quasi-religious set of answers to

6. The same difficulty of relating a concept of the basis of solidarity to the mechanism of implementation, which Rousseau could not solve, is present here. Thus the "general will" could justify Jacobin dictatorship. Similarly, the "proletariat" has become an abstraction used to justify Communist party dictatorship.

the problems of teleological meaning; and, at another level, inculcating loyalty to the party as such and to the governments established under its control. There is some question of just how this set of normative elements, as common value-orientations and loyalties, fits in the framework of Marxist theory; but there is no doubt of its practical importance to the revolutionary movement.

No American authors are included in this preliminary section of the Reader. This is because, in this preliminary period, there were no American works of importance comparable to the European ones on which we have drawn. It may be stated, however, that the general trend of American social thought was, as would be expected, far closer to the utilitarian individualistic trend than either of the versions of the collectivistic trend discussed above. In this trend, understandably, the version associated with Locke, economics, and the ideas of liberal political democracy were most prominent. The Hobbesian version, with its tendency to association with rigidly authoritarian collectivism, has been minimized.

As shown in Section B, and to some extent in Section C of Part One, the distinctively American contribution has been mainly in the area of "social psychology," which, in the frame of reference used in this Introduction, lies mostly in the borderline between the utilitarian version of individualistic "rationalism" and the more biologically oriented analysis of the factors involved in the individual's behavior. However, at least one branch of American thought was less concerned than its British counterpart with a set of postulates on whose basis the macroscopic functioning of the economy and the political system could be analyzed, and more concerned with the determinants of the individual's behavior and its relations to the more intimate contexts of interaction in which he was placed. It was in this area of greater flexibility that it became possible to take explicit account of the normative components of the determination of social interaction. The most important men in this area were Cooley, G. H. Mead, and, later, W. I. Thomas. The background of their role will be further discussed in the Foreword to Section B.

The trends of social thought reviewed in this Foreword were, with few exceptions, not based on empirical research in the present sense. Perhaps the most notable exception was Malthus' survey of the relation of kinship structure and property-holding in several European countries, reported in later editions of his *Principle of Population*. There was also some historical research, and, on the part of the economists, statistical investigation. Only in the most limited sense, however, could these works be considered as representing a science, which necessarily relates deliberately designed empirical research and theory. Most of it consists in "reflection on experience."

This reflection, however—including acute, though unsystematic, observations of empirical phenomena—is the stuff of which the *beginnings* of a science are made. What emerged from the complicated and often conflicting movements of these philosophical, semi-philosophical, ideological, and very partially scientifically oriented movements of thought was a relatively determinate *structure of problems* which, in a later generation, could be handled through more systematic empirical observation and a higher level of theoretical analysis.

The first of these great problems is that of order in Hobbes's sense—which, though stated and discussed as a problem of how to guarantee order in a practical sense, could also be treated as a scientific problem, namely, of how to specify the conditions on which the empirically observed levels of social order depended. While utilitarianism yielded rich returns in the intermediate sphere of economic analysis, the logic of the problem drove thinking in two directions, whose eventual convergence is very important in our universe of discourse. The first direction was the question of what normative components of the social system must be understood to operate, in order to explain social order without abandoning the whole voluntaristic and, in a sense, rationalistic concept of action which the utilitarians had assumed, by accepting the "reductionist" line of argument. In the "voluntarist" direction this problem led inevitably to convergence with the "collectivist" trend of thought. The one traced, through Rousseau and Comte, to Durkheim, was the one of major present significance.

On the other hand, demonstrating the empirical existence and the functional necessity of these normative components did not solve the problem of mechanisms, of how in fact such components entered into the determination of the individual's behavior. Hence the other end of the utilitarian problem-range: the problem of what scientifically analyzable phenomena underlay the early postulates of the "rational pursuit of self-interest" was necessarily thrown open to thorough reconsideration. Here a most notable convergence occurred—on the one hand, Durkheim, stating from the "collectivistic" end, was forced to consider the motivation of the individual, and eventually arrived at the concept of the internalization of normative culture. On the other hand, Freud, starting from what may be called the "medical" version of biological determinism, arrived, through his theory of the significance of "object-relations," at the complementary view—a view at which the Americans cited above, from a more "social" version of psychology, also arrived.

When problems are considered on this level of generality, it is easy to forget that a society, above all a modern society, is very complex and highly differentiated. Durkheim took an essential step to cover this difficulty by not, like Comte, speaking only of consensus in general; he dealt directly with the problem of solidarity in the type of differentiated system characterized by an advanced division of labor.

Once there was a clear focus on the importance of a "collective" normative component, the problem of its basis in human experience became progressively more salient. The tradition of French thought provided a basis for a far more explicit emphasis on its importance, but less for its further analysis. Rousseau went directly into the problems of practical politics, and Comte came to rest on science as such. In this connection, however, German Idealism was in a position to develop a more differentiated basis for analyzing "culture." For Western empiricism, this trend represented a distressing dissociation from the "realities" of economic and political interest—to say nothing of the biological level. But it presented the beginning of a more differentiated analysis of an essential set of components. Hegel is important specifically because his version is more differentiated than that of other "classical idealists" or of his "historicist" successors. From the sociological point of view, Marx worked out a premature synthesis between the two traditions; he ignored the problem of how the "realistic" elements of "economic interest" and the "idealistic" elements of the normative component of an ordered social system could belong together, unresolved, in a single system. One is forced to conclude that order is possible only in the ferment of the transition from an inherently conflict-filled previous society to an undefined presumptive future society; the only Marxist order is the order of the revolutionary process. Weber's later excursion from the idealistic into the "realistic" realm seems far more successful than Marx's, from a scientific point of view. Its key question was how the normative component (in Weber's case, rooted in religious commitments) could operate through the motivation of individuals in both "revolutionary" and stable social situations—this completed the circle by converging with Durkheim and with Freud.

The bearing of the above summary on the organization of the materials in this Reader should be clear. After presenting the fundamentals in Part One, we proceed to presenting problems of the internal structure of social systems themselves in Part Two. This may be considered the area of primarily "Durkheimian" emphasis. We feel that the "institutionalization" of normative culture is, for sociology, the keynote of social structure. Second, however, a very important set of problems is concerned with the motivation of social action. This area leads us into the problems associated with the relation of the individual to the social system. Here Freud's work, and various other schools and trends of "individual" and "social" psychology, are paramount. "Normative Culture," as institutionalized in the values and norms of social systems, cannot be dissociated from a variety of other aspects of the development of culture, e.g., religious movements, science, art, etc. Part Four is devoted primarily to selections bearing on this range of problems. Weber is the theorist who contributed more in this area than anyone else. Part Five is devoted to the relatively few notable ideas which have emerged on the question of the patterns and processes of change which social systems, constituted as we think they are, may be thought to undergo.

# 1. *On Hatreds and Dissensions in the Republic*

BY NICCOLO MACHIAVELLI

IT WAS my intention when I first resolved upon writing the things done by the Florentine people, within and without their city, to begin my narrative with the year 1434 of the Christian era, at which time the family of the Medici, by the merits of Cosimo and his father Giovanni, exercised more authority in Florence than any one else. For I thought to myself that Messer Lionardo d'Arezzo and Messer Poggio, two excellent historians, had related all the events that had occurred previous to that time. But having afterwards diligently read their writings to see in what order and manner they had proceeded, so that by imitating them our history might be the more approved by the reader, I found that in their descriptions of the wars carried on by the Florentines with foreign princes and peoples they had been most diligent; but of their civil discords and internal dissensions, and of the effects resulting therefrom, they had in part been silent, and in part had described them very briefly, which to the reader could be neither useful nor agreeable. I believe they did so because these facts seemed to them so unimportant that they judged them unworthy of being recorded in history, or because they feared to offend the descendants of those who took part in them, and who by the narration of these facts might have deemed themselves calumniated. These two reasons (be it said with their leave) seemed to me wholly unworthy of such great men; because if anything delights or instructs in history, it is that which is described in detail; and if any lesson is useful to the citizens who govern republics, it is that which demonstrates the causes of the hatreds and dissensions in the republic, so that, having learned wisdom from the perils experienced by others, they may maintain themselves united. And if the divisions of any republic were ever noteworthy, those of Florence certainly are most so, because the greater part of the other republics of which we have any knowledge were content with one division, by which, according to chance, they either increased or ruined their city. But Florence, not content with one division, had many. In Rome, as everybody knows, after the expulsion of the kings, a division arose between the nobles and the people, and with that she maintained herself until her downfall. So did Athens, and so all the republics that flourished in those times. But in Florence, the first division was amongst the nobles, afterwards between the nobles and the citizens, and finally between the citizens and the populace; and many times it happened that one of the parties that remained in power again divided in two. These divisions caused so many deaths, so many exiles, so much destruction of so many families, as never occurred in any other city of which we have any record. And truly no other circumstance so much illustrates the power of our city as that which resulted from these divisions, which would have been enough to destroy any other great and powerful republic.

Ours, nevertheless, seems always to have increased in power; such was the virtue of her citizens and the strength of their genius and courage to make themselves and their country great, that the many who remained untouched by so many evils could by their virtues exalt their city more than the malignity of those events that diminished her greatness could have oppressed her. And doubtless if Florence had had so much good fortune that, after having freed herself from the Empire, she could have adopted a form of government that would have kept her united, I know not what republic, modern or ancient, would have been her superior, such abundance of power of arms and industry would she in that case have possessed. For it will be seen that after she had expelled the Ghibellines in such numbers that Tuscany and Lombardy were full of them, the Guelfs, together with those who remained in Florence, drew from the city, and of her own citizens, twelve hundred mounted men and twelve thousand infantry for the war against Arezzo, one year before the battle of Campaldino.

Afterwards, in the war against Filippo Visconti, Duke of Milan, having to make trial of her own resources, but not of her own troops (for they had exhausted them at that time), it will be seen that she spent during the five years that this war lasted the sum of three and a half millions of florins; and after that war was finished they were not satis-

---

Reprinted from Niccolo Machiavelli, Preface to *The History of Florence*, in *The Historical, Political and Diplomatic Writings of Niccolo Machiavelli*, trans. Christian E. Detmold (Boston: James R. Osgood & Co., 1882), I, 7–9.

fied to remain at peace, but took the field against Lucca. I cannot see therefore what reasons there can be why these divisions should not be worthy of being particularly described. And if those most noble writers were withheld from doing so by fear of offending the memory of those of whom they would have to speak, they deceive themselves in that respect, and show that they little know the ambition of men, and the desire they have to perpetuate the names of their ancestors and their own. And they do not remember that many, not having had the opportunity of acquiring fame by any praiseworthy acts, have endeavored to acquire it by disgraceful ones. Nor have they considered how the actions that have inherent greatness, such as those of governments and states, however they may have originated, or whatever their object may have been, always bring more honor than discredit to the actors. But I, having considered these things, have been induced thereby to change my purpose, and have resolved to begin my history from the origin of our city. And as it is not my intention to occupy the same ground as others, I shall describe particularly only those things up to the year 1434 that occurred within the city, and of the foreign relations I shall say no more than what may be necessary for a proper understanding of the internal affairs. From and after the year 1434, however, I shall fully describe both the one and the other. Beyond that, for the better understanding of each period, before I treat of Florence I shall relate by what means Italy came to be under the rule of those potentates who governed her at that time.

## 2. *Of the Natural Conditions of Mankind*

BY THOMAS HOBBES

NATURE hath made men so equall, in the faculties of body, and mind; as that though there bee found one man sometimes manifestly stronger in body, or of quicker mind then another; yet when all is reckoned together, the difference between man, and man, is not so considerable, as that one man can thereupon claim himselfe any benefit, to which another may not pretend, as well as he. For as to the strength of body, the weakest has strength enough to kill the strongest, either by secret machination, or by confederacy with others, that are in the same danger with himselfe.

And as to the faculties of the mind, (setting aside the arts grounded upon words, and especially that skill of proceeding upon generall, and infallible rules, called Science; which very few have, and but in few things; as being not a native faculty, born with us; nor attained, (as Prudence,) while we look after somewhat els,) I find yet a greater equality amongst men, than that of strength. For Prudence, is but Experience; which equall time, equally bestowes on all men, in those things they equally apply themselves unto. That which may perhaps make such equality incredible, is but a vain conceipt of ones owne wisdome, which almost all men think they have in a greater degree, than the Vulgar; that is, than all men but themselves, and a few others, whom by Fame, or for concurring with themselves, they approve. For such is the nature of men, that howsoever they may acknowledge many others to be more witty, or more eloquent, or more learned; Yet they will hardly believe there be many so wise as themselves: For they see their own wit at hand, and other mens at a distance. But this proveth rather that men are in that point equall, than unequall. For there is not ordinarily a greater signe of the equall distribution of any thing, than that every man is contented with his share.

From this equality of ability, ariseth equality of hope in the attaining of our Ends. And therefore if any two men desire the same thing, which neverthelesse they cannot both enjoy, they become enemies; and in the way to their End, (which is principally their own conservation, and sometimes their delectation only,) endeavour to destroy, or subdue one an other. And from hence it comes to passe, that where an Invader hath no more to feare, than an other mans single power; if one plant, sow, build, or possesse a convenient Seat, others may

Reprinted from Thomas Hobbes, *Leviathan* (Oxford: James Thornton, 1881), chap. xiii, pp. 91–96.

probably be expected to come prepared with forces united, to dispossesse, and deprive him, not only of the fruit of his labour, but also of his life, or liberty. And the Invader again is in the like danger of another.

And from this diffidence of one another, there is no way for any man to secure himselfe, so reasonable, as Anticipation; that is, by force, or wiles, to master the persons of all men he can, so long, till he see no other power great enough to endanger him: And this is no more than his own conservation requireth, and is generally allowed. Also because there be some, that taking pleasure in contemplating their own power in the acts of conquest, which they pursue farther than their security requires; if others, that otherwise would be glad to be at ease within modest bounds, should not by invasion increase their power, they would not be able, long time, by standing only on their defence, to subsist. And by consequence, such augmentation of dominion over men, being necessary to a mans conservation, it ought to be allowed him.

Againe, men have no pleasure, (but on the contrary a great deale of griefe) in keeping company, where there is no power able to over-awe them all. For every man looketh that his companion should value him, at the same rate he sets upon himselfe: And upon all signes of contempt, or undervaluing, naturally endeavours, as far as he dares (which amongst them that have no common power to keep them in quiet, is far enough to make them destroy each other,) to extort a greater value from his contemners, by dommage; and from others, by this example.

So that in the nature of man, we find three principall causes of quarrell. First, Competition; Secondly, Diffidence, Thirdly, Glory.

The first, maketh men invade for Gain; the second, for Safety; and the third, for Reputation. The first use Violence, to make themselves Masters of other mens persons, wives, children, and cattell; the second, to defend them; the third, for trifles, as a word, a smile, a different opinion, and any other signe of undervalue, either direct in their Persons, or by reflexion in their Kindred, their Friends, their Nation, their Profession, or their Name.

Hereby it is manifest, that during the time men live without a common Power to keep them all in awe, they are in that condition which is called Warre; and such a warre, as is of every man, against every man. For WARRE, consisteth not in Battell onely, or the act of fighting; but in a tract of time, wherein the Will to contend by Battell is sufficiently known: and therefore the notion of *Time,* is to be considered in the nature of Warre; as it is in the nature of Weather. For as the nature of Foule weather, lyeth not in a showre or two of rain; but in an inclination thereto of many dayes together: So the nature of War, consisteth not in actuall fighting; but in the known disposition thereto, during all the time there is no assurance to the contrary. All other time is PEACE.

Whatsoever therefore is consequent to a time of Warre, where every man is Enemy to every man; the same is consequent to the time, wherein men live without other security, than what their own strength, and their own invention shall furnish them withall. In such condition, there is no place for Industry; because the fruit thereof is uncertain: and consequently no Culture of the Earth; no Navigation, nor use of the commodities that may be imported by Sea; no commodious Building; no Instruments of moving, and removing such things as require much force; no Knowledge of the face of the Earth; no account of Time; no Arts; no Letters; no Society; and which is worst of all, continuall feare, and danger of violent death; And the life of man, solitary, poore, nasty, brutish, and short.

It may seem strange to some man, that has not well weighed these things; that Nature should thus dissociate, and render men apt to invade, and destroy one another: and he may therefore, not trusting to his Inference, made from the Passions, desire perhaps to have the same confirmed by Experience. Let him therefore consider with himselfe, when taking a journey, he armes himselfe, and seeks to go well accompanied; when going to sleep, he locks his dores; when even in his house he lockes his chests; and this when he knowes there bee Lawes, and publike Officers, armed, to revenge all injuries shall bee done him; what opinion he has of his fellow subjects, when he rides armed; of his fellow Citizens, when he locks his dores; and of his children, and servants, when he locks his chests. Does he not there as much accuse mankind by his actions, as I do by my words? But neither of us accuse mans nature in it. The Desires, and other Passions of man, are in themselves no Sin. No more are the Actions, that proceed from those Passions, till they know a Law that forbids them: which till Lawes be made they cannot know: nor can any Law be made, till they have agreed upon the Person that shall make it.

It may peradventure be thought, there was never such a time, nor condition of warre as this; and I believe it was never generally so, over all the world: but there are many places, where they live so now. For the savage people in many places of *America,* except the government of small Families, the concord whereof dependeth on naturall lust, have no government at all; and live at this day in that brutish manner, as I said before. Howsoever, it may be perceived what manner of life there would be, where there were no common Power to feare; by the manner of life, which men that have formerly lived under a peaceful government, use to degenerate into, in a civil Warre.

But though there had never been any time, wherein particular men were in a condition of warre one against another; yet in all times, Kings, and Persons of Soveraigne authority, because of their Independency, are in continuall jealousies, and in the state and posture of Gladiators; having their weapons pointing, and their eyes fixed on one another; that is, their Forts, Garrisons, and Guns upon the Frontiers of their Kingdomes; and continuall Spyes upon their neighbours; which is a posture of War. But because they uphold thereby, the Industry of their Subjects; there does not follow from it, that misery, which accompanies the Liberty of particular men.

To this warre of every man against every man, this also is consequent; that nothing can be Unjust. The notions of Right and Wrong, Justice and Injustice have there no place. Where there is no common Power, there is no Law: where no Law, no Injus'ice. Force, and Fraud, are in warre the two Cardinall vertues. Justice, and Injustice are none of the Faculties neither of the Body, nor Mind. If they were, they might be in a man that were alone in the world, as well as his Senses, and Passions. They are Qualities, that relate to men in Society, not in Solitude. It is consequent also to the same condition, that there be no Propriety, no Dominion, no *Mine* and *Thine* distinct; but onely that to be every mans, that he can get; and for so long, as he can keep it. And thus much for the ill condition, which man by meer Nature is actually placed in; though with a possibility to come out of it, consisting partly in the Passions, partly in his Reason.

The Passions that encline men to Peace, are Feare of Death; Desire of such things as are necessary to commodious living; and a Hope by their Industry to obtain them. And Reason suggesteth convenient Articles of Peace, upon which men may be drawn to agreement. These Articles, are they, which otherwise are called the Lawes of Nature: whereof I shall speak more particularly, in the two following Chapters.

# 3. *Of the State of Nature*

BY JOHN LOCKE

TO UNDERSTAND political power right, and derive it from its original, we must consider, what state all men are naturally in, and that is, *a state of perfect freedom* to order their actions, and dispose of their possessions and persons, as they think fit, within the bounds of the law of nature, without asking leave, or depending upon the will of any other man.

A *state* also *of equality,* wherein all the power and jurisdiction is reciprocal, no one having more than another; there being nothing more evident, than that creatures of the same species and rank, promiscuously born to all the same advantages of nature, and the use of the same faculties, should also be equal one amongst another without subordination or subjection, unless the lord and master of them all should, by any manifest declaration of his will, set one above another, and confer on him, by an evident and clear appointment, an undoubted right to dominion and sovereignty.

But though this be *a state of liberty,* yet *it is not a state of license:* though man in that state have an uncontroulable liberty to dispose of his person or possessions, yet he has not liberty to destroy himself, or so much as any creature in his possession, but where some nobler use than its bare preservation calls for it. The *state of nature* has a law of nature to govern it, which obliges every one: and reason, which is that law, teaches all mankind, who

---

Reprinted from John Locke, *Second Treatise of Civil Government,* chap. ii, secs. 4, 6–8, 11–14, in *Two Treatises on Government* (London: Printed for R. Butler, Bruton-Street, Berkeley-Square; W. Reid, Charing-Cross; W. Sharpe, King-Street, Covent Garden; and John Bumpas, Holborn Bars, 1821), pp. 189–93, 195–99.

will but consult it, that being all *equal and independent,* no one ought to harm another in his life, health, liberty, or possessions: for men being all the workmanship of one omnipotent, and infinitely wise maker; all the servants of one sovereign master, sent into the world by his order, and about his business; they are his property, whose workmanship they are, made to last during his, not one another's pleasure: and being furnished with like faculties, sharing all in one community of nature, there cannot be supposed any such *subordination* among us, that may authorize us to destroy one another, as if we were made for one another's uses, as the inferior ranks of creatures are for ours. Every one, as he is *bound to preserve himself,* and not to quit his station wilfully, so by the like reason, when his own preservation comes not in competition, ought he, as much as he can, to *preserve the rest of mankind,* and may not, unless it be to do justice on an offender, take away, or impair the life, or what tends to the preservation of the life, the liberty, health, limb, or goods of another.

And that all men may be restrained from invading others rights, and from doing hurt to one another, and the law of nature be observed, which willeth the peace and *preservation of all mankind,* the *execution* of the law of nature is, in that state, put into every man's hands, whereby every one has a right to punish the transgressors of that law to such a degree, as may hinder its violation: for the *law of nature* would, as all other laws that concern men in this world, be in vain, if there were nobody that in the state of nature had a *power to execute* that law, and thereby preserve the innocent and restrain offenders. And if any one in the state of nature may punish another for any evil he has done, every one may do so: for in that *state of perfect equality* where naturally there is no superiority or jurisdiction of one over another, what any may do in prosecution of that law, every one must needs have a right to do.

And thus, in the state of nature, *one man comes by a power over another;* but yet no absolute or arbitrary power, to use a criminal, when he has got him in his hands, according to the passionate heats, or boundless extravagancy of his own will; but only to retribute to him, so far as calm reason and conscience dictate, what is proportionate to his transgression, which is so much as may serve for *reparation* and *restraint:* for these two are the only reasons, why one man may lawfully do harm to another, which is that we call *punishment.* In transgressing the law of nature, the offender declares himself to live by another rule than that of reason and common equity, which is that measure God has set to the actions of men, for their mutual security; and so he becomes dangerous to mankind, the tye, which is to secure them from injury and violence, being slighted and broken by him. Which being a trespass against the whole species, and the peace and safety of it, provided for by the law of nature, every man upon this score, by the right he hath to preserve mankind in general, may restrain, or where it is necessary, destroy things noxious to them, and so may bring such evil on any one, who hath transgressed that law, as may make him repent the doing of it, and thereby deter him, and by his example others, from doing the like mischief. And in this case, and upon this ground, *every man hath a right to punish the offender, and be executioner of the law of nature.*

* * *

From* these *two distinct rights,* the one of *punishing* the crime *for restraint,* and preventing the like offence, which right of punishing is in every body; the other of taking *reparation,* which belongs only to the injured party, comes it to pass that the magistrate, who by being magistrate hath the common right of punishing put into his hands, can often, where the public good demands not the execution of the law, *remit* the punishment of criminal offences by his own authority, but yet cannot *remit* the satisfaction due to any private man for the damage he has received. That, he who has suffered the damage has a right to demand in his own name, and he alone can remit: the damnified person has this power of appropriating to himself the goods or service of the offender, *by right of self-preservation,* as every man has a power to punish the crime, to prevent its being committed again, *by the right he has of preserving all mankind,* and doing all reasonable things he can in order to that end: and thus it is, that every man, in the state of nature, has a power to kill a murderer, both *to deter* others from doing the like injury, which no reparation can compensate, by the example of the punishment that attends it from every body, and also to secure men from the attempts of a criminal, who having renounced reason, the common rule and measure God hath given to mankind, hath, by the unjust violence and slaughter he hath committed upon one, declared war against all mankind, and therefore may be destroyed as a *lion* or a *tyger,* one of those wild savage beasts, with whom men can have no society nor security: and upon this is grounded that great law of nature, "Whoso sheddeth man's blood, by man shall his blood be shed." And Cain was so fully convinced, that every one had a right to destroy such a criminal, that after the murder of his

* This section reprinted from pp. 195–99.

brother, he cries out, *Every one that findeth me shall slay me;* so plain was it writ in the hearts of all mankind.

By the same reason may a man in the state of nature *punish the lesser breaches* of that law. It will perhaps be demanded, with death? I answer, each transgression may be *punished* to that *degree,* and with so much *severity,* as will suffice to make it an ill bargain to the offender, give him cause to repent, and terrify others from doing the like. Every offence, that can be committed in the state of nature, may in the state of nature be also punished equally, and as far forth as it may, in a commonwealth: for though it would be besides my present purpose, to enter here into the particulars of the law of nature, or its *measures of punishment;* yet, it is certain there is such a law, and that too, as intelligible and plain to a rational creature, and a studier of that law, as the positive laws of commonwealths: nay, possibly plainer; as much as reason is easier to be understood, than the fancies and intricate contrivances of men, following contrary and hidden interests put into words; for so truly are a great part of the *municipal* laws of countries, which are only so far right, as they are founded on the law of nature, by which they are to be regulated and interpreted.

To this strange doctrine, *viz.* That *in the state of nature every one has the executive power* of the law of nature, I doubt not but it will be objected, that it is unreasonable for men to be judges in their own cases, that self-love will make men partial to themselves and their friends: and on the other side, that ill-nature, passion and revenge will carry them too far in punishing others; and hence nothing but confusion and disorder will follow; and that therefore God hath certainly appointed government to restrain the partiality and violence of men. I easily grant, that *civil government* is the proper remedy for the inconveniences of the state of nature, which must certainly be great, where men may be judges in their own case, since it is easy to be imagined, that he who was so unjust as to do his brother an injury, will scarce be so just as to condemn himself for it; but I shall desire those who make this objection, to remember, that *absolute monarchs* are but men; and if government is to be the remedy of those evils, which necessarily follow from men's being judges in their own cases, and the state of nature is therefore not to be endured, I desire to know what kind of government that is, and how much better it is than the state of nature, where one man, commanding a multitude, has the liberty to be judge in his own case, and may do to all his subjects whatever he pleases, without the least liberty to any one to question or controul those who execute his pleasure? and in whatsoever he doth, whether led by reason, mistake or passion, must be submitted to? much better it is in the state of nature, wherein men are not bound to submit to the unjust will of another; and if he that judges, judges amiss in his own, or any other case, he is answerable for it to the rest of mankind.

It is often asked as a mighty objection, *where are,* or ever were there any *men in such a state of nature?* To which it may suffice as an answer at present, that since all princes and rulers of *independent* governments all through the world, are in a state of nature, it is plain the world never was, nor ever will be, without numbers of men in that state. I have named all governors of *independent communities,* whether they are, or are not, in league with others: for it is not every compact that puts an end to the state of nature between men, but only this one of agreeing together mutually to enter into one community, and make one body politic; other promises, and compacts, men may make one with another, and yet still be in the state of nature. The promises and bargains for truck, &c. between the two men in the desert island, mentioned by Garcilasso de la Vega, in his history of Peru; or between a Swiss and an Indian, in the woods of America, are binding to them, though they are perfectly in a state of nature, in reference to one another: for truth and keeping of faith belongs to men, as men, and not as members of society.

# 4. *Of the Principle Which Gives Occasion to the Division of Labour*

BY ADAM SMITH

THIS DIVISION of labour, from which so many advantages are derived, is not originally the effect of any human wisdom, which foresees and intends that general opulence to which it gives occasion. It is the necessary, though very slow and gradual, consequence of a certain propensity in human nature which has in view no such extensive utility; the propensity to truck, barter, and exchange one thing for another.

Whether this propensity be one of those original principles in human nature, of which no further account can be given; or whether, as seems more probable, it be the necessary consequence of the faculties of reason and speech, it belongs not to our present subject to enquire. It is common to all men, and to be found in no other race of animals, which seem to know neither this nor any other species of contracts. Two greyhounds, in running down the same hare, have sometimes the appearance of acting in some sort of concert. Each turns her towards his companion, or endeavours to intercept her when his companion turns her towards himself. This, however, is not the effect of any contract, but of the accidental concurrence of their passions in the same object at that particular time. Nobody ever saw a dog make a fair and deliberate exchange of one bone for another with another dog. Nobody ever saw one animal by its gestures and natural cries signify to another, this is mine, that yours; I am willing to give this for that. When an animal wants to obtain something either of a man, or of another animal, it has no other means of persuasion but to gain the favour of those whose service it requires. A puppy fawns upon its dam, and a spaniel endeavours by a thousand attractions to engage the attention of its master who is at dinner, when it wants to be fed by him. Man sometimes uses the same arts with his brethren, and when he has no other means of engaging them to act according to his inclinations, endeavours by every servile and fawning attention to obtain their good will. He has not time, however, to do this upon every occasion. In civilized society he stands at all times in need of the co-operation and assistance of great multitudes, while his whole life is scarce sufficient to gain the friendship of a few persons. In almost every other race of animals, each individual, when it is grown up to maturity, is entirely independent, and in its natural state has occasion for the assistance of no other living creature. But man has almost constant occasion for the help of his brethren, and it is in vain for him to expect it from their benevolence only. He will be more likely to prevail if he can interest their self-love in his favour, and shew them that it is for their own advantage to do for him what he requires of them. Whoever offers to another a bargain of any kind, proposes to do this: Give me that which I want, and you shall have this which you want, is the meaning of every such offer; and it is in this manner that we obtain from one another the far greater part of those good offices which we stand in need of. It is not from the benevolence of the butcher, the brewer, or the baker, that we expect our dinner, but from their regard to their own interest. We address ourselves, not to their humanity but to their selflove, and never talk to them of our own necessities but of their advantages. Nobody but a beggar chuses to depend chiefly upon the benevolence of his fellow-citizens. Even a beggar does not depend upon it entirely. The charity of well-disposed people, indeed, supplies him with the whole fund of his subsistence. But though this principle ultimately provides him with all the necessaries of life which he has occasion for, it neither does nor can provide him with them as he has occasion for them. The greater part of his occasional wants are supplied in the same manner as those of other people, by treaty, by barter, and by purchase. With the money which one man gives him he purchases food. The old cloaths which another bestows upon him he exchanges for other old cloaths which suit him better, or for lodging, or for food, or for money, with which he can buy either food, cloaths, or lodging, as he has occasion.

As it is by treaty, by barter, and by purchase, that we obtain from one another the greater part of those mutual good offices which we stand in

---

Reprinted from Adam Smith, *An Inquiry into the Nature and Causes of the Wealth of Nations* (7th ed.; London, 1793), Book I, chap. ii, pp. 19–25.

need of, so it is this same trucking disposition which originally gives occasion to the division of labour. In a tribe of hunters or shepherds a particular person makes bows and arrows, for example, with more readiness and dexterity than any other. He frequently exchanges them for cattle or for venison with his companions; and he finds at last that he can in this manner get more cattle and venison, than if he himself went to the field to catch them. From a regard to his own interest, therefore, the making of bows and arrows grows to be his chief business, and he becomes a sort of armourer. Another excels in making the frames and covers of their little huts or moveable houses. He is accustomed to be of use in this way to his neighbours, who reward him in the same manner with cattle and with venison, till at last he finds it his interest to dedicate himself entirely to this employment, and to become a sort of house-carpenter. In the same manner a third becomes a smith or a brazier; a fourth a tanner or dresser of hides or skins, the principal part of the cloathing of savages. And thus the certainty of being able to exchange all that surplus part of the produce of his own labour, which is over and above his own consumption, for such parts of the produce of other men's labour as he may have occasion for, encourages every man to apply himself to a particular occupation, and to cultivate and bring to perfection whatever talent or genius he may possess for that particular species of business.

The difference of natural talents in different men is, in reality, much less than we are aware of; and the very different genius which appears to distinguish men of different professions, when grown up to maturity, is not upon many occasions so much the cause, as the effect of the division of labour. The difference between the most dissimilar characters, between a philosopher and a common street porter, for example, seems to arise not so much from nature, as from habit, custom, and education. When they came into the world, and for the first six or eight years of their existence, they were, perhaps, very much alike, and neither their parents nor playfellows could perceive any remarkable difference. About that age, or soon after, they come to be employed in very different occupations. The difference of talents comes then to be taken notice of, and widens by degrees, till at last the vanity of the philosopher is willing to acknowledge scarce any resemblance. But without the disposition to truck, barter, and exchange, every man must have procured to himself every necessary and conveniency of life which he wanted. All must have had the same duties to perform, and the same work to do, and there could have been no such difference of employment as could alone give occasion to any great difference of talents.

As it is this disposition which forms that difference of talents, so remarkable among men of different professions, so it is this same disposition which renders that difference useful. Many tribes of animals acknowledged to be all of the same species, derive from nature a much more remarkable distinction of genius, than what, antecedent to custom and education, appears to take place among men. By nature a philosopher is not in genius and disposition half so different from a street porter, as a mastiff is from a greyhound, or a greyhound from a spaniel, or this last from a shepherd's dog. Those different tribes of animals, however, though all of the same species, are of scarce any use to one another. The strength of the mastiff is not in the least supported either by the swiftness of the greyhound, or by the sagacity of the spaniel, or by the docility of the shepherd's dog. The effects of those different geniuses and talents, for want of the power or disposition to barter and exchange, cannot be brought into a common stock, and do not in the least contribute to the better accommodation and conveniency of the species. Each animal is still obliged to support and defend itself, separately and independently, and derives no sort of advantage from that variety of talents with which nature has distinguished its fellows. Among men, on the contrary, the most dissimilar geniuses are of use to one another; the different produces of their respective talents, by the general disposition to truck, barter, and exchange, being brought, as it were, into a common stock, where every man may purchase whatever part of the produce of other men's talents he has occasion for.

# 5. *Of Systems of Equality*

BY THOMAS R. MALTHUS

IN READING Mr. Godwin's ingenious and able work on political justice, it is impossible not to be struck with the spirit and energy of his style, the force and precision of some of his reasonings, the ardent tone of his thoughts, and particularly with that impressive earnestness of manner which gives an air of truth to the whole. At the same time, it must be confessed, that he has not proceeded in his enquiries with the caution that sound philosophy seems to require. His conclusions are often unwarranted by his premises. He fails sometimes in removing the objections which he himself brings forward. He relies too much on general and abstract propositions which will not admit of application. And his conjectures certainly far outstrip the modesty of nature.

The system of equality which Mr. Godwin proposes, is, without doubt, by far the most beautiful and engaging of any that has yet appeared. An amelioration of society to be produced merely by reason and conviction, wears much more the promise of permanence, than any change effected and maintained by force. The unlimited exercise of private judgment, is a doctrine inexpressibly grand and captivating, and has a vast superiority over those systems where every individual is in a manner the slave of the public. The substitution of benevolence as the master-spring, and moving principle of society, instead of self-love, is a consummation devoutly to be wished. In short, it is impossible to contemplate the whole of this fair structure, without emotions of delight and admiration, accompanied with ardent longing for the period of its accomplishment. But, alas! that moment can never arrive. The whole is little better than a dream, a beautiful phantom of the imagination. These "gorgeous palaces" of happiness and immortality, these "solemn temples" of truth and virtue will dissolve, "like the baseless fabric of a vision," when we awaken to real life, and contemplate the true and genuine situation of man on earth.

Mr. Godwin, at the conclusion of the third chapter of his eighth book, speaking of population, says, "There is a principle in human society, by which population is perpetually kept down to the level of the means of subsistence. Thus among the wandering tribes of America and Asia, we never find through the lapse of ages that population has so increased as to render necessary the cultivation of the earth." This principle, which Mr. Godwin thus mentions as some mysterious and occult cause, and which he does not attempt to investigate, will be found to be the grinding law of necessity; misery, and the fear of misery.

The great error under which Mr. Godwin labours throughout his whole work, is, the attributing almost all the vices and misery that are seen in civil society to human institutions. Political regulations, and the established administration of property, are with him the fruitful sources of all evil, the hotbeds of all the crimes that degrade mankind. Were this really a true state of the case, it would not seem a hopeless task to remove evil completely from the world; and reason seems to be the proper and adequate instrument for effecting so great a purpose. But the truth is, that though human institutions appear to be the obvious and obstrusive causes of much mischief to mankind; yet, in reality, they are light and superficial, they are mere feathers that float on the surface, in comparison with those deeper seated causes of impurity that corrupt the springs, and render turbid the whole stream of human life.

Mr. Godwin, in his chapter on the benefits attendant on a system of equality, says, "The spirit of oppression, the spirit of servility, and the spirit of fraud, these are the immediate growth of the established administration of property. They are alike hostile to intellectual improvement. The other vices of envy, malice, and revenge, are their inseparable companions. In a state of society, where men lived in the midst of plenty, and where all shared alike the bounties of nature, these sentiments would inevitably expire. The narrow principle of selfishness would vanish. No man being obliged to guard his little store, or provide with anxiety and pain for his restless wants, each would lose his individual existence in the thought of the general good. No man would be an enemy to his neighbour, for they would have no subject of contention; and, of consequence, philanthropy would resume the empire which reason assigns her. Mind would be delivered

---

Reprinted from Thomas R. Malthus, *An Essay on the Principle of Population* (London: J. Johnson, 1798), chap. x, pp. 173–207; chap. xi, pp. 210–18.

from her perpetual anxiety about corporal support, and free to expatiate in the field of thought, which is congenial to her. Each would assist the enquiries of all."

This would, indeed, be a happy state. But that it is merely an imaginary picture, with scarcely a feature near the truth, the reader, I am afraid, is already too well convinced.

Man cannot live in the midst of plenty. All cannot share alike the bounties of nature. Were there no established administration of property, every man would be obliged to guard with force his little store. Selfishness would be triumphant. The subjects of contention would be perpetual. Every individual mind would be under a constant anxiety about corporal support; and not a single intellect would be left free to expatiate in the field of thought.

How little Mr. Godwin has turned the attention of his penetrating mind to the real state of man on earth, will sufficiently appear from the manner in which he endeavours to remove the difficulty of an overcharged population. He says, "The obvious answer to this objection, is, that to reason thus is to foresee difficulties at a great distance. Three fourths of the habitable globe is now uncultivated. The parts already cultivated are capable of immeasurable improvement. Myriads of centuries of still increasing population may pass away, and the earth be still found sufficient for the subsistence of its inhabitants."

I have already pointed out the error of supposing that no distress and difficulty would arise from an overcharged population before the earth absolutely refused to produce any more. But let us imagine for a moment Mr. Godwin's beautiful system of equality realized in its utmost purity, and see how soon this difficulty might be expected to press under so perfect a form of society. A theory that will not admit of application cannot possibly be just.

Let us suppose all the causes of misery and vice in this island removed. War and contention cease. Unwholesome trades and manufactories do not exist. Crowds no longer collect together in great and pestilent cities for purposes of court intrigue, of commerce, and vicious gratifications. Simple, healthy, and rational amusements take place of drinking, gaming and debauchery. There are no towns sufficiently large to have any prejudicial effects on the human constitution. The greater part of the happy inhabitants of this terrestrial paradise live in hamlets and farm-houses scattered over the face of the country. Every house is clean, airy, sufficiently roomy, and in a healthy situation. All men are equal. The labours of luxury are at end. And the necessary labours of agriculture are shared amicably among all. The number of persons, and the produce of the island, we suppose to be the same as at present. The spirit of benevolence, guided by impartial justice, will divide this produce among all the members of the society according to their wants. Though it would be impossible that they should all have animal food every day, yet vegetable food, with meat occasionally, would satisfy the desires of a frugal people, and would be sufficient to preserve them in health, strength, and spirits.

Mr. Godwin considers marriage as a fraud and a monopoly. Let us suppose the commerce of the sexes established upon principles of the most perfect freedom. Mr. Godwin does not think himself that this freedom would lead to a promiscuous intercourse; and in this I perfectly agree with him. The love of variety is a vicious, corrupt, and unnatural taste, and could not prevail in any great degree in a simple and virtuous state of society. Each man would probably select himself a partner, to whom he would adhere as long as that adherence continued to be the choice of both parties. It would be of little consequence, according to Mr. Godwin, how many children a woman had, or to whom they belonged. Provisions and assistance would spontaneously flow from the quarter in which they abounded, to the quarter that was deficient. And every man would be ready to furnish instruction to the rising generation according to his capacity.

I cannot conceive a form of society so favourable upon the whole to population. The irremediableness of marriage, as it is at present constituted, undoubtedly deters many from entering into that state. An unshackled intercourse on the contrary, would be a most powerful incitement to early attachments: and as we are supposing no anxiety about the future support of children to exist, I do not conceive that there would be one woman in a hundred, of twenty-three, without a family.

With these extraordinary encouragements to population, and every cause of depopulation, as we have supposed, removed, the numbers would necessarily increase faster than in any society that has ever yet been known. I have mentioned, on the authority of a pamphlet published by a Dr. Styles, and referred to by Dr. Price, that the inhabitants of the back settlements of America doubled their numbers in fifteen years. England is certainly a more healthy country than the back settlements of America; and as we have supposed every house in the island to be airy and wholesome, and the encouragements to have a family greater even than with the back settlers, no probable reason can be assigned, why the population should not double itself in less, if possible, than fifteen years. But to be quite sure that we do not go beyond the truth, we will only suppose the period of doubling to be twenty-five years, a ratio of increase, which is well known to have taken place throughout all the Northern States of America.

There can be little doubt, that the equalization of property which we have supposed, added to the circumstance of the labour of the whole community being directed chiefly to agriculture, would tend greatly to augment the produce of the country. But to answer the demands of a population increasing so rapidly, Mr. Godwin's calculation of half an hour a day for each man, would certainly not be sufficient. It is probable that the half of every man's time must be employed for this purpose. Yet with such, or much greater exertions, a person who is acquainted with the nature of the soil in this country, and who reflects on the fertility of the lands already in cultivation, and the barrenness of those that are not cultivated, will be very much disposed to doubt, whether the whole average produce could possibly be doubled in twenty-five years from the present period. The only chance of success would be the ploughing up all the grazing countries, and putting an end almost entirely to the use of animal food. Yet a part of this scheme might defeat itself. The soil of England will not produce much without dressing; and cattle seem to be necessary to make that species of manure, which best suits the land. In China, it is said, that the soil in some of the provinces is so fertile, as to produce two crops of rice in the year without dressing. None of the lands in England will answer to this description.

Difficult, however, as it might be, to double the average produce of the island in twenty-five years, let us suppose it effected. At the expiration of the first period therefore, the food, though almost entirely vegetable, would be sufficient to support in health, the doubled population of fourteen millions.

During the next period of doubling, where will the food be found to satisfy the importunate demands of the increasing numbers. Where is the fresh land to turn up? where is the dressing necessary to improve that which is already in cultivation? There is no person with the smallest knowledge of land, but would say, that it was impossible that the average produce of the country could be increased during the second twenty-five years by a quantity equal to what it at present yields. Yet we will suppose this increase, however improbable, to take place. The exuberant strength of the argument allows of almost any concession. Even with this concession, however, there would be seven millions at the expiration of the second term, unprovided for. A quantity of food equal to the frugal support of twenty-one millions, would be to be divided among twenty-eight millions.

Alas! what becomes of the picture where men lived in the midst of plenty: where no man was obliged to provide with anxiety and pain for his restless wants: where the narrow principle of selfishness did not exist: where Mind was delivered from her perpetual anxiety about corporal support, and free to expatiate in the field of thought which is congenial to her. This beautiful fabric of imagination vanishes at the severe touch of truth. The spirit of benevolence, cherished and invigorated by plenty, is repressed by the chilling breath of want. The hateful passions that had vanished, reappear. The mighty law of self-preservation, expels all the softer and more exalted emotions of the soul. The temptations to evil are too strong for human nature to resist. The corn is plucked before it is ripe, or secreted in unfair proportions; and the whole black train of vices that belong to falsehood are immediately generated. Provisions no longer flow in for the support of the mother with a large family. The children are sickly from insufficient food. The rosy flush of health gives place to the pallid cheek and hollow eye of misery. Benevolence yet lingering in a few bosoms, makes some faint expiring struggles, till at length self-love resumes his wonted empire, and lords it triumphant over the world.

No human institutions here existed, to the perverseness of which Mr. Godwin ascribes the original sin of the worst men. No opposition had been produced by them between public and private good. No monopoly had been created of those advantages which reason directs to be left in common. No man had been goaded to the breach of order by unjust laws. Benevolence had established her reign in all hearts: and yet in so short a period as within fifty years, violence, oppression, falsehood, misery, every hateful vice, and every form of distress, which degrade and sadden the present state of society, seem to have been generated by the most imperious circumstances, by laws inherent in the nature of man, and absolutely independent of all human regulations.

If we are not yet too well convinced of the reality of this melancholy picture, let us but look for a moment into the next period of twenty-five years; and we shall see twenty-eight millions of human beings without the means of support; and before the conclusion of the first century, the population would be one hundred and twelve millions, and the food only sufficient for thirty-five millions, leaving seventy-seven millions unprovided for. In these ages want would be indeed triumphant, and rapine and murder must reign at large: and yet all this time we are supposing the produce of the earth absolutely unlimited, and the yearly increase greater than the boldest speculator can imagine.

This is undoubtedly a very different view of the difficulty arising from population, from that which Mr. Godwin gives, when he says, "Myriads of centuries of still increasing population may pass away, and the earth be still found sufficient for the subsistence of its inhabitants."

I am sufficiently aware that the redundant twenty-eight millions, or seventy-seven millions, that I have mentioned, could never have existed. It is a perfectly just observation of Mr. Godwin, that, "There is a principle in human society, by which population is perpetually kept down to the level of the means of subsistence." The sole question is, what is this principle? Is it some obscure and occult cause? Is it some mysterious interference of heaven, which at a certain period, strikes the men with impotence, and the women with barrenness? Or is it a cause, open to our researches, within our view, a cause, which has constantly been observed to operate, though with varied force, in every state in which man has been placed? Is it not a degree of misery, the necessary and inevitable result of the laws of nature, which human institutions, so far from aggravating, have tended considerably to mitigate, though they never can remove?

It may be curious to observe, in the case that we have been supposing, how some of the laws which at present govern civilized society, would be successively dictated by the most imperious necessity. As man, according to Mr. Godwin, is the creature of the impressions to which he is subject, the goadings of want could not continue long, before some violations of public or private stock would necessarily take place. As these violations increased in number and extent, the more active and comprehensive intellects of the society would soon perceive, that while population was fast increasing, the yearly produce of the country would shortly begin to diminish. The urgency of the case would suggest the necessity of some immediate measures to be taken for the general safety. Some kind of convention would then be called, and the dangerous situation of the country stated in the strongest terms. It would be observed, that while they lived in the midst of plenty, it was of little consequence who laboured the least, or who possessed the least, as every man was perfectly willing and ready to supply the wants of his neigbour. But that the question was no longer, whether one man should give to another, that which he did not use himself; but whether he should give to his neighbour the food which was absolutely necessary to his own existence. It would be represented, that the number of those that were in want very greatly exceeded the number and means of those who should supply them: that these pressing wants, which from the state of the produce of the country could not all be gratified, had occasioned some flagrant violations of justice: that these violations had already checked the increase of food, and would, if they were not by some means or other prevented, throw the whole community in confusion: that imperious necessity seemed to dictate that a yearly increase of produce should, if possible, be obtained at all events: that in order to effect this first, great, and indispensible purpose, it would be adviseable to make a more complete division of land, and to secure every man's stock against violation by the most powerful sanctions, even by death itself.

It might be urged perhaps by some objectors, that, as the fertility of the land increased, and various accidents occurred, the share of some men might be much more than sufficient for their support, and that when the reign of self-love was once established, they would not distribute their surplus produce without some compensation in return. It would be observed, in answer, that this was an inconvenience greatly to be lamented; but that it was an evil which bore no comparison to the black train of distresses, that would inevitably be occasioned by the insecurity of property: that the quantity of food which one man could consume, was necessarily limited by the narrow capacity of the human stomach: that it was not certainly probable that he should throw away the rest; but that even if he exchanged his surplus food for the labour of others, and made them in some degree dependent on him, this would still be better than that these others should absolutely starve.

It seems highly probable, therefore, that an administration of property, not very different from that which prevails in civilized States at present, would be established, as the best, though inadequate, remedy, for the evils which were pressing on the society.

The next subject that would come under discussion, intimately connected with the preceding, is, the commerce between the sexes. It would be urged by those who had turned their attention to the true cause of the difficulties under which the community laboured, that while every man felt secure that all his children would be well provided for by general benevolence, the powers of the earth would be absolutely inadequate to produce food for the population which would inevitably ensue: that even, if the whole attention and labour of the society were directed to this sole point, and if, by the most perfect security of property, and every other encouragement that could be thought of, the greatest possible increase of produce were yearly obtained; yet still, that the increase of food would by no means keep pace with the much more rapid increase of population: that some check to population therefore was imperiously called for: that the most natural and obvious check seemed to be, to make every man provide for his own children: that this would operate in some respect, as a measure and guide, in the increase of population; as it might be expected that no man would bring beings into the world, for whom he could not find the means of support: that where this notwithstanding was the case, it seemed necessary, for the example of others, that the disgrace and inconvenience attending such a conduct, should fall upon that individual, who had thus inconsiderately plunged himself and innocent children in misery and want.

The institution of marriage, or at least, of some express or implied obligation on every man to support his own children, seems to be the natural result of these reasonings in a community under the difficulties that we have supposed.

The view of these difficulties, presents us with a very natural origin of the superior disgrace which attends a breach of chastity in the woman, than in the man. It could not be expected that women should have resources sufficient to support their own children. When therefore a woman was connected with a man, who had entered into no compact to maintain her children; and aware of the inconveniences that he might bring upon himself, had deserted her, these children must necessarily fall for support upon the society, or starve. And to prevent the frequent recurrence of such an inconvenience, as it would be highly unjust to punish so natural a fault by personal restraint or infliction, the men might agree to punish it with disgrace. The offence is besides more obvious and conspicuous in the woman, and less liable to any mistake. The father of a child may not always be known, but the same uncertainty cannot easily exist with regard to the mother. Where the evidence of the offence was most complete, and the inconvenience to the society at the same time the greatest, there, it was agreed, that the largest share of blame should fall. The obligation on every man to maintain his children, the society would enforce, if there were occasion; and the greater degree of inconvenience or labour, to which a family would necessarily subject him, added to some portion of disgrace which every human being must incur, who leads another into unhappiness, might be considered as a sufficient punishment for the man.

That a woman should at present be almost driven from society, for an offence, which men commit nearly with impunity, seems to be undoubtedly a breach of natural justice. But the origin of the custom, as the most obvious and effectual method of preventing the frequent recurrence of a serious inconvenience to a community, appears to be natural, though not perhaps perfectly justifiable. This origin, however, is now lost in the new train of ideas which the custom has since generated. What at first might be dictated by state necessity, is now supported by female delicacy; and operates with the greatest force on that part of society, where, if the original intention of the custom were preserved, there is the least real occasion for it.

When these two fundamental laws of society, the security of property, and the institution of marriage, were once established, inequality of conditions must necessarily follow. Those who were born after the division of property, would come into a world already possessed. If their parents, from having too large a family, could not give them sufficient for their support, what are they to do in a world where every thing is appropriated? We have seen the fatal effects that would result to a society, if every man had a valid claim to an equal share of the produce of the earth. The members of a family which was grown too large for the original division of land appropriated to it, could not then demand a part of the surplus produce of others, as a debt of justice. It has appeared, that from the inevitable laws of our nature, some human beings must suffer from want. These are the unhappy persons who, in the great lottery of life, have drawn a blank. The number of these claimants would soon exceed the ability of the surplus produce to supply. Moral merit is a very difficult distinguishing criterion, except in extreme cases. The owners of surplus produce would in general seek some more obvious mark of distinction. And it seems both natural and just, that except upon particular occasions, their choice should fall upon those, who were able, and professed themselves willing, to exert their strength in procuring a further surplus produce; and thus at once benefiting the community, and enabling these proprietors to afford assistance to greater numbers. All who were in want of food would be urged by imperious necessity to offer their labour in exchange for this article so absolutely essential to existence. The fund appropriated to the maintenance of labour, would be, the aggregate quantity of food possessed by the owners of land beyond their own consumption. When the demands upon this fund were great and numerous, it would naturally be divided in very small shares. Labour would be ill paid. Men would offer to work for a bare subsistence, and the rearing of families would be checked by sickness and misery. On the contrary, when this fund was increasing fast; when it was great in proportion to the number of claimants; it would be divided in much larger shares. No man would exchange his labour without receiving an ample quantity of food in return. Labourers would live in ease and comfort; and would consequently be able to rear a numerous and vigorous offspring.

On the state of this fund, the happiness, or the degree of misery, prevailing among the lower classes of people in every known State, at present chiefly depends. And on this happiness, or degree of misery, depends the increase, stationariness, or decrease of population.

And thus it appears, that a society constituted according to the most beautiful form that imagination can conceive, with benevolence for its moving principle, instead of self-love, and with every evil disposition in all its members corrected by reason and not force, would, from the inevitable laws of nature, and not from any original depravity of man, in a very short period, degenerate into a society, constructed upon a plan not essentially different from that which prevails in every known State at present; I mean, a society divided into a class of proprietors, and a class of labourers, and with self-love for the main-spring of the great machine.

* * *

We* have supposed Mr. Godwin's system of society once completely established. But it is supposing an impossibility. The same causes in nature which would destroy it so rapidly, were it once established, would prevent the possibility of its establishment. And upon what grounds we can presume a change in these natural causes, I am utterly at a loss to conjecture. No move towards the extinction of the passion between the sexes has taken place in the five or six thousand years that the world has existed. Men in the decline of life have, in all ages, declaimed against a passion which they have ceased to feel, but with as little reason as success. Those who from coldness of constitutional temperament have never felt what love is, will surely be allowed to be very incompetent judges, with regard to the power of this passion, to contribute to the sum of pleasurable sensations in life. Those who have spent their youth in criminal excesses, and have prepared for themselves, as the comforts of their age, corporal debility, and mental remorse, may well inveigh against such pleasures as vain and futile, and unproductive of lasting satisfaction. But the pleasures of pure love will bear the contemplation of the most improved reason, and the most exalted virtue. Perhaps there is scarcely a man who has once experienced the genuine delight of virtuous love, however great his intellectual pleasures may have been, that does not look back to the period, as the sunny spot in his whole life, where his imagination loves to bask, which he recollects and contemplates with the fondest regrets, and which he would most wish to live over again. The superiority of intellectual, to sensual pleasures, consists rather, in their filling up more time, in their having a larger range, and in their being less liable to satiety, than in their being more real and essential.

Intemperance in every enjoyment defeats its own purpose. A walk in the finest day, through the most beautiful country, if pursued too far, ends in pain and fatigue. The most wholesome and invigorating food, eaten with an unrestrained appetite, produces weakness, instead of strength. Even intellectual pleasures, though certainly less liable than others to satiety, pursued with too little intermission, debilitate the body, and impair the vigour of the mind. To argue against the reality of these pleasures from their abuse, seems to be hardly just. Morality, according to Mr. Godwin, is a calculation of consequences, or, as Archdeacon Paley very justly expresses it, the will of God, as collected from general expediency. According to either of these definitions, a sensual pleasure, not attended with the probability of unhappy consequences, does not offend against the laws of morality: and if it be pursued with such a degree of temperance, as to leave the most ample room for intellectual attainments, it must undoubtedly add to the sum of pleasurable sensations in life. Virtuous love, exalted by friendship, seems to be that sort of mixture of sensual and intellectual enjoyment particularly suited to the nature of man, and most powerfully calculated to awaken the sympathies of the soul, and produce the most exquisite gratifications.

Mr. Godwin says, in order to shew the evident inferiority of the pleasures of sense, "Strip the commerce of the sexes of all its attendant circumstances, and it would be generally despised." He might as well say to a man who admired trees; strip them of their spreading branches and lovely foliage, and what beauty can you see in a bare pole? But it was the tree with the branches and foliage, and not without them, that excited admiration. One feature of an object, may be as distinct, and excite as different emotions, from the aggregate, as any two things the most remote, as a beautiful woman, and a map of Madagascar. It is "the symmetry of person, the vivacity, the voluptuous softness of temper, the affectionate kindness of feelings, the imagination and the wit" of a woman that excite the passion of love, and not the mere distinction of her being a female. Urged by the passion of love, men have been driven into acts highly prejudicial to the general interests of society; but probably they would have found no difficulty in resisting the temptation, had it appeared in the form of a woman, with no other attractions

* This section reprinted from chap. xi, pp. 210–18.

whatever but her sex. To strip sensual pleasures of all their adjuncts, in order to prove their inferiority, is to deprive a magnet of some of its most essential causes of attraction, and then to say that it is weak and inefficient.

In the pursuit of every enjoyment, whether sensual or intellectual, Reason, that faculty which enables us to calculate consequences, is the proper corrective and guide. It is probable therefore that improved reason will always tend to prevent the abuse of sensual pleasures, though it by no means follows that it will extinguish them.

I have endeavoured to expose the fallacy of that argument which infers an unlimited progress from a partial improvement, the limits of which cannot be exactly ascertained. It has appeared, I think, that there are many instances in which a decided progress has been observed, where yet it would be a gross absurdity to suppose that progress indefinite. But towards the extinction of the passion between the sexes, no observable progress whatever has hitherto been made. To suppose such an extinction, therefore, is merely to offer an unfounded conjecture, unsupported by any philosophical probabilities.

It is a truth, which history I am afraid makes too clear, that some men of the highest mental powers, have been addicted not only to a moderate, but even to an immoderate indulgence in the pleasures of sensual love. But allowing, as I should be inclined to do, notwithstanding numerous instances to the contrary, that great intellectual exertions tend to diminish the empire of this passion over man; it is evident that the mass of mankind must be improved more highly than the brightest ornaments of the species at present, before any difference can take place sufficient sensibly to affect population. I would by no means suppose that the mass of mankind has reached its term of improvement; but the principal argument of this essay tends to place in a strong point of view, the improbability, that the lower classes of people in any country, should ever be sufficiently free from want and labour, to attain any high degree of intellectual improvement.

# 6. *The Civic Community*

BY GEORG W. F. HEGEL

182. THE CONCRETE PERSON, who as particular is an end to himself, is a totality of wants and a mixture of necessity and caprice. As such he is one of the principles of the civic community. But the particular person is essentially connected with others. Hence each establishes and satisfies himself by means of others, and so must call in the assistance of the form of universality. This universality is the other principle of the civic community. . . .

*  *  *

183. The self-seeking end is conditioned in its realization by the universal. Hence is formed a system of mutual dependence, a system which interweaves the subsistence, happiness, and rights of the individual with the subsistence, happiness, and right of all. The general right and well-being form the basis of the individual's right and well-being, which only by this connection receives actuality and security. This system we may in the first instance call the external state, the state which satisfies one's needs, and meets the requirements of the understanding.

*  *  *

187. Individuals in the civic community are private persons, who pursue their own interests. As these interests are occasioned by the universal, which appears as a means, they can be obtained only in so far as individuals in their desire, will, and conduct, conform to the universal, and become a link in the chain of the whole. The interest of the idea as such does not, it is true, lie in the consciousness of the citizens; yet it is not wholly wanting. It is found in the process, by means of which the individual, through necessity of nature and the caprice of his wants, seeks to raise his individual natural existence into formal freedom and the formal universality of knowing and willing.

Reprinted from Georg W. F. Hegel, *The Philosophy of Right,* trans. S. W. Dyde (London: George Bell & Sons, 1896), secs. 182–83, 187–88, 190–93, 196–99, 201, 207, 209–10, 229–32, 235, 249, 252, 256–57, 259, with omissions.

Thus, without departing from its particular nature, the individual's character is enlarged.

*Note.*—The view that civilization is an external degenerate form of life is allied to the idea that the natural condition of uncivilized peoples is one of unsophisticated innocence. So also the view that civilization is a mere means for the satisfaction of one's needs, and for the enjoyment and comfort of one's particular life, takes for granted that these selfish ends are absolute. Both theories manifest ignorance of the nature of spirit and the end of reason. Spirit is real only when by its own motion it divides itself, gives itself limit and finitude in the natural needs and the region of external necessity, and then, by moulding and shaping itself in them, overcomes them, and secures for itself an objective embodiment. The rational end, therefore, is neither the simplicity of nature nor the enjoyments resulting from civilization through the development of particularity. It rather works away from the condition of simple nature, in which there is either no self or a crude state of consciousness and will, and transcends the naïve individuality, in which spirit is submerged. Its externality thus in the first instance receives the rationality, of which it is capable, namely, the form of universality characteristic of the understanding. Only in this way is spirit at home and with itself in this externality as such. Hence in it the freedom of spirit is realized. Spirit, becoming actualized in an element, which of itself was foreign to its free character, has to do only with what is produced by itself and bears its own impress.—In this way the form of universality comes into independent existence in thought, a form which is the only worthy element for the existence of the idea.

Culture or education is, as we may thus conclude, in its ultimate sense a liberation, and that of a high kind. Its task is to make possible the infinitely subjective substantiality of the ethical life. In the process we pass upwards from the direct and natural existence to what is spiritual and has the form of the universal.—In the individual agent this liberation involves a struggle against mere subjectivity, immediate desire, subjective vanity, and capricious liking. The hardness of the task is in part the cause of the disfavor under which it falls. None the less is it through the labour of education that the subjective will itself wins possession of the objectivity, in which alone it is able and worthy to be the embodiment of the idea.—At the same time the form of universality, into which particularity has moulded itself and worked itself up, gives rise to that general principle of the understanding, in accordance with which the particular passes upward into the true, independent existence of the individual. And since the particular gives to the universal its adequate content and unconditioned self-direction, it even in the ethical sphere is infinitely independent and free subjectivity. Education is thus proved to be an inherent element of the absolute, and is shown to have infinite value. . . .

188. The civic community contains three elements:

A. The recasting of want, and the satisfaction of the individual through his work, through the work of all others, and through the satisfaction of their wants. This is a system of wants.

B. Actualization of the general freedom required for this, *i.e.*, the protection of property by the administration of justice.

C. Provision against possible mischances, and care for the particular interest as a common interest, by means of police and the corporation. . . .

WANT AND ITS SATISFACTION

190. The animal has a limited range of ways and means for satisfying his limited wants. Man in his dependence proves his universality and his ability to become independent, firstly, by multiplying his wants and means, and, secondly, by dissecting the concrete want into parts. The parts then become other wants, and through being specialized are more abstract than the first.

*Note.*—The object is in right a person, in morals a subject, in the family a member, in the city generally a burgher (*bourgeois*); and here, at the standpoint of want, he is the concrete product of picture-thought which we call man. Here, and properly only here, is it that we first speak of man in this sense. . . .

191. The means for satisfying the specialized wants are similarly divided and increased. These means become in their turn relative ends and abstract wants. Hence the multiplication expands into an infinite series of distinctions with regard to these phases, and of judgments concerning the suitability of the means to their ends. This is refinement. . . .

192. The satisfaction of want and the attainment of means thereto become a realized possibility for others, through whose wants and labour satisfaction is in turn conditioned. The abstraction, which becomes a quality of wants and means (§ 191), helps to determine the mutual relation of individuals. This general recognition of others is the element which makes the isolated abstract wants and means concrete and social. . . .

193. The social element is a special instrument both of the simple acquisition of the means, and

also of the reduplication of the ways by which want is satisfied. Further, it contains directly the claim of equality with others. Both the desire for equality, including the imitation of others, and also the desire of each person to be unique, become real sources of the multiplication and extension of wants.

* * *

LABOUR

196. The instrument for preparing and acquiring specialized means adequate to specialized wants is labour. By labour the material, directly handed over by nature for these numerous ends, is specialized in a variety of ways. This fashioning of the material gives to the means value and purpose, so that in consumption it is chiefly human products and human effort that are used up.

*Addition.*—The direct material, which requires no working up, is small. Even air must be acquired, since it has to be made warm. Perhaps water is the only thing which man can use, simply as it is. Human sweat and toil win for men the means for satisfying their wants.

197. Training on its theoretical side is developed by the great variety of objects and interests, and consists not only in numberless picture-thoughts and items of knowledge, but also in mobility and quickness of imagination, a mental alertness in passing from one image, or idea, to another, and in the apprehension of intricate general relations. This is the training of the understanding, with which goes the development of language. Practical training, or training by labour, consists in habituation to an employment, which satisfies a self-caused want. Its action is limited partly by the nature of the material, but chiefly by the caprice of others. It involves an habitual use of skill acquired by practice and implying objective conditions.

* * *

198. The universal and objective in work is to be found in the abstraction which, giving rise to the specialization of means and wants, causes the specialization also of production. This is the division of labour. By it the labour of the individual becomes more simple, his skill in his abstract work greater, and the amount he produces larger. The result of the abstraction of skill and means is that men's interdependence or mutual relation is completed. It becomes a thorough necessity. Moreover, the abstraction of production causes work to be continually more mechanical, until it is at last possible for man to step out and let the machine take his place.

WEALTH

199. Through the dependence and co-operation involved in labour, subjective self-seeking is converted into a contribution towards the satisfaction of the wants of all others. The universal so penetrates the particular by its dialectic movement, that the individual, while acquiring, producing, and enjoying for himself, at the same time produces and acquires for the enjoyment of others. This is a necessity, and in this necessity arising out of mutual dependence is contained the fact of a general and permanent wealth. In it each person may share by means of his education and skill. Each, too, is by it assured of subsistence, while the results of his labour preserve and increase the general wealth.

* * *

201. The infinitely varied means and their infinitely interlacing play of mutual production and exchange are gathered together by virtue of the universality inherent in their content, and become divided into general masses. The whole is thus formed into particular systems of wants, means, and labour, ways and methods of satisfaction, and theoretical and practical training. Amongst these systems the individuals are apportioned, and compose a cluster of classes or estates.

* * *

207. The particularity of the individual becomes definitely and actually realized, only by his limiting himself exclusively to one of the particular spheres of want. In this system the ethical sense is that of rectitude or class-honour. It involves the decision of the individual by means of his own native activity, diligence, and skill to make himself a member of one of these classes, preserve himself in it, and provide for himself only through the instrumentality of the universal. He should acknowledge this position, and also claim to have it recognized by others.—Morality has its peculiar place in this sphere, where the ruling factor is reflection upon one's action, or consideration of the end involved in particular wants and in well-being. Here also the element of chance in satisfying these ends makes random and individual assistance a duty.

*Note.*—Youth is specially apt to struggle against the proposal that it should decide upon a particular vocation, on the ground that any decision is a limitation of its universal scope and a mere external necessity. This aloofness is a product of the abstract thinking, which clings to the universal and unreal. It fails to recognize that the conception must experience a division into conception and its reality, if it is to have a definite and particular realization, and to win for itself reality and ethical objectivity.

*Addition.*—By the sentence that a man must be something we understand that he must belong to a definite class; for this something signifies a substantive reality. A human being without a vocation is a mere private person, who has no place in any real universal. Still, the individual in his exclusiveness may regard himself as the universal, and may fancy that when he takes a trade or profession, he is sinking to a lower plane. That is the false notion that a thing, when it attains the realization which properly belongs to it, limits itself and gives up its independence.

* * *

## *Administration of Justice*

209. The relative principle of the mutual exchange of wants and labour for their satisfaction has in the first instance its return into itself in the infinite personality generally, *i.e.,* in abstract right. Yet it is the very sphere of the relative which in the form of education gives embodiment to right, by fixing it as something universally acknowledged, known, and willed. The relative also, through the interposition of knowledge and will, supplies right with validity and objective actuality.

*Note.*—It is the essence of education and of thought, which is the consciousness of the individual in universal form, that the I should be apprehended as a universal person, in whom all are identical. Man must be accounted a universal being, not because he is a Jew, Catholic, Protestant, German, or Italian, but because he is a man. This thinking or reflective consciousness, is of infinite importance. It is defective only when it plumes itself upon being cosmopolitan, in opposition to the concrete life of the citizen. . . .

210. The objective actuality of right consists partly in existing for consciousness, or more generally in its being known, and partly in having, and being generally recognized as having, the validity and force of a reality.

* * *

229. In the civic community the idea is lost in particularity, and dispersed by the separation of inner and outer. But in the administration of justice the community is brought back to the conception, that is, to the unity of the intrinsic universal with subjective particularity. But as subjective particularity is present only as one single case, and the universal only as abstract right, the unification is in the first instance relative. The realization of this relative unity over the whole range of particularity is the function of the police, and within a limited but concrete totality constitutes the corporation.

*Addition.*—In the civic community universality is only necessity. In the relation of wants, right as such is the only steadfast principle. But the sphere of this right is limited, and refers merely to the protection of what I have. To right as such, happiness is something external. Yet in the system of wants well-being is an essential element. The universal, which is at first only right, has to spread itself over the whole field of particularity. Justice, it is true, is a large factor in the civic community. The state will flourish, if it has good laws, of which free property is the fundamental condition. But since I am wholly environed by my particularity, I have a right to demand that in connecting myself with others I shall further my special happiness. Regard to my particular well-being is taken by the police and the corporation.

## *Police and Corporation*

230. In the system of wants the subsistence and happiness of every individual is a possibility, whose realization is conditioned by the objective system of wants. By the administration of justice compensation is rendered for injury done to property or person. But the right, which is actualized in the particular individual, contains the two following factors. It asks firstly that person and property should be secured by the removal of all fortuitous hindrances, and secondly that the security of the individual's subsistence and happiness, his particular well-being should be regarded and actualized as a right.

### POLICE

231. So far as the particular will is the principle of a purpose, the force by which the universal guarantees security is limited to the realm of mere accident, and is an external arrangement.

232. Crimes are in their nature contigent or casual, taking the form of capricious choice of evil, and must be prevented or brought to justice by the general force. Apart from them, however, arbitrary choice must be allowed a place in connection with acts in themselves lawful, such as the private use of property. Here it comes into external relation with other individuals, and also with public institutions for realizing a common end. In this way a private act is exposed to a haphazard play of circumstances, which take it beyond my control. It thus may or actually does effect an injury or wrong to others.

* * *

235. Although everyone relies on the untrammelled possibility of satisfying his daily wants, yet,

when in the indefinite multiplication and limitation of them it is sought to procure or exchange the means and it is desired to expedite the transaction, there comes into sight a common interest, which makes the business of one subverse the interest of all. There appear, likewise, ways and means, which may be of public utility. To oversee and foster the ways and means calculated to promote the public welfare is the function of a public power.

* * *

249. The universal, which is contained in the particularity of the civic community, is realized and preserved by the external system of police supervision, whose purpose is simply to protect and secure the multitude of private ends and interests subsisting within it. It has also the higher function of caring for the interests which lead out beyond the civic community (§ 246). In accordance with the idea particularity itself makes the universal, which exists in its special interests, the end and object of its will and endeavour. The ethical principle thus comes back as a constituent element of the civic community. This is the corporation.

* * *

252. In keeping with this view, the corporation, under the oversight of the public authority, has the right to look after its own clearly-defined interests, according to the objective qualifications of skill and rectitude to adopt members, whose number is determined by the general system, to make provision for its adherents against fortuitous occurrences, and to foster the capacity necessary in any one desiring to become a member. In general it must stand to its members as a second family, a position which remains more indefinite than the family relation, because the general civic community is at a farther remove from individuals and their special needs.

*Note.*—The tradesman is different from the day-labourer, as well as from him who is ready for any casual employment. The trader, be he employer or employee, is a member of an association, not for mere accidental gain but for the whole circuit of gain, or the universal involved in his particular maintenance. The privileges, which are rights of a corporate branch of the civic community, are not the same as special privileges in the etymological sense of the term. Special privileges are haphazard exceptions to a general law, but the other privileges are legal phases of the particularity of an essential branch of the community. . . .

* * *

256. The limited and finite end of the corporation has its truth in the absolutely universal end and the absolute actuality of this end. This actualized end is also the truth of the division involved in the external system of police, which is merely a relative identity of the divided elements. Thus, the sphere of the civic community passes into the state.

*Note.*—City and country are the two as yet ideal constituents, out of which the state proceeds. The city is the seat of the civic society, and of the reflection which goes into itself and causes separation. The country is the seat of the ethical, which rests upon nature. The one comprises the individuals, who gain their livelihood by virtue of their relation to other persons possessed of rights. The other comprises the family. The state is the true meaning and ground of both.

The development of simple ethical observance into the dismemberment marking the civic community, and then forward into the state, which is shown to be the true foundation of these more abstract phases, is the only scientific proof of the conception of the state.—Although in the course of the scientific exposition the state has the appearance of a result, it is in reality the true foundation and cause. This appearance and its process are provisional, and must now be replaced by the state in its direct existence. In actual fact the state is in general primary. Within it the family grows into the civic community, the idea of the state being that which sunders itself into these two elements. In the development of the civic community the ethical substance reaches its infinite form, which contains the following elements:—(1) infinite differentation even to the point at which consciousness as it is in itself exists for itself, and (2) the form of universality, which in civilization is the form of thought, that form by which spirit is itself in its laws and institutions. They are its thought will, and it and they together become objective and real in an organic whole.

## *The State*

257. The state is the realized ethical idea or ethical spirit. It is the will which manifests itself, makes itself clear and visible, substantiates itself. It is the will which thinks and knows itself, and carries out what it knows, and in so far as it knows. The state finds in ethical custom its direct and unreflected existence, and its indirect and reflected existence in the self-consciousness of the individual and in his knowledge and activity. Self-consciousness in the form of social disposition has its substantive freedom in the state, as the essence, purpose, and product of its activity.

*Note.*—The Penates are the inner and lower order of gods; the spirit of a nation, Athene, is the divinity which knows and wills itself. Piety is feeling, or ethical behaviour in the form of feeling;

political virtue is the willing of the thought-out end, which exists absolutely.

* * *

259. (*a*) The idea of the state has direct actuality in the individual state. It, as a self-referring organism, is the constitution or internal state-organization or polity.

(*b*) It passes over into a relation of the individual state to other states. This is its external organization or polity.

(*c*) As universal idea, or kind, or species, it has absolute authority over individual states. This is the spirit which gives itself reality in the process of world-history.

# 7. *The Functions of Government in General*

BY JOHN STUART MILL

IN ATTEMPTING to enumerate the necessary functions of government, we find them to be considerably more multifarious than most people are at first aware of, and not capable of being circumscribed by those very definite lines of demarcation, which, in the inconsiderateness of popular discussion, it is often attempted to draw round them. We sometimes, for example, hear it said that governments ought to confine themselves to affording protection against force and fraud: that, these two things apart, people should be free agents, able to take care of themselves, and that so long as a person practises no violence or deception, to the injury of others in person or property, legislatures and governments are in no way called on to concern themselves about him. But why should people be protected by their government, that is, by their own collective strength, against violence and fraud, and not against other evils, except that the expediency is more obvious? If nothing, but what people cannot possibly do for themselves, can be fit to be done for them by government, people might be required to protect themselves by their skill and courage even against force, or to beg or buy protection against it, as they actually do where the government is not capable of protecting them: and against fraud every one has the protection of his own wits. But without further anticipating the discussion of principles, it is sufficient on the present occasion to consider facts.

Under which of these heads, the repression of force or of fraud, are we to place the operation, for example, of the laws of inheritance? Some such laws must exist in all societies. It may be said, perhaps, that in this matter government has merely to give effect to the disposition which an individual makes of his own property by will. This, however, is at least extremely disputable; there is probably no country by whose laws the power of testamentary disposition is perfectly absolute. And suppose the very common case of there being no will: does not the law, that is, the government, decide on principles of general expediency, who shall take the succession? and in case the successor is in any manner incompetent, does it not appoint persons, frequently officers of its own, to collect the property and apply it to his benefit? There are many other cases in which the government undertakes the administration of property, because the public interest, or perhaps only that of the particular persons concerned, is thought to require it. This is often done in cases of litigated property; and in cases of judicially declared insolvency. It has never been contended that in doing these things, a government exceeds its province.

Nor is the function of the law in defining property itself, so simple a thing as may be supposed. It may be imagined, perhaps, that the law has only to declare and protect the right of every one to what he has himself produced, or acquired by the voluntary consent, fairly obtained, of those who produced it. But is there nothing recognised as property except what has been produced? Is there not the earth itself, its forests and waters, and all other natural riches, above and below the surface? These are the inheritance of the human race, and there must be regulations for the common enjoyment of it. What rights, and under what conditions, a person shall be allowed to exercise over any portion of this com-

---

Reprinted from John Stuart Mill, *Principles of Political Economy* (London: Longman, Green, Longman, Robertson, Green, 1865), Book V, chap. i, sec. 2, pp. 480–82.

mon inheritance, cannot be left undecided. No function of government is less optional than the regulation of these things, or more completely involved in the idea of civilized society.

Again, the legitimacy is conceded of repressing violence or treachery; but under which of these heads are we to place the obligation imposed on people to perform their contracts? Non-performance does not necessarily imply fraud; the person who entered into the contract may have sincerely intended to fulfil it: and the term fraud, which can scarcely admit of being extended even to the case of voluntary breach of contract when no deception was practised, is certainly not applicable when the omission to perform is a case of negligence. Is it no part of the duty of governments to enforce contracts? Here the doctrine of non-interference would no doubt be stretched a little, and it would be said, that enforcing contracts is not regulating the affairs of individuals at the pleasure of government, but giving effect to their own expressed desire. Let us acquiesce in this enlargement of the restrictive theory, and take it for what it is worth. But governments do not limit their concern with contracts to a simple enforcement. They take upon themselves to determine what contracts are fit to be enforced. It is not enough that one person, not being either cheated or compelled, makes a promise to another. There are promises by which it is not for the public good that persons should have the power of binding themselves. To say nothing of engagements to do something contrary to law, there are engagements which the law refuses to enforce, for reasons connected with the interest of the promiser, or with the general policy of the state. A contract by which a person sells himself to another as a slave, would be declared void by the tribunals of this and of most other European countries. There are few nations whose laws enforce a contract for what is looked upon as prostitution, or any matrimonial engagement of which the conditions vary in any respect from those which the law has thought fit to prescribe. But when once it is admitted that there are any engagements which for reasons of expediency the law ought not to enforce, the same question is necessarily opened with respect to all engagements. Whether, for example, the law should enforce a contract to labour, when the wages are too low, or the hours of work too severe: whether it should enforce a contract by which a person binds himself to remain, for more than a very limited period, in the service of a given individual: whether a contract of marriage, entered into for life, should continue to be enforced against the deliberate will of the persons, or of either of the persons, who entered into it. Every question which can possibly arise as to the policy of contracts, and of the relations which they establish among human beings, is a question for the legislator; and one which he cannot escape from considering, and in some way or other deciding.

Again, the prevention and suppression of force and fraud afford appropriate employment for soldiers, policemen, and criminal judges; but there are also civil tribunals. The punishment of wrong is one business of an administration of justice, but the decision of disputes is another. Innumerable disputes arise between persons, without *mala fides* on either side, through misconception of their legal rights, or from not being agreed about the facts, on the proof of which those rights are legally dependent. Is it not for the general interest that the State should appoint persons to clear up these uncertainties and terminate these disputes? It cannot be said to be a case of absolute necessity. People might appoint an arbitrator, and engage to submit to his decision; and they do so where there are no courts of justice, or where the courts are not trusted, or where their delays and expenses, or the irrationality of their rules of evidence, deter people from resorting to them. Still, it is universally thought right that the State should establish civil tribunals; and if their defects often drive people to have recourse to substitutes, even then the power held in reserve of carrying the case before a legally constituted court, gives to the substitutes their principal efficacy.

Not only does the State undertake to decide disputes, it takes precautions beforehand that disputes may not arise. The laws of most countries lay down rules for determining many things, not because it is of much consequence in what way they are determined, but in order that they may be determined somehow, and there may be no question on the subject. The law prescribes forms of words for many kinds of contract, in order that no dispute or misunderstanding may arise about their meaning: it makes provision that if a dispute does arise, evidence shall be procurable for deciding it, by requiring that the document be attested by witnesses and executed with certain formalities. The law preserves authentic evidence of facts to which legal consequences are attached, by keeping a registry of such facts; as of births, deaths, and marriages, of wills and contracts, and of judicial proceedings. In doing these things, it has never been alleged that government oversteps the proper limits of its functions.

Again, however wide a scope we may allow to the doctrine that individuals are the proper guardians of their own interests, and that government owes nothing to them but to save them from being interfered with by other people, the doctrine can never be applicable to any persons but those who are capable of acting in their own behalf. The individual may be an infant, or a lunatic, or fallen into imbecility. The law surely must look after the interests of such persons. It does not necessarily do this through officers of its own. It often devolves the trust upon some relative or connexion. But in doing so is its duty ended? Can it make over the interests of one person to the control of another, and be excused from supervision, or from holding the person thus trusted, responsible for the discharge of the trust?

There is a multitude of cases in which governments, with general approbation, assume powers and execute functions for which no reason can be assigned except the simple one, that they conduce to general convenience. We may take as an example, the function (which is a monopoly too) of coining money. This is assumed for no more recondite purpose than that of saying to individuals the trouble, delay, and expense of weighing and assaying. No one, however, even of those most jealous of state interference, has objected to this as an improper exercise of the powers of government. Prescribing a set of standard weights and measures is another instance. Paving, lighting, and cleansing the streets and thoroughfares, is another; whether done by the general government, or, as is more usual, and generally more advisable, by a municipal authority. Making or improving harbours, building lighthouses, making surveys in order to have accurate maps and charts, raising dykes to keep the sea out, and embankments to keep rivers in, are cases in point.

Examples might be indefinitely multiplied without intruding on any disputed ground. But enough has been said to show that the admitted functions of government embrace a much wider field than can easily be included within the ring-fence of any restrictive definition, and that it is hardly possible to find any ground of justification common to them all, except the comprehensive one of general expediency; nor to limit the interference of government by any universal rule, save the simple and vague one that it should never be admitted but when the case of expediency is strong.

# 8. *On the Social Contract*

BY JEAN JACQUES ROUSSEAU

## *On the Necessity of Recurring Always to the Primitive Convention*

ON THE SUPPOSITION, that I should grant to be true what I have hitherto disproved, the advocate for despotism would, however, profit but little. There will be always a great difference between subjecting a multitude, and governing a society. Let individuals, in any number whatever, become severally and successively subject to one man, they are all, in that case, nothing more than master and slaves; they are not a people governed by their chief; they are an Aggregate if you will, but do not form an association; there subsists among them neither commonwealth nor body politic. Such a superior, though he should become the master of half the world, would be still a private person, and his interest, separate and distinct from that of his people, would be still no more than a private interest. When such a person dies, also the empire over which he presided is dissolved, and its component parts remain totally unconnected, just as an oak falls into a heap of ashes, when it is consumed by the fire.

A people, says Grotius, may voluntarily bestow themselves on a king: according to Grotius, therefore, a people are a people before they thus give themselves up to regal authority. Even this gift, however, is an act of society, and presupposes a public deliberation on the matter. Hence, before we examine into the act, by which a people make choice of a king, it is proper to examine into that by which a people became a people, for, on this, which is necessarily prior to the other, rests the true foundation of society.

For, if, in fact, there be no prior convention, whence arises (unless indeed the election was unanimous) the obligation of the smaller number to sub-

Reprinted from Jean Jacques Rousseau, *A Treatise on the Social Compact,* Book I, chaps. v–ix, and Book II, chaps. i–iii, in *The Miscellaneous Works of Mr. J. J. Rousseau* (London: T. Becket and P. A. DeHondt, 1767), pp. 16–37.

mit to the choice of the greater? and whence comes it, that an hundred persons, for instance, who might desire to have a master, had a right to vote for ten others who might desire to have none? The choice by a plurality of votes is itself an establishment of convention, and supposes, that unanimity must at least for once have subsisted among them.

### *On the Social Pact or Covenant*

I suppose mankind arrived at that term, when the obstacles to their preservation, in a state of nature, prevail over the endeavours of individuals, to maintain themselves in such a state. At such a crisis this primitive state therefore could no longer subsist, and the human race must have perished, if they had not changed their manner of living.

Now as men cannot create new powers, but only compound and direct those which really exist, they have no other means of preservation, than that of forming, by their union, an accumulation of forces, sufficient to oppose the obstacles to their security, and of putting these in action by a first mover, capable of making them act in concert with each other.

This general accumulation of power cannot arise but from the concurrence of many particular forces; but the force and liberty of each individual being the principal instruments of his own preservation, how is he to engage them in the common interest, without hurting his own, and neglecting the obligations he lies under to himself? This difficulty, being applied to my present subject, may be expressed in the following terms:

"To find that form of association which shall protect and defend, with the whole force of the community, the person and property of each individual, and in which each person, by uniting himself to the rest, shall nevertheless be obedient only to himself, and remain as fully at liberty as before." Such is the fundamental problem, of which the social compact gives the solution.

The clauses of this compact are so precisely determined by the nature of the act, that the least restriction or modification renders them void and of no effect; in so much, that, although they may perhaps never have been formally promulgated, they are yet universally the same, and are every where tacitly acknowledged and received. When the social pact, however, is violated, individuals recover their natural liberty, and are re-invested with their original rights, by losing that conventional liberty for the sake of which they had renounced them.

Again; these clauses, well understood are all reducible to one, *viz.* the total alienation of every individual, with all his rights and privileges, to the whole community. For, in the first place, as every one gives himself up entirely and without reserve, all are in the same circumstances, so that no one can be interested in making their common connection burthensome to others.

Besides, as the alienation is made without reserve, the union is as perfect as possible, nor hath any particular associate any thing to reclaim; whereas, if they should severally retain any peculiar privileges, there being no common umpire to determine between them and the public, each being his own judge in some cases, would, in time, pretend to be so in all, the state of nature would still subsist, and their association would necessarily become tyrannical or void.

In fine, the individual, by giving himself up to all, gives himself to none; and, as he acquires the same right over every other person in the community, as he gives them over himself, he gains an equivalent for what he bestows, and still a greater power to preserve what he retains.

If, therefore, we take from the social compact every thing that is not essential to it, we shall find it reduced to the following terms: "We, the contracting parties, do jointly and severally submit our persons and abilities, to the supreme direction of the general will of all, and, in a collective body, receive each member into that body, as an indivisible part of the whole."

This act of association accordingly converts the several individual contracting parties into one moral collective body, composed of as many members as there are votes in the assembly, which receives also from the same act its unity and existence. This public personage, which is thus formed by the union of all its members, used formerly to be denominated a CITY,[1] and, at present, takes the name of a *repub-*

1. The true sense of this word is almost entirely perverted among the moderns; most people take a town for a city, and an house-keeper for a citizen. Such are ignorant, however, that, though houses may form a town, it is the citizens only that constitute a city. This same errour formerly cost the Carthaginians very dear. I do not remember, in the course of my reading, to have ever found the title of *Cives* given to the subjects of a prince, not even formerly to the Macedonians, nor, in our times, to the English, though more nearly bordering on liberty than any other nation. The French are the only people who familiarly take on themselves the name of *citizens,* because they have no just idea of its meaning, as may be seen in their dictionaries; for, were it otherwise, indeed, they would be guilty of high treason in assuming it. This term is with them rather expressive of a virtue than a privilege. Hence, when Bodin spoke of the citizens and inhabitants of Geneva, he committed a wretched blunder, in mistaking one for the other. Mr. d'Alembert indeed has avoided this mistake in the Encyclopoedia, where he has properly distinguished the four orders of people (and even five, reckoning mere strangers) that are found in our city, and of which two only compose the republic: No other French author that I know of hath ever comprehended the meaning of the word *citizen.*

*lic,* or *body politic.* It is also called, by its several members, a *state,* when it is passive; the *sovereign,* when it is active; and simply a *power,* when it is compared with other bodies of the same nature. With regard to the associates themselves, they take collectively the name of the *people,* and are separately called *citizens,* as partaking of the sovereign authority, and *subjects,* as subjected to the laws of the state. These terms, indeed, are frequently confounded, and mistaken one for the other; it is sufficient, however, to be able to distinguish them, when they are used with precision.

## *Of the Sovereign*

It is plain from the above formula, that the act of association includes a reciprocal engagement between particulars and the public; and that each individual, in contracting, if I may so say, with himself, is laid under a twofold engagement, *viz.* as a member of the sovereignty toward particular persons, and as a member of the state toward the sovereign. That maxim of the civil law, however, is inapplicable here, which says, that no one is bound by the engagements he enters into with himself; for, there is a wide difference between entering into a personal obligation with one's self, and with a whole, of which one may constitute a part.

It is farther to be observed, that the public determination, which is obligatory on the subject, with regard to the sovereign, on account of the twofold relation by which each stands contracted, is not, for the contrary reason, obligatory on the supreme power towards itself: and that it is consequently inconsistent with the nature of the body politic, that such supreme power should impose a law, which it cannot break. For, as the sovereign stands only in a single relation, it is in the same case as that of an individual contracting with himself; whence it is plain, that there neither is, nor can be, any fundamental law obligatory on the whole body of a people, even the social compact itself not being such. By this, however, it is not meant, that such a body cannot enter into engagements with others, in matters that do not derogate from this contract; for, with respect to foreign objects, it is a simple and individual person.

But, as the body politic, or the sovereign, derives its very existence from this inviolable contract, it can enter into no lawful engagement, even with any similar body, derogatory from the tenour of this primitive act; such as that of alienating any part of itself, or of submitting itself intirely to a foreign sovereign. To violate the act whereby it exists would be to annihilate itself, and from nothing can arise nothing.

No sooner are a multitude of individuals thus united in a body, than it becomes impossible to act offensively against any of the members, without attacking the whole, and still less to offend the whole body, without injuring the members. Hence both duty and interest equally oblige the two contracting parties to assist each other, and the same persons ought to endeavour to include, within this twofold relation, all the advantages which depend on it.

Now the sovereign, being formed only by the several individuals of which the state is composed, can have no interest contrary to theirs; of course the supreme power stands in no need of any guarantee toward the subjects, because it is impossible, that the body should be capable of hurting all its members; and we shall see hereafter, that it can as little tend to injure any of them in particular. Hence the sovereign is necessarily, and for the same reason that it exists, always such as it ought to be.

The case is different, however, as to the relation in which the subjects stand to the sovereign; as, notwithstanding their common interest, the latter can have no security that the former will discharge their engagements, unless means be found to engage their fidelity.

In fact, every individual may, as a man, entertain a particular will, either contradictory or dissimilar to his general will, as a citizen. His private interest may influence him, in a manner diametrically opposite to the common interest of the society. Reflecting on his own existence as positive and naturally independent, he may conceive what he owes to the common cause, to be a free and gratuitous contribution, the want of which will be less hurtful to others, than the discharge of it will be burthensome to himself; and, regarding the moral person of the state as an imaginary being, because it is not a man, he may be desirous of enjoying all the privileges of a citizen without fulfilling his engagement as a subject; an injustice, that, in its progress, must necessarily be the ruin of the body politic.

To the end, therefore, that the social compact should not prove an empty form, it tacitly includes this engagement, which only can enforce the rest, *viz.* that whosoever refuses to pay obedience to the general will, shall be liable to be compelled to it by the force of the whole body. And this is in effect nothing more, than that they may be compelled to be free; for such is the condition which, in uniting every citizen to the state, secured him from all personal dependence; a condition, which forms the whole artifice and play of the political machine: it is this alone that renders all social engagements just and equitable which, without it, would be absurd, tyrannical, and subject to the most enormous abuses.

## *Of Civil Society in General*

The transition of man from a state of nature to a state of society is productive of a very remarkable change in his being, by substituting justice instead of instinct, as the rule of his conduct, and attaching that morality to his actions, of which they were before destitute. It is in immediate consequence of this change, when the voice of duty succeeds to physical impulse and the law of appetite, that man, who hitherto regarded only his own gratification, finds himself obliged to act on other principles, and to consult his reason, before he follows the dictates of his passions. Although, by entering into a state of society, he is deprived also of many advantages which depend on that of nature, he gains by it others so very considerable, his faculties exert and expand themselves, his ideas are enlarged, his sentiments ennobled, and his whole soul is elevated to so great a degree, that, if the abuses of this new state do not degrade him below the former, he ought incessantly to bless that happy moment in which he was rescued from it, and converted from a stupid and ignorant animal into an intelligent and wise Being.

To state the balance of what is lost and gained by this change, we shall reduce it to comparative terms. By entering into the social compact, man gives up his natural liberty, or unlimited right to every thing which he is desirous of, and can attain. In return for this, he gains social liberty, and an exclusive property in all those things of which he is possessed. To avoid any mistake, however, in the nature of these compensations, it is necessary to make a just distinction between natural liberty, which is limited by nothing but the inabilities of the individual, and social liberty, which is limited by the general will of the community; and also, between that possession, which is only effected by force, or follows the right of prior occupancy, and that property, which is founded only on a positive title.

To the preceding also may be added, as the acquisition of a social state, moral liberty, which only renders a man truly master of himself: for to be under the direction of appetite alone is to be in a state of slavery, while to pay obedience only to those laws which we prescribe to ourselves, is liberty. But I have said too much already on this subject, the philosophical meaning of the word Liberty, being, in this place, out of the question.

## *Of Real Demesnes*

Each member of the community, in becoming such, devotes himself to the public from that moment, in such a state as he then is, with all his power and abilities, of which abilities his possessions make a part. Not that in consequence of this act the possession changes its nature, by changing hands, and becomes actual property in those of the sovereignty; but as the power of the community is incomparably greater than that of an individual, the public possession is in fact more fixed and irrevocable, without being more lawful, at least with regard to foreigners. For every state is, with respect to its members, master of all their possessions, by virtue of the social compact, which, in a state, serves as the basis of all other rights; but, with regard to other powers or states, it is master of them only, by the right of prior occupancy, which it derives from individuals.

The right of prior occupancy, although more real than that of the strongest, becomes not an equitable right, till after the establishment of property. Every man hath naturally a right to every thing which is necessary for his subsistence; but the positive act by which he is made the proprietor of a certain possession excludes him from the property of any other. His portion being assigned him, he ought to confine himself to that, and hath no longer any right to a community of possession. Hence it is that the right of prior occupancy, though but of little force in a state of nature, is so respectable in that of society. The point to which we are chiefly directed in the consideration of this right, is rather what belongs to another, than what does not belong to us.

To define the right of prior occupancy in general terms, it is founded on the following conditions. It is requisite, in the first place, that the lands in question should be unoccupied; secondly, that no greater quantity of it should be occupied than is necessary for the subsistence of the occupiers; and, in the third place, that possession should be taken of it, not by a vain ceremony, but by actual cultivation, the only mark of property, which, in defect of judicial titles, should be at all respected.

To allow the first occupier a right to as much territory as he may cultivate, and is necessary to his subsistence, is certainly carrying the matter as far as is reasonable. Otherwise we know not how to set bounds to this right. Is it sufficient for a man to set foot on an uninhabited territory, to pretend immediately an exclusive right to it? Is it sufficient for him to have power enough at one time to drive others from the spot, to deprive them for ever afterwards of the right of returning to it? How can a man, or even a whole people, possess themselves of an immense territory, and exclude from it the rest of mankind, without being guilty of an illegal usurpation, since, by so doing, they deprive the rest of mankind of an habitation, and those means of subsistence, which nature hath given in common to them all? When Nunez Balbao stood on the sea-shore, and, in the name of the crown of Castile, took possession of the Pacific Ocean, and of all South America, was this sufficient to dispossess all the inhabitants of that vast country, and exclude all the other sovereigns in the world? On such a supposition, the like idle ceremonies might have been ridiculously multiplied, and his Catholic Majesty would have had no more to do, than to have taken possession in his closet of all the countries in the world, and to have afterwards only deducted from his empire such as were before possessed by other princes.

It is easy to conceive, how the united and contiguous estates of individuals become the territory of the public, and in what manner the right of sovereignty, extending itself from the subjects to the lands they occupy, becomes at once both real and personal; a circumstance which lays the possessors under a state of the greatest dependence, and makes even their own abilities a security for their fidelity. This is an advantage which does not appear to have been duly attended to, by sovereigns among the ancients, who, by stiling themselves only kings of the Persians, the Scythians, the Macedonians, seemed to look on themselves only as chief of men, rather than as masters of a country. Modern princes more artfully stile themselves the kings of England, France, Spain, *&c.* and thus, by claiming the territory itself, are secure of the inhabitants.

What is very singular in this alienation is, that the community, in accepting the possessions of individuals, is so far from despoiling them there-of, that, on the contrary, it only confirms them in such possessions, by converting an usurpation into an actual right, and a bare possession into a real property. The possessors also being considered as the depositaries of the public wealth, while their rights are respected by all the members of the state, and maintained by all its force against any foreign power, they acquire, if I may so say, by a cession advantageous to the public, and still more so to themselves, every thing they ceded by it: a paradox which is easily explained by the distinction to be made between the rights which the sovereign and the proprietor have in the same fund, as will be seen hereafter.

It may also happen, that men may form themselves into a society, before they have any possessions; and that, acquiring a territory sufficient for all, they may possess it in common, or divide it among them, either equally, or in such different proportions as may be determined by the sovereign. Now, in whatsoever manner such acquisition may be made, the right which each individual has to his own estate, must be always subordinate to the right which the community hath over the possessions of all; for, without this, there would be nothing binding in the social tie, nor any real force in the exercise of the supreme power.

I shall end this book, with a remark, that ought to serve as the basis of the whole social system: and this is, that, instead of annihilating the natural equality among mankind, the fundamental compact substitutes, on the contrary, a moral and legal equality, to make up for that natural and physical difference which prevails among individuals, who, though unequal in personal strength and mental abilities, become thus all equal by convention and right.[2]

## *That the Sovereignty Is Unalienable*

The first and most important consequence to be drawn from the principles already established, is, that the general *will* only can direct the forces of the state agreeable to the end of its original institution, which is the common good; for, though the opposition of private interests might make the establishment of societies necessary, it must have been through the coalition of those interests, that such establishment became possible. The bonds of society must have been formed out of something common to those several interests, for, if there had been no point to which they could have been reconciled, no society could possibly have subsisted. Now it is only on these points that the government of society should be founded.

I say, therefore, that the sovereignty, being only the exertion of the general will, cannot be alienated, and that the sovereign, which is only a collective being, cannot be represented but by itself: the power of a people may be transmitted or delegated, but not their will.

It may not be absolutely impossible, that the will of an individual should agree, in some particular point, with the general will of a whole people; it is, however, impossible, that such agreement should be constant and durable, for the will of particulars always tends to make distinctions of preference,

2. This equality, indeed, is under some governments merely apparent and delusive, serving only to keep the poor still in misery, and favour the oppression of the rich. And, in fact, the laws are always useful to persons of fortune, and hurtful to those who are destitute: whence it follows, that a state of society is advantageous to mankind in general, only when they all possess something, and none of them have anything too much.

and the general will to a perfect equality. It is further still more impossible, supposing such agreement might always subsist, to have any security that it would do so, as it could never be the effect of art, but of chance. The sovereign may say, My will is now agreeable to the will of such an individual, or at least to what he pretends to be his will; but it cannot pretend to say, I agree to whatever may be the will of such individual to morrow; as it is absurd for the will to lay itself under any restraint regarding the future, and as it is impossible for the will to consent to any thing contrary to the interest of the being whose will it is. Should a people therefore enter into the engagement of simply promising obedience, they would lose their quality, as a people, and be virtually dissolved by that very act. The moment there exists a master, there can be no longer a sovereign, the body politic being thereby destroyed.

I would not be understood to mean, that the orders of a chief may not pass for the dictates of the general will, when the sovereign, though at liberty to contradict, does not oppose it. In such a case, it is to be presumed, from the universal silence of the people, that they give their consent. This will be farther explained in the end.

## *That the Sovereignty Is Indivisible*

For the same reason that the sovereignty is unalienable, it is also indivisible; for the will is general,[3] or it is not; it is that of the body of the people, or only that of a part. In the first case, this will, when declared, is an act of sovereignty, and becomes a law: in the second, it is only a particular will, or an act of the magistracy, and is at most a decree.

But our politicians, incapable of dividing the sovereignty in its first principles, divide it in its object; they distinguish it into power and will; into a legislative and executive power; into the prerogatives of taxation, of executing justice, and of making war; into departments of domestic and foreign administration. Sometimes they blend all these confusedly together, and, at others, consider them as distinct and separate, making out the sovereign to be a fantastic compound, just as if they should compose a man out of several bodies, of which one should have only eyes, another arms, a third feet, and nothing more. It is said of the jugglers in Japan, that they will take a child, and cut it into pieces in the presence of the spectators, then, throwing up its dismembered limbs one after another into the air, they are united, and the child descends alive, and well as before. The legerdemain of our modern politicians greatly resembles this trick of the Japonese; for they, after having dismembered the body politic with equal dexterity, bring all its parts together by *hocus pocus* again, and represent it the same as before.

This error arises from their not having formed precise ideas of the sovereign authority, and from their mistaking the simple emanations of this authority, for parts of its essence. Thus, for instance, the acts of declaring war and making peace are usually regarded as acts of sovereignty, which they are not; for neither of these acts are laws, but consist only of the application of the law. Each is a particular act, determinate only of the meaning of the law in such case, as will be seen more clearly, when the idea attached to the word *law* shall be precisely settled.

By tracing, in like manner, their other divisions, we shall find, that we are constantly mistaken, whenever we think the sovereignty divided; and that the prerogatives, which are supposed to be parts of the sovereignty, are all subordinate to it, and always suppose the predetermination of a superior will, which those prerogatives only serve to put in execution.

It is impossible to say, in how much obscurity this want of precision hath involved the reasonings of authors, on the subject of political law, when they came to examine into the respective rights of kings and people, on the principles they had established. By turning to the third and fourth chapters of the first book of Grotius, the reader may see, how that learned author and his translator, Barbeyrac, bewildered and entangled themselves in their own sophisms, thro' fear of saying too much or too little for their purpose, and of making those interests clash, which it was their business to reconcile. Grotius being dissatisfied with his own countrymen, a refugee in France, and willing to pay his court to Lewis XIII. to whom his book is dedicated, spared no art nor pains to strip the people of their privileges, and to invest kings with prerogative. Barbeyrac also wrote with a similar view, dedicating his translation to George I. of England. But, unluckily, the expulsion of James II. which he calls an abdication, obliged him to be much on the reserve, to turn and wind about, as he saw occasion, in order not to make William III. an usurper. Had these two writers adopted true principles, all these difficulties would have vanished, and they would have written consistently; in such a case, however, they could only, in sober sadness, have told the truth, and would have paid their court only to the people. Now, to tell the

3. In order that this will should be general, it is not always necessary it should be unanimous: it is necessary, however, that every individual should be permitted to vote; every formal exclusion infringing the generality.

truth, is not the way to make a fortune; nor are ambassadors appointed, or places and pensions given away by the populace.

### *Whether the General Will Can Be in the Wrong*

It follows, from what has been said, that the general Will is always in the right, and constantly tends to the public good; it does not follow, however, that the deliberations of the people will always be attended with the same rectitude. We are ever desirous of our own good, but we do not always distinguish in what it consists. A whole people never can be corrupted, but they may be often mistaken, and it is in such a case only that they appear to seek their own disadvantage.

There is often a considerable difference between the will of all the members and the general will of the whole body; the latter regards only the common interest, the other respects the private interest of individuals, and is the aggregated sum of their particular wills; but, if we take from this sum those contradictory wills that mutually destroy each other,[4] the sum of the remaining differences is the general will.

4. *Each interest,* says the Marquis d'A. *has different principles. A coalition between two particular interests may be formed, out of opposition to that of a third.* He might have added, that a coalition of all is formed out of opposition to the interest of each. Were there no different and clashing interests, that of the whole would be hardly distinguishable, as it would meet with no obstacle. All things would go regularly on of their own accord, and civil policy would cease to be an art.

If a people, sufficiently informed of the nature of the subject under their consideration, should deliberate, without having any communication with each other, the general will would always result from the greater number of their little differences, and their deliberation would be such as it ought to be. But when they enter into cabals, and form partial associations, at the expence of the general one, the will of each of these associations becomes general, with regard to the particular members of each, and, in itself, particular, with regard to the state. In such a case, therefore, it may be said, there is no longer as many voters as individuals, but only as many voices as there are associations. The differences then become less numerous, and give a less general result. Again, should one of these partial associations be so great, as to influence all the rest, the result would no longer be the sum of many little differences, but that of one great one; in which case, a general will would no longer subsist.

It is requisite, therefore, in order that each resolution may be dictated by the general will, that no such partial societies should be formed in a state, and that each citizen should think for himself. Such was the sublime institution of the great Lycurgus. But, if such partial societies must and will exist, it is then expedient to multiply their number, and prevent their inequality, as was done by Solon, Numa, and Servius. These are the only salutary precautions that can be taken, in order that the general will may be properly informed, and the people not be mistaken as to their true interest.

# *9. Society and Government*

BY AUGUSTE COMTE

HAVING NOW ascertained the fundamental position of the problems of political philosophy, and thus obtained guidance as to the scientific aim to be attained, the next step is to exhibit the general spirit of Social Physics, whose conditions we have been deciding.

Reprinted from Auguste Comte, *The Positive Philosophy,* freely translated and condensed by Harriet Martineau (London: George Bell & Sons, 1896), Vol. II, Book VI, chap. iii, pp. 218–32, and chap. v, pp. 275, 280–81, 289–98.

SPIRIT OF SOCIAL SCIENCE.

The philosophical principle of the science being that social phenomena are subject to natural laws, admitting of rational prevision, we have to ascertain what is the precise subject, and what the peculiar character of those laws. The distinction between the Statical and Dynamical conditions of the subject must be extended to social science; and I shall treat of the conditions of social existence as, in biology, I treated of organization under the head of anatomy; and then of the laws of social movement, as in biology of those of life, under the head of physiology. This division, necessary for exploratory purposes, must not be stretched beyond that use: and, as we saw in Biology, that the distinction becomes weaker with the advance of science, so shall we see that when the science of social physics is fully constituted, this division will remain for analytical purposes, but not as a real separation of the science into two parts. The distinction is not between two classes of facts, but between two aspects of a theory. It corresponds with the double conception of order and progress: for order consists (in a positive sense) in a permanent harmony among the conditions of social existence; and progress consists in social development; and the conditions in the one case, and the laws of movement in the other, constitute the statics and dynamics of social physics.—And here we find again the constant relation between the science and the art,—the theory and the practice. A science which proposes a positive study of the laws of order and of progress cannot be charged with speculative rashness by practical men of any intelligence, since it offers the only rational basis for the practical means of satisfying the needs of society, as to order and progress; and the correspondence in this case will be found to be analogous to that which we have seen to exist between biological science and the arts which relate to it,—the medical art especially.—One view of the deepest interest in this connection is that the ideas of order and progress which are in perpetual conflict in existing society, occasioning infinite disturbance, are thus reconciled, and made necessary to each other, becoming as truly inseparable as the ideas of organization and life in the individual being. The further we go in the study of the conditions of human society, the more clearly will the organizing and progressive spirit of the positive philosophy become manifest.

The statistical study of sociology consists in the investigation of the laws of action and reaction of the different parts of the social system,—apart, for the occasion, from the fundamental movement which is always gradually modifying them. In this view, sociological prevision, founded upon the exact general knowledge of those relations, acts by judging by each other the various statical indications of each mode of social existence, in conformity with direct observation,—just as is done daily in the case of anatomy. This view condemns the existing philosophical practice of contemplating social elements separately, as if they had an independent existence; and it leads us to regard them as in mutual relation, and forming a whole which compels us to treat them in combination. By this method, not only are we furnished with the only possible basis for the study of social movement, but we are put in possession of an important aid to direct observation; since many social elements which cannot be investigated by immediate observation may be estimated by their scientific relation to others already known. When we have a scientific knowledge of the interior relation of the parts of any science or art; and again, of the relations of the sciences to each other: and again, of the relations of arts to their respective sciences, the observation of certain portions of the scheme enables us to pronounce on the state of other portions, with a true philosophical security. The case is the same when, instead of studying the collective social phenomena of a single nation, we include in the study those of contemporary nations, whose reciprocal influence cannot be disputed, though it is much reduced in modern times, and, as in the instance of western Europe and eastern Asia, apparently almost effaced.

SOCIAL ORGANIZATION.

The only essential case in which this fundamental relation is misconceived or neglected is that which is the most important of all,—involving, as it does, social organization, properly so called. The theory of social organization is still conceived of as absolute and isolated, independent altogether of the general analysis of the corresponding civilization, of which it can, in fact, constitute only one of the principle elements. [This vice is chargeable in an almost equal degree upon the most opposite political schools, which agree in abstract discussions of political systems, without thinking of the coexisting state of civilization, and usually conclude with making their immutable political type coincide with an infantile state of human development.] If we ascend to the philosophical source of this error, we shall find it, I think, in the great theological dogma of the Fall of Man. This fundamental dogma, which reappears, in one form or another, in all religions, and which is supported in its intellectual influence by the natural propensity of men to admire the past, tends, directly and necessarily, to make the continuous deterioration of society coincide with the extension of civilization. We have noticed before how, when it passes from the theological into the metaphysical state, this dogma takes the form of the celebrated hypothesis of a chimerical state of nature, superior to the social state, and the more remote, the further we advance in civilization. We cannot fail to perceive the extreme seriousness, in a political as well as a philosophical sense, of an error so completely incorporated with existing doctrines, and so deeply influencing in an unconscious way, our collective social speculations,—the more disastrously perhaps for not being expressly maintained as a general principle.—If it were so presented, it must immediately give way before sound philosophical discussion; for it is in direct contradiction to many ideas in political philosophy which, without having attained any scientific consistency, are obtaining some intellectual ascendancy, through the natural course of events, or the expansion of the general mind. For instance, all enlightened political writers acknowledge more or less mutual relation between political institutions; and this is the first direct step towards the rational conception of the agreement of the special system of institutions with the total system of civilization. We now see the best thinkers admitting a constant mutual connection between the political and the civil power: which means, in scientific language, that preponderating social forces always end in assuming the direction of society. Such partial advances towards a right view,—such fortunate feeling after the right path, must not, however, induce us to relax in our requirements of a true philosophical conception of that general social agreement which can alone constitute organization. Desultory indications, more literary than scientific, can never supply the place of a strict philosophical doctrine, as we may see from the fact that, from Aristotle downwards, (and even from an earlier period,) the greater number of philosophers have constantly reproduced the famous aphorism of the necessary subordination of laws to manners, without this germ of sound philosophy having had any effect on the general habit of regarding institutions as independent of the coexisting state of civilization,—however strange it may seem that such a contradiction should live through twenty centuries. This is, however, the natural course with intellectual principles and philosophical opinions, as well as with social manners and political institutions. When once they have obtained possession of men's minds, they live on, notwithstanding their admitted impotence and inconvenience, giving occasion to more and more serious inconsistencies, till the expansion of human reason originates new principles, of equivalent generality and superior rationality. We must not therefore take for more than their worth the desultory attempts that we see made in the right direction, but must insist on the principle which lies at the heart of every scheme of social organization,—the necessary participation of the collective political *régime* in the universal consensus of the social body.

The scientific principle of the relation between the political and the social condition is simply this;—that there must always be a spontaneous harmony between the whole and the parts of the social system, the elements of which must inevitably be, sooner or later, combined in a mode entirely conformable to their nature. It is evident that not only must political institutions and social manners on the one hand, and manners and ideas on the other, be always mutually connected; but, further, that this consolidated whole must be always connected, by its nature, with the corresponding state of the integral development of humanity, considered in all its aspects, of intellectual, moral, and physical activity: and the only object of any political system whatever, temporal or spiritual, is to regulate the spontaneous expansion so as best to direct it towards its determinate end. Even during revolutionary periods, when the harmony appears furthest from being duly realized, it still exists: for without it there would be a total dissolution of the social organism. During those exceptional seasons, the political *régime* is still, in the long run, in conformity with the corresponding state of civilization, as the disturbances which are manifest in the one proceed from equivalent derangements in the other. It is observable that when the popular theory attributes to the legislator the permanent power of infringing the harmony we are speaking of, it supposes him to be armed with a sufficient authority. But every social power, whether called authority or anything else, is constituted by a corresponding assent, spontaneous or deliberate, explicit or implicit, of various individual wills, resolved, from certain preparatory convictions, to concur in a common action, of which this power is first the organ, and then the regulator. Thus, authority is derived from concurrence, and not concurrence from authority, (setting aside the necessary reaction:) so that no great power can arise otherwise than from the strongly prevalent disposition of the society in which it exists: and when there is no strong preponderance, such powers as exist are weak accordingly: and the more extensive the society, the more irresistible is the correspondence. On the other hand, there is no denying the influence which, by a necessary reaction, the political system, as a whole, exercises over the general system of civilization, and which is so often exhibited in the action, fortunate or disastrous, of institutions, measures, or purely political events, even upon the course of the sciences and arts, in all ages of society, and especially the earliest. We need not dwell on this; for no one denies it. The common error, indeed, is to exaggerate it, so as to place the reaction before the primary action. It is evident, considering their scientific relation to each other, that both concur in creating that fundamental agreement of the social organism which I propose to set forth in a brief manner, as the philosophical principle of statical sociology. We shall have to advert repeatedly to the subject of the general correspondence between the political *régime* and the contemporary state of civilization, in connection with the question of the necessary limits of political action, and in the chapter which I must devote to social statics: but I did not think fit to wait for these explanations before pointing out that the political system ought always to be regarded as relative. The relative point of view, substituted for the absolute tendency of the ordinary theories, certainly constitutes the chief scientific character of the positive philosophy in its political application. If, on the one hand, the conception of this connection between government and civilization presents all ideas of political good or evil as necessarily relative and variable (which is quite another thing than being arbitrary), on the other hand, it provides a rational basis for a positive theory of the spontaneous order of human society, already vaguely perceived, in regard to some minor relations, by that part of the metaphysical polity which we call political economy; for, if the value of any political system can consist in nothing but its harmony with the corresponding social state, it follows that in the natural course of events, and in the absence of intervention, such a harmony must necessarily be established.

INTERCONNECTION OF THE SOCIAL ORGANISM.

There are two principal considerations which induce me to insist on this elementary idea of the radical consensus proper to the social organism: first, the extreme philosophical importance of this master-thought of social statics, which must, from its nature, constitute the rational basis of any new political philosophy; and, secondly, in an accessory way, that dynamical considerations of sociology must prevail throughout the rest of this work, as being at present more interesting, and therefore better understood; and it is, on that account, the more necessary to characterize now the general spirit of social statics, which will henceforth be treated only in an indirect and implicit way. As all artificial and voluntary order is simply a prolongation of the natural and involuntary order to which all human society tends, every rational political institution must rest upon an exact preparatory analysis of corresponding spontaneous tendencies, which alone can furnish a sufficiently solid basis. In brief, it is our business to contemplate order, that we may perfect it; and not to create it; which would be impossible. In a scientific view, this master-thought of universal social interconnection becomes the consequence and complement of a fundamental idea established, in our view of biology, as eminently proper to the study of living bodies. Not that this idea of interconnection is peculiar to that study: it is necessarily common to all phenomena; but amidst immense differences in intensity and variety, and therefore in philosophical importance. It is, in fact, true that wherever there is any system whatever, a certain interconnection must exist. The purely mechanical phenomena of astronomy offer the first suggestion of it; for the perturbations of one planet may sensibly affect another, through a modified gravitation. But the relation becomes closer and more marked in proportion to the complexity and diminished generality of the phenomena, and thus, it is in organic systems that we must look for the fullest mutual connection. Hitherto, it had been merely an accessory idea; but then it becomes the basis of positive conceptions; and it becomes more marked, the more compound are the organisms, and the more complex the phenomena in question, —the animal interconnection being more complete than the vegetable, and the human more than the brute; the nervous system being the chief seat of the biological interconnection. The idea must therefore be scientifically preponderant in social physics, even more than in biology, where it is so decisively recognized by the best order of students. But the existing political philosophy supposes the absence of any such interconnection among the aspects of society: and it is this which has rendered it necessary for me now to establish the point,—leaving the illustration of it to a future portion of the volume. Its consideration is, in fact, as indispensable in assigning its encyclopædic rank to social science as we before saw it to be in instituting Social Physics a science at all.

It follows from this attribute that there can be no scientific study of society, either in its conditions or its movements, if it is separated into portions, and its divisions are studied apart. I have already remarked upon this, in regard to what is called political economy. Materials may be furnished by the observation of different departments; and such observation may be necessary for that object: but it cannot be called science. The methodical division of studies which takes place in the simple inorganic sciences is thoroughly irrational in the recent and complex science of society, and can produce no results. The day may come when some sort of subdivision may be practicable and desirable; but it is impossible for us now to anticipate what the principle of distribution may be; for the principle itself must arise from the development of the science; and that development can take place no otherwise than by our formation of the science as a whole. The complete body will indicate for itself, at the right season, the particular points which need investigation; and then will be the time for such special study as may be required. By any other method of proceeding, we shall only find ourselves encumbered with special discussions, badly instituted, worse pursued, and accomplishing no other purpose than that of impeding the formation of real science. It is no easy matter to study social phenomena in the only right way,—viewing each element in the light of the whole system. It is no easy matter to exercise such vigilance as that no one of the number of contemporary aspects shall be lost sight of. But it is the right and the only way; and we may perceive in it a clear suggestion that this lofty study should be reserved for the highest order of scientific minds, better prepared than others, by wise educational discipline, for sustained speculative efforts, aided by an habitual subordination of the passions to the reason. There is no need to draw out any lengthened comparison between this state of things as it should be and that which is. And no existing degree of social disturbance can surprise us when we consider how intellectual anarchy is at the bottom of such disturbance, and see how anarchical our intellectual condition appears in the presence of the principle I have laid down.

ORDER OF STATICAL STUDY.

Before we go on to the subject of social dynamics, I will just remark that the prominent interconnection we have been considering prescribes a procedure in organic studies different from that which suits inorganic. The metaphysicians announce as an aphorism that we should always, in every kind of study, proceed from the simple to the compound: whereas, it appears most rational to suppose that we should follow that or the reverse method, as may best suit our subject. There can be no absolute merit in the method enjoined, apart from its suitableness. The rule should rather be (and there probably was a time when the two rules were one) that we must proceed from the more known to the less. Now, in the inorganic sciences, the elements are much better known to us than the whole which they constitute: so that in that case we must proceed from the simple to the compound. But the reverse method is necessary in the study of Man and of Society; Man and Society as a whole being better known to us, and more accessible subjects of study, than the parts which constitute them. In exploring the universe, it is as a whole that it is inaccessible to us; whereas, in investigating Man or Society, our difficulty is in penetrating the details. We have seen, in our survey of biology, that the general idea of animal nature is more distinct to our minds than the simpler notion of vegetable nature; and that man is the biological unity; the idea of Man being at once the most compound, and the starting-point of speculation in regard to vital existence. Thus, if we compare the two halves of natural philosophy, we shall find that in the one case it is the last degree of composition, and, in the other, the last degree of simplicity, that is beyond the scope of our research. As for the rest, it may obviate some danger of idle discussion to say that the positive philosophy, subordinating all fancies to reality, excludes logical controversies about the absolute value of this or that method, apart from its scientific application. The only ground of preference being the superior adaptation of any means to the proposed end, this philosophy may, without any inconsistency, change its order of proceeding when the one first tried is found to be inferior to its converse:—a discovery of which there is no fear in regard to the question we have now been examining.

DYNAMICAL STUDY.

Passing on from statical to dynamical sociology, we will contemplate the philosophical conception which should govern our study of the movement of society. Part of this subject is already despatched, from the explanations made in connection with statics having simplified the chief difficulties of the case. And social dynamics will be so prominent throughout the rest of this work, that I may reduce within very small compass what I have to say now under that head.

Though the statical view of society is the basis of sociology, the dynamical view is not only the more interesting of the two, but the more marked in its philosophical character, from its being more distinguished from biology by the master-thought of continuous progress, or rather, of the gradual development of humanity. If I were writing a methodical treatise on political philosophy, it would be necessary to offer a preliminary analysis of the individual impulsions which make up the progressive force of the human race, by referring them to that instinct which results from the concurrence of all our natural tendencies, and which urges man to develop the whole of his life, physical, moral, and intellectual, as far as his circumstances allow. But this view is admitted by all enlightened philosophers; so that I must proceed at once to consider the continuous succession of human development, regarded in the whole race, as if humanity were one. For clearness, we may take advantage of Condorcet's device of supposing a single nation to which we may refer all the consecutive social modifications actually witnessed among distinct peoples. This rational fiction is nearer the reality than we are accustomed to suppose; for, in a political view, the true successors of such or such a people are certainly those who, taking up and carrying out their primitive endeavours, have prolonged their social progress, whatever may be the soil which they inhabit, or even the race from which they spring. In brief, it is political continuity which regulates sociological succession, though the having a common country must usually affect this continuity in a high degree. As a scientific artifice merely, however, I shall employ this hypothesis, and on the ground of its manifest utility.

SOCIAL CONTINUITY.

The true general spirit of social dynamics then consists in conceiving of each of these consecutive social states as the necessary result of the preceding, and the indispensable mover of the following, according to the axiom of Leibnitz,—*the present is big with the future*. In this view, the object of science is to discover the laws which govern this continuity, and the aggregate of which determines the course of human development. In short, social dynamics studies the laws of succession, while social statics inquires into those of co-existence; so that the use of the first is to furnish the true theory of progress to political practice, while the second performs the same service in regard to order; and this suitability to the needs of modern society is a strong confirmation of the philosophical character of such a combination.

PRODUCED BY NATURAL LAWS.

If the existence of sociological laws has been established in the more difficult and uncertain case of the statical condition, we may assume that they will not be questioned in the dynamical province. In all times and places, the ordinary course of even our brief individual life has disclosed certain remarkable modifications which have occurred, in various ways, in the social state; and all the most ancient representations of human life bear unconscious and most interesting testimony to this, apart from all systematic estimate of the fact. Now it is the slow, continuous accumulation of these successive changes which gradually constitutes the social movement, whose steps are ordinarily marked by generations, as the most appreciable elementary variations are wrought by the constant renewal of adults. At a time when the average rapidity of this progression seems to all eyes to be remarkably accelerated, the reality of the movement cannot be disputed, even by those who most abhor it. The only question is about the constant subjection of these great dynamical phenomena to invariable natural laws, a proposition about which there is no question to any one who takes his stand on positive philosophy. It is easy however to establish, from any point of view, that the successive modifications of society have always taken place in a determinate order, the rational explanation of which is already possible in so many cases that we may confidently hope to recognize it ultimately in all the rest. So remarkable is the steadiness of this order, moreover, that it exhibits an exact parallelism of development among distinct and independent populations, as we shall see when we come to the historical portion of this volume. Since, then, the existence of the social movement is unquestionable, on the one hand, and, on the other, the succession of social states is never arbitrary, we cannot but regard this continuous phenomenon as subject to natural laws as positive as those which govern all other phenomena, though more complex. There is in fact no intellectual alternative; and thus it is evident that it is on the ground of social science that the great conflict must soon terminate which has gone on for three centuries between the positive and the theologico-metaphysical spirit. Banished for ever from all other classes of speculation, in principle at least, the old philosophies now prevail in social science alone; and it is from this domain that they have to be excluded, by the conception of the social movement being subject to invariable natural laws, instead of to any will whatever.

Though the fundamental laws of social interconnection are especially verified in this condition of movement, and though there is a necessary unity in this phenomenon, it may be usefully applied, for preparatory purposes, to the separate elementary aspects of human existence, physical, moral, intellectual and, finally, political,—their mutual relation being kept in view. Now, in whichever of these ways we regard, as a whole, the movement of humanity, from the earliest periods till now, we shall find that the various steps are connected in a determinate order; as we shall hereafter see, when we investigate the laws of this succession. I need refer here only to the intellectual evolution, which is the most distinct and unquestionable of all, as it has been the least impeded and most advanced of any, and has therefore been usually taken for guidance. The chief part of this evolution, and that which has most influenced the general progression, is no doubt the development of the scientific spirit, from the primitive labours of such philosophers as Thales and Pythagoras to those of men like Lagrange and Bichat. Now, no enlightened man can doubt that, in this long succession of efforts and discoveries, the human mind has pursued a determinate course, the exact preparatory knowledge of which might have allowed a cultivated reason to foresee the progress proper to each period. Though the historical considerations cited in my former volume were only incidental, any one may recognize in them numerous and indisputable examples of this necessary succession, more complex perhaps, but not more arbitrary than any natural law, whether in regard to the development of each separate science, or to the mutual influence of the different branches of natural philosophy. In accordance with the principles laid down at the beginning of this work, we have already seen in various signal instances, that the chief progress of each period, and even of each generation, was a necessary result of the immediately preceding state; so that the men of genius, to whom such progression has been too exclusively attributed, are essentially only the proper organs of a predetermined movement, which would, in their absence, have found other issues. We find a verification of this in history, which shows that various eminent men were ready to make the same great discovery at the same time, while the discovery required only one organ. All the parts of the human evolution admit of analogous observations, as we shall presently see, though they are more complex and less obvious than that which I have just cited. The natural progression of the arts of life is abundantly evident; and in our direct study of social dynamics we shall find an explanation of the apparent exception of the fine arts, which will be found to oppose no contradiction to the general course of human progression. As to that part of the movement which appears at present to be least reducible to natural laws, the political movement (still supposed to be governed by wills of adequate power), it is clear as in any other case that political systems have exhibited an historical succession, according to a traceable filiation, in a determinate order, which I am prepared to show to be even more inevitable than that of the different states of human intelligence.

The interconnection which we have examined and established in a statical view may aid us in developing the conception of the existence of positive laws in social dynamics. Unless the movement was determined by those laws, it would occasion the entire destruction of the social system. Now, that interconnection simplifies and strengthens the preparatory indications of dynamic order; for, when it has once been shown in any relation, we are authorized to extend it to all others; and this unites all the partial proofs that we can successively obtain of the reality of this scientific conception. In the choice and the application of these verifications, we must remember that the laws of social dynamics are most recognizable when they relate to the largest societies, in which secondary disturbances have the smallest effect. Again, these fundamental laws become the more irresistible, and therefore the more appreciable, in proportion to the advancement of the civilization upon which they operate, because the social movement becomes more distinct and certain with every conquest over accidental influences. As for the philosophical co-ordination of these preparatory evidences, the combination of which is important to science, it is clear that the social evolution must be more inevitably subject to natural laws, the more compound are the phenomena, and the less perceptible therefore the irregularities which arise from individual influences. This shows how inconsistent it is, for instance, to suppose the scientific movement to be subject to positive laws, while the political movement is regarded as arbitrary; for the latter, being more composite, must overrule individual disturbances, and be therefore more evidently predetermined than the former, in which individual genius must have more power. Any paradoxical appearance which this statement may exhibit will disappear in the course of further examination.

* * *

THREE ASPECTS.

Every sociological analysis supposes three classes of considerations, each more complex than the preceding: viz., the conditions of social existence of the individual, the family, and society; the last comprehending, in a scientific sense, the whole of the human species, and chiefly, the whole of the white race. . . .

* * *

THE FAMILY.

As every system must be composed of elements of the same nature with itself, the scientific spirit forbids us to regard society as composed of individuals. The true social unit is certainly the family,—reduced, if necessary, to the elementary couple which forms its basis. This consideration implies more than the physiological truth that families become tribes, and tribes become nations: so that the whole human race might be conceived of as the gradual development of a single family, if local diversities did not forbid such a supposition. There is a political point of view from which also we must consider this elementary idea, inasmuch as the family presents the true germ of the various characteristics of the social organism. Such a conception is intermediate between the idea of the individual and that of the species, or society. There would be as many scientific inconveniences in passing it over in a speculative sense as there are dangers in practice in pretending to treat of social life without the inevitable preparation of the domestic life. Whichever way we look at it, this necessary transition always presents itself, whether in regard to elementary notions of fundamental harmony, or for the spontaneous rise of social sentiment. It is by this avenue that Man comes forth from his mere personality, and learns to live in another, while obeying his most powerful instincts. . . .

* * *

SOCIETY.

The third head of our statical analysis brings us to the consideration of society, as composed of families and not of individuals, and from a point of view which commands all times and places.

The main cause of the superiority of the social to the individual organism is, according to an established law, the more marked speciality of the various functions fulfilled by organs more and more distinct, but interconnected; so that unity of aim is more and more combined with diversity of means. We cannot, of course, fully appreciate a phenomenon which is for ever proceeding before our eyes, and in which we bear a part; but if we withdraw ourselves in thought from the social system, and contemplate it as from afar, can we conceive of a more marvellous spectacle, in the whole range of natural phenomena, than the regular and constant convergence of an innumerable multitude of human beings, each possessing a distinct and, in a certain degree, independent existence, and yet incessantly disposed, amidst all their discordance of talent and character, to occur in many ways in the same general development, without concert, and even consciousness on the part of most of them, who believe that they are merely following their personal impulses? This is the scientific picture of the phenomenon: and no temporary disturbances can prevent its being, under all circumstances, essentially true. This reconciliation of the individuality of labour with co-operation of endeavours, which becomes more remarkable as society grows more complex and extended, constitutes the radical character of human operations when we rise from the domestic to the social point of view. The degree of association that we observe among the superior animals has something voluntary in it, but there is no organization which can make it resemble the human: and the first individual specializing of common functions is seen in our simple domestic life, which is thus a type of the social organization. The division of labour can never, however, be very marked in the family, because the members are few; and yet more because such a division would soon show itself to be hostile to the spirit of the institution; for domestic training, being founded on imitation, must dispose the children to follow parental employments, instead of undertaking new ones: and again, any very marked separation in the employments of the members must impair the domestic unity which is the aim of the association. The more we look into the subject, the more we shall see that the appropriation of employments, which is the elementary principle of general society, cannot hold anything like so important a place in the family. In fact, the domestic relations do not constitute an association, but a *union,* in the full force of the term; and, on account of this close intimacy, the domestic connection is of a totally different nature from the social. Its character is essentially moral, and only incidentally intellectual; or, in anatomical language, it corresponds more to the middle than to the anterior part of the brain. Founded chiefly upon attachment and gratitude, the domestic union satisfies, by its mere existence, all our sympathetic instincts, quite apart from all idea of active and continuous co-operation towards any end, unless it be that of its own institution. Though more or less co-ordination of different employments must exist, it is so secondary an affair that when, unhappily, it remains the only principle of connection, the domestic union degenerates into mere association, and is even too likely to dissolve altogether. In society the elementary economy presents an inverse character, the sentiment of co-operation becoming preponderant, and the sympathetic instinct, without losing its steadiness, becoming secondary. No doubt there are a multitude of men well enough organized to love their fellow-labourers, however numerous or remote they may be, and however indirect may be their co-operation; but such a sentiment, arising from the reaction of the reason upon the social feelings, could never be strong enough to guide social life. Even under the best circumstances the intellectual mediocrity of the majority of men does not allow them to form any distinct idea of relations which are too extensive, too indirect, and too foreign to their own occupations to impart any sympathetic stimulus which could be of permanent use. It is only in domestic life that Man can habitually seek the full and free expansion of his social affections; and perhaps this is the chief reason why it is the last indispensable preparation for social life; for concentration is as necessary to the feelings as generalization to the thoughts. Even the most eminent men, who direct their sympathetic instincts upon their race at large or the society in which they live, are usually impelled to this by the moral disappointments of a domestic life which has failed in some of its conditions; and however genial the imperfect compensation may be to them, this abstract love of their species admits of nothing like that satisfaction of the affections which arises from a very limited, and especially an individual attachment. However this may be, such cases are besides too evidently exceptional to affect any inquiry into the social economy. Thus, though the sympathetic instinct exists wherever there is association, more or less, the principle of co-operation is that which must prevail, when we pass on from the consideration of the family to the general co-ordination of families. To attribute to it the formation of the social state, as it was the fashion of the last century to do, is a capital error; but, when the association has once begun, there is nothing like this principle of co-operation for giving consistency and character to the combination. In the lower stages of savage life we see families combining for a temporary purpose, and then returning, almost like the brutes, to their isolated independence, as soon as the expedition, which is usually one of war or the chase, is ended, though already some common opinions, expressed in a certain uniform language, are preparing them for permanent union in tribes, more or less numerous. It is upon the principle of co-operation, then, spontaneous or concerted, that we must found our analysis of the last division of social statics.

DISTRIBUTION OF DEVELOPMENTS.

We must include in our view of the division of employments something much more extensive than the material arrangements which the expression is usually understood to convey. We must include under it all human operations whatever, regarding not only individuals and classes, but also, in many ways, different nations, as participating in a special mode and degree, in a vast common work, the gradual development of which connects the fellow-labourers with the whole series of their predecessors, and even with their successors. This is what is meant when we speak of the race being bound up together by the very distribution of their occupations; and it is this distribution which causes the extent and growing complexity of the social organism, which thus appears as comprising the whole of the human race. Man can hardly exist in a solitary state: the family can exist in isolation, because it can divide its employments and provide for its wants in a rough kind of way: a spontaneous approximation of families is incessantly exposed to temporary rupture, occasioned by the most trifling incidents. But when a regular division of employments has spread through any society, the social state begins to acquire a consistency and stability which place it out of danger from particular divergencies. The habit of partial co-operation convinces each family of its close dependence on the rest, and, at the same time, of its own importance, each one being then justified in regarding itself as fulfilling a real public function, more or less indispensable to the general economy, but inseparable from the system as a whole. In this view the social organization tends more and more to rest on an exact estimate of individual diversities, by so distributing employments as to appoint each one to the destination he is most fit for, from his own nature (which however is seldom very distinctly marked), from his education and his position, and, in short, from all his qualifications; so that all individual organizations, even the most vicious and imperfect (short of monstrosity), may be finally made use of for the general good. Such is, at least, the social type which we conceive of as the limit of the existing social order, and to which we may be for ever approximating, though without the hope of ever attaining it; and it is, in fact, a reproduction, with a large extension, of the domestic organism, with less power, in proportion to its extent, of appointing a due destination to every member; so that the social discipline must always be more artificial, and therefore more imperfect, than the domestic, which nature herself ordains and administers.

The necessities of this co-ordination and distribution of special offices, cause inconvenience which I am compelled to advert to; for it is in the investigation of these that we find the scientific germ of the relation between the idea of society and that of government.

INCONVENIENCES.

Some economists have pointed out, but in a very inadequate way, the evils of an exaggerated division of material labour; and I have indicated, in regard to the more important field of scientific labour, the mischievous intellectual consequences of the spirit of speciality which at present prevails. It is necessary to estimate directly the principle of such an influence, in order to understand the object of the spontaneous system of requisites for the continuous preservation of society. In decomposing, we always disperse; and the distribution of human labours must occasion individual divergencies, both intellectual and moral, which require a permanent discipline to keep them within bounds. If the separation of social functions develops a useful spirit of detail, on the one hand, it tends, on the other, to extinguish or to restrict what we may call the aggregate or general spirit. In the same way, in moral relations, while each individual is in close dependence on the mass, he is drawn away from it by the expansion of his special activity, constantly recalling him to his private interest, which he but very dimly perceives to be related to the public. On both grounds the inconveniences of the division of functions increase with its characteristic advantages, without their being in the same relation, throughout the spontaneous course of the social evolution. The growing speciality of habitual ideas and familiar relations must tend to restrict the understanding more and more, while sharpening it in a certain direction, and to sever more and more the private interest from a public interest which is for ever becoming more vague and indirect; while, at the same time, the social affections, gradually concentrated among individuals of the same profession, become more and more alienated from all other classes, for want of a sufficient analogy of ways and ideas. Thus it is that the principle by which alone general society could be developed and extended, threatens, in another view, to decompose it into a multitude of unconnected corporations, which almost seem not to belong to the same species; and hence it is that the gradual expansion of human ability seems destined to produce such minds as are very common among civilized peoples, and prodigiously admired by them,—minds which are very able in some one respect and monstrously incapable in all others. If we have been accustomed to deplore the spectacle, among the artisan class of a workman occupied during his whole life in nothing else but making knife-handles or pins' heads, we may find something quite as lamentable in the intellectual class, in the exclusive employment of a human brain in resolving some equations, or in classifying insects. The moral effect is, unhappily, analogous in the two cases. It occasions a miserable indifference about the general course of human affairs, as long as there are equations to resolve and pins to manufacture. This is an extreme case of human automatism; but the frequency, and the growing frequency, of the evil gives a real scientific importance to the case, as indicating the general tendency, and warning us to restrain it. Thus it appears to me that the social destination of government is to guard against and restrain the fundamental dispersion of ideas, sentiments, and interests, which is the inevitable result of the very principle of human development, and which, if left to itself, would put a stop to social progression in all important respects.

BASIS OF THE TRUE THEORY OF GOVERNMENT.

Here we have, in my opinion, the basis of the elementary and abstract theory of government, regarded in its complete scientific extension; that is, as characterized by the universal necessary reaction,—first spontaneous and then regulated,—of the whole upon the parts. It is clear that the only way of preventing such a dispersion is by setting up this reaction as a new special function, which shall intervene in the performance of all the various functions of the social economy, to keep up the idea of the whole, and the feeling of the common interconnection: and the more energetically, the more individual activity tends to dissolve them. Not itself affecting any determinate social progress, it contributes to all that society can achieve, in any direction whatever, and which society could not achieve without its concentrating and protective care. The very nature of its action indicates that it cannot be merely material, but also, and much more, intellectual and moral; so as to show the double necessity of what has been called the temporal and spiritual government, the rational subordination of which was the best feature of the social organization that was happily effected in its day, under the influence of the prevalent Catholicism. Moreover, this ruling function must become more, instead of less necessary, as human development proceeds, because its essential principle is inseparable from that of the development itself.—Thus, it is the habitual predominance of the spirit of the whole which constitutes government, in whatever way it is regarded. The next consideration is, how such an action arises, independently of all systematic combination, in the natural course of the social economy.

ELEMENTARY SUBORDINATION.

If the dispersive tendency arising from the distribution of functions naturally propagates itself, it is clear that any influence capable of neutralizing it must also be constantly expanding. In fact, an elementary subordination must always be growing out of the distribution of human operations, which gives birth to government, in the bosom of society itself, as we could easily discover by analyzing any marked subdivision which has just taken place in any employment whatever. This subordination is not only material, but yet more intellectual and moral; that is, it requires, besides practical submission, a corresponding degree of real confidence in both the capacity and the probity of the special organs to whom a function, hitherto universal, is confided. Every one of us relies, even for life itself, on the aptitude and the morality of a multitude of almost unknown agents, whose folly or wickedness might affect the welfare of vast numbers of human beings. Such a condition belongs to all modes of social existence. If it is especially attributed to industrial societies, it is only because it must be most conspicuous where the division of labour goes furthest; and it is as certainly to be found in purely military societies; as the statical analysis of an army, a man-of-war, or any other active corporation shows in a moment.

This elementary subordination discloses its own law; which is, that the various operations in which individuals are engaged fall naturally under the direction of those which are next above them in generality. We may easily convince ourselves of this by analysing any special occupation at the moment when it assumes a separate character: because the task thus separated is necessarily more special than the function from which it proceeds, and to which its own fulfilment must be subordinated. This is not the occasion on which to expatiate on this law; but its political bearing concerns us here, —indicating as it does the germ of a true classification of social functions. We shall hereafter meet with a full verification of this law in regard to the industrial life of modern societies: the eminent regularity of military associations renders the law obvious at once; and when the law is once admitted, it discloses the spontaneous connection of this elementary social subordination with that political subordination, properly so called, which is the basis of government, and which presents itself as the last degree in the hierarchy formed by the subjection of the more special to the more general classes of phenomena. For, as the various particular functions of the social economy are naturally implicated in relations of greater generality, all must at length be subject to the direction of the most general function of all, which is characterized, as we have seen, by the constant action of the whole upon the parts. On the other hand, the organs of this direction must be much strengthened by the encouragement afforded to intellectual and moral inequality under a system of division of employments. It is clear that while men were obliged to do everything for themselves, they must have been confined to domestic life, devoting all their activity to supply the wants of the family; and there could be little expansion of individual ability and character. Though marked individuality must always have made itself felt, in every state of society, the division of labour, and the leisure which it brings, have been needful to the conspicuous development of that intellectual superiority on which all political ascendancy must mainly rest. We must observe, moreover, that there can be no such division of intellectual as of material labour; so that the intellectual functions must be less affected than the industrial by the dispersive tendencies of such a division. We are familiar with the effect of civilization in developing moral, and yet more, intellectual inequalities; but we must bear in mind that moral and intellectual forces do not admit, like the physical, of being accumulated and compounded: so that, eminently as they can occur, and clearly as they are the creators of social concurrence, they are much less adapted for direct cooperation. A sufficient coalition of the most insignificant individuals can easily carry any point of physical conflict, or of acquisition of wealth, against the highest superiority in an individual or a family; so that, for example, the most enormous private fortune cannot sustain any competition with the financial power of a nation, whose treasury is filled by a multitude of the smallest contributions. But, on the contrary, if the enterprise depends on a high intellectual power, as in the case of a great scientific or poetical conception, there can be no association of ordinary minds, however extensive, which can compete with a Descartes or a Shakspere. It is the same in the moral case; as, for instance, if society is in need of any great resource of devotedness, the want cannot be supplied by accumulating any amount of moderate zeal furnished by individuals. The only use of a multitude in such a case is that it improves the chance of finding the *unique* organ of the proposed function; and when that singular agent is once found, there is no degree of multitude which can weigh down its preponderance. It is through this privilege that intellectual and moral forces tend to an ever-increasing social authority, from the time when a due division of employments admits of their proper development.

TENDENCY OF SOCIETY TO GOVERNMENT.

Such is, then, the elementary tendency of all human society to a spontaneous government. This tendency accords with a corresponding system, inherent in us as individuals, of special dispositions towards command in some, and towards obedience in others. We must not, with regard to the first, confound the desire to rule with the fitness to do so; though the desire is one element of the fitness:

and, on the other hand, there is a much stronger inclination to obedience in the generality of men than it is customary in our day to suppose. If men were as rebellious as they are at present represented, it would be difficult to understand how they could ever have been disciplined: and it is certain that we are all more or less disposed to respect any superiority, especially any intellectual or moral elevation, in our neighbours, independently of any view to our own advantage: and this instinct of submission is, in truth, only too often lavished on deceptive appearances. However excessive the desire of command may be in our revolutionary day, there can be no one who, in his secret mind, has not often felt, more or less vividly, how sweet it is to obey when he can have the rare privilege of consigning the burdensome responsibility of his general self-conduct to wise and trustworthy guidance: and probably the sense of this is strongest in those who are best fitted for command. In the midst of political convulsion, when the spirit of revolutionary destruction is abroad, the mass of the people manifest a scrupulous obedience towards the intellectual and moral guides from whom they accept direction, and upon whom they may even press a temporary dictatorship, in their primary and urgent need of a preponderant authority. Thus do individual dispositions show themselves to be in harmony with the course of social relations as a whole, in teaching us that political subordination is as inevitable, generally speaking, as it is indispensable. And this completes the elementary delineation of Social Statics.

My sketch has perhaps been so abstract and condensed that the conceptions of this chapter may appear obscure at present; but light will fall upon them as we proceed. We may already see, however, the practical advantage which arises from the scientific evolution of human relations. The individual life, ruled by personal instincts; the domestic, by sympathetic instincts; and the social, by the special development of intellectual influences, prepare for the states of human existence which are to follow: and that which ensues is, first, personal morality, which subjects the preservation of the individual to a wise discipline; next, domestic morality, which subordinates selfishness to sympathy; and lastly, social morality, which directs all dividual tendencies by enlightened reason, always having the general economy in view, so as to bring into concurrence all the faculties of human nature, according to their appropriate laws.

# 10. *The Material Forces and the Relations of Production*

BY KARL MARX

THE SUBJECT of our discussion is first of all *material* production by individuals as determined by society, naturally constitutes the starting point. The individual and isolated hunter or fisher who forms the starting point with Smith and Ricardo, belongs to the insipid illusions of the eighteenth century. They are Robinsonades which do not by any means represent, as students of the history of civilization imagine, a reaction against over-refinement and a return to a misunderstood natural life. They are no more based on such a naturalism than is Rousseau's "contrat social," which makes naturally independent individuals come in contact and have mutual intercourse by contract. They are the fiction and only the æsthetic fiction of the small and great Robinsonades. They are, moreover, the anticipation of "bourgeois society," which had been in course of development since the sixteenth century and made gigantic strides towards maturity in the eighteenth. In this society of free competition the individual appears free from the bonds of nature, etc., which in former epochs of history made him a part of a definite, limited human conglomeration. To the prophets of the eighteenth century, on whose shoulders Smith and Ricardo are still standing, this eighteenth century individual, constituting the joint product of the dissolution of the feudal form of society and of the new forces of production which had developed since the sixteenth century, appears

---

Reprinted from Karl Marx, *A Contribution to the Critique of Political Economy,* Trans. N. I. Stone, from the 2d German ed. (New York: International Library Publishing Co., 1904), Appendix, secs. 1, 2, pp. 265–69, 291–92, Author's Preface, pp. 11–13.

as an ideal whose existence belongs to the past; not as a result of history, but as its starting point.

Since that individual appeared to be in conformity with nature and [corresponded] to their conception of human nature, [he was regarded] not as a product of history, but of nature. This illusion has been characteristic of every new epoch in the past. Steuart, who, as an aristocrat, stood more firmly on historical ground, contrary to the spirit of the eighteenth century, escaped this simplicity of view. The further back we go into history, the more the individual and, therefore, the producing individual seems to depend on and constitute a part of a larger whole: at first it is, quite naturally, the family and the clan, which is but an enlarged family; later on, it is the community growing up in its different forms out of the clash and the amalgamation of clans. It is but in the eighteenth century, in "bourgeois society," that the different forms of social union confront the individual as a mere means to his private ends, as an outward necessity. But the period in which this view of the isolated individual becomes prevalent, is the very one in which the inter-relations of society (general from this point of view) have reached the highest state of development. Man is in the most literal sense of the word a *zoon politikon* not only a social animal, but an animal which can develop into an individual only in society. Production by isolated individuals outside of society—something which might happen as an exception to a civilized man who by accident got into the wilderness and already dynamically possessed within himself the forces of society—is as great an absurdity as the idea of the development of language without individuals living together and talking to one another. We need not dwell on this any longer. It would not be necessary to touch upon this point at all, were not the vagary which had its justification and sense with the people of the eighteenth century transplanted in all earnest into the field of political economy by Bastiat, Carey, Proudhon and others. Proudhon and others naturally find it very pleasant, when they do not know the historical origin of a certain economic phenomenon, to give it a quasi historical-philosophical explanation by going into mythology. Adam or Prometheus hit upon the scheme cut and dried, whereupon it was adopted, etc. Nothing is more tediously dry than the dreaming *locus communis.*

Whenever we speak, therefore, of production, we always have in mind production at a certain stage of social development, or production by social individuals. Hence, it might seem that in order to speak of production at all, we must either trace the historical process of development through its various phases, or declare at the outset that we are dealing with a certain historical period, as, e.g., with modern capitalistic production which, as a matter of fact, constitutes the subject proper of this work. But all stages of production have certain landmarks in common, common purposes. *Production in general* is an abstraction, but it is a rational abstraction, in so far as it singles out and fixes the common features, thereby saving us repetition. Yet these general or common features discovered by comparison constitute something very complex, whose constituent elements have different destinations. Some of these elements belong to all epochs, others are common to a few. Some of them are common to the most modern as well as to the most ancient epochs. No production is conceivable without them; but while even the most completely developed languages have laws and conditions in common with the least developed ones, what is characteristic of their development are the points of departure from the general and common. The conditions which generally govern production must be differentiated in order that the essential points of difference be not lost sight of in view of the general uniformity which is due to the fact that the subject, mankind, and the object, nature, remain the same. The failure to remember this one fact is the source of all the wisdom of modern economists who are trying to prove the eternal nature and harmony of existing social conditions.

* * *

The result we arrive at is not that production, distribution, exchange, and consumption are identical, but that they are all members of one entity, different sides of one unit. Production predominates not only over production itself in the opposite sense of that term, but over the other elements as well. With it the process constantly starts over again. That exchange and consumption can not be the predominating elements is self evident. The same is true of distribution in the narrow sense of distribution of products; as for distribution in the sense of distribution of the agents of production, it is itself but a factor of production. A definite [form of] production thus determines the [forms of] consumption, distribution, exchange, and *also the mutual relations between these various elements.* Of course, production *in its one-sided form* is in its turn influenced by other elements; e.g. with the expansion of the market, i.e. of the sphere of exchange, production grows in volume and is subdivided to a greater extent.

With a change in distribution, production undergoes a change; as e.g. in the case of concentration of capital, of a change in the distribution of population in city and country, etc. Finally, the demands of consumption also influence production. A mutual interaction takes place between the various elements. Such is the case with every organic body.

* * *

In the social production which men carry on they enter into definite relations that are indispensable and independent of their will; these relations of production correspond to a definite stage of development of their material powers of production. The sum total of these relations of production constitutes the economic structure of society—the real foundation, on which rise legal and political superstructures and to which correspond definite forms of social consciousness. The mode of production in material life determines the general character of the social, political and spiritual processes of life. It is not the consciousness of men that determines their existence, but, on the contrary, their social existence determines their consciousness. At a certain stage of their development, the material forces of production in society come in conflict with the existing relations of production, or—what is but a legal expression for the same thing—with the property relations within which they had been at work before. From forms of development of the forces of production these relations turn into their fetters. Then comes the period of social revolution. With the change of the economic foundation the entire immense superstructure is more or less rapidly transformed. In considering such transformations the distinction should always be made between the material transformation of the economic conditions of production which can be determined with the precision of natural science, and the legal, political, religious, æsthetic or philosophic—in short ideological forms in which men become conscious of this conflict and fight it out. Just as our opinion of an individual is not based on what he thinks of himself, so can we not judge of such a period of transformation by its own consciousness: on the contrary, this consciousness must rather be explained from the contradictions of material life, from the existing conflict between the social forces of production and the relations of production. No social order ever disappears before all the productive forces, for which there is room in it, have been developed; and new higher relations of production never appear before the material conditions of their existence have matured in the womb of the old society. Therefore, mankind always takes up only such problems as it can solve; since, looking at the matter more closely, we will always find that the problem itself arises only when the material conditions necessary for its solution already exist or are at least in the process of formation. In broad outlines we can designate the Asiatic, the ancient, the feudal and the modern bourgeois methods of production as so many epochs in the progress of the economic formation of society. The bourgeois relations of production are the last antagonistic form of the social process of production—antagonistic not in the sense of individual antagonism, but of one arising from conditions surrounding the life of individuals in society; at the same time the productive forces developing in the womb of bourgeois society create the material conditions for the solution of that antagonism. This social formation constitutes, therefore, the closing chapter of the prehistoric stage of human society.

# *11. On Status and Contract*

BY SIR HENRY SUMNER MAINE

THE MOVEMENT of the progressive societies has been uniform in one respect. Through all its course it has been distinguished by the gradual dissolution of family dependency and the growth of individual obligation in its place. The individual is steadily substituted for the Family, as the unit of which civil laws take account. The advance has been accomplished at varying rates of celerity, and there are societies not absolutely stationary in which the collapse of the ancient organisation can only be perceived by careful study of the phenomena they present. But, whatever its pace, the change has not been subject to reaction or recoil, and apparent

Reprinted from Sir Henry Sumner Maine, *Ancient Law* (New York: H. Holt & Co., 1885; from the 5th London edition), chap. v, pp. 163–65.

retardations will be found to have been occasioned through the absorption of archaic ideas and customs from some entirely foreign source. Nor is it difficult to see what is the tie between man and man which replaces by degrees those forms of reciprocity in rights and duties which have their origin in the Family. It is Contract. Starting, as from one terminus of history, from a condition of society in which all the relations of Persons are summed up in the relations of Family, we seem to have steadily moved towards a phase of social order in which all these relations arise from the free agreement of individuals. In Western Europe the progress achieved in this direction has been considerable. Thus the status of the Slave has disappeared—it has been superseded by the contractual relation of the servant to his master. The status of the Female under Tutelage, if the tutelage be understood of persons other than her husband, has also ceased to exist; from her coming of age to her marriage all the relations she may form are relations of contract. So too the status of the Son under Power has no true place in the law of modern European societies. If any civil obligation binds together the Parent and the child of full age, it is one to which only contract gives its legal validity. The apparent exceptions are exceptions of that stamp which illustrate the rule. The child before years of discretion, the orphan under guardianship, the adjudged lunatic, have all their capacities and incapacities regulated by the Law of Persons. But why? The reason is differently expressed in the conventional language of different systems, but in substance it is stated to the same effect by all. The great majority of Jurists are constant to the principle that the classes of persons just mentioned are subject to extrinsic control on the single ground that they do not possess the faculty of forming a judgment on their own interests; in other words, that they are wanting in the first essential of an engagement by Contract.

The word Status may be usefully employed to construct a formula expressing the law of progress thus indicated, which, whatever be its value, seems to me to be sufficiently ascertained. All the forms of Status taken notice of in the Law of Persons were derived from, and to some extent are still coloured by, the powers and privileges anciently residing in the Family. If then we employ Status, agreeably with the usage of the best writers, to signify these personal conditions only, and avoid applying the term to such conditions as are the immediate or remote result of agreement, we may say that the movement of the progressive societies has hitherto been a movement *from Status to Contract.*

# 12. *The Nature of Society*

BY HERBERT SPENCER

212. THIS QUESTION has to be asked and answered at the outset. Until we have decided whether or not to regard a society as an entity; and until we have decided whether, if regarded as an entity, a society is to be classed as absolutely unlike all other entities or as like some others; our conception of the subject-matter before us remains vague.

It may be said that a society is but a collective name for a number of individuals. Carrying the controversy between nominalism and realism into another sphere, a nominalist might affirm that just as there exist only the members of a species, while the species considered apart from them has no existence; so the units of a society alone exist, while the existence of the society is but verbal. Instancing a lecturer's audience as an aggregate which by disappearing at the close of the lecture, proves itself to be not a thing but only a certain arrangement of persons, he might argue that the like holds of the citizens forming a nation.

But without disputing the other steps of his argument, the last step may be denied. The arrangement, temporary in the one case, is permanent in the other; and it is the permanence of the relations among component parts which constitutes the individuality of a whole as distinguished from the individualities of its parts. A mass broken into fragments ceases to be a thing; while, conversely, the

---

Reprinted from Herbert Spencer, *The Principles of Sociology* (New York: D. Appleton & Co., 1898), Vol. II, Book II, secs. 212–17, 223, 270–71, pp. 447–53, 456, 593–97.

stones, bricks, and wood, previously separate, become the thing called a house if connected in fixed ways.

Thus we consistently regard a society as an entity, because, though formed of discrete units, a certain concreteness in the aggregate of them is implied by the general persistence of the arrangements among them throughout the area occupied. And it is this trait which yields our idea of a society. For, withholding the name from an ever-changing cluster such as primitive men form, we apply it only where some constancy in the distribution of parts has resulted from settled life.

213. But now, regarding a society as a thing, what kind of thing must we call it? It seems totally unlike every object with which our senses acquaint us. Any likeness it may possibly have to other objects, cannot be manifest to perception, but can be discerned only by reason. If the constant relations among its parts make it an entity; the question arises whether these constant relations among its parts are akin to the constant relations among the parts of other entities. Between a society and anything else, the only conceivable resemblance must be one due to *parallelism of principle in the arrangement of components.*

There are two great classes of aggregates with which the social aggregate may be compared—the inorganic and the organic. Are the attributes of a society in any way like those of a not-living body? or are they in any way like those of a living body? or are they entirely unlike those of both?

The first of these questions needs only to be asked to be answered in the negative. A whole of which the parts are alive, cannot, in its general characters, be like lifeless wholes. The second question, not to be thus promptly answered, is to be answered in the affirmative. The reasons for asserting that the permanent relations among the parts of a society, are analogous to the permanent relations among the parts of a living body, we have now to consider.

## A Society Is an Organism

214. When we say that growth is common to social aggregates and organic aggregates, we do not thus entirely exclude community with inorganic aggregates. Some of these, as crystals, grow in a visible manner; and all of them, on the hypothesis of evolution, have arisen by integration at some time or other. Nevertheless, compared with things we call inanimate, living bodies and societies so conspicuously exhibit augmentation of mass, that we may fairly regard this as characterizing them both. Many organisms grow throughout their lives; and the rest grow throughout considerable parts of their lives. Social growth usually continues either up to times when the societies divide, or up to times when they are overwhelmed.

Here, then, is the first trait by which societies ally themselves with the organic world and substantially distinguish themselves from the inorganic world.

215. It is also a character of social bodies, as of living bodies, that while they increase in size they increase in structure. Like a low animal, the embryo of a high one has few distinguishable parts; but while it is acquiring greater mass, its parts multiply and differentiate. It is thus with a society. At first the unlikenesses among its groups of units are inconspicuous in number and degree; but as population augments, divisions and sub-divisions become more numerous and more decided. Further, in the social organism as in the individual organism, differentiations cease only with that completion of the type which marks maturity and precedes decay.

Though in inorganic aggregates also, as in the entire Solar System and in each of its members, structural differentiations accompany the integrations; yet these are so relatively slow, and so relatively simple, that they may be disregarded. The multiplication of contrasted parts in bodies politic and in living bodies, is so great that it substantially constitutes another common character which marks them off from inorganic bodies.

216. This community will be more fully appreciated on observing that progressive differentiation of structures is accompanied by progressive differentiation of functions.

The divisions, primary, secondary, and tertiary, which arise in a developing animal, do not assume their major and minor unlikenesses to no purpose. Along with diversities in their shapes and compositions go diversities in the actions they perform: they grow into unlike organs having unlike duties. Assuming the entire function of absorbing nutriment at the same time that it takes on its structural characters, the alimentary system becomes gradually marked off into contrasted portions; each of which has a special function forming part of the general function. A limb, instrumental to locomotion or prehension, acquires divisions and sub-divisions which perform their leading and their subsidiary shares in this office. So is it with the parts into which a society divides. A dominant class arising does not simply become unlike the rest, but assumes control over the rest; and when this class separates into the more and the less dominant, these, again, begin to discharge distinct parts of the entire control. With the classes whose actions are controlled it is the same. The various groups into which they fall have various occupations: each of such groups also, within itself, acquiring minor contrasts of parts along with minor contrasts of duties.

And here we see more clearly how the two classes of things we are comparing, distinguish themselves from things of other classes; for such differences of structure as slowly arise in inorganic aggregates, are not accompanied by what we can fairly call differences of function.

217. Why in a body politic and in a living body, these unlike actions of unlike parts are properly regarded by us as functions, while we cannot so regard the unlike actions of unlike parts in an inorganic body, we shall perceive on turning to the next and most distinctive common trait.

Evolution establishes in them both, not differences simply, but definitely-connected differences—differences such that each makes the others possible. The parts of an inorganic aggregate are so related that one may change greatly without appreciably affecting the rest. It is otherwise with the parts of an organic aggregate or of a social aggregate. In either of these, the changes in the parts are mutually determined, and the changed actions of the parts are mutually dependent. In both, too, this mutuality increases as the evolution advances. The lowest type of animal is all stomach, all respiratory surface, all limb. Development of a type having appendages by which to move about or lay hold of food, can take place only if these appendages, losing power to absorb nutriment directly from surrounding bodies, are supplied with nutriment by parts which retain the power of absorption. A respiratory surface to which the circulating fluids are brought to be ærated, can be formed only on condition that the concomitant loss of ability to supply itself with materials for repair and growth, is made good by the development of a structure bringing these materials. Similarly in a society. What we call with perfect propriety its organization, necessarily implies traits of the same kind. While rudimentary, a society is all warrior, all hunter, all hut-builder, all tool-maker: every part fulfils for itself all needs. Progress to a stage characterized by a permanent army, can go on only as there arise arrangements for supplying that army with food, clothes, and munitions of war by the rest. If here the population occupies itself solely with agriculture and there with mining—if these manufacture goods while those distribute them, it must be on condition that in exchange for a special kind of service rendered by each part to other parts, these other parts severally give due proportions of their services.

This division of labour, first dwelt on by political economists as a social phenomenon, and thereupon recognized by biologists as a phenomenon of living bodies, which they called the "physiological division of labour," is that which in the society, as in the animal, makes it a living whole. Scarcely can I emphasize enough the truth that in respect of this fundamental trait, a social organism and an individual organism are entirely alike. When we see that in a mammal, arresting the lungs quickly brings the heart to a stand; that if the stomach fails absolutely in its office all other parts by-and-by cease to act; that paralysis of its limbs entails on the body at large death from want of food, or inability to escape; that loss of even such small organs as the eyes, deprives the rest of a service essential to their preservation; we cannot but admit that mutual dependence of parts is an essential characteristic. And when, in a society, we see that the workers in iron stop if the miners do not supply materials; that makers of clothes cannot carry on their business in the absence of those who spin and weave textile fabrics; that the manufacturing community will cease to act unless the food-producing and food-distributing agencies are acting; that the controlling powers, governments, bureaux, judicial officers, police, must fail to keep order when the necessaries of life are not supplied to them by the parts kept in order; we are obliged to say that this mutual dependence of parts is similarly rigorous. Unlike as the two kinds of aggregates otherwise are, they are unlike in respect of this fundamental character, and the characters implied by it.

* * *

223. From this last consideration, which is a digression rather than a part of the argument, let us now return and sum up the reasons for regarding a society as an organism.

It undergoes continuous growth. As it grows, its parts become unlike: it exhibits increase of structure. The unlike parts simultaneously assume activities of unlike kinds. These activities are not simply different, but their differences are so related as to make one another possible. The reciprocal aid thus given causes mutual dependence of the parts. And the mutually-dependent parts, living by and for one another, form an aggregate constituted on the same general principle as is an individual organism. The analogy of a society to an organism becomes still clearer on learning that every organism of appreciable size is a society; and on further learning that in both, the lives of the units continue for some time if the life of the aggregate is suddenly arrested, while if the aggregate is not destroyed by violence, its life greatly exceeds in duration the lives of its units. Though the two are contrasted as respectively discrete and concrete, and though there results a difference in the ends subserved by the organization, there does not result a difference in the laws of the organization: the required mutual influences of the parts, not transmissible in a direct way, being, in a society, transmitted in an indirect way.

Having thus considered in their most general forms the reasons for regarding a society as an organism, we are prepared for following out the comparison in detail. . . .

* * *

270. But now let us drop this alleged parallelism between individual organizations and social organizations. I have used the analogies elaborated, but as a scaffolding to help in building up a coherent body of sociological inductions. Let us take away the scaffolding: the inductions will stand by themselves.

We saw that societies are aggregates which grow; that in the various types of them there are great varieties in the growths reached; that types of successively larger sizes result from the aggregation and re-aggregation of those of smaller sizes; and that this increase by coalescence, joined with interstitial increase, is the process through which have been formed the vast civilized nations.

Along with increase of size in societies goes increase of structure. Primitive hordes are without established distinction of parts. With growth of them into tribes habitually come some unlikenesses; both in the powers and occupations of their members. Unions of tribes are followed by more unlikenesses, governmental and industrial—social grades running through the whole mass, and contrasts between the differently-occupied parts in different localities. Such differentiations multiply as the compounding progresses. They proceed from the general to the special. First the broad division between ruling and ruled; then within the ruling part divisions into political, religious, military, and within the ruled part divisions into food producing classes and handi-craftsmen; then within each of these divisions minor ones, and so on.

Passing from the structural aspect to the functional aspect, we note that so long as all parts of a society have like natures and activities, there is hardly any mutual dependence, and the aggregate scarcely forms a vital whole. As its parts assume different functions they become dependent on one another, so that injury to one hurts others; until, in highly-evolved societies, general perturbation is caused by derangement of any portion. This contrast between undeveloped and developed societies, arises from the fact that with increasing specialization of functions comes increasing inability in each part to perform the functions of other parts.

The organization of every society begins with a contrast between the division which carries on relations, habitually hostile, with environing societies, and the division which is devoted to procuring necessaries of life; and during the earlier stages of development these two divisions constitute the whole. Eventually there arises an intermediate division serving to transfer products and influences from part to part. And in all subsequent stages, evolution of the two earlier systems of structures depends on evolution of this additional system.

While the society as a whole has the character of its sustaining system determined by the character of its environment, inorganic and organic, the respective parts of this system differentiate in adaptation to local circumstances; and, after primary industries have been thus localized and specialized, secondary industries dependent on them arise in conformity with the same principle. Further, as fast as societies become compounded and re-compounded, and the distributing system develops, the parts devoted to each kind of industry, originally scattered, aggregate in the most favourable localities; and the localized industrial structures, unlike the governmental structures, grow regardless of the original lines of division.

Increase of size, resulting from the massing of groups, necessitates means of communication; both for achieving combined offensive and defensive actions, and for exchange of products. Faint tracks, then paths, rude roads, finished roads, successively arise; and as fast as intercourse is thus facilitated, there is a transition from direct barter to trading carried on by a separate class; out of which evolves a complex mercantile agency of wholesale and retail distributors. The movement of commodities effected by this agency, beginning as a slow flux to and re-flux from certain places at long intervals, passes into rhythmical, regular, rapid currents; and materials for sustentation distributed hither and thither, from being few and crude become numerous and elaborated. Growing efficiency of transfer with greater variety of transferred products, increases the mutual dependence of parts at the same time that it enables each part to fulfil its function better.

Unlike the sustaining system, evolved by converse with the organic and inorganic environments, the regulating system is evolved by converse, offensive and defensive, with environing societies. In primitive headless groups temporary chieftainship results from temporary war; chronic hostilities generate permanent chieftainship; and gradually from the military control results the civil control. Habitual war, requiring prompt combination in the actions of parts, necessitates subordination. Societies in which there is little subordination disappear, and leave outstanding those in which subordination is great; and so there are produced, societies in which the habit fostered by war and surviving in peace, brings about permanent submission to a government. The centralized regulating thus evolved, is in early stages the sole regulating system. But in large societies which have become predominantly industrial, there is added a decentralized regulating system for the industrial structures; and this, at first subject in every way to the original system, acquires at length substantial independence. Finally there arises for the distributing structures also, an independent controlling agency.

Societies fall firstly into the classes of simple, compound, doubly-compound, trebly-compound; and from the lowest the transition to the highest is through these stages. Otherwise, though less definitely, societies may be grouped as militant and industrial; of which the one type in its developed form is organized on the principle of compulsory co-operation, while the other in its developed form is organized on the principle of voluntary co-operation. The one is characterized not only by a despotic central power, but also by unlimited political control of personal conduct; while the other is characterized not only by a democratic or representative central power, but also by limitation of political control over personal conduct.

Lastly we noted the corollary that change in the predominant social activities brings metamorphosis. If, where the militant type has not elaborated into so rigid a form as to prevent change, a considerable industrial system arises, there come mitigations of the coercive restraints characterizing the militant type, and weakening of its structures. Conversely, where an industrial system largely developed has established freer social forms, resumption of offensive and defensive activities causes reversion towards the militant type.

271. And now, summing up the results of this general survey, let us observe the extent to which we are prepared by it for further inquiries.

The many facts contemplated unite in proving that social evolution forms a part of evolution at large. Like evolving aggregates in general, societies show *integration,* both by simple increase of mass and by coalescence and re-coalescence of masses. The change from *homogeneity* to *heterogeneity* is multitudinously exemplified; up from the simple tribe, alike in all its parts, to the civilized nation, full of structural and functional unlikenesses. With progressing integration and heterogeneity goes increasing *coherence.* We see the wandering group dispersing, dividing, held together by no bonds; the tribe with parts made more coherent by subordination to a dominant man; the cluster of tribes united in a political plexus under a chief with sub-chiefs; and so on up to the civilized nation, consolidated enough to hold together for a thousand years or more. Simultaneously comes increasing *definiteness.* Social organization is at first vague; advance brings settled arrangements which grow slowly more precise; customs pass into laws which, while gaining fixity, also become more specific in their applications to varieties of actions; and all institutions, at first confusedly intermingled, slowly separate, at the same time that each within itself marks off more distinctly its component structures. Thus in all respects is fulfilled the formula of evolution. There is progress towards greater size, coherence, multiformity, and definiteness.

Besides these general truths, a number of special truths have been disclosed by our survey. Comparisons of societies in their ascending grades, have made manifest certain cardinal facts respecting their growths, structures, and functions—facts respecting the systems of structures, sustaining, distributing, regulating, of which they are composed; respecting the relations of these structures to the surrounding conditions and the dominant forms of social activities entailed; and respecting the metamorphoses of types caused by changes in the activities. The inductions arrived at, thus constituting in rude outline an Empirical Sociology, show that in social phenomena there is a general order of co-existence and sequence; and that therefore social phenomena form the subject-matter of a science reducible, in some measure at least, to the deductive form.

Guided, then, by the law of evolution in general, and, in subordination to it, guided by the foregoing inductions, we are now prepared for following out the synthesis of social phenomena. We must begin with those simplest ones presented by the evolution of the family.

*Section B*

# The Elements of Social Interaction: Roles and Collectivities

EDITORIAL FOREWORD

# Interaction: Roles and Collectivities

*by Kaspar D. Naegele*

(i)

AMONG THEM, THE THREE sections of Part One of this Reader provide a view of the character of society. More than one such view is possible. For example, Emerson, the American transcendentalist, would see it as a form of mutual discovery. The Church fathers would see it as part of the sinful world. The medieval believer would see it in orders of rank ordained by God. Plato and Aristotle would combine a distinction between nature and convention with a fusion of social and political distinctions: they would see society fully embodied in the city-state.

The history of such views itself can be a part of the study of society. But the study of society is possible only with certain views of it. Our concern is with the possibility and growth of this study, entailing, we believe, efforts in *three* directions: (1) The continuous *distinction* between "normative" and "existential" questions, *so that* the *relation* between them can become evident. (2) The continuous revision of a *differentiated* view of society *both* as a reality *sui generis* and as an order involved with such other orders as those of *culture, personality* and the several realms of *nature* (from the weather to the organism). (3) The continuous balance between a view of differentiated society as *also* a *coherent* order (whatever the strategic elements of this coherence may be, such as conflict, ritual, consensus, and loyalty) *and* as an order *with a history*.

Parts Two and Three deal with many of the issues implied by the view that society is a differentiated phenomenon involving other *orders* of coherence. Part Four concerns some of the questions posed by the relation of social and other orders. All these questions cut across the Reader as a whole. They emerge from the materials that the first section of this part has just presented. Part One of this Reader is, however, primarily concerned with establishing the basic issues that confront and constitute efforts to make the study of social phenomena a scientific, and hence a cumulative enterprise. There are various kinds of cumulative enterprises. In a sense, technology is one, as are the Roman Catholic Church and language. We are concerned with the growth of explanation of facts defined as social facts. Such explanations—as distinct from wise and indispensable assertions or primarily reasoned proposals (in the realm of social phenomena)—have a shorter history than explanations in the realm of physical phenomena. We believe that the distinctions—between the questions of rightness and the questions of "so-ness" implied by the previous section—are necessary for a cumulative study of society; moreover, they probably could not have arisen until social arrangements themselves presented a certain division and rivalry of fundamental positions. We want to avoid the old fallacy, *post hoc, ergo propter hoc*. Neither the Greeks nor the Church fathers, neither the thirteenth century nor the seventeenth, really embarked on the empirical study of social phenomena. As the previous section has shown, it took the criss-cross of alternative and yet convergent positions—like those of Machiavelli and Hobbes, Smith and Malthus, Hegel and Comte, Locke and Marx, Maine and Spencer—to set the stage for work that could confront the tasks of empirical research.

It is sometimes difficult to remember this remarkable dialogue in a form helpful in solving questions we want to pose now. The Foreword to the foregoing section stressed several themes; among them, that to study social phenomena is to study, among other things, what men believe. What men believe includes their commitments to ideals. It includes, as will be discussed, a whole range of understandings and preferences concerning *appropriateness.*

Sociologists want to see what men consider appropriate, why they draw the lines of appropriateness and inappropriateness as they do, and what the consequences are of these facts. They want to see into the character of the various corporate bodies of which individuals come to see themselves as members. They want to help explain the nature of the relation that individuals have to the *public life*. This life—with its involvement in such phenomena as "the state," "the church," "society," "rights," "the community"—is constituted through invisible matters. These, however, become *represented:* in royal courts and courts of law, church buildings and banks, the stock exchange and legal documents. The first section of this Reader has presented some rival proposals for the analysis of the nature of the public life. It has dealt with some possible questions about it. It has shown how, within the same domain of questions, different thinkers, in order to raise questions at all, must assume that other matters have been provisionally answered. None of the contributors of this section, for instance, seeks to dissect "human nature": instead, they all make assumptions about it. Their view, in the main, is "outward" into the realm of the political economy, of law, of the wide divisions—like social class—of the division of labor and of authority. At the same time, they keep "the individual" in mind. They have a sense of history. We may not be able to agree with their formulations nor even understand these formulations in their authors' terms. But their formulations, somehow surrounded by the tranquility that the distance of time seems to bestow, help to give direction and root to our immediate labors, even if these must—to lead farther—assume the risks of departure. As Whitehead reminds us, "A science which hesitates to forget its founders is lost."

Still, among them, the thirteen men—and it is interesting to speculate about how equally endowed women would have formulated these matters, if in those times they had been free to do so—represent, in the medium of abstractions, a sense of the *order* and its development that *surrounds* us. In one respect, they are all *political* thinkers. Yet they recognize this surrounding order as, at least in some ways, *distinct* from the mechanical coherence of the utterly impersonal world. Though the state may be a matter of fate or of history, it is never consistently and responsibly considered as though it were in no important respects different from the weather. Similarly, yet quite unequally, there is implied in these previous selections a view of public order as an *organization:* as a coherence that comprehends such diverse matters as rulers and ruled, private interests and covenants, rival classes and alternative ways of settling economic transactions.

(ii)

Sociological analysis proceeded by applying, again and again, the distinction between concrete and analytic uses of the same term, such as "individualism" and "collectivism," to what then become recognizable as the spheres and groupings of society. A society thus becomes the matrix of kinship and religion, stratification and government, of an economy and an educational system. When seen as a historic phenomenon within the wider context of nature, it becomes the ground and resultant of the processes of work and play carried on by people who can both learn and contribute in relation to others who learn and contribute before and after them. Words like "political" and "economic" come to refer alike to the *spheres* of (national) societies with their representative institutions, electoral bodies, civil service, corporations, free or regulated enterprise, etc., *and* to the component features of the *relations* between individuals. Historically, the study of society involved a *separation* of politics, economics, and law, considered as disciplines, from the disciplined study of social relations.

This history helps to give the word "social" an ambiguity that exceeds the ambiguity of terms like "legal," "political," "economic," or "psychological." "Social" stands for those spheres of human life which are neither biological nor among these latter four. To the extent to which the first three classifications deal with specific institutions and the processes associated with them, the social then deals with the institutions "left over," e.g., voluntary associations, the kinship system, religious organizations. It soon becomes clear, however, that *any* institution has economic and political and legal features. These are understood as matters dealing with the production and distribution of resources, of power, and of legal justice respectively. Indeed, the term *social institution* thus becomes redundant, in the sense that there are no non-social institutions. This adds a further meaning to "social." It becomes a matter of two opposing concerns: with *organization* and *consensus;* and with *conduct* in the *presence* (imagined or actual) of *another* person who can (now or later) similarly act with reference to another person. In either case, "social" includes a temporal dimension which combines two features: repetition and innovation. This dimension of social facts and social arrangements will be discussed in later sections of this Reader, particularly in Part Five. Yet the historic character of all social facts, whether it be acknowledged or not, is, for the editors at least, part of the settled matter of social scientific analysis. Meanwhile, we must turn directly to the developing meaning of the term "social" itself, in order to link the analyses of public matters with the more immediately "personal" analyses provided, especially by the first two selections of this section.

Already we have distinguished four "layers" to the term "social": most generally conceived, it refers to the problem of *order* as such, as this arises through *two* facts: the mutual dependence of human beings on one another, made possible by their relative freedom from a pattern of specific instincts; and the capacity, however differently and unequally developed, to think of one's self as different from others. George Herbert Mead makes much of these facts. As facts, they raise additional questions of the mutual relations among common values, different roles, similar conduct, and consensus. As we saw in Section A, these apparently private facts of dependence and difference were seen in their public and political form by those who provided the first great impetus for the growth of knowledge concerning phenomena considered under the aspect of their social structure and development. "Social" means an inclusive order in or against which any individual acts—but without which he cannot act at all. The *forms* this order takes (*Gemeinschaft* versus *Gezellschaft*, etc.), the differentiations which can occur within it (modes of political and economic patterns, their mutual relation, etc.), and the alternate ways in which individuals can be seen to be *related* to it (under the aspect of their dependence on it, autonomy from it, contribution to it, or victimization by it) thus become chronic issues that are dealt with in every page of this Reader. In that form, "social" refers to the *coherence*—individually experienced as common membership in a historic enterprise—that can be discovered among the arrangements by which people live out their lives; and to the *severalness* of spheres and groupings that marks all but the most primitive self-sufficient groupings that can contain, in principle, the whole of the life spans of all of their members. This coherence, however, is a matter of function and of meaning. Even in its most inclusive sense, the term "social" is not free from ambiguity: it refers alike to the discoverable interconnections among arrangements, like politics and stratification, even when these connections are not perceived by those whom they affect or from whose intentions they are in fact created; *and* to the agreements marking or underlying the enterprises by which people carry on, be it in the market place or at home, in a factory or at a pub. Curiously, the social as the province of sociology required, for its systematic dissection, the *addition* of another discipline to the company of economics, political science, psychology, and anthropology. The subject matter of this discipline is old. The new material, particularly through the works of Weber and of Durkheim, was the dissection of the special character of social relations and institutions with reference to the question: What existential ideas are most necessary and suitable to analyze—and, eventually, explain—the alternative ways in which human beings organize themselves into such corporate enterprises as societies, religious groups, political parties, occupational associations, and the like?

The "additional" and "residual" characters of the social dimension—elegantly reversed by Durkheim's famous dictum that society is a reality *sui generis*—had, as we already saw, two consequences: it made of the social something that lies behind (or "in," as it might be better put today) *all* human enterprises, including those that appear to be analyzable apart from it (e.g., economic systems, political arrangements, or religious institutions); and it made accessible for respectable study those features of immediate and contemporary life which were less formal than economic, political, or legal arrangements and yet on a plane other than psychological processes of individuals.

This ambiguity of "social" suggests the second level of its meaning—its reference to the *membership* aspect of human phenomena; its reference, in other words, to the phenomenon of organization. On the first level, the experiential counterpart to the abstract notion of social was, as we have seen, the *sense of consensus* or of common commitment. On the second level, we find the sense of belonging. The first deals with a wide mold of agreements, including the agreements about "rights" to disagree. Given a variety of historic circumstance, the social on this plane may appear in the first instance as an "antithetical" matter; society as constraint ranged against the individual and his freedom. The character of the tensions between individual and collectivity have been traced in the Foreword to Section A. It was shown there that there are two different uses of this distinction; one is analytic and the other concrete. Both usages affect the progress of the study of society, even if sociology can itself grow only to the extent to which it is neutral in the moral debate about the "proper" balance among the rival claims for the enhancement and limitation of different kinds of freedom and obligations. Under the aspect of inclusive commitment, the social appears, however, as the condition of corporate or individual freedom. In this sense, analysis and experience often part company. This inclusive sense of the social is generally a matter of *a* (national) society—of a politically more or less autonomous unit in which membership is a matter of citizenship. Still, separating the terms "political" and "social," "state" and "society," was indispensable for studying society. This separation poses the fruitful problem of the alternative relations between different political and social patterns. In that case, "political" refers primarily to the distribution of "public" power, and "social," to the *range* of *different* webs of relationships (and their mutual traversibility by any one person) found within any one society. Politics constitutes a *sphere* of action within a society, while all actions within it are social. Similarly, all actions are accessible to political analysis. The political is thus gathered into a separate sphere (in one aspect called government) in a way in which the social is not—with the possible exception of sociability, about which Simmel speaks in the first selection below, which will be discussed later.

The foregoing was intended to show a link between the levels of commitment and of organization, as these terms have been used here. The terms themselves are not important. On this second plane, social refers to the "corporateness" of much human enterprise. Two variable facts immediately occur in that connection: their formality, and their size. The multiplicity of definite corporate enterprises within modern human society is an obvious fact. Most of us work in an organizational context, be it corporations, small businesses, hospitals, or educational institutions. Most of us spend some time in one or more voluntary organizations: trade unions, professional bodies, political parties, religious groupings. We can immediately think of a whole host of characteristics of these structures—among them, the fact that they can be experienced or described as structures, since in some measure they are arranged in a recurrent way. This makes the social dimension of human enterprise a chronically second fact. The first fact about such enterprises seems to be the ends they are to accomplish: the provision of work, salvation, profits, entertainment, edification, security. Their pursuit usually involves some order of *concerted* activity, which constitutes the social character of human enterprise. It always involves coherence and differentiation. One aspect of the latter is the establishment of a boundary, however permeable, between being part of a social system and being outside it. Another aspect is the phenomenon of the division of labor, responsibility, and power that is part of any organization.

These issues will be more systematically treated elsewhere in this Reader. At present, we are concerned only with seeing the emergent aspect of the social dimension of phenomena. While pursuing their ends, men establish relations with one another that confront them with further issues. These issues bear no simple relations to the ends whose pursuit brought them into prominence. They arise out of an irreducible set of exigencies created when two or more persons want to *sustain* (or impose), on themselves or others, an arrangement affecting conduct. In that respect, the social aspect of phenomena involves the settlement of a variety of issues, including how the ends and the rules governing the means necessary to implement such ends should be related. Ends can be various—e.g., the attainment of salvation, maximization of profit, insurance against premature death, accomplishment of national independence. Should they be committed to paper (in the form of written constitutions, contracts, etc.)? Should they be "left" to general consensus? Or, in other words: organizations become comprehensible only to the extent they are perceived as historic arrangements involved in pursuing ends that necessarily exceed the ends that they set themselves. In that respect, ostensibly dissimilar social systems, such as the Roman Catholic Church and General Motors, are necessarily involved in solving quite similar issues. Social organizations may be compared to musical compositions: the elements of their composition are few; their alternative combinations are many.

We have made a double shift. We began with the notion of the social applicable to that order in which one participates as a citizen. In one respect, it is this order to which the first selections were ultimately addressed. It is the order in which the political and social meet most completely. Yet for all their generality and invisibility and consequent reliance on mediation through various symbols—from flags to anthems to votes—subsequent thought has tended to consider national societies as a particular instance of a more general and more "analytic" usage of "social." Sociology, after all, began in a complex society. Persistent coherences involving the notion of membership—sometimes referred to as social systems—thus become the major illustrative phenomena through which the term "social" received its distinct meaning. Social systems are less inclusive than societies, concretely speaking, and more inclusive, logically speaking. All societies are examples of social systems; but the reverse does not hold. Social systems, moreover, are obviously not of a piece, as Part Two of the Reader shows. Quite apart from their ends, groups vary in their corporateness and their size, and also in the coincidence or limitation of grounds on which they establish their inclusiveness or their exclusiveness. Circles of friends, cabals, secret societies, sects, seminars—all these are forms of social groupings, which are also sometimes parts of more encompassing and more formal organizations.

It is time to move to the third plane on this framework. If our readings had begun with the Greeks, we would have seen that they confined "social" to the realm of private and "natural" bonds, and that there was thus a contrast between the social and political realms. In time, a horizontal distinction has become a vertical one.[1] The distinctions between private and public, social and political, have had to be rearranged. The status of the terms of these distinctions has become complicated by the difference, applicable to them all, between their "analytic" and "concrete" uses. By this logic, each of these terms refers alike to *realms of* activities and to *elements in* the relations among men. Other distinctions have been added—e.g., those between formal and informal, communal and associational. Yet ultimately, "social" always stands for a nexus. This Reader begins with writers who have contributed to a tradition of thought which would claim this nexus to be fully intelligible in its own right. Unless properly qualified, this statement may easily claim too much. The "social," as that which is given by the fact that human beings sustain relations to one another regardless of what these relations are about, obviously *involves* the psychological dispositions of the parties to such relations. The nature of this involvement is taken up in Part Three. The Introduction to that part will also discuss whether "social" considerations can be reduced to "psychological" ones. Similarly, Part Four will show that social relations involve commitments to normative and existential ideas. These always involve some form of "ultimacy" and hence of belief, including religious positions. Yet it is inherent, in the distinctions and proposals that make up this Reader, that the relations among men and the connections arising from them are comprehensible without commitments to specific religious (non-empirical) positions—even if such commitments are themselves to be taken seriously in any attempt at accounting for the genesis, maintenance, and change characterizing these relations. Furthermore, though the social is constituted by relatedness, relatedness obviously takes more than a social form. It can be logical, meaningful, stylistic, mechanical, spacial, temporal, and so forth. Watches sustain no social relations to arms, nor do wheels to carts.

A nexus is social, then, to the degree to which it involves the possibilities and facts of *mutual* orientation by two or more people. Such mutual orientation is always "about something": employment, love, common beliefs, feuds. Like any bonds, these require their appropriate occasions: conversation, exchange of goods and money, obedience to orders, formulation of policy, declaration of love. They require enactment, occurring within the confines of time and space, within some created situation, recurrent or new. Yet social relations are less confined than social situations: they have a past and a future. Social situations are the necessary *samples* of the (changing) character of someone's relation to his brother or his boss or his father or his son. These relations, while created only in the occasions without which we cannot act, are not a matter only of these occasions. Their qualities of love and hate, inclusiveness and limitation, intensity or peripheralness, exceed the possibilities of any one occasion and require a succession of occasions. The character of this succession requires resources that are not fully contained in any one social occasion. Respect for an expert and affection for a father, dependence on an employer and love for a woman—these are examples of *social* relations. They are *known,* to their parties or their observers, only within the disclosures contained by particular occasions. Yet they are *constituted* by acts and memories, commitments and expectations, ideas and feelings, which do not disappear with the situation in which they are displayed and are not always displayed on every occasion. On this plane, moreover, the "social" appears as the generic feature of *all* human relations. The latter involve some reciprocity of two or more people whose *difference,* as individuals, is in some measure also an aspect of their mutual involvement. In that sense the "social" is a very open concept: it includes relations of conflict and of cooperation; arrangements that are exclusive—like emotions; and arrangements of coherence that are, in principle, indefinitely inclusive, as, e.g., recognizing another as a human being.

The fourth plane of "social" is now apparent. Social relations are constituted through social acts. To act is to make a difference; to act socially is to make this difference with some intended reference to another person or category or collectivity about whom one believes (or knows) that now or later (if not previously) he too can act socially.

The wider detour is now complete. It was necessary in order to remember the drastic difference between the characters of the dissections of social and individual life demonstrated in the works of most of the authors from whose writings the rest of the Reader has been selected and the work which constitutes the first section. The distinction is not invidious. It concerns merely the relative emphasis, beginning primarily with Weber and Durkheim, on

1. For many illuminating observations on this and diverse related matters, see, in particular, Hannah Arendt's beautiful book, *The Human Condition* (Chicago: University of Chicago Press, 1958).

a pattern of concepts which can guide specific efforts of research. Ideally, such research would *explain* discoverable relations within or among the several planes of socialness that the previous discussion has suggested.

The difference is not absolute. It is accompanied by important, though easily forgotten *continuities* between the more autonomous and self-contained claims and interpretations of the thinkers of the nineteenth, eighteenth, and seventeenth centuries, and those of the twentieth. The continuities lie in the plane of the questions asked and the distinctions proposed to enable someone to find an answer. To ask about government and its functions, about the structure of status or contract, or about the significance of sovereignty, is, after all, to have a phenomenon already in view. Questions presuppose answers to previous questions.

Three of the selections in this section are concerned with the two last planes of the social—relatedness, and action. They almost constitute a triangle, with Mead's account and Weber's definition as the two corners of the base. Simmel's dissection of one type of occasion is a more concrete exercise in analyzing the mutual involvement of concepts dealing with social relations, roles, acts, and actors. In the following section we move toward and on the two other planes, social organization and society. The discussion continues thus, being at the same time much involved in the further dissection of the structure of social relations. Chronology, from now on, is likely to be in reverse order. Contributions are grouped around themes and arranged in some succession of logical priority. In the main, our ordering is intended to be continuous with the more general proposals of the two introductory essays at the beginning of the Reader.

(iii)

Simmel asked about society what Kant asked about knowledge: how is it possible? Hidden in such a question, even though it may be an attempt to leave it behind, is usually the additional question: *What* is society like? Spencer has already provided one explicit answer to this question. Simmel has been discussed at perhaps too great length in one of the introductory essays. The selection used here is one attempt to state the generic character of the "social." To do so, it makes use of a most important group of distinctions, those inherent in the fact that, in relating to one another for any reason, we must make use, simultaneously, of both ideas and feelings. These create contrasts, as well as themselves being part of the contrast between two or more persons that the notion of social relation implies.

In Western tradition, contrasts are usually expressed as dichotomies: essence and accident, body and mind, environment and heredity, true and false, absolute and relative. This tendency toward dualism provides much opportunity for efforts to dissolve these as mere artifacts of language. There is, for instance, no heredity without an environment, and vice versa. For many people, willing to grant the *difference* between ideas and matter, this is again a contrast which at least, from the point of view of ideas, depends on the existence of the other side. An extraordinary amount has been written about these issues. Yet all known societies —however differently they might view them—recognize many contrasts, such as those of day and night, old and young, male and female. They may think of them as matters of degree, as variations on a few themes. They may consider them as embodied, as the previous contrasts are, in diurnal, anatomic, and physiological differentiation of nature itself. Embodiment, however, is an ambiguous term; it leaves undistinguished, e.g., the extent to which the contrast between male and female is given by the fact that human bodies "come" in two forms or by the fact that as a contrast, it is socially elaborated within the limits of these forms but not in a uniform manner. One may also think of contrasts in a number of spheres: landscapes, cities, culture, lines of work, periods in a lifetime. One may think of them as alternatives or as complements.

Male and female are not alternatives for individuals. They are stubborn contrasts. As "roles," with certain exceptions, they are virtually social absolutes, paralleling in their immutability within any one society the more general immutability of anatomy and biological function.

Simmel addresses himself to a different order of contrast: that between art or play, and "reality" (real life). To a degree, this is an exercise in applying a distinction which plays a cardinal role in all his work: the distinction between form and content. In some ways this is not too fortunate a distinction; or, at least, it is not too fortunate a definition of it, especially since we think of form as "empty" or as "outside," much as we think of the bowl containing the rising dough. This is not what is meant. Forms, like play, conflict, or subordination, are both modes of association among people and elements within any association. In the second capacity, they vary in their importance in relation to the other elements with which they help constitute any specific social constellation, be it a specific occasion or some durable organization.

Simmel is neither consistent nor systematic in this regard. Yet he introduces a far-reaching reminder of a chronic contrast in social affairs: the contrast between the concatenated events of real and everyday life and the more isolated occasions of play, as these parallel the contrast between daily actions of work and sleep and the phenomena of art. The selection will speak for itself. The contrast on which it depends is certainly an ambiguous one, for it involves the relations and differences between such terms as serious, real, and consequential, and playful, fictitious, and isolated. One specific form of this contrast—the divergence between the round of life and drama, as one representation of life—has been most influential in a great deal of sociological analysis. The next selection from Mead's work also shows this. The weakness of contrasting play and life or art and life is in the first instance a logical one, since life presumably includes what is said to differ from it. Substantively, however, the essay (originally a lecture) brings to the fore a variety of questions and themes that, from now on, will in different fashion be part of most of the other selections of this Reader.

Schematically described, these questions and themes include the following:

*The differentiation of society.* The selection suggests that the occasion of sociability differs from other occasions. This is self-evident. Yet through Simmel's eyes, and thence through the compounded interpretations that can extend farther what he saw with them, this difference can become fruitfully problematic. It is a difference among the differences of social occasions. These, as already suggested, are samples of social arrangements: necessary and particular encounters in definite places and at definite times, which include, in their meaning both to those included and, potentially, to many then excluded, commitments and consequences that transcend them. The differentiation of occasions within society proceeds along a variety of axes. Simmel, in the present instance, is concerned with the relative prominence of the motive of association for its own sake. Occasions differ, in other words, precisely in the manner in which their social encounters are means or ends. They differ, further, in either sphere. They can be means to the ends of bargaining or cure, learning or eating. Their ends can involve play or ritual. The chances are that any occasion contains *all* the basic themes—but in a typical combination. The differentiation of occasions, moreover, requires certain conditions. In the case of sociability, it requires notions of guest and host. These are terms for social roles; individuals are differentiated—reciprocally, to some extent, to social arrangements—by a set or repertoire of roles. This is a plausible observation, but one which theoretically has turned out to be as fruitful as it is equivocal. The same individual, on different occasions, can be host or guest. Yet the occasions of sociability require the difference between guest and host. The selection suggests, therefore, that in the term "role," whatever difficulty there may be in reaching consensus and clarity about its definition, we may have a way to spring the trap of the long dialogue concerning the relation between individuals and their circles, groups, and institutional contexts.

Simmel introduces another aspect of differentiation, that between form and motive—how one behaves at a party is one question; why one goes is another. The same occasion can include a variety of motives, yet it imposes limits on their expression—while also, conceivably, producing or liberating motives which were not wittingly, at least, part of one's reasons for coming.

Simmel emphasizes the "isolation" of sociability from all other spheres of activity. He conceives this isolation to be part of its meaning to its participants. Without taking pains to make the distinction persistent, he combines, in his analysis, an attempt to represent the concrete meanings the social occasion of sociability has for its participants with the question of what analytic distinctions are needed by me as an observer, to observe and state the character of social interaction between people at a party which allow me to describe what goes on and to account for what does not go on. In another essay (not included in this Reader), he complements his present emphasis by an analysis of the meal. We all must eat, but how and with whom and when and what we eat are social questions. Their answers help the process of differentiating the social from a natural order.

There are several planes to the concern with differentiation: it applies to the differences *between* social and non-social facts; the differences (in occasions, roles, and, as we shall see, institutional patterns) *within and among* social systems; and to the differences between the patterns of distinctions which as persons and citizens we *need* or *create* as we *live* and act within societies, and the pattern of distinctions we require in order to *account* for social facts. Having to do with *inter*-action or with mutual expectation, social facts ultimately always involve a severalness that points to a relation, but a relation with an "inwardness." Yet the complementary or parallel inwardness of guests and host are addressed to conversation or to games—to activities seriously limiting the simultaneous pursuit of other kinds of activities, except eating, dancing, or singing. More than that, Simmel attributes to this particular occasion an element of *fictitiousness.*

*The representational character of society.* Fictitiousness is one aspect of the phenomenon of symbolism. Mead, in the next selection, will return to the question of gestures and symbols, just as Durkheim in another selection writes about representations. Play and art are other cognate phenomena. Societies are deeply affected by the stubborn realities of the material, including the organic, world. The facts that we have only two eyes, that we walk upright, that we have to eat, that we must die, that we are not, as a rule, born in litters, etc., are deep in the arrangements by which we carry on. Our carrying on also involves ideas and beliefs, agreements and disagreements. Our experience implies awareness, which necessarily involves a recognition of what is so and of what could be so. Recognition of the possible carries the implication of fiction, which is facilitated by the paradox that our relations to one another involve our differences. Differences among people involve the recognition of varieties of experience—and these varieties, in becoming known, form the other side of our recognition of the difference between an inwardness and an outwardness. It is one of several kinds of discrepancies related to one another. We do not or cannot always say what we mean, do what we intend, or want what we have. Besides, what binds us in our differences has to transcend these, as symbols and art do. Through them, we express and elaborate the contrast between word and thing, actual and possible, or real and fictitious. Since symbols and art are part of the real world—in that people cannot move in that world without them—it follows that what we call social intercourse requires the use of metaphor and analogy. The social and the use of expression become mutually implicated. But self-expression—just talking to another, reading a story, etc.—a form of social action, as we shall discuss presently, is also an element, in another sense, of all actions. In this way, the social and the self-expressive introduce a contrast. Further, social occasions differ from one another by virtue of the order of contrast each assumes toward all other occasions.

*The coherence of society.* Simmel's analysis of sociability also indicates the role in social occasions of what others have called the common definition of the situation. This combines host and guests, though their respective roles differ. Simmel does not use the word "role," but he describes its phenomena. Any one role always implies at least one other with which it somehow becomes reciprocal. There can be no host without guests. Such differentiation also relates them. Simmel sees the differentiation of roles as a way by which occasions hang together; he also indicates, in this selection, the importance of agreed standards. Though he says little about them, such standards include the notion of invitation. The occasion coheres by virtue of the absence of the uninvited.

Simmel treats sociability as an occasion to be analyzed in its own right. He could have asked questions about the contribution of such occasions to other social arrangements, or he could have asked about the history of sociability and the shifts within it in some given society. In the West, at least, this is one occasion in which one combines the fictions that Simmel indicates with being absorbed by the occasion. It may be true that sociability demands that its guests and hosts be deliberately restricted in their involvement: "doing business," "talking shop," displaying one's personal problems—potentially any of these may be inappropriate. Yet, by its freedom from the serious and consequential life, sociability also constitutes a form of freedom. Since it is an occasion addressed to mutual conversation, the freedom generated within it—however stylized its expression—would become expressive of one's personality. It is not fortuitous that the man who wrote about sociability also wrote about letter writing. For the reasons above, the study of sociable occasions by participant observers would seem doubly inappropriate. Simmel's analysis is a speculative conspectus. It provides perspective; it moves into manageable focus the contrasts of serious and playful, and real and fictitious, without which the study of society may easily become trivial and false. It establishes links between the work of the artist and the scientist, without confusing them.

The selection from George Herbert Mead deals with an old problem: the phenomenon of the self. Nietzsche spoke of it as a grammatical illusion. As it stands, the sense of the self, with its inevitable indication of a cognate sense of being different from others, would appear to limit sociological analysis as such. Mead meets the problem directly, by conceiving the self as itself a social phenomenon. There are various ways of understanding his analysis. As we read it today, fortified by Freud and others, we may find it impossible to assess the full import of Mead's analysis. It is deeply influenced by the cardinal importance of communication, particularly of language. The concern with communication in this sense is a peculiarly modern one, though the study of language is certainly old, Mead seeks to cope with the experienced contrast of self and group, or self and others, by starting with the very character of this contrast and considering it as comprehending what, from the point of view of any one person, appear as gaps and divergences.

In previous selections, the divergence between self and organization, self and society, or self and state was primarily considered as one aspect of the question of order. It thus is, in this case, a moral problem. In Mead's case, it is primarily considered as a cognitive matter. He wants to know how it occurs that I think of myself *as* myself. He takes seriously the observation that I can, in fact, think of myself. I can make myself my own object. In that respect, I am a duality. The duality of I and Other has its emergent counterpart in the duality of I and Me, about which the selection speaks in detail. From that point of view, the self as the seat of one's aloneness, of one's irreducible sense of difference from all others, is indeed a social emergent. We think of ourselves precisely because, in the company of others, we have learned to think of ourselves as they think of us. They think of us as they have learned to think of themselves, namely, as persons each of whom has a self. As we internalize their view of us, we become linked to them in a web of relations, and aware that we are different from them. Our very sense of difference is, then, a social product.

Today, this account has ramifications in several directions. It may be associated with some of the observations on the patterns of inner striving and equilibrium that Freud and others have indicated. It might also be suggested that we do not think of ourselves as others think of us, but as we *think* others think of us. Still, Mead's questions and proposals belong to the chronic and ultimate issues that are revealed by any persistent thought about the possibilities of studying society.

The *self* may be one of those concepts about which there cannot be any clear consensus and without which much social research cannot proceed. Mead certainly addressed himself to some very fundamental and very immediate issues when he inquired about the self. He asked, as suggested, because he was very much impressed by the pervasive importance of social phenomena, which he felt were the necessary matrix for *any* thought. He began to think about not only the self, but also about symbolism as one aspect of the wider phenomenon of communication. A concern with gestures as well as with language became central for him. The fertile puzzle of conversations as accomplished facts was his working grounds.

Mead had predecessors—Baldwin and Cooley, especially, in the sociological tradition. (If not for the space limitations in this Reader, it would have included more writings from these authors.) Their important contributions were, logically at least, incorporated in Mead's analysis of the self and its emergent character. This emergence provided incisive commentaries about the distinction between play and games. When Simmel, in the earlier selection, discusses sociability as a play form of society, he means what Mead, in the present selection, would discuss as the *game*. The game is play with shared rules. Thus, again and again, perceptions of similar phenomena by two different people become mutually disconnected through the use of different terms.

Mead, unlike Simmel, goes into detail about the concept of role. The self is constituted in the act of adopting attitudes of others. I assume them, I perceive as they perceive. In a measure, to perceive as they do is to be them. To be another is to play his role—play, for they take it seriously that we are not them. For Mead, it follows from all this that there is no human nature outside society. The mind and the self "are without residue social emergents." This is made possible by language, in the broadest sense of that term. Language mediates. Language, as Mead says, is a principle of social organization making the distinctively human society possible. Mead links this possibility closely with the facts of the organism, including, in the human case, the dependence of the organism on other organisms and on an environing context in which organisms are sustained. One might conceivably call Mead a biosocial theorist.

Mead's formulations provide as many solutions as they do problems. The I and the Me are perceived as engaged in an inner dialogue to which the I contributes an unpredictable and creative element. The Me is an ambiguous concept, compounded of the I as object, and of the incorporated social attitudes. The "generalized other," as a term, opens many vistas for the way in which we structure our social world, though it obscures some distinctions made by other thinkers. We would distinguish between persons and patterns within the social world; or between a meaningful world, to which we can respond because it responds to us, and a wider environment, which we must treat as though it were not human.

Mead's belief in the "normalcy of multiple personality" may parallel in importance Durkheim's concept of the normalcy of crime. In any case, this selection represents part of the thought of a man who, perhaps more than any other, has helped define the opportunities of social psychology. He proposes the dimensions that help constitute the facts of someone's action when he is in the presence of others.

The selection by Max Weber begins with the concept of social act. Weber clarifies and begins to classify the concept of social action, which is logically part of any sociological analysis. As such, the phenomenon of social action has really not been subject to much direct research, possibly because actions are both the immediate events of social arrangements and the ultimate facts to which one can refer them.

As events, social actions are a particular class. Max Weber proposes a way of describing the anatomy of this class as well as the forms that social actions can take. Judged by their languages, all known human societies recognize action. From a sociological perspective, actions become relevant when they occur with reference to another person. Social acts are more easily analyzed and classified than circumscribed. They imply an agent whose presence makes some difference to another agent with whom he shares the particular occasion, or else whose conduct within an occasion he considers to be affected by the presence of that other agent. Such presence may be imaginary. Without agents there are no acts, but acting is only one kind of accomplishment of a particular actor, an accomplishment involving some order of intent. The nature of the relation between agents and their acts is far from simple. Today we would speak of unconscious and conscious acts, of acts involving responsibility and of acts not involving it. The concept *agent* has ceased to be simple. Agents are perceived as subject to influence, just as acts, in Weber's discussion, are seen to be unequally related to matters of tradition, impulse, interest, custom, etc. In line with Mead's reasoning, acts may be considered as both outward and inward phenomena—then the distinction between contemplation and action is one of a classification of actions as such. Similarly, in their structure, actions involve some distinction between ends and means; yet acts differ in the relation between means and ends. The distinction may well be applicable to all acts; but we would recognize a difference between shaking someone's hand, and putting money into his hand because we define him as a salesman in a department store. From one point of view, both actions are means; but they stand for quite different relations between the two persons in the two cases. In the first instance, we may, as Simmel did in the first selection, speak about an association for its own sake. In its context, the handshake is a gesture of recognizing this association. In the second case, we can speak about an economic transaction: it involves one person's relation to another as primarily a means. The consideration of social actions thus raises virtually the whole range of questions which link the variety of selections within this bulky Reader. Moreover, it is not clear, except to the extent to which we do not think about it pedantically, where actions begin and stop. Nor is it clear what we mean by the difference between who one is and what one does, once actions are perceived as the accomplishments of agents. Still, as Linton and others indicate in the next section, for social arrangements, the distinction between person and actor is strategic.

These selections, then, share a concern with those phenomena which appear when one considers immediate encounters between two or more persons. Each represents a group of explicit proposals surrounded by tacit assumptions and recognitions. Mead suggests that social phenomena are facilitated by language, the instrument of meaning *par excellence. Social* phenomena imply the issues of meaning. Weber and Simmel point, in particular, to the normative aspects of meaning with regard to their strategic significance for the possibilities of social interaction. The normative, as the dimension of appropriateness and inappropriateness, is the ground for characterizing the differences between occasions, between roles, or between one social system and another. Appropriateness includes not only the matter of the ends that people seek or with which they begin their seeking (whatever new ends may then appear to them). It refers also to the question of means by which, within given occasions, they hope to accomplish some end. Democracy as a pattern of equality becomes the means for the apparent purity of association within occasions of sociability.

The obviousness of a handshake, of a cocktail party, of a conversation among two or three people —these would seem, at first thought, to be ill served by such abstraction. Yet the questions of how these occasions are possible, what kinds of occasions one can possibly distinguish, and how one can account for their occurrence and their sequences, require this detour to the platform of more general ideas, from which one can then return to the occasions of social life.

The third selection, from Marcel Mauss's essay on *The Gift,* deals with social reciprocity as it transcends particular encounters among individuals in each other's presence. Mauss sees society contained by the obligations of giving and receiving. We may think of receiving—in contrast to giving— as a privilege; yet as we know from our experience of unwelcome invitations or presents, they too must be "received." Reciprocity, then, proceeds with reference to three obligations: to give, to receive, and to repay.

Mauss makes two further points. Gifts seem to stand in sharp, even moral, contrast to self-interested and calculating acts. Unlike the latter, they seem to represent spontaneous and disinterested concerns. This contrast raises the old and persistent question of self-interest. Mauss argues that if by economically self-interested activities we refer to utilitarian and rational calculations, then the previous contrast is by no means simple. Gifts are not just spontaneous. They represent the recognition, at least, of ultimate obligations and sanctions. Further, gifts typically take a material form. They are part of an on-going process of exchange. The medium of exchange may be concrete and calculable. The meaning of exchange, however, involves personal intentions and social agreements. Thus, economic acts have kinship with gifts, and gifts contain economic elements.

In other words, a society must traffic in things: "everything is stuff to be given away and repaid." But this exchange issues from persons; and these persons are not simply individuals in their own right—they are also representatives and members of various corporate groupings whose character further affects the process of exchange. By linking material and nonmaterial, spontaneous and obligatory, immediately reciprocal and enduringly consequential *aspects* of social interaction, Mauss fittingly rounds out this Section of the Reader.

# *1. The Sociology of Sociability*

BY GEORG SIMMEL

THERE IS an old conflict over the nature of society. One side mystically exaggerates its significance, contending that only through society is human life endowed with reality. The other regards it as a mere abstract concept by means of which the observer draws the realities, which are individual human beings, into a whole, as one calls trees and brooks, houses and meadows, a "landscape." However one decides this conflict, he must allow society to be a reality in a double sense. On the one hand are the individuals in their directly perceptible existence, the bearers of the processes of association, who are united by these processes into the higher unity which one calls "society"; on the other hand, the interests which, living in the individuals, motivate such union: economic and ideal interests, warlike and erotic, religious and charitable. To satisfy such urges and to attain such purposes, arise the innumerable forms of social life, all the with-one-another, for-one-another, in-one-another, against-one-another, and through-one-another, in state and commune, in church and economic associations, in family and clubs. The energy effects of atoms upon each other bring matter into the innumerable forms which we see as "things." Just so the impulses and interests, which a man experiences in himself and which push him out toward other men, bring about all the forms of association by which a mere sum of separate individuals are made into a "society."

Within this constellation, called society, or out of it, there develops a special sociological structure corresponding to those of art and play, which draw their form from these realities but nevertheless leave their reality behind them. It may be an open question whether the concept of a play impulse or an artistic impulse possesses explanatory value; at least it directs attention to the fact that in every play or artistic activity there is contained a common element not affected by their differences of content. Some residue of satisfaction lies in gymnastics, as in card-playing, in music, and in plastic, something which has nothing to do with the peculiarities of music or plastic as such but only with the fact that both of the latter are art and both of the former are play. A common element, a likeness of psychological reaction and need, is found in all these various things—something easily distinguishable from the special interest which gives each its distinction. In the same

Reprinted from Georg Simmel, "The Sociology of Sociability," trans. Everett C. Hughes, *American Journal of Sociology,* LV, No. 3 (November, 1949), 254–61, by permission of the University of Chicago Press. Copyright 1949 by the University of Chicago. A translation of "Soziologie der Geselligkeit," the opening speech at the first meeting of the German Sociological Society (*Verhandlungen des Ersten Deutschen Soziologentages vom 19–20 Oktober, 1910, in Frankfurt A.M.* [Tübingen: J. C. B. Mohr, 1911], pp. 1–16).

sense one may speak of an impulse to sociability in man. To be sure, it is for the sake of special needs and interests that men unite in economic associations or blood fraternities, in cult societies or robber bands. But, above and beyond their special content, all these associations are accompanied by a feeling for, by a satisfaction in, the very fact that one is associated with others and that the solitariness of the individual is resolved into togetherness, a union with others. Of course, this feeling can, in individual cases, be nullified by contrary psychological factors; association can be felt as a mere burden, endured for the sake of our objective aims. But typically there is involved in all effective motives for association a feeling of the worth of association as such, a drive which presses toward this form of existence and often only later calls forth that objective content which carries the particular association along. And as that which I have called artistic impulse draws its form from the complexes of perceivable things and builds this form into a special structure corresponding to the artistic impulse, so also the impulse to sociability distils, as it were, out of the realities of social life the pure essence of association, of the associative process as a value and a satisfaction. It thereby constitutes what we call sociability in the narrower sense. It is no mere accident of language that all sociability, even the purely spontaneous, if it is to have meaning and stability, lays such great value on form, on good form. For "good form" is mutual self-definition, interaction of the elements, through which a unity is made; and since in sociability the concrete motives bound up with life-goals fall away, so must the pure form, the free-playing, interacting interdependence of individuals stand out so much the more strongly and operate with so much the greater effect.

And what joins art with play now appears in the likeness of both to sociability. From the realities of life play draws its great, essential themes: the chase and cunning; the proving of physical and mental powers, the contest and reliance on chance and the favor of forces which one cannot influence. Freed of substance, through which these activities make up the seriousness of life, play gets its cheerfulness but also that symbolic significance which distinguishes it from pure pastime. And just this will show itself more and more as the essence of sociability; that it makes up its substance from numerous fundamental forms of serious relationships among men, a substance, however, spared the frictional relations of real life; but out of its formal relations to real life, sociability (and the more so as it approaches pure sociability) takes on a symbolically playing fulness of life and a significance which a superficial rationalism always seeks only in the content. Rationalism, finding no content there, seeks to do away with sociability as empty idleness, as did the savant who asked concerning a work of art, "What does that prove?" It is nevertheless not without significance that in many, perhaps in all, European languages, the word "society" (Gesellschaft) indicates literally "togetherness." The political, economic, the society held together by some purpose is, nevertheless, always "society." But only the sociable is a "society" without qualifying adjective, because it alone presents the pure, abstract play of form, all the specific contents of the one-sided and qualified societies being dissolved away.

Sociability is, then, the play-form of association and is related to the content-determined concreteness of association as art is related to reality. Now the great problem of association comes to a solution possible only in sociability. The problem is that of the measure of significance and accent which belongs to the individual as such in and as against the social milieu. Since sociability in its pure form has no ulterior end, no content, and no result outside itself, it is oriented completely about personalities. Since nothing but the satisfaction of the impulse to sociability—although with a resonance left over—is to be gained, the process remains, in its conditions as in its results, strictly limited to its personal bearers; the personal traits of amiability, breeding, cordiality, and attractiveness of all kinds determine the character of purely sociable association. But precisely because all is oriented about them, the personalities must not emphasize themselves too individually. Where real interests, co-operating or clashing, determine the social form, they provide of themselves that the individual shall not present his peculiarities and individuality with too much abandon and aggressiveness. But where this restraint is wanting, if association is to be possible at all, there must prevail another restriction of personal pushing, a restriction springing solely out of the form of the association. It is for this reason that the sense of tact is of such special significance in society, for it guides the self-regulation of the individual in his personal relations to others where no outer or directly egoistic interests provide regulation. And perhaps it is the specific function of tact to mark out for individual impulsiveness, for the ego and for outward demands, those limits which the rights of others require. A very remarkable sociological structure appears at this point. In sociability, whatever the personality has of objective importance, of features which have their orientation toward something outside the circle, must not interfere. Riches and social position, learning and fame, exceptional capacities and merits of the individual have no role in sociability or, at most, as a slight nuance of that immateriality with which alone reality dares penetrate into the artificial structure of sociability. As these objective qualities which gather about the personality, so also must the most purely and deeply personal qualities be excluded from sociability. The most personal things—character, mood, and fate—have thus no place in it. It is tactless to bring in personal humor, good or ill, excitement and depression, the light and shadow of one's inner life. Where a connection, begun on the sociable level—and not necessarily a superficial or conventional one—finally comes to center about personal values, it loses the essential quality of sociability and becomes an association determined by a content—not unlike a business or religious relation, for which contact, exchange, and speech are but instruments for ulterior ends, while for sociability they are the whole meaning and content of the social processes. This exclusion of the personal reaches into even the most external matters; a lady would not want to appear in such extreme *décolletage* in a really personal, intimately friendly situation with one or two men as she would in a large company without any embarrassment. In the latter she would not feel herself personally involved in the same measure and could therefore abandon herself to the impersonal freedom of the mask. For she is, in the larger company, herself, to be sure, but not quite completely herself, since she is only an element in a formally constituted gathering.

A man, taken as a whole, is, so to speak, a somewhat unformed complex of contents, powers, potentialities; only according to the motivations and relationships of a changing existence is he articulated into a differentiated, defined structure. As an economic and political agent, as a member of a family or of a profession, he is, so to speak, an *ad hoc* construction; his life-material is ever determined by a special idea, poured into a special mold, whose relatively independent life is, to be sure, nourished from the common but somewhat undefinable source of energy, the ego. In this sense, the man, as a social creature, is also a unique structure, occurring in no other connection. On the one hand, he has removed all the objective qualities of the personality and entered into the structure of sociability with nothing but the capacities, attractions, and interests of his pure humanity. On the other hand, this structure stops short of the purely subjective and inward parts of his personality. That discretion which is one's first demand upon others in sociability is also required of one's own ego, because a breach of it in either direction causes the sociological artifact of sociability to break down into a sociological naturalism. One can therefore speak of an upper and a lower sociability threshold for the individual. At the moment when people direct their association toward objective content and purpose, as well as at the moment when the absolutely personal and subjective matters of the individual enter freely into the phenomenon, sociability is no longer the central and controlling principle but at most a formalistic and outwardly instrumental principle.

From this negative definition of the nature of sociability through boundaries and thresholds, however, one can perhaps find the positive motif. Kant set it up as the principle of law that everyone should have that measure of freedom which could exist along with the freedom of every other person. If one stands by the sociability impulse as the source or also as the substance of sociability, the following is the principle according to which it is constituted: everyone should have as much satisfaction of this impulse as is consonant with the satisfaction of the impulse for all others. If one expresses this not in terms of the impulse but rather in terms of success, the principle of sociability may be formulated thus: everyone should guarantee to the other that maximum of sociable values (joy, relief, vivacity) which is consonant with the maximum of values he himself receives. As justice upon the Kantian basis is thoroughly democratic, so likewise this principle shows the democratic structure of all sociability, which to be sure every social stratum can realize only within itself, and which so often makes sociability between members of different social classes burdensome and painful. But even among social equals the democracy of their sociability is a play. Sociability creates, if one will, an ideal sociological world, for in it—so say the enunciated principles—the pleasure of the individual is always contingent upon the joy of others; here, by definition, no one can have his satisfaction at the cost of contrary experiences on the part of others. In other forms of association such lack of reciprocity is excluded only by the ethical imperative which govern them but not by their own immanent nature. This world of sociability, the only one in which a democracy of equals is possible without friction, is an *artificial* world, made up of beings who have renounced both the objective and the purely personal features of the intensity and extensiveness of life in order to bring about among themselves a pure interaction, free of any disturbing material accent. If we now have the conception that we enter into sociability purely as "human beings," as that which we really are, lacking all the burdens, the agitations, the inequalities with which real life disturbs the purity of our picture, it is because modern life is overburdened with objective content and material demands. Ridding ourselves of this burden in sociable circles, we believe we return to our natural-personal being and overlook the fact that this personal aspect also does not consist in its full uniqueness and natural completeness, but only in a certain reserve and stylizing of the sociable man. In earlier epochs, when a man did not depend so much upon the purposive, objective content of his associations, his "formal personality" stood out more clearly against his personal existence: hence personal bearing in the society of earlier times was much more ceremonially rigidly and impersonally regulated than now. This reduction of the personal periphery of the measure of significance which homogeneous interaction with others allowed the individual has been followed by a swing to the opposite extreme; a specific attitude in society is that courtesy by which the strong, outstanding person not only places himself on a level with the weaker but goes so far as to assume the attitude that the weaker is the more worthy and superior. If association is interaction at all, it appears in its purest and most stylized form when it goes on among equals, just as symmetry and balance are the most outstanding forms of artistic stylizing of visible elements. Inasmuch as sociability is the abstraction of association—an abstraction of the character of art or of play—it demands the purest, most transparent, most engaging kind of interaction—that among *equals*. It must, because of its very nature, posit beings who give up so much of their objective content, who are so modified in both their outward and their inner significance, that they are sociably equal, and every one of them can win sociability values for himself only under the condition that the others, interacting with him, can also win them. It is a game in which one "acts" as though all were equal, as though he especially esteemed everyone. This is just as far from being a lie as is play or art in all their departures from reality. But the instant the intentions and events of practical reality enter into the speech and behavior of sociability, it does become a lie—just as a painting does when it attempts, panorama fashion, to be taken for reality. That which is right and proper within the self-contained life of sociability, concerned only with the immediate play of its forms, becomes a lie when this is mere pretense, which in reality is guided by purposes of quite another sort than the sociable or is used to conceal such purposes—and indeed sociability may easily get entangled with real life.

It is an obvious corollary that everything may be subsumed under sociability which one can call sociological play-form; above all, play itself, which assumes a large place in the sociability of all epochs. The expression "social game" is significant in the deeper sense which I have indicated. The entire interactional or associational complex among men: the desire to gain advantage, trade, formation of parties and the desire to win from another, the movement between opposition and co-operation, outwitting and revenge—all this, fraught with purposive content in the serious affairs of reality, in play leads a life carried along only and completely by the stimulus of these functions. For even when play turns about a money prize, it is not the prize, which indeed could be won in many other ways, which is the specific point of the play; but the attraction for the true sportsman lies in the dynamics and in the chances of that sociologically significant form of activity itself. The social game has a deeper double meaning—that it is played not only *in* a society as its outward bearer but that *with* the society actually "society" is played. Further, in the sociology of the sexes, eroticism has elaborated a form of play: coquetry, which finds in sociability its lightest, most playful, and yet its widest realization. If the erotic question between the sexes turns about consent or denial (whose objects are naturally of endless variety and degree and by no means only of strictly physiological nature), so is it the essence of feminine coquetry to play hinted consent and hinted denial against each other to draw the man on without letting matters come to a decision, to rebuff him without making him lose all hope. The coquette brings her attractiveness to its climax by letting the man hang on the verge of getting what he wants without letting it become too serious for herself; her conduct swings between yes and no, without stopping at one or the other. She thus playfully shows the simple and pure form of erotic decision and can bring its polar opposites together in a quite integrated behavior, since the decisive and fateful content, which would bring it to one of the two decisions, by definition does not enter into coquetry. And this freedom from all the weight of firm content and residual reality gives coquetry that character of vacillation, of distance, of the ideal, which allows one to speak with some right of the "art"—not of the "arts"—of coquetry. In order, however, for coquetry to spread as so natural a growth on the soil of sociability, as experience shows it to be, it must be countered by a special attitude on the part of men. So long as the man denies himself the stimulation of coquetry, or so long as he is—on the contrary—merely a victim who is involuntarily carried along by her vacillations from a half-yes to a half-no—so long does coquetry lack the adequate structure of sociability. It lacks that free interaction and equivalence of the elements which is the fundamental condition of sociability. The latter appears only when the man desires nothing more than this free moving play, in which something definitively erotic lurks only as a remote symbol, and when he does not get his pleasure in these gestures and preliminaries from erotic desire or fear of it. Coquetry, as it unfolds its grace on the heights of sociable cultivation, has left behind the reality of erotic desire, of consent or denial, and becomes a play of shadow pictures of these serious matters. Where the latter enter or lurk, the whole process becomes a private affair of the two persons, played out on the level of reality; under the sociological sign of sociability, however, in which the essential orientation of the person to the fulness of life does not enter, coquetry is the teasing or even ironic play with which eroticism has distilled the pure essence of its interaction out from its substantive or individual content. As sociability plays at the forms of society, so coquetry plays out the forms of eroticism.

In what measure sociability realizes to the full the abstraction of the forms of sociological interaction otherwise significant because of their content and gives them—now turning about themselves, so to speak—a shadow body is revealed finally in that most extensive instrument of all human common life, conversation. The decisive point is expressed in the quite banal experience that in the serious affairs of life men talk for the sake of the content which they wish to impart or about which they want to come to an understanding—in sociability talking is an end in itself; in purely sociable conversation the content is merely the indispensable carrier of the stimulation, which the lively exchange of talk as such unfolds. All the forms with which this exchange develops: argument and the appeals to the norms recognized by both parties; the conclusion of peace through compromise and the discovery of common convictions; the thankful acceptance of the new and the parrying-off of that on which no understanding is to be hoped for—all these forms of conversational interaction, otherwise in the service of innumerable contents and purposes of human intercourse, here have their meaning in themselves; that is to say, in the excitement of the play of relations which they establish between individuals, binding and loosening, conquering and being vanquished, giving and taking. In order that this play may retain its self-sufficiency at the level of pure form, the content must receive no weight on its own account; as soon as the discussion gets business-like, it is no longer sociable; it turns its compass point around as soon as the verification of a truth becomes its purpose. Its character as sociable converse is disturbed just as when it turns into a serious argument. The form of the common search of the truth, the form of the argument, may occur; but it must not permit the seriousness of the momentary content to become its substance any more than one may put a piece of three-dimensional reality into the perspective of a painting. Not that the content of sociable conversation is a matter of indifference; it must be interesting, gripping, even significant—only it is not the purpose of the conversation that these qualities should square with objective results, which stand by definition outside the conversation. Outwardly, therefore, two conversations may run a similar course, but only that one of them is sociable in which the subject matter, with all its value and stimulation, finds its justification, its place, and its purpose only in the functional play of conversation as such, in the form of repartee with its special unique significance. It therefore inheres in the nature of sociable conversation that its object matter can change lightly and quickly; for, since the matter is only the means, it has an entirely interchangeable and accidental character which inheres in means as against fixed purposes. Thus sociability offers, as was said, perhaps the only case in which talk is a legitimate end in itself. For by the fact that it is two-sided—indeed with the possible exception of looking-each-other-over the purest and most sublimated form of mutuality among all sociological phenomena—it becomes the most adequate fulfilment of a relation, which is, so to speak, nothing but relationship, in which even that which is otherwise pure form of interaction is its own self-sufficient content. It results from this whole complex that also the telling of tales, witticisms, anecdotes, although often a stopgap and evidence of conversational poverty, still can show a fine tact in which all the motives of sociability are apparent. For, in the first place, the conversation is by this means kept above all individual intimacy, beyond everything purely personal which would not fit into the categories of sociability. This objective element is brought in not for the sake of its content but in the interest of sociability; that something is said and accepted is not an end in itself but a mere means to maintain the liveliness, the mutual understanding, the common consciousness of the group. Not only thereby is it given a content which all can share but it is a gift of the individual to the whole, behind which the giver can remain invisible; the finest sociably told story is that in which the narrator allows his own person to remain completely in the background; the most effective story holds itself in the happy balance of the sociable ethic, in which the subjectively individual as well as the objectively substantive have dissolved themselves completely in the service of pure sociability.

It is hereby indicated that sociability is the play-form also for the ethical forces of concrete society. The great problems placed before these forces are that the individual has to fit himself into a whole system and live for it: that, however, out of this system values and enhancement must flow back to him, that the life of the individual is but a means for the ends of the whole, the life of the whole but an instrument for the purposes of the individual. Sociability carries the seriousness, indeed the frequent tragedy of these requirements, over into its shadow world, in which there is no friction, because shadows cannot impinge upon one another. If it is, further, the ethical task of association to make the coming-together and the separation of its elements an exact and just expression of their inner relations, determined by the wholeness of their lives, so within sociability this freedom and adequacy are freed of their concrete and substantively deeper limitations; the manner in which in a "society" groups form and break up, conversation spins itself out, deepens, loosens, cuts itself off purely according to impulse and opportunity, that is a miniature picture of the social ideal that man might call the freedom of bondage.

If all association and separation shall be the strictly appropriate representation of inner realities, so are the latter here fallen by the way, and only the former phenomenon is left, whose play, obedient to its own laws, whose closed charm, represents *aesthetically* that moderation which the seriousness of realities otherwise demands of its ethical decisions.

This total interpretation of sociability is evidently realized by certain historical developments. In the earlier German Middle Ages we find knightly fraternities which were founded by friendly patrician families. The religious and practical ends of these unions seem to have been lost rather early, and in the fourteenth century the chivalrous interests and conduct remain their only specific content. Soon after, this also disappears, and there remain only purely sociable unions of aristocratic strata. Here the sociability apparently develops as the residuum of a society determined by a content—as the residuum which, because the content has been lost, can exist only in form and in the forms of with-one-another and for-one-another. That the essential existence of these forms can have only the inner nature of play or, reaching deeper, of art appears even more clearly in the court society of the *ancien régime*. Here by the falling-off of the concrete life-content, which was sucked away from the French aristocracy in some measure by the monarchy, there developed free-moving forms, toward which the consciousness of this class was crystallized—forms whose force, definitions, and relations were purely sociable and in no way symbols or functions of the real meanings and intensities of persons and institutions. The etiquette of court society became an end in itself; it "etiquetted" no content any longer but had elaborated immanent laws, comparable to those of art, which have validity only from the viewpoint of art and do not at all have the purpose of imitating faithfully and strikingly the reality of the model, that is, of things outside art.

With this phenomenon, sociability attains its most sovereign expression but at the same time verges on caricature. To be sure, it is its nature to shut out realities from the interactive relations of men and to build its castle in air according to the formal laws of these relations which move within themselves and recognize no purpose outside themselves. But the deep-running source, from which this empire takes its energies, is nonetheless to be sought not in these self-regulating forms but only in the vitality of real individuals, in their sensitivities and attractions, in the fulness of their impulses and convictions. All sociability is but a symbol of life, as it shows itself in the flow of a lightly amusing play; but, even so, a symbol of *life,* whose likeness it only so far alters as is required by the distance from it gained in the play, exactly as also the freest and most fantastic art, the furthest from all reality, nourishes itself from a deep and true relation to reality, if it is not to be empty and lying. If sociability cuts off completely the threads which bind it to real life and out of which it spins its admittedly stylized web, it turns from play to empty farce, to a lifeless schematization proud of its woodenness.

From this context it becomes apparent that men can complain both justly and unjustly of the superficiality of social intercourse. It is one of the most pregnant facts of mental life that, if we weld certain elements taken from the whole of being into a realm of their own, which is governed by its own laws and not by those of the whole, this realm, if completely cut off from the life of the whole, can display in its inner realization an empty nature suspended in the air; but then, often altered only by imponderables, precisely in this state of removal from all immediate reality, its deeper nature can appear more completely, more integrated and meaningful, than any attempt to comprehend it realistically and without taking distance. Accordingly as the former or the latter experience predominates, will one's own life, running its own course according to its own norms, be a formal, meaningless dead thing—or a symbolic play, in whose aesthetic charm all the finest and most highly sublimated dynamics of social existence and its riches are gathered. In all art, in all the symbolism of the religious life, in great measure even in the complex formulations of science, we are thrown back upon this belief, upon this feeling, that autonomies of mere parts of observed reality, that the combinations of certain superficial elements possess a relation to the depth and wholeness of life, which, although often not easy to formulate, makes such a part the bearer and the representative of the fundamental reality. From this we may understand the saving grace and blessing effect of these realms built out of the pure forms of existence, for in them we are released from life but have it still. The sight of the sea frees us inwardly, not in spite of but because of the fact that in its rushing up only to recede, its receding only to rise again, in the play and counterplay of its waves, the whole of life is stylized to the simplest expression of its dynamic, quite free from all reality which one may experience and from all the baggage of individual fate, whose final meaning seems nevertheless to flow into this stark picture. Just so art perhaps reveals the secret of life; that we save ourselves not by simply looking away from it but precisely in that in the apparently self-governing play of its forms we construct and experience the meaning and the forces of its deepest reality but without the reality itself. Sociability would not hold for so many thoughtful men who feel in every moment the pressure of life, this emancipating and saving exhilaration if it were only a flight from life, the mere momentary lifting of its seriousness. It can often enough be only this negative thing, a conventionalism and inwardly lifeless exchange of formulas; so perhaps in the *ancien régime,* where gloomy anxiety over a threatening reality drove men into pure escape, into severance from the powers of actual life. The freeing and lightening, however, that precisely the more thoughtful man finds in sociability is this; that association and exchange of stimulus, in which all the tasks and the whole weight of life are realized, here is consumed in an artistic play, in that simultaneous sublimation and dilution, in which the heavily freighted forces of reality are felt only as from a distance, their weight fleeting in a charm.

## 2. *The I and the Me*

BY GEORGE H. MEAD

WE WERE SPEAKING of the social conditions under which the self arises as an object. In addition to language we found two illustrations, one in play and the other in the game, and I wish to summarize and expand my account on these points. I have spoken of these from the point of view of children. We can, of course, refer also to the attitudes of more primitive people out of which our civilization has arisen. A striking illustration of play as distinct from the game is found in the myths and various of the plays which primitive people carry out, especially in religious pageants. The pure play attitude which we find in the case of little children may not be found here, since the participants are adults, and undoubtedly the relationship of these play processes to that which they interpret is more or less in the minds of even the most primitive people. In the process of interpretation of such

---

Reprinted from George H. Mead, in *Mind, Self, and Society,* ed. Charles Morris (Chicago: University of Chicago Press, 1934), Part III, sec. 20, pp. 152–64, with the permission of the University of Chicago Press. 

rituals, there is an organization of play which perhaps might be compared to that which is taking place in the kindergarten in dealing with the plays of little children, where these are made into a set that will have a definite structure or relationship. At least something of the same sort is found in the play of primitive people. This type of activity belongs, of course, not to the everyday life of the people in their dealing with the objects about them—there we have a more or less definitely developed self-consciousness—but in their attitudes toward the forces about them, the nature upon which they depend; in their attitude toward this nature which is vague and uncertain, there we have a much more primitive response; and that response finds its expression in taking the role of the other, playing at the expression of their gods and their heroes, going through certain rites which are the representation of what these individuals are supposed to be doing. The process is one which develops, to be sure, into a more or less definite technique and is controlled; and yet we can say that it has arisen out of situations similar to those in which little children play at being a parent, at being a teacher—vague personalities that are about them and which affect them and on which they depend. These are personalities which they take, roles they play, and in so far control the development of their own personality. This outcome is just what the kindergarten works toward. It takes the characters of these various vague beings and gets them into such an organized social relationship to each other that they build up the character of the little child. The very introduction of organization from outside supposes a lack of organization at this period in the child's experience. Over against such a situation of the little child and primitive people, we have the game as such.

The fundamental difference between the game and play is that in the latter the child must have the attitude of all the others involved in that game. The attitudes of the other players which the participant assumes organize into a sort of unit, and it is that organization which controls the response of the individual. The illustration used was of a person playing baseball. Each one of his own acts is determined by his assumption of the action of the others who are playing the game. What he does is controlled by his being everyone else on that team, at least in so far as those attitudes affect his own particular response. We get then an "other" which is an organization of the attitudes of those involved in the same process.

The organized community or social group which gives to the individual his unity of self may be called "the generalized other." The attitude of the generalized other is the attitude of the whole community.[1] Thus, for example, in the case of such a social group as a ball team, the team is the generalized other in so far as it enters—as an organized process or social activity—into the experience of any one of the individual members of it.

If the given human individual is to develop a self in the fullest sense, it is not sufficient for him merely to take the attitudes of other human individuals toward himself and toward one another within the human social process, and to bring that social process as a whole into his individual experience merely in these terms: he must also, in the same way that he takes the attitudes of other individuals toward himself and toward one another, take their attitudes toward the various phases or aspects of the common social activity or set of social undertakings in which, as members of an organized society or social group, they are all engaged; and he must then, by generalizing these individual attitudes of that organized society or social group itself, as a whole, act toward different social projects which at any given time it is carrying out, or toward the various larger phases of the general social process which constitutes its life and of which these projects are specific manifestations. This getting of the broad activities of any given social whole or organized society as such within the experiential field of any one of the individuals involved or included in that whole is, in other words, the essential basis and prerequisite of the fullest development of that individual's self: only in so far as he takes the attitudes of the organized social group to which he belongs toward the organized, co-operative social activity or set of such activities in which that group as such is engaged, does he develop a complete self or possess the sort of complete self he has developed. And on the other hand, the complex co-operative processes and activities and institutional functionings of or-

1. It is possible for inanimate objects, no less than for other human organisms, to form parts of the generalized and organized—the completely socialized—other for any given human individual, in so far as he responds to such objects socially or in a social fashion (by means of the mechanism of thought, the internalized conversation of gestures). Any thing—any object or set of objects, whether animate or inanimate, human or animal, or merely physical—toward which he acts, or to which he responds, socially, is an element in what for him is the generalized other; by taking the attitudes of which toward himself he becomes conscious of himself as an object or individual, and thus develops a self or personality. Thus, for example, the cult, in its primitive form, is merely the social embodiment of the relation between the given social group or community and its physical environment—an organized social means, adopted by the individual members of that group or community, of entering into social relations with that environment, or (in a sense) of carrying on conversations with it; and in this way that environment becomes part of the total generalized other for each of the individual members of the given social group or community.

ganized human society are also possible only in so far as every individual involved in them or belonging to that society can take the general attitudes of all other such individuals with reference to these processes and activities and institutional functionings, and to the organized social whole of experiential relations and interactions thereby constituted—and can direct his own behavior accordingly.

It is in the form of the generalized other that the social process influences the behavior of the individuals involved in it and carrying it on, i.e., that the community exercises control over the conduct of its individual members; for it is in this form that the social process or community enters as a determining factor into the individual's thinking. In abstract thought the individual takes the attitude of the generalized other[2] toward himself, without reference to its expression in any particular other individuals; and in concrete thought he takes that attitude in so far as it is expressed in the attitudes toward his behavior of those other individuals with whom he is involved in the given social situation or act. But only by taking the attitude of the generalized other toward himself, in one or another of these ways, can he think at all; for only thus can thinking—or the internalized conversation of gestures which constitutes thinking—occur. And only through the taking by individuals of the attitude or attitudes of the generalized other toward themselves is the existence of a universe of discourse, as that system of common or social meanings which thinking presupposes at its context, rendered possible.

The self-conscious human individual, then, takes or assumes the organized social attitudes of the given social group or community (or of some one section thereof) to which he belongs, toward the social problems of various kinds which confront that group or community at any given time, and which arise in connection with the correspondingly different social projects or organized co-operative enterprises in which that group or community as such is engaged; and as an individual participant in these social projects or co-operative enterprises, he governs his own conduct accordingly. In politics, for example, the individual identifies himself with an entire political party and takes the organized attitudes of that entire party toward the rest of the given social community and toward the problems which confront the party within the given social situation; and he consequently reacts or responds in terms of the organized attitudes of the party as a whole. He thus enters into a special set of social relations with all the other individuals who belong to that political party; and in the same way he enters into various other special sets of social relations, with various other classes of individuals respectively, the individuals of each of these classes being the other members of some one of the particular organized subgroups (determined in socially functional terms) of which he himself is a member within the entire given society or social community. In the most highly developed, organized, and complicated human social communities—those evolved by civilized man—these various socially functional classes or subgroups of individuals to which any given individual belongs (and with the other individual members of which he thus enters into a special set of social relations) are of two kinds. Some of them are concrete social classes or subgroups, such as political parties, clubs, corporations, which are all actually functional social units, in terms of which their individual members are directly related to one another. The others are abstract social classes or subgroups, such as the class of debtors and the class of creditors, in terms of which their individual members are related to one another only more or less indirectly, and which only more or less indirectly function as social units, but which afford or represent unlimited possibilities for the widening and ramifying and enriching of the social relations among all the individual members of the given society as an organized and unified whole. The given individual's membership in several of these abstract social classes or subgroups makes possible his entrance into definite social relations (however indirect) with an almost infinite number of other individuals who also belong to or are included within one or another of these abstract social classes or subgroups cutting across functional lines of demarcation which divide different human social communities from one another, and including individual members form several (in some cases from all) such communities. Of these abstract social classes or subgroups of human individuals the one which is most inclusive and extensive is, of course, the one defined by the logical universe of discourse (or sys-

2. We have said that the internal conversation of the individual with himself in terms of words or significant gestures—the conversation which constitutes the process or activity of thinking—is carried on by the individual from the standpoint of the "generalized other." And the more abstract that conversation is, the more abstract thinking happens to be, the further removed is the generalized other from any connection with particular individuals. It is especially in abstract thinking, that is to say, that the conversation involved is carried on by the individual with the generalized other, rather than with any particular individuals. Thus it is, for example, that abstract concepts are concepts stated in terms of the attitudes of the entire social group or community; they are stated on the basis of the individual's consciousness of the attitudes of the generalized other toward them, as a result of his taking these attitudes of the generalized other and then responding to them. And thus it is also that abstract propositions are stated in a form which anyone—any other intelligent individual—will accept.

tem of universally significant symbols) determined by the participation and communicative interaction of individuals; for of all such classes or subgroups, it is the one which claims the largest number of individual members, and which enables the largest conceivable number of human individuals to enter into some sort of social relation, however, indirect or abstract it may be, with one another—a relation arising from the universal functioning of gestures as significant symbols in the general human social process of communication.

I have pointed out, then, that there are two general stages in the full development of the self. At the first of these stages, the individual's self is constituted simply by an organization of the particular attitudes of other individuals toward himself and toward one another in the specific social acts in which he participates with them. But at the second stage in the full development of the individual's self that self is constituted not only by an organization of these particular individual attitudes, but also by an organization of the social attitudes of the generalized other or the social group as a whole to which he belongs. These social or group attitudes are brought within the individual's field of direct experience, and are included as elements in the structure or constitution of his self, in the same way that the attitudes of particular other individuals are; and the individual arrives at them, or succeeds in taking them, by means of further organizing, and then generalizing, the attitudes of particular other individuals in terms of their organized social bearings and implications. So the self reaches its full development by organizing these individual attitudes of others into the organized social or group attitudes, and by thus becoming an individual reflection of the general systematic pattern of social or group behavior in which it and the others are all involved—a pattern which enters as a whole into the individual's experience in terms of these organized group attitudes which, through the mechanism of his central nervous system, he takes toward himself, just as he takes the individual attitudes of others.

The game has a logic, so that such an organization of the self is rendered possible: there is a definite end to be obtained; the actions of the different individuals are all related to each other with reference to that end so that they do not conflict; one is not in conflict with himself in the attitude of another man on the team. If one has the attitude of the person throwing the ball he can also have the response of catching the ball. The two are related so that they further the purpose of the game itself. They are interrelated in a unitary, organic fashion. There is a definite unity, then, which is introduced into the organization of other selves when we reach such a stage as that of the game, as over against the situation of play where there is a simple succession of one role after another, a situation which is, of course, characteristic of the child's own personality. The child is one thing at one time and another at another, and what he is at one moment does not determine what he is at another. That is both the charm of childhood as well as its inadequacy. You cannot count on the child; you cannot assume that all the things he does are going to determine what he will do at any moment. He is not organized into a whole. The child has no definite character, no definite personality.

The game is then an illustration of the situation out of which an organized personality arises. In so far as the child does take the attitude of the other and allows that attitude of the other to determine the thing he is going to do with reference to a common end, he is becoming an organic member of society. He is taking over the morale of that society and is becoming an essential member of it. He belongs to it in so far as he does allow the attitude of the other that he takes to control his own immediate expression. What is involved here is some sort of an organized process. That which is expressed in terms of the game is, of course, being continually expressed in the social life of the child, but this wider process goes beyond the immediate experience of the child himself. The importance of the game is that it lies entirely inside of the child's own experience, and the importance of our modern type of education is that it is brought as far as possible within this realm. The different attitudes that a child assumes are so organized that they exercise a definite control over his response, as the attitudes in a game control his own immediate response. In the game we get an organized other, a generalized other, which is found in the nature of the child itself, and finds its expression in the immediate experience of the child. And it is that organized activity in the child's own nature controlling the particular response which gives unity, and which builds up his own self.

What goes on in the game goes on in the life of the child all the time. He is continually taking the attitudes of those about him, especially the roles of those who in some sense control him and on whom he depends. He gets the function of the process in an abstract sort of a way at first. It goes over from the play into the game in a real sense. He has to play the game. The morale of the game takes hold of the child more than the larger morale of the whole community. The child passes into the game and the game expresses a social situation in which he can completely enter; its morale may have a greater hold on him than that of the family to which he belongs or the community in which he lives. There are all sorts of social organizations, some of which are fairly lasting, some temporary, into which the child is entering, and he is playing a sort of social game in them. It is a period in which he likes "to belong," and he gets into organizations which come into existence and pass out of existence. He becomes a something which can function in the organized whole, and thus tends to determine himself in his relationship with the group to which he belongs. That process is one which is a striking stage in the development of the child's morale. It constitutes him a self-conscious member of the community to which he belongs.

Such is the process by which a personality arises. I have spoken of this as a process in which a child takes the role of the other, and said that it takes place essentially through the use of language. Language is predominantly based on the vocal gesture by means of which co-operative activities in a community are carried out. Language in its significant sense is that vocal gesture which tends to arouse in the individual the attitude which it arouses in others, and it is this perfecting of the self by the gesture which mediates the social activities that gives rise to the process of taking the role of the other. The latter phrase is a little unfortunate because it suggests an actor's attitude which is actually more sophisticated than that which is involved in our own experience. To this degree it does not correctly describe that which I have in mind. We see the process most definitely in a primitive form in those situations where the child's play takes different roles. Here the very fact that he is ready to pay out money, for instance, arouses the attitude of the person who receives money; the very process is calling out in him the corresponding activities of the other person involved. The individual stimulates himself to the response which he is calling out in the other person, and then acts in some degree in response to that situation. In play the child does definitely act out the role which he himself has aroused in himself. It is that which gives, as I have said, a definite content in the individual which answers to the stimulus that affects him as it affects somebody else. The content of the other that enters into one personality is the response in the individual which his gesture calls out in the other.

We may illustrate our basic concept by a reference to the notion of property. If we say "This is my property, I shall control it," that affirmation calls out a certain set of responses which must be the same in any community in which property exists. It involves an organized attitude with reference to property which is common to all the members of the community. One must have a definite attitude of control of his own property and respect for the property of others. Those attitudes (as organized sets of responses) must be there on the part of all, so that when one says such a thing he calls out in himself the response of the others. He is calling out the response of what I have called a generalized other. That which makes society possible is such common responses, such organized attitudes, with reference to what we term property, the cults of religion, the process of education, and the relations of the family. Of course, the wider the society the more definitely universal these objects must be. In any case there must be a definite set of responses, which we may speak of as abstract, and which can belong to a very large group. Property is in itself a very abstract concept. It is that which the individual can control himself and nobody else can control. The attitude is different from that of a dog toward a bone. A dog will fight any other dog trying to take the bone. The dog is not taking the attitude of the other dog. A man who says "This is my property" is taking an attitude of the other person. The man is appealing to his rights because he is able to take the attitude which everybody else in the group has with reference to property, thus arousing in himself the attitude of others.

What goes to make up the organized self is the organization of the attitudes which are common to the group. A person is a personality because he belongs to a community, because he takes over the institutions of that community into his own conduct. He takes its language as a medium by which he gets his personality, and then through a process of taking the different roles that all the others furnish he comes to get the attitude of the members of the community. Such, in a certain sense, is the structure of a man's personality. There are certain common responses which each individual has toward certain common things, and in so far as those common responses are awakened in the individual when he is affecting other persons he arouses his own self. The structure, then, on which the self is built is this response which is common to all, for one has to be a member of a community to be a self. Such responses are abstract attitudes, but they constitute just what we term a man's character. They give him what we term his principles, the acknowledged attitudes of all members of the community toward what are the values of that community. He is putting himself in the place of the generalized other, which represents the organized responses of all the members of the group. It is that which guides conduct controlled by principles, and a person who has such an organized group of responses is a man whom we say has character, in the moral sense.

It is a structure of attitudes, then, which goes to make up a self, as distinct from a group of habits. We all of us have, for example, certain groups of habits, such as the particular intonations which a person uses in his speech. This is a set of habits of vocal expression which one has but which one does not know about. The sets of habits which we have of that sort mean nothing to us; we do not hear the intonations of our speech that others hear unless we are paying particular attention to them. The habits of emotional expression which belong to our speech are of the same sort. We may know that we have expressed ourselves in a joyous fashion but the detailed process is one which does not come back to our conscious selves. There are whole bundles of such habits which do not enter into a conscious self, but which help to make up what is termed the unconscious self.

After all, what we mean by self-consciousness is an awakening in ourselves of the group of attitudes which we are arousing in others, especially when it is an important set of responses which go to make up the members of the community. It is unfortunate to fuse or mix up consciousness, as we ordinarily use that term, and self-consciousness. Consciousness, as frequently used, simply has reference to the field of experience, but self-consciousness refers to the ability to call out in ourselves a set of definite responses which belong to the others of the group. Consciousness and self-consciousness are not on the same level. A man alone has, fortunately or unfortunately, access to his own toothache, but that is not what we mean by self-consciousness.

I have so far emphasized what I have called the structures upon which the self is constructed, the framework of the self, as it were. Of course we are not only what is common to all: each one of the selves is different from everyone else; but there has to be such a common structure as I have sketched in order that we may be members of a community at all. We cannot be ourselves unless we are also members in whom there is a community of attitudes which control the attitudes of all. We cannot have rights unless we have common attitudes. That which we have acquired as self-conscious persons makes us such members of society and gives us selves. Selves can only exist in definite relationships to other selves. No hard-and-fast line can be drawn between our own selves and the selves of others, since our own selves exist and enter as such into our experience only in so far as the selves of others exist and enter as such into our experience also. The individual possesses a self only in relation to the selves of the other members of his social group; and the structure of his self expresses or reflects the general behavior pattern of this social group to which he belongs, just as does the structure of the self of every other individual belonging to this social group.

## 3. *Reciprocity*

BY MARCEL MAUSS

WE INTEND in this book to isolate one important set of phenomena: namely, prestations which are in theory voluntary, disinterested and spontaneous, but are in fact obligatory and interested. The form usually taken is that of the gift generously offered; but the accompanying behaviour is formal pretence and social deception, while the transaction itself is based on obligation and economic self-interest. We shall note the various principles behind this necessary form of exchange (which is nothing less than the division of labour itself), but we shall confine our detailed study to the enquiry: *In primitive or archaic types of society what is the principle whereby the gift received has to be repaid? What force is there in the thing given which compels the recipient to make a return?* We hope, by presenting enough data, to be able to answer this question precisely, and also to indicate the direction in which answers to cognate questions might be sought. We shall also pose new problems. Of these, some concern the morality of

---

Reprinted from Marcel Mauss, *The Gift,* trans. Ian Cunnison (Glencoe, Ill.: The Free Press, 1954), pp. 1–2, 3, 10–12, 69–77, with the permission of The Free Press.

the contract: for instance, the manner in which today the law of things remains bound up with the law of persons; and some refer to the forms and ideas which have always been present in exchange and which even now are to be seen in the idea of individual interest.

* * *

In the systems of the past we do not find simple exchange of goods, wealth and produce through markets established among individuals. For it is groups, and not individuals, which carry on exchange, make contracts, and are bound by obligations; the persons represented in the contracts are moral persons—clans, tribes, and families; the groups, or the chiefs as intermediaries for the groups, confront and oppose each other. Further, what they exchange is not exclusively goods and wealth, real and personal property, and things of economic value. They exchange rather courtesies, entertainments, ritual, military assistance, women, children, dances, and feasts; and fairs in which the market is but one element and the circulation of wealth but one part of a wide and enduring contract. Finally, although the prestations and counter-prestations take place under a voluntary guise they are in essence strictly obligatory, and their sanction is private or open warfare. We propose to call this the system of *total prestations*.

* * *

## *The Obligation to Give and the Obligation to Receive*

To appreciate fully the institutions of total prestation and the potlatch we must seek to explain two complementary factors. Total prestation not only carries with it the obligation to repay gifts received, but it implies two others equally important: the obligation to give presents and the obligation to receive them. A complete theory of the three obligations would include a satisfactory fundamental explanation of this form of contract among Polynesian clans. For the moment we simply indicate the manner in which the subject might be treated.

It is easy to find a large number of facts on the obligation to receive. A clan, household, association or guest is constrained to demand hospitality, to receive presents, to barter or to make blood and marriage alliances. The Dayaks have even developed a whole set of customs based on the obligation to partake of any meal at which one is present or which one has seen in preparation.

The obligation to give is no less important. If we understood this, we should also know how men came to exchange things with each other. We merely point out a few facts. To refuse to give, or to fail to invite, is—like refusing to accept—the equivalent of a declaration of war; it is a refusal of friendship and intercourse. Again, one gives because one is forced to do so, because the recipient has a sort of proprietary right over everything which belongs to the donor. This right is expressed and conceived as a sort of spiritual bond. Thus in Australia the man who owes all the game he kills to his father- and mother-in-law may eat nothing in their presence for fear that their very breath should poison his food. We have seen above that the *taonga* sister's son has customs of this kind in Samoa, which are comparable with those of the sister's son (*vasu*) in Fiji.

In all these instances there is a series of rights and duties about consuming and repaying existing side by side with rights and duties about giving and receiving. The pattern of symmetrical and reciprocal rights is not difficult to understand if we realize that it is first and foremost a pattern of spiritual bonds between things which are to some extent parts of persons, and persons and groups that behave in some measure as if they were things.

All these institutions reveal the same kind of social and psychological pattern. Food, women, children, possessions, charms, land, labour, services, religious offices, rank—everything is stuff to be given away and repaid. In perpetual interchange of what we may call spiritual matter, comprising men and things, these elements pass and repass between clans and individuals, ranks, sexes and generations.

* * *

## *Political and Economic Conclusions*

Our facts do more than illumine our morality and point out our ideal; for they help us to analyse economic facts of a more general nature, and our analysis might suggest the way to better administrative procedures for our societies.

We have repeatedly pointed out how this economy of gift-exchange fails to conform to the principles of so-called natural economy or utilitarianism. The phenomena in the economic life of the people we have studied (and they are good representatives of the great neolithic stage of civilization) and the survivals of these traditions in societies closer to ours and even in our own custom, are disregarded in the schemes adopted by the few economists who have tried to compare the various forms of economic life. We add our own observations to those of Malinowski who devoted a whole work to ousting the prevalent doctrines on primitive economics.

Here is a chain of undoubted fact. The notion of value exists in these societies. Very great surpluses, even by European standards, are amassed; they are expended often at pure loss with tremendous extravagance and without a trace of mercenariness; among things exchanged are tokens of wealth, a kind of money. All this very rich economy is nevertheless imbued with religious elements; money still has its magical power and is linked to clan and individual. Diverse economic activities—for example, the market—are impregnated with ritual and myth; they retain a ceremonial character, obligatory and efficacious; they have their own ritual and etiquette. Here is the answer to the question already posed by Durkheim about the religious origin of the notion of economic value. The facts also supply answers to a string of problems about the forms and origins of what is so badly termed exchange—the barter or *permutatio* of useful articles. In the view of cautious Latin authors in the Aristotelian tradition and their *a priori* economic history, this is the origin of the division of labour. On the contrary, it is something other than utility which makes goods circulate in these multifarious and fairly enlightened societies. Clans, age groups and sexes, in view of the many relationships ensuing from contacts between them, are in a state of perpetual economic effervescence which has little about it that is materialistic; it is much less prosaic than our sale and purchase, hire of services and speculations.

We may go farther than this and break down, reconsider and redefine the principal notions of which we have already made use. Our terms 'present' and 'gift' do not have precise meanings, but we could find no others. Concepts which we like to put in opposition—freedom and obligation; generosity, liberality, luxury on the one hand and saving, interest, austerity on the other—are not exact and it would be well to put them to the test. We cannot deal very fully with this; but let us take an example from the Trobriands. It is a complex notion that inspires the economic actions we have described, a notion neither of purely free and gratuitous prestations, nor of purely interested and utilitarian production and exchange; it is a kind of hybrid.

Malinowski made a serious effort to classify all the transactions he witnessed in the Trobriands according to the interest or disinterestedness present in them. He ranges them from pure gift to barter with bargaining, but this classification is untenable. Thus according to Malinowski the typical 'pure gift' is that between spouses. Now in our view one of the most important acts noted by the author, and one which throws a strong light on sexual relationships, is the *mapula,* the sequence of payments by a husband to his wife as a kind of salary for sexual services. Likewise the payments to chiefs are tribute; the distributions of food (*sagali*) are payments for labour or ritual accomplished, such as work done on the eve of a funeral. Thus basically as these gifts are not spontaneous so also they are not really disinterested. They are for the most part counter-prestations made not solely in order to pay for goods or services, but also to maintain a profitable alliance which it would be unwise to reject, as for instance partnership between fishing tribes and tribes of hunters and potters. Now this fact is widespread—we have met it with the Maori, Tsimshian and others. Thus it is clear wherein this mystical and practical force resides, which at once binds clans together and keeps them separate, which divides their labour and constrains them to exchange. Even in these societies the individuals and the groups, or rather the sub-groups, have always felt the sovereign right to refuse a contract, and it is this which lends an appearance of generosity to the circulation of goods. On the other hand, normally they had neither the right of, nor interest in, such a refusal; and it is that which makes these distant societies seem akin to ours.

The use of money suggests other considerations. The Trobriand *vaygu'a,* armshells and necklaces, like the North-West American coppers and Iroquois *wampum,* are at once wealth, tokens of wealth, means of exchange and payment, and things to be given away or destroyed. In addition they are pledges, linked to the persons who use them and who in turn are bound by them. Since, however, at other times they serve as tokens of money, there is interest in giving them away, for if they are transformed into services or merchandise that yield money then one is better off in the end. We may truly say that the Trobriand or Tsimshian chief behaves somewhat like the capitalist who knows how to spend his money at the right time only to build his capital up again. Interest and disinterestedness taken together explain this form of the circulation of wealth and of the circulation of tokens of wealth that follows upon it.

Even the destruction of wealth does not correspond to the complete disinterestedness which one might expect. These great acts of generosity are not free from self-interest. The extravagant consumption of wealth, particularly in the potlatch, always exaggerated and often purely destructive, in which goods long stored are all at once given away or destroyed, lends to these institutions the appearance of wasteful expenditure and child-like prodigality. Not only are valuable goods thrown away and foodstuffs consumed to excess but there is destruction for its own sake—coppers are thrown into the sea or broken. But the motives of such excessive gifts and reckless consumption, such mad losses and destruction of wealth, especially in these potlatch societies, are in no way disinterested. Between vassals and chiefs, between vassals and their henchmen, the hierarchy is established by means of these gifts. To give is to show one's superiority, to show that one is something more and higher, that one is *magister*. To accept without returning or repaying more is to face subordination, to become a client and subservient, to become *minister*.

The magic ritual in the *kula* known as *mwasila* contains spells and symbols which show that the man who wants to enter into a contract seeks above all profit in the form of social—one might almost say animal—superiority. Thus he charms the betelnut to be used with his partners, casts a spell over the chief and his fellows, then over his own pigs, his necklaces, his head and mouth, the opening gifts and whatever else he carries; then he chants, not without exaggeration: 'I shall kick the mountain, the mountain moves . . . the mountain falls down. . . . My spell shall go to the top of Dobu Mountain. . . . My canoe will sink. . . . My fame is like thunder, my treading is like the roar of flying witches. . . . Tudududu.' The aim is to be the first, the finest, luckiest, strongest and richest and that is how to set about it. Later the chief confirms his *mana* when he redistributes to his vassals and relatives what he has just received; he maintains his rank among the chiefs by exchanging armshells for necklaces, hospitality for visits, and so on. In this case wealth is, in every aspect, as much a thing of prestige as a thing of utility. But are we certain that our own position is different and that wealth with us is not first and foremost a means of controlling others?

Let us test now the notion to which we have opposed the ideas of the gift and disinterestedness: that of interest and the individual pursuit of utility. This agrees no better with previous theories. If similar motives animate Trobriand and American chiefs and Andaman clans and once animated generous Hindu or Germanic noblemen in their giving and spending, they are not to be found in the cold reasoning of the business man, banker or capitalist. In those earlier civilizations one had interests but they differed from those of our time. There, if one hoards, it is only to spend later on, to put people under obligations and to win followers. Exchanges are made as well, but only of luxury objects like clothing and ornaments, or feasts and other things that are consumed at once. Return is made with interest, but that is done in order to humiliate the original donor or exchange partner and not merely to recompense him for the loss that the lapse of time causes him. He has an interest but it is only analogous to the one which we say is our guiding principle.

Ranged between the relatively amorphous and disinterested economy within the sub-groups of Australian and North American (Eastern and Prairie) clans, and the individualistic economy of pure interest which our societies have had to some extent ever since their discovery by Greeks and Semites, there is a great series of institutions and economic events not governed by the rationalism which past theory so readily took for granted.

The word 'interest' is recent in origin and can be traced back to the Latin *interest* written on account books opposite rents to be recovered. In the most epicurean of these philosophies pleasure and the good were pursued and not material utility. The victory of rationalism and mercantilism was required before the notions of profit and the individual were given currency and raised to the level of principles. One can date roughly—after Mandeville and his *Fable des Abeilles*—the triumph of the notion of individual interest. It is only by awkward paraphrasing that one can render the phrase 'individual interest' in Latin, Greek or Arabic. Even the men who wrote in classical Sanskrit and used the word *artha,* which is fairly close to our idea of interest, turned it, as they did with other categories of action, into an idea different from ours. The sacred books of ancient India divide human actions into the categories of law *(dharma),* interest *(artha)* the desire *(kama)*. But *artha* refers particularly to the political interest of king, Brahmins and ministers, or royalty and the various castes. The considerable literature of the *Niticastra* is not economic in tone.

It is only our Western societies that quite recently turned man into an economic animal. But we are not yet all animals of the same species. In both lower and upper classes pure irrational expenditure is in current practice: it is still characteristic of some French noble houses. *Homo oeconomicus* is not behind us, but before, like the moral man, the man of duty, the scientific man and the reasonable man. For a long time man was something quite different; and it is not so long now since be became a machine —a calculating machine.

In other respects we are still far from frigid utilitarian calculation. Make a thorough statistical analysis, as Halbwachs did for the working classes, of the consumption and expenditure of our middle classes and how many needs are found satisfied? How many desires are fulfilled that have utility as their end? Does not the rich man's expenditure on luxury, art, servants and extravagances recall the expenditure of the nobleman of former times or the savage chiefs whose customs we have been describing?

It is another question to ask if it is good that this should be so. It is a good thing possibly that there exist means of expenditure and exchange other than economic ones. However, we contend that the best economic procedure is not to be found in the calculation of individual needs. I believe that we must become, in proportion as we would develop our wealth, something more than better financiers, accountants and administrators. The mere pursuit of individual ends is harmful to the ends and peace of the whole, to the rhythm of its work and pleasures, and hence in the end to the individual.

We have just seen how important sections and groups of our capital industries are seeking to attach groups of their employees to them. Again all the syndicalist groups, employers' as much as wage-earners', claim that they are defending and representing the general interest with a fervour equal to that of the particular interests of their members, or of the interests of the groups themselves. Their speeches are burnished with many fine metaphors. Nevertheless, one has to admit that not only ethics and philosophy, but also economic opinion and practice, are starting to rise to this 'social' level. The feeling is that there is no better way of making men work than by reassuring them of being paid loyally all their lives for labour which they give loyally not only for their own sakes but for that of others. The producer-exchanger feels now as he has always felt—but this time he feels it more acutely—that he is giving something of himself, his time and his life. Thus he wants recompense, however modest, for this gift. And to refuse him this recompense is to incite him to laziness and lower production.

We draw now a conclusion both sociological and practical. The famous Sura LXIV, 'Mutual Deception,' given at Mecca to Mohammed, says:

15. Your possessions and your children are only a trial and Allah it is with whom is a great reward.

16. Therefore be careful [of your duty to] Allah as much as you can, and hear and obey and spend (*sadaqa*), it is better for your souls; and whoever is saved from the greediness of his soul, these it is that are the successful.

17. If you set apart from Allah a goodly portion, He will double it for you and forgive you; and Allah is the multiplier of rewards, forebearing.

18. The knower of the unseen and the seen, the mighty, the wise.

Replace the name of Allah by that of the society or professional group, or unite all three; replace the concept of alms by that of co-operation, of a prestation altruistically made; you will have a fair idea of the practice which is now coming into being. It can be seen at work already in certain economic groups and in the hearts of the masses who often enough know their own interest and the common interest better than their leaders do.

## *Sociological and Ethical Conclusions*

We may be permitted another note about the method we have used. We do not set this work up as a model; it simply proffers one or two suggestions. It is incomplete: the analysis could be pushed farther. We are really posing questions for historians and anthropologists and offering possible lines of research for them rather than resolving a problem and laying down definite answers. It is enough for us to be sure for the moment that we have given sufficient data for such an end.

This being the case, we would point out that there is a heuristic element in our manner of treatment. The facts we have studied are all 'total' social phenomena. The word 'general' may be preferred although we like it less. Some of the facts presented concern the whole of society and its institutions (as with potlatch, opposing clans, tribes on visit, etc.); others, in which exchanges and contracts are the concern of individuals, embrace a large number of institutions.

These phenomena are at once legal, economic, religious, æsthetic, morphological and so on. They are legal in that they concern individual and collective rights, organized and diffuse morality; they may be entirely obligatory, or subject simply to praise or disapproval. They are at once political and domestic, being of interest both to classes and to clans and families. They are religious; they concern true religion, animism, magic and diffuse religious mentality. They are economic, for the notions of value, utility, interest, luxury, wealth, acquisition, accumulation, consumption and liberal and sumptuous expenditure are all present, although not perhaps in their modern senses. Moreover, these institutions have an important æsthetic side which we have left unstudied; but the dances performed, the songs and shows, the dramatic representations given between camps or partners, the objects made, used, decorated, polished, amassed and transmitted with affection, received with joy, given away in triumph, the feasts in which everyone participates—all these, the food, objects and services, are the source of æsthetic emotions as well as emotions aroused by interest. This is true not only of Melanesia but also, and particularly, of the potlatch of North-West America and still more true of the market-festival of the Indo-European world. Lastly, our phenomena are clearly morphological. Everything that happens in the course of gatherings, fairs and markets or in the feasts that replace them, presupposes groups whose duration exceeds the season of social concentration, like the winter potlatch of the Kwakiutl or the few weeks of the Melanesian maritime expeditions. Moreover, in order that these meetings may be carried out in peace, there must be roads or water for transport and tribal, inter-tribal or international alliances—*commercium* and *connubium*.

# 4. *Social Action and Its Types*

BY MAX WEBER

## *The Definition of Sociology and of Social Action*

1. SOCIOLOGY (in the sense in which this highly ambiguous word is used here) is a science which attempts the interpretive understanding of social action in order thereby to arrive at a causal explanation of its course and effects. In "action" is included all human behaviour when and in so far as the acting individual attaches a subjective meaning to it. Action in this sense may be either overt or purely inward or subjective; it may consist of positive intervention in a situation, or of deliberately refraining from such intervention or passively acquiescing in the situation. Action is social in so far as, by virtue of the subjective meaning attached to it by the acting individual (or individuals), it takes account of the behaviour of others and is thereby oriented in its course.[1] . . .

### THE CONCEPT OF SOCIAL ACTION

1. Social action, which includes both failure to act and passive acquiescence, may be oriented to the past, present, or expected future behaviour of others. Thus it may be motivated by revenge for a past attack, defence against present, or measures of defence against future aggression. The "others" may be individual persons, and may be known to the actor as such, or may constitute an indefinite plurality and may be entirely unknown as individuals. Thus "money" is a means of exchange which the actor accepts in payment because he orients his action to the expectation that a large but unknown number of individuals he is personally unacquainted with will be ready to accept it in exchange on some future occasion.

2. Not every kind of action, even of overt action, is "social" in the sense of the present discussion. Overt action is non-social if it is oriented solely to the behaviour of inanimate objects. Subjective attitudes constitute social action only so far as they are oriented to the behaviour of others. For example, religious behaviour is not social if it is simply a matter of contemplation or of solitary prayer. The economic activity of an individual is

---

Reprinted from Max Weber, *The Theory of Social and Economic Organization*, trans. A. M. Henderson and Talcott Parsons, ed. Talcott Parsons (Glencoe, Ill.: The Free Press, 1947), Part I, secs. 1–4, pp. 88, 112–23. 

1. In this series of definitions Weber employs several important terms which need discussion. In addition to *Verstehen*, which has already been commented upon, there are four important ones: *Deuten, Sinn, Handeln,* and *Verhalten*. *Deuten* has generally been translated as "interpret." As used by Weber in this context it refers to the interpretation of subjective states of mind and the meanings which can be imputed as intended by an actor. Any other meaning of the word "interpretation" is irrelevant to Weber's discussion. The term *Sinn* has generally been translated as "meaning"; and its variations, particularly the corresponding adjectives, *sinnhaft, sinnvoll, sinnfremd,* have been dealt with by appropriately modifying the term meaning. The reference here again is always to features of the content of subjective states of mind or of symbolic systems which are ultimately referable to such states of mind.

The terms *Handeln* and *Verhalten* are directly related. *Verhalten* is the broader term referring to any mode of behaviour of human individuals, regardless of the frame of reference in terms of which it is analysed. "Behaviour" has seemed to be the most appropriate English equivalent. *Handeln*, on the other hand, refers to the concrete phenomenon of human behaviour only in so far as it is capable of "understanding," in Weber's technical sense, in terms of subjective categories. The most appropriate English equivalent has seemed to be "action." This corresponds to the editor's usage in *The Structure of Social Action* and would seem to be fairly well established. "Conduct" is also closely similar and has sometimes been used. *Deuten, Verstehen,* and *Sinn* are thus applicable to human behaviour only in so far as it constitutes action or conduct in this specific sense.—ED.

only social if, and then only in so far as, it takes account of the behaviour of someone else. Thus very generally in formal terms it becomes social in so far as the actor's actual control over economic goods is respected by others. Concretely it is social, for instance, if in relation to the actor's own consumption the future wants of others are taken into account and this becomes one consideration affecting the actor's own saving. Or, in another connexion, production may be oriented to the future wants of other people.

3. Not every type of contact of human beings has a social character; this is rather confined to cases where the actor's behaviour is meaningfully oriented to that of others. For example, a mere collision of two cyclists may be compared to a natural event. On the other hand, their attempt to avoid hitting each other, or whatever insults, blows, or friendly discussion might follow the collision, would constitute "social action."

4. Social action is not identical either with the similar actions of many persons or with action influenced by other persons. Thus, if at the beginning of a shower a number of people on the street put up their umbrellas at the same time, this would not ordinarily be a case of action mutually oriented to that of each other, but rather of all reacting in the same way to the like need of protection from the rain. It is well known that the actions of the individual are strongly influenced by the mere fact that he is a member of a crowd confined within a limited space. Thus, the subject matter of studies of "crowd psychology," such as those of Le Bon, will be called "action conditioned by crowds." It is also possible for large numbers, though dispersed, to be influenced simultaneously or successively by a source of influence operating similarly on all the individuals, as by means of the press. Here also the behaviour of an individual is influenced by his membership in the crowd and by the fact that he is aware of being a member. Some types of reaction are only made possible by the mere fact that the individual acts as part of a crowd. Others become more difficult under these conditions. Hence it is possible that a particular event or mode of human behaviour can give rise to the most diverse kinds of feeling—gaiety, anger, enthusiasm, despair, and passions of all sorts—in a crowd situation which would not occur at all or not nearly so readily if the individual were alone. But for this to happen there need not, at least in many cases, be any meaningful relation between the behaviour of the individual and the fact that he is a member of a crowd. It is not proposed in the present sense to call action "social" when it is merely a result of the effect on the individual of the existence of a crowd as such and the action is not oriented to that fact on the level of meaning. At the same time the borderline is naturally highly indefinite. In such cases as that of the influence of the demagogue, there may be a wide variation in the extent to which his mass clientele is affected by a meaningful reaction to the fact of its large numbers; and whatever this relation may be, it is open to varying interpretations.

But furthermore, mere "imitation" of the action of others, such as that on which Tarde has rightly laid emphasis, will not be considered a case of specifically social action if it is purely reactive so that there is no meaningful orientation to the actor imitated. The borderline is, however, so indefinite that it is often hardly possible to discriminate. The mere fact that a person is found to employ some apparently useful procedure which he learned from someone else does not, however, constitute, in the present sense, social action. Action such as this is not oriented to the action of the other person, but the actor has, through observing the other, become acquainted with certain objective facts; and it is these to which his action is oriented. His action is then *causally* determined by the action of others, but not meaningfully. On the other hand, if the action of others is imitated because it is "fashionable" or traditional or exemplary, or lends social distinction, or on similar grounds, it is meaningfully oriented either to the behaviour of the source of imitation or of third persons or of both. There are of course all manner of transitional cases between the two types of imitation. Both the phenomena discussed above, the behaviour of crowds and imitation, stand on the indefinite borderline of social action. The same is true, as will often appear, of traditionalism and charisma. The reason for the indefiniteness of the line in these and other cases lies in the fact that both the orientation to the behaviour of others and the meaning which can be imputed to the actor himself, are by no means always capable of clear determination and are often altogether unconscious and seldom fully self-conscious. Mere "influence" and meaningful orientation cannot therefore always be clearly differentiated on the empirical level. But conceptually it is essential to distinguish them, even though merely "reactive" imitation may well have a degree of sociological importance at least equal to that of the type which can be called social action in the strict sense. Sociology, it goes without saying, is by no means confined to the study of "social action"; this is only, at least for the kind of sociology being developed here, its central subject matter, that which may be said to be decisive for its status as a science. But this does not imply any judgment on the comparative importance of this and other factors.

## *The Types of Social Action*

Social action, like other forms of action, may be classified in the following four types according to its mode of orientation: (1) in terms of rational orientation to a system of discrete individual ends (*zweckrational*), that is, through expectations as to the behaviour of objects in the external situation and of other human individuals, making use of these expectations as "conditions" or "means" for the successful attainment of the actor's own rationally chosen ends; (2) in terms of rational orientation to an absolute value (*wertrational*); involving a conscious belief in the absolute value of some ethical, aesthetic, religious, or other form of behaviour, entirely for its own sake and independently of any prospects of external success; (3) in terms of affectual orientation, especially emotional, determined by the specific affects and states of feeling of the actor; (4) traditionally oriented, through the habituation of long practice.[2]

1. Strictly traditional behaviour, like the reactive type of imitation discussed above, lies very close to the borderline of what can justifiably be called meaningfully oriented action, and indeed often on the other side. For it is very often a matter of almost automatic reaction to habitual stimuli which guide behaviour in a course which has been repeatedly followed. The great bulk of all everyday action to which people have become habitually accustomed approaches this type. Hence, its place in a systematic classification is not merely that of a limiting case because, as will be shown later, attachment to habitual forms can be upheld with varying degrees of self-consciousness and in a variety of senses. In this case the type may shade over into number two (*Wertrationalität*).

2. Purely affectual behaviour also stands on the borderline of what can be considered "meaningfully" oriented, and often it, too, goes over the line. It may, for instance, consist in an uncontrolled reaction to some exceptional stimulus. It is a case of sublimation when affectually determined action occurs in the form of conscious release of emotional tension. When this happens it is usually, though not always, well on the road to rationalization in one or the other or both of the above senses.

3. The orientation of action in terms of absolute value is distinguished from the affectual type by its clearly self-conscious formulation of the ultimate values governing the action and the consistently planned orientation of its detailed course to these values. At the same time the two types have a common element, namely that the meaning of the action does not lie in the achievement of a result ulterior to it, but in carrying out the specific type of action for its own sake. Examples of affectual action are the satisfaction of a direct impulse to revenge, to sensual gratification, to devote oneself to a person or ideal, to contemplative bliss, or, finally, toward the working off of emotional tensions. Such impulses belong in this category regardless of how sordid or sublime they may be.

Examples of pure rational orientation to absolute values would be the action of persons who, regardless of possible cost to themselves, act to put into practice their convictions of what seems to them to be required by duty, honour, the pursuit of beauty, a religious call, personal loyalty, or the importance of some "cause" no matter in what it consists. For the purposes of this discussion, when action is oriented to absolute values, it always involves "commands" or "demands" to the fulfilment of which the actor feels obligated. It is only in cases where human action is motivated by the fulfilment of such unconditional demands that it will be described as oriented to absolute values. This is empirically the case in widely varying degrees, but for

---

2. The two terms *zweckrational* and *wertrational* are of central significance to Weber's theory, but at the same time present one of the most difficult problems to the translator. Perhaps the keynote of the distinction lies in the absoluteness with which the values involved in *Wertrationalität* are held. The sole important consideration to the actor becomes the realization of the value. In so far as it involves ends, rational considerations, such as those of efficiency, are involved in the choice of means. But there is no question either of rational weighing of this end against others, nor is there a question of 'counting the cost' in the sense of taking account of possible results other than the attainment of the absolute end. In the case of *Zweckrationalität,* on the other hand, Weber conceives action as motivated by a plurality of relatively independent ends, none of which is absolute. Hence, rationality involves on the one hand the weighing of the relative importance of their realization, on the other hand, consideration of whether undesirable consequences would outweigh the benefits to be derived from the projected course of action. It has not seemed possible to find English terms which would express this distinction succinctly. Hence the attempt has been made to express the ideas as clearly as possible without specific terms.

It should also be pointed out that, as Weber's analysis proceeds, there is a tendency of the meaning of these terms to shift, so that *Wertrationalität* comes to refer to a system of ultimate ends, regardless of the degree of their absoluteness, while *Zweckrationalität* refers primarily to considerations respecting the choice of means and ends which are in turn means to further ends, such as money. What seems to have happened is that Weber shifted from a classification of ideal types of action to one of elements in the structure of action. In the latter context "expediency" is often an adequate rendering of *Zweckrationalität.* This process has been analysed in the editor's *Structure of Social Action,* chap. xvi.

The other two terms *affektuell* and *traditional* do not present any difficulty of translation. The term affectual has come into English psychological usage from the German largely through the influence of psychoanalysis.

the most part only to a relatively slight extent. Nevertheless, it will be shown that the occurrence of this mode of action is important enough to justify its formulation as a distinct type; though it may be remarked that there is no intention here of attempting to formulate in any sense an exhaustive classification of types of action.

4. Action is rationally oriented to a system of discrete individual ends (*zweckrational*) when the end, the means, and the secondary results are all rationally taken into account and weighed. This involves rational consideration of alternative means to the end, of the relations of the end to other prospective results of employment of any given means, and finally of the relative importance of different possible ends. Determination of action, either in affectual or in traditional terms, is thus incompatible with this type. Choice between alternative and conflicting ends and results may well be determined by considerations of absolute value. In that case, action is rationally oriented to a system of discrete individual ends only in respect to the choice of means. On the other hand, the actor may, instead of deciding between alternative and conflicting ends in terms of a rational orientation to a system of values, simply take them as given subjective wants and arrange them in a scale of consciously assessed relative urgency. He may then orient his action to this scale in such a way that they are satisfied as far as possible in order of urgency, as formulated in the principle of "marginal utility." The orientation of action to absolute values may thus have various different modes of relation to the other type of rational action, in terms of a system of discrete individual ends. From the latter point of view, however, absolute values are always irrational. Indeed, the more the value to which action is oriented is elevated to the status of an absolute value, the more "irrational" in this sense the corresponding action is. For, the more unconditionally the actor devotes himself to this value for its own sake, to pure sentiment or beauty, to absolute goodness or devotion to duty, the less is he influenced by considerations of the consequences of his action. The orientation of action wholly to the rational achievement of ends without relation to fundamental values is, to be sure, essentially only a limiting case.

5. It would be very unusual to find concrete cases of action, especially of social action, which were oriented *only* in one or another of these ways. Furthermore, this classification of the modes of orientation of action is in no sense meant to exhaust the possibilities of the field, but only to formulate in conceptually pure form certain sociologically important types, to which actual action is more or less closely approximated or, in much the more common case, which constitute the elements combining to make it up. The usefulness of the classification for the purposes of this investigation can only be judged in terms of its results.

## *The Concept of Social Relationship*

The term "social relationship" will be used to denote the behaviour of a plurality of actors in so far as, in its meaningful content, the action of each takes account of that of the others and is oriented in these terms. The social relationship thus *consists* entirely and exclusively in the existence of a *probability* that there will be, in some meaningfully understandable sense, a course of social action. For purposes of definition there is no attempt to specify the basis of this probability.

1. Thus, as a defining criterion, it is essential that there should be at least a minimum of mutual orientation of the action of each to that of the others. Its content may be of the most varied nature; conflict, hostility, sexual attraction, friendship, loyalty, or economic exchange. It may involve the fulfilment, the evasion, or the denunciation of the terms of an agreement; economic, erotic, or some other form of "competition"; common membership in national or class groups or those sharing a common tradition of status. In the latter cases mere group membership may or may not extend to include social action; this will be discussed later. The definition, furthermore, does not specify whether the relation of the actors is "solidary" or the opposite.

2. The "meaning" relevant in this context is always a case of the meaning imputed to the parties in a given concrete case, on the average or in a theoretically formulated pure type—it is never a normatively "correct" or a metaphysically "true" meaning. Even in cases of such forms of social organization as a state, church, association, or marriage, the social relationship consists exclusively in the fact that there has existed, exists, or will exist a probability of action in some definite way appropriate to this meaning. It is vital to be continually clear about this in order to avoid the "reification" of these concepts. A "state," for example, ceases to exist in a sociologically relevant sense whenever there is no longer a probability that certain kinds of meaningfully oriented social action will take place. This probability may be very high or it may be negligibly low. But in any case it is only in the sense and degree in which it does exist or can be estimated that the corresponding social relationship exists. It is impossible to find any other clear meaning for the statement that, for instance, a given "state" exists or has ceased to exist.

3. The subjective meaning need not necessarily be the same for all the parties who are mutually oriented in a given social relationship; there need not in this sense be "reciprocity." "Friendship," "love," "loyalty," "fidelity to contracts," "patriotism," on one side, may well be faced with an entirely different attitude on the other. In such cases the parties associate different meanings with their actions and the social relationship is in so far objectively "asymmetrical" from the points of view of the two parties. It may nevertheless be a case of mutual orientation in so far as, even though partly or wholly erroneously, one party presumes a particular attitude toward him on the part of the other and orients his action to this expectation. This can, and usually will, have consequences for the course of action and the form of the relationship. A relationship is objectively symmetrical only as, according to the typical expectations of the parties, the meaning for one party is the same as that for the other. Thus the actual attitude of a child to its father may be at least approximately that which the father, in the individual case, on the average or typically, has come to expect. A social relationship in which the attitudes are completely and fully corresponding is in reality a limiting case. But the absence of reciprocity will, for terminological purposes, be held to exclude the existence of a social relationship only if it actually results in the absence of a mutual orientation of the action of the parties. Here as elsewhere all sorts of transitional cases are the rule rather than the exception.

4. A social relationship can be of a temporary character or of varying degrees of permanence. That is, it can be of such a kind that there is a probability of the repeated recurrence of the behaviour which corresponds to its subjective meaning, behaviour which is an understandable consequence of the meaning and hence is expected. In order to avoid fallacious impressions, let it be repeated and continually kept in mind, that it is *only* the existence of the probability that, corresponding to a given subjective meaning complex, a certain type of action will take place, which constitutes the "existence" of the social relationship. Thus that a "friendship" or a "state" exists or has existed means this and only this: that we, the observers, judge that there is or has been a probability that on the basis of certain kinds of known subjective attitude of certain individuals there will result in the average sense a certain specific type of action. For the purposes of legal reasoning it is essential to be able to decide whether a rule of law does or does not carry legal authority, hence whether a legal relationship does or does not "exist." This type of question is not, however, relevant to sociological problems.

5. The subjective meaning of a social relationship may change, thus a political relationship, once based on solidarity, may develop into a conflict of interests. In that case it is only a matter of terminological convenience and of the degree of continuity of the change whether we say that a new relationship has come into existence or that the old one continues but has acquired a new meaning. It is also possible for the meaning to be partly constant, partly changing.

6. The meaningful content which remains relatively constant in a social relationship is capable of formulation in terms of maxims which the parties concerned expect to be adhered to by their partners, on the average and approximately. The more rational in relation to values or to given ends the action is, the more is this likely to be the case. There is far less possibility of a rational formulation of subjective meaning in the case of a relation of erotic attraction or of personal loyalty or any other affectual type than, for example, in the case of a business contract.

7. The meaning of a social relationship may be agreed upon by mutual consent. This implies that the parties make promises covering their future behaviour, whether toward each other or toward third persons. In such cases each party then normally counts, so far as he acts rationally, in some degree on the fact that the other will orient his action to the meaning of the agreement as he (the first actor) understands it. In part, they orient their action rationally to these expectations as given facts with, to be sure, varying degrees of subjectively "loyal" intention of doing their part. But in part also they are motivated each by the value to him of his "duty" to adhere to the agreement in the sense in which he understands it. This much may be anticipated.

## *Modes of Orientation of Social Action*

It is possible in the field of social action to observe certain empirical uniformities. Certain types, that is, of action which correspond to a typically appropriate subjective meaning attributable to the same actors, are found to be wide-spread, being frequently repeated by the same individual or simultaneously performed by many different ones. Sociological investigation is concerned with these typical modes of action. Thereby it differs from history, the subject of which is rather the causal explanation of important individual events; important, that is, in having an influence on human destiny.

An actually existent probability of a uniformity in the orientation of social action will be called "usage" (*Brauch*), if and in so far as the probability of its maintenance among a group of persons is determined entirely by its actual practice. Usage will be called "custom" (*Sitte*) if the actual performance rests on long familiarity. On the other hand, a uniformity of action may be said to be "determined by the exploitation of the opportunities of his situation in the self-interest of the actor." This type of uniformity exists in so far as the probability of its empirical performance is determined by the purely rational (*zweckrational*) orientation of the actors to similar ulterior expectations.[3]

1. Usage also includes "fashion" (*Mode*). As distinguished from custom and in direct contrast to it, usage will be called fashion so far as the mere fact of the novelty of the corresponding behaviour is the basis of the orientation of action. Its place is closely related to that of "convention,"[4] since both of them usually spring from a desire for social prestige. It will not, however, be further discussed here.

2. As distinguished from both "convention" and "law," "custom" refers to rules devoid of any external sanction. The actor conforms with them of his own free will, whether his motivation lies in the fact that he merely fails to think about it, that it is more comfortable to conform, or whatever else the reason may be. But always it is a justified expectation on the part of the members of the group that a customary rule will be adhered to. Thus custom is not "valid"[5] in anything like the legal sense; conformity with it is not "demanded" by anybody. Naturally, the transition from this to validly enforced convention and to law is gradual. Everywhere what has been traditionally handed down has been an important source of what has come to be enforced. To-day it is customary every morning to eat a breakfast which, within limits, conforms to a certain pattern. But there is no obligation to do so, except possibly for hotel guests ("American plan"), and it has not always been customary. On the other hand, the current mode of dress, even though it has partly originated in custom, is to-day very largely no longer customary alone, but conventional.

3. Many of the especially notable uniformities in the course of social action are not determined by orientation to any sort of norm which is held to be valid, nor do they rest on custom, but entirely on the fact that the corresponding type of social action is in the nature of the case best adapted to the normal interests of the actors as they themselves are aware of them. This is above all true of economic action, for example, the uniformities of price determination in a "free" market, but is by no means confined to such cases. The dealers in a market thus treat their own actions as means for obtaining the satisfaction of the ends defined by what they realize to be their own typical economic interests, and similarly treat as conditions the corresponding typical expectations as to the prospective behaviour of others. The more strictly rational their action is, the more will they tend to react similarly to the same situation. In this way there arise similarities, uniformities, and continuities in their attitudes and actions which are often far more stable than they would be if action were oriented to a system of norms and duties which were considered binding on the members of a group. This phenomenon—the fact that orientation to the situation in terms of the pure self-interest of the individual and of the others to whom he is related can bring about results which are very similar to those which an authoritarian agency, very often in vain, has attempted to obtain by coercion—has aroused a lively interest, especially in economic affairs. Observation of this has, in fact, been one of the important sources of economics as a science. But it is true in all other spheres of action as well. This type, with its clarity of self-consciousness and freedom from subjective scruples, is the polar antithesis of every sort of unthinking acquiescence in customary ways, as well as, on the other hand, of devotion to norms consciously accepted as absolute values. One of the most important aspects of the process of "rationalization" of action is the substitution for the unthinking acceptance of ancient custom, of deliberate adaptation to situations

3. In the above classification as well as in some of those which follow, the terminology is not standardized either in German or in English. Hence, just as there is a certain arbitrariness in Weber's definitions, the same is true of any corresponding set of definitions in English. It should be kept in mind that all of them are modes of orientation of action to patterns which contain a normative element. "Usage" has seemed to be the most appropriate translation of *Brauch* since, according to Weber's own definition, the principal criterion is that "it is done to conform with the pattern." There would also seem to be good precedent for the translation of *Sitte* by "custom." The contrast with fashion, which Weber takes up in his first comment, is essentially the same in both languages. The term *Interessenlage* presents greater difficulty. It involves two components: the motivation in terms of self-interest and orientation to the opportunities presented by the situation. It has not seemed possible to use any single term to convey this meaning in English and hence, a more roundabout expression has had to be resorted to.—ED.

4. The term "convention" in Weber's usage is narrower than *Brauch*. The difference consists in the fact that a normative pattern to which action is oriented is conventional only in so far as it is regarded as part of a legitimate order, whereas the question of moral obligation to conformity which legitimacy implies is not involved in "usage." The distinction is closely related to that of W. G. Sumner between "mores" and "folkways." It has seemed best to retain the English term closest to Weber's own. —ED.

5. The German term which has been translated as "validity" is *Geltung*. The primary use of this term is in a legal context and hence the validity in question is not empirical or logical validity, but legal. A legal rule is "valid" in so far as it is judged binding upon those who recognize the legitimacy of the legal order.—ED.

in terms of self-interest. To be sure, this process by no means exhausts the concept of rationalization of action. For in addition this can proceed in a variety of other directions; positively in that of a conscious rationalization of ultimate values; or negatively, at the expense not only of custom, but of emotional values; and, finally, in favour of a morally sceptical type of rationality, at the expense of any belief in absolute values. The many possible meanings of the concept of rationalization will often enter into the discussion.[6] Further remarks on the analytical problem will be found below.[7]

4. The stability of merely customary action rests essentially on the fact that the person who does not adapt himself to it is subjected to both petty and major inconveniences and annoyances as long as the majority of the people he comes in contact with continue to uphold the custom and conform with it.

Similarly, the stability of action in terms of self-interest rests on the fact that the person who does not orient his action to the interests of others, does not "take account" of them, arouses their antagonism or may end up in a situation different from that which he had foreseen or wished to bring about. He thus runs the risk of damaging his own interests.

6. It is, in a sense, the empirical reference of this statement which constitutes the central theme of Weber's series of studies in the Sociology of Religion. In so far as he finds it possible to attribute importance to "ideas" in the determination of action, the most important differences between systems of ideas are not so much those in the degree of rationalization as in the direction which the process of rationalization in each case has taken. This series of studies was left uncompleted at his death, but all the material which was in a condition fit for publication has been assembled in the three volumes of the *Gesammelte Aufsätze zur Religionssoziologie*.—Ed.

7. It has not been possible to identify this reference of Weber's. It refers most probably to a projected conclusion of the whole work which was never written.—Ed.

*Section C*

# The Modes of the Institutionalization of Action

# The Institutionalization of Action

*by Kaspar D. Naegele*

THE FOLLOWING SECTION APpropriately concludes Part One of this Reader. It returns to some themes underlying the selections in Section A. More particularly, it concentrates on a question prominent for Hobbes, Marx, and Maine: What *kinds* of social relations is it necessary to distinguish? It asks: how can we describe the important differences in the relations between individuals in such a way that we can state as clearly as possible what we experience as recurrent contrasts? These contrasts can be contained within one society at one time. They can refer, e.g., to the differences that we recognize in our dealings with the milkman and our dealings with our brothers. Or, more generally, they can refer to the contrasts between spheres of social life, such as kinship, economic activities, or religion. Often we see these as actually separate matters. To describe these contrasts even more generally—they can as well be those which we recognize between contemporary times and a previous period, like the Middle Ages.

The foregoing section has linked a concern with social relations with the logically necessarily related interests in both social acts, and social systems and societies. In addition, the Introduction to Section A has emphasized the difference between concrete and analytic distinctions—a difference that the analysis of social phenomena requires as much as it makes it difficult. One major source of this difficulty has also been suggested: social phenomena are themselves partially constituted by the distinctions people make. If we then contrast a business relation between two men with a friendship relation or, what may be the same thing, try to understand what is meant by the maxim that we should not do business with our friends, we are asking quite a number of questions. (1) How can we describe the norms that govern these two relations? (2) In what ways might *one* set of distinctions state the differences between these relations? and (3) Of what import is it to be able to distinguish friendship from business?

This all sounds descriptive and classifying. It also sounds mundane. Yet progressive refinement within a persistent effort at characterizing the "essential" and "typical" differences among the governing features of social relations has been a durable part of virtually all sociological analysis, and has provided the opportunity for the convergence of ideas partially documented in this section. It has provided, because of this and additional reasons still to be discussed, an encouraging impetus to keep sociology comparative. Often the wish to compare, among societies or among periods or sectors of the same society, has been relegated to background, or dropped. It is, nevertheless, a stubborn wish.

Four authors have been chosen to show solutions available for the analytical sorting out of social relations. Among them, the six selections of the section provide the essential dimensions of the issue which more recent analysis has found necessary.

The sequence of the selections reflects the fact that the classification of social relations, in starting in "the middle" as it were, is both a matter of characterizing the very coherence of different societies—of contrasting sections of it, if such there be—and of specifying roles available to specific individuals. Ultimately, such an enterprise leads back to the logically prior question: what "elements" of social relations can be used for a classification? We have ended the section with material from Max Weber's fundamental proposals concerning the categories necessary for sociological analysis, that discusses this last question.

We have begun with Toennies. In the history

of sociological analysis, he probably provides the clearest beginning of an extended analysis of "paired comparison." His distinction of *Gemeinschaft* and *Gesellschaft* has become famous and productive. It brings into view, if only as a reminder, the contrasts between industrial and feudal society, city and village, business and friendship, impersonal market and kinship, complex and simple divisions of labor, impersonal and personal encounters with other people. How are these paired contrasts related? In mentioning one side of a contrast—e.g., distant, impersonal, instrumental—what becomes of the other side? Is it a "residual" category and as such less clear and more heterogeneous than what is now its opposite? Are close, personal, and expressive just other terms for not distant, not impersonal, not instrumental?

For all their difficulties, dichotomous contrasts of this kind are made easy for us by experience and language. True and false, male and female, old and young, past and future, in and out—these are among the fundamental categories by which we order the world. Toennies was not the first to propose a dichotomous way of ordering the multiplicity and succession of inclusive social arrangements and of cultures. We have seen cognate contrasts drawn by Spencer, Maine, and, in a sense, by Marx, in Section A above. Again, Toennies' proposals are parallel, in some respects, to those of Durkheim, who wrote after him. *Gemeinschaft* and mechanical solidarity differ respectively from *Gesellschaft* and organic solidarity. Unfortunately, Toennies' description of *Gemeinschaft,* of a personal nexus in which persons appear to one another more as ends and less as means, is close to what might be, for other reasons, spontaneously described as an "organic" state of affairs. Once this terminological "crossing" is recognized, it can be dismissed again.

Toennies used the facts of industrial society as his point of departure. He saw them embedded in a conflicting heterogeneity of values, that easily obscures the extent of consensus also marking and binding this society. He wrote in the Germany of the 1880's. He wrote his famous book as a young man. He died in 1936.

His starting point is the individual involved in the "rational pursuit of his self interest." This is "society," as different from "community." It is a positive form of social relation, characterized by the coincidence of a number of facts. As a social relation, it is typically sustained as a means to the ends of otherwise separate individuals. Each needs the other, as, e.g., a man making a person-to-person long-distance call still needs an operator. The relation is limited to the facilitation of interest, and excludes the personalities of the involved parties. Characteristically, it can be studied when people are involved in economic exchange or in forming associations—*Vereine*—to establish some rather specific purpose.

According to Toennies, relations divide into those of equality and those of authority. This division cuts across the previous distinctions. Still, *Gesellschaft* is characterized by *Kuerwille:* deliberate choice, planning, voluntary association, segmental encounters. *Gemeinschaft* involves *Wesenswille:* the acting out of consensus and tradition—by contrast, it allows for much less individual scope. Relations of the *Gemeinschaft* type are more inclusive: persons confront each other as ends; they cohere more durably. They thus constitute a more "organic" nexus. Their coherence in the other case is, instead, a matter of compromising between divergent, if not conflicting, interests. Such compromises are adjudicated by a variety of standards and rules defining obligations. In *Gemeinschaft,* one shares a common fate: men then are not islands unto themselves. In *Gesellschaft,* their mutual regard is circumscribed by a sense of specific, if not formal, obligation. They are bound, in the extreme case, by contract, by agreements which set up relatively clear boundaries of obligation. *Gemeinschaft* nexi cannot be so clearly specified. Obligations ramify. Coherence itself becomes a valued matter. Specific acts—unlike the specific acts of buying and selling—are simultaneously both *means,* in relation to the daily or physical exigencies of some given solidarity, and *expressions* of past intentions and future attitudes. Friendship and parenthood, examples of relations of *Gemeinschaft,* are constituted by expectations of respect, reliability, generosity, wisdom, or whatever—in any case, they involve qualities cutting across specific acts. Specific acts express them. Social acts, especially in this context, require their wider setting. This is also true within the context of *Gesellschaft.* But the relations between specific acts and their contexts differ. In the *Gesellschaft* case, e.g., a transaction requires rules; a contract implies promises and sanctions. Yet the transaction can occur without any other encounters, leaving both parties virtually anonymous. In the *Gemeinschaft* case, specific acts tend to be consequential for a state of social relatedness between specific persons. *Gemeinschaft* militates against anonymity.

These reminders of some, and by no means of all, of Toennies' classifying accomplishment should suffice to show its importance. This importance is not diminished by its difficulties, or the necessary revisions others have introduced into it. Besides, classification, as a form of description, is not yet explanation—even if, as is sometimes true, certain kinds of explanations first require classification.

The associated elements of Toennies' dichotomy are a compound of logic and observation, of definition and interpretation. Some of the contrasts clearly intersect, rather than oppose, each other. The coercive quality of *Gemeinschaft,* for instance, is questionable when one considers marriage in our society. Presumably, no one *must* get married. The fact that marriage is normatively conditional for certain privileges and accomplishments, given additional regulations of sexuality and parenthood, is a different matter.

It is not fortuitous that Toennies' distinction between *Gemeinschaft* and *Gesellschaft* has persisted. It is concerned alike with the major distinctions among social relations, the components of social relations, and the history of society. Subsequent developments, as the Epilogue to this Reader will show, have involved far-reaching revisions and criticism of this dichotomy; but they have not discredited it as such. The nature of social bonds, and hence the question of their kinds, remains a perennial issue. Toennies' distinctions, as they stand, are not sufficient for an adequate distinction between the coherences represented by such pairs as mothers and daughters, businessmen and buyers, doctors and patients, priests and confessors, employers and employees, teachers and pupils. Yet any attempt to state the differences between the members of these pairs, with reference to the least number of elements necessary for their distinction, usually involves recourse to the contrast between the personal and the impersonal as modes of relatedness among persons.

Toennies' contribution also raises the question of the ultimate unit of sociological analysis. This implies a number of things. Genes and morphemes, phonemes and particles of matter—these are examples of some ultimate units in other universes. In sociology, there has as yet been no stability in this regard. Still, it is possible to demonstrate that a concept of the social act generally runs through most sociological analysis of the kind represented in this Reader. One can also begin, as Toennies did, with the notion of social relation. In that case, acts themselves become different by virtue of their relation to social relations; and relations, in turn, can be contrasted precisely through the manner in which specific acts come to represent them.

Social relations have an inner structure, composed of mutually related elements—this is also true of genes. One possible mark of an ultimate unit could be that it both ends and begins analysis. In the case of social phenomena and social facts, we are also often searching for an illustrative, simple, yet significant model which would characterize the nature of social coherence. A chess game or a conversation, an economic transaction or a religious ritual—as occasions, these cut across the distinction of personal and impersonal nexus; though each involves the simultaneous presences of actors. Yet the social goes beyond this. It often involves mediated coherence—in contrast to which, as we shall see in the subsequent section, we begin to think of primary or small groups.

Durkheim returns to these themes in the two important selections that continue this section. Another author, however, intervenes between selections from Toennies and Durkheim. Ralph Linton's discussion of the difference between ascription and achievement, as principles for the distribution of social privilege or social opportunity, concerns, on the level of role, one of the several ideas included in Toennies' distinction. Linton's discussion suggests a further contrast that has become indispensable to all subsequent analysis. This may be described crudely as the contrast between inheritance and accomplishment, both considered within the context of social orders. In our society, to be someone's son is an ascribed fact; to be someone else's doctor is an accomplishment. This distinction leads to the distinction between open and closed, a contrast used by Weber in his discussion of social relations. The contrast between open and closed can be applied on a variety of planes, including that of large societies. As a dimension, it refers to the extent to which any one acknowledged status in a specific social arrangement is or is not available to a variety of others who were not born into this status.

As suggested, the distinction between inheritance and accomplishment has the merits of being applicable on a variety of planes. Within the sphere of kinship, for instance, at least in our society, the roles of son and daughter may be ascribed; the role of husband, and in a sense the role of father and the comparable roles of wife and mother, are achieved. Yet their achievement differs from that of the roles of banker, fireman, barber, or politician. The sphere of kinship and the sphere of the occupational world seem to involve a contrast of ascription and achievement. Our system of stratification, by contrast to the classical Indian caste system, appears to involve differences in proportion within each of the ascribed and the achieved positions and possibilities. Ascribed social status involves the act of bestowal. This leads to the very heart of social orders. Since society involves a membership, however unequal or differentiated it may be in any one case, it is an order which must find a place for all those born to it. In the case of national, contemporary, industrialized societies, this problem has been solved by the concept of citizenship, which involves various combinations of the social interpretation of place and of parenthood. Typically, the kinship system is one way of distributing social positions to the newborn. We make this legitimate or illegitimate through the institutions of marriage. In addition, we simultaneously bestow upon the infant both a position within society and a position within a family—as though we balanced the absence of any choice about being born with the automatic privilege of thereby being part of a relational nexus.

The principle of ascription means the enhancement of those considerations which would have us think of others by virtue of their embeddedness in a variety of social connections. From this point of view, the British monarchy is a matter of hereditary ascription. It is not open to achievement. The same is true of the Norwegian monarchy, though the descendants of Haakon V are descendants of a king who demanded a popular election, and who wanted to combine bestowal with the possibility of accomplishment. Bestowal of privilege and obligation involves also its opposites—possible exclusion and rejection. Bestowal and exclusion need not be confined to relational matters. The notion of second-class citizenship, for instance, is often a matter of the invidious comparison of classifications, through membership in what is socially defined as a different category of person.

The distinction between achievement and ascription intersects, therefore, the important additional distinction underlying the way in which we think about other persons. This involves the contrast between thinking of them by virtue of their social connectedness, or the lack thereof, to others, or by virtue of their membership in a logically defined class. One can think of another person as someone's son, or someone's plumber, as tall, or as someone's sister or brother. Ascribed statuses are those which make use of relational or classifying attributes that, as such, involve bestowal rather than individual or collective efforts. It is quite a different matter that such efforts, which then lead to achieved statuses, may in some ultimate sense involve previously ascribed positions whence a person starts. In other words, no society can be wholly free of either of these principles. Societies differ in the proportion between them and in the relative prominence of either in the different spheres together constituting that society.

Ascribed statuses cannot be sought; but they can, in a sense, be lost. They share a certain conditionality. The latter differs from the more extensive conditionality of effort that characterizes achieved statuses. The son can become wicked and be disowned. Yet the ascribed statuses within the sphere of kinship particularly belong to a kind of irrevocable social position that is characteristically absent from the achieved social positions within the sphere of economic success or social mobility. These achieved positions are contingent on effort; they presuppose, therefore, freedom to make the effort. Achievement also demands that positions be occupied primarily by virtue of characteristics which can be acquired. In these terms, the position of guest that Simmel discussed in a previous selection occupies an interesting intermediary position. One can manipulate social affairs to become part of certain social occasions. Yet the guest's role is still contingent upon an invitation. Invitations are one form of social bestowal.

As a principle, ascription makes prominent relational qualities in the occupation of social positions and the performance of their implied roles. By contrast, achievement emphasizes individual or collective striving, and the deliberate acquisition of skills, resources, or other attributes deemed necessary for a certain position. The term obscures, for other than logical reasons, the fact that social arrangements emphasizing achievement imply agreed freedoms as well as recognizing successful striving. The doctor, as an achieved role, implies both validation and acknowledgment. It implies judges, in the form of patients and colleagues, who are willing to attribute competence. If the counterpart to ascription is rejection, the counterpart to achievement is failure.

All these elaborations of Linton's distinction, many of them contained in his own discussion, are intended to illustrate the cardinal importance of this particular distinction when it is used as a starting point for restating the characteristic issues that social orders create and solve.

The two selections from Durkheim constitute a classic illustration of a sequence of conceptual analysis and specific empirical research, both carried forward by a persistent theoretic concern with the character of social facts. The first selection starts with a vague contrast of present (i.e., the nineteenth- and early twentieth-century French milieu) and past society. Within this, he proposes a keen, sharp distinction between mechanical and organic solidarity—a distinction that closely parallels Toennies' distinction between *Gemeinschaft* and *Gesellschaft;* it complements Toennies' in many respects, some of which are "extra-scientific," though they have a bearing on the pursuit of sociological analysis per se. Toennies' distinction between *Gemeinschaft* and *Gesellschaft* is often more than disinterested and conceptual. It can easily become transformed into a moral preference—if it does not actually originate in one. The personalness of *Gemeinschaft* is often favorably contrasted with the impersonalness of society. Sociological theorizing—as an attempt to make explicit the elements from which social arrangements, including cherished examples of it, are built—must tend toward a criticism of the analyzed phenomena. Self-consciousness and questioning about arrangements by which people historically have wished to live are almost automatically an order of critique. In addition, the questioning necessary for understanding and explaining social facts is likely to be facilitated in minds feeling themselves somehow out of tune. Besides facilitating that analysis, such distance also often distorts it.

In any case, the *Gemeinschaft-Gesellschaft* distinction is not always easily disentangled from a critique of the competitive, impersonal individualism of capitalist, industrialized, contemporary society. A logical irony which has not impeded such criticism is that people who extol the virtues of *Gemeinschaft* often also jealously argue for the preservation of individuality and private freedoms.

Durkheim goes beyond such controversy, by adding a concern with individuality and individual happiness to a concern for the available alternatives of social orders. He is interested in "peace of mind," as he calls it in lectures on professional ethics and civic morality. Yet he is equally interested in the systematic analysis of social facts considered as real and intelligible regularities open to the same order of systematic inquiry possible within the realm of natural phenomena. Like Toennies, he distinguishes two forms of solidarity, forms that represent a historic succession as well as a formulation of elements constituting social relations or larger social units. In other words, both Toennies and Durkheim address themselves to the tasks of characterizing actual relations and of proposing distinctions necessary for the analytical separation of simultaneous relations in which any one person may be involved.

Durkheim's contrast between mechanical and organic solidarity involves him simultaneously in elaborating indices of social orders, and in proposing the mutual relations between numbers, individuality, division of labor, and the role of common moral values. For all his belief in the hard and "tangible" character of social phenomena—a belief that, at least in his earlier writing, he finds necessary for the scientific study of society—he is never blind to their essential invisibility. As the Book of Common Prayer would say, he is in search of outward and visible signs for these inward and invisible matters. Consistent with his concern with the peculiar character of social facts, Durkheim regards law as one of the main indicators of social arrangement. Law, as one form of norm and sanction, reveals, together with other sanctions, the peculiar character of social phenomena—their moral constitution. Mechanical and organic solidarity—as two forms of social, i.e., moral orders—differ by virtue of the relative role of repressive and restitute law, the amount of division of labor, the degree of individuality, possible within them, and the immediate conspicuousness of a binding social consensus constraining the members of this order. Moral consensus under conditions of organic solidarity is less conspicuous. Durkheim insists that conspicuousness and importance must not be confused. Population growth is the engine of change which would have organic solidarity grow out of mechanical solidarity and which in fact presupposes the latter. Such growth makes for differentiation, which leads to specialization and enhancement of individual variety, but also to misunderstanding of the moral consensus on which such individuality in fact depends. Sociology, then, becomes the study of complex social arrangements involved in a poignant dilemma of combining a consensus necessary for the development of individuality with enhancing such individuality.

In other words, Durkheim considers the problem of order that has accompanied the writing of the men who open Section A above. His concern with moral issues, however, is carried forward by questions opening these issues to systematic exploration. In one respect, these questions fall into two main classes. Durkheim wants to know both about the history of social arrangements and about the function of any one of them within the context of a given society. He combines what have often since then become arraigned as rival perspectives. He shows, furthermore, how the division of labor—with its concomitant mutual distance between individuals and the specialization and intensification of their faculties—provides a cohesive function. It makes for mediated interdependence. Today, we would add that those who tend to depend on it are likely to take such interdependence for granted, and that it is clearly noticed only in the face of crises, like strikes or unemployment, when the mutual relations among the disparate spheres of society become painfully visible.

In his work on suicide, Durkheim considers in greater detail the relative advantages and costs of different forms of social solidarity. He is interested in the questions of both social and personal stability. Perhaps for the first time in history, Durkheim, in his classic monograph on suicide, provides a model for sociological research involving the deliberate gathering or interpretation of quantitative facts outside the realm of economic transaction or of demographic development. The importance of his monograph on suicide is manifold. It continues the discussion of the elements of solidarity. It calls for the distinction between the analysis of rates and the analysis of the individual case, while showing that such interests are related, and that their proper relation depends on their proper distinction. It begins with the unequivocal fact of self-inflicted death, and immediately asks two questions: What is the relative distribution of this phenomenon among persons differing in their typical relation to others? And, in what sense is this simple fact a single fact?

He answers the first question by taking religious membership as an index of typical differences among possible relations between a person and a surrounding social circle, organization, or group. After eliminating explanations preceding his own, he looks to these dimensions as resources for explanations in the given variation of suicides within a given population.

With regard to the second question, Durkheim suggests that the single fact of suicide must be understood with relation to the social evaluation of suicide as such. He remembers that, as an event, it can be permitted or forbidden. Obviously, he does not suggest that it does not occur where it is forbidden. On the contrary—he is struck by the fact that while Catholics, Protestants, and Jews agree in disapproving of suicide, they differ in the frequency with which their members engage in it. He relates this difference to his earlier distinction between mechanical and organic solidarity. The notion of mechanical solidarity helps him formulate the concept of altruistic suicide. Under conditions of mechanical solidarity, individual, private interests are subordinate to collective concerns. In this connection, Durkheim recognizes the fact that in the army, e.g., officers have a higher rate of suicide than enlisted men. In other words, attachment to an order in which individual survival is subordinated to honor enhances one's inclination to suicide when faced with some loss of esteem. In this sense, altruistic suicide differs from two other forms: egoistic and anomic. Durkheim suggests a fourth form, fatalistic, but does not develop it. If one can end one's life because of one's involvement in an organization whose honor is compromised by one's own survival, one can similarly add to one's chances of suicide by being part of a social circle which values the enhancement of personal responsibility. Such circles are likely to differ in their chances of generating suicide to the extent to which they do not provide social support in the face of guilt and failure.

From this point of view, the terms Catholic, Protestant, and Jewish are indices for alternative solutions (or lack thereof) of the question of social support in the face of failure. The Protestant, more than the Catholic and the Jew, is burdened by an order of unsupported responsibility which facilitates his managing failure by death. Today, psychodynamic considerations would be added to Durkheim's description of the typical relations between Protestants, Catholics, and Jews, and their co-believers. This would provide additional links between the private and the public spheres; it would not undo Durkheim's analysis. In any case, in Durkheim's analysis, the higher rate of Protestant suicides is a reflection of a relative lack of social support in the face of the burdens and strivings that are the result of social membership. This is one possible cost of organic solidarity, with its emphasis on enhancing individual personality. Organic solidarity, as discussed above, is characterized by the greater generality of its binding consensus. Such generality is necessary when individual difference and variation become valued accomplishments.

Both altruistic and egoistic suicides occur under conditions of clear rules. Whatever despair either may involve, it is not the despair of uncertainty; it is, if anything, the despair of a disproportion between the desirable and the actual. Typically organic solidarity, however, contains another possibility. The ends which people seek within its confines and the norms governing their pursuit can become elusive. Within the fluctuations of its economic change, organic solidarity can give rise to the possibilities of other forms of social discontinuities, including social mobility. It can lead to a moral vacuum. Durkheim uses the word *anomie* to describe this state of affairs. The term is ambiguous, since it seems sometimes to refer to a conflict in the ends that men seek, and sometimes to the absence of a clear view of any end that they might wish to attain.

In any case, Durkheim faces the fact that economic depression, as well as sudden economic prosperity, is often accompanied by an increase in suicide. Later research may have shown his statistics to be faulty; but his ideas have remained productive. Both situations are cases of a more general phenomenon. Both demonstrate that people's actions and stability are contingent on commitments to standards and beliefs making life meaningful and providing bases of choice among alternative courses of conduct. Sudden change in any direction—enhancing or undermining one's fortune—is in fact constituted by new conditions, in which one often lacks the requisite guides for necessary action. Whether, by *anomie,* one means the attrition of a landscape of ends toward which one wishes to proceed, or of standards by which one can choose when one comes to road-forks, it constitutes an individual or collective situation making action difficult. Yet Durkheim's analysis, particularly of suicide, assumes that the pursuit of ends is a constitutive element of personality itself. This position provides a restatement of the question of the relation between individuals and social arrangements.

In Durkheim's analysis, in spite of its ambiguity and shift over time, the social becomes simultaneously an order of external constraint and support, and part of the necessary inner resources constituting personality as such. Anomic suicide is, so to speak, the empirical answer to the logical fallacy of an original human nature. Isolated from ends, human nature could not have arisen; and in facing the attrition of ends, it is once more helped toward decay.

These comments are intended to provide some continuity among the necessarily select and disparate passages in this Reader. Our purpose throughout is to let the passages speak for themselves, while we justify our having selected them.

This section is logically concluded by Max Weber's dissection of the elements of social action, social relations, social organization, and legitimate order. Like Durkheim, Weber began by facing concrete historic circumstances and wishing to impose some approximate first order on them. Linton developed one strand of distinction. Max Weber, in this section, is more concerned with the logically complementary question of what conceptual distinctions must be made in order to be just to the known and experienced complexity of social orders and their historic succession. He is concerned, in this context, with the clarification of categories. In his case, this accompanied a huge enterprise of historic analysis, with particular reference to the mutual relations between religiosity and economic systems. About Durkheim's selection preceding the two by Max Weber, one may ask what validity the proposed explanations have, and to what other regularities Durkheim's proposals about suicide could be applied. Of Weber's specific contributions it is necessary to inquire how clear the distinctions he proposes are, what alternative distinctions could have been made, and what kind of research such distinctions facilitate. This Reader is not directly concerned with providing answers, but with raising questions; it cannot be reiterated too often that the assembling of materials for it has primarily been guided by the aim of documenting and suitably arranging the resources available for sociological analysis, so that the continuity among sociologists' works can be enhanced.

Max Weber suspends a huge panoply of distinctions between the two poles of social action and social order. This panoply is intended to make social change and stability intelligible. It proceeds from the assumption that the systematic (scientific) inquiry into social phenomena, which are also historic phenomena, is always a matter of both stability and change. Like Durkheim's simultaneous interest in history and function, Weber's simultaneous interest in stability and change has often become a matter of rival perspective, as will be discussed again in the introductory material to the last part of this Reader.

The selections from Max Weber rounding out this section follow directly from the Weber selection that completed Section B above. While elaborating his monumental gridwork of distinctions, Max Weber interrupts a discussion of the difference between open and closed social relations with the comment that this laborious effort at defining everyday facts may well appear to be a dry and useless enterprise. On the other hand, the enterprise demonstrates that what we take as self-evident is least likely to be thought through. The present section represents part of this rich thinking process. It leads to a variety of cardinal ideas which help constitute the universe of sociological analysis. Readers of this Reader will come to different conclusions about the worth and importance of such an enterprise; about the relations, in Max Weber's case, between his theoretic distinctions and the history of his own more specific empirical work.

One of the admitted shortcomings of this or any anthology should once more become apparent: Even though we have often quoted from Max Weber throughout these volumes and even if all his selections were seen only in their mutual relation, this would still not provide an adequate representation of his total work. The same is true for all the other authors from whom we have taken selections. In Max Weber's case, it is particularly serious. His is one of the few cases in which the work of one man comes to assume a fragmentary hugeness which is visible only when one sees it as a whole. Freud, Durkheim, and Simmel, from this point of view, represent quite different configurations of accomplishment. In any event, the two selections dealing with the constitutive elements of social organization and legitimate orders can be read as a circumspect, tough, and discriminating effort to propose a latticework of distinctions which are as much a summary of a man's knowledge as they are a statement of his intentions. Durkheim returned again and again to the moral quality of social facts; Weber was equally insistent on their meaningful character. His category is perhaps the wider one; his efforts are more those of a universal historian. Durkheim preferred, as a method of analysis, the progressive elimination of alternative perspectives in relation to a specified and delimited phenomenon, like suicide, religious ritual, or division of labor; Max Weber, like him, also has a guiding and single focus—the rationalization of the world.

He also wishes to formulate a categorical arsenal for coming to terms with the properties of social phenomena on four levels: social action, social relations, regularities of choice, and legitimate orders. He tries to outline the generic features of social acts or of social relations, of such regularities as convention and fashion, or of legitimate orders. He also seeks to distinguish *kinds* of each of these coherences. If a social act is an act involving mutual orientation, he distinguishes four forms of such orientation: those concerned with the implementation of specific ends or consequences; those concerned with the expression of moral positions; those issuing from affective dispositions; and those arising from tradition. One may be quite critical of such a classification, as it seems to lack an explicit principle of differentiation. Still, the proposal reminds one of the constituted dimensions of social interaction, and releases one from imprisonment by the immediately experienced. Similarly, on the plane of social relations, Weber proposes both variables of their inner structure, and a classification of their concrete forms. For example, he distinguishes the mutability of a relation, or its durability, from its definability, or its definability from its degree of formality. He separates open and closed relations on the basis of their accessibility, or lack of it, to others also interested in the intended meaning of a given social relation. He uses this distinction to cut across the previous differentiation between conflict, communal and associational relations. Again, we may be critical and wonder whether concrete and analytical matters have been properly separated. Too, we are reminded of a continuity among Toennies, Durkheim, and Weber. Considering action, Weber distinguishes between usage, interest, and legitimate order. He then inquires seriously how the legitimacy of action can be guaranteed and how legitimacy is attributed to it. This leads him to distinguish kinds of sanctions. He proposes terms like "convention" and "legal order," to bring into line the experienced difference between disapproval and legal coercion. Such distinctions become related to his analysis of authority and power. Max Weber's primary concern is with the bases on which power—i.e., the chances of imposing one's will successfully—becomes justified or justifiable. Weber distinguishes between power and authority, for he considers power to be sociologically amorphous. By contrast, in his work, authority becomes more precise: it refers to the chances that an order meets obedience among specifiable persons.

Weber acknowledges the continuity between his efforts and the accomplishments of the past. He wishes to enhance self-consciousness in using the ideas necessary for an account of the structure and history of social arrangements. Given the serious center of meaning, the co-ordinates of his analysis typically involve the contrasts of reason and tradition, emotion and interest, felt coherence and calculating association, legal requirement and charismatic demand. Distributed over the several planes of social action, social relation, social regularity, and legitimate order, such contrasts soon return him to a concern with the social constellations that indicate law as a form of obligatory order—distinct from convention, which leads to disapproval. Law requires a bureaucratic staff.

Max Weber extends his ordering of social constellations by sorting out kinds of corporate groups. This sorting is facilitated by his concern with authority, power, and representation.

In summary: like Toennies, Linton, and Durkheim, Max Weber in the following selections is concerned with consensus, and with the regulative principles through which a variety of disparate persons come to produce the regularities among their acts that are not explicable on the basis either of their biological constitutions or of purely economic considerations.

# 1. *Gemeinschaft and Gesellschaft*

BY FERDINAND TOENNIES

## *Subject*

RELATIONS BETWEEN HUMAN WILLS—GEMEINSCHAFT (COMMUNITY) AND GESELLSCHAFT (SOCIETY) FROM A LINGUISTIC POINT OF VIEW[1]

HUMAN WILLS stand in manifold relations to one another. Every such relationship is a mutual action, inasmuch as one party is active or gives while the other party is passive or receives. These actions are of such a nature that they tend either towards preservation or towards destruction of the other will or life; that is, they are either positive or negative. This study will consider as its subject of investigation only the relationships of mutual affirmation. Every such relationship represents unity in plurality or plurality in unity. It consists of assistance, relief, services, which are transmitted back and forth from one party to another and are to be considered as expressions of wills and their forces. The group which is formed through this positive type of relationship is called an association (*Verbindung*) when conceived of as a thing of being which acts as a unit inwardly and outwardly. The relationship itself, and also the resulting association, is conceived of either as real and organic life—this is the essential characteristic of the *Gemeinschaft* (community),—or as imaginary and mechanical structure—this is the concept of *Gesellschaft* (society).

Through the application of these two terms we shall see that the chosen expressions are rooted in their synonymic use in the German language. But to date in scientific terminology they have been customarily confused and used at random without any distinction. For this reason, a few introductory remarks may explain the inherent contrast between these two concepts. All intimate, private, and exclusive living together, so we discover, is understood as life in Gemeinschaft (community). Gesellschaft (society) is public life—it is the world itself. In Gemeinschaft (community) with one's family, one lives from birth on bound to it in weal and woe. One goes into Gesellschaft (society) as one goes into a strange country. A young man is warned against bad Gesellschaft (society), but the expression bad Gemeinschaft (community) violates the meaning of the word. Lawyers may speak of domestic (*häusliche*) Gesellschaft (society) thinking only of the legalistic concept of a social association, but the domestic Gemeinschaft (community) or home life with its immeasurable influence upon the human soul has been felt by everyone who ever shared it. Likewise, each member of a bridal couple knows that he or she goes into marriage as a complete Gemeinschaft (community) of life (*communio totius vitae*). A Gesellschaft (society) of life would be a contradiction in and of itself. One keeps or enjoys another's Gesellschaft (society or company) but not his Gemeinschaft (community) in this sense. One becomes a part of a religious Gemeinschaft (community); religious Gesellschaften (associations, or societies) like any other groups formed for given purposes, exist only in so far as they, viewed from without, take their places among the institutions of a political body or as they represent conceptual elements of a theory; they do not touch upon the religious Gemeinschaft as such. There exists a Gemeinschaft (community) of language, of folkways, or mores, or of beliefs; but, by way of contrast, Gesellschaft (society or company) exists in the realm of business, travel, or sciences. So of special importance are the commercial Gesellschaften (societies or companies), whereas, even though a certain familiarity and Gemeinschaft (community) may exist among business partners, one could indeed hardly speak of commercial Gemeinschaft (community). To make the word combination, "joint-stock Gemeinschaft," would be abominable. On the other hand, there exists a Gemeinschaft (community) of ownership in fields, forest, and pasture. The Gemeinschaft (community) of property between man and wife cannot be called Gesellschaft

---

Reprinted from Ferdinand Toennies, *Community and Society* (*Gemeinschaft und Gesellschaft,* trans. and introduced by Charles P. Loomis (East Lansing, Mich.: Michigan State University Press, 1957) Book I, secs. 1, 2, pp. 33–40, 42–44, 46–48, 64–69, 75–78, with the permission of Michigan State University Press.

1. The parenthetical English renditions of the words *Gemeinschaft* and *Gesellschaft* found in this section indicate the difficulty which would be encountered if one attempted their translation by any one pair of terms. Elsewhere in the text these two substantives and their adjective forms are not translated when they are used in the ideal typological sense.

(society) of property. Thus many differences become apparent.

In the most general way, one could speak of a Gemeinschaft (community) comprising the whole of mankind, such as the church wishes to be regarded. But human Gesellschaft (society) is conceived as mere coexistence of people independent of each other. Recently, the concept of Gesellschaft as opposed to and distinct from the state has been developed. This term will also be used in this treatise, but can only derive its adequate explanation from the underlying contrast to the Gemeinschaft of the people.

Gemeinschaft (community) is old; Gesellschaft (society) is new as a name as well as a phenomenon. This has been recognized by an author who otherwise taught political science in all its aspects without penetrating to its fundamentals. "The entire concept of Gesellschaft (society) in a social and political sense," says Bluntschli (*Staatswörterbuch* IV), "finds its natural foundation in the folkways, mores, and ideas of the third estate. It is not really the concept of a people (*Volks-Begriff*) but the concept of the third estate . . . Its Gesellschaft has become the origin and expression of common opinions and tendencies . . . Wherever urban culture blossoms and bears fruits, Gesellschaft appears as its indispensable organ. The rural people know little of it." On the other hand, all praise of rural life has pointed out that the Gemeinschaft (community) among people is stronger there and more alive; it is the lasting and genuine form of living together. In contrast to Gemeinschaft, Gesellschaft (society) is transitory and superficial. Accordingly, Gemeinschaft (community) should be understood as a living organism, Gesellschaft (society) as a mechanical aggregate and artifact.

### ORGANIC AND MECHANICAL FORMATIONS

Everything real is organic in so far as it can be conceived only as something related to the totality of reality and defined in its nature and movements by this totality. Thus attraction in its manifold forms makes the universe, in so far as it is accessible to our knowledge, into a totality, the action of which expresses itself in the movements by which any two bodies change their mutually held positions. But for observation and scientific theory based thereupon, a totality must be limited to be effective, and each such totality will consist of smaller totalities which have a certain direction and speed in relation to each other. Attraction itself remains either unexplained (as force in space) or is understood as mechanical force (by exterior contact) making itself effective, perhaps in some unknown manner.

Thus the masses of matter may be divided into homogeneous molecules which attract each other with more or less energy and which in their aggregate state appear as bodies. The molecules are divided into dissimilar (chemical) atoms, the dissimilarity of which remains to be explained by further analysis of the different arrangement which similar atom constituents take within the atom. Pure theoretical mechanics, however, presupposes the existence of centers of force without dimension as sources of real actions and reactions. The concept of these centers is very close to the concept of metaphysical atoms and it excludes from the calculation all influence of the movements, or tendencies thereto, of the parts. For all practical applications the physical molecules, when thought of in relation to the same body as their systems, can be considered equally well as carriers of energy, as substance itself, since these molecules are equal in size and no attention is given to their possible subdivision. All real masses may be compared by weight and expressed as quantities of a similar definite substance when their parts are conceived as being in a perfectly solid state of aggregation.

In every case the unit, which is assumed as the subject of a movement or as an integral part of a totality (a higher unit), is the product of a fiction necessary for scientific analysis. Strictly speaking, only the ultimate units, metaphysical atoms, could be accepted as their adequate representatives: somethings which are nothings or nothings which are somethings (*Etwasse, welche Nichtse, oder Nichtse, welche Etwasse sind*). But in so reasoning, the relative meaning of all concepts of size must be kept in mind.

In reality, however, even if they may be anomalies in the mechanical concept, there exist bodies other than these combinable and combining particles of matter conceived of as dead. Such bodies appear to be natural totalities which, as totalities, have movement and action in relation to their parts. These are the organic bodies. To these we human beings, who strive for knowledge and understanding, ourselves belong. Each of us has, in addition to imparted knowledge of all possible bodies, an immediate knowledge of his own. We are driven to the conclusion that psychic life is connected with every living body, existing as an entity in the same way as we know ourselves to exist. But objective observation teaches not less clearly that in the case of a living body we deal each time with a totality which is not a mere aggregation of its parts but one which is made up of these parts in such a manner that they are dependent upon and conditioned by the totality, and that such a body as a totality and hence as a form possesses reality and substance.

As human beings we are able to produce only

inorganic things from organic materials, dividing and recombining them. In the same way things are also made into a unity through scientific manipulation and are a unity in our concepts. Naïve interpretation or attitudes and artistic imagination, folk belief, and inspired poetry lend life to the phenomena. This creative element is also apparent in the fictions of science. But science also reduces the living to the dead in order to grasp its relations and conditions. It transforms all conditions and forces into movements and interprets all movements as quantities of labor performed, i.e., expended energy, in order to comprehend processes as similar and commensurable. This last is true to the same extent that the assumed units are realities, and the possibility for thought is unlimited. Thus understanding, as an end, is attained, and therewith other objectives.

However, the tendencies and inevitableness of organic growth and decay cannot be understood through mechanical means. In the organic world the concept itself is a living reality, changing and developing as does the idea of the individual being. When science enters this realm it changes its own nature and develops from a logical and rational to an intuitive and dialectic interpretation; it becomes philosophy. However, the present study does not deal with genus and species, i.e., in regard to human beings it is not concerned with race, people, or tribe as biological units. Instead, we have in mind their sociological interpretation, which sees human relationships and associations as living organisms or, in contrast, mechanical constructions. This has its counterpart and analogy in the theory of individual will, and in this sense to present the psychological problem will be the text of the second book of this treatise.

## *Theory of Gemeinschaft*

### EMBRYO OR EMERGENT FORMS

In accordance with the preliminary explanations, the theory of Gemeinschaft starts from the assumption of perfect unity of human wills as an original or natural condition which is preserved in spite of actual separation. This natural condition is found in manifold forms because of dependence on the nature of the relationship between individuals who are differently conditioned. The common root of this natural condition is the coherence of vegetative life through birth and the fact that the human wills, in so far as each one of these wills is related to a definite physical body, are and remain linked to each other by parental descent and by sex, or by necessity become so linked. This close interrelation as a direct and mutual affirmation is represented in its most intense form by three types of relationships, namely: (1) the relation between a mother and her child; (2) the relation between husband and wife in its natural or general biological meaning; (3) the relation among brothers and sisters, that is, at least among those who know each other as being the offspring of the same mother. If in the relations of kindred individuals one may assume the embryo of Gemeinschaft or the tendency and force thereto, rooted in the individual wills, specific significance must be attributed to the three above-mentioned relationships, which are the strongest and most capable of development. Each, however, is important in a special way:

(A) The relation between mother and child is most deeply rooted in liking or in pure instinct. Also, in this case the transition from an existing physical to a purely psychic bond is evident. But the physical element is the more apparent the closer the relation remains to its origin (birth). The relationship implies long duration as the mother has to feed, protect, and educate the child until it becomes capable of doing this alone. With this development the relation loses in essentiality, and separation of mother and child becomes more probable. This tendency toward separation, however, can be counterbalanced, or at least restrained, by other tendencies, namely, through the mother and child becoming accustomed to one another and through remembrance of the pleasures which they have given each other, especially the gratitude of the child for the care and painstaking attention of the mother. To these direct mutual relations other common and indirectly binding relations involving other things are added: pleasure, habit, remembrance of objects in the environments which were, or have become, pleasant. The same holds also of shared remembrances of intimate, helpful, beloved persons such as the father, if he lives with the mother, or the brothers and sisters of the mother or child, etc.

(B) The sexual instinct does not in any way necessitate a permanent living together. Moreover, in the beginning it does not lead so much to a fixed mutual relationship as to one-sided subjugation of the woman, who, weaker by nature, can be reduced to an object of mere possession or to servitude. For this reason the relationship between man and wife, if considered independent from kinship and from all social forces based thereupon, has to be supported mainly by habituation to one another in order that the relationship may shape itself into one of mutual affirmation. Besides this, there are, as will be readily understood, the other previously mentioned factors which assist in strengthening the bond. Especially in this connection may be mentioned the relationship to the children as common possession, and, further, the common possessions and household.

(C) Among brothers and sisters there is no such innate and instinctive affection and natural liking or preference as between mother and children or between husband and wife. This is true even though the husband-wife relationship may resemble that among brothers and sisters, and there are many reasons to believe that this has frequently been the case with some tribes in an earlier period in the history of man. It must be remembered, however, that among such tribes, as long as descent was reckoned only from the mother, the relationship between brothers and sisters was extended in name, as well as in its emotional aspects, to the corresponding generations of cousins. This practice was so general that the more limited meaning of the concept was, as in many other cases, developed only in a later period. It was through a similar development in the most important ethnic groups that marriage between brothers and sisters came to be regarded as illicit, and where exogamy prevailed, marriage and clan membership (but not kinship) also became mutually exclusive. Therefore, one is justified in considering love between brother and sister, although essentially based upon blood kinship, as the most "human" relationship between human beings. The intellectual quality of this relationship as compared to the two others discussed above is also apparent from the fact that while instinct plays only a small part, the intellectual force of memory is the foremost in creating, conserving, and consolidating this bond of hearts. For where children of the same mother, in living with her, are also living together with each other, the reminiscences of each of them about pleasant impressions and experiences will necessarily include the person and the activities of the other one. This all the more so, the more closely the group is tied together, especially where, endangered from the outside, it is compelled to strive and act in unison. Thus habit makes such life easier and dearer. At the same time the greatest possible *similarity* of nature and equality of strength may be expected among brothers even though the differences in intelligence and experience, as a purely human or mental element, may easily be perceived.

### THEIR UNITY

Many other less intimate relationships are linked to those most fundamental and familiar types. They find their unity and perfection in the relationships between father and children. The existence of an organic basis which keeps the intelligent being connected with the offspring of his body makes this relationship in the most important aspect similar to the first one mentioned (A), from which it differs in that the instinctive part of it is so much weaker. Thus it resembles more closely the husband-wife relationship and is, therefore, more readily conceived as merely coercive. But while the affection of the husband, as to duration more than as to intensity, is inferior to that of the mother, the love of a father differs from the love of a mother in the opposite direction. If present to any considerable degree, therefore, it is similar through its spiritual nature to the affection among brothers and sisters, but, in contrast to the latter, it is defined by an inequality of nature, especially that of age and intellectual power.

Thus the idea of authority is, within the Gemeinschaft, most adequately represented by fatherhood or paternity. However, authority, in this sense, does not imply possession and use in the interest of the master; it means education and instruction as the fulfilment of procreation, i.e., sharing the fullness of one's own life and experiences with the children who will grow gradually to reciprocate these gifts and thus to establish a truly mutual relationship. In this regard the first-born son has a natural preference—he is the closest to the father and will occupy the place which the aging father leaves. The full authority of the father is, therefore, at least implicitly, passed on to the first-born son at his very birth. Thus the idea of an ever-renewed vital force finds its expression in the continuous succession of fathers and sons. We know that this rule of inheritance is not the original one. Apparently the patriarchate has been preceded by the matriarchate and the rule of the brother on the mother's side, and even if collateral succession (the system of tanistry) has precedence over primogeniture, this precedence is based only on the relation to a former generation: the succeeding brother does not derive his right from the brother but from the common father.

* * *

### GEMEINSCHAFT BY BLOOD—OF PLACE—OF MIND. KINSHIP—NEIGHBORHOOD—FRIENDSHIP

The Gemeinschaft by blood, denoting unity of being, is developed and differentiated into Gemeinschaft of locality, which is based on a common habitat. A further differentiation leads to the Gemeinschaft of mind which implies only co-operation and co-ordinated action for a common goal. Gemeinschaft of locality may be conceived as a community of physical life, just as Gemeinschaft of mind expresses the community of mental life. In conjunction with the others, this last type of Gemeinschaft represents the truly human and supreme form of community. The first or kinship Gemeinschaft signifies a common relation to, and share in, human beings themselves, while in the second one such a common relation is established through collective ownership of land, and in the third the common bond is represented by sacred places and worshiped deities. All three types of Gemeinschaft are closely interrelated in space as well as in time. They are, therefore, also related in all such single phenomena and in their development as well as in general human culture and its history. Wherever human beings are related through their wills in an organic manner and affirm each other, we find Gemeinschaft of one or another of the three types. Either the earlier type involves the later one, or the later type has developed to relative independence from some earlier one. It is, therefore, possible to deal with (1) kinship, (2) neighborhood, and (3) friendship as definite and meaningful derivations of these original categories.

The house constitutes the realm and, as it were, the body of kinship. Here people live together under one protecting roof, here they share their possessions and their pleasures; they feed from the same supply, they sit at the same table. As invisible spirits the dead are venerated here, as if they were still powerful and held a protecting hand over their family. Thus common fear and common honor ensure with greater certainty peaceful living and co-operation. The will and spirit of kinship is not confined within the walls of the house nor bound up with physical proximity; but where it is strong and alive in the closest and most intimate relationship, it can live on itself, thrive on memory alone, and overcome any distance by its feeling and its imagination of nearness and common activity. But, nevertheless, it seeks all the more for physical proximity and is loath to give it up, because such nearness alone will fulfill the desire for love. The ordinary human being, therefore—in the long run and for the average of cases—feels best and most cheerful if he is surrounded by his family and relatives. He is among his own (*chez soi*).

Neighborhood describes the general character of living together in the rural village. The proximity of dwellings, the communal fields, and even the mere contiguity of holdings necessitate many contacts of human beings and cause inurement to and intimate knowledge of one another. They also necessitate co-operation in labor, order, and management, and lead to common supplication for grace and mercy to the gods and spirits of land and water who bring blessing or menace with disaster. Although essentially based upon proximity of habitation, this neighborhood type of Gemeinschaft can nevertheless persist during separation from the locality, but it then needs to be supported still more than before by well-defined habits of reunion and sacred customs.

Friendship is independent of kinship and neighborhood, being conditioned by and resulting from similarity of work and intellectual attitude. It comes most easily into existence when callings or crafts are the same or of similar character. Such a tie, however, must be made and maintained through easy and frequent meetings, which are most likely to take place in a town. A worshiped deity, created out of a common mentality, has an immediate significance for the preservation of such a bond, since only, or at least mainly, this deity is able to give it living and lasting form. Such good spirit, therefore, is not bound to any place but lives in the conscience of its worshipers and accompanies them on their travels into foreign countries. Thus, those who are brethren of such a common faith feel, like members of the same craft or rank, everywhere united by a spiritual bond and the co-operation in a common task. Urban community of life may be classified as neighborhood, as is also the case with a community of domestic life in which nonrelated members or servants participate. In contradistinction, spiritual friendship forms a kind of invisible scene or meeting which has to be kept alive by artistic intuition and creative will. The relations between human beings themselves as friends and comrades have the least organic and intrinsically necessary character. They are the least instinctive and they are based less upon habit of neighborhood. They are of a mental nature and seem to be founded, therefore, as compared with the earlier relationships, upon chance or free choice.

* * *

### AUTHORITY AND SERVICE—INEQUALITY AND ITS LIMITS

All authority is characterized by particular and enhanced freedom and honor, and thus represents a specific sphere of will. As such it must be derived from the general and equal share of will of the Gemeinschaft. It finds its corollary in service as a particular and diminished freedom and honor. Each authority can be regarded as service and each service as authority, provided the particularity involved is taken into consideration. The realm of will and therefore the will of the Gemeinschaft is a mass of determined force, power, or right. And right is, in essence, will as being able or being allowed and will as obligation or duty. This is the nature of all derived realms of will in which rights and duties are the two corresponding aspects of the same thing, or nothing but the subjective modalities of the same objective substance of right or force. In this way, through increased and diminished duties and rights, real inequalities exist and develop within the Gemeinschaft through its will. These inequalities can be increased only to a certain limit, however, because beyond this limit the essence of the Gemeinschaft as the unity of unequal beings would be dissolved: In case the superiors' legal power would become too great, their relation to the common sphere of right would become indifferent and without value and the inferiors' legal power would become too small and their relationship thereto unreal and insignificant.

The less human beings who remain or come into contact with each other are bound together in relation to the same Gemeinschaft, the more they stand opposite each other as free agents of their wills and abilities. The less this freedom is dependent upon a preconditioned will of the individual himself, which is to say the less this will is dependent upon or influenced by a common will, the greater is the freedom. For, besides the inherited forces and instincts, the influence of a community as an educating and guiding will is the most important factor determining the condition and formation of every individual habit and disposition. Especially is the family spirit (*Familiengeist*) important, but so also is every spirit (*Geist*) which is similar to it and has the same effects.

COMMON WILL—UNDERSTANDING—NATURAL LAW—LANGUAGE—MOTHER TONGUE—CONCORD

Reciprocal, binding sentiment as a peculiar will of a Gemeinshaft we shall call understanding (*consensus*).[2] It represents the special social force and sympathy which keeps human beings together as members of a totality. As everything instinctive in the man is related to reasons and requires the capacity of speech, this mentality can be regarded also as the reason and significance of such a relationship. This mentality exists, for instance, between the parent and the child only to the degree in which the child is conceived as possessing speech, intellect, and reason. In the same way it can be said that everything that conforms to the conception of a Gemeinschaft relationship and what in and for this situation has meaning, forms its laws. Everything that conforms to the conception of this Gemeinschaft relationship is to be considered as the proper and real will of those bound together. In so far as enjoyment and labor are differentiated according to the very nature and capability of individuals, especially in such a manner that one part is entitled to guidance, the other bound to obedience, this constitutes a natural law as an order of group life, which assigns a sphere and function, incorporating duties and privileges, to every will. Understanding is based upon intimate knowledge of each other in so far as this is conditioned and advanced by direct interest of one being in the life of the other, and readiness to take part in his joy and sorrow. For that reason understanding is the more probable, the more alike the constitution and experience or the more the natural disposition, character, and intellectual attitude are similar or harmonize.

The real organ of understanding, through which it develops and improves, is language. Language given by means of gestures and sounds enables expressions of pain and pleasure, fear and desire, and all other feelings and emotions to be imparted and understood. Language has—as we all know—not been invented and, as it were, agreed upon as a means and tool by which one makes oneself understood. It is itself the living understanding both in its content and in its form. Similar to all other conscious activities of expression, the manifestation of language is the involuntary outcome of deep feelings and prevailing thoughts. It is not merely an artificial means of overcoming a natural lack of understanding, nor does it serve merely the purpose of enabling one to make oneself understood. Language can be used, however, among those who do understand each other, as a mere system of symbols, the same as other symbols which have been agreed upon. All these manifestations can be expressions of hostile as well as friendly passions. This justifies the general statement that friendly and hostile moods and passions underlie the same or very similar conditions. We must, however, distinguish between the hostility which springs from the rupture or loosening of natural and existing ties and the other type of hostility which is based upon strangeness, misunderstanding, and distrust. Both are instinctive, but the first one is anger, hatred, displeasure; the second one is fear, abhorrence, dislike. The first one is acute, the second one chronic. Of course language, like any other means of communication between minds, did not spring from either of these two kinds of hostility—which is only an unnatural and diseased state—but from intimacy, fondness, and affection. Especially from the deep understanding between mother and child, mother tongue should develop most easily and vigorously. Underlying the open hostility associated with an intimate understanding, on the contrary, we can always think of a certain friendship and unity.

The real foundation of unity, and consequently the possibility of Gemeinschaft, is in the first place

2. *Verständnis* is translated "understanding." The concept as here used should also carry the meaning of mutual understanding and possession of similar sentiments, hopes, aspirations, desires, attitudes, emotions, and beliefs.

closeness of blood relationship and mixture of blood, secondly physical proximity, and finally—for human beings—intellectual proximity. In this gradation are, therefore, to be found the sources of all kinds of understanding.

We may now establish the great main laws of Gemeinschaft. (1) Relatives and married couples love each other or easily adjust themselves to each other. They speak together and think along similar lines. Likewise do neighbors and other friends. (2) Between people who love each other there is understanding. (3) Those who love and understand each other remain and dwell together and organize their common life. A mixed or complex form of common determinative will, which has become as natural as language itself and which consists of a multitude of feelings of understanding which are measured by its norm, we call concord (*Eintracht*) or family spirit (*concordia* as a cordial allegiance and unity). Understanding and concord are one and the same thing; namely, will of the Gemeinschaft in its most elementary forms, including understanding in their separate relations and actions and concord in their total force and nature.

* * *

## *Theory of Gesellschaft*

### THE FUNDAMENTAL CHARACTERISTIC OF THE GESELLSCHAFT, A NEGATION—EQUALITY OF VALUE—THE OBJECTIVE JUDGMENT

The theory of the Gesellschaft deals with the artificial construction of an aggregate of human beings which superficially resembles the Gemeinschaft in so far as the individuals peacefully live and dwell together. However, in the Gemeinshaft they remain essentially united in spite of all separating factors, whereas in the Gesellschaft they are essentially separated in spite of all uniting factors. In the Gesellschaft, as contrasted with the Gemeinschaft, we find no actions that can be derived from an a priori and necessarily existing unity; no actions, therefore, which manifest the will and the spirit of the unity even if performed by the individual; no actions which, in so far as they are performed by the individual, take place on behalf of those united with him. In the Gesellschaft such actions do not exist. On the contrary, here everybody is by himself and isolated, and there exists a condition of tension against all others. Their spheres of activity and power are sharply separated, so that everybody refuses to everyone else contacts with and admittance to his sphere; i.e., intrusions are regarded as hostile acts. Such a negative attitude towards one another becomes the normal and always underlying relation of these power-endowed individuals, and it characterizes the Gesellschaft in the condition of rest; nobody wants to grant and produce anything for another individual, nor will he be inclined to give ungrudgingly to another individual, if it be not in exchange for a gift or labor equivalent that he considers at least equal to what he has given. It is even necessary that it be more desirable to him than what he coud have kept himself; because only for the sake of receiving something that seems better to him will he be moved to give away a good. Inasmuch as each and every one is possessed of such will it is self-evident that for the individual "B" the object "a" may possibly be better than the object "b," and correspondingly, for the individual "A" the object "b" better than the object "a"; it is, however, only with reference to these relations that "a" is better than "b" and at the same time "b" is better than "a." This leads us to the question, With what meaning may one speak of the worth or of the value of things, independently of such relationships?

The answer runs as follows: In the concept presented here, all goods are conceived to be separate, as are also their owners. What somebody has and enjoys, he has and enjoys to the exclusion of all others. So, in reality, something that has a common value does not exist. Its existence may, however, be brought about through fiction on the part of the individuals, which means that they have to invent a common personality and his will, to whom this common value has to bear reference. Now, a manipulation of this kind must be warranted by a sufficient occasion. Such an occasion is given when we consider the simple action of the delivery of an object by one individual and its acceptance by another one. For there a contact takes place and there is brought into existence a common sphere which is desired by both individuals and lasts through the same length of time as does the "transaction." This period of time may be so small as to be negligible, but, on the other hand, it may also be extended indefinitely. At any rate, during this period the piece which is getting separated from the sphere of, for example, the individual "A" has ceased to be under the exclusive dominion of "A" and has not yet begun to be entirely under the dominion of "B": it is still under the partial dominion of "A" and already under the partial dominion of "B." It is still dependent upon both individuals, provided that their wills with reference to it are in accord. This is, however, the case as long as the act of giving and receiving continues. During this time it is a common good and represents a social value. Now the will that is directed to this common good is combined and mutual and *can* also be regarded as homogeneous in that it keeps demanding from either individual the execution of the twofold act until it is entirely completed. This will *must* however, be regarded as a unity inasmuch as it is conceived as a personality or inasmuch as a personality is assigned to it; for to conceive something as existing or as a thing is the same as conceiving it as a unity. There, however, we must be careful to discern whether and to what extent such an *ens fictivum* (artificial being) exists only in the theory, i.e., in scientific thinking, or whether and under which conditions it is also implanted in the thinking of the individuals who are its thinking agents. This last-mentioned possibility presupposes, of course, that the individuals are already capable of common willing and acting. For, again, it is quite a different proposition if they are imagined to be only participants in the authorship of something that is conceived as objective in the scientific sense because it is that which under given conditions "each and every one" is compelled to think.

Now, it is to be admitted that each act of giving and receiving implicitly includes a social will, in the way just indicated. These acts are, furthermore, not conceivable except in connection with their purpose or end, i.e., the receipt of the compensating gift. As, however, this latter act is conditioned in like manner, neither act can precede the other; they must concur. Or, expressing the same thought in other words, the acceptance equals the delivery of an accepted compensation. Thus, the exchange itself, considered as a united and single act, represents the content of the assumed social will. With regard to this will the exchanged goods are of equal value. This equality is the judgment of the will and is valid for both individuals, since they have passed it when their wills were in concord; hence it is binding only for the moment in which the act of exchange takes place or for the space of time during which it continues. In order that the judgment may even with this qualification become objective and universally valid, it must appear as a judgment passed by "each and every one." Hence, each and every one must have this single will; in other words, the will of the exchange becomes universal; i.e., each and every one becomes a participant in the single act and he confirms it; thus it becomes an absolute and public act. On the contrary, the Gesellschaft may deny this act and declare "a" is not equal to "b," but smaller than "b" or greater than "b," i.e., the objects are not being exchanged according to their true values. The true value is explained as that value which each and every one attributes to a thing that we thus regard as a general Gesellschaft-conditioned good. Hence, the true value is ascertained if there is nobody who estimates either object as higher or lower in terms of the other. Now, a general consensus of each and every one that is not accidental, but necessary, will be effected only with reference to what is sensible, right, and true. Since all individuals are thus of one mind we may imagine them as concentrated in the person of a measuring, weighing, and knowing judge who passes the objective judgment. The judgment must be recognizable by each and every one, and each and every one must conform to it inasmuch as they themselves are endowed with judgment and objective thinking, or, figuratively speaking, as they use the same yardstick or weigh with the same scales.

### VALUE AS AN OBJECTIVE QUALITY—QUANTITIES OF NECESSARY LABOR

We are now confronted with the following question: What shall we consider to be the yardstick or balances in this procedure of deliberative comparing? We know the "quality" which is to be determined quantitatively by means of this constant tester, and we call it "value." Value must not, however, be identified with "worth," since worth is a quality which is perceived by the real individual. Moreover, the very difference of worth as it is sensed by real individuals, in relation to the same object, is the basis of a reasonable exchange. We, however, are concerned to find equality of value in objective judgment of different objects. In natural and naïve evaluation one takes things of the same category in order to compare them. The evaluation takes the form of a question, the answer to which consists of an affirmation or negation, in a stronger or lesser degree, according as the objects submit to the idea of such a comparison. In this sense we may establish a general category of serviceable (or useful) things. Some may be considered as necessary, some as superfluous, some may be given prominence as very useful, and others rejected as very harmful. In this connection humanity would have to be pictured as a whole, or at least as a Gemeinschaft of human beings which —like the real individual—lives and therefore has needs; it has to be regarded as uniform in its will, so that it shares profit and loss (since the judgment is at the same time considered as a subjective one).

Now, if one asserts the equality of value of two exchanged objects, this does not at all mean that they are equally useful and necessary for an aggregate being. Otherwise the possibility of someone buying absolutely harmful things would have to be set up. But that would be monstrous and utopian. One may assert on good grounds that a judgment is wrong when conditioned by desire, so that many a one acquires through exchange an object that is harmful to himself. But it is self-evident that the same liquor which is harmful to the workman is positively useful to the owner of the distillery, since he does not drink it but sells it. In order that a thing may be at all of value in the Gesellschaft, it is only necessary that it be possessed by one party to the exclusion of another and be desired by one or another individual of this latter party. Apart from this requirement all its other characteristics are insignificant. Saying that a thing has a certain value does not mean that it is endowed with an equal amount of usefulness. Value is an objective quality; as length is an objective quality for the senses of vision and of touch, and as weight for the muscular sense and the sense of touch, so value is an objective quality for the understanding that examines and comprehends social facts. This understanding takes note of and examines the objects as to whether they can be manufactured quickly, or whether they require much time; as to whether they can be easily provided, or whether they require toil and drudgery. In other words, the understanding analyzes the actuality of the objects by examining the possibility of their existence, and it then determines their probability. For determining value the probability of existence is the only test, being subjective in regard to the sensible exchanging individual, and objective in regard to the Gesellschaft. This dictum in the first place carries only the following purport: if a sensible individual is confronted with objects being offered for sale, the thought comes (must come) to him that those objects naturally have a cost in order to be there at all, and particularly to be at that special place at that special time, be this cost represented by other objects against which they have been exchanged, or by labor, or by both items. However, the Gesellschaft, as it is an *ens fictivum* (artificial being) does not exchange anything, unless it be conceived of as an individual person, which here is quite out of the question. Therefore, since the exchange takes place only between human individuals, there is no being that could confront the Gesellschaft. From the viewpoint of the Gesellschaft the cost of the objects is, therefore, represented only by toil and labor. Robbery, as well as exchange, when considered as a means of acquiring objects, is based upon the assumption that goods already exist. Only producing, nurturing, creating, and fashioning labor is to be considered in this connection as the cause of the existence of things at a particular time. To this inherent labor can be added the extraneous labor of movement in space, as the cause of the existence of a given good at a particular place.

Things are considered as equal in so far as each object or each quantity of objects stands merely for a certain quantity of necessary labor. Thus the Gesellschaft disregards the fact that some producers work faster or with better yield (more productively) than others, so that with greater skill or better tools the same objects can be produced with less labor. All such individual differences can be reduced to a common denominator. This process becomes all the more complete in the degree that the exchange of commodities becomes general or Gesellschaft-like. That is to say: each individual offers his commodity to everyone else, and all are capable of producing the same commodities, but everyone, through his own insight and free choice, confines himself to that commodity which presents the least difficulties to him. Thus we exclude here the case of a work which is essentially Gemeinschaft-like but which is divided or divides itself up so that special arts are developed, inherited, and taught. But here we rather have in mind that each individual takes that piece of work which most closely approaches the price that the Gesellschaft attributes to it; that is to say, a piece of work which requires as little extra labor as possible. Thus the Gesellschaft can be imagined to be in reality composed of such separate individuals all of whom are busy for the general Gesellschaft inasmuch as they seem to be active in their own interests and who are working for their own interests while they seem to be working for the Gesellschaft. As a consequence of repeated dividing (of labors) and of indefinite exercise of free choice, there finally falls to each individual an actually equal and simple or elementary labor, representing an atom that he contributes and which forms an integrating part of the total labor of the Gesellschaft. By means of exchange each individual disposes of value not useful to him in order to acquire an equal value that he can use. The present investigation will show what relationship the real structure of the Gesellschaft bears to the concept presented here.

* * *

### ACTIVITY AS OBJECT OF A PROMISE—POWER TO ENFORCE IT—RELATION—NATURAL LAW—CONVENTION

In every exchange the place of a perceivable object can be taken by an activity. The activity itself is given and received. It must be useful or agreeable to the receiver as a commodity. This activity is thought of as a commodity the production and consumption of which coincide in time.

Although the performance which is not given but only promised may be contrasted with the thing which is not given and only promised, the result in both cases is similar. It belongs to the receiver legally; after the term expires he can force the promising party legally to perform the activity promised, just as he could legally force the debtor to give that which is owed or have it taken with force. A performance which is owed can be acquired only by force. The promise of a performance can as well be mutual as one-sided; therefore, resulting rights to coercion can also be mutual or one-sided as the case may be. In this respect several people can bind themselves for a certain equal activity in such a manner that everyone uses the performance of the other as an aid to himself. Finally, several people can agree to regard their association as an existing and independent being of the same individual nature as they are themselves, and to grant this fictitious person a special will and the capacity to act and therefore to make contracts and to incur obligations. Like all other things related to contracts, this so-called person is to be conceived as objective and real only in so far as the Gesellschaft seems to co-operate with it and to confirm its existence. Only in this way is this so-called person a thinking agent of the legal order of the Gesellschaft, and it is called a society, an association or special-interest group, a corporation, or any such name. The natural content of such an order can be comprised in the one formula: "*Pacta esse observanda*"—contracts must be executed. This includes the presupposition of a condition of separate realms or spheres of will so that an accepted and consequently legal change of each sphere can take place by contract in favor or in disfavor of spheres which are outside the system, or within the system. This means that the agreement of all is involved. Such concurrence of wills is according to its nature momentarily punctual so that the change, as creation of a new situation, does not have to have a duration in time. This necessitates no modification of the most important rule, that everyone can do legally within his realm that which he wishes, but nothing outside. If, however, a common realm originates, as might be the case in a lasting obligation and in an organization, freedom itself, as the total of rights to act freely, must be divided and altered or a new artificial or fictitious form of freedom created. The simple form of the general will of the Gesellschaft, in so far as it postulates this law of nature, I call *convention*. Positive definitions and regulations of all kinds, which according to their origin are of a very different style, can be recognized as conventional, so that convention is often understood as a synonym for tradition and custom. But what springs from tradition and custom or the folkways and mores is conventional only in so far as it is wanted and maintained for its general use, and in so far as the general use is maintained by the individual for his use. Convention is not, as in the case of tradition, kept as sacred inheritance of the ancestors. Consequently, the words tradition, customs, or folkways and mores, are not adequate to convey the meaning of convention.

### BOURGEOIS SOCIETY (*bürgerliche Gesellschaft*)—EVERYONE A MERCHANT—UNIVERSAL COMPETITION—GESELLSCHAFT IN A MORAL SENSE

Gesellschaft, an aggregate by convention and law of nature, is to be understood as a multitude of natural and artificial individuals, the wills and spheres of whom are in many relations with and to one another, and remain nevertheless independent of one another and devoid of mutual familiar relationships. This gives us the general description of "bourgeois society" or "exchange Gesellschaft," the nature and movements of which legislative economy attempts to understand; a condition in which, according to the expression of Adam Smith, "Every man . . . becomes in some measure a merchant, . . ." Where merchants, companies, or firms or associations deal with one another in international or national markets and exchanges, the nature of the Gesellschaft is erected as in a concave mirror or as in an extract.

The generality of this situation is by no means, as the famous Scotchman imagined, the immediate or even probable result of the innovation that labor is divided and products exchanged. It is more a remote goal with respect to which the development of the Gesellschaft must be understood. To the extent that this goal is realized, the existence of a Gesellschaft in the sense that it is used here is real at a given time. It is something in the process of becoming, something which should be conceived here as personality of the general will or the general reason, and at the same time (as we know) it is fictitious and nominal. It is like an emanation, as if it had emerged from the heads of the persons in whom it rests, who join hands eagerly to exchange across all distances, limits, and scruples, and establish this speculative Utopia as the only country, the only city, in which all fortune seekers and all merchant adventurers have a really common interest. As the fiction of money is represented by metal or paper, it is represented by the entire globe, or by a circumscribed territory.

In the conception of Gesellschaft the original or natural relations of human beings to each other must be excluded. The possibility of a relation in the Gesellschaft assumes no more than a multitude of mere persons who are capable of delivering something and consequently of promising something. Gesellschaft as a totality to which a system of conventional rules applies is limitless; it breaks through its chance and real boundaries constantly. In Gesellschaft every person strives for that which is to his own advantage and affirms the actions of others only in so far as and as long as they can further his interest. Before and outside of convention and also before and outside of each special contract, the relation of all to all may therefore be conceived as potential hostility or latent war. Against this condition all agreements of the will stand out as so many treaties and peace pacts. This conception is the only one which does justice to all facts of business and trade where all rights and duties can be reduced to mere value and definitions of ability to deliver. Every theory of pure private law or law of nature understood as pertaining to the Gesellschaft has to be considered as being based upon this conception. Buyer and seller in their manifold types stand in relation one to the other in such a manner that each one, for as little of his own wealth as possible, desires and attempts to obtain as much of the wealth of others as possible. The real commercial and business people race with each other on many sprinting tracks, as it were, trying each to get the better of the other and to be the first to reach the goal: the sale of their goods and of as large a quantity as possible. Thus they are forced to crowd each other out or to trip each other up. The loss of one is the profit of the other, and this is the case in every individual exchange, unless owners exchange goods of actually equal value. This constitutes general competition which takes place in so many other spheres, but is nowhere so evident and so much in the consciousness of people as in trade, to which, consequently, the conception is limited in its common use. Competition has been described by many pessimists as an illustration of the war of all against all, which a famous thinker has conceived as the natural state of mankind.

However, even competition carries within it, as do all forms of such war, the possibility of being ended. Even enemies like these—although among these it may be the least likely—recognize that under certain conditions it is to their advantage to agree and to spare each other. They may even unite themselves together for a common purpose (or also—and this is the most likely—against a common enemy). Thus competition is limited and abolished by coalition.

In analogy to this situation, based upon the exchange of material goods, all conventional society life, in the narrower sense of the word, can be understood. Its supreme rule is politeness. It consists of an exchange of words and courtesies in which everyone seems to be present for the good of everyone else and everyone seems to consider everyone else as his equal, whereas in reality everyone is thinking of himself and trying to bring to the fore his importance and advantages in competition with the others. For everything pleasant which someone does for someone else, he expects, even demands, at least an equivalent. He weighs exactly his services, flatteries, presents, and so on, to determine whether they will bring about the desired result. Formless contracts are made continuously, as it were, and constantly many are pushed aside in the race by the few fortunate and powerful ones.

Since all relations in the Gesellschaft are based upon comparison of possible and offered services, it is evident that the relations with visible, material matters have preference, and that mere activities and words form the foundation for such relationships only in an unreal way. In contrast to this, Gemeinschaft as a bond of "blood" is in the first place a physical relation, therefore expressing itself in deeds and words. Here the common relation to the material objects is of a secondary nature and such objects are not exchanged as often as they are used and possessed in common.

# 2. *Status and Role*

BY RALPH LINTON

IN THE PRECEDING CHAPTER we discussed the nature of society and pointed out that the functioning of societies depends upon the presence of patterns for reciprocal behavior between individuals or groups of individuals. The polar positions in such patterns of reciprocal behavior are technically known as *statuses.* The term *status,* like the term *culture,* has come to be used with a double significance. *A status,* in the abstract, is a position in a particular pattern. It is thus quite correct to speak of each individual as having many statuses, since each individual participates in the expression of a number of patterns. However, unless the term is qualified in some way, *the status* of any individual means the sum total of all the statuses which he occupies. It represents his position with relation to the total society. Thus the status of Mr. Jones as a member of his community derives from a combination of all the statuses which he holds as a citizen, as an attorney, as a Mason, as a Methodist, as Mrs. Jones's husband, and so on.

A status, as distinct from the individual who may occupy it, is simply a collection of rights and duties. Since these rights and duties can find expression only through the medium of individuals, it is extremely hard for us to maintain a distinction in our thinking between statuses and the people who hold them and exercise the rights and duties which constitute them. The relation between any individual and any status he holds is somewhat like that between the driver of an automobile and the driver's place in the machine. The driver's seat with its steering wheel, accelerator, and other controls is a constant with ever-present potentialities for action and control, while the driver may be any member of the family and may exercise these potentialities very well or very badly.

A *role* represents the dynamic aspect of a status. The individual is socially assigned to a status and occupies it with relation to other statuses. When he puts the rights and duties which constitute the status into effect, he is performing a role. Role and status are quite inseparable, and the distinction between them is of only academic interest. There are no roles without statuses or statuses without roles. Just as in the case of *status,* the term *role* is used with a double significance. Every individual has a series of roles deriving from the various patterns in which he participates and at the same time *a role,* general, which represents the sum total of these roles and determines what he does for his society and what he can expect from it.

Although all statuses and roles derive from social patterns and are integral parts of patterns, they have an independent function with relation to the individuals who occupy particular statuses and exercise their roles. To such individuals the combined status and role represent the minimum of attitudes and behavior which he must assume if he is to participate in the overt expression of the pattern. Status and role serve to reduce the ideal patterns for social life to individual terms. They become models for organizing the attitudes and behavior of the individual so that these will be congruous with those of the other individuals participating in the expression of the pattern. Thus if we are studying football teams in the abstract, the position of quarter-back is meaningless except in relation to the other positions. From the point of view of the quarter-back himself it is a distinct and important entity. It determines where he shall take his place in the line-up and what he shall do in various plays. His assignment to this position at once limits and defines his activities and establishes a minimum of things which he must learn. Similarly, in a social pattern such as that for the employer-employee relationship the statuses of employer and employee define what each has to know and do to put the pattern into operation. The employer does not need to know the techniques involved in the employee's labor, and the employee does not need to know the techniques for marketing or accounting.

It is obvious that, as long as there is no interference from external sources, the more perfectly the members of any society are adjusted to their statuses and roles the more smoothly the society will function. In its attempts to bring about such adjustments every society finds itself caught on the horns of a dilemma. The individual's formation of

---

habits and attitudes begins at birth, and, other things being equal, the earlier his training for a status can begin the more successful it is likely to be. At the same time, no two individuals are alike, and a status which will be congenial to one may be quite uncongenial to another. Also, there are in all social systems certain roles which require more than training for their successful performance. Perfect technique does not make a great violinist, nor a thorough book knowledge of tactics an efficient general. The utilization of the special gifts of individuals may be highly important to society, as in the case of the general, yet these gifts usually show themselves rather late, and to wait upon their manifestation for the assignment of statuses would be to forfeit the advantages to be derived from commencing training early.

Fortunately, human beings are so mutable that almost any normal individual can be trained to the adequate performance of almost any role. Most of the business of living can be conducted on a basis of habit, with little need for intelligence and none for special gifts. Societies have met the dilemma by developing two types of statuses, the *ascribed* and the *achieved*. *Ascribed* statuses are those which are assigned to individuals without reference to their innate differences or abilities. They can be predicted and trained for from the moment of birth. The *achieved* statuses are, as a minimum, those requiring special qualities, although they are not necessarily limited to these. They are not assigned to individuals from birth but are left open to be filled through competition and individual effort. The majority of the statuses in all social systems are of the ascribed type and those which take care of the ordinary day-to-day business of living are practically always of this type.

In all societies certain things are selected as reference points for the ascription of status. The things chosen for this purpose are always of such a nature that they are ascertainable at birth, making it possible to begin the training of the individual for his potential statuses and roles at once. The simplest and most universally used of these reference points is sex. Age is used with nearly equal frequency, since all individuals pass through the same cycle of growth, maturity, and decline, and the statuses whose occupation will be determined by age can be forecast and trained for with accuracy. Family relationships, the simplest and most obvious being that of the child to its mother, are also used in all societies as reference points for the establishment of a whole series of statuses. Lastly, there is the matter of birth into a particular socially established group, such as a class or caste. The use of this type of reference is common but not universal. In all societies the actual ascription of statuses to the individual is controlled by a series of these reference points which together serve to delimit the field of his future participation in the life of the group.

The division and ascription of statuses with relation to sex seems to be basic in all social systems. All societies prescribe different attitudes and activities to men and to women. Most of them try to rationalize these prescriptions in terms of the physiological differences between the sexes or their different roles in reproduction. However, a comparative study of the statuses ascribed to women and men in different cultures seems to show that while such factors may have served as a starting point for the development of a division the actual ascriptions are almost entirely determined by culture. Even the psychological characteristics ascribed to men and women in different societies vary so much that they can have little physiological basis. Our own idea of women as ministering angels contrasts sharply with the ingenuity of women as torturers among the Iroquois and the sadistic delight they took in the process. Even the last two generations have seen a sharp change in the psychological patterns for women in our own society. The delicate, fainting lady of the middle eighteen-hundreds is as extinct as the dodo.

When it comes to the ascription of occupations, which is after all an integral part of status, we find the differences in various societies even more marked. Arapesh women regularly carry heavier loads than men "because their heads are so much harder and stronger." In some societies women do most of the manual labor; in others, as in the Marquesas, even cooking, housekeeping, and baby-tending are proper male occupations, and women spend most of their time primping. Even the general rule that women's handicap through pregnancy and nursing indicates the more active occupations as male and the less active ones as female has many exceptions. Thus among the Tasmanians seal-hunting was women's work. They swam out to the seal rocks, stalked the animals, and clubbed them. Tasmanian women also hunted opossums, which required the climbing of large trees.

Although the actual ascription of occupations along sex lines is highly variable, the pattern of sex division is constant. There are very few societies in which every important activity has not been definitely assigned to men or to women. Even when the two sexes coöperate in a particular occupation, the field of each is usually clearly limited. Thus in Madagascar rice culture the men make the seed beds and terraces and prepare the fields for transplanting. The women do the work of transplanting, which is hard and back-breaking. The women weed the crop, but the men harvest it. The women then carry it to the threshing floors, where the men thresh it while the women winnow it. Lastly, the women pound the grain in mortars and cook it.

When a society takes over a new industry, there is often a period of uncertainty during which the work may be done by either sex, but it soon falls into the province of one or the other. In Madagascar, pottery is made by men in some tribes and by women in others. The only tribe in which it is made by both men and women is one into which the art has been introduced within the last sixty years. I was told that during the fifteen years preceding my visit there had been a marked decrease in the number of male potters, many men who had once practised the art having given it up. The factor of lowered wages, usually advanced as the reason for men leaving one of our own occupations when women enter it in force, certainly was not operative here. The field was not overcrowded, and the prices for men's and women's products were the same. Most of the men who had given up the trade were vague as to their reasons, but a few said frankly that they did not like to compete with women. Apparently the entry of women into the occupation had robbed it of a certain amount of prestige. It was no longer quite the thing for a man to be a potter, even though he was a very good one.

The use of age as a reference point for establishing status is as universal as the use of sex. All societies recognize three age groupings as a minimum: child, adult, and old. Certain societies have emphasized age as a basis for assigning status and have greatly amplified the divisions. Thus in certain African tribes the whole male population is divided into units composed of those born in the same years or within two- or three-year intervals. However, such extreme attention to age is unusual, and we need not discuss it here.

The physical differences between child and adult are easily recognizable, and the passage from childhood to maturity is marked by physiological events which make it possible to date it exactly for girls and within a few weeks or months for boys. However, the physical passage from childhood to maturity does not necessarily coincide with the social transfer of the individual from one category to the other. Thus in our own society both men and women remain legally children until long after they are physically adult. In most societies this difference between the physical and social transfer is more clearly marked than in our own. The child becomes a man not when he is physically mature but when he is formally recognized as a man by his society. This recognition is almost always given ceremonial expression in what are technically known as puberty rites. The most important element in these rites is not the determination of physical maturity but that of social maturity. Whether a boy is able to breed is less vital to his society than whether he is able to do a man's work and has a man's knowledge. Actually, most puberty ceremonies include tests of the boy's learning and fortitude, and if the aspirants are unable to pass these they are left in the child status until they can. For those who pass the tests, the ceremonies usually culminate in the transfer to them of certain secrets which the men guard from women and children.

The passage of individuals from adult to aged is harder to perceive. There is no clear physiological line for men, while even women may retain their full physical vigor and their ability to carry on all the activities of the adult status for several years after the menopause. The social transfer of men from the adult to the aged group is given ceremonial recognition in a few cultures, as when a father formally surrenders his official position and titles to his son, but such recognition is rare. As for women, there appears to be no society in which the menopause is given ceremonial recognition, although there are a few societies in which it does alter the individual's status. Thus Comanche women, after the menopause, were released from their disabilities with regard to the supernatural. They could handle sacred objects, obtain power through dreams and practise as shamans, all things forbidden to women of bearing age.

The general tendency for societies to emphasize the individual's first change in age status and largely ignore the second is no doubt due in part to the difficulty of determining the onset of old age. However, there are also psychological factors involved. The boy or girl is usually anxious to grow up, and this eagerness is heightened by the exclusion of children from certain activities and knowledge. Also, society welcomes new additions to the most active division of the group, that which contributes most to its perpetuation and well-being. Conversely, the individual who enjoys the thought of growing old is atypical in all societies. Even when age brings respect and a new measure of influence, it means the relinquishment of much that is pleasant. We can see among ourselves that the aging usually refuse to recognize the change until long after it has happened.

In the case of age, as in that of sex, the biological factors involved appear to be secondary to the cultural ones in determining the content of status. There are certain activities which cannot be ascribed to children because children either lack the necessary strength or have not had time to acquire the necessary technical skills. However, the attitudes between parent and child and the importance given to the child in the family structure vary enormously from one culture to another. The status of the child among our Puritan ancestors, where he was seen and not heard and ate at the second table, represents one extreme. At the other might be placed the status of the eldest son of a Polynesian chief. All the *mana* (supernatural power) of the royal line converged upon such a child. He was socially superior to his own father and mother, and any attempt to discipline him would have been little short of sacrilege. I once visited the hereditary chief of a Marquesan tribe and found the whole family camping uncomfortably in their own front yard, although they had a good house built on European lines. The eldest son, aged nine, had had a dispute with his father a few days before and had tabooed the house by naming it after his head. The family had thus been compelled to move out and could not use it again until he relented and lifted the taboo. As he could use the house himself and eat anywhere in the village, he was getting along quite well and seemed to enjoy the situation thoroughly.

The statuses ascribed to the old in various societies vary even more than those ascribed to children. In some cases they are relieved of all heavy labor and can settle back comfortably to live off their children. In others they perform most of the hard and monotonous tasks which do not require great physical strength, such as the gathering of firewood. In many societies the old women, in particular, take over most of the care of the younger children, leaving the younger women free to enjoy themselves. In some places the old are treated with consideration and respect; in others they are considered a useless incumbrance and removed as soon as they are incapable of heavy labor. In most societies their advice is sought even when little attention is paid to their wishes. This custom has a sound practical basis, for the individual who contrives to live to old age in an uncivilized group has usually been a person of ability and his memory constitutes a sort of reference library to which one can turn for help under all sorts of circumstances.

In certain societies the change from the adult to the old status is made more difficult for the individual by the fact that the patterns for these statuses ascribe different types of personality to each. This was the case among the Comanche, as it seems to have been among most of the Plains tribes. The adult male was a warrior, vigorous, self-reliant, and pushing. Most of his social relationships were phrased in terms of competition. He took what he could get and held what he had without regard to any abstract rights of those weaker than himself. Any willingness to arbitrate differences or to ignore slights was a sign of weakness resulting in loss of prestige. The old man, on the other hand, was expected to be wise and gentle, willing to overlook slights and, if need be, to endure abuse. It was his task to work for the welfare of the tribe, giving sound advice, settling feuds between the warriors, and even preventing his tribe from making new enemies. Young men strove for war and honor, old men strove for peace and tranquillity. There is abundant evidence that among the Comanche the transition was often a difficult one for the individual. Warriors did not prepare for old age, thinking it a better fate to be killed in action. When waning physical powers forced them to assume the new role, many of them did so grudgingly, and those who had strong magic would go on trying to enforce the rights which belonged to the younger status. Such bad old men were a peril to young ones beginning their careers, for they were jealous of them simply because they were young and strong and admired by the women. The medicine power of these young men was still weak, and the old men could and did kill them by malevolent magic. It is significant that although benevolent medicine men might be of any age in Comanche folklore, malevolent ones were always old.

Before passing on, it might be well to mention still another social status which is closely related to the foregoing. This is the status of the dead. We do not think of the dead as still members of the community, and many societies follow us in this, but there are others in which death is simply another transfer, comparable to that from child to adult. When a man dies, he does not leave his society; he merely surrenders one set of rights and duties and assumes another. Thus a Tanala clan has two sections which are equally real to its members, the living and the dead. In spite of rather half-hearted attempts by the living to explain to the dead that they are dead and to discourage their return, they remain an integral part of the clan. They must be informed of all important events, invited to all clan ceremonies, and remembered at every meal. In return they allow themselves to be consulted, take an active and helpful interest in the affairs of the community, and act as highly efficient guardians of the group's mores. They carry over into their new status the conservatism characteristic of the aged, and their invisible presence and constant watchfulness does more than anything else to ensure the good behavior of the living and to discourage innovations. In a neighboring tribe there are even individual statuses among the dead which are open to achievement. Old Betsileo men and women will often promise that, after their deaths, they will give the living specific forms of help in return for specified offerings. After the death of one of these individuals, a monument will be erected and people will come to pray and make offerings there. If the new ghost performs his functions successfully, his worship may grow into a cult and may even have a priest. If he fails in their performance, he is soon forgotten.

Biological relationships are used to determine some statuses in all societies. The mere fact of birth immediately brings the individual within the scope of a whole series of social patterns which relate him to his parents, either real or ascribed, his brothers and sisters, and his parents' relatives. The biological basis for the ascription of these family statuses is likely to blind us to the fact that the physiological factors which may influence their content are almost exactly the same as those affecting the content of sex and age statuses. While there is a special relationship between the young child and its mother, based on the child's dependence on nursing, even this is soon broken off. After the second year any adult woman can do anything for the child that its mother can do, while any adult male can assume the complete role of the father at any time after the child is conceived. Similarly, the physiological factors which might affect the statuses of uncle and nephew, uncle and niece, or brother and sister are identical with those affecting the relations of persons in different age or sex groupings. This lack of physiological determinants may be responsible in part for the extraordinarily wide range of variation in the contents of the statuses ascribed on the basis of biological relationships in various societies.

* * *

The bulk of the ascribed statuses in all social systems are parceled out to individuals on the basis of sex, age, and family relationships. However, there are many societies in which purely social factors are also used as a basis of ascription. There seems to be a general tendency for societies to divide their component individuals into a series of groups or categories and to ascribe to such categories differing degrees of social importance. Such divisions may originate in many different ways. They may grow out of individual differences in technical skill or other abilities, as in the case of craft groups or the aristocracies of certain Indian tribes, membership in which was determined by the individual's war record. They may also originate through the conscious formation of some social unit, such as the first college fraternity or the first business men's club, which is usually followed by the formation of a series of similar units organized upon nearly the same lines. Lastly, such divisions may originate through the subjugation of one society by another society, with the subsequent fusion of both into a single functional unit, as in the case of Old World aristocracies deriving from conquest. Even when the social divisions originate in individual differences of ability, there seems to be a strong tendency for such divisions to become hereditary. The members of a socially favored division try to transmit the advantages they have gained to their offspring and at the same time to prevent the entry into the division of individuals from lower divisions. In many cases these tendencies result in the organization of the society into a series of hereditary classes or castes. Such hereditary units are always used as reference points for the ascription of status.

The factor of social class or caste rarely if ever replaces the factors of sex, age, and biological relationship in the determination of status. Rather, it supplements these, defining the roles of individuals still more clearly. Where the class system is strong, each class becomes almost a society in itself. It will have a series of sex, age, and relationship statuses which are peculiar to its members. These will differ from the statuses of other classes even when both are determined by the same biological factors. Not only is the commoner debarred from the occupation of aristocratic statuses, but the aristocrat is similarly debarred from the occupation of common statuses. It may be mentioned in passing that this arrangement is not always entirely to the advantage of the members of the upper class. During the nineteenth century the aristocratic prohibition against engaging in trade condemned many aristocrats to genteel poverty.

Feudal Europe offers an excellent example of the ascription of statuses on the basis of social class. A man born into the noble class could look forward to being a bachelor, in the technical sense of a boy beginning his training for knighthood, a squire, and lastly a knight and lord of a manor. The performance of the roles connected with the final status required a long and arduous training both in the use of arms and in administration. The woman born into the same class could also look forward to being lady of a manor, a task which entailed special knowledge and administrative ability fully on a par with that of her husband. A man born into the peasant class could look forward only to becoming a tiller of the soil. He would pass through no statuses corresponding to those of bachelor or squire, and although he might be trained to the use of weapons, these would be different weapons from those used by the knight. The woman born in this class could only look forward to becoming a simple housewife, and her necessary training for this status was limited to a knowledge of housekeeping and baby-tending. The third class in medieval society, the burghers, also had its own series of statuses, the boy looking forward to becoming first an apprentice and then a master training apprentices in turn. All these divergent, class-determined statuses were mutually interdependent, and all contributed to the successful functioning of medieval society. The noble provided protection and direction, the peasant provided food, and the burgher took care of trade and manufactures.

Ascribed statuses, whether assigned according to biological or to social factors, compose the bulk of all social systems. However, all these systems also include a varying number of statuses which are open to individual achievement. It seems as though many statuses of this type were primarily designed to serve as baits for socially acceptable behavior or as escapes for the individual. All societies rely mainly on their ascribed statuses to take care of the ordinary business of living. Most of the statuses which are thrown open to achievement do not touch this business very deeply. The honored ones are extremely satisfying to the individuals who achieve them, but many of them are no more vital to the ordinary functioning of the society than are honorary degrees or inclusions in "Who's Who" among ourselves.

Most societies make only a grudging admission of the fact that a limited number of statuses do require special gifts for their successful performance. Since such gifts rarely manifest themselves in early childhood, these statuses are, of necessity, thrown open to competition. At the same time, the pattern of ascribing all vital statuses is so strong that all societies limit this competition with reference to sex, age, and social affiliations. Even in our own society, where the field open to individual achievement is theoretically unlimited, it is strictly limited in fact. No woman can become President of the United States. Neither could a Negro nor an Indian, although there is no formal rule on this point, while a Jew or even a Catholic entering the presidential race would be very seriously handicapped from the outset. Even with regard to achievable statuses which are much less social importance and which, perhaps, require more specific gifts, the same sort of limited competition is evident. It would be nearly if not quite impossible for either a woman or a Negro to become conductor of our best symphony orchestra, even if better able to perform the duties involved than anyone else in America. At the same time, no man could become president of the D.A.R., and it is doubtful whether any man, unless he adopted a feminine *nom de plume,* could even conduct a syndicated column on advice to the lovelorn, a field in which our society assumes, *a priori,* that women have greater skill.

These limitations upon the competition for achieved statuses no doubt entail a certain loss to society. Persons with special talents appear to be mutants and as such are likely to appear in either sex and in any social class. At the same time, the actual loss to societies through this failure to use their members' gifts to the full is probably a good deal less than persons reared in the American tradition would like to believe. Individual talent is too sporadic and too unpredictable to be allowed any important part in the organization of society. Social systems have to be built upon the potentialities of the average individual, the person who has no special gifts or disabilities. Such individuals can be trained to occupy almost any status and to perform the associated role adequately if not brilliantly. The social ascription of a particular status, with the intensive training that such ascription makes possible, is a guarantee that the role will be performed even if the performance is mediocre. If a society waited to have its statuses filled by individuals with special gifts, certain statuses might not be filled at all. The ascription of status sacrifices the possibility of having certain roles performed superlatively well to the certainty of having them performed passably well.

When a social system has achieved a good adjustment to the other sectors of the group's culture and, through these, to the group's environment, it can get along very well without utilizing special gifts. However, as soon as changes within the culture or in the external environment produce maladjustments, it has to recognize and utilize these gifts. The development of new social patterns calls for the individual qualities of thought and initiative, and the freer the rein given to these the more quickly new adjustments can be arrived at. For this reason, societies living under new or changing conditions are usually characterized by a wealth of achievable statuses and by very broad delimitations of the competition for them. Our own now extinct frontier offered an excellent example of this. Here the class lines of the European societies from which the frontier population had been drawn were completely discarded and individuals were given an unprecedented opportunity to find their place in the new society by their own abilities.

As social systems achieve adjustment to their settings, the social value of individual thought and initiative decreases. Thorough training of the component individuals becomes more necessary to the survival and successful functioning of society than the free expression of their individual abilities. Even leadership, which calls for marked ability under conditions of change, becomes largely a matter of routine activities. To ensure successful training, more and more statuses are transferred from the achieved to the ascribed group, and the competition for those which remain is more and more rigidly delimited. To put the same thing in different terms, individual opportunities decrease. There is not an absolute correlation between the degree of adjustment of a social system to its setting and the limitation of individual opportunity. Thus if the group attaches a high value to individual initiative and individual rights, certain statuses may be left open to competition when their ascription would result in greater social efficiency. However, well-adjusted societies are, in general, characterized by a high preponderance of ascribed over achieved statuses, and increasing perfection of adjustment usually goes hand in hand with increasing rigidity of the social system.

# 3. *On Mechanical and Organic Solidarity*

BY EMILE DURKHEIM

THIS WORK had its origins in the question of the relations of the individual to social solidarity. Why does the individual, while becoming more autonomous, depend more upon society? How can he be at once more individual and more solidary? Certainly, these two movements, contradictory as they appear, develop in parallel fashion. This is the problem we are raising. It appeared to us that what resolves this apparent antinomy is a transformation of social solidarity due to the steadily growing development of the division of labor. That is how we have been led to make this the object of our study.

* * *

The social relations to which the division of labor gives birth have often been considered only in terms of exchange, but this misinterprets what such exchange implies and what results from it. It suggests two beings mutually dependent because they are each incomplete, and translates this mutual dependence outwardly. It is, then, only the superficial expression of an internal and very deep state. Precisely because this state is constant, it calls up a whole mechanism of images which function with a continuity that exchange does not possess. The image of the one who completes us becomes inseparable from ours, not only because it is frequently associated with ours, but particularly because it is the natural complement of it. It thus becomes an integral and permanent part of our conscience, to such a point that we can no longer separate ourselves from it and seek to increase its force. That is why we enjoy the society of the one it represents, since the presence of the object that it expresses, by making us actually perceive it, sets it off more. On the other hand, we will suffer from all circumstances which, like absence or death, may have as effect the barring of its return or the diminishing of its vivacity.

As short as this analysis is, it suffices to show that this mechanism is not identical with that which serves as a basis for sentiments of sympathy whose source is resemblance. Surely there can be no solidarity between others and us unless the image of others unites itself with ours. But when the union results from the resemblance of two images, it consists in an agglutination. The two representations become solidary because, being indistinct, totally or in part, they confound each other, and become no more than one, and they are solidary only in the measure which they confound themselves. On the contrary, in the case of the division of labor, they are outside each other and are linked only because they are distinct. Neither the sentiments nor the social relations which derive from these sentiments are the same in the two cases.

We are thus led to ask if the division of labor would not play the same role in more extensive

---

Reprinted from Emile Durkheim, *The Division of Labor in Society,* trans. George Simpson (Glencoe, Ill.: The Free Press, 1949), Preface, pp. 37–38; Book I, chap. i, 61–62, 64–65, 68–69; chap. ii, pp. 109–10; chap. iii, pp. 111–15, 127–31, with the permission of The Free Press.

groups, if, in contemporary societies where it has developed as we know, it would not have as its function the integration of the social body to assure unity. It is quite legitimate to suppose that the facts which we have just observed reproduce themselves here, but with greater amplitude, that great political societies can maintain themselves in equilibrium only thanks to the specialization of tasks, that the division of labor is the source, if not unique, at least principal, of social solidarity.

* * *

But social solidarity is a completely moral phenomenon which, taken by itself, does not lend itself to exact observation nor indeed to measurement. To proceed to this classification and this comparison, we must substitute for this internal fact which escapes us an external index which symbolizes it and study the former in the light of the latter.

This visible symbol is law. In effect, despite its immaterial character, wherever social solidarity exists, it resides not in a state of pure potentiality, but manifests its presence by sensible indices. Where it is strong, it leads men strongly to one another, frequently puts them in contact, multiplies the occasions when they find themselves related. To speak correctly, considering the point our investigation has reached, it is not easy to say whether social solidarity produces these phenomena, or whether it is a result of them, whether men relate themselves because it is a driving force, or whether it is a driving force because they relate themselves. However, it is not, at the moment, necessary to decide this question; it suffices to state that the two orders of fact are linked and vary at the same time and in the same sense. The more solidary the members of a society are, the more they sustain diverse relations, one with another, or with the group taken collectively, for, if their meetings were rare, they would depend upon one another only at rare intervals, and then tenuously. Moreover, the number of these relations is necessarily proportional to that of the juridical rules which determine them. Indeed, social life, especially where it exists durably, tends inevitably to assume a definite form and to organize itself, and law is nothing else than this very organization in so far as it has greater stability and precision. The general life of society cannot extend its sway without juridical life extending its sway at the same time and in direct relation. We can thus be certain of finding reflected in law all the essential varieties of social solidarity.

* * *

To proceed scientifically, we must find some characteristic which, while being essential to juridical phenomena, varies as they vary. Every precept of law can be defined as a rule of sanctioned conduct. Moreover, it is evident that sanctions change with the gravity attributed to precepts, the place they hold in the public conscience, the role they play in society. It is right, then, to classify juridical rules according to the different sanctions which are attached to them.

They are of two kinds. Some consist essentially in suffering, or at least a loss, inflicted on the agent. They make demands on his fortune, or on his honor, or on his life, or on his liberty, and deprive him of something he enjoys. We call them repressive. They constitute penal law. It is true that those which are attached to rules which are purely moral have the same character, only they are distributed in a diffuse manner, by everybody indiscriminately, whereas those in penal law are applied through the intermediary of a definite organ; they are organized. As for the other type, it does not necessarily imply suffering for the agent, but consists only of *the return of things as they were,* in the reestablishment of troubled relations to their normal state, whether the incriminated act is restored by force to the type whence it deviated, or is annulled, that is, deprived of all social value. We must then separate juridical rules into two great classes, accordingly as they have organized repressive sanctions or only restitutive sanctions. The first comprise all penal law; the second, civil law, commercial law, procedural law, administrative and constitutional law, after abstraction of the penal rules which may be found there.

* * *

There exists a social solidarity which comes from a certain number of states of conscience which are common to all the members of the same society. This is what repressive law materially represents, at least in so far as it is essential. The part that it plays in the general integration of society evidently depends upon the greater or lesser extent of the social life which the common conscience embraces and regulates. The greater the diversity of relations wherein the latter makes its action felt, the more also it creates links which attach the individual to the group; the more, consequently, social cohesion derives completely from this source and bears its mark. But the number of these relations is itself proportional to that of the repressive rules. In determining what fraction of the juridical system penal law represents, we, at the same time, measure the relative importance of this solidarity. It is true that in such a procedure we do not take into account certain elements of the collective conscience which, because of their smaller power or their indeterminateness, remain foreign to repressive law while contributing to the assurance of social harmony.

These are the ones protected by punishments which are merely diffuse. But the same is the case with other parts of law. There is not one of them which is not complemented by custom, and as there is no reason for supposing that the relation of law and custom is not the same in these different spheres, this elimination is not made at the risk of having to alter the results of our comparison.

## *Organic Solidarity Due to the Division of Labor*

The very nature of the restitutive sanction suffices to show that the social solidarity to which this type of law corresponds is of a totally different kind.

What distinguishes this sanction is that it is not expiatory, but consists of a simple *return in state*. Sufferance proportionate to the misdeed is not inflicted on the one who has violated the law or who disregards it; he is simply sentenced to comply with it. If certain things were done, the judge reinstates them as they would have been. He speaks of law; he says nothing of punishment. Damage-interests have no penal character; they are only a means of reviewing the past in order to reinstate it, as far as possible, to its normal form. Tarde, it is true, has tried to find a sort of civil penality in the payment of costs by the defeated party. But, taken in this sense, the word has only a metaphorical value. For punishment to obtain, there would at least have to be some relation between the punishment and the misdeed, and for that it would be necessary for the degree of gravity of the misdeed to be firmly established. In fact, however, he who loses the litigation pays the damages even when his intentions were pure, even when his ignorance alone was his culpability. The reasons for this rule are different from those offered by Tarde: given the fact that justice is not rendered gratuitously, it appears equitable for the damages to be paid by the one who brought them into being. Moreover, it is possible that the prospect of such costs may stop the rash pleader, but that is not sufficient to constitute punishment. The fear of ruin which ordinarily follows indolence or negligence may keep the negotiant active and awake, though ruin is not, in the proper sense of the word, the penal sanction for his misdeeds.

Neglect of these rules is not even punished diffusely. The pleader who has lost in litigation is not disgraced, his honor is not put in question. We can even imagine these rules being other than they are without feeling any repugnance. The idea of tolerating murder arouses us, but we quite easily accept modification of the right of succession, and can even conceive of its possible abolition. It is at least a question which we do not refuse to discuss. Indeed, we admit with impunity that the law of servitudes or that of usufructs may be otherwise organized, that the obligations of vendor and purchaser may be determined in some other manner, that administrative functions may be distributed according to different principles. As these prescriptions do not correspond to any sentiment in us, and as we generally do not scientifically know the reasons for their existence, since this science is not definite, they have no roots in the majority of us. Of course, there are exceptions. We do not tolerate the idea that an engagement contrary to custom or obtained either through violence or fraud can bind the contracting parties. Thus, when public opinion finds itself in the presence of such a case, it shows itself less indifferent than we have just now said, and it increases the legal sanction by its censure. The different domains of the moral life are not radically separated one from another; they are, rather, continuous, and, accordingly, there are among them marginal regions where different characters are found at the same time. However, the preceding proposition remains true in the great majority of cases. It is proof that the rules with a restitutive sanction either do not totally derive from the collective conscience, or are only feeble states of it. Repressive law corresponds to the heart, the centre of the common conscience; laws purely moral are a part less central; finally, restitutive law is born in very ex-centric regions whence it spreads further. The more it becomes truly itself, the more removed it is.

This characteristic is, indeed, made manifest by the manner of its functioning. While repressive law tends to remain diffuse within society, restitutive law creates organs which are more and more specialized: consular tribunals, councils of arbitration, administrative tribunals of every sort. Even in its most general part, that which pertains to civil law, it is exercised only through particular functionaries: magistrates, lawyers, etc., who have become apt in this role because of very special training.

But, although these rules are more or less outside the collective conscience, they are not interested solely in individuals. If this were so, restitutive law would have nothing in common with social solidarity, for the relations that it regulates would bind individuals to one another without binding them to society. They would simply be happenings in private life, as friendly relations are. But society is far from having no hand in this sphere of juridical life. It is true that, generally, it does not intervene of itself and through its own movements; it must be solicited by the interested parties. But, in being called forth, its intervention is none the less the essential cog in the machine, since it alone makes it function. It propounds the law through the organ of its representatives.

It has been contended, however, that this role has nothing properly social about it, but reduces itself to that of a conciliator of private interests; that, consequently, any individual can fill it, and that, if society is in charge of it, it is only for commodious reasons. But nothing is more incorrect than considering society as a sort of third-party arbitrator. When it is led to intervene, it is not to put to rights some individual interests. It does not seek to discover what may be the most advantageous solution for the adversaries and does not propose a compromise for them. Rather, it applies to the particular case which is submitted to it general and traditional rules of law. But law is, above all, a social thing and has a totally different object than the interest of the pleaders. The judge who examines a request for divorce is not concerned with knowing whether this separation is truly desirable for the married parties, but rather whether the causes which are adduced come under one of the categories foreseen by the law.

But better to appreciate the importance of social action, we must observe it, not only at the moment when the sanction is applied, when the troubled relation is adjudicated, but also when it is instituted.

It is, in effect, necessary either to establish or to modify a number of juridical relations which this law takes care of and which the consent of the interested parties suffices neither to create nor to change. Such are those, notably, which concern the state of the persons. Although marriage is a contract, the married persons can neither form it nor break it at their pleasure. It is the same with all the other domestic relations and, with stronger reason, with all those which administrative law regulates. It is true that obligations properly contractual can be entered into and abrogated solely through the efforts of those desiring them. But it must not be forgotten that, if the contract has the power to bind, it is society which gives this power to it. Suppose that society did not sanction the obligations contracted for. They become simply promises which have no more than moral authority.[1] Every contract thus supposes that behind the parties implicated in it there is society very ready to intervene in order to gain respect for the engagements which have been made. Moreover, it lends this obligatory force only to contracts which have in themselves a social value, which is to say, those which conform to the rules of law. We shall see that its intervention is sometimes even more positive. It is present in all relations which restitutive law determines, even in those which appear most completely private, and its presence, though not felt, at least in normal circumstances, is none the less essential.[2]

Since rules with restitutive sanctions are strangers to the common conscience, the relations that they determine are not those which attach themselves indistinctly everywhere. That is to say, they are established immediately, not between the individual and society, but between restricted, special parties in society whom they bind. But, since society is not absent, it must be more or less directly interested, it must feel the repercussions. Thus, according to the force with which society feels them, it intervenes more or less concomitantly and more or less actively, through the intermediary of special organs charged with representing it. These relations are, then, quite different from those which repressive law regulates, for the latter attach the particular conscience to the collective conscience directly and without mediation; that is, the individual to society.

* * *

To sum up: the relations governed by co-operative law with restitutive sanctions and the solidarity which they express, result from the division of social labor. We have explained, moreover, that, in general, co-operative relations do not convey other sanctions. In fact, it is in the nature of special tasks to escape the action of the collective conscience, for, in order for a thing to be the object of common sentiments, the first condition is that it be common, that is to say, that it be present in all consciences and that all can represent it in one and the same manner. To be sure, in so far as functions have a certain generality, everybody can have some idea of them. But the more specialized they are, the more circumscribed the number of those cognizant of each of them. Consequently, the more marginal they are to the common conscience. The rules which determine them cannot have the superior force, the transcendent authority which, when offended, demands expiation. It is also from opinion that their authority comes, as is the case with penal rules, but from an opinion localized in restricted regions of society.

Moreover, even in the special circles where they apply and where, consequently, they are represented in people, they do not correspond to very active sentiments, nor even very often to any type of emotional state. For, as they fix the manner in which the different functions ought to concur in diverse combinations of circumstances which can arise, the objects to which they relate themselves are not always present to consciences. We do not always have

1. And even this moral authority comes from custom, which is to say, from society.

2. We must restrict ourselves to general indications, common to all the norms of restitutive law.

to administer guardianship, trusteeship,[3] or exercise the rights of creditor or buyer, etc., or even exercise them in such and such a condition. But the states of conscience are strong only in so far as they are permanent. The violation of these rules reaches neither the common soul of society in its living parts, nor even, at least not generally, that of special groups, and, consequently, it can determine only a very moderate reaction. All that is necessary is that the functions concur in a regular manner. If this regularity is disrupted, it behooves us to re-establish it. Assuredly, that is not to say that the development of the division of labor cannot be affective of penal law. There are, as we already know, administrative and governmental functions in which certain relations are regulated by repressive law, because of the particular character which the organ of common conscience and everything that relates to it has. In still other cases, the links of solidarity which unite certain social functions can be such that from their break quite general repercussions result invoking a penal sanction. But, for the reason we have given, these counter-blows are exceptional.

This law definitely plays a role in society analogous to that played by the nervous system in the organism. The latter has as its task, in effect, the regulation of the different functions of the body in such a way as to make them harmonize. It thus very naturally expresses the state of concentration at which the organism has arrived, in accordance with the division of physiological labor. Thus, on different levels of the animal scale, we can measure the degree of this concentration according to the development of the nervous system. Which is to say that we can equally measure the degree of concentration at which a society has arrived in accordance with the division of social labor according to the development of co-operative law with restitutive sanctions. We can foresee the great services that this criterion will render us.

Since negative solidarity does not produce any integration by itself, and since, moreover, there is nothing specific about it, we shall recognize only two kinds of positive solidarity which are distinguishable by the following qualities:

1. The first binds the individual directly to society without any intermediary. In the second, he depends upon society, because he depends upon the parts of which it is composed.

2. Society is not seen in the same aspect in the two cases. In the first, what we call society is a more or less organized totality of beliefs and sentiments common to all the members of the group: this is the collective type. On the other hand, the society in which we are solidary in the second instance is a system of different, special functions which definite relations unite. These two societies really make up only one. They are two aspects of one and the same reality, but none the less they must be distinguished.

3. From this second difference there arises another which helps us to characterize and name the two kinds of solidarity.

The first can be strong only if the ideas and tendencies common to all the members of the society are greater in number and intensity than those which pertain personally to each member. It is as much stronger as the excess is more considerable. But what makes our personality is how much of our own individual qualities we have, what distinguishes us from others. This solidarity can grow only in inverse ratio to personality. There are in each of us, as we have said, two consciences: one which is common to our group in its entirety, which, consequently, is not ourself, but society living and acting within us; the other, on the contrary, represents that in us which is personal and distinct, that which makes us an individual.[4] Solidarity which comes from likenesses is at its maximum when the collective conscience completely envelops our whole conscience and coincides in all points with it. But, at that moment, our individuality is nil. It can be born only if the community takes smaller toll of us. There are, here, two contrary forces, one centripetal, the other centrifugal, which cannot flourish at the same time. We cannot, at one and the same time, develop ourselves in two opposite senses. If we have a lively desire to think and act for ourselves, we cannot be strongly inclined to think and act as others do. If our ideal is to present a singular and personal appearance, we do not want to resemble everybody else. Moreover, at the moment when this solidarity exercises its force, our personality vanishes, as our definition permits us to say, for we are no longer ourselves, but the collective life.

The social molecules which can be coherent in this way can act together only in the measure that they have no actions of their own, as the molecules of inorganic bodies. That is why we propose to call this type of solidarity mechanical. The term does not signify that it is produced by mechanical and artificial means. We call it that only by analogy to the cohesion which unites the elements of an inanimate body, as opposed to that which makes a unity out of the elements of a living body. What justifies

3. That is why the law which governs the relations of domestic functions is not penal, although these functions are very general.

4. However, these two consciences are not in regions geographically distinct from us, but penetrate from all sides.

this term is that the link which thus unites the individual to society is wholly analogous to that which attaches a thing to a person. The individual conscience, considered in this light, is a simple dependent upon the collective type and follows all of its movements, as the possessed object follows those of its owner. In societies where this type of solidarity is highly developed, the individual does not appear, as we shall see later. Individuality is something which the society possesses. Thus, in these social types, personal rights are not yet distinguished from real rights.

It is quite otherwise with the solidarity which the division of labor produces. Whereas the previous type implies that individuals resemble each other, this type presumes their difference. The first is possible only in so far as the individual personality is absorbed into the collective personality; the second is possible only if each one has a sphere of action which is peculiar to him; that is, a personality. It is necessary, then, that the collective conscience leave open a part of the individual conscience in order that special functions may be established there, functions which it cannot regulate. The more this region is extended, the stronger is the cohesion which results from this solidarity. In effect, on the one hand, each one depends as much more strictly on society as labor is more divided; and, on the other, the activity of each is as much more personal as it is more specialized. Doubtless, as circumscribed as it is, it is never completely original. Even in the exercise of our occupation, we conform to usages, to practices which are common to our whole professional brotherhood. But, even in this instance, the yoke that we submit to is much less heavy than when society completely controls us, and it leaves much more place open for the free play of our initiative. Here, then, the individuality of all grows at the same time as that of its parts. Society becomes more capable of collective movement, at the same time that each of its elements has more freedom of movement. This solidarity resembles that which we observe among the higher animals. Each organ, in effect, has its special physiognomy, its autonomy. And, moreover, the unity of the organism is as great as the individuation of the parts is more marked. Because of this analogy, we propose to call the solidarity which is due to the division of labor, organic.

# *4. Types of Suicide*

BY EMILE DURKHEIM

WE HAVE thus successively set up the three following propositions:

*Suicide varies inversely with the degree of integration of religious society.*
*Suicide varies inversely with the degree of integration of domestic society.*
*Suicide varies inversely with the degree of integration of political society.*

This grouping shows that whereas these different societies have a moderating influence upon suicide, this is due not to special characteristics of each but to a characteristic common to all. Religion does not owe its efficacy to the special nature of religious sentiments, since domestic and political societies both produce the same effects when strongly integrated. This, moreover, we have already proved when studying directly the manner of action of different religions upon suicide. Inversely, it is not the specific nature of the domestic or political tie which can explain the immunity they confer, since religious society has the same advantage. The cause can only be found in a single quality possessed by all these social groups, though perhaps to varying degrees. The only quality satisfying this condition is that they are all strongly integrated social groups. So we reach the general conclusion: suicide varies inversely with the degree of integration of the social groups of which the individual forms a part.

But society cannot disintegrate without the individual simultaneously detaching himself from social life, without his own goals becoming preponderant over those of the community, in a word without his personality tending to surmount the collective personality. The more weakened the groups to which he belongs, the less he depends

Reprinted from Emile Durkheim, *Suicide,* trans. John A. Spaulding and George Simpson (Glencoe, Ill.: The Free Press, 1951), Book II, chap. iii, pp. 208–16; chap. iv, p. 217, 221–22, 227–28, 239–40.

on them, the more he consequently depends only on himself and recognizes no other rules of conduct than what are founded on his private interests. If we agree to call this state egoism, in which the individual ego asserts itself to excess in the face of the social ego and at its expense, we may call egoistic the special type of suicide springing from excessive individualism.

But how can suicide have such an origin?

First of all, it can be said that, as collective force is one of the obstacles best calculated to restrain suicide, its weakening involves a development of suicide. When society is strongly integrated, it holds individuals under its control, considers them at its service and thus forbids them to dispose wilfully of themselves. Accordingly it opposes their evading their duties to it through death. But how could society impose its supremacy upon them when they refuse to accept this subordination as legitimate? It no longer then possesses the requisite authority to retain them in their duty if they wish to desert; and conscious of its own weakness, it even recognizes their right to do freely what it can no longer prevent. So far as they are the admitted masters of their destinies, it is their privilege to end their lives. They, on their part, have no reason to endure life's sufferings patiently. For they cling to life more resolutely when belonging to a group they love, so as not to betray interests they put before their own. The bond that unites them with the common cause attaches them to life and the lofty goal they envisage prevents their feeling personal troubles so deeply. There is, in short, in a cohesive and animated society a constant interchange of ideas and feelings from all to each and each to all, something like a mutual moral support, which instead of throwing the individual on his own resources, leads him to share in the collective energy and supports his own when exhausted.

But these reasons are purely secondary. Excessive individualism not only results in favoring the action of suicidogenic causes, but it is itself such a cause. It not only frees man's inclination to do away with himself from a protective obstacle, but creates this inclination out of whole cloth and thus gives birth to a special suicide which bears its mark. This must be clearly understood for this is what constitutes the special character of the type of suicide just distinguished and justifies the name we have given it. What is there then in individualism that explains this result?

It has been sometimes said that because of his psychological constitution, man cannot live without attachment to some object which transcends and survives him, and that the reason for this necessity is a need we must have not to perish entirely. Life is said to be intolerable unless some reason for existing is involved, some purpose justifying life's trials. The individual alone is not a sufficient end for his activity. He is too little. He is not only hemmed in spatially; he is also strictly limited temporally. When, therefore, we have no other object than ourselves we cannot avoid the thought that our efforts will finally end in nothingness, since we ourselves disappear. But annihilation terrifies us. Under these conditions one would lose courage to live, that is, to act and struggle, since nothing will remain of our exertions. The state of egoism, in other words, is supposed to be contradictory to human nature and, consequently, too uncertain to have chances of permanence.

In this absolute formulation the proposition is vulnerable. If the thought of the end of our personality were really so hateful, we could consent to live only by blinding ourselves voluntarily as to life's value. For if we may in a measure avoid the prospect of annihilation we cannot extirpate it; it is inevitable, whatever we do. We may push back the frontier for some generations, force our name to endure for some years or centuries longer than our body; a moment, too soon for most men, always comes when it will be nothing. For the groups we join in order to prolong our existence by their means are themselves mortal; they too must dissolve, carrying with them all our deposit of ourselves. Those are few whose memories are closely enough bound to the very history of humanity to be assured of living until its death. So, if we really thus thirsted after immortality, no such brief perspectives could ever appease us. Besides, what of us is it that lives? A word, a sound, an imperceptible trace, most often anonymous,[1] therefore nothing comparable to the violence of our efforts or able to justify them to us. In actuality, though a child is naturally an egoist who feels not the slightest craving to survive himself, and the old man is very often a child in this and so many other respects, neither ceases to cling to life as much or more than the adult; indeed we have seen that suicide is very rare for the first fifteen years and tends to decrease at the other extreme of life. Such too is the case with animals, whose psychological constitution differs from that of men only in degree. It is therefore untrue that life is only possible by its possessing its rationale outside of itself.

Indeed, a whole range of functions concern only the individual; these are the ones indispensable for

1. We say nothing of the ideal protraction of life involved in the belief in immortality of the soul, for (1) this cannot explain why the family or attachment to political society preserves us from suicide; and (2) it is not even this belief which forms religion's prophylactic influence, as we have shown above.

physical life. Since they are made for this purpose only, they are perfected by its attainment. In everything concerning them, therefore, man can act reasonably without thought of transcendental purposes. These functions serve by merely serving him. In so far as he has no other needs, he is therefore self-sufficient and can live happily with no other objective than living. This is not the case, however, with the civilized adult. He has many ideas, feelings and practices unrelated to organic needs. The roles of art, morality, religion, political faith, science itself are not to repair organic exhaustion nor to provide sound functioning of the organs. All this supra-physical life is built and expanded not because of the demands of the cosmic environment but because of the demands of the social environment. The influence of society is what has aroused in us the sentiments of sympathy and solidarity drawing us toward others; it is society which, fashioning us in its image, fills us with religious, political and moral beliefs that control our actions. To play our social role we have striven to extend our intelligence and it is still society that has supplied us with tools for this development by transmitting to us its trust fund of knowledge.

Through the very fact that these superior forms of human activity have a collective origin, they have a collective purpose. As they derive from society they have reference to it; rather they are society itself incarnated and individualized in each one of us. But for them to have a raison d'etre in our eyes, the purpose they envisage must be one not indifferent to us. We can cling to these forms of human activity only to the degree that we cling to society itself. Contrariwise, in the same measure as we feel detached from society we become detached from that life whose source and aim is society. For what purpose do these rules of morality, these precepts of law binding us to all sorts of sacrifices, these restrictive dogmas exist, if there is no being outside us whom they serve and in whom we participate? What is the purpose of science itself? If its only use is to increase our chances for survival, it does not deserve the trouble it entails. Instinct acquits itself better of this role; animals prove this. Why substitute for it a more hesitant and uncertain reflection? What is the end of suffering, above all? If the value of things can only be estimated by their relation to this positive evil for the individual, it is without reward and incomprehensible. This problem does not exist for the believer firm in his faith or the man strongly bound by ties of domestic or political society. Instinctively and unreflectively they ascribe all that they are and do, the one to his Church or his God, the living symbol of the Church, the other to his family, the third to his country or party. Even in their sufferings they see only a means of glorifying the group to which they belong and thus do homage to it. So, the Christian ultimately desires and seeks suffering to testify more fully to his contempt for the flesh and more fully resemble his divine model. But the more the believer doubts, that is, the less he feels himself a real participant in the religious faith to which he belongs, and from which he is freeing himself; the more the family and community become foreign to the individual, so much the more does he become a mystery to himself, unable to escape the exasperating and agonizing question: to what purpose?

If, in other words, as has often been said, man is double, that is because social man superimposes himself upon physical man. Social man necessarily presupposes a society which he expresses and serves. If this dissolves, if we no longer feel it in existence and action about and above us, whatever is social in us is deprived of all objective foundation. All that remains is an artificial combination of illusory images, a phantasmagoria vanishing at the least reflection; that is, nothing which can be a goal for our action. Yet this social man is the essence of civilized man; he is the masterpiece of existence. Thus we are bereft of reasons for existence; for the only life to which we could cling no longer corresponds to anything actual; the only existence still based upon reality no longer meets our needs. Because we have been initiated into a higher existence, the one which satisfies an animal or a child can satisfy us no more and the other itself fades and leaves us helpless. So there is nothing more for our efforts to lay hold of, and we feel them lose themselves in emptiness. In this sense it is true to say that our activity needs an object transcending it. We do not need it to maintain ourselves in the illusion of an impossible immortality; it is implicit in our moral constitution and cannot be even partially lost without this losing its raison d'etre in the same degree. No proof is needed that in such a state of confusion the least cause of discouragement may easily give birth to desperate resolutions. If life is not worth the trouble of being lived, everything becomes a pretext to rid ourselves of it.

But this is not all. This detachment occurs not only in single individuals. One of the constitutive elements of every national temperament consists of a certain way of estimating the value of existence. There is a collective as well as an individual humor inclining peoples to sadness or cheerfulness, making them see things in bright or sombre lights. In fact, only society can pass a collective opinion on the value of human life; for this the individual is incompetent. The latter knows nothing but himself and his own little horizon; thus his experience is too limited to serve as a basis for a general appraisal. He may indeed consider his own life to be aimless; he can say nothing applicable to others. On the contrary, without sophistry, society may generalize its own feeling as to itself, its state of health or lack of health. For individuals share too deeply in the life of society for it to be diseased without their suffering infection. What it suffers they necessarily suffer. Because it is the whole, its ills are communicated to its paths. Hence it cannot disintegrate without awareness that the regular conditions of general existence are equally disturbed. Because society is the end on which our better selves depend, it cannot feel us escaping it without a simultaneous realization that our activity is purposeless. Since we are its handiwork, society cannot be conscious of its own decadence without the feeling that henceforth this work is of no value. Thence are formed currents of depression and disillusionment emanating from no particular individual but expressing society's state of disintegration. They reflect the relaxation of social bonds, a sort of collective asthenia, or social malaise, just as individual sadness, when chronic, in its way reflects the poor organic state of the individual. Then metaphysical and religious systems spring up which, by reducing these obscure sentiments to formulae, attempt to prove to men the senselessness of life and that it is self-deception to believe that it has purpose. Then new moralities originate which, by elevating facts to ethics, commend suicide or at least tend in that direction by suggesting a minimal existence. On their appearance they seem to have been created out of whole cloth by their makers who are sometimes blamed for the pessimism of their doctrines. In reality they are an effect rather than a cause; they merely symbolize in abstract language and systematic form the physiological distress of the body social.[2] As these currents are collective, they have, by virtue of their origin, an authority which they impose upon the individual and they drive him more vigorously on the way to which he is already inclined by the state of moral distress directly aroused in him by the disintegration of society. Thus, at the very moment that, with excessive zeal, he frees himself from the social environment, he still submits to its influence. However individualized a man may be, there is always something collective remaining—the very depression and melancholy resulting from this same exaggerated individualism. He effects communion through sadness when he no longer has anything else with which to achieve it.

Hence this type of suicide well deserves the name we have given it. Egoism is not merely a contributing factor in it; it is its generating cause. In this case the bond attaching man to life relaxes because that attaching him to society is itself slack. The incidents of private life which seem the direct inspiration of suicide and are considered its determining causes are in reality only incidental causes. The individual yields to the slightest shock of circumstance because the state of society has made him a ready prey to suicide.

Several facts confirm this explanation. Suicide is known to be rare among children and to diminish among the aged at the last confines of life; physical man, in both, tends to become the whole of man. Society is still lacking in the former, for it has not had the time to form him in its image; it begins to retreat from the latter or, what amounts to the same thing, he retreats from it. Thus both are more self-sufficient. Feeling a lesser need for self-completion through something not themselves, they are also less exposed to feel the lack of what is necessary for living. The immunity of an animal has the same causes. We shall likewise see in the next chapter that, though lower societies practice a form of suicide of their own, the one we have just discussed is almost unknown to them. Since their social life is very simple, the social inclinations of individuals are simple also and thus they need little for satisfaction. They readily find external objectives to which they become attached. If he can carry with him his gods and his family, primitive man, everywhere that he goes, has all that his social nature demands.

This is also why woman can endure life in isolation more easily than man. When a widow is seen to endure her condition much better than a widower and desires marriage less passionately, one is led to consider this ease in dispensing with the family a mark of superiority; it is said that woman's affective faculties, being very intense, are easily employed outside the domestic circle, while her devotion is indispensable to man to help him endure life. Actually, if this is her privilege it is because her sensibility is rudimentary rather than highly developed. As she lives outside of community existence more than man, she is less penetrated by it; society is less necessary to her because she is less impregnated with sociability. She has few needs in this direction and satisfies them easily. With a few devotional practices and some animals to care for, the old unmarried woman's life is full. If she remains faithfully attached to religious traditions and thus finds ready protection against sui-

2. This is why it is unjust to accuse these theorists of sadness of generalizing personal impressions. They are the echo of a general condition.

cide, it is because these very simple social forms satisfy all her needs. Man, on the contrary, is hard beset in this respect. As his thought and activity develop, they increasingly overflow these antiquated forms. But then he needs others. Because he is a more complex social being, he can maintain his equilibrium only by finding more points of support outside himself, and it is because his moral balance depends on a larger number of conditions that it is more easily disturbed.

## *Altruistic Suicide*

In the order of existence, no good is measureless. A biological quality can only fulfill the purposes it is meant to serve on condition that it does not transgress certain limits. So with social phenomena. If, as we have just seen, excessive individuation leads to suicide, insufficient individuation has the same effects. When man has become detached from society, he encounters less resistance to suicide in himself, and he does so likewise when social integration is too strong.

* * *

We thus confront a type of suicide differing by incisive qualities from the preceding one. Whereas the latter is due to excessive individuation, the former is caused by too rudimentary individuation. One occurs because society allows the individual to escape it, being insufficiently aggregated in some parts or even in the whole; the other, because society holds him in too strict tutelage. Having given the name of *egoism* to the state of the ego living its own life and obeying itself alone, that of *altruism* adequately expresses the opposite state, where the ego is not its own property, where it is blended with something not itself, where the goal of conduct is exterior to itself, that is, in one of the groups in which it participates. So we call the suicide caused by intense altruism *altruistic suicide*. But since it is characteristically performed as a duty, the terminology adopted should express this fact. So we will call such a type *obligatory altruistic suicide*.

The combination of these two adjectives is required to define it; for not every altruistic suicide is necessarily obligatory. Some are not so expressly imposed by society, having a more optional character. In other words, altruistic suicide is a species with several varieties.

* * *

We have thus constituted a second type of suicide, itself consisting of three varieties: obligatory altruistic suicide, optional altruistic suicide, and acute altruistic suicide, the perfect pattern of which is mystical suicide. In these different forms, it contrasts most strikingly with egoistic suicide. One is related to the crude morality which disregards everything relating solely to the individual; the other is closely associated with the refined ethics which sets human personality on so high a pedestal that it can no longer be subordinated to anything. Between the two there is, therefore, all the difference between primitive peoples and the most civilized nations.

However, if lower societies are the theatre par excellence of altruistic suicide, it is also found in more recent civilizations. Under this head may notably be classified the death of some of the Christian martyrs. All those neophytes who without killing themselves, voluntarily allowed their own slaughter, are really suicides. Though they did not kill themselves, they sought death with all their power and behaved so as to make it inevitable. To be suicide, the act from which death must necessarily result need only have been performed by the victim with full knowledge of the facts. Besides, the passionate enthusiasm with which the believers in the new religion faced final torture shows that at this moment they had completely discarded their personalities for the idea of which they had become the servants. Probably the epidemics of suicide which devastated the monasteries on several occasions during the Middle Ages, apparently caused by excesses of religious fervor, were of this nature.

In our contemporary societies, as individual personality becomes increasingly free from the collective personality, such suicides could not be widespread. Some may doubtless be said to have yielded to altruistic motives, such as soldiers who preferred death to the humiliation of defeat, like Commandant Beaurepaire and Admiral Villeneuve, or unhappy persons who kill themselves to prevent disgrace befalling their family. For when such persons renounce life, it is for something they love better than themselves. But they are isolated and exceptional cases. Yet even today there exists among us a special environment where altruistic suicide is chronic: namely, the army.

* * *

It may now be better understood why we insisted on giving an objective definition of suicide and on sticking to it.

Because altruistic suicide, though showing the familiar suicidal traits, resembles especially in its most vivid manifestations some categories of action which we are used to honoring with our respect and even admiration, people have often refused to consider it as self-destruction. It is to be remembered that the deaths of Cato and of the

Girondins were not suicides for Esquirol and Falret. But if suicides with the spirit of renunciation and abnegation as their immediate and visible cause do not deserve the name, it can be no more appropriate for those springing from the same moral disposition, though less apparently; for the second differ by only a few shades from the first. If the inhabitant of the Canary Islands who throws himself into an abyss to do honor to his god is not a suicide, how give this name to a Jain sectary who kills himself to obtain entry to oblivion; to the primitive who, under the influence of the same mental state, renounces life for a slight insult done him or merely to express his contempt for existence; to the bankrupt who prefers not to survive his disgrace; and finally to the many soldiers who every year increase the numbers of voluntary deaths? All these cases have for their root the same state of altruism which is equally the cause of what might be called heroic suicide. Shall they alone be placed among the ranks of suicides and only those excluded whose motive is particularly pure? But first, according to what standard will the division be made? When does a motive cease to be sufficiently praiseworthy for the act it determines to be called suicide? Moreover, by separating these two classes of facts radically from each other, we inevitably misjudge their nature. For the essential characteristics of the type are clearest in obligatory altruistic suicide. Other varieties are only derivative forms. Either a considerable number of instructive phenomena will be eliminated or, if not all are eliminated, not only will a purely arbitrary choice be the only one possible among them, but it will be impossible to detect the common stock to which those that are retained belong. Such is the risk we incur in making the definition of suicide depend on the subjective feelings it inspires.

Besides, not even the reasons for the sentiment thought to justify this exclusion are well founded. The fact is stressed that the motives of certain altruistic suicides reappear in slightly different forms as the basis of actions regarded by everyone as moral. But is egoistic suicide any different? Has not the sentiment of individual autonomy its own morality as well as the opposite sentiment? If the latter serves as foundation to a kind of courage, strengthening and even hardening the heart, the other softens and moves it to pity. Where altruistic suicide is prevalent, man is always ready to give his life; however, at the same time, he sets no more value on that of another. On the contrary, when he rates individual personality above all other ends, he respects it in others. His cult for it makes him suffer from all that minimizes it even among his fellows. A broader sympathy for human suffering succeeds the fanatical devotions of primitive times. Every sort of suicide is then merely the exaggerated or deflected form of a virtue. In that case, however, the way they affect the moral conscience does not sufficiently differentiate them to justify their being separated into different types.

# 5. *Types of Social Organization*

BY MAX WEBER

## *Types of Solidary Social Relationships*

A SOCIAL RELATIONSHIP will be called "communal"[1] if and so far as the orientation of social action—whether in the individual case, on the average, or in the pure type—is based on a subjective feeling of the parties, whether affectual

Reprinted from Max Weber, *The Theory of Social and Economic Organization,* trans. A. H. Henderson and Talcott Parsons, ed. Talcott Parsons (Glencoe, Ill.: The Free Press, 1947), Chap. i, secs. 9–17, pp. 136–57, with the permission of The Free Press. Copyright 1947 by Oxford University Press.

1. The two types of relationship which Weber distinguishes in this section he himself calls *Vergemeinschaftung* and *Vergesellschaftung.* His own usage here is an adaptation of the well-known terms of Toennies, *Gemeinschaft* and *Gesellschaft,* and has been directly influenced by Toennies' work. Though there has been much discussion of them in English, it is safe to say that no satisfactory equivalent of Toennies' terms have been found. In particular, "community" and either "society" or "association" are unsatisfactory, since these terms have quite different connotations in English. In the context, however, in which Weber uses his slightly altered terms, that of action within a social relationship, the adjective forms "communal" and "associative" do not seem to be objectionable. Their exact meanings should become clear from Weber's definitions and comments.—ED.

or traditional, that they belong together. A social relationship will, on the other hand, be called "associative" if and in so far as the orientation of social action within it rests on a rationally motivated adjustment of interests or a similarly motivated agreement, whether the basis of rational judgment be absolute values or reasons of expediency. It is especially common, though by no means inevitable, for the associative type of relationship to rest on a rational agreement by mutual consent. In that case the corresponding action is, at the pole of rationality, oriented either to a rational belief in the binding validity of the obligation to adhere to it, or to a rational expectation that the other party will live up to it.[2]

1. The purest cases of associative relationships are: (a) rational free market exchange, which constitutes a compromise of opposed but complementary interests; (b) the pure voluntary association based on self-interest,[3] a case of agreement as to a long-run course of action oriented purely to the promotion of specific ulterior interests, economic or other, of its members; (c) the voluntary association of individuals motivated by an adherence to a set of common absolute values,[4] for example, the rational sect, in so far as it does not cultivate emotional and affective interests, but seeks only to serve a "cause." This last case, to be sure, seldom occurs in anything approaching the pure type.

2. Communal relationships may rest on various types of affectual, emotional, or traditional bases. Examples are a religious brotherhood, an erotic relationship, a relation of personal loyalty, a national community, the *esprit de corps* of a military unit. The type case most conveniently illustrated by the family. But the great majority of social relationships has this characteristic to some degree, while it is at the same time to some degree determined by associative factors. No matter how calculating and hard-headed the ruling considerations in such a social relationship—as that of a merchant to his customers—may be, it is quite possible for it to involve emotional values which transcend its utilitarian significance. Every social relationship which goes beyond the pursuit of immediate common ends, which hence lasts for long periods, involves relatively permanent social relationships between the same persons, and these cannot be exclusively confined to the technically necessary activities. Hence in such cases as association in the same military unit, in the same school class, in the same workshop or office, there is always some tendency in this direction, although the degree, to be sure, varies enormously.[5] Conversely, a social relationship which is normally considered primarily communal may involve action on the part of some or even all of the participants, which is to an important degree oriented to considerations of expediency. There is, for instance, a wide variation in the extent to which the members of a family group feel a genuine community of interests or, on the other hand, exploit the relationship for their own ends. The concept of communal relationship has been intentionally defined in very general terms and hence includes a very heterogeneous group of phenomena.

3. The communal type of relationship is, according to the usual interpretation of its subjective meaning, the most radical antithesis of conflict. This should not, however, be allowed to obscure the fact that coercion of all sorts is a very common thing in even the most intimate of such communal relationships if one party is weaker in character than the other. Furthermore, a process of the selection of types leading to differences in opportunity and survival, goes on within these relationships just the same as anywhere else. Associative relationships, on the other hand, very often consist only in compromises between rival interests, where only a part of the occasion or means of conflict has been eliminated, or even an attempt has been made to do so. Hence, outside the area of compromise, the conflict of interests, with its attendant competition for supremacy, remains unchanged. Conflict and communal relationships are relative concepts. Conflict varies enormously according to the means employed, especially whether they are violent or peaceful, and to the ruthlessness with which they are used. It has already been pointed out that any type of order governing social action in some way leaves room for a process of selection among various rival human types.

4. It is by no means true that the existence of common qualities, a common situation, or common modes of behaviour imply the existence of a communal social relationship. Thus, for instance, the possession of a common biological inheritance by virtue of which persons are classified as belonging to the same "race," naturally implies no sort of

---

2. This terminology is similar to the distinction made by Ferdinand Toennies in his pioneering work, *Gemeinschaft und Gesellschaft;* but for his purposes, Toennies has given this distinction a rather more specific meaning than would be convenient for purposes of the present discussion.

3. *Zweckverein.*

4. *Gesinnungsverein.*

5. Weber's emphasis on the importance of these communal elements even within functionally specific formal organizations like industrial plants has been strongly confirmed by the findings of research since this was written. One important study which shows the importance of informal organization on this level among the workers of an industrial plant is reported in Roethlisberger and Dickson, *Management and the Worker.*—ED.

communal social relationship between them. By restrictions on social intercourse and on marriage persons may find themselves in a similar situation, a situation of isolation from the environment which imposes these distinctions. But even if they all react to this situation in the same way, this does not constitute a communal relationship. The latter does not even exist if they have a common "feeling" about this situation and its consequences. It is only when this feeling leads to a mutual orientation of their behaviour to each other that a social relationship arises between them, a social relationship to each other and not only to persons in the environment. Furthermore, it is only so far as this relationship involves feelings of belonging together that it is a "communal" relationship. In the case of the Jews, for instance, except for Zionist circles and the action of certain associations promoting specifically Jewish interests, there thus exist communal relationships only to a relatively small extent; indeed, Jews often repudiate the existence of a Jewish "community."

Community of language, which arises from a similarity of tradition through the family and the surrounding social environment, facilitates mutual understanding, and thus the formation of all types of social relationships, in the highest degree. But taken by itself it is not sufficient to constitute a communal relationship, but only for the facilitation of intercourse within the groups concerned, thus for the development of associative relationships. In the first place, this takes place between *individuals,* not because they speak the same language, but because they have other types of interests. Orientation to the rules of a common language is thus primarily important as a means of communication, not as the content of a social relationship. It is only with the emergence of a consciousness of difference from third persons who speak a different language that the fact that two persons speak the same language, and in that respect share a common situation, can lead them to a feeling of community and to modes of social organization consciously based on the sharing of the common language.

Participation in a "market" is still another kind. It encourages association between the individual parties to specific acts of exchange and a social relationship, above all that of competition, between the individual participants who must mutually orient their action to each other. But no further modes of association develop except in cases where certain participants enter into agreements in order to better their competitive situations, or where they all agree on rules for the purpose of regulating transactions and of securing favourable general conditions for all. It may further be remarked that the market and the competitive economy resting on it form the most important type of the reciprocal determination of action in terms of pure self-interest, a type which is characteristic of modern economic life.

## *Open and Closed Relationships*

A social relationship, regardless of whether it is communal or associative in character, will be spoken of as "open" to outsiders if and in so far as participation in the mutually oriented social action relevant to its subjective meaning is, according to its system of order, not denied to anyone who wishes to participate and who is actually in a position to do so. A relationship will, on the other hand, be called "closed" against outsiders so far as, according to its subjective meaning and the binding rules of its order, participation of certain persons is excluded, limited, or subjected to conditions. Whether a relationship is open or closed may be determined traditionally, affectually, or rationally in terms of values or of expediency. It is especially likely to be closed, for rational reasons, in the following type of situation: a social relationship may provide the parties to it with opportunities for the satisfaction of various interests, whether the satisfactions be spiritual or material, whether the interest be in the end of the relationship as such or in some ulterior consequence of participation, or whether it is achieved through co-operative action or by a compromise of interests. If the participants expect that the admission of others will lead to an improvement of their situation, an improvement in degree, in kind, in the security or the value of the satisfaction, their interest will be in keeping the relationship open. If, on the other hand, their expectations are of improving their position by monopolistic tactics, their interest is in a closed relationship.

There are various ways in which it is possible for a closed social relationship to guarantee its monopolized advantages to the parties. Such advantages may be left free to competitive struggle within the group; they may be regulated or rationed in amount and kind, or they may be appropriated by individuals or sub-groups on a permanent basis and become more or less inalienable. The last is a case of closure within, as well as against, outsiders. Appropriated advantages will be called "rights." As determined by the relevant order, appropriation may be for the benefit of the members of particular communal or associative groups (for instance, household groups), or for the benefit of individuals. In the latter case, the individual may enjoy his rights on a purely personal basis or in such a way that in case of his death one or more other persons related to the holder of the right by birth (kinship), or by some other social relationship, may inherit the rights in question. Or the rights may pass to one or more individuals specifically designated by the holder. Finally, it may be that the holder is more or less fully empowered to alienate his rights by voluntary agreement, either to other specific persons or to anyone he chooses. This is "alienable" appropriation. A party to a closed social relationship will be called a "member";[6] in case his participation is regulated in such a way as to guarantee him appropriated advantages, a "privileged" member. Appropriated rights which are enjoyed by individuals through inheritance or by hereditary groups, whether communal or associative, will be called the "property" of the individual or of groups in question; and, in so far as they are alienable, "free" property.

The apparently gratuitous tediousness involved in the elaborate definition of the above concepts is an example of the fact that we often neglect to think out clearly what seems to be "obvious," because it is intuitively familiar.

1. (a) Examples of communal relationships, which tend to be closed on a traditional basis, are those membership in which is determined by family relationship.

(b) Personal emotional relationships are usually affectually closed. Examples are erotic relationships and, very commonly, relations of personal loyalty.

(c) Closure on the basis of rational commitment to values is usual in groups sharing a common system of explicit religious belief.

(d) Typical cases of rational closure on grounds of expediency are economic associations of a monopolistic or a plutocratic character.

A few examples may be taken at random. Whether a group of people engaged in conversation is open or closed depends on its content. General conversation is apt to be open, as contrasted with intimate conversation or the imparting of official information. Market relationships are in most, or at least in many, cases essentially open. In the case of many relationships, both communal and associative, there is a tendency to shift from a phase of expansion to one of exclusiveness. Examples are the guilds and the democratic city-states of Antiquity and the Middle Ages. At times these groups sought to increase their membership in the interest of improving the security of their position of power by adequate numbers. At other times they restricted their membership to protect the value of their monopolistic position. The same phenomenon is not uncommon in monastic orders and religious sects which have passed from a stage of religious proselytizing to one of restriction in the interest of the maintenance of an ethical standard or for the protection of material interests. There is a similar close relationship between the extension of market relationships in the interest of increased turnover on the one hand, their monopolistic restriction on the other. The promotion of linguistic uniformity is to-day a natural result of the interests of publishers and writers, as opposed to the earlier, not uncommon, tendency for class groups to maintain linguistic peculiarities or even for secret languages to be built up.

2. Both the extent and the methods of regulation and exclusion in relation to outsiders may vary widely, so that the transition from a state of openness to one of regulation and closure is gradual. Various conditions of participation may be laid down; qualifying tests, a period of probation, requirement of possession of a share which can be purchased under certain conditions, election of new members by ballot, membership or eligibility by birth or by virtue of achievements open to anyone. Finally, in case of closure and the appropriation of rights within the group, status may be dependent on the acquisition of an appropriated right. There is a wide variety of different degrees of closure and of conditions of participation. Thus regulation and closure are relative concepts. There are all manner of gradual shadings as between an exclusive club, a theatrical audience the members of which have purchased tickets, and a party rally to which the largest possible number has been urged to come; similarly, from a church service open to the general public through the rituals of a limited sect to the mysteries of a secret cult.

3. Similarly, closure within the group as between the members themselves and in their relations with each other may also assume the most varied forms. Thus a caste, a guild, or a group of stock exchange brokers, which is closed to outsiders, may allow to its members a perfectly free competition for all the advantages which the group as a whole monopolizes for itself. Or it may assign every member strictly to the enjoyment of certain advantages, such as claims over customers or particular business opportunities, for life or even on a hereditary basis. This is particularly characteristic of India. Similarly a closed group of settlers may allow its members free use of the resources of its area or may restrict them rigidly to a plot assigned to each individual household. A closed group of colonists may allow free use of the land or sanction and guarantee permanent appropriation of separate holdings. In such cases all conceivable transitional and intermediate

6. *Rechtsgenosse.*

forms can be found. Historically, the closure of eligibility to fiefs, benefices, and offices within the group, and the appropriation on the part of those enjoying them, have occurred in the most varied forms. Similarly, the establishment of rights to and possession of particular jobs on the part of workers may develop all the way from the "closed shop" to a right to a particular job. The first step in this development may be to prohibit the dismissal of a worker without the consent of the workers' representatives. The development of the "works councils" in Germany after 1918 might be a first step in this direction, though it need not be.[7]

All the details must be reserved to particular studies. The most extreme form of permanent appropriation is found in cases where particular rights are guaranteed to an individual or to certain groups of them, such as households, clans, families, in such a way that it is specified in the order either that, in case of death, the rights descend to specific heirs, or that the possessor is free to transfer them to any other person at will. Such a person thereby becomes a party to the social relationship so that, when appropriation has reached this extreme within the group, it becomes to that extent an open group in relation to outsiders. This is true so long as acquisition of membership is not subject to the ratification of the other, prior members.

4. The principal motives for closure of a relationship are: (a) The maintenance of quality, which is often combined with the interest in prestige and the consequent opportunities to enjoy honour, and even profit. Examples are communities of ascetics, monastic orders, especially, for instance, the Indian mendicant orders, religious sects like the Puritans, organized groups of warriors, of retainers (*Ministerialen*) and other functionaries, organized citizen bodies as in the Greek states, craft guilds; (b) orientation to the scarcity of advantages in their bearing on consumption needs (*Nahrungsspielraum*).[8] Examples are monopolies of consumption, the most developed form of which is a self-subsistent village community; (c) orientation to the scarcity of opportunities for acquisition (*Erwerbsspielraum*). This is found in trade monopolies such as the guilds, the ancient monopolies of fishing rights, and so on. Usually motive (a) is combined with (b) or (c).

## *Representation and Responsibility*

The order which governs a social relationship by tradition or by virtue of its legal establishment, may determine that certain types of action of some of the parties to the relationship will have consequences which affect the others. It may be that all are held responsible for the action of *any* one. In that case they will be spoken of as "solidary" members. Or, on the other hand, the action of certain members, the "representatives," may be binding upon the others. That is, the resulting advantages will go to them, they will enjoy the benefits, or conversely bear the resulting losses.

Representative authority (*Vertretungsgewalt*) may be conferred in accordance with the binding order in such a way (a) that it is completely appropriated in all its forms—the case of "independent" authority; or (b) it may be conferred in accordance with particular criteria, permanently or for a limited term; or (c) it may be conferred by specific acts of the members or of outside persons, again permanently or for a limited term—the case of appointment. There are many different conditions which determine the ways in which social relationships, communal or associative, develop relations of solidarity, or of representation. In general terms, it is possible only to say that one of the most decisive is the extent to which the action of the group is oriented to violent conflict or to peaceful exchange as its end. Besides these, many special circumstances, which can only be discussed in a detailed analysis, may be of crucial importance. It is not surprising that this development is least conspicuous in groups which pursue purely ideal ends by peaceful means. Often the degree of closure against outsiders is closely related to the development of solidarity or of representation. But this is by no means always the case.

1. This "imputation" of responsibility may in practice involve both active and passive solidarity. All the participants may be held responsible for the action of any one just as he himself is, and similarly may be entitled to enjoy any benefits resulting from his action. This responsibility may be owed to spirits or gods, that is, involve a religious orientation. Or, on the other hand, it may be responsibility to other human beings, as regulated by convention or by law. Examples of regulation by convention are

7. This is a reference to the *Betriebsräte* which were formed in German industrial plants during the Revolution of 1918–19 and were organized in the Weimar Constitution as entitled to representation in the Federal Economic Council.—Ed.

8. Weber here refers to *Nahrungsspielraum*. The concept refers to the scope of economic resources and opportunities on which the standard of living of an individual or a group is dependent. By contrast with this, *Erwerbsspielraum* is a similar scope of resources and economic opportunities seen from the point of view of their possible role as sources of profit. The basic distinction implied in this contrast is of central importance to Weber's analysis later on.—Ed.

blood revenge carried out against or with the help of members of the kin-groups, reprisals against the inhabitants of the town or the country of the offender; of the legal type, formal punishment of relatives, members of the household or fellow-members of a communal group, instead of, or in addition to, the actual offender, and personal liability of members of a household or of a commercial partnership for each other's debts. Solidarity in relation to gods has also had very significant historical results. For instance, in the covenant of Israel with Jahveh, in early Christianity, and in the early Puritan community.

On the other hand, the imputation of solidarity may mean no more than that the participants in a closed social relationship, by virtue of the traditional or legal order, are held legally entitled to enjoy some kind of access to advantages and benefits, especially economic, which a representative has procured. Examples are the control over the powers exercised by the "executive committee" of a club or association, or by the responsible agent of a political or economic association over resources which, as specified in the order, are meant to serve the corporate purpose of the group.

2. Solidarity is typically found in the following cases: (a) In traditional, communal groups based on birth or the sharing of a common life; for example, the household and the kinship unit; (b) in closed relationships which maintain a monopolized position, and control over the corresponding benefits by their own power. The typical case is corporate political groups, especially in the past. But the same situation exists to-day to a high degree, most strikingly in time of war; (c) in profit-making organizations where the participants personally conduct the business. The type case is the business partnership; (d) in some cases, in labour organizations. An example is the Artel. Representation is most frequently found in associations devoted to specific purposes and in legally organized groups, especially when funds have been collected and must be administered in the interests of the group. This will be further discussed in the Sociology of Law.

3. Representative authority is conferred according to "criteria" (see above) in such cases as when it goes by seniority or some other such rule.

4. It is not possible to carry the analysis of this subject further in general terms. Its elaboration must be reserved to detailed investigation of particular fields. The most ancient and most universal phenomenon in this field is that of reprisal, meant either as revenge or as a means of gaining control of hostages, or some other kind of security against future injury.

## *The Concept of "Corporate Group" and Its Types*

A social relationship which is either closed or limits the admission of outsiders by rules, will be called a "corporate group" (*Verband*)[9] so far as its order is enforced by the action of specific individuals whose regular function this is, of a chief or "head" (*Leiter*) and usually also an administrative staff. These functionaries will normally also have representative authority. The incumbency of a directing position or participation in the functions of the administrative staff constitute "governing authority" (*Regierungsgewalt*). This may be appropriated, or it may be assigned in accordance with the binding rules of the association according to specific criteria or procedures. It may be assigned permanently, for a term, or for dealing with a specific situation. "Corporate action" is either the action of the administrative staff, which by virtue of its governing or representative authority is oriented to carrying out the terms of its order, or it is the action of the members as directed by the administrative staff.

1. It is indifferent, so far as the concept is concerned, whether the relationship is of a communal or associative character. It is sufficient for there to be a person or persons in authority—the head of a family, the executive committee of an association, a managing director, a prince, a president, the head of a church—whose action is concerned with carrying into effect the order governing the corporate group. This criterion is decisive because it is not merely a matter of action which is *oriented* to an order, but which is specifically directed to its *enforcement*. Sociologically this adds to the concept of a closed social relationship, a further element, which is of far-reaching empirical importance. For by no means every closed communal or associative relationship is a corporate group. For instance, this is not true of an erotic relationship or of a kinship group without a formalized system of authority.

2. Whether or not a corporate group exists is entirely a matter of the presence of a person in authority, with or without an administrative staff. More precisely, it exists so far as there is a proba-

9. The term *Verband*, which is one of the most important in Weber's scheme, has, in the technical sense defined in this paragraph, been translated as "corporate group." "Association" has not been used because it does not imply the formal differentiation between a head or chief and ordinary members. A "corporation" is, from this point of view, one specific kind of corporate group. The term *Leiter* is not readily translatable. "Chief" has most frequently been used because it seems to have less objectionable connotations than any alternative. Thus we speak of the "chief" of the medical staff of a hospital and use the term in other similar connexions.

bility that certain persons will act in such a way as to tend to carry out the order governing the group; that is, that persons are present who can be counted on to act in this way whenever the occasion arises. For purposes of definition, it is indifferent what is the basis of the relevant expectation, whether it is a case of traditional or affectual devotion to duty, or a case of devotion by virtue of rational values, any of which may be involved in feudal fealty, loyalty to an office or to a service. It may, on the other hand, be a matter of expediency, as, for instance, a pecuniary interest in the attached salary. Thus for purposes of the terminology of this discussion, the corporate group does not "exist" apart from the probability that a course of action oriented in this way will take place. If there is no probability of this type of action on the part of a particular group of persons or of a given individual, there is in these terms a social relationship, but no corporate group. On the other hand, so long as there is a probability of such action, the corporate group, as a sociological phenomenon, continues to exist, in spite of the fact that the specific individuals whose action is oriented to the order in question, may have been completely changed. The concept has been defined intentionally to include precisely this phenomenon.

3. It is possible (a) that, in addition to the action of the administrative staff itself or that which takes place under its direction, there may be other cases where action of the members is intended to uphold the authority of the order; for instance, contributions or "liturgies"[10] and certain types of personal services, such as jury service or military service. It is also possible (b) for the binding order to include norms to which it is expected that the action of the members of a corporate group will be oriented in respects other than those pertaining to the affairs of the corporate group as a unit. For instance, the law of the state includes rules governing private economic relations which are not concerned with the enforcement of the state's legal order as such, but with action in the service of private interests. This is true of most of the "civil" law. In the first case (a) one may speak of action "oriented to corporate affairs" (*Verbandsbezogenes Handeln*); in the second (b) of action "subject to corporate regulation" (*Verbandsgeregeltes Handeln*). It is only in the cases of the action of the administrative staff itself and of that deliberately directed by it that the term "corporate action" (*Verbandshandeln*) will be used. Examples of corporate action would be participation in any capacity in a war fought by a state, or a contribution paid in accordance with a levy authorized by the executive committee of an association, or a contract entered into by the person in authority, the validity of which is recognized by the members and its consequences carried out by them. Further, all administration of justice and administrative procedure belongs in this category.

A corporate group may be either autonomous or heteronomous, either autocephalous or heterocephalous. Autonomy means that the order governing the group has been established by its own members on their own authority, regardless of how this has taken place in other respects. In the case of heteronomy, it has been imposed by an outside agency. Autocephaly means that the chief and his staff act by the authority of the autonomous order of the corporate group itself, not, as in the case of heterocephaly, that they are under the authority of outsiders. Again, this is regardless of any other aspects of the relationship.

A case of heterocephaly is the appointment of the governors of the Canadian provinces by the central government of the Dominion. It is possible for a heterocephalous group to be autonomous and an autocephalous group to be heteronomous. It is also possible in both respects for a corporate group to have both characters at the same time in different spheres. The member-states of the German Empire, a federal state, were autocephalous. But in spite of this, within the sphere of authority of the Reich, they were heteronomous; whereas, within their own sphere, in such matters as religion and education, they were autonomous. Alsace-Lorraine was, under German jurisdiction, in a limited degree autonomous, but at the same time heterocephalous in that the governor was appointed by the Kaiser. All these elements may be present in the same situation to some degree. A corporate group, which is at the same time completely heteronomous and completely heterocephalous, is usually best treated as a "part" of the more extensive group, as would ordinarily be done with a "regiment" as part of an army. But whether this is the case depends on the actual extent of independence in the orientation of action in the particular case. For terminological purposes, it is entirely a question of convenience.

## *Types of Order in Corporate Groups*

The legally-established order of an associative relationship may originate in one of two ways: by voluntary agreement, or by being imposed (*oktroyi-*

10. Weber here uses the term "liturgies" not in the current religious sense but in that of the institution characteristic of the classical Greek city state. This consisted in the provision of entertainments or services for the public ostensibly as a voluntary gift of an individual, but which were in fact obligatory on persons occupying a given status or office. Weber later uses this term in a technical sense which is defined in chapter ii, sec. 12.—Ed.

*ert*) and acquiesced in. The governing authority of a corporate group may claim a legitimate right to impose new rules. The "constitution" (*Verfassung*) of a corporate group is the empirically existing probability, varying in extent, kind, and conditions, that rules imposed by the governing authority will be acceded to. The system of order may, among these conditions, in particular specify that certain groups or sections of the members must consent, or at least have been heard. Besides this, there may be any number of other conditions.

The system of order of a corporate group may be imposed, not only on its members, but also on non-members who conform to certain criteria. This is especially likely to be true in so far as people are related to a given territorial area, by virtue of residence, birth, or the performance of certain actions within the area. An order which controls by virtue of these criteria possesses "territorial validity" (*Gebietsgeltung*). A corporate group, the governing order of which is in principle concerned with territorial validity, will be called a "territorial corporate group" (*Gebietsverband*). This usage will be employed regardless of how far the claim to the authority of its order over its own members is confined to matters pertaining to the area. Such limitation is possible[11] and certainly occurs to some extent.

1. For purposes of this investigation, an order is always "imposed" to the extent that it does not originate from a voluntary personal agreement of all the individuals concerned. The concept of imposition hence includes "majority rule," in that the minority must submit. For that reason there have been long periods when the legitimacy of majority rule has either not been recognized at all, or been held doubtful. This was true in the case of the estates of the Middle Ages, and in very recent times, in the Russian *Obschtschina*. This will be further discussed in the Sociology of Law and of Authority.

2. Even in cases where there is formally "voluntary" agreement, it is very common, as is generally known, for there to be a large measure of imposition. This is true of the *Obschtschina*. In that case, it is the actual state of affairs which is decisive for sociological purposes.

3. The concept of constitution made use of here is that also used by Lassalle. It is not the same as what is meant by a "written" constitution, or indeed by "constitution" in any sort of legal meaning. The only relevant question for sociological purposes is when, for what purposes, and *within what limits,* or possibly under what special conditions (such as the approval of gods or priests or the consent of electors), the members of the corporate group will submit to the governing authority. Furthermore, under what circumstances in these respects the administrative staff and the corporate action of the group will be at the disposal of the supreme authority when it issues orders, or, in particular, imposes new rules.

4. The best cases of the imposition of an order within a territory are the precepts of criminal law and various other legal rules. In such cases political corporate groups use the criteria of whether the actor was resident, born, performed or completed the action, within the area controlled by the corporate group, to decide on the applicability of the rules.

## *Types of Order Governing Action in Corporate Groups*

A system of order which governs corporate action as such, will be called an "administrative" order (*Verwaltungsordnung*). A system of order which governs other kinds of social action and thereby protects the actors in enjoyment of the benefits derived from their relation to the order, will be called a "regulative" order (*Regulierungsordnung*). So far as a corporate group is solely oriented to the first type of order, it will be called an "administrative" group (*Verwaltungsverband*). So far as it is oriented to the second type, a "regulative" group.

1. It goes without saying that the majority of actual corporate groups partake of both characteristics. The type of state, which was the ideal of the theory of absolute laissez faire, would be an example of a purely regulative corporate group. This would, however, assume that the control of the monetary system was left entirely to private enterprise.

2. On the concept of "corporate action," see above, sec. 12, para. 3. Under the concept of administrative order would be included all the rules which govern, not only the action of the administrative staff, but also that of the members in their direct relations to the corporate group. This latter type consists in action in the service of ends, the attainment of which is made mandatory in the system of order governing the group, and for which a positive course of action has deliberately been laid down in advance with directions for its execution by the

11. The concept "objective possibility" (*objektive Möglichkeit*) plays an important technical role in Weber's methodological studies. According to his usage, a thing is "objectively possible" if it "makes sense" to conceive it as an empirically existing entity. It is a question of conforming with the formal, logical conditions. The question whether a phenomenon which is in this sense "objectively possible" will actually be found with any significant degree of probability or approximation, is a logically distinct question.—Ed.

administrative staff and by the members. In a completely communistic economic system, a situation would be approximated where all social action was of this character. In a laissez-faire state, on the other hand, it would include only the functions of judges, police authorities, jurors, soldiers, legislators, and of the general public in the capacity of voters. The distinction between administrative and regulative order coincides in its broad lines, though not always in detail, with the distinction of political theory between public and private law. All further details are treated in the Sociology of Law.

## *Types of Organization and of Corporate Groups*

An "organization" (*Betrieb*) is a system of continuous purposive activity of a specified kind. A "corporate organization" (*Betriebsverband*) is an associative social relationship characterized by an administrative staff devoted to such continuous purposive activity.

A "voluntary association" (*Verein*) is a corporate group originating in a voluntary agreement and in which the established order claims authority over the members only by virtue of a personal act of adherence.

A "compulsory association" (*Anstalt*) is a corporate group the established order of which has, within a given specific sphere of activity, been successfully imposed on every individual who conforms with certain specific criteria.[12]

1. The administration of political and ecclesiastical affairs and of the business of associations is included in the concept of "organization" so far as it conforms to the criterion of continuity.

2. Voluntary and compulsory associations are both types of corporate groups where action is subject to a rationally established order. Or, more accurately, so far as a corporate group has a rationally established order, it will be called a voluntary or compulsory association. The type case of a compulsory association is the state, along with all its subsidiary heterocephalous groups. But, so far as its order is rationally established, the church[13] is also included. The order governing a compulsory association claims to be binding on all persons to whom the particular relevant criteria apply—such as birth, residence, or the use of certain facilities. It makes no difference whether the individual has, as in the case of a voluntary association, personally assumed the obligation; nor does it matter whether he has taken any part in establishing the order. It is thus a case of imposed order in the most definite sense. One of the most important fields of the compulsory association is the control of territorial areas.

3. The distinction between voluntary and compulsory associations is relative in its empirical application. The rules of a voluntary association may affect the interests of non-members, and recognition of the validity of these rules may be imposed upon them by usurpation or by the exercise of the naked power of the association, as well as by processes of legal promulgation, as in the case of the law governing corporate securities.

4. It is hardly necessary to emphasize that the concepts of voluntary and compulsory associations are by no means exhaustive of all conceivable types of corporate groups. Furthermore, they are to be thought of only as "polar" antitheses. In the religious sphere, the corresponding types are "sect" and "church."

## *Power, Authority, and Imperative Control*

"Power" (*Macht*) is the probability that one actor within a social relationship will be in a position to carry out his own will despite resistance, regardless of the basis on which this probability rests.

"Imperative control" (*Herrschaft*)[14] is the probability that a command with a given specific content will be obeyed by a given group of persons. "Discipline" is the probability that by virtue of habituation a command will receive prompt and automatic obedience in stereotyped forms, on the part of a given group of persons.

---

12. *Betrieb* is a word which in German has a number of different meanings in different contexts. It is only in the present technical use that it will be translated by "organization." It should, however, be recognized that the term "organization" is here also used in a technical sense which conforms with Weber's explicit definition. The distinction of *Verein* and *Anstalt* is one of far-reaching sociological importance, which has not become established in English usage. The terms "voluntary" and "compulsory" association seem to be as adequate as any available terms. They should, however, not be interpreted on a common-sense basis but referred to Weber's explicit definitions.—ED.

13. "Church" (*Kirche*) also is here used in a technical sense. We speak of the "Baptist Church," but in Weber's technical terms this is not a church but a sect. The Roman Catholic Church, on the other hand, since it claims jurisdiction over all children of Catholic parents, *is* a church in the technical sense.—ED.

14. As has already been noted, the term *Herrschaft* has no satisfactory English equivalent. The term "imperative control," however, as used by N. S. Timasheff in his *Introduction to the Sociology of Law* is close to Weber's meaning and has been borrowed for the most general purposes. In a majority of instances, however, Weber is concerned with *legitimate Herrschaft,* and in these cases "authority" is both an accurate and a far less awkward translation. *Macht,* as Weber uses it, seems to be quite adequately rendered by "power."—ED.

1. The concept of power is highly comprehensive from the point of view of sociology. All conceivable qualities of a person and all conceivable combinations of circumstances may put him in a position to impose his will in a given situation. The sociological concept of imperative control must hence be more precise and can only mean the probability that a *command* will be obeyed.

2. The concept of "discipline" includes the "habituation" characteristic of uncritical and unresisting mass obedience.

The existence of imperative control turns only on the actual presence of one person successfully issuing orders to others; it does not necessarily imply either the existence of an administrative staff, or, for that matter, of a corporate group. It is, however, uncommon to find it not associated with at least one of these. A corporate group, the members of which are by virtue of their membership subjected to the legitimate exercise of imperative control, that is to "authority," will be called an "imperatively coordinated" group[15] (*Herrschaftsverband*).

1. The head of a household exercises authority without an administrative staff. A Beduin chief, who levies contributions from the caravans, persons, and shipments of goods which pass his stronghold, exercises imperative control over the total group of changing and indeterminate individuals who, though they are not members of any corporate group as such, have gotten themselves into a particular common situation. But to do this, he needs a following which, on the appropriate occasions, serves as his administrative staff in exercising the necessary compulsion. This type of imperative control is, however, conceivable as carried out by a single individual without the help of any administrative staff.

2. If it possesses an administrative staff, a corporate group is always, by virtue of this fact, to some degree imperatively co-ordinated. But the concept is relative. The usual imperatively co-ordinated group is at the same time an administrative organization. The character of the corporate group is determined by a variety of factors: the mode in which the administration is carried out, the character of the personnel, the objects over which it exercises control, and the extent of effective jurisdiction of its authority. The first two factors in particular are dependent in the highest degree on the way in which the authority is legitimized.

15. In this case imperative control is confined to the legitimate type, but it is not possible in English to speak here of an "authoritarian" group. The citizens of any state, no matter how "democratic," are "imperatively controlled" because they are subject to law.—Ed.

### *Political and Religious Corporate Groups*

An imperatively co-ordinated corporate group will be called "political" if and in so far as the enforcement of its order is carried out continually within a given *territorial* area by the application and threat of physical force on the part of the administrative staff. A compulsory political association with continuous organization (*politischer Anstaltsbetrieb*) will be called a "state" if and in so far as its administrative staff successfully upholds a claim to the *monopoly* of the *legitimate* use of physical force in the enforcement of its order. A system of social action, especially that of a corporate group, will be spoken of as "politically oriented" if and in so far as it aims at exerting influence on the directing authorities of a corporate political group; especially at the appropriation, expropriation, redistribution or allocation of the powers of government.

An imperatively co-ordinated corporate group will be called a "hierocratic" group (*hierokratischer Verband*) if and in so far as for the enforcement of its order it employs "psychic" coercion through the distribution or denial of religious benefits ("hierocratic coercion"). A compulsory hierocratic association with continuous organization will be called a "church" if and in so far as its administrative staff claims a monopoly of the legitimate use of hierocratic coercion.

1. It goes without saying that the use of physical force is neither the sole, nor even the most usual, method of administration of political corporate groups. On the contrary, their heads have employed all conceivable means to bring about their ends. But, at the same time, the threat of force, and in case of need its actual use, is the method which is specific to political association and is always the last resort when others have failed. Conversely, physical force is by no means limited to political groups even as a legitimate method of enforcement. It has been freely used by kinship groups, household groups, the medieval guilds under certain circumstances, and everywhere by all those entitled to bear arms. In addition to the fact that it uses, among other means, physical force to enforce its system of order, the political group is further characterized by the fact that the authority of its administrative staff is claimed as binding within a territorial area and this claim is upheld by force. Whenever corporate groups which make use of force are also characterized by the claim to territorial jurisdiction, such as village communities or even some household groups, federations of guilds

or of trade unions, they are by definition to that extent political groups.

2. It is not possible to define a political corporate group, including the state, in terms of the end to which its corporate action is devoted. All the way from provision for subsistence to the patronage of art, there is no conceivable end which *some* political corporation has not at some time pursued. And from the protection of personal security to the administration of justice, there is none which *all* have recognized. Thus it is possible to define the "political" character of a corporate group only in terms of the *means* peculiar to it, the use of force. This means is, however, in the above sense specific, and is indispensable to its character. It is even, under certain circumstances, elevated into an end in itself.

This usage does not exactly conform to everyday speech. But the latter is too consistent to be used for technical purposes. We speak of the "open market" policy[16] of a central bank, of the "financial" policy of an association, of the "educational" policy of a local authority, and mean the systematic treatment and control of a particular problem. It comes considerably closer to the present meaning when we distinguish the "political" aspect or implication of a question. Thus there is the "political" official, the "political" newspaper, the "political" revolution, the "political" club, the "political" party, and the "political" consequences of an action, as distinguished from others such as the economic, cultural, or religious aspect of the persons, affairs or processes in question. In this usage we generally mean by "political," things that have to do with relations of authority within what is, in the present terminology, a political organization, the state. The reference is to things which are likely to uphold, to change or overthrow, to hinder or promote, the interests of the state, as distinguished from persons, things, and processes which have nothing to do with it. This usage thus seeks to bring out the common features of the various *means* of exercising authority which are used within the state in enforcing its order, abstracting them from the ends they serve. Hence it is legitimate to claim that the definition put forward here is only a more precise formulation of what is meant in everyday usage in that it gives sharp emphasis to what is the most characteristic of these means, the actual or threatened use of force. It is, of course, true that everyday usage applies the term "political," not only to groups which are the direct agents of the legitimate use of force itself, but also to other, often wholly peaceful groups, which attempt to influence politically corporate action. It seems best for present purposes to distinguish this type of social action, "politically oriented" action, from political action as such, the actual *corporate* action of political groups.

3. Since the concept of the state has only in modern times reached its full development, it is best to define it in terms appropriate to the modern type of state, but at the same time, in terms which abstract from the values of the present day, since these are particularly subject to change. The primary formal characteristics of the modern state are as follows: It possesses an administrative and legal order subject to change by legislation, to which the organized corporate activity of the administrative staff, which is also regulated by legislation, is oriented. This system of order claims binding authority, not only over the members of the state, the citizens, most of whom have obtained membership by birth, but also to a very large extent, over all action taking place in the area of its jurisdiction. It is thus a compulsory association with a territorial basis. Furthermore, to-day, the use of force is regarded as legitimate only so far as it is either permitted by the state or prescribed by it. Thus the right of a father to discipline his children is recognized—a survival of the former independent authority of the head of a household, which in the right to use force has sometimes extended to a power of life and death over children and slaves. The claim of the modern state to monopolize the use of force is as essential to it as its character of compulsory jurisdiction and of continuous organization.

4. In formulating the concept of a hierocratic corporate group, it is not possible to use the character of the religious sanctions it commands, whether worldly or other-worldly, material or spiritual, as the decisive criterion. What is important is rather the fact that its control over these sanctions can form the basis of a system of spiritual imperative control over human beings. What is most characteristic of the church, even in the common usage of the term, is the fact that it is a rational, compulsory association with continuous organization and that it claims a monopolistic authority. It is normal for a church to strive for complete imperative control on a territorial basis and to attempt to set up the corresponding territorial or parochial organization. So far as this takes place, the means by which this claim to monopoly is upheld, will vary from case to case. But historically, its control over terri-

16. The German is *Devisenpolitik.* Translation in this context is made more difficult by the fact that the German language does not distinguish between "politics" and "policy," *Politik* having both meanings. The remarks which Weber makes about various kinds of policy would have been unnecessary, had he written originally in English.—Ed.

torial areas has not been nearly so essential to the church as to political corporations; and this is particularly true to-day. It is its character as a compulsory association, particularly the fact that one becomes a member of the church by birth, which distinguishes a church from a "sect." It is characteristic of the latter that it is a voluntary association and admits only persons with specific religious qualifications. This subject will be further discussed in the Sociology of Religion.[17]

17. This reference is presumably to the section entitled *Religionssoziologie* which is published as part ii, chap. iv of *Wirtschaft und Gesellschaft,* but is not included in the present translation. In it Weber attempted a systematic typological analysis of the social aspects of religious phenomena. This chapter should not be confused with the three volumes of the *Gesammelte Aufsätze zur Religionssoziologie* which consist of a series of comparative empirical studies of particular religious systems in terms of their bearing on the development of modern capitalism. In the section of *Wirtschaft und Gesellschaft* to which he refers, Weber has attempted a more connected and complete typological analysis than is to be found in the comparative study.—Ed.

# *6. Legitimate Order and Types of Authority*

BY MAX WEBER

## *The Concept of Legitimate Order*

ACTION, especially social action which involves social relationships, may be oriented by the actors to a *belief* (*Vorstellung*) in the existence of a "legitimate order." The probability that action will actually empirically be so oriented will be called the "validity" (*Geltung*) of the order in question.[1]

1. Thus, orientation to the validity of an *order* (*Ordnung*) means more than the mere existence of a uniformity of social action determined by custom or self-interest. If furniture movers regularly advertise at times of the large-scale expiration of leases, this uniformity is determined by self-interest in the exploitation of opportunities. If a salesman visits certain customers on particular days of the month or the week, it is either a case of customary behaviour or a product of some kind of self-interested orientation. But when, on the other hand, a civil servant appears in his office daily at a fixed time, it may involve these elements, but is not determined by custom or self-interest alone, for with these he is at liberty to conform or not as he pleases. As a rule such action in addition is determined by his subjection to an order, the rules governing the department which impose obligations on him, which he is usually careful to fulfil, partly because disobedience would carry disadvantageous consequences to him, but usually also in part because it would be abhorrent to the sense of duty, which, to a greater or lesser extent, is an absolute value to him.

2. The subjective meaning of a social relationship will be called an "order" only if action is approximately or on the average oriented to certain determinate "maxims" or rules. Furthermore, such an order will only be called "valid" if the orientation to such maxims includes, no matter to what actual extent, the recognition that they are binding on the actor or the corresponding action constitutes a desirable model for him to imitate. Naturally, in concrete cases, the orientation of action to an order involves a wide variety of motives. But the circumstance that along with the other sources of conformity the order is also held by at least part of the actors to define a model or to be binding, naturally increases the probability that action will in fact conform to it, often to a very considerable degree. An order which is adhered to from motives of pure expediency is generally much less stable than one upheld on a purely customary basis through the fact that the corresponding behaviour has become habitual. The latter is much the most common type of subjective attitude. But even this type of order is in turn much less stable than an order which enjoys the

Reprinted from Max Weber, *The Theory of Social and Economic Organization,* trans. A. M. Henderson and Talcott Parsons, ed. Talcott Parsons (Glencoe, Ill.: The Free Press, 1947), chap. i, secs. 5–8, pp. 124–35; chap. iii, secs. 1–2, pp. 328–29. 

1. The term *Gelten* has already been dealt with. From the very use of the term in this context it is clear that by "order" (*Ordnung*) Weber here means a *normative* system. The pattern for the concept of "order" is not, as in the law of gravitation, the "order of nature," but the order involved in a system of law.

prestige of being considered binding, or, as it may be expressed, of "legitimacy." The transitions between orientation to an order from motives of tradition or of expediency on the one hand to the case where on the other a belief in its legitimacy is involved, are naturally empirically gradual.

3. It is possible for action to be oriented to an order in other ways than through conformity with its prescriptions, as they are generally understood by the actors. Even in the cases of evasion of or deliberate disobedience to these prescriptions, the probability of its being recognized as a valid norm may have an effect on action. This may, in the first place, be true from the point of view of sheer expediency. A thief orients his action to the validity of the criminal law in that he acts surreptitiously. The fact that the order is recognized as valid in his society is made evident by the fact that he cannot violate it openly without punishment. But apart from this limiting case, it is very common for violation of an order to be confined to more or less numerous partial deviations from it, or for the attempt to be made, with varying degrees of good faith, to justify the deviation as legitimate. Furthermore, there may exist at the same time different interpretations of the meaning of the order. In such cases, for sociological purposes, each can be said to be valid in so far as it actually determines the course of action. The fact that, in the same social group, a plurality of contradictory systems of order may all be recognized as valid, is not a source of difficulty for the sociological approach. Indeed, it is even possible for the same individual to orient his action to contradictory systems of order. This can take place not only at different times, as is an everyday occurrence, but even in the case of the same concrete act. A person who fights a duel orients his action to the code of honour; but at the same time, in so far as he either keeps it secret or conversely gives himself up to the police, he takes account of the criminal law.[2] To be sure, when evasion or contravention of the generally understood meaning of an order has become the rule, the order can be said to be "valid" only in a limited degree and, in the extreme case, not at all. Thus for sociological purposes there does not exist, as there does for the law, a rigid alternative between the validity and lack of validity of a given order. On the contrary, there is a gradual transition between the two extremes; and also it is possible, as it has been pointed out, for contradictory systems of order to exist at the same time. In that case each is "valid" precisely to the extent that there is a probability that action will in fact be oriented to it.[3]

2. When this was written (probably about 1913), duelling was still a relatively common practice in Germany and, in certain circles, was regarded as a definite obligation of honour in the face of some kinds of provocation. It was, however, at the same time an explicitly punishable offence under the criminal law.—ED.

## *The Types of Legitimate Order*

The legitimacy of an order may be guaranteed or upheld in two principal ways:[4] (1) from purely

3. Those familiar with the literature of this subject will recall the part played by the concept of "order" in the brilliant book of Rudolf Stammler, which was cited in the prefatory note, a book which, though like all his works it is very able, is nevertheless fundamentally misleading and confuses the issues in a catastrophic fashion. The reader may compare the author's critical discussion of it, which was also cited in the same place, a discussion which, because of the author's annoyance at Stammler's confusion, was unfortunately written in somewhat too acrimonious a tone.

Stammler fails to distinguish the normative meaning of "validity" from the empirical. He further fails to recognize that social action is oriented to other things beside systems of order. Above all, however, in a way which is wholly indefensible from a logical point of view, he treats order as a "form" of social action and then attempts to bring it into a type of relation to "content," which is analogous to that of form and content in the theory of knowledge. Other errors in his argument will be left aside. But actually, action which is, for instance, primarily economic, is oriented to knowledge of the relative scarcity of certain available means to want satisfaction, in relation to the actor's state of needs and to the present and probable action of others, in so far as the latter affects the same resources. But at the same time, of course, the actor in his choice of economic procedures naturally orients himself *in addition* to the conventional and legal rules which he recognizes as valid, or of which he knows that a violation on his part would call forth a given reaction of other persons. Stammler succeeds in introducing a state of hopeless confusion into this very simple empirical situation, particularly in that he maintains that a causal relationship between an order and actual empirical action involves a contradiction in terms. It is true, of course, that there is no causal relationship between the *normative* validity of an order in the legal sense and any empirical process. In that context there is only the question of whether the order as correctly interpreted in the legal sense "applies" to the empirical situation. The question is whether in a *normative* sense it *should* be treated as valid and, if so, what the content of its normative prescriptions for this situation should be. But for sociological purposes, as distinguished from legal, it is only the probability of orientation to the subjective *belief* in the validity of an order which constitutes the valid order itself. It is undeniable that, in the ordinary sense of the word "causal," there is a causal relationship between this probability and the relevant course of economic action.

4. The reader may readily become confused as to the basis of the following classification, as compared with that presented in the next section. The first classification is one of motives for maintaining a legitimate order in force, whereas the second is one of motives for attributing legitimacy to the order. This explains the inclusion of self-interested motives in the first classification, but not in the second. It is quite possible, for instance, for irreligious persons to support the doctrine of the divine right of kings, because they feel that the breakdown of an order which depends on this would have undesirable consequences. This is not, however, a possible motive on which to base a direct sense of personal moral obligation to conform with the order.—ED.

disinterested motives, which may in turn be (a) purely affectual, consisting in an emotionally determined loyalty; or (b) may derive from a rational belief in the absolute validity of the order as an expression of ultimate values,[5] (*Wertrational*) whether they be moral, esthetic or of any other type; or (c) may originate in religious attitudes, through the belief in the dependence of some condition of religious salvation on conformity with the order; (2) also or entirely by self-interest, that is, through expectations of specific ulterior consequences, but consequences which are, to be sure, of a particular kind.

A system of order will be called *convention* so far as its validity is externally guaranteed by the probability that deviation from it within a given social group will result in a relatively general and practically significant reaction of disapproval. Such an order will be called *law* when conformity with it is upheld by the probability that deviant action will be met by physical or psychic sanctions aimed to compel conformity or to punish disobedience, and applied by a group of men especially empowered to carry out this function.

1. The term convention will be employed to designate that part of the custom followed within a given social group which is recognized as "binding" and protected against violation by sanctions of disapproval. As distinguished from "law" in the sense of the present discussion, it is not enforced by a functionally specialized agency. Stammler distinguishes convention from law in terms of the entirely voluntary character of conformity. This is not, however, in accord with everyday usage and does not even fit the examples he gives. Conformity with convention in such matters as the usual forms of greeting, the mode of dress recognized as appropriate or respectable, and various of the rules governing the restrictions on social intercourse, both in form and content, is very definitely expected of the individual and regarded as binding on him. It is not, as in the case of certain ways of preparing food, a mere usage, which he is free to conform to or not as he sees fit. A violation of conventional rules—such as standards of "respectability"—often leads to the extremely severe and effective sanction of an informal boycott on the part of members of one's group. This may actually be a more severe punishment than any legal penalty. The only thing lacking is the group of men with the specialized function of maintaining enforcement of the order, such as judges, prosecuting attorneys, and administrative officials. The transition, however, is gradual. The case of conventional guarantee of an order which most closely approaches the legal, is the application of a formally threatened and organized boycott. For terminological purposes, this is best considered a form of legal compulsion. Conventional rules may, in addition to mere disapproval, also be upheld by other means; thus domestic authority may be employed to deal with behaviour in defiance of convention. This fact is not, however, important in the present context. The decisive point is that the individual, by virtue of the existence of conventional disapproval, applies these sanctions, however drastic, on his own authority, not as a member of an organized group endowed with a specific authority for this purpose.

2. For the purposes of this discussion the concept "law" will be made to turn on the presence of a group of men engaged in enforcement, however useful it might be to define it differently for other purposes. The character of this agency naturally need not be at all similar to what is at present familiar. In particular it is not necessary that there should be any specifically "judicial" authority. The clan, as an agency of blood revenge and of the prosecution of feuds, is such an enforcing agency if there exist any sort of rules which governs its behaviour in such situations. But this is on the extreme borderline of what can be called legal enforcement. As is well known it has often been denied that international law could be called law, precisely because there is no legal authority above the state capable of enforcing it. In terms of the present terminology this would be correct, for a system of order the sanctions of which consisted wholly in expectations of disapproval and of the reprisals of injured parties, which is thus guaranteed entirely by convention and self-interest without the help of a specialized enforcement agency, is not a case of legal order. But for purposes of legal terminology exactly the opposite usage might well be acceptable.

In any case the means of coercion are irrelevant. Even a "friendly admonition," such as has been used in various religious sects as a form of gentle pressure on sinners, is to be included if it is carried out according to rules by a specially designated group. Another case is the use of the censure as a means of enforcing norms of moral conduct. Psychic coercion has indeed become the specific disciplinary technique of the church. It is thus

5. The antithesis *innerlich-äusserlich* as applied to elements of motivation does not have any direct English counterpart. The aspect of *innerlich*, however, which is most important in the present context seems to be adequately expressed by the term "disinterested." The essential point is that the object of such motivation is valued for its own sake or as a direct expression of ultimate values rather than as a means to some "ulterior" end.—ED.

naturally just as much a case of "law" whether an order is upheld by ecclesiastical or by a political organization, whether in conformity with the rules of an association or by the authority of the head of a household. Even the rules contained in a commentary may be regarded, for this terminology, as law. Article 888, sec. 2, of the German Code of Civil Procedure (*Reichs-Zivil-Prozess-Ordnung*) dealing with unenforceable rights, is a case in point. The *leges imperfectae,* and the category of "natural obligations," are forms of legal terminology which express indirectly limits of conditions of the application of compulsion. In the same sense a trade practice which is compulsorily enforced is also law.[6]

3. It is not necessary for a valid order to be of a general and abstract character. The distinction between a legal precept and the decision in a concrete case, for instance, has not always and everywhere been as clearly made as we have to-day come to expect. An "order" may thus occur simply as the order governing a single concrete situation. The details of this subject belong in the sociology of law.[7] But for present purposes, unless otherwise specified, the modern distinction between a precept and a specific decision will be taken for granted.

4. A system of order which is guaranteed by external sanctions may at the same time be guaranteed by disinterested subjective attitudes. The relations of law, convention, and "ethics" do not constitute a problem for sociology. From a sociological point of view an "ethical" standard is one to which men attribute a certain type of value and which, by virtue of this belief, they treat as a valid norm governing their action. In this sense it can be spoken of as defining what is ethically good in the same way that action which is called beautiful is measured by aesthetic standards. It is possible for ethically normative beliefs of this kind to have a profound influence on action in the absence of any sort of external guarantee. This is often the case when the interests of others would be little affected by their violation.

Such ethical beliefs are also often guaranteed by religious motives, but they may at the same time in the present terminology be upheld to an important extent by disapproval of violations and the consequent boycott, or even legally with the corresponding sanctions of the criminal law, police measures, or civil penalties. Every system of ethics which has in a sociological sense become validly established is likely to be upheld to a large extent by the probability that disapproval will result from its violation, that is, by convention. On the other hand, it is by no means necessary that all conventionally or legally guaranteed forms of order should claim the authority of ethical norms. Legal rules, much more often than conventional, may have been established entirely on grounds of expediency. Whether a belief in the validity of an order as such, which is current in a social group, is to be regarded as belonging to the realm of "ethics" or is a mere convention or a mere legal norm, cannot, for sociological purposes, be decided in general terms. It must be treated as relative to the conception of what values are treated as "ethical" in the social group in question. What these are is, in the relevant respect, not subject to generalization.

## *The Bases of Legitimacy of an Order*

Legitimacy may be ascribed to an order by those acting subject to it in the following ways:—

(a) By tradition; a belief in the legitimacy of what has always existed; (b) by virtue of affectual attitudes, especially emotional, legitimizing the validity of what is newly revealed or a model to imitate; (c) by virtue of a rational belief in its absolute value (*Wertrational*), thus lending it the validity of an absolute and final commitment; (d) because it has been established in a manner which is recognized to be *legal*. This legality may be treated as legitimate in either of two ways: on the one hand, it may derive from a voluntary agreement of the interested parties on the relevant terms. On the other hand, it may be imposed on the basis of what is held to be a legitimate authority over the relevant persons and a corresponding claim to their obedience.

All further details, except for a few other concepts to be defined below, belong in the sociology of law and the sociology of authority. For the present, only a few remarks are necessary.

1. The derivation of the legitimacy of an order from a belief in the sanctity of tradition is the most universal and most primitive case. The fear of magical penalties confirms the general psychological inhibitions against any sort of change in customary modes of action. At the same time the multifarious vested interests which tend to become attached to upholding conformity with an order,

---

6. See secs. 157 and 242 of the German Civil Code. *Bürgerliches Gesetz-Buch* on the concept of "common law obligations," that is, obligations arising out of community standards of acceptable behaviour which come to be sanctioned by law. See the paper of Max Rümelin in *Schwäbische Heimatsgabe für Theodor Häring.*

7. An extended discussion of this subject is included in the German edition of *Wirtschaft und Gesellschaft,* part ii, chap. vii, pp. 386–512. It is not, however, included in the present translation.—ED.

once it has become established, have worked in the same direction.[8]

2. Conscious departures from tradition in the establishment of a new order have originally been due almost entirely to prophetic oracles or at least to pronouncements which have been sanctioned as prophetic. This was true as late as the statutes of the Greek Aisymnetes. Conformity has then depended on belief in the legitimacy of the prophet. In times of strict traditionalism a new order, that is one which was *regarded* as new, could, without being revealed in this way, only become legitimized by the claim that it had actually always been valid though not yet rightly known, or that it had been obscured for a time and was now being restored to its rightful place.

3. The type case of legitimacy by virtue of rational belief in an absolute value is that of "Natural Law." However limited its actual effect, as compared with its ideal claims, it cannot be denied that its logically developed reasoning has had an influence on actual action which is far from negligible. This mode of influence should be clearly distinguished from that of a revealed law, of one imposed by authority, or of one which is merely traditional.

4. To-day the most usual basis of legitimacy is the belief in legality, the readiness to conform with rules which are formally correct and have been imposed by accepted procedure. The distinction between an order derived from voluntary agreement and one which has been imposed is only relative. For so far as the agreement underlying the order is not unanimous, as in the past has often been held necessary for complete legitimacy, its functioning within a social group will be dependent on the willingness of individuals with deviant wishes to give way to the majority. This is very frequently the case and actually means that the order is imposed on the minority. At the same time, it is very common for minorities, by force or by the use of more ruthless and far-sighted methods, to impose an order which in the course of time comes to be regarded as legitimate by those who originally resisted it. In so far as the ballot is used as a legal means of altering an order, it is very common for the will of a minority to attain a formal majority and for the majority to submit. In this case majority rule is a mere illusion. The belief in the legality of an order as established by voluntary agreement is relatively ancient and is occasionally found among so-called primitive peoples; but in these cases it is almost always supplemented by the authority of oracles.

5. So far as it is not derived merely from fear or from motives of expediency, a willingness to submit to an order imposed by one man or a small group, always in some sense implies a belief in the legitimate *authority* of the source imposing it.

6. Submission to an order is almost always determined by a variety of motives; by a wide variety of interests and by a mixture of adherence to tradition and belief in legality, unless it is a case of entirely new regulations. In a very large proportion of cases, the actors subject to the order are of course not even aware how far it is a matter of custom, of convention, or of law. In such cases the sociologist must attempt to formulate the typical basis of validity.

## *The Concept of Conflict*

A social relationship will be referred to as "conflict" (*Kampf*) in so far as action within it is oriented intentionally to carrying out the actor's own will against the resistance of the other party or parties. The term "peaceful" conflict will be applied to cases in which actual physical violence is not employed. A peaceful conflict is "competition" in so far as it consists in a formally peaceful attempt to attain control over opportunities and advantages[9] which are also desired by others. A competitive process is "regulated" competition to the extent that its ends and means are oriented to an order. The struggle, often latent, which takes place between human individuals or types of social status, for advantages and for survival, but without a meaningful mutual orientation in terms of conflict, will be called "selection." In so far as it is a matter of the relative opportunities of individuals during their own lifetime, it is "social selection"; in so far as it concerns differential chances for the survival of inherited characteristics, "biological selection."

1. There are all manner of continuous transitions ranging from the bloody type of conflict which, setting aside all rules, aims at the destruction of the adversary, to the case of the battles of medieval chivalry, bound as they were to the

8. The term "authority" is used to translate *Herrschaft*. It is not adequate for all purposes, but a discussion of the difficulties will be deferred to the point at which the concept becomes of primary importance. See below, sec. 16, p. 152. Weber dealt with this range of problems systematically in two different places, one of which is chapter iii of the present volume. The material of that chapter, however, is expanded and copiously illustrated in part iii of the German edition of *Wirtschaft und Gesellschaft* which is not included in the present translation. This part, like many other parts of the work, was left uncompleted at Weber's death.—ED.

9. *Chancen*. This usage of the term is to be distinguished from that translated as probability or likelihood. —ED.

strictest conventions, and to the strict regulations imposed on sport by the rules of the game. A classic example of conventional regulation even in war is the herald's call before the battle of Fontenoy: "Messieurs les Anglais, tirez les premiers." There are transitions such as that from unregulated competition of, let us say, suitors for the favour of a woman to the competition for economic advantages in exchange relationships, bound as that is by the order governing the market, or to strictly regulated competitions for artistic awards or, finally, to the struggle for victory in election campaigns. The treatment of conflict involving the use of physical violence as a separate type is justified by the special characteristics of the employment of this means and the corresponding peculiarities of the sociological consequences of its use.

2. All typical struggles and modes of competition which take place on a large scale will lead, in the long run, despite the decisive importance in many individual cases of accidental factors and luck, to a selection of those who have in the higher degree, on the average, possessed the personal qualities important to success. What qualities are important depends on the conditions in which the conflict or competition takes place. It may be a matter of physical strength or of unscrupulous cunning, of the level of mental ability or mere lung power and skill in the technique of demagoguery, of loyalty to superiors or of ability to flatter the masses, of creative originality, or of adaptability, of qualities which are unusual, or of those which are possessed by the mediocre majority. *Among* the decisive conditions, it must not be forgotten, belong the systems of order to which the behaviour of the parties is oriented, whether traditionally, as a matter of rationally disinterested loyalty, or of expediency. Each type of order influences opportunities in the process of social selection differently.

Not every process of social selection is, in the present sense, a case of conflict. Social selection, on the contrary, means only in the first instance that certain types of behaviour, and hence of the corresponding personal qualities, are more favourable than others in procuring differential advantages in attaining to certain social relationships, as in the role of "lover," "husband," "member of parliament," "official," "contractor," "managing director," "successful business man," and so on. But the concept does not specify whether this differential advantage in selection for social success is brought to bear through conflict or not, neither does it specify whether the biological chances of survival of the type are affected one way or the other. It is only where there is a genuine competitive process that the term conflict will be used.

It is only in the sense of "selection" that it seems, according to our experience, that conflict is empirically inevitable, and it is furthermore only in the sense of *biological* selection that it is inevitable in principle. Selection is inevitable because apparently no way can be worked out of eliminating it completely. It is possible even for the most strictly pacific order to eliminate means of conflict and the objects of and impulses to conflict only in that it deals with each type individually. But this means that other modes of conflict would come to the fore, possibly in processes of open competition. But even on the utopian assumption that all competition were completely eliminated, conditions would still lead to a latent process of selection, biological or social, which would favour the types best adapted to the conditions, whether their relevant qualities were mainly determined by heredity or by environment. On an empirical level the elimination of conflict cannot go beyond a point which leaves room for some social selection, and in principle a process of biological selection necessarily remains.

3. From the struggle of individuals for personal advantages and survival, it is naturally necessary to distinguish the "conflict" and the "selection" of social relationships. It is only in a metaphorical sense that these concepts can be applied to the latter. For relationships exist only as systems of human action with particular subjective meanings. Thus a process of selection or a conflict between them means only that one type of action has in the course of time been displaced by another, whether it is action by the same persons or by others. This may occur in various ways. Human action may in the first place be consciously aimed to alter certain social relationships—that is, to alter the corresponding action—or it may be directed to the prevention of their development or continuance. Thus a "state" may be destroyed by war or revolution, or a conspiracy may be broken up by savage suppression; prostitution may be suppressed by police action; "shady" business practices, by denial of legal protection or by penalties. Furthermore, social relationships may be influenced by the creation of differential advantages which favour one type over another. It is possible either for individuals or for organized groups to pursue such ends. Secondly, it may, in various ways, be an unanticipated consequence of a course of social action and its relevant conditions that certain types of social relationships (meaning, of course, the corresponding actions) will be adversely affected in their opportunities to maintain themselves or to

arise. All changes of natural and social conditions have some sort of effect on the differential probabilities of survival of social relationships. Anyone is at liberty to speak in such cases of a process of "selection" of social relationships. For instance, he may say that among several states the "strongest," in the sense of the best "adapted," is victorious. It must, however, be kept in mind that this so-called "selection" has nothing to do with the selection of types of human individuals in either the social or the biological sense. In every case it is necessary to inquire into the reasons which have led to a change in the chances of survival of one or another form of social action or social relationship, which has broken up a social relationship or which has permitted it to continue at the expense of other competing forms. The explanation of these processes involves so many factors that it does not seem expedient to employ a single term for them. When this is done, there is always a danger of introducing uncritical value-judgments into empirical investigation. There is, above all, a danger of being primarily concerned with justifying the success of an individual case. Since individual cases are often dependent on highly exceptional circumstances, they may be in a certain sense "fortuitous." In recent years there has been more than enough of this kind of argument. The fact that a given specific social relationship has been eliminated for reasons peculiar to a particular situation, proves nothing whatever about its "fitness to survive" in general terms.

There are three pure types of legitimate authority. The validity of their claims to legitimacy may be based on:

1. Rational grounds—resting on a belief in the "legality" of patterns of normative rules and the right of those elevated to authority under such rules to issue commands (legal authority).
2. Traditional grounds—resting on an established belief in the sanctity of immemorial traditions and the legitimacy of the status of those exercising authority under them (traditional authority); or finally,
3. Charismatic grounds—resting on devotion to the specific and exceptional sanctity, heroism or exemplary character of an individual person, and of the normative patterns or order revealed or ordained by him (charismatic authority).

In the case of legal authority, obedience is owed to the legally established impersonal order. It extends to the persons exercising the authority of office under it only by virtue of the formal legality of their commands and only within the scope of authority of the office. In the case of traditional authority, obedience is owed to the *person* of the chief who occupies the traditionally sanctioned position of authority and who is (within its sphere) bound by tradition. But here the obligation of obedience is not based on the impersonal order, but is a matter of personal loyalty within the area of accustomed obligations. In the case of charismatic authority, it is the charismatically qualified leader as such who is obeyed by virtue of personal trust in him and his revelation, his heroism or his exemplary qualities so far as they fall within the scope of the individual's belief in his charisma.

1. The usefulness of the above classification can only be judged by its results in promoting systematic analysis. The concept of "charisma" ("the gift of grace") is taken from the vocabulary of early Christianity. For the Christian religious organization Rudolf Sohm, in his *Kirchenrecht,* was the first to clarify the substance of the concept, even though he did not use the same terminology. Others (for instance, Hollin, *Enthusiasmus und Bussgewalt*) have clarified certain important consequences of it. It is thus nothing new.

2. The fact that none of these three ideal types, the elucidation of which will occupy the following pages, is usually to be found in historical cases in "pure" form, is naturally not a valid objection to attempting their conceptual formulation in the sharpest possible form. In this respect the present case is no different from many others. Later on the transformation of pure charisma by the process of routinization will be discussed and thereby the relevance of the concept to the understanding of empirical systems of authority considerably increased. But even so it may be said of every empirically historical phenomenon of authority that it is not likely to be "as an open book." Analysis in terms of sociological types has, after all, as compared with purely empirical historical investigation, certain advantages which should not be minimized. That is, it can in the particular case of a concrete form of authority determine what conforms to or approximates such types as "charisma," "hereditary charisma," "the charisma of office," "patriarchy," "bureaucracy," the authority of status groups, and in doing so it can work with relatively unambiguous concepts. But the idea that the whole of concrete historical reality can be exhausted in the conceptual scheme about to be developed is as far from the author's thoughts as anything could be.

# PART TWO

## *Differentiation and Variation in Social Structures*

# Introduction

## BY TALCOTT PARSONS

PART TWO DEALS WITH THE MATERIAL that, for the generation with which we are concerned, was probably the core subject-matter of sociology—and which will probably continue to be so for some time. Broadly speaking, this is the structural morphology of social systems. In the first instance, it is the kinds of groupings of persons in roles that, combined with their complex interlacings and criss-crossings, constitute the structure of societies. When dealing with the larger patterns of form and bases of differentiation of social systems, it becomes necessary to consider, in addition to the morphology of collectivities and roles, general systems of institutionalized values and complex systems of norms, of the types outlined in the General Introduction.

The material dealing with structure has been placed first in the arrangement of selections. This is because we believe, first, that this material had reached a higher level of maturity at an earlier stage of the development of thought than had those parts of the theoretical structure devoted primarily to problems of dynamics and change. In this, as in other respects, we think that the development of the social sciences is analogous to that of the biological. It is easier to observe morphological patterns than the phenomena of process; and such observations can be more readily codified into an intelligible set of patterns.

Second, we believe that the properties most distinctive of social systems as distinguished from the other subsystems of action, notably culture and personalities, can be identified and characterized in the area of structure. The treatment of social structure has been the most important means of separating the analytical independence of the social system from the complex matrix of the phenomena of action in general, particularly culture. Dynamic processes, particularly those involving change in the structure of social systems, involve intimately the interdependence of social and cultural factors, and of social and psychological and organic factors. Since we believe that the analytical separation of these subsystems of action is a very important theoretical task, we feel that the analysis of social structure has been perhaps the most important single "sieve" through which this sifting has been possible and fruitful.

### THE FRAME OF REFERENCE OF STRUCTURAL MORPHOLOGY

The frame of reference within which we have organized the selections in Part Two is both comparative and evolutionary. Our emphasis on the comparative needs little justification. Every segment of knowledge about the range of variation of structural types in the social field helps clarify the formulation of the problems which dynamic theory faces. This knowledge of range is of little theoretical significance unless the data can be codified in terms of relatively definite classifications. Such classifications are the first-order statements of the existence and nature of systematic relations of interdependence between the factors and variables involved in the processes of social interaction. As such, they are the indispensable preliminaries to attempting deeper penetration.

A good example is the incest taboo, i.e., the series of prohibitions of marriage and sexual relations between persons related by kinship. Before the development of modern anthropology, it was generally simply taken for granted that people did not marry close relatives—though there was very little awareness of the reasons for this; it was considered a matter of "nature" or divine decree. Increasing knowledge of non-literate societies, however, showed that, in many such societies, the prohibitions were extended to lengths that seemed extreme to Western eyes—so that as many as three-fourths of the members of the opposite sex in the society might be included in the prohibition. On the other hand, sometimes the prohibition of marriage to distant relatives—so distant that in our society their relationship would not be recognized at all—was accompanied by mandatory cross-cousin marriage well within what, in most Western tradition, have been prohibited degrees of relationship. Development of considerable sophistication in the structural analysis of kinship systems was necessary before these accumulating data made sense—particularly when they showed such phenomena as the mandatory Egyptian and Inca brother-sister marriages in royal and aristocratic subgroups.

Only within our own generation has the emphasis on the special importance of certain types of solidarity of kinship units—a solidarity structurally variable over a wide range—been identified as a major aspect of the problem. In this context, the nuclear family has gradually been perceived to be a very special case because, though there are certain secondary variations, it comes nearer than any other unit of kinship structure to having universal structural significance. Eventually, from an ostensible chaos of evidence—that produced, e.g., the fantastic "primitive promiscuity" hypothesis—a certain amount of order has begun to emerge. The order is greatly strengthened by psychological considerations whose appreciation goes back to Freud far more than to any other source. These considerations concern particularly the role of infantile eroticism in the process of socializing the child, and the necessity of overcoming the attachments the child originally forms within his own family of orientation—overcoming them is necessary if he is to be motivated to the higher-order role-performance of the adult. In this connection, the incest taboo within the nuclear family has become perceived—in spite of certain peripheral exceptions—as a principal universal of human social organization and as very deeply involved in the motivational processes by which social systems are maintained. The clarification which we feel is progressing could not occur without the morphological evidence that comparative research—in this case mostly in anthropology—has accumulated and systematized.

This same example has special relevance to the other dimension of our treatment of structural morphology, namely, the evolutionary dimension. In the Introduction to Section A of Part One, we discussed the importance of the concept of social evolution in the generations immediately preceding the one concerning this Reader. During the period of our attention, there was a strong reaction against the oversimplified aspects of the concept, in the versions put forward in the name of sociology by Comte and Spencer especially, but also by a number of other writers usually classified as anthropologists. Then, particularly in anthropology, radically anti-evolutionist views emerged, taking either the form of the extreme "diffusionism" of discrete cultural traits, or the form of cultural relativity, regarding the socio-cultural world as composed of an indefinite plurality of discrete total cultures, each with its own special individuality without genetic or systematic interrelations. In their more extreme forms, both doctrines seem to negate the possibility of comparative study, through insisting on the uniqueness of the unit of analysis.

The connection between this anti-evolutionist trend and the methodological positions deriving from German Idealist "historicism" is clear.[1] In American sociology, however, interest in evolutionary ideas faded away rather than becoming involved in a dramatic clash of fundamental views. Ward and Sumner failed to hold the central attention of the major figures in the profession during the earlier part of the present century. This was associated with the writings of, e.g., Cooley, Mead, Thomas, and Park, focusing primary attention on smaller-scale structures and processes within the society. For the most part, the "historical" status of American society was not problematical to the last generation of American sociologists.

The most eminent European figures at the turn of the century were, however, much concerned with the problem of social evolution. Though they introduced very important modifications into the earlier versions, they were all fundamentally evolutionists. This statement applies least directly to Pareto, who evinced relatively little concern with any problems of structural morphology—this is one reason that his influence has not been greater. However, he had a strong historical interest concerning Western society and its relations to classical antiquity, as demonstrated in the two final chapters (the entire Volume IV in the English translation) of his *Treatise*.

Though Freud was far more important to our field as a psychologist than as a sociologist, his serious concern with evolutionary problems on the social level is significant. Many of his ideas must

1. Probably the most important connecting link between German thought and American anthropology was Franz Boas, himself of German origin.

be drastically revised. But they contained elements of striking insight; and Freud was clearly aware that a coherent theory in this field was a necessary component of the general theory of human behavior to which he contributed so much. Durkheim was one of the most cogent critics, in the relevant respects, of Comte and Spencer. But Durkheim never suggested abandoning the general evolutionary frame of reference, and his last major work, the *Elementary Forms,* was explicitly oriented to this problem. He never attempted to trace main lines of development or to delineate the main pattern of branches of the tree of social evolution; but the problem was always dominant in his thought.[2]

Max Weber was, however, the most striking figure in this connection. In one sense, Weber's primary emphasis could be described as comparative. In his later work, his central program of research was concerned with the relation of the great religious movements to the characters of the societies which developed under their influence. He analyzed the orientations and values of the religious movements themselves, and developed an elaborate system of ideal types—dealing with many phases of social structure, especially the economic and political—that, taken as a whole, is by far the most highly developed framework for comparative analysis yet available in the field. Only very recently have equally serious attempts again been made.

Seen in its larger context, Weber's scheme is evolutionary as well as comparative. He was deeply concerned with the stages by which the various principal civilizations developed from the periods in which their major religious orientations first crystallized. He was also concerned with a total picture of world history, however far he was from having worked out a complete or generally satisfactory morphological account of it. In a sense, the present task of comparative and evolutionary sociology is to resume the problem where Weber left it.

The comparative and the evolutionary perspectives are vital to sociology, and they are inseparable from each other. In the social world, as in the organic, there is a general direction, so that societies are more or less advanced in the scientifically objective and not merely the ethical senses. There is differentiation, both between types of society, and in the internal structure of each. This does not imply that the evolution of social structure is unilinear in the traditional sense: the "branching tree" model that has become generally accepted in biology seems much closer to the facts.

There is both a direct empirical continuity and a basic similarity of pattern between biological, social, and cultural evolution. The world of action is one primary aspect of the larger world of life phenomena; and the whole is subject to common principles of organization and process. However, some aspects of systems of action are not salient or not present in other parts of the life process, and these become increasingly prominent in human social and cultural evolution. Hence, the theory of social evolution is not simply a matter of applied biology in the most general sense, as some of the early social evolutionists thought. Sociology, in particular, must develop its own autonomous analysis and classifications from its own frame of reference. In this respect, we agree with the objections so frequently raised against the use of organic analogies by various earlier writers (e.g., Spencer)—society certainly is not, in the naïve sense, "an organism."

One very important feature of the evolution of human societies derives from culture's special role in them. In this case, there is some truth in the diffusionist theories of the last generation—structural components can, under certain conditions, be transferred from one social system to others which are genetically (in the historical sense) unrelated to it. The different kinds of this type of transmission and the circumstances under which it can occur constitute a crucial problem area for the sociologist. We shall return to this problem in the Introduction to Part Four, when discussing the general relations of society and culture, and in the Introduction to Part Five, which deals with social change.

## *The Classification of Structural Materials*

From the above considerations, it follows that a theoretically adequate scheme of structural morphology should be capable of systematizing data in three different reference contexts: comparison of different types of society at any given time; delineation of the genetic sequences by which one type becomes transformed into another; and delineation of the differentiated subsystems which, in relation to each other, constitute the structure internal to any given society. Ideally, all three aspects of structural morphology must be integrated in one conceptual scheme. Since all these aspects are ultimately based in the same set of premises, the choice of one among them to serve as the primary point of reference is arbitrary.

2. This aspect of Durkheim's thought has recently been thoroughly reviewed by Robert N. Bellah, "Durkheim and History" *American Sociological Review,* Vol. 24, p. 447, 1959. Dr. Bellah's paper brings out this aspect so strongly that it can probably never again be seriously claimed that Durkheim's main tendency was to "static," ahistorical analysis.

We have given primacy to the third aspect, since work within it has been most highly developed. Most of the material bearing on genetic sequences is included in Part Five rather than Part Two; and what is available is distressingly fragmentary. In Part Two, we have deliberately included a good deal of comparative material.

If the internal structure of a given society is the primary point of reference, the problem of classifying structural components is difficult and troublesome. Theory in this field has not yet reached a satisfactory state—especially in any sense which could be the common property of the professional groups concerned with the field.[3] For this reason, and because of this problem's involvement with those of the relation of social systems to culture and to the individual, arranging the selections in Part Two and dividing it from Parts Three and Four posed a difficult problem.

The best procedure might have been to use the available classification with the most general theoretical merit—e.g., along the lines outlined in the second essay in the General Introduction above. However, there is one serious objection to this procedure. In the period from which the selections have been taken, thinking in terms of this kind of classification did not occur—Weber's work comes closest to our own conceptions, but is still considerably removed. Inevitably, we had to use a compromise, constituting a relative approximation to what we considered an adequate basis for ordering this type of materials.

Let us try to develop the rationale for our classification in its relations both to our own preferred scheme and to the nature of the materials we are presenting. First, the most general principle of organization is, in a modified form, that hierarchy of control relations outlined in the General Introduction—from the lowest level to the highest in that hierarchy. Since this principle must be intersected by others, we have applied it in a broad way.

The two other principal bases of our classification are the categories of economic and political structures. These categories are the least ambiguous of the conventional list of "institutions"; we will discuss later certain ambiguities which should be remembered in orienting to such materials.

"Ascriptive solidarities" are at the bottom of the classification, and "religion," in its structural aspect for society, is at the top.[4] In the middle, between the economic and the political categories, we have placed social stratification; it is, perhaps, the central focus of internal social conflict in sociological thinking, and hence is the most crucial single point at which existing integrative mechanisms can be expected to focus.

As noted, the fundamental point of reference for this classification is the relation to the hierarchy of control; but, because of the inherent multidimensional character of social systems, this relation alone cannot be adequate. For further analysis of these cross-cutting relations, the evolutionary concept is the most convenient point of reference.

## *Ascriptive Solidarity as a Point of Departure*

*Kinship.* In the structure of primitive or relatively undifferentiated societies, ascriptive components are overwhelmingly predominant. The first focus of the ascriptive structure is generally kinship. But kinship is not, as such, a factor or a causal category —except in the special methodological sense in which any structure can be treated as such. Kinship is structurally (in the sense of defining the patterning of social relationships) the most salient and tangible aspect of a functionally diffuse, i.e., relatively undifferentiated, system. Though the kinship system is itself relatively complex—a result in part of the incest taboo—the situation approximates one in which the total status of the individual in the society is determined by his kinship statuses. But structurally and functionally, this includes far more than is involved in kinship in a modern society. As recent anthropological work has shown, it involves the whole complex of territorial references involved in status—residence;[5] the territorial relational context in which "work" is done, i.e., the prototype of later occupational functions; the jurisdictional focus of organization in its legal and political aspects; and the modes of communicative interrelationship which can exist, including messages and the movements of persons and commodities.

The kinship system is, thus, the focus of what in more differentiated contexts would be called the economic and technological aspects of social function. In other words, roles in these functional connections are performed by given persons in given ways by virtue of their places in the ascribed net-

3. The author of this Introduction is now struggling with the problem in connection with an attempt to analyze American society as a total social system. The currently preferred classifications, such as are found in even the best general textbooks, seem seriously unsatisfactory for the purpose. I therefore expect to use a rather radically revised one, which is partly foreshadowed above in Part Two of the General Introduction.

4. We will deal with the other principal aspect of religion in Part Four.

5. See G. P. Murdock, *Social Structure,* N. Y., Macmillan Co., 1949, for an illuminating analysis of the complex interrelations of kinship status, in the sense of biological-affinal relatedness, and residential location.

work of kinship relations. The same applies to the more central functions on behalf of societies as systems. Its most tangible focus is the organization of political authority. Such institutions as clan eldership, chieftainship, etc., are universally associated with kinship status. Whatever primitive equivalent of law there is in such a society is clearly organized at the kinship and religious levels. This last is also generally associated with the same functionally diffuse matrix. The classic analysis based on this general supposition is Durkheim's study of the Australian society (in the *Elementary Forms*).

Whatever differentiations on other levels may underlie the structure of a primitive, kinship-centered society—in the patterns of differentiation which become of primary significance to the comparative study of social structures at more advanced levels—there is a common base, the ascriptive embeddedness in a kinship nexus of all major societal functions.

For this reason, our first major category of structural components of societies has a dual significance. First, it is meant to present some particularly important examples of the description and analysis of types of general social organization in which this ascriptive component clearly dominates all others. Second, it concerns this component's continuing significance, through all the various vicissitudes of the modes of structural differentiation that have occurred from the base line of ascriptive embeddedness. If our concern were only with the primitive base line, we could have confined our selections to the first subsection.[6] It was necessary to add three other rubrics, because, in the further process of differentiation, aspects of the more general ascriptive complex become differentiated both from each other and from non-ascriptive components.

In more general theoretical terms, the category of ascriptive solidarity is the primary, though not the exclusive, base point of the interrelations between the social system and the individual. There are two primary foci of this relationship. The first is the basic connection between sexual reproduction as a biological mechanism, and the family as the primary agency of the process of socialization. The family is primary in that it is the first social agency powerfully to affect the child; it hence lays the foundation of personality structure. Although many imposing social structures are independent of the specificities of the kinship base, there is no tendency to eliminate this base. In social evolution, the principal trend has been toward enhancing the generality of the foundations thereby laid down, not toward eliminating their necessity or even the most general location of the mechanisms of their construction. There is, here, a close analogy with the role of genetic factors in the determination of behavior. The plasticity of the human organism is not an example of the elimination of the relevance of genetic factors; it is an example of a special type of organization of such factors.

*Ethnic Solidarity*. Kinship, with special reference to the nuclear family, is the continuing base for the socialization of the individual's personality. Two other subcategories in our classification of components of ascriptive solidarity may be considered as extensions, in different directions, from this point of reference. One concerns ethnic solidarity. In the more undifferentiated situation, ethnic solidarity is simply taken for granted. It is the unity of a collectivity whose members are bound together by kinship ties—that is, where the member acquires ascriptively, by birth, his membership in the relevant collectivities. Our concern here, however, is the operation of the same principle within a larger structural context involving more than one ethnic group. This pluralism constitutes a fundamental difference from the primitive situation. On the general evolutionary scale, one major reference point is the necessity of juxtaposing those groups who differ in allegiance at this level within another setting of imperatives.

In Western history, the Jews provide the most salient example of this—the problem of the status of the diaspora groups within the wider societies of which they have become parts. If Jewishness had been, in the sectarian sense, a special religious adherence, the problem would have been different. But the Jewish pattern was one of religio-social community, in which membership was by hereditary ascription and to which loyalties were diffuse. By extending the pattern of kinship ascription to a subcommunity within a larger one, a special pattern of differentiated social organization was evolved. The Jews in medieval and early modern Europe were a special and rather extreme case, but they illustrate the principle vividly. The ethnic group and the social class, as bases of organization, share some important common elements, which will be discussed later.

*The Primary Group*. The other extension from kinship ascription as such is the primary group. This is not a direct application of the principle of kin-

6. It might be debated whether concern with the very important types of difference and ranges of variation *within* this base line category of "primitive" society was primarily a function of sociology, or of the anthropologists, who have made vitally important contributions to it. Apart from this jurisdictional question between disciplines, the problems of differentiation beyond this base line are sufficiently formidable, and have played a sufficient part in the preoccupations of the main figures of sociological theory, so that we are justified in concentrating our attention on them.

ship ascription, but is classified with it because they have the common factor of functionally diffuse involvement of the personality. The nuclear family is the prototype of all primary groups. The principle of solidarity based on relatively particularized "personal" loyalty can, however, be extended to types of relation which are more specialized in their functions for the wider society, even up to the case of occupational groups. The relations between these levels, exemplified in the selections of Section A-III will be discussed further in the introduction to that section.

*Territorial Groupings.* The second of the two primary foci of the individual's anchorage in social processes is the territorial location of activities and, with that, the territorial incidence of the jurisdictional application of systems of normative order. As already noted, the more primitive focus of this is the mutual involvement of kinship structure and residential location. With further differentiation, the locations of many activities become progressively more separated from place of residence, and responsibility for both jurisdiction and communication becomes segregated from kinship grouping as such. Just as in the case of biological relatedness, the complex concerned with territorial location, though progressively differentiating, is an indispensable foundation for structuring the basis of the individual's participation in social relationships—including the control of such participation. Like kinship, it can be superseded only in that it may become more "plastic"—a more generalized base permitting wider and more flexible ranges of variation for the individual. Territorial mobility of populations is largely a main trend of general social development, however prominent the exceptions may be.

## *Primary Differentiation from the Ascription Nexus*

Partly because of the importance of this set of exigencies of the individual's foundation in the social system, a complementary set of imperatives concerned with the integration of these many persons in a larger social system always exists at the same time. On the lowest evolutionary levels, this is closely associated with, or embedded in, the general kinship structure itself. The imperative is demonstrated by the incest taboo and, relative to the nuclear family, by the cross-cutting nexus of extended kin groupings. Such groupings are, as noted, agencies defining and enforcing territorially extended systems of normative order, and regulating systems of communication and movement. In other connections, they are the focus of defining and symbolizing values, and of whatever societal goal-orientation occurs.

The most frequent and important differentiation proceeding immediately from this base is that between the diffuse matrix and the structural elements organized about higher-order, more nearly society-wide functional exigencies. The diffuse matrix remains more directly concerned with maintaining the masses of the population, and their reproduction, economic provision, etc.

The most salient of these society-wide exigencies are either religious or political. The religious are concerned primarily with maintaining the basic cultural tradition, with special reference to its value content—i.e., values for the society as a system. The political have primary reference to maintaining cohesion and conformity with the traditionally defined institutionalized order. The paramount political exigencies are those associated with quite specific goals affecting the whole society, like defense, certain society-wide problems of economic production (e.g., the famous irrigation system), and the maintenance of internal loyalty to the institutionalized order. In general, law forms a bridge between these two major components of differentiated societal responsibility.

As a general rule, however much the emphasis on the religious and the political functions may vary, the agencies responsible for them do not, in early stages and at the higher levels, readily become structurally differentiated from each other. Aristocracies and royal lineages are usually *both* political and religious elites; and responsibility for law as general normative prescription, whether it emphasizes the political or the religious more, is vested in the same groups. Usually, these upper groups are differentiated from the lower as ascriptively hereditary kinship groups. Therefore the tendency to differentiate a functionally diffuse leadership element from the diffuse kinship nexus also tends to become the basis of a generalized pattern of social stratification which *includes* a kinship component.

Though complicated, this broad basis of earlier structural differentiation corresponds roughly to the main axis of our organization of materials. Kinship per se cannot be the major basis of this type of differentiation, nor can the other components of the ascriptive complex. Only as kinship groups—or, more rarely, ethnic groups—become specialized with reference to responsibility for societal functions of this order, can they become systematically distinguished from the general run of such groups. The central focus of stratification lies in differentiation for society-wide function. The degree to which this differentiation is institutionalized is variable.

In general, clear differentiation of economic production from a functionally diffuse matrix is a late development in structural evolution. With certain exceptions, some one kinship unit or combination of kinship units remains the principal agency of the productive process. Differentiation in terms of the political and religious functions discussed above, however, requires a higher order of consumption than the production of the kinship units to which the incumbents belong can provide. In transitional cases, like the polygyny of the Trobriand chief described by Malinowski, a predominant position within a particularly wide nexus of kinship relations can provide for this. But usually, more specialized bases of insuring an income to the higher groups of the society develop. There are two alternative emphases. The far commoner is to leave most of the organization of production itself to lower-order units, but to institutionalize, for various types of higher groups, rights to some fraction of the proceeds. Perhaps the commonest example of this is the institutionalization of some sort of rent rights—i.e., to a share of the produce of the land for "owning" groups, as distinct from the cultivators themselves. The second alternative is to put the productive process itself directly under the control of the ruling elements. Various versions of the *oikos* pattern of organization belong in this category, as do the *latifundia* of the Roman upper class. Cases like this should not, however, be considered "economic enterprises" in the usual sense. They do not typically constitute production for an indefinite market; they are modes of providing for the *specific* economic needs of units of the upper groups, that, as such, have a status of diffuse political and religious superiority.

Thus, though in one aspect, this relation between elite and non-elite elements, however one-sided, may be treated as "economic exchange," under these conditions it is never closely analogous to such exchange in a "free market" economy—the economic element is still embedded in a more diffuse matrix whose other elements are primarily non-economic.[7] Similar statements may be made about the factors of political power and support as they operate in such relationships. Because the political component stands at a higher level than the economic in the hierarchy of control relations, within the type of diffuse matrix under consideration, in general, political rather than economic superiority is paramount, in a more analytical sense. On this type of broad two-class basis, those groups enjoying positions of marked economic superiority are very directly integrated in the upper political structure of the society.

The more directly political functions concern the capacity to mobilize societal resources through mechanisms which are not a simple function of the institutionalized obligations of a seamless web of kinship relations as such. Understandably, military service is important in this respect, as is providing economic income for maintaining the upper groups' style of life. In general, this style of life includes a variety of components which have direct symbolic significance for the integration of the society and the expression of its values. It also includes provision for the primary centralized religious functions of the society, and the obligation to enforce internal order in relation to some sort of normative system.

These political components are typically embedded in a diffuse matrix of integrative and pattern-maintenance functions. In this context, the pattern-maintenance functions appear most conspicuously in the religious status of the upper groups, which are nearly universally accorded some special prerogatives—though special subgroups often have more differentiated religious functions. The most conspicuous manifestation of the integrative component is kinship's involvement in the general differentiation. In other words, membership in the upper groups is almost universally mostly hereditary; their lineages become differentiated from those of the lower ranks—even though certain types of mobility may be possible, e.g., through military channels. Political and economic superiority would not be viable without the legitimation provided by integrating a religious tradition with its institutional forms, and without institutionalizing the superiority of the relevant kinship units as such as a superior class or caste. When we speak of a "ruling class," we refer to a differentiated group which enjoys superiority in *all* of these functional respects—though there may be different emphases in subgroups within it, and the characteristics of ruling classes may differ in different societies.

One important case in this area is that where the upper group is ethnically distinct from the lower. Some sociologists, like Franz Oppenheimer, have gone so far as to contend that differentiated political authority and landlordism can arise only through conquest. This seems contrary to the facts; but foreign rule has been a common phenomenon.

In its essentials, this case need not differ much from one whose stratification arises by a process of internal differentiation. The primacy of the political factor over the economic is more marked; economic superiority is achieved and maintained largely through the use of political power. It is a somewhat more subtle point that the needs for legitimation

7. Karl Polanyi, Conrad Arensberg, and Harry Pearson, *Trade and Market in the Early Empires* (Glencoe, Ill.: Free Press, 1957).

and integration are even more acute in this type of case than in the other—as Max Weber made particularly clear. An alliance between foreign political elites and indigenous religious groups is not uncommon—with the latter performing the function, in particular, of "domestication." If such a regime is stable over a long period, a general process of amalgamation is likely to occur, to a point where the ethnic basis of difference disappears. Thus, in England, the uniqueness of the Norman French element was gradually attenuated, so that eventually the use of French and other signs of the ethnic distinction vanished—though they left important residues, like the large French component in the modern English vocabulary.

In medieval English society, this problem of integration was an important focus of the processes by which the Common Law developed and eventually became a highly distinctive system. The fact that the Norman regime was foreign and established by conquest was involved in the early centralization of the English monarchy. But in the conditions of feudalism, the Common Law developed above all in the area of the relations between lord and tenant. In the upper strata of the system, both parties to any conflict were usually French; but lower on the social scale, relations between French and Anglo-Saxon were involved. Probably the ethnic line was the most important single focus of conflict in the system. The Common Law, spreading under royal sponsorship, introduced mechanisms for regulating such conflicts, especially through its procedural emphases. In strict feudal law, a tenant had no rights that could be enforced in the King's courts against his lord. The celebrated rights of Englishmen became institutionalized by a process of encroaching on this privileged relationship. The law increasingly protected the individual from arbitrary action by the lord, usually in the local area. Also, the lords' rights were increasingly freed from the more or less personal basis of feudal tenancy, and institutionalized as rights of property and of local jurisdiction. The general tendency was toward stabilizing the system, and also toward allowing certain types of mobility not possible in a strictly feudal society.

The keynote of the above discussion has been that political and economic functions, in the earlier stages of structural social evolution, are embedded in the three-fold matrix of ascriptive solidarities (notably of kinship and ethnic group, but also of relative territorial fixity), of religion, and of stratification with its introduction of hierarchically differentiated ascriptions. The political functions tend to be more specialized in upper groups and more closely associated with society-wide religious leadership; and economic functions tend to be more segmented and distributed among the masses of the population organized in largely ascriptive units.

## POLITICAL FOCI OF FURTHER DIFFERENTIATION

*Bureaucracy.* In general, two types of sources provide the impetus to further differentiation. The more obvious and more frequently considered centers in the political sphere and is primarily concerned (with respect to one main subtype) with the extension of various types of bureaucratic organization, both military and civil. The second is the development of modes of religious organization and orientation that are autonomous in relation to the more general social structure, particularly its upper echelons.

The essential point about bureaucratization is that it frees the necessary resources from ascriptive ties, which would prevent their disposability, for collective goals according to the exigencies which arise. The most obvious of these ascriptive ties are extended kinship and the kinds of decentralized territorial jurisdiction associated, for example, with feudal systems. The crucial resource in this case is the services of persons, organized in such a way that their loyalty to the implementing political organization takes precedence over other loyalties.

Though top political authority usually remains embedded in the lineage structures of kinship, in and below ministerial and high command levels there may be more or less free disposability of personnel for the goals of higher authority. This process is, however, subject to a series of complex exigencies. The most important such contingency is probably the "internal" problem of the patterning of the organizational structure itself. Others are the problems of economic provision; of integration with other structures, with special reference to the bases on which personnel in the bureaucratic structure are given "security" in relation to conflicting claims on their loyalty; and of the basis of making legitimate such extensive claims on the societal resources.

Different sorts of organizational tasks vary widely. The military looms large in many societies, and usually the line between defense and offense is a thin one. But the great, economically significant public works of earlier eras belong mainly in this category—e.g., the irrigation and canal works of the river valley civilizations. Such projects may also be oriented to goals concerned with religion and/or integrative symbolization. Two cases of this are the enormous mobilization of resources for building temples and other religio-political monuments, like the pyramids of Egypt; and building palaces, which are both utilitarian facilities and symbols of the regimes' greatness and contributions to the society.

Necessarily qualified, Weber's dictum that bureaucracy is the most effective administrative instrument ever developed may be adopted as our point of reference. Internally, bureaucracy's principal characteristics as an ideal type consist in an adequate balance between competence and responsibility on the part of its various units. The requisite standards of competence vary with the nature of the task, and are connected with the related evolution of culture in the instrumental fields, the various technologies, etc. It is only very late that full-fledged science becomes an important component of competence. Responsibility concerns primarily the effectiveness with which units can be co-ordinated in the service of any organization task. Responsibility is associated especially with the nature of the authority and leadership operating within the organization. The fundamental problem is balancing the two essentially independent elements of competence and authority.

The effectiveness of internal organization is dependent on the external relations of a bureaucratic organization, in proportion to the large-scale and formidable character of the task. The factors of economic provision and security come to a head in the problem of the degrees of approximation to the institutionalization of occupational roles. The crucial problem is that of the ways in which and the degrees to which the performance of service can be made independent of involvement in relational contexts external to the organization, when organizational interests conflict potentially with the external interest. As Weber has made clear, the optimum arrangement is full money remuneration, so that neither the operative organization nor any of its subunits need have any claim or stake in the *sources* of economic provision; conversely, the structures constituting these sources need not have control over the organization's operation. This involves complex conditions, two of the most important being the extent of market systems and the feasibility of money taxation. Anything approximating a full system of money remuneration for a large-scale bureaucratic apparatus is found only in a few historical cases. Anything less than a full system, however, imposes severe constraints on the independence of the bureaucratic organization; even more important, where subunits are independently provided for through fiefs, benefices, etc., a powerful centrifugal force tends to arise that easily threatens the internal authority structure of the organization.

The problem of security is closely related to this. The fortunes of the organization may be subject to severe and unexpected vicissitudes; and the status of the individual or subunit within the organization may be seriously insecure. The specialization of bureaucratic roles *ipso facto* means that other, more particularistic bases of security must be sacrificed; because, in general, these involve a diffuse fusion with non-bureaucratic bases of status. Only through the very wide extension of occupational organization through the society as a whole can a close and stable approximation to Weber's ideal type of bureaucracy be achieved.

The famous Chinese Mandarin bureaucracy is an illuminating example of a "compromise" formation. In the society as a whole, this stood virtually alone. The individual had no alternative "occupational" career. Yet there was considerable risk in the process of qualification for office through the examination system, in part as a direct consequence of its universalistic rigor. Furthermore, once qualified, the individual's career chances were still uncertain. This situation influenced strongly the co-existence, over so many centuries, of the bureaucratic system and the social predominance of a landed gentry with full political control at the local levels. The gentry lineage was the security base from which it was possible to take the risks of an official career, and to which were fed back the proceeds of success. This was a mutually profitable symbiosis; but the functional necessity of the security base was a fundamental barrier to the further rationalization of Chinese bureaucracy.

Extreme predominance of the security base over organizational obligations is demonstrated in the military organization of Western feudalism. The leadership of military contingents was so strongly based in their own local feudal nexus that a central command could be sure of commanding their loyalty only within very narrow limits. A truly national level of military organization was not possible without structurally segregating military roles from the feudal network.

For present purposes, the most significant aspect of the problem of the legitimation of bureaucratic organizations and their operations is the relation of bureaucratic organization to any generalized system of law existing in the society. In other words, under certain circumstances groups who are somehow recognized as authorities on what is "normatively correct" in the society tend to become dominant in directing and operating bureaucracies. Another aspect of the Chinese case demonstrates this: the famous Confucian literati were essentially "lawyers";

they were trained in the "proprieties"; they knew what conduct was right and proper for the superior man. Their expert status took in this respect precedence over any standards of technical competence or even organizational effectiveness, thus providing another very severe set of limitations on the rationalization of the bureaucracy.

Another example is the prominent role played by legally trained personnel in the civil bureaucracies of Continental Europe in modern times, particularly in Germany. In general, emancipation from the restrictive aspects of "legalism" while not yet having attained adequate legitimation presents a serious set of problems. Often, the alternative to such legalistic restriction has been a Machiavellian power-orientation by the bureaucracy that has led to severe problems of integration in another direction.[8]

*Political Democracy*. There is a second mode of differentiating the political components of social structure from their diffuse matrices. Bureaucratic organization concerns the *implementation* of goal-oriented decisions and leadership. The other case concerns the mechanisms for arriving at such decisions and for structuring the support for leadership. The development of "political democracy" in classical antiquity is the great example of emancipation from ascription. In the bureaucratic empires, political allegiance remained, as in primitive societies, in virtually all respects ascribed to the "legitimate" authority structure—generally including a generous component of prescription by force. But in Greece and Rome, the institutionalization of the role of citizenship, though restricted to privileged minorities of the total population, included the right to participate in collective decision- and policy-making, and hence the right to allocate support between alternative leadership elements rather than restriction to the one legitimate authority. It is obvious that the stability of such a system would be precarious; it is not surprising that this pattern appeared only under special circumstances and in small-scale units. However, its importance as the basic model for modern political enfranchisement is clear.

It is important that the differentiation of the political from other elements was still incomplete in classical Greece and Rome. In the Greek *polis* and the Roman *urbs,* no clear differentiation between political and religious functions developed. The *polis* was both church and state, though, through certain types of secularization, its political aspect tended to become predominant. For present purposes, the essential point that a considerable proportion of the population were enfranchised, that is, they were freed from specific ascriptive allegiances *within* (not *to*) the *polis*. It is significant that this development did not occur originally in societies which developed complex bureaucratic structures, and that, in Rome, as the *urbs* increased in scale, the incidence of the development became greatly attenuated. This set of circumstances, because of Rome's historical background as a city-state, probably played an important part in the acuteness of the problem of legitimacy in later Rome.

*Law*. The same general social complex—classical antiquity—is the most important source of development of an *independent* system of law. As noted, the legal element was central in the Chinese development; but it took a form which did not readily become differentiated from either the political or the religious—on the contrary, it formed the focus of a special kind of codification of the religio-political fusion. There was thus essentially no pattern of institutionalization of legal rights *against* the state or religion.

The Greek legal system was similar, except that the all-important democratic element institutionalized rights, within the state, to participate in decision-making. In Greece, the legal system did not become generalized on an independent basis. In Rome, whose political dominion grew while internally the democratic element declined in importance, relations to the populations of the Empire became structured in dual form: the extension of the privileges of Roman citizenship to larger and larger circles throughout the Empire; and the development of the *jus gentium* as a legal system applicable to all under Roman jurisdiction. Though administered by political authority and backed by religious sanctions, the system of Roman Law became an independent entity in a unique sense. Roman Law, in addition to classical culture, was clearly one of the most important legacies from antiquity to the modern Western world.

This aspect of law should be distinguished from the types of religious law, to be discussed briefly below, institutionalized in Judaism and Islam. The most important achievement of Roman Law was its type of differentiation of law from religion and from political leadership. In Judaism and Islam, religious sanction was lent to detailed prescriptions of con-

8. The same essential sociological principles apply to the cases of economic and of political bureaucracy; the firm, though oriented to economic production, has a prominent "political" (in the analytical sense) component in its organization. In this context, the association of the family firm with a kinship lineage has had functions similar to those of the gentry lineages in Chinese bureaucracy. The market is, like the official career, a field of serious risk-taking; and family property and the continuity of kinship status in the community have provided an important cushion underlying the risk. Only with the development of a very extensive occupational system in recent times could stable economic and political bureaucracy exist without some such cushion.

duct—this made the Roman type of differentiation impossible. To this day, this is a central problem in Islamic societies.

## TYPES OF RELIGIOUS AUTONOMY

The other massive basis of a further process of structural differentiation toward the upper end of the control hierarchy is the development of religious collectivities and movements which can be considered "autonomous" relative to the main structure of the social system. Our previous generalization that various functional performances are embedded in ascribed matrices, characteristically in primitive societies, especially those organized around kinship, applies to religion as much as to any other principal aspect of the social system. Religious beliefs are typically shared throughout the society, and rituals are symbolically integrated in the social system itself. There is no religious point of view which opposes the point of view assumed to be institutionalized; the only behavior condemned in the name of religion is what is socially deviant, in a general sense. Though there are individual classes of specialists in religious (including magical) matters, no religiously specialized collectivity is structurally distinct from others.

As noted, this fusion tends strongly to be maintained when a marked hierarchical differentiation takes place. Elites are usually both political and religious at the same time.[9]

Religion's position high on the hierarchy of control in the social system implies that it should provide, under favorable conditions, the most powerful source of leverage for structural change in societies. Cases where this leverage has operated fairly autonomously seem rather rare historically and difficult to identify or analyze. Tendencies to religious innovation seem to be generally kept under tighter controls than is the case with other components of the social system.[10]

*Interstitial Autonomy*. In general, the earliest types of religious orientation that are significantly autonomous in relation to the main structure of societies are found in situations interstitial to societies. A typical example is the "holy place." In early Semitic religion, as analyzed by Robertson Smith, the society was largely nomadic. However, it maintained some kind of permanent installation at a holy place—usually an oasis—and a socially separate group, functioning as its custodians, readily developing into a kind of priesthood. This group was an interstitial subsociety, enjoying but dependent upon the tolerance and protection of the major societal powers in the region. These priesthoods of holy places are thought to have played an important part in developing the patterns of religious autonomy that came to fruition in Judaism and later in Islam. A different but related example is the special status of the Oracles in the Hellenic world, situated outside the structure of the *polis*.

Other movements, like early Buddhism in India and Taoism in China, could develop within the structure of a society; but they quickly became isolated as internally interstitial elements, taking the form of special religious subcommunities deprived of any major status in the central social structure. This trend was easiest when the religious movement itself was built on the devaluation of worldly concerns. The early Christian communities within the society of the Eastern part of the Roman Empire show this. "Rendering unto Caesar the things that are Caesar's" meant, in these circumstances, accepting the position of not belonging in the secular society, of being "in it but not of it," hence expecting only to be tolerated within it. The connection of this orientation with the eschatological hopes of early Christianity is clear.

Movements like this, which started out in an internally interstitial position within the society, might ultimately, if they spread far enough, have profound consequences for the society's main course of development. This was particularly true of Christianity.

*Monastic Orders and Sects*. There is an important range of transition from this kind of internally interstitial religious autonomy to that involving rather direct influence over the character of the society itself. One of the most common patterns in which the interstitial type could find relative stability is that of religious orders, usually consisting of adults of one sex living in segregation from the secular society. This pattern was particularly prominent in Buddhism and Taoism in the Orient, where such groups never become wholly independent of the surrounding society. They are dependent on other sources for recruitment, for political protection, and generally for economic subsistence. Moreover,

9. It is notable that the two most important sociologists of religion of our central generation, Durkheim and Weber, both postulated the generality of an embedded type of primitive religion from which more differentiated types might evolve.

10. Religion is placed primarily in the cultural, rather than the social, system. Because, however, of its special relation to the problem of values and the stabilization of value-orientations, it is crucial to the highest level of social structure. The general relation is interpenetration. Generally speaking, the less differentiated both the social and the cultural systems, the more comprehensive the range of interpretation, and hence the more important the more direct forms of social control over religion, and vice versa.

they are rarely content to be completely isolated. They generally wish somehow to take their religious message to the outside world, to share their religious good fortunes with others. Their withdrawal in the name of religion is, with wide variations, always to some extent a withdrawal with intent to return.

An important difference occurs when the group organized about an autonomous religious orientation is composed primarily of families, i.e., of both sexes and all ages living in household units. This is the "sect," in Weber's and Troeltsch's sense; the early Christian communities were of this type. It should be distinguished from a discipleship or "brotherhood," which leads into the monastic order type. The sect is characterized by commitment to make its religion the unequivocally dominant consideration in its members' lives. It therefore involves strong pressure to establish real communities consisting exclusively of believers attempting to lead a religiously ideal life. Two outstanding examples of this are the Anabaptists in the Reformation period in Europe, and the Mormons in nineteenth-century America. Since the religiously ideal pattern of social life is likely to be very different from that of the surrounding general society, the problem of the relation between the two is likely to be acute. Sects thus form the most persistent foci of phenomena of religious persecution, because a genuinely serious conflict at the level of societal values is likely. Many compromises are possible and found in actuality; one important line of accommodation, which will be discussed presently, is that leading from sect to denomination in the modern sense.

*Religious Control of a Total Society*. The importance of the type of social system in which religious and political components were essentially fused has been stressed. It is possible for a movement that is functionally classified as "religiously autonomous" to capture control of such a structure without establishing a structurally differentiated organization of religion. Then the socio-religious structure, especially its elite elements, will tend to give primacy to religious considerations in their general and diffuse functioning.

The Semitic world provides examples of this, in both Judaism and Islam. In Judaism, it apparently occurred in two distinct phases. The first is the one culminating in the Mosaic pattern, in which the Israelites, as Jahweh's chosen people, embarked on the conquest of the Promised Land and the establishment of a society which was conceived as directly governed by Divine Law. The second phase was the Prophetic, during which, under the direct and terrible threat of political disaster, the total Jewish community was enjoined to continue being loyal to religious commitments, even at the sacrifice of political independence. Here, the religion was a kind of lever controlling the development of the whole real society. The Islamic case is, in this respect, very similar. Mohammed, as the Prophet of God, became the religio-political leader of the Arab community; and from then on the community as a whole was conceived as an instrument of the Divine Will, to be guided exclusively by God's law as formulated in the Koran.

*The Differentiation of Religious and Political Structures*. The second possibility for religion is exemplified by Christianity's evolution beyond the sect, namely, to the "church" in the Weber-Troeltsch sense. The values of the religion, specifically as formulated by and institutionalized in the autonomous religious collectivity, the church, are assumed to be binding both on and in the secular society of which the church is a part. However, there is a structural differentiation between religious and secular collectivities that does not exist in Judaism and Islam. "Church" and "state" are no longer one, but "politically organized society" —the "state," in the medieval sense—is, though unequivocally Christian, still autonomous from the Church as a collectivity organization. Pope Innocent III's claim, that the Emperor was a feudal vassal of the Pope was short-lived. In religious terms, the "temporal arm" was conceived as ordained directly by God and responsible directly to God, and not requiring mediation through the Church. Coronation by a religious authority was a recognition of common Christianity, not of Papal suzerainty.

For present purposes, the most significant aspect of this development was its institutionalization of a primary differentiation between these two crucial aspects of the cultural system, and the social. The common Christianity of Church and state designated an area of interpenetration. A certain rigidity involved in their fusion, in collectivity structure, could be broken down on this basis, with far-reaching consequences for wide ranges of social and of cultural freedom and mobility.

Western Christianity gave rise to a series of sect movements, both before and after the Reformation, and to the development of at least two major new church types, the Lutheran and the Calvinistic. These Reformation churches, however, shared, with the Catholic, the concept of the established church—which, ideally, meant that membership in and hence subjection to the normative jurisdiction of both political state and church were coextensive.

In other areas, and particularly in the United States, a somewhat different type of church has emerged within Protestantism; this is the "denomination." It shares with the sect type the purely voluntary basis of membership and the expectation that its members will be responsible for its own affairs, including financial support. It shares, with the church type, however, the status and expectation of being not only in but of the society. That is, it recognizes legitimacy of a secular sphere which is not, in the collectivity sense, under religious control; and it assumes that its members will, on the whole, participate normally in this secular life. Membership in the religious collectivity is only one role, genuinely differentiated from the other roles in which the same individuals are involved. In America, there is the important feature of a plurality of denominational groups which are recognized as legitimate, not only by secular authority, but by each other mutually on the religious plane. The distinction has been made between a generally legitimate religious orientation, and the particularities of a specific denominational position. To be authentically religious, it is no longer necessary to subscribe to one religious group's credally or traditionally specific beliefs and practices.

The great difference of the denomination from the sect and from the interstitial movement lies in its recognition of the secular society's *legitimacy*. It is not set against a "world" defined as inherently evil if not incorporated into the system of explicitly religious control; but it is differentiated *from* the secular world, thus remaining part of the same more generally legitimate system.[11]

Religion has been included, in Part Two of the Reader, as one of our five main major categories of social structure because, seen in the broadest comparative and evolutionary perspective, it is the focal point of articulation between social and cultural systems—notably, that at which the role of value components is most directly involved. Here, only the relation of religion as a focus of values to the structure of the society is primarily at issue. Religion will, however, appear again—both in the general treatment of the relations of society and culture in Part Four, and in the treatment of social change in Part Five.

Other components of culture, which will be discussed in more detail in the Introduction to Part Four, are of great empirical significance. The "secular intellectual culture," whose two principal forms are philosophy and science, but that also involves ideology and technology, is paramount. In this area, there have been problems of relative autonomy vis-à-vis both religion and various sectors of the secular structure, notably the political. Autonomous intellectual culture is one of the most striking features of Western society; the conditions underlying this are necessarily of particular importance in any general sociological analysis of this great complex of societies.

11. I have the impression that, different as the general situation has been from the West, many of the Shinto and Buddhist sects of Japan, at least from the Tokugawa period on, approach the status of being denominations in this sense.

## THE BASES OF ECONOMIC AUTONOMY

In our dialectical progression among the complexities of the five categories of social structure, let us now consider the economic, seen in the context of its relations to the political and religious, and to the ascriptive solidarities.

As emphasized, any large-scale differentiation of the primary functions of economic production from the matrix of ascriptive solidarity occurs later in the general pattern of societal evolution, and it depends on rather specific conditions. In general, first "consumption" and then exchange become economically specialized, before the impetus reaches back to the productive levels. The two major trends noted above, in the economic relations between an upper politico-religious elite class and the mass of the population, may be regarded in this framework. One basis of the more general differentiation is the lower groups' specialization for economically providing for the needs of the larger collectivity and/or of the upper groups. This usually takes the form of continuing the productive process within the framework of a system of ascriptive solidarities, especially of kinship and of the village community. The upper groups—landlords, etc.—receive an important share of the product. The alternative would be to move an important share of economic production into the framework of collective organization somehow directly controlled by the upper groups themselves.

In the latter type of case, the result is not differentiated economic enterprise, except in a highly qualified sense. Religio-political collectivities control the process, though these collectivities may have branches whose primary concern is with economic production. Such branches may be landed estates raising food-stuffs, or they may be workshops producing luxury goods or armaments. They may also involve requisitioning labor for various kinds of public works. Also, a very substantial economic factor is involved in the direct provision of more or less personalized service in the complex households of various types of magnates.

As Durkheim showed, the more specifically economic aspect of functional specialization is deeply involved with the development of the division of labor; this may be considered its focal point of development. The division of labor, however, directly implies the necessity of developing and institutionalizing relationships between the consequent differentiated functional units—in the first instance, between producing and consuming units.

In all primitive societies where division of labor exists, the exchange relationship is always embedded in a network of diffuse ascriptive solidarity, one part of which is usually some mutuality of obligations involving terms which could be called "economic." Under these circumstances, this is the fundamental basis of the "traditionalization" of economic relations. The same general pattern is likely to obtain when the first major step in structural differentiation, separating the religio-political upper classes from the general population, has occurred. The producing elements usually have diffuse relations of dependency, involving especially political protection to the recipients of their surplus production.

A familiar example is the relation between land ownership, hence "rent"-paying, and paternalistic solidarity, in the manorial communities of Western feudalism. The landlord was much more than a property holder; he was a political suzerain and the general protector of his community. This was the meaning of the legal formula that a tenant had no rights against his lord—no outside agency could legitimately intervene in this diffuse solidary relationship.

*The Emergence of Money and Markets: Contract.* There is a vital connection between the breakdown of this kind of relation of diffuse solidarity through differentiation, and the emergence of money and markets. This exists because very severe limitations on differentiation are imposed by the directness of the relations between producer and consumer, that are necessitated by patterns of organization unmediated by any generalized medium of exchange and measure of value.

Differentiating exchange relationships from the diffuse ascribed matrix requires first the institutionalization of patterns governing the field of contract (in the broad sociological sense of the term). To a point, this can proceed independently of money, as a set of expectations of the conditions under which ad hoc agreements can be made. The extent of a contractual system is, however, greatly dependent on the development and acceptance of the medium itself; hence they can be discussed together. Money, as an institutional phenomenon, may be regarded as a special case of the institutionalization of contract.

As noted, the institution of contract consists in a complex of norms independent of the ad hoc content of any particular agreements. The complex is based on some concept of the societal interest in the kinds of contractual agreements that are and can be made, including the kinds that must be prohibited—such as, in our society, any contract infringing the personal freedoms of any individuals, including the contracting parties themselves. From this central focus, rules are defined about the content of permitted and prohibited contracts, with the means for securing the other party's assent either sanctioned or prohibited—i.e., the prohibition of fraud and coercion—and for unforeseen consequences, since the essence of the contractual relation is that rights and obligations must extend over a period of time.

From this point of view, money is a special kind of generalization of such a system of expectations. It advances one step beyond institutionalizing barter, by setting up a system of rules saying that, independent of any specific commitments from any specific contracting parties, the expectations of an as yet undefined set of contractural relations can be formulated, concerned with the expectation that suppliers of potentially wanted goods or services will, over a range of suppliers of the same object and also of types of object, be ready to purvey them in exchange for money. Furthermore, the expectation is that this probability is not specifically limited to any particular time or to any particular terms of exchange.

Two primary sets of problems are concerned with the institutionalization of contract and money. One of these involves regulating the basis for settling terms in cases where there is no ascribed basis on which it is understood that this must occur. The other set concerns the "prior" questions of the terms on which exchangeables will be available for disposal on any terms, or of various sorts of ad hoc arrangement.

The earliest development of markets is, understandably, limited to tangible physical goods. The simplest case is one where the goods "just happen" to be available; that is, where the process of their exchange is not associated with any specific orientation of production to the prospect of exchange. Possibilities under these assumptions are severely limited, and the really important cases are associated with production for the market, i.e., in the expectation of exchanging products for money. Such a situation implies a ramified *system* of markets, since accepting money in exchange for products is meaningful only if it can be spent advantageously in markets other than the one in which it was received.

The more mobile the physical object is, the more readily it can become an object of market exchange. Limiting cases in this respect are land, and permanent fixtures, like buildings and other improvements, which are physically inseparable from land. The fixed position of land and buildings means, in general, that they are involved in a diffuse matrix of relationships making their segregation for purposes of exchange difficult. Alienability of land is likely to be a late development in economic evolution; various kinds of tenancy arrangements are common much earlier. They must fit into a variety of patterns of more or less diffuse solidarity; in many respects, they are thus parallel to relations of employment. The modern type of tenancy, almost purely an arrangement to permit utilization of land and permanent fixtures without other involvements, is nearly as late a development as alienability of land itself.

*Property and Money*. The general problem of the conditions under which physical objects are available for market transactions is very closely associated with that of the institutionalization of property. Probably no society is almost completely lacking in institutionalized rights of individual property in "personal possessions," such as clothing, trinkets, some tools, weapons, ritual objects, etc. These and the most immediate products of the individual's own labor are presumably the most easily marketable commodities. There is, however, a range, from these objects in the direction of those of greater general importance or of greater fixity. Land is at the extreme in the latter respect; and "private" property in land—by whose virtue its uses and tenancy may be prescribed and its ownership may be freely alienated (and bequeathed)—is generally a product of late stages of development. The final result of this general process of differentiating property rights from the diffuse matrix is the institution of ownership, in which the rights of use, control, and disposal or alienation are brought together in the same hands, thereby maximizing the disposability of the physical object and its uses as a mobile resource.[12]

Two other special cases besides land should be discussed briefly. First, the human individual is in one major aspect a physical object, and rights in him may, to a greater or lesser extent, be assimilated to the general pattern of ownership of physical objects. The extreme of this institution is chattel slavery. It has played an important part in certain phases of economic development, especially in classical antiquity and in the relations of the early modern West with colonial areas. It implies a particularly strong accentuation of the bureaucratic type of authority over individuals; and it is an inherently unstable type, because it conflicts with the complex dealing with the importance of the individual's motivational commitment to autonomous role-performance. Weber was right in emphasizing the importance of the institutionalization of "formally free" labor as the paramount "human" factor of production.

The second special case is money. The essential point here is the relation of money to the general category of commodities. Until recently, most economists have considered that money should be treated as a special class of commodity. Today this is an unrealistic view; money is essentially a mechanism of a specialized type of communication, with respect to which the "medium" is relatively indifferent. This situation is the result of a long and complex evolution. The monetary metals have, historically, been valued in their own right as well as in their capacities as media of exchange—significantly, an important part of this valuation has had a "ritual" basis. As the myth of Midas shows, gold cannot be eaten—and, though it can be worn, this is more as a decoration than a matter of "utility." The monetary metals have, as commodities, been prestige symbols much more than utilitarian objects.

The very human aspect of the monetary problem is the concrete variability of pieces of money as physical objects: the problems of standardizing alloy content and weights of individual coins, the problem of clipping, and the like. It was difficult to arrive at the point where the unit of money unequivocally became a symbolic abstraction, whose most adequate expression was a set of notations on a piece of paper—and the still later form, the entry in an account book. Only when this point is reached is the differentiation of money from the general run of commodities complete. And only after the completion of this differentiation can money assume its place as the central controlling apex of the general system of property—the abstract unit which is the equivalent of a unit of economic valuation of *any* commodity or service.

*The Alienability of Human Services*. The above discussion has deliberately concentrated on physi-

12. This statement, like many others in this essay, should not be taken without qualification. Thus, with special reference to land, it seems probable, as indicated in the selection from Pollock and Maitland below, that English law was more favorable to economic development than was Continental law at the time, in spite of the fact that Continental law had adopted more fully the Roman institution of ownership, particularly in land. There seems, however, to be little doubt that in the long run the single ownership is the most favorable to high mobility of productive facilities, which is the central point at issue here.

cal objects as the negotiables of market exchange. There is, however, a second major category, namely, the services of human beings. The problem of institutionalizing the marketing of human services has involved far greater difficulties than the marketing of physical objects, because of considerations of time and context. The sale and purchase of a commodity can be completed in a single transaction, leaving no continuing concern. A "contract of employment," on the other hand, establishes a continuing relationship, between employer and employee, at least until the service contracted for is completed. This relationship is necessarily part of a larger social system and cannot be isolated in the same sense that the usual commodity transaction is isolated. (The case of land as physical object approaches closest to service, because the plot of land remains an object of human evaluation almost indefinitely and cannot be abstracted from a larger context.)

To a limited extent, human services can be purveyed in a labor market on a relatively ad hoc basis. To a somewhat greater extent, they can be specifically oriented to such a market without disturbing the context of solidary relations within which the individual worker is embedded—notably, his household. But in a larger sense, although ownership of a particular commodity can be merely transferred from one subsystem of the society to another, in the case of employment the worker must maintain a *continuing* balanced set of involvements both in the collectivities which "produce" him, *and* in the one (or more) which utilizes his services. Typically, human services establish a *solidary* relation between provider and consumer of the service—whether the latter be an individual, as in fee-for-service professional practice, or a collectivity, as in the more usual category of the contract of employment. The "alienation" of labor presents a quite different order of functional problem in social systems than does the alienation of commodities. The alienation of land is, as noted, in some respects an intermediate case.

*Mobility of the Factors of Production.* Related to the above line of analysis, though not identical with it, is the distinction between access, through the market mechanism, to "consumables," whether they be commodities or services, and to the factors of production. This is much involved with the problem of the extent to which the *producing* unit can become differentiated in its orientation to economic considerations.

This essential process has two aspects. Negatively, it is the process of differentiation—of resources as factors of production becoming sufficiently emancipated from the diffuse nexus to be mobilized through the market mechanism. For commodities as physical objects, this concerns extending what, in the technical economic sense, has been called the "capitalistic" method of production, i.e., the production of many goods which then become instruments of further production. Raw materials thus are produced by special enterprises for the markets on which they are bought—perhaps through a series of intermediaries—by manufacturers. Producing plant and equipment become specialized industries.

The more serious problems concern the element of human service, on both an individual level and an organizational one. The general pattern of the process of differentiation from the bottom is that of the specialization of *collective* segmental units of the social structure in one or another field of economic production. That is, *kinship units* become the units of production for the market; as such, they become mobile factors of production. One of the most familiar examples is that of peasant agriculture. There, the combination of subsistence-orientation and manorial payments in kind and service, in a local setting of diffuse solidarity, gives way to production for a more impersonal market, initially very often in a nearby urban community, then possibly spreading to more distant markets requiring merchant mediation.

It is highly important that the main framework of organization tends to remain embedded in the kinship nexus for so long. This is exemplified in the family firm, the dominant type of organization for economic production in "classical" capitalism. It involves re-directing the whole kinship unit, generally in terms emphasizing continuity over an indefinite series of generations, in the direction of economic function. Family property and firm property are not differentiated, and positions of leadership and authority in the producing organization are ascribed on a kinship basis. From this point of view, the classical entrepreneur may be regarded mostly as the founder of a family enterprise who expects it to be continued under the direction of his heirs. Only in a highly qualified sense is this an "individual" occupational role.

In this general process of development, the early approaches to the occupational type tend to come at or near the bottom of the hierarchy. Labor roles, not technical or managerial roles, are first institutionalized on this basis, involving the differentiation of the organizational setting of work, regulated through the contract of employment, from the household and its various concerns, including premises, property interests, etc.[13] As the scale of organization and the involvement of higher levels of technical competence increase, the occupational role type spreads upward. In the Western world, it has only in the past fifty years reached the managerial levels on a large scale.[14] It has been dependent on a sufficiently extensive occupational system so that failure in business did not necessarily mean a loss of fundamental social status.

The above are the barest essentials of the process by which differentiated economic organization, oriented to the market, may be considered to develop from a diffuse nexus independently of political organization. A concomitant process is the differentiation of types of productive unit by industries—a matter of more interest to the economist and economic historian than to the sociologist. One major aspect of this differentiation concerns the stages in the productive process as it becomes more elaborate and more "capitalistic." Such differentiation necessitates more transportation, more specialization in marketing functions, etc. Thus shipping, canals, railways, etc., become very important.

Another fundamental basis of differentiation is functional in the more purely economic sense. The complex of arrangements concerned with financing assume a central place. The extension of time periods involved, and the lack of direct contact between producers at various stages and the ultimate consumers, necessitate such arrangements. Specialized financial agencies develop, especially in insurance and banking, and the fundamental phenomenon of credit emerges. It is particularly important that banking becomes involved with the constitution of the monetary system itself. Banking and credit constitute the principal paths for emancipating money from its origins in the category of commodities.

It is thus probably more than a quaint historical accident that English banking seems to have originated, at least partially, in the activities of the London goldsmiths. Gold was a semi-sacred symbol of high status, as manifested by, e.g., the requirement that a royal crown be made of gold. It was very difficult to substitute "worthless" promises for this crucial commodity as a circulating medium. The function of the goldsmiths as custodians of gold for safekeeping seems to have been a particularly important step in the process—after all, the gold was not being abandoned as the "real" money; it was being protected against risk of loss. It was not a very great additional step for the goldsmiths to lend on the security of gold holdings, thus issuing credit against which a reserve was held. Even so, Schumpeter was fond of suggesting that banking originated in "crime"—in making available to borrowers what in fact did not "belong" to the lender.

In any case, the invention of credit was a fundamental step in the evolution of economic institutions; it meant the definitive emancipation of the allocation of fluid resources that could operate through the communication of mutual expectations alone. Money became more than the medium of exchange of classic theory; it was, in the form of expandable credit, the primary mechanism for facilitating investment, that is, of autonomous development of economic production.

Finally, the processes of mobilizing the factor of organization within the collective unit—in this case, the firm—through making its managerial functions occupational, must be articulated with processes in the structuring of the organizational environment in which these units operate. Since, in the context presently relevant, these are "independent" units and are not incorporated in larger collectivities, the most essential part of this environment consists in the institutionalized norms to which their operations are subject. This returns us to the institutions of contract, property, and occupation or employment discussed at the beginning of our treatment of the division of labor and economic production. In the structure of the society, the focus of these norms is found in the legal system.

## *Law and Economic Autonomy*

The civilizations in which ramified differentiation of economic function has developed on the basis of private enterprise have been those in which relatively firm and specialized legal systems have also existed. Commercial development reached a relatively high point in Roman society in the late Republic and the Empire. This was made possible largely by the systematization of Roman Law, especially the *jus gentium* mediating the relations of ethnically distinct groups. Then, with the European

13. A very illuminating analysis of the stages and process by which this differentiation can take place, from "domestic" or "putting-out" forms of organization, has been given by Neil J. Smelser, in *Social Change in the Industrial Revolution, 1780–1840* (Chicago: University of Chicago Press, 1959).

14. It is important to note that the Marxian picture of the structure of capitalism is asymmetrical in this respect. Against the occupationally "alienated" labor class, it sets the bourgeoisie, composed of owning-managing kinship groups. The generalization of the occupational role-type to the whole structure (economic "bureaucracy," in Weber's sense) and the virtual disappearance of kinship as a basis of control of the larger business firms, has occurred in the "capitalistic" world without the revolution postulated as necessary by Marx. A rather sketchy analysis of the process of differentiation at the top, with special reference to American industry, is given in Parsons and Smelser, *Economy and Society,* Chapter V.

economic revival that followed the Middle Ages, economic development coincided broadly with the revival of Roman Law and, in England, the development of the Common Law. Private enterprise could develop only within a framework of legal order which above all could protect enterprise against ad hoc political interventions.[15]

It is highly important that the development of these legal systems was by no means a simple function of the business groups' economic interests. One important aspect of their development was the role of relatively autonomous legal professions which were, to a significant degree, independent of *both* political authority and business interest.

The above discussion has been concerned with the process of differentiation "from the bottom up," i.e., essentially independent of the main political-religious leading elements and the more tightly organized collectivity structures under their control. There has also been a process of differentiation from the top down. Probably the most important has been utilizing political bureaucracy, as discussed above, for public works of considerable economic significance for the society as a whole, like irrigation systems, canals, etc. Using the Roman Legions to build the famous Roman roads is another important example. Where political organization itself has been decentralized, as in more or less feudal types of society the same kind of phenomena could occur in smaller-scale, local units of government. On occasion, such enterprises could be oriented to market systems—as when members of the landed nobility in late medieval or early modern Europe engaged in mining.

These developments have been very important in furthering the mobility of resources—particularly human services, through occupational types of role; but, perhaps even more frequently, in some form of requisitioning or serfdom. However, a central difficulty has generally prevented the process of differentiation starting from this point from going through to a full conclusion. This difficulty involves the differentiation of the economic component from the controlling political structure itself. This, in turn, is concerned with the controlling effects of the power interests of political groups, which cause predisposition to shorter-run interests.

For reasons associated with these considerations, the greatest economic "break-through" of all, the Industrial Revolution, did not occur in one of the highly "bureaucratized" early empires like China, Egypt, or Assyria-Babylonia. It is probably significant that the Industrial Revolution did not occur even in the mercantilist France of Louis XIV, which in certain respects was considerably more "advanced" than England; it occurred in England, which, by Continental standards, had a much more rudimentary governmental administrative system. But crucial sectors of England's population had the ethic of ascetic Protestantism; and England had a particularly favorable system of law, as well as a sea-faring tradition and hence access to distant markets and sources of material.

(Parenthetically, it may be remarked that innovation of the most radical kind of economic development is probably independent of the guidance of collective authority—indeed, flourishes best when institutionally protected against such authority. This probably applies just as much to radical cultural developments, particularly to science. This will be discussed more fully in the Introduction to Part Four.)

Though the initial development of industrialization is most favored in a setting of "free enterprise" within a legal order, it does not follow that, once the model is in existence, the same is true of its diffusion to other societies. The process by which the pattern of industrialization has spread from its British point of origin shows a substantially larger participation of political authority in the cases of "imitation." This was true both of Continental Europe and of the United States, and even more, outside this area, for Japan and still more the Soviet Union. A large component of political participation seems very much the rule in this process in the underdeveloped areas today.[16]

## SOCIAL STRATIFICATION

The final topic to be discussed here is the one placed in the middle of our classification series, that of social stratification with special reference to its relation to the problems of the integration of societies. In our initial discussion of the classification we noted that a good deal of social theory has held that this was the primary focus of integrative strain in societies. We do not believe that matters

15. A vivid example of the economic consequences of such intervention is pre-communist China, where no enterprise could survive without specific political "protection."

16. Further discussion of these problems is found in "Some Reflections on the Institutional Framework of Economic Development," *The Challenge of Development* (Jerusalem: Hebrew University, 1958), and "The Principal Characteristics of Industrial Societies," in *The Transformation of Russian Society Since 1861* (ed., C. E. Black; Cambridge: Harvard University Press, 1960). Both are reprinted in Parsons, *Structure and Process in Modern Society* (Glencoe, Ill.: Free Press, 1959). I am also greatly indebted to Professor David S. Landes, of the University of California (Berkeley), for much stimulating insight in this field.

are quite so simple; but this idea is a convenient point of departure.

First, in systems of social interaction tendencies toward polarization are definitely present, on a very general basis. Almost any source of conflict can become a focus around which opposing parties choose sides and draw less directly involved elements into the conflict. Then the premium on effectiveness presents an incentive to resort to progressively more drastic means of promoting one's own interest—the resort to the use of physical force is the ultimate result of this vicious circle.

Second, a strong tendency exists, particularly in the early stages of structural differentiation, toward developing polarization internally along a hierarchical axis. As noted, this focuses most on two problems: the problem of political leadership, and the problem of legitimation in the society with reference to its religion-based values. In general, these two functional references are fused together in the establishment of a politico-religious elite which is set up over the "masses" of the society. When such a process of differentiation (possibly originating in conquest) has begun, it is extremely likely that it will result in (or originate in) the bifurcation of the structure of ascriptive solidarity in the society, in that the elite groups will consist in kinship units, and not in "individuals"—the individual's status remains primarily ascribed. Furthermore, the economic organization is likely to be one where the great bulk of economic production is dispersed in highly segmented ascribed units of the peasant agriculture variety. In this case, the elite groups are usually in a position to claim an important share of the proceeds, both because of the general high prestige of their station, reinforced by legitimation, and because of political power. Hence, in terms of consumption, they are usually far wealthier than the masses. Political centralization, however, usually results in various types of bureaucratically organized enterprises and public works; the relatively centralized political authority controls a disproportionate share of the factors of production.

We are outlining a polarized society whose hierarchical dimension of stratification involves all the other four major bases or organization of social structure. The superior groups are superior on every count—legitimized prestige; political power; control of economic resources; and the prestige of the ascribed solidarities themselves, especially kinship, but sometimes generalized on an ethnic basis. It follows that there are approximations to this pattern on many different levels of structural development. In spite of considerably complicating factors, this was true of the peasantry-gentry structure of classical Chinese society; of the upper- and lower-class differentiation that appeared, in a number of different forms, in classical antiquity; and of eighteenth- and nineteenth-century Western Europe, where the rising bourgeoisie tended to ally and partially amalgamate themselves with the older hereditary aristocracies while, lower down, the humbler rural groups (generally, the "peasants,") tended to become allied with the urban and industrial "working classes."

Perhaps the most pervasive common factor in these tendencies to polarization is the involvement of kinship units as such; upper- or lower-class status is then the status of kinship units involving both sexes and all ages—though considerable mobility between the classes may be possible. However, it must be remembered that the kinship structure itself is not a constant. There has been a historic trend to whittle down the size of kinship units, in the general direction of isolating the nuclear family. In general, in cases where the dichotomy of the class structure is more advanced, the significant units have been lineages which spanned several generations, and not "families" in the modern sense.

*Polarization* vs. *Differentiation.* These considerations suggest, however, that there are tendencies toward invalidating the concept of a simple one-dimensional scale of stratification that could be polarized into a dichotomous antagonism or "class struggle" at a convenient "cutting point." We have already mentioned the most important points of departure for such processes of differentiation.

*Religious Autonomy and Stratification: Four Cases.* Let us consider the principal types already reviewed from this point of view: first, the differentiation, focusing at or near the top of the power structure, of political from religious bases of autonomous organization. Regarded from the religious side first, the most important consideration concerns ways by which religious developments have occurred that would establish bases of high valuation of strata independent of the politico-religious fusion; and would also shake up some of religion's traditionist stereotyping influence on the higher-status structure, thus facilitating political innovation.

Without leading to a major differentiation between "church" and "state" at the collectivity level, this has occurred to an important degree in a number of historical cases, most clearly in those associated with the developments underlying the "world religions." The problem of the nature and type of law as a generalized normative system is intimately involved in them.

In China, the general religious ferment—of

which Taoism and Confucianism were the nearly contemporary outcomes—was a source of a major loosening of the Chou pattern of social structure. By this structure, a kind of religio-political feudalism, tempered with a limited "patrimonial" level of bureaucracy, had become established on a river-valley basis. The Taoist wing of the religious movement led away from the institutionalization of any form of social responsibility; its only direct structural outcome was the establishment of rather unstable types of monastic collectivities and temple priesthoods. It must, however, have had a very important influence in freeing important higher-level population groups from unquestioned allegiance to the older order.

The Confucian wing of the religious movement became the positive source of a pattern of restructuring the society. The Confucians' general integrative doctrine began to set the tone for the society as a whole; they made an orderly polity under a morally responsible dynasty legitimate—with the Confucian priests, as Mandarin officials, assuming the main governing responsibility. On this basis, there was a tendency toward a consolidation of the special Chinese version of the two-class system, since under the Confucian definition of the system there was only one basic type of "superiority," that embodied in the socially responsible scholar-official. To state an apparent paradox: it was an extraordinary case of the "rationalization of traditionalism."

In India, religious autonomy reinforced traditionalism much more radically. Buddhism, at least in its earlier versions, was in this respect like Taoism, though it seems to have been more radical. Salvation lay in complete rejection of all worldly interests—including any kind of social responsibility. The only possible positive social organization sanctioned by Buddhism was the monastic community, composed of fellow-seekers of salvation. In relation to the general society, Buddhism's effect was mostly negative, since it tended to withdraw religious sanction from *any* sort of temporal social organization, including caste.

This problem probably underlay the bifurcation of the major Indian religious tradition into its Hindu and Buddhist streams, and led eventually to the virtual elimination of Buddhism from India. Hinduism took another path, sanctioning the traditional society as the base of departure for the quest for individual salvation. The Brahman priesthood, as the custodians of the historic religious tradition and of the main basis of legitimation of the social order, functioned to uphold consistently a traditional social order, in the most conservative sense. He who felt qualified might, with the Brahmans' positive encouragement, embark on the radical search for personal salvation—but only in the Buddhist manner, by renouncing all worldly responsibilities and interests.

The compromise between the two essential components of the Hindu tradition is expressed in the doctrine of the stages of life. According to this, the individual should spend part of his life fulfilling the traditional obligations of his social status. But later, typically when he has a mature son to take over these obligations, he should renounce the world and seek salvation. In a sense far more radical than that applying to Confucianism, Hinduism renounced any interest in exerting leverage over society on the basis of religious values. Thus the Indian conception of salvation was far more radical than China's—but its extreme otherworldliness meant, in one crucial context, a more drastic positive sanctioning of traditionalism.

In the ancient Greek and Semitic worlds, things were very different. The Greek movement developed in terms of a pattern of rationalization of the immanent order of the world, including the social world. In general, it did not break the fusion of religious and political components; but it made several new processes of differentiation possible. Culturally it laid the foundations of all subsequent Western philosophy and science—the foundations of what eventually became a main framework of secular culture. On a more direct social level it was, as noted, the major source of political democracy, and, in its Roman extension, of an independent, largely secularized legal system.

The keynote of the Greek contribution was a mode of rationalization very different from the Chinese, which could develop a dynamism independent of the structure of the given society. Under the conditions of antiquity, the spread of political democracy seemed inherently limited. But Greek secular culture and the Roman politico-legal system eventually permeated what for that time was an immense population, with an immense diversity of ethnic origins and character, and welded these into a relatively stable society. This society still retained the broad two-class pattern of stratification, but had an immensely greater range of diversification of components with varying characteristics. In religion, it was a "free" society in a sense that had not applied to any other historical case, and would not again be applicable until very modern times. One of its important features was its provisions of a ground in which a movement like Christianity could spread; it also contributed essential ingredients to it.

In the Semitic world, the most extreme source of religious leverage over social development originated—transcendental monotheism as institutionalized in Judaism, Christianity, and Islam. Christianity was to be the sole independent source of a very fundamental pattern of structural differentiation, the differentiation of church and state, that came to its first fruition within the framework of a generally Christian society only in the European Middle Ages and has undergone a series of complex developments since then.

Though this process of differentiation did not occur independently in either Judaism or Islam, in both movements the special emphasis on religion, and its character as stressing the commandments of a transcendental God, caused the high status and high sophistication of a class of experts in religious law. This is certainly one of the most important sources of a specialized commitment to intellectual values in the history of culture, besides the Indian religious intellectualism and the intellectualism originating in Greece.

*Secular Elite Groups.* In Christianity, perhaps the most important consequence of the differentiation of church and state was that it allowed the development of secular elite groups who did not have to, or could not, base the legitimation of their status on religious qualifications. Legitimation in relation to religious *values* was necessary; but this is very different from qualification for the performance of religious functions as such. This development, combined with the dynamism inherent in the Semitic type of religious transcendentalism, constituted a major impetus to the dynamic development of secular society independent of the traditionalizing influence which, in the long run, seems inherent in the fusion of religious and secular leadership.

Initially, the secular elite would necessarily be political, in a diffuse sense. But with the further development of secular society, other foci of differentiation could assume a prominent position—the foci based on legal as distinct from political competence and functions, on secular intellectual competence, and on functions in economic production.

*Legal Professionalism.* As noted above, legal experts emerged as a specialized elite group in the later history of Rome—for the first time in history, on a clearly secular basis. This model was fundamental to the re-emergence of Roman Law in post-medieval Europe. On the Continent, two important developments of partial differentiation occurred. The Catholic Church itself became an elaborately differentiated and rationalized system, whose most important aspects included the technical development of the Canon Law, heavily influenced by Roman Law. Within the Church, there were specialists in Canon Law. Though religiously committed, these specialists were in a very different category from the ordinary priest, whose primary functions were sacramental and pastoral, or the Bishop, with his directly administrative functions. In the secular world, however, the legally trained expert civil servant eventually occupied a special place in the structure of the emerging territorial state. There was a virtual fusion of the higher administrative bureaucracy and one main branch of the legal profession. The revival of Roman Law in a secular context, in the Italian universities first, established a crucial connection between a branch of secular learning, the legal system, and the structure of governmental organization.

Law's independence from government, became most fully developed in England, which established patterns for the English-speaking world and beyond. The Continental type of civil service developed late in England, and when developed, it was largely dissociated from legal professionalism. The legal profession became established as an independent entity much earlier in England than on the Continent, and has a firm monopoly of access to judicial office, and its own corporate control of the bar through the Inns of Court. In contrast with this development on the Continent, in England it occurred essentially independently of the universities. In Europe generally, and particularly in England, the legal profession thus became a secular element of great consequence in social affairs—it was not a simple branch or organ of central political authority.

*Bureaucratic Elites.* Of the two more specifically political components of differentiation and hence of potential elite status, the bureaucratic is usually the first to develop a relative independence; it then divides into two branches, military and civil. In these terms, it is extremely difficult to establish and institutionalize a basis of independent elite status—independent above all of the central basis of political organization at the top level. The primary limitation here rests on what Weber called the problem of legitimation in a system of rational-legal authority.

The military is probably more problematical than the civil. This is concerned with the facts that (1) the use of physical force is itself in general ethically problematical; and (2) in most societies, war cannot be presumed a normal state of affairs, and therefore a military force necessarily spends a large part of the time not doing what it is trained to do. In many societies, activation of military forces is widely interpreted as a disastrous breakdown of normal order.

There is, perhaps, no major component of social structure that has such an ambiguous status. Societies often depend greatly on their military organization; and this dependence is peculiarly dramatic because of the emergency character and high immediate stakes of war. Command of organized force is often a crucial factor in the internal balance of a society, the more so the more unstable the society's balance is in other respects. Therefore, the military components tend to occupy a prominent, if not a dominant, place in political elites. On the other hand, there are problems: first, a particularly acute problem of legitimation; and second, the severe limitations of functional orientation to other problems in the society. As Weber indicated, from many points of view, notably the economic, war is specifically "irrational." These reasons probably cause the rarity of fully "professional" military forces in history, even at the officer level; and they probably underlie the strong tendency for military status to fuse with general hereditary upper-class status. This fusion has been prominent in medieval and post-medieval European history, where a military role was often a generally ascribed role of the male aristocrat. The connection has lasted, until very recent times, in the concept that an officer was a "gentleman" in the specific aristocratic sense.

In certain circumstances, this fusion could give the whole upper class a strongly militaristic cast. Japan, through a good deal of its history, and Prussia provide prominent examples of this. However, the fusion can also act as a strong brake on the militarization of the state. Early modern England, favored by her insular position, provides a good example of this. In the non-militaristic direction, the most important alternative to military professionalization has been treating the military role on an "amateur" basis, as a simple aspect of citizenship. A classic instance of this is the military organization of the Greek *polis;* in this case Sparta could become, as a political organization, virtually a professional army—but a very special kind of one. This militia pattern was also important in the American colonies.

Making high civil bureaucracies legitimate has posed a somewhat parallel problem. The moral problems are not so acute; but civil bureaucracy does not possess the dramatic possibilities of the military, nor can it seize control in emergency situations. These weaknesses are rooted in its primarily instrumental character, as symbolized by the concept of the civil "servant." Hence the articulation of civil bureaucracy with the top level of political structure has always been highly problematical. In general it has, therefore, been associated with "fusions," such as that of the Chinese Mandarins with gentry status, or the English method of honoring the highest civil servants with knighthoods and other titles, in some sense and to some degree thus assimilating them to the aristocracy. If the civil servant were not originally a "gentleman," by being sufficiently successful he could eventually become one. Civil service's connection with legal training on the Continent was another example of this fusion. In general, an extensive civil service built up on a relatively strict "occupational" basis can be a major stable component of the upper political structure only when it is part of a much more extensive occupational system. This condition has been fulfilled only in the modern West, in very recent times.

*Politicians.* Politically elite elements based mainly on leadership in the democratic type of politics have emerged into prominence only in the modern West. This phenomenon appeared on a very small scale in Greece and Rome, but it was never very fully dissociated from ascribed class status, and it still proved unstable. To some degree, it re-emerged in the Italian city-states and in northern Europe during the Renaissance; but its big development occurred only in the late eighteenth and the nineteenth centuries in the West. Here the problem of legitimation is severe, because it is inseparable from the concept of "party," and hence contributes to *division* within the political community while purporting to serve it and its integration. The most successful examples seem to be the British (including the Dominions), the Scandinavian-Dutch, and the American. The first two have solved the dilemma by differentiating between an institutionalized sovereign who is above party, and a politically responsible government dependent on party backing. In America, the place of the sovereign is occupied by the written Constitution, which is held in equal sanctity.

Modern political democracy, especially in reference to its leadership component, is precarious and cannot be expected to operate without favoring conditions. In the British and Scandinavian cases, these conditions include the civil service's partial fusion with the aristocracy, along with the British custom of elevating prominent politicians to the Peerage, whatever their party affiliation or social origin. In America, the most important condition is probably the vast extension of the upper occupational system and the associated cushion of private wealth, which mean that any prominent politician usually can, in case of political difficulty, find "jobs" of acceptable status. In both systems, the legal profession is a special case. A large number of politicians—particularly members of Parliament, of Congress, and of state legislatures—are lawyers. This is caused by the lawyer's special "expertness" in politics, and by the fact that a legal practice can be conducted relatively easily on a part-time basis—an individual can neglect it and then resume it, leaving its conducting to his partners while he is otherwise engaged. This is a functional equivalent of the *Honoratiorenherrschaft,* which Weber considered important and which is by no means dead today.

The "breakdown," or reversion, of modern political democracy in the totalitarian (as distinguished from the "legitimist") direction seems related to the strains of differentiating a "politician" elite from other elite components. This eases the strains involved in openly institutionalized division and factionalism, but does so at the expense of driving the conflicts of interest, and their underlying orientation, underground. In this situation, the totalitarian party, because of the urgency of its problem of legitimation, tends to assume at least a quasi-religious status. Relative to the general process of differentiation under analysis, it represents at least a partial "de-differentiation."

*Secular Cultural Elites.* Another important kind of differentiation focusing near the top of the status hierarchy is the one centering about the role of secular intellectual and aesthetic culture. In an important sense, in the Western world the element of rational theology, derived largely from Greece, contains at least the seeds of this differentiation. Thus in the medieval Church, theology and Scholastic philosophy, originally almost indistinguishable from each other, each became the basis of a specialized professional group, distinct from the Church hierarchy's sacramental and administrative functions. To a certain degree, the same was applicable to the semi-independence of Canon Law within the Church.

The origins of the Western university are associated with the relative secularization of philosophy and letters, oriented particularly to the classical heritage, and with secular law. In general, the universities included theology, but in a separate faculty. Then they added medicine; and as the natural sciences emerged, they could find a place. The problems of the independence of universities, and of various types of private scholars and artists, have been subtle and difficult, with the patterning taking many forms. In certain cases, emancipation from Church control meant only falling under the control of political authority. Another important pattern is patronage by noblemen. But by and large, whatever the source of economic support, the general trend has been toward establishing a complex of mostly autonomous professional groups definitely belonging to the upper social strata, though usually not to the hereditary aristocracy. After about 1850, with the development of science to a position of major social importance, this has become one of the few major points of reference for the organization of the general system of social stratification.

There has always been an important connection between some order of formal education and the conduct of the leadership functions in the society as a whole. In earlier phases, the main foci of learning have been in groups of religious specialists—even the Confucian literati can be counted in this category, if one recognizes that they were also a political elite. The classical intellectual traditions disseminated literary culture to an extent unattained by any prior civilization; and its revival in the Renaissance established one major cultural foundation of Western society. But in the nineteenth century, with the advent of social and political democracy and the development of science, for the first time in history general literacy and increasingly higher levels of mass education appeared. The university system constitutes the main institutionalized focus of trusteeship of this great development of secular knowledge and learning. It is perhaps the most important structural component of modern societies that had no direct counterpart in earlier types of society.

The institutionalization of intellectual culture includes both "pure" scholars and scientists, and also the applied professions. The oldest of these are theology and law; medicine emerges quite early, in spite of the deficiencies in its scientific base. In the earlier stages even of the Industrial Revolution, most technological innovation—to say nothing of routine administration of processes—was in the hands of "inventors" who were not scientifically, often not even academically, trained. During the last two generations, however, these modes of competence have converged; and with this convergence has come the enormously increased practical importance of personnel with high intellectual training, especially in the sciences. Recently, in an unmistakably significant way, this has begun to be extended to the disciplines dealing scientifically with human behavior and social relationships.

*The Business Class: Entrepreneurship and Management.* The last of the primary bases of differentiation that enters importantly into the structure of stratification systems is the economic. As noted, the economic base, as an independent focus, on a large scale, has been a late development, and it has come mainly from "below." Its operation as a mass phenomenon forming a major independent focus of the social structure is confined to the modern West. In terms of economic structure as such, the crucial focus is the extension of "private enterprise" into the field of manufacturing, as distinguished both from commerce and from primary or "extractive" production.

It is essential to distinguish two main phases of the process, each having quite different consequences for stratification. The first phase is the emergence in manufacturing of "family firm" capitalism—where, though the main "labor force" was composed of "employees" standing in widely varying modes of relation to their employers, the ownership and managerial functions were fused in a kinship unit, in which status was, once the firm had been "founded," definitely ascriptive. It was a kind of petty monarchy, flanked by a hereditary aristocracy, within its own little sphere. Because of the common organization in lineage terms, members of the bourgeois class fitted, in this area, into a pattern which was structurally isomorphic with that of the aristocracies already occupying the top positions of prestige in their own societies. Consequently, there was powerful ambition to secure acceptance as aristocratic lineages; and through much of Europe, a good deal of actual fusion of these two population elements did occur. This was probably most successful in England, but the strong focus on it was most persistent in France.[17] This structural pattern obviously bears on the plausibility of treating the Western class system after the Industrial Revolution on a polarized basis.

This situation has been fundamentally changed by the "occupationalizing" of the management of economic production. As noted, managerial functions have been dissociated from the property interests of owning groups—particularly tightly held property complexes. Concomitantly, a managerial class has developed whose status is not dependent on a personal property stake in the enterprise nor on an ascribed position in an owning lineage. Business administration has become a career line, comparable to civil service or a profession. In close association with this development, a much larger contingent of professional experts occupying more strategic positions than ever before have become involved in industrial and governmental bureaucracies. The role of lawyers is relatively old in both connections, though its importance has increased. The roles of engineers, and more lately of research scientists, on any comparable scale, are a relatively recent development. In the United States, and increasingly in Western Europe, the main control of productive wealth through kinship lineage, which was a continuation from the feudal background of the Western class system, has, for practical purposes, been broken for the pace-setting large business element of the economy.

In terms of social stratification, this has meant a shift from an upper group, primarily organized about the prestige of kinship lineages, to one primarily organized about occupational status. Since the family remains the primary unit of class structure, continuity of status between adjacent generations is a very important factor. But the link to the *particular* organizational unit of production has largely been broken; and, especially if there is general expansion, and hence considerable upward mobility. The system of formal education has been becoming increasingly significant as the major channel of this mobility.

*Occupational Differentiation and Stratification.* For the higher-level structures of the stratification system, the fact that the occupational system itself has become so highly differentiated in its upper levels is most important. A complex network of upper "groups" (which it is somewhat dangerous to reify) has developed. There are the great organizations—in civil and military government; in business with many different branches; in education, science, and research; in health care; and in religion. In addition, *cross-cutting* the differentiation of organizations, there is occupational differentiation between executives and administrators, the various types of professional people at levels dealing with science and learning as such and with many different applied fields. There are politicians and promoters of many kinds of causes, including organizers of associations. It is certainly a stratified society; but it no longer has anything like a unitary elite based on lineages, on wealth, on political power, or on monopoly of religious legitimation.

A crucial development has also occurred in the lower levels of the stratification system—the great historic dichotomy between urban lower classes and peasantry has been virtually eliminated. Only 10 per cent of the labor force is engaged in agriculture now in the United States—one of the greatest of all agricultural societies. Furthermore, agriculture itself has become much more assimiliated to the rest of economic production; it is no longer anything approaching a "peasant" type of production. The whole lower range of the social structure has become urbanized and, in a very broad sense, "industrialized"—but definitely *not,* in the Marx-

17. The concept that the driving motive of the entrepreneur was to establish a "family dynasty" has been perhaps most forcefully put forward by Schumpeter in *Capitalism, Socialism and Democracy,* N.Y. & London: Harper & Bros., 1942. For an illuminating analysis of an earlier phase see Elinor Barber, *The Bourgeoisie in Eighteenth-Century France,* Princeton Univ. Press, 1955, also Jesse R. Pitts, "The Bourgeois Family and French Economic Retardation," Ph.D thesis, Harvard Univ., 1958.

ian sense, "proletarianized." The proportion of the population engaged in industrial labor (narrowly defined) has declined; and there has been an enormous development of the "tertiary" sector of the economy. Even more important, the lower fringe of the early industrial labor role has been almost eliminated by the general upgrading process, in which mechanization and education have played primary parts.

Modern industrial society has, probably for the first time in the history of complex societies, developed a situation making simple polarization of the social structure in terms of the opposing interests of generalized upper and lower groups impossible. Ironically, the most modern version of a theory of radical two-class conflict became prominent just at the time when a social structure to which this theory was drastically inapplicable began to develop. The appeal of radical Marxism has been in roughly inverse proportion to the level of industrialization of the society in question—exactly the contrary of Marx's own prediction.

The irony can be carried a step farther. Various observers have noted that, in certain structural respects, there were a series of characteristics common to all industrial societies—both the capitalist or free enterprise type of the West, and the socialist type of the Soviet Union. These characteristics especially concern the occupational structure, in the sense just outlined, and particularly the development of an occupational managerial class and of a class of professional technical experts in many different fields. The important difference between the two types of society concerns the relation of the economy to the political structure, and the latter's character. In the West the problems are the stability of political democracy, and the legal and normative maintenance of the relative independence of economic organization from government. Both these structural patterns are deeply rooted in the long-run evolutionary trends of social development.

In the U.S.S.R., the primary problem concerns the long-run status of the Communist Party—can this quasi-religious structure remain differentiated from the "state" and still maintain a very tight control over it? This question involves both the status of religion (in the more analytical sense), and the possibilities of relaxing control in the direction of political democratization. The major problem is closely linked to the latter—it is the question of bases of genuine autonomy, relative to both party and state, of non-political spheres of organization; notably both of the economy, and of the professions and the services in which they are involved. At present, the most acute focus of tendencies to seek this type of autonomy is the "intellectuals"—in what sense may science and the arts be treated as the simple handmaidens of the Party?

In the long run (though perhaps not in the near future), we feel that the pressures to genuine structural differentiation in the upper levels may well be irresistible—though it is difficult to anticipate the exact ways this differentiation can occur. In any case, in the present, Western "capitalism" cannot be described in Marxian terms as a two-class society; nor can Soviet society be described as a one-class society, least of all if that one class is claimed to be the "proletariat." Each society has been becoming progressively more highly differentiated, in two ways: in terms of the number of levels in a scale of stratification; and, more important, in terms of a cross-cutting web of relations of the *qualitative* differentiation of collectivities and role-types that must be integrated with each other by mechanisms other than the simple maintenance of hierarchical control. This differentiation is most important in the higher strata. Concepts like hierarchical polarization, and the differentiation of the "masses" from "power-elites" and from controllers of capital are not adequate for analyzing the integration of such a society.

## CONCLUSION

The above outline of comparative social structure has been sketched from a frankly evolutionary frame of reference. We have taken the concept of ascriptive solidarities as not merely designating one structural type, but as a broad evolutionary base line. In the process, old ascriptive solidarities are "whittled away," and in a wide variety of ways, new ones are created—e.g., those of feudalism, which are certainly not primitive, and of such structures as the Communist party. However, the *relative* importance of ascriptive solidarity tends to decline, though the process is uneven and reversions are common—the fall of the Roman Empire was such a reversion, and on the largest scale.

Within this framework, there are two keynotes of the evolutionary process. One is the very broad leadership role of innovation in the field of cultural orientation. In earlier stages of innovation, this leadership is usually carried by a diffuse religio-political elite. But a critically important phenomenon is the emergence of the type of autonomous religious orientation which is in a position to exert generalized leverage on the development of a society or complex of societies. The

Semitic religious complex provides the grandest-scale example of this.

A very important innovating role can be played by other types of structural component—especially by the political, as it is differentiated from the religious, the legal, the non-religious aspects of culture (notably science), and the economic. Our broad conviction, however, is that the primary significance of these latter components lies in the context of differentiation, rather than in the context of the broadest leadership of structural innovation, i.e., at the level of values.

We are concerned with differentiation in the structure of the society as a system. We presume a multiple origin of human societies, or at least great dispersion of small units which became socially, culturally, and biologically segmented or differentiated from one another. Partly because of independent origins, partly because of fissions and amalgamations, a variety of societies have existed in the world at any one time, in widely varying degrees and modes of contact with each other. But there has been a process of differentiation within societies as well as among them. We have attempted to outline the place of the principal elements in each of the five main categories of our classification of selections in terms of their relation to various aspects and phases of that process.

In outlining these relations, we have tried to work on intermediate ground. With a great deal more work than has gone into this introductory essay, it might have been possible to attempt a far more strictly systematic morphological analysis than that presented here. Such an analysis would have started from the broad conceptual scheme of the social system presented in the second essay of the General Introduction, and then attempted to work it through in the relevant contexts. But this would have been a very onerous task; and it would have involved departing much farther from the level of the selections which follow, and would have made their mutual relevance difficult for the reader to see.

On the other hand, the selections themselves do not contain any single consistent morphological scheme. Such a scheme did not exist in the generation when these selections were written—though Weber had made great advances toward one. Hence it has seemed advisable to attempt to be as systematic and consistent as possible without attempting to be rigorously formal. Our purpose is to present, as a guide to the interpretation of the selections, a general picture consistent both with the best theory we have and with the present level of empirical knowledge, but to do so without the complex paraphernalia of a highly technical and detailed analytical procedure.

There will be a very brief Foreword to each of the five sections of selections below. These are meant to give the reader a general guide to the nature of the selections, and to explain why they were chosen and organized as they are.

# *Section A*

# Ascriptive Solidarities

EDITORIAL FOREWORD

# Ascriptive Solidarities

*by Talcott Parsons*

As observed in the introduction to this Part of the Reader, the analysis of ascriptive solidarities is the point of departure for the treatment of the structure of social systems with which we are concerned. The importance of these reference points has always been known and appreciated. Until the generation with which we are concerned, however, they had received very little of the kind of attention which can be a source of genuinely technical analysis—though we are including selections from two authors of an earlier period, Morgan and Maine, who laid important foundations for such analysis.

The two major foci of the problem are biological relatedness as the ascriptive basis of kinship structure, and the territorial location of persons and their activities. These foci converge at the concept of residence. Because of limitations on the technology of communication and transportation, the earlier the society's stage of evolution, the more closely its territorial organization is bound to the residential locations and distribution of populations.

The most important development of the structural analysis of kinship occurred after the period most represented in these volumes. The leaders were the group of British social anthropologists, and a few others, like Levy-Strauss in France. We have included only a few samples of the most important contributions to initiating this development. Morgan may be regarded as the founder of the technical analysis of kinship. He was the first to consider seriously the problems presented by the existence of kinship systems differing radically from those taken for granted in the intellectual traditions of the Western world. These differing systems were presented to him in material on American Indians but were also becoming recognized as widely distributed among non-literate societies in many parts of the world.

Kroeber's famous paper on classificatory systems brought Morgan up to date by purging him of many associations with now untenable evolutionary ideas, and relating the problem to the growing body of research, in which Kroeber himself played a prominent part. Certainly, in American anthropology Kroeber's paper was the major starting point of truly modern analysis of kinship.

Malinowski's paper is selected partly because of Malinowski's general importance in this field.[1] But it is included particularly because of his contribution to recognizing the importance of the broadest type of pattern of descent, apart from "classificatory" components as such, contrasting violently with the common sense of Western social studies, namely, matrilineal descent. By the latter part of the generation concerned, this problem had become a central preoccupation of the analysis of kinship systems in general.

That generation's contribution in this field culminated in the work of Radcliffe-Brown. Though it was written after our terminal point, we would have liked to include his classic Introduction to the volume *African Systems of Kinship and Marriage* (London: Oxford University Press, 1950). Because of its length and the impossibility of making a meaningful selection from it, we have reluctantly included instead an earlier statement, taken from *Structure and Function in Primitive Society*. No other writer of the period reached a level of general analysis in the kinship field comparable with Radcliffe-Brown's.

1. See Meyer Fortes, "Malinowski and the Study of Kinship," in Raymond Firth (ed.), *Man and Culture* (London: Routledge, Kegan & Paul, 1957).

Max Weber was not an expert in the analysis of kinship. His major interests were in a different set of aspects of the structure of social systems. In spite of this, however, he was unusually sensitive to the importance of kinship problems. A brief selection from his work is included here, for this reason, and also because it is one of the best works written in that generation on the significance of the household as a residential unit, linking kinship with territorial location. This is a theme of great importance, which Murdock has probably most fully developed so far. It should receive increasing attention in the future.

We have treated ethnic solidarity as an extension of the reference point of kinship. Though it is a very important theme in social analyses, there have been few attempts to treat it in really general terms. We have selected, from a very large and diffuse literature bearing on the subject, only two samples—a brief selection from Weber that belongs in a very general comparative setting, and one from the late Louis Wirth that deals with the problem in recent phases of development of American society. Because the available space here is so limited, only a token recognition of the importance of the problem was possible.

The subject of primary groups is included here, not because they are in the strict sense ascriptive in structural focus, but because of the direct psychological continuity between kinship and all other primary group structures. The keynote is the base in social structure for the individual's psychological security. In all societies, this security is rooted in the kinship system, especially the nuclear family—first of orientation, then of procreation. In the process of social differentiation, however, it can be generalized from this base to non-kin groups.

The selections relevant in this area illustrate a variety of this type of possibilities. Cooley's famous general statement that introduced the concept of the primary group into sociology is the inevitable starting point. Simmel's essay on secrecy indicates the importance of the ways in which primary groups erect barriers to communication with outsiders and thereby protect their internal solidarity. For Simmel, secrecy shades into important problems of privileged communication and privacy. Schmalenbach was one of the first to analyze the importance of "fraternal" groupings, e.g., "brotherhoods" of various kinds and the one-sex peer group. In certain respects, they may be described as deriving, by affective generalization, from the sibling relationship.

Later research has been particularly concerned with the importance of these types of relation in the area ordinarily associated with Toennies' *Gesellschaft*. The Western Electric studies made at the very end of that generation present a classic instance of the development of primary groups within modern occupational contexts under the heading of "informal organization." Durkheim's famous Introduction to the second edition of his *Division of Labor* proposes that principles somehow related to this context may be extended to larger units of social solidarity. The more general theoretical problems associated with personal security and its relation to the personality's regressive substructures will be discussed more fully in Part Three; and the way they fit the analysis of social structure will be discussed in the Introductions to that and its subsections.

The last subsection of Section A concerns the territorial reference point of ascriptive solidarity. Its relation to the residence of the household unit of kinship was recognized in Section A, Subsection I, fifth selection—Weber's statement. This is taken for granted. The importance of a wider territorial principle in primitive societies has, however, been widely neglected. Lowie, in the *Origin of the State,* was one of the first to indicate clearly the importance of this principle—even in that prototype of primitiveness, the Australian society. Then Sir Henry Maine, through his studies in India, was one of the first to emphasize the village community's importance as a general pattern of social organization oriented to a territorial base. Weber, far more than any other writer, has helped to clarify the problems of the nature of urban communities on a comparative basis. The two last selections deal with the higher-order integration of populations in politically organized societies with reference to territoriality—these selections are Marc Bloch's classic delineation of this aspect of European feudalism, and Lord Acton's famous discussion of the nationality principle.

The connection between the territorial principle and the general field of political organization and jurisdiction is of paramouut importance. The last subsection of Section A should be regarded as leading into the materials of Section D, on Political Organization and Authority. Their connection will be discussed again in the Introduction to Section D.

## I–KINSHIP

# 1. *Systems of Consanguinity*

BY LEWIS H. MORGAN

IN CONSIDERING the elements of a system of consanguinity the existence of marriage between single pairs must be assumed. Marriage forms the basis of relationships. In the progress of the inquiry it may become necessary to consider a system with this basis fluctuating, and, perhaps, altogether wanting. The alternative assumption of each may be essential to include all the elements of the subject in its practical relations. The natural and necessary connection of *consanguinei* with each other would be the same in both cases; but with this difference, that in the former the lines of descent from parent to child would be known, while in the latter they would, to a greater or less extent, be incapable of ascertainment. These considerations might affect the form of the system of consanguinity.

The family relationships are as ancient as the *family*. They exist in virtue of the law of derivation, which is expressed by the perpetuation of the species through the marriage relation. A system of consanguinity, which is founded upon a community of blood, is but the formal expression and recognition of these relationships. Around every person there is a circle or group of kindred of which such person is the centre, the *Ego*, from whom the degree of the relationship is reckoned, and to whom the relationship itself returns. Above him are his father and his mother and their ascendants, below him are his children and their descendants; while upon either side are his brothers and sisters and their descendants, and the brothers and sisters of his father and of his mother and their descendants, as well as a much greater number of collateral relatives descended from common ancestors still more remote. To him they are nearer in degree than other individuals of the nation at large. A formal arrangement of the more immediate blood kindred into lines of descent, with the adoption of some method to distinguish one relative from another, and to express the value of the relationship, would be one of the earliest acts of human intelligence.

Should the inquiry be made how far nature suggests a uniform method or plan for the discrimination of the several relationships, and for the arrangement of kindred into distinct lines of descent, the answer would be difficult, unless it was first assumed that marriage between single pairs had always existed, thus rendering definite the lines of parentage. With this point established, or assumed, a natural system, numerical in its character, will be found underlying any form which man may contrive; and which, resting upon an ordinance of nature, is both universal and unchangeable. All of the descendants of an original pair, through intermediate pairs, stand to each other in fixed degrees of proximity, the nearness or remoteness of which is a mere matter of computation. If we ascend from ancestor to ancestor in the lineal line, and again descend through the several collateral lines until the widening circle of kindred circumscribes millions of the living and the dead, all of these individuals, in virtue of their descent from common ancestors, are bound to the "*Ego*" by the chain of consanguinity.

The blood relationships, to which specific terms have been assigned, under the system of the Aryan family, are few in number. They are grandfather and grandmother, father and mother, brother and sister, son and daughter, grandson and granddaughter, uncle and aunt, nephew and niece, and cousin. Those more remote in degree are described either by an augmentation or by a combination of these terms. After these are the affineal or marriage relationships, which are husband and wife, father-in-law and mother-in-law, son-in-law and daughter-in-law, brother-in-law and sister-in-law, step-father and step-mother, step-son and step-daughter, and step-brother and step-sister; together

Reprinted from Lewis H. Morgan, *Systems of Consanguinity and Affinity* ("Smithsonian Contributions to Knowledge," Vol. XVII [Washington, D.C.: Smithsonian Institute, 1870]), Part I, chap. ii, pp. 10–11; Part III, chap. vi, pp. 470–72.

with such of the husbands and wives of blood relatives as receive the corresponding designation by courtesy. These terms are barely sufficient to indicate specifically the nearest relationships, leaving much the largest number to be described by a combination of terms.

So familiar are these ancient household words, and the relationships which they indicate, that a classification of kindred by means of them, according to their degrees of nearness, would seem to be not only a simple undertaking, but, when completed, to contain nothing of interest beyond its adaptation to answer a necessary want. But, since these specific terms are entirely inadequate to designate a person's kindred, they contain in themselves only the minor part of the system. An arrangement into lines, with descriptive phrases to designate such relatives as fall without the specific terms, becomes necessary to its completion. In the mode of arrangement and of description diversities may exist. Every system of consanguinity must be able to ascend and descend in the lineal line through several degrees from any given person, and to specify the relationship of each to *Ego;* and also from the lineal, to enter the several collateral lines and follow and describe the collateral relatives through several generations. When spread out in detail and examined, every scheme of consanguinity and affinity will be found to rest upon definite ideas, and to be framed, so far as it contains any plan, with reference to particular ends. In fine, a system of relationship, originating in necessity, is a domestic institution, which serves to organize a family by the bond of consanguinity. As such it possesses a degree of vitality and a power of self-perpetuation commensurate with its nearness to the primary wants of man.

* * *

Do these systems of relationship rest upon and embody clearly defined ideas and principles; and do they contain the essential requisites of a domestic institution?

Some method of distinguishing the different degrees of consanguinity is an absolute necessity for the daily purposes of life. The invention of terms to express the primary relationships, namely, those for father and mother, brother and sister, son and daughter, and husband and wife, would probably be one of the earliest acts of human speech. With these terms all of the remaining relatives, both by blood and marriage, may be described by using the possessive case of the several terms. The Erse and Gaelic systems were never carried beyond this stage. After a descriptive system was adopted it would have a form, a method of distinguishing relatives one from another, and, as a consequence, an arrangement of kindred into lines of descent. The application of this method involves a series of conceptions which become, at the same time, clothed with definite forms. If this simple plan of consanguinity became permanently introduced into practical use, its transmission, through a few generations, would convert it into an indurated system capable of resisting radical innovations. The Erse and Gaelic are illustrations in point. The ideas embodied are few in number, but their association in fixed relations creates a system, as well as organizes a family. In its connection with the family, and in its structure as a system, its power of self-perpetuation resides. By these considerations it is raised to the rank of a domestic institution.

The invention of terms for collateral relationships must of necessity have been extremely difficult under the descriptive system. This is shown by the present condition of these forms in the several Aryan and Semitic nations, none of which developed their system far beyond the Erse. In process of time the relationship of paternal and maternal *uncle* and *aunt* might be turned from the descriptive into the concrete form by the invention of special terms, making each of the four distinct. This is the extent of the advance made in the Arabic and Hebraic forms. The discrimination of the relationships of *nephew* and *niece* in the concrete would be still more difficult, since it involves a generalization of the children of an individual's brothers and sisters into one class, and the turning of two descriptive phrases into a single concrete term with a masculine and feminine form. These relationships, as now used, were reached among such of the Aryan nations as possess them within the modern period. That of *cousin* was still more difficult of attainment, as it involved a generalization of four different classes of persons into a single class, and the invention of a term to express it in the concrete. Amongst the nations of the Aryan family the Roman and the German alone reached this, the ultimate stage of the system. Such of the remaining nations as possess this relationship borrowed it, with the term, from the Roman source; and it is probable that the Germans derived the conception from the same quarter, although their term was indigenous in the German speech. These terms were designed to relieve the inconvenience of the descriptive method as far as they applied. In so far as they were founded upon generalizations they failed, with some exceptions, to indicate with accuracy the manner of the relationships; whence it became necessary to resort to explanatory words, or to the descriptive method, to be specific. These considerations tend still further to show the stability of the system as a domestic institution, although the ideas which it embodies are limited in number.

In marked contrast with the *descriptive* is the *classificatory* system, which is complex in its structure, elaborate in its discriminations, and opulent in its nomenclature. A very different and more striking series of ideas and principles here present themselves, without any existing causes adequate for their interpretation or explanation. With marriage between single pairs, with the family in a modified sense, with the tribal organization still unimpaired in certain nations and abandoned in others, with polygamy, polyandria and the Hawaiian custom either unknown or of limited practice, and with promiscuous intercourse substantially eradicated, the classificatory system of relationship still exists in full vigor in a large portion of the human family, ages upon ages after the sequence of customs and institutions in which it apparently originated have ceased to exercise any influence upon its form or upon its preservation. This system as it now stands is seen to magnify the bond of consanguinity into stupendous proportions, and to use it as an organic instrument for the formation of a communal family upon the broadest scale of numbers. Differences in the degree of nearness are made to yield to the overmastering strength of the kindred tie. Its generalizations traverse the natural lines of descent, as they now exist through the marriage of single pairs, disregard equalities in the degree of nearness of related persons, and create relationships in contravention of those actually existing. There are upwards of twenty of these particulars, each of which develops a distinct idea, all uniting in the formation of a coherent intelligible and systematic plan of consanguinity. From the excessive and intricate specializations embodied in the system it might be considered difficult of practical use; but it is not the least singular of its characteristics that it is complicated without obscurity, diversified without confusion, and understood and applied with the utmost facility. With such a number of distinct ideas associated together in definite relations, a system has been created which must be regarded as a domestic institution in the highest sense of this expression. No other can properly characterize a structure the framework of which is so complete, and the details of which are so rigorously adjusted.

## 2. *Classificatory Systems of Relationship*

BY ALFRED L. KROEBER

THE DISTINCTION between classificatory and descriptive systems of relationship has been widely accepted, and has found its way into handbooks and general literature. According to the prevalent belief the systems of certain nations or languages group together distinct relationships and call them by one name, and are therefore classifying. Other systems of consanguinity are said to indicate secondary differences of relationship by descriptive epithets added to their primary terms and to be therefore descriptive.

Nothing can be more fallacious than this common view. A moment's reflection is sufficient to show that every language groups together under single designations many distinct degrees and kinds of relationship. Our word brother includes both the older and the younger brother and the brother of a man and of a woman. It therefore embraces or classifies four relationships. The English word cousin denotes both men and women cousins; cousins on the father's or on the mother's side; cousins descended from the parent's brother or the parent's sister; cousins respectively older or younger than one's self, or whose parents are respectively older or younger than the speaker's parents; and cousins of men or women. Thirty-two different relationships are therefore denoted by this one English word. If the term is not strictly limited to the significance of first cousin, the number of distinct ideas that it is capable of expressing is many times thirty-two. Since then it is not only primitive people that classify or fail to distinguish relationships, the suspicion is justified that the current distinction between the two classes or systems of indicating rela-

Reprinted from Alfred L. Kroeber, *The Nature of Culture* (Chicago: University of Chicago Press, 1952), sec. 19, pp. 175–81, with the permission of the University of Chicago Press. 

tionship is subjective, and has its origin in the point of view of investigators, who, on approaching foreign languages, have been impressed with their failure to discriminate certain relationships between which the languages of civilized Europe distinguish, and who, in the enthusiasm of formulating general theories from such facts, have forgotten that their own languages are filled with entirely analogous groupings or classifications which custom has made so familiar and natural that they are not felt as such.

The total number of different relationships which can be distinguished is very large, and reaches at least many hundred. No language possesses different terms for all of these or even for any considerable proportion of them. In one sense it is obvious that a language must be more classificatory as the number of its terms of relationship is smaller. The number of theoretically possible relationships remaining constant, there must be more ideas grouped under one term in proportion as the number of terms is less. Following the accepted understanding of what constitutes classificatory consanguinity, English, with its twenty terms of relationship, must be not less but more classificatory than the languages of all primitive people who happen to possess twenty-five, thirty, or more terms.

It is clear that if the phrase classificatory consanguinity is to have any meaning it must be sought in some more discriminating way. The single fact that another people group together various relationships which our language distinguishes does not make their system classificatory. If there is a general and fundamental difference between the systems of relationship of civilized and uncivilized people, its basis must be looked for in something more exact than the rough-and-ready expressions of subjective point of view that have been customary.

It is apparent that what we should try to deal with is not the hundreds or thousands of slightly varying relationships that are expressed or can be expressed by the various languages of man, but the principles or categories of relationship which underlie these. Eight such categories are discernible.

1. *The Difference between Persons of the Same and of Separate Generations.*—The distinctions between father and grandfather, between uncle and cousin, and between a person and his father, involve the recognition of this category.

2. *The Difference between Lineal and Collateral Relationship.*—When the father and the father's brother are distinguished, this category is operative. When only one term is employed for brother and cousin, it is inoperative.

3. *Difference of Age within One Generation.*—The frequent distinction between the older and the younger brother is an instance. In English this category is not operative.

4. *The Sex of the Relative.*—This distinction is carried out so consistently by English, the one exception being the foreign word cousin, that the discrimination is likely to appear self-evident. By many people, however, many relationships are not distinguished for sex. Grandfather and grandmother, brother-in-law and sister-in-law, father-in-law and mother-in-law, and even such close relationships as son and daughter, are expressed respectively by single words.

5. *The Sex of the Speaker.*—Unrepresented in English and most European languages, this category is well known to be of importance in many other languages. The father, mother, brother, sister, and more distant relatives may receive one designation from a man and another from his sister.

6. *The Sex of the Person through Whom Relationship Exists.*—English does not express this category. In consequence we frequently find it necessary to explain whether an uncle is a father's or a mother's brother, and whether a grandmother is paternal or maternal.

7. *The Distinction of Blood Relatives from Connections by Marriage.*—While this distinction is commonly expressed by most languages, there are occasional lapses; just as in familiar English speech the father-in-law is often spoken of as father. Not strictly within the domain of relationship, but analogous to the occasional failure to express this category, is the frequent ignoring on the part of primitive people of the difference between actual relatives and fictitious clan or tribal relatives.

8. *The Condition of Life of the Person through Whom Relationship Exists.*—The relationship may be either of blood or by marriage; the person serving as the bond of relationship may be alive or dead, married or no longer married. Many North American Indians refrain from using such terms as "father-in-law" and "mother-in-law" after the wife's death or separation. Some go so far as to possess terms restricted to such severed relationship. It is natural that the uncle's relation to his orphaned nephew should tend to be somewhat different from his relation to the same boy while his natural protector, his father, was living. Distinct terms are therefore sometimes found for relatives of the uncle and aunt group after the death of a parent.

The adjoined table indicates the representation of the eight categories, and the degree to which they find expression, respectively in English and in several of the Indian languages of North America.

It appears that English gives expression to only four categories. With the exception, however, of the one and foreign word cousin, every term in Eng-

| | ENGLISH | N.A. INDIAN | | | | | CALIFORNIA INDIAN | | | | | | |
|---|---|---|---|---|---|---|---|---|---|---|---|---|---|
| | | Arapaho | Dakota | Pawnee | Skokomish | Chinook | Yuki | Pomo | Washo | Miwok | Yokuts | Luiseño | Mohave |
| No. of terms | 21* | 20 | 31 | 19 | 18 | 28 | 24 | 27 | 28 | 24 | 28 | 34 | 35 |
| Generation | 21 | 20 | 31 | 11 | 13 | 23 | 24 | 21 | 27 | 24 | 22 | 30 | 26 |
| Blood or marriage | 21 | 19 | 31 | 17 | 18 | 26 | 24 | 27 | 28 | 24 | 28 | 32 | 34 |
| Lineal or collateral | 21 | 10 | 20 | 5 | 11 | 25 | 24 | 21 | 28 | 18 | 26 | 34 | 28 |
| Sex of relative | 20 | 18 | 29 | 17 | 2 | 12 | 16 | 21 | 20 | 20 | 17 | 18 | 22 |
| Sex of connecting relative | 0 | 6 | 6 | 2 | 0 | 20 | 13 | 13 | 14 | 10 | 14 | 19 | 21 |
| Sex of speaker | 0 | 3 | 18 | 4 | 0 | 15 | 3 | 3 | 10 | 2 | 12 | 10 | 14 |
| Age in generation | 0 | 3 | 7 | 2 | 2 | 2 | 3 | 4 | 4 | 4 | 4 | 12 | 8 |
| Condition of connecting relative | 0 | 0 | 0 | 0 | 8 | 1 | 0 | 0 | 0 | 0 | † | 0 | 1 |

* All terms are omitted, such as great-grandfather, great-uncle, and second cousin, which are not generally used in ordinary speech and exist principally as a reserve available for specific discrimination on occasion.

† Terms denoting relatives by marriage undergo a vocalic change to indicate the death of the connecting relative.

lish involves the recognition of each of these four categories. All the Indian languages express from six to eight categories. Almost all of them recognize seven. But in all the Indian languages the majority of the categories occurring are expressed in only part of the terms of relationship found in the language. There are even Indian languages, such as Pawnee and Mohave, in which not a single one of the seven or eight categories finds expression in every term. While in English the degree of recognition which is accorded the represented categories is indicable by a percentage of 100 in all cases but one, when it is 95, in Pawnee corresponding percentages range variously from about 10 to 90, and in Mohave from 5 to 95. All the other Indian languages, as compared with English, closely approach the condition of Pawnee and Mohave.

It is clear that this difference is real and fundamental. English is simple, consistent, and so far as it goes, complete. The Indian systems of relationship all start from a more elaborate basis but carry out their scheme less completely. This is inevitable from the fact that the total number of terms of relationship employed by them is approximately the same as in English. The addition of only one category to those found in English normally doubles the number of terms required to give full expression to the system; and the presence of three additional categories multiplies the possible total by about eight. As the number of terms occurring in any of the Indian languages under consideration is not much more than half greater than in English, and sometimes is not greater at all, it is clear that at least some of their categories must find only very partial expression.

In short, as far as the expression of possible categories is concerned, English is less complete than any of the Indian languages; but as regards the giving of expression to the categories which it recognizes, English is more complete. In potentiality, the English scheme is poorer and simpler; but from its own point of view it is both more complete and more consistent. As English may evidently be taken as representative of European languages, it is in this point that the real difference is to be found between the systems that have been called classificatory and those that have been called descriptive.

The so-called descriptive systems express a small number of categories of relationship completely; the wrongly-named classificatory systems express a larger number of categories with less regularity. Judged from its own point of view, English is the less classificatory; looked at from the Indian point of view it is the more classificatory, inasmuch as in every one of its terms it fails to recognize certain distinctions often made in other languages; regarded from a general and comparative point of view, neither system is more or less classificatory.

In short, the prevalent idea of the classificatory system breaks down entirely under analysis. And in so far as there is a fundamental difference between the languages of European and of less civilized peoples in the method of denoting relationship, the difference can be determined only on the basis of the categories described and can be best expressed in terms of the categories.

A tendency toward reciprocal expression is sometimes of importance and may influence the degree to which categories are given expression. Reciprocal terms are such that all the persons included in the relationship expressed by one term call by one name all the persons who apply this term to them. In the most extreme form of reciprocity the two groups of relatives use the same term. The paternal grandparents call their sons' children, whether boys or girls, by the same term which these children, both boys and girls, apply to their fathers' parents. Nevertheless, the reciprocal relation is just as clear, though less strikingly expressed, when each of the groups uses a different term for the other. Our English words father and child, or brother and sister, are not reciprocal, for the term child is employed also by the mother, and brother is used by the brother as well as by the sister. In fact the only reciprocal term in English is cousin. The tendency toward reciprocal expression is developed in many Indian languages. It is particularly strong in California. In some languages this tendency has brought it about that different categories are involved in the terms applied to a pair of mutual relationships. The term father's sister indicates the sex of the relative but not of the speaker. The exact reciprocal of father's sister is woman's brother's child. This term, however, does not recognize the sex of the relative indicated, but does imply the sex of the speaker. The two reciprocal terms therefore each involve a category which the other does not express. If the same categories were represented in the two terms, brother's daughter would correspond to father's sister and exact reciprocity would be impossible. When, therefore, the terms found are father's sister and woman's brother's child, it is clear that the tendency toward the establishment of exactly reciprocal terms has been stronger than the feeling favoring the consistent use or neglect of certain categories; in other words, the extent to which certain categories are expressed has been determined by the vigor of the reciprocal tendency.

The categories serve also to indicate the leading characteristics of systems of the same general order. It is obvious, for instance, that the most important difference between Dakota and Arapaho is the strong tendency of the former to recognize the sex of the speaker. Chinook is notable for laying more stress on the sex of the speaker and of the connecting relation than on the sex of the relative—no doubt owing to the fact that the sex of the relative is indicable by purely grammatical means. General differences such as naturally occur between the languages of one region and of another can also be expressed in terms of the categories. All the California systems, for instance, lay much more stress upon the sex of the connecting relative than do any of the Plains languages examined. The Plains systems are conspicuous for their weak development of the distinction between lineal and collateral relationship, this finding expression in two-thirds of all cases in Dakota, half in Arapaho, one-fourth in Pawnee. In seven California languages the corresponding values lie between three-fourths and complete expression. The method can be applied successfully even in the case of smaller and contiguous geographical areas. Of the seven California languages Luiseño and Mohave are spoken in southern California. Their systems show a unity as compared with the systems of the five languages from northern and central California. Both the southern California languages have a greater number of terms; both are stronger in the expression of the categories of the sex of the connecting relative and of age within the same generation; and both are weaker in the category of sex of the relative, than the others. Again, Chinook and Skokomish, both of the North Pacific Coast, are alike in indicating the condition of the connecting relative and in failing, on account of the possession of grammatical sex gender, to distinguish the sex of relatives themselves in many terms of relationship. There is a very deep-going difference between them, however, in the fact that Skokomish is as free as English from recognizing the sex of the speaker and of connecting relatives, while Chinook generally expresses both categories. In short, the categories present a means of comparing systems of terms of relationship along the basic lines of their structure and of expressing their similarities and differences without reference to individual terms or details.

The reason why the vague and unsatisfactory idea of a classificatory system of consanguinity has found such wide acceptance is not to be sought in any primary interest in designations of relationship as such, but in the fact that terms of relationship have usually been regarded principally as material from which conclusions as to the organization of society and conditions of marriage could be inferred. If it had been more clearly recognized that terms of relationship are determined primarily by linguistic factors, and are only occasionally, and then indirectly, affected by social circumstances, it would probably long ago have been generally realized that the difference between descriptive and classificatory systems is subjective and superficial. Nothing is more precarious than the common method of deducing the recent existence of social or marital institutions from a designation of relationship. Even when the social condition agrees perfectly with expressions of relationship, it is unsafe to conclude without corroborative evidence that these expressions are a direct reflection or result of the condition.

In the Dakota language, according to Riggs, there is only one word for grandfather and father-in-law. Following the mode of reasoning sometimes employed, it might be deduced from this that these two relationships were once identical. Worked out to its implications, the absurd conclusion would be that marriage with the mother was once customary among the Sioux.

In the same language the words for woman's male cousin and for woman's brother-in-law have the same radical, differing only in a suffix. Similar reasoning would induce in this case that marriage of cousins was or had been the rule among the Sioux, a social condition utterly opposed to the basic principles of almost all Indian society.

The use of such identical or similar terms for distinct relationships is due to a considerable similarity between the relationships. A woman's male cousin and her brother-in-law are alike in sex, are both of opposite sex from the speaker, are of the same generation as herself, and are both collateral, so that they are similar under four categories. In view of the comparative paucity of terms as compared with possible relationships, it is entirely natural that the same word, or the same stem, should at times be used to denote two relationships having as much in common as these two.

No one would assume that the colloquial habit in modern English of speaking of the brother-in-law as brother implies anything as to form of marriage, for logically the use of the term could only be an indication of sister marriage. It is easily conceivable that in the future development of English the more cumbersome of these two terms might come into complete disuse in daily life and the shorter take its place, without the least change in social or marital conditions.

The causes which determine the formation, choice, and similarities of terms of relationship are primarily linguistic. Whenever it is desired to regard terms of relationship as due to sociological causes and as indicative of social conditions, the burden of proof must be entirely with the propounder of such views.

Even the circumstances that the father's brother is frequently called father is not necessarily due to or connected with the custom of the levirate; nor can group marriage be inferred from the circumstance that there is frequently no other term for mother's sister than mother. A woman and her sister are more alike than a woman and her brother, but the difference is conceptual, in other words linguistic, as well as sociological. It is true that a woman's sister can take her place in innumerable functions and relations in which a brother cannot; and yet a woman and her sister, being of the same sex, agree in one more category of relationship than the same woman and her brother, and are therefore more similar in relationship and more naturally denoted by the same term. There are so many cases where the expression of relationship cannot have been determined by sociological factors and must be purely psychological, as in the instances just discussed, that it is fair to require that the preference be given to the psychological cause, or that this be admitted as of at least equal probability, even in cases where either explanation is theoretically possible and supporting evidence is absent.

On the whole it is inherently very unlikely in any particular case that the use of identical terms for similar relationships can ever be connected with such special customs as the levirate or group marriage. It is a much more conservative view to hold that such forms of linguistic expression and such conditions are both the outcome of the unalterable fact that certain relationships are more similar to one another than others. On the one hand this fact has led to certain sociological institutions; on the other hand, to psychological recognitions and their expression in language. To connect the institutions and the terms causally can rarely be anything but hazardous. It has been an unfortunate characteristic of the anthropology of recent years to seek in a great measure specific causes for specific events, connection between which can be established only through evidence that is subjectively selected. On wider knowledge and freedom from motive it is becoming increasingly apparent that causal explanations of detached anthropological phenomena can be but rarely found in other detached phenomena, and that it is even difficult to specify the most general tendencies that actuate the forms taken by culture as the immediate causes of particular phenomena.

The following conclusions may be drawn:

1. The generally accepted distinction between descriptive and classificatory systems of terms of relationship cannot be supported.

2. Systems of terms of relationship can be properly compared through an examination of the categories of relationship which they involve and of the degree to which they give expression to these categories.

3. The fundamental difference between systems of terms of relationship of Europeans and of American Indians is that the former express a smaller number of categories of relationship than the latter and express them more completely.

4. Terms of relationship reflect psychology, not sociology. They are determined primarily by language and can be utilized for sociological inferences only with extreme caution.

# 3. *The Complex of Mother-Right*

BY BRONISLAW MALINOWSKI

WE HAVE BEEN comparing the two civilizations, the European and the Melanesian, and we have seen that there exist deep differences, some of the forces by which society moulds man's biological nature being essentially dissimilar. Though in each there is a certain latitude given to sexual freedom, and a certain amount of interference with and regulation of the sex instinct, yet in each the incidence of the taboo and the play of sexual liberty within its prescribed bounds are entirely different. There is also a quite dissimilar distribution of authority within the family, and correlated with it a different mode of counting kinship. We have followed in both societies the growth of the average boy or girl under these divergent tribal laws and customs. We have found that at almost every step there are great differences due to the interplay between biological impulse and social rule which sometimes harmonize, sometimes conflict, sometimes lead to a short bliss, sometimes to an inequilibrium fraught, however, with possibilities for a future development. At the final stage of the child's life-history, after it has reached maturity, we have seen its feelings crystallize into a system of sentiments towards the mother, father, brother, sister, and in the Trobriands, the maternal uncle, a system which is typical of each society, and which, in order to adapt ourselves to psycho-analytic terminology, we called the "Family Complex" or the "nuclear complex."

Now allow me to restate briefly the main features of these two "complexes." The Oedipus complex, the system of attitudes typical of our patriarchal society, is formed in early infancy, partly during the transition between the first and second stages of childhood, partly in the course of the latter. So that, towards its end, when the boy is about five or six years old, his attitudes are well formed, though perhaps not finally settled. And these attitudes comprise already a number of elements of hate and suppressed desire. In this, I think, our results do not differ to any extent from those of psycho-analysis. [I have come to realize since the above was written that no orthodox or semi-orthodox psycho-analyst would accept my statement of the "complex," or of any aspect of the doctrine.]

In the matrilineal society at that stage, though the child has developed very definite sentiments towards its father and mother, nothing suppressed, nothing negative, no frustrated desire forms a part of them. Whence arises this difference? As we saw, the social arrangements of the Trobriand matriliny are in almost complete harmony with the biological course of development, while the institution of father-right found in our society crosses and represses a number of natural impulses and inclinations. To trace it more in detail, there is the passionate attachment to the mother, the bodily desire to cling close to her, which in patriarchal institutions is in one way or another broken or interfered with; the influence of our morality, which condemns sexuality in children; the brutality of the father, especially in the lower strata, the atmosphere of his exclusive right to mother and child acting subtly but strongly in the higher strata, the fear felt by the wife of displeasing her husband—all these influences force apart parents and children. Even where the rivalry between father and child for the mother's personal attention is reduced to a minimum, or to naught, there comes, in the second period, a distinct clash of social interests between father and child. The child is an encumbrance and an obstacle to the parental freedom, a reminder of age and decline and, if it is a son, often the menace of a future social rivalry. Thus, over and above the clash of sensuality, there is ample room for social friction between father and child. I say advisedly "child" and not "boy," for, according to our results, the sex difference between the children does not play any great part at this stage, nor has a closer relation between father and daughter as yet made its appearance.

All these forces and influences are absent from the matrilineal society of the Trobriands. First of all—and that has, *bien entendu,* nothing to do with matriliny—there is no condemnation of sex or of sensuality as such, above all, no moral horror at the idea of infantile sexuality. The sensuous clinging of the child to his mother is allowed to take its natural course till it plays itself out and is diverted by other

Reprinted from Bronislaw Malinowski, *Sex and Repression in Savage Society* (New York: Harcourt, Brace & Co.; and London: Kegan Paul, Trench, Trubner & Co., 1927), chap. iv, pp. 74–82, with the permission of Humanities Press, Inc., and Kegan Paul, Trench, Trubner & Co.

bodily interests. The attitude of the father to the child during these two early periods is that of a near friend and helper. At the time when our father makes himself pleasant at best by his entire absence from the nursery, the Trobriand father is first a nurse and then a companion.

The development of pre-sexual life at this stage also differs in Europe and Melanesia; the repressions of the nursery among us, especially in the higher classes, develop a tendency towards clandestine inquisitions into indecent things, especially excretory functions and organs. Among the savages we find no such period. Now this infantile pregenital indecency establishes distinctions between the decent-indecent, the pure-impure, and the indecent, parent-proof compartment reinforces and gives additional depth to the taboo which is suddenly cast over certain relations to the mother, that is to the premature banishment from her bed and bodily embraces.

So that here also the complications of our society are not shared by the children in the Trobriands. At the next stage of sexuality we find a no less relevant difference. In Europe there is a latency period more or less pronounced, which implies a breach of continuity in the sexual development and, according to Freud, serves to reinforce many of our repressions and the general amnesia, and to create many dangers in the normal development of sex. On the other hand, it also represents the triumph of other cultural and social interests over sexuality. Among the savages at this stage, sex in an early genital form—a form almost unknown among ourselves—establishes itself foremost among the child's interests, never to be dislodged again. This, while in many respects it is culturally destructive, helps the gradual and harmonious weaning of the child from the family influences.

With this we have entered already into the second half of the child's development, for the period of sexual latency in our society belongs to this part. When we consider these two later stages which form the second half of the development, we find another profound difference. With us during this early period of puberty, the Oedipus complex, the attitudes of the boy towards his parents, only solidify and crystallize. In Melanesia, on the other hand, it is mainly during this second epoch, in fact almost exclusively then, that any complex is formed. For only at this period is the child submitted to the system of repressions and taboos which begin to mould his nature. To these forces, he responds, partly by adaptation, partly by developing more or less repressed antagonisms and desires, for human nature is not only malleable but also elastic.

The repressing and moulding forces in Melanesia are twofold—the submission to matriarchal tribal law, and the prohibitions of exogamy. The first is brought about by the influence of the mother's brother, who, in appealing to the child's sense of honour, pride and ambition, comes to stand to him in a relation in many respects analogous to that of the father among us. On the other hand, both the efforts which he demands and the rivalry between successor and succeeded introduce the negative elements of jealousy and resentment. Thus an "ambivalent" attitude is formed in which veneration assumes the acknowledged dominant place, while a repressed hatred manifests itself only indirectly.

The second taboo, the prohibition of incest, surrounds the sister, and to a lesser degree other female relatives on the maternal side, as well as clanswomen, with a veil of sexual mystery. Of all this class of women, the sister is the representative to whom the taboo applies most stringently. We noted that this severing taboo, entering the boy's life in infancy, cuts short the incipient tenderness towards his sister which is the natural impulse of a child. This taboo also, since it makes even an accidental contact in sexual matters a crime, causes the thought of the sister to be always present, as well as consistently repressed.

Comparing the two systems of family attitudes briefly, we see that in a patriarchal society, the infantile rivalries and the later social functions introduce into the attitude of father and son, besides mutual attachment, also a certain amount of resentment and dislike. Between mother and son, on the other hand, the premature separation in infancy leaves a deep, unsatisfied craving which, later on, when sexual interests come in, is mixed up in memory with the new bodily longings, and assumes often an erotic character which comes up in dreams and other fantasies. In the Trobriands there is no friction between father and son, and all the infantile craving of the child for its mother is allowed gradually to spend itself in a natural, spontaneous manner. The ambivalent attitude of veneration and dislike is felt between a man and his mother's brother, while the repressed sexual attitude of incestuous temptation can be formed only towards his sister. Applying to each society a terse, though somewhat crude formula, we might say that in the Oedipus complex there is the repressed desire to kill the father and marry the mother, while in the matrilineal society of the Trobriands the wish is to marry the sister and to kill the maternal uncle.

With this, we have summarized the results of our detailed inquiry, and given an answer to the first problem set out at the beginning, that is, we have studied the variation of the nuclear complex with the constitution of the family, and we have shown in what manner the complex depends upon some of the features of family life and sexual morals.

We are indebted to psycho-analysis for the discovery that there exists a typical configuration of sentiments in our society, and for a partial explanation, mainly concerned with sex, as to why such a complex must exist. In the foregoing pages we were able to give an outline of the nuclear complex of another society, a matrilineal one, where it has never been studied before. We found that this complex differs essentially from the patriarchal one, and we have shown why it must differ and what social forces bring it about. We have drawn our comparison on the broadest basis, and, without neglecting sexual factors, we have also systematically drawn in the other elements. The result is important, for, so far, it has never been suspected that another type of nuclear complex might be in existence. By my analysis, I have established that Freud's theories not only roughly correspond to human psychology, but that they follow closely the modification in human nature brought about by various constitutions of society. In other words, I have established a deep correlation between the type of society and the nuclear complex found there. While this is in a sense a confirmation of the main tenet of Freudian psychology, it might compel us to modify certain of its features, or rather to make some of its formulae more elastic. To put it concretely, it appears necessary to draw in more systematically the correlation between biological and social influences; not to assume the universal existence of the Oedipus complex, but in studying every type of civilization, to establish the special complex which pertains to it.

# 4. *The Study of Kinship Systems*

BY A. R. RADCLIFFE-BROWN

## *I*

FOR SEVENTY-FIVE YEARS the subject of kinship has occupied a special and important position in social anthropology. I propose in this address to consider the methods that have been and are being used in that branch of our studies and the kinds of results that we may reasonably expect to arrive at by those methods. I shall consider and compare two methods which I shall speak of as that of conjectural history and that of structural or sociological analysis.

One of these methods was first applied to some social institutions by French and British (mostly Scots) writers of the eighteenth century. It was of this method that Dugald Stewart wrote in 1795: "To this species of philosophical investigation, which has no appropriated name in our language, I shall take the liberty of giving the title of *Theoretical* or *Conjectural History;* an expression which coincides pretty nearly in its meaning with that of *Natural History,* as employed by Mr. Hume (see his *Natural History of Religion*), and with what some French writers have called *Histoire Raisonnée.*" I shall accept Dugald Stewart's suggestion and shall use the name "conjectural history."

The method of conjectural history is used in a number of different ways. One is to attempt to base on general considerations, on what Dugald Stewart calls "known principles of human nature," conjectures as to first beginnings—of political society (Hobbes), of language (Adam Smith), of religion (Tylor), of the family (Westermarck), and so on. Sometimes an attempt is made to deal with the whole course of development of human society, as in the works of Morgan, Father Schmidt and Elliot Smith. Sometimes we are offered a conjectural history of the development of a particular institution, as in Robertson Smith's treatment of sacrifice. The special form of the method with which we shall be concerned in what follows is the attempt to explain a particular feature of one or more social systems by a hypothesis as to how it came into existence.

An early example of the method of conjectural history applied to kinship is to be found in the essay on *Primitive Marriage* published by John F. M'Lennan in 1865. You will remember the two principal theses put forward in that book: the origin of the custom of exogamy from marriage by capture, and

Reprinted from A. R. Radcliffe-Brown, *Structure and Function in Primitive Society* (Gencoe, Ill.: The Free Press, 1952), chap. iii, pp. 49–89, with the permission of The Free Press.

the proposition that "the most ancient system in which the idea of blood relationship was embodied was a system of kinship through females only." Six years later there appeared *The Systems of Consanguinity and Affinity* of Lewis Morgan, a monument of scholarly, patient research in the collection of data, to be followed in 1877 by his *Ancient Society,* in which he offered a conjectural outline history of the whole course of social development. These works of M'Lennan and Morgan were followed by a considerable mass of literature, which has continued to be produced down to the present day, in which the method of conjectural history has been applied in different forms to various features of kinship organisation.

As I think you know, I regard the pursuit of this method as one of the chief obstacles to the development of a scientific theory of human society. But my position has often been misunderstood. My objection to conjectural history is not that it is historical, but that it is conjectural. History shows us how certain events or changes in the past have led to certain other events or conditions, and thus reveals human life in a particular region of the world as a chain of connected happenings. But it can do this only when there is direct evidence for both the preceding and succeeding events or conditions and also some actual evidence of their interconnection. In conjectural history we have direct knowledge about a state of affairs existing at a certain time and place, without any adequate knowledge of the preceding conditions and events, about which we are therefore reduced to making conjectures. To establish any probability for such conjectures we should need to have a knowledge of laws of social development which we certainly do not possess and to which I do not think we shall ever attain.

My own study of kinship began in 1904 under Rivers, when I was his first and at that time his only student in social anthropology, having for three years previously studied psychology under him. I owe a great deal to that contact with Rivers, and more rather than less because from the outset it appeared that we disagreed on the subject of method. For Rivers followed the method of conjectural history, at first under the influence of Morgan, and later in the form of what he called ethnological analysis, as exemplified in his *History of Melanesian Society* (1914*a*). But in his field work Rivers had discovered and revealed to others the importance of the investigation of the behaviour of relatives to one another as a means of understanding a system of kinship. In what follows I shall be criticising one side of Rivers' work, but the position I now hold is the one I held in my friendly discussions with him during a period of ten years, ending in an agreement to go on disagreeing. My esteem for Rivers as man, as teacher, and as scientist, is in no way diminished by the fact that I find myself obliged to criticise adversely his use of the method of conjectural history.

At the outset it is necessary to give a definition. I shall use the term "kinship system" as short for a system of kinship and marriage or kinship and affinity. It is a pity that there is no inclusive term in English for all relationships which result from the existence of the family and marriage. It would be very tiresome to speak all the time of a system of kinship and affinity. I hope, therefore, that my use of the term will be accepted. It need not lead to ambiguity.

The unit of structure from which a kinship system is built up is the group which I call an "elementary family," consisting of a man and his wife and their child or children, whether they are living together or not. A childless married couple does not constitute a family in this sense. Children may be acquired, and thus made members of an elementary family, by adoption as well as by birth. We must also recognise the existence of compound families. In a polygynous family there is only one husband with two or more wives and their respective children. Another form of compound family is produced in monogamous societies by a second marriage, giving rise to what we call step-relationships and such relationships as that of half-brothers. Compound families can be regarded as formed of elementary families with a common member.

The existence of the elementary family creates three special kinds of social relationship, that between parent and child, that between children of the same parents (siblings), and that between husband and wife as parents of the same child or children. A person is born or adopted into a family in which he or she is son or daughter and brother or sister. When a man marries and has children he now belongs to a second elementary family, in which he is husband and father. This interlocking of elementary families creates a network of what I shall call, for lack of any better term, genealogical relations, spreading out indefinitely.

The three relationships that exist within the elementary family constitute what I call the first order. Relationships of the second order are those which depend on the connection of two elementary families through a common member, and are such as father's father, mother's brother, wife's sister, and so on. In the third order are such as father's brother's son and mother's brother's wife. Thus we can trace, if we have genealogical information, relationships of the fourth, fifth or *n*th order. In any given society a certain number of these relationships are recognised for social purposes, i.e. they have attached to them certain rights and duties, or certain distinctive modes of behaviour. It is the relations that are recognised in this way that constitute what I am calling a kinship system, or, in full, a system of kinship and affinity.

A most important character of a kinship system is its range. In a narrow range system, such as the English system of the present day, only a limited number of relatives are recognised as such in any way that entails any special behaviour or any specific right and duties. In ancient times in England the range was wider, since a fifth cousin had a claim to a share of the *wergild* when a man was killed. In systems of very wide range, such as are found in some non-European societies, a man may recognise many hundreds of relatives, towards each of whom his behaviour is qualified by the existence of the relationship.

It must be noted also that in some societies persons are regarded as being connected by relationships of the same kind although no actual genealogical tie is known. Thus the members of a clan are regarded as being kinsmen, although for some of them it may not be possible to show their descent from a common ancestor. It is this that distinguishes what will here be called a clan from a lineage.

Thus a kinship system, as I am using the term, or a system of kinship and affinity if you prefer so to call it, is in the first place a system of dyadic relations between person and person in a community, the behaviour of any two persons in any of these relations being regulated in some way, and to a greater or less extent, by social usage.

A kinship system also includes the existence of definite social groups. The first of these is the domestic family, which is a group of persons who at a particular time are living together in one dwelling, or collection of dwellings, with some sort of economic arrangement that we may call joint housekeeping. There are many varieties of the domestic family, varying in their form, their size, and the manner of their common life. A domestic family may consist of a single elementary family, or it may be a group including a hundred or more persons, such as the *zadruga* of the Southern Slavs or the *taravad* of the Nayar. Important in some societies is what may be called a local cluster of domestic families. In many kinship systems unilinear groups of kindred—lineage groups, clans and moieties—play an important part.

By a kinship system, then, I mean a network of social relations of the kind just defined, which thus constitutes part of that total network of social relations that I call social structure. The rights and duties of relatives to one another and the social usages that they observe in their social contacts, since it is by these that the relations are described, are part of the system. I regard ancestor-worship, where it exists, as in a real sense part of the kinship system, constituted as it is by the relations of living persons to their deceased kindred, and affecting as it does the relations of living persons to one another. The terms used in a society in addressing or referring to relatives are a part of the system, and so are the ideas that the people themselves have about kinship.

You will perceive that by using the word "system" I have made an assumption, an important and far-reaching assumption; for that word implies that whatever it is applied to is a complex unity, an organised whole. My explicit hypothesis is that between the various features of a particular kinship system there is a complex relation of interdependence. The formulation of this working hypothesis leads immediately to the method of sociological analysis, by which we seek to discover the nature of kinship systems as systems, if they be really such. For this purpose we need to make a systematic comparison of a sufficient number of sufficiently diverse systems. We must compare them, not in reference to single, superficial, and therefore immediately observable characters, but as wholes, as systems, and in reference, therefore, to general characters which are only discovered in the process of comparison. Our purpose is to arrive at valid abstractions or general ideas in terms of which the phenomena can be described and classified.

I propose to illustrate the two methods, that of conjectural history and that of system analysis, by means of a particular example, and for this purpose I select a peculiar feature of the kinship terminology of a number of scattered tribes. When Morgan made his study of the terminology of kinship in North American tribes, he noted certain peculiarities in the terms for cousins. In the Choctaw tribe he found that a man calls his father's sister's son by the same term of relationship that he applies to his own father and his father's brother. We may say that the father's sister's son is thus treated in the terminology as though he were a younger brother of the father. Reciprocally a man calls his mother's brother's son by the term for "son." Consistently with this he applies one term of relationship to his father's sister and her daughter, and speaks of his mother's brother's daughter as a "daughter." In the Omaha tribe, on the other hand, Morgan found that a man calls his mother's brother's son "uncle," i.e. mother's brother, and calls his mother's brother's daughter "mother," so that reciprocally he speaks of his father's sister's son by the term that he uses for his sister's son, and a woman uses a single term for her own son, her sister's son and her father's sister's

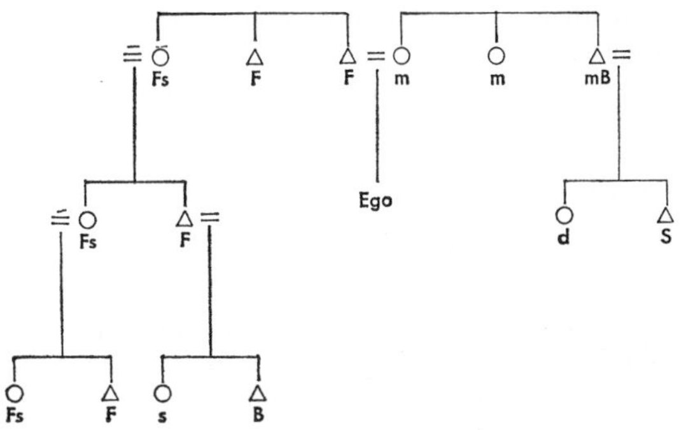


Fig. 1—Choctaw

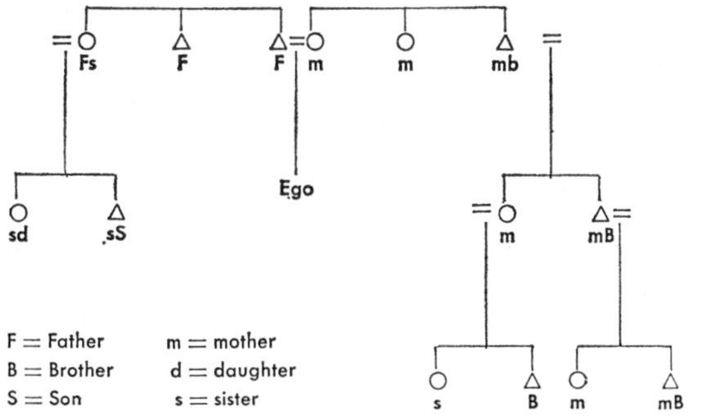


Fig. 2—Omaha

son. Figs. 1 and 2 will help to make these terminologies clear.

Terminologies similar to the Omaha are found in a number of regions: (1) in the Siouan tribes related to the Omaha, such as the Osage, Winnebago, etc.; (2) in certain Algonquian tribes, of which we may take the Fox Indians as an example; (3) in an area of California which includes the Miwok; (4) in some tribes of East Africa, both Bantu and non-Bantu, including the Nandi and the BaThonga; (5) amongst the Lhota Nagas of Assam; and (6) in some New Guinea tribes. Terminologies similar to the Choctaw are found: (1) in other south-eastern tribes of the United States, including the Cherokee; (2) in the Crow and Hidatsa tribes of the Plains area; (3) amongst the Hopi and some other Pueblo Indians; (4) in the Tlingit and Haida of the north-west coast of America; (5) in the Banks Islands in Melanesia; and (6) in one Twi-speaking community of West Africa.

There are some who would regard this kind of terminology as "contrary to common sense," but that means no more than that it is not in accordance with our modern European ideas of kinship and its terminology. It ought to be easy for any anthropologist to recognise that what is common sense in one society may be the opposite of common sense in another. The Choctaw and Omaha terminologies do call for some explanation; but so does the English terminology, in which we use the word "cousin" for all children of both brothers and sisters of both mother and father—a procedure which would probably seem to some non-Europeans to be contrary not only to common sense but also to morals. What I wish to attempt, therefore, is to show you that the Choctaw and Omaha terminologies are just as reasonable and fitting in the social systems in which they occur as our own terminology is in our own social system.

I would point out that the Choctaw system and the Omaha system exhibit a single structural principle applied in different ways, in what we may perhaps call opposite directions. We shall therefore consider them together, as varieties of a single species.

Attempts have been made to explain these terminologies by the method of conjectural history. The first was that of Kohler in 1897, in his essay "Zur Urgeschichte der Ehe." Kohler set out to defend Morgan's theory of group-marriage, and used the Choctaw and Omaha systems for his argument. He explained the Choctaw terminology as the result of marriage with the mother's brother's wife, and the Omaha system as the result of a custom of marriage with the wife's brother's daughter. Kohler's essay was reviewed by Durkheim (1898) in what was an important, if brief, contribution to the theory of kinship. He rejected Kohler's hypotheses, and pointed out the connection of the Choctaw and Omaha systems with matrilineal and patrilineal descent respectively.

The subject was considered again by Rivers in reference to the Banks Islands, and, without bringing in, as Kohler had done, the question of group-marriage, he explained the Banks Islands terminology as resulting from a custom of marriage with the mother's brother's widow. Gifford (1916), having found the characteristic feature of the Omaha system in the Miwok of California, followed the lead of Kohler and Rivers, and explained it as the result of the custom of marriage with the wife's brother's daughter. About the same time, and independently, Mrs. Seligman (1917) offered the same explanation of the Omaha feature as it occurs in the Nandi and other tribes of Africa.

Let me summarise the argument with reference to the Omaha type. The hypothesis is that in certain societies, mostly having a definite patrilineal organisation, a custom was for some reason adopted of permitting a man to marry his wife's brother's daughter. Referring to Fig. 3, this means that D

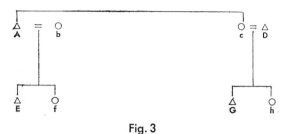


Fig. 3

*Note—A and c are brother and sister*

would be allowed to marry f. When such a marriage occurred, then for G and h, f, who is their mother's brother's daughter, would become their step-mother, and E, their mother's brother's son, would become the brother of their step-mother. The hypothesis then assumes that the kinship terminology was so modified as to anticipate this form of marriage wherever it might occur. G and h will call f, their mother's brother's daughter and therefore their possible future step-mother, "mother," and her brother E they will call "mother's brother." Reciprocally f will call G "son" and E will call him "sister's son." There is an exactly parallel argument for the Choctaw system. A custom arises by which a man may occasionally marry the widow of his mother's brother. In the figure, G would marry b, the wife of his mother's brother A. Thus E and f would become his step-children. If this marriage is anticipated in the terminology, then E and f will call G "father" and h "father's sister."

Let us note that in the Omaha tribe and in some others having a similar terminology it is regarded as permissible for a man to marry his wife's brother's daughter. Marriage with the mother's brother's widow does not seem to occur regularly with the Choctaw terminology, and does certainly occur without it, even in tribes with an Omaha terminology such as the BaThonga.

The basis of what we may call the Kohler hypothesis is the obvious fact that in each of the two varieties the terminology and the special form of marriage are consistent; the two things fit together in what may be called a logical way. This, I think, anyone can see by inspection of the data. But the hypothesis goes far beyond this. It supposes that there is some sort of causal connection such that the marriage custom can be said to have caused, produced, or resulted in, the special terminology. No evidence is adduced that this is actually the way in which things happened. The argument is entirely *a priori*. It is the essential weakness of conjectural history that its hypotheses cannot be verified. Thus this hypothesis cannot be considered as anything more than a speculation or conjecture as to how things might have happened.

Now it would be equally plausible to suggest that the special form of marriage is the result of the terminology. If, as in the terminology of the Omaha type, I treat my wife's brother's daughter as being the younger sister of my wife, and, by the custom of the sororate, it is considered proper for me to marry my wife's younger sister, then I might well be permitted to marry the woman who, in the terminological system, is treated as such, namely her brother's daughter. This hypothesis is, of course, equally lacking in proof. If we adopt the Kohler hypothesis the terminology is conceived to be in some sense explained, but there is no explanation of the marriage custom. By the alternative hypothesis the marriage custom is explained, but the terminology is not. I do not see how there can be any ground for a choice of one of these two hypotheses in preference to the other except purely personal predilection.

However, while we could conceive of the marriage custom as being the immediate result of the terminology in a society which already has sororal polygyny, the terminology cannot be the immediate result of the marriage custom without the concomitant action of some other undetermined factor. We have examples of societies in which a man sometimes marries the widow of his mother's brother, but only uses the terminology which this marriage makes appropriate after the marriage has taken place. Although we have no recorded instance of this procedure in marriage with the wife's brother's daughter it is at least conceivable that it might occur. What is lacking in the hypothesis we are examining is some reason why the whole terminology should be adjusted so as to fit a particular form of marriage which only occasionally occurs.

Let us now leave the hypothesis and examine the structural principles of those kinship systems in which this terminology occurs, whether in the Choctaw or the Omaha form. It is necessary, however, to say something on the subject of kinship terminologies, about which there has been a great deal of controversy. Morgan's first interest in the subject was as an ethnologist, i.e. one seeking to discover the historical relations of the peoples of the earth. He thought that by collecting a sufficient sample of terminologies and comparing them he could reveal the historical relation of the American Indians (the Ganowanian peoples as he called them) to the peoples of Asia. In the course of his work, however, he decided that these terminologies could be used to infer the former existence of forms of social organisation. He supposed that the classificatory terminology which he found in North American tribes such as the Iroquois was inconsistent with the form of social organisation with which it is actually found, and therefore could not have arisen in a society so organised, but must be a "survival" from some different kind of social system.

This was, of course, pure assumption, but it is the kind of assumption that the method of conjectural history encourages us to make, often unconsciously or implicitly. Morgan was thus led to a hypothesis that is one of the most fantastic in a subject that is full of fantastic hypotheses. The truth is that he had quite failed to understand the nature and function of the classificatory terminology. There is nothing that so effectively prevents the perception and understanding of things as they are as hypotheses of conjectural history, or the desire to invent such hypotheses.

One of Morgan's early critics, Starcke (1889), was, I believe, the first to maintain the position which has always been my own. He held that in general a kinship nomenclature is "the faithful reflection of the juridical relations which arise between the nearest kinsfolk in each tribe." He condemned as unsound the attempt to use such nomenclatures to make historical reconstructions of past societies. It would be interesting to consider why it is that Starcke has had so few followers and Morgan so many, but that I cannot here undertake.

In 1909 Kroeber published in our *Journal* a paper on "Classificatory Systems of Relationship." To the contentions of that paper Rivers made a reply in his lectures on *Kinship and Social Organisation* (1914*b*), and Kroeber answered the criticisms of Rivers in his *California Kinship Systems* (1917).

I discussed Kroeber's paper with Rivers when it appeared and found myself in the position of disagreeing with both sides of the controversy. Kroeber wrote: "Nothing is more precarious than the common method of deducing the recent existence of social or marital institutions from a designation of relationship." This is a restatement of Starcke's contention of 1889, and with it I was, and still am, in complete agreement, thereby disagreeing with Rivers. Kroeber also wrote: "It has been an unfortunate characteristic of the anthropology of recent years to seek in a great measure specific causes for specific events, connection between which can be established only through evidence that is subjectively selected. On wider knowledge and freedom from motive it is becoming increasingly apparent that causal explanations of detached anthropological phenomena can be but rarely found in other detached phenomena." With this statement I am in agreement.

But both Kroeber and Rivers seemed to agree that causal explanations are necessary for the constitution of what Kroeber calls "true science." For Rivers anthropology is a true science because, or to the extent that, it can show causal connections; for Kroeber it is not a true science. Here I disagree with both Kroeber and Rivers, holding that a pure theoretical science (whether physical, biological or social) is not concerned with causal relations in this sense. The concept of cause and effect belongs properly to applied science, to practical life and its arts and techniques and to history.

This brings us to the crux of the Rivers-Kroeber debate. Rivers held that the characteristics of a kinship nomenclature are determined by social or sociological factors, that particular features of terminology result from particular features of social organisation. Against this Kroeber held that the features of a system of terminology "are determined primarily by language" and "reflect psychology not sociology." "Terms of relationship," he wrote, "are determined primarily by linguistic factors and are only occasionally, and then indirectly, affected by social circumstances." But in his later paper Kroeber explains that what he calls psychological factors "are social or cultural phenomena as thoroughly and completely as institutions, beliefs or industries are social phenomena." His thesis is therefore concerned with a distinction between two kinds of social phenomena. One of these he calls institutional, defined as "practices connected with marriage, descent, personal relations, and the like." These are what he called in his first paper "social factors." The other kind he speaks of as the "psyche" of a culture, "that is, the ways of thinking and feeling characteristic of the culture." These constitute what he calls the psychological factors.

Thus Kroeber's thesis, on its positive side, is that similarities and differences of kinship nomenclature are to be interpreted or understood by reference to similarities and differences of kinship nomenclature of thought." On its negative side, and it is with this that we are concerned, Kroeber's thesis is that there is no regular close connection between similarities and differences of kinship nomenclature and similarities and differences of "institutions," i.e. practices connected with marriage, descent and personal relations. He admits, in 1917, the existence of "undoubted correspondence of terminology and social practice in certain parts of Australia and Oceania," but denies that such are to be found in California. It may be pointed out that in Australia and Oceania they have been deliberately looked for, in California they have not. It may well be that in the remnants of Californian tribes it is now too late to look for them.

In opposition to Kroeber, and in a certain sense in agreement with Rivers, I hold that all over the world there are important correspondences between kinship nomenclature and social practices. Such correspondences are not to be simply assumed; they must be demonstrated by field work and comparative analysis. But their absence may not be assumed either; and Kroeber's arguments from their alleged absence in California remain, I think, entirely unconvincing.

For Kroeber the kinship nomenclature of a people represents their general manner of thought as it is applied to kinship. But the institutions of a people also represent their general manner of thought about kinship and marriage. Are we to suppose that in Californian tribes the way of thinking about kinship as it appears on the one hand in the terminology and on the other hand in social customs are not merely different but are not connected? This seems to be in effect what Kroeber is proposing.

Kroeber pointed out in 1917 that his original paper represented "a genuine attempt to understand kinship systems as kinship systems." But by "kinship system" Kroeber means only a system of nomenclature. Moreover, Kroeber is an ethnologist, not a social anthropologist. His chief, if not his sole, interest in the subject is in the possibility of discovering and defining the historical relations of peoples by comparison of their systems of nomenclature.

My own conception is that the nomenclature of kinship is an intrinsic part of a kinship system, just as it is also, of course, an intrinsic part of a language. The relations between the nomenclature and the rest of the system are relations within an ordered whole. My concern, both in field work in various parts of the world and in comparative studies, has been to discover the nature of these relations.

In the actual study of a kinship system the nomenclature is of the utmost importance. It affords the best possible approach to the investigation and analysis of the kinship system as a whole. This, of course, it could not do if there were no real relations of interdependence between the terminology and the rest of the system. That there are such relations I can affirm from my own field work in more than one region. It will be borne out, I believe, by any anthropologist who has made a thorough field study of a kinship system.

I have dealt with the controversy between Kroeber and Rivers because, as both the controversialists point out, the real issue is not simply one concerning kinship terms, but is a very important question of the general method of anthropological studies. It seemed to me that I could best make clear my own position by showing you how it differs from that of Rivers on the one side and that of Kroeber on the other.

Kinship systems are made and re-made by man, in the same sense that languages are made and re-made, which does not mean that they are normally constructed or changed by a process of deliberation and under control of conscious purpose. A language has to work, i.e. it has to provide a more or less adequate instrument for communication, and in order that it may work it has to conform to certain general necessary conditions. A morphological comparison of languages shows us the different ways in which these conditions have been compiled with by using different morphological principles such as inflection, agglutination, word order, internal modification or the use of tone or stress. A kinship system also has to work if it is to exist or persist. It has to provide an orderly and workable system of social relations defined by social usage. A comparison of different systems shows us how workable kinship systems have been created by utilising certain structural principles and certain mechanisms.

One common feature of kinship systems is the recognition of certain categories or kinds into which the various relatives of a single person can be grouped. The actual social relation between a person and his relative, as defined by rights and duties or socially approved attitudes and modes of behaviour, is then to a greater or less extent fixed by the category to which the relative belongs. The nomenclature of kinship is commonly used as a means of establishing and recognising these categories. A single term may be used to refer to a category of relatives and different categories will be distinguished by different terms.

Let us consider a simple example from our own system. We do what is rather unusual in the general run of kinship systems: we regard the father's brother and the mother's brother as relatives of the same kind of category. We apply a single term originally denoting the mother's brother (from the Latin *avunculus*) to both of them. The legal relationship in English law, except for entailed estates and titles of nobility, is the same for a nephew and either of his uncles; for example, the nephew has the same rights of inheritance in case of intestacy over the estate of either. In what may be called the socially standardised behaviour of England it is not possible to note any regular distinction made between the maternal and the paternal uncle. Reciprocally the relation of a man to his different kinds of nephews is in general the same. By extension, no significant difference is made between the son of one's mother's brother and the son of one's father's brother.

In Montenegro, on the contrary, to take another European system, the father's brothers constitute one category and the mother's brothers another. These relatives are distinguished by different terms, and so are their respective wives, and the social relations in which a man stands to his two kinds of uncles show marked differences.

There is nothing "natural" about the English attitude towards uncles. Indeed many peoples in many parts of the world would regard this failure to distinguish between relatives on the father's side and those on the mother's side as unnatural and even improper. But the terminology is consistent with our whole kinship system.

The kinship systems with which we shall be concerned here all have certain forms of what Morgan called the "classificatory" terminology. What Morgan meant by this term is quite clear from his writings, but his definition is often ignored, perhaps because people do not bother to read him. A nomenclature is classificatory when it uses terms which primarily apply to lineal relatives, such as "father," to refer also to collateral relatives. Thus, by Morgan's definition, the English word "uncle" is not a classificatory term, but the very opposite, since it is used only for collateral relatives. Kroeber (1909) criticises Morgan and rejects his conception of classificatory terminologies, and then proceeds to make use of the same distinction by taking as one of the important features of terminologies the extent to which they separate or distinguish lineal from collateral relatives. It seems to be merely the word "classificatory" that Kroeber does not like. Doubtless it is not the ideal word; but it has long been in use and no better one has been suggested, though others have been put forward.

I do not propose to deal with all systems in which the classificatory principle is applied in the terminology, but only with a certain widespread type. In these systems the distinction between lineal and collateral relatives is clearly recognised and is of great importance in social life, but it is in certain respects subordinated to another structural principle, which can be spoken of as the principle of the solidarity of the sibling group. A group of siblings is constituted by the sons and daughters of a man and his wife in monogamous societies, or of a man and his wives where there is polygyny, or of a woman and her husbands in polyandrous communities. The bond uniting brothers and sisters together into a social group is everywhere regarded as important, but it is more emphasised in some societies than in others. The solidarity of the sibling group is shown in the first instance in the social relations between its members.

From this principle there is derived a further principle which I shall speak of as that of the unity of the sibling group. This refers not to the internal unity of the group as exhibited in the behaviour of members to one another, but to its unity in relation

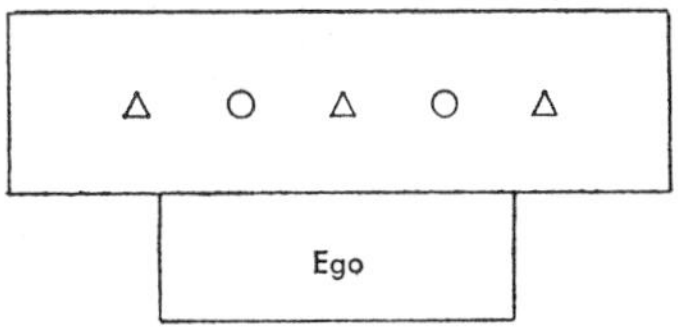


Fig. 4

to a person outside it and connected with it by a specific relation to one of its members.

A diagram may help the discussion. Fig. 4 represents a sibling group of three brothers and two sisters, to which Ego is related by the fact that he is the son of one of the three men. In the kinship systems with which I am now dealing, Ego regards himself as standing in the same general kind of relation to all the members of the group. For him it constitutes a unity. His relation to the brothers and sisters of his father is conceived as being of the same general kind as his relation to his father. Within the group, however, there are two principles of differentiation, sex and seniority, which have to be taken into account. In systems in which seniority is not emphasised a man treats his father's brothers, both older and younger, as being like his father. He refers to them or addresses them by the same term of kinship that he applies to his own father, and in certain important respects his behaviour towards them is similar to his behaviour towards his own father. What defines this behaviour is, of course, different in different systems. Where seniority is strongly emphasised, a man may distinguish between the senior brother and the junior brother either in behaviour alone or both in behavior and terminology, but there still remains a common element in the pattern of behaviour towards all "fathers."

The difference of sex is more important than the difference of seniority, and in this matter there is considerable variation in the systems we are considering. But in quite a considerable number of systems, in different parts of the world, there are certain features of a man's relationship to his father's sister which can be correctly described by saying that he regards her as a sort of female father. In some of these systems he actually calls her "female father," or some modification of the term for father. If it seems to you impossible that a man should regard his father's sister as a relative of the same kind as his own father, this is because you are thinking, not about social relationships as defined by modes of behaviour, with which we are here concerned, but about the physiological relationship, which is irrelevant.

The same kind of thing happens with the sibling group of the mother. The mother's sisters are treated as relatives of the same kind as the mother, both in terminology and in certain principles of behaviour or attitude. In a number of systems the mother's brother is also treated as a relative of the same kind as the mother. He may be called "male mother," as in Bantu tribes of Africa and in Tonga in the Pacific. If the principle of seniority is stressed, the mother's brothers may be distinguished according as they are older or younger than the mother.

Those of you who have never had any direct contact with systems of this kind find it difficult to comprehend how a father's sister can be regarded as a female father or a mother's brother as a male mother. This is due to the difficulty of dissociating the terms "father" and "mother" from the connotations they have in our own social system. It is absolutely essential to do this if the kinship systems of other societies are ever to be understood. Perhaps it will help somewhat if I refer to another terminology which seems to us peculiar. Most of the systems with which I am now dealing have a word for "child," or words for "son" and "daughter," which a man applies to his own children and his brother's children, and a woman applies to her own children and her sister's children. But in some Australian tribes there are two different words for "child." One is used by a man for his own child (or his brother's child) and by a woman for her brother's child; the other is used by a woman for her own or her sister's child, and by a man for his sister's child. I think you will see that this is another way of expressing in the terminology the unity that links brother and sister in relation to the child of either of them. I am called by one term by my father and his brothers and sisters; and by another term by my mother and her sisters and brothers.

The same principle, that of the unity of the sibling group, is applied to other sibling groups. Thus the father's father's brother is regarded as belonging to the same category as the father's father, with the result that his son is a somewhat more distant relative of the same kind as the father and his brothers. By means of such extension of the basic principle, a very large number of collateral relatives of different degrees of distance can be brought under a limited number of categories. A man may have many, even hundreds, of relatives whom he thus classifies as "fathers," "brothers," "mother's brothers" and so on. But there are different ways in which this extension of the basic classificatory principle can be applied, so that there result systems of different types. What is common to them all is that they make some use of this structural principle which I have briefly illustrated.

What I am trying to show you is that the classificatory terminology is a method of providing a wide-range kinship organisation, by making use of the unity of the sibling group in order to establish a few categories of relationship under which a very large number of near and distant relatives can be included. For all the relatives who are denoted by one term, there is normally some element of attitude or behaviour that is regarded as appropriate to them and not to others. But within a category there may be and always are important distinctions. There is, first, the very important distinction between one's own father and his brother. There are distinctions within the category between nearer and more distant relatives. There is sometimes an important distinction between relatives of a certain category who belong to other clans. There are other distinctions that are made in different particular systems. Thus the categories represented by the terminology never give us anything more than the skeleton of the real ordering of relatives in the social life. But in every system that I have been able to study they do give us this skeleton.

If this thesis is true, if this is what the classificatory terminology actually is in the tribes in which it exists, it is obvious that Morgan's whole theory is entirely ungrounded. The classificatory system, as thus interpreted, depends upon the recognition of the strong social ties that unite brothers and sisters of the same elementary family, and the utilisation of this tie to build up a complex orderly arrangement of social relations amongst kin. It could not come into existence except in a society based on the elementary family. Nowhere in the world are the ties between a man and his own children or between children of one father stronger than in Australian tribes, which, as you know, present an extreme example of the classificatory terminology.

The internal solidarity of the sibling group, and its unity in relation to persons connected with it, appear in a great number of different forms in different societies. I cannot make any attempt to deal with these, but for the sake of the later argument I will point out that it is in the light of this structural principle that we must interpret the customs of sororal polygyny (marriage with two or more sisters), the sororate (marriage with the deceased wife's sister), adelphic polyandry (marriage of a woman with two or more brothers, by far the commonest form of polyandry), and the levirate (marriage with the brother's widow). Sapir, using the method of conjectural history, has suggested that the classificatory terminology may be the result of the customs of the levirate and sororate. That the two things are connected is, I think, clear, but for the supposed causal connection there is no evidence whatever. Their real connection is that they are different ways of applying or using the principle of the unity of the sibling group, and they may therefore exist together or separately.

An organisation into clans or moieties is also based on the principle of the solidarity and unity of the sibling group in combination with other principles. Tylor suggested a connection between exogamous clans and the classificatory terminology. Rivers put this in terms of conjectural history, and argued that the classificatory terminology must have had its origin in the organisation of society into exogamous moieties.

## *II*

It is necessary, for our analysis, to consider briefly another aspect of the structure of kinship systems, namely the division into generations. The distinction of generation has its basis in the elementary family, in the relation of parents and children. A certain generalising tendency is discoverable in many kinship systems in the behaviour of relatives of different generations. Thus we find very frequently that a person is expected to adopt an attitude of more or less marked respect towards all his relatives of the first ascending generation. There are restraints on behaviour which maintain a certain distance or prevent too close an intimacy. There is, in fact, a generalised relation of ascendancy and subordination between the two generations. This is usually accompanied by a relation of friendly equality between a person and his relatives of the second ascending generation. The nomenclature for grandparents and grandchildren is of significance in this connection. In some classificatory systems, such as those of Australian tribes, the grandparents on the father's side are distinguished, in terminology and in behaviour, from those on the mother's side. But in many classificatory systems the generalising tendency results in all relatives of the generation being classed together as "grandfathers" and "grandmothers."

We may note in passing that in classificatory terminologies of what Morgan called the Malayan type and Rivers the Hawaiian type, this generalising process is applied to other generations, so that all relatives of the parents' generation may be called "father" and "mother" and all those of one's own generation may be called "brother" and "sister."

There are many kinship systems in various parts of the world that exhibit a structural principle which I shall speak of as the combination of alternate generations. This means that relatives of the grandfather's generation are thought of as combined with those of one's own generation over against the relatives of the parents' generation. The extreme development of this principle is to be seen in Australian tribes. I shall refer to this later.

While some systems emphasise the distinction of generations in their terminology or in their social structure, there are also systems in which relatives of two or more generations are included in a single category. So far as I have been able to make a comparative study, the various instances of this seem to fall into four classes.

In one class of instances the term of relationship does not carry a connotation referring to any particular generation and is used to mark off a sort of marginal region between non-relatives and those close relatives towards whom specific duties and over whom specific rights are recognised. The application of the term generally only implies that since the other person is recognised as a relative he or she must be treated with a certain general attitude of friendliness and not as a stranger. A good example is provided by the terms *ol-le-sotwa* and *en-e-sotwa* in Masai. I would include the English word "cousin' 'in this class.

A second class of instances includes those in which there is conflict or inconsistency between the required attitude towards a particular relative and the required general attitude towards the generation to which he belongs. Thus in some tribes in South-East Africa there is conflict between the general rule that relatives of the first ascending generation are to be treated with marked respect and the custom of privileged disrespect towards the mother's brother. This is resolved by placing the mother's brother in the second ascending generation and calling him "grandfather." An opposite example is found in the Masai. A man is on terms of familiarity with all his relatives of the second descending generation, who are his "grandchildren." But it is felt that the relation between a man and the wife of his son's son should be one not of familiarity but of marked reserve. The inconsistency is resolved by a sort of legal fiction by which she is moved out of her generation and is called "son's wife."

A third class of instances are those resulting from the structural principle, already mentioned, whereby alternate generations are combined. Thus the father's father may be called "older brother" and treated as such, and the son's son may be called "younger brother." Or a man and his son's son may be both included in a single category of relationship. There are many illustrations of this in Australian tribes and some elsewhere. An example from the Hopi will be given later.

The fourth class of instances includes the systems of Choctaw and Omaha type and also certain others, and in these the distinction between generations is set aside in favour of another principle, that of the unity of the lineage group.

Since the word lineage is often loosely used, I must explain what I mean by it. A patrilineal or agnatic lineage consists of a man and all his descendants through males for a determinate number of generations. Thus a minimal lineage includes three generations, and we can have lineages of four, five or *n* generations. A matrilineal lineage consists of a woman and all her descendants through females for a determinate number of generations. A lineage group consists of all the members of a lineage who are alive at a particular time. A clan, as I shall use the term here, is a group which, though not actually or demonstrably (by genealogies) a lineage, is regarded as being in some ways similar to a lineage. It normally consists of a number of actual lineages. Lineages, both patrilineal and matrilineal, exist implicitly in any kinship system, but it is only in some systems that the solidarity of the lineage group is an important feature in the social structure.

Where lineage groups are important we can speak of the solidarity of the group, which shows itself in the first instance in the internal relations between the members. By the principle of the unity of the lineage group I mean that for a person who does not belong to the lineage but is connected with it through some important bond of kinship or by marriage, its members constitute a single category, with a distinction within the category between males and females, and possibly other distinctions also. When this principle is applied in the terminology a person connected with a lineage from outside applies to its members, of one sex, through at least three generations, the same term of relationship. In its extreme development, as applied to the clan, a person connected with a clan in a certain way applies a single term of relationship to all members of the clan. An example will be given later.

The Omaha type of terminology may be illustrated by the system of the Fox Indians, which has been carefully studied by Dr. Sol Tax (1937). The features of the system that are relevant to the argument are illustrated in the accompanying diagrams (Figs. 5–9).*

* In these diagrams △ represents a male person and ○ a female. The sign = connects a man and his wife and the lines descending from it indicate their children. The letters (capitals for males and lower case for females) stand for the kinship terms of a classificatory system, in which the same term is applied to a number of relatives. GF stands for the term used in referring to a grandfather, and similarly gm for grandmother; the others are F, father, m. mother, ms, mother's sister, fs, father's sister, MB, mother's brother, FL, father-in-law, ml, mother-in-law, B, brother, sis ,sister, BL, brother-in-law, sl, sister-in-law, S, son, d, daughter, N, nephew (strictly speaking sister's son) n, niece (sister's daughter of a male) GC or gc, grandchild.

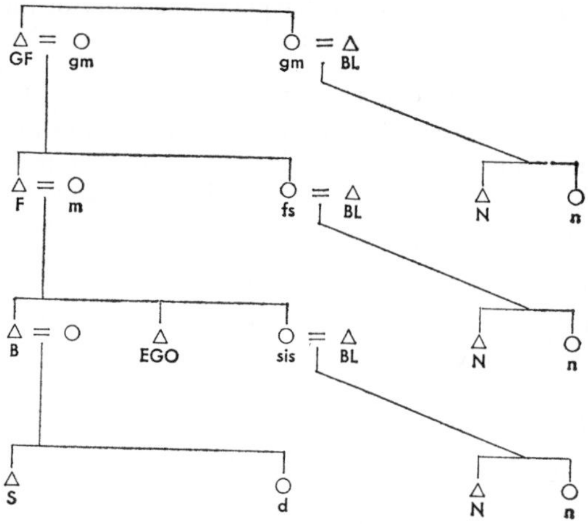


Fig. 5—Fox

Father's Lineage

In his own patrilineal lineage a man distinguishes his relatives according to generation as "grandfather" (GF), "father" (F), "older or younger brother" (B), "son" (S), "grandmother" (gm), "father's sister" (fs), "sister" (sis) and "daughter" (d). I would draw your attention to the fact that he applies a single term, "brother-in-law" (BL), irrespective of generation, to the husbands of the women of the lineage through three generations (his own and the two ascending generations), and that he calls the children of all these women by the same terms, "nephew" (N) and "niece" (n). Thus the women of Ego's own lineage of these generations constitute a sort of group, and Ego regards himself as standing in the same relationship to the children and hus-

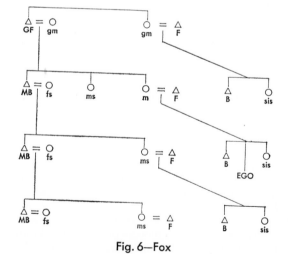

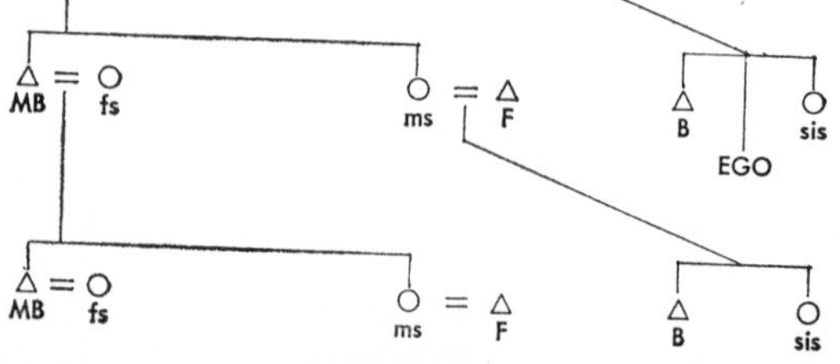


Fig. 6—Fox

Mother's Lineage

bands of all of them, although these persons belong to a number of different lineages.

Turning to the mother's patrilineal lineage, it can be seen that a man calls his mother's father "grandfather," but calls all the males of the lineage in the three succeeding generations "mother's brother" (MB). Similarly he calls the women of these three generations, except his own mother, by a term translated as "mother's sister" (ms). He applies the term "father" (F) to the husbands of all the women of the lineage through four generations (including the husband of the mother's father's sister) and the children of all these women are his "brothers" and "sisters." He is the son of one particular woman of a unified group, and the sons of the other women of the group are therefore his "brothers."

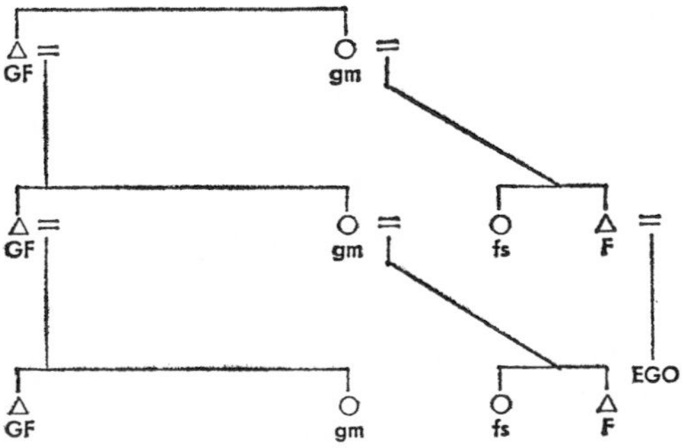


Fig. 7—Fox

Father's Mother's Lineage

In his father's mother's lineage Ego calls all the men and women throughout three generations "grandfather" and "grandmother." The children of these "grandmothers" are all his "fathers" and "father's sisters," irrespective of generation. In his mother's mother's lineage he also calls all the males "grandfather" and the females "grandmother," but I have not thought it necessary to include a figure to show this.

In his wife's lineage a man calls his wife's father by a term which we will translate "father-in-law" (FL). It is a modification of the word for "grandfather."* The sons and brother's sons of the "fathers-in-law" are "brothers-in-law" (BL), and the daughters are "sisters-in-law" (sl). The children of a "brother-in-law" are again "brother-in-law" and "sister-in-law." Thus these two terms are applied to

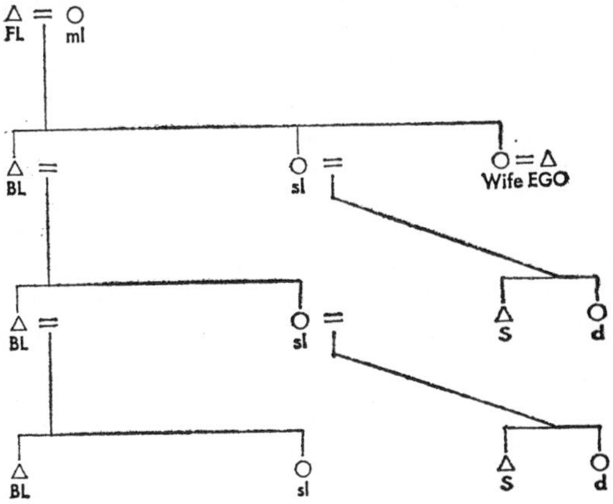


Fig. 8—Fox

Wife's Lineage

the men and women of a lineage through three generations. The children of all these "sisters-in-law" are "sons" and "daughters."

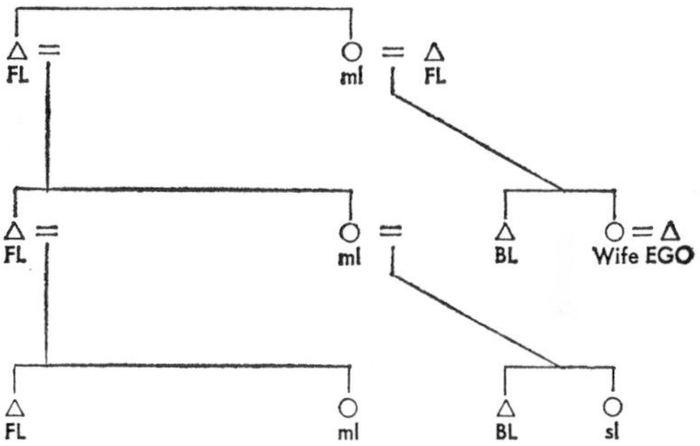


Fig. 9—Fox

Wife's Mother's Lineage

Fig. 9 shows the lineage of the wife's mother. In this lineage, through three generations, all the men are called "father-in-law" and all the women "mother-in-law."

Is the classification of relatives in the Fox terminology simply a matter of language, as some would have us believe? Dr. Tax's observations (1937) enable us to affirm that it is not. He writes:

> The kinship terminology is applied to all known relatives (even in some cases where the genealogical relationship is not traceable) so that the entire tribe is divided into a small number of types of relationship pairs. Each of these types carries with it a more or less distinct traditional pattern of behaviour. Generally speaking, the behaviour of close relatives follows the pattern in its greatest intensity, that of farther relatives

* The Fox terms for father-in-law and mother-in-law are modifications of the terms for grandfather and grandmother. In the Omaha tribe the terms for grandparents, without modification, are apploed to the parents-in-law and to those who are called "father-in-law" and "mother-in-law" in the Fox tribe.

in lesser degree; but there are numerous cases where, for some reason, a pair of close relatives "do not behave towards each other at all as they should."

Dr. Tax goes on to define the patterns of behaviour for the various types of relationship. Thus the classification of relatives into categories, carried out by means of the nomenclature, or therein expressed, appears also in the regulation of social behaviour. There is good evidence that this is true of other systems of Omaha type, and, contrary to Kroeber's thesis, we may justifiably accept the hypothesis that it is probably true of all.

Charts similar to those given here for the Fox Indians can be made for other systems of the Omaha type. I think that a careful examination and comparison of the various systems shows that, while there are variations, there is a single structural principle underlying both the terminology and the associated social structure. A lineage of three (or sometimes more) generations is regarded as a unity. A person is related to certain lineages at particular points: in the Fox tribe to the lineages of his mother, his father's mother, his mother's mother, his wife, and his wife's mother. In each instance he regards himself as related to the succeeding generations of the lineage in the same way as he is related to the generation with which he is actually connected. Thus all the men of his mother's lineage are his "mother's brothers," those of his grandmother's lineage his "grandfathers," and those of his wife's lineage are his "brothers-in-law."

This structural principle of the unity of the patrilineal lineage is not a hypothetical cause of the terminology. It is a principle that is directly discoverable by comparative analysis of systems of this type; or, in other words, it is an immediate abstraction from observed facts.

Let us now examine a society in which the principle of the unity of the lineage group is applied to matrilineal lineages. For this I select the system of the Hopi Indians, which has been analysed in a masterly manner by Dr. Fred Eggan (1950). The most significant features of the system are illustrated in the accompanying figures.

A man's own lineage is, of course, that of his mother. He distinguishes the women of his lineage by generation as "grandmother" (gm), "mother" (m), "sister" (sis), "niece" (n), and "grandchild" (gc). Amongst the men of his lineage he distinguishes his "mother's brothers" (MB), "brothers" (B) and "nephews" (N). But he includes his mother's mother's brother and his sister's daughter's son in the same category as his brothers. The structural principle exhibited here is that already referred to as the combination of alternative generations. It should be noted that a man includes the children of

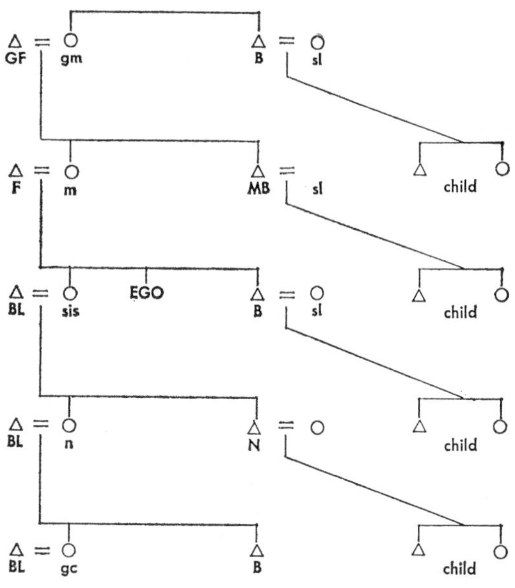


Fig. 10—Hopi
Mother's Lineage

all men of his own lineage, irrespective of generation, in the same category as his own children. Fig. 10 should be carefully compared with Fig. 5, for the Fox Indians, as the comparison is illuminating.

In his father's lineage a man calls all the male

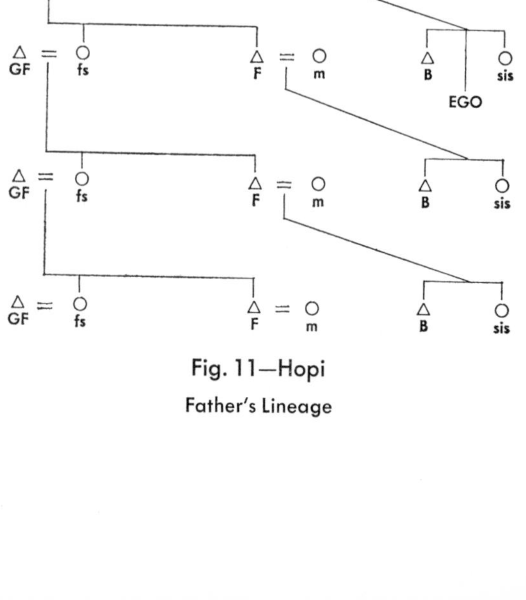

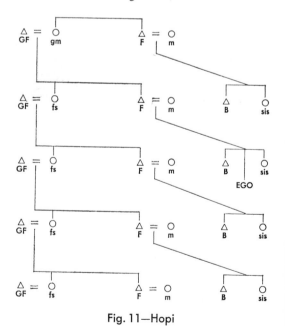


Fig. 11—Hopi
Father's Lineage

members through five generations "father" and, with the exception of his father's mother (his "grandmother"), he calls all the women "father's sister." The husband of any woman of the lineage is a "grandfather," and the wife of any man of the lineage is a "mother." The children of his "fathers" are "brothers" and "sisters." Fig. 11 should be carefully compared with Fig. 6.

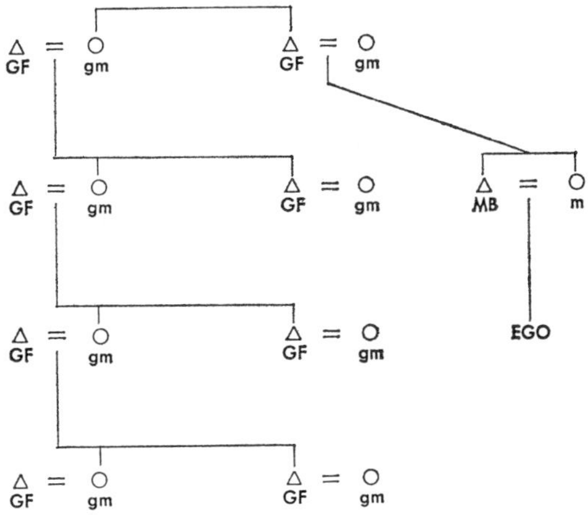


Fig. 12—Hopi

Mother's Father's Lineage

In his mother's father's lineage a man calls all the men and women through four generations "grandfather" and "grandmother."

The Hopi do not regard a man as related to his father's father's lineage as a whole, and the principle is therefore not applied to it. He does call his own father's father "grandfather."

Dr. Eggan has shown that for the Hopi this classification of relatives into categories is not simply a matter of terminology or language, but is the basis of much of the regulation of social life.

What is, I think, clearly brought out by a comparison of the Fox and Hopi systems is their fundamental similarity. By the theories of conjectural history this similarity is the accidental result of different historical processes. By my theory it is the result of the systematic application of the same structural principle, in one instance to patrilineal and in the other to matrilineal lineages.

I cannot, of course, discuss all the various systems of Choctaw and Omaha type. The variations that they show in certain features are very interesting and important. If you wish to test my theory you will examine them, or some of them, for yourselves, and the easiest way to analyse any system is to reduce it to a set of lineage charts similar to those given here for the Fox and the Hopi. For any system such a set of charts will reveal the exact way in which the general principle of the unity of the lineage is applied. The manner of application varies somewhat, but the principle appears in each system of the type.

You will doubtless already have noticed that in these systems there are an extraordinary number of relatives of all ages to whom a man applies the terms "grandfather" and "grandmother." There is, I believe, a good reason for this, which should be briefly indicated. It is a general rule in societies having a classificatory terminology that for all the various relatives included under a single term there is some more or less definite pattern of behaviour which is regarded as normal or appropriate. But there are important differences in this matter. In certain instances the pattern can be defined by reference to specific rights and duties, or by specific modes of behaviour. For example, in the Kariera tribe of Australia a man must practice the most careful avoidance of all women who are included in the category of "father's sister," of whom there are very many and of whom his wife's mother is one. But in other instances all that the application of a term implies is a certain general attitude rather than any more specific relation. Within such a category there may be a specific jural or personal relation to a particular individual. In many classificatory systems the terms for grandfather and grandmother are used in this way, as implying a general attitude of friendliness, relatively free from restraint, towards all persons to whom they are applied. Grandparents and grandchildren are persons with whom one can be on free and easy terms. This is connected with an extremely widespread, indeed almost universal, way of organising the relation of alternate generations to one another.

In the Fox and Hopi systems all the members of the lineage of a grandparent are included in one category with the grandparents and the attitude that is appropriate towards a grandparent is extended to them. This does not imply any definite set of rights and duties, but only a certain general type of behaviour, of a kind that is regarded as appropriate towards relatives of the second ascending generation in a great many societies not belonging to the Choctaw and Omaha type.

I should have liked to discuss this further and to have dealt with those varieties of the Omaha type (such as the VaNdau) in which the mother's brother and the mother's brother's son are called "grandfather." But I have only time to draw your attention to a special variety of the Choctaw type which is of great interest in this connection. The Cherokee were divided into seven martrilineal clans. In the father's clan a man called all the men and women of his father's and all succeeding generations "father" and "father's sister," and this clan and all its individual members had to be treated with great respect. A man could not marry a woman of his father's clan, and of course he could not marry into his own clan. In the clan of his father's father and that of his mother's father a man calls all the women of all generations "grandmother." He thus treats, not the lineage, but the whole clan as a unity, although a clan must have numbered many hundreds of persons. With any woman whom he calls "grandmother" a man is allowed to be on free and easy terms. It was regarded as particularly appropriate that a man should marry a "grandmother," i.e. a woman of his mother's father's or father's father's clan.

Let us now return to a brief consideration of the special customs of marriage that have been proposed as causes of the Choctaw and Omaha terminologies respectively. Marriage with the wife's brother's daughter is theoretically possible and does perhaps actually, though only occasionally, occur in some of the tribes having a system of Omaha type. Though there has been no marriage of this kind in the Fox tribe in recent times it is spoken of as a custom that formerly existed. We have seen that the marriage custom and the terminology fit consistently. The reason for this should now be easy to understand, for a little consideration will show that this particular marriage is an application of the principle of the unity of the lineage combined with the custom of the sororate or sororal polygyny. In the usual form of these customs we are concerned only with the principle of the unity of the sibling group. A man marries one woman of a particular sibling group and thereby establishes a particular relation to that group as a unity. The men are now permanently his brothers-in-law. Towards one of the women he stands in a marital relationship, and therefore towards the others he is conceived as standing in a similar relationship which may be called a quasi-marital relationship. For instance, they will regard his children as being their "children." Thus it is appropriate that when he takes a second wife, whether before or after the death of his first, he should marry his wife's sister.

I am quite aware that sororal polygyny can be attributed to the fact that co-wives who are sisters are less likely to quarrel seriously than two who are not so related, and that the sororate may similarly be justified by the fact that a stepmother is more likely to have proper affection for her stepchildren if they are the children of her own sister. These propositions do not conflict with my explanation but support it, for the principle of the unity of the sibling group as a structural principle is based on the solidarity of brothers and sisters within one family.

When we turn to systems of the Omaha type, we see that in place of the unity of the sibling group we now have a unity of the larger group, the lineage group of three generations. When a man marries one woman of this group he enters into a relation with the group as a unity, so that all the men are now his brothers-in-law, and he at the same time enters into what I have called a quasi-marital relationship with all the women, including not only his wife's sisters but also his wife's brother's daughters, and in some systems his wife's father's sisters. The group within which, by the principle of the sororate, he may take a second wife without entering into any new social bonds is thus extended to include his wife's brother's daughter; and the custom of marriage with this relative is simply the result of the application of the principle of the unity of the lineage in a system of patrilineal lineages. The special form of marriage and the special system of terminology, where they occur together, are directly connected by the fact that they are both applications of the one structural principle. There is no ground whatever for supposing that one is the historical cause of the other.

The matter is much more complex when we come to the custom of marriage with the mother's brother's widow. This form of marriage is found associated with terminology of the Choctaw type in the Banks Islands, in the tribes of North-West America and in the Twi-speaking Akim Abuakwa. But it is also found in many other places where that type of terminology does not exist. Nor is it correlated with matrilineal descent, for it is to be found in African societies that are markedly patrilineal in their institutions. There does not seem to be any theoretical explanation that will apply to all the known instances of this custom. There is no time on this occasion to discuss this subject by an analysis of instances.

I must briefly refer to another theory, which goes back to Durkheim's review (1898) of Kohler, and by which the Choctaw and Omaha terminologies are explained as being the direct result of emphasis on matrilineal and patrilineal descent respectively. We have, fortunately, a crucial instance to which we can refer in this connection, in the system of the Manus of the Admiralty Islands, of which we have an excellent analysis by Dr. Margaret Mead (1934). The most important feature of the Manus system is the existence of patrilineal clans (called by Dr. Mead "gentes") and the major emphasis is on patrilineal descent. The solidarity of the patrilineal lineage is exhibited in many features of the system, but not in the terminology. However this emphasis on patrilineal descent is to a certain extent counter-balanced by the recognition of matrilineal lineages, and this does appear in the terminology in features that make it similar to the Choctaw type. Thus a single term, *pinpapu,* is applied to the father's father's sister and to all her female descendants in the female line, and a single term, *patieye,* is applied to the father's sister and all her descendants in the female line. The unity of the matrilineal lineage is exhibited not only in the use of these terms, but also in the general social relation in which a person stands to the members of it, and is an important feature of the total complex kinship structure.

One of the strange ideas that has been, and I fear still is, current is that if a society recognises lineage at all it can only recognize either patrilineal or matrilineal lineage. I believe the origin of this absurd notion, and its persistence in the face of known facts, are the result of that early hypothesis of conjectural history that matrilineal descent is more primitive, i.e. historically earlier, than patrilineal descent. From the beginning of this century we have been acquainted with societies, such as the Herero, in which both matrilineal and patrilineal lineages are recognised; but these were dismissed as being "transitional" forms. This is another example of the way in which attachment to the method and hypotheses of conjectural history prevents us from seeing things as they are. It was this, I think, that was responsible for Rivers' failing to discover that the Toda system recognises matrilineal lineage as well as patrilineal, and that the islands of the New Hebrides have a system of patrilineal groups in addition to their matrilineal moieties. Apart from the presuppositions of the method of conjectural history, there is no reason why a society should not build its kinship system on the basis of both patrilineal and matrilineal lineage, and we know that there are many societies that do exactly this.

In my criticism of the method of conjectural history I have insisted on the need for demonstration in anthropology. How then am I to demonstrate that my interpretation of the Choctaw-Omaha terminologies is the valid one? There are a number of possible arguments, but I have time for only one, which I hope may be considered sufficient. This is drawn from the existence of terminologies in which the unity of lineage or clan is exhibited, but which do not belong to either the Choctaw or the Omaha type; and I will mention one example, that of the Yaralde tribe of South Australia.

The Yaralde are divided into local patrilineal totemic clans. A man belongs to his father's clan, and we will consider his relation to three other clans: those of his mother, his father's mother and his mother's mother. The Yaralde, like many other Australian tribes, such as the Aranda, have four terms for grandparents, each of which is applied to both men and women. The term *maiya* is applied to the father's father and his brothers and sisters and to all members of a man's own clan of the second ascending generation. A second term, *ŋaitja,* is applied to the mother's father and his brothers and sisters, i.e. to persons of the mother's clan of the appropriate generation. The third term, *mutṣa,* is applied not only to the father's mother and her brothers and sisters, but to all persons belonging to the same clan, of all generations and of both sexes. The clan is spoken of collectively as a man's *mutṣaurui.* Similarly the term *baka* is applied to the mother's mother and her brothers and sisters and to all members of her clan of all generations, the clan being spoken of as a man's *bakaurui.* The structural principle here is that for the outside related person the clan constitutes a unity within which distinctions of generation are obliterated. Compare this with the treatment of lineages or clans of grandparents in the Fox, Hopi and Cherokee systems.

The Yaralde terminology for relatives in the mother's clan is shown in Fig. 13. It will be noted that the mother's brother's son and daughter are not called mother's brother (*wano*) and mother (*neŋko*) as in Omaha systems. But the son's son and daughter of the mother's brother are called "mother's brother" and "mother." If we wish to explain this by a special form of marriage it would have to be

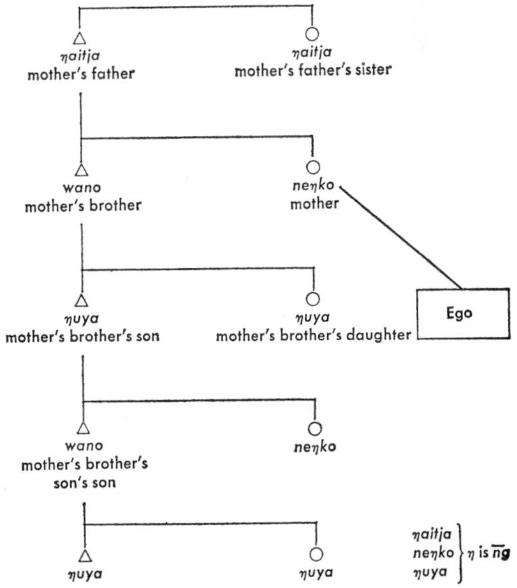


Fig. 13—Yaralde
Mother's Lineage

marriage with the wife's brother's son's daughter. I am not certain that such a marriage would be prohibited by the Yaralde system, but I am quite sure that it is not a custom so regular as to be regarded as an effective cause in producing the Yaralde terminology, and it would afford no explanation whatever for the terminological unification of the clans of the father's mother and the mother's mother. The structural principle involved is obviously that of the merging of alternate generations, which is of such great importance in Australia, and which we have also seen in the Hopi system. A system very similar to the Yaralde is found in the Ungarinyin tribe of North-West Australia, but I will not do more than refer to it.

Earlier in this address I said that I would try to show you that the Omaha type of terminology is just as reasonable and fitting in those social systems in which it is found as our own terminology is in our system. I hope I have succeeded in doing this. On the basis of the elementary family and the genealogical relationships resulting therefrom, we English have constructed for ourselves a certain kinship system which meets the necessities of an ordered social life and is fairly self-consistent. The Fox or the Hopi have on the same basis constructed a relatively self-consistent system of a different type which provides for the needs of social cohesion in a different way and over a wider range. We understand the terminology in each instance as soon as we see it as part of an ordered system. The obvious connection of the Omaha terminology with the custom of marriage with the wife's brother's daughter is seen as a relation between two parts of a self-consistent working system, not as a relation of cause and effect.

If you ask the question, "How is it that the Omaha (or any other of the tribes we have considered) have the system that they do?" then it is obvious that the method of structural analysis does not afford an answer. But neither does conjectural history. The proffered but purely hypothetical explanation of the Omaha terminology is that it resulted from the adoption of a certain unusual custom of marriage. This obviously gives us no explanation until we know why the Omaha and other tribes came to adopt this custom. The only possible way of answering the question why a particular society has the social system that it does have is by a detailed study of its history over a sufficient period, generally several centuries. For the tribes with which we are here concerned the materials for such a history are entirely lacking. This is, of course, very regrettable, but there is nothing that we can do about it. If you want to know how England comes to have its present system of constitutional monarchy and parliamentary government, you will go to the history books, which will give you the details of the growth of the system. If there were no records at all of this historical development, would the anthropologists think it worth while to spend their time in making conjectures as to what it might have been?

Even when there are historical records, they only enable us to discover how a particular system has grown out of a somewhat different particular system. Thus it would be possible to write a historical account of the changes of the kinship system of England during the past ten centuries. This would take us back to the Teutonic bilateral sib system, as exhibited in the institution of *wergild*. But we still should not know why the Teutonic peoples had this kind of system, while the Romans had a different system of agnatic lineages. The great value of history for a science of society is that it gives us materials for the study of how social systems change. In this respect conjectural history is absolutely worthless.

But if you ask, not how the English kinship system or the English political system came into existence, but how it works at the present time, that is a question that can be answered by research of the same kind as anthropological field-work, and historical considerations are relatively, if not absolutely, unimportant. Such knowledge of how social systems work is of great value for any understanding of human life. It often has been and still is neglected by anthropologists who consider it their principal task to write the history of peoples or institutions that have no history.

If you accept the analysis that I have given, but still wish to apply the method of conjectural history, what you have to conjecture is why all the tribes that have been enumerated elected to construct their kinship systems on the basis of the unity of the lineage.

What kind of results can we expect to obtain from the method of sociological analysis? Nothing, of course, that will be acceptable as significant by those who demand that any explanation of a social phenomenon must be a historical explanation, or by those who demand what is called psychological explanation, i.e. explanation in terms of the individual and his motives. I suggest that the results that we may reasonably expect are as follows:

1. It will enable us to make a systematic classification of kinship systems. Systematic classification is an essential in any scientific treatment of any class of phenomena, and such classification must be in terms of general properties.

2. It enables us to understand particular features of particular systems. It does this in two ways: (*a*) by revealing the particular feature as a part of an

organised whole; (*b*) by showing that it is a special example of a recognisable class of phenomena. Thus I have tried to show that the Choctaw and Omaha terminologies belong to a class which also includes the Yaralde terminology, and that these are all special applications of the general principle of the solidarity and continuity of the lineage, which appears in many other forms in a great number of different societies.

3. It is the only method by which we can hope ultimately to arrive at valid generalisations about the nature of human society, i.e. about the universal characteristics of all societies, past, present, and future. It is, of course, such generalisations that are meant when we speak of sociological laws.

In the method of conjectural history single problems are usually considered in isolation. On the other hand, the method of structural analysis aims at a general theory, and a great many different facts and problems are, therefore, considered together and in relation to one another. It is obvious that in this address, inordinately long as it has been, I have only been able to touch on a few points in the general theory of kinship structure. I have dealt briefly with one or two other points in earlier publications. That particular part of the general theory which has occupied us today may be said to be the theory of the establishment of type relationships. I have mentioned the tendency present in many societies to set up a type relationship between a person and all his relatives of the parents' generation, and the even more marked tendency to establish a type relationship, usually one of free and easy behaviour, towards the relatives of the grandparents' generation. I have not tried to deal with this except incidentally. The major part of the exposition has been concerned with two structural principles which are themselves examples of a more general structural principle or class of principles. By the principle of the unity of the sibling group a type relationship is set up between a given person and all the members of a sibling group to which he is related in a certain way. It is by reference to this principle, I hold, that we must interpret the classificatory terminology and such customs as the sororate and levirate. By the principle of the unity of the lineage group a type relationship is set up between a given person and all the members of a lineage group to which he is related in a certain way. It is by reference to this principle, I hold, that we must interpret the terminologies of the Fox, the Hopi and the Yaralde, and other similar systems in many scattered parts of the world.

If you will take the time to study two or three hundred kinship systems from all parts of the world you will be impressed, I think, by the great diversity that they exhibit. But you will also be impressed by the way in which some particular feature, such as an Omaha type of terminology, reappears in scattered and widely spread regions. To reduce this diversity to some sort of order is the task of analysis, and by its means we can, I believe, find, beneath the diversities, a limited number of general principles applied and combined in various ways. Lineage solidarity in one form or another is found in a majority of kinship systems. There is nothing at all surprising in the fact that terminologies of the Choctaw and Omaha type, in which it finds what may be called an extreme development, should be encountered in separated regions of America, Africa, Asia and Oceania, in many different families of languages, and in association with many different types of "culture."

Last year I explained in general terms how I conceive the study of social structure (Radcliffe-Brown, 1940*b*). In this address, by means of a particular example, I have tried to show you something of the nature of a certain method of investigation. But do not think that this method can be applied only to the study of kinship. It is applicable in one way or another to all social phenomena, for it is simply the method of abstractive generalisation by the comparison of instances, which is the characteristic method of the inductive sciences.

"Why all this fuss about method?" some of you may perhaps ask. We cannot reach agreement as to the validity or the value of results unless we first reach some agreement as to objectives and the proper methods of attaining them. In the other natural sciences there is such agreement; in social anthropology there is not. Where we disagree, it should be the first purpose of discussion to define as precisely as possible the ground of difference. I have put my case before you, without, I hope, any unfairness towards those with whom I disagree. It is for you to judge which of the two methods that I have compared is most likely to provide that kind of scientific understanding of the nature of human society which it is the accepted task of the social anthropologist to provide for the guidance of mankind.

## *References*

Durkheim, E. (1898). "Zur Urgeschichte der Ehe. Prof. J. Kohler," Analysis III, La Famille, *Année Sociologique*, Vol. I, pp. 306–319.

Eggan, F. (1950). *Social Organisation of the Western Pueblos*. Chicago University Press.

Gifford, E. W. (1916). "Miwok Moieties," *Arch and Ethn. Publ., Univ. California*, Vol. XII, No. 4.

Gilbert, William H., Jr. (1937). "Eastern Cherokee Social Organisation," in *Social Anthropology of North American Tribes* (ed. Fred Eggan). Chicago University Press, pp. 283–338.

Kohler, J. (1897). "Zur Urgeschichte der Ehe," *Zeitschrift für Vergleichende Rechtswissenschaft* (Stuttgart), Bd. 11.

Kroeber, A. L. (1909). "Classificatory Systems of Relationship," *F. R. Anthrop. Inst.*, Vol XXXIX, pp. 77–84.

———, (1917). "California Kinship Systems," *Arch. and Ethn. Publ. Univ. California*, Vol. XII, No. 9.

Mead, Margaret (1934). "Kinship in the Admiralty Islands," *Anthrop. Papers Amer. Mus. Nat. History*, Vol. XXXIV, Pt. II, pp. 181–358.

M'Lennan, John F. (1865). *Primitive Marriage*. Edinburgh: Adam & Charles Black.

Morgan, Lewis H. (1871). "The Systems of Consanguinity and Affinity," *Smithsonian Institution Contributions to Knowledge*, Vol. XVII.

———, (1877). *Ancient Society or Researches in the Lines of Human Progress from Savagery to Civilisation*. London: Macmillan; New York: Henry Holt.

Opler, M. E., (1937*a*). "Chiricahau Apache Social Organisation," in *Social Anthropology of North American Tribes*. (ed. Fred Eggan), Chicago University Press.

———, (1937*b*). "Apache Data Concerning the Relation of Kinship Terminology to Social Classification," *Amer. Anthrop.*, Vol. XXXIX, pp. 201–212.

Radcliffe-Brown, A. R. (1918). "Notes on the Social Organisation of Australian Tribes," Pt. I, *F. R. Anthrop. Inst.*, Vol. XLVIII, pp. 222–253.

———, (1924). "The Mother's Brother in South Africa," *South African F. Science*, Vol. XXI.

———, (1930–31). "The Social Organisation of Australian Tribes," Pts. I–III, *Oceania*, Vol. I, pp. 34–63, 206–246, 322–341, 426–456.

———, (1935). "Patrilineal and Matrilineal Succession," *Iowa Law Review*, Vol. XX, No. 2.

———, (1940*a*). "On Joking Relationships," *Africa*, Vol XIII, No. 3, pp. 195–210.

———, (1940*b*). "On Social Structure," *F. R. Anthrop Inst.*, Vol. LXX, pp. 1–12.

Rivers, W. H. R. (1907). "On the Origin of the Classificatory System of Relationship," in *Anthropological Essays Presented to Edward Burnett Tyler*. Oxford: Clarendon Press. (Reprinted in *Social Organisation*. London: Kegan Paul, 1924, App. 1, pp. 175–192.)

———, (1914*a*). *History of Melanesian Society*. Cambridge University Press.

———, (1941*b*). *Kinship and Social Organisation*. London: London School of Economics.

Seligman, Brenda Z. (1917). "The Relationship Systems of the Nandi Masai and Thonga," *Man*, Vol. XVII, 46.

Starcke, C. N. (1889). *The Primitive Family* (The International Scientific Series, Vol. LXVI). London: Kegan Paul.

Stewart, Dugald (1795). Introduction to *Essays of Adam Smith*.

Tax, Sol (1937). "The Social Organisation of the Fox Indians," in *Social Anthropology of North American Tribes* (ed. Fred Eggan). Chicago University Press, pp. 241–282.

# 5. *The Household Community*

BY MAX WEBER

THE EXAMINATION of the specific, often highly complex effects of the ways in which human communities satisfy their economic requirements will not be undertaken in the following general review, and concrete individual instances will be considered merely as examples.

While abandoning any attempt to systematically classify community types according to their structure, content, and means of communal action—a task which belongs to general sociology—we turn to a brief elucidation of those types of community which are of the greatest importance for our argument. Only the relationship of the economy to society in general—that is to say, the general structural forms of human communities—will be discussed here and not the relationship between the economic sphere and specific areas of culture—literature, art, science, etc. Contents and directions of communal action are discussed only in so far as they give rise to specifically patterned forms of communal action that are also economically relevant. The resulting boundary is no doubt quite fluid. At any rate, we shall be concerned only with certain universal types of communities. What follows next is only a general characterization. Concrete historical forms of these types of communities will be discussed in greater detail in a later part of this work, devoted to authority.

The relationships between father, mother, and children, established by a stable sexual grouping [*sexuelle Dauergemeinschaft*], appear to us today as

Translated by Ferdinand Kolegar, from Max Weber, "Die Hausgemeinschaft," "Die sexuellen Beziehungen in der Hausgemeinschaft," "Die Entwicklung zum 'Oikos,'" "Die Aufloesung der Hausgemeinschaft: Aenderungen ihrer funktionellen Stellung und zunehmende 'Rechenhaftigkeit.' Entstehung der modernen Handelsgesellschaften," in *Wirtschaft und Gesellschaft* (Tübingen: J. C. B. Mohr [Paul Siebeck], 1947), I, 212–15, 218–19, 230–34, 226–30, with the permission of J. C. B. Mohr.

particularly fundamental relationships. However, separated from the extended kinship household as a producing unit, the sexually based relationship between husband and wife, and the physiologically determined relationships between father and children are wholly unstable and tenuous. The father relationship cannot exist without a producing household unit of father and mother; even where there is such a unit the father relationship may not always be of great import. Of all the communal relationships arising on the basis of sexual intercourse, only the mother-child relationship is fundamental, because it is a household unit whose biologically based stability is sufficient to cover the period until the child is able to search for means of subsistence on his own. Thereupon comes the community of experience of siblings brought up together. In this connection, it may be noted that the Greeks spoke of *homogalaktes* (literally: persons suckled with the same milk; hence, foster brothers or sisters) to denote the closest kin. Here, too, the decisive thing is not the fact of the common mother, but the existence of the extended kinship household as a producing unit. Criss-crossing of communal, sexual, and physiological relationships occurs particularly in the family as a specific social institution. Historically, the concept of the family had several meanings and it is useful only if its particular meaning is always clearly defined. More will be said later on about this.

Although the maternal grouping, i.e., the subgroup within the nuclear family formed by mother and children, must be regarded as (in the present sense) the most primitive community of familial character, it does not mean—indeed, it is unimaginable—that there ever were human forms of existence in which maternal groupings were the only communities. As far as it is known, wherever the maternal grouping prevails as a family type, communal relationships, economic and military, exist among men as well, and so do those of men with women (relationships of both sexual and economic nature). The pure maternal grouping as a normal, but obviously secondary, form of community is often found precisely where men's everyday life is confined to the stable community of a "men's house," at first for military purposes, later on for other reasons. Men's houses [*Männerhäuser*] can be found in various countries as a specific concomitant and a resultant of militaristic development.

One cannot think of marriage as a mere combination of the sexual community and the community of experience of father, mother, and children. The concept of marriage can be defined only with reference to other communities and relationships besides these. Marriage as a social institution comes into existence everywhere only as an antithesis to sexual relationships which are *not* regarded as marriage. The existence of a marriage means that (1) a relationship formed against the will of the wife's or the husband's kin will not be tolerated and may even be avenged by a corporate group, such as in olden times the kinsmen of the husband or of the wife or both. (2) It means especially that only children born of stable sexual relationships within a more inclusive economic, political, religious, or other community to which one or both parents belong will be treated, by virtue of their descent, as equal members of a corporate group—house, village, kin, political group, status group, religious group; while descendants who are a product of other sexual relationships will not be treated in such a manner. It should be noted that this is the meaning of the distinction between birth in wedlock and out of wedlock. The prerequisites of a legitimate marriage, the classes of persons not allowed to enter into stable relationships with each other, the kinds of permission and kinds of kinship or other corporate connections required for their validity, the usages which must be observed—all these matters are regulated by "sacred" traditions and orders of those corporate groups. Thus, it is the regulations of communal groups other than mere sexual groupings and sibling communities of experience which endow the marriage with its specific quality. We do not intend to expound here the anthropologically very significant development of these regulations, since it is only their most important economic aspects which concern us.

Sexual relationships and the relationships between children based on the fact of their common parent or parents can engender communal action only by becoming the normal, though not the only, bases of a specific economic corporate group: the household community.

The household community cannot be regarded as simply a primitive institution. Its prerequisite is not a "household" in the present-day sense of the word, but rather a certain degree of organized cultivation of soil. The household community does not seem to have existed in a primitive economy of hunters and nomads. However, even under the conditions of a technically well-advanced agriculture, the household community is often secondary with respect to a preceding state which accorded more power to the inclusive communal groups of kinship and neighborhood on the one hand, and more freedom to the individual vis-à-vis the community of parents, children, grandchildren, and siblings on the other hand. The almost complete separation of the husband's and wife's means and belongings, which was very frequent especially where social differentiation was low, seems to point in this direction, as does the occasional custom according to which man and wife were seated back to back during their meals or even took their meals separately, and the fact that even within the political corporate group there existed independent organizations of women with female chieftains alongside the men's organizations. However, one should not infer from such facts the existence of an individualistic primitive condition.

Conditions that are due to a certain type of military organization, such as the man's absence from the house for his military service, lead to a "manless" household management by the wives and mothers. Such conditions were in part preserved in the family structure of the Spartans, which was based on man's absence from home and separation of belongings. The size and inclusiveness of the household community varies. But it is the most widespread economic group [*Wirtschaftsgemeinschaft*] and involves a continuous and intensive communal action. It is the fundamental basis of loyalty and authority, which in turn is the basis of many other human communal groups. This "authority" is of two kinds: (1) the authority derived from superior strength; and (2) the authority derived from practical knowledge and experience. It is, thus, the authority of men as against women and children; of the able-bodied and brave as against those of lesser capability; of the adult as against the child; of the old as against the young. The "loyalty" again unites those who are subjected to an authority against those who yield authority, but it also binds one to the other. As reverence for ancestors, it finds its way into religion; as a loyalty of the patrimonial official, retainer, or vassal, it becomes a part of the relationships originally having a domestic character.

In terms of economic and personal relationships, the household community in its "pure," though not necessarily primitive, form implies solidarity in dealing with the outside and communism of property and consumption of everyday goods (household communism) within the household. The principle of solidarity in facing the outside world was still found in its pure form in the periodically contractually regulated household communities as enterpreneurial units in the medieval cities of northern and central Italy, especially those most advanced in capitalist economy. All members of the household, including at times even the clerks and apprentices who were by contract members of the community, were jointly responsible to the creditors. This is the historic source of the joint liability of the owners of a private company for the debts incurred by the firm. This concept of joint liability was of great importance in the subsequent development of the legal forms of modern capitalism.

There was nothing corresponding to our law of inheritance in the old household communism. In its place there was, rather, the simple idea that the household community is "immortal." If one of its members dies, or is expelled (after committing an inexpiable ill deed), or is permitted to join another household community (by adoption), or is dismissed (*emancipatio*), or leaves out of his own accord (where this is permitted), he cannot possibly lay claim to his "share." By leaving the household community he has relinquished his share. If a member of the household dies, the communal economy of the survivors simply goes on. The Swiss communes [*Gemeinderschaft*] operate in such a way to the present day.

The principle of household communism, according to which everybody contributes what he can and takes what he needs (as far as the supply of goods suffices), constitutes even today the essential feature of our family household, but is limited in the main to household consumption.

Common residence is an essential attribute of the pure type of household community. Increase in size brings about a division and creation of separate household communities. In order to keep the property and the labor force intact, a compromise based on local dencentralization without partition could be adopted. Granting some special privileges to the individual household is an inevitable consequence of such a solution. Such a partition can be carried to a complete legal separation and independence in the control of the business, yet a surprisingly large measure of household communism can still be preserved. It often happens in Europe, particularly in the Alps (cf. Swiss hotel-keepers' families), and also in the large family firms of international trade that, while the household community and household authority have outwardly completely disappeared, a communism of risk and profit, i.e., sharing of profit and loss of otherwise altogether independent business managements, continues to exist.

I have been told about conditions in international houses with earnings amounting to millions, whose capital belongs for the most part, but not exclusively, to relatives of varying degree and whose management is predominantly, but not solely, in the hands of the members of the family. The individual establishments operate in very diverse and everchanging lines of business; they possess highly variable amounts of capital and labor force; and they achieve widely variable profits. In spite of this, after the deduction of the usual interest on capital, the annual returns of all the branches are simply thrown into one hopper, divided into equal por-

:ions, and allotted according to an amazingly simɔle formula (often by the number of heads). The ɿousehold communism on this level is being preserved for the sake of mutual economic support, which guarantees a compensation of capital requirements and capital surplus between the business establishments and spares them from having to solicit credit from outsiders. The calculating of gain ceases once the point of balance of assets and liabilities is reached. This calculability is practiced only within the establishment which makes the profit. But there it is applied without exception: even a close relative without capital and working as an employee will not be paid more than any other employee, because calculated costs of operation cannot be arbitrarily altered in favor of one individual without creating dissatisfaction in others.

## *Sexual Relationships in the Household Community*

We now return to the household community as the most fundamental type of communal action that is "closed against outsiders." The typical course of development from the old full-fledged household communism is the exact opposite of the previously discussed development, in which the productive unit is preserved in spite of the outward separation of the households, namely internal relaxation of communism and progressive "closure" of the community within, while the outward unity of the household is preserved.

The earliest decline of the continuous household authority evidently does not stem directly from economic motives but from the development of exclusive sexual claims of the household partners on the women who are subject to the common household jurisdiction. This has led to an often highly casuistic regulation of sexual relationships, but, considering the low degree of rationalization of the communal action, these regulations were very strictly observed. Sometimes there exist "communistic" (polyandric) sexual rights. But these polyandrically shared rights, as far as it is known, invariably represent only a relative communism, i.e., a joint possession of a woman by a circumscribed group of persons (brothers or inmates of a "men's house"), from which all outsiders are excluded.

Nowhere, not even where sexual relationships among siblings are institutionalized, does one find complete sexual promiscuity within the household. At least not as a norm. On the contrary, a communistic freedom of sexual intercourse is banished from those households which practice communism in the possession of goods. This was made possible and customary by the attenuation of sexual excitation brought about by living together from childhood on. The "normalization" of this state was obviously in the interest of securing the house solidarity and freedom from rivalry in the household. Wherever the household inmates were assigned to different clans through "clan exogamy," and when the principles of clan exogamy thus made sexual intercourse within the household permissible, certain members of the household had to avoid each other. Household exogamy is an older institution than clan exogamy and continues to exist along with it. Household exogamy, brought about by "associations for the exchange of women" [*Frauentauschkartelle*], of household and kinship communities may be regarded as the beginning of regulated exogamy. At any rate, the conventional disapproval of sexual intercourse applies also to those close relatives who are not excluded from it by the clan's kinship code, e.g., very close paternal relatives in case of exclusive matrilineal succession in kinship exogamy. The institution of marriage among siblings and relatives, on the other hand, is usually confined to socially prominent families, especially royal families. Here it is instrumental to maintaining the household's economic means of power, as well as eliminating political struggles among pretenders, and preserving purity of blood.

Normally, when a man brings a wife into his household community or when, lacking the necessary means, he moves into her own household community, he acquires exclusive sexual rights to that woman. In reality, these exclusive rights are quite often precarious when compared with those enjoyed by an autocratic possessor of household power. For instance, the privileges enjoyed by the father-in-law within the extended family in Russia until modern times are notorious.

However, the household community becomes, as a rule, subdivided into stable sexual groupings, composed of a man, his wife. and their children. The community of parents with their children, their domestics, and unmarried relatives is the normal size of the household community in our society. The household communities of the earlier epochs were not always very large structures. On the contrary, they were often rather small units, especially when the way of earning a livelihood made dispersion necessary. In the past, there were large household communities which, while rooted in the parent and children relationship, extended far beyond it, including grandsons, brothers, cousins, and sometimes also non-kin, to a degree which is very rare among civilized peoples today (*viz.*, extended family). Extensive kinship households prevail where mass labor is employed, e.g., in intensive agricultural economies, but also in aristocratic and plutocratic strata, where, in order to preserve social and economic power positions, it is necessary to keep the property intact.

Apart from the early prohibition of sexual intercourse within the household community, the sexual sphere in an otherwise undeveloped culture is very often curbed by social structures that cut across the household authority in such a fashion that one can say that the first decisive break of the limitless household authority occurs in this area. With increasing attention paid to "blood relationship," the concept of incest extends beyond the household to wider circles of blood relatives living away from the household and becomes subject to clan regulation.

## *The Development to "Oikos"*

In this section we are not particularly concerned with those forms of economic enterprise that became separated from the household community, and which represent the foundation of capitalistic enterprise. Rather, we are interested in the evolution of the household community that took an opposite course. We can distinguish between two lines of development. On the one hand, there is the internal dissolution of household authority and household community by means of "exchange with the outside world" (in the broadest sense of the term), and the consequences of this exchange up until the birth of capitalistic enterprise. On the other hand, there is the development in the opposite direction: the internal differentiation of the household community, its development to *oikos,* to use the term of Rodbertus. *Oikos* in the technical sense is not simply any extended household community or any group which produces on its own various products, industrial or agricultural. Rather, *oikos* refers to the authoritatively governed, expanded household of a prince, great landowner, or a patrician, the principle of which is not to earn money but to produce enough to satisfy the needs of the master through income received in kind. To this end, the master may use any means, including exchange. That the formative principle for him is the utilization of property for consumption needs and not as capital assets is of crucial importance. The essence of *oikos* is in the systematic satisfying of needs rather than in working for profit, even though individual industrial establishments oriented to profit-making may be attached to an *oikos.*

Between these two principles there is, of course, a whole range of gradual transitions and a frequent overlapping between the two. Actually, *oikos* in the sense of a pure collective economy is seldom necessary once material culture reaches some appreciable degree of development. The *oikos* in its pure form i.e., with the exclusion of exchange for profit, is possible only in "autarkic" economy, i.e., as an independent economic unit with a minimum of exchange. A staff of workers dependent on the household, often with highly specialized skills, is engaged in providing the master's economic, military, and sacramental goods and services. His own fields provide the master with all the necessary raw materials; his workshops and workers produce all the required goods; his own domestic servants, clerks, house priests, and warriors provide the rest. The only purpose of exchange, then, is to get rid of occasional surpluses and secure what the household itself cannot produce. This state of affairs is closely approximated by the royal economies of the Orient, especially of Egypt, and, to a lesser degree, by the economy of the noblemen and princes of the Homeric type. The royal households of the Persian and Franconian kings are closely related to it. The development of the landed proprietorships of the Roman Empire took this direction as their size and the bureaucratic and liturgical restrictions upon capitalistic acquisition increased and the influx of slaves decreased. The opposite tendency took place in the Middle Ages, with the growing importance of transportation of goods, cities, and money economy.

*Oikos* was never entirely autarkic in either of these types. The pharaohs and most of the kings and noblemen of the Mediterranean area, especially the primitive ones, were engaged in foreign trade; their treasures depended to a considerable extent on the revenues from this trade. The revenues of the landlords, as early as the Franconian Empire, included a large amount of money or valuable stock and incomes of all sorts. The capitularies of the Franconian law presuppose as a common occurrence the sale of the surpluses of the royal *fisci* not needed by the court and the army.

The unfree laborers of the large land- and slaveholders were usually only partly integrated into the economic organization controlled by the landlord. In the strict sense, this is true for personal servants and for those workers engaged in the economy satisfying the needs of the lord and who were fully taken care of by him ("autarkic units"). Yet, it is also true for those unfree laborers who worked for the master in his own enterprise for the market, in the same manner as the slaves of the landlords of Carthage, Sicily, and Rome worked on their plantations; or the slaves of Demosthenes' father worked in his two *ergasteria;* or, in modern times, Russian peasants worked in their landlords' factories ("market-oriented economy").

A large proportion of these slaves on plantations and in *ergasteria* were purchased in the market and were not "home-grown." Unfree laborers born in a household presuppose the existence of unfree families, i.e., a decentralization of the dependence on the household and usually a partial relinquishment by the lord of his total exploitation of the labor power.

The overwhelming majority of hereditarily unfree laborers is not used in centralized enterprises, and only a part of their productive power is at the disposal of the lord. These laborers pay him taxes, in kind or in money, fixed at a more or less arbitrary or traditional level. The question of how to use this labor force most profitably determines whether the lord will prefer to use the unfree labor as a working force or as a source of rent. In order to have a supplementary labor force of slaves without families lodged in barracks [*familienlose Kasernensklaven*], a cheap and continuous supply of slaves is necessary. Presuppositions of this are wars of slavery [*Menschenraubkriege*] and the availability of cheap food for the slaves, in other words, a southern climate.

Peasants in hereditary dependence can pay feudal dues in money only when they can bring their produce to an accessible—which means, generally, local—market, and when the towns of the area are sufficiently developed. Where cities are insufficiently developed and where crops can be sold only through export, the employment of peasants by way of *corvée* on the landlord's own estate was often the only way of using their labor force with profit. This was the case in eastern Germany and eastern Europe, in contrast to western Europe, in the beginning of the modern era, and in the Russian "black earth" area in the nineteenth century.

These conditions gave rise to the development of a large-scale agricultural enterprise within the *oikos*. The creation of large-scale industrial enterprises with unfree labor, or with the aid or exclusive use of hired free or unfree labor in his own or rented *ergasteria*, can make the manager of an *oikos* very much like a capitalistic entrepreneur, or can change him into one. This is exactly what happened, for instance, with the founders of the industrial system of the *starostas** in Silesia.

Utilizing the existing property so as to produce income is characteristic of the *oikos*. This, from the managerial point of view, can be actually indistinguishable from, and can finally become identical with, the enterpriser's own capital. Certain features of the *starostas* industry, as are to be found in Silesia, remind one of manorial economy. One such is the combination of various enterprises, as, for instance, huge forestries with brick-yards, distilleries, sugar factories, and coal mines. These works are not linked with one another in the same way as a cluster of enterprises is united in a single modern enterprise ("combined" or "mixed"), by virtue of the fact that they represent different stages in the manufacture of certain raw material (including utilization of by-products and waste) or because they are connected by market conditions. The landlord who affiliates a foundry and perhaps even a steel mill with his coal mines, or who attaches sawmills and cellulose factory to his forestry, can achieve practically the same result; the difference then lies only in the point of departure, not in the outcome.

The beginnings of combinations of workshops based on the possession of a certain raw material can be found as early as the *ergasteria* of antiquity. The father of Demosthenes, coming from an Attic merchant family, was an importer and salesman (τῷβουλομένῳ) of ivory, which could be used as an inlay in both knife handles and in furniture. Having already begun to let his own trained slaves manufacture knives in his workshop, he had to take over the *ergasterion* of an insolvent cabinet-maker, including the slaves working in that *ergasterion*. He owned then a cutler's and a cabinet-maker's *ergasterion*.

The development of *ergasteria* progressed in the Hellenistic, especially Alexandrine, and old-Islamic civilizations. Utilizing unfree industrial labor as a source of income was quite common in oriental and classic antiquity, in the early Middle Ages, and in Russia before the abolition of serfdom. The master used to lease his slaves as labor force. Nikias did so on a large scale, hiring out his untrained slaves to the mine-owners. Ultimately, he had the slaves taught some craft in order to utilize them more efficiently. We find this situation through all antiquity, beginning with a contract naming prince Cambyses an owner of a tutor up until the Pandects. The same phenomenon existed in Russia in the eighteenth and nineteenth centuries. After having them trained, the master may leave it up to the slaves to work as craftsmen on their own. Should they do so, they were obliged to pay him rent (in Greek, *apophora;* in Babylonian, *mandaku;* in German, *Halssteuer;* in Russian, *obrok*). The master may also provide a workshop for them and supply them with machinery (*peculium*) and capital (*merx peculiaris*). In the master's enterprise, there is a wide variety of all conceivable gradations that are historically documented, from almost complete freedom of movement to a complete caserne-like regimentation. The economic details and peculiarities of the "enterprises" that arose on the basis of the *oikos*, managed

* *Starosta* (in Poland) is a nobleman holding an estate of the Crown, with or without jurisdiction. Translator's note.

either by the lord or by his subordinates, belong within another context. The development and transformation of the *oikos* into patrimonial authority will be examined later, in connection with our analysis of the types of authority.

## *The Dissolution of the Household Community; Its Changing Function and Increasing "Calculability": The Origin of Modern Trading Companies*

In the course of cultural development, the internal and external determinants of the weakening of household authority gain ascendancy. Operating from within, and correlated with the quantitative growth of economic means and resources, is the development and differentiation of abilities and wants. With the improvement and multiplication of life chances and opportunities, the individual becomes less and less content with being bound to rigid and undifferentiated forms of life prescribed by the community. Increasingly he desires to shape his life as an individual and to enjoy the fruits of his own abilities and labor as he himself wishes.

The dissolution of the household authority is furthered by a number of outside factors. One of them is the fiscal interest in a more intensive exploitation of the individual tax-paying capacity. While this is in favor of fitness for military service, it may work contrary to the interests in keeping one's property intact.

The usual consequence of these disintegrative tendencies is, in the first place, the increasing likelihood of division of household communities in case of inheritance or marriage of children. In the early times of relatively primitive agriculture without tools, employment of mass labor was the only means of increasing productivity. As a result, the household communities grew in size. The historical development and the concomitant development of individualized production brought about a decrease in the size of household communities, which continued until the family unit of parents and children reached its normal size today.

The function of the household community has changed so much that it is becoming increasingly inopportune for an individual to join a large communistic household. An individual no longer gets protection from the household and kinship groups but rather from the corporate political authority, which exercises compulsory jurisdiction. Furthermore, household and occupation became ecologically separated, and the household is no longer a unit of common production but a unit of common consumption. Moreover, the individual receives his entire education increasingly from agencies outside his home and by means which are supplied not by his home but by various institutions of the larger society: schools, bookstores, theaters, concert halls, clubs, public lectures, meetings, etc. He cannot thus regard the household community as the bearer of those cultural values in whose service he places himself.

This decrease in the size of household communities is not due to a growing "subjectivism" but to the objective determinants of its growth. It should not be overlooked that there exist also hindrances to this development, particularly on the highest levels of the economic scale. In agriculture, the possibility of unrestricted splitting up of landed estates is tied in with certain technological conditions. An estate of circular shape, even a large one, with valuable buildings on it, can be partitioned only at a loss. The division is technically facilitated by a sort of common farming, in which the various holdings lie side by side in strips, and by village settlement. Isolated location makes such a partition difficult. Separate farms and large estates, operated with an intensive expenditure of capital, therefore tend to be inherited by one individual. A small farm, operated with intensive expenditure of labor and whose holdings lie side by side without footpaths, so that a particular holding can only be reached by crossing that of a neighbor, has a tendency to continuous splintering. In addition, the separate farm and large estate are much more suitable objects from which to extract tributary taxes on movable property in the form of long-term mortgages and pawns, and they are thus kept intact for the benefit of the creditors.

Large property-holding, being a determinant of position and prestige, is conducive to the desire to keep it intact in the family. A small farm, on the other hand, is merely a place where work is done. There is an appositeness between the seigniorial standard of life, with its fixed conventions, and the large household communities. Given the spaciousness of, say, a castle and the almost inevitable "inner distance" even between the closest members, these large household communities do not restrain the freedom that the individual demands to such an extent as does the middle-class household, which may consist of an equally large number of persons but occupies a smaller space and lacks the aristocratic sense of distance. Today, the large household community provides an appropriate way of life, aside from the seigniorial one, only for an intense ideological community of a religious sect, or a social-ethical sect, or an artistic coterie—corresponding to the monasteries and cloister-like communities of the past.

Even where the household unit remains outwardly intact, the process of internal dissolution of household communism goes on irresistibly along with the growing "calculability." We shall now examine the consequences of this factor in somewhat greater detail.

In the large capitalistic household communities of medieval cities—for example, in Florence—every person has his own account. He has pocket money (*danari borsinghi*) at his free disposal. Specific upper limits are set for certain expenditures—for example, visitors staying at the house upon invitation. He has to settle his account in the same way as do partners in any modern trading company. He has capital shares "within" the community, and he has property (*fuori della compagnia*) deposited with the community, on which he draws interest but which is not regarded as capital and therefore does not share in the profit. Participation in the communal action of the household, with its advantages and obligations, which one is "born into" has thus been replaced by a rational consociation [*Vergesellschaftung*]. The individual is "born into" the household community, but even as a child he is already a potential commercial clerk and business partner of the rationally ordered business enterprise. It is evident that such conduct became possible only within the framework of a money economy; the development of the money economy therefore plays a crucial role in the internal dissolution of the household community. The money economy makes possible an objective calculation both of the productive performances and of the consumption of the individuals, and it makes it possible for them to satisfy their individual wants by "indirect exchange," through the medium of money.

The parallelism of the money economy and the attenuation of household authority is, of course, far from complete. Household authority and household community are economically "irrational" institutions independent of economic conditions of a particular period. In fact, their historical structure exercises considerable influence on the economic relationships. The socio-economic, political, and religious factors—such as the interest in keeping the property of a noble house intact; the military organization according to kinship and presumably household groups; the father's position as a house-priest—determined the origin of the *patria potestas* wielded by the Roman head of the family all his life. But it has persisted throughout the most diverse stages of economic development, until it attenuated in the period of Roman Empire.

A similar situation has been brought about in China by the principle of filial piety, reinforced by the code of duties and bolstered by the state authority and the Confucian bureaucratic ethic, for the purpose of maintaining political control over the subjects—among other things. This principle of filial piety in practice led to a number of undesirable consequences, both economically and politically. Regulations concerning mourning were one case in point. For example, frequent vacancies of offices occurred, because piety to the deceased head of the household—originally fear of the dead man's envy—forbade the use of his property and the occupation of his office. The economic factors originally determine whether a property is inherited by one person or principal heir or whether it is divided. This practice varies with economic influences, but it cannot be explained solely by economic factors, and especially not by contemporary economic conditions. This was demonstrated particularly in the recent studies of Sering. Under identical conditions and in contiguous areas, there exist often quite disparate systems, affected especially by different ethnic composition, e.g., Poles and Germans. The far reaching economic consequences of these differing structures were caused by factors that could be regarded as "irrational" from the economic point of view at the very beginning, or that became irrational as a consequence of changes in economic conditions.

In spite of all, the economic realities intervene in a compelling manner. First, there are characteristic differences depending on whether economic gain is attributed to common work or to common property. If the former situation obtains, the household authority is usually basically unstable, no matter how autocratic it may be. Mere separation from the parental household and the establishment of an independent household is sufficient for a person to be set free from the household authority. This is mostly the case in the large household communities of primitive agricultural peoples. The *emancipatio legis Saxonicae* of the German law clearly has its economic foundation in the recognition of the importance of personal work performance, which antedated the formulation of this law.

On the other hand, the household authority is typically stable wherever ownership of livestock, and property in general, forms the prime basis of existence. This is particularly true when land ceases to be abundant and becomes a scarce commodity. For reasons already alluded to, family and lineage cohesion is generally an attribute of the landed aristocracy. The man without any landed property or with only little of it is also without the corporate lineage group.

The same difference is to be found in the capitalistic stage of development. The large household communities of Florence and other parts of northern Italy practiced the principle of joint responsibility and of maintaining the property intact. In the trading places of the Mediterranean, especially in Sicily and southern Italy, the exact opposite was the case: each adult member of the household could at any time request the apportionment and his share while the legator was still alive. Nor did joint personal liability to the outsiders exist. In the family enterprises of northern Italy, the inherited capital represented the basis of economic power position to a greater degree than did the personal business activities of the partners. The opposite was true in southern Italy, where common property was treated as a product of common work. With the increasing importance of capital, the former practice gained ascendancy.

In terms of a hypothetical sequence of developmental stages starting with the continuous communal action, the "later" stage, i.e., capitalistic type of economy, determines a theoretically "earlier" structure, in which the members of the household are more tightly bound to the household and subjected to the household authority.

A far more significant transformation of household authority and household community, one which is characteristic of the Occident, took place in the household communities oriented to capitalistic enterprise, in Florence and other cities. The entire economic life of such a large household community was periodically regulated by contracts. Whereas, originally, the personal funds and the business organization were regulated by the same set of rules, the situation gradually changed. The conduct of continuous capitalistic enterprise became a special occupation, performed in a special undertaking [*Betrieb*], which became increasingly separated from the activity of the household community, in such a way that the old identity of household, workshop, and office fell apart. The household community ceased to exist as a necessary basis of rational consociation or associative relationship in business. Henceforth, the business partner is not necessarily—or typically—an inmate of the household. Consequently, it was mandatory to separate the business assets from the private property of the partners. Similarly, distinction began to be made between the employees of the business and the personal domestic servants. Above all, distinction had to be made between the debts of the commercial house and the private household debts of the individual partners. The joint responsibility of the partners was limited to the debts of the company, which were identified as such by being transacted under the "firm." i.e., under the name of the business company. This whole development is obviously a precise parallel to the separation of the bureaucratic office as occupation from the private life; the separation of the "bureau" from the private household of the official; the separation of assets and liabilities of the office from the official's private property; and of the official dealings from private dealings. The capitalistic business organization, whose seeds are within the household community, is thus already related to the "bureau," and thus also to the now obvious bureaucratization of the private economic life.

But the factor of decisive importance in this development is not the spatial differentiation or separation of the household from the workshop and the store. This is rather typical of the bazaar system of the Islamic cities in the Orient, which rests throughout on the separation of the borough (*Kasbeh*), bazaar (*suk*), and residence. What is crucial is the separation of household and business for accounting and legal purposes; and the development of a suitable body of laws, such as the commercial register, elimination of dependence of the association and the firm upon the family, and the creation of appropriate laws on bankruptcy. This fundamental development is the characteristic feature of the Occident, and it is worthy of note that the legal forms of our present commercial law were almost all developed as early as the Middle Ages—whereas they were almost entirely foreign to the law of antiquity with its capitalism which was quantitatively sometimes much more developed. This is one of the many phenomena characterizing most clearly the qualitative uniqueness of the development of modern capitalism, since both the concentration of the family property for the purpose of mutual economic support and the development of a "firm" from a family name existed, for example, in China as well. There, too, the joint liability of the family stands behind the debts of the individual. The name used by a company in commercial transactions does not provide information about the actual proprietor: there, too, the "firm" is related to the business organization and not to the household. But the laws on private property and bankruptcy as they were developed in Europe seem to be absent in China. Two things are of special relevance: Association and credit, until the modern era, were to a large degree dependent on the kinship group. Likewise, the keeping of the property intact in the well-to-do kinship groups and the mutual granting of credit within the kinship groups served different purposes. They were concerned not with capitalistic profit but with raising money to cover the costs of family members' preparation for the examinations and afterwards for the purchase of an office. The incumbency of the office then offered the relatives an opportunity to recover their expenses with a profit from the legal and illegal revenues that the office afforded. Furthermore, these relatives could benefit from the protection of the office-holder. It was the chances of the politically rather than economically determined gain that were conducive to the "capitalistic" cohesion of the family, especially one that was well-off economically.

The capitalistic type of association, which corresponds to our joint-stock company and is completely detached, at least formally, from kinship and personal ties, has its antecedents in antiquity only in the area of politically oriented capitalism, i.e., in companies of tax farmers. In the Middle Ages, these were the companies organized partly for colonizing ventures—such as the big branches of the Maone in Genoa—and partly for state credit—such as the Genoese association of creditors, which actually managed the municipal finances. In the area of private enterprise, the strictly commercial and capitalistic association is at first developed merely as an *ad hoc* company (*commenda*) for distant trading, in the manner of occasional business according to varying circumstances, which existed already in the old Babylonian empire. An investor gave money to a traveling salesman for a specific trip, and they both then shared profit and loss. Enterprises that were endowed with monopolistic privilege by the state, especially joint-stock-company-type of colonial enterprises, formed then the transition to the application of these kinds of enterprises in private business.

## II–ETHNIC SOLIDARITIES

# 1. *Ethnic Groups*

BY MAX WEBER

THE QUESTION of whether conspicuous "racial" differences are based on biological heredity or on social and cultural tradition is usually of no importance as far as their effect on mutual attraction or repulsion is concerned. This is true of the development of endogamous conjugal groups, and even more so of attraction and repulsion in other kinds of social intercourse, i.e., of whether all sorts of friendly, companionable, or economic relationships between such groups are established easily and on the footing of mutual trust and respect, or whether such relationships are established with difficulty and with precautions that betray mistrust.

Groups within which easy social intercourse is possible may have their source and beginning in the most superficial differences of outward habits of life, which were formed due to some historical accident, just as well as in inherited racial characteristics. That the deviant custom is not understood in its subjective meaning since the key to it is lacking, is almost as decisive as the peculiarity of the deviant customs as such. But, as we shall soon see, not all repulsion is attributable to the absence of mutual understanding. Differences in the style of beard and hairdo, clothes, food and eating habits, division of labor between the sexes, and all kinds of visible differences can, in some cases, give rise to repulsion and contempt for the bearers of these strangely different ways. In their effect on the feeling of attraction or repulsion, there are as few distinctions between the importance or unimportance of the above-mentioned differences as in the primitive travel descriptions, or in the Histories of Herodotus, or in the old prescientific ethnography. Seen from their positive aspect, however, these differences may give rise to a consciousness of kind. This consciousness of kind may then become the bearer of communal social relationships. Likewise, every type of community, from a household group or neighborhood group to a political or religious community, typically becomes a bearer of shared customs. All differences of custom can sustain a specific sense of

Translated by Ferdinand Kolegar, from Max Weber, "Entstehung ethnischen Gemeinsamkeitsglaubens. Sprach- und Kultgemeinschaft," in *Wirtschaft und Gesellschaft* (Tüebingen: J. C. B. Mohr [Paul Siebeck], 1947), I, 234–40, with the permission of J. C. B. Mohr.

"honor" or "dignity" in their practitioners. The original motives or reasons for the inception of different habits of life are forgotten and the contrasts are then perpetuated as conventions.

Any community can create customs, and it can also effect, in certain circumstances very decisively, the selection of anthropological types. This it can do by breeding, by providing favorable chances of life, survival, and reproduction for certain hereditary qualities and traits. This holds both for internal assimilation and for external differentiation.

Any aspect or cultural trait, no matter how superficial, can serve as a starting point for the familiar tendency to monopolistic closure. The universal force of imitation has the general effect of only gradually changing both the anthropological types through racial mixing and the traditional customs and usages. Sharp boundaries between areas of externally observable styles of life often arose by conscious monopolistic closure. This started from small differences, which were then purposely cultivated and intensified. Or they arose when, as a result of either peaceful or warlike migrations, communities that had previously lived far from each other and had accommodated themselves to their heterogeneous conditions of existence now came to live side by side. Similarly, sharply different racial types, which came into being by breeding in isolation, may come into close mutual contact either because of monopolistic closure or because of migration.

Similarity and contrast of physical type and of custom have the same effect on formation of a community and are subject in their origin and change to identical conditions of communal life, regardless of whether they are biologically inherited or culturally transmitted. The difference lies partly in their differential instability, depending on whether they are biologically inherited or transmitted by tradition, partly in the fixed (though often unknown) limit to engendering new hereditary qualities. Compared to this, the scope for assimilation of new customs is incomparably greater, although there are considerable variations in the transmissibility of traditions.

Almost any kind of similarity or contrast of physical type and of habits can induce the belief that a tribal affinity or disaffinity exists between groups that attract or repel each other. Not every belief in tribal affinity, however, is founded on the resemblance of customs or of physical type. But, in spite of great variations in this area, such a belief can exist and can develop community-forming powers when it is buttressed by a memory of an actual migration, be it colonization or individual migration. The persistent effect of the old and traditional ways and of childhood reminiscences can be a source of a homeland or native-country sentiment [*Heimatsgefuehl*] among emigrants, even when they have become so thoroughly adjusted to the new country that return to their homeland would be intolerable (this being the case of most German-Americans, for example).

In colonies, the attachment to the colonists' homeland survives despite considerable mixing with the inhabitants of the colonial land and despite profound changes in tradition and hereditary type as well. In case of political colonization, the decisive factor is the need of political support. In general, the continuation of relationships created by marriage is important, and so are the market relationships, provided that the "customs" remained unchanged. These market relationships between the homeland and the colony may be very close, especially when colonies are in an almost absolutely alien environment and within an alien political territory.

The belief in tribal kinship, regardless of whether it has any objective foundation, can have important consequences especially for the formation of a political community. Those human groups that entertain a subjective belief in their common descent —because of similarities of physical type or of customs or both, or because of memories of colonization and migration—in such a way that this belief is important for the continuation of nonkinship communal relationship, we shall call "ethnic" groups, regardless of whether an objective blood relationship exists or not. The ethnic group differs from the kinship community precisely in being a group (which believes in its common descent) but not a community, unlike the kinship group which is characterized by actual communal action. In our present sense, the ethnic community itself is not a community; it only facilitates communal relationships. It facilitates and promotes all types of communal relationships, particularly in the political sphere. On the other hand, it is primarily the political community, no matter how artificial, that inspires the belief in common ethnicity. This belief tends to persist even after the disintegration of the political community, unless drastic differences in the custom, physical type, or, above all, language exist among its members.

This artificial origin of the belief in common ethnicity is in full accord with the already described schema of transmutation of rational associative relationships into personalized communal relationships. In the relative absence of rational associative action, almost any, even a purely rational, consociation can attract communal consciousness in the form of personal confraternity based on the belief in common ethnicity. The Greeks still viewed even the arbitrary divisions of the *polis* in terms of personal "corporate groups," with a distinct community of cult and claiming a common artificial ancestor. The twelve tribes of Israel were subdivisions of a political community, and they alternated in performing certain functions on a monthly basis. The same holds for the Greek tribes (*phyle*) and their subdivisions. But even the latter are regarded as units of common ethnic descent. The original division may have been induced by political or actual ethnic differences. The effect, however, was the same, even where such a division was made quite purposely and on the basis of rational considerations, after the break-up of old corporate groups and relinquishment of local cohesion, as it was done by Cleisthenes. This does not mean that, as a rule, the Greek *polis* was actually or originally a tribal or dynastic state. But it is, in general, a sign of the rather low degree of rationalization of Greek communal [political] life. Conversely, it is a symptom of the greater rationalization of the Roman political community that its old schematic subdivisions (*curiae*) took on religious importance with a pretense to ethnic origin to only a small degree.

The belief in common ethnicity is very often, though not always, an obstacle to the existence of groups where easy social intercourse [*soziale Verkehrsgemeinschaften*] is possible. Such groups are not identical with the endogamous conjugal groups, since both of them can be of varying scope and range. But they both rest on a similar basis, which is the belief in a specific "honor" of their members, not shared by the outsiders, i.e., the sense of ethnic honor. Later on we shall discuss how it is related to the sense of honor of a distinctive social group [*staendische Ehre*]. At this point a few remarks will suffice. A rigorous sociological investigation would have to make a much finer distinction between these concepts than we have done for our limited purpose here.

Communities can engender sentiments of community [*Gemeinsamkeitsgefuehle*], which will persist even after the community itself has disappeared and which will have an "ethnic" connotation. The political community in particular can produce such an effect. This is especially so in the case of that type of a community which is the bearer of a specific "culture value of the masses" [*Massenkulturgut*] and which makes mutual understanding possible or easier, namely, the community of language.

Wherever the memory of the origin of an *émigré* community by peaceful secession or emigration ("colony," *ver sacrum*, and the like) from a mother community remains for some reason continually alive, there undoubtedly exists a very specific and often extremely powerful sense of ethnic community. This sense of ethnic community is determined by several factors: by the shared political "memory" or, even more importantly in the earlier times, by the existence of ties with the old cult-communities; and by unceasing strengthening of the kinship groups and other communal relationships by means of pervasive and ever felt relations between the old and the new community. Where these relationships are lacking, or once they cease to exist, the sense of ethnic community is absent, regardless of how close the kinship may be.

Apart from the community of language, which may or may not coincide with objective or subjectively believed consanguinity, and apart from common religious belief, which is also independent of consanguinity, and apart from the effect of common political fortunes and the memories thereof, which at least objectively have nothing to do with consanguinity, the ethnic differences that remain are, on the one hand, aesthetically conspicuous differences of the external physical appearance and, on the other hand and of equal weight, the perceptible differences in the conduct of everyday life. Of special importance are precisely those items which may otherwise seem to be of small social relevance, since when ethnic differentiation is concerned it is always the outward conspicuous differences that come into play.

The community of language and, along with it, the identity of the "ritual regimentation of life," as determined by shared religious beliefs, obviously are universal elements of feelings of ethnic affinity [*ethnische Verwandtschaftsgefuehle*], especially since the meaningful "intelligibility" [*sinnhafte Verstaendlichkeit*] of the behavior of others is the most fundamental presupposition of communal relationship. But since we shall not consider these two elements in the present context, we ask: what is it that remains? It must be admitted that palpable differences in dialect and differences of religion in themselves do not exclude sentiments of common ethnicity.

Next to pronounced differences in the style of economic life, the belief in ethnic affinity has at all times been affected by outward differences in clothes, in the style of housing, food and eating habits, the division of labor between the sexes, and between the free and the unfree. That is to say, these things concern one's conception of what is correct and proper and, above all, of what affects the individual's sense of honor and dignity. All those things we shall find later on as objects of specific differences between "status" groups. The conviction of the excellence of one's own customs and the inferiority of alien ones, a conviction which sustains the sense of ethnic honor, is actually quite analogous to the sense of honor of distinctive status groups.

The sense of ethnic honor is a specific honor of the masses [*Massenehre*], for it is accessible to anybody who belongs to the subjectively believed community of descent. The "poor white trash," i.e., the propertyless and, in the absence of free work opportunities, very often destitute white inhabitants of the southern states of the United States of America in the period of slavery, were the actual bearers of racial antipathy, which was quite foreign to the planters. This was so because the social honor of the "poor whites" was dependent upon the social *déclassement* of the Negroes.

And behind all ethnic diversities there is somehow naturally the notion of the "chosen people," which is nothing else but a counterpart of status differentiation translated into the plane of horizontal coexistence. The idea of a chosen people derives its popularity from the fact that it can be claimed to an equal degree by any and every member of the mutually despising groups, in contrast to status differentiation which always rests on subordination. Consequently, ethnic repulsion may take hold of all conceivable differences between the notions of propriety and transforms them into "ethnic conventions."

Besides the previously mentioned elements, which were still more or less closely related to the economic order, conventionalization (a term to be expounded later) may take hold of such things as a hairdo or style of beard and the like. The differences thereof have an "ethnically" repulsive effect, because they are thought of as symbols of ethnic membership. The repulsion naturally is not based merely on the "symbolic" character of the distinguishing traits. The fact that the Scythian women oiled their hair with butter, which then gave off a rancid odor, while Greek women used perfumed oil to achieve the same purpose, thwarted—according to an ancient report—all attempts at social intercourse between the aristocratic ladies of these two groups. The smell of butter certainly had a more compelling effect than even the most prominent racial differences, or than—as far as I could see—the "odor of Negroes," of which so many fables are told. In general, racial qualities are effective as limiting factors in giving rise to the belief in common ethnicity, such as in case of an excessively heterogeneous and aesthetically unaccepted physical type; they are not positively "community-forming."

Pronounced differences of custom, which play a role equal to that of inherited physical type in the creation of feelings of common ethnicity and ideas of kinship, are usually caused, in addition to linguistic and religious differences, by the diverse economic and political conditions of various human social groups. If we ignore clear-cut linguistic boundaries and sharply demarcated political or religious communities as a basis of differences of custom—and these in fact are lacking in wide areas of the African and South American continents—then there are only gradual transitions of custom and no immutable ethnic frontiers, except those due to gross geographical differences. The sharp demarcation of areas wherein ethnically relevant customs predominate, which were not conditioned either by political or economic or religious factors, usually came into existence by way of migration or expansion, when groups of people that had previously lived in complete or partial isolation from each other and became accommodated to heterogeneous conditions of existence came to live side by side. As a result, the obvious contrast usually evokes, on both sides, the idea of blood disaffinity or "foreignness" [*Blutsfremdheit*], regardless of the objective state of affairs.

It is understandably difficult to determine in general—and it is of questionable importance even in a concrete individual case—what influence specific ethnic factors (i.e., the belief in a blood relationship, or its opposite, which rests on similarities, or differences, of a person's physical appearance and style of life) have on the formation of a community.

There is no difference between the ethnically relevant customs and customs in general, as far as their effect is concerned. The belief in affiliation of descent [*Abstammungsverwandtschaft*], in combination with a similarity of customs, is likely to promote the diffusion of communal action among those allied by ethnic ties, because "imitation" is generally encouraged by the consciousness of community. This is especially true of the propaganda of religious communities. But these are all-too-vague statements. The content of communal action that is possible on an ethnic basis remains indefinite. There is a corresponding ambiguity of concepts denoting ethnically determined communal action, i.e., determined by the belief in blood relationship. Such concepts are "clan," "tribe," "nation," each of which is ordinarily used in the sense of an ethnic subdivision of the following one (although the first two may be used in reversed order). Using such terms, one usually tacitly assumed either the existence of a contemporary political community, be it even a loose one; or memories of an extinct political community, such as they are preserved in epic tales and legends; or the existence of a linguistic community; or, finally, of a religious community.

Certain religious communities especially were the typical concomitants of a tribal or national consciousness based on a belief in blood relationship. But in the absence of the political community, present or past, the external delimitation of such a community was usually rather indistinct. The religious communities of Germanic tribes, as late as the late Burgundian period, were rudiments of political communities and therefore apparently firmly delimited. The Delphian oracle was an undoubted cultic sign of the national identity of the Greek world. But God revealed information even to the barbarians and accepted their adulation, too, and only few segments of Greeks, and none of their most powerful communities, took part in the "societalized" administration of this cult. The community of cult as an index of "tribalism" is thus generally either a remnant of a largely political type of community, which once existed but was destroyed by disunion and colonization, or it is—as in the case of Delphian Apollo—a product of a "culture-community" brought about by other than purely ethnic conditions, and which in its turn gives rise to the belief in blood relationship. All history shows how easily political communal action can give rise to the idea of blood relationship, unless gross differences of anthropological type are there to impede it.

## 2. *The Problem of Minority Groups*

BY LOUIS WIRTH

WE MAY DEFINE a minority as a group of people who, because of their physical or cultural characteristics, are singled out from the others in the society in which they live for differential and unequal treatment, and who therefore regard themselves as objects of collective discrimination. The existence of a minority in a society implies the existence of a corresponding dominant group enjoying higher social status and greater privileges. Minority status carries with it the exclusion from full participation in the life of the society. Though not necessarily an alien group, the minority is treated and regards itself as a people apart.

To understand the nature and significance of minorities it is necessary to take account of their objective as well as their subjective position. A minority must be distinguishable from the dominant group by physical or cultural marks. In the absence of such identifying characteristics it blends into the rest of the population in the course of time. Minorities objectively occupy a disadvantageous position in society. As contrasted with the dominant group they are debarred from certain opportunities —economic, social and political. These deprivations circumscribe the individual's freedom of choice and self-development. The members of minority groups are held in lower esteem and may even be objects of contempt, hatred, ridicule, and violence. They are generally socially isolated and frequently spatially segregated. Their subordinate position becomes manifest in their unequal access to educational opportunities and in their restricted scope of occupational and professional advancement. They are not as free as other members of society to join the voluntary associations that express their interests. They suffer from more than the ordinary amount of social and economic insecurity. Even as concerns public policy they are frequently singled out for special treatment; their property rights may be restricted; they may not enjoy the equal protection of the laws; they may be deprived of the right of suffrage and may be excluded from public office.

Aside from these objective characteristics by which they are distinguished from the dominant group and in large measure as a result of them, minorities tend to develop a set of attitudes, forms of behavior, and other subjective characteristics which tend further to set them apart. One cannot long discriminate against people without generating in them a sense of isolation and of persecution and without giving them a conception of themselves as more different from others than in fact they are. Whether, as a result of this differential treatment, the minority

Reprinted from Louis Wirth, "The Problem of Minority Groups," in Ralph Linton (ed.), *The Science of Man in the World Crisis* (New York: Columbia University Press, 1945), pp. 347–52, 354–56, 358–60, 361–64, with the permission of Columbia University Press.

comes to suffer from a sense of its own inferiority or develops a feeling that it is unjustly treated—which may lead to a rebellious attitude—depends in part upon the length of time that its status has existed and in part upon the total social setting in which the differential treatment operates. Where a caste system has existed over many generations and is sanctioned by religious and other sentiments, the attitude of resignation is likely to be dominant over the spirit of rebellion. But in a secular society where class rather than caste pervades the stratification of people, and where the tradition of minority status is of recent origin, minorities, driven by a sense of frustration and unjustified subordination, are likely to refuse to accept their status and their deprivation without some effort to improve their lot.

When the sentiments and attitude of such a disadvantaged group become articulate, and when the members become conscious of their deprivations and conceive of themselves as persons having rights, and when they clamor for emancipation and equality, a minority becomes a political force to be reckoned with. To the individual members of such a group the most onerous circumstance under which they have to labor is that they are treated as members of a category, irrespective of their individual merits. Hence, it is important to recognize that membership in a minority is involuntary; our own behavior is irrelevant. Many of us are identified with political, social, and intellectual groups which do not enjoy the favor of the dominant group in society, but as long as we are free to join and to leave such groups at will we do not by virtue of our membership in them belong to a minority. Since the racial stock from which we are descended is something over which we have perhaps least control and since racial marks are the most visible and permanent marks with which we are afflicted, racial minorities tend to be the most enduring minorities of all.

It should be noted further that a minority is not necessarily an alien group. Indeed, in many parts of the world it is the native peoples who constitute the minority, whereas the invaders, the conquerors, or the newcomers occupy the status of dominant groups. In the United States the indigenous Indians occupy the position of a minority. In Canada the earlier French settlers are a minority in relation to the more recent English migrants. In almost all colonial countries it is the "foreigners" who are dominant and the indigenous populations who are subordinate.

Nor should it be assumed that the concept is a statistical one. Although the size of the group may have some effect upon its status and upon its relationship to the dominant group, minorities are not to be judged in terms of numbers. The people whom we regard as a minority may actually, from a numerical standpoint, be a majority. Thus, there are many parts of the South in the United States where the Negroes are the overwhelming majority of the inhabitants but, nevertheless, are an unmistakable minority in the sense that they are socially, politically, and economically subordinate.

It may even be true that a people may attain the status of a minority even though it does not become the object of disesteem, discrimination, and persecution. If it considers itself the object of such inferior treatment, an oppression psychosis may develop. If a group sets itself apart from others by a distinctive culture and perpetuates itself in this isolated condition long enough, the social distances between itself and others may grow so great as to lead to the accumulation of suspicion and non-intercourse which will make it virtually impossible for members of these groups to carry on a truly collective life. Lack of intimate knowledge of and contact with others may in the course of time generate an incapacity for mutual understanding and appreciation which allows mental stereotypes to arise which the individual cannot escape. What matters, then, about minorities is not merely their objective position but the corresponding patterns of behavior they develop and the pictures they carry around in their heads of themselves and of others. While minorities more often than not stand in a relationship of conflict with the dominant group, it is their nonparticipation in the life of the larger society, or in certain aspects thereof, that more particularly marks them as a minority people and perpetuates their status as such.

It is easy enough to catalog the minority peoples in various parts of the world in accordance with a set of criteria such as race, national origin, language, religion, or other distinctive cultural traits. Thus it is possible to define the areas of the world where one or another racial, ethnic, linguistic, or religious group occupies a subordinate status with reference to some other group. In different parts of the world different groups are consigned to minority status. A given racial, ethnic, linguistic, or religious group may be dominant in one area and be the minority in another. Similar variations are found throughout history. Groups which in one epoch were dominant may in another be reduced to subordinate status. Because of the colonizing enterprises of some of the nation-states of Western Europe a large part of the rest of the world has been subordinated to their political rule, their economic control, and the technology and culture which the European settlers managed to superimpose upon the peoples and areas which they brought under their domain. On a world scale, therefore, there is an extraordinarily close association between the white Western Europeans as colonizers and conquerors and their status as dominant groups. Correspondingly, there is a close association between the nonwhite peoples of the world as the conquered and enslaved peoples and their status as minority groups. There are notable exceptions, however, both in time and in space. In an earlier period of European history the yellow peoples of the East overran vast stretches of the European continent and for a time at least reduced the natives to inferior status. There had been similar, though temporary, invasions of Europe from Africa in the course of which Negroid groups became dominant over the white Europeans. Similarly, the enterprise and military prowess of the Japanese has led to the subjugation of vast stretches of the Orient beyond their island empire which contain many areas and great populations of non-Japanese stock, including European whites. On the whole, however, the expansion of European civilization to the ends of the earth has been so irresistible that from a racial standpoint, virtually the world over, the whites constitute the dominant group and the colored peoples the minorities.

We are less concerned, however, in this analysis, with racial minorities than with ethnic minorities, and hence it will be well to examine in some detail the linguistic, religious, and national minorities within the white group in Europe and in America. The existence of such groups in virtually every European and American country calls attention to the fact that the modern nation-states into which we are accustomed to divide the world and to which we are wont to ascribe a high degree of ethnic homogeneity are far from being as closely knit by intermarriage, in-breeding, social intercourse, and freedom of opportunity for everyone as the stereotypes of national cultures appear to indicate.

In Europe and in America there are today vast differences between the status of different ethnic groups from country to country and from region to region. In pre-war Poland under the Czarist regime the Poles were a distinct ethnic minority. When they gained their independence at the end of the first World War, they lost their minority status but reduced their Jewish fellow Poles to the status of a minority. As immigrants to the United States the Poles again became themselves a minority. During the brief period of Nazi domination the Sudeten Germans of Czechoslovakia reveled in their position of dominance over the Czechs among whom they had only recently been a minority. The European immigrants to the United States from such dominantly Catholic countries as Italy and Poland, for instance, find themselves reduced from a dominant to a minority group in the course of their immigration. It is not the specific characteristics, therefore, whether racial or ethnic, that mark a people as a minority but the relationship of their group to some other group in the society in which they live. The same characteristics may at one time and under one set of circumstances serve as marks of dominant status and at another time and under another set of circumstances symbolize identification with a minority.

It is much more important, therefore, to understand the nature and the genesis of the relationship between dominant group and minority group than it is to know the marks by the possession of which people are identified as members of either. Once we know that almost any distinctive characteristics, whether it be the physical marks of race, or language, religion, and culture, can serve as criteria of membership in a minority we will not be inclined to construct a typology of minorities upon the marks by which they are identified. A fruitful typology must rather be useful in delineating the kinds of relationships between minorities and dominant groups and on the kinds of behavior characteristically associated with these types of relationships.

An adequate typology of minorities must, therefore, take account of the general types of situations in which minorities find themselves and must seek to comprehend the *modus vivendi* that has grown up between the segments of those societies in which minority problems exist. There are a number of axes alongside of which the problems of minorities range themselves. Among these are: (1) the number and size of distinct minorities in the society in question; (2) the degree to which minority status involves friction with the dominant group or exclusion from participation in the common life of the society; (3) the nature of the social arrangement governing the relationship between minority and dominant group; and, (4) the goals toward which the minority and dominant groups are striving in quest of a new and more satisfactory equilibrium. A survey of historical and contemporary minority problems along these lines will probably not cover the whole range of minority problems and to that extent the typology will be partial. At the same time it should be understood that as long as the relations between minority and dominant group are fluid—and wherever they do not rest upon long-accepted and settled premises—any rigid typology will prove unsatisfactory. Conversely where the minority's relationship to the dominant group is definitely structuralized and embedded in the mores, laws, and institutions a typological approach may be highly rewarding.

* * *

While the above criteria might give us a basis for the classification of minorities, they do not come as close to the actual minority problems that plague the modern world as we can come by analyzing the major goals toward which the ideas, the sentiments, and the actions of minority groups are directed. Viewed in this way minorities may conveniently be typed into: (1) pluralistic; (2) assimilationist; (3) secessionist; and (4) militant.

A pluralistic minority is one which seeks toleration for its differences on the part of the dominant group. Implicit in the quest for toleration of one's group differences is the conception that variant cultures can flourish peacefully side by side in the same society. Indeed, cultural pluralism has been held out as one of the necessary preconditions of a rich and dynamic civilization under conditions of freedom. It has been said in jest that "tolerance is the suspicion that the other fellow might be right."

Toleration requires that the dominant group shall feel sufficiently secure in its position to allow dissenters a certain leeway. Those in control must be convinced either that the issues at stake are not too vital, or else they must be so thoroughly imbued with the ideal of freedom that they do not wish to deny to others some of the liberties which they themselves enjoy. If there is a great gulf between their own status and that of the minority group, if there is a wide difference between the two groups in race or origin, the toleration of minorities may go as far as virtually to perpetuate several subsocieties within the larger society.

Even in the "sacred" society of medieval Europe dominated by the Church, there were long periods when heretics were tolerated, although at other times they faced the alternatives of conformity or extermination. The history of the Jews in medieval Europe offers ample evidence of the ability of a minority to survive even under minimum conditions of toleration. It should be noted, however, that at times the margin of safety was very narrow and that their ultimate survival was facilitated by the fact that they formed an alien cultural island within the larger Christian world and performed useful functions such as trade and commerce in which the creed of the dominant group would not allow its own members to engage. The coexistence of the Jews and Christians in the same countries often did not transcend the degree of mutuality characteristic of the symbiotic relations existing between different species of plants and animals occupying the same habitat but which are forced by their differential structure to live off one another. It involved a minimum of consensus.

The range of toleration which a pluralistic minority seeks may at first be quite narrow. As in the case of the Jews in medieval Europe, or the Protestants in dominantly Catholic countries, it may be confined to freedom to practice a dissenting religion. Or, as in the case of the ethnic minorities of Czarist Russia and the Austro-Hungarian empire of the Hapsburgs, it may take the form of the demand for the recognition of a language as the official medium of expression for the minority and the right to have it taught in their schools. While on the one hand the pluralistic minority craves the toleration of one or more of its cultural idiosyncrasies, on the other hand it resents and seeks protection against coerced absorption by the dominant group. Above all it wishes to maintain its cultural identity.

The nationalities of Europe, which in the nineteenth and early twentieth centuries embarked upon a course of achieving national independence, began their careers as pluralistic minorities bent merely upon attaining cultural autonomy. Some of these minorities had enjoyed national independence at an earlier period and merely wished to recover and preserve their cultural heritage. This was the case in Poland, for instance, which sought to recover from Czarist Russia a measure of religious and linguistic autonomy. Czech and Irish nationalism was initiated under similar historic circumstances.

It would be an error, however, to infer that the claims for cultural autonomy are generally pursued independently of other interests. Coupled with the demand, and often precedent to it there proceeds the struggle for economic and political equality or at least equalization of opportunity. Although the pluralistic minority does not wish to merge its total life with the larger society, it does demand for its members a greater measure of economic and political freedom if not outright civic equality. Ever since the revolutionary epoch of the late eighteenth century the economic and political enfranchisement of minorities has been regarded not merely as inherent in the "rights of man" but as the necessary instrument in the struggle for cultural emancipation. Freedom of choice in occupations, rights of landownership, entry into the civil service, access to the universities and the professions, freedom of speech, assembly, and publication, access to the ballot with a view to representation of minority voices in parliament and government—these and other full privileges of citizenship are the foundation upon which cultural freedom rests and the instruments through which it must be achieved and secured.

* * *

Whereas a pluralistic minority, in order to maintain its group integrity, will generally discourage intermarriage and intimate social intercourse with the dominant group, the assimilationist minority puts no such obstacles in the path of its members but looks upon the crossing of stocks as well as the blending of cultures as wholesome end products. Since assimilation is a two-way process, however, in which there is give and take, the mergence of an assimilationist minority rests upon a willingness of the dominant group to absorb and of the minority group to be absorbed. The ethnic differences that exist between the minority and the dominant group are not necessarily an obstacle to assimilation as long as the cultural traits of each group are not regarded as incompatible with those of the other and as long as their blending is desired by both. The "melting pot" philosophy in the United States which applied to the ethnic minorities but excluded the racial minorities, notably the Negro, in so far as it was actually followed, tended to develop both among immigrants and natives an atmosphere conducive to the emergence of a crescive American culture to which both the dominant and minority groups contributed their share. This new culture, which is still in the process of formation, comprises cultural elements derived from all the ethnic groups constituting the American people, but integrates them into a new blend.

The success with which such an experiment proceeds depends in part upon the relative numbers involved and the period of time over which the process extends. Although since the beginning of the nineteenth century the United States absorbed some 38 million immigrants from abroad, the influx was relatively gradual and the vast spaces and resources of the continent facilitated the settlement and absorption of the newcomers. America was a relatively young country, dominated by the spirit of the frontier and by a set of laws and social ideals strongly influenced by the humanistic, liberalistic doctrines of religious toleration and the rights of man. This, together with the great need for labor to exploit the vast resources of the continent, contributed to keeping American culture fluid and its people hospitable to the newcomers and the heritages they brought with them. No one group in the United States had so much power and pride of ancestry as to be able to assert itself as superior to all others.

Nevertheless as the immigrants came in great waves, and as the wide margin of economic opportunity shrank periodically, outbursts of intolerant and sometimes violent nativism and antialien feeling became manifest here too. As newer immigrant groups followed older waves the latest comers increasingly became the objects of prejudice and discrimination on the part of natives and older immigrants alike. Moreover, as the various ethnic groups concentrated in specific areas and in large urban colonies and thus conspicuously unfolded their old world cultural heritages, their life became virtually autonomous and hence, by isolating themselves, their contact with the broad stream of American culture was retarded. In addition, their very success in competing with native and older settlers in occupations, professions, and business provoked antipathies which found expression in intolerance movements and in the imposition of official and unofficial restrictions and handicaps.

Although the ethnic minorities in the United States suffer mainly from private prejudices rather than restrictive public policies, their path of assimilation is not without its serious obstacles. The distinctive cultures of the various ethnic groups are not merely assemblages of separable traits but historically welded wholes. Each immigrant group not only has its own language or dialect which serves as a barrier to intergroup communication and to the sharing of common ideas and ideals, but also its own religious, social, and even political institutions which tend to perpetuate group solidarity and to inhibit social intercourse with members of the "out" group. Moreover, each ethnic group in the United States, especially in the early period after its arrival, tends to occupy a characteristic niche in the economy which generates certain definite similarities among its members in occupation, standard of living, place of residence, and mode of life. On the basis of such likenesses within the group and differences without, stereotypes are built up and fixed attitudes arise which inhibit contact and develop social distances and prejudices. Overanxiety about being accepted sometimes results in a pattern of conduct among minorities that provokes a defense reaction on the part of the dominant group; these defense reactions may take the form of rebuffs which are likely to accentuate minority consciousness and thus retard assimilation.

No ethnic group is ever unanimous in all of its attitudes and actions, and minority groups are no exception. They, too, have their internal differentiations, their factions and ideological currents and movements. It should be understood, therefore, that the difference between a pluralistic and an assimilationist minority must be sought in the characteristic orientation and directing social movement of these groups. The Jews furnish an excellent illustration of a minority which especially in modern times has vacillated between these two types. When the "out" group was favorably disposed toward the Jews, assimilation proceeded apace, even in the face of occasional rebuffs and persistent discrimination. When the dominant group made entry of the Jews difficult, when intolerance movements became powerful and widespread, and when persecution came to be the order of the day, the Jews as a minority group generally withdrew into themselves and by virtue of being excluded became clannish. The most conspicuous example of this transformation is to be found in the shift in the attitude of the German Jews who—before the anti-Semitic wave climaxed by the Hitler epic—could have been correctly characterized as an assimilationist minority and whose optimum longing upon the advent of Hitler was for even a modicum of toleration. Among Jews in this country a similar differentiation is contemporaneously found. The older settlers and those who have climbed the economic and social scale seek on the whole full incorporation into the larger society and may truly be regarded as an assimilationist minority; but the later comers and those whose hopes have been frustrated by prejudice, those who through generations of persecution in the Old World retain a more orthodox ritual and a more isolated and self-sufficient community life, generally do not seek full cultural identification with American society at large. To be sure they aspire to full social and economic equality with the rest of the population, but they seek to retain a degree of cultural autonomy.

* * *

The principal and ultimate objective of such a minority is to achieve political as well as cultural independence from the dominant group. If such a group has had statehood at an earlier period in its career, the demand for recognition of its national sovereignty may be based upon the cultivation among its members of the romantic sentiments associated—even if only in the imagination—with its former freedom, power, and glory. In such a case the minority's cultural monuments and survivals, its language, lore, literature, and ceremonial institutions, no matter how archaic or reminiscent of the epoch of the group's independence, are revivified and built up into moving symbols of national grandeur.

In this task the intellectuals among the minority group play a crucial role. They can find expression for their talents by recovering, disseminating, and inspiring pride in the group's history and civilization and by pleading its case before world public opinion. Having been rejected by the dominant group for higher positions of leadership, and often having been denied equal opportunity and full participation in the intellectual, social, economic and political life of the larger society, the intellectuals of such minorities tend to be particularly susceptible to a psychic malady bordering on an oppression psychosis. They find their compensation by plunging into the life of the smaller but more hospitable world of their minority.

The Irish, Czech, Polish, Lithuanian, Esthonian, Latvian and Finnish nationalistic movements culminating in the achievement of independent statehood at the end of the first World War were examples of secessionist minority groups. The case of the Jews may also be used to illustrate this type of minority. Zionism in its political, as distinguished from its cultural variety, has acquired considerable support as a result of the resurgence of organized anti-Semitic movements. The forced wholesale migration out of the countries practicing violent persecution and extermination has changed the conception of Palestine from a haven of refuge in which Jews are tolerated to a homeland to which Jews lay official claim.

The protest against the dominant group, however, does not always take the form of separatism and secessionism. It may, under certain circumstances express itself in movements to get out from under the yoke of a dominant group in order to join a group with whom there exists a closer historical and cultural affinity. This is particularly true of minorities located near national frontiers. Wars, and the accompanying repeated redefinitions of international boundaries rarely fail to do violence to the traditions and wishes of some of the populations of border territories. It is generally true that these marginal ethnic groups exhibit more fervid nationalistic feelings than those who have not been buffeted about by treaty-makers.

Secessionist minorities occupying border positions, moreover, generally can count upon the country with which they seek reunion for stimulation of minority consciousness. When France lost Alsace and Lorraine at the end of the Franco-Prussian war in 1871, the French culture of these "lost provinces" became the object of special interest on the part of Frenchmen in and out of these territories. And when these same provinces were lost to Germany at the end of the first World War, a similar propaganda wave on the German side was set in motion. When the Nazis came to power and embarked upon their imperialistic adventures they made the "reunion with the Fatherland" of such territories as the Saar, Alsace, Lorraine, Eupen-et-Malmédy; Sudetenland and the Danzig Corridor an object of frenzied agitation. By every means at their command they revived the flagging or dormant secessionist spirit among these ethnic groups. The created incidents wherever the slightest pretext existed to provoke violent outbreaks so as to elicit from the neighboring governments countermeasures that could be exploited for the purpose of creating a world opinion that the German minorities in these territories were suffering from extreme persecution and were anxiously waiting to be rescued by the armed might of the Fatherland.

The solidarity of modern states is always subject to the danger of the undermining influence of secessionist minorities, but it becomes particularly vulnerable if the minorities are allied with neighboring states which claim them as their own. Out of such situations have arisen many of the tensions which have provoked numerous wars in recent times.

There is a fourth type of minority which may be designated as militant. Its goal reaches far beyond toleration, assimilation, and even cultural and political autonomy. The militant minority has set domination over others as its goal. Far from suffering from feelings of inferiority, it is convinced of its own superiority and inspired by the lust for conquest. While the initial claims of minority movements are generally modest, like all accessions of power, they feed upon their own success and often culminate in delusions of grandeur.

Thus, for instance, the Sudeten Germans, aided and abetted by the Nazi propaganda, diplomatic, and military machine, made claims on the Czecho-Slovak republic which, if granted, would have reduced the Czechs to a minority in their own country. The story, let us hope it is legendary, of the slave who upon his emancipation immediately proceeded to buy himself a slave, suggests a perverse human tendency which applies to minorities as well. No imperialism is as ruthless as that of a relatively small upstart nation. Scarcely had Italy escaped the humiliation of utter defeat in the first World War when she embarked upon the acquisition of *Italia Irredenta* far beyond her own borders across the Adriatic. In recent times, the rise of the relatively obscure Prussian state to a position of dominance in Central Europe is illustrative of the dynamics of a militant minority in quest not merely of a secure basis of national existence but of empire. The none too generous treatment accorded by the newly emancipated Poles between the two World Wars to the Ukrainian, White Russian, Lithuanian, Jewish, and other minorities allotted to the Polish state offers another case of the lack of moderation characteristic of militant minorities once they arrive at a position of power.

The problem of finding a suitable formula for self-government in India would probably have been solved long ago if the Hindu "majority," which considers itself a minority in relation to British imperial rule, could have been satisfied with an arrangement which stopped short of Hindu domination over Moslems. Similarly the problem of Palestine could be brought much nearer a sensible solution if certain elements among Jewish and Arab groups were less militant and did not threaten, in case either were given the opportunity, to reduce the other to the status of a minority.

The justification for singling out the four types of minorities described above for special delineation lies in the fact that each of them exhibits a characteristic set of collective goals among historical and contemporary minority groups and a corresponding set of motives activating the conduct of its members. These four types point to significant differences between actual minority movements. They may also be regarded as marking crucial successive stages in the life cycle of minorities generally.

## III–PRIMARY GROUPS

# 1. *Primary Groups*

BY CHARLES H. COOLEY

MEANING OF PRIMARY GROUPS—FAMILY, PLAYGROUND, AND NEIGHBORHOOD—HOW FAR INFLUENCED BY LARGER SOCIETY—MEANING AND PERMANENCE OF "HUMAN NATURE"—PRIMARY GROUPS, THE NURSERY OF HUMAN NATURE

BY *primary groups* I mean *those characterized by intimate face-to-face associations and cooperation.* They are primary in several senses, but chiefly in that they are fundamental in forming the social nature and ideals of the individual. The result of intimate association, psychologically, is a certain fusion of individualities in a common whole, so that one's very self, for many purposes at least, is the common life and purpose of the group. Perhaps the simplest way of describing this wholeness is by

Reprinted from Charles H. Cooley, *Social Organization* (Glencoe, Ill.: The Free Press, 1956), chap. iii, pp. 23–31, with the permission of The Free Press.

saying that it is a "we"; it *involves the sort of sympathy and mutual identification for which "we" is the natural expression.* One lives in the feeling of the whole and finds the chief aims of his will in that feeling.

It is not to be supposed that the unity of the primary group is one of mere harmony and love. It is always a differentiated and usually a competitive unity, admitting of self-assertion and various appropriative passions; but these passions are socialized by sympathy, and come, or tend to come, under the discipline of a common spirit. *The individual will be ambitious, but the chief object of his ambition will be some desired place in the thought of the others, and he will feel allegiance to common standards of service and fair play.* So the boy will dispute with his fellows a place on the *team,* but above such disputes will place the common glory of his class and school.

The most important spheres of this intimate association and cooperation—though by no means the only ones—are the *family, the play-group of children, and the neighborhood or community group of elders.* These are practically universal, belonging to all times and all stages of development; and are accordingly a chief basis of what is universal in human nature and human ideals. The best comparative studies of the family, such as those of Westermarck[1] or Howard,[2] show it to us as not only a universal institution, but as more alike the world over than the exaggeration of exceptional customs by an earlier school had led us to suppose. Nor can any one doubt the general prevalence of play-groups among children or of informal assemblies of various kinds among their elders. Such association is clearly the nursery of human nature in the world about us, and there is no apparent reason to suppose that the case has anywhere or at any time been essentially different.

As regards play, I might, were it not a matter of common observation, multiply illustrations of the universality and spontaneity of the group discussion and cooperation to which it gives rise. The general fact is that children, especially boys after about their twelfth year, live in fellowships in which their sympathy, ambition, and honor are engaged even more, often, than they are in the family. Most of us can recall examples of the endurance by boys of injustice and even cruelty, rather than appeal from their fellows to parents or teachers—as, for instance, in the hazing so prevalent at schools, and so difficult, for this very reason, to repress. And how elaborate the discussion, how cogent the public opinion, how hot the ambitions in these fellowships.

Nor is this facility of juvenile association, as is sometimes supposed, a trait peculiar to English and American boys; since experience among our immigrant population seems to show that the offspring of the more restrictive civilizations of the continent of Europe form self-governing play-groups with almost equal readiness. Thus, Miss Jane Addams, after pointing out that the "gang" is almost universal, speaks of the interminable discussion which every detail of the gang's activity receives, remarking that "in these social folk-motes, so to speak, the young citizen learns to act upon his own determination."[3]

Of the neighborhood group it may be said, in general, that from the time men formed permanent settlements upon the land, down, at least, to the rise of modern industrial cities, it has played a main part in the primary, heart-to-heart life of the people. Among our Teutonic forefathers the village community was apparently the chief sphere of sympathy and mutual aid for the commons all through the "dark" and Middle Ages, and for many purposes it remains so in rural districts at the present day. In some countries we still find it with its ancient vitality, notably in Russia, where the *mir,* or self-governing village group, is the main theatre of life, along with the family, for perhaps fifty millions of peasants.

In our own life the intimacy of the neighborhood has been broken up by the growth of an intricate mesh of wider contacts which leaves us strangers to people who live in the same house. And even in the country the same principle is at work, though less obviously, diminishing our economic and spiritual community with our neighbors. How far this change is a healthy development, and how far a disease, is perhaps still uncertain.

*Besides these almost universal kinds of primary association, there are many others whose form depends upon the particular state of civilization; the only essential thing,* as I have said, *being a certain intimacy and fusion of personalities. In our own society, being little bound by place, people easily form clubs, fraternal societies, and the like, based on congeniality, which may give rise to real intimacy.* Many such relations are formed at school and college, and among men and women brought together in the first instance by their occupations—as workmen in the same trade, or the like. Where there is a little common interest and activity, kindness grows like weeds by the roadside.

But the fact that the family and neighborhood

1. *The History of Human Marriage.*
2. *A History of Matrimonial Institutions.*
3. *Newer Ideals of Peace,* p. 177.

groups are ascendant in the open and plastic time of childhood makes them even now incomparably more influential than all the rest.

Primary groups are primary in the sense that they give the individual his earliest and most complete experience of social unity, and also in the sense that they do not change in the same degree as more elaborate relations, but form a comparatively permanent source out of which the latter are ever springing. Of course they are not independent of the larger society, but to some extent reflect its spirit; as the German family and the German school bear somewhat distinctly the print of German militarism. But this, after all, is like the tide setting back into creeks, and does not commonly go very far. Among the German, and still more among the Russian, peasantry are found habits of free cooperation and discussion almost uninfluenced by the character of the state; and it is a familiar and well-supported view that the village commune, self-governing as regards local affairs and habituated to discussion, is a very widespread institution in settled communities, and the continuator of a similar autonomy previously existing in the clan. "It is man who makes monarchies and establishes republics, but the commune seems to come directly from the hand of God."[4]

In our own cities the crowded tenements and the general economic and social confusion have sorely wounded the family and the neighborhood, but it is remarkable, in view of these conditions, what vitality they show; and there is nothing upon which the conscience of the time is more determined than upon restoring them to health.

These groups, then, are springs of life, not only for the individual but for social institutions. They are only in part moulded by special traditions, and, in larger degree, express a universal nature. The religion or government of other civilizations may seem alien to us, but the children or the family group wear the common life, and with them we can always make ourselves at home.

By human nature, I suppose, we may understand those sentiments and impulses that are human in being superior to those of lower animals, and also in the sense that they belong to mankind at large, and not to any particular race or time. It means, particularly, sympathy and the innumerable sentiments into which sympathy enters, such as love, resentment, ambition, vanity, hero-worship, and the feeling of social right and wrong.[5]

Human nature in this sense is justly regarded as a comparatively permanent element in society. Always and everywhere men seek honor and dread ridicule, defer to public opinion, cherish their goods and their children, and admire courage, generosity, and success. It is always safe to assume that people are and have been human.

It is true, no doubt, that there are differences of race capacity, so great that a large part of mankind are possibly incapable of any high kind of social organization. But these differences, like those among individuals of the same race, are subtle, depending upon some obscure intellectual deficiency, some want of vigor, or slackness of moral fibre, and do not involve unlikeness in the generic impulses of human nature. In these, all races are very much alike. The more insight one gets into the life of savages, even those that are reckoned the lowest, the more human, the more like ourselves, they appear. Take for instance the natives of central Australia, as described by Spencer and Gillen,[6] tribes having no definite government or worship and scarcely able to count to five. They are generous to one another, emulous of virtue as they understand it, kind to their children and to the aged, and by no means harsh to women. Their faces as shown in the photographs are wholly human and many of them attractive.

And when we come to a comparison between different stages in the development of the same race, between ourselves, for instance, and the Teutonic tribes of the time of Caesar, the difference is neither in human nature nor in capacity, but in organization, in the range and complexity of relations, in the diverse expression of powers and passions essentially much the same.

There is no better proof of this generic likeness of human nature than in the ease and joy with which the modern man makes himself at home in literature depicting the most remote and varied phases of life—in Homer, in the Nibelung tales, in the Hebrew Scriptures, in the legends of the American Indians, in stories of frontier life, of soldiers and sailors, of criminals and tramps, and so on. The more penetratingly any phase of human life is studied, the more an essential likeness to ourselves is revealed.

To return to primary groups: the view here maintained is that human nature is not something existing separately in the individual, but a *group-nature or primary phase of society,* a relatively

4. De Tocqueville, *Democracy in America,* Vol. I, chap. v.

5. These matters are expounded at some length in the writer's *Human Nature and the Social Order.*

6. *The Native Tribes of Central Australia.* Compare also Darwin's views and examples given in chap. vii of his *Descent of Man.*

simple and general condition of the social mind. It is something more, on the one hand, than the mere instinct that is born in us—though that enters into it—and something less, on the other, than the more elaborate development of ideas and sentiments that makes up institutions. It is the nature which is developed and expressed in those simple, face-to-face groups that are somewhat alike in all societies; groups of the family, the playground, and the neighborhood. In the essential similarity of these is to be found the basis, in experience, for similar ideas and sentiments in the human mind. In these, everywhere, human nature comes into existence. Man does not have it at birth; he cannot acquire it except through fellowship, and it decays in isolation.

If this view does not recommend itself to common sense I do not know that elaboration will be of much avail. It simply means the application at this point of the idea that society and individuals are inseparable phases of a common whole, so that wherever we find an individual fact we may look for a social fact to go with it. If there is a universal nature in persons there must be something universal in association to correspond to it.

What else can human nature be than a trait of primary groups? Surely not an attribute of the separate individual—supposing there were any such thing—since its typical characteristics, such as affection, ambition, vanity, and resentment, are inconceivable apart from society. If it belongs, then, to man in association, what kind or degree of association is required to develop it? Evidently nothing elaborate, because elaborate phases of society are transient and diverse, while human nature is comparatively stable and universal. In short, the family and neighborhood life is essential to its genesis and nothing more is.

Here, as everywhere in the study of society, we must learn to see mankind in psychical wholes, rather than in artificial separation. We must see and feel the communal life of family and local groups as immediate facts, not as combinations of something else. And perhaps we shall do this best by recalling our own experience and extending it through sympathetic observation. What, in our life, is the family and the fellowship; what do we know of the we-feeling? Thought of this kind may help us to get a concrete perception of that primary group-nature of which everything social is the outgrowth.

## 2. *Secrecy and Group Communication*

BY GEORG SIMMEL

BEFORE COMING to the secret in the sense of a consciously desired concealment, one must note the different degrees to which various relationships leave the reciprocal knowledge of the total personalities of their members outside their province.

### INTEREST GROUPS

Among the various groups still involving direct interaction, the most important is the association based on some particular interest [*Zweckverband*], more especially that which involves completely objective member contributions, determined by mere membership. The purest form here is monetary contribution. In this case, interaction, solidarity, and the pursuit of common purposes do not depend on everybody's psychological knowledge of everybody else. As a group member, the individual is only the executor of a certain function. Questions concerning those individual motives which determine this performance, or the sort of total personality in which his conduct is imbedded, are completely irrelevant. The association based on some particular interest is the discreet sociological form *par excellence*. Its members are psychologically anonymous. In order to form the association, all they have to know of one another is precisely this fact—that they form it. The increasing objectification of our culture, whose phenomena consist more and more of impersonal elements and less and less absorb the

---

Reprinted from *The Sociology of Georg Simmel*, trans. and ed. Kurt H. Wolff (Glencoe, Ill.: The Free Press, 1950), pp. 317–29, 361–76, with the permission of The Free Press.

subjective totality of the individual (most simply shown by the contrast between handicraft and factory work), also involves sociological structures. Therefore, groups into which earlier man entered in his totality and individuality and which, for this reason, required reciprocal knowledge far beyond the immediate, objective content of the relationship —these groups are now based exclusively on this objective content, which is neatly factored out of the whole relation.

### CONFIDENCE UNDER MORE AND LESS COMPLEX CONDITIONS

This development also gives a peculiar evolution to an antecedent or subsequent form of knowledge about a human being, namely, confidence in him. Confidence, evidently, is one of the most important synthetic forces within society. As a hypothesis regarding future behavior, a hypothesis certain enough to serve as a basis for practical conduct, confidence is intermediate between knowledge and ignorance about a man. The person who knows completely need not trust; while the person who knows nothing can, on no rational grounds, afford even confidence.[1] Epochs, fields of interest, and individuals differ, characteristically, by the measures of knowledge and ignorance which must mix in order that the single, practical decision based on confidence arise.

The objectification of culture has decisively differentiated the quanta of knowledge and ignorance necessary for confidence. The modern merchant who enters business with another; the scholar who together with another embarks upon an investigation; the leader of a political party who makes an agreement with the leader of another party concerning matters of election or the treatment of pending bills; all these know (if we overlook exceptions and imperfections) only exactly *that* and no more about their partner which they *have* to know for the sake of the relationship they wish to enter. The traditions and institutions, the power of public opinion and the definition of the position which inescapably stamps the individual, have become so solid and reliable that one has to know only certain external facts about the other person in order to have the confidence required for the common action. The question is no longer some foundation of personal qualities on which (at least in principle) a modification of behavior within the relation might be based: motivation and regulation of this behavior have become so objectified that confidence no longer needs any properly personal knowledge. Under more primitive, less differentiated conditions, the individual knows much more about his partner in regard to personal matters, and much less in regard to his purely objective competence. The two belong together: in order to produce the necessary confidence despite a lack of knowledge in objective matters, a much higher degree of knowledge in personal matters is necessary.

The purely general knowledge, which extends only to the objective elements of the person and leaves its secret—the personal-individual area—untouched, must be supplemented considerably by the knowledge of this very area, whenever the interest group is of essential significance to the total existence of its members. The mercant who sells grain or oil needs to know only whether his correspondent is good for the price. But if he takes him as his associate, he must not only know his financial standing and certain of his very general qualities, but he must have thorough insight into him as a personality; he must know whether he is decent, compatible, and whether he has a daring or hesitant temperament. Upon such reciprocal knowledge rest not only the beginning of the relationship, but also its whole development, the daily common actions, and the division of functions between the partners. Today the secret of the personality is sociologically more limited. In view of the large extent to which the interest in the common pursuit is borne by personal qualities, the personal element can no longer be so autonomous.

### "ACQUAINTANCE"

Aside from interest groups but aside, equally, from relationships rooted in the total personality, there is the sociologically highly peculiar relation which, in our times, among educated strata, is desig-

1. There is, to be sure, also another type of confidence. But since it stands outside the categories of knowledge and ignorance, it touches the present discussion only indirectly. This type is called the *faith* of one man in another. It belongs in the category of religious faith. Just as nobody has ever believed in God on the basis of any "proof of the existence of God," since, on the contrary, these proofs are *post-festum* justifications or intellectual mirrors of a completely immediate, affective attitude, so one "believes" in a particular man without justifying this faith by proofs of his worthiness, and often even in spite of proofs to the contrary. This confidence, this inner unreservedness in regard to another individual, is mediated neither by experiences nor by hypotheses; it is a primary, fundamental attitude toward the other. In an entirely pure form, detached from any empirical consideration, this state of faith probably exists only within religion. In regard to men, it always, presumably, needs some stimulation or confirmation by the knowledge or expectation mentioned above. On the other hand, even in the social forms of confidence, no matter how exactly and intellectually grounded they may appear to be, there may yet be some additional affective, even mystical, "faith" of man in man. Perhaps what has been characterized here is a fundamental category of human conduct, which goes back to the metaphysical sense of our relationships and which is realized in a merely empirical, accidental, fragmentary manner by the conscious and particular reasons for confidence.

nated simply as "acquaintance." Mutual "acquaintance" by no means is *knowledge* of one another; it involves no actual insight into the individual nature of the personality. It only means that one has taken notice of the other's existence, as it were. It is characteristic that the idea of acquaintance is suggested by the mere mentioning of one's name, by "introducing oneself": "acquaintance" depends upon the knowledge of the *that* of the personality, not of its *what*. After all, by saying that one is acquainted, even well acquainted, with a particular person, one characterizes quite clearly the lack of really intimate relations. Under the rubric of acquaintance, one knows of the other only what he is toward the outside, either in the purely social-representative sense, or in the sense of that which he shows us. The degree of knowledge covered by "being well acquainted with one another," refers not to the other *per se;* not to what is essential in him, intrinsically, but only to what is significant for that aspect of him which is turned toward others and the world.

DISCRETION

Acquaintance in this social sense is, therefore, the proper seat of "discretion." For, discretion consists by no means only in the respect for the secret of the other, for his specific will to conceal this or that from us, but in staying away from the knowledge of all that the other does not expressly reveal to us. It does not refer to anything particular which we are not permitted to know, but to a quite general reserve in regard to the total personality. Discretion is a special form of the typical contrast between the imperatives, "what is not prohibited is allowed," and "what is not allowed is prohibited." Relations among men are thus distinguished according to the question of mutual knowledge—of either "what is not concealed may be known," or "what is not revealed must not be known."

To act upon the second of these decisions corresponds to the feeling (which also operates elsewhere) that an ideal sphere lies around every human being. Although differing in size in various directions and differing according to the person with whom one entertains relations, this sphere cannot be penetrated, unless the personality value of the individual is thereby destroyed. A sphere of this sort is placed around man by his "honor." Language very poignantly designates an insult to one's honor as "coming too close": the radius of this sphere marks, as it were, the distance whose trespassing by another person insults one's honor.

Another sphere of the same form corresponds to what is called the "significance" of a personality. In regard to the "significant" ["great"] man, there is an inner compulsion which tells one to keep at a distance and which does not disappear even in intimate relations with him. The only type for whom such distance does not exist is the individual who has no organ for perceiving significance. For this reason, the "valet" knows no such sphere of distance; for him there is no "hero"; but this is due, not to the *hero*, but to the valet. For the same reason, all importunity is associated with a striking lack of feeling for differences in the significance of men. The individual who fails to keep his distance from a great person does not esteem him highly, much less too highly (as might superficially appear to be the case); but, on the contrary, his importune behavior reveals lack of proper respect. The painter often emphasizes the significance of a figure in a picture that contains many figures by arranging the others in a considerable distance from it. In an analogous fashion, the sociological simile of significance is the distance which keeps the individual outside a certain sphere that is occupied by the power, will, and greatness of a person.

The same sort of circle which surrounds man—although it is value-accentuated in a very different sense—is filled out by his affairs and by his characteristics. To penetrate this circle by taking notice, constitutes a violation of his personality. Just as material property is, so to speak, an extension of the ego,[2] and any interference with our property is, for this reason, felt to be a violation of the person, there also is an intellectual private-property, whose violation effects a lesion of the ego in its very center. Discretion is nothing but the feeling that there exists a right in regard to the sphere of the immediate life contents. Discretion, of course, differs in its extension with different personalities, just as the positions of honor and of property have different radii with respect to "close" individuals and to strangers and indifferent persons. In the case of the above-mentioned, more properly "social" relations, which are most conveniently designated as "acquaintances," the point to which discretion extends is, above all, a very typical boundary: beyond it, perhaps there *are* not even any jealously guarded secrets; but conventionally and discreetly, the other individual, nevertheless, does not trespass it by questions or other invasions.

The question where this boundary lies cannot be answered in terms of a simple principle; it leads into the finest ramifications of societal formation. For, in an absolute sense, the right to intellectual private-property can be affirmed as little as can the

2. Property is that which obeys the will of the owner, as, for instance (with a difference of degree only), our body which is our first "property."

right to material property. We know that, in higher civilizations, material private-property in its essential three dimensions—acquisition, insurance, increase—is never based on the individual's own forces alone. It always requires the conditions and forces of the social milieu. From the beginning, therefore, it is limited by the right of the whole, whether through taxation or through certain checks on acquisition. But this right is grounded more deeply than just in the principle of service and counter-service between society and individual: it is grounded in the much more elementary principle, that the part must sustain as great a restriction upon its autonomous existence and possessiveness as the maintenance and the purposes of the whole require.

This also applies to the inner sphere of man. In the interest of interaction and social cohesion, the individual *must* know certain things about the other person. Nor does the other have the right to oppose this knowledge from a moral standpoint, by demanding the discretion of the first: he cannot claim the entirely undisturbed possession of his own being and consciousness, since this discretion might harm the interests of his society. The businessman who contracts long-range obligations with another; the master who employs a servant (but also the servant before entering the service); the superior who advances a subordinate; the housewife who accepts a new member into her social circle: all these must have the right to learn or infer those aspects of the other's past and present, temperament, and moral quality on the basis of which they can act rationally in regard to him, or reject him. These are very crude instances of the case where the duty of discretion—to renounce the knowledge of all that the other does not voluntarily show us—recedes before practical requirements. But even in subtler and less unambiguous forms, in fragmentary beginnings and unexpressed notions, all of human intercourse rests on the fact that everybody knows somewhat more about the other than the other voluntarily reveals to him; and those things he knows are frequently matters whose knowledge the other person (were he aware of it) would find undesirable.

All this may be considered indiscretion in the individual sense: in the social sense, it is a condition necessary for the concrete density and vitality of interaction. Nevertheless, it is extremely difficult to trace the legal limit of this trespass into intellectual private-property. In general, man arrogates to himself the right to know all he can find out through mere observation and reflection, without applying externally illegitimate means. As a matter of fact, however, indiscretion practiced in this fashion can be just as violent and morally inadmissible as listening behind closed doors and leering at a stranger's letters. To the man with the psychologically fine ear, people innumerable times betray their most secret thoughts and qualities, not only *although,* but often *because,* they anxiously try to guard them. The avid, spying grasp of every inconsiderate word, the boring reflection on what this or that tone of voice might mean, how such and such utterances might be combined, what blushing on mentioning a certain name might betray—none of this transcends the limits of external discretion; it is entirely the work of one's own intellect and, for this reason, one's apparently indisputable right. And all the more so, since such an abuse of psychological superiority often occurs quite involuntarily: often we simply cannot check our interpretation of the other, our construction of his inner nature. No matter how much every decent person tells himself that he must not muse on what the other hides, that he must not exploit the slips and helplessnesses of the other; knowledge, nevertheless, occurs often so automatically, and its result confronts us with such striking suddenness, that mere good will has no power over it. Where the doubtlessly impermissible can yet be so inevitable, the boundary between what is allowed and what is not, is all the more blurred. How far discretion must refrain from touching even intellectually "all that is his"; how far, on the other hand, the interests of interaction and the interdependence of the members of society limit this duty—this is a question for whose answer neither moral tact nor knowledge of objective conditions and their requirements alone is sufficient, since *both* are needed. The subtlety and complexity of this question relegate it to the individual decision which cannot be prejudiced by any general norm—to a much higher degree than does the question of private property in the material sense.

### FRIENDSHIP AND LOVE

In this pre-form or complementation of the secret, the point is not the behavior of the individual who keeps a secret, but the behavior of another individual: within the mixture of reciprocal knowledge of ignorance, the accent is more on the degree of knowledge than of ignorance. We now come to a totally different configuration. It is found in those relationships which, in contrast to the ones discussed, do not center around clearly circumscribed interests that must be fixed objectively if only because of their "superficiality." Instead, they are built, at least in their idea, upon the person in its totality. The principal types here are friendship and marriage.

To the extent that the ideal of friendship was received from antiquity and (peculiarly enough) was developed in a romantic spirit, it aims at an absolute psychological intimacy, and is accompanied by the notion that even material property should be common to friends. This entering of the whole undivided ego into the relationship may be more plausible in friendship than in love for the reason that friendship lacks the specific concentration upon one element which love derives from its sensuousness. To be sure, by virtue of the fact that *one* among the total range of possible reasons for a relation takes the lead, these reasons attain a certain organization, as a group does through leadership. A particularly strong relational factor often blazes the trail on which the rest follow it, when they would otherwise remain latent; and undoubtedly, for most people, sexual love opens the doors of the total personality more widely than does anything else. For not a few, in fact, love is the only form in which they can give their ego in its totality, just as to the artist the form of his art offers the only possibility for revealing his whole inner life. Probably, this observation can be made especially often of women (although the very differently understood "Christian love" is also designed to achieve the same result). Not only because they love do women unreservedly offer the total remainder of their being and having; but all of this, so to speak, is chemically dissolved in love, and overflows to the other being exclusively and entirely in the color, form, and temperament of love. Yet, where the feeling of love is not sufficiently expansive, and the remaining psychological contents of the relationship are not sufficiently malleable, the preponderance of the erotic bond may suppress, as I have already suggested, the other contacts (practical-moral, intellectual), as well as the opening-up of those reservoirs of the personality that lie outside the erotic sphere.

Friendship lacks this vehemence, but also the frequent unevenness, of this abandon. It may be, therefore, more apt than love to connect a whole person with another person in its entirety; it may melt reserves more easily than love does—if not as stormily, yet on a larger scale and in a more enduring sequence. Yet such complete intimacy becomes probably more and more difficult as differentiation among men increases. Modern man, possibly, has too much to hide to sustain a friendship in the ancient sense. Besides, except for their earliest years, personalities are perhaps too uniquely individualized to allow full reciprocity of understanding and receptivity, which always, after all, requires much creative imagination and much divination which is oriented only toward the other. It would seem that, for all these reasons, the modern way of feeling tends more heavily toward differentiated friendships, which cover only one side of the personality, without playing into other aspects of it.

Thus a very special type of friendship emerges, which is of the greatest significance for our problem (the degrees of invasion and reserve within the friendship relation). These differentiated friendships which connect us with one individual in terms of affection, with another, in terms of common intellectual aspects, with a third, in terms of religious impulses, and with a fourth, in terms of common experiences—all these friendships present a very peculiar synthesis in regard to the question of discretion, of reciprocal revelation and concealment. They require that the friends do not look into those mutual spheres of interest and feeling which, after all, are not included in the relation and which, if touched upon, would make them feel painfully the limits of their mutual understanding. But the relation which is thus restricted and surrounded by discretions, may yet stem from the center of the total personality. It may yet be reached by the sap of the ultimate roots of the personality, even though it feeds only part of the person's periphery. In its idea, it involves the same affective depth and the same readiness for sacrifice, which less differentiated epochs and persons connect only with a common *total* sphere of life, for which reservations and discretions constitute no problem.

### MARRIAGE

The measures of self-revelation and self-restraint, with their complements of trespass and discretion, are much more difficult to determine in the case of marriage. Their ratio here belongs in a very general problem area of extreme importance to the sociology of intimate relations. This problem area centers around the question whether the maximum of common values can be attained under the condition that the personalities reciprocally relinquish their autonomies altogether, or under the condition of reserve: the question whether, perhaps, they do not belong *more* to one another qualitatively if, quantitatively, they do so less. This question can be answered, of course, only along with the other question as to how, within the total communicability of man, one can draw the line where restraint and respect of the other begin. The advantage of modern marriage—which, certainly, can answer both questions only from case to case—is that this line is not fixed from the beginning, as it is in other and earlier civilizations. In earlier cultures particularly, marriage is not an erotic but, in principle, only a social and economic institution. The satisfaction of the desire for love is only accidentally connected with it; it is contracted (with exceptions, of course), not only on the basis of individual attraction, but on the ground of family connections, working conditions, and descendants. In this respect, the Greeks achieved a particularly clear differentiation—according to Demosthenes: "We have hetaerae for pleasure; concubines for our daily needs; and wives to give us legitimate children and take care of the interior of the house." In such a mechanical relationship, the psychic center is obviously put out of function. Nevertheless (incidentally), this kind of marriage is constantly illustrated, though with certain modifications, by history and by the observation of actual contemporary marriages. There probably exists in it neither the need for any intimate, reciprocal self-revelation, nor the possibility of it. On the other hand, there is probably an absence of certain reserves of delicacy and chastity which, in spite of their seemingly negative character, are yet the flower of a fully internalized and personal, intimate relation.

The same tendency to exclude, *a priori* and by super-individual decree, certain life-contents from the common features of marriage lies in the variety of marriage forms which may coexist among the same people. Prior to entering marriage, the prospective spouses must choose among these forms, which variously distinguish economic, religious, and domestic-legal interests in their bearing upon matrimony. We find this among many nature peoples, as well as among the Hindus and Romans. Nobody will deny, of course, that even in modern life, marriage is probably contracted overwhelmingly from conventional or material motives. Yet no matter how often it is actualized, the sociological *idea* of modern marriage is the commonness of all life-contents, insofar as they determine the value and fate of the personality, immediately or through their effects. Nor is the nature of this ideal requirement without results: often enough it allows, or even stimulates, an initially quite imperfect union to develop into an ever more comprehensive one. But, whereas the very interminability of this process is the instrument of the happiness and inner vitality of the relationship, its reversal usually entails grave disappointments—namely, when absolute unity is anticipated from the beginning, when neither demand nor revelation knows restraint, not even the restraint which, for all finer and deeper natures, remains locked in the obscurity of the soul even where it seems to pour itself out before the other entirely.

During the first stages of the relationship there is a great temptation, both in marriage and in marriage-like free love, to let oneself be completely absorbed by the other, to send the last reserves of the soul after those of the body, to lose oneself to the other without reservation. Yet, in most cases, this abandon probably threatens the future of the relationship seriously. Only those individuals can give themselves *wholly* without danger who *cannot* wholly give themselves, because their wealth consists in a continuous development in which every abandon is at once followed by new treasures. Such individuals have an inexhaustible reservoir of latent psychological possessions, and hence can no more reveal and give them away at one stroke than a tree can give away next year's fruits with those of the season. But other individuals are different. With every flight of feeling, with every unconditional abandonment, with every revelation of their inner life, they make inroads (as it were) into their capital, because they lack the mainspring of ever renewed psychic affluence which can neither be exhaustively revealed nor be separated from the ego. In these cases, the spouses have a good chance of coming to face one another with empty hands; and the Dionysian bliss of giving may leave behind it an impoverishment which, unjustly, but no less bitterly for that, belies in retrospect even past abandons and their happiness.

We are, after all, made in such a way that we need not only a certain proportion of truth and error as the basis of our lives (as was pointed out earlier), but also a certain proportion of distinctness and indistinctness in the image of our life-elements. The other individual must give us not only gifts we may accept, but the possibility of our giving *him*—hopes, idealizations, hidden beauties, attractions of which not even *he* is conscious. But the place where we deposit all this, which *we* produce, but produce for *him,* is the indistinct horizon of his personality, the interstitial realm, in which faith replaces knowledge. But it must be strongly emphasized that this is, by no means, only a matter of illusions and optimistic or amorous self-deceptions, but that portions even of the persons closest to us must be offered us in the form of indistinctness and unclarity, in order for their attractiveness to keep on the same high level.

It is in this way that the majority of people replace the attraction values, which the minority possess in the inexhaustibility of their inner life and growth. The mere fact of absolute knowledge, of a psychological having-exhausted, sobers us up, even without prior drunkenness; it paralyzes the vitality of relations and lets their continuation really appear pointless. This is the danger of complete and (in more than an external sense) shameless abandon, to which the unlimited possibilities of intimate relations tempt us. These possibilities, in fact, are easily felt as a kind of duty—particularly where there exists no absolute certainty of one's own feeling; and the fear of not giving the other enough leads to giving him too much. It is highly probable that many marriages founder on this lack of reciprocal discretion—discretion both in taking and in giving. They lapse into a trivial habituation without charm, into a matter-of-factness which has no longer any room for surprises. The fertile depth of relations suspects and honors something even more ultimate behind every ultimateness revealed; it daily challenges us to reconquer even secure possessions. But this depth is only the reward for that tenderness and self-discipline which, even in the most intimate relation that comprises the total individual, respects his inner private property, and allows the right to question to be limited by the right to secrecy.

* * *

The essence of the secret society, as such, is autonomy. But this autonomy approaches anarchy: the consequences of leaving the general normative order easily are rootlessness and the absence of a stable life-feeling and of a norm-giving basis. The fixed and minute character and the ritual helps to overcome this lack. In this, we see once more how much man needs a certain ratio between freedom and law; and how, when he does not receive it from *one* source, he seeks to supplement what he obtains of the one by the missing quantity of the other, no matter from what additional source, until he has the ratio he needs. In ritual, the secret society voluntarily imposes upon itself a formal coercion, a complement required by its material separateness and autonomy. It is characteristic that, among the Freemasons, precisely those who enjoy the greatest political freedom, namely, the Americans, request of all their lodges the most rigorous uniformity of work procedure and ritual, whereas in Germany the practice involves a greater autonomy of the individual lodge: here, Freemasonry is so integrated with the general society that it does not demand such freedoms as would easily lead to the counterclaim of their being curtailed. In short, in the secret society the nature of ritual—objectively often quite senseless and schematically coercive—is by no means inconsistent with that group freedom which resembles anarchy, with severance from the norms of the inclusive society. On the contrary: just as the widespread diffusion of secret societies is usually a proof of public un-freedom, of a tendency toward police regimentation, and of political oppression, in short, just as it is a reaction stemming from the need for freedom—so, conversely, the internal, ritual regimentation of secret societies reflects a measure of freedom and severance from society at large which entails the counter-norm of this very schematism, in order to restore the equilibrium of human nature.

### FEATURES OF THE SECRET SOCIETY AS QUANTITATIVE MODIFICATIONS OF GENERAL GROUP FEATURES

These last considerations suggest the methodological principle on the basis of which I wish to analyze those traits of the secret society which have not yet been discussed. The question is, to what extent can they be shown to be essentially quantitative modifications of the typical features of sociation in general? The justification of this conception of the secret society leads once more to a consideration of its position in the whole complex of sociological forms.

The secret element in societies is a primary sociological fact, a particular kind and shading of togetherness, a formal quality of relationship. In direct or indirect interaction with other such qualities, it determines the shape of the group member or of the group itself. Yet, from a historical standpoint, the secret society is a secondary phenomenon; that is, it always develops only within a society already complete in itself. To put it differently: the secret society is characterized by its secrecy in the same way in which other societies (or even secret societies themselves) are characterized by their superordination and subordination, or by their aggressive purposes, or by their imitative character; but, that it can develop with these characteristics is possible only on the condition that a society already exists. Within this larger circle, it opposes it as a narrower one; whatever the purpose of the society, this opposition has, at any rate, the sense of exclusion. Even the altruistic secret society, which merely wants to render a certain service to the total group and intends to disband after achieving it, evidently considers temporary separation from this total group a technique unavoidable in view of its purpose.

*Separateness, Formality, Consciousness.*—Among the many smaller groups which are included in larger ones, there is none whose sociological constellation forces it to emphasize its formal self-sufficiency to the same extent as it does the secret society. Its secret surrounds it like a boundary outside of which there is nothing but materially, or at least formally, opposite matter, a boundary which therefore fuses, within itself, the secret society into a perfect unity. In groups of every other sort, the *content* of group life, the actions of the members in terms of rights and duties, can so occupy the members' consciousness that, normally, the formal fact of sociation plays scarcely any role at all. The secret society, on the other hand, cannot allow its members to forget the distinct and emphatic consciousness that they form a *society*. In comparison with other associations, it here is the passion of secrecy—always felt and always to be preserved—which gives the group-form, depending on it, a significance that is far superior to the significance of content. The secret society completely lacks organic growth, instinctive expansions, and, on the part of its members, all naïve, matter-of-fact feeling of belonging together and forming a unit. However irrational, mystical, or emotional its contents may be, the way in which it is formed is thoroughly conscious and intentional. In its *consciousness* of being a society—a consciousness which is constantly emphasized during its formative period and throughout its lifetime—it is the opposite of all spontaneous groups, in which the joining is only the expression, more or less, of elements which have grown together like roots. Its social-psychological form clearly is that of the interest group [*Zweckverband*]. This constellation makes it understandable why the formal characteristics of group formation in general are specifically pointed up in the secret society, and why some of its essential sociological traits develop as mere quantitative intensifications of very general types of relationship.

*Seclusion: Signs of Recognition.*—One of these has already been indicated, namely, the characterization as well as the cohesion of the secret society by means of seclusion against the social environment. This is the function of the often complicated signs of recognition through which the individual legitimates himself as a member. It should be noted that, prior to the more general diffusion of writing, these signs were more indispensable than later, when their other sociological uses became more important than those of mere legitimation. As long as there were no credentials of acceptance, notifications, or written descriptions of persons, an association with branches in several different places, had nothing but such signs for excluding unauthorized persons, and for having only individuals entitled to them receive its benefits or communications. These signs were revealed only to the legitimate members who, by means of them, were able to legitimate themselves wherever the group existed, and who had the duty to keep them secret.

The *purpose of seclusion* is clearly illuminated by the development of certain secret orders among nature peoples, especially in Africa and among the Indians. These orders are composed only of men. Their essential purpose is to emphasize the differentiation of men from women. Whenever their members act in this capacity, they appear in masks, and women are usually forbidden on severe penalty to approach them. Yet sometimes women succeed in discovering the secret that the horrible apparitions are not ghosts but their husbands. When this happens, the orders often lose their whole significance and become harmless mummeries. The man of nature with his undifferentiated, sensuous conception, cannot imagine a more perfect separateness, such as he wants to emphasize, than for those who wish it and are entitled to it to *hide* themselves, to make themselves invisible. This is the crudest and, externally, most radical manner of concealment; not only a particular act of man, but all of man at once, is concealed—the group does not do something secret, but the totality of its members makes *itself* into a secret. This form of the secret society is perfectly in line with that primitive stage of mind in which the whole personality is still absorbed in every particular activity, and in which the activity is not yet sufficiently objectified to have any character that the whole personality does not automatically share. It is also understandable, therefore, why the whole separateness becomes invalid once the secret of the mask is broken, and why, then, the secret society loses its inner significance along with its means and its expression.

*The Aristocratic Motive; Aristocracy.*—The separateness of the secret society expresses a value: people separate from others because they do not want to make common cause with them, because they wish to let them feel their superiority. This motive leads everywhere to group formations, which evidently are very different from those undertaken for objective purposes. By joining one another, those who want to distinguish themselves give rise to the development of an aristocracy, which strengthens and (so to speak) enlarges their position and self-consciousness by the weight of their own sum. Separation and group formation are thus connected through the aristocratizing motive. In many cases, this connection gives separation itself the stamp of something "special," in an honorific sense. Even in school classes, it can be observed how small, closely integrated cliques of classmates think of themselves as the elite over against the others who are not organized—merely because of the formal fact of constituting a special group; and the others, through their hostility and envy, involuntarily acknowledge this higher value. In these cases, secrecy and mystification amount to heightening the wall toward the outside, and hence to strengthening the aristocratic character of the group.

This significance of the secret society as the intensification of sociological exclusiveness in general, is strikingly shown in political aristocracies. Secrecy has always been among the requisites of their regime. In the first place, by trying to conceal the numerical insignificance of the ruling class, aristocracies exploit the psychological fact that the unknown itself appears to be fearsome, mighty, threatening. In Sparta, the number of warriors was kept secret as much as possible. In Venice, the same end was intended by the decree that all *nobili* [noblemen] had to wear a simple black costume: no striking dress was to call the small number of men in power to the attention of the people. This was even carried to the point where the group of the highest elite was concealed completely: the names of the three state inquisitors were unknown to everybody except the council of ten who elected them. In some Swiss aristocracies, one of the most important authorities was simply called "the Secret Ones"; and in Freiburg, the aristocratic families were known as "the secret lineages" [*die heimlichen Geschlechter*]. The democratic principle, on the contrary, is associated with the principle of publicity and, in the same sense, with the tendency toward general and basic laws. For, these laws apply to an unlimited number of subjects and are, therefore, public in their very essence. Conversely, the use of secrecy by aristocratic regimes is only the extreme intensification of the social exclusiveness and exemption which, ordinarily, make aristocracies opposed to general, fundamentally fixed legislations.

Where the aristocratic idea does not characterize the policies of a group but the disposition of an individual, the relation between exclusiveness and secrecy manifests itself on a very different plane. The morally and intellectually distinguished person despises all concealment, because his inner certainty makes him indifferent to what others know or do not know of him, and to the question whether he is appraised correctly or falsely by them, or held in high or low esteem. For him, secrecy is a concession to outsiders; secrecy is dependence of conduct upon regard for others. For this reason, the "mask" which many consider sign and proof of an aristocratic personality that is turned away from the multitude, on the contrary proves the importance of the multitude to the wearer of the mask. The "mask" of the truly noble person is that even when he shows himself without disguise, the many do not understand him, do not even see him, so to speak.

*Degrees of Initiation: Formal and Material Separation from the Outside.*—This exclusion of everything outside the group is a general formal-sociological fact, which merely uses secrecy as a more pointed technique. It attains a particular nuance in the plurality of degrees in which it is customary for initiation into the secret society, down to its last mysteries, to take place. The existence of such degrees threw light earlier upon another sociological feature of the secret society. As a rule, before he is even accepted into the first degree, the novice must give a solemn promise of secrecy concerning everything he may experience, whereby the absolute, *formal* separation, achievable by secrecy, is effected. Yet, inasmuch as the actual content or purpose of the society becomes accessible to the neophyte only gradually—whether this purpose is the perfect purification and sanctification of the soul through the consecration of the mysteries, or the absolute suspension of every moral barrier, as among the Assassins and other criminal societies—the *material* separation is achieved differently, in a more continuous, relative manner. In this material respect, the neophyte is still closer to the status of non-participant, from which testing and education eventually lead him to grasp the totality or core of the association. This core, evidently, thus gains a protection and isolation from the outside far beyond those by means of the oath upon entrance. It is seen to (as has already been shown in the example of the Druids) that the still untried neophyte does not have much he could betray: within the general secrecy that encompasses the group as a whole, the graduated secrecy produces an elastic sphere of protection (as it were) around its innermost essence.

The contrast between exoteric and esoteric members, such as is attributed to the Pythagorean order, is the most poignant form of this protective measure. The circle composed of those only partially initiated formed a sort of buffer region against the non-initiates. It is everywhere the dual function of the "middler" to connect and to separate, or, actually, rather to play only one role which, according to our perceptual categories and our viewpoint, we designate as connecting or as separating. In the same way, the real unity of superficially contradictory activities is here seen in its clearest light: precisely because the lower grades of the order mediate the transition to the center of the secret, they create a gradual densification of the sphere of repulsion which surrounds this center and which protects it more securely than could any abrupt and radical alternative between total inclusion and total exclusion.

*Group Egoism.*—In practice, sociological autonomy presents itself as group egoism: the group pursues its own purposes with the same inconsiderateness for all purposes outside itself which, in the case of the individual, is precisely called egoism. Usually, to be sure, this inconsiderateness is morally justified in the consciousness of the individual members by the fact that the group purposes themselves have a super-individual, objective character; that it is often impossible to name any particular individual who profits from the group's egoistic behavior; and that, as a matter of fact, this behavior often requires the group members' selflessness and sacrifice. But the point here is not to make any ethical valuation, but only to stress the group's separation from its environment, which is brought about or characterized by the egoism of the group. However, in the case of a small circle, which intends to preserve and develop itself within a larger one, this egoism has certain limits as long as it exists publicly. An open association, no matter how violently it fights against other associations within the same larger society, or against the general foundations of this society itself, must always maintain that the realization of its own ultimate purposes is to the advantage of the whole; and the necessity of this outward assertion somewhat restricts the actual egoism of its actions. This necessity does not exist in the case of secret societies, which always therefore, at least potentially, can afford to be hostile to other groups or to the whole. Non-secret groups cannot admit such a hostility, and, therefore, cannot unconditionally practice it. Nothing symbolizes, or possibly promotes, the separation of the secret society from its social environment as decisively as the elimination of the hypocrisy, or of the actual condescension, by means of which the non-secret society is inevitably integrated with the teleology of its environment.

*Inclusiveness and Exclusiveness as Group Principles.*—In spite of the actual quantitative delimitation of every true community, there exists a considerable number of groups whose inner tendency is to include all those who are not explicitly excluded. Within certain political, religious, and status limits, everybody is considered immediately as "belonging" so long as he satisfies certain external conditions, which are usually not a matter of his will, but are given with his existence itself. All people, for instance, who are born within the territory of a given state, are members, unless particular circumstances make exceptions of them, of the (often very complex) civic society. The member of a given social class is included, as a matter of course, in the social conventions and forms of connection of this class, unless he becomes a voluntary or involuntary outsider. The extreme case is the claim of a church that it includes all mankind; and that, if any individuals are excluded from the religious association, which, ideally, is valid also for them, it is only through historical accident, sinful stubbornness, or God's special intention.

We note here the distinction of two principles, which clearly indicate a basic differentiation of the sociological significance of groups generally, no matter how much practice may mix them and make the difference lose some of its sharpness. On the one hand, there is the principle of including everybody who is not explicitly excluded; and, on the other, there is the principle of excluding everybody who is not explicitly included. The second type is represented in greatest purity by the secret society. The unconditional character of its separation, which is borne by the consciousness of it at every step of the group's development, causes, and is caused by, the fact that those who are not explicitly accepted, are for this simple reason explicitly excluded. The Masonic order could no better have supported its recent emphatic assertion that it is not a "secret order," properly speaking, than by simultaneously professing its ideal of including *all* men, of representing humanity.

*Seclusion Against the Outside and Internal Cohesion.*—Here, as everywhere else, the intensified seclusion against the outside is associated with the intensification of cohesion internally: we have here two sides, or external forms, of the same sociological attitude. A purpose which occasions an individual to enter into secret association with others, excludes almost always such an overwhelming part of his general social circle from participation, that the potential and real participants gain rarity value. He must keep on good terms with them because it is much more difficult to replace them here than (other things being equal) in a legitimate association. Furthermore, every discord inside the secret society brings danger of betrayal, which usually both the self-preservation of the individual and that of the group are interested in avoiding.

Finally, the isolation of the secret society from the surrounding social syntheses removes a number of occasions for conflict. Among all the bonds of the individual, the bond of secret sociation always has an exceptional position. In comparison with it, the official bonds—familial, civic, religious, economic, through rank and friendship—no matter how varied their contents, touch contact surfaces of a very different kind and measure. Only the contrast with the secret societies makes it clear that their claims criss-cross one another, because they lie (so to speak) in the same plane. Since these claims openly compete for the individual's strength and interests, individuals collide within any one of these circles: each individual is simultaneously claimed by the interests of other groups.

The sociological isolation of the secret society greatly limits such collisions. In accordance with its purpose and operation, competing interests of open-society origin are shut out. Every secret society—if only because it usually fills its own sphere alone (the same individual hardly ever belongs to more than one secret society)—exercises over its members a sort of absolute dominion, which gives them little opportunity to engage in conflicts such as result from the coordination of the plurality of spheres that represent open groups. The "king's peace," which really ought to reign within every association, is promoted in a formally unsurpassable manner, by the peculiar and exceptional conditions of the secret society. In fact, it seems as if, aside from the more realistic reason in favor of the "king's peace," the mere form of secrecy itself kept the members freer from other influences and disturbances, and thus facilitated their accord. A certain English politician found the basis for the strength of the English cabinet in the secrecy which surrounds it: everybody who has ever been active in public life, he suggested, knows that a small number of people can be brought to agree the more easily, the more secret are its negotiations.

*Centralization.*—Corresponding to the outstanding degree of cohesion within the secret society is the thoroughness of its centralization. The secret society offers examples of unconditional and blind obedience to leaders who—although, naturally, they may also be found elsewhere—are yet particularly remarkable in view of the frequent anarchic character of the secret society that negates all other law. The more criminal its purposes, the more unlimited, usually, is the power of the leaders and the cruelty of its exercise. The Assassins in Arabia; the Chauffeurs, a predatory band with a widely ramified organization which raged, particularly, in eighteenth-century France; the Gardunas in Spain, a criminal society that had relations with the Inquisition from the seventeenth to the beginning of the nineteenth century—all these, whose very nature was lawlessness and rebellion, unconditionally and without any criticism submitted to chiefs whom they themselves (as least in part) appointed.

The interrelation between the needs for freedom and for a bond operates here; it appears in the rigor of ritual, which combines the extremes of both: for the sake of a balanced life-feeling, the excess of freedom from all otherwise valid norms must be brought into equilibrium by a similarly excessive submission and renunciation of the will. Yet more essential, probably, is the necessity of centralization, which is the life condition of the secret society. It is especially important for that type—for instance, the criminal band—which lives off surrounding groups, interferes with them through all kinds of radiations and actions, and thus is gravely threatened by treason and the distraction of interests, once it is no longer governed by the most intransigent cohesion with its point of origin in its own center.

Secret societies which, for whatever reasons, fail to develop a tightly solidifying authority are, therefore, typically exposed to very grave dangers. Originally, the Waldenses were not a secret society; they became one in the thirteenth century, only because of external pressure to keep themselves hidden. This made it impossible for them to meet regularly, which in turn deprived their doctrine of its unity. A number of branches arose, which lived and developed separately, and were often hostile to one another. The order declined because it lacked the necessary complement of the secret society: uninterruptedly effective centralization. Freemasonry, probably, owes the evident lag in its power behind its diffusion and means, to the considerable autonomy of its parts, which have neither a unified organization nor a central authority. Their common features merely cover principles and signs of recognition, and thus are traits of equality and of relations between person and person only, not of centralization, which holds the energies of the members together and is the complement of separation.

It is merely an exaggeration of this formal motive of centralization that secret societies are often directed by *unknown* leaders: the lower echelons are not to know whom they obey. To be sure, this occurs, above all, for the sake of preserving the secret. With this intention, it was developed to an extraordinary degree in the organization of an early nineteenth-century Italian secret society, the Welfic Knights, which worked for the liberation and unification of Italy. At each of their various branches, the Knights had a highest council of six persons, who did not know one another and communicated only by means of an intermediary, called "The Visible One." But the preservation of secrecy is by no means the only purpose of unknown leaders. Instead, they exemplify the most extreme and abstract sublimation of dependence upon a center: the tension between dependent and leader reaches the highest degree when the leader becomes invisible. All that remains then, is the pure fact of obedience —merciless, as it were, and unmodified by any personal nuances—out of which the superordinate as a subject has vanished. If obedience to impersonal authority, to mere office, to the executor of an objective law, has the character of invincible strength, it is intensified to the point of an uncanny absoluteness when the ruling personality remains, in principle, hidden. For if, with the visibility and familiarity of the ruler, the individual suggestion and the power of personality are removed from the relationship or domination, domination also loses all attenuations, all relative and "human" elements inherent in the empirical, unique personality. Obedience is thus colored by the feeling of subjection to an intangible power, whose limits cannot be traced, and which can nowhere be seen, but must, for this reason, be suspected everywhere. In the secret society with an unknown leader, the general sociological cohesion of a group through the unity of its ruling authority is transferred, as it were, into an imaginary focus, and thus attains its purest, most intense form.

*De-individualization.*—De-individualization is the sociological character which, in the individual member, corresponds to this centralistic subordination. Where the immediate concern of the society is not the interests of its elements; where the society rather transcends itself (as it were) by using its members as means for purposes and actions extraneous to them—the secret society shows, once more, a heightened measure of leveling of the individuality, of "de-selfing" [*Entselbstung*]. *Some* measure of this is characteristic of everything social, generally. But the secret *society* uses de-individualization to compensate for the above-mentioned individualizing and differentiating character of the *secret*. This begins with the secret orders of nature peoples, whose appearance and activities are accompanied almost everywhere by the wearing of masks—so that an outstanding expert suggested that the presence of masks among a nature people should at once make one suspect the existence of secret societies. It is, of course, in the nature of the secret order for its members to conceal themselves. But, when a particular individual appears and acts unambiguously as a member of a secret order, and merely does not show what individuality (which is normally well known) is associated with him, the disappearance of personality behind its role is most strongly emphasized. In the Irish conspiracy which was organized under the name of Clan-na-gael in America in 1870, the individual members were never designated by their names, but only by numbers. This, too, of course, was done for the practical purpose of secrecy; but, at the same time, it proves how much this purpose suppresses individuality. Leadership can proceed with much greater inconsiderateness and indifference to individual wishes and capacities of persons who appear only as numbers and who may not be known by their personal names even to the other members (which at least occurred in groups similar to the Clan-na-gael), than it can if the group includes each member as a personal entity. No less effective, toward the same end, is the comprehensive role and strength of ritual, which always indicates the fact that the objective organization has overcome the personal element in the members' activities and contributions to the group. The hierarchical order admits the individual only as the discharger of a predetermined role; for each member, it holds ready a stylized garb in which his personal outlines disappear.

*Equality of Members.*—It is merely another name for this elimination of the differentiated personality if secret societies practice great relative equality among their members. This does not contradict the despotic character of their organization: in all kinds of other groups, too, despotism is correlated with the leveling of the ruled. Within the secret society, there often is a brotherly equality among the members, which constitutes a sharp and tendentious contrast to their differences in their other life situations. Characteristically, this is most noticeable in secret societies of a religio-ethical nature—which strongly accentuate brotherhood—and, on the other hand, in those of an illegal character. In his memoirs, Bismarck writes of a pederastic organization, wide-spread in Berlin, with which he became acquainted as a young justiciary; he stresses "the *equalizing* effect throughout all strata of the collective practice of the forbidden."

This de-personalization, wherein the secret group exaggerates in a one-sided manner a typical relationship between individual and society, appears, finally, as characteristic *irresponsibility*. Here, too, the mask is the most primitive phenomenon. Most African secret orders are represented by a man disguised as a spirit of the woods, who commits all violations, including robbery and murder, against anyone he happens to meet. He is not held responsible for his crimes—obviously, only because of his mask. The mask is the somewhat clumsy form in which these groups let the personalities of their members disappear, and without which the members would undoubtedly be overtaken by revenge and punishment. But responsibility is so immediately connected with the ego (philosophically, too, the whole problem of responsibility belongs in the problem of the ego), that, for such naïve feeling, the disguise of the person suspends all responsibility.

This connection is used no less in political finesse. In the North American House of Representatives, actual decisions are made in the standing committees, with which the House is almost always in agreement. But the transactions of these committees are secret; thus, the most important part of legislative activity is hidden from the public. In large measure, this seems to extinguish the political responsibility of the delegates, since nobody can be held responsible for uncontrollable procedures. Inasmuch as individual contributions toward a particular decision remain hidden, the decision appears to be made by some super-individual authority. Here, too, irresponsibility is the consequence or the symbol of the intensified sociological de-individualization, which corresponds to the secrecy of group action. This also hold for all directorates, faculties, committees, administrations, etc., whose transactions are secret: the individual, as a person, disappears as the quasi-nameless group member, and with his disappearance as a person disappears the responsibility that cannot be imagined to inhere in a being whose concrete activities are intangible.

*The Secret Society and the General Government.*—This one-sided intensification of general sociological features is confirmed, finally, by the danger with which society at large believes, rightly or wrongly, secret societies threaten it. Where the over-all aim of the general society is strong (particularly political) centralization, it is antagonistic to all special associations, quite irrespective of their contents and purposes. Simply by being units, these groups compete with the principle of centralization which alone wishes to have the prerogative of fusing individuals into a unitary form. The preoccupation of the central power with "special associations" runs through all of political history—a point which is relevant in many respects to the present investigations and has already been stressed. A characteristic type of this preoccupation is suggested, for instance, by the Swiss Convention of 1481, according to which no separate alliances were permitted between any of the ten confederated states. Another example is the persecution of apprentices' associations by the despotism of the seventeenth and eighteenth centuries. A third is the tendency to disenfranchise local political communities which is so often demonstrated by the modern state.

The secret society greatly increases this danger which the special association presents to the surrounding totality. Man has rarely a calm and rational attitude toward what he knows only little or vaguely. Instead, his attitude consists in part in levity, which treats the unknown as if it did not exist, and in part in anxious fantasy, which, on the contrary, inflates it into immense dangers and terrors. The secret society, therefore, appears dangerous by virtue of its mere secrecy. It is impossible to know whether a special association might not one day use its energies for undesirable purposes, although they were gathered for legitimate ones: this fear is the main source of the basic suspicion which central powers have of all associations among their subjects.

In regard to groups which make it their principle to conceal themselves, the suspicion that their secrecy hides dangers is all the more readily suggested. The Orange Societies which were organized in England, in the beginning of the nineteenth century, for the suppression of Catholicism, avoided all public discussion, working only in secret, through personal connections and correspondence. But this very secrecy let them appear as a public danger: the suspicion arose "that men, who shrank from appealing to public opinion, mediated a resort to force." Purely on the grounds of its secrecy, the secret order thus appears dangerously close to a conspiracy against the reigning powers. How much this is only an intensification of the general political questionability of special associations is clearly shown in a case like the following. The oldest German guilds offered their members effective legal protection, and thus replaced the protection of the state. For this reason, the Danish kings promoted them, since they saw in them a support of the public order. But, on the other hand, for the very same reason, the guilds also were considered to be *competitors* of the state: they were condemned in this capacity by the Frankish capitularies—more particularly, because they were designated as *conspiracies*. The secret society is so much considered an enemy of the central power that, even conversely, every group that is politically rejected, is called a secret society.

# 3. *The Sociological Category of Communion*

BY HERMAN SCHMALENBACH

FOR Ferdinand Toennies, the family, particularly the peasant and small-town family, is the prime example of a human community. The basis of family bonds is a natural and physical coherence. Such coherence is generated by proximity and consanguinity. Like other natural phenomena, families are situated in time and space. They can be located. Yet, social relations are more than physical. They are "psychical" phenomena as well. The natural features of the family are, it would seem, merely external: They only establish the possibilities for the emergence of community. Even consanguinity does not generate social relations unless a commonality is recognized "by the persons concerned." Community, then, can be characterized as that order of social coherence which develops on the basis of natural interdependence.

This is often misunderstood. We speak of "beginning life in earnest," as in the case of youth, but we actually refer to several matters: separation from one's home and the style of life of one's parents, the impulsive entry into a free and open world, and joining with others in association and friendship. Such associations are nowadays referred to as communities. But is this appropriate? Are such "communities" constituted by natural bonds? Are not the original and natural bonds that joined child to family rent asunder?

Perhaps our version of the concept of community represents an illegitimate narrowing of that term. Surely, there are conflicts between community and community, between peer group and family. The real problem is whether such conflicts represent special peculiarities of unique relations or general characteristics of social relations. We do not have to prove here that the wish to separate oneself from one's home and to wander far afield is independent of specific features of one's family of origin. Neither is it solely a matter of desiring to repudiate such origins, although it may be manifest in that form. Nor are such wishes merely symptomatic of specific periods when the generations as such appear to be in sharp conflict. Again, these wishes are not exclusively confined to those sectors of the population that are relatively emancipated from the demands of tradition. Apprentices of every calling have always had their time of travel. Admittedly there are times and circles that value the settled life more than others. Yet the desire for travel arises in any young person about the time he is twenty. Such desire need not necessarily be confined to the short and temporarily impulsive period of romantic youth. Associations and friendships formed as part of this process can be anything but transitory. When they are taken seriously, such friendships even exhibit an affinity to religious phenomena. At any rate, religious associations seem originally always to have been communions.

Innumerable friendships develop among people in their youth. As such, they may be quite free from any religious motives, while betraying, at the same time, the general religious affinity just described. Such an affinity is especially characteristic of all associations that are taken very seriously by their members. In any case, the general yearning, found all through the world these days, for some human community clearly seems to be associated

---

Translated by Kaspar D. Naegele and Gregory P. Stone, from Herman Schmalenbach, *Die Dioskuren* ("Die Soziologische Kategorie des Bundes," Vol. I).

This is a free translation. Besides the usual complicated German sentence structure, the original contains passages from the poetry of Stefan George. These have been omitted, as have the extensive footnotes and references, which are often not essential to the main argument. References to Max Weber at the end of the essay are, for the most part, to the first chapter of his *Wirtschaft und Gesellschaft,* now available in translation. Because the references are so well known to sociologists, they have not been documented. We have attempted to restrict our translation only to those portions of the original which carry forward the author's plea for supplementing Toennies' familiar distinction between *Gemeinschaft* and *Gesellschaft* with the concept, *Bund,* so that the objective relations of *Gemeinschaft* will not be confused with relations built on sentiment and affect.

There is no ready English equivalent for Schmalenbach's concept or for Toennies' concepts. For the latter, we have employed "community" and "society," and we ask the reader always to interpret the translations in the particular usage of Toennies. Both terms have a multiplicity of referents in sociology, any of which could confuse the main issues of the essay. *Bund* refers to those social relations in which persons are characteristically *en rapport.* It carries with it the notion of a sympathetic comradeship—a camaraderie. Yet such relations are not always sustained by positive emotions. Persons may be caught up with one another as they share in any and all manner of sentiment—love and hate, joy and despair. Thus, the term reminds us of Cooley's early effort to propose the communion as a general mode of human association. We have selected Cooley's term to translate the concept, *Bund,* in the somewhat arbitrary and forced effort to establish some continuity beween American and German thinking on these matters.

with religious yearning as well. One can see this in the cult of friendship as practiced by the Romantics. Even where all this is not manifestly the case, an element of religiosity (which I hesitate to call "religious") seems to bind deeply some social relations and impart to them a profoundly sacred character. You can observe this in the collective enthusiasm of youth for high ideals, in their national loyalties, in the patriotic concern with national symbols on the part of the youth of a country, or in the mutual devotion of Communist young people. But, just as such communions present the aspect of religiosity, so do religious groupings present the aspect of communion at their inception.

All natural bonds may be torn asunder by the formation of associations, brotherhoods, fraternities, and the like. In line with this, Max Weber and, following him, Ernest Troeltsch formulated the important distinction between church and sect. The church is a community, and may become a society. Sect is a pure communion. Max Weber did not exploit his discovery to transform the basic categories of sociology from the dichotomy presented by Toennies into a necessary trichotomy. Still he came close to it. He distinguished, within community, between traditional and affective or emotional bonds. It is indeed the case that communions are borne along by waves of emotion, reaching ecstatic heights of collective enthusiasm, rising from the depths of love or hate. This raises the question: are such communions merely a subform of community or an alternative social form altogether, differing both from community and from society?

## *Community and Communion*

It may be too narrow to characterize community as an association based on the natural coherence of its members. Even Toennies admitted that habit and memory can constitute communal ties in the absence of blood ties, although communal ties are strengthened by blood bonds. Max Weber suggested that the basis of communal ties frequently lies in tradition. Yet, ties of blood and matters of tradition are surely separate issues. Presumably ties of blood can establish communities in the absence of habits and common memories among the individuals concerned, but this presupposes cultural traditions and, at some point, a knowledge of "common ancestry." The father comes immediately to stand in a characteristic relation to his son when he returns after a decade or more from foreign parts and, for the first time, meets a son born during his absence. Such an encounter need not involve floods of emotion. It is not necessarily influenced by the attitudes of the mother (who may already be dead), nor does it require memories of a mother even though this may be part of the whole matter. Even love seems to be dispensable. Any creature that recognizes "ties of blood" will be responsive accordingly when it becomes aware of them, or first senses or suspects them. It will respond with a kind of communal consciousness.

This is a precarious term. Still, I must admit that it belongs to the natural features of community. We often refer to a village, a province, or a country as handing down patterns of values. The natural, then, includes all those attributes that one has inherited collectively, into which one has grown and been born, and through which one has grown together with others. It happens that what appear to be bonds of blood are also a matter of common usage, a matter of custom and of shared modes of thought or expression, all of which have no other sanction than tradition.

Even the purely local neighborhood seems, in the past at least, to have had features in common with a kinship system. This does not mean that there have to be memories stretching far back. Still, where this is the case, the natural coherence of the neighborhood becomes much more firmly established. Less intense forms of neighborly community can become established by the sheer fact that individuals have lived the adult portion of their life in one place. Indeed, there are forms of community that can be sustained between the salesman and the customer in shops that one frequents with some regularity. One can sustain a kind of community even with the silent passerby whom one sees frequently on the street. In general, even the shortest of encounters can, as a limiting case, become the basis of subsequent community, if a trace of those contacts is impressed on the mind. Such encounters leave a latent remnant, which later can re-emerge. It is essential in this connection simply to admit the assertion that social phenomena are based on natural conditions. But, as soon as other than natural facts provide the social ferment, human associations take on a noncommunal character.

Included in the natural realm are not only matters of locality or space but also matters of time. Time and space, after all, lack qualitative features only on the plane of abstract thought. The precondition for the formation of human community consists only in the chance that the qualitative features of time and place operate not as such, but exclusively as a consequence of their translation into a socially spatial and temporal contiguity.

Spatial and temporal contiguity, then, seem to be an essential basis of that order of coalescence which we call community. If one were to attempt to specify this more closely, one would have to enumerate all "the basic conditions of life." Yet this could never suffice, for only socially consequential conditions can lead to community. It is as though the conditions of community are independent of us, while we are dependent on them; as though, in fact, we cannot purposely act to create community.

At best this is a tentative way of speaking about the matter. It is not quite true that one cannot deliberately act to bring about community. One can, inadvertently or intentionally, do something toward the formation of community by pursuing any course of action. One may produce, as an intentional by-product, a state of community, or at least a basis for it, in the hope or anticipation that a community has been initiated. Such action, to be sure, is often indirect. Still, in some respects, the conditions of community are dependent on what individuals do. In contrast and for opposite reasons, the conditions of communion may be so completely independent of us that we cannot intervene and must adapt ourselves to them as given. In that case, the distinguishing characteristics of community are simply the natural qualities of its basis and the fact that only communities have such natural bases. But even these must be qualified so that they include tradition, custom, etc. By contrast, communions are likely to take such categories of nature, give them metaphysical and other forms of exaggerated interpretations, and in turn claim them for themselves in the name of a concept of "true" nature.

One additional consideration is essential for the proper characterization of community. It is in this connection that I have decided to regard ties of blood as an archetype of community, as it were. In this respect my argument begins at the same point as Toennies', but we end in opposite places. I have already skirted the issue: how do primarily natural occasions become transformed into social relations, given the fact that, after all, social phenomena are psychic? I have argued that ties of blood have to become recognized as such. Their sheer existence is not sufficient to establish those social phenomena that, nevertheless, depend on them. However, this might lead one to consider all forms of mutual attraction—which, in turn, one might see as part of the nature of things—as the equivalent of sympathy and then consider sympathy as the basis of community. After all, do we not *feel* close or related, consider ourselves bound to others through some secret bond? If that is the case, does not the distinction between community and communion become rather ambiguous? Yet communal bonds, even in the unconscious, are psychic phenomena. The bases of community are psychic whether they be unconscious or not. More important, unconscious processes, too, are psychic and can, as such, be part of the basic community. Objective knowledge about ties of blood is indeed not sufficient. The recognition of such bonds must be accompanied by a simultaneous sense of inner or psychic coherence.

Such a sense of coherence may have an unconscious component. One may know of it and about it, but, even in that case, the knowledge takes the form of an inner glow in a clouded stream which shimmers below and is neither comprehensive nor totally elucidating. The murkiness is never fully dispelled. The "unconscious" is not directly comparable to the "conscious," but to another idea—the "condition of consciousness"—the same content in a different form (I refer to Eduard von Hartmann, and also to Fechner). This is extremely important, because it follows that the unconscious may be known but never entirely revealed. The unconscious remains "generically there," or better "existentially there." (Although it can be detected, analyzed, and perhaps confirmed consciously, certainly the total unconscious can not be lifted into consciousness and remain the same.)[1]

1. The conscious and unconscious are not construed here as opposites. Actually there are two conceptions of the condition of consciousness. Actual "knowing," as knowledge *of* something, is always only knowledge of circumstances (I know that . . .). The circumstances are "there" (phenomenologically) and the conditions of existence in which they occur are independent of "knowing." Only "then," in such a way, can they be known, and they cannot be disclosed otherwise. Thus, there is an unmediated directly perceived apprehension of the conditions of existence itself and, beyond those objective circumstances, lies the question of the relation of knowledge to them in so far as the existence of knowledge as a phenomenon of its own kind has not been considered. Knowledge may or may not affect the "unconscious." It remains "the unconscious." As long as we "know" it is real, it remains real. The matter of "consciousness," then, is raised along with "the unconscious." Understandably this too can become an object of knowing—in spite of its usefulness the expression is certainly awkward. However, this is not essential: the expression "unconscious consciousness"—or better "unknown consciousness"—is not nonsense. One can live predominantly in "the bright light of awareness" without ever being aware, for example, of that fact. Moreover, someone else may be very much aware of the many peculiarities of such a person's "unconscious." For the most part "ignorance" belongs to the "unknown consciousness," as do those things that have readily disappeared from consciousness while being preserved in the "unconscious," or, in any case, functioning there, even if they are then quite something else. On the whole, the conscious is more closely related to the process of knowing than is the "unconscious." Knowing is a function of the conscious, although occasionally knowing may affect the unconscious. (Only as a function of consciousness can knowing destroy the unconscious. The impact of the unconscious upon knowing and upon the conscious is highly problematical and complicated in any case.) I believe that these allusions are needed here. Perhaps I should also have emphasized that the unconscious, if you will, is a phenomenon of consciousness or, better, something directly known as well as something that may be revealed.

The formative conditions of community ordinarily are unconscious and are not exclusively in the province of the external and the physical (consequently they become primarily social). Not only common blood ties—which are advanced here as the prototype—but also common ancestry of all other kinds, and the acquisitions of one's personal and more or less "waking" life may be activated as the formative conditions of community upon a relatively brief spatial and temporal contact. I suggest that these things leave behind them a "trace" in the "unconscious." To be sure, we may "know" about these things, but, apart from the fact that expressed knowledge is by no means an irrelevant matter here, the formulation upon which community rests is not recognition, but a modification that the "unconscious" has established as part of our psychic make-up. Moreover, we may even consciously resist acknowledging community by interpreting it as fortuitous, unreal, and consequently incredible. This, too, may have consequences.

Principally, we have, as it were, surrendered ourselves to our unconscious; we have surrendered without resistance. The consideration of the psychic "substance" on which community is based establishes, in a profound sense, the manner in which the foundations for such a relationship are actually constituted by conditions and states of which "we" are "independent" but upon which "we" "depend." The "unconscious" suggests a matter far different from the fact that natural and innate conditions are antithetical to psychic conditions, because it affects the "psyche" in somewhat the same way as the natural and innate does—similar to the way nature affects plants or unthinking vegetables.

Speaking experimentally, this is what differentiates community from communion: community implies the recognition of something taken for granted and the assertion of the self-evident. Generally speaking, one will not expressly sanction or condemn those communities to which one belongs. One is usually not fully aware of them. They are given. They simply exist. As a rule we are not likely to take much notice of our membership in them, even when it is a question of our membership in far-flung communities—such as commonalities of language, of ethnicity, or of the fact of a common humanity. The communal circles of which we are part reach into imponderable distances and cover connections of all kinds. One cannot be aware of all of them. Yet, as persons, we are always affected by them. Our own unconscious is directly or indirectly constituted in and through them. Only through contrasts and disturbances does a community become an object of attention for its members. Often this merely takes the form of coming to their notice. At least this is so when fate strikes, provided it strikes not wholly unexpectedly, and without radically contravening a legitimate order.

In the event of death of the next of kin, especially when the person concerned is already old or has been ill for a long time, a peasant does not undergo especially disturbing experiences, at least not consciously. Rather, he turns to the task to be done. In other respects, however, communal disturbances can give rise to strong emotions, particularly when daily routines are suddenly and profoundly disturbed. This is particularly the case when one faces a threat, especially an avoidable one. When the threat is absolutely inescapable, then people, very much bound to their communal existence, accept their fate. Their thought is blanketed by sentiment. Where there is a choice, emotions seethe, and sometimes considerable violence ensues. As a rule, the disturbance itself becomes the object of these emotions. In that case, they take on a negative character. Such emotions, indeed, take the shape of rage, anger, hatred and, in the case of success, of triumph. In the case of failure, there arise spite, bitterness. resentment. and, eventually perhaps, sorrow, regret, and pain. Positive feelings oriented toward community are much rarer. They too constitute reactions to disturbances, particularly successfully managed disturbances, or, at least, disturbances limited in their import. They also arise in the presence of outsiders.

However, disturbances can also come from within. A young person, for instance, may demand to leave home. Should this be considered unwarranted, a father might respond to it with the words, "Here you are, and here you will remain, for you belong here." All the person knows then is that he belongs; there is little in the way of positive communal emotion. Filial devotion, parental love, or the love of siblings—these are for the most part simply forms of speech or perhaps expressions that derive their meaning more from the spirit of communion. In the case of a community, one just belongs and generally irrevocably so. One *is* mutually related; one need never feel or think it so. Children of two families simply know that one belongs to one family and the other to the other family. That is all that they know about families as such. None of these experiences are attended by any specific emotions. Nowadays, however, one is inclined to consider a consciousness of kind or of community as a matter of feeling. It must be remembered that the feeling of communal belonging always presupposes a conscious recognition of community.

To belong together and to be tied to one another,

perhaps irrevocably, is the essential matter. One need not feel anything in particular. Still, sense of community might lead to experiences of tenderness, happiness, or pride. Nevertheless, it is characteristic of the peasant, who is after all the best example of a person typically bound to the community, to become uncomfortable when emotions are displayed. They seem alien to him. Similarly, cosmopolitan people, but for opposite reasons, shy away from emotionality. It seems irrational to them. To the peasant, emotionality is to be avoided because it gives psychic processes too much autonomy. Often a peasant is considered sparse and dour in his emotional expressions. He is even said to lack feeling for nature. On the other hand, people argue that he not so much lacks feeling as words for its expression. Actually, peasants probably do "have" extraordinarily few of these feelings by way of conscious experience. This is not because they do not have them at all, but because, being unconsciously tied both to community and to nature, emotional experiences do not articulate a peasant's relations to the world around him.

It is really strange that, given these facts, one should think of community as something both represented among peasants and based on feeling. This simply constitutes a sentimentalizing of peasantry. Urban people are prone to such distortions. They reflect the rootlessness of the person who lives his life in urban society. Actually they are an expression of a desire for communion. Such a desire tends to combine a wish for belongingness with a high valuation of peasantry, of community, and of nature. In itself it does not, of course, constitute community, nor does it lead to a proper understanding of community. Instead, it confuses community with communion.

There are many instances of such sentimental proclivities. A contemporary yearning for community, which is genuine, though romantic, is one form of this attitude. Even Toennies exhibited it in some measure. He emphasized community so much that he must bear the responsibility for the confusion. Toennies (and everyone else) knows that rural neighbors may become mortal enemies when, for example, a boundary is disputed, just as brothers may become enemies when an inheritance is challenged. Despite this, neighbors and brothers always remain neighbors and brothers. Neighborliness and brotherhood persist psychically. There is probably no better example anywhere to demonstrate how minor a role "feelings" play as a basis of community.

Often feelings are construed as the basis of community relations, because they are erroneously thought to be "deeper," or "nearer" the unconscious, than rational thought. However, all mental activity, including thought, has an unconscious component. Now, it is precisely in this context that the fundamental difference between community and communion may be established. The reality and basis of community do not consist in feeling. Nevertheless, a community does exhibit quite specific emotions, some of them directed toward itself, even if the community does not owe its reality or its basis to these feelings. Such sentiments include the sense of tenderness for the other members of the community, or for the community as such, the feeling of happiness in knowing of one's belonging, or even a sense of pride. The essence of community is association constituted in the unconscious. Community, as an organic and natural coalescence, precedes emotional recognition of it by its members. Feelings are simply subsequent forms of experience at the level of consciousness. They are *products* of community. To speak this way is not simply to speak in the language of interpretative psychology, but to proceed phenomenologically. Our very feelings tell us these things.

As you examine general feelings of community you generally discover an element of gratitude. Gratitude necessarily presupposes a relationship that already exists, and it arises as mutual concessions and generosity are recognized, just as tenderness, happiness, or pride also develop in response to extant social relations. In all of its forms, feelings associated with community or directed toward it, be they positive or negative, presuppose something that already exists. They are addressed to a world that is considered to precede them. Even if someone insisted stubbornly that the reality of community is positivistically equated with the feltness of it, he would find, in examining such feelings, that they always point to something that pre-existed.

In the case of human communion this is radically different. Emotional experiences are the very stuff of the relationship. They are, in fact, their basis. Jubilant followers who swarm around a leader chosen in an inspired flood of passion do not intend (at least their "feelings" do not intend) to be bound up with him and with one another on the basis of characteristics they naturally have in common. They are bound together by the feeling actually experienced. Indeed, each one is *en rapport*. Admittedly, feelings are conditioned for us all by our character and our disposition, of whatever kind these may be, and character and disposition lie in the unconscious. Still, though the unconscious is, as it were, the precondition of all emotionality, it does not as yet contain human communion. The unconscious contains potential emotions and as such enables the individuals to enter into communion. Yet, that communion is founded beyond the unconscious. The stuff of which it is made—the basis of its sustenance—is actually the cognitive recognition of feeling.

It may seem questionable that feelings are in fact constitutive of communions. Some may argue that a religious congregation, for instance, is kept together not so much by the several feelings of its individual members as by the deity to whom they pray. No doubt the primary objects of religious feelings are not so much the social structure of the religious community or some combination of parts of that structure, but the noumenal objects of their religious orientation. And yet the noumenal must be felt, if religious and established social phenomena are to appear. At least it must be received with some kind of religious feeling. Then the religious congregation becomes in fact a communion. It is feelings that hold it together. To put it another way, it is their deity as a felt object that gives the religious group its coherence. This does not mean that religion is completely reduced to subjective dispositions.

Conventionally, feelings are regarded as only subjective phenomena. This is an error. Feelings can be intentional and, as such, oriented toward objects. This leaves open the question whether such objects in fact exist or not. Primary religious feelings are in this sense intentional, for religion surely arises only when a religion has established patterns of the noumenal and the human world that can be experienced. Feelings are the psychic organs for such experience. But feelings, as we have argued, embrace the objects to which they are directed. Admittedly, to the religious person, it is less his feelings and more the phenomena he experiences that are all important. In that connection, there seems to be a general aversion toward even the term "experience" because, plausibly enough, it suggests subjectivity, as does the term "emotion."

For sociologists, quite apart from psychologists, it is, however, psychic events that constitute primary data. They too would err if, in their analysis of religious objects, they were not to take into account the feelings directed to such objects. Only such psychic matters can constitute the basis of communion. Sociologically speaking, however, psychic reality in the case of religion is not a deity, but the believer. This is not to deny that a deity may not, in turn, be considered as a formal psychic reality; but, in that case, it constitutes an objective psychic reality, while the sociologist is primarily concerned with the subjective psychic existence of deities from the standpoint of those who accept them. The study of primary religious feelings in terms of their "cognitive recognition" has much to teach a sociologist concerned with communion. In the primary central religious experience, the soul is absolutely alone with its god. The individual returns from this encounter with a strange and new perspective. He then enters a new set of social relations. Through these, his religious experiences are reaffirmed in a spirit of closeness and compassion. A communion is established. Originally this is the case even in the extreme instances of Calvinistic and Jesuitic religious experience.

The social transformation of religious events need not always take this form. Despite the oneness of the soul in its absolute dedication to a god, it frequently senses simultaneously the presence of others. It is as though religious attention were encircled by a recognition of one's relatedness to others, much as light is encircled by a halo. And yet, in that case, the social is logically secondary to the center of original religiosity. Still, to the extent to which the social plays a role at all, it does so through feelings. These found and help constitute a communion.

Actually the feelings founding a communion need not, in the first instance, refer to specific other members of such a communion. Youths, collectively enthused by some high ideal, coalesce into one organization, even if they do not specifically concern themselves one with the other. Still, the awareness of one's emotions is likely, if coherently, to be accompanied by a felt connectedness. More frequently, however, friends, like like-minded religious persons, are prone to develop a kind of enthusiastic solidarity with one another.

Now it would seem that in the case of religious communion, as well as community, feelings point to a condition previously established. In the case of religious groupings, the precondition is a deity. The succession of the two events (of the recognition of the noumenal and the development of the social) once more suggests the pre-existence of objects toward which feelings can be developed. But if the precondition is not psychic, or, at any rate, is not social, then what is given beforehand is a deity. The deity, admittedly, to the extent that it is recognized as such, must be a felt deity. In that case feeling and object go together. The psychic fact also pre-exists. Thus, the original givenness is still not social, as we ordinarily use the term. In the experience of a deity, it can be assumed that those who have this experience have it as separate individuals whose individual religious feelings have not yet forged a felt community. Their solidarity develops only as these individuals, with their several religious experiences, encounter one another, recognize the general and similar direction of their feelings, and, on the basis of this recognition, kindle still further enthusiasm in one another. This, in turn, creates a new dimension of feeling. Only this dimension includes a social component and can be characterized as the emotion of communion.

In contrast, a community pre-exists as such and is experienced as pre-existing. Subsequent communal emotions may, nevertheless, arise. In that case one finds not only the conditions for a conscious "coming together," but also sees the community itself as already existing, whereas communion arises only through the actual and experienced recognition of a mutual sense of belonging. On the other hand, one has to admit that the similarity of direction in religious feelings that characterizes individuals who otherwise stand in no mutual relation with each other constitutes more than a mere coincidence of parallel sentiments. It involves an element of the social. In that event the social too is part of the givenness of things. It will be discovered by those who meet after having previously succumbed to religious experience in similar ways. Then they will recognize their solidarity. In that case the so-called social element appears not as communion, but as community.

This is true in other instances as well. There are a variety of structures within the context of community that allow no unequivocal classification into community or communion. In their case too one might think that the original state of coherence consists in consensus, and that the recognition of such a consensus, in turn, helps constitute community. In fact, recognition only means that community becomes visible. In other words, community makes its appearance in this fashion, but does not derive its existence thereby.

Nationals meeting each other abroad, for instance, do not first have to enter into communion. They acknowledge each other as members of one circle to which they belong. The same can be the case with coreligionists, although this is likely to occur only in the case of well-established religions. When one deals with ecstatic or orgiastic notions of features of fundamentalist religions, the encounters of previously unacquainted coreligionists are different. They become aware of their pre-existing ties. These have, in fact, the form of community. On the basis of such coherence they establish a deliberate communion that differs radically from the natural coherence provided by the sheer existence of those religions as communities.

It is self-evident that one can be a member of a community and in addition sustain special relations of a different kind with selected members of that community or, in fact, the community as a whole. Such relations constitute communions. In that sense, brothers can be close friends. This, however, can lead to difficulties: the essential features of such social relations as kinship and friendship are in potential conflict.

When the sense of belonging together characteristic of community is not so deeply rooted, as in newly established religions, the opportunities for establishing communions are increased. It is quite possible to imagine a group of established and mature men meeting one another as adherents of the same still-young religion. Under these circumstances their community becomes apparent; their conduct is now oriented toward their mutual coherence. A communion may not arise at all. Conduct in this case may well be consciously a matter of community behavior. The odds are, though, that their conduct will more often issue from unconscious dispositions, even if the first cause of such conduct lies in a recognition of their membership in the same religious community. It is an unconscious response leading simply to a sense of belonging. The unconscious, in other words, is modified by the conditions of community; in turn, community becomes incorporated in the unconsciousness. There, it is considered virtually a matter of nature. Communal facts both penetrate the unconscious and modify it. This is surely the case with great experiences, such as religious ones. Nevertheless, it is more likely that such encounters will rekindle original and primary religious sentiments. In that case, a communion may arise, for communion is formed by an actual experience of common feeling. At the same time, every experience of communion has the effect of establishing communal bonds. Communion, after all, is constituted by a complex of emotions, the central objects of which need not be other people. The objects can also be external manifestations, including a deity. That might lead one to think that the communion is, as it were, only a secondary by-product whose valence is less than the valence of the objects toward which feelings are primarily directed. This would be erroneous. Such feelings are consciously experienced, but they are somewhat removed from the center of one's awareness.

In this connection, too, the absolute difference between community and communion once more appears. It may be quite easy for enthusiastic apologists of one kind of communion to claim that members passionately devoted to some solidarity such as a religious sect must, for that reason, belong with the whole of their beings, with all of what they are, so to speak, including their unconscious dispositions. Actually a superficial kind of emotionality, indeed, leads only to a superficial sort of communion. Still, it does lead to a communion.

This superficiality can have a variety of sources. It may come from the fact that the feelings in question are in fact not deeply rooted in the unconscious regions of the persons concerned, or that their consequences exert less influence on the unconscious. After all, it is part of the question of the depth of a feeling—whence it comes, and where it leads. Truly, a communion will be all the more tightly knit, the more the feelings that are constituted in it mobilize the unconscious dispositions of the members in question. In any case, conscious experiences of emotion are still wholly involved. Only such experiences can inflame unconscious dispositions when, in an ultimate sense, the very condition of experience in turn is rooted in the unconscious. But, to repeat, only feelings establish communions. The consequences of these feelings include not only the formation of the communion, but also that of a community.

It does not follow from this, however, that a more deeply established communion must for that very reason constitute a community. Such a communion indeed may lead to community and will, in fact, do so, but only to the extent to which the communion is then left behind. This possibility is, however, limited. We must distinguish between, as it were, the inclination of unconscious attitudes and the establishment, within the unconscious, of social relations. Where we have the former, feelings are likely to appear and reappear. Only where periodic excitement calms down once more—perhaps even dies out—and is then replaced by a kind of coalescence between emotion and unconscious disposition, can one speak of community. It is for this reason that, in the case of younger religions, the meetings of similarly excited persons are more likely to lead to communion than to community.

Perhaps I might add here, too, that the apologists for communion should remember that community is typically marked by a certain settled quietness and persistence. It is a structure taken for granted. The qualities tend not to be overly appreciated by the apologists of communion. I should also add, however, that the feelings constitutive of communion, while not necessarily focused on other persons, but rather on a variety of impersonal or other sorts of objects, may nevertheless be directly concerned with persons. Where one analyzes feelings oriented toward community, both these concerns are simultaneously present. It is quite possible to become related to a community in a double sense, as a community and as a communion. There are certain strains and antinomies involved in such a relation. A deep conflict between community and communion remains. It is the hidden reason why those who are very much part of a community distrust those others whose relations include the elements of communion. It is also noteworthy that those social relations within a community that suggest communion are the ones preferred by people who are not in fact members of a community. Much of the present-day yearning for communal coherence assumes this character. Such yearning is usually less directed toward a specific community than toward coherence as such.

In all this there occurs a frequent misuse of the word community. Even though the character of community is properly understood, those yearning for it would probably not be able to live within it. They are, after all, often people of developed sensitivities and differentiated emotions who, as such, are not likely to be capable of complete immersion in a communal relationship.

There is another matter that also obscures the boundary between community and communion. We feel attracted to someone, feel close or related to someone, feel tied to him by some secret or silent bond. Is this any different from feeling a social relation involving ties of blood? Are we dealing here only with a matter of degree? In any case, it would appear not to be a matter of community but of communion. When one feels sympathy, this is distinctly a matter of communion. Similarly, when one recognizes ties of blood or feels them, the extent to which genuine emotions are indeed involved raises a question not only of community but also of communion. Feelings emanating from a sense of kin provide one also with a sense of the organic, genetic, and pre-existing character of community. In that case, community dominates; one's feelings are relatively insignificant. True, someone who feels attracted to someone else similarly feels a givenness, and hence a communal bond. Yet this only constitutes an invitation for the development of communion. The main thing is not so much a pre-existing community as a yet-to-be-founded communion. Still, there are limiting cases. One may speak about communities of sympathy that are constituted only in manifest behavior. They differ in degree from proper ties of blood.

These things should not, however, obscure the fundamental difference between the types of social relations we have been trying to analyze. Admittedly, in our experience of the real world, conceptual distinctions always become blurred. Artificial differentiations are not to be developed to the point where one is no longer able to see their mutual relations. We do not wish to provide a perspective that apprehends the world as an either-or proposition and becomes an inappropriate and scholastic confusion of concepts and reality.

This line of analysis may appear rather forced.

Some may raise objections to any claim of absolute difference between community and communion, since it is not a difference to be found as such in social life, itself. Others may agree that there are differences of direction among social groupings, that these go deep, and that it becomes important to distinguish them conceptually. But—so the counterargument may continue—this is simply a matter of conceptual distinctions, the justification for which lies in their usefulness. I can only say by way of general rebuttal to this argument that part of the great importance of more recent philosophy, especially as found in the work of Edmund Husserl, lies in the rediscovery of the Platonic idea (eidos). The whole notion of "species," for instance, is not just a more-or-less adequate crutch for the reconstruction of a more-or-less adequate notion of the order of things. The term species is not deduced from experience. The latter would indeed deny its validity. Rather, within the realm of ideas itself, various fundamental lines of cleavage appear. Reality has no choice but to "follow" the same lines. Still it may be quite true that within reality it is often not at all easy to see the lines of distinction that our concepts in fact draw. One can speak about intermediate cases only where such cases are themselves posited by our conceptual schemes. Perhaps my argument will become clearer and more plausible, if I now add a third term—the notion of society—to the previous distinction between community and communion.

## *Community, Communion, and Society*

The respective differences among these three terms should make exposition of this last term less difficult. The essential character of society, in contrast to community, lies in the priority of individual over social existence. Society refers to those relations that are entered into by previously unrelated individuals. In the case of community, its parts are bound from the very beginning as are the parts of an organic whole. One has, of course, to admit that the autonomy of independent individuals whence society develops simply does not exist in isolation and cannot ever exist in that way. Society is a form of relatedness that presupposes the essential separateness of individuals, although it may well be that their very individuality presupposes membership in a variety of other social relations. The old antithesis of the priority of the whole over its parts, or of the parts over its whole, is repeated in the contrast between society and community. Yet, even this contrast needs to be complemented by the reminder that the essential separateness of the individual in the case of society remains intact within society. Though individuals may have to or may want to bind themselves in a variety of societies, they remain separable and separate individuals even after they have accomplished this. They continue to sustain a mutual distance. They bridge this mutual distance with various connections. These connections, however, remain visible and hence rational, just as the totality of societal relations is only indeed a relational matter. The spirit of society is inspired by the ethos of a cool reserve.

The members of community, then, are originally interdependent. The parts of a society are originally apart. The comrades of a communion have, in the first instance, no joint interest. Communions develop only as members meet or when a community is already formed. The experiences leading to their creation are individual experiences. It follows in this regard that communion and society are more like each other, because the interpersonal basis of communion is so narrow and specified.

A friend is an alter ego. We feel his pain and pleasure as our own pain and pleasure. The waning of such a relation hurts. While we may speak about coalescence in this regard—as we have used the term in connection with community—one may speak about a perhaps more intensive mutual fusion. Such a fusion can, of course, take on a variety of forms and degrees, but it emphasizes the principle of "separateness." From this point of view, community and society form a straight line. Communion lies between them. But, in another respect, community and society are alike and differ from communion. Or, to put it yet another way: one can think of a series starting with society, leading to community, and hence to communion; or of one starting with community, continuing with society, and ending with communion.

Society is characterized by the fact that its constitutive relations involve reciprocity: every action as a rule takes place on behalf of some counter action and in the expectation of it. Contract is representative of society, it is alien to community. The members of a family cannot be bound to one another merely by the instrument of contract. In that situation contract plays only a subordinate role. It arises in connection with specific matters. In the case of the thought-ways of peasants one finds a perspective different from the type of mentality that calculates. Communion, on the other hand, cherishes and perhaps even demands unreserved devotion, complete sacrifice and unreserved giving not only of material things, but also of one's self. At least this would be the extreme case. The other cases are simply deviations in degree from this ideal.

Society, then, is characterized by the relation of parts or members to the whole and by the role of exchange. Communal bonds, in contrast, are by their very nature enduring. They might become loosened over time, but their original tendency is to endure. Even the simplest and most peripheral of memories suffices for the resurrection of any community including one that seems to have died. On the other hand, societal relations are oriented toward momentary, definite, perhaps even unique occurrences. In their case, when the business is settled, individuals go their separate ways. Yet the "business" with respect to which people convene and disperse in this way recurs, unless there are some definite obstacles. People often wish to resume once more those relations that have brought satisfaction in the past. Even society, then, appears to be molded by a seeming quality of duration, but the connectedness of society is constituted, in fact, only by a sequence of single and repeated acts.

Communion, on the other hand, is a precarious or unstable structure by its very nature. As long as it persists, it persists in single and discrete acts, never outside those acts. Thus, we have spoken of fusion rather than coalescence. After all, the character of human communion requires fairly intense mutual involvement, and the emotional ecstasy on which communions depend is a fleeting thing. The emotions come and go like tides of the sea. Their power may be great. They can shake us to the very root, destroy us, or even drive us to distraction or madness, but they do not endure. In excitement or drunkenness, emotions may engender much, but they also are displaced once more by soberness. The affective qualities of one's awareness decline or are replaced by other matters. These contrasts of the three structures flow directly from their respective essential differences.

It is equally evident that communions always tend to become transformed into societal or communal structures. The main reason for this is their previously mentioned lability. One instance of this lability is provided by "the vow of eternal love." It has provided subject matter for humor even in ancient times. It reflects the inner contradiction of communion as well as the remedy used to resolve the contradiction. The vow, after all, contains the seeds of societal organization. Still, with its intention to create an enduring arrangement, it also is a step toward community. In this way, through these two links, in turn, communion contradicts itself.

More generally stated, it is the ethos of loyalty by means of which communions try to overcome their inherent precariousness. In doing this, communions are subject to partly societal, partly communal tendencies. Today we consider marriage as one of the most important communions. Every marriage begins with a sacred promise of mutual faithfulness and loyalty. This institution, involving monogamous and patrimonial arrangements, could probably only become established historically by transforming obligations of mutual loyalty into definitely binding expectations. We find similar situations among religions. They demand that children who begin their religious life as members of a community into which they are born (baptism) should voluntarily swear loyalty to their church (confirmation) at a time when they reach the age when their social relations are frequently characterized by the impulse toward communion. Religious ties are, then, ties of communion and are exposed to all the risks of communion.

Faithfulness, when more precisely analyzed—as Simmel noted—is a "substitution for love." As long as one loves, one need not be concerned about faithfulness. Love is its own guarantee. Yet, through loyalty and the pledge of loyalty, bonds of love, originally constituted as a communion, are transformed in part into a communal arrangement and in part into a societal one. Society, too, requires faithfulness. Virtue in the case of society is tantamount to honoring one's contracts. Contracts made for long periods of time require some assurance that the parties involved cannot withdraw from their mutual obligations. Such obligations were voluntarily undertaken in the first instance but subsequently constitute a constraint on the freedom of the parties concerned. A promise is the seed of contract. Promises as such, or promises taken in the abstract, are in fact pledges of loyalty. In a sense every promise promises faithfulness toward those who have been promised. To promise loyalty is simply a promise in principle, specifying nothing in particular. This, certainly, represents an attitude characteristic of communion. But only persons who are in fact free, unconstrained, and not hampered by irrational ties can make promises or sign contracts. Otherwise they would be subject to quite unpredictable conflicts. Only a man autonomous in his decision, free from all irrational bonds, can be expected not to promise or to make commitments he cannot keep. To be in this position requires that one is at all times thoroughly cognizant of one's various obligations. Similarly, only people who *remain* free and do not become the victims of irrational forces or superior powers at some later date can, in fact, sustain promises or sign agreements. Contract requires a persistent comprehensibility of social affairs. Contract, therefore, proceeds within a relational context. Faithfulness, thus, is a societal phenomenon. Only where faithfulness is taken for granted, is it possible for arrangements as a whole to be, in fact, societal. Indeed, it is only then that one can speak about society and yet there are traces of societal arrangements on all planes of culture.

It appears that, whenever one deals with economic or juridical arrangement, in fact where one deals with any arrangements that demand some frame of reference and some durability, elements of society are present. Sometimes, such arrangements have not become differentiated and autonomous; they may still have the aspect of community or communion. However, in these cases, for societal features to emerge, they require particular guarantees against the irrational factors that might otherwise prevent individuals from meeting the impersonal demands of societal arrangements. Similarly, it is necessary that freedom from irrational demands not merely be achieved for the moment, but become an established fact, so that contract obligations can, in effect, be entered into. It is for these reasons that ceremony and ritual accompanied juridical and even economic arrangements in earlier times. Yet, at this very point, societal demands become converted into communal ones, for, in this instance, people have not yet reached the point where they can take societal kinds of expectations for granted. They are not yet free. They do not face irrational forces in an autonomous fashion. Accordingly, we surround juridical and economic proceedings with an appropriate dignity. In this way, such arrangements become memorable and remembered, and, as such, they also become part of a communal routine of life. Even communions, then, can become transformed alike into societal and communal structures through various kinds of votes and oaths on the basis of which members promise mutual loyalty.

Other forms of the expression of mutual loyalty are even more illustrative of these processes. The founding of blood bonds by drinking a few drops of one another's blood constitutes an attempt to found a communion of such intense loyalty that it has, in fact, all the features of community as such. In that connection one should mention, too, that the term "brother" is often transferred to people jointly belonging to the same communal communion. However, wherever communions persist or are intended to persist, they come to assume characteristics of both community and society. This is partly intentional; partly it is a matter of automatic unintended development. This is particularly true of religious associations. The history of Christianity furnishes one outstanding example in this regard. Christianity had to take on the features of statutory coherence in order, in fact, to become an enduring phenomenon. Every enduring communion needs some kind of formal agreement that permits little or no deviation and that requires further agreement for its abrogation. Only momentary social arrangements, like leaving for a day's outing, can dispense with some kind of formal agreement.

To be sure, religious institutions are primarily of religious significance. Still, in their social consequence they lead to the creation of societal structures. This, in turn, brings with it the danger of spiritless rigidity. In the case of the Roman Catholic Church, the quasi-military establishment of the ancient Romans played its role. This process, with its orientation toward durable and taken-for-granted features, leads to a further transformation into communal forms. For later generations, previous associations are givens: they are forms incorporated in their unconscious. The most eminent symbol of the transformation of a religious communion into a religious community is provided by infant baptism. Yet religious movements take periodical cognizance of the fact that the essence of their religious attitude is most appropriately expressed through the social relations of communion and not through those of a community or a society.

Christianity, for instance, calls its adherents back again and again to consider the demands of love. It asks them to replace the processes of calculation and other forms of societal conduct with love for their neighbors. At least periodical attempts are made to persuade genuine believers not to become immersed in the distracting obligations imposed by community affiliations. This is the social meaning of celibacy among priests or priestesses (or, as in the case of the Roman Catholic Church, among monks). In the context of Christianity we again see very clearly that the character of communion conflicts fundamentally with the respective characteristics of community and society.

It is at this point also that the essential sociological differences between church and sect appear. With the help of sects the source of communion in individual religious experience can become enlivened again. Sects displace the inarticulate givenness of community and the calculating coolness of society. The marks of such processes of rejuvenation are provided by an emphasis on a communistic ethic of love and by adult baptism. Socially speaking then, religion is originally a matter of communions. Hence, religious renewal requires sectarian movements. Yet, in the course of their establishment they incorporate societal elements, while they persist only in the form of community structures. (Incidentally, the question of original and genuine religiosity is not for debate at this point. The two terms are certainly not to be equated.

This discussion seeks to by-pass judgments of value.)

Even with regard to loyalty, communions become mindful of their actual character. Loyalty easily becomes "sheer loyalty" or "cold faithfulness." In fact, communions might counter the threat of a transformation into communal or societal structures with a positive emphasis on the complementary threat to their lability. At any rate, lability may be deliberately valued. Some people, deeply attached to the characteristic qualities of communions, go so far as to keep themselves open to ever-new communions. Artists, for instance, sometimes develop a distinct distaste for small town Philistinism and urban heartlessness. Such distaste is the other side of a positive attachment to communions. For them, community has a negative ring. It appears stale, superficial, and narrow. To remain confined by it seems hypocritical. At the same time, society is experienced primarily as a kind of calculating and mechanized state of affairs. Under these circumstances, the uncertain, transitory, and discontinuous features of communion become positively valued. Such people see in various parts of the world a reservoir of new and beckoning adventurous possibilities. They look for new enthusiasms and happenings, for the see-saw of new friendships or love affairs.

For the systematic development of sociology, then, the categories of community, society, and communion are of basic importance. They are general and modal categories. They do not constitute species of concrete structures, such as are represented by the terms, "peasantry," "bourgeoisie," "nobility," or even by such expressions as "family," "clan," and the like. Rather, they are forms of being that may or may not be assumed by such concrete structures.

All this, however, has to be further limited and specified. Certain specific social structures have a particular affinity for one or the other of these three modes of social organization. We have already discussed this in connection with religious organizations. We have argued, too, that economic and judicial relations are essentially of a societal character. They cannot be fully developed among peasants, among villagers, or among friends, lovers, or coreligionists. They are prevented from full development there by the work of counterforces that precede economic and juridical matters while, of course, being related to them as well.

Contrariwise, the family is by its very nature a community. Families that present themselves as communions appear affected and artificial, at least to families with obvious roots in a common past. Where the members of a family regard each other with the distance characteristic of society, the coherence typical of kinship seems to have been lost. When conflicts arise concerning inheritance, it is considered a sign of family breakdown to go to a court of law for a decision, even if this might be the most expeditious procedure. Such a decision, nevertheless, would seem worse than a feud. Similarly, the peasantry and even villagers are, like a family, preferably linked by communal ties.

In addition to showing a special affinity between new religious structures and communions as such, I might have also referred to the camaraderie of the military. The clearest models, however, in each case are as follows: For society, judicial and economic relations; for community, the family; for communion, friendship. Admittedly, there are friendships of all kinds. One can find friendship in the realm of business as well as in the sphere of politics. Such relations may indeed involve elements of perfection and mutual good will. Yet their bases remain economic and political. It seems almost like a misuse of the term to apply the notion of friendship in this connection. It is true that genuine friendships become communities through enduring and frequent encounters. But this can also be a matter of embarrassment. Often it is wise for friends to sustain some temporary separation, particularly if the suspicion arises that the relation is a communal one rather than a true communion. If upon meeting again they find that a community has, in fact, replaced friendship, there is bound to be some disappointment.

All these examples show that actual, concrete social structures are, up to a point, indifferent to the modes of organization that we have distinguished. At the same time, they show selective affinities for one or the other of these basic categories. The categories, in turn, are mutually independent. This is true not only on the plane of ideas, but points to a more essential analytic independence, which can be implemented to explain the mixtures and transitions of concrete social relations.

Society does not develop in a simple or straight line from community. A specific ethos underlies it, and that some ethos, particularly when it first appears, may be consolidated by communion. The rise of capitalism and the modern state had its age of heroes. Predatory warfare, patriotism, and religious enthusiasm have culminated in the birth of "society." Actually society was possible only as people slowly realized—and this in anything but a continuous fashion—that their ethos, as ethos, conflicted with its content. Even today a great deal of entrepreneurial activity is accomplished in the spirit of communion.

The family, too, provides an instance of community developing for communion, for the family consists, in the first instance, in marriage. Young marriages are perhaps not yet real marriages or, at any rate, not yet families. Permanently childless marriages seem incomplete. It is only through children that spouses are really brought together. Still, the family necessarily begins with marriage. Matriarchal arrangements are no exceptions. Now, at the time of its consummation, marriage can have a strong community character, and it is always undertaken as a community. Spouses find each other as members of circles that have similar values, mores, or styles of life. Admittedly, in the case of certain individuals or even in the case of certain circles or status groupings, one finds a preference for selecting mates from the widest possible sphere so as to provide distance and unfamiliarity. At the other extreme, there are courtship arrangements that completely determine the selection of spouses. Marital selection seems to involve the demand for some kind of status endogamy, while involving economic calculations as well. For the most part these demands are simply external manifestations of community relations. Finally, one can find virtually all kinds of "societal" marital arrangements, including the use of professional marriage brokers, newspapers, advertisements, and the like. Yet, even here, spouses concerned with becoming genuinely married or founding families must develop community bonds. As a rule such "societally contracted" marriages tend to keep their origins a secret, since impersonal selection procedures are felt to be poignantly incongruous with the communal character of kinship arrangements. Such incongruity would also be felt, were marriages to derive exclusively from considerations of community.

In all times the ideal of marriage has been the marriage of love, an idea that has been realized to some extent, anyway. Perhaps this reflects a misunderstanding deriving from the extension of those attitudes appropriate for communion into fields where they are actually inappropriate. Young people sometimes consider marriage a profane affair and contrast it rather prosaically with love and the bonds of love. In fact, a fair amount of experience seems to teach that love, in the specific sense of actual feelings, dies in marriage. Love finds this painful and rejects the transformation of itself into a community arrangement. Marriages of love are not always happy in the face of daily and enduring routine. Marriages and, even more so, families must of necessity become what in fact they naturally are: communities. This is so much the case that spouses often take one another for granted. This taking-things-for-granted, this everydayness, is disliked by persons who are brought together in the spirit of communion. Yet, what they respond to negatively has positive value for a community. From the point of view of community, a taken-for-granted establishment of social arrangements symbolizes its fullness and maturity. Still, we tend at times to value social relations based on spontaneous love more than arrangements that exhibit qualities of endurance or reliability that love, in this sense, does not necessarily imply. In the reverse direction, community and societal structures exert pressures at least on some people that, in turn, give rise to a desire for communion.

Community becomes transformed into society. Society coalesces into a community. In a sense the three modes of organization sustain a mutual dependence. Further, the very relations of society and communion require for their existence the elements of community such as language, shared values, similarity of age, or other commonalties that are, as it were, given by nature. And, by the same logic, communion and community cannot persist in the absence of societal forces. To complete the chain, community and society arise out of the conditions of communion. I would call juridical and economic relations the earliest elements of society that can be discovered in the contexts of the community and the communion. I have supposed too that these societal beginnings are originally thoroughly embedded in the context of community. There is also an aspect of communion and sentiment provided by the dignified atmosphere of ceremony. These, in turn, imbue the social relation with enhanced status. Yet even where society, as a form, predominates, it has been preceded by communion. At any rate, the three modal forms are qualified reciprocally from the first.

## *Implications for Max Weber's Types of Social Action*

Toennies' distinction between community and society treated communion as a sublimation, so to speak, of community. The problem of communion was also not differentiated in Toennies' psychology. He treated the phenomenon of community simultaneously in a naturalistic organic—namely, an unconscious—setting and in the context of pure instinct or pleasure. Thus, mother and child were construed to be in communion, because they constituted a community.

Yet, empirical observation has already led to the more precise analyses of Max Weber, setting "traditional" bonds apart from the "affective," particularly the emotional bonds that are sometimes found in communities. That Max Weber, in this case, reached an impasse is explained by his biased perspective. First, he located the subject matter of sociology in "social action," that is, in the "ideal-typical constructions" of social life rather than in social life itself. Second, he restricted "understanding" to such an extent that only acts of "consciousness" were included.

To me "understanding" implies a "*Geisteswissenschaftliche* sociology," rather than a "*Verstehende sociology*." This is the sense in which Dilthey constructed the meaning of the term, "understanding." Weber, on the other hand, referred to Jaspers and then to Simmel and Rickert. Thus, he erred, in that only "subjectively intended meaning" in the sense of the "conscious import of social action" is interpreted as capable of study. A misunderstanding of Husserl has probably produced the confusion, as we shall see. The consequence is, as Weber put it, that "a very significant part of sociologically relevant conduct, especially purely traditional action, is treated as being on the margin" of incomprehensibility. This is an absurdity of Max Weber's epistomological asceticism. Although he strained for methodological precision, his methodology was not always profound. The implication is that the pure and genuine community should, in the strict sense, be interpreted as unanalyzable, in spite of its sociological relevance as well as the wealth of knowledge that Max Weber himself had of that social form. Only that aspect of community manifested explicitly in consciousness can be studied. Now this is often a "consciousness of feeling." Yet, for sociological study, "comprehensible meaning" must be abstracted from feeling, in Weber's sense, and then the distinctions between "traditional" action—in so far as it is still "comprehensible"—and "affective-emotional" action, between community and communion, become fluid and intermingle.

We can see this difficulty clearly in Weber's own writing:

> Predominantly traditional conduct—just as that which is merely mimetic response—stands wholly and absolutely on the borderline of and often beyond that which can be called a "meaningfully" oriented action, because it is very frequently only a hollow response in the direction of a long and firmly established attitude or resigned reaction to a customary stimulus. The bulk of all long established daily routine approaches this type, which belongs in the theoretical system not only as a marginal case, . . . but also, therefore, because the tie to customary ways of doing things can be preserved in different degrees and senses.

In this case, the type approaches that of affective conduct. Therefore, there is really a transition between these things, because Max Weber's position on consciousness takes community into consideration only at that point where there is an interpreted meaning that is "comprehensible" for him—the point where community merges over into communion. Indeed, Weber knows that even the "meaning of social action," in his sense, as well as "comprehensible meaning," often and frequently lie, for the most part, in the unconscious:

> Evident "motives" and "repressions" often directly disguise . . . actions and even the real context of the performance of action. . . . In this case sociology is confronted with the task of defining, explaining, and confirming the context, whether or not it has entirely or in part been raised into consciousness or concretely "intended."

As a matter of fact, the entire methodology of Max Weber breaks down at this "marginal instance of meaningful interpretation." And it leads at the same time to a point where central social phenomena are excluded from possible observation: "All traditional actions and broad categories of charisma, almost but not quite," are comprised "by fragments of comprehensibility." Max Weber himself was not entirely satisfied with the matter; and he revealed the premises that led to the difficulty; yet this does not permit any alternative judgment about the matter. He writes:

> Actual conduct is carried on, in the large part of its manifestation, in semiconsciousness or unconsciousness of its "intended meaning." Action carried on instinctually or habitually "feels" more uncertain in the majority of cases than that which is cognitive or has "made itself clear." In the case of most such conduct, only rarely and often only in individual instances, will a meaning (whether rational or irrational) of an act emerge into consciousness. Genuinely effective, that is wholly and clearly apprehended, meaningful action is in reality always only a marginal case. Every historical and sociological observation will always have to take these considerations into account in analyzing reality. However, that should not preclude the fact that sociology forms its concepts through the classification of objectively possible intended meaning, *all the more so, whether or not conscious conduct is carried on in a meaningfully oriented manner.*

This last (italicized) suggestion (which I oppose) permits the speculation that its consequences are already suspect to Weber himself. Surely, sociological concepts must have the breadth to comprehend all objectively possible reality. An ideal-type ought never to establish "exceptions," but always only "deviations."

Max Weber did not heed his own proscription at all, at least not completely: concepts like "affective," "emotional" are not at all "derived from the classification of intended meaning," but are types of psychic *acts* (they are acts in themselves, not in their "intent")! The phrase, "intended meaning," is the place, in principle, where the misunderstanding of Husserl has produced confusion.

I am so close to the perspective of Weber's "*Verstehende* sociology" that I deplore the fact that I cannot agree with it completely. The concept, "intended meaning," is exceedingly ambiguous. Max Weber's "intent of consciousness" concerns him only slightly if at all. It doesn't belong in sociology where Weber has put it. But, how sociological he is in his actions! Weber tries at last to exclude the most fundamental social phenomena from the concept of "social action."

Finally, it follows that Max Weber's "*Verstehende* sociology"—*nolens volens*—is rationalistic! Weber has various misgivings about "irrational understandings" and "irrational meaning." For example, he writes:

> Predominantly affective behavior belongs also [like "traditional"] on the border of and often beyond that which is meaningfully oriented; it can be an impulsive response to an unusual stimulus. It is a sublimation when affectively conditioned behavior erupts as a conscious discharge of a feeling-state. For then it is already on the way (not always) to rationalization.

In fact an "intended meaning," in the sense employed by Weber, precludes the irrational from "conscious-import" in the case of "affective behavior." An inquiry in terms of "intended meaning" is always obliged either to fall short of its purpose or to rationalize its operation after the fact in an artificial manner.

Therefore, there is, in any case, no final solution. Weber's examples are entirely rational *and* entirely irrational in their basic motive. What can be more *rational* than to counteract irritability by chopping wood! What is more *irrational* than striving for relaxation! What Weber really has in mind is the "meaning of the act" and the "intent of the act." "Consciousness" is completely irrelevant to these things. His entire position is altered by this observation. Moreover, it has ramifications in completely different directions. Rationalism impressed Weber conclusively and in a completely positive way. He meant perhaps that "all irrational, affectively conditioned, meaningful contexts of conduct are most clearly represented and studied as 'deviations' from a constructed purely rational purposeful course"! Even if reality is preponderantly irrational, the method of "*Verstehende* sociology" must be "rationalistic" in the construction of concepts!

Of course, there is, by virtue of another theory of Max Weber, a dichotomy of "social action" within the "rational society." In that case, it is still dubious whether what he calls "value-rational" and "rational-purposeful" activity may not legitimately provide a nice parallel dichotomy within community—a dichotomy within a dichotomy.

"Value" and "purpose" are closely related. This may be presumed wherever there is ultimate purpose or self-interest (which may freely convert into one another). At least in the case of ultimate purpose, "irrationality" and "value" both enter into the "rational-purposeful" act. Accordingly, Weber has necessarily indicated that "rational-purposeful action" is always dependent upon purposes that lie beyond the act itself and refer to external matters. As opposed to this, "value-rational action" should be characterized in such a way that—seen in the perspective of "purpose," which is dissipated in the act—it is self-contained. Then "purpose" is truly tied to "value," but "value" is not truly tied to "purpose." Here, consequently, Weber's terminology is vindicated. "Rational-purposeful" refers, first of all, to purpose; "value-rational," to unmediated value, but the latter is always valued and, therefore, irrational.

If a thing has value in itself, then it may be asked whether this distinction constitutes anything more than a difference in degree. "Irrational" and "externally given," "proffered," "demanded" value is in any case indispensable, whether it is affixed only to the "purpose" and consequently to results, or whether to the "intrinsic value" of the action irrespective of the consequences. Beyond this, however, as has been uniquely demonstrated by Weber himself, that action which he calls "rational-purposeful" likewise has its own distinctive and irrational value, and in this case is pervaded by it, not only from the standpoint of "purpose," but also in the action itself. To be sure, this is the case, not only for the contents of the act, which are only indirectly significant here, since they are "value-rational," but also for "rationality"—rationality as such. Moreover, in the case of "rational-purposeful activities," the "purpose" is neither the basic nor the only source of "value," and, in such a case, the "purpose" as well as the results can even be highly irrelevant.

This can be seen by assessing the "good intentions" in so many theoretical as well as practical moral systems of "rational-purposeful" modes of thought. Those whose "intentions" were "good" are not censured. Their failure results only in chagrin. Even a rational painstaking attempt to achieve a "purpose" whose "value" seems imprudent or unintelligible to a "rational-purposeful" critic is rejected as odd or foolish or droll or ultimately as mad, whereas an act not really "rational" meets up with ethical aversion. In all of these cases there is certainly a difference between "value-rational" and "rational-purposeful" activity. The "rational-purposeful" act is that which I have elsewhere called "autarchic rationality." One can even call the difference absolute. However, the contrary case of "nonautarchic rationality" means precisely that which is not totally uninhibited, whether it is found in community or in communion. And, instead of a category, there is a mixed type.

Nowhere may "rational-purposeful" and "value-rational" acts be separated conceptually. Only in one respect is a basic difference established, if not conceived conceptually. It is established within the category "society." This is accomplished by virtue of the fact that the "irrational," the rationality of which is always necessarily required, can be given and legitimated "emotionally-affectively" or "traditionally"—better "naturally" (comprehending the "traditional" act). With only an imperceptible nuance, Weber's terms (though to be sure he is difficult to understand) may be applied to the actual difference. "Purposes," therefore, lie within "value-rational" activities, and these, above all, are irrationally rational or "emotional-affective." Thus, they appear in collective experience as "values" of "action." In "rational-purposeful" activities, they are more precisely "purposes." Still the "claims" and "precepts" of "rationality" are "traditional" and "natural." Consequently, they are taken for granted and remain unemphasized.

There is no gainsaying the fact that Max Weber's exposition did not specify this distinction but rather the distinction discussed earlier. However, it appears that his discussion ultimately leads to the present distinction. In this view, "rational-purposeful" and "value-rational" acts, as far as their distinction can have lasting significance, are both merely agencies by which society is transformed in one instance into community, in the other into communion. They are not merely different categories of action that are incidentally there, but agencies of transformation. Thence it follows that, if we confront the distinction between community and communion and the vastly different dichotomy of "rational" action with the contrast provided by rational and irrational domains, we arrive at a fourfold over-all classification. In actuality "rational" and "irrational" action do not exhaust the possibilities, but, when considered along with "emotional" action and the "unconscious," they form a trichotomy in which both areas of consciousness as well perhaps as both areas of irrational action are included.

Moreover, this exhibits again, by its very resistance to manipulation, a weighty justification for the analytical separation of community and communion.

Weber's strangely terse statements about "value-rational" and "rational-purposeful" action may be clear to him. They are not completely clear to us. However, he saw at least that the irrational in its relationship to purpose does permeate "rational-purposeful" action: "action, therefore, is rational-purposeful only in the means employed." To be sure, there are purposes "simply as given subjectively regnant necessities." Weber appeared to regard these as admittedly not rational, but neither did he regard them as irrational. He never made up his mind. Yet, in the end, he did say that "absolute rational-purposeful action" is "only in reality one constructed marginal case." Actually, it is not even that. As opposed to "value-rational" action, one might think that such action must be manifested as rational only in the attitude adopted to the consideration of means for accomplishing purposes. In any case, that is the impression conveyed by all the examples of the type proffered by Weber. However, "value-rational" action can often be included with action that is "rational-purposeful only in its means," and consequently "rational-purposeful" action may be included with it!

With respect to that which Weber *abstractly* asserts to be the essence of "value-rational" action, one is certanly not led, in the first instance at least, to consider the attainment of ends in trying to assess the value of such action. Furthermore, it is not necessary to take ends into account in assessing the rationality of an act. When one meets a specified number of obligations, one acts in a "value-rational" but *purpose*less way. Ideally, the obligations are never weighed, nor are affirmations sought from others; only spontaneous gratitude may arise. Whether there can be complete freedom from "purpose" in "autarchical rationality," or in rational-purposeful action, to use Weber's term, remains an open question. There are certainly instances of "autarchical rationality" where the end in view has no relevance. Examples are bureaucratic memoranda, filing and tabulation, classification of all kinds, military exercises, and the academic mania for filing data. Stamp collecting is another example of "autarchical rationality devoid of purpose." Many children's games belong here, as do most forms of play. In the case of "dedicated" rational-purposeful action, then, it is not necessary to place a "value" upon the end in view or to consider its accomplishment.

In other respects, one might well speak of "autarchical rationality" as a "constructed marginal case." Nevertheless, we are dealing with analytic, not substantive, distinctions. Weber's distinction is, again, different. Concerning an "action that is only rational-purposeful in its choice of means," he contrasts value-rationally given ends with long established ends that are "given simply as regnant subjective necessities." These latter obviously do not appear "more rational" to him, but "more commensurate with rationality" (thus, superficial considerations lead him to a logical impossibility).

This really adds nothing to the matter, although it may appear to do so. It introduces the notion of "self-evident" ends. Yet, Weber must certainly realize that "self-evidence" is something very subjective. It means one thing for a person in one culture and something else for another person in another culture! "Self-evidence" is always only evidence to which we have become accustomed. Rational-purposeful action is, therefore, only an aspect of rationality transformed by community. However, if there were universal self-evidence of a natural kind, then it is fitting to allude to Weber's "regnant subjective necessities" as a part of nature, otherwise they would be included by him in the narrower sense of natural as always preferably "traditional." Economic efficiency, which Weber cites most frequently to illustrate a purely "rational-purposeful" end, has certainly been shown earlier by Weber to be in no way "self-evident" at all times or in all places. Economics is, as I have pointed out, only coincident with rationalism. Rational action as such, however, was not always self-evident: it had its heroes and age of communions; only then did it become "self-evident." For Weber himself, the affairs of Puritanism—already characterized by "autarchical rationality"!—are justly regarded as a prime example of "value-rational" activity.

Be that as it may, some qualification is needed here. In a later part of his systematic treatise, where the obstacles of a distorted methodology and the related distorted conceptualization have become less imposing, Max Weber deals with a special, yet very important, social phenomenon. He apprehended precisely the trichotomy of fundamental sociological categories we have proposed. I speak of his types of authority:

> There are three pure types of legitimate authority. Their legitimate value is, so to speak, primarily: (1) rational in character . . . , (2) traditional in character . . . , (3) charismatic in character: on the basis of unusual devotion to the sacredness, the heroic power, or the mimesis of a person and the order revealed or created by him.

With reference to charismatic authority Weber emphasized above all its *unusual* character. This allows him to show, in a fundamental and excellent manner, the abrupt contrasts between charismatic and "rational" authority on the one hand and "traditional" authority on the other ("both are specifically everyday forms of authority"). Weber realized that charismatic authority manifests above all "an emotional tendency toward community." Beyond its unusual character, he notes further that charismatic authority is intrinsically transitory. To overcome this fact, "charismatic authority which, so to speak, occurs in its ideal-typical form only *in statu nascendi* must alter its essential character: it is traditionalized or rationalized." Thus, like the forms of social relations I have proposed, the three types of authority merge into and give rise to one another.

[*Translators' Postscript:* The original essay is much longer than this extract. It concludes with an attempt to link the three modalities to history. Our present situation, as a kind of world-wide economy and communication system, is seen as the logical extension of the notion of society. At the same time, Schmalenbach argues that the extension of society provokes new enthusiasms for the founding of all the more intimate communions. He sees contemporary society as a kind of syncretistic mixture of a variety of quite extreme contrasts. From this mixture he promises himself some fertile new developments.]

# 4. *The Organization of the Primary Working Group*

BY F. J. ROETHLISBERGER AND WILLIAM J. DICKSON

THE PROBLEM of analyzing the data usually proves to be more difficult than obtaining it. The questions our investigators were asking of their data, more particularly of the observation material, can be stated as follows: Do we have here just so many "individuals," or are they related to one another in such a way that they form a group or configuration? If they do form a configuration, how are they differentiated from or integrated with other groups? In short, do we have here evidences of social organization? Clearly, the method of analyzing the data had to be designed to bring out whatever evidences of social organization there might be. The procedure may be summarized briefly.

First, each person entering into the study, whether operator, inspector, or supervisor, was considered separately. The observation material and interview material were examined carefully and every entry in which a particular person was mentioned or referred to was lifted out and listed under his name. Through this method of classification, the degree and kind of social participation of each individual in the Bank Wiring Observation Room became apparent.

Secondly, the material thus listed for each person was examined for evidence of the extent of his participation. Two questions were asked: (1) To whom do this person's relations extend? Does he associate with everyone in the group, or are his social activities restricted to a few? (2) Does he enter a great deal or relatively little into social relations with the people with whom he associates? In other words, if $S_1$ converses and associates with the men in his soldering unit to the exclusion of everyone else, does he do so frequently or infrequently?

Thirdly, an attempt was made to determine the kind of participation manifested by each person. Such questions as the following were considered: Does he assume a superordinate or subordinate role? Does he strive for leadership? If so, is he permitted to do so, or are his attempts in that direction opposed by others? Are most of his social contacts related to his job, or are they in the nature of arguments, conversations, or games which have no immediate relation to his work?

Fourthly, each occurrence in which a person entered into association with another person was examined to see whether the relation thus manifested expressed an antagonism, a friendship, or was merely neutral. Each incident, of course, had to be related to its social context before its significance could be determined. Take, for example, the following entry: "$S_4$ spent most of his spare time today drawing pictures. He drew an elaborate picture of a ship which he called 'Old Ironsides.'" A conclusion which might be drawn from this statement as it stands is that $S_4$ apparently preferred to spend his time in drawing pictures rather than in mingling with the other operators. This, then, might be construed to reflect a negative relation between $S_4$ and the group, that is, that he preferred his own company to theirs. But when considered in connection with other factors in the situation, this interpretation is seen to be the opposite of that finally assigned to it by the investigators. $S_4$ at the time was a newcomer, having just replaced $S_3$. He was not well acquainted with anyone in the group. Furthermore, after he had been in the room a week and had become better acquainted, he no longer spent his spare time drawing pictures. The investigators concluded, therefore, that drawing pictures was a means by which $S_4$ attracted attention to himself, excited comment, and thus tended to integrate himself with the group. It was a way of approach rather than of avoidance.

In the two preceding chapters the results obtained from analyzing the material according to this procedure have been given. The participation of each individual in the social activities of the group has been described. After having analyzed the data in this manner, however, the question arises: Are there any similarities in the participation of certain individuals? For example, does $W_1$ almost always associate with $W_2$ and $W_3$ to the exclusion of $W_7$, $W_8$, and $W_9$, and, likewise, do $W_2$ and $W_3$ both associate with $W_1$ to the exclusion of $W_7$, $W_8$, and $W_9$? Do the members of one occupational group look up to or down upon the members of another? Do the employees arrange themselves in any social

Reprinted by permission of the publishers from Fritz Jules Roethlisberger and W. J. Dickson, *Management and the Worker* (Cambridge, Mass.: Harvard University Press, 1939), chap. xxi, pp. 493–510. 

order with regard to games, job trading, controversies over windows, and other matters? In this chapter these and similar questions will be considered.

## *Relations between Nonsupervisory Occupational Groups*

The first question the investigators asked was this: There are four occupational groups in the department: wiremen, soldermen, inspectors, and trucker. From a purely technical standpoint the members of these groups are all "operators," that is, they are of nonsupervisory rank. Are they differentiated only from the standpoint of the jobs they perform, or have these technical divisions of labor become the basis of a social stratification? Do workmen in one group look upon themselves as superior or inferior to workmen in another group and, if so, how is this social distinction manifested? In order to answer this question, similarities in the behavior of different people in each occupational group, which could be said to be independent of the personalities involved, were noted. Wiremen as a group were considered in relation to soldermen as a group, and so on.

### CONNECTOR WIREMEN IN RELATION TO SELECTOR WIREMEN

The wiremen in the department worked upon two types of equipment, one type called "connectors," the other "selectors." The technique of wiring was exactly the same for both types. The only differences, apart from the names, were (1) that a connector equipment might be and usually was eleven banks long, whereas a selector equipment was never more than ten, and (2) that a connector fixture weighed only about half as much as a selector fixture. In the observation room $W_7$, $W_8$, and $W_9$ ordinarily worked on selectors, and the other operators worked on connectors.

Some of the wiremen interviewed in the regular department expressed a preference for connector wiring. The reasons given usually related to the lightness of the fixture. In reality, however, the weight of the fixture was inconsequential. The fixtures were easily lifted, and only two of them had to be carried during an average day. The effort required was scarcely great enough to be felt by healthy young men who frequently engaged in strenuous sports after work. This explanation, therefore, could hardly be taken as the reason for their preference. Further study revealed the real significance of the preference for connector wiring. In the department the connector wiremen were all placed together toward the front of the room, the direction the men faced while working, and the selector wiremen were located back of them. They were, therefore, spatially arranged in such a way as to suggest that the connector wiremen, since they were in front, were somewhat superior to those to whom their backs were turned. From talking to the supervisors and some of the wiremen the investigators learned that the newer members of the wiring group and some of the slower ones were located "in back." As these men "in back" acquired proficiency and new men were added, they were moved forward. Inasmuch as increases in efficiency were usually rewarded by increases in hourly rates, this meant that the people who were moving forward spatially were also moving upward socially. An individual's location roughly reflected his relative standing in efficiency, earnings, and the esteem of his supervisors. The connector wiremen represented the elite. Indeed, some of the wiremen looked upon "going on connectors" as a promotion even if their hourly rates were not changed. Conversely, some of the connector wiremen felt injured if they were "put back on selectors" and regarded such a change as a demotion even though their hourly rates were not changed. Here, then, a minor technical distinction had become so elaborated that it provided a basis upon which the wiremen were in some measure socially differentiated.

### WIREMEN IN RELATION TO SOLDERMEN

The position of wireman was regarded in the department as somewhat superior to that of solderman. Beginners were usually started as soldermen, and from soldering they passed on to wiring. The change in job was usually accompanied by an increase in hourly rate. This, together with the fact that the wireman's job required more specialized abilities than that of the solderman, gave the wiremen a slightly higher status in the department, which was expressed in numerous ways, some of which will be described below.

One of the most frequent ways in which the wiremen demonstrated their superior standing was in job trading. Theoretically, there was supposed to be no job trading. Wiremen were supposed to wire and soldermen were supposed to solder. The purpose of this rule was, of course, to promote efficiency through specialization. In spite of the rule, however, the men did trade jobs. The important point here is that in practically every case the request for trading originated with a wireman and the soldermen almost always traded without protest. Sometimes the wiremen presented their requests to trade to the group chief but more frequently they did not. Though occasionally the soldermen protested over trading, they usually gave in. In other words, the wiremen ordered and the soldermen obeyed.

In the task of getting lunches for the group the difference of status between wiremen and soldermen was apparent. It was common practice in the department for one of the men to go out to one of the near-by lunch counters and get lunches for those in the department who wanted them. This practice prevented congestion at the lunch counters, and it saved the people in the department a great deal of trouble. The person who got the lunches was called the "lunch boy," even though he was a grown man and was not assigned the duties of an office boy. When the men were moved to the observation room, they continued with this practice until the regular "lunch boy" was transferred. The group chief, after announcing the transfer, asked if anyone in the group wanted to take over the job. After some discussion $S_1$ said that he would. On the first day the group chief went with $S_1$ to assist him. On the second day, however, the group chief refused to go, saying that there was no use in wasting two men's time. As long as the group chief lent his prestige to the task the group said nothing, but as soon as the solderman had to go alone they started "kidding" him. $S_1$ kept on getting the lunches for about a week, and then $S_4$ started getting them as a regular part of his job. Toward the end of the study, when $S_4$ was moved out to the department, the job reverted to $S_1$. He kept the job until the group chief himself took it over. The group chief, however, was careful to explain to the observer that he was not actually getting the lunches but merely taking the orders and giving them to a man in the department. He apparently felt that the job was a bit below his dignity. In the observer's record there was no instance of a wireman's getting the lunches. One day $W_1$ went around and took the orders for lunches and collected the money, but when he had done so he turned the orders over to $S_1$. As soon as $W_1$ started taking the orders, $I_1$ shouted, "Look who's getting the lunches today," which may be taken as an indication that it was an unusual thing for a wireman to do. $W_1$ continued taking the orders for some time, but $S_1$ always bought the food and brought it back to the room.

The following illustration also serves to show that the wiremen felt themselves a little superior.

The section chief came in and found $S_1$ soldering without goggles. He told $S_1$ to stop until he put them on. $S_1$ had mislaid them and spent about five minutes looking for them. He grumbled about having to wear goggles as he looked for them.

*$S_1$:* "I don't know where the hell those glasses are. I suppose one of you guys hid them. There ain't no sense to wearing them anyway. I soldered for four years before they ever thought of glasses. Now you've gotta keep them on. There ain't no solder gonna splash in a fellow's eye. That's just the damn fool notion somebody's got. I've gotta go around here all day in a fog just because some damn fool wants us to wear goggles."

*SC:* "Never mind why you've got to wear them, just get them and put them on."

*$W_2$:* "I worked on a job for three years where I had to wear goggles and it didn't kill me."

*$S_1$:* "Yes, and I suppose you wore them all the time."

*$W_2$:* "Well maybe I didn't, but it didn't hurt me to wear them when I had to. There's one thing you have to remember, $S_1$. Do you hear? Don't do as I do—do as I say. Get that?"

*$S_1$:* "Why don't you guys wear glasses when you fix repairs?"

*$W_3$:* "We don't have to put them on for that little bit of soldering, but you're a solderman. You've got to wear them."

*$S_1$:* "Aw, you guys are all a bunch of damn fools."

#### WIREMEN AND SOLDERMEN IN RELATION TO THE TRUCKER

The trucker's job was to keep the group supplied with piece parts and to remove completed equipments from the room. Before loading the completed units on his truck, which was pushed by hand, he stamped each one with an identification number, the purpose of which was to enable the Inspection Branch to trace the work back to the inspector who had passed upon it.

During the first few weeks nothing happened to indicate the relation the trucker had with the group. However, when the men felt more at ease in the presence of the observer, certain events began to occur which seemed to reflect the trucker-operator relation. For example, the group started referring to the trucker as a gigolo and as "Goofy." They annoyed him in numerous small ways: by spitting on the place where the identification number was supposed to be stamped, by jogging his arm just as he was about to affix the stamp, by holding the truck when he tried to push it out of the room, or by tickling him in the ribs while he was lifting an equipment onto the truck. That these incidents reflected a relation between occupational groups and not special personal relations is attested to by the fact that most of the wiremen and soldermen behaved in the same way toward the trucker, and by the fact that they displayed the same attitude toward a second trucker who replaced the first one about the middle of the study. Their general attitude was independent of the personalities involved.

WIREMEN AND SOLDERMEN IN RELATION TO THE INSPECTORS

The inspectors belonged to an outside organization, the Inspection Branch. They reported to a different set of supervisors, were paid on an hourly basis, and on the whole had more education than the men whose work they inspected. Their function as inspectors gave them a superordinate position to the operators. This was manifested in many ways. For example, when the wiremen and soldermen came to be interviewed they invariably appeared in their shirt sleeves, or, if it were chilly, in sweaters. The inspectors, however, always came dressed in coats and vests. The significance of this cannot be understood without knowing something about the subtle distinctions in dress in the Operating Branch. The foreman and his assistant usually wore ordinary business suits with coats and vests, the vest being optional. The section chiefs and group chiefs usually wore vests but not coats. Their shirts were usually white, and they wore neckties. Operators as a rule wore neither coats nor vests. They might wear white shirts and a necktie, but ordinarily left their shirts open at the throat, or if they wore a tie, the knot was not pulled up tightly around the neck and the collar button was usually left unfastened. This was the general pattern. There were many exceptions and deviations from it, but the fact remains that dress did have some social significance. Thus, the fact that the inspectors wore coats and vests when they came to be interviewed might be taken as a reflection of their social status in the company.

The inspectors were considered outsiders, and this was indicated in many ways other than by the fact that they did not report to the Operating Branch supervisors. That they did not trade jobs or go for lunches was evidence of this relation between the operators and the inspectors, but perhaps the best demonstration of it was in the matter of control over the windows. The wiremen who were situated on the side of the room facing the court took a proprietary interest in the windows opposite their workbenches. If $W_6$, for example, wanted the window open, he opened it even though other people protested. The people who were farthest removed from the windows protested a great deal because the draft was thrown on their side of the room. Endless controversy resulted. The point to be brought out here is that an inspector entered into one of these controversies only on one occasion, and it was this one occasion which demonstrated clearly the relation between operators and inspectors. The inspector involved was a man who was substituting for $I_3$. He complained that the room was cold. Someone had turned the heat off and one of the windows was open. Since his complaint went unheeded, he walked over to close the window. As he was about to release the chain which held it open, $W_9$ ordered him to leave it open and seized the chain. The inspector then tried to turn on the heat, but $W_9$ scuffled with him and finally took the handle off the valve. During all this the other men lent $W_9$ their verbal support. Finally, after the operators had convinced the inspector that he had no jurisdiction over the window and he had given up, one of the soldermen walked over and closed the window. The inspector thanked him, and the controversy ended. Wiremen and soldermen might fix the windows if they pleased, but the inspectors could not do so without getting into trouble. The other inspectors probably sensed the situation and never attempted to overstep.

SOCIAL STRATIFICATION IN THE OBSERVATION GROUP

The foregoing analysis of the relations among the occupational groups in the observation room shows that social significance did attach to the occupations the several groups performed. An ordering process had taken place in the organization of the human element in the department, and social significance had become attached to the various tasks. From an informal standpoint, then, the observation group was differentiated into five gradations, ranging from highest to lowest in the following order: inspectors, connector wiremen, selector wiremen, soldermen, and trucker.

## *The Informal Organization of the Observation Group*

The first question the investigators asked of their data was answered in the affirmative: the workmen were socially differentiated along occupational lines. But did this mean that only the people within each occupational group tended to associate together? Did the workmen tend to form occupational cliques, or were they organized on some other basis? If occupation was not the basis of their integration, just how were they organized? The answer to this question, it was thought, could be obtained by observing how the members of the group were differentiated in terms of such informal social activities as games, controversies over the windows, job trading, and helping one another.

GAMES

From the beginning of the study the observer noted and recorded a variety of activities which may be subsumed under this heading. For the most part, these were games of chance which included the following: matching coins, lagging coins, shooting craps, card games, bets on combination of digits in the serial numbers on their weekly pay checks, pools on horse racing, baseball, and quality records, chipping in to purchase candy, and "binging." The men usually engaged in these games during brief respites from work or during lulls in activity resulting from interruptions in the flow of work. The games were extremely varied and were seemingly elaborated spontaneously with reference to anything into which the element of chance entered. Financial gain was not the main inducement, for most of the wagers were small, ranging from one to ten cents. However, those who participated in the betting on the horse races usually did so seriously. They dubbed their favorite the "Test Room Horse" and bet on him fairly consistently.

Figure 1 shows the people who joined in these games and the people with whom each person participated. The symbols indicating the different operators are enclosed in small circles. The operators are arranged roughly by soldering units, which are indicated by the spacing of the wiremen. Thus, $W_1$, $W_2$, $W_3$, and $S_1$ constitute soldering unit A; $W_4$, $W_5$, $W_6$, and $S_2$ constitute soldering unit B; and $W_7$, $W_8$, $W_9$, and $S_4$ constitute soldering unit C. The inspectors are placed above the groups for which they inspected. The arrows connecting the different circles indicate that the people thus connected participated in one or more games either as pairs or as members of a larger group.

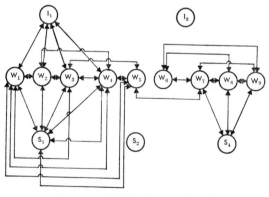

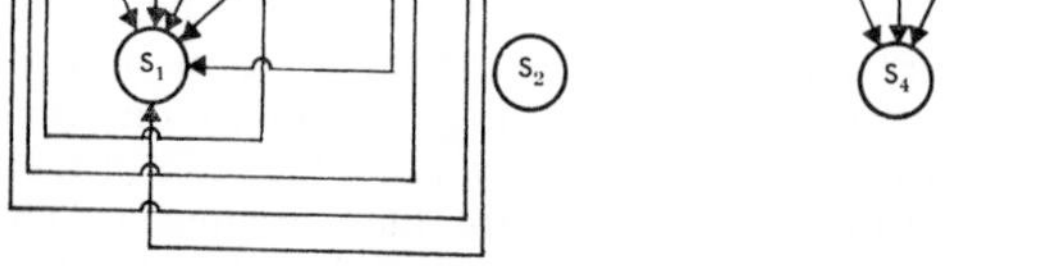


Figure 1

Participation in Games

BANK WIRING OBSERVATION ROOM

The significant point brought out in Figure 1 is that participation in games was confined to two groups and, furthermore, that each group participated to the exclusion of the other. One group, which for convenience will be referred to as group A, comprised $W_1$, $W_2$, $W_3$, $W_4$, $W_5$, $S_1$, and $I_1$. These people were in adjacent work positions and were all located toward the front of the room. The other group, referred to as group B, was composed of $W_6$, $W_7$, $W_8$, $W_9$, and $S_4$. These people were also in adjacent work positions and were located toward the rear of the room. Two people, $S_2$ and $I_3$, never took part in these activities. Although the frequency with which each person participated in games is not shown in this diagram, it should be stated that $W_5$ participated in only one game with the people in group A, whereas all the others in group A took part in a variety of games. It should also be noted that $W_5$ on one occasion took part with $W_7$. He was the only person in group A who participated with a member of group B.

Participation in games, then, was not at random. It was confined to two groups, which suggests that in this way the interpersonal relations among the people in the observation room were finding expression. This suggestion is strengthened by the fact that the kinds of games in which the two groups participated also tended to differentiate them. For example, all the gambling games occurred in group A, and all the "binging" occurred in group B. Both groups purchased candy from the Club store, but the purchases were made separately, and neither group shared with the other.

CONTROVERSIES ABOUT WINDOWS

It has already been mentioned that the wiremen who were stationed nearest the windows took a proprietary interest in them and that a great deal of controversy resulted over whether the windows should be open or closed. That this activity also expressed the interpersonal relations in the group is apparent from the following excerpt from the observer's record:

$W_6$ had his window open and $W_5$ closed it.

*$W_6$:* "You leave that window open. I want some fresh air in here."

*$W_5$:* "It's too cold. I want it closed."

*$W_6$:* "You take care of your own window. This one is mine and if I open it, it's going to stay open."

They opened and closed the window several times and had a heated argument over it. $W_6$ told $W_5$ that if he closed it again he would punch him in the nose.

*$S_1$:* (From the side lines) "That's right, $W_6$, stick up for your rights. If he closes it again, hang one on him. We've got to have a good fight in here before long."

$W_5$ left the window alone. This disappointed $S_1$, so he implied that $W_5$ was yellow.

*$S_1$:* "I'll tell you what you had better do if he closes that window again, $W_6$, sue him. He won't fight, so the only way you can do anything with him is to sue him."

The group had a lot of fun over this. $W_5$ and $W_6$ did not speak to each other during the rest of the morning.

This quarrel between $W_5$ and $W_6$ not only expressed their mutual antagonism but also gave $S_1$ an opportunity to express his antagonism toward $W_5$.

Figure 2 shows the men who joined in these controversies and those with whom they participated. This diagram is to be interpreted in the

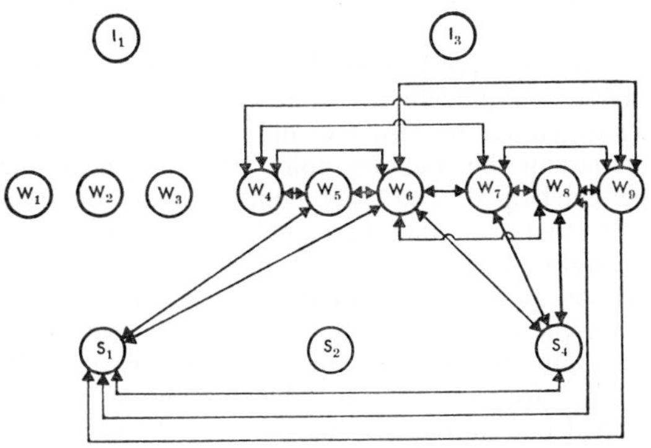


Figure 2

Participation in Controversies about Windows

BANK WIRING OBSERVATION ROOM

same way as that for games. A person was judged to be involved in these disputes even though he participated only verbally. The chief point brought out in this diagram is that most of the controversies over windows centered in group B ($W_6$, $W_7$, $W_8$, $W_9$, and $S_4$). The quarrels among the members of this group and between this group and other people in the observation room accounted for 90 per cent of the controversies. Their quarrels with people outside of their group were with $S_1$, $W_4$, and $W_5$. There was very little controversy over the windows among the members of group A, and what little there was occurred between $W_4$ and $W_5$ and between $S_1$ and $W_5$.

### JOB TRADING

Job trading has already been mentioned in connection with the relation between wiremen and soldermen. Accurate records of this activity were kept throughout the study and are summarized graphically in Figure 3.[1] The inspectors are omitted from this diagram because they did not participate. The arrows point from the person who initiated the request to trade to the person who accepted the request. The numbers alongside the arrows show the number of times the people so designated traded.

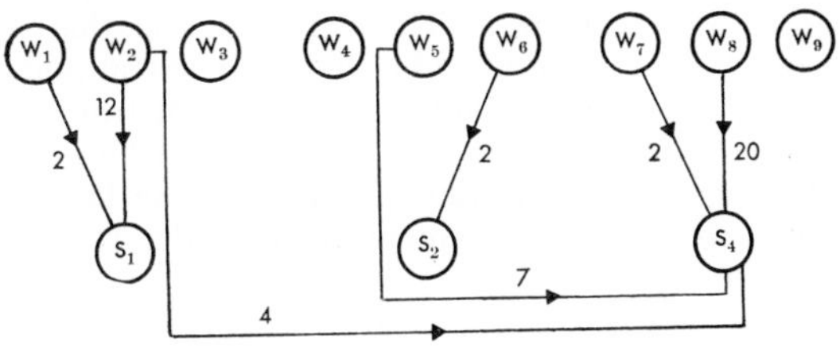


Figure 3

Participation in Job Trading

BANK WIRING OBSERVATION ROOM

Perhaps the most interesting point brought out in this diagram is that most of the trading was requested of $S_4$, the solderman for the three selector wiremen. Thirty-three of the forty-nine times job trading occurred were with $S_4$. Furthermore, it will be noted that, whereas connector wiremen from soldering units A and B traded with $S_4$, none of the selector wiremen ($W_7$, $W_8$, and $W_9$) ever traded outside of their own soldering unit. In other words, the connector wiremen apparently felt free to change jobs either with their own soldermen or with the soldermen for the selector wiremen, but the latter did not feel free to trade outside of their own unit.

### HELPING ONE ANOTHER

While there was no written rule to this effect, helping one another, like job trading, was in practice forbidden.[2] In spite of this rule, however, it

1. For the sake of simplicity, trading between wiremen and $S_3$, who was in the observation room only a short time, and trading between wiremen while one of them was soldering have been omitted from this figure. These omissions do not alter in any way the conclusions to be drawn from this figure.

2. The operators were permitted to help one another only when for observable technical reasons, such as a shortage of parts, they were prevented from working on their own equipments. The reason for this rule was that a wireman should be able to work faster when unmolested by another wireman's presence. In practice there were very few occasions when helping one another was technically justified and for this reason the greater part of this activity was against the rules.

was done a good deal when technically there was no justification for it. The wiremen said that it made them feel good to be helped. Their attitude is best expressed in the following excerpt from an interview with $W_4$. $W_4$ had just said that he liked working in the observation room because he felt more free to move around than in the regular department.

*Int:* "You do move around quite a bit, do you? Then you don't always work on your own equipment?"

*$W_4$:* "Oh no, not always, but most of the time. That is, once in a while if a fellow gets behind someone will go over and help him out."

*Int:* "Do they do that for anyone who is behind?"

*$W_4$:* "No. You know, it's a funny thing about that gang. It seems like if a fellow is loafing and gets behind, nobody will help him out, but if he is making an honest effort he will be helped. I've seen that happen time and again. Somebody who has been working along hard all day and has had a lot of tough luck will be helped out."

*Int:* "Do you find that certain people help certain other people all the time, or do they change around quite a bit?"

*$W_4$:* "Well, some people are friendlier than others, you know, and where that's the case you will find them helping each other out. Once in a while a fellow will get behind who ordinarily is a good worker. That sometimes happens to anyone. I know one fellow down there who did that and two other fellows went over and started helping him out. That was around a quarter to four. They had their job done and thought they would give him a hand. He didn't say anything, he let them go ahead and help him out, but you know he never helps anyone else out. Since then he has never given a hand to anybody. Do you think they would help him out again? No sir! They're off of him. They don't like a guy that does that. I think it's a good idea to help a fellow out once in a while. I know I appreciate it. It makes all the difference in the world. It's a funny thing, I'll be working along and be behind, and I'll feel all fagged out. Then somebody comes over and starts in wiring on my equipment with me, and you know I perk up to beat the band. I don't know; it just seems to put new life in you, no matter if he only helps you for a couple of levels. I can pick up and work like the deuce then, up till quitting time."

*Int:* "I wonder why."

*$W_4$:* "I don't know why it is. You have a feeling when you're behind that you've got so much work behind it's going to be impossible to get it done, anyway. Then when somebody helps you out it gives you a fresh start, sort of."

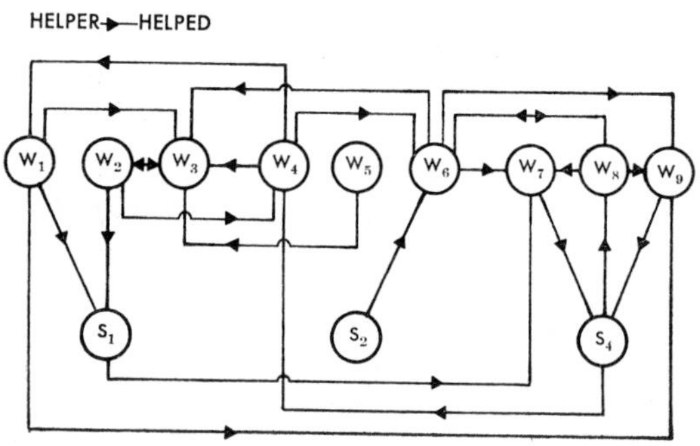


Figure 4

Participation in Helping

BANK WIRING OBSERVATION ROOM

Records were kept of this activity and are summarized graphically in Figure 4. The inspectors are again omitted because they did not participate. The arrows in the diagram point from helper to the person helped. The chief points brought out are, first, that everyone participated in helping and, secondly, that it was not confined within work groups. In these two respects this activity differed from the others thus far described. It seemed to integrate the whole group rather than parts of it.

The frequency with which different people helped one another is not shown in Figure 4 because only two people stood out from the group in this respect. They were $W_3$ and $W_6$. $W_3$ was helped out more than anyone else in the observation room, even though he did not need it. $W_1$, $W_2$, $W_4$, $W_5$, and $W_6$ helped him at one time or another. They liked to work with him. $W_6$, on the other hand, gave more help than anyone else in the room. His help was always accepted but it was rarely reciprocated. Two people, $W_5$ and $S_2$, gave help a few times, but on no occasion did they receive help.

### FRIENDSHIPS AND ANTAGONISMS

To summarize the friendships and antagonisms which existed in this group, Figures 5 and 6 have been prepared. Figure 5 shows friendships; Figure 6 shows antagonisms. The three soldering units are arranged as in the previous diagrams.

Looking first at Figure 5, representing friendships, it will be seen that they tend to cluster in two groups. One group includes five people who were in the front of the room, $W_1$, $W_3$, $W_4$, $S_1$, and $I_1$. The other group comprises the members of soldering unit C, the four people in the rear of the room. Outside of these two groups the only strong friendship was that between $S_1$ and $W_7$. Five people, $W_2$,

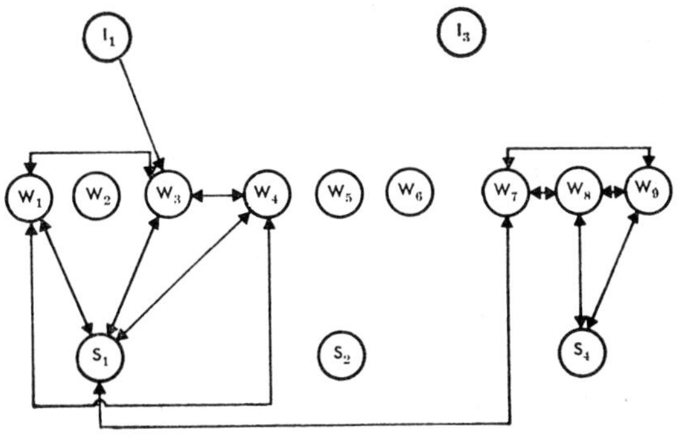


Figure 5

Friendships

BANK WIRING OBSERVATION ROOM

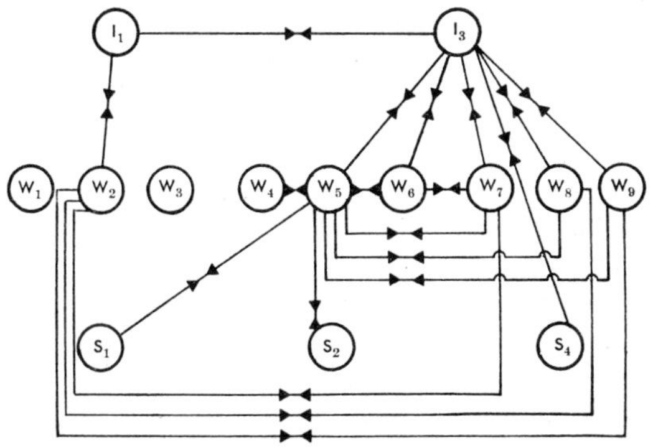


Figure 6

Antagonisms

BANK WIRING OBSERVATION ROOM

$W_5$, $W_6$, $S_2$, and $I_3$, were not bound by any strong friendships.

Looking next at the diagram representing antagonisms, Figure 6, it will be seen that they originated chiefly from the wiremen in soldering unit C and were directed by these people as a group toward $W_2$, $W_5$, and $I_3$, three of the people who were not bound by any strong friendships. Antagonisms arising outside of soldering unit C were directed chiefly toward $W_5$ and $I_3$, the two people who aroused more antagonism than anyone else in the group. It is also apparent that there were no antagonisms between the people in the front of the room who were bound together by friendships and people with whom they were not especially friendly. $I_1$ was antagonistic toward $I_3$ and $W_2$, $S_1$ toward $W_5$, and $W_4$ toward $W_5$, but there were no antagonisms directed from $W_1$, $W_3$, $W_4$, $S_1$, and $I_1$ as a group toward anyone. In this respect the wiremen in soldering unit C were unique: they possessed an internal solidarity, a certain cohesion among themselves, and strong external antagonism or opposition to certain persons outside of their group.

## *The Two Cliques*

On the basis of the material just reviewed some conclusion can now be drawn as to the informal organization of this group of workmen. In the first place, it is quite apparent that the question raised at the beginning of the preceding section must be answered in the negative: these people were not integrated on the basis of occupation; they did not form occupational cliques. In the second place, it is equally apparent that there did exist certain configurations of relations in this group. With one exception, every record examined seemed to be telling something about these configurations. Whether the investigators looked at games, job trading, quarrels over the windows, or friendships and antagonisms, two groups seemed to stand out. One of these groups was located toward the front of the room, the other toward the back. "The group in front" and "the group in back" were common terms of designation among the workmen themselves. The first of these groups will be referred to as clique A, the second, the group toward the rear of the room, as clique B.

What was the membership of these two cliques? This question can be answered only approximately. Clique A included $W_1$, $W_3$, $W_4$, $S_1$, and $I_1$, and clique B included $W_7$, $W_8$, $W_9$, and $S_4$. $W_5$, $S_2$, and $I_3$ were outside either clique. With $W_2$ and $W_6$, however, the situation was not so clear. $W_2$ participated in the games of clique A, but beyond this the similarity of his behavior to theirs ceased. He entered very little into their conversations and tended to isolate himself from them. Much of his behavior suggested that he did not feel his position in the group to be secure. He was the only wireman in soldering unit A who traded jobs with $S_4$, the solderman in clique B, and he traded jobs with his own solderman more than anyone else did. In so far as the social function of job trading was to differentiate wiremen from soldermen, this could be interpreted as meaning that $W_2$ felt rather keenly the necessity of constantly emphasizing his position by subordinating the soldermen. Taking all the evidence into consideration, then, it may be concluded that $W_2$ was not a bona fide member of clique A. $W_6$ tended to participate in clique B. He was continually "horsing around" with the selector wiremen and had relatively little to do with the members of clique A.

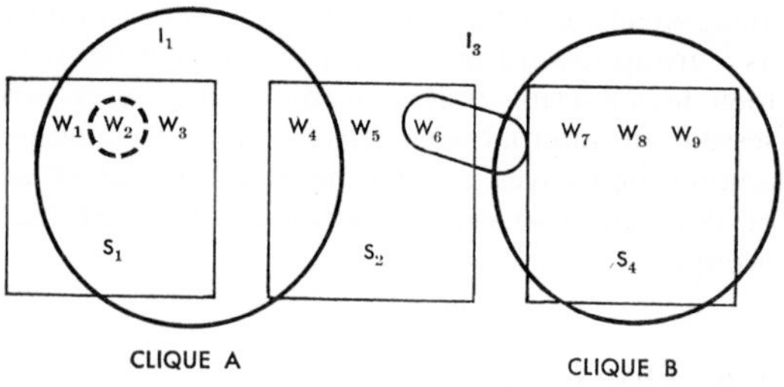


Figure 7

The Internal Organization of the Group

BANK WIRING OBSERVATION ROOM

That he was not entirely accepted in clique B was shown in many ways, chief of which was the way in which clique B co-operated in resisting his attempts to dominate anyone in their group. Yet he participated in clique B much more than $W_2$ did in clique A. It may be concluded that althongh $W_6$ tended to participate in clique B, he was still in many ways an outsider.

As a means of summarizing the results of this inquiry, Figure 7 has been prepared to represent diagrammatically the internal organization of the observation group. The soldering units into which the members of the group were divided are shown by the three rectangles. The two large circles demarcate the two cliques, A and B. There were three individuals, $I_3$, $W_5$, and $S_2$, who were clearly outside either clique.[3] The line around $W_6$ has been made to intersect that of clique B to indicate his partial participation in it. The instability of $W_2$'s position is indicated by the broken circle around his number.

That the members of clique A regarded themselves as superior to clique B was indicated in many ways. Clique A did or refrained from doing certain things which were done by clique B. They did not trade jobs nearly so much, and on the whole they did not enter into the controversies about the windows. Clique A engaged in games of chance, whereas clique B engaged more often in "binging." Both groups purchased candy from the Club store, but purchases were made separately and neither clique shared with the other. Clique A bought chocolate candy in small quantities, whereas clique B bought a less expensive kind in such large quantities that $W_9$ one time became ill from eating too much. Clique A argued more and indulged in less noise and horseplay than clique B. The members of clique A felt that their conversations were on a higher plane than those which went on in clique B; as $W_4$ said, "We talk about things of some importance."

3. Perhaps a word of caution is necessary here. When it is said that this group was divided into two cliques and that certain people were outside either clique, it does not mean that there was no solidarity between the two cliques or between the cliques and the outsiders. There is always the danger, in examining small groups intensively, of overemphasizing differentiating factors. Internal solidarity thus appears to be lacking. That this group, as a whole, did have very strong sentiments in common has already been shown in discussing their attitudes toward output and will be brought out more clearly in the next chapters. It should also be said that position in the group is not so static as one might assume from this diagram. Had the study continued longer, membership in the cliques might have shifted. Also, if the group had been larger, or if the group had been allowed to remain in the regular department, it is quite probable that the people who appear to be outsiders here would have formed cliques with others who had similar sentiments.

# 5. *The Solidarity of Occupational Groups*

BY EMILE DURKHEIM

IF ALL CORPORATIVE ORGANIZATION is not necessarily an historical anachronism, is there any reason for believing that it may play, in contemporary societies, the great role we have attributed to it? For, if it be indispensable, it is not because of the economic services it can render, but because of the moral influence it can have. What we especially see in the occupational group is a moral power capable of containing individual egos, of maintaining a spirited sentiment of common solidarity in the consciousness of all the workers, of preventing the law of the strongest from being

Reprinted from Emile Durkheim, *The Division of Labor in Society,* trans. George Simpson (Glencoe, Ill.: The Free Press, 1947), pp. 10–18, 22–31, with the permission of The Free Press.

brutally applied to industrial and commercial relations. It is now thought to be unsuitable for such a role. Because it had its origin in short-lived interests, it appears that it can be used only for utilitarian ends, and the mementos left by corporations of the old regime seem only to confirm this impression. They are gratuitously represented in the future as they were during the last days of their existence, particularly busy in maintaining or increasing their privileges and their monopolies; and it cannot be seen how interests so narrowly occupational can have a favorable effect on the ethics of the body or its members.

But what has been true of certain corporations for a very short space of their development cannot be applied to all the corporative regime. Far from having acquired a sort of moral infirmity from its constitution, it has especially played a moral role during the major part of its history. This is particularly evident in the Roman corporations. "The corporations of workers," says Waltzing, "were, with the Romans, far from having an occupational character as pronounced as in the Middle Ages; we find there neither regulation of methods, nor imposed apprenticeship, nor monopoly; nor was their end to unite the necessary elements to exploit an industry."[1] To be sure, the association gave them more force in time of need for safeguarding their common interests. But that was only one of the useful consequences produced by the institution; that was not its *raison d'être,* its principal function. Above all, the corporation was a religious organization. Each one had its particular god whose cult was celebrated in a special temple when the means were available. In the same way as each family had its *Lar familiaris;* each city its *Genius publicus,* each organization had its protecting god, *Genius collegii.* Naturally, this occupational cult did not dispense with celebrations, with sacrifices and banquets in common. All sorts of circumstances were used as reasons for these joyful gatherings. Moreover, distribution of food-stuffs and money often took place at the community's expense. There have been questions as to whether the corporation had a sick-fund; if it regularly helped those members who were in need. Opinions on this point are divergent.[2] But what lends interest and import to this discussion is that these common banquets, more or less periodic, and the distribution accompanying them, often took the place of help, and formed a bureau of indirect assistance. Thus, the unfortunate knew they could count on this disguised aid. As corollary to this religious character, the organization of workmen was, at the same time, a burial society. United in a cult during their lives, like the *Gentiles,* the members of these corporations also wished to rest together after death. All the fairly rich corporations had a collective *columbarium* where, when the organization had not the funds to buy a burial plot, there was at least the certainty that its members would have honorable burial at the expense of the common fund.

A common cult, common banquets, a common cemetery, all united together—are these not all the distinctive characteristics of the domestic organization at the time of the Romans? Thus, it has been said that the Roman corporation was a "great family." "No word," says Waltzing, "better indicates the nature of the relations uniting the brotherhood, and a great many indications prove a great fraternity reigned in their midst."[3] The community of interests took the place of the community of blood. "The members looked upon themselves as brothers, even to the extent of calling themselves by that name." The most ordinary expression, as a matter of fact, was that of *sodales,* but even that word expresses a spiritual relationship implying a narrow fraternity. The protectors of the organization often took the names of father and mother. "A proof of the devotion the brothers had for their organization lies in the bequests and donations they made. There are also funereal monuments upon which are found: *Pius in collegio,* he was faithful towards his organization, as if one said, *Pius in suos.*"[4] This familial life was so developed that Boissier makes it the principal aim of all the Roman corporations. "Even in the workers' corporations," he says, "there was association principally for the pleasure of living together, for finding outside oneself distractions from fatigue and boredom, to create an intimacy less restrained than the family, and less extensive than the city, and thus to make life easier and more agreeable."[5]

As Christian societies belong to a social type very different from the city-state, the corporations of the Middle Ages do not exactly resemble the Roman corporations. But they also constitute a moral environment for their members. "The corporation," says Levasseur, "united people of the same occupation by strong bonds. Rather often they were established in the parish house, or in a particular chapel and put themselves under the invocation of a saint who became the patron saint of all the community. . . . There they gathered, attended with great ceremony the solemn masses; after which the

1. *Etude historique sur les corporations professionelles chez les Romains,* I, p. 194.
2. The majority of historians believe that certain organizations, at least, were mutual-aid societies.

3. *Op. cit.,* I, p. 330.
4. *Op. cit.,* I, p. 331.
5. *La Religion romaine,* II, pp. 287–288.

members of the brotherhood went, all together, to end their day in joyous feasting. In this way the corporations of the Middle Ages closely resembled those of Roman times."[6] The corporation, moreover, often used part of its budgetary funds for charity.

Moreover, precise rules fixed the respective duties of employers and workmen, as well as the duties of employers toward each other, for each occupation. There are, to be sure, regulations not in accord with our present ideas, but judgment must be made according to the ethics of the time, since that is what the rules express. What is indisputable is that they are all inspired by zeal, not for individuals, but for corporative interest, whether poorly or well understood. Now the subordination of private utility to common utility, whatever it may be, always has a moral character, for it necessarily implies sacrifice and abnegation. In addition, a great many of these rules proceeded from moral sentiments still ours today.[7] The valet was protected from the caprices of his master who could not dismiss him at will. It is true that the obligation was reciprocal; but besides this reciprocity being just in itself, it is still more justified by reason of the important privileges the worker enjoyed then. Thus, masters were forbidden to negate his *right to work,* which allowed him to seek assistance from his neighbors, or even their wives. In short, as Levasseur says, "these regulations concerning the apprentices and workmen are worthy of consideration by historian and economist. They are the work of a barbarous century. They carry the mark of worth-while minds and good, common sense, worthy of observation."[8] Finally, a system of rules was designed to guarantee occupational honesty. All sorts of precautions were taken to prevent the merchant or workman from deceiving the buyer, to compel him "to perform good, loyal work."[9] To be sure, a time came when the rules became uselessly complicated, when the masters were a great deal busier safeguarding their privileges than caring about the good name of the occupation and the honesty of their members. But there is no institution which, at some given moment, does not degenerate, either because it does not know how to change and mobilize anew, or because it develops unilaterally, overdoing some of its activities. This makes it unsuited to furnish the services with which it is charged. That is reason to seek its reformation, not to declare it forever useless, nor to destroy it.

Whatever it may be from this standpoint, the preceding facts sufficiently prove that the occupational group is not incapable of exerting moral action. . . . The considerable place that religion took in life, in Rome as well as in the Middle Ages, makes particularly evident the true nature of its functions, for all religious community then constituted a moral milieu, in the same way as all moral discipline tended forcibly to take a religious form. And besides, this character of corporative organization comes from very general causes that can be seen acting in other circumstances. When a certain number of individuals in the midst of a political society are found to have ideas, interests, sentiments, and occupations not shared by the rest of the population, it is inevitable that they will be attracted toward each other under the influence of these likenesses. They will seek each other out, enter into relations, associate, and thus, little by little, a restricted group, having its special characteristics, will be formed in the midst of the general society. But once the group is formed, a moral life appears naturally carrying the mark of the particular conditions in which it has developed. For it is impossible for men to live together, associating in industry, without acquiring a sentiment of the whole formed by their union, without attaching themselves to that whole, preoccupying themselves with its interests, and taking account of it in their conduct. This attachment has in it something surpassing the individual. This subordination of particular interests to the general interest is, indeed, the source of all moral activity. As this sentiment grows more precise and determined, applying itself to the most ordinary and the most important circumstances of life, it is translated into definitive formulae, and thus a body of moral rules is in process of establishment.

At the same time that this result is produced of itself and by the force of circumstances, it is useful and the feeling of its utility lends confirmation to it. Society is not alone in its interest in the formation of special groups to regulate their own activity, developing within them what otherwise would become anarchic; but the individual, on his part, finds joy in it, for anarchy is painful to him. He also suffers from pain and disorder produced whenever inter-individual relations are not submitted to some regulatory influence. It is not good for man to live with the threat of war in the midst of his immediate companions. This sensation of general hostility, the mutual defiance resulting from it, the tension it necessitates, are difficult states when they are chronic. If we love war, we also love the joys of

6. *Les classes ouvrières en France jusqu'a la Révolution,* I, pp. 217–218.

7. *Op. cit.,* I, p. 221.—See, on the same moral character of the corporation in Germany, Gierke, *Das Deutsche Genossenschaftswesen,* I, p. 384; for England, Ashley, *An Introduction to English Economic History and Theory.*

8. *Op. cit.,* p. 238.

9. *Op. cit.,* pp. 240–261.

peace, and the latter are of more worth as men are more profoundly socialized, which is to say (for the two words are synonymous) more profoundly civilized. Common life is attractive as well as coercive. Doubtless, constraint is necessary to lead man to surpass himself, to add to his physical nature another; but as he learns the charm of this new life, he contracts the need for it, and there is no order of activity in which he does not seek it passionately. That is why when individuals who are found to have common interests associate, it is not only to defend these interests, it is to associate, that is, not to feel lost among adversaries, to have the pleasure of communing, to make one out of many, which is to say, finally, to lead the same moral life together.

Domestic morality is not otherwise formed. Because of the prestige the family has in our eyes, it seems to us that if it has been, and if it is always, a school of devotion, of abnegation, the place *par excellence* of morality, it is because of quite particular, intrinsic characteristics found nowhere else. It is believed that consanguinity is an exceptionally powerful cause of moral relationship. But we have often had the occasion for showing[10] that consanguinity has not the extraordinary efficacy attributed to it. The proof is that in many societies the non-blood relations are found in numbers in the centre of the family; the so-called relationship is then contracted with great facility, and it has all the effects of a blood-tie. Inversely, it often happens that very near blood relations are, morally or juridically, strangers to each other; for example, the case of cognates in the Roman family. The family does not then owe its virtues to the unity of descent; it is quite simply a group of individuals who find themselves related to one another in the midst of political society by a particularly strong community of ideas, of sentiments and interests. Consanguinity facilitates this concentration, for it causes mutual adaptation of consciences. But a great many other factors come into play: material neighborhood, solidarity of interests, the need of uniting against a common danger, or simply to unite, are other powerful causes of relationship.

Now, they are not special to the family, but they are found, although in different forms, in the corporation. If, then, the first of these groups has played so considerable a role in the moral history of humanity, why should the second be incapable of doing the same? To be sure, there is always this difference between them, that members of a family live their lives together, while members of a corporation live only their occupational lives together. The family is a sort of complete society whose action controls our economic activity as well as our religious, political, scientific activities. Anything significant we do, even outside the house, acts upon it, and provokes appropriate reactions. The sphere of influence of a corporation is, in a sense, more restricted. Still, we must not lose sight of the increasingly important position the occupation takes in life as work becomes more specialized, for the field of each individual activity tends steadily to become delimited by the functions with which the individual is particularly charged. Moreover, if familial action extends everywhere, it can only be general; detail escapes it. Finally, the family, in losing the unity and indivisibility of former times, has lost with one stroke a great part of its efficacy. As it is today broken up with each generation, man passes a notable part of his existence far from all domestic influence. The corporation has none of these disturbances; it is as continuous as life. The inferiority that it presents, in comparison with the family, has its compensation.

If we find it necessary thus to bring together the family and the corporation, it is not simply to establish an instructive parallel between them, but because the two institutions are closely connected. This is observable in the history of Roman corporations. We have seen, indeed, that they were formed on the model of domestic society, of which they were at first only a new and enlarged form. But, the occupational group would not, at this point, recall the familial group, if there were not some bond of relation between them. And, indeed, the corporation has been, in a sense, the heir of the family. As long as industry is exclusively agricultural, it has, in the family and in the village, which is itself only a sort of great family, its immediate organ, and it needs no other. As exchange is not, or is very little, developed, the farmer's life does not extend outside the familial circle. Economic activity, having no consequences outside the family, is sufficiently regulated by the family, and the family itself thus serves as occupational group. But the case is no longer the same once trades exist. For to live by trade, customers are necessary, and going outside the house to find them is necessary, as is having relations with competitors, fighting against them, coming to an understanding with them. In addition, trades demand cities, and cities have always been formed and recruited principally from the ranks of immigrants, individuals who have left their native homes. A new form of activity was thus constituted which burst from the old familial form. In order not to remain in an unorganized state, it was necessary to create a new form, which would be fitting to it; or otherwise said, it was necessary for a secondary group of a new kind to be formed. This is the origin of the corporation; it was substituted for

10. See especially *Année sociologique,* I, pp. 313 ff.

the family in the exercise of a function which had been domestic, but which could no longer keep this character. Such an origin does not allow us to attribute to it that sort of constitutional amorality which is generally gratuitously bestowed upon it. Just as the family has elaborated domestic ethics and law, the corporation is now the source of occupational ethics and law.

* * *

But there is more knowledge to be gathered from the summary we have just made.

First of all, it shows us how the corporation has fallen into discredit for about two centuries, and, consequently, what it must become in order to take its place again among our public institutions. We have just seen, indeed, that in the form it had in the Middle Ages it was narrowly bound to the organization of the commune. This solidarity was without inconvenience as long as the trades themselves had a communal character. While, as originally, merchants and workers had only the inhabitants of the city or its immediate environs for customers, which means as long as the market was principally local, the bodies of trades, with their municipal organization, answered all needs. But it was no longer the same once great industry was born. As it had nothing especially urban about it, it could not adapt itself to a system which had not been made for it. First, it does not necessarily have its centre in a city; it can even be established outside all preexisting rural or urban agglomerations. It looks for that territory where it can best maintain itself and thrive. Thus, its field of action is limited to no determined region; its clientele is recruited everywhere. An institution so entirely wrapped up in the commune as was the old corporation could not then be used to encompass and regulate a form of collective activity which was so completely foreign to the communal life.

And, indeed, as soon as great industry appeared, it was found to be outside the corporative regime, and that was what caused the bodies of trades to do all in their power to prevent industry's progress. Nevertheless, it was certainly not freed of all regulation; in the beginning the State played a role analogous to that which the corporations played for small-scale commerce and urban trades. At the same time as the royal power accorded the manufacturers certain privileges, in return it submitted them to its control. That is indicated in the title of royal manufacturers. But as it is well known how unsuited the State is for this function, this direct control could not fail to become oppressive. It was almost impossible from the time great industry reached a certain degree of development and diversity; that is why classical economists demanded its suppression, and with good cause. But if the corporation, as it then existed, could not be adapted to this new form of industry, and if the State could not replace the old corporative discipline, it does not follow that all discipline would be useless thenceforward. It simply meant that the old corporation had to be transformed to continue to fill its role in the new conditions of economic life. Unfortunately, it had not enough suppleness to be reformed in time; that is why it was discarded. Because it did not know how to assimilate itself to the new life which was evolving, it was divorced from that life, and, in this way, it became what it was upon the eve of the Revolution, a sort of dead substance, a strange body which could maintain itself in the social organism only through inertia. It is then not surprising that a moment came when it was violently expelled. But to destroy it was not a means of giving satisfaction to the needs it had not satisfied. And that is the reason the question still remains with us, and has become still more acute after a century of groping and fruitless experience.

The work of the sociologist is not that of the statesman. We do not have to present in detail what this reform should be. It will be sufficient to indicate the general principles as they appear from the preceding facts.

What the experience of the past proves, above all, is that the framework of the occupational group must always have relations with the framework of economic life. It is because of this lack of relationship that the corporative regime disappeared. Since the market, formerly municipal, has become national and international, the corporations must assume the same extension. Instead of being limited only to the workers of a city, it must enlarge in such a way as to include all the members of the occupation scattered over the territory,[11] for in whatever region they are found, whether they live in the city or the country, they are all solidary, and participate in a common life. Since this common life is, in certain respects, independent of all territorial determinations, the appropriate organ must be created that expresses and regularizes its function. Because of these dimensions, such an organ would necessarily be in direct contact with the central organ of the collective life, for the rather important events which interest a whole category of industrial enterprises

11. We do not have to speak of international organization which, in consequence of the international character of the market, would necessarily develop above this national organization, for the latter alone can actually constitute a juridical institution. The first, under present European law, can result only in freely concluded arrangements between national corporations.

in a country necessarily have very general repercussions of which the State cannot fail to take cognizance; hence it intervenes. Thus, it is not without reason that royal power tended instinctively not to allow great industry outside its control when it did appear. It was impossible for it not to be interested in a form of activity which, by its very nature, can always affect all society. But this regulatory action, if it is necessary, must not degenerate into narrow subordination, as happened in the seventeenth and eighteenth centuries. The two related organs must remain distinct and autonomous; each of them has its function, which it alone can take care of. If the functioning of making general principles of industrial legislation belongs to the governmental assemblies, they are incapable of diversifying them according to the different industries. It is this diversification which constitutes the proper task of the corporation[12] This unitarian organization for a whole country in no way excludes the formation of secondary organs, comprising workers of the same region, or of the same locality, whose role would be to specialize still more the occupational regulation according to the local or regional necessities. Economic life would thus be regulated and determined without losing any of its diversity.

For that very reason, the corporative regime would be protected against that tendency towards immobility that it has often been charged with in the past, for it is a fault which is rooted in the narrowly communal character of the corporation. As long as it was limited to the city, it was inevitable for it to become a prisoner of tradition as the city itself. As, in a group so restricted, the conditions of life are almost invariable, habit exercises a terrific effect upon people, and even innovations are dreaded. The traditionalism of the corporations was thus only an aspect of the communal traditionalism, and had the same qualities. Then, once it was ingrained in the mores, it survived the causes which had produced and originally justified it. That is why, when the material and moral concentration of the country, and great industry which is its consequence, had opened minds to new desires, awakened new needs, introduced into the tastes and fashions a mobility heretofore unknown, the corporation, which was obstinately attached to its old customs, was unable to satisfy these new exigencies. But national corporations, by virtue of their dimension and complexity, would not be exposed to this danger. Too many diverse minds would be in action for stationary uniformity to be established. In a group formed of numerous and varied elements, new combinations are always being produced. There would then be nothing rigid about such an organization, and it would consequently find itself in harmony with the mobile equilibrium of needs and ideas.

Besides, it must not be thought that the entire function of the corporation is to make rules and apply them. To be sure, where a group is formed, a moral discipline is formed too. But the institution of this discipline is only one of the many ways through which collective activity is manifested. A group is not only a moral authority which dominates the life of its members; it is also a source of life *sui generis*. From it comes a warmth which animates its members, making them intensely human, destroying their egotisms. Thus, in the past, the family was the legislator of law and ethics whose severity went to extremes of violence, at the same time that it was the place where one first learned to enjoy the effusions of sentiment. We have also seen how the corporation, in Rome and in the Middle Ages, awakened these same needs and sought to satisfy them. The corporations of the future will have a complexity of attributes still greater, by reason of their increased growth. Around their proper occupational functions others which come from the communes or private societies will be grouping themselves. The functions of assistance are such that, to be well filled, they demand feelings of solidarity between assistants and assisted, a certain intellectual and moral homogeneity such as the same occupation produces. A great many educational institutions (technical schools, adult education, etc.) equally seem to have to find their natural environment in the corporation. It is the same for aesthetic life, for it appears in the nature of things that this noble form of sport and recreation develops side by side with the serious life which it serves to balance and relieve. In fact, there are even now syndicates which are at the same time societies of mutual aid; others found common houses where there are organized courses, concerts, and dramatic presentations. The corporative activity can thus assume the most varied forms.

12. This specialization could be made only with the aid of selected assemblies charged to represent the corporation. In the present state of industry, these assemblies, in the same way as tribunals charged with applying the occupational regulations, should evidently be comprised of representatives of employees and representatives of employers, as is already the case in the tribunals of skilled trades; and that, in proportions corresponding to the respective importance attributed by opinion to these two factors in production. But if it is necessary that both meet in the directing councils of the corporations, it is no less important that at the base of the corporative organization they form distinct and independent groups, for their interests are too often rival and antagonistic. To be able to go about their ways freely, they must go about their ways separately. The two groups thus constituted would then be able to appoint their representatives to the common assemblies.

There is even reason to suppose that the corporation will become the foundation or one of the essential bases of our political organization. We have seen, indeed, that if it first begins by being outside the social system, it tends to fix itself in it in proportion to the development of economic life. It is, therefore, just to say that if progress continues to be made in this direction, it will have to take a more prominent and more predominant place in society. It was formerly the elementary division of communal organization. Now that the commune, heretofore an autonomous organism, has lost its place in the State, as the municipal market did in the national market, is it not fair to suppose that the corporation also will have to experience a corresponding transformation, becoming the elementary division of the State, the fundamental political unity? Society, instead of remaining what it is today, an aggregate of juxtaposed territorial districts, would become a vast system of national corporations. From various quarters it is asked that elective assemblies be formed by occupations, and not by territorial divisions; and certainly, in this way, political assemblies would more exactly express the diversity of social interests and their relations. They would be a more faithful picture of social life in its entirety. But to say that the nation, in becoming aware of itself, must be grouped into occupations,—does not this mean that the organized occupation or corporation should be the essential organ of public life?

Thus the great gap in the structure of European societies we elsewhere point to would be filled. It will be seen, indeed, how, as advances are made in history, the organization which has territorial groups as its base (village or city, district, province, etc.) steadily becomes effaced. To be sure, each of us belongs to a commune, or a department, but the bonds attaching us there became daily more fragile and more slack. These geographical divisions are, for the most part, artificial and no longer awaken in us profound sentiments. The provincial spirit has disappeared never to return; the patriotism of the parish has become an archaism that cannot be restored at will. The municipal or departmental affairs affect and agitate us in proportion to their coincidence with our occupational affairs. Our activity is extended quite beyond these groups which are too narrow for it, and, moreover, a good deal of what happens there leaves us indifferent. There is thus produced a spontaneous weakening of the old social structure. Now, it is impossible for this organization to disappear without something replacing it. A society composed of an infinite number of unorganized individuals, that a hypertrophied State is forced to oppress and contain, constitutes a veritable sociological monstrosity. For collective activity is always too complex to be able to be expressed through the single and unique organ of the State. Moreover, the State is too remote from individuals; its relations with them too external and intermittent to penetrate deeply into individual consciences and socialize them within. Where the State is the only environment in which men can live communal lives, they inevitably lose contact, become detached, and thus society disintegrates. A nation can be maintained only if, between the State and the individual, there is intercalated a whole series of secondary groups near enough to the individuals to attract them strongly in their sphere of action and drag them, in this way, into the general torrent of social life. We have just shown how occupational groups are suited to fill this role, and that is their destiny. One thus conceives how important it is, especially in the economic order, for them to emerge from that state of inconsistency and disorganization in which they have remained for a century, since these occupations today absorb the major part of our collective forces.[13]

Perhaps now we shall be better able to explain the conclusions we reached at the end of our book, *Suicide*.[14] We were already proposing there a strong corporative organization as a means of remedying the misfortune which the increase in suicides, together with many other symptoms, evinces. Certain critics have found that the remedy was not proportionate to the extent of the evil, but that is because they have undervalued the true nature of the corporation, and the place to which it is destined in social life, as well as the grave anomaly resulting from its disappearance. They have seen only an utilitarian association whose effect would at best bring order to economic interests, whereas it must really be the essential element of our social

13. We do not mean that the territorial divisions are destined to disappear entirely, but only that they will become of less importance. The old institutions never vanish before the new without leaving any traces of themselves. They persist, not only through sheer force of survival, but because there still persists something of the needs they once answered. The material neighborhood will always constitute a bond between men; consequently, political and social organization with a territorial base will certainly exist. Only, they will not have their present predominance, precisely because this bond has lost its force. Moreover, we have shown above, that even at the base of the corporation, there will always be found geographical divisions. Furthermore, between the diverse corporations of the same locality or region there will necessarily be special relations of solidarity which will, at all times, demand appropriate organization.

14. *Suicide,* trans. John A. Spaulding and George Simpson; ed. George Simpson (Glencoe, Ill.: The Free Press, 1951).

structure. The absence of all corporative institution creates, then, in the organization of a people like ours, a void whose importance it is difficult to exaggerate. It is a whole system of organs necessary in the normal functioning of the common life which is wanting. Such a constitutive lack is evidently not a local evil, limited to a region of society; it is a malady *totius substantiae,* affecting all the organism. Consequently, the attempt to put an end to it cannot fail to produce the most far reaching consequences. It is the general health of the social body which is here at stake.

That does not mean, however, that the corporation is a sort of panacea for everything. The crisis through which we are passing is not rooted in a single and unique cause. To put an end to it, it is not sufficient to regulate it where necessary. Justice must prevail. Now, as we shall say further on, "as long as there are rich and poor at birth, there cannot be just contract," nor a just distribution of social goods. But if the corporative reform does not dispense with the others, it is the first condition for their efficacy. Let us imagine that the primordial condition of ideal justice may be realized; let us suppose that men enter life in a state of perfect economic equality, which is to say, that riches have entirely ceased being hereditary. The problems in the environment with which we were struggling would not be solved by that. Indeed, there will always be an economic apparatus, and various agents collaborating in its functioning. It will then be necessary to determine their rights and duties, and that, for each form of industry. It will be necessary that in each occupation a body of laws be made fixing the quantity of work, the just remuneration of the different officials, their duties toward each other, and toward the community, etc. Life will be just as complex as ever. Because riches will not be transmitted any longer as they are today will not mean that the state of anarchy has disappeared, for it is not a question as to the ownership of riches, but as to the regulation of the activity to which these riches give rise. It will not regulate itself by magic, as soon as it is useful, if the necessary forces for the institution of this regulation have not been aroused and organized.

Moreover, new difficulties will arise which will remain insoluble without a corporative organization. Up to now, it was the family which, either through collective property or descendence, assured the continuity of economic life, by the possession and exploitation of goods held intact, or, from the time the old familial communism fell away, the nearest relatives received the goods of the deceased.[15] In the case of collective property, neither death nor a new generation changed the relations of things to persons; in the case of descent, the change was made automatically, and the goods, at no time, remained unowned and unused. But if domestic society cannot play this role any longer, there must be another social organ to replace its exercise of this necessary function. For there is only one way of preventing the periodic suspension of any activity: a group, perpetual as the family, must possess goods and exploit them itself, or, at the death of the owner, receive them and send them to some other individual holder to improve them. But as we have shown, the State is poorly equipped to supervise these very specialized economic tasks. There is, then, only the occupational group which can capably look after them. It answers, indeed, two necessary conditions; it is so closely connected with the economic life that it feels its needs, at the same time having a perpetuity at least equal to the family. But to fill this role, it must exist and be mature enough to take care of the new and complex role which devolves upon it.

If the problem of the corporation is not the only one demanding public attention, there is certainly none more urgent, for the others can be considered only when this has been solved. No modification, no matter how small, can be introduced into the juridical order, if one does not begin by creating the necessary organ for the institution of the new law. That is why it is vain to delay by seeking precisely what this law must be, for in the present state of knowledge, our approximation will be clumsy and always open to doubt. How much more important it is to put ourselves at once to work establishing the moral forces which alone can determine its realization!

15. It is true that where a will is permitted the proprietor can determine the transmission of his property. But a will only gives the right to act contrary to the law of succession. This law is the norm according to which the transfers are made. These cases are very generally limited and are always exceptional.

## IV–TERRITORIAL COMMUNITY

# 1. *On the Origins of the State*

BY ROBERT H. LOWIE

IN 1861, Sir Henry Sumner Maine, the father of comparative jurisprudence, sharply separated two principles of uniting individuals for governmental purposes,—the blood tie and the territorial tie. He further combined this conceptual distinction with an *historical* theory, to wit, that in less advanced or earlier societies "kinship in blood is the sole possible ground of community in political functions." No revolution, he argued, could be "so startling and so complete as the change which is accomplished when some other principle—such as that, for instance, of *local contiguity*—establishes itself for the first time as the basis of common political action." And, again, he writes: ". . . the idea that a number of persons should exercise political rights in common simply because they happened to live within the same topographical limits was utterly strange and monstrous to primitive antiquity." Where members of alien lineage were taken into the fold it was at least on the basis of a legal fiction that they were "descended from the same stock as the people on whom they were engrafted."[1]

When Lewis H. Morgan developed his own scheme of "Ancient Society" (1877), he not only adopted Maine's basic distinction but also gave greater definiteness to the views of his predecessor, especially in point of chronology. All forms of government, he argued, belonged to one of two categories,—they were either founded on persons and personal relations or on territory and property. Ranged on one side were such units as the gens (clan, sib) and phratry; on the other, the series comprising the ward, township, county, province, and national domain. Political, that is, territorial organization was declared to have been unknown prior to classical antiquity. It was in 594 B.C. that Solon took the initial step of breaking up the patrilineal gentes (clans, sibs) of the Athenians by a property classification, and in 507 B.C. Cleisthenes completed the advance by substituting for the traditional gentile organization purely local lines of division, by cutting up the old noble lineages and assigning the fragments to different local groups. Henceforth every citizen was registered, taxed, and given a vote as a member not of a clan but of a township, that is, of a territorial unit.

This classical distinction between "social" or "tribal," and "political" or "territorial," organization is significant and unexceptionable. That is to say, there *is* a fundamental difference between the two principles discriminated, and of both the history of human society provides abundant examples. It is not the logical but the historical aspect of the theory that evokes doubt. Why should the peoples of the world, after contentedly living for millennia under a government based on the blood tie, engage in that startling revolution described by Maine, of substituting the totally novel alignment of persons by locality? Neither author provides an adequate solution. Must we here break with the notion of continuous evolution? That certainly grates on the sensibilities of latter-day historical-mindedness. In the presence of overwhelming positive evidence we should be willing to cast Continuity on the rubbish heap of exploded fictions, but without such rigorous demonstration we shall do well to cling to it and seek an alternative interpretation. Nor is it difficult to outline the avenue of approach. If 507 or 594 B.C. does *not* mark an abrupt departure from past tradition, then older and simpler communities must have displayed the local bond along with the consanguineal tie. The two principles, in other words, however antithetical, are not of necessity mutually exclusive. It is then possible to satisfy the postulate of Continuity. We are no longer face to face with the miracle of a spontaneous generation but with the scientific problem of how an originally weak but

---



1. *Ancient Law,* Chapter V, 124–126.

perceptible territorial sentiment, at first subordinate to the blood tie, was intensified to the point of assuming the dominant role.

Whether this interpretation is warranted, is of course a question to be determined by empirical facts.

In fairness we must, first of all, concede that these yield considerable justification for the position maintained by Maine and Morgan. Again and again, in going over the descriptive literature of social anthropology, the reader must be struck by the prominence of personal relationship in governmental affairs, such as the administration of justice. What, for instance, is the significance of the blood feud, which outside of Africa is such a common mode of adjusting misunderstandings? From the present angle it is simply a negation of the state: it implies the doctrine that persons living in the same village or country are not by such juxtaposition jointly subordinate to some transcendent local authority but have claims upon and obligations to their kin only, each lineage standing towards any other in the same relationship as, say, the United States to France or England,—perhaps actually at amity, yet at any time potentially shifting into a state of avowed hostility.

The condition thus abstractly defined is best illustrated by a series of examples taken from different parts of the primitive world.

Let us begin with the Yurok of northwestern California. We have already commented on the smallness of their political units; at present we are concerned with their composition. Examining one of the typical hamlets, such as Weitspus on the Klamath River, we find an aggregation of less than 200 souls, the male population comprising mainly or exclusively blood kindred. The women generally come from other settlements; apart from this tendency to "local exogamy," the village is a self-contained, independent center of population lacking a sense of attachment to any equivalent units, or of subordination to a major whole, and to that extent comparable with an Andamanese camp. Of adjacent settlements in a group, one "was sometimes involved in a feud while another directly across the river looked on." Indeed, even within the hamlet itself a communal sense is lacking: the individual Weitspus recognizes no duty to his fellow-townsfolk, no executive or judicial authority; his obligations are to his kin and his kin only, so that "all so-called wars were only feuds that happened to involve large groups of kinsmen, several such groups, or unrelated fellow townsmen of the original participants." Notwithstanding the complete absence of administrative and legal officials, the Yurok have a definite code of customary laws; yet all "rights, claims, possessions, and privileges are individual and personal, and all wrongs are against individuals. There is no offense against the community, no duty owing it, no right or power of any sort inhering in it." And, as a corollary to this proposition, punishment of a public character is likewise wanting. "Each side to an issue presses and resists vigorously, exacts all it can, yields when it has to, continues the controversy when continuance promises to be profitable or settlement is clearly suicidal, and usually ends in compromising more or less."[2]

This description is, *mutatis mutandis,* wholly applicable to the Angami Naga, who occupy the hills between Assam and Burma. Though living in a village, the Angami looks upon the sib (clan) as the real unit of organization. "So distinct is the clan from the village that it forms almost a village in itself, often fortified within the village inside in its own boundaries and not infrequently at variance almost amounting to war with other clans in the same village. Under normal circumstances there are sporadic riots due to the internal dissensions between the kin groups since in most disputes between two men of different clans the clansmen on each side appear as partisans and foment the discord." Even in times of war clan jealousies prove a disruptive force.[3]

Perhaps a still more striking illustration is supplied by the Ifugao of northern Luzon, precisely because these Philippine Islanders exemplify the paradox of an exceedingly complicated body of customary law coupled with a condition of virtual anarchy. Our principal source, Dr. R. F. Barton,[4] is quite clear-cut on the subject. He represents the natives as acting with complete disregard of any considerations outside of relationship. An individual owes support to his kindred against all other kin groups, and in proportion to the proximity of his relationship, while he is free from any obligations to the remainder of the local group. This group has no authorized official to arrange disputes between distinct bodies of kindred; there is merely a go-between with purely advisory functions. According to the author's explicit interpretation the political life of the Ifugao rests on consanguinity, and on consanguinity only.

The three examples cited in some measure justify the views of Maine and Morgan. Here are three peoples remote from one another and described by as many independent witnesses, whose testimony

2. Kroeber, *Handbook of the Indians of California* (1925), 3, 8–15, 20, 49.
3. J. H. Hutton, *The Angami Nagas* (1921), 109.
4. *Ifugao Law*, in *Univ. of Cal. Pub. in Amer. Arch. and Ethnol.* (1919), XV: 1–127.

agrees as to the point at issue. Nevertheless, a closer scrutiny of the evidence reveals in each and every one of these instances that while the blood tie is the conspicuous one the local bond is by no means wholly in abeyance.

Let us begin by examining the Ifugao, on whom the descriptive material is most abundant. We find, first of all, that throughout Ifugao territory there is substantial agreement as to customary law. The principles on which a go-between intermediating between warring families renders his decision enjoy general acceptance, even though they may be warped in particular applications. In cases of adultery a fine is imposed on the offender, the amount varying with the relative status in society of the aggrieved and the guilty party. That *some* penalty should be inflicted, is acknowledged even by the offender and his relatives; they are merely leagued together to shield him from bodily harm and beat down exorbitant demands for indemnity. Even if the adulterer is a prominent man supported by a host of henchmen he does not seek wholly to evade punishment but only to reduce it to a minimum. In short, there *is* definite recognition of some obligations to *un*related members of the same community. This rudimentary sense of duty toward the local group stands forth most clearly in the treatment of thieves. If Barton's picture of Ifugao society were to be taken literally, we should expect the same punishment to be meted out to *any* person outside the aggrieved party's kindred. But this inference does not tally with the facts reported. Theft committed by a fellow villager is mulcted by a traditional fine; a marauding outsider, however, is almost certain to be slain forthwith. Similarly, the principle of collective responsibility is extended beyond the circle of consanguinity so as to embrace the neighborhood group. If a creditor remains unsatisfied, he may on occasion appropriate buffalo belonging not only to his tardy debtor or his kin but those of any person inhabiting the same village.

Finally, there is a tacit understanding among different kin groups that internecine strife should be discountenanced lest the *territorial* unit be unduly weakened as compared with corresponding units; and the individual Ifugao is expected to comport himself in such fashion as not to entangle his neighbors in hostilities with other *local* groups. In short, the apparently exclusive potency of blood relationship is seen to be appreciably limited by the recognition of local contiguity as a basis for political action and sentiment.

What is true of the Ifugao, holds likewise for the equally "anarchic" Yurok. Professor Kroeber successfully disproves the existence of any *national* sentiment among them in his account of their so-called wars, which would fail to unite more than one tenth of the whole "tribe" against, say, the Hupa. But the same narratives also show that local affiliations of lesser scope were operative: "under threat of attack from a remote and consolidated alien foe, village might adhere to village in joint war, just as, in lesser feuds, town mates, impelled by bonds of association or imperiled by their common residence, would sometimes unite with the group of individuals with whom the feud originated." Our author adds that "these are occasions such as draw neighbors together the world over, be they individuals, districts, or nations." But that is precisely my contention, to wit, that even in extreme cases of separatism the neighborhood tie becomes a significant element in governmental activity, not perhaps in itself adequate for the institution of what we call "political" organization but providing the germ from which such an organization may develop.

This factor is strengthened by two features. For one thing, the men of a settlement are united by the institution of the sudatory, where they both sweat and sleep together throughout the winter and often in the summer, "passing the evenings in talk and smoking." The type of social unit thus created will be discussed more fully in the following chapter. Secondly, the local tie clearly appears in ritualistic activity. Not only is each ceremony riveted to a particular spot but, what is far more important in the present context, the association with localities serves to knit people together. Every main performance is conducted by competing parties representing as many villages. "These match and outdo one another, as the rich man of each village gradually hands over more and more of his own and his followers' and friends' valuables to the dancers to display." Moreover, it may be said that the very fact of such amicable rivalry in some manner counteracts the excessive particularism described above. It might have paved the way, though apparently among the Yurok it never did, for a more extensive union of local bodies.[5]

Angami conditions are amazingly like those reported for the Yurok and the Ifugao. On the one hand, the same centrifugal tendency is expressed in exaggeratedly tangible form, so that one clan in the village may be separated from the rest by a wall twelve feet in thickness. Murder leads to a vendetta waged by the clans concerned rather than to the expulsion of the criminal by a judicial authority, and in cases of misunderstanding between persons of different villages the blood feud might be restricted to the kindred of the two parties "and it would be quite possible for all the

5. Kroeber, *op. cit.*, 15, 50, 55, 81.

other clans in both villages to be friendly, while the clans of the respective parties to the vendetta were on head-taking terms." Nevertheless, when a serious breach of the social code occurs "the clans in almost any village would be found agreed"; military operations are certainly carried on by villagers as such; and many important magico-religious observances are communal in character.[6]

The Yurok, Ifugao and Angami are *a fortiori* instances: they represent the maximum conceivable lack of governmental coördination of the kin groups occupying the same habitat. If even here the traditional theory of the exclusiveness of the blood tie breaks down, the presence of the local bond will have to be admitted for less extreme cases. However, it is possible to go further and to turn the tables on Maine and Morgan. Not only do local ties coexist with those of blood kinship, but it may be contended that the bond of relationship when defined in sociological rather than biological terms is itself in no small part a *derivative* of local contiguity. This view is so contrary to accepted notions that some evidence must be adduced in its defense.

Let us once more turn to the Angami Naga. Like many of the ruder peoples, they are divided into moieties, each child being reckoned from birth either a Pezoma or a Pepfüma according to his father's half of the tribe. This dual organization is traced to two legendary brothers, whose respective descendants the members of the two subdivisions are believed to be. But unlike such lineages elsewhere, the Angami moieties are not exogamous at the present time: often the population of a village is composed wholly of persons of one moiety and no objection is voiced against the marriage of fellow members. It is credibly stated by Mr. Hutton's informants that the customary taboo once held sway, but in course of time there seems to have been a constant shift of the marriage regulating function to lesser and lesser fragments of the moiety. Thus, the village of Kohima is inhabited exclusively by Pepfüma people, who freely intermarry so far as they belong to distinct sibs. Of these, at one time within native tradition, there were only two, *viz.*, the Cherama and the Pferonoma. These, accordingly, were at that time to all intents and purposes exogamous moieties on the familiar pattern, as Pezoma and Pepfüma are reputed to have once been. But while Cherama persisted unsegmented, its mate was broken up into six sections, making (with Cherama) seven sibs in all at the present time. The exogamous unit of Kohima has thus been repeatedly redefined: at first it was presumably the archaic Pepfüma moiety, whose members were forced to seek spouses outside their own village; subsequently fellow-Pepfüma might marry, provided the union was that of a Cherama with a Pferonoma; and finally, a Pferonoma of sib *a* might marry either a Cherama or a Pferonoma of sibs *b, c, d, e, f*.

Nevertheless, so far there is no deviation from the widespread principle that marriage is regulated by *some* sort of kinship body, though the incest group, to use a convenient term, has materially shrunk in course of time. When, however, we scrutinize the data of Mr. Hutton's genealogical tables and his accompanying text, a new fact of the utmost importance emerges. *Permissible intermarriage is a function of locality no less than of consanguinity*. That is to say, the more inclusive kinship taboo is relaxed only in so far as the individuals concerned are not coresidents in the same community. To quote some striking sentences from our author's report:

"The marriage in the present generation is Pezoma-Pezoma, but *between different villages*."

"Here there is a Pezoma-Pezoma marriage in the last generation and a Pepfüma-Pepfüma marriage in the generation before, but in the latter case *between persons of different villages*."

The Cherhechima division "may not intermarry within itself *in the same village*."[7]

The kin group, in short, is not a marriage regulating group simply because it is a kin group but partly, at least, because it is a local group.

This interpretation, however, may be challenged on the ground that the territorial factor came to be stressed at a relatively late stage, while in the earlier periods the patrilineal kin group was the sole principle regulating sex relations. It might also be contended that even today the intrusion of the local factor is incidental or derivative: exogamy is local only because within the settlement there is certainty as to blood kinship while people living elsewhere are either not known to be related or known to be only remotely related. This argument is plausible enough, and in order to meet it we must proceed to a critique of the kinship concept itself.

While kinship is universally recognized between a child and both his parents, this resulting "bilateral" kin group corresponding to our own family is frequently supplemented among the simpler peoples of the globe by the familiar "unilateral" kin. That is to say, the child is linked either with the father *or* the mother, the Angami illustrating the patrilineal, the Hopi of Arizona the matrilineal variety of unilateral reckoning. Since the bilateral

6. Hutton, *op. cit.* 45, 109, 150 *seq.*, 193.

7. Hutton, *op. cit.*, 110 *seq.*, 125–132, 418 *seq.* The italics are mine.

family is omnipresent, this may seem to involve a contradiction, which, nevertheless, is more apparent than real. The bilateral family may, for instance, center in certain economic duties and sentimental attachments, while political functions —say, the blood feud—are connected solely with the patrilineal group.

Now, my contention is that both the bilateral (family) and the unilateral (clan, sib, moiety) unit are rooted in a local as well as a consanguine factor. Let us begin by considering the unilateral kin group, which in some quarters is still regarded as a distinguishing badge of primitive society generally.

Among the unilaterally organized tribes there are some in which the kin and the territorial group coincide. This is true of large sections of California. Mr. Gifford has recently shown that the Miwok, who live near the center of the state, were formerly split up into minute paternal lineages, each politically autonomous, each bearing a local name and owning a definite tract of land. Closely conforming to this model, the South Californian Diegueño were organized into patrilineal groups controlling areas so definitely circumscribed that it has been possible to plot their respective holdings. Similarly, in West Australia the local group embraces a body of blood relatives related through their fathers, and it is this small group, simultaneously consanguine and territorial, that acts as a miniature state, for example, by waging war.[8]

Now, what makes a group of this type cohere? It is easy to say that the sense of blood relationship is primary, but very difficult to prove; for what we observe is not such priority but the inextricable union of the consanguine and the local bond. Each unit in West Australia feels itself indissolubly linked with a definite locality by mystical ties. Why? Because of the reverence felt for the paternal ancestry settled there? But why *should* the paternal ancestry be singled out for reverential treatment? Is it not possible to invert the cheap and obvious explanation? It may be that the aborigines do not view a locality reverently because it is connected with their paternal ancestors but that they esteem their ancestors in so far as they are linked with a certain locality.

This leads us directly to the core of the clan problem. Why, we ask, do people ever feel a more special affiliation with one side of the family than with the other? It cannot be the kinship factor that accounts for the differential relationship, for that factor would operate equally for the paternal and the maternal kindred. The clue to the solution was long ago supplied by E. B. Tylor.[9] Let us assume the rule of marriage that obtains among the Hopi of Arizona,—matrilocal residence. By this the bridegroom takes up his abode with his wife's parents, that is to say, since there is female house ownership, with his mother-in-law, to whom her other daughters likewise bring their several husbands. This explains forthwith why kinsfolk biologically on a par are discriminated sociologically. Between the mother's brother, who sees his sisters' children grow up under his own mother's roof, and his nephews and nieces there naturally develops a sentiment of attachment that cannot possibly obtain between them and the father's brother. Similarly, the mother's sister becomes a closer relation than the paternal aunt, who cannot possibly be a coresident. It is equally clear why there is a discrimination between different types of cousin. A Hopi grows up with the children of his mother's sister, while the children of his *father's* sister are reared in another house. In corresponding fashion the scales are weighted in favor of the *paternal* kin wherever patrilocal residence takes the place of matrilocalism. In short, spatial segregation accounts to a large extent for the alignment of relatives found in a tribe organized into clans.

It is true that residence after marriage is not always rigidly or permanently fixed, and in such cases supplementary factors must be invoked. For instance, a paternal lineage may be lined, as in northeastern North America, by common utilization of a hunting territory. Again, as in sections of Australia, a maternal kin group may cohere through exploitation of the same seed gathering tract; or, as among the Hidatsa, by the joint cultivation of a plot by a mother, her daughters, and her daughters' daughters. But in each of these instances, the ultimate determinant of cohesion is evidently not mere kinship but kinship enforced by propinquity.

So far I have considered the blood bond only with reference to the unilateral kinship group which looms so large in the discussions of ancient law. At present, however, it is recognized by all ethnologists open to argument that the unilateral principle is not a primeval one but was superimposed at a relatively late period upon the bilateral principle, which invariably accompanies it. The evidence from nearly all the unequivocally simplest tribes of the globe, such as the Shoshoneans of Utah and Nevada, the Yahgan of Tierra del Fuego, the Andamanese of the Bay of Bengal,

8. E. W. Gifford, *Miwok Lineages and the Political Unit in Aboriginal California,* in *American Anthropologist* (1926), 389–401. L. Spier, *Southern Diegueño Customs,* in *Univ. Cal. Publs. Amer. Arch. and Ethnol.,* (1923), XX: 296–308. R. H. Lowie, *Primitive Society* (1920), 393.

9. *The Matriarchal Family System,* in *Nineteenth Century* (1896), 91–96.

and the Chukchi of northeastern Siberia seems to dispose of the hoary dogma that the clan is a truly archaic institution.[10] If, then, the basic importance of the local element is to be established, it must be demonstrated not only in association with the unilateral clan but with the bilateral family.

The very attempt to do this may seem fantastic; for how can anything claim equal rank with those fundamental blood ties upon which our very existence depends? Here, however, we must stress a point of the utmost importance, which has been recently expressed by Dr. Malinowski. Biological and sociological kinship are two distinct concepts. The one is based on instinctive response in accordance with biological utility; the other, however dependent for its origin on the former, is never wholly derived from it and may diverge from it very appreciably. As Malinowski insists, the maternal *instinct* ceases with the discharge of its biological functions; it becomes a *sociologically* creative force only when it has ripened into a specifically human "sentiment" in Shand's sense of the term. But what is it, I should ask, that fosters the sentiment unless it is the constant association during childhood,—prolonged in primitive communities by the generally extended period of lactation? Eliminate the element of contiguity, and the family as a *social* unit tends to disappear. Borgoras's graphic picture of Chukchi life introduces us to lone boys wandering away from home never to return. In what sense do they remain members of their families? Evidently only in a biological sense; sociologically the tie snaps when it fails to be reënforced by spatial proximity.

As for the bond between father and child, we have that whole range of usages which obscure biological paternity while in no way affecting the social or legal kinship. The case of the Bánaro, who live along the Potter's River in New Guinea, has been thoroughly elucidated by Dr. Thurnwald and may serve for purposes of illustration.[11] A Bánaro bride is not initiated into the mysteries of sex life by her husband, but by a friend of her husband's father and, subsequently, by her father-in-law. These activities take place in the so-called spirit hall of the village, and the men themselves are said to impersonate a spirit. As for the groom, he is not permitted access to his wife until after the birth of a child, which is designated as a "spirit's child" (*Geisterkind*) but is adopted by his mother's husband. Owing to the ceremonial laxity of sex relations during great tribal festivals, the husband cannot even be certain of his paternity in the case of subsequent issue. But, as our authority again and again assures us, this is a matter of complete indifference to the natives: "*Ob der Gatte der wirkliche Vater der Kinder ist, kommit bei diesem System nicht in Betracht.*" The concept of fatherhood is linked with that not of procreator but of educator, provider and protector. It is the husband's cohabitation with the mother—in the etymological no less than in the customary sense of the term—that stamps him sociologically as a parent and makes the children members of *his* clan. Kinship is not kinship in its own right, but as a derivative of a local factor. As Dr. Malinowski has put it, there seems to be a "tendency in the human species, on the part of the male to feel attached to the children born by a woman with whom he has mated, has been living permanently and has kept watch over during her pregnancy."[12]

Dr. Thurnwald's Papuan case is but a special sample of the wider category of adoption,—that legal fiction by which children who need not even be related may become, for all social purposes, as their adoptive parents' real offspring. Whatever may be the motive in different areas, which presumably varies considerably, the psychological concomitant is usually a sentimental relationship that approximates, if it does not attain, the natural emotions. The data from other areas seem to me to corroborate my personal impression among the Crow Indians, that there is a generic love of children—no matter whose—which merely requires to be particularized in a definite instance by constant association in order to develop into a full-fledged parental sentiment.

To sum up our argument. The traditional distinction established by Maine and Morgan retains its validity in so far as conceptually a union of neighbors is different from a union of kinsmen. It must even be conceded that the blood tie is frequently the overshadowing element in the governmental activities of primitive peoples. Yet, though it often dwarfs the territorial factor, it never succeeds in eliminating it. Nay, if we inquire into the bond of consanguinity itself, we find lurking in the background a spatial determinant of the sentiments underlying it. Abstractly separated by a chasm, the two types of union are in reality intertwined. The basic problem of the state is thus not that of explaining the somersault by which ancient peoples achieved the step from a government by personal relations to one by territorial contiguity only. The question is rather to show what processes strengthened the local tie which must be recognized as not less ancient than the rival principle.

10. R. H. Lowie, *Primitive Society* (1920), 150 *seq.* W. Schmidt, *Völker und Kulturen* (1924), 79 *seq.*

11. Thurnwald, *Die Gemeinde der Bánaro* (Stuttgart, 1921), pp. 21 *seq.*, 37 *f.*, 99 *seq.*

12. B. Malinowski, *Crime and Custom in Savage Society* (1926), 107.

# 2. *The Village Community*

BY SIR HENRY SUMNER MAINE

THE STUDENT of legal antiquities who has once convinced himself that the soil of the greatest part of Europe was formerly owned and tilled by proprietary groups, of substantially the same character and composition as those which are still found in the only parts of Asia which are open to sustained and careful observation, has his interest immediately drawn to what, in truth, is the great problem of legal history. This is the question of the process by which the primitive mode of enjoyment was converted into the agrarian system, out of which immediately grew the land-law prevailing in all Western Continental Europe before the first French Revolution, and from which is demontrably descended our own existing real-property law. For this newer system no name has come into general use except Feudalism, a word which has the defect of calling attention to one set only of its characteristic incidents. We cannot reasonably doubt that one partial explanation of its origin is, so far as it goes, correct. It arose from or was greatly influenced by the Benefices, grants of Roman provincial land by the chieftains of the tribes which overran the Roman Empire; such grants being conferred on their associates upon certain conditions, of which the commonest was military service. There is also tolerably universal agreement that somewhere in Roman law (though *where*, all are not agreed) are to be found the rules which determined the nature of these beneficiary holdings. This may be called the theory of the official origin of feudalism, the enjoyment of land being coupled with the discharge of certain definite duties; and there are some who complete the theory by asserting that among the Teutonic races, at all events, there was an ineradicable tendency in all offices to become hereditary, and that thus the Benefices, which at first were held for life, became at last descendible from father to son.

There is no question, as I said, that this account is more than probable, and that the Benefices either began or hastened the changes which led ultimately to feudalism. Yet I think that nobody whose mind has dwelt on the explanation, has brought himself to regard it as complete. It does not tell us how the Benefices came to have so extraordinary a historical fortune. It does not account for the early, if partial, feudalisation of countries like Germany and England, where the cultivated soil was in the hands of free and fully organised communities, and was not, like the land of Italy or Gaul, at the disposal of a conquering king—where the royal or national grants which resembled the Benefices were probably made out of waste land—and where the influence of Roman law was feebly felt or not at all.

The feudalisation of any one country in Europe must be conceived as a process including a long series of political, administrative, and judicial changes; and there is some difficulty in confining our discussion of it to changes in the condition of property which belong more properly to this department of study. But I think we may limit our consideration of the subject by looking at it in this way. If we begin with modern English real-property law, and, by the help of its records and of the statutes affecting it, trace its history backwards, we come upon a period at which the soil of England was occupied and tilled by separate proprietary societies. Each of these societies is, or bears the marks of having been, a compact and organically complete assemblage of men, occupying a definite area of land. Thus far it resembles the old cultivating communities, but it differs from them in being held together by a variety of subordinate relations to a feudal chief, single or corporate, the Lord. I will call the new group the Manorial group, and though my words must not be taken as strictly correct, I will say that a group of tenants, autocratically organised and governed, has succeeded a group of households of which the organisation and government were democratic. The new group, as known to our law, is often in a state of dissolution, but, where it is perfect, it consists of a number of persons holding land of the Lord by free tenures, and of a number of persons holding land of the Lord by tenures capable of being shown to have been, in their origin, servile—the authority of the Lord being exercised over both classes, although in different ways, through the agency of a peculiar tribunal, the Court Baron. The lands held by the first description of tenants are technically known as the Tene-

Reprinted from Sir Henry Sumner Maine, *Village Communities in the East and West* (New York: Henry Holt & Co., 1889), Lect. IV, pp. 131–71.

mental lands; those held by the second class constitute the Lord's Domain. Both kinds of land are essential to the completeness of the Manorial group. If there are not Tenemental lands to supply a certain minimum number of free tenants to attend the Court Baron, and, according to the legal theory, to sit with the lord as its judges, the Court Baron can no longer in strictness be held; if it be continued under such circumstances, as it often was in practice, it can only be upheld as a Customary Manorial Court, sitting for the assessment and receipt of customary dues from the tenants of the Domain. On the other hand, if there be no Domain, or if it be parted with, the authority of the Lord over the free tenants is no longer Manorial; it becomes a Seignory in gross, or mere Lordship.

Since much of the public waste land of our country is known to have passed by national or royal grant to individuals or corporations, who, in all probability, brought it extensively under cultivation from the first by servile labour, it cannot be supposed that each of the new Manorial groups takes the place of a Village group which at some time or other consisted of free allodial proprietors. Still, we may accept the belief of the best authorities that over a great part of England there has been a true succession of one group to the other. Comparing, then, the two, let us ask what are the specific changes which have taken place? The first, and far the most important of all, is that, in England as everywhere in Western Europe, the waste or common-land of the community has become the lord's waste. It is still ancillary to the Tenemental lands; the free tenants of the lord, whom we may provisionally take to represent the freemen of the village-community, retain all their ascertained rights of pasture and gathering firewood, and in some cases similar rights have been acquired by other classes; but, subject to all ascertained rights, the waste belongs, actually or potentially, to the lord's domain. The lord's "right of approvement," affirmed by the Statute of Merton, and extended and confirmed by subsequent statutes, permits him to enclose and appropriate so much of the waste as is not wanted to satisfy other existing rights; nor can it be doubted that he largely exercises this right, reclaiming part of the waste for himself by his personal dependents and adding it to whatever share may have belonged to him from the first in the cultivated land of the community, and colonising other portions of it with settlements of his villeins who are on their way to become copyholders. The legal theory has altogether departed from the primitive view; the waste is now the lord's waste; the commoners are for the most part assumed to have acquired their rights by sufferance of the lord, and there is a visible tendency in courts and text-writers to speak of the lord's rights, not only as superior to those of the commoners, but as being in fact of greater antiquity.

When we pass from the waste to the grass lands which were intermediate between the common land and the cultivated area, we find many varieties in the degree of authority acquired by the lord. The customs of manors differ greatly on the point. Sometimes, the lord encloses for his own benefit from Candlemas to Midsummer or Lammas, and the common right belongs during the rest of the year to a class of burgesses, or to the householders of a village, or to the persons inhabiting certain ancient tenements. Sometimes, the lord only regulates the inclosure, and determines the time of setting up and removing the fences. Sometimes, other persons enclose, and the lord has the grass when the several enjoyment comes to an end. Sometimes, his right of pasture extends to the baulks of turf which separate the common arable fields; and probably there is no manorial right which in later times has been more bitterly resented than this, since it is practically fatal to the cultivation of green crops in the arable soil.

Leaving the meadows and turning to the lands under regular tillage, we cannot doubt that the free holders of the Tenemental lands correspond in the main to the free heads of households composing the old village-community. The assumption has often been made, and it appears to be borne out by the facts which can be established as to the common fields still open or comparatively lately enclosed. The tenure of a certain number of these fields is freehold; they are parcelled out, or may be shown to have been in the last century parcelled out, among many different owners; they are nearly always distributed into three strips, and some of them are even at this hour cultivated according to methods of tillage which are stamped by their very rudeness as coming down from a remote antiquity. They appear to be the lands of a class which has never ceased to be free, and they are divided and cultivated exactly as the arable mark of a Teutonic township can be inferred by a large induction, to have been divided and tilled. But, on the other hand, many large tracts of intermixed land are still, or were till their recent enfranchisement, copyhold of particular manors, and some of them are held by the intermediate tenure, known as customary freehold, which is confined by the legal theory to lands which once formed part of the King's Domain. I have not been able to ascertain the proportion of common lands held by these base tenures to freehold lands of the same kind, but there is no doubt that much commonable or intermixed land is found, which is not freehold. Since the descent of copyhold and customary freehold tenures from the holdings of servile classes appears to be well established, the frequent occurrence of intermixed lands of this nature seems to bear out the inference suggested by Sir H. Ellis's enumeration of the conditions of men referred to in Domesday Book, that, during the long process of feudalism, some of the free villagers sank to the status, almost certainly not a uniform status, which was implied in villenage. (See also Mr. Freeman's remark, "Hist. Norm. Conq." i. 97.) But evidence, supplied from quarters so wide apart as British India and the English settlements in North America, leads me to think that, at a time when a system of customary tillage widely prevailed, assemblages of people planted on waste land would be likely to copy the system literally; and I conjecture that parts of the great wastes undoubtedly reclaimed by the exercise of the right afterwards called the lord's "right of approvement" were settled by servile colonies modelled on the ancient Teutonic township.

The bond which kept the Manorial group together was evidently the Manorial Court, presided over by the lord or his representative. Under the name of Manorial Court three courts are usually included, which legal theory keeps apart, the Court Leet, the Court Baron, and the Customary Court of the Manor. I think there cannot be reasonable doubt of the legitimate descent of all three from the assembly of the Township. Besides the wide criminal and civil jurisdiction which belonged to them, and which, though it has been partly abolished, has chiefly lost its importance through insensible decay, they long continued in the exercise of administrative or regulative powers which are scarcely distinguishable from legislation. Other vestiges of powers exerted by the collective body of free owners at a time when the conceptions of legislative and judicial authority had not yet been separated, remained in the functions of the Leet Jury; in the right asserted for the free tenants of sitting as Judges in the Court Baron; and in the election of various petty officers. It is true that, as regards one of these Courts, the legal theory of its character is to a certain extent inconsistent with the pedigree I have claimed for it. The lawyers have always contended that the Court Leet only existed through the King's grant, express or implied; and in pursuance of the same doctrine they have laid down that, whereas the lord might himself sit in the Court Baron, he must have a person of competent legal learning to represent him in the Court Leet. But this only proves that the Court Leet, which was entrusted with the examination of the Frankpledge, had more public importance than the other Manorial Courts, and was therefore more distinctly brought under the assumption which had geen gradually forming itself, that royal authority is the fountain of all justice. Even in the last extremity of decline, the Manorial Courts have not wholly ceased to be regarded as the tie which connects the common interests of a definite group of persons engaged in the cultivation of the soil. Marshall ("Rural Economy of Yorkshire," i. 27) mentions the remarkable fact that these Courts were sometimes kept up at the beginning of the century by the voluntary consent of the neighbourhood in certain districts where, from the disappearance of the servile tenures which had enabled the Customary Courts to be continued, the right to hold them had been forfeited. The manorial group still sufficiently cohered for it to be felt that some common authority was required to regulate such matters as the repair of minor roads, the cleansing of rivulets, the ascertainment of the sufficiency of ring-fences, the assessment of the damages of impounded cattle, the removal of nuisances, and the stocking of commons.

On the whole, the comparison of the Village group with the English group which I have called Manorial rather than Feudal, suggests the following general observations. Wherever that collective ownership of land which was a universal phenomenon in primitive societies has dissolved, or gone far to dissolve, into individual property, the individual rights thus formed have been but slightly affected by the process of feudalisation. If there are reasons for thinking that some free village societies fell during the process into the predial condition of villenage—whatever that condition may really have implied—a compensating process began at some unknown date, under which the base tenant made a steady approach to the level of the freeholder. Even rights which savoured of the collective stage of property were maintained comparatively intact, provided that they were ascertained: such as rights of pasture on the waste and rights of several or of common enjoyment (as the case might be) in the grass land. The encroachments of the lord were in proportion to the want of certainty in the rights of the community. Into the grass land he intruded more than into the arable land; into the waste much more than into either. The conclusion suggested to my mind is that, in succeeding to the legislative power of the old community, he was enabled to appropriate to himself such of its rights as were not immediately valuable, and which, in the event of their becoming valuable, required legislative adjustment to settle the mode of enjoying them. Let me add that the general truth of my description of the character of the change which somehow took place, is perhaps rendered antecedently more probable by the comparison of a mature, but non-feudal, body of jurisprudence, like the Roman law, with any deeply feudalised legal system. You will remember the class of enjoyable objects which the Roman lawyers call *res nullius, res publici usûs, res omnium* or *universorum;* these it reserves to the entire community, or confers on the first taker. But, under feudalised law, nearly all these objects which are capable of several enjoyment belong to the lord of the manor, or to the king. Even Prize of War, the most significant of the class, belongs theoretically to the sovereign in the first instance. By a very singular anomaly, which has had important practical results, Game is not strictly private property under English law; but the doctrine on the subject is traceable to the later influence of the Roman law.

There must be a considerable element of conjecture in any account which may be given of a series of changes which took place for the most part in remote antiquity, and which probably were far from uniform either in character or in rate of advance. It happens, however, that the vestiges of the earlier stages of the process of feudalisation are more discernible in Germany than elsewhere, both in documentary records and on the face of the land; owing in part no doubt to the comparatively feeble action of that superior and central authority which has obliterated or obscured so much in our own country. A whole school of writers, among whom Von Maurer has the first place, has employed itself in restoring and interpreting these traces of the Past. How did the Manor rise out of the Mark?—this is their way of stating the problem. What were the causes of indigenous growth which, independently of grants of land by royal or national authority, were leading to a suzerainty or superiority of one cultivating community over another, or of one family over the rest of the families composing the village-community? The great cause in the view of these writers was the exceeding quarrelsomeness of these little societies, and the consequent frequency of intertribal war. One community conquers another, and the spoil of war is generally the common mark or waste of the worsted community. Either the conquerors appropriate and colonise part of the waste so taken, or they take the whole domain and restore it to be held in dependence on the victor-society. The change from one of these systems to another occurred, you will remember, in Roman history, and constitutes an epoch in the development of the Roman Law of Property. The effect of the first system on the Teutonic communities was inequality of property; since the common land appropriated and occupied does not seem to have been equally divided, but a certain preference was given to the members of the successful community who had most effectually contributed to the victory. Under the second system, when its land was restored to the conquered society, the superiority over it which remained to the victor, bore the strongest analogy to a suzerainty or lordship. Such a suzerainty was not, however, exclusively created by success in war. Sometimes a community possessed of common land exceptionally extensive or exceptionally fertile would send colonies of families to parts of it. Each of these new communities would receive a new arable mark, but such of the land as remained unappropriated would still be the common land of all the townships. At the head of this sort of confederacy there would, however, be the original mother community from which the colonists proceeded, and there seems no doubt that in such a state of things she claimed a superiority or suzerainty over all the younger townships.

But, even if we had the fullest evidence of the growth of suzerainties in this inchoate shape, we should still have advanced a very little way in tracing the transmutation of the village system into the manorial system, if it were not for another phenomenon to which Landau has more particularly called attention. The Teutonic communities, though their organisation (if modern language must be employed) can only be described as democratic, appear nevertheless to have generally had an abiding tradition that in some one family, or in some families, the blood which ran in the veins of all the freemen was purest; probably because the direct descent of such family or families from a common ancestor was remembered or believed in. From the members of these families, the leader for a military expedition would as a rule be chosen; but as in this stage of thought the different varieties of power were not distinguished from one another, the power acquired by the chieftain would be a combination of political, military, and judicial power. The choice of the leader would in great emergencies be a true election, but on less serious occasions would tend to become an acquiesence in the direction of the eldest male agnate of the family which had the primacy of the township. Similarly, the power which had at first been more military than anything else, would in more peaceful times tend rather to assume a political and judicial form. The leader thus taken from the privileged family would have the largest share of the lands appropriated from conquered village-societies; and there is ground for supposing that he was sometimes rewarded by an exceptionally large share of the common land belonging to the society which he had headed. Everything in fact which disturbed the peaceful order of the village system led to the aggrandisement of the leading family and of its chief. Among the privileges which he obtained was one of which the importance did not show itself till much later. He became powerful enough in his own township to sever his own plot of land from the rest, and, if he thought fit, to enclose it; and thus to break up or enfeeble that system of common cultivation under rules of obligatory custom which depended mainly on the concurrence of all the villagers.

There were therefore, in the cultivating communities of the German and Scandinavian races, causes at work which were leading to inequality of property in land. There were causes at work which were leading to the establishment of superiorities or suzerainties of one township over another. There were causes at work which tended to place the benefits of an unequal proprietary system and the enjoyment of these suzerainties in the hands of particular families, and consequently of their chiefs for the time being. Here you have all the elements of the system we are compelled to call feudal. But the system in its ultimate development was the result of a double set of influences. One set, which I have been describing, were of primitive growth. Another showed themselves when powerful Teutonic monarchies began to be formed, and consisted in grants of national waste land or of the soil of conquered provinces. Doubtless some of the grantees were chiefs of families already risen to power under indigenous Teutonic conditions; but in any case a Beneficiary would be a chieftain of a peculiarly powerful class. The cultivators of his land would either be persons settled on it by himself, or they would be vanquished provincials who had no rights which he did not choose to recognise or concede. It is not, therefore, surprising that there should have been a completer constitution of feudalism in the countries which at the time of conquest were filled with Romanised populations. The mould would be Teutonic, but the materials would be unusually plastic, and here would more especially come into play the influence of Roman law, giving precision to relations which under purely Teutonic social conditions may have been in a high degree vague and indefinite. It is well known that this systematic feudalism reacted upon the more purely Teutonic societies and gave an impulse to changes which were elsewhere proceeding at a slower pace.

I have very briefly summarised the results of a very long and laborious enquiry, and only so far as is necessary for my immediate purpose. Merely remarking that I can see little or nothing in the conclusions of these eminent German writers which is out of harmony with the account given by English scholars of the parallel phenomena of change manifested in England before the Conquest, I proceed to ask, following the scheme of these Lectures, whether the experience of Englishmen in India throws any light or has any bearing upon the questions which have been occupying us? It is not too much to say that the phenomena observed in the East, and those established in the West by historical research, illustrate one another at every point. In India these dry bones live. Not only, as I have told you, is the Village-Community the basis of British administration in those provinces in which the art of government has to be practised with skill and caution, but a number of controversies turning on the mode of transition from the village system to what I have called the manorial system are as earnestly, and sometimes even as violently, debated by our countrymen in the East as are the great aspects of politics among ourselves. All Indian disputes take, I should explain, a historical or antiquarian shape. The assumption universally made is that the country must be governed in harmony with the established usages of the natives, and each administrative school has therefore to justify its opinions by showing that the principles to which it adheres are found in some sense or other to underlie the known customary law of India. The extravagance of partisanship which here shows itself in unqualified assertion of the universal applicability of general propositions has its Indian counterpart in unqualified assertion of the universal existence of particular customs. The Indian controversy is, however, a controversy about facts which, though they are more complex than the disputants suppose, are nevertheless much simpler than the material of English political controversy; and the results are therefore proportionately more instructive to the bystander who has entire sympathy with neither party.

Let us suppose a province annexed for the first time to the British Indian Empire. The first civil act of the new government is always to effect a settlement of the land revenue; that is, to determine the amount of that relatively large share of the produce of the soil, or of its value, which is demanded by the sovereign in all Oriental States, and out of which all the main expenses of government are defrayed. Among the many questions upon which a decision must be had, the one of most practical importance is, "Who shall be settled with?" —with whom shall the settlement be made? What persons, what bodies, what groups, shall be held responsible to the British Government for its land revenue? What practically has to be determined is the unit of society for agrarian purposes; and you find that, in determining it, you determine everything, and give its character finally to the entire political and social constitution of the province. You are at once compelled to confer on the selected class powers co-extensive with its duties to the sovereign. Not that the assumption is ever made that new proprietary powers are conferred on it, but what are supposed to be its rights in relation to all other classes are defined; and in the vague and floating order of primitive societies, the mere definition of a right immensely increases its strength. As a matter of fact, it is found that all agrarian rights, whether superior or subordinate to those of the person held responsible to Government, have a steady tendency to decay. I will not ask you to remember the technical names of the various classes of persons "settled with" in different parts of India—Zemindars, Talukdars, Lumberdars—names which doubtless sound uncouth, and which, in fact, have not an identical meaning throughout the country—but I dwell on the fact that the various interests in the soil which these names symbolise are seen to grow at the expense of all others. Do you, on entering on the settlement of a new province, find that a peasant proprietary has been displaced by an oligarchy of vigorous usurpers, and do you think it expedient to take the government dues from the once oppressed yeomen? The result is the immediate decline, and consequently bitter discontent, of the class above them, who find themselves sinking to the footing of mere annuitants on the land. Such was the land settlement of Oudh, which was shattered to pieces by the Sepoy mutiny of 1857, and which greatly affected its course. Do you, reversing this policy, arrange that the superior holder shall be answerable to Government? You find that you have created a landed aristocracy which has no parallel in wealth or power except the proprietors of English soil. Of this nature is the more modern settlement of the province of Oudh, only recently consummated; and such will ultimately be the position of the Talukdars, or Barons, among whom its soil has been divided. Do you adopt a policy different from either of those which I have indicated and make your arrangements with the representative of the village-community? You find that you have arrested a process of change which was steadily proceeding. You have given to this peculiar proprietary group a vitality which it was losing, and a stiffness to the relations of the various classes composing it which they never had before.

It would be a mere conceit to try to establish any close analogy between the Teutonic Kings and the British government of India. Yet, so much as this is true and instructive. The only owner of the soil of India with whom the English Government has any relations, is, in its eyes, a mere functionary. It chooses him where it pleases, and extracts from him services, chiefly pecuniary, but to a certain small extent personal. It is found, however, that when an official appointed by a powerful government acts upon the loose constitution of a primitive society he crushes down all other classes and exalts that to which he himself belongs. But for recent legislation this process would have gone to any length in India, and would have assuredly affected many other provinces than those which were its immediate theatre. It may, at least, be said that by observing it we gain a clearer conception of the effect of beneficiary gifts on the general tenure of land, and that we better understand the enormous power acquired by the chieftains who rendered immediate services to the Teutonic kings.

The English in India appear to have started with the assumption of the Mahometans that the sovereign might lawfully select anybody he pleased as the collector of his revenue; but they soon accepted the principle that the class to be "settled with" was the class best entitled to be regarded as having rights of property in the soil. At a later date they discovered that, even when this class was determined, they had to decide what it was that proprietary rights over Indian land implied, and what powers they carried with them. No questions fuller of inherent difficulties were ever proposed for solution. As regards the first of them, the functionaries administering India might, with some eminent exceptions, but still not unfairly, be distributed into two great schools—the partisans of the theory that the soil belongs to the peasantry either as individuals or as organised in groups; and the partisans of the theory that ownership of the soil ought to be, and but for British influence would be, everywhere in India vested in some sort of native aristocracy. As regards the second question, the Indian officials are much more exactly divided into those who contend that the highest right of property acknowledged to exist over the soil carries with it the same powers which attach to an English owner in fee-simple of the present day, and into those who are of opinion that, if these powers are to square with native idea and custom, they must be more or less limited and controlled. The controversies on these two points are the most vehemently debated of Indian disputes; and none ever presented greater difficulties to the person who tries to form an opinion on their merits, not from his own knowledge but upon the evidence supplied to him by others. He finds men of the utmost experience, of trained power of observation, and of the most unquestionable good faith, stating precisely opposite conclusions with precisely equal positiveness. But if he avail himself of the advantage given him by the parallel facts of European tenure, he will, perhaps, venture to have an opinion, and to think that in these, as in many other fierce disputes, both sides are right and both sides are wrong.

There is no doubt that the first point at issue was much obscured, and attention diverted to irrelevant matter, by the unlucky experiment tried at the end of the last century by Lord Cornwallis. A province, like Bengal Proper, where the village system had fallen to pieces of itself, was the proper field for the creation of a peasant proprietary; but Lord Cornwallis turned it into a country of great estates, and was compelled to take his landlords from the tax-gatherers of his worthless predecessors. The political valuelessness of the proprietary thus created, its failure to obtain any wholesome influence over the peasantry, and its oppression of all inferior holders, led not only to distrust of the economical principles implied in its establishment, but to a sort of reluctance to believe in the existence of any naturally privileged class in the provinces subsequently acquired and examined. The most distinguished public servants of that day have left much on record which implies an opinion that no ownership of Indian land was discoverable, except that of the village-communities, subject to the dominion of the State.

But in fact it appears that, of all the landmarks on the line of movement traced by German and English scholars from the Village group to the Manorial group, there is not one which may not be met with in India, saving always the extreme points at either end. I have not had described to me any village-community under the unmodified collective government of the heads of households, but there are those who think they find the vestiges of the original constitution in a sort of democratic spirit and habit of free criticism which prevail even when the government has passed to an hereditary officer. If any thoroughly authenticated example could be produced of a community exercising absolute liberty of choice in electing its Headman, it would point still more significantly to an unmodified original equality; but the preference alleged to be invariably shown to the members of particular families appears to show that these elections belong really to the phenomena of hereditary succession. It is not, however, disputed that villages are found in great numbers in which the government is lodged with a council, neither claiming to be nor regarded as being anything more than a representation of the entire cultivating body. The instances, however, in which the authority has passed to some particular family or families are extremely numerous. Sometimes the office of Headman belongs absolutely to the head of a particular family; sometimes it belongs to him primarily, but he may be set aside for incapacity or physical blemish; sometimes there is a power of choosing him limited to an election between the members of one or more privileged households. The powers which he enjoys—or which it perhaps should be said, he would enjoy under native conditions of society—are also very various. But the judicial power of mediating in disputes and of interpreting customs appears to be certainly vested in him, together with the duty of keeping order; and, independently of the functions which he discharges with the consent of his neighbours, the British Government often expressly confides to him a certain amount of regular jurisdiction and of regular authority in matters of police.

There is no question that many of the families whom the English have recognised as owners of villages were privileged families enjoying the primacy of the township; but the widest difference of opinion has prevailed as to the nature and origin of the rights claimed by certain families for their chiefs over whole tracts of country, embracing the domain of several village-communities. It has been strongly contended on one side that these great proprietors are nothing but the descendants of farmers of the revenue under Native Governments; on the other it is asserted that in some cases at all events they were Chieftains of Clans who were selected by preference to represent the Royal or Imperial native government in districts in which they had an hereditary influence. There appears to me reasonable evidence that this last theory is true of certain localities in India. Clan society is also in Europe the Celtic form of the family organisation of society; and, for myself, I have great difficulty in conceiving the origin of customary law otherwise than by assuming the former existence of larger groups, under patriarchal chieftains, which at a later date dissolved into the independent collections of families forming the cultivating communities of the Teutonic (including the Scandinavian) races and of the Hindoos.

If it be taken for granted that the English in India were bound to recognise rights of property somewhere, their selection of the persons in whom these rights should vest does not seem to have been as absurd as the adherents of one Indian school are in the habit of hinting, if not of asserting. Claims to some sort of superior right over land in fact existed which corresponded to every single stage through which the conception of proprietorship has passed in the Western world, excepting only the later stages. The variety of these claims was practically infinite, and not only did not diminish, but greatly increased, as native customs and ideas were more accurately examined. Even when the village-communities were allowed to be in some sense the proprietors of the land which they tilled, they proved on careful inspection not to be simple groups, but highly composite bodies, composed of several sections with conflicting and occasionally with irreconcilable claims. The English officials solved a problem of almost hopeless perplexity by registering all the owners of superior rights as landowners, their conception of ownership being roughly taken from their own country; but the fundamental question very soon revived under another form in the shape of the second issue disputed between the Indian administrative schools, which is, whether proprietorship in India is to be taken to be the same assemblage of powers which constitutes the modern English ownership of land in fee-simple.

It seems to me that the error of the school which asserts the existence of strong proprietary rights in India lies much less in merely making this assertion than in assuming the existence of a perfect analogy between rights of property as understood in India and as understood in this country. The presumption is strongly against the reality of any such correspondence. The rights of property are, in the eye of the jurist, a bundle of powers, capable of being mentally contemplated apart from one another and capable of being separately enjoyed. The historical enquirer can also, whenever there are materials for a history of the past, trace the gradual growth of the conception of absolute property in land. That conception appears to me, for reasons which I shall afterwards assign, to have grown out of the ownership of the lord in that portion of his domain which he cultivated by his immediate personal dependants, and therefore to be a late and gradually matured fruit of the feudalisation of Europe. A process closely resembling feudalisation was undoubtedly once at work in India; there are Indian phenomena answering to the phenomena of nascent absolute ownership in England and Europe; but then these Indian phenomena, instead of succeeding one another, are all found existing together at the present moment. The feudalisation of India, if so it may be called, was never in fact completed. The characteristic signs of its consummation are wanting. It may be doubted whether in any single instance the whole power of regulating the affairs of the village-community has passed to an hereditary official when the English entered the country; on the other hand, in the enormous majority of examples there are peculiarities of organisation which show conclusively that the village-group is either unmodified or has not yet nearly passed into the manorial group. Even, however, were we at liberty to believe that India has been completely feudalised, we should still be as far as possible from being entitled to assume that the highest Indian form of ownership corresponds to the absolute ownership of the English holder in fee-simple. It has been said that many persons talk and write as if all the Englishmen who lived between the Norman Conquest and the Reformation lived at exactly the same time; but this Indian assumption implies that there has been no change in our conception of landed property between the epoch at which England became completely feudal and the epoch (let us say) at which the Corn-laws were repealed. Yet during all these centuries England has been legislatively and to a great extent judicially centralised, and has been acted on by economical influences of very great uniformity. India, from the earliest ages till the British entered it, was under the dominion of comparatively powerful kings, who swept away the produce of the labour of the village-communities and carried off the young men to serve in their wars, but did not otherwise meddle with the cultivating societies. This was doubtless the great cause of their irregular development. Intertribal wars soon gave way to the wars of great kings leading mercenary armies, but these monarchs, with few and doubtful exceptions, neither legislated nor centralised. The village-communities were left to modify themselves separately in their own way.

This subject is one of much practical importance, and I propose to treat of the more difficult problems which it raises in the next Lecture; at present I will content myself with repeating that there seems to me the heaviest presumption against the existence in any part of India of a form of ownership conferring the exact rights on the proprietor which are given by the present English ownership in fee-simple. There are now, however, a vast number of vested rights in the country, fully recognised by the English Government, which assume the identity of Indian and English proprietorship, and neither justice nor policy permits them to be disturbed. Moreover it is abstractedly possible that further observation of particular localities by accurate observers may, so far as regards those localities, rebut the presumption of which I have spoken, provided that the enquirer be acquainted with the parallel phenomena which belong to European legal history, and provided that he possess the faculty, not very common among us, of distinguishing the rudimentary stages of legal thought from its maturity. The way in which, among the unlettered members of a primitive society, law and morality run into one another ought especially to be studied. The subordinate holder who in India states that the superior holder has the power to do a certain act, but that he ought not to do it, does not make an admission; he raises a question of the utmost difficulty.

It has been usual to speak of the feudalisation of Western Europe as if it had been an unmixed evil, and there is but too much reason to believe that it was accompanied in its course by a great amount of human suffering. But there are some facts of Indian experience which may lead us to think that the advantage of some of the economical and juridical results which it produced has been underrated. If the process indeed had really consisted, as some of the enthusiasts for its repetition in India appear to suppose that it did, merely in the superposition of the lord over the free owners of land, with power to demand such services or dues as he pleased and to vary his demands at pleasure, very little indeed could be said for it. But this picture of it is certainly untrue of our own country. We are not at liberty to assume that the obligations incurred by the free owner of land who *commended* himself to a lord were other than, within certain limits, fixed and definite services; and the one distinguishing characteristic which the English feudists discover in that free Socage tenure for which the English villagers most probably exchanged their allodial ownership is certainty, regularity and permanence of service. The great novelties which the transition from one form of property to another produced were, the new authority over the waste which the lord acquired (and which was connected with the transfer to him of the half judicial, half legislative, powers of the collective community) and the emancipation of the lord within his own domains from the fetters of obligatory agricultural custom. Now Europe was then full of great wastes, and the urgent business in hand was to reclaim them. Large forests were to be felled, and wide tracts of untilled land had to be brought under cultivation. In England, inexorably confined within natural boundaries, there pressed with increasing force the necessity for adopting the methods of agriculture which were fitted to augment the total supply of food for a growing population. But for this work society organised in village-communities is but little adapted. The Indian administrators who regard the cultivating groups with most favour, contend that they secure a large amount of comfort and happiness for the families included within them, that their industry is generally, and that their skill is occasionally, meritorious. But their admirers certainly do not claim for them that they readily adopt new crops and new modes of tillage, and it is often admitted that they are grudging and improvident owners of their waste-land. The British Government, as I before stated, has applied a remedy to this last defect by acting on the right to curtail excessive wastes which it inherited from its predecessors; and of late years it has done its utmost to extend and improve the cultivation of one great staple, Cotton—amid difficulties which seem to be very imperfectly understood by those who suppose that in order to obtain the sowing of a new crop, or the sowing of an old crop in a new way, from a peasant in bondage to hereditary custom, it is enough to prove to him that it is very likely to be profitable. There is Indian evidence that the forms of property imitated from modern English examples have a value of their own, when reclamation has to be conducted on a large scale, or novelties in agriculture have to be introduced. The Zemindars of Lower Bengal, the landed proprietary established by Lord Cornwallis, have the worst reputation as landlords, and appear to have frequently deserved it; but the grants of land originally made to them included great uncultivated tracts, and at the time when their power over subordinate holders was least limited they brought large areas of waste-land under tillage by the colonies of peasants which they planted there. The proprietorship conferred on them has also much to do with the introduction into Lower Bengal, nearly alone among Indian provinces, of new and vast agricultural industries, which, if they had been placed under timely regulation (which unfortunately they were not) would have added as much to the comfort of the people as they have added to the wealth of the country.

It appears therefore to me to be highly probable that the autocratically governed manorial group is better suited than the village group for bringing under cultivation a country in which waste-lands are extensive. So also does it seem to me likely to have been at all times more tolerant of agricultural novelties. It is a serious error to suppose that the non-feudal forms of property which characterised the cultivating communities had any real resemblance to the absolute property of our own day. The land was free only in the sense of being free from feudal services, but it was enslaved to custom. An intricate net of usage bound down the allodial owner, as it now binds the Indian peasant, to a fixed routine of cultivation. It can hardly be said that in England or Germany these usages had ceased to exercise a deadening influence even within living memory, since very recent writers in both countries complain of the bad agriculture, perpetuated by custom in the open common fields. The famous movement against Inclosures under the Tudor reigns was certainly in part provoked by inclosures of plots in the three common fields made with the intention of breaking the custom and extending the systematic cultivation of grasses; and it is curious to find the witnesses examined before the Select Committee of 1844 using precisely the same language which was employed by the writers who in the sixteenth century took the unpopular side, and declaring that the value and produce of the intermixed lands might be very greatly increased if the owner, instead of having one plot in each field, had three plots thrown together in one field and dealt with them as he pleased. As I said before, it seems to me a plausible conjecture that our absolute form of property is really descended from the proprietorship of the lord in the domain which—besides planting it with the settlements of "unfree" families—he tilled, when it was close to his castle or manor-house, by his own dependants under his own eye. He was free from the agricultural customs which shackled those below him, and the services exacted from above were not of a kind to affect his management of the land which he kept in his hands. The English settlers on the New England coast did not, as I shall point out, at first adopt this form of property, but they did so very shortly, and we unquestionably owe to it such an achievement as the cultivation of the soil of North America.

If, however, a society organised in groups on the primitive model is ineffective for Production, so also if left to develop itself solely under primitive influences it fails to secure any considerable improvement in Distribution. Although it is hardly possible to avoid speaking of the Western village groups as in one stage democratically governed, they were really oligarchies, as the Eastern communities always tend to become. These little societies had doubtless anciently a power of absorption, when men were of more value than land. But this they lose in time. There is plenty of evidence that, when Western Europe was undergoing feudalisation, it was full of enthralled classes; and I imagine that the authority acquired by the feudal chief over the waste was much more of an advantage than the contrary to these classes, whom he planted largely there in colonies which have probably been sometimes mistaken for assemblages of originally free villagers. The status of the slave is always deplorable; the status of the predial slave is often worse than that of the personal or household slave; but the lowest depth of miserable subjection is reached when the person enthralled to the land is at the mercy of peasants, whether they exercise their powers singly or in communities.

Whether the Indian village-communities had wholly lost their capacity for the absorption of strangers when the British dominion began, is a point on which I have heard several contradictory opinions; but it is beyond doubt that the influence of the British Government, which in this respect is nothing more than the ordinary influence of settled authority, has tended steadily to turn the communities into close corporations. The definition of rights which it has effected through its various judicial agencies—the process of law by which it punishes violations of right—above all the money value which it has given to all rights by the security which it has established from one end of India to another—have helped to make the classes in possession of vested rights cling to them with daily increasing tenacity. To a certain small extent this indirect and unintended process of shutting the door to the acquisition of new communal rights has been counteracted by a rough rule introduced by the English, and lately engrafted on the written law, under which the cultivator of the soil who has been in possession of it for a period of years is in some parts of India protected against a few of the extreme powers which attach to ownership of the modern English type. But the rule is now in some discredit, and the sphere of its operation has of late been much curtailed. And my own opinion (which I shall state more at length in the next Lecture) is, that even if the utmost effect were given to it, it would not make up for some of the inequalities of distribution between classes actually included in the village group which have made their way into it through the influence of economical ideas originating in the West. On the whole the conclusion which I have arrived at concerning the village-communities is that, during the primitive struggle for existence they were expansive and elastic bodies, and these properties may be perpetuated in them for any time by bad government. But tolerably good government takes away their absorptive power by its indirect effects, and can only restore it by direct interposition.

It was part of my design to append to these Lectures an epitome of the work in which Professor Nasse has attempted to connect the actual condition of landed property in much of England at the end of the last century as shown in the various publications of Marshall, with the early English forms of tenure and cultivation as known to us through the labours of English and German scholars. But I have abandoned my intention on learning that Nasse's book is likely to be made generally accessible through an English translation. The undertaking is one which presents considerable difficulties. Nasse complains of the unusual scarcity of English records bearing on tenure and agricultural custom, but in this place we may note another class of difficulties having its source in those abundant technicalities of English real-property law which are so hard to read by anybody except the professional lawyer; and yet another in the historical theory of their land law which almost all English lawyers have adopted, and which colours all English treatises and all the decisions of English Courts—a theory which, it is not unjust to say, practically regards the manorial system as having no ascertainable antecedents, and all rights *primâ facie* inconsistent with it as having established themselves through prescription and by the sufferance of the lord. I may be allowed to say that the book in which Nasse has knotted together the two ends of the historical thread is a very extraordinary one to be written by a foreigner. Much of it deals with matter which can only be discussed appropriately in other departments of study; but I may notice in this place one set of causes, of a purely juridical nature, which, besides those assigned by Nasse, tended in later times to throw small or yeoman properties into the hands of large landowners. The popular opinion much exaggerates the extent to which this accumulation of landed properties had proceeded before the great inclosures of the last century, but still it had gone some length, and undoubtedly one cause was the influence, not at first strongly felt, of the Statute of Devises. Each landed proprietor ultimately acquired the power—within limits certainly, but very wide ones—to create a private law for his own estate. The efforts of English judges to introduce order into this chaos made it rather worse; for the expedient which they adopted for the purpose was to give a forced technical meaning to the popular language of testators. One large and complex branch of English law is still concerned with the rules for construing in a technical sense the loose popular expressions found in wills. Every estate, willed away by a testator technically unlearned, was in danger of being burdened with a mass of conflicting rights and interests, for the most part never contemplated by the testator himself. There was only one way of insuring oneself against this consequence, and that was the employment of an expert to make the will; but there is reason to believe that the wholesale employment of legal experts which is now one of the singularities of this country is of comparatively modern date, since it is one of the traditions of the English Bar, derived from the last generation of lawyers, that among the great sources of litigation were at one time wills made by village schoolmasters. Estates thus burdened could only be held by very rich men; as they alone could provide and insure against the technical traps which abounded in the private law under which the land was held, or could render them innocuous by continued possession ending in a prescriptive title. It is impossible not to see that the practice of unshackled devise tended to bring small estates into the market as unprofitable to the holders through the complication of interests in them, and at the same time tended to make them purchaseable by rich men only.

The simple truth is that, if a system of small or peasant holdings is to continue, the power of testators must be severely restrained in order to produce simplicity in the law of the estate. It does not at all follow that the restrictions must be those of the Code Napoleon; but restrictions there must be, and I venture to think that a not unsatisfactory solution of the problem is to be found in the law by which the Indian Government has recently sought to control the power of will-making, which the early English judges either introduced into India or invested with proportions which had never belonged to it before.

# 3. *The Urban Community*

BY MAX WEBER

## *Economic Character of the City: Market Settlement*

THE MANY definitions of the city have only one element in common: namely that the city consists simply of a collection of one or more separate dwellings but is a relatively closed settlement. Customarily, though not exclusively, in cities the houses are built closely to each other, often, today, wall to wall. This massing of elements interpenetrates the everyday concept of the "city" which is thought of quantitatively as a large locality. In itself this is not imprecise for the city often represents a locality and dense settlement of dwellings

Reprinted from Max Weber, *The City,* trans. and ed. Don Martindale and Gertrud Neuwirth (Glencoe, Ill.: The Free Press, 1958), chap. i, pp. 65–75, with the permission of The Free Press.

forming a colony so extensive that personal reciprocal acquaintance of the inhabitants is lacking. However, if interpreted in this way only very large localities could qualify as cities; moreover it would be ambiguous, for various cultural factors determine the size at which "impersonality" tends to appear. Precisely this impersonality was absent in many historical localities possessing the legal character of cities. Even in contemporary Russia there are villages comprising many thousands of inhabitants which are, thus, larger than many old "cities" (for example, in the Polish colonial area of the German East) which had only a few hundred inhabitants. Both in terms of what it would include and what it would exclude size alone can hardly be sufficient to define the city.

Economically defined, the city is a settlement the inhabitants of which live primarily off trade and commerce rather than agriculture. However, it is not altogether proper to call all localities "cities" which are dominated by trade and commerce. This would include in the concept "city" colonies made up of family members and maintaining a single, practically hereditary trade establishment such as the "trade villages" of Asia and Russia. It is necessary to add a certain "versatility" of practiced trades to the characteristics of the city. However, this in itself does not appear suitable as the single distinguishing characteristic of the city either.

Economic versatility can be established in at least two ways: by the presence of a feudal estate or a market. The economic and political needs of a feudal or princely estate can encourage specialization in trade products in providing a demand for which work is performed and goods are bartered. However, even though the *oikos* of a lord or prince is as large as a city, a colony of artisans and small merchants bound to villein services is not customarily called a "city" even though historically a large proportion of important "cities" originated in such settlements. In cities of such origin the products for a prince's court often remained a highly important, even chief, source of income for the settlers.

The other method of establishing economic versatility is more generally important for the "city"; this is the existence in the place of settlement of a regular rather than an occasional exchange of goods. The market becomes an essential component in the livelihood of the settlers. To be sure, not every "market" converted the locality in which it was found into a city. The periodic fairs and yearly foreign-trade markets at which traveling merchants met at fixed times to sell their goods in wholesale or retail lots to each other or to consumers often occurred in places which we would call "villages."

Thus, we wish to speak of a "city" only in cases where the local inhabitants satisfy an economically substantial part of their daily wants in the local market, and to an essential extent by products which the local population and that of the immediate hinterland produced for sale in the market or acquired in other ways. In the meaning employed here the "city" is a market place. The local market forms the economic center of the colony in which, due to the specialization in economic products, both the non-urban population and urbanites satisfy their wants for articles of trade and commerce. Wherever it appeared as a configuration different from the country it was normal for the city to be both a lordly or princely residence as well as a market place. It simultaneously possessed centers of both kinds, *oikos* and market and frequently in addition to the regular market it also served as periodic foreign markets of traveling merchants. In the meaning of the word here, the city is a "market settlement."

Often the existence of a market rests upon the concessions and guarantees of protection by a lord or prince. They were often interested in such things as a regular supply of foreign commercial articles and trade products, in tolls, in moneys for escorts and other protection fees, in market tariffs and taxes from law suits. However, the lord or prince might also hope to profit from the local settlement of tradesmen and merchants capable of paying taxes and, as soon as the market settlement arose around the market, from land rents arising therefrom. Such opportunities were of especial importance to the lord or prince since they represented chances for monetary revenues and the increase in his treasure of precious metal.

However, the city could lack any attachment, physical or otherwise, to a lordly or princely residence. This was the case when it originated as a pure market settlement at a suitable intersection point (*Umschlageplatz*) where the means of transportation were changed by virtue of concession to nonresident lords or princes or usurpation by the interested parties themselves. This could assume the form of concessions to entrepreneurs—permitting them to lay out a market and recruit settlers for it. Such capitalistic establishment of cities was especially frequent in medieval frontier areas, particularly in East, North, and Central Europe. Historically, though not as a rule, the practice has appeared throughout the world.

Without any attachment to the court of a prince or without princely concessions, the city could arise through the association of foreign invaders, naval warriors, or commercial settlers or, finally, native parties interested in the carrying trade. This occurred frequently in the early Middle Ages. The resultant city could be a pure market place. However, it is more usual to find large princely or patrimonial households and a market conjoined. In this case the eminent household as one contact point of the city could satisfy its wants either primarily by means of a natural economy (that is by villein service or natural service or taxes placed upon the artisans and merchants dependent on it) or it could supply itself more or less secondarily by barter in the local market as that market's most important buyer. The more pronounced the latter relation the more distinct the market foundation of the city looms and the city ceases by degrees to be a mere appendaged market settlement alongside the *oikos*. Despite attachment to the large household it then became a market city. As a rule the quantitative expansion of the original princely city and its economic importance go hand in hand with an increase in the satisfaction of wants in the market by the princely household and other large urban households attached to that of the prince as courts of vassals or major officials.

## *Types of Consumer and Producer City*

Similar to the city of the prince, the inhabitants of which are economically dependent upon the purchasing power of noble households are cities in which the purchasing power of other larger consumers, such as rentiers, determines the economic opportunities of resident tradesmen and merchants. In terms of the kind and source of their incomes such larger consumers may be of quite varied types. They may be officials who spend their legal and illegal income in the city or lords or other political power holders who spend their non-urban land rents or politically determined incomes there. In either of these cases the city closely approximates the princely city for it depends upon patrimonial and political incomes which supply the purchasing power of large consumers. Peking was a city of officials; Moscow, before suspension of serfdom, was a land-rent city.

Different in principle are the superficially similar cities in which urban land-rents are determined by traffic monopolies of landed property. Such cities originate in the trade and commerce consolidated in the hands of an urban aristocracy. This type of development has always been widespread: it appeared in Antiquity; in the Near East until the Byzantine Empire; and in the Middle Ages. The city that emerges is not economically of a rentier type but is, rather, a merchant or trade city the rents of which represent a tribute of acquisitors to the owners of houses. The conceptual differentiation of this case from the one in which rents are not determined by tributary obligations to monopolists but by non-urban sources, should not obscure the interrelation in the past of both forms. The large consumers can be rentiers spending their business incomes (today mainly interest on bonds, dividends or shares) in the city. Whereupon purchasing power rests on capitalistically conditioned monetary rentier sources as in the city of Arnheim. Or purchasing power can depend upon state pensions or other state rents as appears in a "pensionopolis" like Wiesbaden. In all similar cases one may describe the urban form as a consumer city, for the presence in residence of large consumers of special economic character is of decisive economic importance for the local tradesmen and merchants.

A contrasting form is presented by the producer city. The increase in population and purchasing power in the city may be due, as for example in Essen or Bochum, to the location there of factories, manufactures, or home-work industries supplying outside territories—thus representing the modern type. Or, again, the crafts and trades of the locality may ship their goods away as in cities of Asiatic, Ancient, and Medieval types. In either case the consumers for the local market are made up of large consumers if they are residents and/or entrepreneurs, workers and craftsmen who form the great mass, and merchants and benefactors of land-rent supported indirectly by the workers and craftsmen.

The trade city and merchant city are confronted by the consumer city in which the purchasing power of its larger consumers rests on the retail for profit of foreign products on the local market (for example, the woolen drapers in the Middle Ages), the foreign sale for profit of local products or goods obtained by native producers (for example, the herring of the Hansa) or the purchase of foreign products and their sale with or without storage at the place to the outside (intermediate commercial cities). Very frequently a combination of all these economic activities occurred: the *commenda* and *societas maris* implied that a *tractator* (travelling merchant) journied to Levantine markets with products purchased with capital entrusted to him by resident capitalists. Often the *tractator* traveled entirely in ballast. He sold these products in the East and with the proceeds he purchased oriental articles brought back for sale in the local market. The profits of the undertaking were then divided between *tractator* and capitalist according to prearranged formulas.

The purchasing power and tax ability of the commercial city rested on the local economic establishment as was also the case for the producers' city in contrast to the consumers' city. The economic opportunities of the shipping and transport trade and of numerous secondary wholesale and retail activities were at the disposal of the merchants. However the economic activity of these establishments was not entirely executed for the local retail trade but in substantial measure for external trade. In principle, this state of affairs was similar to that of the modern city, which is the location of national and international financiers or large banks (London, Paris, Berlin) or of joint stock companies or cartels (Dusseldorf). It follows that today more than ever a predominant part of the earnings of firms flow to localities other than the place of earning. Moreover, a growing part of business proceeds are not consumed by their rightful receivers at the metropolitan location of the business but in suburban villas, rural resorts or international hotels. Parallel with these developments "city-towns" or city-districts consisting almost exclusively of business establishments are arising.

There is no intention here of advancing the further casuistic distinctions required by a purely economic theory of the city. Moreover, it hardly needs to be mentioned that actual cities nearly always represent mixed types. Thus, if cities are to be economically classified at all, it must be in terms of their prevailing economic component.

## *Relation of the City to Agriculture*

The relation of the city to agriculture has not been clear cut. There were and are "semi-rural cities" (*Ackerburgerstaedte*) localities which while serving as places of market traffic and centers of typically urban trade, are sharply separated from the average city by the presence of a broad stratum of resident burghers satisfying a large part of their food needs through cultivation and even producing food for sale. Normally the larger the city the less the opportunity for urban residents to dispose of acreage in relation to their food needs at the same time without controlling a self-sufficient pasture and wood lot in the manner of the village. Cologne, the largest German city in the Middle Ages, almost completely lacked the *Allmende* (commons) from the beginning though the commons was not absent from any normal village of the time. Other German and foreign medieval cities at least placed considerable pastures and woods at the disposal of their burghers.

The presence of large acreages accessible to the urbanite is found more frequently as one turns attention to the south or back toward antiquity. While today we justly regard the typical "urbanite" as a man who does not supply his own food need on his own land, originally the contrary was the case for the majority of typical ancient cities. In contrast to the medieval situation, the ancient urbanite was quite legitimately characterized by the fact that a *kleros, fundus* (In Israel: *chelek*) which he called his own, was a parcel of land which fed him. The full urbanite of antiquity was a semi-peasant.

In the Medieval period, as in Antiquity, agricultural property was retained in the hands of merchant strata. This was more frequently the case in the south than in the north of Europe. In both medieval and ancient city states agricultural properties, occasionally of quite exorbitant size, were found widely scattered, either being politically dominated by municipal authorities of powerful cities or in the possession of eminent individual citizen landlords. Examples are supplied by the Cheronesic domination of the Miltiades or the political or lordly estates of medieval aristocratic families, such as the Genoese Grimaldi, in the provinces or overseas.

As a general rule inter-local estates and the sovereign rights of individual citizens were not the objects of an urban economic policy. However, mixed conditions at times arose such that according to the circumstances estates were guaranteed to individuals by the city. In the nature of the case this only occurred when the individuals whose estates were guaranteed by the city belonged to the most powerful patricians. In such cases the estate was acquired and maintained through indirect help of civic power which in turn might share in its economic and political usufruct. This was frequently the case in the past.

The relation of the city as agent of trade and commerce to the land as producer of food comprises one aspect of the "urban economy" and forms a special "economic stage" between the "household economy" on the one hand and the "national economy" on the other. When the city is visualized in this manner, however, politico-economic aspects are conceptually fused with pure economic aspects and conceived as forming one whole. The mere fact that merchants and tradesmen live crowded together carrying on a regular satisfaction of daily needs in the market does not exhaust the concept of the "city." Where only the satisfaction of agricultural needs occurs within closed settlements and where—what is not identical with it—agricultural production appears in relation to non-agricultural acquisition, and when the presence or absence of markets constitutes the difference, we speak of trade and commercial localities and of small market-towns, but not of cities. There were, thus, hidden non-economic dimensions in the phenomena brought under review in the previous sections. It is time to expand the concept of the "city" to include extra-economic factors.

## *The Politico-Administrative Concept of the City*

Beside possessing an accumulation of abodes the city also has an economic association with its own landed property and a budget of receipts and expenditure. Such an economic association may also appear in the village no matter how great the quantitative differences. Moreover, it was not peculiar to the city alone, at least in the past, that it was both an economic and a regulatory association. Trespass restrictions, pasture regulations, the prohibition of the export of wood and straw, and similar regulations are known to the village, constituting an economic policy of the association as such.

The cities of the past were differentiated only by the kinds of regulations which appeared. Only the objects of political economic regulation on behalf of the association and the range of characteristic measures embraced by them were peculiar. It goes without saying that measures of the "urban economic policy" took substantial account of the fact that under the transportation conditions of the time the majority of all inland cities were dependent upon the agricultural resources of the immediate hinterland. As shown by the grain policies of Athens and Rome this was true for maritime cities. In a majority, not all, of urban trades areas, opportunity was provided for the natural "play of the market." The urban market supplied the normal, not the sole, place for the exchange of products, especially food.

Account also must be taken of the fact that production for trade was predominantly in the form of artisan technology organized in specialized small establishments. Such production operated without or with little capital and with strictly limited numbers of journeymen who were trained in long apprenticeships. Such production was economically in the form of wage worker as price work for customers. Sale to the local retailers was largely a sale to customers.

The market conditions of the time were the kind that would naturally emerge, given the above facts. The so-called "urban economic policy" was basically characterized by its attempt to stabilize the conditions of the local urban economy by means of economic regulations in the interest of permanently and cheaply feeding the masses and standardizing the economic opportunities of tradesmen and merchants. However, as we shall see, economic regulation was not the sole object of the urban economic policy nor, when it historically appears, was it fully developed. It emerges only under the political regime of the guild. Finally it can not be proved to be simply a transitional stage in the development of all cities. In any case, the urban economic policy does not represent a universal stage in economic evolution.

On the basis of customer relations and specialized small establishments operating without capital, the local urban market with its exchange between agricultural and non-agricultural producers and resident merchants, represents a kind of economic counterpart to barter as against systematically divided performances in terms of work and taxes of a specialized dependent economy in connection with the *oikos,* having its basis in the accumulation and integration of work in the manner, without exchange occurring inside. Following out the parallel: the *regulation* (urban economic policy) of the exchange and production conditions in the city represent the counterpart to the *organization* (traditional and feudal-contractual) of activities united in the economy of the *oikos.*

The very fact that in drawing these distinctions we are led to use the concepts of an "urban economic area" and "urban area," and "urban authority," already indicates that the concept of the "city" can and must be examined in terms of a series of concepts other than the purely economic categories so far employed.

The additional concepts required for analysis of the city are political. This already appears in the fact that the urban economic policy itself may be the work of a prince to whom political dominion of the city with its inhabitants belongs. In this case when there is an urban economic policy it is determined *for* the inhabitants of the city not *by* them. However even when this is the case the city must still be considered to be a partially autonomous association, a "community" with special political and administrative arrangements.

The economic concept previously discussed must be entirely separated from the political-administrative concept of the city. Only in the latter sense may a special *area* belong to the city. A locale can be held to be a city in a political-administrative sense though it would not qualify as a city economically. In the Middle Ages there were areas legally defined as "cities" in which the inhabitants derived ninety percent or more of their livelihood from agriculture, representing a far larger fraction of their income than that of the inhabitants of many localities legally defined as "villages."

Naturally, the transition from such semi-rural cities to consumers', producers' or commercial cities is quite fluid. In those settlements which differ administratively from the village and are thus dealt with as cities only one thing, namely, the kind of regulations of land-owning, is customarily different from rural land-owning forms. Economically such cities are differentiated by a special kind of rent situation presented in urban real estate which consists in house ownership to which land ownership is accessory. The position of urban real estate is connected administratively with special taxation principles. It is bound even more closely to a further element decisive for the political-administrative concept of the city and standing entirely outside the purely economic analysis, namely, the fortress.

### *Fortress and Garrison*

It is very significant that the city in the past, in Antiquity and the Middle Ages, outside as well as within Europe, was also a special fortress or garrison. At present this property of the city has been entirely lost, but it was not universal even in the past. In Japan, for example, it was not the rule. Administratively one may, with Rathgen, doubt the existence of cities at all. In contrast to Japan, in China every city was surrounded with a gigantic ring of walls. However, it is also true that many economically rural localities which were not cities in the administrative sense, possessed walls at all times. In China such places were not the seat of state authorities.

In many Mediterranean areas such as Sicily a man living outside the urban walls as a rural worker and country resident is almost unknown. This is a product of century-long insecurity. By contrast in old Hellas the Spartan polis sparkled by the absence of walls, yet the property of being a "garrison-town" was met. Sparta despised walls for the very reason that it was a permanent open military camp.

Though there is still dispute as to how long Athens was without walls, like all Hellenic cities except Sparta it contained in the Acropolis a castle built on rock in the same manner as Ekbantama and Persepolis which were royal castles with surrounding settlements. The castle or wall belonged normally to Oriental as well as to ancient Mediterranean and ordinary medieval cities.

# *4. European Feudalism*

BY MARC BLOCH

THE ADJECTIVE *feodalis* (relating to the fief) and the French substantive *féodalité,* used in the restricted sense of a quality peculiar to a fief, date the first from the Middle Ages, the second probably from the sixteenth century. But it was not before the eighteenth century that the custom arose of using for the designation of a whole system of social organization either compound expressions like feudal regime, government or system or, a little later, abstract substantives such as *féodalité* or feudalism. German historians in general have adopted *Lehnwesen* from *Lehn,* the German equivalent of fief. The extension of the use of a word derived from a particular institution, the fief, which can scarcely be considered the central and only significant institution of feudalism, to characterize the social regime prevailing widely during the Middle Ages, and more particularly from the tenth to the thirteenth centuries, in the greater part of western and central Europe is mainly attributable to the influence of Montesquieu. Although Montesquieu considered the establishment in Europe of "feudal laws" a phenomenon *sui generis,* "an event occurring once in the world and destined perhaps never to occur again," modern sociologists and comparative historians have detected in other civilizations the existence of institutions analogous to those of the Middle Ages. Consequently the term feudalism has come to be applied to a mode of social organization that may recur in divers forms in differing periods and environments. Mediaeval European feudalism nevertheless remains the model of all feudal systems as well as the best known.

The origins of the European feudal regime have too frequently been discussed under the form of an ethnic dilemma: are they Roman or Germanic? As a matter of fact the social type that is called feudalism was born in Europe of conditions peculiar to the society from which it sprang. Since feudal society did not stamp itself upon a clean slate, but

---

Reprinted from Marc Bloch, "European Feudalism," in *Encyclopaedia of the Social Sciences* (New York: Macmillan Co., 1931), VI, 203–10, with the permission of the Macmillan Co.

evolved little by little through the slow adaptation and modification of older usages, it is not difficult to discover in it traces of earlier systems of organization. But these elements were borrowed from very diverse environments. The feudal vocabulary itself, which combines Roman elements—one of them, the term vassal, taken by the Romans from the Celts—with Germanic elements by its very medley represents the singularly mixed character of the society in which feudalism took its rise.

The most remarkable characteristic of the western world at the beginning of the Middle Ages was the fact that it had been constituted by the encounter and fusion of civilizations existing at very unequal stages of evolution. On the one hand, there was the Roman or Romano-Hellenic world, itself hardly a unit in its foundations. For under the apparent uniformity of the imperial façade many local usages persisted which imposed conditions of life at times quite dissimilar upon the various social groups. On the other hand, there was the still comparatively primitive civilization of the peoples of ancient Germany, who had invaded the Roman domains and carved kingdoms out of it.

The bankruptcy of the state represents the most potent fact during this period. Whatever care the kingdoms of the barbarians may have taken to turn to their profit the formidable administrative system of ancient Rome—already, moreover, far advanced in decay at the time of the great invasions—however remarkable an effort at rehabilitation the monarchy of the first Carolingians may have represented after a century of extreme disorder, the powerlessness of the central government to exercise an effective control over a territory much too extensive for the forces at its disposal betrayed itself more and more glaringly, and for a long period after the middle of the ninth century, in a manner truly irremediable. Undoubtedly the reenforcement accruing from the Germanic traditions was not in this regard entirely negligible; the conception of royalty as the appanage of a sacred family, which derived from the most primitive notions of ancient Germany, resulted in a dynastic perpetuity better established than any that the Roman Empire had ever known. The idea of the state—or, more accurately, the idea of royalty—never entirely vanished. Likewise the institutions codified by the Carolingians long continued, more or less deformed, to exercise an influence. Men, however, lost the habit of expecting protection from a too distant sovereign. They sought it elsewhere and supplanted their obedience to the more remote ruler by other ties of dependence. The state tax ceased to be collected and the administration of justice was parceled out among a crowd of local authorities that had little or no connection with a central organism.

Less apparent but not less grave was the disturbance among social groups founded but lately upon a kinship more or less remote and fictitious, such as clan or tribe. It is impossible to ascertain to what degree the tradition of the old clannish relations had been able to survive in Roman Gaul and Italy, although in Great Britain the history of the imperfectly Romanized Celtic lands at the beginning of the Middle Ages shows them still very strong. On the other hand, it cannot be doubted that this kind of social group was of great importance among the German peoples during the period immediately preceding that of the invasions. But the great turmoil of the conquest, together, no doubt, with certain tendencies from within, weakened these ties. Not that kinship relations ceased during the entire Middle Ages to be a human bond of immense strength. The numerous family feuds which jeopardized the active and passive solidarity of groups in all grades of the social hierarchy bear witness to the strength of these ties. So do various institutions juridical and economic. But these ties came to apply only to a comparatively restricted group whose common descent was easy to establish, namely, the family in the strict sense of the word and no longer the clan or the tribe. This group, which made room for paternal as well as maternal kinship, was not very clearly defined and most of the obligations or modes of living imposed upon its members resulted rather from habits and feelings than from legally defined constraints. The ties of kinship continued to exist very powerfully in the feudal society but they took their place beside new ties after which they tended to pattern themselves and to which they were at times considered inferior.

The social environment in which the feudal relations developed was characterized by an economic system in which exchange although not entirely absent was comparatively rare and in which the not very abundant specie played but a restricted role. It has sometimes been said that at that time land was the only form of wealth. This statement needs explanation and qualification. It cannot be denied that the paucity of commercial relations caused the very existence of every man to depend narrowly upon his possibility of disposing in some way of the resources furnished by a portion of the soil placed under his control. But an important fraction of the population drew its revenue from the land only indirectly under the form of personal service in money or in kind for the use of the land. Moreover, the possession of superior rights to the land was for the possessor in many respects but a means of exercising an effective power of command over the men to whom he conceded or permitted the direct enjoyment of the fields. One of the essential characteristics of feudalism is that prestige and social worth sprang less from the free disposal of property than from the free disposal of human forces. But the difficulty of commercial exchange had a considerable effect upon the structure of society. The absence of an easy flow of sales and purchases such as exists in present day societies prevented the formation of agricultural or industrial salaried classes and of any body of functionaries remunerated periodically in money.

In the absence then of a strong state, of blood ties capable of dominating the whole life and of an economic system founded upon money payments there grew up in Carolingian and post-Carolingian society relations of man to man of a peculiar type. The superior individual granted his protection and divers material advantages that assured a subsistence to the dependent directly or indirectly; the inferior pledged various prestations or various services and was under a general obligation to render aid. These relations were not always freely assumed nor did they imply a universally satisfactory equilibrium between the two parties. Built upon authority, the feudal regime never ceased to contain a great number of constraints, violences and abuses. However, this idea of the personal bond, hierarchic and synallagmatic in character, dominated European feudalism.

Societies before the rise of feudalism already contained examples of relations of this sort. These did not, however, play the preponderant role that they were to assume later. Rural lordship existed in the Roman world and also at least in germ in the Germanic world. Roman society never ceased to give a large place to patron and client relationship. Around the powerful surged a great crowd of persons—at times themselves of high rank—who commended themselves to them. In addition these clienteles included as a general rule numerous former slaves freed by their masters in exchange for certain obligations of an economic nature and a general duty of fidelity (*obsequium*). Celtic society before the conquest also contained similar groups. In Germany alongside the normal relations that united the freeman to his family, his clan and his people others more transitory had grown up in the form of bands of faithful men of every origin gathered around a chief. Nourished in his dwelling, receiving from him horses and armor, they accompanied him to battle and constituted his strength and prestige. In this way people became accustomed to a certain conception of social bonds which developing in a favorable environment were to give rise to feudalism proper.

The leading features of feudalism in its fully developed form are the system of vassalage and the institution of the fief. As early as the Frankish and Lombard periods a great number of freemen of all ranks felt the need of seeking the protection of someone more powerful than themselves or of securing a decent livelihood by offering their military services to a superior. The poorest became slaves or simply tenants. But all who could clung to their dignity as men legally free and preferred not to lower themselves to the less honorable services which burdened the tenant liable to the corvée. They "commended" themselves *ingenuili ordine*. Exalted persons, on the other hand, sought to surround themselves with loyal people who should be attached to them by solid bonds. Thus arose the contract of dependence most characteristic of the feudal system.

In Frankish law, at least, the relations of vassalage were established by means of a formal act to which a little later the name homage was applied (in German *Mannschaft* or *Hulde*). The future vassal placed his hands in the lord's joined hands while repeating a few words promising loyalty, after which lord and vassal kissed each other on the mouth. As this ceremony, probably borrowed from old German traditions, gave no place to any religious elements, the custom early arose of following it up with an oath of fealty taken by the vassal on the Gospel or on relics.

The obligations created by homage and fealty held as long as both contracting parties were alive. They were extinguished upon the death of either. When heredity later came into play it undermined the whole system of vassalage. But heredity itself, as applying to the vassalic bonds, always remained rather a matter of practise than of law. In case of the death of lord or vassal a new offer of homage was in every case considered necessary to revive the tie. Being attached to concrete forms the vassalic right held bound only the two persons whom the ceremony brought face to face.

The reciprocal obligations of lord and vassal rested upon general simple principles susceptible in their details of infinite modifications and regulated with an increasing precision by local custom. The vassal owed the lord fidelity, obedience in the face of the whole world and aid in all circumstances in which the lord might need it. He supported him with his counsel, assisted him on occasion in his judicial functions and opened his purse to him in case of necessity. Little by little the cases in which this pecuniary aid—also called tallage—was legitimately exactable tended to become more defined and restricted to such occasions as the celebration of the knighthood of the lord's eldest son and of the marriage of his eldest daughter, ransom and so on. Above all the vassal owed the lord military service. This form of aid gradually came to predominate over all others.

In return the lord owed his man his protection; he assumed his defense before the tribunals, when there still were state tribunals; he avenged his wrongs and cared for his orphans until they became of age. Besides he assured him a livelihood in various ways and especially in the form of an economic grant generally known as a fief.

In the absence of a salary system there existed but two means of remunerating services. The master could receive his dependents in his own house, assure them food and shelter (*provende*), even clothe them; or he could assign them a piece of land upon which they might support themselves either directly or through returns received from those allowed to work it.

Of "provided" vassals nurtured in the lord's dwelling there were certainly a great number in the ninth and tenth centuries. They were still to be met with in the France of Philip Augustus. But vassals and lords early agreed in preferring the system of allotments of land, which provided the former with a greater independence and relieved the latter from the responsibility of looking after the support—particularly difficult under a rudimentary economic regime—of numerous and at times turbulent bands. Gradually most of the vassals found themselves "housed" (*chasés, casati*). The land assigned to them derived its peculiar features from the fact that it carried with it certain clearly defined services that were to be performed for the grantor. The property thus granted was at first called *beneficium*. Then little by little in the countries of Romanic speech which had adopted Frankish customs this term was supplanted (to such an extent that it has left not a trace in the Gallo-Roman dialects) by a term of Germanic origin: fief (*fevum* or *feodum*). The possession of land without obligation to any superior was, after the Frankish period, called alodial tenure. When a freeholder of this kind felt the need of commending himself he was in most cases forced to turn over his holding to the lord and receive it back as a fief. With the more complete feudalization of society these alodia decreased in number.

As the tenure service was a general institution of the economy of the period, there always existed a very great number of fiefs whose holders were not vassals: fiefs of artisans attached to the lord, such as painters and carpenters; of servants, such as cooks and doorkeepers; of officials charged with the administration of the manors, such as mayors and provosts. But any land granted to a vassal could be only a fief. Little by little, in proportion as the class of vassals tended to be transformed into nobility their fiefs appeared of a superior condition to those that were encumbered with humbler services, and eventually the jurists inclined to regard them as the only true fiefs. The institution of the fief, like that of homage, retained its personal character and was effective only for the lifetime of the contracting parties. Whenever either of them died the concession had to be renewed in the form of the symbolic tradition of investiture. With the establishment of the hereditary principle this ceremony became the means whereby the lord collected a sum of money (relief) as the price for the renewal of the fief.

On the other hand, it frequently happened that the vassal himself disposed of the very fiefs he held from a superior lord as fiefs for his own men. This subinfeudation, in principle, presumed the assent of the grantor of the original fief, but social necessities made it more and more customary to dispense with this. Thus alongside of and to a large extent parallel to the chains of personal dependence there arose chains of landed dependence. Mediaeval law in contrast with the Roman and modern notions of landed property conceived the soil as being subject to a great number of real rights differing among themselves and superimposed. Each of them had the value of a possession protected by custom (*saisine*, seisin, *Gewehr*) and none was clothed with that absolute character which the word property carries with it.

The seigniory, or manor, was the fundamental unit of the feudal regime. Under the name of villa it was very widespread in Gaul and in Roman Italy and in both cases doubtless went back to very old traditions such as those of village or clan chieftains. The seigniory usually consisted of several small farms. The cultivators were not the owners of the land but owed various duties and services to a lord who exercised over them a general power of command and from whom they held their lands on condition of a renewal of the investiture and the payment of a certain sum with every mutation. Generally in the Frankish period the lord also possessed a vast farm, the demesne, whose cultivation was assured in large part by the corvées due from the tenants. After the twelfth century these demesnes, chopped up into small farms, decreased in importance, first in France and Italy, more slowly in Germany, and the lord tended to become a mere receiver of land rents.

In gathering round the seigniory humble folk obeyed the same need of protection that men of a higher rank sought to satisfy in vassalage. The small peasant handed over his alodium to the lord and received it back under the form of a tenure with dues and corvées attached. Often he pledged his person and that of his descendants by the same act, thus entering into personal service. The life of the seigniory was regulated by custom. As the lords had every interest in keeping their lands peopled, the habit speedily arose of considering the peasant tenures, even the servile ones, as hereditary. Again, the seigniory fortified itself in the feudal period by appropriating a great number of state functions and by assuring the remuneration of the military class, which tended to rise above the others.

The churches figured among the principal possessors of seigniories. Some of them from the end of the Roman Empire obtained the right to retain the taxes levied upon their subjects. These privileges, confirmed and extended to churches more and more by the Frankish sovereigns, were the first form of immunity. This soon carried with it another advantage: the prohibition of representatives of the law—exacting and prone to be tyrannical—from trespassing upon immunized land to exercise their functions, notably their judicial powers. Analogous immunities were early obtained by lay lords.

In theory the men who lived upon a seigniory thus privileged remained answerable to the royal courts; their lord was responsible for their appearance. In reality the lord more and more tended to become a judge; he always had been so for his slaves, who at least in their relations to one another and to their master were answerable by the nature of things only to him. On the other hand, his role as protector seemed to confer upon him the right to maintain good order among his free tenants and his vassals. Under Charlemagne the state itself considered his intervention a guaranty of good order. After the fall of the Carolingian state the judicial power of the lord found a new lease of life in the usurpation of public functions, itself the consequence of the utilization of vassalage by the sovereigns.

In the Frankish period all freemen were liable to military service. But more and more the strength of armies seemed to center in horsemen equipped with complete armor and serving as leaders for little bands of other horsemen and of footmen. To remunerate the services of these knights, who accompanied them to the royal army or aided them in their blood feuds, the noblemen had acquired the habit of distributing fiefs among them; and, to make sure of their fidelity, of requesting homage. The sovereigns soon did the same. Notably Charles Martel, engrossed in his struggle against the Arabs and domestic enemies, created numerous military fiefs, carved largely from the domains of the churches which he usurped. Commendation, which had in the beginning been a sure means for men of every class to find a protector, tended thus to become a social tie peculiar to a class of military vassals (of the king or the nobles), who were at the same time possessors of seigniories. By a parallel tendency the old ceremony of the delivery of arms, a heritage from Germanic traditions originally distinguishing the majority of all freemen, now applied only to specialized warriors. This was the "dubbing"; whoever had received it could give it in his turn and thereby make knights. This class, until the twelfth century still open to adventurers of every origin, had an ethics of its own, a code of honor and fidelity tinged more and more with religious ideas, and felt itself to be virtually an order.

On the other hand, to reward their representatives throughout the country, in particular the counts, the kings, not being able to put them on salary, distributed fiefs among them consisting either of lands or of a share of the royal revenues in the provinces. To bind them by a tie that had some strength they chose them from among their vassals or exacted homage of them. The royal vassals in their turn and the churches surrounded themselves with their own vassals and confided to them a part of their functions and the administration of a part of their property.

Social and economic conditions thus made for decentralization and produced a veritable parceling out of all the powers of the state, such as justice, the right to coin money, tolls and the like. The profits accruing from these powers fell not only to the former direct representatives of the state, such as the counts, or to the immunized churches, but also by a sort of secondary appropriation to the representatives of these first usurpers.

The introduction of the principle of heredity into the feudal system was of paramount importance. The lord, who had need of men, sought to retain the services of the dead vassal's sons. The vassal's son was usually quite willing to do homage to his father's lord, in whom he found a natural protector. Above all it was at this price alone that he could keep the ancestral fief. In fact heredity was adopted little by little as a rule of conduct demanded first by public opinion, then by custom, and the lord who demurred ran the risk of offending his men. Charles the Bald considered it to be normal. In Italy the emperor Conrad II established it as law for fiefs below those of a count. Neither in France nor in Germany was it ever the subject of any legislation. In France it was early made general with but few exceptions and in Germany it was adopted more quickly for fiefs of a lower order and more slowly for fiefs of greater importance.

At the same time that they became hereditary the fiefs tended to become alienable. Of course the lord's assent would always be necessary for alienation. But it became less and less admissible to refuse it. The fiefs, together with the authority attaching to them and with the fragments of state functions that often went along with them, became hereditary, resulting in a confusion of powers over men and things. Heredity, however, while it put a seal on the feudal system certainly compromised its very foundations.

In all consistency the vassal system would have required each vassal to have but one lord. That was the very condition of the entire devotion which was the first of his duties, and the Caroligian legislation had so decided. But it was a great temptation to take fiefs wherever one could get them; when the fiefs had become patrimonial it sometimes happened that a vassal received by inheritance or purchase a fief that was held from some lord other than the one to whom he had first done homage. Cases of vassals of two or more lords are found from the tenth century and they become more numerous in the later period. How was one to apportion obligations to the various masters? In France in the eleventh century the custom arose of choosing one of these allegiances as more binding than the others. This was called liege (pure) homage. But in the thirteenth century this system, in its turn, was rendered ineffectual by the very multiplication of the liege homages offered by the same vassal to different lords. One was then reduced to consider, among the liege homages, which always took the first place, and, among the simple ones, the first homage in date, or sometimes the one attached to the greater fief as the strongest. In Germany and Italy, where the liege homage never took root, these classifications by dates or according to the importance of the fiefs had always been in vogue. But such multifarious allegiances could no longer count for much.

An essential characteristic of the feudal contract was the theory that if one of the two contracting parties broke his pledges he thereby freed the other party from all obligations. But precise definition as to the circumstances under which non-fulfilment of the contract, whether on the part of the lord or of the vassal, justified the rupture was completely wanting. In spite of the efforts of Carolingian legislation this salient point remained vague. The absence of all recognized superior authority left it to the interested parties to arbitrate the particular case. This uncertainty, the unforeseen consequence of the synallagmatic character of the bond, smoothed the way for all kinds of felony.

Although the salient features of the feudal regime were very nearly the same in all countries of western Europe there were, nevertheless, certain national differences and peculiarities. Thus in France the parceling out of the powers of the state, notably the appropriation of justice, was carried farthest. There too the military class became most solidly constituted and developed its chivalrous code, which from there spread over all Europe. In Germany feudal conceptions did not pervade the judicial life so profoundly, and two codes of customary law developed side by side, the general laws of the different countries (*Landrecht*) and the laws of fiefs (*Lehnrecht*). The alodia there, as in Italy and the south of France, persisted in greater numbers than elsewhere. The exclusive right to invest the superior judges who dealt with criminal cases involving the death penalty remained in the hands of the royal power. The emperors also maintained a long and effective struggle against the inheritance of the great fiefs. But they had to accept the obligation to enfeoff again the fiefs having the powers of earldoms when they were left without heirs or had been confiscated. This, unlike the case of France, prevented the increase of the royal domain itself. In Italy the previous importance of the cities and the urban habits of a great part of the knights themselves early created a formidable rivalry to the powers of the landed lords.

In Russia a real feudal regime was in full process of development up to the moment when it was stifled by the power of the Muscovite state. As in the west, the vassalage of the boyars became transformed into a state nobility. They were, however, more strictly subject to the czar since the synallagmatic character of the contract of service had always been less marked than in the west. The seigniory, vigorously constituted, survived for a long time. In the Byzantine state of the first centuries there existed tenures burdened with military service for the state but these were tenures of peasant soldiers. The emperors viewed these free peasants as constituting the strength of the army and struggled against their being crushed by the seigniories. From the eleventh century their resistance weakened and finally the seigniory, favored with immunities and obliged by way of compensation to furnish soldiers to the state, became the keystone of the military organization. But these seigniories were not themselves subdivided in hierarchical form by bonds of fiefs and vassalage; so that one of the essential characteristics of feudalism—that gradation of obligations which in Europe preserved the homogeneity of the political organization—was always lacking in Byzantium. The Scandinavian peninsula offers a clear case of a country in which for want of one of the primary elements of feudal organization, that of seigniorial economy, a real feudalism failed to arise.

Much more significant is the distinction between countries in which feudalism had grown up spontaneously and those in which it had been planted by conquest. In the former the feudal regime was never able to attain that systematic character that hardly belongs to any but institutions formed fully accoutered and thereby unembarrassed with survivals. It appears, on the contrary, as a much more symmetrical edifice in the countries in which it was planted by conquest, such as the Latin states of the Holy Land, the Norman kingdom of southern Italy and especially England.

The social condition of England at the time of the conquest was in many respects analogous to that of Frankish Gaul at the time when the feudal system began to take shape. Both were marked by a slow absorption of the free peasants in the framework of a seigniory whose dependents still obeyed juridical statutes of extreme variety, by a tendency toward the generalization of dependent relations, by the appropriation of justice by the powerful, by the existence of tenures burdened with military service and called as in Germany *Laen,* and by the importance of the thanes, a class fairly similar to that of the Frankish royal vassals. But all that was poorly coordinated and the fusion of the relations of fief and vassalage had not been effected. The Norman kings imposed upon the country a feudal system conceived to their advantage. The boundaries of the seigniories (called manors) were definitely fixed; a sort of serfdom was introduced which, however, was in the course of time to evolve in a very different direction from the French; in spite of the much greater power of royal justice than in France the English lords were considered the exclusive judges of their tenants in their relations with them, which was finally to prevent the inheritance of tenures. Above all, the kings divided the whole country into military fiefs according to a system brought over from their Norman duchy. The tenants in chief were each to furnish the king with a certain number of knights. To be able to do so they distributed fiefs in their return. But these chains of dependence soon becoming practically hereditary all led back to the king, from whom in the last analysis all land was held, even that of the church (under the form of the "free alms"). The alodium, a foreign body in the feudal world of the continent, did not exist at all in England. Finally, the king could demand the oath of fealty of his vassals' vassals.

At the end of the twelfth century a profound change took place in European society characterized by the formation of classes, economic transformations and the development of the state. In the tenth or eleventh century society consisted primarily of groups of dependents. As the sense of personal ties wore away, the human mass tended to organize itself in large classes arranged in a hierarchy. Knighthood became hereditary and changed into nobility. In England indeed the noble never had precise lawful privileges clearly separating him from the freeman. In Italy, habituated to a kind of life increasingly urban, he was hardly to be distinguished from the rich burgher. In France, on the contrary, the nobility made of itself a single closed class to which only the king could introduce new members. In Germany a whole hierarchy established itself within the nobility, and according to the theory of the *Heerschild* no member of one of these subclasses could without derogation accept a fief from a man occupying a lower grade.

Beginning in the twelfth century economic exchange became more active. The cities developed and relations quite foreign to the feudal type came to light. Bound to his fellow townsmen by an oath of mutual aid, which unlike the vassal oath united equals, the townsman needed no other protector than the community to which he belonged. His social code too was quite different from that of the military vassal. Moreover, the advent of a new economic regime founded upon exchange and money payment permitted the extension of the salaried class and at every step of the social scale took away from the fief and the enfeoffment any *raison d'être* for their functions.

This economic transformation in turn contributed to the rebirth of the state. Hired troops took the place of the vassals, who nearly everwhere had greatly succeeded in limiting their obligations. Corps of salaried officials subject to dismissal were formed. Such concentration of power did not redound solely to the advantage of the kings. In France and Germany certain royal vassals had brought under their control a great number of earldoms and multiform seigniorial rights and exalted their power above the crowd of lesser seigniories. While in France the great principalities thus formed were at last absorbed by the royal power, in Germany they well nigh annihilated it. In Italy the states formed around and by leading cities chiefly benefited from this movement. Everywhere the state, whatever its nature, was henceforth a master and protector. He who now depended only on it without "commending" himself to anyone no longer felt isolated.

The rural seigniory lasted much longer. Being adapted to the needs of the capitalistic era it still continued to flourish throughout the sixteenth, seventeenth and eighteenth centuries; it was transplanted by Europeans into various colonies, notably French Canada. It was not abolished in France until the revolution; it disappeared definitely from Germany—aside from a few survivals—in 1848; in England it disappeared but very slowly from the statute book and left behind a very strong imprint on the constitution of rural society.

The same needs from which vassalage took its rise long continued to make themselves felt, at least intermittently in troubled periods. The homage, now but an empty rite, had its substitutes. The English liverymen in the time of the Wars of the Roses are reminiscent of the mesne tenants of the early Middle Ages. In the France of the seventeenth century to belong to a great lord afforded the gentry the best means of getting on. The orders of knighthood were invented by the princes at the close of the Middle Ages to insure the fidelity of those admitted to them; Napoleon himself in establishing the Legion of Honor had much the same idea. But those orders that have survived, as well as their contemporary imitations, have lost every role but that of honorific distinction.

In the last centuries of the Middle Ages the states had sought to turn to account the old feudal organization, requiring of vassals if not an active military service at least a compensatory tax. But these attempts had little success. In England a law of the Commonwealth in 1656, confirmed by the Restoration in 1660, abolished all distinction between the fiefs of knights and the free tenures (socages). The fiction that all land is held from the crown, the use of the word fee to designate the highest form of landed rights, are relics of the systematic organization introduced by the Norman kings; primogeniture applied in the absence of a will to all succession in real estate is a legacy of the law of fiefs. In certain German states, such as Prussia under Frederick William I, the fiefs were transformed into alodia in the eighteenth century by legislative action. France waited until the revolution of 1789 to abolish fiefs and vassalage, which had ceased to bring any considerable revenue to the coffers of lords and king. In the nineteenth century these antiquated institutions finally disappeared in Europe. The class of military vassals had given birth to the nobility. In France the latter saw its privileges completely abolished along with the feudal organization itself, and by the same act its social role was doomed to extinction. But in some other countries it has long outlived the fiefs both in fact and in law.

The clearest legacy of feudalism to modern societies is the emphasis placed upon the notion of the political contract. The reciprocity of obligations which united lord and vassal and caused with every grave dereliction by the superior the release of the inferior in the eyes of the law was transferred in the thirteenth century to the state. Practically everywhere, but with peculiar clearness in England and Aragon, the idea was expressed that the subject is bound to the king only so long as the latter remains a loyal protector. This sentiment counterbalanced the tradition of royal sanctity and finally triumphed over it.

# 5. *Nationality*

BY LORD ACTON

WHENEVER GREAT INTELLECTUAL cultivation has been combined with that suffering which is inseparable from extensive changes in the condition of the people, men of speculative or imaginative genius have sought in the contemplation of an ideal society a remedy, or at least a consolation, for evils which they were practically unable to remove. Poetry has always preserved the idea, that at some distant time or place, in the Western islands or the Arcadian region, an innocent and contented people, free from the corruption and restraint of civilised life, have realised the legends of the golden age. The office of the poets is always nearly the

Reprinted from Lord Acton, *Essays on Freedom and Power* (Glencoe, Ill.: The Free Press, 1949), chap. vi, pp. 166–95, with the permission of The Free Press.

same, and there is little variation in the features of their ideal world; but when philosophers attempt to admonish or reform mankind by devising an imaginary state, their motive is more definite and immediate, and their commonwealth is a satire as well as a model. Plato and Plotinus. More and Campanella, constructed their fanciful societies with those materials which were omitted from the fabric of the actual communities, by the defects of which they were inspired. The Republic, the Utopia, and the City of the Sun were protests against a state of things which the experience of their authors taught them to condemn, and from the faults of which they took refuge in the opposite extremes. They remained without influence, and have never passed from literary into political history, because something more than discontent and speculative ingenuity is needed in order to invest a political idea with power over the masses of mankind. The scheme of a philosopher can command the practical allegiance of fanatics only, not of nations; and though oppression may give rise to violent and repeated outbreaks, like the convulsions of a man in pain, it cannot mature a settled purpose and plan of regeneration, unless a new notion of happiness is joined to the sense of present evil.

The history of religion furnishes a complete illustration. Between the later mediæval sects and Protestantism there is an essential difference, that outweighs the points of analogy found in those systems which are regarded as heralds of the Reformation, and is enough to explain the vitality of the last in comparison with the others. Whilst Wycliffe and Hus contradicted certain particulars of the Catholic teaching, Luther rejected the authority of the Church, and gave to the individual conscience an independence which was sure to lead to an incessant resistance. There is a similar difference between the Revolt of the Netherlands, the Great Rebellion, the War of Independence, or the rising of Brabant, on the one hand, and the French Revolution on the other. Before 1789, insurrections were provoked by particular wrongs, and were justified by definite complaints and by an appeal to principles which all men acknowledged. New theories were sometimes advanced in the cause of controversy, but they were accidental, and the great argument against tyranny was fidelity to the ancient laws. Since the change produced by the French Revolution, those aspirations which are awakened by the evils and defects of the social state have come to act as permanent and energetic forces throughout the civilised world. They are spontaneous and aggressive, needing no prophet to proclaim, no champion to defend them, but popular, unreasoning, and almost irresistible. The Revolution effected this change, partly by its doctrines, partly by the indirect influence of events. It taught the people to regard their wishes and wants as the supreme criterion of right. The rapid vicissitudes of power, in which each party successively appealed to the favour of the masses as the arbiter of success, accustomed the masses to be arbitrary as well as insubordinate. The fall of many governments, and the frequent redistribution of territory, deprived all settlements of the dignity of permanence. Tradition and prescription ceased to be guardians of authority; and the arrangements which proceeded from revolutions, from the triumphs of war, and from treaties of peace, were equally regardless of established rights. Duty cannot be dissociated from right, and nations refuse to be controlled by laws which are no protection.

In this condition of the world, theory and action follow close upon each other, and practical evils easily give birth to opposite systems. In the realms of free-will, the regularity of natural progress is preserved by the conflict of extremes. The impulse of the reaction carries men from one extremity towards another. The pursuit of a remote and ideal object, which captivates the imagination by its splendour and the reason by its simplicity, evokes an energy which would not be inspired by a rational, possible end, limited by many antagonistic claims, and confined to what is reasonable, practicable, and just. One excess or exaggeration is the corrective of the other, and error promotes truth, where the masses are concerned, by counterbalancing a contrary error. The few have not strength to achieve great changes unaided; the many have not wisdom to be moved by truth unmixed. Where the disease is various, no particular definite remedy can meet the wants of all. Only the attraction of an abstract idea, or of an ideal state, can unite in a common action multitudes who seek a universal cure for many special evils, and a common restorative applicable to many different conditions. And hence false principles, which correspond with the bad as well as with the just aspirations of mankind, are a normal and necessary element in the social life of nations.

Theories of this kind are just, inasmuch as they are provoked by definite ascertained evils, and undertake their removal. They are useful in opposition, as a warning or a threat, to modify existing things, and keep awake the consciousness of wrong. They cannot serve as a basis for the reconstruction of civil society, as medicine cannot serve for food; but they may influence it with advantage, because they point out the direction, though not the measure, in which reform is needed. They oppose an order of things which is the result of a selfish and violent abuse of power by the ruling classes, and of artificial restriction on the natural progress of the world, destitute of an ideal element or a moral purpose. Practical extremes differ from the theoretical extremes they provoke, because the first are both arbitrary and violent, whilst the last, though also revolutionary, are at the same time remedial. In one case the wrong is voluntary, in the other it is inevitable. This is the general character of the contest between the existing order and the subversive theories that deny its legitimacy. There are three principal theories of this kind, impugning the present distribution of power, of property, and of territory, and attacking respectively the aristocracy, the middle class, and the sovereignty. They are the theories of equality, communism, and nationality. Though sprung from a common origin, opposing cognate evils, and connected by many links, they did not appear simultaneously. Rousseau proclaimed the first, Babœuf the second, Mazzini the third; and the third is the most recent in its appearance, the most attractive at the present time, and the richest in promise of future power.

In the old European system, the rights of nationalities were neither recognised by governments nor asserted by the people. The interest of the reigning families, not those of the nations, regulated the frontiers; and the administration was conducted generally without any reference to popular desires. Where all liberties were suppressed, the claims of national independence were necessarily ignored, and a princess, in the words of Fénelon, carried a monarchy in her wedding portion. The eighteenth century acquiesced in this oblivion of corporate rights on the Continent, for the absolutists cared only for the State, and the liberals only for the individual. The Church, the nobles, and the nation had no place in the popular theories of the age; and they devised none in their own defence, for they were not openly attacked. The aristocracy retained its privileges, and the Church her property; and the dynastic interest, which overruled the natural inclination of the nations, and destroyed their independence, nevertheless maintained their integrity. The national sentiment was not wounded in its most sensitive part. To dispossess a sovereign of his hereditary crown, and to annex his dominions, would have been held to inflict an injury upon all monarchies, and to furnish their subjects with a dangerous example, by depriving royalty of its inviolable character. In time of war, as there was no national cause at stake, there was no attempt to rouse national feeling. The courtesy of the rulers towards each other was proportionate to the contempt for the lower orders. Compliments passed between the commanders of hostile armies; there was no bitterness, and no excitement; battles were fought with the pomp and pride of a parade. The art of war became a slow and learned game. The monarchies were united not only by a natural community of interests, but by family alliances. A marriage contract sometimes became the signal for an interminable war, whilst family connections often set a barrier to ambition. After the wars of religion came to an end in 1648, the only wars were those which were waged for an inheritance or a dependency, or against countries whose system of government exempted them from the common law of dynastic States, and made them not only unprotected but obnoxious. These countries were England and Holland, until Holland ceased to be a republic, and until, in England, the defeat of the Jacobites in the forty-five terminated the struggle for the Crown. There was one country, however, which still continued to be an exception; one monarch whose place was not admitted in the comity of kings.

Poland did not possess those securities for stability which were supplied by dynastic connections and the theory of legitimacy, wherever a crown could be obtained by marriage or inheritance. A monarch without royal blood, a crown bestowed by the nation, were an anomaly and an outrage in that age of dynastic absolutism. The country was excluded from the European system by the nature of its institutions. It excited a cupidity which could not be satisfied. It gave the reigning families of Europe no hope of permanently strengthening themselves by intermarriage with its rulers, or of obtaining it by request or by inheritance. The Hapsburgs had contested the possession of Spain and the Indies with the French Bourbons, of Italy with the Spanish Bourbons, of the empire with the house of Wittelsbach, of Silesia with the house of Hohenzollern. There had been wars between rival houses for half the territories of Italy and Germany. But none could hope to redeem their losses or increase their power in a country to which marriage and descent gave no claim. Where they could not permanently inherit they endeavoured, by intrigues, to prevail at each election, and after contending in support of candidates who were their partisans, the neighbours at last appointed an instrument for the final demolition of the Polish State. Till then no nation had been deprived of its political existence by the Christian Powers, and whatever disregard had been shown for national interests and sympathies, some care had been taken to conceal the wrong by a hypocritical perversion of law. But the partition of Poland was an act of wanton violence, committed in open defiance not only of popular feeling but of public law. For the first time in modern history a great State was suppressed, and a whole nation divided among its enemies.

The famous measure, the most revolutionary act

of the old absolutism, awakened the theory of nationality in Europe, converting a dormant right into an aspiration, and a sentiment into a political claim. "No wise or honest man," wrote Edmund Burke, "can approve of that partition, or can contemplate it without prognosticating great mischief from it to all countries at some future time."[1] Thenceforward there was a nation demanding to be united in a State,—a soul, as it were, wandering in search of a body in which to begin life over again; and, for the first time, a cry was heard that the arrangement of States was unjust—that their limits were unnatural, and that a whole people was deprived of its right to constitute an independent community. Before that claim could be efficiently asserted against the overwhelming power of its opponents,—before it gained energy, after the last partition, to overcome the influence of long habits of submission, and of the contempt which previous disorders had brought upon Poland,—the ancient European system was in ruins, and a new world was rising in its place.

The old despotic policy which made the Poles its prey had two adversaries,—the spirit of English liberty, and the doctrines of that revolution which destroyed the French monarchy with its own weapons; and these two contradicted in contrary ways the theory that nations have no collective rights. At the present day, the theory of nationality is not only the most powerful auxiliary of revolution, but its actual substance in the movements of the last three years. This, however, is a recent alliance, unknown to the first French Revolution. The modern theory of nationality arose partly as a legitimate consequence, partly as a reaction against it. As the system which overlooked national division was opposed by liberalism in two forms, the French and the English, so the system which insists upon them proceeds from two distinct sources, and exhibits the character either of 1688 or of 1789. When the French people abolished the authorities under which it lived, and became its own master, France was in danger of dissolution: for the common will is difficult to ascertain, and does not readily agree. "The laws," said Vergniaud, in the debate on the sentence of the king, "are obligatory only as the presumptive will of the people, which retains the right of approving or condemning them. The instant it manifests its wish the work of the national representation, the law, must disappear." This doctrine resolved society into its natural elements, and threatened to break up the country into as many republics as there were communes. For true republicanism is the principle of self-government in the whole and in all the parts. In an extensive country, it can prevail only by the union of several independent communities in a single confederacy, as in Greece, in Switzerland, in the Netherlands, and in America; so that a large republic not founded on the federal principle must result in the government of a single city, like Rome and Paris, and in a less degree, Athens, Berne, and Amsterdam; or, in other words, a great democracy must either sacrifice self-government to unity, or preserve it by federalism.

The France of history fell together with the French State, which was the growth of centuries. The old sovereignty was destroyed. The local authorities were looked upon with aversion and alarm. The new central authority needed to be established on a new principle of unity. The state of nature, which was the ideal of society, was made the basis of the nation; descent was put in the place of tradition, and the French people was regarded as a physical product: an ethnological, not historic, unit. It was assumed that a unity existed separate from the representation and the government, wholly independent of the past, and capable at any moment of expressing or of changing its mind. In the words of Siéyès, it was no longer France, but some unknown country to which the nation was transported. The central power possessed authority, inasmuch as it obeyed the whole, and no divergence was permitted from the universal sentiment. This power, endowed with volition, was personified in the Republic One and Indivisible. The title signified that a part could not speak or act for the whole,—that there was a power supreme over the State, distinct from, and independent of, its members; and it expressed, for the first time in history, the notion of an abstract nationality. In this manner the idea of the sovereignty of the people, uncontrolled by the past, gave birth to the idea of nationality independent of the political influence of history. It sprang from the rejection of the two authorities,—of the State and of the past. The kingdom of France was, geographically as well as politically, the product of a long series of events, and the same influences which built up the State formed the territory. The Revolution repudiated alike the agencies to which France owed her boundaries and those to which she owed her government. Every effaceable trace and relic of national history was carefully wiped away,—the system of administration, the physical divisions of the country, the classes of society, the corporations, the weights and measures, the calendar. France was no longer bounded by the limits she had received from the condemned influence of her history; she could recognise only those which were set by nature. The definition of the nation was borrowed from the material world, and, in order to avoid

1. "Observations on the Conduct of the Minority," *Works,* V, 112.

a loss of territory, it became not only an abstraction but a fiction.

There was a principle of nationality in the ethnological character of the movement, which is the source of the common observation that revolution is more frequent in Catholic than in Protestant countries. It is, in fact, more frequent in the Latin than in the Teutonic world, because it depends partly on a national impulse, which is only awakened where there is an alien element, the vestige of a foreign dominion, to expel. Western Europe has undergone two conquests—one by the Romans and one by the Germans, and twice received laws from the invaders. Each time it rose again against the victorious race; and the two great reactions, while they differ according to the different characters of the two conquests, have the phenomenon of imperialism in common. The Roman republic laboured to crush the subjugated nations into a homogeneous and obedient mass; but the increase which the proconsular authority obtained in the process subverted the republican government, and the reaction of the provinces against Rome assisted in establishing the empire. The Cæsarean system gave an unprecedented freedom to the dependencies, and raised them to a civil equality which put an end to the dominion of race over race and of class over class. The monarchy was hailed as a refuge from the pride and cupidity of the Roman people; and the love of equality, the hatred of nobility, and the tolerance of despotism implanted by Rome became, at least in Gaul, the chief feature of the national character. But among the nations whose vitality had been broken down by the stern republic, not one retained the materials necessary to enjoy independence, or to develop a new history. The political faculty which organises states and finds society in a moral order was exhausted, and the Christian doctors looked in vain over the waste of ruins for a people by whose aid the Church might survive the decay of Rome. A new element of national life was brought to that declining world by the enemies who destroyed it. The flood of barbarians settled over it for a season, and then subsided; and when the landmarks of civilisation appeared once more, it was found that the soil had been impregnated with a fertilising and regenerating influence, and that the inundation had laid the germs of future states and of a new society. The political sense and energy came with the new blood, and was exhibited in the power exercised by the younger race upon the old, and in the establishment of a graduated freedom. Instead of universal equal rights, the actual enjoyment of which is necessarily contingent on, and commensurate with, power, the rights of the people were made dependent on a variety of conditions, the first of which was the distribution of property. Civil society became a classified organism instead of a formless combination of atoms, and the feudal system gradually arose.

Roman Gaul had so thoroughly adopted the ideas of absolute authority and undistinguished equality during the five centuries between Cæsar and Clovis, that the people could never be reconciled to the new system. Feudalism remained a foreign importation, and the feudal aristocracy an alien race, and the common people of France sought protection against both in the Roman jurisprudence and the power of the crown. The development of absolute monarchy by the help of democracy is the one constant character of French history. The royal power, feudal at first, and limited by the immunities and the great vassals, became more popular as it grew more absolute; while the suppression of aristocracy, the removal of the intermediate authorities, was so particularly the object of the nation, that it was more energetically accomplished after the fall of the throne. The monarchy which had been engaged from the thirteenth century in curbing the nobles, was at last thrust aside by the democracy, because it was too dilatory in the work, and was unable to deny its own origin and effectually ruin the class from which it sprang. All those things which constitute the peculiar character of the French Revolution,—the demand for equality, the hatred of nobility and feudalism, and of the Church which was connected with them, the constant reference to pagan examples, the suppression of monarchy, the new code of law, the breach with tradition, and the substitution of an ideal system for everything that had proceeded from the mixture and mutual action of the races,—all these exhibit the common type of a reaction against the effects of the Frankish invasion. The hatred of royalty was less than the hatred of aristocracy; privileges were more detested than tyranny; and the king perished because of the origin of his authority rather than because of its abuse. Monarchy unconnected with aristocracy became popular in France, even when most uncontrolled; whilst the attempt to reconstitute the throne, and to limit and fence it with its peers, broke down, because the old Teutonic elements on which it relied—hereditary nobility, primogeniture, and privilege—were no longer tolerated. The substance of the ideas of 1789 is not the limitation of the sovereign power, but the abrogation of intermediate powers. These powers, and the classes which enjoyed them, come in Latin Europe from a barbarian origin; and the movement which calls itself liberal is essentially national. If liberty were its object, its means would be the establishment of great independent authorities not derived from the State, and its model would be England. But its object is equality; and it seeks, like France in 1789, to cast out the elements of inequality which were introduced by the Teutonic race. This is the object which Italy and Spain have had in common with France, and herein consists the natural league of the Latin nations.

This national element in the movement was not understood by the revolutionary leaders. At first, their doctrine appeared entirely contrary to the idea of nationality. They taught that certain general principles of government were absolutely right in all States; and they asserted in theory the unrestricted freedom of the individual, and the supremacy of the will over every external necessity or obligation. This is in apparent contradiction to the national theory, that certain natural forces ought to determine the character, the form, and the policy of the State, by which a kind of fate is put in the place of freedom. Accordingly the national sentiment was not developed directly out of the revolution in which it was involved, but was exhibited first in resistance to it, when the attempt to emancipate had been absorbed in the desire to subjugate, and the republic had been succeeded by the empire. Napoleon called a new power into existence by attacking nationality in Russia, by delivering it in Italy, by governing in defiance of it in Germany and Spain. The sovereigns of these countries were deposed or degraded; and a system of administration was introduced which was French in its origin, its spirit, and its instruments. The people resisted the change. The movement against it was popular and spontaneous, because the rulers were absent or helpless; and it was national, because it was directed against foreign institutions. In Tyrol, in Spain, and afterwards in Prussia, the people did not receive the impulse from the government, but undertook of their own accord to cast out the armies and the ideas of revolutionised France. Men were made conscious of the national element of the revolution by its conquests, not in its rise. The three things which the Empire most openly oppressed—religion, national independence, and political liberty—united in a short-lived league to animate the great uprising by which Napoleon fell. Under the influence of that memorable alliance a political spirit was called forth on the Continent, which clung to freedom and abhorred revolution, and sought to restore, to develop, and to reform the decayed national institutions. The men who proclaimed these ideas, Stein and Görres, Humboldt, Müller, and De Maistre,[2] were as hostile to Bonapartism as to the absolutism of the old governments, and insisted on the national rights, which had been invaded equally by both, and which they hoped to restore by the destruction of the French supremacy. With the cause that triumphed at Waterloo the friends of the Revolution had no sympathy, for they had learned to identify their doctrine with the cause of France. The Holland House Whigs in England, the Afrancesados in Spain, the Muratists in Italy, and the partisans of the Confederation of the Rhine, merging patriotism in their revolutionary affections, regretted the fall of the French power, and looked with alarm at those new and unknown forces which the War of Deliverance had evoked, and which were as menacing to French liberalism as to French supremacy.

But the new aspirations for national and popular rights were crushed at the restoration. The liberals of those days cared for freedom, not in the shape of national independence, but of French institutions; and they combined against the nations with the ambition of the governments. They were as ready to sacrifice nationality to their ideal as the Holy Alliance was to the interests of absolutism. Talleyrand indeed declared at Vienna that the Polish question ought to have precedence over all other questions, because the partition of Poland had been one of the first and greatest causes of the evils which Europe had suffered; but dynastic interests prevailed. All the sovereigns represented at Vienna recovered their dominions, except the King of Saxony, who was punished for his fidelity to Napoleon; but the States that were unrepresented in the reigning families—Poland, Venice, and

2. There are some remarkable thoughts on nationality in the State Papers of the Count de Maistre: "En premier lieu les nations sont quelque chose dans le monde, il n'est pas permis de les compter pour rien, de les affliger dans leurs convenances, dans leurs affections, dans leurs intérêts les plus chers.... Or le traité du 30 mai anéantit complétement la Savoie; il divise l'indivisible; il partage en trois portions une malheureuse nation de 400,000 hommes, une par la langue, une par la religion, une par le caractère, une par l'habitude invétérée, une enfin par les limites naturelles. . . . L'union des nations ne souffre pas de difficultés sur la carte géographique; mais dans la réalité, c'est autre chose; il y a des nations *immiscibles*. . . . Je lui parlai par occasion de l'esprit italien qui s'agite dans ce moment; il (Count Nesselrode) me répondit: 'Oui, Monsieur; mais cet esprit est un grand mal, car il peut gêner les arrangements de l'Italie.' "—*Correspondance Diplomatique de J. de Maistre,* II, 7, 8, 21, 25. In the same year, 1815, Görres wrote: "In Italien wie allerwarts ist das Volk gewecht; es will etwas grossartiges, es will Ideen haben, die, wenn es sie auch nicht ganz begreift, doch einen freien unendlichen Gesichtskreis seiner Einbildung eröffnen. . . . Es ist reiner Naturtrieb, dass ein Volk, also scharf und deutlich in seine natürlichen Gränzen eingeschlossen, aus der Zerstreuung in die Einheit sich zu sammeln sucht."—*Werke,* II, 20.

Genoa—were not revived, and even the Pope had great difficulty in recovering the Legations from the grasp of Austria. Nationality, which the old *régime* had ignored, which had been outraged by the revolution and the empire, received, after its first open demonstration, the hardest blow at the Congress of Vienna. The principle which the first partition had generated, to which the revolution had given a basis of theory, which had been lashed by the empire into a momentary convulsive effort, was matured by the long error of the restoration into a consistent doctrine, nourished and justified by the situation of Europe.

The governments of the Holy Alliance devoted themselves to suppress with equal care the revolutionary spirit by which they had been threatened, and the national spirit by which they had been restored. Austria, which owed nothing to the national movement, and had prevented its revival after 1809, naturally took the lead in repressing it. Every disturbance of the final settlements of 1815, every aspiration for changes or reforms, was condemned as sedition. This system repressed the good with the evil tendencies of the age; and the resistance which it provoked, during the generation that passed away from the restoration to the fall of Metternich, and again under the reaction which commenced with Schwarzenberg and ended with the administrations of Bach and Manteuffel, proceeded from various combinations of the opposite forms of liberalism. In the successive phases of that struggle, the idea that national claims are above all other rights gradually rose to the supremacy which it now possesses among the revolutionary agencies.

The first liberal movement, that of the Carbonari in the south of Europe, had no specific national character, but was supported by the Bonapartists both in Spain and Italy. In the following years the opposite ideas of 1813 came to the front, and a revolutionary movement, in many respects hostile to the principles of revolution, began in defence of liberty, religion, and nationality. All these causes were united in the Irish agitation, and in the Greek, Belgian, and Polish revolutionists. Those sentiments which had been insulted by Napoleon, and had risen against him, rose against the governments of the restoration. They had been oppressed by the sword, and then by the treaties. The national principle added force, but not justice, to this movement, which, in every case but Poland, was successful. A period followed in which it degenerated into a purely national idea, as the agitation for repeal succeeded emancipation, and Panslavism and Panhellenism arose under the auspices of the Eastern Church. This was the third phase of the resistance to the settlement of Vienna, which was weak, because it failed to satisfy national or constitutional aspirations, either of which would have been a safeguard against the other, by a moral if not by a popular justification. At first, in 1813, the people rose against their conquerors, in defence of their legitimate rulers. They refused to be governed by usurpers. In the period between 1825 and 1831, they resolved that they would not be misgoverned by strangers. The French administration was often better than that which it displaced, but there were prior claimants for the authority exercised by the French, and at first the national contest was a contest for legitimacy. In the second period this element was wanting. No dispossessed princes led the Greeks, the Belgians, or the Poles. The Turks, the Dutch, and the Russians were attacked, not as usurpers, but as oppressors,—because they misgoverned, not because they were of a different race. Then began a time when the text simply was, that nations would not be governed by foreigners. Power legitimately obtained, and exercised with moderation, was declared invalid. National rights, like religion, had borne part in the previous combinations, and had been auxiliaries in the struggles for freedom, but now nationality became a paramount claim, which was to assert itself alone, which might put forward as pretexts the rights of rulers, the liberties of the people, the safety of religion, but which, if no such union could be formed, was to prevail at the expense of every other cause for which nations make sacrifices.

Metternich is, next to Napoleon, the chief promoter of this theory; for the anti-national character of the restoration was most distinct in Austria, and it is in opposition to the Austrian Government that nationality grew into a system. Napoleon, who, trusting to his armies, despised moral forces in politics, was overthrown by their rising. Austria committed the same fault in the government of her Italian provinces. The kingdom of Italy had united all the northern part of the Peninsula in a single State; and the national feelings, which the French repressed elsewhere, were encouraged as a safeguard of their power in Italy and in Poland. When the tide of victory turned, Austria invoked against the French the aid of the new sentiment they had fostered. Nugent announced, in his proclamation to the Italians, that they should become an independent nation. The same spirit served different masters, and contributed first to the destruction of the old States, then to the expulsion of the French, and again, under Charles Albert, to a new revolution. It was appealed to in the name of the most contradictory principles of government, and served all parties in succession, because it was one in which all could unite. Beginning by a protest against the dominion of race over race, its mildest and least-developed form, it grew into a condemnation of every State that included different races, and finally became the complete and consistent theory, that the State and the nation must be co-extensive. "It is," says Mr. Mill, "in general a necessary condition of free institutions, that the boundaries of governments should coincide in the main with those of nationalities."[3]

The outward historical progress of this idea from an indefinite aspiration to be the keystone of a political system, may be traced in the life of the man who gave to it the element in which its strength resides,—Giuseppe Mazzini. He found Carbonarism impotent against the measures of the governments, and resolved to give new life to the liberal movement by transferring it to the ground of nationality. Exile is the nursery of nationality, as oppression is the school of liberalism; and Mazzini conceived the idea of Young Italy when he was a refugee at Marseilles. In the same way, the Polish exiles are the champions of every national movement; for to them all political rights are absorbed in the idea of independence, which, however they may differ with each other, is the one aspiration common to them all. Towards the year 1830 literature also contributed to the national idea. "It was the time," says Mazzini, "of the great conflict between the romantic and the classical school, which might with equal truth be called a conflict between the partisans of freedom and of authority." The romantic school was infidel in Italy, and Catholic in Germany; but in both it had the common effect of encouraging national history and literature, and Dante was as great an authority with the Italian democrats as with the leaders of the mediæval revival at Vienna, Munich, and Berlin. But neither the influence of the exiles, nor that of the poets and critics of the new party, extended over the masses. It was a sect without popular sympathy or encouragement, a conspiracy founded not on a grievance, but on a doctrine; and when the attempt to rise was made in Savoy, in 1834, under a banner with the motto "Unity, Independence, God and Humanity," the people were puzzled at its object, and indifferent to its failure. But Mazzini continued his propaganda, developed his *Giovine Italia* into a *Giovine Europa,* and established in 1847 the international league of nations. "The people," he said, in his opening address, "is penetrated with only one idea, that of unity and nationality. . . . There is no international question as to forms of government, but only a national question."

The revolution of 1848, unsuccessful in its national purpose, prepared the subsequent victories of nationality in two ways. The first of these was the restoration of the Austrian power in Italy, with a new and more energetic centralisation, which gave no promise of freedom. Whilst that system prevailed, the right was on the side of the national aspirations, and they were revived in a more complete and cultivated form by Manin. The policy of the Austrian Government, which failed during the ten years of the reaction to convert the tenure by force into a tenure by right, and to establish with free institutions the condition of allegiance, gave a negative encouragement to the theory. It deprived Francis Joseph of all active support and sympathy in 1859, for he was more clearly wrong in his conduct than his enemies in their doctrines. The real cause of the energy which the national theory has acquired is, however, the triumph of the democratic principle in France, and its recognition by the European Powers. The theory of nationality is involved in the democratic theory of the sovereignty of the general will. "One hardly knows what any division of the human race should be free to do, if not to determine with which of the various collective bodies of human beings they choose to associate themselves."[4] It is by this act that a nation constitutes itself. To have a collective will, unity is necessary, and independence is requisite in order to assert it. Unity and nationality are still more essential to the notion of the sovereignty of the people than the cashiering of monarchs, or the revocation of laws. Arbitrary acts of this kind may be prevented by the happiness of the people or the popularity of the king, but a nation inspired by the democratic idea cannot with consistency allow a part of itself to belong to a foreign State, or the whole to be divided into several native States. The theory of nationality therefore proceeds from both the principles which divide the political world,—from legitimacy, which ignores its claims, and from the revolution, which assumes them; and for the same reason it is the chief weapon of the last against the first.

In pursuing the outward and visible growth of the national theory we are prepared for an examination of its political character and value. The absolutism which has created it denies equally that absolute right of national unity which is a product of democracy, and that claim of national liberty which belongs to the theory of freedom. These two views of nationality, corresponding to the French and to the English systems, are connected in name

3 Mill's *Considerations on Representative Government,* p. 298.

4. Mill's *Considerations,* p. 296.

only, and are in reality the opposite extremes of political thought. In one case, nationality is founded on the perpetual supremacy of the collective will, of which the unity of the nation is the necessary condition, to which every other influence must defer, and against which no obligation enjoys authority, and all resistance is tyrannical. The nation is here an ideal unit founded on the race, in defiance of the modifying action of external causes, of tradition, and of existing rights. It overrules the rights and wishes of the inhabitants, absorbing their divergent interests in a fictitious unity; sacrifices their several inclinations and duties to the higher claim of nationality, and crushes all natural rights and all established liberties for the purpose of vindicating itself.[5] Whenever a single definite object is made the supreme end of the State, be it the advantage of a class, the safety or the power of the country, the greatest happiness of the greatest number, or the support of any speculative idea, the State becomes for the time inevitably absolute. Liberty alone demands for its realisation the limitation of the public authority, for liberty is the only object which benefits all alike, and provokes no sincere opposition. In supporting the claims of national unity, governments must be subverted in whose title there is no flaw, and whose policy is beneficent and equitable, and subjects must be compelled to transfer their allegiance to an authority for which they have no attachment, and which may be practically a foreign domination. Connected with this theory in nothing except in the common enmity of the absolute state, is the theory which represents nationality as an essential, but not a supreme element in determining the forms of the State. It is distinguished from the other, because it tends to diversity and not to uniformity, to harmony and not to unity; because it aims not at an arbitrary change, but at careful respect for the existing conditions of political life, and because it obeys the laws and results of history, not the aspirations of an ideal future. While the theory of unity makes the nation a source of despotism and revolution, the theory of liberty regards it as the bulwark of self-government, and the foremost limit to the excessive power of the State. Private rights, which are sacrificed to the unity, are preserved by the union of nations. No power can so efficiently resist the tendencies of centralisation, of corruption, and of absolutism, as that community which is the vastest that can be included in a State, which imposes on its members a consistent similarity of character, interest, and opinion, and which arrests the action of the sovereign by the influence of a divided patriotism. The presence of different nations under the same sovereignty is similar in its effect to the independence of the Church in the State. It provides against the servility which flourishes under the shadow of a single authority, by balancing interests, multiplying associations, and giving to the subject the restraint and support of a combined opinion. In the same way it promotes independence by forming definite groups of public opinion, and by affording a great source and centre of political sentiments, and of notions of duty not derived from the sovereign will. Liberty provokes diversity, and diversity preserves liberty by supplying the means of organisation. All those portions of law which govern the relations of men with each other, and regulate social life, are the varying result of national custom and the creation of private society. In these things, therefore, the several nations will differ from each other; for they themselves have produced them, and they do not owe them to the State which rules them all. This diversity in the same State is a firm barrier against the intrusion of the government beyond the political sphere which is common to all into the social department which escapes legislation and is ruled by spontaneous laws. This sort of interference is characteristic of an absolute government, and is sure to provoke a reaction, and finally a remedy. That intolerance of social freedom which is natural to absolutism is sure to find a corrective in the national diversities, which no other force could so efficiently provide. The co-existence of several nations under the same State is a test, as well as the best security of its freedom. It is also one of the chief instruments of civilisation; and, as such, it is in the natural and providential order, and indicates a state of greater advancement than the national unity which is the ideal of modern liberalism.

The combination of different nations in one State is as necessary a condition of civilised life as the combination of men in society. Inferior races are raised by living in political unions with races intellectually superior. Exhausted and decaying nations are revived by the contact of a younger vitality. Nations in which the elements of organisation and the capacity for government have been lost, either through the demoralising influence of despotism, or the disintegrating action of democracy, are restored and educated anew under the discipline of a stronger and less corrupted race.

---

5. "Le sentiment d'indépendance nationale est encore plus général et plus profondément gravé dans le cœur des peuples que l'amour d'une liberté constitutionnelle. Les nations les plus soumises au despotisme éprouvent ce sentiment avec autant de vivacité que les nations libres; les peuples les plus barbares le sentent même encore plus vivement que les nations policées."—*L'Italie au Dix-neuvième Siècle,* p. 148, Paris, 1821.

This fertilising and regenerating process can only be obtained by living under one government. It is in the cauldron of the State that the fusion takes place by which the vigour, the knowledge, and the capacity of one portion of mankind may be communicated to another. Where political and national boundaries coincide, society ceases to advance, and nations relapse into a condition corresponding to that of men who renounce intercourse with their fellow-men. The difference between the two unites mankind not only by the benefits it confers on those who live together, but because it connects society either by a political or a national bond, gives to every people an interest in its neighbours, either because they are under the same government or because they are of the same race, and thus promotes the interests of humanity, of civilisation, and of religion.

Christianity rejoices at the mixture of races, as paganism identifies itself with their differences, because truth is universal, and errors various and particular. In the ancient world idolatry and nationality went together, and the same term is applied in Scripture to both. It was the mission of the Church to overcome national differences. The period of her undisputed supremacy was that in which all Western Europe obeyed the same laws, all literature was contained in one language, and the political unit of Christendom was personified in a single potentate, while its intellectual unity was represented in one university. As the ancient Romans concluded their conquests by carrying away the gods of the conquered people, Charlemagne overcame the national resistance of the Saxons only by the forcible destruction of their pagan rites. Out of the mediæval period, and the combined action of the German race and the Church, came forth a new system of nations and a new conception of nationality. Nature was overcome in the nation as well as in the individual. In pagan and uncultivated times, nations were distinguished from each other by the widest diversity, not only in religion, but in customs, language, and character. Under the new law they had many things in common; the old barriers which separated them were removed, and the new principle of self-government, which Christianity imposed, enabled them to live together under the same authority, without necessarily losing their cherished habits, their customs, or their laws. The new idea of freedom made room for different races in one State. A nation was no longer what it had been to the ancient world,—the progeny of a common ancestor, or the aboriginal product of a particular region,—a result of merely physical and material causes,—but a moral and political being; not the creation of geographical or physiological unity, but developed in the course of history by the action of the State. It is derived from the State, not supreme over it. A State may in course of time produce a nationality; but that a nationality should constitute a State is contrary to the nature of modern civilisation. The nation derives its rights and its power from the memory of a former independence.

The Church has agreed in this respect with the tendency of political progress, and discouraged wherever she could the isolation of nations, admonishing them of their duties to each other, and regarding conquest and feudal investitude as the natural means of raising barbarous or sunken nations to a higher level. But though she has never attributed to national independence an immunity from the accidental consequences of feudal law, of hereditary claims, or of testamentary arrangements, she defends national liberty against uniformity and centralisation with an energy inspired by perfect community of interests. For the same enemy threatens both; and the State which is reluctant to tolerate differences, and to do justice to the peculiar character of various races, must from the same cause interfere in the internal government of religion. The connection of religious liberty with the emancipation of Poland or Ireland is not merely the accidental result of local causes; and the failure of the Concordat to unite the subjects of Austria is the natural consequence of a policy which did not desire to protect the provinces in their diversity and autonomy, and sought to bribe the Church by favours instead of strengthening her by independence. From this influence of religion in modern history has proceeded a new definition of patriotism.

The difference between nationality and the State is exhibited in the nature of patriotic attachment. Our connection with the race is merely natural or physical, whilst our duties to the political nation are ethical. One is a community of affections and instincts infinitely important and powerful in savage life, but pertaining more to the animal than to the civilised man; the other is an authority governing by laws, imposing obligations, and giving a moral sanction and character to the natural relations of society. Patriotism is in political life what faith is in religion, and it stands to the domestic feelings and to homesickness as faith to fanaticism and to superstition. It has one aspect derived from private life and nature, for it is an extension of the family affections, as the tribe is an extension of the family. But in its real political character, patriotism consists in the development of the instinct of self-preservation into a moral duty which may involve self-sacrifice. Self-preservation is both an instinct and a duty, natural and involuntary in one respect, and at the same time a moral obligation. By the first it produces the family; by the last the State. If the nation could exist without the State, subject only to the instinct of self-preservation, it would be incapable of denying, controlling, or sacrificing itself; it would be an end and a rule to itself. But in the political order moral purposes are realised and public ends are pursued to which private interests and even existence must be sacrificed. The great sign of true patriotism, the development of selfishness into sacrifice, is the product of political life. That sense of duty which is supplied by race is not entirely separated from its selfish and instinctive basis; and the love of country, like married love, stands at the same time on a material and a moral foundation. The patriot must distinguish between the two causes or objects of his devotion. The attachment which is given only to the country is like obedience given only to the State—a submission to physical influences. The man who prefers his country before every other duty shows the same spirit as the man who surrenders every right to the State. They both deny that right is superior to authority.

There is a moral and political country, in the language of Burke, distinct from the geographical, which may be possibly in collision with it. The Frenchmen who bore arms against the Convention were as patriotic as the Englishmen who bore arms against King Charles, for they recognised a higher duty than that of obedience to the actual sovereign. "In an address to France," said Burke, "in an attempt to treat with it, or in considering any scheme at all relative to it, it is impossible we should mean the geographical, we must always mean the moral and political, country. . . . The truth is, that France is out of itself—the moral France is separated from the geographical. The master of the house is expelled, and the robbers are in possession. If we look for the corporate people of France, existing as corporate in the eye and intention of public law (that corporate people, I mean, who are free to deliberate and to decide, and who have a capacity to treat and conclude), they are in Flanders and Germany, in Switzerland, Spain, Italy, and England. There are all the princes of the blood, there are all the orders of the State, there are all the parliaments of the kingdom. . . . I am sure that if half that number of the same description were taken out of this country, it would leave hardly anything that I should call the people of England."[6] Rousseau draws nearly the same distinction between the country to which we happen to belong and that which fulfils towards us the political functions of the State. In the *Emile* he has a sentence of which it is not easy in a translation to convey the point: "Qui n'a pas une patrie a du moins un pays." And in his tract on Political Economy he writes: "How shall men love their country if it is nothing more for them than for strangers, and bestows on them only that which it can refuse to none?" It is in the same sense he says, further on, "La patrie ne peut subsister sans la liberté."[7]

The nationality formed by the State, then, is the only one to which we owe political duties, and it is, therefore, the only one which has political rights. The Swiss are ethnologically either French, Italian, or German; but no nationality has the slightest claim upon them, except the purely political nationality of Switzerland. The Tuscan or the Neapolitan State has formed a nationality, but the citizens of Florence and of Naples have no political community with each other. There are other States which have neither succeeded in absorbing distinct races in a political nationality, nor in separating a particular district from a larger nation. Austria and Mexico are instances on the one hand, Parma and Baden on the other. The progress of civilisation deals hardly with the last description of States. In order to maintain their integrity they must attach themselves by confederations, or family alliances, to greater Powers, and thus lose something of their independence. Their tendency is to isolate and shut off their inhabitants, to narrow the horizon of their views, and to dwarf in some degree the proportions of their ideas. Public opinion cannot maintain its liberty and purity in such small dimensions, and the currents that come from larger communities sweep over a contracted territory. In a small and homogeneous population there is hardly room for a natural classification of society, or for inner groups of interests that set bounds to sovereign power. The government and the subjects contend with borrowed weapons. The resources of the one and the aspirations of the other are derived from some external source, and the consequence is that the country becomes the instrument and the scene of contests in which it is not interested. These States, like the minuter communities of the Middle Ages, serve a purpose, by constituting partitions and securities of self-government in the larger States;

6. Burke's "Remarks on the Policy of the Allies," *Works,* V. 26, 29, 30.

7. *Œuvres,* I, 593, 595; 11, 717. Bossuet, in a passage of great beauty on the love of country, does not attain to the political definition of the word: "La société humaine demande qu'on aime la terre où l'on habite ensemble, ou la regarde comme une mère et une nourrice commune. . . . Les hommes en effet se sentent liés par quelque chose de fort, lorsqu'ils songent, que le même terre qui les a portés et nourris étant vivants, les recevra dans son sein quand ils seront morts." "Politique tirée de l'Ecriture Sainte," *Œuvres,* X, 317.

but they are impediments to the progress of society, which depends on the mixture of races under the same governments.

The vanity and peril of national claims founded on no political tradition, but on race alone, appear in Mexico. There the races are divided by blood, without being grouped together in different regions. It is, therefore, neither possible to unite them nor to convert them into the elements of an organised State. They are fluid, shapeless, and unconnected, and cannot be precipitated, or formed into the basis of political institutions. As they cannot be used by the State, they cannot be recognised by it; and their peculiar qualities, capabilities, passions, and attachments are of no service, and therefore obtain no regard. They are necessarily ignored, and are therefore perpetually outraged. From this difficulty of races with political pretensions, but without political position, the Eastern world escaped by the institution of castes. Where there are only two races there is the resource of slavery; but when different races inhabit the different territories of one Empire composed of several smaller States, it is of all possible combinations the most favourable to the establishment of a highly developed system of freedom. In Austria there are two circumstances which add to the difficulty of the problem, but also increase its importance. The several nationalities are at very unequal degrees of advancement, and there is no single nation which is so predominant as to overwhelm or absorb the others. These are the conditions necessary for the very highest degree of organisation which government is capable of receiving. They supply the greatest variety of intellectual resource; the perpetual incentive to progress which is afforded not merely by competition, but by the spectacle of a more advanced people; the most abundant elements of self-government, combined with the impossibility for the State to rule all by its own will; and the fullest security for the preservation of local customs and ancient rights. In such a country as this, liberty would achieve its most glorious results, while centralisation and absolutism would be destruction.

The problem presented to the government of Austria is higher than that which is solved in England, because of the necessity of admitting the national claims. The parliamentary system fails to provide for them, as it presupposes the unity of the people. Hence in those countries in which different races dwell together, it has not satisfied their desires, and is regarded as an imperfect form of freedom. It brings out more clearly than before the differences it does not recognise, and thus continues the work of the old absolutism, and appears as a new phase of centralisation. In those countries, therefore, the power of the imperial parliament must be limited as jealously as the power of the crown, and many of its functions must be discharged by provincial diets, and a descending series of local authorities.

The great importance of nationality in the State consists in the fact that it is the basis of political capacity. The character of a nation determines in great measure the form and vitality of the State. Certain political habits and ideas belong to particular nations, and they vary with the course of the national history. A people just emerging from barbarism, a people effete from the excesses of a luxurious civilisation, cannot possess the means of governing itself; a people devoted to equality, or to absolute monarchy, is incapable of producing an aristocracy; a people averse to the institution of private property is without the first element of freedom. Each of these can be converted into efficient members of a free community only by the contact of a superior race, in whose power will lie the future prospects of the State. A system which ignores these things, and does not rely for its support on the character and aptitude of the people, does not intend that they should administer their own affairs, but that they should simply be obedient to the supreme command. The denial of nationality, therefore, implies the denial of political liberty.

The greatest adversary of the rights of nationality is the modern theory of nationality. By making the State and the nation commensurate with each other in theory, it reduces practically to a subject condition all other nationalities that may be within the boundary. It cannot admit them to an equality with the ruling nation which constitutes the State, because the State would then cease to be national, which would be a contradiction of the principle of its existence. According, therefore, to the degree of humanity and civilisation in that dominant body which claims all the rights of the community, the inferior races are exterminated, or reduced to servitude, or outlawed, or put in a condition of dependence.

If we take the establishment of liberty for the realisation of moral duties to be the end of civil society, we must conclude that those states are substantially the most perfect which, like the British and Austrian Empires, include various distinct nationalities without oppressing them. Those in which no mixture of races has occurred are imperfect; and those in which its effects have disappeared are decrepit. A State which is incompetent to satisfy different races condemns itself; a State which labours to neutralise, to absorb, or to expel them, destroys its own vitality; a State which does not include them is destitute of the chief basis of self-government. The theory of nationality, therefore, is a retrograde step in history. It is the most advanced form of the revolution, and must retain its power to the end of the revolutionary period, of which it announces the approach. Its great historical importance depends on two chief causes.

First, it is a chimera. The settlement at which it aims is impossible. As it can never be satisfied and exhausted, and always continues to assert itself, it prevents the government from ever relapsing into the condition which provoked its rise. The danger is too threatening, and the power over men's minds too great, to allow any system to endure which justifies the resistance of nationality. It must contribute, therefore, to obtain that which in theory it condemns,—the liberty of different nationalities as members of one sovereign community. This is a service which no other force could accomplish; for it is a corrective alike of absolute monarchy, of democracy, and of constitutionalism, as well as of the centralisation which is common to all three. Neither the monarchical nor the revolutionary, nor the parliamentary system can do this; and all the ideas which have excited enthusiasm in past times are impotent for the purpose except nationality alone.

And secondly, the national theory marks the end of the revolutionary doctrine and its logical exhaustion. In proclaiming the supremacy of the rights of nationality, the system of democratic equality goes beyond its own extreme boundary, and falls into contradiction with itself. Between the democratic and the national phase of the revolution, socialism had intervened, and had already carried the consequences of the principle to an absurdity. But that phase was passed. The revolution survived its offspring, and produced another further result. Nationality is more advanced than socialism, because it is a more arbitrary system. The social theory endeavours to provide for the existence of the individual beneath the terrible burdens which modern society heaps upon labour. It is not merely a development of the notion of equality, but a refuge from real misery and starvation. However false the solution, it was a reasonable demand that the poor should be saved from destruction; and if the freedom of the State was sacrificed to the safety of the individual, the more immediate object was, at least in theory, attained. But nationality does not aim either at liberty or prosperity, both of which it sacrifices to the imperative necessity of making the nation the mould and measure of the State. Its course will be marked with material as well as mortal ruin, in order that a new invention may prevail over the works of God and the interests of mankind. There is no principle of change, no phase of political speculation conceivable, more comprehensive, more subversive, or more arbitrary than this. It is a confutation of democracy, because it sets limits to the exercise of the popular will, and substitutes for it a higher principle. It prevents not only the division, but the extension of the State, and forbids to terminate war by conquest, and to obtain a security for peace. Thus, after surrendering the individual to the collective will, the revolutionary system makes the collective will subject to conditions which are independent of it, and rejects all law, only to be controlled by an accident.

Although, therefore, the theory of nationality is more absurd and more criminal than the theory of socialism, it has an important mission in the world, and marks the final conflict, and therefore the end, of two forces which are the worst enemies of civil freedom,—the absolute monarchy and the revolution.

# *Section B*

# Occupation and Economy

EDITORIAL FOREWORD

# Occupation and Economy

*by Talcott Parsons*

THE SELECTIONS IN THIS SECTION deal with the economic aspect of the structure of societies in connection with the theme of occupational roles—the most important focus of the entrance of the services of human individuals in roles into the economic process. We are essentially concerned with analyzing the ways in which this economic aspect of social structure has become differentiated from other aspects. Here, at least as much as anywhere else, we have had to make a few selections from a very large literature. Our two principal criteria were the "classic" character of the statement, and its specific relevance to the sociological, as distinguished from the economic, aspects of the concrete problem areas.

We have classified the materials according to this criterion of sociological relevance. The first subsection is simply a statement of the economist's major frame of reference. The one selection in this subsection is from Alfred Marshall's *Principles*, which was certainly that generation's most influential general treatment of economic theory. The second subsection deals with the institutional framework of a more or less differentiated economy, as that concept was established in the General Introduction to the Reader, and also elaborated in the Introduction to Part Two. The crucial concepts in this area are the division of labor, contractual relations, property, and their relations to the problem of solidarity or integration of the social system. The third subsection deals with the ways in which an economy's structurally differentiated units can be related to each other, so far as the mechanisms are primarily economic. The fourth subsection returns to materials concerning the character of the units themselves. The fifth subsection includes two classic statements concerning problems of change in economic structure.

We have utilized a few sources written earlier than our main period because, in the present subject matter, they set a tone which has been seriously superseded in only a few respects. Adam Smith's famous statement about the division of labor was included in Part One, as one of the critical documents of utilitarian social thought. The second subsection begins with another selection from Smith. It deals with a crucial theme of the institutional setting of classical economic analysis: what the utilitarians considered the primary functional axis of differentiation in the economy—that between "capital," in their specific theoretical sense, and "labor." The problem of organizing the firm as a productive unit was not salient at that time; the primary concern was with financing production, with capital conceived as "making advances to labor." Smith's statement of this theme is followed by a classic statement by Malthus, in certain respects generalizing it into a pattern of differentiating the whole society into classes, on the basis of economic function. This theme leads directly into that of social stratification, particularly through the type of influence exerted on Marx by the classical economists.

The morphology of economic differentiation as such—of the forms taken by the division of labor—is an aspect of comparative social structure that has not been much considered. Here, as in so many areas, Weber's work stands almost alone in its analytical elaboration and comprehensiveness. As an example of the greater complication of the problems and the advance made over the simple classical framework, we present a selection from Weber's economic sociology[1] on types of the divi-

1. By the term "Weber's economic sociology," we refer to Chapter II of *The Theory of Social and Economic Organization*.

sion of labor. This provides many starting points for the structural analysis of occupational roles.

Sociologists have neglected the institution of property. Economic historians have paid some attention to it, but on the whole the best treatments are found in the works of legal historians. From the extensive literature, we have chosen a selection from Pollock and Maitland's *History of English Law* that deals with the earlier phases of the legal development which led eventually to the modern institution of ownership in land. This selection is obviously a very fragmentary representation of a large and important subject.

As noted in the two more general Introductions above, contract is the master institution in the economic field. Sir Henry Maine, as a legal historian with an evolutionary perspective, was probably most important in putting the problem into the center of social thinking.[2] He regarded contract as a positive institution, and not simply in the more negative terms common in the utilitarian tradition. However, Durkheim, above all, placed contract in a central position in the theoretical analysis of modern society, as well as in the structure of theory as such. The last selection in the second subsection (chapter 7 of Book I of his *Division of Labor*) is a classic of sociological theory. Polemically oriented to Spencer's concept of contractual relations, it is the definitive critique of utilitarianism from the point of view of the problem of order or social integration; and he built his own theory of organic solidarity on this foundation.

There is a direct transition from the institutional structure of contract to the organization of the more specifically economic modes of contractual relations in markets. Sociologists have also seriously neglected the market, tending to regard it as the subject matter of the economist; however, the latter has tended to neglect the market's sociological aspects. In the period under consideration, Weber's brief statement on the nature and types of markets is the most penetrating and comprehensive in the literature.

The subject of markets leads directly to the subject of the different modes of orientation to the problem of monetary proceeds—the more or less direct analytical sense in which we can speak of "capitalism." Again, Weber, in a brief selection from his economic sociology, presents the most penetrating discussion of this.

The Introduction to Part Two is concerned with the nature of money itself, as an institutionalized mechanism performing the two functions defined by the classical economists as constituting a "measure of value" and as constituting a "medium of exchange." However, it is difficult to find a more general analysis of the nature of money that links its economic characteristics with its institutional foundations. In this area, at the end of the period, a new level was reached in Keynes's famous *General Theory*. We have included the chapter from it that summarizes the principal characteristics of and presuppositions about money.

Finally, we have included Frank Knight's paper, though it verges on being too recent, as a general statement of the nature of a "free enterprise" economy. Though Professor Knight was not, in this Reader's terms, considering the economy as a subsystem of the total society, his delineation of it fits very well with this concept.

The fourth subsection returns to the consideration of structural units in the society. Rather earlier than most of our authors, Le Play made a classic study of European workers' households that provides a general account of the setting of the development of the recruitment of the "worker" level of the labor force in the course of the industrial revolution. This selection is followed by two selections from Weber's economic sociology. The first deals with the theme of "economic bureaucracy"—i.e., with the firm as a social organization, as distinguished from a "combinatorial mechanism" for the factors of production. For Weber, harnessing the mechanisms of bureaucracy to privately controlled economic production was the principal characteristic, structurally speaking, of "rational bourgeois capitalism," as distinguished from the other types described in the second selection in the third subsection. Weber in part directly analyzed and in part foresaw the trend of "occupationalizing" the process of production. The second Weber selection here deals with what he considered the two crucial types of orientation of such units to the market—orientation to profit, and orientation to "budgetary management." Structurally speaking, this is the line dividing orientation toward self-interest and orientation toward collective interest—alternatives often erroneously considered "psychological." Weber correctly treats this as a structural feature of organizational units involved in the economy, and not as a question of individuals' motivations.

A selection from Alfred Marshall on the problem of organization in industry completes this subsection. More than any other economic theorist, Marshall introduced organization, as a fourth factor of production, into the threefold classical

2. In relatively direct relation, that is, to sociological interests. The immense literature on the "social contract" preceding this belongs rather to political theory. See the Introduction to Part One, Section A.

scheme of land, labor, and capital. Marshall supported this important theoretical decision with a very shrewd survey of relatively empirical aspects of economic organization. The sociological relevance of this problem is evident; through the organizational factor, one of the major aspects of the society's institutional structure impinges on the economic process as such.

The final subsection essentially consists of a recognition of the problems of structural evolution and change in the economic field. It comprises two selections. The first, written by the Austrian economic historian Karl Bücher, served for long as the classic typology of modes of organization of production in the industrial field. The other is Joseph Schumpeter's famous concept of entrepreneurship, which has had a profound influence on studies of economic development, and is clearly as much sociological as economic in its theoretical orientation.

## I–GENERAL CONSIDERATIONS

# *Wants in Relation to Activities*

BY ALFRED MARSHALL

HUMAN WANTS AND DESIRES are countless in number and very various in kind. The uncivilized man indeed has not many more than the brute animal; but every step in his progress upwards increases the variety of his needs together with the variety in his methods of satisfying them. Thus though the brute and the savage alike have their preferences for chioce morsels, neither of them cares much for variety for its own sake. As, however, man rises in civilization, as his mind becomes developed, and even his animal passions begin to associate themselves with mental activities, his wants become rapidly more subtle and more various; and in the minor details of life he begins to desire change for the sake of change, long before he has consciously escaped from the yoke of custom. The first great step in this direction comes with the art of making a fire: gradually he gets to accustom himself to many different kinds of food and drink cooked in many different ways; and before long monotony begins to become irksome to him, and he finds it a great hardship when accident compels him to live for a long time exclusively on one or two kinds of food.

As a man's riches increase his food and drink becomes more various and costly, but his appetite is limited by nature, and when his expenditure on food is extravagant it is more often to gratify the desires of hospitality and display than to indulge his own senses.

This brings us to remark with Senior that "Strong as is the desire for variety, it is weak compared with the desire for distinction: a feeling which if we consider its universality, and its constancy, that it affects all men and at all times, that it comes with us from the cradle and never leaves us till we go into the grave, may be pronounced to be the most powerful of human passions." This great half-truth is well illustrated by a comparison of the desire for choice and various food with that for choice and various dress.

That need for dress which is the result of natural causes varies with the climate and the season of year, and a little with the nature of a person's occupations. But in dress conventional wants overshadow those which are natural. Thus in many of the earlier stages of civilization the sumptuary mandates of Law and Custom have rigidly prescribed to the members of each caste or industrial grade, the style and the standard of expense up to which their dress must reach and beyond which they may not go; and part of the substance of these mandates remains now, though subject to rapid change. In Scotland, for instance, in Adam Smith's time many persons were allowed by custom to go abroad without shoes and stockings who may not do so now; and many may still do it in Scotland who

Reprinted from Alfred Marshall, *Principles of Economics* (2d ed.; London: Macmillan and Co., 1891), chap. ii, pp. 144–48.

might not in England. Again, in England now a well-to-do labourer is expected to appear on Sunday in a black coat and, in some places, in a silk hat; though these would have subjected him to ridicule but a short time ago. In all the lower ranks of life there is a constant increase both in that variety and expensiveness which custom requires as a minimum, and in that which it tolerates as a maximum; and the efforts to obtain distinction by dress are extending themselves throughout the lower grades of English society.

But in the upper grades, though the dress of women is still various and costly, that of men is simple and inexpensive as compared with what it was in Europe not long ago, and is to-day in the East. For those men who are most truly distinguished on their own account, have a natural dislike to seem to claim attention by their dress; and they have set the fashion.[1]

House room satisfies the imperative need for shelter from the weather: but that need plays very little part in the effective demand for house room. For though a small but well-built cabin gives excellent shelter, its stifling atmosphere, its necessary uncleanliness, and its want of the decencies and the quiet of life are great evils. It is not so much that they cause physical discomfort as that they tend to stunt the faculties, and limit people's higher activities. With every increase in these activities the demand for larger house room becomes more urgent.[2]

And therefore relatively large and well appointed house room is, even in the lowest social ranks, at once a "necessary for efficiency," and the most convenient and obvious way of advancing a material claim to social distinction. And even in those grades in which everyone has house room sufficient for the higher activities of himself and his family, a yet further and almost unlimited increase is desired as a requisite for the exercise of many of the higher social activities.

It is again the desire for the exercise and development of activities, spreading through every rank of society, which leads not only to the pursuit of science, literature and art for their own sake, but to the rapidly increasing demand for the work of those who pursue them as professions. This is one of the most marked characteristics of our age; and the same may be said of the growing desire for those amusements, such as athletic games and travelling, which develop activities, rather than indulge any sensuous craving.[3]

For indeed the desire for excellence for its own sake, is almost as wide in its range as the lower desire for distinction. As that graduates down from the ambition of those who may hope that their names will be in men's mouths in distant lands and in distant times, to the hope of the country lass that the new ribbon she puts on for Easter may not pass unnoticed by her neighbours; so the desire for excellence for its own sake graduates down from that of a Newton, or a Stradivarius, to that of the fisherman who, even when no one is looking and he is not in a hurry, delights in handling his craft well, and in the fact that she is well built and responds promptly to his guidance. Desires of this kind exert a great influence on the Supply of the highest faculties and the greatest inventions; and they are not unimportant on the side of Demand. For a large part of the demand for the most highly skilled professional services and the best work of the mechanical artisan, arises from the delight that people have in the training of their own faculties, and in exercising them by aid of the most delicately adjusted and responsive implements.

Speaking broadly therefore, although it is man's wants in the earliest stages of his development that give rise to his activities, yet afterwards each new step upwards is to be regarded rather as the development of new activities giving rise to new wants, than that of new wants giving rise to new activities.

We see this clearly if we look away from healthy conditions of life, where new activities are constantly being developed; and watch the West Indian negro, using his new freedom and wealth not to get the means of satisfying new wants, but in idle stagnation that is not rest; or again look at that rapidly lessening part of the English working classes, who have no ambition and no pride or delight in the growth of their faculties and activities,

1. A woman may display wealth, but she may not display only her wealth, by her dress; or else she defeats her ends. She must also suggest some distinction of character as well as of wealth: for though her dress may owe more to her dressmaker than to herself, yet there is a traditional assumption that, being less busy than man with external affairs, she can give more time to taking thought as to her dress. Even under the sway of modern fashions, to be "well dressed"—not "expensively dressed"—is a reasonable minor aim for those who desire to be distinguished for their faculties and abilities; and this will be still more the case if the evil dominion of the wanton vagaries of fashion should pass away. For to arrange costumes beautiful in themselves, various and well-adapted to their purposes is an object worthy of high endeavour; it belongs to the same class, though not to the same rank in that class, as the painting of a good picture.

2. It is true that many active minded working men prefer cramped lodgings in a town to a roomy cottage in the country; but that is because they have a strong taste for those activities for which a country life offers little scope.

3. As a minor point it may be noticed that those drinks which stimulate the mental activities are largely displacing those which merely gratify the senses. The consumption of tea is increasing very fast while that of alcohol is stationary; and there is in all ranks of society a diminishing demand for the grosser and more immediately stupefying form of alcohol.

and spend on drink whatever surplus their wages afford over the bare necessities of a squalid life.

It is not true therefore that "the Theory of Consumption is the scientific basis of economics." For much that is of chief interest in the Science of Wants, is borrowed from the Science of Efforts and Activities. These two supplement one another; either is incomplete without the other. But if either, more than the other, may claim to be the interpreter of the history of man, whether on the economic side or any other, it is the Science of Activities and not that of Wants; and McCulloch indicated their true relations when, discussing "the Progressive Nature of Man," he said:—"The gratification of a want or a desire is merely a step to some new pursuit. In every stage of his progress he is destined to contrive and invent, to engage in new undertakings; and, when these are accomplished to enter with fresh energy upon others."

From this it follows that such a discussion of Demand as is possible at this stage of our work, must be confined to an elementary analysis of an almost purely formal kind. The higher study of Consumption must come after, and not before, the main body of economic analysis; and, though it may have its beginning within the proper domain of economics, it cannot find its conclusions there, but must extend far beyond.

## II–ECONOMIC INSTITUTIONS

# 1. *Capitalists and Laborers*

BY ADAM SMITH

THE PRODUCE of labour constitutes the natural recompence or wages of labour.

In that original state of things, which precedes both the appropriation of land and the accumulation of stock, the whole produce of labour belongs to the labourer. He has neither landlord nor master to share with him.

Had this state continued, the wages of labour would have augmented with all those improvements in its productive powers, to which the division of labour gives occasion. All things would gradually have become cheaper. They would have been produced by a smaller quantity of labour; and as the commodities produced by equal quantities of labour would naturally in this state of things be exchanged for one another, they would have been purchased likewise with the produce of a smaller quantity.

But though all things would have become cheaper in reality, in appearance many things might have become dearer than before, or have been exchanged for a greater quantity of other goods. Let us suppose, for example, that in the greater part of employments the productive powers of labour had been improved to tenfold, or that a day's labour could produce ten times the quantity of work which it had done originally; but that in a particular employment they had been improved only to double, or that a day's labour could produce only twice the quantity of work which it had done before. In exchanging the produce of a day's labour in the greater part of employments, for that of a day's labour in this particular one, ten times the original quality of work in them would purchase only twice the original quantity in it. Any particular quantity in it, therefore, a pound weight, for example, would appear to be five times dearer than before. In reality, however, it would be twice as cheap. Though it required five times the quantity of other goods to purchase it, it would require only half the quantity of labour either to purchase or to produce it. The acquisition, therefore, would be twice as easy as before.

But this original state of things, in which the labourer enjoyed the whole produce of his own labour, could not last beyond the first introduction of the appropriation of land and the accumulation of stock. It was at an end, therefore, long before the

Reprinted from Adam Smith, *An Inquiry into the Nature and Causes of the Wealth of Nations* (7th ed.; London: A. Strahan & T. Cadell, 1793), chap. viii, pp. 96–111.

most considerable improvements were made in the productive powers of labour, and it would be to no purpose to trace further what might have been its effects upon the recompence or wages of labour.

As soon as land becomes private property, the landlord demands a share of almost all the produce which the labourer can either raise, or collect from it. His rent makes the first deduction from the produce of the labour which is employed upon land.

It seldom happens that the person who tills the ground has wherewithal to maintain himself till he reaps the harvest. His maintenance is generally advanced to him from the stock of a master, the farmer who employs him, and who would have no interest to employ him, unless he was to share in the produce of his labour, or unless his stock was to be replaced to him with a profit. This profit makes a second deduction from the produce of the labour which is employed upon land.

The produce of almost all other labour is liable to the like deduction of profit. In all arts and manufactures the greater part of the workmen stand in need of a master to advance them the materials of their work, and their wages and maintenance till it be completed. He shares in the produce of their labour, or in the value which it adds to the materials upon which it is bestowed; and in this share consists his profit.

It sometimes happens, indeed, that a single independent workman has stock sufficient both to purchase the materials of his work, and to maintain himself till it be completed. He is both master and workman, and enjoys the whole produce of his own labour, or the whole value which it adds to the materials upon which it is bestowed. It includes what are usually two distinct revenues, belonging to two distinct persons, the profits of stock, and the wages of labour.

Such cases, however, are not very frequent, and in every part of Europe, twenty workmen serve under a master for one that is independent; and the wages of labour are every where understood to be, what they usually are, when the labourer is one person, and the owner of the stock which employs him another.

What are the common wages of labour, depends every where upon the contract usually made between those two parties, whose interests are by no means the same. The workmen desire to get as much, the masters to give as little as possible. The former are disposed to combine in order to raise, the latter in order to lower the wages of labour.

It is not, however, difficult to foresee which of the two parties must, upon all ordinary occasions, have the advantage in the dispute, and force the other into a compliance with their terms. The masters, being fewer in number, can combine much more easily; and the law, besides, authorises, or at least does not prohibit their combinations, while it prohibits those of the workmen. We have no acts of parliament against combining to lower the price of work; but many against combining to raise it. In all such disputes the masters can hold out much longer. A landlord, a farmer, a master manufacturer, or merchant, though they did not employ a single workman, could generally live a year or two upon the stocks which they have already acquired. Many workmen could not subsist a week, few could subsist a month, and scarce any a year without employment. In the long-run the workman may be as necessary to his master as his master is to him; but the necessity is not so immediate.

We rarely hear, it has been said, of the combinations of masters, though frequently of those of workmen. But whoever imagines, upon this account, that masters rarely combine, is as ignorant of the world as of the subject. Masters are always and every where in a sort of tacit, but constant and uniform, combination, not to raise the wages of labour above their actual rate. To violate this combination is every where a most unpopular action, and a sort of reproach to a master among his neighbors and equals. We seldom, indeed, hear of this combination, because it is the usual, and one may say, the natural state of things which nobody ever hears of. Masters too sometimes enter into particular combinations to sink the wages of labour even below this rate. These are always conducted with the utmost silence and secrecy, till the moment of execution, and when the workmen yield, as they sometimes do, without resistance, though severely felt by them, they are never heard of by other people. Such combinations, however, are frequently resisted by a contrary defensive combination of the workmen; who sometimes too, without any provocation of this kind, combine of their own accord to raise the price of their labour. Their usual pretenses are, sometimes the high price of provisions; sometimes the great profit which their masters make by their work. But whether their combinations be offensive or defensive, they are always abundantly heard of. In order to bring the point to a speedy decision, they have always recourse to the loudest clamour, and sometimes to the most shocking violence and outrage. They are desperate, and act with the folly and extravagance of desperate men, who must either starve, or frighten their masters into an immediate compliance with their demands. The masters upon these occasions are just as clamorous upon the other side, and never cease to call aloud for the assistance of the civil magistrate, and the rigorous execution of those laws which have been enacted with so much severity against the combinations of servants, labourers, and journeymen. The workmen, accordingly, very seldom derive any advantage from the violence of those tumultuous combinations, which, partly from the interposition of the civil magistrate, partly from the superior steadiness of the masters, partly from the necessity which the greater part of the workmen are under of submitting for the sake of present subsistence, generally end in nothing, but the punishment or ruin of the ringleaders.

But though in disputes with their workmen, masters must generally have the advantage, there is however a certain rate, below which it seems impossible to reduce, for any considerable time, the ordinary wages even of the lowest species of labour.

A man must always live by his work, and his wages must at least be sufficient to maintain him. They must even upon most occasions be somewhat more; otherwise it would be impossible for him to bring up a family, and the race of such workmen could not last beyond the first generation. Mr. Cantillon seems, upon this account, to suppose that the lowest species of common labourers must every where earn at least double their own maintenance, in order that one with another they may be enabled to bring up two children; the labour of the wife, on account of her necessary attendance on the children, being supposed no more than sufficient to provide for herself. But one half the children born, it is computed, die before the age of manhood. The poorest labourers, therefore, according to this account, must, one with another, attempt to rear at least four children, in order that two may have an equal chance of living to that age. But the necessary maintenance of four children, it is supposed, may be nearly equal to that of one man. The labour of an able-bodied slave, the same author adds, is computed to be worth double his maintenance; and that of the meanest labourer, he thinks, cannot be worth less than that of an able-bodied slave. Thus far at least seems certain, that, in order to bring up a family, the labour of the husband and wife together must, even in the lowest species of common labour, be able to earn something more than what is precisely necessary for their own maintenance; but in what proportion, whether in that above mentioned, or in any other, I shall not take upon me to determine.

There are certain circumstances, however, which sometimes give the labourers an advantage, and enable them to raise their wages considerably above this rate; evidently the lowest which is consistent with common humanity.

When in any country the demand for those who live by wages, labourers, journeymen, servants of every kind, is continually increasing; when every year furnishes employment for a greater number than had been employed the year before, the workmen have no occasion to combine in order to raise their wages. The scarcity of hands occasions a competition among masters, who bid against one another, in order to get workmen, and thus voluntarily break through the natural combination of masters not to raise wages.

The demand for those who live by wages, it is evident, cannot increase but in proportion to the increase of the funds which are destined to the payment of wages. These funds are of two kinds: first, the revenue which is over and above what is necessary for the maintenance; and, secondly, the stock which is over and above what is necessary for the employment of their masters.

When the landlord, annuitant, or monied man, has a greater revenue than what he judges sufficient to maintain his own family, he employs either the whole or a part of the surplus in maintaining one or more menial servants. Increase this surplus, and he will naturally increase the number of those servants.

When an independent workman, such as a weaver or shoemaker, has got more stock than what is sufficient to purchase the materials of his own work, and to maintain himself till he can dispose of it, he naturally employs one or more journeymen with the surplus, in order to make a profit by their work. Increase this surplus, and he will naturally increase the number of his journeymen.

The demand for those who live by wages, therefore, necessarily increases with the increase of the revenue and stock of every country, and cannot possibly increase without it. The increase of revenue and stock is the increase of national wealth. The demand for those who live by wages, therefore, naturally increases with the increase of national wealth, and cannot possibly increase without it.

It is not the actual greatness of national wealth, but its continual increase, which occasions a rise in the wages of labour. It is not, accordingly, in the richest countries, but in the most thriving, or in those which are growing rich the fastest, that the wages of labour are highest. England is certainly, in the present times, a much richer country than any part of North America. The wages of labour, however, are much higher in North America than in any part of England. In the province of New York, common labourers earn* three shillings and sixpence currency, equal to two shillings

* This was written in 1773, before the commencement of the late disturbances.

sterling, a day; ship carpenters, ten shillings and sixpence currency, with a pint of rum worth sixpence sterling, equal in all to six shillings and sixpence sterling; house carpenters and bricklayers, eight shillings currency, equal to four shillings and sixpence sterling; journeymen taylors, five shillings currency, equal to about two shillings and ten pence sterling. These prices are all above the London price; and wages are said to be as high in the other colonies as in New York. The price of provisions is every where in North America much lower than in England. A dearth has never been known there. In the worst seasons, they have always had a sufficiency for themselves, though less for exportation. If the money price of labour, therefore, be higher than it is any where in the mother country, its real price, the real command of the necessaries and conveniences of life which it conveys to the labourer, must be higher in a still greater proportion.

But though North America is not yet so rich as England, it is much more thriving, and advancing with much greater rapidity to the further acquisition of riches. The most decisive mark of the prosperity of any country is the increase of the number of its inhabitants. In Great Britain, and most other European countries, they are not supposed to double in less than five hundred years. In the British colonies in North America, it has been found, that they double in twenty or five-and-twenty years. Nor in the present times is this increase principally owing to the continual importation of new inhabitants, but to the great multiplication of the species. Those who live to old age; it is said, frequently see there from fifty to a hundred, and sometimes many more, descendants from their own body. Labour is there so well rewarded, that a numerous family of children, instead of being a burthen, is a source of opulence and prosperity to the parents. The labour of each child, before it can leave their house, is computed to be worth a hundred pounds clear gain to them. A young widow with four or five young children, who, among the middling or inferior ranks of people in Europe, would have so little chance for a second husband, is there frequently courted as a sort of fortune. The value of children is the greatest of all encouragements to marriage. We cannot, therefore, wonder that the people in North America should generally marry very young. Notwithstanding the great increase occasioned by such early marriages, there is a continual complaint of the scarcity of hands in North America. The demand for labourers, the funds destined for maintaining them, increase, it seems, still faster than they can find labourers to employ.

Though the wealth of a country should be very great, yet if it has been long stationary, we must not expect to find the wages of labour very high in it. The funds destined for the payment of wages, the revenue and stock of its inhabitants, may be of the greatest extent; but if they have continued for several centuries of the same, or very nearly of the same extent, the number of labourers employed every year could easily supply, and even more than supply, the number wanted the following year. There could seldom be any scarcity of hands, nor could the masters be obliged to bid against one another in order to get them. The hands, on the contrary, would, in this case, naturally multiply beyond their employment. There would be a constant scarcity of employment, and the labourers would be obliged to bid against one another in order to get it. If in such a country the wages of labour had ever been more than sufficient to maintain the labourer, and to enable him to bring up a family, the competition of the labourers and the interest of the masters would soon reduce them to this lowest rate which is consistent with common humanity. China has been long one of the richest, that is, one of the most fertile, best cultivated, most industrious, and most populous countries in the world. It seems, however, to have been long stationary. Marco Polo, who visited it more than five hundred years ago, describes its cultivation, industry, and populousness, almost in the same terms in which they are described by travellers in the present times. It had, perhaps, even long before his time, acquired that full complement of riches which the nature of its laws and institutions permits it to acquire. The accounts of all travellers, inconsistent in many other respects, agree in the low wages of labour, and in the difficulty which a labourer finds in bringing up a family in China. If by digging the ground a whole day he can get what will purchase a small qauntity of rice in the evening, he is contented. The condition of artificers is, if possible, still worse. Instead of waiting idolently in their work-houses, for the calls of their customers, as in Europe, they are continually running about the streets, with the tools of their respective trades, offering their service, and as it were begging employment. The poverty of the lower ranks of people in China far surpasses that of the most beggarly nations in Europe. In the neighbourhood of Canton many hundred, it is commonly said, many thousand families have no habitation on the land, but live constantly in little fishing boats upon the rivers and canals. The subsistence which they find there is so scanty that they are eager to fish up the nastiest garbage thrown overboard from any European ship. Any carrion, the carcase of a dead dog or cat, for example, though half putrid and stinking, is as welcome to them as the most wholesome food to the people of other countries. Marriage is encouraged in China, not by the profitableness of children, but by the liberty of destroying them. In all great towns several are every night exposed in the street, or drowned like puppies in the water. The performance of this horrid office is even said to be the avowed business by which some people earn their subsistence.

China, however, though it may perhaps stand still, does not seem to go backwards. Its towns are no where deserted by their inhabitants. The lands which had once been cultivated, are nowhere neglected. The same, or very nearly the same, annual labour must therefore continue to be performed, and the funds destined for maintaining it must not, consequently, be sensibly diminished. The lowest class of labourers, therefore, notwithstanding their scanty subsistence, must some way or another make shift to continue their race so far as to keep up their usual numbers.

But it would be otherwise in a country where the funds destined for the maintenance of labour were sensibly decaying. Every year the demand for servants and labourers would, in all the different classes of employments, be less than it had been the year before. Many who had been bred in the superior classes, not being able to find employment in their own business, would be glad to seek it in the lowest. The lowest class being not only overstocked with its own workmen, but with the overflowings of all the other classes, the competition for employment would be so great in it, as to reduce the wages of labour to the most miserable and scanty subsistence of the labourer. Many would not be able to find employment even upon these hard terms, but would either starve, or be driven to seek a subsistence either by begging, or by the perpetration perhaps of the greatest enormities. Want, famine, and mortality, would immediately prevail in that class, and from thence extend themselves to all the superior classes, till the number of inhabitants in the country was reduced to what could easily be maintained by the revenue and stock which remained in it, and which had escaped either the tyranny or calamity which had destroyed the rest. This perhaps is nearly the present state of Bengal, and of some other of the English settlements in the East Indies. In a fertile country which had before been much depopulated, where subsistence, consequently, should not be very difficult, and where, notwithstanding, three or four hundred thousand people die of hunger in one year, we may be assured that the funds destined for the maintenance of the labouring poor are fast decaying. The difference between the genius of the British constitution which protects and governs North America, and that of the mercantile company which oppresses and domineers in the East Indies, cannot perhaps be better illustrated than by the different state of those countries.

The liberal reward of labour, therefore, as it is the necessary effect, so it is the natural symptom of increasing national wealth. The scanty maintenance of the labouring poor, on the other hand, is the natural symptom that things are at a stand, and their starving condition that they are going fast backwards.

# 2. *The Division of Society into Classes*

BY THOMAS R. MALTHUS

DR. ADAM SMITH has very justly observed, that nations, as well as individuals, grow rich by parsimony, and poor by profusion; and that, therefore, every frugal man was a friend, and every spendthrift an enemy to his country. The reason he gives is, that what is saved from revenue is always added to stock, and is therefore taken from the maintenance of labour that is generally unproductive, and employed in the maintenance of labour that realizes itself in valuable commodities. No observation can be more evidently just. The subject of Mr. Godwin's essay is a little similar in its first appearance, but in essence is as distinct as possible. He considers the mischief of profusion, as an ac-

Reprinted from Thomas R. Malthus, *First Essay on Population* (1798), reprinted for the Royal Economic Society (London: Macmillan Co., 1926), pp. 282–301, with the permission of the Macmillan Co.

knowledged truth; and therefore makes his comparison between the avaricious man, and the man who spends his income. But the avaricious man of Mr. Godwin, is totally a distinct character, at least with regard to his effect upon the prosperity of the state, from the frugal man of Dr. Adam Smith. The frugal man in order to make more money, saves from his income, and adds to his capital; and this capital he either employs himself in the maintenance of productive labour, or he lends it to some other person, who will probably employ it in this way. He benefits the state, because he adds to its general capital; and because wealth employed as capital, not only sets in motion more labour, than when spent as income, but the labour is besides of a more valuable kind. But the avaricious man of Mr. Godwin locks up his wealth in a chest, and sets in motion no labour of any kind, either productive or unproductive. This is so essential a difference, that Mr. Godwin's decision in his essay, appears at once as evidently true. It could not, indeed, but occur to Mr. Godwin, that some present inconvenience might arise to the poor, from thus locking up the funds destined for the maintenance of labour. The only way, therefore, he had of weakening this objection, was to compare the two characters chiefly with regard to their tendency to accelerate the approach of that happy state of cultivated equality, on which he says we ought always to fix our eyes as our polar star.

I think it has been proved in the former parts of this essay, that such a state of society is absolutely impracticable. What consequences then are we to expect from looking to such a point, as our guide and polar star, in the great sea of political discovery? Reason would teach us to expect no other, than winds perpetually adverse, constant but fruitless toil, frequent shipwreck, and certain misery. We shall not only fail in making the smallest real approach towards such a perfect form of society; but by wasting our strength of mind and body, in a direction in which it is impossible to proceed, and by the frequent distress which we must necessarily occasion by our repeated failures, we shall evidently impede that degree of improvement in society, which is really attainable.

It has appeared that a society constituted according to Mr. Godwin's system, must, from the inevitable laws of our nature, degenerate into a class of proprietors, and a class of labourers; and that the substitution of benevolence, for self-love, as the moving principle of society, instead of producing the happy effects that might be expected from so fair a name, would cause the same pressure of want to be felt by the whole of society, which is now felt only by a part. It is to the established administration of property, and to the apparently narrow principle of self-love, that we are indebted for all the noblest exertions of human genius, all the finer and more delicate emotions of the soul, for every thing, indeed, that distinguishes the civilized, from the savage state; and no sufficient change, has as yet taken place in the nature of civilized man, to enable us to say, that he either is, or ever will be, in a state, when he may safely throw down the ladder by which he has risen to this eminence.

If in every society that has advanced beyond the savage state, a class of proprietors, and a class of labourers,[1] must necessarily exist, it is evident, that, as labour is the only property of the class of labourers, every thing that tends to diminish the value of this property, must tend to diminish the possessions of this part of society. The only way that a poor man has of supporting himself in independence, is by the exertion of his bodily strength. This is the only commodity he has to give in exchange for the necessaries of life. It would hardly appear then that you benefit him, by narrowing the market for this commodity, by decreasing the demand for labour, and lessening the value of the only property that he possesses.

Mr. Godwin would perhaps say, that the whole system of barter and exchange, is a vile and iniquitous traffic. If you would essentially relieve the poor man, you should take a part of his labour upon yourself, or give him your money, without exacting so severe a return for it. In answer to the first method proposed, it may be observed, that even if the rich could be persuaded to assist the poor in this way, the value of the assistance would be comparatively trifling. The rich, though they think themselves of great importance, bear but a small proportion in point of numbers to the poor, and would, therefore, relieve them but of a small part of their burdens by taking a share. Were all those that are employed in the labours of luxuries, added to the number of those employed in producing necessaries; and could these necessary labours be amicably divided among all, each man's share might indeed be comparatively light; but desireable as such an amicable division would undoubtedly be, I can-

1. It should be observed, that the principal argument of this essay, only goes to prove the necessity of a class of proprietors, and a class of labourers, but by no means infers, that the present great inequality of property, is either necessary or useful to society. On the contrary, it must certainly be considered as an evil, and every institution that promotes it, is essentially bad and impolitic. But whether a government could with advantage to society actively interfere to repress inequality of fortunes, may be a matter of doubt. Perhaps the generous system of perfect liberty, adopted by Dr. Adam Smith, and the French œconomists, would be ill exchanged for any system of restraint.

not conceive any practical principle[2] according to which it could take place. It has been shewn, that the spirit of benevolence, guided by the strict impartial justice that Mr. Godwin describes, would, if vigorously acted upon, depress in want and misery the whole human race. Let us examine what would be the consequence, if the proprietor were to retain a decent share for himself; but to give the rest away to the poor, without exacting a task from them in return. Not to mention the idleness and the vice that such a proceeding, if general, would probably create in the present state of society, and the great risk there would be, of diminishing the produce of land, as well as the labours of luxury, another objection yet remains.

It has appeared that from the principle of population, more will always be in want than can be adequately supplied. The surplus of the rich man might be sufficient for three, but four will be desirous to obtain it. He cannot make this selection of three out of the four, without conferring a great favour on those that are the objects of his choice. These persons must consider themselves as under a great obligation to him, and as dependent upon him for their support. The rich man would feel his power, and the poor man his dependence; and the evil effects of these two impressions on the human heart are well known. Though I perfectly agree with Mr. Godwin therefore in the evil of hard labour; yet I still think it a less evil, and less calculated to debase the human mind, than dependence; and every history of man that we have ever read, places in a strong point of view, the danger to which that mind is exposed, which is intrusted with constant power.

In the present state of things, and particularly when labour is in request, the man who does a days work for me, confers full as great an obligation upon me, as I do upon him. I possess what he wants; he possesses what I want. We make an amicable exchange. The poor man walks erect in conscious independence; and the mind of his employer is not vitiated by a sense of power.

Three or four hundred years ago, there was undoubtedly much less labour in England, in proportion to the population, than at present; but there was much more dependence: and we probably should not now enjoy our present degree of civil liberty, if the poor, by the introduction of manufactures, had not been enabled to give something in exchange for the provisions of the great Lords, instead of being dependent upon their bounty. Even the greatest enemies of trade and manufactures, and I do not reckon myself a very determined friend to them, must allow, that when they were introduced into England, liberty came in their train.

Nothing that has been said, tends in the most remote degree to undervalue the principle of benevolence. It is one of the noblest and most godlike qualities of the human heart, generated perhaps, slowly and gradually from self-love; and afterwards intended to act as a general law, whose kind office it should be, to soften the partial deformities, to correct the asperities, and to smooth the wrinkles of its parent: and this seems to be the analogy of all nature. Perhaps there is no one general law of nature that will not appear, to us at least, to produce partial evil; and we frequently observe at the same time, some bountiful provision, which acting as another general law, corrects the inequalities of the first.

The proper office of benevolence is to soften the partial evils arising from self-love, but it can never be substituted in its place. If no man were to allow himself to act, till he had completely determined, that the action he was about to perform, was more conducive than any other to the general good, the most enlightened minds would hesitate in perplexity and amazement; and the unenlightened, would be continually committing the grossest mistakes.

As Mr. Godwin, therefore, has not laid down any practical principle, according to which the necessary labours of agriculture might be amicably shared among the whole class of labourers; by general invectives against employing the poor, he appears to pursue an unattainable good through much present evil. For if every man who employs the poor, ought to be considered as their enemy, and as adding to the weight of their oppressions; and if the miser is, for this reason, to be preferred to the man who spends his income, it follows, that any number of men who now spend their incomes, might, to the advantage of society, be converted into misers. Suppose then, that a hundred thousand persons who now employ ten men each, were to lock up their wealth from general use, it is evident, that a million of working men of different kinds would be completely thrown out of all employment. The extensive misery that such an event would produce in the present state of society, Mr. Godwin himself could hardly refuse to acknowledge; and I question whether he might not find some difficulty in proving, that a conduct of this kind tended more than the conduct of those who spend their incomes to

2. Mr. Godwin seems to have but little respect for practical principles; but I own it appears to me, that he is a much greater benefactor to mankind, who points out how inferior good may be attained, than he who merely expiates on the deformity of the present state of society, and the beauty of a different state, without pointing out a practical method, that might be immediately applied, of accelerating our advances from the one, to the other.

"place human beings in the condition in which they ought to be placed."

But Mr. Godwin says, that the miser really locks up nothing; that the point has not been rightly understood; and that the true development and definition of the nature of wealth have not been applied to illustrate it. Having defined therefore wealth, very justly, to be the commodities raised and fostered by human labour, he observes, that the miser locks up neither corn, nor oxen, nor clothes, nor houses. Undoubtedly he does not really lock up these articles, but he locks up the power of producing them, which is virtually the same. These things are certainly used and consumed by his contemporaries, as truly, and to as great an extent, as if he were a beggar; but not to as great an extent, as if he had employed his wealth, in turning up more land, in breeding more oxen, in employing more taylors, and in building more houses. But supposing, for a moment, that the conduct of the miser did not tend to check any really useful produce, how are all those, who are thrown out of employment, to obtain patents which they may shew in order to be awarded a proper share of the food and raiment produced by the society? This is the unconquerable difficulty.

I am perfectly willing to concede to Mr. Godwin that there is much more labour in the world than is really necessary; and that, if the lower classes of society could agree among themselves never to work more than six or seven hours in the day, the commodities essential to human happiness might still be produced in as great abundance as at present. But it is almost impossible to conceive that such an agreement could be adhered to. From the principle of population, some would necessarily be more in want than others. Those that had large families, would naturally be desirous of exchanging two hours more of their labour for an ampler quantity of subsistence. How are they to be prevented from making this exchange? It would be a violation of the first and most sacred property that a man possesses, to attempt, by positive institutions, to interfere with his command over his own labour.

Till Mr. Godwin, therefore, can point out some practical plan according to which the necessary labour in a society might be equitably divided; his invectives against labour, if they were attended to, would certainly produce much present evil, without approximating us to that state of cultivated equality to which he looks forward as his polar star; and which, he seems to think, should at present be our guide in determining the nature and tendency of human actions. A mariner guided by such a polar star is in danger of shipwreck.

Perhaps there is no possible way in which wealth could, in general, be employed so beneficially to a state, and particularly to the lower orders of it, as by improving and rendering productive that land, which to a farmer would not answer the expence of cultivation. Had Mr. Godwin exerted his energetic eloquence in painting the superior worth and usefulness of the character who employed the poor in this way, to him who employed them in narrow luxuries, every enlightened man must have applauded his efforts. The increasing demand for agricultural labour must always tend to better the condition of the poor; and if the accession of work be of this kind, so far is it from being true, that the poor would be obliged to work ten hours, for the same price, that they before worked eight, that the very reverse would be the fact; and a labourer might then support his wife and family as well by the labour of six hours, as he could before by the labour of eight.

# 3. *Types of Division of Labor*

BY MAX WEBER

EVERY TYPE of social action in a group which is oriented to economic considerations and every associative relationship of economic significance involves to some degree a particular mode of division and organization of human services in the interest of production. A mere glance at the facts of economic action reveals that different persons perform different types of work and that these are combined in the service of common ends, with each other and with the non-human means of production, in the most varied ways. The complexity of

Reprinted from Max Weber, *The Theory of Social and Economic Organization,* trans. A. M. Henderson and Talcott Parsons, ed. Talcott Parsons (Glencoe, Ill.: The Free Press, 1947), pp. 218–24. 

these phenomena is extreme, but yet it is possible to distinguish a few types.

Human services for economic purposes may be distinguished as (a) "managerial," or (b) oriented to the instructions of a managerial agency. The latter type will be called "labour" for purposes of the following discussion.

It goes without saying that managerial activity constitutes "labour" in the most definite sense if labour is taken to mean the expenditure of time and effort as such. The use of the term labour in contradistinction to managerial activity has, however, come to be generally accepted for social reasons and this usage will be followed in the present discussion. For more general purposes, the terms "services" or "work" will be used.

Within a social group the ways in which labour or other work may be carried on typically may be classified in the following way: (1) technically, according to the way in which the services of a plurality of co-operating individuals are divided up and combined, with each other and with the non-human means of production, to carry out the technical procedures of production; (2) socially. In the first place, forms of labour may vary according to whether particular services do or do not fall within the jurisdiction of autocephalous and autonomous economic units, and according to the economic character of these units. Closely connected with this is variation according to the modes and extent to which the various services, the non-human means of production, and opportunities for economic profit, used as sources of profit or as means of acquisition, are or are not appropriated. These factors determine the mode of occupational differentiation, a social phenomenon, and the organization of the market, an economic phenomenon; (3) finally, in every case of combination of services with each other and with non-human means of production, it is important, in determining their division among economic units and the modes of appropriation, to know whether they are used in a context of budgetary administration or of profit-making enterprise.

1. It should be emphatically stated that the present discussion is concerned only with a brief summary of the sociological aspects of these phenomena, so far as they are relevant to its context. The economic aspect is included only in so far as it is expressed in what are formally sociological categories. In a substantive sense, the discussion would be economic only if the conditions of price determination and market relationships, which have heretofore been dealt with only on a theoretical level, were introduced into it. It would, however, be possible to treat such substantive aspects of the problem in such a general introduction to the field only in terms which would involve a very unfortunate kind of one-sidedness. Furthermore, attempts to explain these things in *purely* economic terms are both misleading and open to question. To take an example: The Dark Ages in the tenth to the twelfth centuries have been held to be the decisive period for the development of that type of Medieval labour which, though subject to corporate regulations, was in a sense free labour. In particular, it is held that the lords were in a situation of having to compete for the fees and income arising from the control over land, personal status, and jurisdiction; and that this situation permitted peasants, miners, and artisans to profit from the competition of the lords. It is further held that the decisive period for the development of capitalism was that of the great long-drawn-out price revolution of the sixteenth century. This led both to an absolute and a relative increase in the prices of almost all products of the land in the Western World. It is only necessary to apply well-known principles of agricultural economics to see that this both made possible and stimulated the development of enterprises which sold products on the market. This in turn led to the development of large-scale production, in part, as in England, of the capitalistic type; in part, as between the Elbe and Russia, more on the basis of patriarchal estates. Furthermore, it meant, in most cases, an absolute rise of prices, but, relatively in the normal case, a fall in the price of important industrial products. Then, so far as the necessary forms of organization and other conditions, both external and subjective, were given, there would be a stimulus to the development of market enterprises related in a competitive system. These were, to be sure, not present in Germany, but this fact is held to account for the economic decline which started there about that time. The consequence of all this is the development of capitalistic enterprises in the industrial field. Its necessary prerequisite was the development of extensive markets. An indication that this was actually happening is seen in certain changes of English commercial policy, to say nothing of other phenomena.

In order to verify theoretical reasoning about the substantive economic conditions of the development of economic structures, it would be necessary to employ theses, such as these and similar ones. This cannot, however, be attempted in the present discussion. These and numerous other equally controversial theories, even so far as they could be proved not to be wholly erroneous, cannot be incorporated into the present scheme which is intentionally limited to sociological *concepts*. In that the present discussion renounces any attempt to take account of this type of data, however, the following exposition in this chapter explicitly repudiates any claim to concrete "explanation" and restricts itself to working out a sociological typology. The same is true of the previous discussion in that it consciously omitted to develop a theory of money and price determination. This must be strongly emphasized. For the facts of the economic situation provide the flesh and blood for a genuine explanation of the process by which even a sociologically relevant development takes place. What can be done here is only to provide a scaffolding which is adequate to enable the analysis to work with relatively clear and definite concepts.

It is obvious, not only that no attempt is here made to do justice to the empirical historical aspect of economic development, but even the typology of the genetic order of possible forms is neglected. The present aim is only to develop a systematic scheme of classification.

2. A common and correct objection to the usual terminology of economics, is that it fails to make a distinction between the "organization" and the "enterprise."[1] In the field of economically oriented action, "organization" is a technical category which designates the ways in which various types of services are continuously combined with each other and with non-human means of production. Its antithesis is one of two things: either intermittent activity or that which is discontinuous from the technical point of view, as is true empirically of every household. The antithesis of enterprise, denoting as it does a type of economic orientation, namely, profit-making, is the budgetary unit which is oriented to provision for needs. Classification of types of economic orientation in terms of profit-making enterprise and budgetary units is not, however, exhaustive. There are actions oriented to acquisition which are not covered by the concept of enterprise. All cases of seeking earnings from work, like the work of the author, the artist, the official, are neither one nor the other. The receipt and uses of incomes from investment is a clear case of budgetary administration.

Despite the mixture of categories, a profit-making organization (*Erwerbsbetrieb*)[2] is spoken of wherever there is continuous permanent co-ordinated action on the part of an entrepreneur. Such action is in fact unthinkable without an "organization," though, in the limiting case, it may be merely the organization of his own activity, without any help from others. Here it is a matter primarily of distinguishing the budgetary unit from the enterprise and its attendant organization. The term "profit-making organization," instead of a continuous profit-making enterprise is, it may now be noted, to be accepted, because there it is unambiguous, only for the simplest case where the unit of technical organization coincides with the unit of enterprise. But in a market economy, it is possible for a number of technically separate organizations or "plants" to be combined in a single enterprise. The latter receives its unity by no means alone through the personal relationship of the various units to the same entrepreneur, but by virtue of the fact that they are all controlled in terms of some kind of consistent plan in their exploitation for purposes of profit. It is hence possible that there should be transitional forms. Where the term "organization" or "plant" is used by itself, it will always refer to the technically distinct unit consisting in buildings, equipment, labour forces, and technical management. The latter is possibly heterocephalous and heteronomous. This state of affairs would still exist, as even ordinary usage recognizes, in a communistic economy. The term "profit-making organization" will be used from now on only in cases where the technical and the economic unit, the enterprise, coincide.[3]

The relation between organization and enterprise raises particularly difficult terminological questions in the case of such categories as "factory" and "putting-out industry."[4] The latter is clearly a category of enterprise. From the point of view of organization, there are two types of units: The commercial organization and those which are parts of the workers' households without any centralized workshop except in certain cases where a master craftsman organizes one on his own initiative. The organizations in the worker's household perform certain specified functions for the commercial organization, and vice versa. The process is thus not understandable in terms of technical organization alone. It is necessary in addition to employ the categories of market, profit-making enterprise, household (of the individual worker), and exploitation of contracted services for profit.

---

1. *Betrieb* and *Unternehmung*. In a good deal of his discussion, Weber uses the term *Betrieb* in a context where this distinction is not important. Thus he speaks of an *Erwerbsbetrieb;* hence *Betrieb* has often been translated as "enterprise." But where the distinction is important in the context, "organization" is used.—ED.

2. See above note. In most cases it has seemed best to translate *Erwerbsbetrieb* with "enterprise," as to speak of a profit-making organization as distinguished from an enterprise would unduly complicate the terminology without bringing out sufficiently important empirical distinctions. —ED.

3. As has already been noted, it does not seem necessary to introduce this terminological complication into the translation.—ED.

4. *Hausindustrie*. This is often translated as "domestic industry." As Weber points out, however, this term designates the unit of technical organization, namely the household, and not of business enterprise. For this reason such authorities as Professor E. F. Gay prefer the term "putting out industry."—ED.

The concept of "factory" could, as has often been proposed, be defined in entirely non-economic terms as a mode of technical organization, leaving aside consideration of the status of the workers, whether free or unfree, the mode of division of labour, involving the extent of internal technical specialization, and the type of means of production, whether machines or tools. This would make it equivalent to an organized workshop. But besides this, it is neccessary to include in the definition the mode of appropriation in the hands of an owner of the premises and the means of production. Otherwise, the concept becomes confused with that of an "ergasterion."[5] If this distinction is made, it seems more appropriate to define both factory and "putting-out system" as strictly economic categories of capitalistic enterprise. Then, in a strictly socialistic economy, there would neither be factories nor "putting-out" enterprises, but only workshops, buildings, machines, tools, and various types of labour in the shop or at home.

3. The question of stages of economic development will be considered only in so far as it is absolutely necessary, and then only incidentally. The following points will suffice for the present.

It has fortunately become more common lately to distinguish types of economic system from types of economic policy. The stages which Schönberg first suggested, and, which in a somewhat altered form, have become identified with Schmoller's name, "domestic economy," "village economy," the economy of landed estates and royal households, "town economy," "territorial economy," and "national economy,"[6] have been formulated according to the type of corporate group regulating economic activity. But there is no implication of any specific mode of variation even in the type of regulation to which economic activity has been subjected by the different corporate groups thus classified in terms of the extent of their jurisdiction. Thus the territorial economic policies of the German states consisted to a large extent simply in taking over the measures developed in the town economy. Furthermore, their innovations were not greatly different from the "mercantilistic" policies, which were typical of those of the patrimonial states which had already achieved a relatively high level of rationality. They were thus similar to "national economic policies," to use the common term, which is, however, not very appropriate. This classification, futher, clearly does not imply that the inner structure of the economic system, the modes in which work roles were assigned, differentiated and combined, the ways in which these different functions were divided between independent economic units, and the modes of appropriation of control over labour, means of production, and opportunities for profit, in any way ran parallel to the extent of jurisdiction of the corporate group, which might be responsible for economic policy. Above all, it does not imply that this structure was a simple function of the extent of corporate jurisdiction. To demonstrate the untenability of this view, it is only necessary to compare the Western World with Asia and the situation in modern Europe with that of Antiquity. At the same time, in considering economic structure, it is by no means legitimate to ignore the existence or absence of corporate groups with substantive powers of regulation of economic activity, nor to ignore the essential purposes of their regulation. The modes of profit-making activity are strongly influenced by such regulation, but it is by no means only political corporations which are important in this respect.

4. In this connexion, as well as others, the purpose of the discussion has been to determine the optimum conditions for the formal rationality of economic activity and its relation to the various types of substantive demands which may be made on the economic system.

5. Weber himself takes over the Greek word, and since the closest English equivalent, "workshop," is too indefinite, it seems best to retain his own term.—ED.

6. The corresponding German terms are: *Hauswirtschaft, Dorfwirtschaft, Stadtwirtschaft, Territorialwirtschaft,* and *Volkswirtschaft.*—ED.

# 4. *Ownership and Possession*

BY SIR FREDERICK POLLACK AND FREDERICK W. MAITLAND

## *Seisin*

IN THE HISTORY of our law there is no idea more cardinal than that of seisin. Even in the law of the present day it plays a part which must be studied by every lawyer; but in the past it was so important that we may almost say that the whole system of our land law was law about seisin and its consequences.

Seisin is possession. A few, but only a few words about etymology may be ventured. The inference has been too hastily drawn that this word speaks to us of a time of violence, when he who seized land was seised of it, when seizing land was the normal mode of acquiring possession. Now doubtless there is an etymological connexion between "seizing" and being "seised," but the nature of that connexion is not very certain. If on the one hand "seisin" is connected with "to seize," on the other hand it is connected with "to sit" and "to set":—the man who is seised is the man who is sitting on land; when he was put in seisin he was set there and made to sit there. Thus seisin seems to have the same root as the German *Besitz* and the Latin *possessio*. To our medieval lawyers the word *seisina* suggested the very opposite of violence; it suggested peace and quiet. It did so to Coke.

* * *

Now in the course of time *seisin* becomes a highly technical word; but we must not think of it having been so always. Few, if any, of the terms in our legal vocabulary have always been technical terms. The licence that the man of science can allow himself of coining new words is one which by the nature of the case is denied to lawyers. They have to take their terms out of the popular speech; gradually the words so taken are defined; sometimes a word continues to have both a technical meaning for lawyers and a different and vaguer meaning for laymen; sometimes the word that lawyers have adopted is abandoned by the laity. Such for a long time past has been the fate of *seisin*.

The process by which words are specified, by which their technical meaning is determined, is to a first glance a curious, illogical process. Legal reasoning seems circular:—for example, it is argued in one case that a man has an action of trespass because he has possession, in the next case that he has possession because he has an action of trespass; and so we seem to be running round from right to remedy and then from remedy to right. All the while, however, our law of possession and trespass is being more perfectly defined. Its course is not circular but spiral; it never comes back to quite the same point as that from which it started. This play of reasoning between right and remedy fixes the use of words. A remedy, called an assize, is given to any one who is disseised of his free tenement:—in a few years lawyers will be arguing that *X* has been "disseised of his free tenement," because it is an established point that a person in his position can bring an assize. The word *seisin* becomes specified by its relation to certain particular remedies.

What those remedies were it will be our duty to consider. But first we may satisfy ourselves that, to begin with, seisin simply meant possession. Of this we may be convinced by two observations. In the first place, it would seem that for at least three centuries after the Norman Conquest our lawyers had no other word whereby to describe possession. In their theoretical discussions, they, or such of them as looked to the Roman books as models of jurisprudence, could use the words *possessio* and *possidere;* but these words are rarely employed in the formal records of litigation, save in one particular context. The parson of a church is "in possession" of the church:—but then this is no matter for our English law or our temporal courts; it is matter for the canon law and the courts Christian; and it is all the more expedient to find some other term than "seised" for the parson, since it may be necessary to contrast the rights of the parson who is possessed of the church with those of the patron who is seised of the advowson.

In the second place, this word "seisin" was used of all manner of things and all manner of permanent rights that could be regarded as things. At a later date to speak of a person as being seised, or in seisin of, a chattel would have been a gross solecism. But throughout the thirteenth century and in the

Reprinted from Sir Frederick Pollack and Frederick W. Maitland, *The History of English Law* (2d ed.; London: Cambridge University Press, 1898), II, 29–30, 31–39, 40–44, 74–79.

most technical documents men are seised of chattels and in seisin of them, of a fleece of wool, of a gammon of bacon, of a penny. People were possessed of these things; law had to recognize and protect their possession; it had no other word than "seisin" and therefore used it freely. It may well be, as some think, that the ideas of seisin and possession are first developed in relation to land; one sits, settles, squats on land, and in early ages, preeminently during the feudal time, the seisin of chattels was commonly interwoven with the seisin of land. Flocks and herds were the valuable chattels; "chattel" and "cattle" are the same word; and normally cattle are possessed by him who possesses the land on which they are levant and couchant. Still when the possession of chattels was severed from the possession of land, when the oxen were stolen or were sold to a chapman, there was no word to describe the possession of this new possessor, this thief or purchaser, save seisin. Sometimes we meet with the phrase "vested and seised," which was common in France; this however seems to mean no more than "seised," and though we may now and then read of "investiture," chiefly in relation to ecclesiastical offices, this does not become one of the technical terms of the common law.

When we say that seisin is possession, we use the latter term in the sense in which lawyers use it, a sense in which possession is quite distinct from, and may be sharply opposed to, proprietary right. In common talk we constantly speak as though possession were much the same as ownership. When a man says "I possess a watch," he generally means "I own a watch." Suppose that he has left his watch with a watchmaker for repair, and is asked whether he still possesses a watch, whether the watch is not in the watchmaker's possession and if so whether both he and the watchmaker have possession of the same watch at the same time, he is perhaps a little puzzled and resents our questions as lawyers' impertinences. Even if the watch has been stolen, he is not very willing to admit that he no longer possesses a watch. This is instructive:—in our non-professional moments *possession* seems much nearer to our lips than *ownership*. Often however we slur over the gulf by means of the conveniently ambiguous verbs "have" and "have got"—I have a watch, the watchmaker has it—I have a watch, but some one else has got it. But so soon as there is any law worthy of the name, right and possession must emerge and be contrasted:—so soon as any one has said "You have got what belongs to me," the germs of these two notions have appeared and can be opposed to each other. Bracton is never tired of emphasizing the contrast. In so doing he constantly makes use of the Roman terms *possessio* on the one hand, *proprietas* or *dominium* on the other. These are not the technical terms of English law; but it has terms which answer a like purpose, *seisina* on the one hand, *ius* on the other. The person who has right may not be seised, the person who is seised may not be seised of right.

The idea of seisin seems to be closely connected in our ancestors' minds with the idea of enjoyment. A man is in seisin of land when he is enjoying it or in a position to enjoy it; he is seised of an advowson (for of "incorporeal things" there may be seisin) when he presents a parson who is admitted to the church; he is seised of freedom from toll when he successfully resists a demand for payment. This connexion is brought out by the interesting word *esplees* (*expleta*). In a proprietary action for land the demandant will assert that he, or some ancestor of his, was "seised of the land in his demesne as of fee and of right, by taking thence esplees to the value of five shillings, as in corn and other issues of the land." The man who takes and enjoys the fruits of the earth thereby "exploits" his seisin, that is to say, he makes his seisin "explicit," visible to the eyes of his neighbours. In order that a seisin may have all its legal effects it must be thus exploited. Still a man must have seisin before he can exploit it, and therefore in a possessory action it is unnecessary for the plaintiff to allege this taking of esplees. The moment at which he acquires his seisin may not be the right moment for mowing hay or reaping corn. Seisin of land therefore is not the enjoyment of the fruits of the earth; it is rather that state of things which in due time will render such an enjoyment possible.

Law must define this vague idea, and it can not find the whole essence of possession in visible facts. It is so now-a-days. We see a man in the street carrying an umbrella; we can not at once tell whether or no he possesses it. Is he its owner, is he a thief, is he a borrower, a hirer, is he the owner's servant? If he is the owner, he possesses it; if he is a thief, he possesses it. If he is the owner's servant, we shall probably deny his possession. If he is a borrower, we may have our doubts; the language of every-day life may hesitate about the matter; law must make up its mind. Before we attribute possession to a man, we must apparently know something about the intentions that he has in regard to the thing, or rather about the intentions that he must be supposed to have when the manner in which he came by the thing has been taken into consideration. Probably the better way of stating the matter is not to speak of his real intentions, which are often beside the mark, nor of the intentions that he must be supposed to have, which are fictions, but to say at once that we require to know how he came by the thing.[1] This being known, problems await us. If the carrier of the umbrella is its owner, he possesses it; if he is a thief making off with a stolen chattel, he possesses it; if he has by mistake taken what he believes to be his own, he probably possesses it; if he has borrowed it or hired it, the case is not so plain; law must decide—and various systems of law will decide differently—whether possession shall be attributed to the borrower or to the lender, to the letter or the hirer.

When deciding to whom it would attribute a seisin, our medieval law had to contemplate a complex mass of facts and rights. In the first place, the actual occupant of the soil, who was cultivating it and taking its fruits, might be so doing in exercise, or professed exercise, of any one of many different rights. He might be there as tenant at will, tenant for term of years, tenant in villeinage, tenant for life, tenant in dower, tenant by the curtesy, tenant in fee simple, guardian of an infant, and so forth. But further, at the same moment many persons might have and be actually enjoying rights of a proprietary kind in the same plot of ground. Giles would be holding in villeinage of Ralph, who held in free socage of the abbot, who held in frankalmoin of the earl, who held by knight's service of the king. There would be the case of the reversioner to be considered and the case of the remainderman.

In the thirteenth century certain lines have been firmly drawn. The royal remedies for the protection of seisin given by Henry II. were given only to those who were seised "of a free tenement": the novel disseisin lies when a man has been disseised *de libero tenemento suo.* Doubtless these words were intended to exclude those who held in villeinage. This is well brought out by a change in the language of Magna Carta. The original charter of 1215 by its most famous clause declares that no free man is to be disseised, unless it be by the lawful judgment of his peers or the law of the land. The charter of 1217 inserts the words "de libero tenemento suo vel libertatibus vel liberis consuetudinibus suis." It is not intended, it would not be suffered, that a man holding in villeinage, even though personally *liber homo,* should have a possession protected by the king's court. Such a tenant is not seised of free tenement, and, as royal justice is now beginning to supplant all other justice, it is said that he has no seisin recognized by the common law. The lord of whom he holds is the person protected by the common law, and is seised *de libero tenemento;* if you eject the villein tenant, you disseise the lord. But within the sphere of manorial justice this tenant is seised—seisin has been delivered to him by the rod according to the custom of the manor—and when he pleads in the manorial court he will say that he is seised according to the custom of the manor. Here then already we have a dual seisin:—the lord seised *quoad* the king's courts and the common law, the tenant seised *quoad* the lord's court and the manorial custom.

In the past the tenant for term of years, though he was in occupation of the soil, had not been considered to be seised of it. In the days of Henry II. when the great possessory remedy, the assize of novel disseisin, was being invented, tenancies for terms of years seem to have been novelties, and the lawyers were endeavouring to treat the "termor"—this is a conveniently brief name for the tenant for term of years—as one who had no right in the land, but merely the benefit of a contract. His lessor was seised; eject the lessee, and you disseise the lessor. Already in Bracton's day, however, this doctrine was losing its foundation; the termor was acquiring a remedy against ejectors. But this remedy was a new action and one which in no wise affected the old assize of novel disseisin. For a while men had to content themselves with ascribing a seisin of a certain sort to both the termor and his lessor. Eject the termor, you lay yourself open to two actions, a *Quare eiecit infra terminum* brought by him, an assize of novel disseisin brought by his lessor. The lessor still has the assize; despite the termor's occupation, he is seised, and seised in demesne, of the land; and he is seised, while the termor is not seised, "of a free tenement"—this is proved by his having the assize. Thus the term "free tenement" is getting a new edge; the termor has no free tenement, no freehold, no seisin of the freehold. At a later date lawyers will meet this difficulty by the introduction of "possession" as a new technical term; they will deny "seisin" of any sort or kind to the termor, and, on the other hand, will allow him possession. But of tenancies for years we shall have more to say hereafter.

An infant's guardian, though the wardship was a profitable, vendible right, was not seised of the infant's land; his occupation of the land was the infant's seisin. It is true that about this matter language might hesitate and fluctuate. It is, for example, common enough to speak of the lord and guardian putting the ward into seisin of the land when he has attained his majority; but for the main purposes of the law the guardian's own right, the *custodia,* is converted into an incorporeal thing, an incorporeal chattel, of which there may be a seisin or possession,

1. A servant who is carrying his master's goods can not become a possessor of them by merely forming the intent to appropriate them. If we say that he must be supposed to have an honest intent until by some act he shows the contrary, we are introducing a fiction.

and for the protection of such a seisin there is a special possessory action. If a person who is in occupation of the land as guardian is ejected from the land, and wishes to make good his own rights, he will complain, not of having been disseised of the land, but of having been ejected from the wardship.

As to the tenant for life—including under that term tenant in dower and tenant by the curtesy—our law seems never to have had any doubt. The tenant for life, if he is in occupation of the land by himself, his servants, his villein tenants or his termors, is seised, seised of the land, seised in demesne, seised of a free tenement. If ejected, he will bring exactly the same possessory action that he would have brought had he been a tenant in fee.

Then we must consider the ascending series of lords and tenants. Let us suppose that Ralph holds in fee and in free socage of the earl, who holds in fee by knight's service of the king. If all is as it should be, then both Ralph and the earl may be said to be seised of the land. Ralph, who is occupying the land by himself, his servants, his villein tenants or his termors, is seised in demesne. The earl, to whom Ralph is paying rent, also is seised; he is seised of the land, not in demesne but in service. We have here to remember that if the feudal idea of seignoral justice has been permitted to develop itself freely, this ascending series of seisins would have had as its counterpart an ascending series of courts. The king's court would have known of no seisin save that of the earl, the tenant in chief. The seisin of Ralph, the earl's immediate tenant, would have found protection—at least in the first instance—only in the earl's court; and so downwards, each seisin being protected by a different court. The seisin of the tenant in villeinage protected only in the manorial court is an illustration of this principle. But then Henry II. had restrained and crippled this principle; he had given a remedy in his own court to every one who could say that he had been disseised of a free tenement. The result of this is for a while a perplexing use of terms. Ralph, the tenant in demesne, he who has no freeholder below him, is indubitably seised of the land, however distant he may be in the feudal scale from the king. Eject him, and he will bring against you the assize of novel disseisin; indeed if his lord, the earl, ejects him or even distrains him outrageously, he will bring the assize against his lord, thus showing that as between him and his lord the seisin of the land is with him. It is possible that at one time by ejecting Ralph, a stranger would have disseised both Ralph and his lord and exposed himself to two actions; but this does not seem to have been the law of Bracton's day. The lord was ceasing to have any interest in what we may call the personality of his tenant. If Ralph is ejected by Roger, the earl can not complain of this; he is in no way bound to accept Roger as a tenant; he can distrain the tenement for the services due to him from Ralph; he is entitled to those services but to nothing else. More and more an incorporeal thing or group of incorporeal things supplants the land as the subject matter of the lord's right and the lord's seisin. He is entitled to and seised of, not the land itself, but a seignory, the services, fealty, homage of a tenant.

* * *

On the whole we may say that the possession of land which the law protects under the name of a "seisin of freehold," is the occupation of land by one who has come to it otherwise than as tenant in villeinage, tenant at will, tenant for term of years or guardian, that occupation being exercised by himself, his servants, guardians, tenants in villeinage, tenants at will or tenants for term of years. This seems the best statement of the matter:—occupation of land is seisin of free tenement unless it has been obtained in one of certain particular ways. If, however, we prefer to look at the other side of the principle, we may say that the *animus* required of the person who is "seised of free tenement" is the intent to hold that land as though he were tenant for life or tenant in fee holding by some free tenure.

More remains to be said of the nature of seisin, especially of that element in it which we have spoken of as occupation; but this can best be said if we turn to speak of the effects of seisin, its protection by law, its relation to proprietary rights.

We may make our task the lighter if for one moment we glance at controversies which have divided the legal theorists of our own day. Why does our law protect possession? Several different answers have been, or may be, given to this question. There is something in it that attracts the speculative lawyer, for there is something that can be made to look like a paradox. Why should law, when it has on its hands the difficult work of protecting ownership and other rights in things, prepare puzzles for itself by undertaking to protect something that is not ownership, something that will from time to time come into sharp collision with ownership? Is it not a main object of law that every one should enjoy what is his own *de iure,* and if so why are we to consecrate that *de facto* enjoyment which is signified by the term *possession,* and why, above all, are we to protect the possessor even against the owner?

It is chiefly, though not solely, in relation to the classical Roman law that these questions have been discussed, and, if any profitable discussion of them is to be had, it seems essential that some definite body of law should be examined with an accurate heed of dates and successive stages of development. If, scorning all relations of space and time, we ask why law protects possession, the only true answer that we are likely to get is that the law of different peoples at different times has protected possession for many different reasons. Nor can we utterly leave out of account motives and aims of which an abstract jurisprudence knows nothing. That simple justice may be done between man and man has seldom been the sole object of legislators; political have interfered with juristic interests. An illustration may make this plainer. We may well believe that Henry II. when he instituted the possessory assizes was not without thought of the additional strength that would accrue to him and his successors, could he make his subjects feel that they owed the beatitude of possession to his ordinance and the action of his court. Still, whatever may be the legislator's motive, judges must find some rational principle which shall guide them in the administration of possessory remedies; and they have a choice between different principles. These may perhaps be reduced in number to four, or may be said to cluster round four types.

In the first place, the protection given to possession may be merely a provision for the better maintenance of peace and quiet. It is a prohibition of self-help in the interest of public order. The possessor is protected, not on account of any merits of his, but because the peace must be kept; to allow men to make forcible entries on land or to seize goods without form of law, is to invite violence. Just so the murderer, whose life is forfeited to law, may not be slain, save in due form of law; in a civilized state he is protected against irregular vengeance, not because he deserves to live, for he deserves to die, but because the permission of revenge would certainly do more harm than good to the community. Were this then the only principle at work, we should naturally expect to find the protection of possession in some chapter of the criminal law dealing with offences against public order, riots, affrays, and the like.

Others would look for it, not in the law of crimes, but in the law of torts or civil injuries. The possessor's possession is protected, not indeed because he has any sort of right in the thing, but because in general one can not disturb his possession without being guilty, or almost guilty, of some injury to his person, some act which, if it does not amount to an assault, still comes so dangerously near to an assault that it can be regarded as an invasion of that sphere of peace and quiet which the law should guarantee to every one of its subjects. This doctrine which found expression in Savigny's famous essay has before now raised an echo in an English court:—"These rights of action are given in respect of the immediate and present violation of possession, independently of rights of property. They are an extension of that protection which the law throws around the person.[2]

A very different theory, that of the great Ihering, has gained ground in our own time. In order to give an adequate protection to ownership, it has been found necessary to protect possession. To prove ownership is difficult, to prove possession comparatively easy. Suppose a land-owner ejected from possession; to require of him to prove his ownership before he can be reinstated, is to require too much; thieves and land-grabbers will presume upon the difficulty that a rightful owner will have in making out a flawless title. It must be enough then that the ejected owner should prove that he was in possession and was ejected; the ejector must be precluded from pleading that the possession which he disturbed was not possession under good title. Possession then is an outwork of property. But though the object of the law in protecting possession is to protect the possession of those who have a right to possess, that object can only be obtained by protecting every possessor. Once allow any question about property to be raised, and the whole plan of affording easy remedies to ousted owners will break down. In order that right may be triumphant, the possessory action must be open to the evil and to the good, it must draw no distinction between the just and the unjust possessor. The protection of wrongful possessors is an unfortunate but unavoidable consequence of the attempt to protect rightful possessors. This theory would make us look for the law of possession, not in the law of crimes, nor in the law of torts, but in very close connexion with the law of property.

There is yet another opinion, which differs from the last, though both make a close connexion between possession and proprietary rights. Possession as such deserves protection, and really there is little more to be said, at least by the lawyer. He who possesses has by the mere fact of his possession more right in the thing than the non-possessor has; he of all men has most right in the thing until someone has asserted and proved a greater right. When a thing belongs to no one and is capable of appropriation, the mere act of taking possession of it gives right against all the world; when a thing belongs to *A*, the mere fact that *B* takes possession of it still gives *B* a right which is good against all who have no better.

2. *Rogers* v. *Spence*, 13 Meeson and Welsby, 581.

An attempt might be made, and it would be in harmony with our English modes of thought, to evade any choice between these various "abstract principles" by a frank profession of the utilitarian character of law. But the success which awaits such an attempt seems very doubtful; for, granted that in some way or another the protection of possession promotes the welfare of the community, the question still arises, why and in what measure this is so. Under what sub-head of "utility" shall we bring this protection? Shall we lay stress on the public disorder which would be occasioned by unrestricted "self-help," on the probability that personal injuries will be done to individuals, on the necessity of providing ready remedies for ousted owners, on the natural expectation that what a man possesses he will be allowed to possess until some one has proved a better title? This is no idle question, for on the answer to it must depend the extent to which and the mode in which possession ought to be consecrated. Measures, which would be quite adequate to prevent any serious danger of general disorder, would be quite inadequate to give the ejected owner an easy action for recovering what is his. If all that we want is peace and quiet, it may be enough to punish ejectors by fine or imprisonment; but this does nothing for ejected possessors, gives them no recovery of the possession that they have lost. Again, let us grant that the ejected possessor should be able to recover the land from the ejector if the latter is still in possession; but suppose that the land has already passed into a third hand; shall the ejected possessor be able to recover it from him to whom the ejector has given or sold it? If to this question we say Yes, we shall hardly be able to justify our answer by any theory which regards injury to the person, or something very like injury to the person, as the gist of the possessory action for here we shall be taking possession away from one who has come to it without violence.

Now we ought—so it seems to us—to see that there well may be a certain truth in all these theories. That the German jurists in their attempts to pin the Roman lawyers down to some one neat doctrine of possession and of the reasons for protecting it, may have been engaged on an impossible task, it is not for us to suggest in this place; but so far as concerns our own English law we make no doubt that at different times and in different measures every conceivable reason for protecting possession has been felt as a weighty argument and has had its influence on rights and remedies. At first we find the several principles working together in harmonious concert; they will work together because as yet they are not sharply defined. Gradually their outlines become clearer; discrepancies between them begin to appear; and, as the result of long continued conflict, some of them are victorious at the expense of others.

* * *

A graduated hierarchy of actions has been established. "Possessoriness" has become a matter of degree. At the bottom stands the novel disseisin, possessory in every sense, summary and punitive. Above it rises the mort d'ancestor, summary but not so summary, going back to the seisin of one who is already dead. Above this again are writs of entry, writs which have strong affinities with the writ of right, so strong that in Bracton's day an action begun by writ of entry may by the pleadings be turned into a final, proprietary action. The writs of entry are not so summary as are the assizes, but they are rapid when compared with the writ of right; the most dilatory of the essoins is precluded; there can be no battle or grand assize. Ultimately we ascend to the writ of right. Actions are higher or lower, some lie "more in the right" than others. You may try one after another; begin with the novel disseisin, go on to the mort d'ancestor, then see whether a writ of entry will serve your turn and, having failed, fall back upon the writ of right.

Now we can not consent to dismiss these rules about writs of entry as though they were matters of mere procedure. They seem to be the outward manifestation of a great rule of substantive law, for this graduated hierarchy of actions corresponds to a graduated hierarchy of seisins and of proprietary rights. The rule of substantive law we take to be this:—Seisin generates a proprietary right—an ownership, we may even say—which is good against all who have no better, because they have no older, right. We have gone far beyond the protection of seisin against violence. The man who obtains seisin obtains thereby a proprietary right that is good against all who have no older seisin to rely upon, a right that he can pass to others by those means by which proprietary rights are conveyed, a right that is protected at every point by the possessory assizes and the writs of entry. At one and the same moment there may be many persons each of whom is in some sort entitled in fee simple to this piece of land: —*C*'s title is good against all but *B* and *A*; *B*'s title is good against all but *A*; *A*'s title is absolute.

But is even *A*'s title absolute? Our law has an action which it says is proprietary—the writ of right. As between the parties to it, this action is conclusive. The vanquished party and his heirs are "abjudged" from the land for ever. In the strongest language that our law knows the demandant has to assert ownership of the land. He says that he, or his ancestor, has been seised of the land as of fee "and of right" and, if he relies on the seisin of an ancestor, he must trace the descent of "the right" from heir to heir into his own person. For all this, we may doubt whether he is supposed to prove a right that is good against all the world. The tenant puts himself upon the grand assize. What, we must ask, will be the question submitted to the recognitors? It will not be this, whether the demandant is owner of the land. It will be this, whether the demandant or the tenant has the greater right to the land. Of absolute right nothing is said; greater right is right enough. Next we must observe that the judgment in this action will not preclude a third person from claiming the land. The judgment if it is followed by inaction on his part for some brief period—ultimately year and day was the time allowed to him—may preclude him, should he be in this country and under no disability; but the judgment itself is no bar. But lastly, as we understand the matter, even in the writ of right the tenant has no means of protecting himself by an assertion that the ownership of the land belongs neither to him nor to the demandant but to some third person. This needs some explanation, for appearances may be against what we have here said.

Clement brings a writ of right against William. He pleads that his grandfather Adam was seised in fee and of right, that from Adam the right descended to Bernard as son and heir, and from Bernard to Clement as son and heir. William may put himself upon battle or upon the grand assize; in the latter case a verdict will decide whether Clement or William has the greater right. But a third course is open. William may endeavour to plead specially and to bring some one question of fact before a jury. In this way he may attack the pedigree that Clement has pleaded at any point; he may, for example, assert that Bernard was not Adam's son or was a bastard. In so doing he may seem at times to be setting up *ius tertii,* to be urging by way of defence for himself the right of a stranger. But really he is not doing this. He is proving that Clement's right is not better than his own. For example, he says: "Bernard was not Adam's heir, for Adam left an elder son, Baldwin by name, who is alive." Now if this be so, Clement has no right in the land whatever; Clement does not allege that he himself has been seised and he is not the heir of any one who has been seised. But what, as we think, William can not do is this, he can not shield himself by the right of a stranger to the action whose title is inconsistent with the statement that Adam was seised in fee and of right. He can not, for example, say, "Adam your ancestor got his seisin by disseising Odo, or by taking a feoffment from Odo's guardian, and Odo, or Odo's heir, has a better right than either of us."[3]

Thus our law of the thirteenth century seems to recognize in its practical working the relativity of ownership. One story is good until another is told. One ownership is valid until an older is proved. No one is ever called upon to demonstrate an ownership good against all men; he does enough even in a proprietary action if he proves an older right than that of the person whom he attacks. In other words, even under a writ of right the common law does not provide for any kind of judgment *in rem.*

The question whether this idea—"the relativity of proprietary right"—should be called archaic, is difficult. A discussion of it might lead us into controversies which are better left to those who have more copious materials for the history of very remote ages than England can produce. For our own part we shall be willing to allow that the evolution of the writs of entry, a process to be explained rather by politics than by jurisprudence, has given to this idea in England a preternatural sharpness. The proprietary action by writ of right is cumbrous and is irrational, for it permits trial by battle. Open attacks upon it can not be made, for it brings some profit to the lords and is supported by a popular sentiment which would gladly refer a solemn question of right to the judgment of the Omniscient. But covert attacks can be made, and they take the form of actions which protect the title begotten by seisin, actions in which artificial limits are set to the right of defence. On the other hand, we can not but think that this idea of relatively good proprietary right came very naturally to Englishmen. It developed itself in spite of cosmopolitan jurisprudence and a romanized terminology. The lawyers themselves believe that there is a wide gulf between possessory and proprietory actions; but they are not certain of its whereabouts. They believe that somewhere or another there must be an absolute ownership. This they call *dreyt dreyt,* mere right, *ius merum.* Apparently they have mistaken the meaning of their own phrases; their *ius merum* is but that *mere dreit* or *ius maius* which the demandant asserts in a writ

3. It is very difficult to offer any direct proof of this doctrine, more especially as Bracton never finished his account of the writ of right. But see the remarkable passage on f. 434b, 435, which culminates in "plura possunt esse iura proprietatis et plures possunt habere maius ius aliis, secundum quod fuerint priores vel posteriores." After reading the numerous cases of writs of right in the Note Book and many others as well, we can only say that we know no case in which the tenant by special plea gets behind the seisin of the demandant's ancestor. As to later times there can be no doubt. See *e.g.* Littleton, sec. 478, quoted below, p. 78. See also Lightwood, Possession of Land, 74.

of right.[4] Bracton more than once protests with Ulpian that possession has nothing in common with property, and yet has to explain how successive possessions beget successive ownerships which all live on together, the younger being invalid against the older. The land law of the later middle ages is permeated by this idea of relativity, and he would be very bold who said that it does not govern us in England at the present day, though the "forms of action" are things of the past and we have now no action for the recovery of land in which a defendant is precluded from relying on whatever right he may have.[5]

We can now say our last word about that curious term "estate." We have seen that the word *status,* which when it falls from Bracton's pen generally means personal condition, is soon afterwards set apart to signify a proprietary right in land or in some other tenement:—John atte Style has an estate of fee simple in Blackacre. We seem to catch the word in the very act of appropriating a new meaning when Bracton says that the estate of an infant whether in corporeal or in incorporeal things must not be changed during his minority. A person already has a status in things; that status may be the status of tenant for life or the status of tenant in fee. It is of course characteristic of this age that a man's status—his general position in the legal scheme—is closely connected with his proprietary rights. The various "estates of men," the various "estates of the realm," are supposed to be variously endowed with land; the baron, for example, ought in theory to be the holder of a barony; he has the status of a baron because he has the estate of a baron. But a peculiar definiteness is given to the term by that theory of possession which we have been examining. Seisin generates title. At one and the same time there may be many titles to one and the same piece of land, titles which have various degrees of validity. It is quite possible that two of these titles should meet in one man and yet maintain an independent existence. If a man demands to be put into the possession of land, he must not vaguely claim a certain piece of land, he must point out some particular title on which he relies, and if he has more than one, he must make his choice between them. For example, he must claim that "status" in the land which his grandfather had and which has descended to him. It becomes possible to raise the question whether a certain possessor of the land was on the land "as of" one status, or "as of" another status; he may have had an ancient title to that land and also a new title acquired by disseisin. What was his status; "as of" which estate was he seised? One status may be heritable, another not heritable; the heritability of a third may have been restricted by the *forma doni.* And so we pass to a classification of estates; some are estates in fee, some are estates for life; some estates in fee are estates in fee simple, others are estates in fee conditional; and so forth. We have come by a word, an idea, in which the elements of our proprietary calculus can find utterance.

4. It is probable that the Latin *ius merum* is a mistaken translation of the Anglo-French *mere dreit,* or as it would stand in Modern French *majeur* (**maire*) *droit.* We have Dr. Murray's authority for this note.

5. Holmes, Common Law, p. 215; Pollock and Wright, Possession, 93–100; Lightwood, Possession of Land, 104–127. One of the most striking statements of this doctrine is in Littleton, sec. 478. "Also if a man be disseised by an infant, who alien in fee, and the alienee dieth seised and his heir entreth, the disseisor being within age, now it is in the election of the disseisor to have a writ of entry *dum fuit infa aetatem* or a writ of right against the heir of the alienee, and, which writ of them he shall choose, he ought to recover by law." In other words, a proprietary action is open to the most violent and most fraudulent of land-grabbers as against one whose title is younger than his own; "and he ought to recover by law."

# 5. *On Contract*

BY SIR HENRY SUMNER MAINE

SOCIAL INQUIRIES, so far as they depend on the consideration of legal phenomena, are in so backward a condition that we need not be surprised at not finding these truths recognised in the commonplaces which pass current concerning the progress of society. These commonplaces answer much more to our prejudices than to our con-

Reprinted from Sir Henry Sumner Maine, *Ancient Law* (New York: Henry Holt Co., 1885, from the 5th London ed.), chap. ix, pp. 297–98, 301–23.

victions. The strong disinclination of most men to regard morality as advancing seems to be especially powerful when the virtues on which Contract depends are in question, and many of us have an almost instinctive reluctance to admitting that good faith and trust in our fellows are more widely diffused than of old, or that there is anything in contemporary manners which parallels the loyalty of the antique world. From time to time, these prepossessions are greatly strengthened by the spectacle of frauds, unheard of before the period at which they were observed, and astonishing from their complication as well shocking from criminality. But the very character of these frauds shows clearly that, before they became possible, the moral obligations of which they are the breach must have been more than proportionately developed. It is the confidence reposed and deserved by the many which affords facilities for the bad faith of the few, so that, if colossal examples of dishonesty occur, there is no surer conclusion than that scrupulous honesty is displayed in the average of the transactions which, in the particular case, have supplied the delinquent with his opportunity. If we insist on reading the history of morality as reflected in jurisprudence, by turning our eyes not on the law of Contract but on the law of Crime, we must be careful that we read it aright. The only form of dishonesty treated of in the most ancient Roman law is Theft. At the moment at which I write, the newest chapter in the English criminal law is one which attempts to prescribe punishment for the frauds of Trustees. The proper inference from this contrast is not that the primitive Romans practised a higher morality than ourselves. We should rather say that, in the interval between their day and ours, morality had advanced from a very rude to a highly refined conception—from viewing the rights of property as exclusively sacred, to looking upon the rights growing out of the mere unilateral reposal of confidence as entitled to the protection of the penal law.

* * *

The favorite occupation of active minds at the present moment, and the one which answers to the speculations of our forefathers on the origin of the social state, is the analysis of society as it exists and moves before our eyes; but, through omitting to call in the assistance of history, this analysis too often degenerates into an idle exercise of curiosity, and is especially apt to incapacitate the inquirer for comprehending states of society which differ considerably from that to which he is accustomed. The mistake of judging the men of other periods by the morality of our own day has its parallel in the mistake of supposing that every wheel or bolt in the modern social machine had its counterpart in more rudimentary societies. Such impressions ramify very widely, and masque themselves very subtly, in historical works written in the modern fashion; but I find the trace of their presence in the domain of jurisprudence in the praise which is frequently bestowed on the little apologue of Montesquieu concerning the Troglodytes, inserted in the *Lettres Persanes*. The Troglodytes were a people who systematically violated their Contracts, and so perished utterly. If the story bears the moral which its author intended, and is employed to expose an anti-social heresy by which this century and the last have been threatened, it is most unexceptionable; but if the inference be obtained from it that society could not possibly hold together without attaching a sacredness to promises and agreements which should be on something like a par with the respect that is paid to them by a mature civilisation, it involves an error so grave as to be fatal to all sound understanding of legal history. The fact is that the Troglodytes have flourished and founded powerful states with very small attention to the obligations of Contract. The point which before all others has to be apprehended in the constitution of primitive societies is that the individual creates for himself few or no rights, and few or no duties. The rules which he obeys are derived first from the station into which he is born, and next from the imperative commands addressed to him by the chief of the household of which he forms a part. Such a system leaves the very smallest room for Contract. The members of the same family (for so we may interpret the evidence) are wholly incapable of contracting with each other, and the family is entitled to disregard the engagements by which any one of its subordinate members has attempted to bind it. Family, it is true, may contract with family, and chieftain with chieftain, but the transaction is one of the same nature, and encumbered by as many formalities, as the alienation of property, and the disregard of one iota of the performance is fatal to the obligation. The positive duty resulting from one man's reliance on the word of another is among the slowest conquests of advancing civilisation.

Neither Ancient Law nor any other source of evidence discloses to us society entirely destitute of the conception of Contract. But the conception, when it first shows itself, is obviously rudimentary. No trustworthy primitive record can be read without perceiving that the habit of mind which induces us to make good a promise is as yet imperfectly developed, and that acts of flagrant perfidy are often mentioned without blame and sometimes described with approbation. In the Homeric literature, for instance, the deceitful cunning of

Ulysses appears as a virtue of the same rank with the prudence of Nestor, the constancy of Hector, and the gallantry of Achilles. Ancient law is still more suggestive of the distance which separates the crude form of Contract from its maturity. At first, nothing is seen like the interposition of law to compel the performance of a promise. That which the law arms with its sanctions is not a promise, but a promise accompanied with a solemn ceremonial. Not only are the formalities of equal importance with the promise itself, but they are, if anything, of greater importance; for that delicate analysis which mature jurisprudence applies to the conditions of mind under which a particular verbal assent is given appears, in ancient law, to be transferred to the words and gestures of the accompanying performance. No pledge is enforced if a single form be omitted or misplaced, but, on the other hand, if the forms can be shown to have been accurately proceeded with, it is of no avail to plead that the promise was made under duress or deception. The transmutation of this ancient view into the familiar notion of a Contract is plainly seen in the history of jurisprudence. First one or two steps in the ceremonial are dispensed with; then the others are simplified or permitted to be neglected on certain conditions; lastly, a few specific contracts are separated from the rest and allowed to be entered into without form, the selected contracts being those on which the activity and energy of social intercourse depend. Slowly, but most distinctly, the mental engagement isolates itself amid the technicalities, and gradually becomes the sole ingredient on which the interest of the jurisconsult is concentrated. Such a mental engagement, signified through external acts, the Romans called a Pact or Convention; and when the Convention has once been conceived as the nucleus of a Contract, it soon becomes the tendency of advancing jurisprudence to break away the external shell of form and ceremony. Forms are thenceforward only retained so far as they are guarantees of authenticity, and securities for caution and deliberation. The idea of a Contract is fully developed, or, to employ the Roman phrase, Contracts are absorbed in Pacts.

The history of this course of change in Roman law is exceedingly instructive. At the earliest dawn of the jurisprudence, the term in use for a Contract was one which is very familiar to the students of historical Latinity. It was *nexum,* and the parties to the contract were said to be *nexi,* expressions which must be carefully attended to on account of the singular durableness of the metaphor on which they are founded. The notion that persons under a contractural engagement are connected together by a strong *bond* or *chain,* continued till the last to influence the Roman jurisprudence of Contract; and flowing thence it has mixed itself with modern ideas. What then was involved in this nexum or bond? A definition which has descended to us from one of the Latin antiquarians describes *nexum* as *omne quod geritur per æs et libram,* "every transaction with the copper and the balance," and these words have occasioned a good deal of perplexity. The copper and the balance are the well-known accomplishments of the Mancipation, the ancient solemnity described in a former chapter, by which the right of ownership in the highest form of Roman Property was transferred from one person to another. Mancipation was a *conveyance,* and hence has arisen the difficulty, for the definition thus cited appears to confound Contracts and Conveyances, which in the philosophy of jurisprudence are not simply kept apart, but are actually opposed to each other. The *jus in re,* right *in rem,* right "availing against all the world," or Proprietary Right, is sharply distinguished by the analyst of mature jurisprudence from the *jus ad rem,* right in *personam,* right "availing against a single individual or group," or Obligation. Now Conveyances transfer Proprietary Rights, Contracts create Obligations —how then can the two be included under the same name or same general conception? This, like many similar embarrassments, has been occasioned by the error of ascribing to the mental condition of an unformed society a faculty which pre-eminently belongs to an advanced stage of intellectual development, the faculty of distinguishing in speculation ideas which are blended in practice. We have indications not to be mistaken of a state of social affairs in which Conveyances and Contracts were practically confounded; nor did the discrepance of the conceptions become perceptible till men had begun to adopt a distinct practice in contracting and conveying.

It may here be observed that we know enough of ancient Roman law to give some idea of the mode of transformation followed by legal conceptions and by legal phraseology in the infancy of Jurisprudence. The change which they undergo appears to be a change from general to special; or, as we might otherwise express it, the ancient conceptions and the ancient terms are subjected to a process of gradual specialisation. An ancient legal conception corresponds not to one but to several modern conceptions. An ancient technical expression serves to indicate a variety of things which in modern law have separate names allotted to them. If, however, we take up the history of Jurisprudence at the next stage, we find that the subordinate conceptions have gradually disengaged themselves, and that the old general names are giving way to special appellations. The old general conception is not obliterated, but it has ceased to cover more than one or a few of the notions which it first included. So too the old technical name remains, but it discharges only one of the functions which it once performed. We may exemplify this phenomenon in various ways. Patriarchal Power of all sorts appears, for instance, to have been once conceived as identical in character, and it was doubtless distinguished by one name. The Power exercised by the ancestor was the same whether it was exercised over the family or the material property—over flocks, herds, slaves, children, or wife. We cannot be absolutely certain of its old Roman name, but there is very strong reason for believing, from the number of expressions indicating shades of the notion of *power* into which the word *manus* enters, that the ancient general term was *manus*. But, when Roman law has advanced a little, both the name and the idea have become specialised. Power is discriminated, both in word and in conception, according to the object over which it is exerted. Exercised over material commodities or slaves, it has become *dominium*—over children it is *Protestas*—over free persons whose services have been made away to another by their own ancestor, it is *mancipium*—over a wife, it is still *manus*. The old word, it will be perceived, has not altogether fallen into desuetude, but is confined to one very special exercise of the authority it had formerly denoted. This example will enable us to comprehend the nature of the historical alliance between Contracts and Conveyances. There seems to have been one solemn ceremonial at first for all solemn transactions, and its name at Rome appears to have been *nexum*. Precisely the same forms which were in use when a conveyance of property was effected seem to have been employed in the making of a contract. But we have not very far to move onwards before we came to a period at which the notion of a Contract has disengaged itself from the notion of a Conveyance. A double change has thus taken place. The transaction "with the copper and the balance," when intended to have for its office the transfer of property, is known by the new and special name of Mancipation. The ancient Nexum still designates the same ceremony, but only when it is employed for the special purpose of solemnising a contract.

When two or three legal conceptions are spoken of as anciently blended in one, it is not intended to imply that some one of the included notions may not be older than the others, or, when those others have been formed, may not greatly predominate over and take precedence over them. The reason why one legal conception continues so long to cover several conceptions, and one technical phrase to do instead of several, is doubtless that practical changes are accomplished in the law of primitive societies long before men see occasion to notice or name them. Though I have said that the Patriarchal Power was not at first distinguished according to the objects over which it was exercised. I feel sure that Power over Children was the root of the old conception of Power; and I cannot doubt that the earliest use of the Nexum, and the one primarily regarded by those who resorted to it, was to give proper solemnity to the alienation of property. It is likely that a very slight perversion of the Nexum from its original functions first gave rise to its employment in Contracts, and that the very slightness of the change long prevented its being appreciated or noticed. The old name remained because men had not become conscious that they wanted a new one; the old notion clung to the mind because nobody had seen reason to be at the pains of examining it. We have had the process clearly exemplified in the history of Testaments. A Will was at first a simple conveyance of Property. It was only the enormous practical difference that gradually showed itself between this particular conveyance and all others which caused it to be regarded separately, and even as it was, centuries elapsed before the ameliorators of law cleared away the useless encumbrance of the nominal mancipation, and consented to care for nothing in the Will but the expressed intentions of the Testator. It is unfortunate that we cannot track the early history of Contracts with the same absolute confidence as the early history of Wills, but we are not quite without hints that contracts first showed themselves through the *nexum* being put to a new use and afterwards obtained recognition as distinct transactions through the important practical consequences of the experiment. There is some, but not very violent, conjecture in the following delineation of the process. Let us conceive a sale for ready money as the normal type of the Nexum. The seller brought the property of which he intended to dispose—a slave, for example—the purchaser attended with the rough ingots of copper which served for money—and an indispensable assistant, the *libripens*, presented himself with a pair of scales. The slave with certain fixed formalities was handed over to the vendee—the copper was weighed by the *libripens* and passed to the vendor. So long as the business lasted it was a *nexum*, and the parties were *nexi;* but the moment it was completed, the *nexum* ended, and the vendor and purchaser ceased to bear the name derived from their momentary relation. But now, let us move a step onward in commercial history. Suppose the slave transferred, but the money was not paid. In *that* case the *nexum* is finished, so far as the seller is concerned, and when he has once handed over his property he is no longer *nexus;* but, in regard to the purchaser, the *nexum* continues. The transaction, as to his part of it, is incomplete, and he is still considered to be *nexus.* It follows, therefore, that the same term described the conveyance by which the right of property was transmitted, and the personal obligation of the debtor for the unpaid purchase-money. We may still go forward, and picture to ourselves a proceeding wholly formal, in which *nothing* is handed over and *nothing* paid; we are brought at once to a transaction indicative of much higher commercial activity, an *executory Contract of Sale.*

If it be true that, both in the popular and in the professional view, a *Contract* was long regarded as an *incomplete Conveyance,* the truth has importance for many reasons. The speculations of the last century concerning mankind in a state of nature, are not unfairly summed up in the doctrine that "in the primitive society property was nothing, and obligation everything"; and it will now be seen that, if the proposition were reversed, it would be nearer the reality. On the other hand, considered historically, the primitive association of Conveyances and Contracts explains something which often strikes the scholar and jurist as singularly enigmatical, I mean the extraordinary and uniform severity of very ancient systems of law to *debtors,* and the extravagant powers which they lodge with *creditors.* When once we understand that the *nexum* was artificially prolonged to give time to the debtor, we can better comprehend his position in the eye of the public and of the law. His indebtedness was doubtless regarded as an anomaly, and suspense of payment in general as an artifice and a distortion of strict rule. The person who had duly consummated his part in the transaction must, on the contrary, have stood in peculiar favour; and nothing would seem more natural than to arm him with stringent facilities for enforcing the completion of a proceeding which, of strict right, ought never to have been extended or deferred.

Nexum, therefore, which originally signified a Conveyance of property, came insensibly to denote a Contract also, and ultimately so constant became the association between this word and the notion of a Contract, that a special term, Mancipium or Mancipatio, had to be used for the purpose of designating the true nexum or transaction in which the property was really transferred. Contracts are therefore now severed from Conveyances, and the first stage in their history is accomplished, but still they are far enough from that epoch of their development when the promise of the contractor has a higher sacredness than the formalities with which it is coupled. In attempting to indicate the character of the changes passed through in this interval, it is necessary to trespass a little on a subject which lies properly beyond the range of these pages, the analysis of Agreement effected by the Roman jurisconsults. Of this analysis, the most beautiful monument of their sagacity, I need not say more than that it is based on the theoretical separation of the Obligation from the Convention or Pact. Bentham and Mr. Austin have laid down that the "two main essentials of a contract are these: first, a signification by the promising party of his *intention* to do the acts or to observe the forbearances which he promises to do or to observe. Secondly, a signification by the promisee that he *expects* the promising party will fulfil the proferred promise." This is virtually identical with the doctrine of the Roman lawyers, but then, in their view, the result of these "significations" was not a Contract, but a Convention or Pact. A Pact was the utmost product of the engagements of individuals agreeing among themselves, and it distinctly fell short of a Contract. Whether it ultimately became a Contract depended on the question whether the law annexed an Obligation to it. A Contract was a Pact (or Convention) *plus* an Obligation. So long as the Pact remained unclothed with the Obligation, it was called *nude* or *naked.*

What was an Obligation? It is defined by the Roman lawyers as "Juris vinculum, quo necessitate adstringimur alicujus solvendæ rei." This definition connects the Obligation with the Nexum through the common metaphor on which they are founded, and shows us with much clearness the pedigree of a peculiar conception. The obligation is the "bond" or "chain," with which the law joins together persons or groups of persons, in consequence of certain voluntary acts. The acts which have the effect of attracting an Obligation are chiefly those classed under the heads of Contract and Delict, of Agreement and Wrong; but a variety of other acts have a similar consequence which are not capable of being comprised in an exact classification. It is to be remarked, however, that the Pact does not draw to itself the Obligation in consequence of any moral necessity; it is the law which annexes it in the plenitude of its power, a point the more necessary to be noted, because a different doctrine has sometimes been propounded by modern interpreters of the Civil Law who had moral or metaphysical theories of their own to support. The image of a *vinculum juris* colours and pervades every part of the Roman law of Contract and Delict. The law bound the parties together, and the *chain* could only be undone by the process called *solutio,* an expression still figurative, to which our word "payment" is only occasionally and incidentally equivalent. The consistency with which the figurative image was allowed to present itself, explains an otherwise puzzling peculiarity of Roman legal phraseology, the fact that "Obligation" signifies rights as well as duties, the right, for example, to have a debt paid as well as the duty of paying it. The Romans kept, in fact, the entire picture of the "legal chain" before their eyes, and regarded one end of it no more and no less than the other.

In the developed Roman law, the Convention, as soon as it was completed, was, in almost all cases, at once crowned with the Obligation, and so became a Contract; and this was the result to which contract-law was surely tending. But for the purpose of this inquiry, we must attend particularly to the intermediate stage—that in which something more than a perfect agreement was required to attract the Obligation. This epoch is synchronous with the period at which the famous Roman classification of Contracts into four sorts—the Verbal, the Literal, the Real, and the Consensual—had come into use, and during which these four orders of Contract constituted the only descriptions of engagement which the law would enforce. The meaning of the fourfold distribution is readily understood as soon as we apprehend the theory which severed the Obligation from the Convention. Each class of contracts was in fact named from certain formalities which were required over and above the mere agreement of the contracting parties. In the Verbal Contract, as soon as the Convention was effected, a form of words had to be gone through before the vinculum juris was attached to it. In the Literal Contract, an entry in a ledger or table-book had the effect of clothing the Convention with the Obligation, and the same result followed, in the case of the Real Contract, from the delivery of the Res or Thing which was the subject of the preliminary engagement. The Contracting parties came, in short, to an understanding in each case; but, if they went no further, they were not *obliged* to one another, and could not compel performance or ask redress for a breach of faith. But let them comply with certain prescribed formalities, and the Contract was immediately complete, taking its name from the particular form which it has suited them to adopt. The exceptions to this practice will be noticed presently.

I have enumerated the four Contracts in their historical order, which order, however, the Roman Institutional writers did not invariably follow. There can be no doubt that the Verbal Contract was the most ancient of the four, and that it is the eldest known descendant of the primitive Nexum. Several species of Verbal Contract were anciently in use, but the most important of all, and the only one treated of by our authorities, was effected by means of a *stipulation,* that is, a Question and Answer; a question addressed by the person who exacted the promise, and an answer given by the person who made it. This question and answer constituted the additional ingredient which, as I have just explained, was demanded by the primitive notion over and above the mere agreement of the persons interested. They formed the agency by which the Obligation was annexed. The old Nexum has now bequeathed to maturer jurisprudence first of all the conception of a chain uniting the contracting parties, and this has become the Obligation. It has further transmitted the notion of a ceremonial accompanying and consecrating the engagement, and this ceremonial has been transmuted into the Stipulation. The conversion of the solemn conveyance, which was the prominent feature of the original Nexum, into a mere question and answer, would be more of a mystery than it is if we had not the analogous history of Roman Testaments to enlighten us. Looking at that history, we can understand how the formal conveyance was first separated from the part of the proceeding which had immediate reference to the business in hand, and how afterwards it was omitted altogether. As then the question and answer of the Stipulation were unquestionably the Nexum in a simplified shape, we are prepared to find that they long partook of the nature of a technical term. It would be a mistake to consider them exclusively recommending themselves to the older Roman lawyers through their usefulness in furnishing persons mediating an agreement with an opportunity for consideration and reflection. It is not to be disputed that they had a value of this kind, which was gradually recognised; but there is proof that their function in respect to Contracts was at first formal and ceremonial in the statement of authorities, that not every question and answer was of old sufficient to constitute a Stipulation, but only a question and answer couched in technical phraseology specially appropriated to the particular occasion.

But although it is essential for the proper appreciation of the history of contract-law that the Stipulation should be understood to have been looked upon as a solemn form before it was recognised as a useful security, it would be wrong on the other hand to shut our eyes to its real usefulness. The Verbal Contract, though it had lost much of its ancient importance, survived to the latest period of Roman jurisprudence; and we may take it for granted that no institution of Roman law had so extended a longevity unless it served some practical advantage. I observe in an English writer some expressions of surprise that the Romans even of the earliest times were content with so meagre a protection against haste and irreflection. But on examining the Stipulation closely, and remembering that we have to do with a state of society in which written evidence was not easily procurable, I think we must admit that this Question and Answer, had it been expressly devised to answer the purpose which it served, would have been justly designated a highly ingenious expedient. It was the *promisee* who, in the character of stipulator, put all the terms of the contract into the form of a question, and the answer was given by the *promisor*. "Do you promise that you will deliver me such and such a slave, at such and such a place, on such and such a day?" "I do promise." Now, if we reflect for a moment, we shall see that this obligation to put the promise interrogatively inverts the natural position of the parties, and, by effectually breaking the tenor of the conversation, prevents the attention from gliding over a dangerous pledge. With us, a verbal promise is, generally speaking, to be gathered exclusively from the words of the promisor. In old Roman law, another step was absolutely required; it was necessary for the promise, after the agreement had been made, to sum up all its terms in a solemn interrogation; and it was of this interrogation, of course, and of the assent to it, that proof had to be given at the trial —*not* of the promise, which was not in itself binding. How great a difference this seemingly insignificant peculiarity may make in the phraseology of contract-law is speedily realised by the beginner in Roman jurisprudence, one of whose first stumbling-blocks is almost universally created by it. When we in English have occasion, in mentioning a contract, to connect it for convenience' sake with one of the parties,—for example, if we wished to speak generally of a contractor,—it is always the promis*or* at whom our words are pointing. But the general language of Roman law takes a different turn; it always regards the contract, if we may so speak, from the point of view of the promis*ee;* in speaking of a party to a contract, it is always the Stipulator, the person who asks the question, who is primarily alluded to. But the serviceableness of the stipulation is most vividly illustrated by referring to the actual examples in the pages of the Latin comic dramatists. If the entire scenes are read down in which these passages occur (ex. gra. Plautus, *Pseudolus,* Act I. sc. 1; Act IV. sc. 6; *Trinummus,* Act V. sc. 2), it will be perceived how effectually the attention of the person meditating the promise must have been arrested by the question, and how ample was the opportunity for withdrawal from an improvident undertaking.

In the Literal or Written Contract, the formal act by which an Obligation was superinduced on the Convention, was an entry of the sum due, where it could be specifically ascertained, on the debit side of a ledger. The explanation of this contract turns on a point of Roman domestic manners, the systematic character and exceeding regularity of bookkeeping in ancient times. There are several minor difficulties of old Roman law, for example, the nature of the Slave's Peculium, which are only cleared up when we recollect that a Roman household consisted of a number of persons strictly accountable to its head, and that every single item of domestic receipt and expenditure, after being entered in waste books, was transferred at stated periods to a general household ledger. There are some obscurities, however, in the descriptions we have received of the Literal Contract, the fact being that the habit of keeping books ceased to be universal in later times, and the expression "Literal Contract," came to signify a form of engagement entirely different from that originally understood. We are not, therefore, in a position to say, with respect to the primitive Literal Contract, whether the obligation was created by a simple entry on the part of the creditor, or whether the consent of the debtor or a correspondent entry in his own books was necessary to give it legal effect. The essential point is however established, that, in the case of this Contract, all formalities were dispensed with on a condition being complied with. This is another step downwards in the history of contract-law.

The Contract which stands next in historical succession, the Real Contract, shows a great advance in ethical conceptions. Whenever any agreement had for its object the delivery of a specific thing—and this is the case with the large majority of simple engagements—the Obligation was drawn down as soon as the delivery had actually taken place. Such a result must have involved a serious innovation on the oldest ideas of Contract; for doubtless, in the primitive times, when a contracting party had neglected to clothe his agreement in a stipulation, nothing done in pursuance of the agreement would be recognised by the law. A person who had paid over money on loan would be unable to sue for its repayment unless he had formally *stipulated* for it. But, in the Real Contract, performance on one side is allowed to impose a legal duty on the other—evidently on ethical grounds. For the first time then moral considerations appear as an ingredient in Contract-law, and the Real Contract differs from its two predecessors in being founded on these, rather than on respect for technical forms or on deference to Roman domestic habits.

We now reach the fourth class, or Consensual Contracts, the most interesting and important of all. Four specified Contracts were distinguished by this name: Mandatum, *i.e.* Commission or Agency; Societas or Partnership; Emtio Venditio or Sale; and Locatio Conductio or Letting and Hiring. A few pages back, after stating that a Contract consisted of a Pact or Convention to which an Obligation had been superadded, I spoke of certain acts or formalities by which the law permitted the Obligation to be attracted to the Pact. I used this language on account of the advantage of a general expression, but it is not strictly correct unless it be understood to include the negative as well as the positive. For, in truth, the peculiarity of these Consensual Contracts is that *no* formalities are required to create them of the Pact. Much that is indefensible, and much more that is obscure, has been written about the Consensual Contracts, and it has even been asserted that in them the *consent* of the Parties is more emphatically given than in any other species of agreement. But the term Consensual merely indicates that the Obligation is here annexed at once to the *Consensus*. The Consensus, or mutual assent of the parties, is the final and crowning ingredient in the Convention, and it is the special characteristic of agreements falling under one of the four heads of Sale, Partnership, Agency, and Hiring, that, as soon as the assent of the parties has supplied this ingredient, there is *at once* a Contract. The Consensus draws with it the Obligation, performing, in transactions of the sort specified, the exact functions which are discharged, in the other contracts, by the *Res* or Thing, by the *Verba* stipulationis, and by the *Literæ* or written entry in a ledger. Consensual is therefore a term which does not involve the slightest anomaly, but is exactly analogous to Real, Verbal, and Literal.

In the intercourse of life the commonest and most important of all the contracts are unquestionably the four stlyed Consensual. The larger part of the collective existence of every community is consumed in transactions of buying and selling, of letting and hiring, of alliances between men for purposes of business, or delegation of business from one man to another; and this is no doubt the consideration which led the Romans, as it has led most societies, to relieve these transactions from technical incumbrance, to abstain as much as possible from clogging the most efficient springs of social movement.

# 6. *Organic Solidarity and Contract*

BY EMILE DURKHEIM

## *I*

IF HIGHER societies do not rest upon a fundamental contract which sets forth the general principles of political life, they would have, or would be considered to have, according to Spencer, the vast system of particular contracts which link individuals as a unique basis. They would depend upon the group only in proportion to their dependence upon one another, and they would depend upon one another only in proportion to conventions privately entered into and freely concluded. Social solidarity would then be nothing else than the spontaneous accord of individual interests, an accord of which contracts are the natural expression. The typical social relation would be the economic, stripped of all regulation and resulting from the entirely free initiative of the parties. In short, society would be solely the stage where individuals exchanged the products of their labor, without any action properly social coming to regulate this exchange.

Is this the character of societies whose unity is produced by the division of labor? If this were so, we could with justice doubt their stability. For if interest relates men, it is never for more than some

Reprinted from Emile Durkheim, *The Division of Labor in Society,* trans. George Simpson (Glencoe, Ill.: The Free Press, 1947), pp. 203–17, 226–29, with the permission of The Free Press.

few moments. It can create only an external link between them. In the fact of exchange, the various agents remain outside of each other, and when the business has been completed, each one retires and is left entirely on his own. Consciences are only superficially in contact; they neither penetrate each other, nor do they adhere. If we look further into the matter, we shall see that this total harmony of interests conceals a latent or deferred conflict. For where interest is the only ruling force each individual finds himself in a state of war with every other since nothing comes to mollify the egos, and any truce in this eternal antagonism would not be of long duration. There is nothing less constant than interest. Today, it unites me to you; tomorrow, it will make me your enemy. Such a cause can only give rise to transient relations and passing associations. We now understand how necessary it is to see if this is really the nature of organic solidarity.

In no respect, according to Spencer, does industrial society exist in a pure state. It is a partially ideal type which slowly disengages itself in the evolutionary process, but it has not yet been completely realized. Consequently, to rightly attribute to it the qualities we have just been discussing, we would have to establish systematically that societies appear in a fashion as complete as they are elevated, discounting cases of regression.

It is first affirmed that the sphere of social activity grows smaller and smaller, to the great advantage of the individual. But to prove this proposition by real instances, it is not enough to cite, as Spencer does, some cases where the individual has been effectively emancipated from collective influence. These examples, numerous as they may be, can serve only as illustrations, and are, by themselves, devoid of any demonstrative force. It is very possible that, in this respect, socal action has regressed, but that, in other respects, it has been extended, and that, ultimately, we are mistaking a transformation for a disappearance. The only way of giving objective proof is not to cite some facts taken at random, but to follow historically, from its origins until recent times, the way in which social action has essentially manifested itself, and to see whether, in time, it has added or lost volume. We know that this is law. The obligations that society imposes upon its members, as inconsequential and unenduring as they may be, take on a juridicial form. Consequently, the relative dimensions of this system permit us to measure with exactitude the relative extent of social action.

But is is very evident that, far from diminishing, it grows greater and greater and becomes more and more complex. The more primitive a code is, the smaller its volume. On the contrary, it is as large as it is more recent. There can be no doubt about this. To be sure, it does not result in making the sphere of individual activity smaller. We must not forget that if there is more regulation in life, there is more life in general. This is sufficient proof that social discipline has not been relaxing. One of its forms tends, it is true, to regress, as we have already seen, but others, much richer and much more complex, develop in its place. If repressive law loses ground, restitutive law, which originally did not exist at all, keeps growing. If society no longer imposes upon everybody certain uniform practices, it takes greater care to define and regulate the special relations between different social functions, and this activity is not smaller because it is different.

Spencer would reply that he had not insisted upon the dimunition of every kind of control, but only of positive control. Let us admit this distinction. Whether it be positive or negative, the control is none the less social, and the principal question is to understand whether it has extended itself or contracted. Whether it be to command or to deny, to say *Do this* or *Do not do that,* if society intervenes more, we have not the right to say that individual spontaneity suffices more and more in all spheres. If the rules determining conduct have multiplied, whether they be imperative or prohibitive, it is not true that it depends more and more completely on private initiative.

But has this distinction itself any foundation? By positive control, Spencer means that which commands action, while negative control commands only abstention. As he says: A man has a piece of land; I cultivate it for him either wholly or in part, or else I impose upon him either wholly or in part the way in which he should cultivate it. This is a positive control. On the other hand, I give him neither aid nor advice about its cultivation; I simply do not molest my neighbor's crop, or trespass upon my neighbor's land, or put rubbish on his clearing. This is a negative control. The difference is very marked between ordering him to follow, as a citizen, a certain course, or suggesting means for the citizen to employ, and, on the other hand, not disturbing the course which some citizen is pursuing. If such is the meaning of these terms, then positive control is not disappearing.

We know, of course, that restitutive law is growing. But, in the large majority of cases, it either points out to a citizen the course he ought to pursue, or it interests itself in the means that this citizen is employing to attain his end. It answers the two following questions for each juridical relation: (1) Under what conditions and in what form does it normally exist? (2) What are the obligations it entails? The determination of the form and the conditions is essentially positive, since it forces the individual to follow a certain procedure in order to attain his end. As for the obligations, if they only forbid, in principle, our troubling another person in the exercise of his functions, Spencer's thesis would be true, at least in part. But they consist most often in the statement of services of a positive nature.

On this point we must go into some detail.

## *II*

It is quite true that contractual relations, which originally were rare or completely absent, multiply as social labor becomes divided. But what Spencer seems to have failed to see is that non-contractual relations develop at the same time.

First, let us examine that part of law which is improperly termed private, and which, in reality, regulates diffuse social functions, or what may be called the visceral life of the social organism.

In the first place, we know that domestic law, as simple as it was in the beginning, has become more and more complex. That is to say, that the different species of juridical relations to which family life gives rise are much more numerous than heretofore. But the obligations which result from this are of an eminently positive nature; they constitute a reciprocity of rights and duties. Moreover, they are not contractual, at least in their typical form. The conditions upon which they are dependent are related to our personal status which, in turn, depends upon birth, on our consanguineous relations, and, consequently, upon facts which are beyond volition.

Marriage and adoption, however, are sources of domestic relations, and they are contracts. But it rightly happens that the closer we get to the most elevated social types, the more also do these two juridical operations lose their properly contractual character.

Not only in lower societies, but in Rome itself until the end of the Empire, marriage remains an entirely private affair. It generally is a sale, real among primitive people, later fictive, but valid only through the consent of the parties duly attested. Neither solemn formalities of any kind nor intervention by some authority were then necessary. It is only with Christianity that marriage took on another character. The Christians early got into the habit of having their union consecrated by a priest. An act of the emperor Leo the Philosopher converted this usage into a law for the East. The Council of Trent sanctioned it likewise for the West. From then on, marriage ceased to be freely contracted, and was concluded through the intermediary of a public power, the Church, and the role that the Church played was not only that of a witness, but it was she and she alone who created the juridical tie which until then the wills of the participants sufficed to establish. We know how, later, the civil authority was substituted in this function for the religious authority, and how at the same time the part played by society and its necessary formalities was extended.*

The history of the contract of adoption is still more instructive.

We have already seen with what facility and on what a large scale adoption was practiced among the Indian tribes of North America. It could give rise to all the forms of kinship. If the adopted was of the same age as the adopting, they became brothers and sisters; if the adopted was already a mother, she became the mother of the one who adopted her.

Among the Arabs, before Mohammed, adoption often served to establish real families. It frequently happened that several persons would mutually adopt one another. They then became brothers and sisters, and the kinship which united them was just as strong as if they had been descended from a common origin. We find the same type of adoption among the Slavs. Very often, the members of different families became brothers and sisters and formed was is called a confraternity (*probatinstvo*). These societies were contracted for freely and without formality; agreement was enough to establish them. Moreover, the tie which binds these elective brothers is even stronger than that which results from natural fraternity.

Among the Germans, adoption was probably quite as easy and frequent. Very simple ceremonies were enough to establish it. But in India, Greece, and Rome, it was already subordinated to determined conditions. The one adopting had to be of a certain age, could not stand in such relation to the age of the adopted that it would be impossible to be his natural father. Ultimately, this change of family became a highly complex juridical operation which necessitated the intervention of a magistrate. At the same time, the number of those who could enjoy the right of adoption became more restricted. Only the father of a family or a bachelor *sui juris* could adopt, and the first could, only if he had no legitimate children.

In our current law the restrictive conditions have been even more multiplied. The adopted must be of age, the adopting must be more than fifty years of age, and have long treated the adopted as his

* Of course, the case is the same for the dissolution of the conjugal bond.

child. We must notice that, thus limited, it has become a very rare event. Before the appearance of the French Code, the whole procedure had almost completely fallen into disuse, and today it is, in certain countries such as Holland and lower Canada, not permitted at all.

At the same time that it became more rare, adoption lost its efficacy. In the beginning, adoptive kinship was in all respects similar to natural kinship. In Rome, the similarity was still very great. It was no longer, however, a perfect identity. In the sixteenth century, the adopted no longer has the right of succession if the adoptive father dies intestate. The French Code has re-established this right, but the kinship to which the adoption gives rise does not extend beyond the adopting and the adopted.

We see how insufficient the traditional explanation is, which attributes this custom of adoption among ancient societies to the need of assuring the perpetuity of the ancestral cult. The peoples who have practiced it in the greatest and freest manner, as the Indians of America, the Arabs, the Slavs, had no such cult, and, furthermore, at Rome and Athens, where domestic religion was at its height, this law is for the first time submitted to control and restrictions. If it was able to satisfy these needs, it was not established to satisfy them, and, inversely, if it tends to disappear, it is not because we have less desire to perpetuate our name and our race. It is in the structure of actual societies and in the place which the family occupies that we must seek the determining cause for this change.

Another proof of the truth of this is that it has become even more impossible to leave a family by an act of private authority than to enter into it. As the kinship-tie does not result from a contract, it cannot be broken as a contract can. Among the Iroquois, we sometimes see a part of a clan leave to go to join a neighboring clan. Among the Slavs, a member of the Zadruga who is tired of the common life can separate himself from the rest of the family and become a juridical stranger to it, even as he can be excluded by it. Among the Germans, a ceremony of some slight complexity permitted every Frank who so desired to completely drop off all kinship-obligations. In Rome, the son could not leave the family of his own will, and by this sign we recognize a more elevated social type. But the tie that the son could not break could be broken by the father. Thus was emancipation possible. Today neither the father nor the son can alter the natural state of domestic relations. They remain as birth determines them.

In short, at the same time that domestic obligations become more numerous, they take on, as is said, a public character. Not only in early times do they not have a contractural origin, but the role which contract plays in them becomes ever smaller. On the contrary, social control over the manner in which they form, break down, and are modified, becomes greater. The reason lies in the progressive effacement of segmental organization. The family, in truth, is for a long time a veritable social segment. In origin, it confounds itself with the clan. If, later, it becomes distinguished from the clan, it is as a part of the whole. It is a product of a secondary segmentation of the clan, identical with that which has given birth to the clan itself, and when the latter has disappeared, it still keeps the same quality. But everything segmental tends to be more and more reabsorbed into the social mass. That is why the family is forced to transform itself. Instead of remaining an autonomous society along side of the great society, it becomes more and more involved in the system of social organs. It even becomes one of the organs, charged with special functions, and, accordingly, everything that happens within it is capable of general repercussions. That is what brings it about that the regulative organs of society are forced to intervene in order to exercise a moderating influence over the functioning of the family, or even, in certain cases, a positively arousing influence.

But it is not only outside of contractual relations, it is in the play of these relations themselves that social action makes itself felt. For everything in the contract is not contractual. The only engagements which deserve this name are those which have been desired by the individuals and which have no other origin except in this manifestation of free will. Inversely, every obligation which has not been mutually consented to has nothing contractual about it. But wherever a contract exists, it is submitted to regulation which is the work of society and not that of individuals, and which becomes ever more voluminous and more complicated.

It is true that the contracting parties can, in certain respects, arrange to act contrary to the dispositions of the law. But, of course, their rights in this regard are not unlimited. For example, the agreement of the parties cannot make a contract valid if it does not satisfy the conditions of validity required by law. To be sure, in the great majority of cases, a contract is no longer restricted to determined forms. Still it must not be forgotten that there are in our Codes solemn contracts. But if law no longer has the formal exigencies of yesterday, it subjects contracts to engagements of a different sort. It refuses all obligatory force to engagements contracted by an incompetent, or without object, or with illicit purpose, or made by a person who cannot sell, or transact over an article which cannot be sold. Among the obligations which it attaches to various contracts, there are some which cannot be changed by any stipulation. Thus, a vendor cannot fail in his obligation to guarantee the purchaser against any eviction which results from something personal to the vendor (art. 1628); he cannot fail to repay the purchase-price in case of eviction, whatever its origin, provided that the buyer has not known of the danger (art. 1629), nor to set forth clearly what is being contracted for (art. 1602). Indeed, in a certain measure, he cannot be exempt from guaranteeing against hidden defects (arts. 1641 and 1643), particularly when known. If it is a question of fixtures, it is the buyer who must not profit from the situation by imposing a price too obviously below the real value of the thing (art. 1674), etc. Moreover, everything that relates to proof, the nature of the actions to which the contract gives a right, the time in which they must be begun, is absolutely independent of individual transactions.

In other cases social action does not manifest itself only by the refusal to recognize a contract formed in violation of the law, but by a positive intervention. Thus, the judge can, whatever the terms of the agreement, grant a delay to a debtor (arts. 1184, 1244, 1655, 1900), or even oblige the borrower to restore the article to the lender before the term agreed upon, if the latter has pressing need of it (art. 1189). But what shows better than anything else that contracts give rise to obligations which have not been contracted for is that they "make obligatory not only what there is expressed in them, but also all consequences which equity, usage, or the law imputes from the nature of the obligation" (art. 1135). In virtue of this principle, there must be supplied in the contract "clauses pertaining to usage, although they may not be expressed therein" (art. 1160).

But even if social action should not express itself in this way, it would not cease to be real. The possibility of derogating the law, which seems to reduce the contractual right to the role of eventual substitute for contracts properly called, is, in the very great majority of cases, purely theoretical. We can convince ourselves of this by showing what it consists in.

To be sure, when men unite in a contract, it is because, through the division of labor, either simple or complex, they need each other. But in order for them to co-operate harmoniously, it is not enough that they enter into a relationship, nor even that they feel the state of mutual dependence in which they find themselves. It is still necessary that the conditions of this co-operation be fixed for the duration of their relations. The rights and duties of each must be defined, not only in view of the situation such as it presents itself at the moment when the contract is made, but with foresight for the circumstances which may arise to modify it. Otherwise, at every instant, there would be conflicts and endless difficulties. We must not forget that, if the division of labor makes interests solidary, it does not confound them; it keeps them distinct and opposite. Even as in the internal workings of the individual organism each organ is in conflict with others while co-operating with them, each of the contractants, while needing the other, seeks to obtain what he needs at the least expense; that is to say, to acquire as many rights as possible in exchange for the smallest possible obligations.

It is necessary therefore to pre-determine the share of each, but this cannot be done according to a preconceived plan. There is nothing in the nature of things from which one can deduce what the obligations of one or the other ought to be until a certain limit is reached. Every determination of this kind can only result in compromise. It is a compromise between the rivalry of interests present and their solidarity. It is a position of equilibrium which can be found only after more or less laborious experiments. But it is quite evident that we can neither begin these experiments over again nor restore this equilibrium at fresh expense every time that we engage in some contractual relation. We lack all ability to do that. It is not at the moment when difficulties surge upon us that we must resolve them, and, moreover, we can neither foresee the variety of possible circumstances in which our contract will involve itself, nor fix in advance with the aid of simple mental calculus what will be in each case the rights and duties of each, save in matters in which we have a very definite experience. Moreover, the material conditions of life oppose themselves to the repetition of such operations. For, at each instant, and often at the most inopportune, we find ourselves contracting, either for something we have bought, or sold, somewhere we are traveling, our hiring of one's services, some acceptance of hostelry, etc. The greater part of our relations with others is of a contractual nature. If, then, it were necessary each time to begin the struggles anew, to again go through the conferences necessary to establish firmly all the conditions of agreement for the present and the future, we would be put to rout. For all these reasons, if we were linked only by the terms of our contracts, as they are agreed upon, only a precarious solidarity would result.

But contract-law is that which determines the juridical consequences of our acts that we have not determined. It expresses the normal conditions of equilibrium, as they arise from themselves or from the average. A résumé of numerous, varied experiences, what we cannot foresee individually is there provided for, what we cannot regulate is there regulated, and this regulation imposes itself upon us, although it may not be our handiwork, but that of society and tradition. It forces us to assume obligations that we have not contracted for, in the exact sense of the word, since we have not deliberated upon them, nor even, occasionally, had any knowledge about them in advance. Of course, the initial acts is always contractual, but there are consequences, sometimes immediate, which run over the limits of the contract. We co-operate because we wish to, but our voluntary co-operation creates duties for us that we did not desire.

From this point of view, the law of contracts appears in an entirely different light. It is no longer simply a useful complement of individual conventions; it is their fundamental norm. Imposing itself upon us with the authority of traditional experience, it constitutes the foundation of our contractual relations. We cannot evade it, except partially and accidentally. The law confers its rights upon us and subjects us to duties deriving from such acts of our will. We can, in certain cases, abandon them or change them for others. But both are none the less the normal type of rights and duties which circumstance lays upon us, and an express act is necessary for their modification. Thus, modifications are relatively rare. In principle, the rule applies; innovations are exceptional. The law of contracts exercises over us a regulative force of the greatest importance, since it determines what we ought to do and what we can require. It is a law which can be changed only by the consent of the parties, but so long as it is not abrogated or replaced, it guards its authority, and, moreover, a legislative act can be passed only in rare cases. There is, then, only a difference of degree between the law which regulates the obligations which that contract engenders and those which fix the other duties of citizens.

Finally, besides this organized, defined pressure which law exercises, there is one which comes from custom. In the way in which we make our contracts and in which we execute them, we are held to conform to rules which, though not sanctioned either directly or indirectly by any code, are none the less imperative. There are professional obligations, purely moral, which are, however, very strict. They are particularly apparent in the so-called liberal professions, and if they are perhaps less numerous in others, there is place for demanding them, as we shall see, if such demand is not the result of a morbid condition. But if this action is more diffuse than the preceding, it is just as social. Moreover, it is necessarily as much more extended as the contractual relations are more developed, for it is diversified like contracts.

In sum, a contract is not sufficient unto itself, but is possible only thanks to a regulation of the contract which is originally social. It is implied, first, because it has for its function much less the creation of new rules than the diversification in particular cases of pre-established rules; then, because it has and can have the power to bind only under certain conditions which it is necessary to define. If, in principle, society lends it an obligatory force, it is because, in general, the accord of particular wills suffices to assure, with the preceding reservations, the harmonious coming together of diffuse social functions. But if it conflicts with social purposes, if it tends to trouble the regular operation of organs, if, as is said, it is not just, it is necessary, while depriving it of all social value, to strip it of all authority as well. The role of society is not, then, in any case, simply to see passively that contracts are carried out. It is also to determine under what conditions they are executable, and if it is necessary, to restore them to their normal form. The agreement of parties cannot render a clause just which by itself is unjust, and there are rules of justice whose violation social justice prevents, even if it has been consented to by the interested parties.

A regulation whose extent cannot be limited in advance is thus necessary. A contract, says Spencer, has for its object assuring the worker the equivalent of the expense which his work has cost him. If such is truly the role of a contract, it will never be able to fulfill it unless it is more minutely regulated than it is today, for it surely would be a miracle if it succeeded in bringing about this equivalence. In fact, it is as much the gain which exceeds the expense, as the expense which exceeds the gain, and the disproportion is often striking. But, replies a whole school, if the gains are too small, the function will be abandoned for others. If they are too high, they will be sought after and this will diminish the profits. It is forgotten that one whole part of the population cannot thus quit its task, because no other is accessible to it. The very ones who have more liberty of movement cannot replace it in an instant. Such revolutions always take long to accomplish. While waiting, unjust contracts, unsocial by definition, have been executed with the agreement of society, and when the equilibrium in this respect has been reestablished, there is no reason for not breaking it for another.

There is no need for showing that this intervention, under its different forms, is of an eminently positive nature, since it has for its purpose the determination of the way in which we ought to cooperate. It is not it, it is true, which gives the impulse to the functions concurring, but once the concourse has begun, it rules it. As soon as we have made the first step towards cooperation, we are involved in the regulative action which society exercises over us. If Spencer qualified this as negative, it is because, for him, contract consists only in exchange. But, even from this point of view, the expression he employs is not exact. No doubt, when, after having an object delivered, or profiting from a service, I refuse to furnish a suitable equivalent, I take from another what belongs to him, and we can say that society, by obliging me to keep my promise, is only preventing an injury, an indirect aggression. But if I have simply promised a service without having previously received remuneration, I am not less held to keep my engagement. In this case, however, I do not enrich myself at the expense of another; I only refuse to be useful to him. Moreover, exchange, as we have seen, is not all there is to a contract. There is also the proper harmony of functions concurring. They are not only in contact for the short time during which things pass from one hand to another; but more extensive relations necessarily result from them, in the course of which it is important that their solidarity be not troubled.

* * *

## *IV*

The following propositions sum up the first part of our work.

Social life comes from a double source, the likeness of consciences and the division of social labor. The individual is socialized in the first case, because, not having any real individuality, he becomes, with those whom he resembles, part of the same collective type; in the second case, because, while having a physiognomy and a personal activity which distinguishes him from others, he depends upon them in the same measure that he is distinguished from them, and consequently upon the society which results from their union.

The similitude of consciences gives rise to juridical rules which, with the threat of repressive measures, impose uniform beliefs and practices upon all. The more pronounced this is, the more completely is social life confounded with religious life, and the nearer to communism are economic institutions.

The division of labor gives rise to juridical rules which determine the nature and the relations of divided functions, but whose violation calls forth only restitutive measures without any expiatory character.

Each of these bodies of juridical rules is, moreover, accompanied by a body of purely moral rules. Where penal law is very voluminous, common morality is very extensive; that is to say, there is a multitude of collective practices placed under the protection of public opinion. Where restitutive law is highly developed, there is an occupational morality for each profession. In the interior of the same group of workers, there exists an opinion, diffuse in the entire extent of this circumscribed aggregate, which, without being furnished with legal sanctions, is rendered obedience. These are usages and customs common to the same order of functionaries which no one of them can break without incurring the censure of the corporation.* This morality is distinguished from the preceding by differences analogous to those which separate the two corresponding types of law. It is localized in a limited region of society. Moreover, the repressive character of the sanctions attaching to it is much less accentuated. Professional misdeeds call forth reprobation much more feeble than attacks against public morality.

The rules of occupational morality and justice, however, are as imperative as the others. They force the individual to act in view of ends which are not strictly his own, to make concessions, to consent to compromises, to take into account interests higher than his own. Consequently, even where society relies most completely upon the division of labor, it does not become a jumble of juxtaposed atoms, between which it can establish only external, transient contacts. Rather the members are united by ties which extend deeper and far beyond the short moments during which the exchange is made. Each of the functions that they exercise is, in a fixed way, dependent upon others, and with them forms a solidary system. Accordingly, from the nature of the chosen task permament duties arise. Because we fill some certain domestic or social function, we are involved in a complex of obligations from which we have no right to free ourselves. There is, above all, an organ upon which we are tending to depend more and more; this is the State. The points at which we are in contact with it multiply as do the occasions when it is entrusted with the duty of reminding us of the sentiment of common solidarity.

Thus, altruism is not destined to become, as Spencer desires, a sort of agreeable ornament to social life, but it will forever be its fundamental basis. How can we ever really dispense with it? Men cannot live together without acknowledging, and,

* This censure, moreover, just as all moral punishment, is translated into external movements (discipline, dismissal of employees, loss of relations, etc.).

consequently, making mutual sacrifices, without tying themselves to one another with strong, durable bonds. Every society is a moral society. In certain respects, this character is even more pronounced in organized societies. Because the individual is not sufficient unto himself, it is from society that he receives everything necessary to him, as it is for society that he works. Thus is formed a very strong sentiment of the state of dependence in which he finds himself. He becomes accustomed to estimating it as its just value, that is to say, in regarding himself as part of a whole, the organ of an organism. Such sentiments naturally inspire not only mundane sacrifices which assure the regular development of daily social life, but even, on occasion, acts of complete self-renunciation and wholesale abnegation. On its side, society learns to regard its members no longer as things over which it has rights, but as co-operators whom it cannot neglect and towards whom it owes duties. Thus, it is wrong to oppose a society which comes from a community of beliefs to one which has a co-operative basis, according only to the first a moral character, and seeing in the latter only an economic grouping. In reality, co-operation also has its intrinsic morality. There is, however, reason to believe, as we shall see later, that in contemporary societies this morality has not yet reached the high development which would now seem necessary to it.

But it is not of the same nature as the other. The other is strong only if the individual is not. Made up of rules which are practiced by all distinctly, it receives from this universal, uniform practice an authority which bestows something super-human upon it, and which puts it beyond the pale of discussion. The co-operative society, on the contrary, develops in the measure that individual personality becomes stronger. As regulated as a function may be, there is a large place always left for personal initiative. A great many of the obligations thus sanctioned have their origin in a choice of the will. It is we who choose our professions, and even certain of our domestic functions. Of course, once our resolution has ceased to be internal and has been externally translated by social consequences, we are tied down. Duties are imposed upon us that we have not expressly desired. It is, however, through a voluntary act that this has taken place. Finally, because these rules of conduct relate, not to the conditions of common life, but to the different forms of professional activity, they have a more temporal character, which, while lessening their obligatory force, renders them more accessible to the action of men.

There are, then, two great currents of social life to which two types of structure, not less different, correspond.

Of these currents, that which has its origin in social similitudes first runs on alone and without a rival. At this moment, it confounds itself with the very life of society; then, little by little, it canalizes, rarefies, while the second is always growing. Indeed, the segmental structure is more and more covered over by the other, but without ever completely disappearing.

## III–ORGANIZATION OF THE ECONOMY

# 1. *The Market*

BY MAX WEBER

BY THE "market situation" (*Marktage*) for any object of exchange is meant all the opportunities of exchanging it for money which are known by the participants in the market situation to be available to them and relevant in orienting their attitudes to prices and to competition.

"Marketability" (*Marktgängigkeit*) is the degree of regularity with which an object tends to be an object of exchange on the market.

"Market freedom" is the degree of autonomy en-

Reprinted from Max Weber, *The Theory of Social and Economic Organization,* trans. A. M. Henderson and Talcott Parsons, ed. Talcott Parsons (2d ed.; Glencoe, Ill.: The Free Press, 1956), pp. 181–86. 

joyed by the parties to market relationships in price determination and in competition.

"Regulation of the market," on the contrary, is the state of affairs where there is a substantive restriction, effectively enforced by the provisions of an order, on the marketability of certain potential objects of exchange or on the market freedom of certain participants. Regulation of the market may be determined (1) traditionally, by the actors' becoming accustomed to traditionally accepted limitations on exchange or to traditional conditions. (2) By convention, through social disapproval of treating certain utilities as marketable or of subjecting certain objects of exchange to free competition and free price determination, in general or when undertaken by certain groups of persons. (3) By law, through legal restrictions on exchange or on the freedom of competition, in general or for particular groups of persons or for particular objects of exchange. Legal regulation may take the form of influencing the market situation of objects of exchange by price regulation or of limiting the possession, acquisition, or exchange of rights of control and disposal over certain goods to certain specific groups of persons. In the latter case it is a legally-guaranteed monopoly or a legal limitation of economic freedom. (4) By voluntary action arising from the play of interests. In this case there is substantive regulation of the market, though the market remains formally free. This type of regulation tends to develop when certain participants in the market are, by virtue of their totally or approximately exclusive control of the possession of or opportunities to acquire certain utilities—that is, of their monopolistic powers—in a position to influence the market situation in such a way as actually to abolish the market freedom of others. In particular, they may make agreements with each other and with typical exchange partners for regulating market conditions. Typical examples are market quota agreements and price cartels.

1. It is convenient, though not necessary, to confine the term "market situation" to cases of exchange for money because it is only then that uniform numerical statements of relationships become possible. Opportunities for exchange *in kind* are best described simply as exchange opportunities. Different kinds of goods are and have been marketable in widely different and variable degrees, even where a money economy was well developed. The details cannot be gone into here. In general, articles produced in standardized form in large quantities and widely consumed have been the most marketable; unusual goods, only occasionally in demand, the least. Durable consumption goods which can be made use of over long periods and means of production with a long or indefinite life, above all, agricultural and forest land, have been marketable to a much less degree than finished goods of everyday use or means of production which are quickly used up, which can be used only once, or which give quick returns.

2. The regulation of markets, as an economically rational policy, has been historically associated with the growth of formal market freedom and the extension of marketability of goods. The original modes of market regulation have been various, partly traditional and magical, partly dictated by kinship relations, by class privileges, by military needs, by welfare policies, and not least by the interests and requirements of the governing authorities of corporate groups. But in each of these cases the dominant interests have not been primarily concerned with maximizing the opportunities of acquisition and economic provision of the participants in the market themselves; have, indeed, often been in conflict with them. (1) Sometimes the effect has been to exclude certain objects from market dealings, either permanently or for a time. This has happened in the magical case, by taboo; in that of kinship, by the hereditary appropriation of property; on the basis of social status, with fiefs. In times of famine the sale of grain has been temporarily prohibited. In other cases permission to sell has been made conditional on a prior offer to certain persons, such as kinsmen, co-members of class groups, and of guilds, or fellow-citizens of a town; or the sale has been limited by maximum prices, as is common in war time, or by minimum prices. Thus in the interests of the dignity of magicians, lawyers, physicians, they have not been allowed to accept fees below a certain minimum. (2) Sometimes certain categories of persons, such as members of the nobility, peasants, or sometimes even artisans, have been excluded from market trade in general or with respect to certain commodities. (3) Sometimes the market freedom of consumers has been restricted by regulations, as in regulations specifying consumption for different classes, rationing in case of war or of famine. (4) Another type is the restriction of the market freedom of potential competitors in the interest of the market position of certain groups, such as the professions or the guilds. Finally, (5) certain economic privileges, such as royal monopolies, have been reserved to the political authorities or to those holding a charter from such authorities. This was typical for the early capitalistic monopolies.

Of all these, the fifth type of market regulation has been the most highly rational in terms of the interests of market participants; the first type, the least. By "rational" in this sense is meant promoting the interests of the various groups whose action is oriented to the market situations as a means to the advantageous purchase and sale of goods, with consideration for the interests of other groups not thus oriented proportionally minimized. The groups which, relative to these forms of regulation have been most interested in the freedom of the market, have been those whose interests lay in the greatest possible extension of the marketability of goods, whether from the point of view of availability for consumption, or of ready opportunities for sale. Voluntary market regulation has not appeared extensively and permanently except where there have been highly developed profit-making interests. With a view to the securing of monopolistic advantages, this could take several forms: (1) the pure regulation of opportunities for purchase and sale, which is typical of the widespread phenomena of trading monopolies; (2) the monopolization of transportation facilities, as in shipping and railways; (3) the monopolization of the production of goods; and (4) that of the extension of credit and of financing. The last two types generally are accompanied by an increase in the regulation of economic activity by corporate groups other than the immediate participants in the market relationships. But unlike the primitive, irrational forms of regulation, this is apt to be deliberately oriented to the market situation. The starting point of voluntary market regulation has naturally in general been the fact that certain groups with a far-reaching degree of actual control over economic resources have been in a position to take advantage of the formal freedom of the market to establish monopolies. Voluntary associations of consumers, such as consumers' co-operative societies, have, on the other hand, tended to originate among those who were in an economically weak position. They have hence often been able to accomplish savings for their members, but only occasionally and in particular localities have they been able to establish an effective system of market regulation.

## *The Formal and Substantive Rationality of Economic Action*

The term "formal rationality of economic action" will be used to designate the extent of quantitative calculation or accounting which is technically possible and which is actually applied. The "substantive rationality," on the other hand, is the degree in which a given group of persons, no matter how it is delimited, is or could be adequately provided with goods by means of an economically oriented course of social action. This course of action will be interpreted in terms of a given set of ultimate values no matter what they may be. There is a variety of different possibilities.

1. The terminology suggested above is thought of merely as a means of securing greater consistency in the use of the word "rational" in this field. It is actually only a more precise form of the meanings which are continually recurring in the discussion of "socialization" and of evaluation in money and in kind.

2. A system of economic activity will be called "formally" rational according to the degree in which the provision for needs, which is essential to every rational economy, is capable of being expressed in numerical, calculable terms, and is so expressed. In the first instance, it is quite independent of the technical form these calculations take, particularly whether estimates are expressed in money or in kind. The concept is thus unambiguous, at least in the sense that expression in money terms yields the highest degree of formal calculability. Naturally, even this is true only relatively, so long as other things are equal.

3. On the other hand, the concept of substantive rationality is full of difficulties. It conveys only one element common to all the possible empirical situations; namely, that it is not sufficient to consider only the purely formal fact that calculations are being made on grounds of expediency by the methods which are, among those available, technically the most nearly adequate. In addition, it is necessary to take account of the fact that economic activity is oriented to ultimate ends (*Forderungen*) of some kind, whether they be ethical, political, utiltarian, hedonistic, the attainment of social equality, or of anything else. Substantive rationality cannot be measured in terms of formal calculation alone, but also involves a relation to the absolute values or to the content of the particular given ends to which it is oriented. In principle, there is an indefinite number of possible standards of value which are "rational" in this sense. Socialistic and communistic standards which, though by no means unambiguous in themselves, always involve elements of social justice and equality, form only one group among the indefinite plurality of possible points of view. Others are action in the interest of a hierarchy of class distinctions or in furtherance of the power of a political unit, particularly by war. All these and many others are of potential "substantive" significance. These points of view are, however, significant only as bases from which to judge the outcome of economic action. In addition, it is possible to criticize the attitude toward the economic activity itself

or toward the means used, from ethical, ascetic, or aesthetic points of view. Of all of these, the merely formal calculation in money terms may seem either of quite secondary importance or even as fundamentally evil in itself, quite apart from the consequences of the modern methods of calculation. There is no question in this discussion of attempting value judgments in this field, but only of determining and delimiting what is to be called "formal." In this context the concept of "substantive" is itself in a certain sense "formal"; that is, it is an abstract, generic concept.

## 2. *The Principal Modes of Capitalistic Orientation*

BY MAX WEBER

THERE ARE a number of qualitatively different modes in which it is possible for the orientation to profit to be determined in a capitalistic manner; that is, in proportion to its rationality in terms of capital accounting.

1. Profit-making activity may be oriented to the exploitation of market advantages in a continuous process of purchase and sale on the market where exchange is free; that is, formally not subject to compulsion and materially, at least relatively, free. Or it may be oriented to the maximization of profit in continuous productive enterprises which make use of capital accounting.

2. It may be oriented to opportunities for profit by trade and speculation in money, taking over debts of all sorts, and creating means of payment. A closely related type is the professional extension of credit, either for consumption or for profit-making purposes.

3. It may be oriented to opportunities for acquiring "booty" from corporate political groups or persons connected with politics. This includes the financing of wars or revolutions and the financing of party leaders by loans and supplies.

4. It may be oriented to opportunities for continuous profit by virtue of domination by force or of a position of power guaranteed by the political authority. There are two main sub-types: colonial capitalism operated through plantations with compulsory payments or compulsory labour and by monopolistic and compulsory trade. On the other hand there is the fiscal type, profit making by farming of taxes and of offices, whether in the home area or in colonies.

5. The orientation to opportunities for profit opened up by unusual transactions with political bodies.

6. The orientation to opportunities for profit of the following types: (a) To purely speculative transactions in standardized commodities or in the securities of an enterprise; (b) by carrying out the continuous financial operations of political bodies; (c) by the promotional financing of new enterprises in the form of sale of securities to investors; (d) by the speculative financing of capitalistic enterprises and of various other types of economic organization with the purpose of a profitable regulation of market situations or of attaining power.

Types (1) and (6) are to a large extent peculiar to the modern Western World. The other types have been common all over the world for thousands of years where the possibilities of exchange, money economy, and money financing have been present. In the Western World they have not had such a dominant importance as modes of profit-making as they had in Antiquity, except in restricted areas and for relatively brief periods, particularly in times of war. Where large areas have been pacified for a long period, as in the Chinese and later Roman Empires, these have tended to decline, leaving only commerce, money changing and lending, as forms of capitalistic acquisition. The capitalistic financing of political activities has always depended on two conditions: a competition of states with one another for power and the corresponding competition for control of capital which was free as between them. All this has ended only with the establishment of large-scale, unified states.

---

Reprinted from Max Weber, *The Theory of Social and Economic Organization,* trans. A. M. Henderson and Talcott Parsons, ed. Talcott Parsons (2d ed.; Glencoe, Ill.: The Free Press, 1956), pp. 279–80. 

It is only in the modern Western World that rational capitalistic enterprises with fixed capital, free labour, the rational specialization and combination of functions, and the allocation of productive functions on the basis of capitalistic enterprises, bound together in a market economy, are to be found. This involves the capitalistic type of organization of labour, which in formal times is purely voluntary, as the typical and dominant mode of providing for the wants of the masses of the population, with expropriation of the workers from the means of production and appropriation of the enterprises by security owners. It is also only here that we find public credit in the form of issues of government securities, the legal form of the business corporation, the issue of securities, and financing carried on as the business of rational enterprises, trade in commodities and securities or organized exchanges, money and capital markets, monopolistic associations as a type of economically rational organization of the production of goods by profit-making enterprises as opposed to the mere trade in them.

This difference calls for an explanation and the explanation cannot be given on economic grounds alone. Types (3) to (5) inclusive will be treated here together as "politically oriented capitalism." The whole of the later discussion will be devoted particularly, though not alone, to the problem of explaining the difference. In general terms, it is possible only to make the following statement:—

1. It is clear from the very beginning that the types of political events and processes which open up the kind of opportunities for profit which are exploited by political capitalism are, seen in economic terms—that is, from the point of view either of orientation to market advantages or of the consumption needs of budgetary units—irrational.

2. It is further clear that purely speculative opportunities for profit and pure consumption credit are, from the point of view both of want satisfaction and of the production of goods, irrational because they are determined by the fortuitous distribution of ownership and of market advantages. The same may also be true of opportunities for promotion and financing, under certain circumstances; but this is by no means necessarily always the case.

Apart from the rational capitalistic enterprise, the modern economic order is unique in its mode of regulation of the monetary system and in the commercialization of bills of exchange and securities.

# 3. *The Essential Properties of Interest and Money*

BY JOHN MAYNARD KEYNES

## *I*

IT SEEMS, then, that the *rate of interest on money* plays a peculiar part in setting a limit to the level of employment, since it sets a standard to which the marginal efficiency of a capital-asset must attain if it is to be newly produced. That this should be so, is, at first sight, most perplexing. It is natural to enquire wherein the peculiarity of money lies as distinct from other assets, whether it is only money which has a rate of interest, and what would happen in a non-monetary economy. Until we have answered these questions, the full significance of our theory will not be clear.

The money-rate of interest—we may remind the reader—is nothing more than the percentage excess of a sum of money contracted for forward delivery, *e.g.* a year hence, over what we may call the "spot" or cash price of the sum thus contracted for forward delivery. It would seem, therefore, that for every kind of capital-asset there must be an analogue of the rate of interest on money. For there is a definite quantity of (*e.g.*) wheat to be delivered a year hence which has the same exchange value to-day as 100 quarters of wheat for "spot" delivery. If the former quantity is 105 quarters, we may say that the wheat-rate of interest is 5 per cent. per annum; and if it is 95 quarters, that it is *minus* 5 per cent. per annum. Thus for every durable commodity we have a rate

---

Reprinted from John Maynard Keynes, *The General Theory of Employment, Interest, and Money* (New York: Harcourt, Brace & Co., 1936), pp. 222–27, 229–42, with the permission of Harcourt, Brace & Co., Professor R. F. Kelin, and Macmillan & Co., London.

of interest in terms of itself,—a wheat-rate of interest, a copper-rate of interest, a house-rate of interest, even a steel-plant-rate of interest.

The difference between the "future" and "spot" contracts for a commodity, such as wheat, which are quoted in the market, bears a definite relation to the wheat-rate of interest, but, since the future contract is quoted in terms of money for forward delivery and not in terms of wheat for spot delivery, it also brings in the money-rate of interest. The exact relationship is as follows:

Let us suppose that the spot price of wheat is £100 per 100 quarters, that the price of the "future" contract for wheat for delivery a year hence is £107 per 100 quarters, and that the money-rate of interest is 5 per cent.; what is the wheat-rate of interest? £100 spot will buy £105 for forward delivery, and £105 for forward delivery will buy $^{105}/_{107}$. 100 (=98) quarters for forward delivery. Alternatively £100 spot will buy 100 quarters of wheat for spot delivery. Thus 100 quarters of wheat for spot delivery will buy 98 quarters for forward delivery. It follows that the wheat-rate of interest is *minus* 2 per cent per annum.

It follows from this that there is no reason why their rates of interest should be the same for different commodities,—why the wheat-rate of interest should be equal to the copper-rate of interest. For the relation between the "spot" and "future" contracts, as quoted in the market, is notoriously different for different commodities. This, we shall find, will lead us to the clue we are seeking. For it may be that it is the *greatest* of the own-rates of interest (as we may call them) which rules the roost (because it is the greatest of these rates that the marginal efficiency of a capital-asset must attain if it is to be newly produced); and that there are reasons why it is the money-rate of interest which is often the greatest (because, as we shall find, certain forces, which operate to reduce the own-rates of interest of other assets, do not operate in the case of money).

It may be added that, just as there are differing commodity-rates of interest at any time, so also exchange dealers are familiar with the fact that the rate of interest is not even the same in terms of two different moneys, *e.g.* sterling and dollars. For here also the difference between the "spot" and "future" contracts for a foreign money in terms of sterling are not, as a rule, the same for different foreign moneys.

Now each of these commodity standards offers us the same facility as money for measuring the marginal efficiency of capital. For we can take any commodity we choose, *e.g.* wheat; calculate the wheat-value of the prospective yields of any capital asset; and the rate of discount which makes the present value of this series of wheat annuities equal to the present supply price of the asset in terms of wheat gives us the marginal efficiency of the asset in terms of wheat. If no change is expected in the relative value of two alternative standards, then the marginal efficiency of a capital-asset will be the same in whichever of the two standards it is measured, since the numerator and denominator of the fraction which leads up to the marginal efficiency will be changed in the same proportion. If, however, one of the alternative standards is expected to change in value in terms of the other, the marginal efficiencies of capital-assets will be changed by the same percentage, according to which standard they are measured in. To illustrate this let us take the simplest case where wheat, one of the alternative standards, is expected to appreciate at a steady rate of $a$ per cent per annum in terms of money; the marginal efficiency of an asset, which is $x$ per cent in terms of money, will then be $x-a$ per cent in terms of wheat. Since the marginal efficiencies of all capital-assets will be altered by the same amount, it follows that their order of magnitude will be the same irrespective of the standard which is selected.

If there were some composite commodity which could be regarded strictly speaking as representative, we could regard the rate of interest and the marginal efficiency of capital in terms of this commodity as being, in a sense, uniquely *the* rate of interest and *the* marginal efficiency of capital. But there are, of course, the same obstacles in the way of this as there are to setting up a unique standard of value.

So far, therefore, the money-rate of interest has no uniqueness compared with other rates of interest, but is on precisely the same footing. Wherein, then, lies the peculiarity of the money-rate of interest which gives it the predominating practical importance attributed to it in the preceding chapters? Why should the volume of output and employment be more intimately bound up with the money-rate of interest than with the wheat-rate of interest or the house-rate of interest?

## *II*

Let us consider what the various commodity-rates of interest over a period of (say) a year are likely to be for different types of assets. Since we are taking each commodity in turn as the standard, the returns on each commodity must be reckoned in this context as being measured in terms of itself.

There are three attributes which different types of assets possess in different degrees; namely, as follows:

(i) Some assets produce a yield or output $q$, measured in terms of themselves, by assisting some process of production or supplying services to a consumer.

(ii) Most assets, except money, suffer some wastage or involve some cost through the mere passage of time (apart from any change in their relative value), irrespective of their being used to produce a yield; *i.e.* they involve a carrying cost $c$ measured in terms of themselves. It does not matter for our present purpose exactly where we draw the line between the costs which we deduct before calculating $q$ and those which we include in $c$, since in what follows we shall be exclusively concerned with $q - c$.

(iii) Finally, the power of disposal over an asset during a period may offer a potential convenience or security, which is not equal for assets of different kinds, though the assets themselves are of equal initial value. There is, so to speak, nothing to show for this at the end of the period in the shape of output; yet it is something for which people are ready to pay something. The amount (measured in terms of itself) which they are willing to pay for the potential convenience or security given by this power of disposal (exclusive of yield or carrying cost attaching to the asset), we shall call its liquidity-premium $l$.

It follows that the total return expected from the ownership of an asset over a period is equal to its yield *minus* its carrying cost *plus* its liquidity-premium, *i.e.* to $q - c + l$. That is to say, $q - c + l$ is the own-rate of interest of any commodity, where $q$, $c$ and $l$ are measured in terms of itself as the standard.

It is characteristic of instrumental capital (*e.g.* a machine) or of consumption capital (*e.g.* a house) which is in use, that its yield should normally exceed its carrying cost, whilst its liquidity-premium is probably negligible; of a stock of liquid goods or of surplus laid-up instrumental or consumption capital that it should incur a carrying cost in terms of itself without any yield to set off against it, the liquidity-premium in this case also being usually negligible as soon as stocks exceed a moderate level, though capable of being significant in special circumstances; and of money that its yield is *nil,* and its carrying cost negligible, but its liquidity-premium substantial. Different commodities may, indeed, have differing degrees of liquidity-premium amongst themselves, and money may incur some degree of carrying costs, *e.g.* for safe custody. But it is an essential difference between money and all (or most) other assets that in the case of money its liquidity-premium much exceeds its carrying cost, whereas in the case of other assets their carrying cost much exceeds their liquidity-premium.

* * *

## *III*

In attributing, therefore, a peculiar significance to the money-rate of interest, we have been tacitly assuming that the kind of money to which we are accustomed has some special characteristics which lead to its own-rate of interest in terms of itself as standard being more reluctant to fall as output increases than the own-rates of interest of any other assets in terms of themselves. Is this assumption justified? Reflection shows, I think, that the following peculiarities, which commonly characterise money as we know it, are capable of justifying it. To the extent that the established standard of value has these peculiarities, the summary statement, that it is the money-rate of interest which is the significant rate of interest, will hold good.

(i) The first characteristic which tends towards the above conclusion is the fact that money has, both in the long and in the short period, a zero, or at any rate a very small, elasticity of production, so far as the power of private enterprise is concerned, as distinct from the monetary authority;—elasticity of production meaning, in this context, the response of the quantity of labour applied to producing it to a rise in the quantity of labour which a unit of it will command. Money, that is to say, cannot be readily produced;—labour cannot be turned on at will by entrepreneurs to produce money in increasing quantities as its price rises in terms of the wage-unit. In the case of an inconvertible managed currency this condition is strictly satisfied. But in the case of a gold-standard currency it is also approximately so, in the sense that the maximum proportional addition to the quantity of labour which can be thus employed is very small, except indeed in a country of which gold-mining is the major industry.

Now, in the case of assets having an elasticity of production, the reason why we assumed their own-rate of interest to decline was because we assumed the stock of them to increase as the result of a higher rate of output. In the case of money, however—postponing, for the moment, our consideration of the effects of reducing the wage-unit or of a deliberate increase in its supply by the monetary authority—the supply is fixed. Thus the characteristic that money cannot be readily produced by labour gives at once some *prima facie* presumption for the view that its own-rate of interest will be relatively reluctant to fall; whereas if money could be grown like a crop or manufactured like a motor-car, depressions would be avoided or mitigated because, if the price of other assets was tending to fall in terms of money, more labour would be diverted into the production of money;—as we see to be the case in gold-mining countries, though for the world as a whole the maximum diversion in this way is almost negligible.

(ii) Obviously, however, the above condition is satisfied, not only by money, but by all pure rent-factors, the production of which is completely inelastic. A second condition, therefore, is required to distinguish money from other rent elements.

The second *differentia* of money is that it has an elasticity of substitution equal, or nearly equal, to zero; which means that as the exchange value of money rises there is no tendency to substitute some other factor for it;—except, perhaps, to some trifling extent, where the money-commodity is also used in manufacture or the arts. This follows from the peculiarity of money that its utility is solely derived from its exchange-value, so that the two rise and fall *pari passu,* with the result that as the exchange value of money rises there is no motive or tendency, as in the case of rent-factors, to substitute some other factor for it.

Thus, not only is it impossible to turn more labour on to producing money when its labour-price rises, but money is a bottomless sink for purchasing power, when the demand for it increases, since there is no value for it at which demand is diverted—as in the case of other rent-factors—so as to slop over into a demand for other things.

The only qualification to this arises when the rise in the value of money leads to uncertainty as to the future maintenance of this rise; in which event, $a_1$ and $a_2$ are increased, which is tantamount to an increase in the commodity-rates of money-interest and is, therefore, stimulating to the output of other assets.

(iii) Thirdly, we must consider whether these conclusions are upset by the fact that, even though the quantity of money cannot be increased by diverting labour into producing it, nevertheless an assumption that its effective supply is rigidly fixed would be inaccurate. In particular, a reduction of the wage-unit will release cash from its other uses for the satisfaction of the liquidity-motive; whilst, in addition to this, as money-values fall, the stock of money will bear a higher proportion to the total wealth of the community.

It is not possible to dispute on purely theoretical grounds that this reaction might be capable of allowing an adequate decline in the money-rate of interest. There are, however, several reasons, which taken in combination are of compelling force, why in an economy of the type to which we are accustomed it is very probable that the money-rate of interest will often prove reluctant to decline adequately:

(*a*) We have to allow, first of all, for the reactions of a fall in the wage-unit on the marginal efficiencies of other assets in terms of money;—for it is the *difference* between these and the money-rate of interest with which we are concerned. If the effect of the fall in the wage-unit is to produce an expectation that it will subsequently rise again, the result will be wholly favourable. If, on the contrary, the effect is to produce an expectation of a further fall, the reaction on the marginal efficiency of capital may offset the decline in the rate of interest.

(*b*) The fact that wages tend to be sticky in terms of money, the money-wage being more stable than the real wage, tends to limit the readiness of the wage-unit to fall in terms of money. Moreover, if this were not so, the position might be worse rather than better; because, if money-wages were to fall easily, this might often tend to create an expectation of a further fall with unfavourable reactions on the marginal efficiency of capital. Furthermore, if wages were to be fixed in terms of some other commodity, *e.g.* wheat, it is improbable that they would continue to be sticky. It is because of money's other characteristics—those, especially, which make it *liquid*—that wages, when fixed in terms of it, tend to be sticky.[1]

(*c*) Thirdly, we come to what is the most fundamental consideration in this context, namely, the characteristics of money which satisfy liquidity-preference. For, in certain circumstances such as will often occur, these will cause the rate of interest to be insensitive, particularly below a certain figure, even to a substantial increase in the quantity of money in proportion to other forms of wealth. In other words, beyond a certain point money's yield from liquidity does not fall in response to an increase in its quantity to anything approaching the extent to which the yield from other types of assets falls when their quantity is comparably increased.

In this connection the low (or negligible) carrying-costs of money play an essential part. For if its carrying-costs were material, they would offset the effect of expectations as to the prospective value of money at future dates. The readiness of the public to increase their stock of money in response to a comparatively small stimulus is due to the advantages of liquidity (real or supposed) having no offset to contend with in the shape of carrying-costs mounting steeply with the lapse of time. In the case of a commodity other than money a modest stock of it may offer some convenience to users of the commodity. But even though a larger stock might have some attractions as representing a store of wealth of stable value, this would be offset by its carrying-costs in the shape of storage, wastage, etc. Hence,

1. If wages (and contracts) were fixed in terms of wheat, it might be that wheat would acquire some of money's liquidity-premium.

after a certain point is reached, there is necessarily a loss in holding a greater stock.

In the case of money, however, this, as we have seen, is not so,—and for a variety of reasons, namely, those which constitute money as being, in the estimation of the public, *par excellence* "liquid." Thus those reformers, who look for a remedy by creating artificial carrying-costs for money through the device of requiring legal-tender currency to be periodically stamped at a prescribed cost in order to retain its quality as money, or in analogous ways, have been on the right track; and the practical value of their proposals deserves consideration.

The significance of the money-rate of interest arises, therefore, out of the combination of the characteristics that, through the working of the liquidity-motive, this rate of interest may be somewhat unresponsive to a change in the proportion which the quantity of money bears to other forms of wealth measured in money, and that money has (or may have) zero (or negligible) elasticities both of production and of substitution. The first condition means that demand may be predominantly directed to money, the second that when this occurs labour cannot be employed in producing more money, and the third that there is no mitigation at any point through some other factor being capable, if it is sufficiently cheap, of doing money's duty equally well. The only relief—apart from changes in the marginal efficiency of capital—can come (so long as the propensity towards liquidity is unchanged) from an increase in the quantity of money, or—which is formally the same thing—a rise in the value of money which enables a given quantity to provide increased money-services.

Thus a rise in the money-rate of interest retards the output of all the objects of which the production is elastic without being capable of stimulating the output of money (the production of which is, by hypothesis, perfectly inelastic). The money-rate of interest, by setting the pace for all the other commodity-rates of interest, holds back investment in the production of these other commodities without being capable of stimulating investment for the production of money, which by hypothesis cannot be produced. Moreover, owing to the elasticity of demand for liquid cash in terms of debts, a small change in the conditions governing this demand may not much alter the money-rate of interest, whilst (apart from official action) it is also impracticable, owing to the inelasticity of the production of money, for natural forces to bring the money-rate of interest down by affecting the supply side. In the case of an ordinary commodity, the inelasticity of the demand for liquid stocks of it would enable small changes on the demand side to bring its rate of interest up or down with a rush, whilst the elasticity of its supply would also tend to prevent a high premium on spot over forward delivery. Thus with other commodities left to themselves, "natural forces," *i.e.* the ordinary forces of the market, would tend to bring their rate of interest down until the emergence of full employment had brought about for commodities generally the inelasticity of supply which we have postulated as a normal characteristic of money. Thus in the absence of money and in the absence—we must, of course, also suppose—of any other commodity with the assumed characteristics of money, the rates of interest would only reach equilibrium when there is full employment.

Unemployment develops, that is to say, because people want the moon;—men cannot be employed when the object of desire (*i.e.* money) is something which cannot be produced and the demand for which cannot be readily choked off. There is no remedy but to persuade the public that green cheese is practically the same thing and to have a green cheese factory (*i.e.* a central bank) under public control.

It is interesting to notice that the characteristic which has been traditionally supposed to render gold especially suitable for use as the standard of value, namely, its inelasticity of supply, turns out to be precisely the characteristic which is at the bottom of the trouble.

Our conclusion can be stated in the most general form (taking the propensity to consume as given) as follows. No further increase in the rate of investment is possible when the greatest amongst the own-rates of own-interest of all available assets is equal to the greatest amongst the marginal efficiencies of all assets, measured in terms of the asset whose own-rate of own-interest is greatest.

In a position of full employment this condition is necessarily satisfied. But it may also be satisfied before full employment is reached, if there exists some asset, having zero (or relatively small) elasticities of production and substitution,[2] whose rate of interest declines more slowly, as output increases, than the marginal efficiencies of capital-assets measured in the terms of it.

## *IV*

We have shown above that for a commodity to be the standard of value is not a sufficient condition for that commodity's rate of interest to be the signif-

2. A *zero* elasticity is a more stringent condition than is necessarily required.

icant rate of interest. It is, however, interesting to consider how far those characteristics of money as we know it, which make the money-rate of interest the significant rate, are bound up with money being the standard in which debts and wages are usually fixed. The matter requires consideration under two aspects.

In the first place, the fact that contracts are fixed, and wages are usually somewhat stable, in terms of money unquestionably plays a large part in attracting to money so high a liquidity-premium. The convenience of holding assets in the same standard as that in which future liabilities may fall due and in a standard in terms of which the future cost of living is expected to be relatively stable, is obvious. At the same time the expectation of relative stability in the future money-cost of output might not be entertained with much confidence if the standard of value were a commodity with a high elasticity of production. Moreover, the low carrying costs of money as we know it play quite as large a part as a high liquidity-premium in making the money-rate of interest the significant rate. For what matters is the *difference* between the liquidity-premium and the carrying-costs; and in the case of most commodities, other than such assets as gold and silver and bank-notes, the carrying-costs are at least as high as the liquidity-premium ordinarily attaching to the standard in which contracts and wages are fixed, so that, even if the liquidity-premium now attaching to (*e.g.*) sterling-money were to be transferred to (*e.g.*) wheat, the wheat-rate of interest would still be unlikely to rise above zero. It remains the case, therefore, that, whilst the fact of contracts and wages being fixed in terms of money considerably enhances the significance of the money-rate of interest, this circumstance is, nevertheless, probably insufficient by itself to produce the observed characteristics of the money-rate of interest.

The second point to be considered is more subtle. The normal expectation that the value of output will be more stable in terms of money than in terms of any other commodity, depends of course, not on wages being arranged in terms of money, but on wages being relatively *sticky* in terms of money. What, then, would the position be if wages were expected to be more sticky (*i.e.* more stable) in terms of some one or more commodities other than money, than in terms of money itself? Such an expectation requires, not only that the costs of the commodity in question are expected to be relatively constant in terms of the wage-unit for a greater or smaller scale of output both in the short and in the long period, but also that any surplus over the current demand at cost-price can be taken into stock without cost, *i.e.* that its liquidity-premium exceeds its carrying-costs (for, otherwise, since there is no hope of profit from a higher price, the carrying of a stock must necessarily involve a loss). If a commodity can be found to satisfy these conditions, then, assuredly, it might be set up as a rival to money. Thus it is not logically impossible that there should be a commodity in terms of which the value of output is expected to be more stable than in terms of money. But it does not seem probable that any such commodity exists.

I conclude, therefore, that the commodity, in terms of which wages are expected to be most sticky, cannot be one whose elasticity of production is not least, and for which the excess of carrying-costs over liquidity-premium is not least. In other words, the expectation of a relative stickiness of wages in terms of money is a corollary of the excess of liquidity-premium over carrying-costs being greater for money than for any other asset.

Thus we see that the various characteristics, which combine to make the money-rate of interest significant, interact with one another in a cumulative fashion. The fact that money has low elasticities of production and substitution and low carrying-costs tends to raise the expectation that money-wages will be relatively stable; and this expectation enhances money's liquidity-premium and prevents the exceptional correlation between the money-rate of interest and the marginal efficiencies of other assets which might, if it could exist, rob the money-rate of interest of its sting.

Professor Pigou (with others) has been accustomed to assume that there is a presumption in favour of real wages being more stable than money-wages. But this could only be the case if there were a presumption in favour of stability of employment. Moreover, there is also the difficulty that wage-goods have a high carrying-cost. If, indeed, some attempt were made to stabilise real wages by fixing wages in terms of wage-goods, the effect could only be to cause a violent oscillation of money-prices. For every small fluctuation in the propensity to consume and the inducement to invest would cause money-prices to rush violently between zero and infinity. That money-wages should be more stable than real wages is a condition of the system possessing inherent stability.

Thus the attribution of relative stability to real wages is not merely a mistake in fact and experience. It is also a mistake in logic, if we are supposing that the system in view is stable, in the sense that small changes in the propensity to consume and the inducement to invest do not produce violent effects on prices.

## *V*

As a footnote to the above, it may be worth emphasising what has been already stated above, namely, that "liquidity" and "carrying-costs" are both a matter of degree; and that it is only in having the former high relatively to the latter that the peculiarity of "money" consists.

Consider, for example, an economy in which there is no asset for which the liquidity-premium is always in excess of the carrying-costs; which is the best definition I can give of a so-called "non-monetary" economy. There exists nothing, that is to say, but particular consumables and particular capital equipments more or less differentiated according to the character of the consumables which they can yield up, or assist to yield up, over a greater or a shorter period of time; all of which, unlike cash, deteriorate or involve expense, if they are kept in stock, to a value in excess of any liquidity-premium which may attach to them.

In such an economy capital equipments will differ from one another (*a*) in the variety of the consumables in the production of which they are capable of assisting, (*b*) in the stability of value of their output (in the sense in which the value of bread is more stable through time than the value of fashionable novelties), and (*c*) in the rapidity with which the wealth embodied in them can become "liquid," in the sense of producing output, the proceeds of which can be re-embodied if desired in quite a different form.

The owners of wealth will then weigh the lack of "liquidity" of different capital equipments in the above sense as a medium in which to hold wealth against the best available actuarial estimate of their prospective yields after allowing for risk. The liquidity-premium, it will be observed, is partly similar to the risk-premium, but partly different;—the difference corresponding to the difference between the best estimates we can make of probabilities and the confidence with which we make them. When we were dealing, in earlier chapters, with the estimation of prospective yield, we did not enter into detail as to how the estimation is made: and to avoid complicating the argument, we did not distinguish differences in liquidity from differences in risk proper. It is evident, however, that in calculating the own-rate of interest we must allow for both.

There is, clearly, no absolute standard of "liquidity" but merely a scale of liquidity—a varying premium of which account has to be taken, in addition to the yield of use and the carrying-costs, in estimating the comparative attractions of holding different forms of wealth. The conception of what contributes to "liquidity" is a partly vague one, changing from time to time and depending on social practices and institutions. The order of preference in the minds of owners of wealth in which at any given time they express their feelings about liquidity is, however, definite and is all we require for our analysis of the behaviour of the economic system.

It may be that in certain historic environments the possession of land has been characterised by a high liquidity-premium in the minds of owners of wealth; and since land resembles money in that its elasticities of production and substitution may be very low,[3] it is conceivable that there have been occasions in history in which the desire to hold land has played the same rôle in keeping up the rate of interest at too high a level which money has played in recent times. It is difficult to trace this influence quantitatively owing to the absence of a forward price for land in terms of itself which is strictly comparable with the rate of interest on a money debt. We have, however, something which has, at times, been closely analogous, in the shape of high rates of interest on mortgages.[4] The high rates of interest from mortgages on land, often exceeding the probable net yield from cultivating the land, have been a familiar feature of many agricultural economies. Usury laws have been directed primarily against encumbrances of this character. And rightly so. For in earlier social organisations where long-term bonds in the modern sense were non-existent, the competition of a high interest-rate on mortgages may well have had the same effect in retarding the growth of wealth from current investment in newly produced capital-assets, as high interest rates on long-term debts have had in more recent times.

That the world after several millennia of steady individual saving, is so poor as it is in accumulated capital-assets, is to be explained, in my opinion, neither by the improvident propensities of mankind, nor even by the destruction of war, but by the high liquidity-premiums formerly attaching to the ownership of land and now attaching to money. I differ

---

3. The attribute of "liquidity" is by no means independent of the presence of these two characteristics. For it is unlikely that an asset, of which the supply can be easily increased or the desire for which can be easily diverted by a change in relative price, will possess the attribute of "liquidity" in the minds of owners of wealth. Money itself rapidly loses the attribute of "liquidity" if its future supply is expected to undergo sharp changes.

4. A mortgage and the interest thereon are, indeed, fixed in terms of money. But the fact that the mortgagor has the option to deliver the land itself in discharge of the debt—and must so deliver it if he cannot find the money on demand—has sometimes made the mortgage system approximate to a contract of land for future delivery against land for spot delivery. There have been sales of lands to tenants against mortgages effected by them, which, in fact, came very near to being transactions of this character.

in this from the older view as expressed by Marshall with an unusual dogmatic force in his *Principles of Economics*, p. 581:—

Everyone is aware that the accumulation of wealth is held in check, and the rate of interest so far sustained, by the preference which the great mass of humanity have for present over deferred gratifications, or, in other words, by their unwillingness to "wait."

# 4. *The Economic Organization*

BY FRANK H. KNIGHT

THE PROBLEM of organization, which sets the problem of economic science, deals with the concrete means or mechanism for dividing the general function of making a living for the people into parts and bringing about the performance of these parts in due proportion and harmony.

More specifically, it is a problem of the social machinery for accomplishing *five fairly distinct functions*. Every system of organization must perform these tasks, and it is its success or failure in discharging these functions which determines its value as a system. Back of the study of economics is the practical need of making the organization better, and we can hope for success in this task only if we proceed to it intelligently, which is to say on the basis of an understanding of the nature of the work which a system of organization has to perform, and of the alternatives open in the way of possible types of organization machinery.

## *The Five Main Functions of an Economic System*

The general task of organizing the economic activity of society may be divided into a number of fundamental functions. These are in fact very much inter-connected and overlapping, but the distinction is useful as an aid to discussing the existing economic order both descriptively and critically, its structure as well as its workings. These functions fall into a more or less logical sequence. The first is to decide what is to be done, that is, what goods and services are to be produced, and in what proportions. It is the function of setting standards, of establishing a social scale of values, or the function of social choice; the second is the function of organizing production, in the narrow sense, of getting done the things settled upon as most worth doing; third is distribution, the apportioning of the product among the members of society; the fourth is really a group of functions having to do with maintaining and improving the social structure, or promoting social progress.

### 1. THE FUNCTION OF FIXING STANDARDS; THE NOTION OF EFFICIENCY

In a world where organizations were absent, where each individual carried on his life activities in isolation and independence of all others, the matter of standards would be simply a matter of individual choice. But when the production of wealth is socialized, there has to be a *social* decision as to the relative importance or different uses of productive power, as to which wants are to be satisfied and which left unsatisfied or to what extent any one is to be satisfied at the expense of any other. In the case of an individual, choice need be made only among his own wants; but in a social system, the wants of different individuals also come into conflict. As far as this is a quantitative question merely, of how far the wants of one are to be gratified at the expense of the wants of another, or left ungratified in favor of another, the problem is one of *distribution*, and will be noticed under another heading (the third function). But to a large and increasing extent, society finds it necessary or advisable further to regulate the individual's regulation of his own want-satisfaction, to enforce a community standard of living. As a matter of fact, these two problems are closely interlaced, the question of *whose* wants and that of *which* wants are to be given preference, and in what measure. It is important to observe that they are

Reprinted from Frank H. Knight, *The Economic Organization* (New York: Augustus M. Kelley, 1951), pp. 7–15, with permission of Augustus M. Kelley.

largely the same question. The difference in the "amount" consumed by different persons is not mainly a difference in the amounts of the same commodities; different persons consume different things, which are quantitatively compared only through the agency of the value scale itself. Nevertheless there seems to be ample justification for a logical separation of the questions of what is to be produced from that of who is to get the product, and for discussing separately the relations between the two phases of organization.

A point of fundamental importance in connection with the question of standards is that of the origin or ultimate source of wants. The system of social organization does more than reduce individual values to a common denominator or scale of equivalence. In large part the individual wants themselves are *created* by social intercourse, and their character is also largely dependent upon the form of organization of the economic system upon which they are dependent for their gratification. The workings of the economic organization in this connection form a problem too large and complex to be discussed at any length in a small book like this one. Indeed, the subject of wants is not only vast in scope but apparently cannot be reduced to scientific terms, except within rather narrow limits, falling rather in the field of art. The scientific discussion of economics has to be restricted in the main to the analysis of the organization of want-satisfaction. In the science of economics the wants are largely taken for granted as facts of the time and place, and the discussion of their origin and formation is left for the most part to the distinct studies of social psychology and cultural anthropology. The deliberate creation or changing of wants for specific commodities as by advertising, is to some extent an exception, but in the main such activities must be regarded as creating a *knowledge* of certain *means* of satisfying wants rather than as changing ultimate *wants*.

The problem of standards or values occupies a key position in Economics. The practical objective of economics, it must be kept in mind, is that of improving the social organization and increasing its efficiency. There is a common misconception that it is possible to measure or discuss efficiency in purely physical terms. The first principles of physics or engineering science teach that this is not true, that the term efficiency involves the idea of value, and some measure of value as well. It is perhaps the most important principle of physical science that neither matter nor energy can be created or destroyed, that whatever goes into any process must come out in some form, and hence as a mere matter of physical quantity, the efficiency of all operations would equal one hundred per cent. The correct definition of efficiency is the ratio, not between "output" and "input" but between *useful* output and total output or input. Hence efficiency, even in the simplest energy transformation, is meaningless without a measure of usefulness or value. In any attempt to understand economic efficiency, the notion of value is more obviously crucial since most economic problems are concerned with a number of kinds both of outlay and of return, and there is no conceivable way of making comparisons without first reducing all the factors to terms of a common measure. It will appear in due course that the science of economics is largely taken up with description and analysis of the process by which this common denominator of things consumed and produced by the economic system is arrived at, that is, with the *problem of measuring values*.

### 2. THE FUNCTION OF ORGANIZING PRODUCTION

The second step, logically speaking, after the ranking and grading of the uses to which productive power may be put, is that of actually putting them to use in accordance with the scale of values thus established. From a social point of view, this process may be viewed under two aspects, (a) the assignment or *allocation* of the available productive forces and materials among the various lines of industry, and (b) the effective *coordination* of the various means of production in each industry into such groupings as will produce the greatest result. The second of these tasks properly belongs to technological rather than to economic science, and is treated in economics only with reference to the interrelations between the organization of society as a whole and the internal organization of the industries.

### 3. THE FUNCTION OF DISTRIBUTION

This third function would not exist at all in an unorganized world. Each individual, acting independently of all others, would simply consume what he produced. But where production is socialized, the separate productive contribution of one participant in the process cannot be directly identified or separated. It is apparent that a modern factory operative, say one who spends all his time putting buttons on shoes or nailing the covers on packing cases, cannot live on his own product, physically interpreted. When we further consider that different individuals contribute to production in fundamentally different ways, many by furnishing land or other "natural resources" or material equipment or money or managerial or supervisory services, or by selling goods, and in other ways which make no identifiable physical change in any product, it is manifest that if everyone is to get a living out of the process some *social mechanism* of distribution is called for.

In this connection should be recalled the close relation between distribution and the control of production. The decision as to what to produce is closely bound up with the decision for whom to produce. There is also a close relation between the third function and the second. In our social system distribution is the chief agency relied upon to control production and stimulate efficiency. Ours is a system of "private property," "free competition" and "contract." This means that every productive resource or agent, including labor power, typically "belongs" to some person who is free within the legal conditions of marketing, to get what he can out of its use. It is assumed, and the course of the argument will show at length why it is true, that there is in some effective sense a real positive connection between the productive contribution made by any productive agent and the remuneration which its "owner" can secure for its use. Hence this remuneration (a distributive share) and the wish to make it as large as possible, constitute the chief reliance of society for an incentive to place the agency into use in the general productive system in such a way as to make it as productive as possible. The strongest argument in favor of such a system as ours is the contention that this direct, selfish motive is the only dependable method, or at least the best method, for guaranteeing that productive forces will be organized and worked efficiently. The argument assumes that in spite of the difficulty above referred to of identifying the particular contribution to the social product made by any person or piece of property, it is possible to separate it out, and measure it, in terms of value and that the distributive system does this with accuracy enough to make remunerations vary in accord with product. If this were not true in the main, remuneration could not really afford an incentive to productive efficiency, and an economic order based on individualism would not function.

4. ECONOMIC MAINTENANCE AND PROGRESS

There is no moral connotation in the term progress; it refers to any persistent cumulative change, whether regarded as good or bad. The principal forms of economic progress include, (1) growth of population and any cumulative change in its composition or education which affects either its productive powers or its wants; (2) the accumulation of material aids to production or "capital" of all kinds, including such permanent sources of satisfaction as newly discovered natural resources and also works of art (destruction and exhaustion of resources not replaced is also a progressive change); (3) improvements in technical processes or changes in the form of business organization. It is to be noted especially that progress has two sorts of significance for the economic organization. First, it is one of the products or values created by the latter, at a cost; i.e., it involves using productive power for this purpose and sacrificing its use for other purposes; and second, it affects and changes the character of the economic system itself and the conditions under which the system works.

This fourth function of organization, especially the provision for progress, cuts across all the other three. It is a matter of standards or values to decide how much progress society can afford or cares to have at the cost of sacrificing present values, and what forms it shall take; it is a matter of productive organization to utilize the determined share of available productive power to bring about progress in the amount and of the kinds decided upon, and it is a problem of distribution to apportion the burdens and benefits of progress among the members of society. We may be reminded also that it is true of progress as of all other lines of human action that it comes within the field of economics just in so far as it is related to the organized system of producing and distributing the means of want-satisfaction.

The first three of these functions (or four, since No. 2 is really double, involving two aspects) are relatively "short-time" in character. They are all aspects of the general problem of an economic society working under "given conditions," in contrast with the fourth function which relates to the problem of improving the given conditions through the course of time. The first three therefore make up the problems of what may be called the "stationary economy." If society either could not or did not try to grow and progress and make improvements, its economic problem would be entirely within this field. But since economic societies do in fact face problems of growth and improvement, and make some effort to solve them intelligently, we have to add the fourth function, or group of functions. Such problems are frequently referred to under the head of "dynamic" economics; for reasons which cannot be given in detail here, this is a seriously misleading use of language, and they should be called simply problems of progress or historical problems.

The "given conditions" of the stationary economy are included under the three heads of *resources, wants,* and *technology,* which may be subdivided and classified in more elaborate ways. The separation is based on the plain and simple fact that with reference to social calculations and plans which look ahead only a few years, these factors, resources, wants and the technological system will not change enough to affect the argument or plans seriously. But looking ahead over historical time they do change, to an indefinite extent, and the production and guidance of changes in them becomes the dominant character of the social economic problem. In the "short-run" (of a few years), the problem is to utilize in the best way the existing resources and technology in the satisfaction of existing wants.

A FIFTH FUNCTION: TO ADJUST CONSUMPTION TO PRODUCTION WITHIN VERY SHORT PERIODS

For completeness, this survey of functions should point out that within *very short* periods society faces still another set of "given conditions," hence still another type of problem, and in consequence its economic organization has still another task or function to perform, though this fifth function is rarely distinguished sharply from those of the "stationary economy" point of view. From this latter point of view, the problem is to adjust production to consumption under the given conditions. But in many cases, production cannot be adjusted quickly, while demand conditions do change rapidly; and in addition, production in many fields is subject to fluctuations from causes beyond control. In consequence, the supply of many commodities is fixed for considerable periods of time, on a level more or less divergent from the best possible adjustment to existing conditions of demand. The supply on hand is of course the result of productive operations in the past, and has to suffice until it can be changed. In agriculture this is conspicuously true. The crop of a given year has to last until the next year's crop is produced (except in so far as other parts of the world having different crop seasons can be drawn upon). In the case of manufactured goods, production is not definitely periodic, but it is still true that the rate of production frequently cannot be changed in a short time, to meet changes in demand, at least not without enormous cost.

It follows that over short periods consumption has to be controlled and distributed with reference to an existing supply or current rate of production, at the same time that adjustment of production to consumption requirements is being made as rapidly as practicable. The existing supply of wheat or potatoes, for example, must be distributed (a) over the season for which it has to suffice and (b) among the different consumers and their different needs. Thus there is a fifth function or organization, the opposite in a sense, of number two in the four above discussed, namely the short-run adjustment of consumption to past or current production.

# IV–UNITS OF THE ECONOMY

## 1. *Household Economy*

BY FRÉDÉRIC LE PLAY

### *The Means of Subsistence of Workers and the Account of Receipts, with the Main Items of This Account*

THE FOUR SOURCES OF RECEIPTS: PROPERTIES, SUBSIDIES, CONSTRUCTION-TYPE WORK, AND COTTAGE INDUSTRIES

THOSE who have observed the living conditions of workers only in the large cities of the West cannot imagine how varied their resources may be in other areas; hence, they do not suspect how important the budgeting of a family's resources must be in a general scheme of observation. The diversity of these resources has two main sources: First, those who hire workers remunerate their services in many ways. They pay for the worker's time or his production, sometimes according to the needs of his family, sometimes according to

Translated by Jesse Pitts, from Frédéric le Play, *Les ouvriers européens* (2nd ed.; Tours: Mame, 1879), chap. x, pp. 240–47.

the work performed. Second, the workers' statuses differ depending upon tradition, occupation, and geographic location. Sometimes they discharge only the lowest functions in society; sometimes, on the contrary, they constitute the very body of the society. Often, they add to their main occupation the roles of property owners, tenants, or master craftsmen, thus supplementing their remuneration from their regular occupation with various sorts of incomes and fees.

Only the accounts of a retainer can be reduced to a few entries. In most cases, these would be merely: the yearly allocation of room and board, plus clothing given to a bachelor, and the yearly salary allowance. Nevertheless, even under these conditions, the study of a remuneration system commensurate to needs is not without complications. Furthermore, certain particular circumstances, closely tied to local tradition, may introduce some variety into the budget of household workers. This happens, for instance, in the case of the Pen-Ty, or retainer of lower Britanny. At first, as merely general helper on the employer's farmstead, he is authorized by local custom to own two cows, which he raises and exploits for his benefit. According to this custom, the employer is obligated to feed, without recompense, the cows of his retainer with his own cattle. These animals and their produce constitute important items in the budget of the retainer and help him to establish himself later as Pen-Ty or tenant chief of his own household.

We see no such complexity in the case of the Carinthian charcoaler; and his budget represents the extreme example, in the Western world, of simplicity in the condition of the unmarried retainer. In the North and East, on the contrary, and in general in countries where the traditional structures of early times—as well as old customs—have been preserved, retainers have a more complex existence. This complication is generally due to two main causes: retainers who marry are allowed to remain in the vicinity of the employer's household; furthermore, through their sideline occupations, they belong, more or less, to the category of tenants or master craftsmen. For example, the retainers in Scandinavia, Russia, and Turkey often undertake on their own account with tools furnished by their employer, a little farming, a little husbandry, the making of cloth or clothing, as well as hunting and fishing and related activities. They may even do some transporting, trading, and speculation. However, since, after all, retainers must give the major part of their time to the service of their employer, they can never give much scope to these undertakings, however varied they may be. This obligation gives to their receipts a simplicity clearly evidenced by the method, and which differentiates at a glance these workers from the other five types. It is enough to peruse the various monographs to appreciate the differences in budget existing between that of the household worker cited above and the ordinary wage-worker. The difference is even more striking when one compares him with a worker-tenant, a master craftsman, or a land owner.

The simplest case in the category of workers who are heads of households would be that in which an entire family lives exclusively on the wage earned by the family head for a simple type of labor, proportional to the days worked. The account of receipts would have only one entry. In order to establish it, it would be enough to know, on the one hand, the quantity of work, that is, the number of days worked, and, on the other hand, the remuneration rates for each day. Several authors who have dealt with the question of wages seem to have taken for granted that European populations were made up of families of this type. This led them to many grievous errors. Such a family type is very rare, if it exists; as far as my own experience is concerned, I have never discovered a single case.

Usually, other members of the family—the wife, the children, and the grandparents who live in the household—are gainfully occupied and draw remunerations that contribute to the family welfare. Furthermore, the most active members—the father, the mother, and the adolescents—commonly undertake several sorts of gainful activities, besides their regular occupations. For instance, for some of the families described in the *Ouvriers européens,* one may count as many as ten such additional activities. It is obvious that the itemization of the revenues derived from these activities introduces into the accounting of receipts a fair amount of complexity.

On the other hand, I have rarely observed in Europe families living exclusively on the wages earned by their members. One may even consider as exceptional the cases in which a family does not add to its regular wages resources derived from three other types of receipts that may be recognized in the budget of European workers: income from properties, subsidies, and the profits of cottage industries. These latter receipts often become the main source of the family's financial security. In the Orient, there exist laboring classes whose vernacular has no word for the type of remuneration described in the West by the word "wage."

The institution of wage payments, i.e., of remuneration proportional to the work done, can develop only in the modern system of temporary work commitments. Whether freely entered into or not, as long as the commitment between master and workman is irrevocable, it is necessary that the latter's daily bread be guaranteed. Whether the worker is free or unfree, remuneration, whatever its nature, is necessarily proportional to the needs of the entire family. Thus is explained the feelings of serenity and the stability that characterized traditional Europe. The same obligation is no longer recognized in the modern world; hence, social peace is endangered. Furthermore, the common people are not sufficiently endowed in intelligence and morality to be self-sufficient. All the Oriental languages, and precisely those that are devoid of a word for wages, describe a remuneration proportional to the family's needs by a special expression that has disappeared from the modern languages of the Western world.

In each rural or industrial collectivity, custom determines once and for all the quantity of goods that enters into the daily consumption pattern of a family. On the other hand, the price of these commodities often fluctuates from year to year and season to season. It is obvious that remuneration in kind gives more security to a family than remuneration in money. No wonder, then, that money wages, common in the West, give rise to dissension; this is rare in the case of remuneration in kind, which is more common in the Orient or the North. The French language, to my knowledge, no longer has an expression covering the various types of remuneration in kind. Hence, I shall use for that purpose the word "subsidy," which includes among its accepted meanings the special meaning I have used in this book. Under this term, I shall henceforth describe all the payments in kind that, not being proportional to the work done, cannot be considered as wages.

The subsidy is usually established on the basis of the family's needs. It is granted regularly each year or only when special needs become manifest. Generally, it is not terminated when work is suspended or slackens, in response to market fluctuations, illness, the early onset of infirmities—which often afflict the working man—or any other cause independent of the latter's will. Often, the benefit of subsidies is extended to the wife, the children, or the grandparents, even when the head of the family shows willful neglect or misconduct.

The wage-earners—heads of working-class families of various categories—especially those who by their application to work and sobriety begin to be identified with the class of proprietors, rarely limit their activity to the work they accomplish for their employer's account: they commonly undertake for their own account some of the cottage industries described above as occasional resources for the retainer. These handicrafts are nearly always practiced with the help of the entire family. Their importance, in the economy of the country, resides precisely in their creating work opportunities for the wife, the children, and the grandparents. Sometimes, when the worker and family head, out of self-interest or necessity, is compelled to give all his time to his regular occupation, these industries will be the exclusive domain of the rest of the family. The cottage industries that families will undertake in these conditions present a variety that cannot be imagined without having thoroughly studied the lives of working men in the various regions of Europe. These industries often absorb considerable time, especially from the higher categories of workers; they always lead, even for the lower categories, to many entries of money and goods. The accounting would become very complicated if we were to include in it all the receipts and expenditures that these industries involve.

The workers who are heads of families are not limited to becoming wage-earners or master craftsmen: they often rise to the status of proprietors. They draw from the ownership of real estate several kinds of income, which should not be confused with the three other types of receipts previously described. Other workers, who as yet do not own real estate, own sums of money or other movable equities which, after having given some additional interest, will serve to acquire the former type of property. Finally, other workers who will not succeed in rising to the status of proprietors—because of their moral weaknesses, local customs, or any other cause—nevertheless own goods other than those serving the specific consumption needs of individuals. The family finds a source of income in these goods, by renting them or by using them in the execution of special construction work, or as resources for cottage industries. Among the movable goods of this sort that workers may ordinarily possess, one must give special mention to domestic animals, tools, and, in general, the specific raw materials of the construction trades and cottage industries. The possession of these goods, like that of real estate, by the fact that it insures an income independent of manual labor, is of great social importance. It links, by a subtle transition, the mores of the workers to those of the upper classes of the society. Hence, it was useful to establish in the account of receipts this subdivision for the income derived from properties.

# 2. The Social Organization of Production

BY MAX WEBER

## *Social Aspects of the Division of Labour*

FROM the social point of view, types of the division of labour may be classified in the following way: In the first place, there is the question of the ways in which qualitatively different, especially complementary functions, are divided between more or less autocephalous and autonomous economic units, which may further be distinguished economically according to whether they are budgetary units or profit-making enterprises. There are two polar possibilities:

(1) A "unitary" economy (*Einheitswirtschaft*) where the specialization of functions is wholly internal, completely heterocephalous and heteronomous and carried out on a purely technical basis. The same would be true of the co-ordination of function. A unitary economy may, from an economic point of view, be either a budgetary unit or a profit-making enterprise.

On the largest possible scale a communistic organization of a national economy would be a unitary budgetary economy. On the smallest scale an example is the primitive family unit, which included all or the great majority of productive functions—a closed household economy. The type case of a profit-making enterprise with a high degree of internal specialization and co-ordination of functions is naturally the great vertical combination[1] which treats with outsiders only as an integrated unit. These two distinctions will suffice for for the moment as a treatment of the development of autonomous economic units; (2) the differentiation of functions may, on the other hand, exist as between autocephalous economic units. (a) It may consist in the specialization or specification of functions between units which are heteronomous, but are autocephalous, which are thus oriented to an order established by agreement or imposed. The order, in turn, may be substantively oriented in a variety of ways. Its main concern may be to provide for the needs of a superior economic unit, which may be the budgetary unit of a lord, an *oikos*, or a profit-making enterprise controlled by a political body. The order may, on the other hand, be concerned with providing for the needs of the members of some organized group. From an economic point of view, this may be accomplished by the organization of subsidiary budgetary units, or of profit-making enterprises. The corporate group in question may exercise any one of a large number of functions. It may be confined to the regulation of economic activity or may, at the same time, be engaged in economic action on its own account. (b) The other main type is the specialization of autocephalous and autonomous units in a market economy, which are oriented on the one hand substantively only to their own self-interest, formally only to the order of a corporate group, such as the laissez-faire state, which enforces only formal, rather than substantive rules.

1. A typical example of the corporate group which, limiting its function to the regulation of economic activity, takes the form of a budgetary unit administered by an association of the members, is the organization of village handicrafts in India. Corporate groups, which are themselves engaged in economic activity, like the household of a great noble, are illustrated by the organizations which provide for the wants of great landlords or slaveowners by means of contributions from the individual holdings of subjects, dependents, serfs, slaves, cottars, or sometimes village craftsmen. These phenomena have been found spontaneously developed in every part of the world. Cases of production of compulsory payments in kind to a landlord or to a town corporation, have, in so far as they have not served substantive, but as has often been the case, only fiscal ends, constituted only the regulation of economic activity. This type of control has served profit-making ends in cases where the services of household industries have been exploited for the benefit of the controlling unit.

The types where there is specialization and spe-

---

Reprinted from Max Weber, *The Theory of Social and Economic Organization*, trans. A. M. Henderson and Talcott Parsons, ed. Talcott Parsons (Glencoe, Ill.: The Free Press, 1947), pp. 228–50. Copyright 1947 by Oxford University Press.

1. What Weber apparently has in mind is the type of "trust" which controls all stages of the process of production from raw material to the finished product. Thus many of our steel enterprises have not only blast furnaces and rolling mills, but coal mines, coke ovens, railways and ships, and iron ore mines. The most notable example in Germany in Weber's time was the Stinnes combine.—ED.

cification of function, as between heteronomous units, are all cases of the imposition of specialized functions. They have been common in many very old small-scale industries. The Solingen metal trade was originally organized in terms of a voluntary association determining the division of labour by agreement. It was only later that it became organized in terms of imperative co-ordination—that is, became a "putting-out industry." The type where the autocephalous economic units are subject only to regulation by a corporate group is illustrated by innumerable cases of the rules established by village communities and town corporations for the regulation of trade, so far at least as these have a substantive influence on the processes of production.

The case of specialization as between units in a market economy is best illustrated by the modern economic order.

2. A few further details may be added. The rules of those corporate groups which attempt to provide for the wants of their members on a budgetary basis, are related to the component budgetary units in a particular way—that is, they are oriented to the prospective needs of the individual members, not of the organized group, such as a village, itself. Specified services of this kind will be called demiurgic liturgies;[2] and this type of provision for needs, correspondingly, demiurgic. It is always a question of corporate regulation governing the division of labour and, in some cases, the ways in which specialized functions are co-ordinated.

This term will not, on the other hand, be applied to a corporate group, whether it is imperatively co-ordinated or based on voluntary co-operation, if it carries on economic activity on its own account, contributions to which are assigned on a specialized basis. The type cases of this category are the specialized and specified contributions in kind of feudal manors, landed estates, and other types of large household units. But assigned obligations are also common in various types of corporate groups which are not primarily oriented to economic ends, such as the households of princes, political groups and the budgetary administration of local communities. These contributions are generally for the benefit of the budgetary needs of the governing authority or for corporate purposes. This way of providing for the needs of a budgetary unit by means of qualitatively specified liturgies and payments in kind on the part of peasants, craftsmen, and merchants, will, when they are owed to a personal superior, be called the *oikos*[3] type of organization. Where they are received by the corporate budgetary unit as such, they will be called "corporate liturgies in kind." The principle governing this mode of provision for the budgetary needs of a corporate group engaged in economic action, is "liturgical" provision. This mode of organization has played an exceedingly important historical role and will have to be discussed frequently. In many political corporations, it has taken the place of modern taxation and, in economic groups, it has made possible a decentralization of the central organization by providing for its needs through agencies which were not included in the single common unit. On the contrary, each unit has managed its own affairs, but has assumed the obligation to fulfil certain functions for the central unit and to that extent has been dependent on it. Examples are peasants and serfs, subject to various kinds of labour services and payments in kind; craftsmen attached to an estate; and a large number of other types. Rodbertus was the first to apply the term "*oikos*" to the large-scale household economies of Antiquity. He used as the principal criterion the tendency to self-sufficiency in provision for needs by using the services of members of the household unit itself or of others dependent on it. In all these cases, the non-human means of production were made available without relation to the market. It is a fact that the landed estates, and still more the royal households of antiquity, especially in the New Kingdom in Egypt, were cases where the greater part of the needs of the unit were provided by services and payments in kind, which were obligations of dependent household units. At the same time, the degree of approach to the pure type varies widely. The same phenomena are to be found at times in China and India, and to a less extent in our own Middle Ages, beginning with the *capitulare de villis.* It is true that exchange with the outside world has generally not been entirely lacking, but has tended to have the character of budgetary exchange. Obligations to money payment have also not been uncommon, but have generally played a subsidiary part in the main provision for needs and have tended to be traditionally fixed. It has also not been uncommon for the economic units subject to liturgical obligations to be involved in exchange relations. The decisive point, however, is that the main emphasis lay on the fact that the subsistence of the members was regarded as a return for the services of the land and equipment the members were privileged

2. The term "demiurgic" is taken over directly from Weber, who introduced it in this technical sense. It is not, apparently, current in the German literature.—ED.

3. The term "*oikos*" is, of course, taken over from the Greek. As Weber notes below, however, it was introduced into economic discussion by Rodbertus and has been used in the German literature ever since.—ED.

to use. There are, of course, many transitional forms. But in each case there is some kind of regulation of functions by a corporate group which is concerned with the mode of division of labour and of its co-ordination.

3. The cases where a corporate group regulating economic activity is oriented to considerations of economic profit, are well illustrated by the economic regulations of the communes of Medieval Europe and by the guilds and castes of China and India. The regulations governed the number of master craftsmen and their functions and also the technique of the craft, thus the way in which labour was oriented in the handicrafts. They belonged to this type so far as the rules were intended not primarily to secure provision for a given standard of living of the craftsmen, but, as was often though not always the case, to secure their market position by maintaining the quality of performance and by dividing up the market. Like every other type of economic regulation, that of the guilds, of course, involved limitations on market freedom and hence on fully autonomous orientation of craftsmen to the maximization of their profits. It was unquestionably intended to maintain the income standards of the existing craft shops and to that extent, in spite of its formal resemblance to profit-making enterprise, still involved a budgetary mode of orientation.

4. The cases where the corporate group carrying on economic activity has been concerned with profit making, are illustrated, apart from the cases of putting-out industry already discussed, by the agricultural estates of north-eastern Germany. These have been carried out by semi-independent tenants bound by a common system of rules. In the north-west it has taken the form of the part-time labour by individuals with small independent holdings (*Heuerlingswirtschaft*). These estates, like the putting-out industries, have been profit-making enterprises of the landlord as were those of the "putter-out." The economic activities of the tenants and of the domestic workers are oriented primarily to the obligations which have been imposed upon them both in the division of functions and in their co-ordination. These obligations determine the organization of labour on the estate as they determine the mode of dependency of the domestic worker. Apart from this, they are budgetary units. Their contribution to the profit-making activity is not autonomous, but is a heteronomous function on behalf of the enterprise of the landlord or the putter-out. According to the degree in which this orientation is substantively standardized, the technical aspects of the division of labour within a single organization may approach the kind which is typical of the factory.

## *Social Aspects of the Division of Labour—(Continued)*

From a social point of view, the modes of the division of labour may be further classified according to the mode in which the economic advantages, which are regarded as returns for the different functions, are appropriated. The objects of appropriation may be opportunities for realizing returns on work, non-human means of production, or opportunities for profit from the exercise of managerial functions.

When the returns from labour services are appropriated, the service may be owed to a particular recipient, such as a lord, or a particular corporate group; or it may be disposed of on the market. In either case, there may be any one of four radically different possibilities: (a) Monopolistic appropriation of opportunities for return by the individual worker—the case of "free guild labour." This may be hereditary but alienable, as for the Indian village craftsman; or personal and inalienable, as for the Medieval craftsman, who in addition disposed of his services on the market. Rights of eligibility for office are personal and inalienable, but not marketable. Or finally, they may be hereditary, but inalienable, as was the case with certain of the rights attached to the Medieval handicrafts, but above all, the Indian handicrafts and various types of Medieval offices. In all these cases the appropriation may be unconditional or subject to various substantive conditions; (b) The second possibility is that the return for labour services should be appropriated by an "owner" of the worker—the case of "unfree labour." There may be free appropriation which is both hereditary and alienable—the case of slavery proper. Or, though it is hereditary and alienable—the case of slavery proper. Or, though it is hereditary, it may not be freely alienable, but may, for instance, be bound to the non-human means of production, particularly the land. This includes serfdom and hereditary dependency (*Erbuntertänigkeit*).

The appropriation of the use of labour by a lord may be limited by substantive conditions, as in serfdom. The worker cannot leave his status of his own free will, but neither can it arbitrarily be taken from him.

The appropriation of returns of labour may be used by the owner for purposes of budgetary administration, as a source of income in kind or in money, or as a source of labour service in the unit, as in the case of domestic slaves or serfs. Or it may be used as a means of profit. In that case the dependent may be obligated to contribute goods or to work on raw materials provided by the owner. The owner will then sell the product. This is unfree domestic industry. He may, finally, be used as a labourer in an organized shop—a slave or serf workshop.

The person herein designated as the "owner" is very generally involved in the work process himself in a managerial capacity or even in part as a worker, but this need not be true. It may be that his position as owner, *ipso facto,* makes him the managing agent. But this is by no means necessary and is very generally not the case.

The use of slaves and serfs, the latter including various types of dependents, as part of a process of budgetary administration and not as workers in a profit-making enterprise, was typical of Antiquity and of the early Middle Ages. There are, for instance, inscriptions which mentioned slaves "of a Persian prince who were bound out as apprentices on the understanding that they might be used for labour services in the household, but might also be allowed, in return for a payment to the owner,[4] to work independently for customers." Though by no means without exception, this tended to be the rule for Greek slaves; and in Rome this type of independent economic activity became a legal institution which involved providing the slave with a *peculium* or *merx peculiaris.* He was naturally obligated to make payments to his owner. In the Middle Ages, body serfdom frequently involved merely a right to claim payments. This was usual in western and southern Germany. In Russia, also, an actual limitation to the receipt of these payments (*obrok*) from an otherwise free serf was, though not universal, very common. Its legal status was, however, precarious.

The use of unfree labour for profit-making purposes has taken the following principal forms, particularly in the domestic industries on the estates of landlords, including various royal estates, among them probably those of the Pharaohs: (1) Unfree obligation to payments in kind—the delivery of goods in kind, the raw material for which was produced by the workers themselves as well as worked on by them. Flax is an example; (2) unfree domestic industry—work on material provided by the lord. The product could be sold at least in part for money by the lord. But in many cases, as in Antiquity, the tendency was to confine market sale to occasional instances. In early modern times, however, particularly in the border regions between the Germans and the Slavs, this was not the case, particularly, though not alone, where domestic industries have developed on the estates of landlords. The use of unfree labour in a continuous organization could take the form of unfree domestic labour or of labour in a workshop. Both forms are common. The latter was one of the various forms of the *Ergasterion* of Antiquity. It also was found on the estates of the Pharaohs, in temple workshops, and from the testimony of the frescoes on tombs, on the estates of private owners or lords. It also existed in the Orient, in Greece (Demosthenes' shop in Athens) in the Roman estate workshops, in Byzantium, in the Carolingian "genitium," and in modern times, for example, in Russian factories operated with serf labour; (c) the third possibility is the absence of every sort of appropriation—in this sense, formally free labour. The services of labour are treated as the subject of a contractual relationship which is formally free on both sides. The contract may, however, be substantively regulated in various ways through a conventional or legal order governing the conditions of labour.

Freely contracted labour may be used in various ways. In the first place, in a budgetary unit, as occasional labour, either in the household of the employer (*stör*) or in that of the worker himself. Or it may be permanent, again performed in the household of the employer, as in the case of domestic service, or in that of the worker, as typical of the colonate. It may, on the other hand, be used for profit, again on an occasional or a permanent basis; and in both cases either in the worker's own home or on premises provided by the employer. The latter is true of workers on an estate or in a workshop, but especially of the factory.

Where the worker is employed in a budgetary unit, he is directly in the service of a consumer who supervises his labour. Otherwise, he is in the service of a profit-making entrepreneur. Though the form is often legally identical, economically the difference is fundamental. Coloni may be in either status; but it is more typical for them to be workers in an *oikos;* (d) the fourth possibility is that opportunities for return for labour services may be appropriated by an association of workers, either without any appropriation by the individual worker or with important limitations on such appropriation. This may involve absolute or relative closure against outsiders and also prohibition of the dismissal of workers from employment by management without consent of the workers, or at least some kind of limitations on power of dismissal.

Examples of the type of appropriation involving closure of the group are castes of workers, the type of miners' association found in the Medieval

4. In Greek, "ἀποφορά"; Russian, "*obrok*"; German, "*Hals*" or "*Leibzips.*"

mining industry, the organized groups or retainers sometimes found at courts, or the threshers on a landed estate. This type of appropriation is found throughout the social history of all parts of the world in an endless variety of forms. The second type involving limitations on powers of dismissal, which is also very widespread, plays an important part in the modern situation in the "closed shop" of trade unions and especially in the "works councils."

Every form of appropriation of jobs by workers in profit-making enterprises, like the converse case of appropriation of the services of workers by owners, involves limitations on the free recruitment of the labour force. This means that workers cannot be selected solely on grounds of their technical efficiency, and to this extent there is a limitation on the formal rationalization of economic activity. These circumstances further impose substantive limitations on technical rationality in so far as: (1) The exploitation of the products of labour is appropriated by an owner. This may occur through the tendency to arbitrary restriction of the production of labour by tradition, by convention, or by contract. Or it may occur by the reduction or complete disappearance of the worker's own interest in maximizing the production. The latter occurs when, as in slavery, the worker is freely appropriated by an owner; (2) limitations on technical rationalization may also result from appropriation on the part of the worker. There may be a conflict of the self-interest of the worker, which lies in the maintenance of his traditional mode of life, with the attempts of his employer to get him to produce at the optimum technical level or to use other modes of production in place of his labour. For employers, there is always the possibility of transforming their exploitation of labour into a mere source of income. The tendency for the exploitation of the products to be appropriated by the workers thus under favourable circumstances generally leads to a more or less complete exclusion of the owner from management. But it also regularly tends to place workers in a state of dependence on people with whom they deal who enjoy a more favourable market position. These, such as putting-out entrepreneurs, then tend to assume a managerial position.

1. The tendency of appropriation of jobs by workers and that of workers by owners are formally antithetical. But in practice they have very similar results. This should not be surprising. In the first place, the two tendencies are very generally formally related. This is true when appropriation of the workers by an owner coincides with appropriation of opportunities for jobs by a closed corporate group of workers, as has happened in feudal courts. In such cases it is natural that exploitation of services should, to a large extent, be stereotyped; hence that production should be restricted and the worker have little interest in maximizing it. The result is generally a successful resistance of workers against any sort of technical innovation. But even where this does not occur, the fact that workers are appropriated by an owner means in practice that he is obliged to make use of this particular labour force. He is not in a position like that of the modern factory manager to select according to technical needs, but must utilize those he has without selection. This is particularly true of slave labour. Any attempt to exact performance from appropriated workers beyond that which has become traditionally established, encounters traditionalistic obstacles. These could only be overcome by the most ruthless methods, which are not without their danger from the point of view of the employer's own self-interest, since they might undermine the traditionalistic bases of his authority. Hence almost universally the production of appropriated workers has shown a tendency to restriction. Even where, as was particularly true of eastern Europe in early modern times, this has been broken up by the power of the propertied classes, the development of much higher technical levels of production has still been impeded by the absence of the selective process and by the absence of any element of self-interest or independent risk on the part of the appropriated workers. When jobs have been formally appropriated by workers, the same result has come about even more rapidly.

2. Appropriation by workers was particularly common in the development of the early Middle Ages, from the tenth to the thirteenth centuries. The Carolingian "beunden" and all the other beginnings of large-scale agricultural enterprise declined and disappeared. The income of feudal lords and landed proprietors became stereotyped at a very low level; and an increasing proportion of the products in kind, in agriculture and mining, and of the money proceeds from the handicrafts, went to the workers. In just this form this development was peculiar to the Western World. The principal circumstances which favoured it were as follows: (a) The fact that the propertied classes were heavily involved in political and military activity; (b) the absence of a suitable administrative staff. These two circumstances made it impossible to treat these workers in any other way than as a source of stereotyped income; (c) the fact that the freedom of movement of workers as between the potential employers competing for their services could not easily be

restricted; (d) the numerous opportunities of opening up new land, new mines, and new local markets; (e) the primitive level of the technical tradition. The more the appropriation of opportunities for profit by the workers took the place of the appropriation of workers by owners, the more the owners became merely recipients of income. Classical examples are the mining industry and the English guilds. But this, even at an early period, tended to go further to the point of repudiation of payments to a lord altogether, as exemplified in the saying, "A townsman is a freeman." Almost immediately all this led to a broadening of opportunities of making profit by market transactions, arising either from within the group of workers themselves or from without through the development of trade.

## *Social Aspects of the Division of Labour—(Continued)*

### THE APPROPRIATION OF THE NON-HUMAN MEANS OF PRODUCTION

The non-human means of production may be appropriated by workers as individuals or as corporate groups, by owners, or by regulating groups consisting of third parties.

When appropriated by workers, it may be by the individual worker who then becomes the "owner" of the non-human means of production; or the appropriation may be carried out by a more or less completely closed group of workers so that, though the individual worker is not the owner, the corporate group is. Such a corporate group may carry out its functions as a unitary economy as on a "communistic" basis, or with appropriation of shares (*Genossenschaftlich*). In all these cases, appropriation may be used for the purposes of budgetary administration or for profit making.

Appropriation by individual workers may exist in a system of completely free market relations, as between small peasants, artisans, boatmen, or taxi-drivers, each owning his own means of production. Where it is not the individual but a corporate group which is the agent of appropriation, there is a wide variety of possibilities, varying particularly with the extent to which the system is of a budgetary or a profit-making character. The household economy, which is in principle neither necessarily primitive nor in fact communistic, may be oriented wholly to provision for its own needs. Or it may, perhaps only occasionally, dispose of surpluses of certain types of raw material accumulated by virtue of a favourable location, or of products derived from some particular technical skill, as a means to better provision. This occasional sale may then develop into a regular system of profit-making exchange. In such cases it is common for "tribal" crafts to develop with an interethnic specialization of function and exchange. Generally speaking, marketability depends on maintaining a monopoly, which in turn is usually secured by inherited secrets. These may develop into wandering craft groups or possibly pariah[5] crafts. It is also possible, as in India, where these groups are united in a political structure and where there are ritual barriers between the ethnic elements, for them to develop into castes.

The case where members of the group possess appropriated shares is that of "producers' co-operation."[6] Household economies may, with the development of money accounting, approach this type. Otherwise, it is only occasionally found, as an organization of workmen. There is, however, one important case closely approaching this type—the mining industry of the early Middle Ages.

Since appropriation by organized groups of workers has already been discussed, appropriation by "owners" or organized groups of them can mean only the expropriation of the workers from the means of production, not merely as individuals, but as a whole. An owner may in this connexion appropriate one or more of the following items: land, including water; subterranean wealth; sources of power; work premises; labour equipment, such as tools, apparatus and machinery; and raw materials. In any given case all these may be concentrated in a single ownership or they may be appropriated by different owners. The owners may employ the means of production they appropriate in a context of budgetary administration, as means to provide for their own needs, or as sources of income by loans. In the latter case, the loans may in turn be used for budgetary purposes or as means for earning a profit, in which case they may be used in a profit-making enterprise without capital accounting, as capital goods in another's enterprise or as capital goods in the owner's own enterprise.

The appropriating agency may be a corporate group engaged in economic activity. In this case, all the alternatives just outlined are open to it. It is, however, also possible that the means of production should be appropriated by a corporate group which only *regulates* economic activity. In

---

5. The term *Paria* is used by Weber in a technical sense to designate a group occupying the same territorial area as others, but separated from them by ritual barriers which severely limit social intercourse between the groups. It has been common for such groups to have specialized occupations, particularly occupations which are despised in the larger society.—ED.

6. What is ordinarily called a "producers' co-operative association" would be included in this type, but Weber conceives the type itself more broadly. In certain respects, for instance, the medieval manor and other types of village community could be considered as examples.—ED.

this case, they are neither used as capital goods nor as a source of income, but are placed at the disposal of the members.

1. When land is appropriated by isolated economic units, it is usually for the period of actual cultivation until the harvest or, so far as, by virtue of clearing or irrigation, land is itself an artifact, for the period of continuous cultivation.

It is only when scarcity of land has become noticeable that it is common for rights of cultivation, pasturage and use of timber to be reserved to the members of a settlement group, and for the extent of their use to be limited: (1) When that happens, appropriation may be carried out by a corporate group. This may be of differing sizes, according to the mode of use to which the land is put—for gardens, meadows, arable land, pastures, or woodland. These have been appropriated by progressively larger groups from the individual household to the whole tribe. Typical cases are the appropriation of arable land, meadows, and pastures by a kinship group or a local community, usually a village. It has been usual for woodland to be appropriated by broader territorial groups, differing greatly in character and extent. The individual household has typically appropriated garden land and the area around the house and has had shares in arable fields and meadows. The assignment of these shares may take various forms. Where a wandering agricultural people takes over new areas, it may involve rigid equality. In a sedentary agricultural regime, there may be a rationally systematic redistribution. This usually occurs only as a consequence of fiscal claims when villagers are collectively responsible for taxes, or of claims of the members to political equality. The unit of technical organization has normally been the household group; (2) the subject of appropriation may be a landlord. This status may, as will be discussed later, be based primarily on the individual's position of authority in a kinship group or as political chieftain with claims to exact labour services, or on fiscal or military authority, or on some form of organization for the systematic exploitation of new land or an irrigation project.

Proprietorship over land may be made a source of utilities by the employment of the unfree labour of slaves or serfs. This, in turn, may be administered as part of a budgetary unit, through deliveries in kind or labour services, as as a means of profit, as a "plantation." On the other hand, it may be exploited with free labour. Here again it may be treated in budgetary terms, drawing income from the land in the form of payments in kind or from share-cropping by tenants or of money rents from tenants. In both cases the equipment used may be provided by the tenant himself or may be loaned to him by the landlord. A landlord may also exploit his holdings as a source of profit in the form of a large-scale rational enterprise.

Where the land is used as part of a budgetary economy with unfree labour, the landlord is apt to be bound traditionally in his exploitation of it, both with respect to his labour personnel, which is not subject to selection, and to their functions. The use of unfree labour in a profit-making organization, the "plantation," has only occurred in a few cases, notably in Antiquity in Carthage and in Rome, and in modern times in the plantations of colonial areas and in the Southern States of North America. Its use in large-scale profit-making enterprises with free labour has occurred only in the modern Western World. It is the mode of development of land proprietorship, in particular the way in which it was broken up, which has been most decisive in determining the modern forms of land appropriation. To-day, only the following pure types are found: the owner of land, the capitalistic tenant, and the propertyless agricultural labourer. The latter type is exceptional, found principally in England.

Sources of wealth adapted to exploitation by mining may be appropriated in the following ways: (a) By the owner of the land, who in the past has usually been a *landlord;* (b) by a political overlord or authority; (c) by any person discovering deposits worthy of mining; (d) by a corporate group of workers and (e) by a profit-making enterprise.

Landlords and political authorities may administer their holdings themselves, as they did occasionally in the early Middle Ages; or they may use them as a source of income, by leasing them to an organized group of workers or to any discoverer whatever or anyone who was a member of a given group. This was the case with the "free mines" of the Middle Ages and was the origin of the institution of "mining freedom" (*Bergbaufreiheit*).

In the Middle Ages, the groups of organized mine workers were typically sharing co-operatives where each member was under obligation either to the owner or to the other solidary members to work in the mine. This obligation was balanced by a right to a share in the products. There was also the type of association of owners which distributed shares of the proceeds and each of whom had to make contributions. The tendency was for the owners to be progressively expropriated in favour of the workers; but these, in turn, as their need for equipment increased, became more and more dependent on groups with command over capital goods. Thus in the end, the appropriation took the form of a capitalistic enterprise, a limited liability company.

2. Means of production which are bound to a fixed position, such as sources of power, particularly water power, "mills" for various different purposes, and workshops, sometimes including the apparatus in them, have in the past, particularly in the Middle Ages, generally been appropriated in one of the following ways: (a) by princes or landlords; (b) by towns (c) by associations of workers, such as guilds, without the development, in any of them, of a unified productive organization.

In the first two cases, they are usually exploited as a source of income, a charge being made for their use. This has often been combined with monopoly position and the compulsory use of the facilities. Each productive unit would make use of the facilities in turn, according to need or, under certain circumstances, it was made the monopoly of a closed, regulative group. Baking ovens, various kinds of grinding mills for grain or oil, fulling mills, polishing equipment, slaughter-houses, dye works, bleaching equipment, forges—which were usually, to be sure, leased—breweries, distilleries, other equipment including particularly shipyards in the possession of the Hanseatic towns, and all kinds of market booths have been appropriated in this way. Under pre-capitalistic conditions, these have all tended to be exploited by allowing workers to use them in return for a payment; thus as part of the budgetary resources of the owner, rather than as capital, whether the owner were an individual or a corporate group, including town corporations. This type of production and budgetary exploitation as a source of investment income for the owning individual or group, or possibly production by a producers' co-operative group, has preceded their transformation into the "fixed capital" of individual business units. Those using such equipment have tended to treat them in part as means of meeting their own needs, especially in the case of baking ovens, but also of equipment for brewing and distilling. In part they have used them in profit-making operations.

3. For maritime commerce the typical arrangement in past times has been the appropriation of the ship by a plurality of owners who have tended to become more and more sharply differentiated from the workers on ships. The organization of maritime enterprise has tended then to develop into a system of sharing risks with shippers in which ship owners, officers, and even the crew, were associated. This did not however, produce any fundamentally new forms of appropriation, but affected only the forms of calculation and hence the distribution of profit and loss.

4. To-day, it is usual for all kinds of equipment and tools to be appropriated under one controlling agency, as is essential to the modern factory; but in earlier times, this has been exceptional. In particular, the economic character of the Greek and Byzantine "ergasterion" and the corresponding Roman "ergastulum" has been highly equivocal, a fact which historians have persistently ignored. It was a "workshop" which might, on the one hand, be a part of a household unit in which slaves might carry out production for the owner's own needs, as on a landed estate. Or it might be a place where slaves carried out some subsidiary process of production of goods for sale. But, on the other hand, the workshop might be used as a source of profit in the ownership of a private individual or of a corporate group, which latter might be a town, as was true of the workshops of the Piraeus. A property would then be leased to individuals or to organized groups of workers in return for payment. Thus when it is stated that people worked in an ergasterion, especially in a town, it is always necessary to inquire further to whom it belonged and who was the owner of the other means of production necessary for the work process. Did it employ free labour? Did they work for their own profit? Or did it employ slaves, in which case it is necessary to know who their owners were and whether they were working on their own account, though making a ἀποφορᾶ payment to their master, or directly for their master. According to the ways in which these questions are answered, the structure would be radically different from an economic point of view. In the great majority of cases, even as late as the Byzantine and Mohammedan types, the ergasterion seems to have been primarily a source of budgetary income and was hence fundamentally different from the modern factory and should not be treated as an early stage of its development. From an economic point of view, this category is, in lack of definiteness, most closely comparable to the various types of mills, found in the Middle Ages.

5. Even in cases where the workshop and the means of production are appropriated by an individual owner who hires labour, the situation is not, from an economic point of view, necessarily what would usually be called a factory to-day. It is necessary in addition to have the use of mechanical power, of machinery, and of an elaborate internal differentiation and combination of functions. The factory to-day is a category of the capitalistic economy. Hence in the present discussion, the concept will be confined to a type of organization which is at least potentially under the control of a profit-making enterprise with fixed capital. It thus takes the form of an organized workshop with internal differentiation of function, with the appro-

priation of all the non-human means of production and with a high degree of mechanization of the work process by the use of mechanical power and machinery. The great workshop of Jack of Newbury, which was famous among its sixteenth-century contemporaries, did not have any of these features. It is alleged to have contained hundreds of hand looms which were his property, and the entrepreneur bought the raw material for the workers, and maintained all manner of welfare arrangements for them. But each worker worked independently as if he were at home. It was possible for an internal differentiation and combination of functions to exist in an ergasterion in which a master employed unfree labourers in Egypt, Greece, Byzantium, and in the Mohammedan world. There is no doubt that such cases have existed. But the Greek texts show clearly that even in such cases it was common for the master to be content with the payment of an ἀποφορά from each worker though perhaps a higher one from persons in a supervisory position. This alone is sufficient to warn us not to consider such a structure economically equivalent to a factory or even to a workshop like that of Jack of Newbury. The closest approximation to the factory in the usual sense is found in royal manufactures, like the imperial Chinese porcelain manufactures and the European manufactures of court luxuries which were modelled on it. The best case of all is the manufacture of military equipment. No one can be prevented from calling these "factories." The Russian workshops operating with serf labour seem at first sight to stand even closer to the modern factory. Here the appropriation of the workers themselves is added to that of the means of production. But for present purposes the concept "factory" will, for the reasons stated, be limited to organized workshops where the non-human means of production are fully appropriated by an owner, but the workers are not; where there is internal specialization of functions, and where mechanical power and machines which must be "tended" are used. All other types of organized workshops will be designated as such with the appropriate additional description.

## *Social Aspects of the Division of Labour—(Concluded)*

### THE APPROPRIATION OF MANAGERIAL FUNCTIONS

In all cases of the management of traditional budgetary units, it is typical for the appropriation of managerial functions to take place either by the titular head himself, such as the head of the family or the kinship group, or by members of an administrative staff appointed for the management of the unit, such as household servants or officials.

In the case of profit-making enterprises, it occurs in the following situations: (a) When management and ordinary labour are entirely or very nearly identical. In this case there is usually also appropriation of the non-human means of production by the worker. This type of appropriation may be unlimited, that is, hereditary and alienable on the part of the individual, with or without a guaranteed market. It may, on the other hand, be appropriated by an organized group, with appropriation of the function by the individual restricted to personal tenure (that is, without rights of inheritance or alienation) or subject to substantive regulation, thus limited and dependent on various conditions. Again, a market may or may not be guaranteed; (b) where management and ordinary work are differentiated, there may be a monopolistic appropriation of entrepreneurial functions in various possible forms, notably by co-operative groups, such as guilds, or monopolies granted by the political authority.

In cases where managerial functions are, from a formal point of view, wholly unappropriated, the appropriation of the means of production or of the credit necessary for securing control over them is, in practice, in a capitalistic form of organization, identical with appropriation of control of management by the owners of the means of production. Owners can, in such cases, exercise their control by personally managing the business or by appointment of the actual managers. Where there is a plurality of owners, they will co-operate in the selection.

Wherever there is appropriation of technically complementary means of production, it generally means, in practice, at least some degree of effective voice in the selection of management and, to a relative extent at least, the expropriation of the workers from management. The expropriation of individual workers does not necessarily imply the expropriation of workers in general. Though they are formally expropriated, it is possible for an association of workers to be in fact in a position to play an effective part in management or in the selection of managing personnel.

## *The Expropriation of Workers from the Means of Production*

The expropriation of the individual worker from ownership of the means of production is in part determined by the following purely technical factors: (a) The fact that sometimes the means of production require the services of many workers, at the same time or successively; (b) the fact that sometimes sources of power can only be rationally exploited by using them simultaneously for many similar types of work under a unified control; (c) the fact that often a technically rational organization of the work process is possible only by combining many complementary processes under continuous common supervision; (d) the fact that sometimes special technical training is needed for the management of co-ordinated processes of labour which, in turn, can only be exploited rationally on a large scale; (e) the fact that, if the means of production and raw materials are under unified control, there is the possibility of subjecting labour to a stringent discipline and thereby controlling both the speed of work and standardization and quality of products.

These factors, however, do not exclude the possibility of appropriation by an organized group of workers, a producers' co-operative. They necessitate only the separation of the *individual* worker from the means of production.

The expropriation of workers in general, including clerical personnel and technically trained persons, from possession of the means of production depends on the following principal economic factors: (a) The fact that, other things being equal, it is generally possible to achieve a higher level of technical efficiency if the management has extensive control over the selection and the modes of use of workers, as compared with the situation created by the appropriation of jobs or the existence of rights to participate in management. These latter conditions produce technically, as well as economically, irrational obstacles to efficiency. In particular, considerations appropriate to small-scale budgetary administration and the immediate interests of consumers are often in conflict with the efficiency of the organization; (b) in a market economy a management which is not hampered by any established rights of the workers, and which enjoys unrestricted control over the goods and equipment which underlie its borrowings, is in a superior credit position. This is particularly true if the management consists in individuals experienced in business affairs and with a good reputation for "safety" derived from their continuous conduct of business; (c) from a historical point of view, the expropriation of labour has developed since the sixteenth century in an economy characterized by a progressive development of the market system, both extensively and intensively, by the sheer technical superiority and actual indispensability of a type of autocratic management oriented to the particular market situations, and by the structure of power relationships in the society.

In addition to these general conditions, the effect of the fact that enterprise has been oriented to the exploitation of market advantages has been to favour such expropriation: (a) As compared with every type of economic attitude which, from the point of view of calculation is less rational, it has favoured the maximum of technical rationality in capital accounting. This, however, has been a function of the complete appropriation of economic resources by owners; (b) it has favoured commercial abilities in management as opposed to the technical. It has also favoured the maintenance of technical and commercial secrets; (c) it has favoured a speculative business policy which again has required expropriation; (d) apart from any considerations of technical rationality, expropriation has been favoured by the bargaining superiority which management, by virtue of its possession of property, has enjoyed, both on the labour market in relation to the worker, and in the commodity market, by virtue of its capital accounting, and its command over capital goods and credit. In these ways it is superior to any type of competitor operating on a lower level of rationality in methods of calculation or less well situated with respect to capital and credit resources. The upshot of all these considerations is that the maximum of formal rationality in capital accounting is possible only where the workers are subjected to the authority of business management. This is a further specific element of substantive irrationality[7] in the modern economic order; (e) finally, free labour and the complete appropriation of the means of production create the most favourable conditions for discipline.

## *The Expropriation of Workers from the Means of Production—(Continued)*

The expropriation of *all* the workers from the means of production may have the following effects in practice: (1) That management is in the hands of the administrative staff of a corporate group. This would be true very particularly of any rationally organized socialistic economy. The expropriation of all the workers would be retained and merely brought to completion by the expropriation of private owners; (2) that the managerial functions are, by virtue of their appropriation of the means of production, exercised by the owners or by persons they appoint. The appropriation of control over the persons exercising managerial authority by the interests of ownership may have the following con-

7. Attention should be called again to Weber's peculiar use of the term "irrational." He means that the maximum of formal rationality in his specific sense can be attained only in a structure which is in conflict with certain important values or ideas of welfare.—ED.

sequences: (a) Management by one or more entrepreneurs who are at the same time owners—the immediate appropriation of managerial functions. This situation, however, does not exclude the possibility that a wide degree of control over the policies of management may rest in hands outside the organization, by virtue of their powers over credit or financing; for instance, the bankers who finance the enterprise; (b) the separation of managerial functions from appropriated ownership, especially through limitations of the functions of owners to the appointment of management and to the free appropriation of shares of the profits, these powers exercised by the owners of capital shares. From this situation to the purely personal type of appropriation there are all manner of gradual transitions. The separation of ownership and management is formally rational in the sense that, as contrasted with the case of permanent and hereditary appropriation of managerial functions, it permits the selection for managerial posts of the persons best qualified from the standpoint of profitability. But this can have various different practical consequences. By virtue of their ownership, control over managerial positions may rest in the hands of property interests outside the organization as such. They may be shareholders who are, above all, concerned with maximizing their investment returns. Or control over managerial positions may lie, by virtue of a temporary market situation, in the hands of speculative interests outside the organization, such as shareholders who are interested in profits from the sale of their shares. Or, finally, control over managerial positions may be in the hands of other business interests, such as banks or others, which by virtue of their power over markets or over credit are in a position to exercise control. These may pursue their own interests, which are often foreign to those of the organization as such.

Interests are spoken of as "outside the firm" so far as they are not primarily oriented to the long-run profitability of the enterprise. This may be true of all sorts of property interests. It is particularly true, however, of interests having control of the plant and capital goods of the enterprise or of a share in it, which is not exercised as a permanent investment, but as a means of making a speculative profit. The types of outside interest which are most readily reconciled with those of the enterprise are those of pure investment; they are, that is, interests in long-run profitability.

The ways in which these outside interests play into the modes of control over managerial position constitutes another specific element of substantive irrationality in the modern economic order. This is the more true the higher the degree of rationality exercised in selection. It is possible for entirely private property interests to exercise control, or others which are oriented to ends having no connexion with the organization, or finally, those concerned only with gambling. By gaining control of shares, these can control the appointment of the managing personnel and, more important, the business policies they pursue. The influence exercised on the market situation, especially that for capital goods, and in turn on the orientation of production of goods for profit, by speculative interests outside the producing organizations themselves, is *one* of the sources of the phenomena known as the "crises" of the modern market economy. This cannot, however, be further discussed here.

# 3. *Budgetary Management and Profit-Making*

BY MAX WEBER

THE RATIONALITY OF MONETARY ACCOUNTING: MANAGEMENT AND BUDGETING

FROM A PURELY technical point of view, money is the most "efficient" means of economic accounting. That is, it is formally the most rational means of orienting economic activity. Accounting in terms of money, and not its actual use, is thus the specific means of rational, economic provision. So far as it is completely rational, money accounting has the following primary consequences:

(1) The valuation of all the means of achieving a productive purpose in terms of the present or expected market situation. This includes everything

---

Reprinted from Max Weber, *The Theory of Social and Economic Organization,* trans. A. M. Henderson and Talcott Parsons, ed. Talcott Parsons (Glencoe, Ill.: The Free Press, 1947), pp. 186–203. 

which is needed at present or it is expected may be needed in the future; everything actually in the actor's control, which he may come to control or may acquire by exchange from the control of others; everything lost, or in danger of damage or destruction; all types of utilities of means of production or any other sort of economic advantages.

(2) The numerical statement of (a) the prospects of every projected course of economic action and (b) assessment of the results of every completed action in the form of an account comparing costs and returns in money and comparing the estimated net profit to be gained from alternative lines of action by means of these calculations.

(3) A periodical comparison of all the goods and other assets controlled by an economic unit at a given time with those controlled at the beginning of a period, both in terms of money.

(4) A previous estimate and subsequent verification of receipts and expenditures, either those in money itself, or those which can be valued in money, which the economic unit is likely to have available for its use during a period, if it maintains the money value of the means at its disposal intact.

(5) The orientation of provision for consumption to these data by the use of money available during the accounting period for the acquisition of the requisite utilities in accordance with the principle of marginal utility.

The continual use and provision by an economic unit, whether through production or exchange, of goods either for its own consumption or to procure other goods to be consumed, will be called "budgetary management" (*Haushalt*).[1] Where rationality is maximized, its basis for an individual or for a group economically oriented in this way is the "budget" (*Haushaltsplan*), which states systematically in what way the means which are expected to be used within the unit for an accounting period—needs for utilities or for means of production—can be covered by the anticipated income.

The "income" of a "budgetary unit" is the total of goods valued in money, which, as estimated according to the principle stated above in number 4, has been available during a previous period or, on the availability of which the unit is likely to be able to count by rational calculations for the present or for a future period. The total estimated value of the goods at the disposal of a budgetary unit, which are normally used immediately or as a source of income, will be called its "resources" (*Vermögen*).[2] The possibility of complete money budgeting for the budgetary unit is dependent on the possibility that its income and resources consist either in money or in goods which are at any time subject to exchange for money; that is, which are in the highest degree marketable.

A rational type of management and budgeting of a budgetary unit is possible where calculation is carried out in kind, as will be further discussed below. It is true that in that case there is no such thing as a single sum of "resources" capable of being estimated in money nor is there a single income. Calculations must be worked out in terms of "possession" of concrete goods and, where acquisition is limited to peaceful means, of concrete "receipts" from the direct outlay of available goods and services. These receipts will then be administered with a view to attaining the optimum provision for the satisfaction of wants. If the wants are strictly given, this involves a comparatively simple problem from the technical point of view so long as the situation does not require a very precise estimate of the comparative utility to be gained from the allocation of the available resources to each of a large number of very heterogeneous modes of use. If the situation is markedly different, even the simple self-sufficient household is faced with problems which are only to a very limited degree subject to a formally exact solution by calculation. The actual solution is usually found partly by the application of purely traditional standards, partly by making very rough estimates, which, however, may be quite adequate where both the wants concerned and the conditions of provision for them are well known and readily comparable. When possessions consist in heterogeneous goods, as must be the case in the absence of exchange, a formally exact calculable comparison of the state of possession at the beginning and the end of a period, or of the comparison of different possible ways of securing receipts, is possible only with categories of goods which are qualitatively similar. The typical result is that all the available goods are treated as forming a totality of possessions in kind and certain goods are treated as available for consumption so long as it appears that this will not in the long run diminish the available re-

1. The concept *Haushalt*, as distinguished from *Erwerb*, is central to Weber's analysis in this context. He means by it essentially what Aristotle meant by the "management of a household" (Jowett's translation). It is a question of rational allocation of resources in providing for a given set of needs. The concept of budget and budgetary management seems to be the closest English equivalent in common use.—Ed.

2. Corresponding to the distinction of *Haushalt* and *Erwerb*, Weber distinguishes *Vermögen* and *Kapital*. They are, of course, classes of property distinguished, however, in terms of their function in the management of an economic unit. There is no English equivalent of *Vermögen* in this sense, and it has seemed necessary to employ the more general term "resources." Where there is danger of confusion, it will be amplified as "budgetary resources." —Ed.

sources. But every change in the conditions of production—as, for instance, through a bad harvest—or any change in wants necessitates a new allocation since it alters the scale of relative marginal utilities. Under conditions which are simple and adequately understood, this adaptation may be carried out without much difficulty. Otherwise, it is technically more difficult than if money terms could be used. For then any change in the price situation in principle influences the satisfaction only of the wants which are marginal on the scale of relative urgency, which are thus met with the final (variable) increments of income.

As far as accounting in kind becomes more and more rational, and is thus emancipated from tradition, the estimation of marginal utilities in terms of the relative urgency of wants encounters grave complications; whereas, if it were carried out in terms of money resources and income, it would be relatively simple. In the latter case the question is merely whether to apply more labour or whether to satisfy or sacrifice, as the case may be, one or more wants, rather than others. For when the problems of budgetary management are expressed in money terms, this is the form that "costs" take. But where calculations are in kind, it is necessary, in addition to having a scale of urgency of wants, to estimate (1) the various possible modes of use of the means of production, including their value in terms of previous labour applied to them; that is, it is necessary to evaluate a variant and changeable relationship between want satisfaction and expenditure of resources. This involves further (2) estimating the amount of labour which it would be necessary to expend in order to secure various forms of new receipts; and (3) the ways in which the various resources could be used in carrying out each of a series of potential productive processes. It is one of the most important tasks of economic theory to analyse the various possible ways in which these evaluations can be rationally carried out. It is, on the other hand, a task for economic history to follow out the ways in which the budgetary management of resources in kind has actually worked out in the course of various historical epochs. In general, the following may be said: (1) that the degree of formal rationality has, generally speaking, fallen short of the level which was even empirically possible, to say nothing of the theoretical maximum. As a matter of necessity, the accounting of nonmonetary budgetary management units has in the great majority of cases remained strongly bound to tradition. (2) In the larger units of this type, precisely because an expansion and refinement of everyday wants has not taken place, there has been a tendency to employ surpluses for uses outside the everyday standard of living, above all, for artistic purposes. This is an important basis of the tendency of societies with an economy on a low level of the use of money to develop cultures with a strong emphasis on style and an artistic type of orientation.

1. The category of "resources" includes more than physical goods. It also includes all the economic advantages over which the budgetary unit has an assured control, whether that control is due to custom, to the play of interests, to convention, or to law. The clientèle of a profit-making organization, whether it be a medical or legal practice, or a retail shop, belongs to the resources of the owner if it is for whatever reason relatively stable. In case such resources are legally appropriated, they may, according to the definition in Chapter 1, sec. 10, constitute part of its property.

2. Money accounting is found without the actual use of money or with its use limited to the settlement of balances which cannot be paid in kind in the goods being exchanged on both sides. Evidence of this is common in the Egyptian and Babylonian records. The use of money accounting as a measure of payments in kind is found in the code of Hammurabi and in the late Roman and early Medieval law, in the permission for a debtor to pay an amount due in whatever form he is able. The establishment of equivalents may in such cases have been carried out on the basis of traditional prices or of prices laid down by decree.

3. Apart from this, the above discussion contains only commonplaces, which are introduced to facilitate the formulation of a precise concept of the rational budgetary unit as distinguished from that of a rational profit-making enterprise—the latter will be discussed presently. It is important to state explicitly that both can take rational forms. The satisfaction of needs is not something more "primitive" than profit-seeking; "resources" is not necessarily a more primitive category than capital; income, than profit. It is, however, true that historically the budgetary unit has been prior and has been the dominant form in most periods of the past.

4. It is indifferent what unit is the bearer of a budgetary management economy. Both the budget of a state and the family budget of a worker fall under the same category.

5. Empirically the administration of budgetary units and profit-making are not mutually exclusive alternatives. The business of a consumers' cooperative, for instance, is normally oriented to the economical provision for wants; but in the form of its activity, it tends to be a profit-making business without being oriented to profit as a substantive end.

In the action of an individual, the two elements may be so intimately intertwined, and in the past have typically been so, that only the conclusion of the course of action, whether its product was sold or consumed, can serve as a basis for interpreting the meaning of the action. This has been particularly true of small peasants. Exchange may well be a part of the process of budgetary management where it is a matter of acquiring consumption goods by exchange and of disposing of surpluses. On the other hand, the budgetary economy of a prince or a landowner may, at least in part in the sense of the following discussion, be a profit-making enterprise. This has been true on a large scale in earlier times. Whole industries have developed out of the heterocephalous and heteronomous enterprises which landowners, monasteries, princes, etc., have established to exploit the products of their lands. All sorts of profit-making enterprises to-day are part of the economy of such units as local authorities or even states. In these cases it is legitimate to include in the "income" of the units, if they are rationally administered, only the net profits of these enterprises. Conversely, it is possible for profit-making enterprises to establish various types of heteronomous budgetary units under their direction for such purposes as providing subsistence for slaves or wage workers—among them are "welfare" organizations, housing and eating facilities. Net profits are money surpluses after the deduction of all money costs. See above, para. 2 of this section.

6. It has been possible here to give only the most elementary starting points for analysing the significance of economic calculations in kind for general social development.

## *The Concept and Types of Profit-Making. The Role of Capital*

"Profit-making" (*Erwerben*)[3] is activity which is oriented to opportunities for seeking new powers of control over goods on a single occasion, repeatedly, or continuously. "Profit-making activity" is activity which is partly oriented to profit-making. Profit-making is economic if it is oriented to acquisition by peaceful methods. It may be oriented to the exploitation of market situations. "Means of profit" (*Erwerbsmittel*) are those goods and other economic advantages which are used in the interests of economic profit-making. Exchange for profit is that which is oriented to market situations in order to increase control over goods, rather than to secure means for consumption. Credit may be extended as a means of increasing control over the necessary requisites of profit-making activity.

There is a form of monetary accounting which is peculiar to rational economic profit-making; namely, "capital accounting." Capital accounting is the valuation and verification of opportunities for profit and of the success of profit-making activity. It involves the valuation of the total assets of the enterprise, whether these consist in goods in kind or in money, at the beginning of a period of activity; and the comparison of this with a similar valuation of the assets still present or newly acquired, at the end of the process. In the case of a profit-making organization operating continuously, it is a matter of accounting periods. But in any case, a balance is drawn between the initial and final states of the enterprise. "Capital" is the sum of money in terms of which the means of profit-making which are available to the enterprise are valued. "Profit," and correspondingly "loss," is the difference between the valuations as revealed by the initial balance and that drawn at the conclusion of the period. "Capital risk" is the estimated probability of loss as expressed in terms of a balance. A profit-making "enterprise" (*Unternehmen*) is a system of action capable of autonomous orientation to capital accounting. This orientation takes place by means of calculation. On the one hand, there is a calculation, prior to actual action, of the probable risks and chances of profit; on the other hand, at the conclusion of a measure, verification of the actual profit or loss resulting. "Profitability" (*Rentabilität*) means, in the rational case, one of two things: (1) the amount of profit estimated as possible by previous calculations, the attainment of which is made an objective of the entrepreneur's activity; or (2) that which an audit shows actually to have been earned in a given period and which is available for the consumption uses of the entrepreneur, without prejudice to his future chances of profit making. In both cases it is usually expressed in ratios—to-day, percentages—in relation to the capital of the initial balance.

Enterprises based on capital accounting may be oriented to the exploitation of opportunities of acquisition afforded by the market or they may be oriented toward other channels of acquisition, such as exploitation of the ability to use force, as in the case of tax farming or the sale of offices.

Each individual operation undertaken by a rational profit-making enterprise is oriented to estimated profitability by means of calculation. In the case of profit-making activities on the market, capital accounting requires: (1) that there exist, subject

3. In common usage the term *Erwerben* would perhaps best be translated as "acquisition." This has not, however, been used as Weber is here using the term in a technical sense as the antithesis of *Haushalten.* "Profit-Making" brings out this specific meaning much more clearly.—ED.

to estimate beforehand, adequately extensive and assured opportunities for sale of the goods which the enterprise produces; that is, normally a high degree of marketability. (2) That, similarly, the means of carrying on the enterprise such as instruments of production and the services of labour are available in the market at costs which can be estimated with an adequate degree of certainty. Finally, (3) that the technical and legal conditions to which the process is subjected, from the acquisition of the means of production to final sale, including transport, manufacturing operations, storage, etc., can be taken account of as calculable money costs.

The extraordinary importance of the highest possible degree of calculability as the basis for efficient capital accounting will be evidenced again and again throughout the discussion of the sociological conditions of economic activity. It is far from the case that only economic factors are important to it. On the contrary, it will be shown that the most various sorts of external and subjective barriers have existed to account for the fact that capital accounting has arisen as a basic form of economic calculation only in the Western World.

As distinguished from the calculation appropriate to a budgetary unit, the capital accounting and calculation of the market entrepreneur, are oriented not to marginal utility, but to profitability. To be sure, the probabilities of profit are in the last analysis dependent on the income of consumption units and, through this, on the marginal utility of the available income of the final consumers of consumption goods. As it is usually put, it depends on their "purchasing power" for the relevant commodities. But from a technical point of view, the accounting calculations of a profit-making enterprise and of a consumption unit differ as fundamentally as do the ends of want satisfaction and of profit-making which they serve. For purposes of economic theory, it is the marginal consumer who determines the direction of production. In actual fact, given the actual distribution of power this is only true in a limited sense for the modern situation. To a large degree, even if the consumer is in a position to buy, his wants are "awakened" and "directed" by the entrepreneur.

In a market economy every form of rational calculation, hence, especially, of capital accounting, is oriented to expectations of prices and their changes as they are determined by the conflicts of interests in bargaining and competition and the resolution of these conflicts. In the estimation of profitability this is made particularly clear by the form of bookkeeping, the double entry type, which is the most highly developed from a technical point of view. For here, in the system of accounting, there is introduced the fiction of exchange transactions between the different parts of a single enterprise; or, between different accounts in order to develop a technique of estimating the bearing of each particular measure on the profitability of the enterprise. Thus the highest degree of rational capital accounting presupposes the existence of competition on a large scale. And this in turn involves a further very specific condition. It is not possible in *any* economic system for subjective wants to correspond directly to effective demand; that is, to that which enters into calculations for provision by the acquisition of goods. For whether or not a subjective want can be satisfied depends, on the one hand, on its place in the scale of relative urgency; on the other hand, on the goods which are actually or potentially estimated to be available for its satisfaction. Satisfaction does not take place if the utilities needed for it are applied to other more urgent uses, or if they either cannot be procured at all, or only by such sacrifices of labour and goods that future wants, which are still, from a present point of view, adjudged more urgent, could not be satisfied. This is true of consumption in every kind of economic system including a communistic one.

In an economy which makes use of capital accounting and which is thus characterized by the appropriation of the means of production by individual units, that is by property, profitability depends on the prices which the "consumers," according to the marginal utility of money in relation to their income, can and will pay. It is only possible to produce profitably for those consumers who, in these terms, have sufficient income. A need may fail to be satisfied, not only when an individual's own demand for other goods takes precedence, but also when the greater purchasing power of others, in relation to any kind of demand, withdraws the relevant good from the market. Thus the fact that competition on the market is an essential condition of the existence of rational money accounting further implies that the outcome of the economic process is decisively influenced by the ability of persons who are plentifully supplied with money to outbid the others, and of those more favourably situated for production to underbid their rivals on the selling side. The latter are particularly those well supplied with goods essential to production or with money. In particular, rational money accounting presupposes the existence of effective prices and not merely of fictitious prices conventionally employed for technical accounting purposes. These, in turn, presuppose money which functions as an effective circulating medium of exchange and in demand as such, and not merely as a technical accounting unit.[4] Thus the orientation of action to money prices and to profit has the following consequences: (1) that the distribution of the amount of money or of marketable goods at the disposal of the different parties in the market is decisive in determining the direction taken by the production of goods, so far as it is carried on by profit-making enterprises. For it is only demand which is made effective through purchasing power which is and can be satisfied. Further, (2) the question, what type of demand is to be satisfied by the production of goods, becomes in turn dependent on the profitability of production itself. Production is, to be sure, in formal terms a rational process of want satisfaction. But it does not respond to actual wants unless their possessors are in a position to make them effective by sufficient purchasing power on the market.

"Capital goods," as distinguished from ordinary possessions or the resources of a budgetary unit, are all such goods as are administered and so long as they are administered on the basis of capital accounting. "Interest on capital," as distinct from various other possible kinds of interest on loans, is: (1) what is estimated to be the minimum normal profitability of the use of material means to profit making; (2) the rate of interest at which profit-making enterprises can obtain money or capital goods.

1. The concept of capital has been defined strictly with reference to the individual enterprise and in accordance with accounting practice, which was, indeed, the most convenient method for present purposes. This usage is much less in conflict with everyday speech than with the usual scientific use of the term, which, furthermore, has by no means been consistent. In order to test the usefulness of the present accounting term, which is being increasingly employed in scientific writings again, it is necessary only to ask the following simple questions: (1) What does it mean when we say that a company has an original capital of a million pounds? When (2) that capital is "written down"? When (3) laws dealing with financing make rules which lay down what may and may not be included in original capital? The first question means that when profit is being divided, it is only when the excess of credits over debits as stated in the balance sheet exceeds a million pounds, that it can be treated as profit and divided among the shareholders to do what they like with. In the case of a one man enterprise, it means that only this surplus may be used for his private expenditures. The second question concerns the situation where there have been heavy losses. It means that the division of profit need not be postponed until a surplus of over a million pounds has been accumulated but that the division of "profits" may begin at a lower figure. In order to do this, it is necessary to "write down" the capital and this is the purpose of the operation. Finally, the purpose of rules as to how capital liability can be "covered" by acquisition of assets and when and how it can be written down or up is to give creditors and shareholders a guarantee that the division of profits will be carried out correctly according to the rules of the enterprise; in such a way, that is, (a) that profitability is maintained, and (b) that the security of the creditors is not impaired. The rules as to what may be entered in the balance sheet are concerned essentially with how objects may be reckoned as capital. (4) What does it mean when we say that as a result of unprofitability "capital turns to other channels of investment"? The statement may refer to the resources of a budgetary unit, for "investment" may be a category of the administration of budgetary resources, as well as of profit-making enterprise. But it may mean that capital goods partly have ceased to be such by being sold, for instance as scrap or junk, partly are transferred to other uses as capital. (5) What is meant when we speak of the "power of capital"? We mean that the possessors of control over the means of production and of economic advantages which can be used as capital goods in a profit-making enterprise enjoy, by virtue of this control and of the orientation of economic action to the principles of capitalistic acquisition, a specific position of power in relation to others.

In the earliest beginnings of rational profit-making activity capital appears, though not under this name, as a sum of money used in accounting. Thus in the "commenda" relationship various types of goods were entrusted to a travelling merchant to sell in a foreign market, and possibly he was also commissioned to purchase other goods wanted for sale at home. The profit or loss was then divided in a particular proportion between the travelling merchant and the entrepreneur who advanced the capital. But for this to take place it was necessary to value the goods in money; that is, to strike balances at the beginning and the conclusion of an enterprise. The "capital" of the commenda relationship or the *societas maris* was simply this

4. Since Weber wrote, there has been an extensive discussion of the problem of whether rational allocation of resources was possible in a completely socialistic economy in which there were no independent, competitively determined prices. The principal weight of technical opinion seems at present to take the opposite position from that which Weber defends here. A recent discussion of the problem will be found in the book on the *Economic Theory of Socialism*, edited by B. E. Lippincott. This book includes a bibliography on the subject.—ED.

money valuation, which served only the purpose of settling accounts between the parties and no other.

What is meant when the term "capital market" is used? It means that goods, especially money, are in demand in order to be used as capital goods. Furthermore, it means that there are profit-making enterprises, especially various kinds of "banks," which make profits by the provision of goods, especially money, for this purpose as a regular business. In the case of so-called "loan capital," which consists in handing over money in lieu of a promise to return the same amount at a later time with or without the addition of "interest," the term capital will only be used if lending is the object of a profit-making enterprise. Otherwise, the term "money loans" will be used. Everyday speech tends to use the term capital in so far as "interest" is paid because the latter is usually reckoned as a proportion of the nominal value of the loan. It is only because of this basis of calculation that we speak of the amount of a loan or a deposit as capital. It is true that this is the origin of the term. *Capitale* was the principal sum of a loan which is said, though it cannot be proved, to derive from the heads counted in a loan of cattle. But this is irrelevant. Even in very early times a loan of goods in kind was reckoned in money terms; and it was on this basis that interest was calculated, so that even in such cases capital goods and capital accounting are typically related, as has been true in later times. In the case of an ordinary loan, which is made simply as a phase in the administration of a budgetary unit and so far as it is employed for the needs of the budgetary unit, the term "loan capital" will not be used. The same, of course, applies to the lender.

The concept of a profit-making enterprise is in accord with ordinary usage, except for the fact that the orientation to capital accounting, which is usually taken for granted, is made explicit. This is done in order to emphasize that not every case of search for profit as such constitutes an "enterprise," but only when it is capable of orientation to capital accounting, regardless of whether it is on a large or a small scale. At the same time it is indifferent whether this capital accounting is in fact rationally carried out according to rational principles. Similarly the terms "profit" and "loss" will be used only as applying to enterprises oriented to capital accounting. The earnings or other modes of acquisition without relation to capital, of such persons as authors, physicians, lawyers, civil servants, professors, clerks, technicians, or workers, is naturally "acquisition" (*Erwerb*), but it is not "profit." Even everyday usage would not call it profit. "Profitability" is a concept which is applicable to every sort of act which is oriented in terms of business accounting technique to profit and loss, such as the employment of a particular worker, the purchase of a new machine, the determination of rest periods in the working day, etc.

It is not expedient in defining the concept of interest on capital to start with interest on any type of loan. If somebody helps out a peasant by giving him seed and demands an increment on its return, or if the same is done in the case of money loaned to a household to be returned with interest, it is not expedient to call this a "capitalistic" process. It is possible, where action is rational, for the lender to secure an additional amount because his creditor is in a position to expect benefits from the use of the loan greater than the amount of the interest he pays; when, that is, the situation is seen in terms of what it would be if he had had to do without the loan. Similarly, the lender, being aware of the situation, is in a position to exploit it, in that for him the marginal utility of his present control over the goods he lends is exceeded by the marginal utility at the relevant future time of the repayment with the addition of the interest. This is essentially a matter of the administration of budgetary units and their resources, not of capital accounting. Even a person who secures a loan for his urgent personal needs from a "usurer" is not for purposes of the present discussion said to be paying interest on capital, nor does the lender receive such interest. It is rather a case of return for the loan. But the person who makes a business of lending calculates interest, in case he acts rationally, in terms of its relation to his business capital, and must consider that he has suffered a "loss" if the returns from loans do not come up to the requisite rate of profitability. This is a case of interest on capital; the former is simply interest. Thus for the present terminological purposes, interest on capital is always that which is calculated on the basis of capital, not that which is a return for capital. It is always oriented to money valuations, and thus to the sociological fact that disposal over means to making profit, whether through the market or not, is in private hands; that is, appropriated. Without this, capital accounting, and thus calculation of interest, would be unthinkable.

In a rational profit-making enterprise, the interest, which is charged on the books to a capital sum, is the minimum of profitability. It is in terms of whether or not this minimum is reached that a judgment of the advisability of this particular mode of use of capital goods is arrived at. Advisability in this context is naturally conceived from the point of view of maximizing profit. The rate for this minimum profitability is, it is well known, only approximately that at which it is possible to secure credit on the capital market at the time. But nevertheless, the existence of the capital market is the reason why calculations are made on this basis, just as the existence of market exchange is the basis for making entries against the different accounts. It is one of the fundamental phenomena of a capitalistic economy that entrepreneurs are permanently willing to pay interest for loans. This phenomenon can only be explained by understanding how it is that the average entrepreneur may hope in the long run to earn a profit, or that entrepeneurs on the average in fact do earn it, over and above what they have to pay as interest on loans.

Economic theory approaches this problem in terms of the relative marginal utilities of goods under present and under future control. No objection is to be made to this procedure. But the sociologist wishes to know in addition how this supposed relation of marginal utilities affects human action so that actors are in a position and willing to make differences in time preference a basis of the payment of interest. For it is by no means obvious that this would happen at all times and places. In fact, it is a phenomenon specific to profit-making economies. The primary basis of it is the economic market structure which mediates between the profit-making enterprises, on the one hand, and the budgetary units on the other, which not only consume the goods offered on the market but also provide certain essential means of production, notably labour. It is only where there is such a market that profit-making enterprises are founded and administered permanently with a capitalistic orientation. Such enterprises are further dependent on an expectation of earning the minimum rate of interest on capital. In terms of economic theory, which is subject to numerous variations, it might well be said that this type of exploitation of the situation was a consequence of positions of power deriving from private property in the means of production and in the products. It is only this type of economically-acting individuals who are in a position to orient their economic activity to interest payments.

2. The budgetary administration of resources and profit-making enterprises may be outwardly so similar as to appear identical. They are in fact in the analysis only distinguishable in terms of the difference in meaningful orientation of the corresponding economic activities. In the one case, it is oriented to maintaining and improving profitability and the market position of the enterprise; in the other, to the security and increase of resources and income. It is, however, by no means necessary that this fundamental orientation should always, in a concrete case, be decisively turned in either direction; and sometimes it is impossible to decide it. In cases where the private resources of the entrepreneur are identical with his business control over its business resources and his private income is identical with the profit of the business, the two things seem to go entirely hand in hand. All manner of personal considerations may in such a case cause the entrepreneur to enter upon business policies which, in terms of the rational maximization of profit, are irrational. But very generally, private resources and those of the business are not identical. Furthermore, such factors as personal indebtedness of the proprietor, his personal demand for a higher present income, and the like, often exert what is, in terms of business considerations, a highly irrational influence on the business. Such situations often lead to measures intended to eliminate these influences altogether, as in the incorporation of family businesses.

The tendency to separate the sphere of private affairs from the business is thus not fortuitous. It is a consequence of the fact that, from the point of view of business interest, the interest in maintaining the private resources of the owner is often irrational, as is his interest in income receipts at any given time from the point of view of the profitability of the enterprise. Considerations relevant to the profitability of a business are also not identical with those governing the private interests of persons who are related to it as workers or as consumers. Conversely, the interests growing out of the private fortunes and income of persons or corporate groups having powers of control over an enterprise, do not necessarily lie in the same direction as the long-run considerations of maximizing its profitability and its market position. This is definitely, even especially, true when a profit-making enterprise is controlled by a producers' cooperative association. The objective interests of rational management of a business enterprise and the personal interest of the individuals who control it, are by no means identical and are often opposed. This fact implies the distinction in principle of the budgetary unit and the enterprise, even where both, with respect to powers of control and objects controlled, are identical.

It is essential for purposes of a clear and convenient terminology to maintain a sharp distinction between the budgetary unit and the profit-making enterprise. The purchase of securities on the part of a private investor who wishes to consume the proceeds, is not an investment of capital but of personal resources. A money loan made by a private individual for obtaining the interest is, when regarded from the standpoint of the lender, entirely different from one made by a bank to the same borrower. On the other hand, a loan made to a consumer and one to an entrepreneur for business purposes are quite different from the point of view of the borrower. The bank is investing capital and the entrepreneur is borrowing capital; but in the first case, it may be for the borrower a matter simply of borrowing for purposes of budgetary management; in the second it may be, for the lender, a case of investment of his private resources. This distinction between private resources and capital, between the budgetary unit and the profit-making enterprise, is of far-reaching importance. In particular, without it, it is impossible to understand the economic development of the ancient world and the limitations on the development of capitalism in those times.

3. By no means all profit-making enterprises with capital accounting are doubly oriented to the market in that they both purchase means of production on the market and sell their product there. Tax farming and all sorts of financial operations have been carried on with capital accounting but without selling any products. The very important consequences of this will be discussed later. It is a case of capitalistic profit-making which is not oriented to the market.

4. For reasons of convenience, acquisitive activity and profit-making enterprise have been distinguished. Anyone is engaged in acquisitive activity so far as he seeks, among other things, in given ways to acquire goods—money or others—which he does not yet possess. Thus it includes the official and the worker, no less than the entrepreneur. But the term "profit-making enterprise" will be confined to those types of acquisitive activity which are continually oriented to market advantages by virtue of the fact that goods are used as means to secure profit, either (a) through the production and sale of goods in demand, or (b) through the offer of services in demand in exchange for money, which may occur through free exchange or through the exploitation of appropriated advantages, as has been pointed out above. The person who is a mere investor is, in the present terminology, not engaged in profit-making, no matter how rationally he administers his resources.

5. It goes without saying that in terms of economic theory the direction in which goods can be profitably produced by profit-making enterprises is determined by their marginal utilities for final consumers in conjunction with the latter's incomes. But from a sociological point of view, it should not be forgotten that, to a large extent, in a capitalistic economy (a) new wants are created and others allowed to disappear and (b) capitalistic enterprises, through their aggressive advertising policies, exercise an important influence on the demand functions of consumers. Indeed, these are essential traits of a capitalistic economy. It is true that this does not apply primarily to wants of the highest degree of necessity, but even types of food provision and housing are importantly determined by the producers in a capitalistic economy.

# *4. Industrial Organization*

BY ALFRED MARSHALL

WRITERS on social science from the time of Plato downwards have delighted to dwell on the increased efficiency which labour derives from organization. But in this, as in other cases, Adam Smith gave a new and larger significance to an old doctrine, by the philosophic thoroughness with which he explained it, and the practical knowledge with which he illustrated it. After insisting on the advantages of the division of labour, and pointing out how they render it possible for increased numbers to live in comfort on a limited territory, he argued that the pressure of population on the means of subsistence tends to weed out those races who through want of organization or for any other cause are unable to turn to the best account the advantages of the place in which they live.

Reprinted from Alfred Marshall, *Principles of Economics* (London: Macmillan & Co., 1890), I, 300–1, 310–11, 314–17, 318–19, 322–25, 339–42, 344–46, 353–56, 359–66, 368–73.

Before Adam Smith's book had yet found many readers, biologists were already beginning to make great advances towards understanding the real nature of the differences in organization which separate the higher from the lower animals; and before two more generations had elapsed Malthus' historical account of man's struggle for existence set Darwin thinking as to the effects of the struggle for existence in the animal world. Since that time biology has more than repaid her debt; and economists have in their turn owed much to the many profound analogies which have been discovered between social and especially industrial organization on the one side, and the physical organization of the higher animals on the other. In a few cases indeed the apparent analogies disappeared on closer inquiry: but many of those which seemed at first sight most fanciful, have gradually been supplemented by others, and have at last established their claim to illustrate a fundamental unity of action between the laws of nature in the physical and in the moral world. This central unity is set forth in the general rule, to which there are not very many exceptions, that the development of the organism, whether social or physical, involves a greater subdivision of functions between its separate parts on the one hand, and on the other a more intimate connection between them. Each part gets to be less and less self-sufficient, to depend for its well-being more and more on other parts, so that no change can take place in any part of a highly developed organism without affecting others also.

This increased subdivision of functions, or "differentiation" as it is called, manifests itself with regard to industry in such forms as the division of labour, and the development of specialized skill, knowledge and machinery: while "integration," that is, a growing intimacy and firmness of the connections between the separate parts of the industrial organism, shows itself in such forms as the increase of security of commercial credit, and of the means and habits of communication by sea and road, by railway and telegraph, by post and printing-press.

* * *

## *The Division of Labour and the Influence of Machinery*

The first condition of an efficient organization of industry is that it should keep every one employed at such work as his abilities and training fit him to do well, and should equip him with the best machinery and other appliances for his work. We shall leave on one side for the present the distribution of functions between those who carry out the details of production on the one hand, and those who manage its general arrangement and undertake its risks on the other; and confine ourselves to the division of labour between different classes of operations, with special reference to the influence of machinery. In the following chapter we shall consider the reciprocal effects of division of labour and localization of industry; in a third chapter we shall inquire how far the advantages of division of labour depend upon the aggregation of large capitals into the hands of single individuals or firms, or, as is commonly said, on production on a large scale; and lastly we shall examine the growing specialization of the work of business management.

Every one is familiar with the fact that "practice makes perfect," that it enables an operation, which at first seemed difficult, to be done after a time with comparatively little exertion, and yet much better than before; and physiology in some measure explains this fact. For it gives reasons for believing that the change is due to the gradual growth of new habits of more or less "reflex" or automatic action. Perfectly reflex actions, such as that of breathing during sleep, are performed by the responsibility of the local nerve centres without any reference to the supreme central authority of the thinking power, which is supposed to reside in the cerebrum. But all deliberate movements require the attention of the chief central authority: it receives information from the nerve centres or local authorities and perhaps in some cases direct from the sentient nerves, and sends back detailed and complex instructions to the local authorities or in some cases direct to muscular nerves, and so co-ordinates their action as to bring about the required results.

* * *

Again, in the wood and the metal industries, a man who has to perform exactly the same operations over and over again on the same piece of material gets into the habit of holding it exactly in the way in which it is wanted, and of arranging the tools and other things which he has to handle in such positions that he is able to bring them to work on one another with the least possible loss of time and of force in the movements of his own body. Accustomed to find them always in the same position and to take them in the same order, his hands work in harmony with one another almost automatically: and as his practice increases, his expenditure of nervous force diminishes even more rapidly than his expenditure of muscular force. But when the action has thus been reduced to routine it has nearly arrived at the stage at which it can be taken over by machinery. The chief difficulty to be overcome is that of getting the machinery to hold the material firmly in exactly the position in which the machine tool can be brought to bear on it in the right way, and without wasting meanwhile too much time in taking grip of it. But this can generally be contrived when it is worth while to spend some labour and expense on it; and then the whole operation can often be controlled by a worker who, sitting before the machine, takes with the left hand a piece of wood or metal from a heap and puts it in a socket, while with the right he draws down a lever, or in some other way sets the machine tool at work, and finally with his left hand throws on to another heap the material which has been cut or punched or drilled or planed exactly after a given pattern. It is in these industries especially that we find the reports of modern trades unions to be full of complaints that unskilled labourers, and even their wives and children, are put to do work which used to require the skill and judgment of a trained mechanic, but which has been reduced to mere routine by the improvement of machinery and the ever-increasing minuteness of the subdivision of labour.

We are thus led to a general rule, the action of which is more prominent in some branches of manufacture than others, but which applies to all. It is, that any manufacturing operation that can be reduced to uniformity, so that exactly the same thing has to be done over and over again in the same way, is sure to be taken over sooner or later by machinery. There may be delays and difficulties; but if the work to be done by it is on a sufficient scale, money and inventive power will be spent without stint on the task till it is achieved.

New machinery, when just invented, generally requires a great deal of care and attention. But the work of its attendant is always being sifted; that which is uniform and monotonous is gradually taken over by the machine, which thus becomes steadily more and more automatic and self-acting; till at last there is nothing for the hand to do, but to supply the material at certain intervals and to take away the work when finished. There still remains the responsibility for seeing that the machinery is in good order and working smoothly; but even this task is often made light by the introduction of an automatic movement, which brings the machine to a stop the instant anything goes wrong.

Nothing could be more narrow or monotonous than the occupation of a weaver of plain stuffs in the old time. But now one woman will manage four or more looms, each of which does many times as much work in the course of the day as the old hand loom did; and her work is much less monotonous and calls for much more judgment than his did. So that for every hundred yards of cloth that are woven, the purely monotonous work done by human beings is probably not a twentieth part of what it was.

Thus the two movements of the improvement of machinery and the growing subdivision of labour have gone together and are in some measure connected. But the connection is not so close as is generally supposed. It is the largeness of markets, the increased demand for great numbers of things of the same kind, and in some cases of things made with great accuracy, that leads to subdivision of labour; the chief effect of the improvement of machinery is to cheapen and make more accurate the work which would anyhow have been subdivided. For instance, "in organizing the works at Soho, Boulton and Watt found it necessary to carry division of labour to the furthest practical point. There were no slide-lathes, planing machines or boring tools, such as now render mechanical accuracy of construction almost a matter of certainty. Everything depended on the individual mechanic's accuracy of hand and eye; yet mechanics generally were much less skilled then than they are now. The way in which Boulton and Watt contrived partially to get over the difficulty was to confine their workmen to special classes of work, and make them as expert in them as possible. By continued practice in handling the same tools and fabricating the same articles, they thus acquired great individual proficiency." Thus machinery constantly supplants and renders unnecessary that purely manual skill, the attainment of which was, even up to Adam Smith's time, the chief advantage of division of labour. But this influence is more than countervailed by its tendency to increase the scale of manufactures and to make them more complex; and therefore to increase the opportunities for division of labour of all kinds, and especially in the matter of business management.

* * *

The influences which machinery exerts over the character of modern industry are well illustrated in the manufacture of watches. A few years ago the chief seat of this business was in French Switzerland; where the subdivision of labour was carried far, though a great part of the work was done by a more or less scattered population. There were about fifty distinct branches of trade each of which did one small part of the work. In almost all of them a highly specialized manual skill was required, but very little judgment; the earnings were generally low, because the trade had been established too long for those in it to have anything like a monopoly, and there was no difficulty in bringing up to it any child with ordinary intelligence. But this industry is now yielding ground to the American system of making watches by machinery, which requires very little specialized manual skill. In fact the machinery is becoming every year more and more automatic, and is getting to require less and less assistance from the human hand. But the more delicate the machine's power, the greater is the judgment and carefulness which is called for from those who see after it. Take for instance a beautiful machine which feeds itself with steelwire at one end, and delivers at the other tiny screws of exquisite form; it displaces a great many operatives who had indeed acquired a very high and specialized manual skill, but who lived sedentary lives, straining their eyesight through microscopes, and finding in their work very little scope for any faculty except a mere command over the use of their fingers. But the machine is intricate and costly, and the person who minds it must have an intelligence, and an energetic sense of responsibility, which go a long way towards making a fine character; and which, though more common than they were, are yet sufficiently rare to be able to earn a very high rate of pay. No doubt this is an extreme case; and the greater part of the work done in a watch factory is much simpler. But a great deal of it requires higher faculties than the old system did, and those engaged in it earn on the average higher wages; at the same time that it has already brought the price of a trustworthy watch within the range of the poorest classes of the community and is showing signs of being able soon to accomplish the very highest class of work.

* * *

Now looking at all this we are struck on the one hand by the power of mechanical and scientific appliances to attain results that would be impossible without them: and on the other hand by the persistent way in which they take over work that used to require manual skill and dexterity, but not much judgment; while they leave for man's hand all those parts which do require the use of judgment, and open up all sorts of new occupations in which there is a great demand for it. Every improvement and cheapening of the printer's appliances increases the demand for the judgment and discretion and literary knowledge of the reader, for the skill and taste of those who know how to set up a good title page, or how to make ready a sheet on which an engraving is to be printed, so that light and shade will be distributed properly. It increases the demand for the gifted and highly-trained artists who draw or engrave on wood and stone and metal, and for those who know how to give an accurate report in ten lines of the substance of a speech that occupied ten minutes—an intellectual feat the difficulty of which we underrate, because it is so frequently performed. And again, it tends to increase the work of photographers and electrotypers, and stereotypers, of the makers of printer's machinery, and many others who get a higher training and a higher income from their work than did those layers on and takers off, and those folders of newspapers who have found their work taken over by iron fingers and iron arms.

We may now pass to consider the effects which machinery has in relieving that excessive muscular strain which a few generations ago was the common lot of more than half the working men even in such a country as England. The most marvellous instances of the power of machinery are seen in large iron works, and especially in those for making armour plates, where the force to be exerted is so great that man's muscles count for nothing, and where every movement, whether horizontal or vertical, has to be effected by hydraulic or steam force, and man stands by governing the machinery and occasionally clearing away ashes or performing some such secondary task. Machinery of this class has increased our command over nature, but it has not directly altered the character of man's work very much; for that which it does he could not have done without it. Let us then look at work such as that of house carpenters who make things of the same kind as those used by our forefathers, but with much less toil for themselves. They now give themselves chiefly to those parts of the task which are most pleasant and most interesting; while in every country town and almost every village there are found steam mills for sawing, planing and moulding, which relieve them of that grievous fatigue which not very long ago used to make them prematurely old.

Facts of this kind are to be found in the recent history of many trades: and they are of great importance when we are considering the way in which the modern organization of industry is tending to narrow the scope of each person's work, and thereby to render it monotonous. For those trades in which the work is most subdivided are those in which the chief muscular strain is most certain to be taken off by machinery; and thus the chief evil of monotonous work is much diminished. As Roscher says, it is monotony of life much more than monotony of work that is to be dreaded: monotony of work is an evil of the first order only when it involves monotony of life. Now when a person's employment requires much physical exertion, he is fit for nothing after his work; and unless his mental faculties are called forth in his work, they have little chance of being developed at all. But the nervous force is not very much exhausted in the ordinary work of a factory, at all events where there is not excessive noise, and where the hours of labour are not too long. The social surroundings in the factory and out of it stimulate mental activity; and even those workers in it whose occupations are seemingly the most monotonous have much more intelligence and mental resource than has been shown by the English agricultural labourer whose employment has more variety. It is true that the American agriculturist is an able man, and that his children rise rapidly in the world. But he has had better social conditions than the English; he has always had to think for himself, and has long had to use and to repair complex machines; and the English agricultural labourer is following in his steps, and is steadily improving his position.

Perhaps the textile industries afford the best instance of work that used to be done by hand and is now done by machinery. They are especially prominent in England, where they give employment to nearly half a million males and more than half a million females, or more than one in ten of those persons who are earning independent incomes. The strain that is taken off human muscles in dealing even with those soft materials is shewn by the fact that for every one of these million operatives there is used about one horse-power of steam, that is, about ten times as much as they would themselves exert if they were all strong men; and the history of these industries will serve to remind us that many of those who perform the more monotonous parts of manufacturing work are as a rule not skilled workers who have come down to it from a higher class of work, but unskilled workers who have risen to it. A great number of those who work in the Lancashire cotton mills have come there from poverty-stricken districts of Ireland, while others are the descendants of paupers and people of weak physique, who were sent there in large numbers early in the century from the most miserable conditions of life in the poorest agricultural districts, where the labourers were fed and housed almost worse than the animals whom they tended. Again, when regret is expressed that the cotton factory hands of New England have not the high standard of culture which prevailed among them a century ago, we must remember that the descendants of those factory workers have moved up to higher and more responsible posts, and include many of the ablest and wealthiest of the citizens of America. Those who have taken their places are in the process of being raised; they are chiefly French Canadians and Irish, who though they may learn in their new homes some of the vices of civilization, are yet much better off and have on the whole better opportunities of developing the higher faculties of themselves and their children than they had in their old homes.

But passing from this inquiry we must proceed to consider what are the conditions under which the economies in production arising from division of labour can best be secured. It is obvious that the efficiency of specialized machinery or specialized skill is but one condition of its economic use; the other is that sufficient work should be found to keep it well employed. As Babbage pointed out, in a large factory "the master manufacturer by dividing the work to be executed into different processes, each requiring different degrees of skill or force, can purchase exactly that precise quantity of both which is necessary for each process; whereas if the whole work were executed by one workman that person must possess sufficient skill to perform the most difficult and sufficient strength to execute the most laborious of the operations into which the work is divided." And it is to be noticed that the economy of production requires not only that each person should be employed constantly in a narrow range of work, but also that, when it is necessary for him to undertake different tasks, each of these tasks should be such as to call forth as much as possible of his skill and ability. Just in the same way the economy of machinery requires that a powerful turning-lathe when specially arranged for one class of work should be kept employed as long as possible on that work; and if after all it is necessary to employ it on other work, that should be such as to be worthy of the lathe, and not such as could have been done equally well by a much smaller machine.

Here then, so far as the economy of production goes, men and machines stand on much the same footing: but while machinery is a mere implement of production, man's welfare is also its ultimate aim. We have already been occupied with the question whether the human race as a whole gains by carrying to an extreme that specialization of function which causes all the most difficult work to be done by a few people: but we have now to consider it more nearly with special reference to the work of business management. The main drift of the next three chapters is to inquire what are the causes which make different forms of business management the fittest to profit by their environment, and the most likely to prevail over others; but it is well that meanwhile we should have in our minds the question, how far they are severally fitted to benefit their environment.

Many of those economies in the use of specialized skill and machinery which are commonly regarded as within the reach of very large establishments, can be secured in a great measure by the concentration of many small businesses of a similar character in particular localities: or, as is commonly said, by the localization of industry. This subject has such important bearings on much of our future work, that it will be worth while to study it with some care.

## *The Concentration of Specialized Industries in Particular Localities*

In an early stage of civilization every place had to depend on its own resources for most of the heavy wares which it consumed; unless indeed it happened to have special facilities for water carriage. But the slowness with which customs changed, made it easy for producers to meet the wants of consumers with whom they had but very little communication; and it enabled comparatively poor people to buy a few expensive goods from a distance, in the security that they would add to the pleasure of festivals and holidays during a life time, or perhaps even during two or three life times. Consequently the lighter and more expensive articles of dress and personal adornment, together with spices and some kinds of metal implements used by all classes, and many other things for the special use of the rich, often came from astonishing distances. Some of these were produced only in a few places, or even only in one place; and they were diffused all over Europe partly by the agency of fairs and professional pedlars, and partly by the producers themselves, who would vary their work by travelling on foot for many thousand miles to sell their goods and see the world. These sturdy travellers took on themselves the risks of their little businesses; they enabled the production of certain classes of goods to be kept on the right track for satisfying the needs of purchasers far away; and they created new wants among consumers, by showing them at fairs or at their own houses new goods from a distant land.

This concentration of special groups of industry in particular localities, or the "localization of industry" as it is commonly called, began at an early stage in the world's history; and gradually prepared the way for many of the modern developments of division of labour in the mechanical arts and in the task of business management. Even now we find industries of a primitive fashion localized in retired villages of central Europe, and sending their simple wares even to the busiest haunts of modern industry. In Russia the expansion of a family group into a village has often been the cause of a localized industry; and there are an immense number of villages each of which carries on only one branch of production, or even only a part of one. There are for instance over 500 villages devoted to various branches of woodwork; one village makes nothing but spokes for the wheels of vehicles, another nothing but the bodies and so on; and indications of a like state of things are found in the histories of oriental civilizations and in the chronicles of mediæval Europe.

The causes by which localized industries have been originated are various. But the chief of them have been physical conditions; such as the character of the climate and the soil, of mines and quarries in the neighbourhood, or within easy access by land or water. Thus metallic industries have generally been either near mines or in places where fuel was cheap. The iron industries in England first sought those districts in which charcoal was plentiful, and afterwards they went to the neighbourhood of collieries. Staffordshire makes many kinds of pottery, all the materials of which are imported from a long distance; but she has cheap coal and excellent clay for making the heavy "seggars" or boxes in which the pottery is placed while being fired. Straw plaiting has its chief home in Bedfordshire, where straw has just the right proportion of silex to give strength without brittleness; and Buckinghamshire beeches have afforded the material for the Wycombe chairmaking. The Sheffield cutlery trade is due chiefly to the excellent grit of which its grindstones are made.

Another chief cause has been the patronage of a court. The rich folk there assembled make a demand for goods of specially high quality, and this attracts skilled workmen from a distance, and educates those on the spot. When an Eastern potentate changed his residence—and, partly for sanitary reasons, this was constantly done—the deserted town was apt to take refuge in the development of a specialized industry, which had owed its origin to the presence of the court. But very often the rulers deliberately invited artisans from a distance and settled them in a group together. Thus the mechanical faculty of Lancashire is said to be due to the influence of Norman smiths who were settled at Warrington by Hugo de Lupus in William the Conqueror's time. While the greater part of England's manufacturing industry before the era of cotton and steam had its course directed by settlements of Flemish and Huguenot artisans; many of which were made under the immediate direction of Plantagenet and Tudor kings. These immigrants taught us how to weave woollen and worsted stuffs, though for a long time we sent our cloths to the Netherlands to be fulled and dyed. They taught us how to cure herrings, how to manufacture silk, how to make lace, glass, and paper, and to provide for many other of our wants.

But how did these immigrants learn their skill? Their ancestors had no doubt profited by the traditional arts of earlier civilizations on the shores of the Mediterranean and in the far East: for nearly all important knowledge has long deep roots stretching downwards to distant times; and so widely spread have been these roots, so ready to send up shoots of vigorous life, that there is perhaps no part of the old world in which there might not long ago have flourished many beautiful and highly skilled industries, if their growth had been favoured by the character of the people, and by their social and political institutions. This accident or that may have determined whether a particular industry flourished in any one town; the industrial character of a whole country even may have been largely influenced by the richness of her soil and her mines, and her facilities for commerce. Such natural advantages may themselves have stimulated free industry and enterprise: but it is the existence of these last, by whatever means they may have been promoted, which has been the supreme condition for the growth of noble forms of the arts of life. In sketching the history of free industry and enterprise we have already incidentally traced the outlines of the causes which have localized the industrial leadership of the world now in this country and now in that. We have seen how physical nature acts on man's energies, how he is stimulated by an invigorating climate, and how he is encouraged to bold ventures by the opening out of rich fields for his work: but we have also seen how the use he makes of these advantages depends on his ideals of life, and how inextricably therefore the religious, political and economic threads of the world's history are interwoven; while together they have been bent this way or that by great political events and the influence of the strong personalities of individuals.

The causes which determine the economic progress of nations will require further study when we come to discuss the problems of international trade. But for the present we must turn aside from these broader movements of the localization of industry; and follow the fortunes of groups of skilled workers who are gathered within the narrow boundaries of a manufacturing town or a thickly peopled industrial district.

When then an industry has once chosen a locality for itself, it is likely to stay there long: so great are the advantages which people following the same skilled trade get from near neighbourhood to one another. The mysteries of the trade become no mysteries; but are as it were in the air, and children learn many of them unconsciously. Good work is rightly appreciated, inventions and improvements in machinery, in processes and the general organization of the business have their merits promptly discussed; if one man starts a new idea it is taken up by others and combined with suggestions of their own; and thus becomes the source of yet more new ideas.

And subsidiary trades grow up in the neighbourhood, supplying it with implements and materials, organizing its traffic, and in many ways conducing to the economy of its material.

Again the economic use of expensive machinery can sometimes be attained in a very high degree in a district in which there is a large aggregate production of the same kind, even though no individual capital employed in the trade be very large. For subsidiary industries devoting themselves each to one small branch of the process of production, and working it for a great many of their neighbours, are able to keep in constant use machinery of the most highly specialized character; and to make it pay its expenses, though its original cost may have been high, and its rate of depreciation very rapid.

Again, in all but the earliest stages of economic development a localized industry gains a great advantage from the fact that it offers a constant market for skill. Employers are apt to resort to any place where they are likely to find a good choice of workers with the special skill which they require; while men seeking employment naturally go to places where they expect to find a good market for their skill, in consequence of the presence of many employers who require its aid. The owner of an isolated factory is often put to great shifts for want of some special skilled labour which has suddenly run short; and a skilled workman, when thrown out of employment in it, has no easy refuge. Social forces here co-operate with economic: there are often strong friendships between employers and employed; but neither side likes to feel that in case of any disagreeable incident happening between them, they must go on rubbing against one another: both sides like to be able easily to break off old associations should they become irksome. These difficulties are still very great, though they are being diminished by the railway, the printing press and the telegraph.

On the other hand a localized industry has some disadvantages as a market for labour if the work done in it is chiefly of one kind, such for instance as can be done only by strong men. In those iron districts in which there are no textile or other factories to give employment to women and children, wages are high and the cost of labour dear to the employer, while the average money earnings of each family are low. But the remedy for this evil is obvious, and is found in the growth in the same neighbourhood of industries of a supplementary character. Thus textile industries are constantly found congregated in the neighbourhood of mining and engineering industries, in some cases having been attracted by almost imperceptible steps; in others, as for instance at Barrow, having been started deliberately on a large scale in order to give variety of employment in a place where previously there had been but little demand for the work of women and children.

The advantages of variety of employment are combined with those of localized industries in some of our manufacturing towns, and this is a chief cause of their continued growth. But on the other hand the value which the central sites of a large town have for trading purposes, enables them to command much higher ground-rents than the situations are worth for factories, even when account is taken of this combination of advantages: and there is a similar competition for dwelling space between the employés of the trading houses, and the factory workers. The result is that factories now congregate in the outskirts of large towns and in manufacturing districts in their neighbourhood rather than in the towns themselves.

A district which is dependent chiefly on one industry is liable to extreme depression, in case of a falling off in the demand for its produce, or of a failure in the supply of the raw material which it uses. This evil again is in a great measure avoided by those large towns, or large industrial districts in which several distinct industries are strongly developed. If one of them fails for a time, the others are likely to support it in many ways, chiefly indirect; one of these being that they keep in heart the local shopkeepers, who are thus enabled to continue their assistance longer than they otherwise could, to the work-people in those trades that happen to be depressed.

Every cheapening of the means of communication, every new facility for the free interchange of ideas between distant places alters the action of the forces which tend to localize industries. Speaking generally we may say that a lowering of tariffs, or of freights for the transport of goods, tends to make each locality buy more largely from a distance what it requires; and thus tends to concentrate particular industries in special localities: but on the other hand every thing that increases people's readiness to migrate from one place to another, tends to bring skilled artisans to ply their crafts near to the consumers who will purchase their wares. These two opposing tendencies are well illustrated by the recent history of the English people.

On the one hand the steady cheapening of freights, the opening of railways from the agricultural districts of America and India to the seaboard, and the adoption by England of a free-trade policy, have led to a great increase in her importation of raw produce. But on the other hand the growing cheapness, rapidity and comfort of foreign travel, are inducing her trained business men and her skilled artisans to pioneer the way for new industries in other lands, and to help them to manufacture for themselves goods which they have been wont to buy from England. English mechanics have taught people in almost every part of the world how to use English machinery, and even how to make the machinery like it; and English miners have opened out mines of ore which have diminished the foreign demand for many of England's products.

One of the most striking movements towards the specialization of a country's industries, which history records, is the rapid increase of the non-agricultural population of England in recent times.

## *Production on a Large Scale*

The advantages of production on a large scale are best shown in manufacture; under which head we may include all businesses engaged in working up material into forms in which it will be adapted for sale in distant markets: the characteristic of manufacturing industries which makes them offer generally the best illustrations of the advantages of production on a large scale, is their power of choosing freely the locality in which they will do their work. They are thus contrasted on the one hand with agriculture and other extractive industries, (mining, quarrying, fishing etc.), the geographical distribution of which is determined by nature; and on the other hand with industries that make or repair things to suit the special needs of individual consumers, from whom they cannot be far removed, at all events without great loss.

The chief advantages of production on a large scale are economy of skill, economy of machinery and economy of materials: but the last of these is rapidly losing importance relatively to the other two. It is true that an isolated workman often throws away a number of small things which would have been collected and turned to good account in a factory; but waste of this kind can scarcely occur in a localized manufacture even if it is in the hands of small men; and there is not very much of it in any branch of industry in modern England, except perhaps in agriculture and in domestic cooking. No doubt many of the most important advances of recent years have been due to the utilizing of what had been a waste product; but this has been generally due to a distinct invention, either chemical or mechanical, the use of which has been indeed promoted by minute subdivision of labour, but has not been directly dependent on it. Again it is true that when a hundred suits of furniture, or of clothing, have to be cut out on exactly the same pattern, it is worth while to spend great care on so planning the cutting out of the boards or the cloth, that only a few small pieces are wasted. But this is properly an economy of skill; one planning is made to suffice for many tasks, and therefore can be done well and carefully. We may pass then to the economy of machinery.

In spite of the aid which subsidiary industries can give to small manufactures, where many in the same branch of trade are collected in one neighbourhood, they are still placed under a great disadvantage by the growing variety and expensiveness of machinery. For in a large establishment there are often many expensive machines each made specially for one small use. Each of them requires space in a good light, and thus stands for something considerable in the rent and general expenses of the factory; and independently of interest and the expense of keeping it in repair a heavy allowance must be made for depreciation in consequence of its being probably improved upon before long. A small manufacturer must therefore have many things done by hand or by imperfect machinery, though he knows how to have them done better and cheaper by special machinery, if only he could find constant employment for it.

But next, a small manufacturer may not always be acquainted with the best machinery for his purpose. It is true that if the industry in which he is engaged has been long established on a large scale, his machinery will be well up to the mark, provided he can afford to buy the best in the market. In agriculture and the cotton industries for instance, improvements in machinery are devised almost exclusively by machine makers, and are accessible to all, at any rate on paying a royalty for patent right. But this is not the case in industries that are as yet in an early stage of development or are rapidly changing their form; such as the chemical industries, the watchmaking industry and some branches of the jute and silk manufactures; and in a host of trades that are constantly springing up to supply some new want or to work up some new material.

In all such trades new machinery and new processes are for the greater part devised by manufacturers for their own use. Each new departure is an experiment which may fail; those which succeed must pay for themselves and for the failure of others; and though a small manufacturer may think he sees his way to an improvement, he must reckon on having to work it out tentatively, at considerable risk and expense and with much interruption to his other work; and even if he should be able to perfect it, he is not likely to be able to make the most of it. For instance, he may have devised a new specialty, which would get a large sale if it could be brought under general notice: but to do this would perhaps cost many thousand pounds; and if so he will probably have to turn his back on it. For it is almost impossible for him to discharge, what Roscher calls the characteristic task of the modern manufacturer, that of creating new wants by showing people something which they had never thought of having before; but which they want to have as soon as the notion is suggested to them. In the pottery trade for example the small manufacturer cannot afford even to make experiments with new patterns and designs except in a very tentative way. His chance is better with regard to an improvement in making things for which there is already a good market. But even here he cannot get the full benefit of his invention unless he patents it; and sells the right to use it; or borrows some capital and extends his business; or lastly changes the character of his business and devotes his capital to that particular stage of the manufacture to which his improvement applies. But after all such cases are exceptional: the growth of machinery in variety and expensiveness presses hard on the small manufacturer everywhere. It has already driven him completely out of some trades and is fast driving him out of others.

* * *

The large manufacturer has a much better chance than a small one has, of getting hold of men with exceptional natural abilities, to do the most difficult part of his work—that on which the reputation of his establishment chiefly depends. This is occasionally important as regards mere handiwork in trades which require much taste and originality, as for instance that of a house decorator, and in those which require exceptionally fine workmanship, as for instance that of a manufacturer of delicate mechanism. But in most businesses, its chief importance lies in the facilities which it gives to the employer for the selection of able and tried men, men whom he trusts and who trust him, to be his foremen and heads of departments. We are thus brought to the central problem of the modern organization of industry, viz. that which relates to the advantages and disadvantages of the subdivision of the work of business management.

The head of a large business can reserve all his strength for the broadest and most fundamental problems of his trade: he must indeed assure himself that his managers, clerks and foremen are the right men for their work, and are doing their work well; but beyond this he need not trouble himself much about details. He can keep his mind fresh and clear for thinking out the most difficult and vital problems of his business; for studying the broader movements of the markets, the yet undeveloped results of current events at home and abroad; and for contriving how to improve the organization of the internal and external relations of his business.

For much of this work the small employer has not the time if he has the ability; he cannot take so broad a survey of his trade, or look so far ahead; he must often be content to follow the lead of others. And yet he must spend much of his time on work that is below him; for if he is to succeed at all, he must have a good deal of originating and organizing force; his mind must be in some respects of a high quality; and his strength is wasted when he occupies himself, as he must do to a great extent, with easy but tedious routine work.

On the other hand the small employer has great advantages of his own. The master's eye is everywhere; there is no shirking by his foremen or workmen. Again by keeping things himself under lock and key, and in other ways, he can save much of the book-keeping, and nearly all of the cumbrous system of checks that are necessary in the business of a large firm. The gain from this source is of very great importance in trades which use the more valuable metals and other expensive materials.

And though he must always remain at a great disadvantage in getting information and in making experiments; yet in this matter the general course of progress is on his side. For newspapers, and trade and technical publications of all kinds are perpetually scouting for him and bringing him much of the knowledge he wants—knowledge which a little while ago would have been beyond the reach of anyone who could not afford to have well-paid agents in many distant parts. Again it is to his interest also that the secrecy of business is on the whole diminishing, and that the most important improvements in method seldom remain secret for long after they have passed from the experimental stage. It is to his advantage that changes in manufacture depend less on mere rules of thumb and more on broad developments of scientific principle; and that many of these are made by students in the pursuit of knowledge for its own sake, and are promptly published in the general interest. Although therefore the small manufacturer can seldom be in the front of the race of progress, he need not be far from it, if he has the time and the ability for availing himself of the modern facilities for obtaining knowledge. But it is true that he must be exceptionally strong if he can do this without neglecting the minor but necessary details of the business.

* * *

## *Business Management*

Business may be taken to include all provision for the wants of others which is made in the expectation of payment direct or indirect from those who are to be benefitted. It is thus contrasted with the provision for our own wants which each of us makes for himself, and with those kindly services which are prompted by family affection and the desire to promote the well-being of others. Business management or undertaking has always had many different forms, and their number and variety was never so great as in England now. Relics remain of almost every form that has ever been in use; while new forms are constantly being developed.

The primitive handicraftsman managed his whole business for himself; but since his customers were with few exceptions his immediate neighbours, since he required very little capital, since the plan of production was arranged for him by custom, and since he had no labour to superintend outside of his own household, these tasks did not involve any very great mental strain. He was far from enjoying unbroken prosperity; war and scarcity were constantly pressing on him and his neighbours, hindering his work and stopping their demand for his wares. But he was inclined to take good and evil fortune, like sunshine and rain, as things beyond his control: his fingers worked on, but his brain was seldom weary.

Even in modern England we find now and then a village artisan who adheres to primitive methods, and makes things on his own account for sale to his neighbours; managing his own business and undertaking all its risks. But such cases are rare: the most striking instances of an adherence to old-fashioned methods of business are supplied by the learned professions; for a physician or a solicitor manages as a rule his own business and does all its work. This plan is not without its disadvantages: much valuable activity is wasted or turned to but slight account by some professional men of first-rate ability, who have not the special aptitude required for obtaining a business connection; they would be better paid, would lead happier lives, and would do more good service for the world if their work could be arranged for them by some sort of a middleman. But yet on the whole things are probably best as they are: there are sound reasons behind the popular instinct which distrusts the intrusion of the middleman in the supply of those services which require the highest and most delicate mental qualities, and which can have their full value only when there is complete personal confidence.

English solicitors however act, if not as employers or undertakers, yet as agents for hiring that branch of the legal profession which ranks highest, and whose work involves the hardest mental strain. Again many of the best instructors of youths sell their services, not directly to the consumer, but to the governing body of a college or school, or to a head master, who arranges for their purchase: the employer supplies to the teacher a market for his labour; and is supposed to give to the purchaser, who may not be a good judge himself, some sort of guarantee as to the quality of the teaching supplied.

Again, artists of every kind, however eminent, often find it to their advantage to employ some one else to arrange for them with customers; while those of less established repute are sometimes dependent for their living on capitalist traders, who are not themselves artists, but who understand how to sell artistic work to the best advantage.

But we have already seen how unsuitable the primitive pattern is for the greater part of the business of the modern world. The task of directing production so that a given effort may be most effective in supplying human wants is so difficult under the complex conditions of modern life, that it has to be broken up and given into the hands of a specialized body of employers, or to use a more general term, of business men; who "adventure" or "undertake" its risks; who bring together the capital and the labour required for the work; who arrange or "engineer" its general plan, and who superintend its minor details. Looking at business men from one point of view we may regard them as a highly skilled industrial grade, from another as middlemen intervening between the manual worker and the consumer.

There are some kinds of business men who undertake great risks, and exercise a large influence over the welfare both of the producers and of the consumers of the wares in which they deal, but who are not to any considerable extent direct employers of labour. The extreme type of these is the dealer on the stock exchange or the produce markets, whose daily purchases and sales are of vast dimensions, and who yet has neither factory nor warehouse, but at most an office with a few clerks in it. The good and the evil effects of the action of speculators such as these are however so complex themselves, and are so intimately interwoven with fluctuations of commercial credit and the changes of the money market that they cannot be conveniently discussed in this place. It is true that there is an element of speculation in almost every kind of business: but in this early stage of our inquiry it is best that we should give our chief attention to those forms of business in which administration counts for most and the subtler forms of speculation for least. Let us then take some illustrations of the more common types of business, and watch the relations in which the undertaking of risks stands to the rest of the work of the business man.

The building trade will serve our purpose well, partly because it adheres in some respects to primitive methods of business, Late in the Middle Ages it was quite common for a private person to build a house for himself without the aid of a master builder; and the habit is not even now altogether extinct. A person who undertakes his own building must hire separately all his workmen, he must watch their work and check their demands for payment; he must buy his materials from many quarters, and he must dispense with the use of expensive machinery unless he happens to be able to hire it. In the result he probably pays more than the current wages; but as others gain what he loses, there is no resultant waste so far. There is however great waste in the time he spends in bargaining with the men and testing and directing their work by his imperfect knowledge; and again in the time that he spends in finding out what kinds and quantities he wants of different materials, and where to get them best, and so on. This waste is avoided by that division of labour which assigns to the professional builder the task of superintending details, and to the professional architect the task of drawing plans.

The division of labour is often carried still further when houses are built not at the expense of those who are to live in them, but as a building speculation. When this is done on a large scale, as for instance in opening out a new suburb, the stakes at issue are so large as to offer an attractive field to powerful capitalists with a very high order of general business ability, but perhaps with not much technical knowledge of the building trade. They rely on their own judgment of the decision as to what are likely to be the coming relations of demand and supply for different kinds of houses; but they intrust to others the management of details. They employ architects and surveyors to make plans in accordance with their general directions; and then enter in to contracts with professional builders for carrying them out. But they themselves undertake the chief risks of the business, and control its general direction.

* * *

When the profits of business are under discussion they are generally connected in people's minds with the employer of labour: "the employer" is often taken as a term practically coextensive with the receiver of business profits. But the instances which we have just considered are sufficient to illustrate the truth that the superintendence of labour is but one side, and often not the most important side of business work; and that the employer who undertakes the whole risks of his business really performs two entirely distinct services on behalf of the community, and requires a twofold ability.

The ideal manufacturer for instance, if he makes goods not to meet special orders but for the general market, must, in his first rôle as merchant and organizer of production, have a thorough knowledge of *things* in his own trade. He must have the power of forecasting the broad movements of production and consumption, of seeing where there is an opportunity for supplying a new commodity that will meet a real want or improving the plan of producing an old commodity. He must be able to judge cautiously and undertake risks boldly; and he must of course understand the materials and machinery used in his trade.

But secondary in his rôle of employer he must be a natural leader of *men*. He must have a power of first choosing his assistants rightly and then trusting them fully; of interesting them in the business and of getting them to trust him, so as to bring out whatever enterprise and power of origination there is in them; while he himself exercises a general control over everything, and preserves order and unity in the main plan of the business.

The abilities required to make an ideal employer are so great and so numerous that very few persons can exhibit them all in a very high degree. Their relative importance however varies with the nature of the industry and the size of the business; and while one employer excels in one set of qualities, another excels in another; scarcely any two owe their success to exactly the same combination of advantages. Some men make their way by the use of none but noble qualities, while others owe their prosperity to qualities in which there is very little that is really admirable except sagacity and strength of purpose.

Such then being the general nature of the work of business management, we have next to inquire what opportunities different classes of people have of developing business ability; and, when they have obtained that, what opportunities they have of getting command over the capital required to give it scope. This inquiry may conveniently be combined with some examination of the different "forms of business management." Hitherto we have considered almost exclusively that form in which the whole responsibility and control rests in the hands of a single individual. But this form is yielding ground to others in which the supreme authority is distributed among several partners or even a great number of shareholders. Private firms and joint stock companies, co-operative societies and public corporations are taking a constantly increasing share in the management of business; and one chief reason of this is that they offer an attractive field to people who have good business abilities, but have not inherited any great business opportunities.

The son of a man already established in business has certainly very great advantages over others. He has from his youth up special facilities for obtaining the knowledge and developing the faculties that are required in the management of his father's business: he learns quietly and almost unconsciously about men and manners in his father's trade and in those from which that trade buys and to which it sells; he gets to know the relative importance and the real significance of the various problems and anxieties which occupy his father's mind: and he acquires a technical knowledge of the processes and the machinery of the trade. Some of what he learns will be applicable only to his father's trade; but the greater part will be serviceable in any trade that is in any way allied with that; while those general faculties of judgment and resource, of enterprise and caution, of firmness and courtesy, which are trained by association with those who control the larger issues of any one trade, will go a long way towards fitting him for managing almost any other trade. Further the sons of successful business men start with more material capital than almost any one else except those who by nurture and education are likely to be disinclined for business and unfitted for it: and if they continue their father's work, they have also the vantage ground of established trade connections. It would therefore at first sight seem likely that business men should constitute a sort of caste; dividing out among their sons the chief posts of command, and founding hereditary dynasties, which should rule certain branches of trade for many generations together. But the actual state of things is very different.

As a matter of fact when a man has got together a great business, his descendants, in spite of all their great advantages, often fail to develop the high abilities and the special turn of mind and temperament required for carrying it on with equal success. He himself was probably brought up by parents of strong earnest character; and was educated by their personal influence and by struggle with difficulties in early life. But his children, at all events if they were born after he became rich, and in any case his grand-children, are perhaps left a good deal to the care of domestic servants who are not of the same strong fibre as the parents by whose influence he was educated. And while his highest ambition was probably success in business, they are likely to be at least equally anxious for social or academic distinction.

For a time indeed all may go well. His sons find a firmly established trade connection and, what is perhaps even more important, a well chosen staff of subordinates with a generous interest in the business. By mere assiduity and caution, availing themselves of the traditions of the firm, they may hold together for a long time. But when a full generation has passed, when the old traditions are no longer a safe guide, and when the bonds that held together the old staff have been dissolved, then the business almost invariably falls to pieces unless it is practically handed over to the management of new men who have meanwhile risen to partnership in the firm.

But in most cases his descendants arrive at this result by a shorter route. They prefer an abundant income coming to them without effort on their part, to one which though twice as large could be earned only by incessant toil and anxiety; and they sell the business to private persons or a joint stock company; or they become sleeping partners in it; that is sharing in its risks and in its profits, but not taking part in its management: in either case the active control over their capital falls chiefly into the hands of new men.

The oldest and simplest plan for renovating the energies of a business is that of taking into partnership some of its ablest employés. The autocratic owner and manager of a large manufacturing or trading concern finds that, as years go on, he has to delegate more and more responsibility to his chief subordinates; partly because the work to be done is growing heavier, and partly because his own strength is becoming less than it was. He still exercises a supreme control, but much must depend on their energy and probity: so, if his sons are not old enough, or for any other reason are not ready to take part of the burden off his shoulders, he decides to stimulate the zeal of one or more of his trusted assistants by taking them into partnership: he thus lightens his own labours, at the same time that he secures that the task of his life will be carried on by those whose habits he has moulded, and for whom he has perhaps acquired something like a fatherly affection. Much of the happiest romance of life, much that is most pleasant to dwell upon in the social history of England from the Middle Ages up to our own day is connected with the story of private partnerships of this class.

But there are now, and there always have been private partnerships on more equal terms, two or more people of about equal wealth and ability combining their resources for a large and difficult undertaking. In such cases there is often a distinct partition of the work of management: in manufactures for instance one partner will sometimes give himself almost exclusively to the work of buying raw material and selling the finished product, while the other is responsible for the management of the factory: and in a trading establishment one partner will control the wholesale and the other the retail department. In these and other ways private partnership is capable of adapting itself to a great variety of problems: it is very strong and very elastic; it has played a great part in the past, and it is full of vitality now.

But the expansion of old trades and the growth of new trades have long tended to outgrow the capitals that can easily be obtained by private companies; and from the end of the Middle Ages to the present time there has been a movement of constantly increasing force towards the substitution of public joint stock companies, the shares of which can be sold to anybody in the open market, for private companies, the shares in which are not transferable without the leave of all concerned; and various plans, with which we need not occupy ourselves just now, have been adopted in different countries for enabling the shareholders to limit their risks to their shares. The effect of this change has been to induce people, many of whom have no special knowledge of trade, to give their capital into the hands of others employed by them: and there has thus arisen a new distribution of the various parts of the work of business management.

The ultimate undertakers of the risks incurred by a joint stock company are the shareholders; but as a rule they do not take much active part in engineering the business and controlling its general policy; and they take no part in superintending its details. After the business has once got out of the hands of its original promoters, the control of it is left chiefly in the hands of Directors; who, if the company is a very large one, probably own but a very small proportion of its shares, while the greater part of them have not much technical knowledge of the work to be done. They are not generally expected to give their whole time to it; but they are supposed to bring wide general knowledge and sound judgment to bear on the broader problems of its policy; and at the same time to make sure that the "Managers" of the company are doing their work thoroughly. To the Managers and their assistants is left a great part of the work of engineering the business, and the whole of the work of superintending it: but they are not required to bring any capital into it; and they are supposed to be promoted from the lower ranks to the higher according to their zeal and ability. Since the joint stock companies in the United Kingdom have an aggregate income of £100,000,000, and do a tenth of the business of all kinds that is done in the country, they offer very large opportunities to men with natural talents for business management, who have not inherited any material capital, or any business connection.

Joint stock companies have great elasticity and can expand themselves without limit when the work to which they have set themselves offers a wide scope; and they are gaining ground in nearly all directions. But they have one great source of weakness in the absence of any adequate knowledge of the business on the part of the shareholders who undertake its chief risks. It is true that the head of a large private firm undertakes the chief risks of the business, while he intrusts many of its details to others; but his position is secured by his power of forming a direct judgment as to whether his subordinates serve his interests faithfully and discreetly. If those to whom he has intrusted the buying or selling of goods for him take commissions from those with whom they deal, he is in a position to discover and punish the fraud. If they show favouritism and promote incompetent relations or friends of their own, or if they themselves become idle and shirk their work, or even if they do not fulfil the promise of exceptional ability which induced him to give them their first lift, he can discover what is going wrong and set it right.

But in all these matters the great body of the shareholders of a joint stock company are, save in a few exceptional instances, almost powerless; though a few of the larger shareholders often exert themselves to find out what is going on; and are thus able to exercise an effective and wise control over the general management of the business. It is a strong proof of the marvellous growth in recent times of a spirit of honesty and uprightness in commercial matters, that the leading officers of great public companies yield as little as they do to the vast temptations to fraud which lie in their way. If they showed an eagerness to avail themselves of opportunities for wrong-doing at all approaching that of which we read in the commercial history of earlier civilization, their wrong uses of the trusts imposed in them would have been on so great a scale as to prevent the development of this democratic form of business. There is every reason to hope that the progress of trade morality will continue, aided in the future as it has been in the past, by a diminution of trade secrecy and by increased publicity in every form; and thus collective and democratic forms of business management may be able to extend themselves safely in many directions in which they have hitherto failed, and may far exceed the great services they already render in opening a large career to those who have no advantages of birth.

The same may be said of the undertakings of governments imperial and local: they also may have a great future before them, but up to the present time the tax-payer who undertakes the ultimate risks has not generally succeeded in exercising an efficient control over the businesses, and in securing officers who will do their work with as much energy and enterprise as is shown in private establishments. The problem of government undertakings involves however many important side issues, which will require our careful attention later on.

* * *

In speaking of the difficulty that a working man has in rising to a post in which he can turn his business ability to full account, the chief stress is commonly laid upon his want of capital: but this is not always his chief difficulty. For instance the co-operative distributive societies have accumulated a vast capital, on which they find it difficult to get a good rate of interest; and which they would be rejoiced to lend to any set of working men who could show that they had the capacity for dealing with difficult business problems. Co-operators who have firstly a high order of business ability and probity, and secondly the "personal capital" of great reputation among their fellows for these qualities, will have no difficulty in getting command of enough material capital for a considerable undertaking: the real difficulty is to convince a sufficient number of those around them that they have these rare qualities. And the case is not very different when an individual endeavours to obtain from the ordinary sources the loan of the capital required to start him in business.

It is true that in almost every business there is a constant increase in the amount of capital required to make a fair start; but there is a much more rapid increase in the amount of capital which is owned by people who do not want to use it themselves, and are so eager to lend it out that they will accept a constantly lower and lower rate of interest for it. Much of this capital passes into the hands of bankers and others, people of keen intellect and restless energy; people who have no class prejudices and care nothing for social distinctions; and who would promptly lend it to any one of whose business ability and honesty they were convinced. To say nothing of the credit that can be got in many businesses from those who supply the requisite raw material or stock in trade, the opportunities for direct borrowing are now so great that an increase in the amount of capital required for a start in business is no very serious obstacle in the way of a person who has once got over the initial difficulty of earning a reputation for being likely to use it well.

And perhaps a greater though not so conspicuous hindrance to the rise of the working man is the growing complexity of business. The head of a business has now to think of many things about which he never used to trouble himself in earlier days; and these are just the kind of difficulties for which the training of the workshop affords the least preparation. Against this must be set the rapid improvement of the education of the working man not only at school, but what is more important, in after life by newspapers and from the work of co-operative societies and trades unions, and in other ways.

About three-fourths of the whole population of England belong to the wage-earning classes; and at all events when they are well fed, properly housed and educated, they have their fair share of that nervous strength which is the raw material of business ability. Without going out of their way they are all consciously or unconsciously competitors for posts of business command. The ordinary workman if he shows ability generally becomes a foreman, from that he may rise to be a manager, and to be taken into partnership with his employer. Or having saved a little of his own he may start one of those small shops which still can hold their own in a working man's quarter, stock it chiefly on credit, and let his wife attend to it by day, while he gives his evenings to it. In these or in other ways he may increase his capital till he can start a small workshop, or factory. Once having made a good beginning he will find the banks eager to give him generous credit. He must have time; and since he is not likely to start in business till after middle age he must have a long as well as a strong life; but if he has this and has also "patience, genius and good fortune" he is pretty sure to command a large capital before he dies. In a factory those who work with their hands, have better opportunities of rising to posts of command than the book-keepers and many others to whom social tradition has assigned a higher place. But in trading concerns it is otherwise; what manual work is done in them has as a rule no educating character, while the experience of the office is better adapted for preparing a man to manage a commercial than a manufacturing business.

There is then on the whole a broad movement from below upwards. There are perhaps not so many who rise at once from the position of working men to that of employers: but there are more who get on sufficiently far to give their sons a good chance of attaining to the highest posts. The complete rise is not so very often accomplished in one generation; it is more often spread over two; but the total volume of the movement upwards is probably greater than it has ever been. And it may be remarked in passing that it is better for society as a whole that the rise should be distributed over two generations. The workmen who at the begining of this century rose in such large numbers to become employers were seldom fit for posts of command: they were too often harsh and tyrannical; they lost their self-control, and were neither truly noble nor truly happy; while their children were often haughty, extravagant, and self-indulgent, squandering their wealth on low and vulgar amusements, having the worst faults of the older aristocracy without their virtues. The foreman or superintendent who has still to obey as well as to command, but who is rising and sees his children likely to rise further, is in some ways more to be envied than the small master. His success is less conspicuous, but his work is often higher and more important for the world, while his character is more gentle and refined and not less strong. His children are well-trained; and if they get wealth, they are likelv to make a fairly good use of it.

When a man of great ability is once at the head of an independent business, whatever be the route by which he has got there, he will with moderate good fortune, soon be able to show such evidence of his power of turning capital to good account as to enable him to borrow in one way or another almost any amount that he may need. Making good profits he adds to his own capital, and this extra capital of his own is a material security for further borrowings; while the fact that he has made it himself tends to make lenders less careful to insist on a full security for their loans. Of course fortune tells for much in business: a very able man may find things going against him; the fact that he is losing money may diminish his power of borrowing. If he is working partly on borrowed capital, it may even make those who have lent it, refuse to renew their loans, and may thus cause him to succumb to what would have been but a passing misfortune, if he had been using no capital but his own: and in fighting his way upwards he may have a chequered life full of great anxieties, and even misfortunes. But he can show his ability in misfortune as well as in success: human nature is sanguine; and it is notorious that men are abundantly willing to lend to those who have passed through commercial disaster without loss to their business reputation. Thus, in spite of vicissitudes, the able business man generally finds that in the long run the capital at his command grows in proportion to his ability.

Meanwhile he, who with small ability is in command of a large capital, speedily loses it: he may perhaps be one who could and would have managed a small business with credit, and left it stronger than he had found it: but if he has not the genius for dealing with large problems, the larger it is the more speedily will he break it up. For as a rule a large business can be kept going only by transactions which, after allowing for ordinary risks, leave but a very small percentage of gain. A small profit on a large turn-over quickly made, will yield a rich income to able men: and in those businesses which are of such a nature as to give scope to very large capitals, competition generally cuts the rate of profits on the turn-over very fine. A village trader may make five per cent. less profits on his turn-over than his abler rival, and yet be able to hold his head above water. But in those large manufacturing and trading businesses in which there is a quick return and a straightforward routine, the whole profits on the turn-over are often so very small that a person who falls behind his rivals by even a small percentage loses a large sum at every turn-over; while in those large businesses which are difficult and do not rely on routine, and which afford high profits on the turn-over to really able management, there are no profits at all to be got by any-one who attempts the task with only ordinary ability.

These two sets of forces, the one increasing the capital at the command of able men, and the other destroying the capital that is in the hands of weaker men, bring about the result that there is a far more close correspondence between the ability of business men and the size of the businesses which they own than at first sight would appear probable. And when to this fact we add all the many routes, which we have already discussed, by which a man of great natural business ability can work his way up high in some private firm or public company, we may conclude that wherever there is work on a large scale to be done in such a country as England, the ability and the capital required for it are pretty sure to be speedily forthcoming.

Further, just as industrial skill and ability are getting every day to depend more and more on the broad faculties of judgment, promptness, resource, carefulness and steadfastness of purpose—faculties which are not specialized to any one trade, but which are more or less useful in all—so it is with regard to business ability. In fact business ability consists more of these general and non-specialized faculties than do industrial skill and ability in the lower grades: and the higher the grade of business ability the more various are its applications.

Since then business ability in command of capital moves with great ease horizontally from a trade which is overcrowded to one which offers good openings for it: and since it moves with great ease vertically, the abler men rising to the higher posts in their own trade, we may conclude than in modern England the supply of business ability in command of capital accommodates itself, as a general rule, to the demand for it.

## V–ECONOMIC DEVELOPMENT

# *1. A Historical Survey of Industrial Systems*

BY KARL BÜCHER

IN ECONOMIC and social matters most people have very definite opinions on what *should be,* often much more definite than on what *is*. What in their view should be is by no means an ideal state of affairs, an imaginative creation that has never been realized. Very frequently indeed it is a conception drawn from the conditions that prevailed in times more or less remote, which long custom has led us to consider normal.

Such is the case, if we mistake not, with many of our contemporaries regarding what we call *handicraft* and the so-called handicraft problem. One has become accustomed to look upon handi-

Reprinted from Karl Bücher, *Industrial Evolution,* trans. S. M. Wickett (New York: Henry Holt & Co., 1901), chap. iv, pp. 150–84.

craft as the normal form of industry, after it has dominated five centuries or more of the life of the burgher class of Germany. The proverb says "Handicraft stands on golden ground"; and observation teaches us that this ground is, according to present-day valuation, no longer golden. We ask ourselves how that happy condition can be restored, how handicraft can be "resuscitated."

But what right has one to regard handicraft as the normal form of industry and thus as it were to strive after an ideal whose realization belongs to the past?

The earlier political economists represent handicraft as the original form of industrial production. "In a tribe of hunters or shepherds," says Adam Smith, "a particular person makes bows and arrows with more readiness and dexterity than any other. He frequently exchanges them for cattle or venison with his companions; and he finds at last he can in this manner get more cattle and venison than if he himself went to the field to catch them." Finally, "the making of bows and arrows grows to be his chief business and he becomes a sort of armourer." If we follow this historical progress a couple of stages further, the original handicraftsman will after a time probably take an apprentice, and when the latter has learned his trade, a second, while the first becomes his journeyman.

Seek as we may, we find nothing added by subsequent development. When we speak of a craftsman to-day we have in mind a business undertaker on a small scale, who has passed by regular stages of transition from apprentice to journeyman and from journeyman to master workman, who produces with his own hand and his own capital for a locally limited circle of customers, and into whose hands flows undiminished the whole product of his labour. Everything that one can demand of an industrial system founded on justice seems realized in the life of the typical craftsman—gradual social progress, independence, an income corresponding to services rendered. And those forms of industry that vary from this primal type, namely, house industry and factory production, may readily appear abnormal; and the social stratification of those employed, and the accompanying unequal distribution of income out of harmony with the idea of economic justice.

Even later economists are rarely free from this popular conception. In contrasting the three industrial systems that they recognise, handicraft, house industry, and factory production, they almost unwittingly draw from the fundamental institutions of handicraft the criterion for judging the others. Until quite recently house industry was for many of them merely a degenerate handicraft or a transitional form, and the factory a necessary evil of the age of machinery. This narrowness of view was prejudicial to the scientific understanding of even modern industrial methods, open as these are to direct observation.

An historically constructive view, such as we will here present, must from the start shake off the idea that any particular form in any department of economic activity can be the norm for all times and peoples. Even handicraft is for it only one phenomenon in the great stream of history, with its origin, continuance, and success dependent upon certain given economic conditions. It is neither the original nor even a necessary form in the historical evolution of industrial production. It is, in other words, just as little necessary that the industry of a country shall have passed through the handicraft phase before arriving at house industry or factory manufacture as that every people shall have been hunters or nomads before passing over to settled agriculture. Among us handicraft has been preceded by other industrial systems, which, indeed, even in Europe, still exist in part.

The great historical significance of these primitive industrial forms in the evolution of economic conditions has hitherto been almost wholly ignored, although they shaped for thousands of years the economic life of the nations and left lasting marks upon their social organizations. Only a comparatively small portion of the history of industry, namely, that part which written laws have enabled us to know, has been at all cleared up; and this, too, much more on its formal side than as regards its inner life, its method of operation. Even the guild handicraft of the Middle Ages, to which in recent times so much persevering and penetrating labour has been devoted, has, on the side of its actual operation, enjoyed scarcely more accurate investigation. In this domain arbitrary theoretical constructions based upon the postulates and concepts of modern commercial economy still widely prevail.

Our "historical" political economy, it is true, has a wealth of material for the economic history of the classical and modern peoples. But it has hardly yet been duly noted that the complex nature of all social phenomena renders it just as difficult for the investigator of to-day to reconstruct the economic conditions of the life of the nations of antiquity and of the Middle Ages as to forecast even with the most lively and powerful imagination the ultimate consequences of the "socialist State of the future." We shall not arrive at an understanding of whole epochs of early economic history until we study the economic side of the life of primitive and uncivilized peoples of the present with the care we to-day devote to Englishmen and Americans. Instead of sending our young political economists on journeys of investigation to these latter, we should rather send them to the Russians, the Rumanians, or the South Slavs; we should study the characteristic features of primitive economic life and the legal conceptions of the peoples of our newly acquired colonies before such features and conceptions disappear under the influence of European trade.

It is almost a fortunate circumstance that such external influences rarely affect deeply the real life of the people, but are confined chiefly to the more privileged classes. Hence it is that in extensive regions of eastern and northern Europe, which the unheeding traveller courses through by rail, there may still be observed among the rural population primitive forms of production that modern commerce has caused to vary but slightly.

In the attempt made in the following pages to give a compact presentation of what we know of the industrial methods of such "backward" tribes and the present conclusions of industrial history, our sole aim is to present in clear outline the chief stages of development. In order to have a guiding thread through the perplexing variety and wealth of forms of individual ethnographical observations, it is most necessary to separate typical and casual, to disregard subsidiary and transitional forms, and to consider a new phase of development as beginning only where changes in industrial technique call forth economic phenomena that imply a radical alteration in the organization of society. In this way we arrive at five main systems of industry. In historical succession they are:

1. Housework (Domestic Work).
2. Wage-work.
3. Handicraft.
4. Commission Work (House Industry).
5. Factory Work.

We shall first attempt to give a concise outline of the characteristic economic peculiarities of these industrial systems, merely indicating the socio-historical import of the whole development. The filling out of occasional gaps and the explanation of the transitions from one system to the other may be left to detailed investigation. In our sketch we shall, naturally, devote most time to the two industrial systems precedent to handicraft, while for the later a brief account may suffice. We begin with housework.

Housework is industrial production in and for the house from raw materials furnished by the household itself. In its original and purest form it presupposes the absence of exchange, and the ability of each household to satisfy by its own labour the wants of its members. Each commodity passes through all the stages of production in the establishment in which it is to be consumed. Production is consequently undertaken only according to the needs of the house itself. There is still neither circulation of goods nor capital. The wealth of the house consists entirely in consumption goods in various stages of completion, such as corn, meal, bread, flax, yarn, cloth, and clothes. It also possesses auxiliary means of production, such as the handmill, the axe, the distaff, and the weaver's loom, but no goods with which it could procure other goods by process of exchange. All it has it owes to its own labour, and it is scarcely possible to separate the operations of the household from those of production.

In the form of housework, industry is older than agriculture. Wherever explorers of new countries have come into contact with primitive peoples, they have found many forms of industrial skill, such as the making of bow and arrow, the weaving of mats and vessels out of reeds, bast, and tough roots, a primitive pottery, tanning skins, crushing farinaceous grains on the grinding-stone, smelting iron ore, the building of houses. To-day the hunting tribes of North America, the fisher tribes of the South Sea, the nomad hordes of Siberia, and the agricultural negro tribes of Africa make similar display of varied technical skill without possessing actual artisans. Even the wretched naked forest tribes of Central Brazil make their clubs and bows and arrows, build houses and bark canoes, make tools of bone and stone, weave baskets for carrying and storing, scoop out gourd dishes, spin, knit, and weave, form artistically ornamented clay vessels without knowledge of the potter's wheel, carve ornamented digging-sticks, stools, flutes, combs, and masks, and prepare many kinds of ornaments out of feathers, skins, etc.

In the temperate and colder countries with the advance to the use of the plough, this activity loses more and more the character of the accidental; the whole husbandry acquires a settled character; the mild period of the year must be devoted to the procuring of raw material and to outdoor work; in winter the working up of this material clusters the members of the household around the hearth. For each kind of work there is developed a definite method which is incorporated into the domestic life according to the natural and imperative demands of economy; about it custom weaves its fine golden ethical thread; it enriches and ennobles the life of men among whom, with its simple technique and archaic forms, it is transmitted from generation to generation. As people labour only for their own requirements, the interest of the producer in the work of his hands long survives the completion of the work. His highest technical skill and his whole artistic sense are embodied in it. It is for this reason that the products of domestic work throughout Germany have become for our age of artistic industry such a rich mine of models of popular style.

The Norwegian peasant is not merely his own smith and joiner, like the Westphalian *Hofschulze* in Immermann's "Münchhausen"; with his own hands he also builds his wooden house, makes his field-implements, wagons and sleighs, tans leather, carves from wood various kinds of house utensils, and even makes metal ones. In Iceland the very peasants are skilful workers in silver. In the Highlands of Scotland, up to the close of last century, every man was his own weaver, fuller, tanner, and shoemaker. In Galicia and Bukowina, in many parts of Hungary and Siebenbürgen, in Rumania, and among the southern Slav peoples there could scarcely be found, down to recent times, any other craftsman than the smith, and he was usually a gypsy. In Greece and other lands of the Balkan peninsula the only additional craftsmen were occasional wandering builders. Numberless examples of a similar kind might be adduced from other peoples. The wonderful adroitness and dexterity of the Russian and Swedish peasants, to cite a striking instance, has its undoubted origin in the varied technical tasks of their own households. The industrial employments of women in ancient and modern times, such as spinning, weaving, baking, etc., are too well known to call for further reference.

In order to obtain an idea of the wealth of domestic industrial skill that characterizes the life of less civilized peoples a detailed description would be necessary. Lack of space unfortunately forbids that here. It will suffice, however, to reproduce the following sentences from an account of household work in Bukowina:

"In the narrow circle of the family, or at least within the limits of his little village, the Bukowina countryman supplies all his own necessaries. In building a house the husband, as a rule, can do the work of carpenter, roofer, etc., while the wife must attend to plastering the woven and slatted walls or stopping the chinks in the log walls with moss, pounding out of the floor, and many other related duties. From the cultivation of the plant from which cloth is spun or the raising of sheep down to the making of bed and other clothes out of linen, wool or furs, leather, felt, or plaited straw, the Bukowina country folk produce everything, including dyes from plants of their own culture, as well as the necessary though, indeed, extremely primitive utensils. The same holds in general of the food-supply. With a rather heavy expenditure of labour the peasant cultivates his field of maize, and with his handmill grinds the kukuruz meal used by him in baking mamaliga, his chief article of food, which resembles polenta. His simple farming implements, the dishes and utensils for household and kitchen, he, or, if not he, some self-taught villager, is also able to make. The working of iron, alone, a substance that the native population uses in exceedingly small quantities, he generally leaves to the gypsies scattered through the country."

Yet whatever the industrial skill developed by the self-sufficing household, such a method of supply was destined to prove inadequate when the household diminished to the smaller circle of blood-relations, which we call the family. The ancient family group, it is true, was broader than our present family; but just at the time when wants are increasing in extent and variety, the tribal organization of many peoples breaks down and a more minute division of labour among the members of the household is rendered impossible. The transition to specialized production and a system of exchange would at this point have been unaviodable had it not been possible, by adopting slaves or by utilizing serf labour, to enlarge artificially the household circle. The greater the number of these unfree members of the household, the easier it is to introduce a varied division of labour among them and to train each person for a definite industrial employment.

Thus we find among the house-slaves of the wealthy Greeks and Romans industrial workers of various kinds; and in the famous instructions of Charles the Great regarding the management of his country estates we have definite rules prescribing what kinds of unfree workers shall be maintained at each villa. "Each steward," we read, "shall have in his service good workmen, such as smiths, workers in gold and silver, shoemakers, turners, carpenters, shield-makers, fishers, fowlers, soap-boilers, brewers of mead *(siceratores),* bakers, and net-makers." Copious evidence of a similar kind is available for the manors of the nobility and the monasteries. The handicraftsmen maintained by them are at their exclusive service; in some cases they are merely domestic servants receiving their board and lodging in the manor-house, in others they are settled and gain their living on their own holdings, and in return render villein services in that branch of labour in which they have special skill. In token that they are engaged to hold their skill at the service of the manor, they bear the title *officiales, officiati,* i.e., officials.

Housework, we see, has here obtained an extensive organization, which allows the lord of the manor a relatively large and varied consumption of industrial products.

But housework does not remain mere production for direct consumption. At a very early stage inequality of natural endowment causes a varied development of technical skill. One tribe produces pottery, stone implements, or arrows, and a neighbouring tribe does not. Such industrial products are then scattered among other tribes as gifts of hospitality, or as spoils of war, and later as the objects of exchange. Among the ancient Greeks wealthy slave-owners caused a considerable number of their dependent labourers, whom they did not need for their own estates, to be trained for a special industry, and then to produce for the market. In a similar fashion peasant families exchange the surplus products of their household industry more frequently than the surpluses from their agriculture or cattle-raising. As in the Old Testament it is one of the good qualities of the virtuous wife to dispose of the wares that her own hands have produced, so to-day the negro wife in Central Africa carries to the weekly market the pots or basketware she produces in order to exchange them for salt or pearls. In like manner, in many parts of Germany the rural population have from the beginning of the Middle Ages sold their linen cloths at the town markets and fairs; and in the era of mercantilism measures were taken by the government in Silesia and Westphalia to facilitate the export of home-made linen. So also in the Baltic provinces during the Middle Ages the coarse woollen cloth, *Vadhmâl,* which is still woven by the peasant women, was one of the best known articles of trade, and actually served as money. Similarly among many African peoples domestic products made by neighbouring tribes serve as general mediums of exchange. In almost every villager's house in Japan yarn is spun and cloth woven out of cotton grown in his own fields, and of this a portion comes into exchange. In Sweden the West Goths and Smalanders wander through almost the whole country offering for sale home-woven stuffs. In Hungary, Galicia, Rumania, and the southern Slav countries, everywhere one can meet with peasants offering for sale at the weekly town markets their earthen and wooden wares, and peasant women selling, along with vegetables and eggs, aprons, embroidered ribbons, and laces which they themselves have made.

It is especially when the land owned by a family becomes divided up and no longer suffices for its maintenance, that a part of the rural population take up a special branch of housework and produce for the market in exactly the same way as our small peasants in South Germany produce wine, hops, or tobacco. At first the necessary raw material is gained from their own land or drawn from the communal forests; later on, if need be, it is also purchased. All sorts of allied branches of production are added; and thus there develops out of housework, as in many parts of Russia, an endlessly varied system of peasant industry on a small scale.

But the evolution may take another course, and an independent professional class of industrial labourers arise, and with them our second industrial system—*wage-work.* Whereas all industrial skill has hitherto been exercised in close association with property in land and tillage, the adept house-labourer now frees himself from this association, and upon his technical skill founds for himself an existence that gradually becomes independent of property in land. But he has only his simple tools for work; he has no business capital. He therefore always exercises his skill upon raw material furnished him by the producer of the raw material, who is at the same time the consumer of the finished product.

Here again two distinct forms of this relationship are possible. In one case the wage-worker is taken temporarily into the house, receives his board and, if he does not belong to the place, his lodging as well, together with the daily wage; and leaves when the needs of his customer are satisfied. In South Germany we call this going on one's intinerancy (*auf die Stör gehen*), and may accordingly designate the whole industrial phase as that of *itinerancy* (*Stör*), and the labourer carrying on work in this manner as the *itinerant* (*Störer*). The dressmakers and seamstresses whom our women in many places are accustomed to take into the house may serve as an illustration.

On the other hand, the wage-worker may have his own place of business, and the raw material be given out to him. For working it up he receives piece-work wage. In the country the linen-weaver, the miller, and the baker working for a wage are examples. We will designate this form of work *home work* (*Heimwerk*). It is met with chiefly in industries that demand permanent means of production difficult to transport, such as mills, ovens, weavers' looms, forges, etc.

Both forms of wage-work are still very common in all parts of the world. Examples might be drawn from India and Japan, from Morocco and the Sudan, and from almost all European countries. The system can be traced in Babylonian temple records and in ancient Egypt; it can be followed in literature from Homer down through ancient and mediæval times to the present day. The whole conception of the relation of the customer to the independent (personally free or unfree) artisan in early Greek and Roman law rests upon wage-work; and only by it are numerous ordinances of mediæval guild law to be explained.

In the Alpine lands it is still the predominant industrial method in the country. The Styrian writer P. K. Rosegger has, in an interesting book, given a picture of his experiences as apprentice to a peripatetic tailor carrying on his trade among the peasants. "The peasant craftsmen," he says in the preface, "such as the cobbler, the tailor, the weaver, the cooper (in other places also the saddler, the wheelwright, the carpenter, and, in general, all artisan builders), are in many Alpine districts a sort of nomad folk. Each of them has, indeed, a definite abode somewhere, either in his own little house or in the rented room of a peasant's home, where his family lives, where he has safekeeping for his possessions, and where he spends his Sundays and holidays. On Monday morning, however, he puts his tools upon his back or in his pocket and starts out upon his rounds; that is, he goes out for work and takes up his quarters in the home of the peasant by whom he has been engaged, and there remains until he has satisfied the household needs. Then he wends his way to another farm. The handicraftsman in his temporary abode is looked upon as belonging to the family." Every peasant's house has a special room with a "handicraftsman's bed" for his quarters overnight; wherever he has been working during the week, he is invited to Sunday dinner.

We find described in almost the same words the industrial conditions of rural Sweden and many parts of Norway. In Russia and the southern Slav countries there are hundreds of thousands of wage-workers, belonging especially to the building and clothing trades, who lead a continuous migratory life and who, on account of the great distances travelled, often remain away from home half a year or more.

From the point of view of development these two forms of wage-work have different origins. Itinerant labour is based upon the exclusive possession of aptitude for a special kind of work, homework upon the exclusive possession of fixed means of production. Upon this basis there now arises all sorts of *mixed forms* between housework and wage-work.

The *itinerant* labourer is at first an experienced neighbour whose advice is sought in carrying out an important piece of work, the actual work, however, still being performed by the members of the household. Even later it is long the practice for the members of the customer's family to give the necessary assistance to the craftsman and his journeyman; and this is still met with in the country, for example, in the raising of a frame building.

In the case of *homework* the later tradesman is at first merely the owner of the business plant and technical director of the production, the customer doing the actual work. This frequently remains true in the country to-day with oil-presses, flax-mills, mills for husking barley and oats, and cider-mills.

In many North German towns the mediæval maltsters and brewers were merely the owners of malt-kilns and brewing-houses, who for a fee gave the citizens the opportunity of malting their own barley and brewing their own beer. In the flour-mills the customer at least supplied the handler who attended to the sifting of the meal. Even to-day it is customary in many localities for the peasant's wife, after kneading the dough, to mould the bread-loaves in her own house; the baker simply places his oven at her disposal, heats it and attends to the baking. In French and western Swiss towns the public washing places are managed in much the same fashion, merely providing their customers with washing-apparatus and hot water, and frequently a drying-place in addition, while the work is done by the servants or female members of the customer's household. These afterwards bring the washed and dried linen to the mangle to be smoothed out, in which process the owner assists by working the handle. Payment is made by the hour. In Posen and West Prussia until recently it was the custom for the owner of a smithy merely to supply fire, tools, and iron, leaving the actual work to his customers.

From the economic point of view the essential feature of the wage-work system is that there is no business capital. Neither the raw material nor the finished industrial product is for its producer ever a means of profit. The character and extent of the production are still determined in every case by the owner of the soil, who produces the raw material; he also superintends the whole process of production. The peasant grows, threshes, and cleans the rye and then turns it over to the miller to be ground, paying him in kind; the meal is given to the baker, who delivers, on receipt of a baker's wage and indemnification for the firing, a certain number of loaves made from it. From the sowing of the seed until the moment the bread is consumed the product has never been capital, but always a mere article for use in course of preparation. No earnings of management and interest charges or middleman's profits attach to the finished product, but only wages for work done.

Under certain social conditions, and where needs are very simple, this is a thoroughly economic method of production and, like housework, secures the excellence of the product and the complete adjustment of supply to demand. It avoids exchange, where this would lead only to a round-about method of supplying the producer of the raw material with wares prepared from his own products. But it also forces the consumer to run the risk attaching to industrial production, as only those needs that can be foreseen can find suitable and prompt satisfaction, while a sudden need must often remain unsatisfied because the wage-worker happens at the very time to be elsewhere engaged. In the case of homework there is the additional danger that a portion of the material furnished may be embezzled or changed. The system has also many disadvantages for the wage-worker. Amongst these are the inconveniences and loss of time suffered in his itinerancy from place to place; also the irregularity of employment, which leads now to the overwork, now to the complete idleness, of the workman. Both forms of wage-work thus act satisfactorily only when the unoccupied hours can be turned to account in some allied branch of agriculture.

In the Middle Ages, when this could be done, wage-work greatly facilitated the emancipation of the artisan from serfdom and feudal obligations, as it required practically no capital to start an independent business. It is a great mistake still common to look upon the class of guild handicraftsmen of the Middle Ages as a class of small capitalists. It was in essence rather an industrial labouring class, distinguished from the labourers of to-day by the fact that each worked not for a single employer but for a large number of consumers. The supplying of the material by the customer is common to almost all mediæval handicrafts; in many instances, indeed, it continues for centuries, even after the customer has ceased to produce the raw material himself and must buy it, as, for example, the leather for the shoemaker and the cloth for the tailor. The furnishing of the material by the master workman is a practice that takes slow root; at first it holds only for the poorer customers, but later for the wealthy as well. Thus arises *handicraft* in the sense in which it is generally understood to-day; but alongside it wage-work maintains itself for a long time, even entering, in many cases, into the service of handicraft. Thus the tanner is wage-worker for the shoemaker and saddler, the miller for the baker, the wool-beater, the dyer, and the fuller wage-workers for the cloth-maker.

In the towns itinerancy is the first of two forms of wage-work to decline. This decline is considerably hastened by the interference of the guilds.[1] The itinerancy was too suggestive of early villenage. In it the workman is, so to speak, only a special kind of day-labourer, who must temporarily become a subordinate member of another household. Consequently from the fourteenth century on we find the guild ordinances frequently prohibiting the master from working in private houses. To the same cause is to be ascribed the hatred displayed by the town craftsmen towards those of the country, because the migratory labour of the latter could not well be forbidden. Eventually *itinerant* or *botcher* (*Bönhase*), becomes a general term of contempt for those who work without regular credentials from the guilds. In the North German towns the guild masters claimed the right of entering the houses of their customers to ferret out the itinerant artisans and call them to account,—the so-called "botcher-hunt"; and the public authorities were often weak enough to wink at this breach of the domestic rights of the citizen.

But the guilds did not everywhere have such an easy task in supplanting one industrial system by another. As early as the middle of the fourteenth century the sovereign authority in the Austrian duchy takes vigorous measures against them. In the statutes of the electorate of Saxony for the year 1482 shoemakers, tailors, furriers, joiners, glaziers, and other handicraftsmen who shall refuse without sufficient reason to work in the house of their customer are made liable to a fine of three florins, a high sum for those times. In Basel a definite statute governing house tailors was enacted in 1526 for the maintenance of "ancient and honourable customs." In many German territories definite ordinances were made regulating the charges of the various kinds of wage-workers. Thus in many crafts, especially in the building trade, wage-work has persisted down to the present time.

In the majority, however, its place has been taken by the industrial system that to-day is customarily designated *handicraft,* whose nature we have indicated at the beginning of the present chapter. It might also be called *price-work* (*Preiswerk*), which would mark the contrast with wage-work. For the handicraftsman is distinguished from the wage-worker only by the fact that he possesses all the means of production, and sells for a definite price the finished article which is the product of his own

1. In this connection it may not be out of place to point out that, in the industrial limitation of those entitled to the privileges of the guild, the old housework was at the same time affected. In very many of the guild ordinances we find the regulation that the non-guildsman may do handicraftsman's work, but only in so far as the needs of his household demand, not for purposes of sale. The surplus house production for the market described above was thereby made impossible.

raw material and his own incorporated labour, while the wage-worker merely receives a recompense for his labour.

All the important characteristics of handicraft may be summed up in the single expression *custom production.* It is the method of sale that distinguishes this industrial system from all later ones. The handicraftsman always works for the consumer of his product whether it be that the latter by placing separate orders affords the occasion for the work, or that the two meet at the weekly or yearly market. Ordered work and work for the market must supplement each other if "dull times" are to be avoided. As a rule the region of sale is local, namely, the town and its more immediate neighbourhood. The customer buys at first hand, the handicraftsman sells to the actual consumer. This assures a proper adjustment of supply and demand and introduces an ethical feature into the whole relationship; the producer in the presence of the consumer feels responsibility for his work.

With the rise of handicraft a wide cleft, so to speak, appears in the economic process of production. Hitherto the owner of the land, though perhaps calling in the aid of other wage-workers, had conducted this whole process; now there are two classes of economic activity, each of which embraces only a part of the process of production, one producing the raw material, the other the manufactured article. It is a principle that handicraft endeavoured to carry out wherever possible—an article should pass through all the stages of its preparation in the same workshop. In this way the needed capital is diminished and frequent additions of profit to price avoided. By the acquisition of an independent business capital the artisan class is changed from a mere wage-earning class of labourers into a capitalistic producing class; and the movable property now, dissociated from landownership, accumulates in its hands and becomes the basis of an independent social and political reputability which is embodied in the burgher class.

The direct relationship between the handicraftsman and the consumer of his products makes it necessary that the business remain small. Whenever any one line of handicraft threatens to become too large, new handicrafts split off from it and appropriate part of its sphere of production. This is the mediæval division of labour, which continually creates new and independent trades and which led later to that jealous delimitation of the spheres of work that caused a large portion of the energy of the guild system to be consumed in internal bickerings.

Handicraft is a phenomenon peculiar to the town. Peoples which, like the Russians, have developed no real town life, know likewise no national handicraft. And this also explains why, with the formation of large centralized States and unified commercial territories, handicraft was doomed to decline. In the seventeenth and eighteenth centuries there was developed a new industrial system, based no longer on the local but on the national and international market. Our ancestors have denoted this system by the two names *manufactories* and *factories,* without distinguishing between the two terms. When viewed more closely these are seen to indicate two quite distinct industrial systems. The one hitherto characterized by the misleading phrase *house industry* we prefer to call the *commission system* (*Verlag*), the other is our *factory system.* Both systems undertake the work of supplying a wide market with industrial products, and both require for this purpose a large number of labourers; they differ only in the manner in which they accomplish the work and organize the labourers.

In this respect the method of the commission system is the simplest. In the first place, it leaves the existing method of production quite undisturbed and confines itself to organizing the market. The business undertaker is a commercial entrepreneur who regularly employs a large number of labourers in their own homes, away from his place of business. These labourers are either former handicraftsmen who now produce for a single *tradesman* instead of for a number of consumers, or former wage-workers who now receive their raw material, not from the consumer, but from the merchant; or, finally, they are peasant families, the former products of whose domestic work are now produced as market wares and by the entrepreneur introduced into the markets of the world.

In some cases the entrepreneur advances to the small producers, who at first enjoy a fairly independent position, the purchase price of their products; in some cases he furnishes them with the raw material, and then pays piecework wage; while in others he owns even the principal machinery, such as the weaver's loom, the embroidering machine, etc. As the small producers have only the *one* customer they gradually sink into ever-greater dependence. The entrepreneur becomes their employer, and they are employees, even when they supply the raw material themselves.

It is scarcely necessary to describe in detail the commission system and its contingent method of work, house industry. We have plenty of examples in the mountain districts of Germany, for instance, the straw-plaiting and the clock and brush industries in the Black Forest, the wood-carving of Upper Bavaria, the toy manufacture in the Meiningen Oberland, the embroidery of the Voigtland, the lace-making of the Erzgebirge, etc. The history and present condition of these industries have been fairly well investigated in recent times. But we can no more enter into them than into the great variety of phases presented by this form of industry.

The essential feature is ever the transformation of the industrial product, before it reaches the consumer, into capital—that is, into a means of acquisition for one or more intermediary merchants. Whether the entrepreneur place the product on the general market, or keep a town wareroom from which to sell it; whether he receive the wares from the houseworker ready for sale, or himself subject them to a last finishing process; whether the workman call himself master and keep journeymen, or whether he be a tiller of the soil as well—the house workman is always far removed from the real market of his product and from a knowledge of market conditions, and therein lies the chief cause of his hopeless weakness.

If under the commission system capital has merely assumed control of the marketing of the products, under the *factory system* it grasps the whole process of production. The former system, in order to accomplish the productive task falling to it, draws loosely together a large number of homogeneous labourers, imparts to their production a definite direction, approximately the same for each, and causes the product of their labour to flow, as it were, into a great reservoir before distributing it in all directions. The factory system organizes the whole process of production; it unites various kinds of workers, by mutual relations of control and subjection, into a compact and well-disciplined body, brings them together in a special business establishment, provides them with an extensive and complex outfit of the machinery of production, and thereby immensely increases their productive power. The factory system is as distinguishable from the commission system as the well-organized, uniformly equipped regular army from the motley volunteer militia.

Just as in an army corps ready for battle, troops of varied training and accoutrement—infantry, cavalry, and artillery regiments, pioneers, engineers, ammunition columns and commissariat are welded into one, so under the factory system groups of workers of varied skill and equipment are united together and enabled to accomplish the most difficult tasks of production.

The secret of the factory's strength as an institution for production thus lies in the *effective utilization of labour*. In order to accomplish this it takes a peculiar road, which at first sight appears circuitous. It divides as far as possible all the work necessary to a process of production into its simplest elements, separates the difficult from the easy, the mechanical from the intellectual, the skilled from the rude. It thus arrives at a system of successive functions, and is enabled to employ simultaneously and successively human powers of the most varied kind—trained and untrained men, women and children, workers with the hand and head, workers possessing technical, artistic and commercial skill. The restriction of each individual to a small section of the labouring process effects a mighty increase in the volume of work turned out. A hundred workmen in a factory accomplish in a given process of production more than a hundred independent master craftsmen, although each of the latter understands the whole process, while none of the former understands more than a small portion of it. As far as the struggle between handicraft and factory is fought out on the ground of technical skill, it is an evidence how the weak overcome the strong when guided by superior intellectual power.

The machine is not the essential feature of the factory, although the *subdivision of work* just described has, by breaking up the sum of labour into simple movements, endlessly assisted and multiplied the application of machinery. From early times machines for performing tasks and for furnishing power have been employed in industry. In connection with the factory, however, their application attained its present importance only when men succeeded in securing a motive power that would work unintermittently, uniformly and ubiquitously, namely, steam; and even here its full importance is felt only in connection with the peculiar industrial form of factory manufacture.

An example will serve to illustrate what has just been said. In the year 1787 the canton of Zurich had 34,000 male and female hand-spinners producing cotton yarn. After the introduction of the English spinning-machines a few factories produced an equal or greater quantity of thread, and the number of their workers (chiefly women and children) fell to scarcely a third of what it had been before. What is the explanation? The machines? But was not the then-existing spinning-wheel a machine? Certainly it was; and, moreover, a very ingenious one. Machine was thus ousted by machine. Or better, what had hitherto been done by the woman hand-spinner with her wheel was now done by successive collaboration of a whole series of various kinds of workers and machines. The entire spinning process had been decomposed into its simplest elements, and perfectly new operations had arisen for which even immature powers could in part be utilized.

In the subdivision of work originate these further peculiarities of factory production—the necessity of manufacture on a large scale, the requirement of a large capital, and the economic dependence of the workman.

With regard to the two last points we easily perceive an important difference between the factory and the commission system. Its *large fixed capital* assures to factory work greater steadiness in production. Under the commission system the house-workers can at any moment be deprived of employment without the entrepreneur running any risk of losing capital; but the manufacturer must in like case go on producing, because he fears loss of interest and shrinkage in the value of his fixed capital, and because he cannot afford to lose his trained body of workmen. This is the reason why it is probable that the commission system will long maintain itself alongside factory production in those branches of industry in which the demand is liable to sudden change, and in which the articles produced are of great variety.

If, in conclusion, we were briefly to characterize these five industrial systems, we might say that housework is production for one's own needs, wage-work is custom work, handicraft is custom production, commission work is decentralized, and factory labour centralized production of wares. As no economic phenomenon stands isolated, each of these systems of industry is at the same time but a section of a great economic and social order. Housework is the transformation of materials in the autonomous household economy; wage-work belongs to the period of transition from independent household economy to town economy; the heyday of handicraft coincides with the period when town economy reached its full development; the commission system is a connecting link between town economy and national economy (independent State economy), and the factory system is the industrial system of fully developed national economy.

It would lead us too far to explain in this chapter how each industrial system fits organically into the contemporary method of production and how it is mutually determined by a series of allied phenomena in the spheres of agriculture, personal services, trade and transportation. It can scarcely escape the observant eye that all the elements of the evolution here broadly sketched are contained in the primitive cell of society, the family; or, in economic phrase, in the conditions of production in the independent household. From this primitive social unit, teeming with life and swallowing up all individual existence, parts have continually detached themselves through differentiation and integration, and become more and more independent. Wage-work is only a sprout from the root of the tree of independent household economy; handicraft still needs its protection in order to flourish; commission work makes the marketing of products a special business, while production sinks back almost to the first stages of development. Factory manufacture, on the other hand, permeates with the entrepreneur principle the whole process of production; it is an independent economic system freed from all elements of consumption, and separated as regards commodities and locality from the household life of those engaged in it.

The position of the worker changes in a similar way. With the commencement of wage-work the industrial worker separates himself personally from the independent household economy of the landed proprietor; with the transition to handicraft he also becomes, through the elimination of business capital, materially free and independent. Through the commission system he enters into a fresh personal subjection, he falls into dependence upon the capitalistic entrepreneur; under the factory system he becomes also materially dependent upon him. By four stages of evolution he passes from manorial servitude to factory servitude.

There is a sort of parallelism in this evolution. The relation between the unfree houseworker and the ancient landowner bears a certain resemblance to the relation between the factory hand and the modern manufacturer; and the wage-worker occupies much the same position with regard to the economy of the landed proprietor that the worker engaged in house industry does to the entrepreneur giving out commission work. In the middle of this ascending and descending series stands handicraft as its foundation and corner-stone. From housework to handicraft we see the gradual emancipation of the worker from the soil and the formation of capital; from handicraft to the factory system a gradual separation of capital from work, and the subjection of the worker to capital.

At the stage of housework capital has not yet emerged; there are only consumption goods at various stages of ripeness. Everything belongs to the household—raw material, tools, the manufactured article, often the worker himself. In the case of wage-work the tools are the only capital in the hands of the worker; the raw and auxiliary materials are household stores not yet ready for consumption; the work-place belongs, under the system of migratory labour, to the domestic establishment that is to consume the finished product, or, under the housework system, to the worker who produces the article. In the case of handicraft the tools, work-place, and raw material are capital in the possession of the worker; the latter is master of the product, though he invariably sells it to the immediate consumer. In the commission system the product also becomes capital—not the capital of the worker, however, but of quite a new figure on the scene, the commercial entrepreneur; the worker either retains all his means of production, or he loses possession successively of his goods, capital, and his implements of production. Thus all the elements of capital finally unite in the hand of the manufacturer, and serve him as a foundation for the reorganization of industrial production. In his hands even the worker's share in the product becomes a part of the business capital.

This share of the worker consists, at the stage of housework, in a participation in the consumption of the finished products; in the case of wage-work it consists in board, together with a time- or piece-work wage, which even at this point includes compensation for wear and tear of tools; in handicraft it consists in the full returns from production. Under the commission system the commercial undertaker takes away a portion of the latter as profit on his business capital; under the factory system all the elements of production which can be turned into capital become crystallizing centres for further profits on capital, while for the worker there remains only the stipulated wage.

We must not, however, imagine the historical evolution of the industrial system to have been such that each new industrial method absolutely superseded its predecessor. That would be just as far astray as, for example, to suppose that a new means of communication supplants those already existing. Railways have done away neither with conveyances on the highways, nor with transportation by means of ships, pack-animals or the human back; they have only confined each of these older methods of transportation to the field in which it can best develop its peculiar advantages: it is probable that not only absolutely but relatively more horses and men are employed in the work of transportation in our civilized countries to-day than there were in the year 1830.

The very same causes that have produced such an enormous increase in traffic are also at work in the sphere of industry; and in spite of the continual improvement of the mechanical means of production they demand an ever-increasing number of persons. From two quarters, however, the sphere of productive industry is constantly receiving accessions; first, from the old household economy and agriculture, from which even to-day parts are always separating themselves and becoming independent branches of industry; secondly, from the continual improvement[2] and increase in range of articles serving for the satisfaction of our wants.

As regards the first point, there have sprung up in the industrial world during the last generation dozens of new trades for taking over such kinds of work as used formerly to fall to the women of the household or to the servants, such as vegetable and fruit preserving, fancy baking and preparation of meats, making and mending women's and children's clothes, cleaning windows, feather beds and curtains, chemical cleaning and dyeing, painting and polishing floors, gas and water installation, etc. Under the heading "Art and Market Gardening," the latest statistics of trades in the German Empire give thirty-five, and under the heading "Stock-raising," thirty-one, independent occupations, many of which are of very recent origin.

With regard to the second point, we will mention only the bicycle industry, which within a short time has not only necessitated the erection of a great number of factories, but has already given rise to special repair-shops and separate establishments for the manufacture of rubber tires, cyclometers and bicycle spokes. A still more striking example is afforded by the application of electricity. In the industrial census of 1895 there are enumerated names of twenty-two electrical occupations that did not exist in 1882. The production of electrical machines, apparatus and plant in the German Empire gave employment in 1895 to 14,494 persons, with 18,449 members of their families and servants—thus furnishing a living for nearly 33,000 persons. In metal-work, in the manufacture of machinery, chemicals, paper, in the building industries, the clothing and cleaning industries the number of recorded occupations more than doubled itself between 1882 and 1895. It is, at the same time, to be remembered not only that specialization has made immense strides, but that in many instances subsidiary articles of production and trade which have hitherto been produced by the businesses using them are the objects of separate enterprises. In these fields industry not only meets demand but frequently outruns it, as has at all times been the case. In the patent lists we find significant expression of this effort to improve the world of commodities; and though many of the new inventions prove deficient in vitality, there

2. In reply to a criticism of this expression in the Revue d'économie politique for November, 1892, (p. 1228, note), we will not omit making it more definite by saying that we do not mean by it the improvement of the quality of already existing species of goods, but the supplanting of existing goods by others which better and more cheaply supply the demand.

always remains a considerable number whereby life is permanently enriched.

If we were able statistically to bring together the whole sum of industrial products produced yearly in Germany in such a way that we could separate the output of factories, of house industry, and of handicraft, wage-work and housework, we should without doubt find that the greater part of the factory wares embraces goods which were never produced under any of the other industrial systems, and that handicraft produces to-day an absolutely greater quantity than ever before. The commission and factory systems, it is true, have completely absorbed some of the lesser handicrafts and robbed many others of portions of their sphere of production. But all the great guild handicrafts that existed at the close of the 18th century with perhaps the single exception of weaving, still exist to-day. Handicraft is constantly being displaced by the more perfect industrial systems, just as in mediæval times housework and wage-work were ousted by handicraft, only now it occurs in a less violent manner, on the field of free competition. This competition of all with all, supported as it is by a perfected system of transportation and communication, often compels the transition from custom to wholesale production, even where from the technical standpoint the former might still have been possible. Many independent master workmen enter the service of the entrepreneur carrying on commission or factory work just as their predecessors a thousand years ago became manorial labourers.

Handicraft has thus been relegated economically and socially to a secondary position. But even if it will no longer flourish in the large towns, it has in compensation spread all the more in the country, and here called forth, in combination with agriculture, numerous industries upon which the eye of the philanthropist can rest with delight. Handicraft, it may be said with certainty, will no more disappear than wage-work and housework have disappeared. What it has won for society in a time of universal feudalization, namely, a robust class of people independent of landed property, whose existence is based upon personal worth and a small amount of movables, and who are a repository of popular morality and uprightness—that will and must remain a lasting possession, even though the existence of those whom these virtues will in future adorn may rest upon a different basis.

In recent times there has been raised with rare persistence a cry for the uprooting of the older industry. Handicraft, house industry, in general all forms of work on a small scale are, we are told, a drag upon the national productive power; they are "antiquated, superseded, rude, not to say socially impeditive methods of production," which in the best interests of those who follow them must be replaced by a "rational and judicious organization and regulation of human activities on a large scale," if the actual national production is not to lag far behind what is technically possible.

This short-sighted economico-political theorizing is not new. There was once a time when every peasant shoemaker who raised his own potatoes and cabbage was looked upon as a sort of enemy to the highest possible national wealth, and when people would have liked to force him by police regulation to stick to his last, even though at the same time he ran the risk of starving. Truly, it has always been much easier to censure than to understand.

If, instead of such dogmatic pronouncements, a willingness had been shown to make an unbiassed investigation of the conditions governing those older and supposedly antiquated systems of production, the conviction would soon have arisen that in the majority of cases where they still persist they are economically and socially justifiable; and the means for the removal of the existing evils would be sought in the soil in which these industrial forms are rooted instead of such drastic remedies being applied to them. In this way we should undoubtedly preserve the good of each of these individual systems and be striving only to remove their disadvantages.

For, after all, the comforting result of every serious consideration of history is, that no single element of culture which has once entered into the life of men is lost; that even after the hour of its predominance has expired, it continues in some more modest position to coöperate in the realization of the great end in which we all believe, the helping of mankind towards more and more perfect forms of existence.

# 2. *The Fundamentals of Economic Development*

BY JOSEPH A. SCHUMPETER

WE NOW come to the third of the elements with which our analysis works, namely the "new combination of means of production," and credit. Although all three elements form a whole, the third may be described as the fundamental phenomenon of economic development. The carrying out of new combinations we call "enterprise"; the individuals whose function it is to carry them out we call "entrepreneurs." These concepts are at once broader and narrower than the usual. Broader, because in the first place we call entrepreneurs not only those "independent" businessmen in an exchange economy who are usually so designated, but all who actually fulfil the function by which we define the concept, even if they are, as is becoming the rule, "dependent" employees of a company, like managers, members of boards of directors, and so forth, or even if their actual power to perform the entrepreneurial function has any other foundations, such as the control of a majority of shares. As it is the carrying out of new combinations that constitutes the entrepreneur, it is not necessary that he should be permanently connected with an individual firm; many "financiers," "promotors," and so forth are not, and still they may be entrepreneurs in our sense. On the other hand, our concept is narrower than the traditional one in that it does not include all heads of firms or managers or industrialists who merely may operate an established business, but only those who actually perform that function. Nevertheless I maintain that the above definition does no more than formulate with greater precision what the traditional doctrine really means to convey. In the first place our definition agrees with the usual one on the fundamental point of distinguishing between "entrepreneurs" and "capitalists"—irrespective of whether the latter are regarded as owners of money, claims to money, or material goods. This distinction is common property to-day and has been so for a considerable time. It also settles the question whether the ordinary shareholder as such is an entrepreneur, and disposes of the conception of the entrepreneur as risk bearer.[1] Furthermore, the ordinary characterisation of the entrepreneur type by such expessions as "initiative," "authority," or "foresight" points entirely in our direction. For there is little scope for such qualities within the routine of the circular flow, and if this had been sharply separated from the occurrence of changes in this routine itself, the emphasis in the definition of the function of entrepreneurs would have been shifted automatically to the latter. Finally there are definitions which we could simply accept. There is in particular the well known one that goes back to J. B. Say: the entrepreneur's function is to combine the productive factors, to bring them together. Since this is a performance of a special kind only when the factors are combined for the first time—while it is merely routine work if done in the course of running a business—this definition coincides with ours. When Mataja (in Unternehmergewinn) defines the entrepreneur as one who receives profit, we have only to add the conclusion of the first chapter, that there is no profit in the circular flow, in order to trace this formulation too back to ours.[2]

Reprinted by permission of the publishers from Joseph A. Schumpeter, *The Theory of Economic Development* (Cambridge, Mass.: Harvard University Press, 1934), pp. 74–94. 

1. Risk obviously always falls on the owner of the means of production or of the money-capital which was paid for them, hence never on the entrepreneur *as such*. A shareholder *may* be an entrepreneur. He may even owe to his holding a controlling interest the power to act as an entrepreneur. Shareholders *per se,* however, are never entrepreneurs, but merely capitalists, who in consideration of their submitting to certain risks participate in profits. That this is no reason to look upon them as anything but capitalists is shown by the facts, first, that the average shareholder has normally no power to influence the management of his company, and secondly, that participation in profits is frequent in cases in which everyone recognises the presence of a loan contract. Compare, for example, the Graeco-Roman *foenus nauticum.* Surely this interpretation is more true to life than the other one, which, following the lead of a faulty legal construction—which can only be explained historically—attributes functions to the average shareholder which he hardly ever thinks of discharging.

2. The definition of the entrepreneur in terms of entrepreneurial profit instead of in terms of the function the performance of which creates the entrepreneurial profit is obviously not brilliant. But we have still another objection to it: we shall see that entrepreneurial profit does not fall to the entrepreneur by "necessity" in the same sense as the marginal product of labor does to the worker.

And this view is not foreign to traditional theory, as is shown by the construction of the *entrepreneur faisant ni bénéfice ni perte,* which has been worked out rigorously by Walras, but is the property of many other authors. The tendency is for the entrepreneur to make neither profit nor loss in the circular flow—that is he has no function of a special kind there, he simply does not exist; but in his stead, there are heads of firms or business managers of a different type which we had better not designate by the same term.

It is a prejudice to believe that the knowledge of the historical origin of an institution or of a type immediately shows us its sociological or economic nature. Such knowledge often leads us to understand it, but it does not directly yield a theory of it. Still more false is the belief that "primitive" forms of a type are also *ipso facto* the "simpler" or the "more original" in the sense that they show their nature more purely and with fewer complications than later ones. Very frequently the opposite is the case, amongst other reasons because increasing specialisation may allow functions and qualities to stand out sharply, which are more difficult to recognise in more primitive conditions when mixed with others. So it is in our case. In the general position of the chief of a primitive horde it is difficult to separate the entrepreneurial element from the others. For the same reason most economists up to the time of the younger Mill failed to keep capitalist and entrepreneur distinct because the manufacturer of a hundred years ago was both; and certainly the course of events since then has facilitated the making of this distinction, as the system of land tenure in England has facilitated the distinction between farmer and landowner, while on the Continent this distinction is still occasionally neglected, especially in the case of the peasant who tills his own soil.[3] But in our case there are still more of such difficulties. The entrepreneur of earlier times was not only as a rule the capitalist too, he was also often—as he still is to-day in the case of small concerns—his own technical expert, in so far as a professional specialist was not called in for special cases. Likewise he was (and is) often his own buying and selling agent, the head of his office, his own personnel manager, and sometimes, even though as a rule he of course employed solicitors, his own legal adviser in current affairs. And it was performing some or all of these functions that regularly filled his days. The carrying out of new combinations can no more be a *vocation* than the making and execution of strategical decisions, although it is this function and not his routine work that characterises the military leader. Therefore the entrepreneur's essential function must always appear mixed up with other kinds of activity, which as a rule must be much more conspicuous than the essential one. Hence the Marshallian definition of the entrepreneur, which simply treats the entrepreneurial function as "management" in the widest meaning, will naturally appeal to most of us. We do not accept it, simply because it does not bring out what we consider to be the salient point and the only one which specifically distinguishes entrepreneurial from other activities.

Nevertheless there are types—the course of events has evolved them by degrees—which exhibit the entrepreneurial function with particular purity. The "promoter," to be sure, belongs to them only with qualifications. For, neglecting the associations relative to social and moral status which are attached to this type, the promoter is frequently only an agent intervening on commission, who does the work of financial technique in floating the new enterprise. In this case he is not its creator nor the driving power in the process. However, he *may* be the latter also, and then he is something like an "entrepreneur by profession." But the modern type of "captain of industry" corresponds more closely to what is meant here, especially if one recognises his identity on the one hand with, say, the commercial entrepreneur of twelfth-century Venice—or, among later types, with John Law—and on the other hand with the village potentate who combines with his agriculture and his cattle trade, say, a rural brewery, an hotel, and a store. But whatever the type, everyone is an entrepreneur only when he actually "carries out new combinations," and loses that character as soon as he has built up his business, when he settles down to running it as other people run their businesses. This is the rule, of course, and hence it is just as rare for anyone always to remain an entrepreneur throughout the decades of his active life as it is for a businessman never to have a moment in which he is an entrepreneur, to however modest a degree.

Because being an entrepreneur is not a profession and as a rule not a lasting condition, entrepreneurs do not form a social class in the technical sense, as, for example, landowners or capitalists or workmen do. Of course the entrepreneurial function will *lead* to certain class

3. Only this neglect explains the attitude of many socialistic theorists towards peasant property. For smallness of the individual possession makes a difference only for the petit-bourgeois, not for the socialist. The criterion of the employment of labor other than that of the owner and his family is economically relevant only from the standpoint of a kind of exploitation theory which is hardly tenable any longer.

positions for the successful entrepreneur and his family. It can also put its stamp on an epoch of social history, can form a style of life, or systems of moral and aesthetic values; but in itself it signifies a class position no more than it presupposes one. And the class position which may be attained is not as such an entrepreneurial position, but is characterised as landowning or capitalist, according to how the proceeds of the enterprise are used. Inheritance of the pecuniary result and of personal qualities may then both keep up this position for more than one generation and make further enterprise easier for descendants, but the function of the entrepreneur itself cannot be inherited, as is shown well enough by the history of manufacturing families.[4]

But now the decisive question arises: why then is the carrying out of new combinations a special process and the object of a special kind of "function"; Every individual carries on his economic affairs as well as he can. To be sure, his own intentions are never realised with ideal perfection, but ultimately his behavior is moulded by the influence on him of the results of his conduct, so as to fit circumstances which do not as a rule change suddenly. If a business can never be absolutely perfect in any sense, yet it in time approaches a relative perfection having regard to the surrounding world, the social conditions, the knowledge of the time, and the horizon of each individual or each group. New possibilities are continuously being offered by the surrounding world, in particular new discoveries are continuously being added to the existing store of knowledge. Why should not the individual make just as much use of the new possibilities as of the old, and, according to the market position as he understands it, keep pigs instead of cows, or even choose a new crop rotation, if this can be seen to be more advantageous? And what kind of special new phenomena or problems, not to be found in the established circular flow, can arise there?

While in the accustomed circular flow every individual can act promptly and rationally because he is sure of his ground and is supported by the conduct, as adjusted to this circular flow, of all other individuals, who in turn expect the accustomed activity from him, he cannot simply do this when he is confronted by a new task. While in the accustomed channels his own ability and experience suffice for the normal individual, when confronted with innovations he needs guidance. While he swims with the stream in the circular flow which is familiar to him, he swims against the stream if he wishes to change its channel. What was formerly a help becomes a hindrance. What was a familiar datum becomes an unknown. Where the boundaries of routine stop, many people can go no further, and the rest can only do so in a highly variable manner. The assumption that conduct is prompt and rational is in all cases a fiction. But it proves to be sufficiently near to reality, if things have time to hammer logic into men. Where this has happened, and within the limits in which it has happened, one may rest content with this fiction and build theories upon it. It is then not true that habit or custom or non-economic ways of thinking cause a hopeless difference between the individuals of different classes, times, or cultures, and that, for example, the "economics of the stock exchange" would be inapplicable say to the peasants of to-day or to the craftsmen of the Middle Ages. On the contrary the same theoretical picture[5] in its broadest contour lines fits the individuals of quite different cultures, whatever their degree of intelligence and of economic rationality, and we can depend upon it that the peasant sells his calf just as cunningly and egotistically as the stock exchange member his portfolio of shares. But this holds good only where precedents without number have formed conduct through decades and, in fundamentals, through hundreds and thousands of years, and have eliminated unadapted behavior. Outside of these limits our fiction loses its closeness to reality.[6] To cling to it there also, as the traditional theory does, is to hide an essential thing and to ignore a fact which, in contrast with other deviations of our assumptions from reality, is theoretically important and the source of the explanation of phenomena which would not exist without it.

Therefore, in describing the circular flow one must treat combinations of means of production (the production-functions) as data, like natural pos-

4. On the nature of the entrepreneurial function also compare my statement in the article "Unternehmer" in the Handwörterbuch der Staatswissenschaften.

5. The same *theoretical* picture, obviously not the same sociological, cultural, and so forth.

6. How much this is the case is best seen to-day in the economic life of those nations, and within our civilisation in the economics of those individuals, whom the development of the last century has not yet completely drawn into its stream, for example, in the economy of the Central European peasant. This peasant "calculates"; there is no deficiency of the "economic way of thinking" (Wirtschaftsgesinnung) in him. Yet he cannot take a step out of the beaten path; his economy has not changed at all for centuries, except perhaps through the exercise of external force and influence. Why? Because the choice of new methods is not simply an element in the concept of rational economic action, nor a matter of course, but a distinct process which stands in need of special explanation.

sibilities, and admit only small[7] variations at the margins, such as every individual can accomplish by adapting himself to changes in his economic environment, without materially deviating from familiar lines. Therefore, too, the carrying out of new combinations is a special function, and the privilege of a type of people who are much less numerous than all those who have the "objective" possibility of doing it. Therefore, finally, entrepreneurs are a special type,[8] and their behavior a special problem, the motive power of a great number of significant phenomena. Hence, our position may be characterised by three corresponding pairs of opposites. First, by the opposition of two real processes: the circular flow or the tendency towards equilibrium on the one hand, a change in the channels of economic routine or a spontaneous change in the economic data arising from within the system on the other. Secondly, by the opposition of two theoretical *apparatuses:* statics and dynamics.[9] Thirdly, by the opposition

7. Small disturbances which may indeed, as mentioned earlier, in time add up to great amounts. The decisive point is that the businessman, if he makes them, never alters his routine. The usual case is one of small, the exception one of great (*uno actu* great), disturbances. Only in this sense is emphasis put upon "smallness" here. The objection that there can be no difference in principle between small and large disturbances is not effective. For it is false in itself, in so far as it is based upon the disregard of the principle of the infinitesimal method, the essence of which lies in the fact that one can assert of "small quantities" under certain circumstances what one cannot assert of "large quantities." But the reader who takes umbrage at the large-small contrast may, if he wishes, substitute for it the contrast adapting-spontaneous. Personally I am not willing to do this because the latter method of expression is much easier to misunderstand than the former and really would demand still longer explanations.

8. In the first place it is a question of a type of *conduct* and of a type of *person* in so far as this conduct is accessible in very unequal measure and to relatively few people, so that it constitutes their outstanding characteristic. Because the exposition of the first edition was reproached with exaggerating and mistaking the peculiarity of this conduct, and with overlooking the fact that it is more or less open to every businessman, and because the exposition in a later paper ("Wellenbewegung des Wirtschaftslebens," Archiv für Sozialwissenschaft) was charged with introducing an intermediate type ("half-static" businessmen), the following may be submitted. The conduct in question is peculiar in two ways. First, because it is directed towards something different and signifies doing something different from other conduct. One may indeed in this connection include it with the latter in a higher unity, but this does not alter the fact that a theoretically relevant difference exists between the two, and that only one of them is adequately described by traditional theory. Secondly, the type of conduct in question not only differs from the other in its object, "innovation" being peculiar to it, but also in that it presupposes aptitudes differing *in kind* and not only in degree from those of mere rational economic behavior.

Now these aptitudes are presumably distributed in an ethically homogeneous population just like others, that is the curve of their distribution has a maximum ordinate, deviations on either side of which become rarer the greater they are. Similiarly we can assume that every healthy man can sing if he will. Perhaps half the individuals in an ethically homogeneous group have the capacity for it to an average degree, a quarter in progressively diminishing measure, and, let us say, a quarter in a measure above the average; and within this quarter, through a series of continually increasing singing ability and continually diminishing number of people who possess it, we come finally to the Carusos. Only in this quarter are we struck in general by the singing ability, and only in the supreme instances can it become the characterising mark of the person. Although practically all men can sing, singing ability does not cease to be a distinguishable characteristic and attribute of a minority, indeed not exactly of a type, because this characteristic—unlike ours—affects the total personality relatively little.

Let us apply this: Again, a quarter of the population may be so poor in those qualities, let us say here provisionally, of economic initiative that the deficiency makes itself felt by poverty of their moral personality, and they play a wretched part in the smallest affairs of private and professional life in which this element is called for. We recognise this type and know that many of the best clerks, distinguished by devotion to duty, expert knowledge, and exactitude, belong to it. Then comes the "half," the "normal." These prove themselves to be better in the things which even within the established channels cannot simply be "dispatched" (erledigen) but must also be "decided" (entscheiden) and "carried out" (durchsetzen). Practically all business people belong here, otherwise they would never have attained their positions; most represent a selection—individually or hereditarily tested. A textile manufacturer travels no "new" road when he goes to a wool auction. But the situations there are never the same, and the success of the business depends so much upon skill and initiative in buying wool that the fact that the textile industry has so far exhibited no trustification comparable with that in heavy manufacturing is undoubtedly partly explicable by the reluctance of the cleverer manufacturers to renounce the advantage of their own skill in buying wool. From there, rising in the scale we come finally into the highest quarter, to people who are a type characterised by super-normal qualities of intellect and will. Within this type there are not only many varieties (merchants, manufacturers, financiers, etc.) but also a continuous variety of degrees of intensity in "initiative." In our argument types of every intensity occur. Many a one can steer a safe course, where no one has yet been; others follow where first another went before; still others only in the crowd, but in this among the first. So also the great political leader of every kind and time is a type, yet not a thing unique, but only the apex of a pyramid from which there is a continuous variation down to the average and from it to the sub-normal values. And yet not only is "leading" a special function, but the leader also something special, distinguishable—wherefore there is no sense in our case in asking: "Where does that type begin then? and then to exclaim: "This is no type at all!"

9. It has been objected against the first edition that it sometimes defines "statics" as a theoretical construction, sometimes as the picture of an actual state of economic life. I believe that the present exposition gives no ground for this opinion. "Static" theory does not assume a stationary economy; it also treats of the effects of changes in data. In itself, therefore, there is no necessary connection between static theory and stationary reality. Only in so far as one can exhibit the fundamental form of the economic course of events with the maximum simplicity in an unchanging economy does this assumption recommend itself to theory. The stationary economy is for uncounted thousands of years, and also in historical times in many places for centuries, an incontrovertible fact, apart from the fact, moreover, which Sombart emphasised, that there

of two types of conduct, which, following reality, we can picture as two types of individuals: mere managers and entrepreneurs. And therefore the "best method" of producing in the theoretical sense is to be conceived as "the most advantageous among the methods which have been empirically tested and become familiar." But it is not the "best" of the methods "possible' at the time. If one does not make this distinction, the concept becomes meaningless and precisely those problems remain unsolved which our interpretation is meant to provide for.

Let us now formulate precisely the characteristic feature of the conduct and type under discussion. The smallest daily action embodies a huge mental effort. Every schoolboy would have to be a mental giant, if he himself had to create all he knows and uses by his own individual activity. And every man would have to be a giant of wisdom and will, if he had in every case to create anew all the rules by which he guides his everyday conduct. This is true not only of those decisions and actions of individual and social life the principles of which are the product of tens of thousands of years, but also of those products of shorter periods and of a more special nature which constitute the particular instrument for performing vocational tasks. But precisely the things the performance of which according to this should involve a supreme effort, in general demand no special individual effort at all; those which should be especially difficult are in reality especially easy; what should demand superhuman capacity is accessible to the least gifted, given mental health. In particular within the ordinary routine there is no need for leadership. Of course it is still necessary to set people their tasks, to keep up discipline, and so forth; but this is easy and a function any normal person can learn to fulfil. Within the lines familiar to all, even the function of directing other people, though still necessary, is mere "work" like any other, comparable to the service of tending a machine. All people get to know, and are able to do, their daily tasks in the customary way and ordinarily perform them by themselves; the "director" has his routine as they have theirs; and his directive function serves merely to correct individual aberrations.

This is so because all knowledge and habit once acquired becomes as firmly rooted in ourselves as a railway embankment in the earth. It does not require to be continually renewed and consciously reproduced, but sinks into the strata of subconsciousness. It is normally transmitted almost without friction by inheritance, teaching, upbringing, pressure of environment. Everything we think, feel, or do often enough becomes automatic and our conscious life is unburdened of it. The enormous economy of force, in the race and the individual, here involved is not great enough, however, to make daily life a light burden and to prevent its demands from exhausting the average energy all the same. But it is great enough to make it possible to meet the ordinary claims. This holds good likewise for economic daily life. And from this it follows also for economic life that every step outside the boundary of routine has difficulties and involves a new element. It is this element that constitutes the phenomena of leadership.

The nature of these difficulties may be focussed in the following three points. First, outside these accustomed channels the individual is without those data for his decisions and those rules of conduct which are usually very accurately known to him within them. Of course he must still foresee and estimate on the basis of his experience. But many things must remain uncertain, still others are only ascertainable within wide limits, some can perhaps only be "guessed." In particular this is true of those data which the individual strives to alter and of those which he wants to create. Now he must really to some extent do what tradition does for him in everyday life, viz. consciously plan his conduct in every particular. There will be much more conscious rationality in this than in customary action, which as such does not need to be reflected upon at all; but this plan must necessarily

---

is a tendency towards a stationary state in every period of depression. Hence it is readily understood how this historical fact and that theoretical construction have allied themselves in a way which led to some confusion. The words "statics" and "dynamics" the author would not now use in the meaning they carry above, where they are simply short expressions for "theory of the circular flow" and "theory of development." One more thing: theory employs two methods of interpretation, which may perhaps make difficulties. If it is to be shown how all the elements of the economic system are determined in equilibrium by one another, this equilibrium system is considered as not yet existing and is built up before our eyes *ab ovo*. This does not mean that its coming into being is genetically explained thereby. Only its existence and functioning are made logically clear by mental dissection. And the experiences and habits of individuals are assumed as existing. How just these productive combinations have come about is not thereby explained. Further, if two contiguous equilibrium positions are to be investigated, then sometimes (not always), as in Pigou's Economics of Welfare, the "best" productive combination in the first is compared with the "best" in the second. And this again need not, but may, mean that the two combinations in the sense meant here differ not only by small variations in quantity but in their whole technical and commercial structure. Here too the coming into being of the second combination and the problems connected with it are not investigated, but only the functioning and the outcome of the already existing combination. Even though justified as far as it goes, this method of treatment passes over our problem. If the assertion were implied that this is also settled by it, it would be false.

be open not only to errors greater in degree, but also to other kinds of errors than those occurring in customary action. What has been done already has the sharp-edged reality of all the things which we have seen and experienced; the new is only the figment of our imagination. Carrying out a new plan and acting according to a customary one are things as different as making a road and walking along it.

How different a thing this is becomes clearer if one bears in mind the impossibility of surveying exhaustively all the effects and counter-effects of the projected enterprise. Even as many of them as could in theory be ascertained if one had unlimited time and means must practically remain in the dark. As military action must be taken in a given strategic position even if all the data potentially procurable are not available, so also in economic life action must be taken without working out all the details of what is to be done. Here the success of everything depends upon intuition, the capacity of seeing things in a way which afterwards proves to be true, even though it cannot be established at the moment, and of grasping the essential fact, discarding the unessential, even though one can give no account of the principles by which this is done. Thorough preparatory work, and special knowledge, breadth of intellectual understanding, talent for logical analysis, may under certain circumstances be sources of failure. The more accurately, however, we learn to know the natural and social world, the more perfect our control of facts becomes; and the greater the extent, with time and progressive rationalisation, within which things can be simply calculated, and indeed quickly and reliably calculated, the more the significance of this function decreases. Therefore the importance of the entrepreneur type must diminish just as the importance of the military commander has already diminished. Nevertheless a part of the very essence of each type is bound up with this function.

As this first point lies in the task, so the second lies in the psyche of the businessman himself. It is not only objectively more difficult to do something new than what is familiar and tested by experience, but the individual feels reluctance to it and would do so even if the objective difficulties did not exist. This is so in all fields. The history of science is one great confirmation of the fact that we find it exceedingly difficult to adopt a new scientific point of view or method. Thought turns again and again into the accustomed track even if it has become unsuitable and the more suitable innovation in itself presents no particular difficulties. The very nature of fixed habits of thinking, their energy-saving function, is founded upon the fact that they have become subconscious, that they yield their results automatically and are proof against criticism and even against contradiction by individual facts. But precisely because of this they become drag-chains when they have outlived their usefulness. So it is also in the economic world. In the breast of one who wishes to do something new, the forces of habit rise up and bear witness against the embryonic project. A new and another kind of effort of will is therefore necessary in order to wrest, amidst the work and care of the daily round, scope and time for conceiving and working out the new combination and to bring oneself to look upon it as a real possibility and not merely as a day-dream. This mental freedom presupposes a great surplus force over the everyday demand and is something peculiar and by nature rare.

The third point consists in the reaction of the social environment against one who wishes to do something new. This reaction may manifest itself first of all in the existence of legal or political impediments. But neglecting this, any deviating conduct by a member of a social group is condemned, though in greatly varying degrees according as the social group is used to such conduct or not. Even a deviation from social custom in such things as dress or manners arouses opposition, and of course all the more so in the graver cases. This opposition is stronger in primitive stages of culture than in others, but it is never absent. Even mere astonishment at the deviation, even merely noticing it, exercises a pressure on the individual. The manifestation of condemnation may at once bring noticeable consequences in its train. It may even come to social ostracism and finally to physical prevention or to direct attack. Neither the fact that progressive differentiation weakens this opposition —especially as the most important cause of the weakening is the very development which we wish to explain—nor the further fact that the social opposition operates under certain circumstances and upon many individuals as a stimulus, changes anything in principle in the significance of it. Surmounting this opposition is always a special kind of task which does not exist in the customary course of life, a task which also requires a special kind of conduct. In matters economic this resistance manifests itself first of all in the groups threatened by the innovation, then in the difficulty in finding the necessary cooperation, finally in the difficulty in winning over consumers. Even though these elements are still effective to-day, despite the fact that a period of turbulent development has accustomed us to the appearance and the carrying out of innovations, they can be best studied in the beginnings of capitalism. But they are so obvious there that it would be time lost for our purposes to dwell upon them.

There is leadership *only* for these reasons—leadership, that is, as a special kind of function and in contrast to a mere difference in rank, which would exist in every social body, in the smallest as in the largest, and in combination with which it generally appears. The facts alluded to create a boundary beyond which the majority of people do not function promptly by themselves and require help from a minority. If social life had in all respects the relative immutability of, for example, the astronomical world, or if mutable this mutability were yet incapable of being influenced by human action, or finally if capable of being so influenced this type of action were yet equally open to everyone, then there would be no special function of leadership as distinguished from routine work.

The specific problem of leadership arises and the leader type appears only where new possibilities present themselves. That is why it is so strongly marked among the Normans at the time of their conquests and so feebly among the Slavs in the centuries of their unchanging and relatively protected life in the marshes of the Pripet. Our three points characterise the nature of the *function* as well as the *conduct* or behavior which constitutes the leader type. It is no part of his function to "find" or to "create" new possibilities. They are always present, abundantly accumulated by all sorts of people. Often they are also generally known and being discussed by scientific or literary writers. In other cases, there is nothing to discover about them, because they are quite obvious. To take an example from political life, it was not at all difficult to see how the social and political conditions of France at the time of Louis XVI could have been improved so as to avoid a breakdown of the *ancien régime*. Plenty of people as a matter of fact did see it. But nobody was in a position to *do* it. Now, it is this "doing the thing," without which possibilities are dead, of which the leader's function consists. This holds good of all kinds of leadership, ephemeral as well as more enduring ones. The former may serve as an instance. What is to be done in a casual emergency is as a rule quite simple. Most or all people may see it, yet they want someone to speak out, to lead, and to organise. Even leadership which influences merely by example, as artistic or scientific leadership, does not consist simply in finding or creating the new thing but in so impressing the social group with it as to draw it on in its wake. It is, therefore, more by will than by intellect that the leaders fulfil their function, more by "authority," "personal weight," and so forth than by original ideas.

Economic leadership in particular must hence be distinguished from "invention." As long as they are not carried into practice, inventions are economically irrelevant. And to carry any improvement into effect is a task entirely different from the inventing of it, and a task, moreover, requiring entirely different kinds of aptitudes. Although entrepreneurs of course *may* be inventors just as they may be capitalists, they are inventors not by nature of their function but by coincidence and vice versa. Besides, the innovations which it is the function of entrepreneurs to carry out need not necessarily be any inventions at all. It is, therefore, not advisable, and it may be downright misleading, to stress the element of invention as much as many writers do.

The entrepreneurial kind of leadership, as distinguished from other kinds of economic leadership such as we should expect to find in a primitive tribe of a communist society, is of course colored by the conditions peculiar to it. It has none of that glamour which characterises other kinds of leadership. It consists in fulfilling a very special task which only in rare cases appeals to the imagination of the public. For its success, keenness and vigor are not more essential than a certain narrowness which seizes the immediate chance and *nothing else*. "Personal weight" is, to be sure, not without importance. Yet the personality of the capitalistic entrepreneur need not, and generally does not, answer to the idea most of us have of what a "leader" looks like, so much so that there is some difficulty in realizing that he comes within the sociological category of leader at all. He "leads" the means of production into new channels. But this he does, not by convincing people of the desirability of carrying out his plan or by creating confidence in his leading in the manner of a political leader—the only man he has to convince or to impress is the banker who is to finance him—but by buying them or their services, and then using them as he sees fit. He also leads in the sense that he draws other producers in his branch after him. But as they are his competitors, who first reduce and then annihilate his profit, this is, as it were, leadership against one's own will. Finally, he renders a service, the full appreciation of which takes a specialist's knowledge of the case. It is not so easily understood by the public at large as a politician's successful speech or a general's victory in the field, not to insist on the fact that he seems to act—and often harshly—in his individual interest alone. We shall understand, therefore, that we do not observe, in this case, the emergence of all those affective values which are the glory of all other kinds of social leadership. Add to this the precariousness of the economic position both of the individual entrepreneur and of entrepreneurs as a group, and the fact that when his economic success raises him socially he has no cultural tradition or attitude to fall back upon, but moves about in society as an upstart, whose ways are readily laughed at, and we shall understand why this type has never been popular, and why even scientific critique often makes short work of it.[10]

We shall finally try to round off our picture of the entrepreneur in the same manner in which we always, in science as well as in practical life, try to understand human behavior, viz. by analysing the characteristic motives of his conduct. Any attempt to do this must of course meet with all those objections against the economist's intrusion into "psychology" which have been made familiar by a long series of writers. We cannot here enter into the fundamental question of the relation between psychology and economics. It is enough to state that those who on principle object to *any* psychological considerations in an economic argument may leave out what we are about to say without thereby losing contact with the argument of the following chapters. For none of the results to which our analysis is intended to lead stands or falls with our "psychology of the entrepreneur," or could be vitiated by any errors in it. Nowhere is there, as the reader will easily satisfy himself, any necessity for us to overstep the frontiers of observable behavior. Those who do not object to *all* psychology but only to the *kind* of psychology which we know from the traditional textbook, will see that we do not adopt any part of the time-honored picture of the motivation of the "economic man."

In the theory of the circular flow, the importance of examining motives is very much reduced by the fact that the equations of the system of equilibrium may be so interpreted as not to imply any psychic magnitudes at all, as shown by the analysis of Pareto and of Barone. This is the reason why even very defective psychology interferes much less with results than one would expect. There may be rational *conduct* even in the absence of rational *motive*. But as soon as we really wish to penetrate into motivation, the problem proves by no means simple. Within given social circumstances and habits, most of what people do every day will appear to them primarily from the point of view of duty carrying a social or a superhuman sanction. There is very little of conscious rationality, still less of hedonism and of *individual* egoism about it, and so much of it as may safely be said to exist is of comparatively recent growth. Nevertheless, as long as we confine ourselves to the great outlines of constantly repeated economic action, we may link it up with wants and the desire to satisfy them, on condition that we are careful to recognise that economic motive so defined varies in intensity very much in time; that it is society that shapes the particular desires we observe; that wants must be taken with reference to the group which the individual thinks of when deciding his course of action—the family or any other group, smaller or larger than the family; that action does not promptly follow upon desire but only more or less imperfectly corresponds to it; that the field of individual choice is always, though in very different ways and to very different degrees, fenced in by social habits or conventions and the like: it still remains broadly true that, within the circular flow, everyone adapts himself to his environment so as to satisfy certain *given* wants—of himself or others—as best he can. In *all* cases, the *meaning* of economic action is the satisfaction of wants in the sense that there would be no economic action if there were no wants. In the case of the circular flow, we may also think of satisfaction of wants as the normal *motive*.

The latter is not true for our type. In one sense, he may indeed be called the most rational and the most egotistical of all. For, as we have seen, conscious rationality enters much more into the carrying out of new plans, which themselves have to be worked out before they can be acted upon, than into the mere running of an established business, which is largely a matter of routine. And the typical entrepreneur is more self-centered than other types, because he relies less than they do on tradition and connection and because his characteristic task—theoretically as well as historically—consists precisely in breaking up old, and creating new, tradition. Although this applies primarily to his economic action, it also extends to the moral, cultural, and social consequences of it. It is, of course, no mere coincidence that the period of the rise of the entrepreneur type also gave birth to Utilitarianism.

But his conduct and his motive are "rational" in no other sense. And in *no* sense is his character-

10. It may, therefore, not be superfluous to point out that our analysis of the rôle of the entrepreneur does not involve any "glorification" of the type, as some readers of the first edition of this book seemed to think. We do hold that entrepreneurs *have* an economic function as distinguished from, say, robbers. But we neither style every entrepreneur a genius or a benefactor to humanity, nor do we wish to express any opinion about the comparative merits of the social organisation in which he plays his rôle, or about the question whether what he does could not be effected more cheaply or efficiently in other ways.

istic motivation of the hedonist kind. If we define hedonist motive of action as the wish to satisfy one's wants, we may indeed make "wants" include any impulse whatsoever, just as we may define egoism so as to include all altruistic values too, on the strength of the fact that they also mean something in the way of self-gratification. But this would reduce our definition to tautology. If we wish to give it meaning, we must restrict it to such wants as are capable of being satisfied by the consumption of goods, and to that kind of satisfaction which is expected from it. Then it is no longer true that our type is acting on a wish to satisfy his wants.

For unless we assume that individuals of our type are driven along by an insatiable craving for hedonist satisfaction, the operations of Gossen's law would in the case of business leaders soon put a stop to further effort. Experience teaches, however, that typical entrepreneurs retire from the arena only when and because their strength is spent and they feel no longer equal to their task. This does not seem to verify the picture of the economic man, balancing probable results against disutility of effort and reaching in due course a point of equilibrium beyond which he is not willing to go. Effort, in our case, does not seem to weigh at all in the sense of being felt as a reason to stop. And activity of the entrepreneurial type is obviously an obstacle to hedonist enjoyment of those kinds of commodity which are usually acquired by incomes beyond a certain size, because their "consumption" presupposes leisure. Hedonistically, therefore, the conduct which we usually observe in individuals of our type would be irrational.

This would not, of course, prove the absence of hedonistic motive. Yet it points to another psychology of non-hedonist character, especially if we take into account the indifference to hedonist enjoyment which is often conspicuous in outstanding specimens of the type and which is not difficult to understand.

First of all, there is the dream and the will to found a private kingdom, usually, though not necessarily, also a dynasty. The modern world really does not know any such positions, but what may be attained by industrial or commercial success is still the nearest approach to medieval lordship possible to modern man. Its fascination is specially strong for people who have no other chance of achieving social distinction. The sensation of power and independence loses nothing by the fact that both are largely illusions. Closer analysis would lead to discovering an endless variety within this group of motives, from spiritual ambition down to mere snobbery. But this need not detain us. Let it suffice to point out that motives of this kind, although they stand nearest to consumers' satisfaction, do not coincide with it.

Then there is the will to conquer: the impulse to fight, to prove oneself superior to others, to succeed for the sake, not of the fruits of success, but of success itself. From this aspect, economic action becomes akin to sport—there are financial races, or rather boxing-matches. The financial result is a secondary consideration, or, at all events, mainly valued as an index of success and as a symptom of victory, the displaying of which very often is more important as a motive of large expenditure than the wish for the consumers' goods themselves. Again we should find countless nuances, some of which, like social ambition, shade into the first group of motives. And again we are faced with a motivation characteristically different from that of "satisfaction of wants" in the sense defined above, or from, to put the same thing into other words, "hedonistic adaptation."

Finally, there is the joy of creating, of getting things done, or simply of exercising one's energy and ingenuity. This is akin to a ubiquitous motive, but nowhere else does it stand out as an independent factor of behavior with anything like the clearness with which it obtrudes itself in our case. Our type seeks out difficulties, changes in order to change, delights in ventures. This group of motives is the most distinctly anti-hedonist of the three.

Only with the first groups of motives is private property as the result of entrepreneurial activity an essential factor in making it operative. With the other two it is not. Pecuniary gain is indeed a very accurate expression of success, especially of *relative* success, and from the standpoint of the man who strives for it, it has the additional advantage of being an objective fact and largely independent of the opinion of others. These and other peculiarities incident to the mechanism of "acquisitive" society make it very difficult to replace it as a motor of industrial development, even if we would discard the importance it has for creating a fund ready for investment. Nevertheless it is true that the second and third groups of entrepreneurial motives may in principle be taken care of by other social arrangements not involving private gain from economic innovation. What other stimuli could be provided, and how they could be made to work as well as the "capitalistic" ones do, are questions which are beyond our theme. They are taken too lightly by social reformers, and are altogether ignored by fiscal radicalism. But they are not insoluble, and may be answered by detailed observation of the psychology of entrepreneurial activity, at least for given times and places.

# *Section C*

# Stratification and Mobility

EDITORIAL FOREWORD

# Stratification and Mobility

*by Talcott Parsons*

THOUGH IT IS PROMINENT IN more recent sociology, particularly in the United States, the subject of social stratification did not, in the earlier phases, produce a large volume of notable literature. This section's relative brevity reflects this fact; there are not many writings which were highly influential.

The modern sociological interest in stratification has taken most of its departure from its reference to economic organization as this took shape in Western society during the Industrial Revolution, and the concept has been amplified from there. Hence the initial selection we present is by Adam Smith, though not, this time, with direct reference to the problem of economic organization, except as implicit background. This selection is concerned with the way in which the problem of the distribution of wealth became focused in the classical economics. There are three shares of income that figure in that analysis; and rent became progressively less important as industrial organization began overshadowing agriculture. Hence it is the relation between the businessman's profit (which, in the classical scheme, included interest) and the worker's wages that formed the focus of the important conflict of interest. This was associated with the assumption, discussed in the general Introduction to Part Two, that there was a relatively simple dichotomy between owning-managing family groups and property-less "workers." As noted in the Introduction to Section B, the owner's function was conceived more as "making advances to labor" than as active management.

Into his concept of class struggle, Marx built this broad picture of the structure of industry and its inherent conflict of interest over proceeds. The *Communist Manifesto* itself is the best statement of the Marxist position, and a selection from that presents the position.

Theoretical development occurred essentially through a process of amplification from this economic point of reference. Goblot presents an analysis concentrating on the style-of-life aspect of social class; occupation becomes an essential component, though not the final criterion, of membership. Possibly the style-of-life aspect of occupation may be more important than its effective contribution to society. He is chiefly interested in showing the consequence of the class function—the stabilization of life chances—for the recruitment process (the barrier) and for the inner structure of the class (the level).

The following three selections vary their emphasis somewhat; instead of concentrating on the most general structural picture, they emphasize a more detailed analysis of components in a society's hierarchical structure. Simmel took the general pattern of super- and sub-ordination as a type case of "social form," and attempted to survey the various modes in which this dimension of social relationships could develop. Like Goblot, Simmel reacted strongly against any simple dichotomy concept which could be applied universally to characterize a whole society; but Simmel extended his analysis to include non-occupational bases of hierarchy.

The selections from Pareto and Veblen deal with somewhat more specialized aspects of the problem. Pareto retains the dichotomy between a system's elite and non-elite components, but he broadens the Marxian analysis. He treats elites with different functional positions in the society as, within limits, independently variable—he recognizes the independent significance of the political process, and does not reduce political leadership in a capitalistic age to the status of the "executive committee of the bourgeoisie." Also, Pareto was one of the early authors to emphasize mobility—genetic continuity in kinship terms is not a given; there are complex processes of differentially selective recruitment of elite groups of different sorts. In this respect, Pareto exemplifies an important phase of the revolt against the exclusive economic Marxian emphasis. For Pareto, it was a revolt primarily in favor of the autonomy of political processes.

Veblen was the most important early American theorist in this field. He shared, though with many qualifications, the broad Marxist view of the main conflict of interest in industrial society, and disparaged the pretensions of the upper groups. His treatment of conspicuous consumption, developed in the *Theory of the Leisure Class,* initiated consideration of the interrelations between the analysis of conflicting economic interest in the Marxian tradition, and the symbolic significance of patterns of the style of life that could be applied on a more broadly comparative basis. Perhaps without knowing it, Veblen was subtly challenging the doctrine of the nearly exclusive predominance of economic interest; otherwise, why should the motive of validation of status through the proper style of life be so powerful? Veblen's interests are obviously connected with the "conformity" problem so prominent in current American social science. Veblen, like Pareto, concentrated on a somewhat special case. Pareto dealt with the instability of the late nineteenth-century alliance between a rising business-oriented bourgeoisie and the controllers of political organization. Veblen was concerned with the status-validation of the American business magnates who had risen during the post-Civil War period. Within a generation, however, these problems were to shift so radically that Pareto's and Veblen's empirical interpretations became dated. But in the history of thought, both raised problems which could not be easily solved within the utilitarian-Marxist frame of reference.

The last two selections in this section treat these problems more generally. In his *Social Mobility,* Sorokin considers social stratification as involving a plurality of relatively independent scales of evaluation, of which the economic was only one. Weber's chapter (from *The Theory of Social and Economic Organization*) is only a fragment, the bare beginning of what was obviously intended to be an extended essay, comparable to the essay on types of authority. The most critical point is the distinction between "class" and "status" as foci of social stratification. Here Weber was consciously attempting to make the Marxian emphasis on economic interest relative, and to place the economic factor in a more comprehensive frame of reference. Both selections present phases of the general reaction against economic determinism in favor of a more general analysis of social systems. There is an evident relation between this shift and the evolutionary and comparative interests stressed in Part Two.

# 1. *Of Wages and Profit in the Different Employments of Labor and Stock*

BY ADAM SMITH

THE whole of the advantages and disadvantages of the different employments of labour and stock, must, in the same neighbourhood, be either perfectly equal, or continually tending to equality. If in the same neighbourhood, there was any employment evidently either more or less advantageous than the rest, so many people would crowd into it in the one case, and so many would desert it in the other, that its advantages would soon return to the level of other employments. This at least would be the case in a society where things were left to follow their natural course, where there was perfect liberty, and where every man was perfectly free both to chuse what occupation he thought proper, and to change it as often as he thought proper. Every man's interest would prompt him to seek the advantageous, and to shun the disadvantageous employment.

Reprinted from Adam Smith, *An Inquiry into the Nature and Causes of the Wealth of Nations* (7th ed.; London: A. Strahan & T. Cadell, 1793), chap. x, pp. 151–84, 188–89, 200–3, 209.

Pecuniary wages and profit, indeed, are every where in Europe extremely different, according to the different employments of labour and stock. But this difference arises partly from certain circumstances in the employments themselves, which, either really, or at least in the imaginations of men, make up for a small pecuniary gain in some, and counter-balance a great one in others; and partly from the policy of Europe, which no-where leaves things at perfect liberty.

The particular consideration of those circumstances and of that policy will divide this chapter into two parts.

## *Inequalities Arising from the Nature of the Employments Themselves*

The five following are the principal circumstances which, so far as I have been able to observe, make up for a small pecuniary gain in some employments, and counter-balance a great one in others: first, the agreeableness or disagreeableness of the employments themselves; secondly, the easiness and cheapness, or the difficulty and expence of learning them; thirdly, the constancy or inconstancy of employment in them; fourthly, the small or great trust which must be reposed in those who exercise them; and fifthly, the probability or improbability of success in them.

First, the wages of labour vary with the ease or hardship, the cleanliness or dirtiness, the honourableness or dishonourableness of the employment. Thus in most places, take the year round, a journeyman taylor earns less than a journeyman weaver. His work is much easier. A journeyman weaver earns less than a journeyman smith. His work is not always easier, but it is much cleanlier. A journeyman blacksmith, though an artificer, seldom earns so much in twelve hours, as a collier, who is only a labourer, does in eight. His work is not quite so dirty, is less dangerous, and is carried on in daylight, and above ground. Honour makes a great part of the reward of all honourable professions. In point of pecuniary gain, all things considered, they are generally under-recompensed, as I shall endeavour to shew by and by. Disgrace has the contrary effect. The trade of a butcher is a brutal and an odious business; but it is in most places more profitable that the greater part of common trades. The most detestable of all employments, that of public executioner, is, in proportion to the quantity of work done, better paid than any common trade whatever.

Hunting and fishing, the most important employments of mankind in the rude state of society, become in its advanced state their most agreeable amusements, and they pursue for pleasure what they once followed from necessity. In the advanced state of society, therefore, they are all very poor people who follow as a trade, what other people pursue as a pastime. Fishermen have been so since the time of Theocritus. A poacher is every-where a very poor man in Great Britain. In countries where the rigour of the law suffers no poachers, the licensed hunter is not in a much better condition. The natural taste for those employments makes more people follow them than can live comfortably by them, and the produce of their labour, in proportion to its quantity, comes always too cheap to market to afford any thing but the most scanty subsistence to the labourers.

Disagreeableness and disgrace affect the profits of stock in the same manner as the wages of labour. The keeper of an inn or tavern, who is never master of his own house, and who is exposed to the brutality of every drunkard, exercises neither a very agreeable nor a very creditable business. But there is scarce any common trade in which a small stock yields so great a profit.

Secondly, the wages of labour vary with the easiness and cheapness, or the difficulty and expence of learning the business.

When any expensive machine is erected, the extraordinary work to be performed by it before it is worn out, it must be expected, will replace the capital laid out upon it, with at least the ordinary profits. A man educated at the expence of much labour and time to any of those employments, which require extraordinary dexterity and skill, may be compared to one of those expensive machines. The work which he learns to perform, it must be expected, over and above the usual wages of common labour, will replace to him the whole expence of his education, with at least the ordinary profits of an equally valuable capital. It must do this too in a reasonable time, regard being had to the very uncertain duration of human life, in the same manner as to the more certain duration of the machine.

The difference between the wages of skilled labour and those of common labour, is founded upon this principle.

The policy of Europe considers the labour of all mechanics, artificers, and manufacturers, as skilled labour; and that of all country labourers as common labour. It seems to suppose that of the former to be of a more nice and delicate nature than that of the latter. It is so perhaps in some cases; but in the greater part it is quite otherwise, as I shall endeavour to shew by and by. The laws and customs of Europe, therefore, in order to qualify any person for exercising the one species of labour, impose the necessity of an apprenticeship, though with different degrees of rigour in different places. They leave the other free and open to every body. During the continuance of the apprenticeship, the whole labour of the apprentice belongs to his master. In the mean time he must, in many cases, be maintained by his parents or relations, and in almost all cases must be cloathed by them. Some money too is commonly given to the master for teaching him his trade. They who cannot give money, give time, or become bound for more than the usual number of years; a consideration which, though it is not always advantageous to the master, on account of the usual idleness of apprentices, is always disadvantageous to the apprentice. In country labour, on the contrary, the labourer, while he is employed about the easier, learns the more difficult parts of his business, and his own labour maintains him through all the different stages of his employment. It is reasonable, therefore, that in Europe the wages of mechanics, artificers, and manufacturers, should be somewhat higher than those of common labourers. They are so accordingly, and their superior gains make them in most places be considered as a superior rank of people. This superiority, however, is generally very small; the daily or weekly earnings of journeymen in the more common sorts of manufactures, such as those of plain linen and woollen cloth, computed at an average, are, in most places, very little more than the day wages of common labourers. Their employment, indeed, is more steady and uniform, and the superiority of their earnings, taking the whole year together, may be somewhat greater. It seems evidently, however, to be no greater than what is sufficient to compensate the superior expence of their education.

Education in the ingenious arts and in the liberal professions, is still more tedious and expensive. The pecuniary recompence, therefore, of painters and sculptors, of lawyers and physicians, ought to be much more liberal: and it is so accordingly.

The profits of stock seem to be very little affected by the easiness or difficulty of learning the trade in which it is employed. All the different ways in which stock is commonly employed in great towns seem, in reality, to be almost equally easy and and equally difficult to learn. One branch either of foreign or domestic trade, cannot well be a much more intricate business than another.

Thirdly, the wages of labour in different occupations vary with the constancy or inconstancy of employment.

Employment is much more constant in some trades than in others. In the greater part of manufactures, a journeyman may be pretty sure of employment almost every day in the year that he is able to work. A mason or bricklayer, on the contrary, can work neither in hard frost nor in foul weather, and his employment at all other times depends upon the occasional calls of his customers. He is liable, in consequence, to be frequently without any. What he earns, therefore, while he is employed, must not only maintain him while he is idle, but make him some compensation for those anxious and desponding moments which the thought of so precarious a situation must sometimes occasion. Where the computed earnings of the greater part of manufacturers, accordingly, are nearly upon a level with the day wages of common labourers, those of masons and bricklayers are generally from one half more to double those wages. Where common labourers earn four and five shillings a week, masons and bricklayers frequently earn seven and eight; where the former earn six, the latter often earn nine and ten, and where the former earn nine and ten, as in London, the latter commonly earn fifteen and eighteen. No species of skilled labour, however, seems more easy to learn than that of masons and bricklayers. Chairmen in London, during the summer season, are said sometimes to be employed as bricklayers. The high wages of those workmen, therefore, are not so much the recompence of their skill, as the compensation for the inconstancy of their employment.

A house carpenter seems to exercise rather a nicer and more ingenious trade than a mason. In most places, however, for it is not universally so, his day-wages are somewhat lower. His employment, though it depends much, does not depend so entirely upon the occasional calls of his customers; and it is not liable to be interrupted by the weather.

When the trades which generally afford constant employment, happen in a particular place not to do so, the wages of the workmen always rise a good deal above their ordinary proportion to those of common labour. In London almost all journeymen artificers are liable to be called upon and dismissed by their masters from day to day, and from week to week, in the same manner as day-labourers in other places. The lowest order of artificers, journeymen taylors, accordingly, earn there half a crown a day, though eighteen pence may be reckoned the wages of common labour. In small towns and country villages, the wages of journeymen taylors frequently scarce equal those of common labour; but in London they are often many weeks without employment, particulary during the summer.

When the inconstancy of employment is combined with the hardship, disagreeableness, and dirtiness of the work, it sometimes raises the wages of the most common labour above those of the most skilful artificers. A collier working by the piece is supposed at Newcastle to earn commonly about double, and in many parts of Scotland about three times the wages of common labour. His high wages arise altogether from the hardship, disagreeableness, and dirtiness of his work. His employment may, upon most occasions, be as constant as he pleases. The coal-heavers in London exercise a trade which in hardship, dirtiness, and disagreeableness, almost equals that of colliers; and from the unavoidable irregularity in the arrivals of coal ships, the employment of the greater part of them is necessarily very inconstant. If colliers, therefore, commonly earn double and triple the wages of common labour, it ought not to seem unreasonable that coal heavers should sometimes earn four and five times those wages. In the enquiry made into their condition a few years ago, it was found that at the rate at which they were then paid, they could earn from six to ten shillings a day. Six shillings are about four times the wages of common labour in London, and in every particular trade, the lowest common earnings may always be considered as those of the far greater number. How extravagant soever those earnings may appear, if they were more than sufficient to compensate all the disagreeable circumstances of the business, there would soon be so great a number of competitors as, in a trade which has no exclusive privilege, would quickly reduce them to a lower rate.

The constancy or inconstancy of employment cannot affect the ordinary profits of stock in any particular trade. Whether the stock is or is not constantly employed depends, not upon the trade, but the trader.

Fourthly, the wages of labour vary according to the small or great trust which must be reposed in the workmen.

The wages of goldsmiths and jewellers are everywhere superior to those of many other workmen, not only of equal, but of much superior ingenuity; on account of the precious materials with which they are intrusted.

We trust our health to the physician; our fortune, and sometimes our life and reputation, to the lawyer and attorney. Such confidence could not safely be reposed in people of a very mean or low condition. Their reward must be such, therefore, as may give them that rank in the society which so important a trust requires. The long time and the great expence which must be laid out in their education, when combined with this circumstance, necessarily enhance still further the price of their labour.

When a person employs only his own stock in trade, there is no trust; and the credit which he may get from other people depends, not upon the nature of his trade, but upon their opinion of his fortune, probity, and prudence. The different rates of profit, therefore, in the different branches of trade, cannot arise from the different degrees of trust reposed in the traders.

Fifthly, the wages of labour in different employments vary according to the probability or improbability of success in them.

The probability that any particular person shall ever be qualified for the employment to which he is educated, is very different in different occupations. In the greater part of mechanic trades, success is almost certain; but very uncertain in the liberal professions. Put your son apprentice to a shoemaker, there is little doubt of his learning to make a pair of shoes: but send him to study the law, it is at least twenty to one if ever he makes such proficiency as will enable him to live by the business. In a perfectly fair lottery, those who draw the prizes ought to gain all that is lost by those who draw the blanks. In a profession where twenty fail for one that succeeds, that one ought to gain all that should have been gained by the unsuccessful twenty. The counsellor at law who, perhaps, at near forty years of age, begins to make something by his profession, ought to receive the retribution, not only of his own so tedious and expensive education, but of that of more than twenty other who are never likely to make any thing by it. How extravagant soever the fees of counsellors at law may sometimes appear, their real retribution is never equal to this. Compute in any particular place what is likely to be annually gained, and what is likely to be annually spent, by all the different workmen in any common trade, such as that of shoemakers or weavers, and you will find that the former sum will generally exceed the latter. But make the same computation with regard to all the counsellors and students of law, in all the different inns of court, and you will find that their annual gains bear but a very small proportion to their annual expence, even though you rate the former as high, and the latter as low, as can well be done. The lottery of the law, therefore, is very far from being a perfectly fair lottery; and that, as well as many other liberal and honourable professions, is, in point of pecuniary gain, evidently under-recompensed.

Those professions keep their level, however, with other occupations, and, notwithstanding these discouragements, all the most generous and liberal spirits are eager to crowd into them. Two different causes contribute to recommend them. First, the desire of the reputation which attends upon superior excellence in any of them; and, secondly, the natural confidence which every man has more or less, not only in his own abilities, but in his own good fortune.

To excel in any profession, in which but few arrive at mediocrity, is the most decisive mark of what is called genius or superior talents. The public admiration which attends upon such distinguished abilities, makes always a part of their reward; a greater or smaller in proportion as it is higher or lower in degree. It makes a considerable part of that reward in the profession of physic; a still greater, perhaps, in that of law; in poetry and philosophy it makes almost the whole.

There are some very agreeable and beautiful talents, of which the possession commands a certain sort of admiration; but of which the exercise for the sake of gain is considered, whether from reason or prejudice, as a sort of public prostitution. The pecuniary recompence, therefore, of those who exercise them in this manner, must be sufficient, not only to pay for the time, labour, and expence of acquiring the talents, but for the discredit which attends the employment of them as the means of subsistence. The exorbitant rewards of players, opera-singers, opera-dancers, &c. are founded upon those two principles; the rarity and beauty of the talents, and the discredit of employing them in this manner. It seems absurd at first sight that we should despise their persons, and yet reward their talents with the most profuse liberality. While we do the one, however, we must of necessity do the other. Should the public opinion or prejudice ever alter with regard to such occupations, their pecuniary recompence would quickly diminish. More people would apply to them, and the competition would quickly reduce the price of their labour. Such talents, though far from being common, are by no means so rare as is imagined. Many people possess them in great perfection, who disdain to make this use of them; and many more are capable of acquiring them, if any thing could be made honourably by them.

The over-weaning conceit which the greater part of men have of their own abilities, is an ancient evil remarked by the philosophers and moralists of all ages. Their absurd presumption in their own good fortune, has been less taken notice of. It is, however, if possible, still more universal. There is no man living, who, when in tolerable health and spirits, has not some share of it. The chance of gain is by every man more or less over-valued, and the chance of loss is by most men under-valued, and by scarce any man, who is in tolerable health and spirits, valued more than it is worth.

That the chance of gain is naturally overvalued, we may learn from the universal success of lotteries. The world neither ever saw, nor ever will see, a perfectly fair lottery; or one in which the whole gain compensated the whole loss; because the undertaker could make nothing by it. In the state lotteries the tickets are really not worth the price which is paid by the original subscribers, and yet commonly sell in the market for twenty, thirty, and sometimes forty per cent. advance. The vain hope of gaining some of the great prizes is the sole cause of this demand. The soberest people scarce look upon it as a folly to pay a small sum for the chance of gaining ten or twenty thousand pounds; though they know that even that small sum is perhaps twenty or thirty per cent. more than the chance is worth. In a lottery in which no prize exceeded twenty pounds, though in other respects it approached much nearer to a perfectly fair one than the common state lotteries, there would not be the same demand for tickets. In order to have a better chance for some of the great prizes, some people purchase several tickets, and others, small shares in a still greater number. There is not, however, a more certain proposition in mathematics, than that the more tickets you adventure upon, the more likely you are to be a loser. Adventure upon all the tickets in the lottery, and you lose for certain; and the greater the number of your tickets, the nearer you approach to this certainty.

That the chance of loss is frequently undervalued, and scarce ever valued more than it is worth, we may learn from the very moderate profit of insurers. In order to make insurance, either from fire or sea-risk, a trade at all, the common premium must be sufficient to compensate the common losses, to pay the expence of management, and to afford such a profit as might have been drawn from an equal capital employed in any common trade. The person who pays no more than this, evidently pays no more than the real value of the risk, or the lowest price at which he can reasonably expect to insure it. But though many people have made a little money by insurance, very few have made a great fortune; and from this consideration alone, it seems evident enough, that the ordinary balance of profit and loss is not more advantageous in this, than in other common trades by which so many people make fortunes. Moderate, however, as the premium of insurance commonly is, many people despise the risk too much to care to pay it. Taking the whole kingdom at an average, nineteen houses in twenty, or rather, perhaps, ninety-nine in a hundred, are not insured from fire. Sea-risk is more alarming to the greater part of people, and the proportion of ships insured to those not insured is much greater. Many fail, however, at all seasons, and even in time of war, without any insurance. This may sometimes perhaps be done without any imprudence. When a great company, or even a great merchant, has twenty or thirty ships at sea, they may, as it were, insure one another. The premium saved upon them all, may more than compensate such losses as they are likely to meet with in the common course of chances. The neglect of insurance upon shipping, however, in the same manner as upon houses, is in most cases, the effect of no such nice calculation, but of mere thoughtless rashness and presumptuous contempt of the risk.

The contempt of risk and the presumptuous hope of success, are in no period of life more active than at the age at which young people chuse their professions. How little the fear of misfortune is then capable of balancing the hope of good luck, appears still more evidently in the readiness of the common people to enlist as soldiers, or to go to sea, than in the eagerness of those of better fashion to enter into what are called the liberal professions.

What a common soldier may lose is obvious enough. Without regarding the danger, however, young volunteers never enlist so readily as at the beginning of a new war; and though they have scarce any chance of preferment, they figure to themselves, in their youthful fancies, a thousand occasions of acquiring honour and distinction which never occur. These romantic hopes make the whole price of their blood. Their pay is less than that of common labourers, and in actual service their fatigues are much greater.

The lottery of the sea is not altogether so disadvantageous as that of the army. The son of a creditable labourer or artificer may frequently go to sea with his father's consent; but if he enlists as a soldier, it is always without it. Other people see some chance of his making something by the one trade: nobody but himself sees any of his making any thing by the other. The great admiral is less the object of public admiration than the great general; and the highest success in the sea service promises a less brilliant fortune and reputation than equal success in the land. The same difference runs through all the inferior degrees of preferment in both. By the rules of precedency a captain in the navy ranks with a colonel in the army: but he does not rank with him in the common estimation. As the great prizes in the lottery are less, the smaller ones must be more numerous. Common sailors, therefore, more frequently get some fortune and preferment than common soldiers; and the hope of those prizes is what principally recommends the trade. Though their skill and dexterity are much superior to that of almost any artificers, and though their whole life is one continual scene of hardship and danger, yet for all this dexterity and skill, for all those hardships and dangers, while they remain in the condition of common sailors, they receive scarce any other recompence but the pleasure of exercising the one and of surmounting the other. Their wages are not greater than those of common labourers at the port which regulates the rate of seamen's wages. As they are continually going from port to port, the monthly pay of those who fail from all the different ports of Great Britain, is more nearly upon a level than that of any other workmen in those different places; and the rate of the port to and from which the greatest number fail, that is, the port of London, regulates that of all the rest. At London the wages of the greater part of the different classes of workmen are about double those of the same classes at Edinburgh. But the sailors who sail from the port of London seldom earn above three or four shillings a month more than those who sail from the port of Leith, and the difference is frequently not so great. In time of peace, and in the merchant service, the London price is from a guinea to about seven-and-twenty shillings the calendar month. A common labourer in London, at the rate of nine or ten shillings a week, may earn in the calendar month from forty to five-and-forty shillings. The sailor, indeed, over and above his pay, is supplied with provisions. Their value, however, may not perhaps always exceed the difference between his pay and that of the common labourer; and though it sometimes should, the excess will not be clear gain to the sailor, because he cannot share it with his wife and family, whom he must maintain out of his wages at home.

The dangers and hair-breadth escapes of a life of adventures, instead of disheartening young people, seem frequently to recommend a trade to them. A tender mother, among the inferior ranks of people, is often afraid to send her son to school at a sea-port town, lest the sight of the ships and the conversation and adventures of the sailors should entice him to go to sea. The distant prospect of hazards, from which we can hope to extricate ourselves by courage and address, is not disagreeable to us, and does not raise the wages of labour in any employment. It is otherwise with those in which courage and address can be of no avail. In trades which are known to be very unwholesome, the wages of labour are always remarkably high. Unwholesomeness is a species of disagreeableness, and its affects upon the wages of labour are to be ranked under that general head.

In all the different employments of stock, the ordinary rate of profit varies more or less with the certainty or uncertainty of the returns. These are in general less uncertain in the inland than in the foreign trade, and in some branches of foreign trade than in others; in the trade to North America, for example, than in that to Jamaica. The ordinary rate of profit always rises more or less with the risk. It does not, however, seem to rise in proportion to it, or so as to compensate it completely. Bankruptcies are most frequent in the most hazardous trades. The most hazardous of all trades, that of a smuggler, though when the adventure succeeds it is likewise the most profitable, is the infallible road to bankruptcy. The presumptuous hope of success seems to act here as upon all other occasions, and to entice so many adventurers into those hazardous trades, that their competition reduces their profit below what is sufficient to compensate the risk. To compensate it completely, the common returns ought, over and above the ordinary profits of stock, not only to make up for all occasional losses, but to afford a surplus profit to the adventurers of the same nature with the profit of insurers. But if the common returns were sufficient for all this, bankruptcies would not be more frequent in these than in other trades.

Of the five circumstances, therefore, which vary the wages of labour, two only affect the profits of stock; the agreeableness or disagreeableness of the business, and the risk or security with which it is attended. In point of agreeableness or disagreeableness, there is little or no difference in the far greater part of the different employments of stock; but a great deal in those of labour; and the ordinary profit of stock, though it rises with the risk, does not always seem to rise in proportion to it. It should follow from all this, that, in the same society or neighbourhood, the average and ordinary rates of profit in the different employments of stock should be more nearly upon a level than the pecuniary wages of the different sorts of labour. They are so accordingly. The difference between the earnings of a common labourer and those of a well employed lawyer or physician, is evidently much greater than that between the ordinary profits in any two different branches of trade. The apparent difference, besides, in the profits of different trades, is generally a deception arising from our not always distinguishing what ought to be considered as wages, from what ought to be considered as profit.

Apothecaries profit is become a bye-word, denoting something uncommonly extravagant. This great apparent profit, however, is frequently no more than the reasonable wages of labour. The skill of an apothecary is a much nicer and more delicate matter than that of any artificer whatever; and the trust which is reposed in him is of much greater importance. He is the physician of the poor in all cases, and of the rich when the distress or danger is not very great. His reward, therefore, ought to be suitable to his skill and his trust, and it arises generally from the price at which he sells his drugs. But the whole drugs which the best employed apothecary, in a large market town, will sell in a year, may not perhaps cost him above thirty or forty pounds. Though he should sell them, therefore, for three or four hundred, or at a thousand per cent. profit, this may frequently be no more than the reasonable wages of his labour charged, in the only way in which he can charge them, upon the price of his drugs. The greater part of the apparent profit is real wages disguised in the garb of profit.

In a small sea-port town, a little grocer will make forty or fifty per cent. upon a stock of a single hundred pounds, while a considerable wholesale merchant in the same place will scarce make eight or ten per cent. upon a stock of ten thousand. The trade of the grocer may be necessary for the conveniency of the inhabitants, and the narrowness of the market may not admit the employment of a larger capital in the business. The man, however, must not only live by his trade, but live by it suitably to the qualifications which it requires. Besides possessing a little capital, he must be able to read, write, and account, and must be a tolerable judge too of, perhaps, fifty or sixty different sorts of goods, their prices, qualities, and the markets where they are to be had cheapest. He must have all the knowledge, in short, that is necessary for a great merchant, which nothing hinders him from becoming but the want of a sufficient capital. Thirty or forty pounds a year cannot be considered as too great a recompence for the labour of a person so accomplished. Deduct this from the seemingly great profits of his capital, and little more will remain, perhaps, than the ordinary profits of stock. The greater part of the apparent profit is, in this case too, real wages.

The difference between the apparent profit of the retail and that of the wholesale trade, is much less in the capital than in small towns and country villages. Where ten thousand pounds can be employed in the grocery trade, the wages of the grocer's labour must be a very trifling addition to the real profits of so great a stock. The apparent profits of the wealthy retailer, therefore, are there more nearly upon a level with those of the wholesale merchant. It is upon this account that goods sold by retail are generally as cheap and frequently much cheaper in the capital than in small towns and country villages. Grocery goods, for example, are generally much cheaper; bread and butcher's meat frequently as cheap. It costs no more to bring grocery goods to the great town than to the country village; but it costs a great deal more to bring corn and cattle, as the greater part of them must be brought from a much greater distance. The prime cost of grocery goods, therefore, being the same in both places, they are cheapest where the least profit is charged upon them. The prime cost of bread and butcher's meat is greater in the great town than in the country village; and though the profit is less, therefore they are not always cheaper there, but often equally cheap. In such articles as bread and butcher's meat, the same cause, which diminishes apparent profit, increases prime cost. The extent of the market, by giving employment to greater stocks, diminishes apparent profit; but by requiring supplies from a greater distance, it increases prime cost. This diminution of the one and increase of the other seem, in most cases, nearly to counter-balance one another; which is probably the reason that, though the prices of corn and cattle are commonly very different in different parts of the kingdom, those of bread and butcher's meat are generally very nearly the same through the greater part of it.

Though the profits of stock both in the wholesale and retail trade are generally less in the capital than in small towns and country villages, yet great fortunes are frequently acquired from small beginnings in the former, and scarce ever in the latter. In small towns and country villages, on account of the narrowness of the market, trade cannot always be extended as stock extends. In such places, therefore, though the rate of a particular person's profits may be very high, the sum or amount of them can never be very great, nor consequently that of his annual accumulation. In great towns, on the contrary, trade can be extended as stock increases, and the credit of a frugal and thriving man increases much faster than his stock. His trade is extended in proportion to the amount of both, and the sum or amount of his profits is in proportion to the extent of his trade, and his annual accumulation in proportion to the amount of his profits. It seldom happens, however, that great fortunes are made even in great towns by any one regular, established, and well-known branch of business, but in consequence of a long life of industry, frugality, and attention. Sudden fortunes, indeed, are sometimes made in such places by what is called the trade of speculation. The speculative merchant exercises no one regular, established, or well-known branch of business. He is a corn merchant this year, and a wine merchant the next, and a sugar, tobacco, or tea merchant the year after. He enters into every trade, when he foresees that it is likely to be more than commonly profitable, and he quits it when he foresees that its profits are likely to return to the level of other trades. His profits and losses, therefore, can bear no regular proportion to those of any one established and well-known branch of business. A bold adventurer may sometimes acquire a considerable fortune by two or three successful speculations; but is just as likely to lose one by two or three unsuccessful ones. This trade can be carried on no where but in great towns. It is only in places of the most extensive commerce and correspondence that the intelligence requisite for it can be had.

The five circumstances above mentioned, though they occasion considerable inequalities in the wages of labour and profits of stock occasion none in the whole of the advantages and disadvantages, real or imaginary, of the different employments of either. The nature of those circumstances is such, that they make up for a small pecuniary gain in some, and counter-balance a great one in others.

In order, however, that this quality may take place in the whole of their advantages or disadvantages, three things are requisite even where there is the most perfect freedom. First, the employments must be well known and long established in the neighbourhood; secondly, they must be in their ordinary, or what may be called their natural state; and, thirdly, they must be the sole or principal employments of those who occupy them.

First, this quality can take place only in those employments which are well known, and have been long established in the neighbourhood.

Where all other circumstances are equal, wages are generally higher in new than in old trades. When a projector attempts to establish a new manufacture, he must at first entice his workmen from other employments by higher wages than they can either earn in their own trades, or than the nature of his work would otherwise require, and a comfortable time must pass away before he can venture to reduce them to the common level. Manufactures for which the demand arises altogether from fashion and fancy, are continually changing, and seldom last long enough to be considered as old established manufactures. Those, on the contrary, for which the demand arises chiefly from use or necessity, are less liable to change, and the same form or fabric may continue in demand for whole centuries together. The wages of labour, therefore, are likely to be higher in manufactures of the former, than in those of the latter kind. Birmingham deals chiefly in manufactures of the former kind; Sheffield in those of the latter; and the wages of labour in those two different places, are said to be suitable to this difference in the nature of their manufactures.

The establishment of any new manufacture, of any new branch of commerce, or of any new practice in agriculture, is always a speculation, from which the projector promises himself extraordinary profits. These profits sometimes are very great, and sometimes, more frequently, perhaps, they are quite otherwise; but in general they bear no regular proportion to those of other old trades in the neighbourhood. If the project succeeds, they are commonly at first very high. When the trade or practice becomes thoroughly established and well known, the competition reduces them to the level of other trades.

Secondly, this equality in the whole of the advantages and disadvantages of the different employments of labour and stock, can take place only in the ordinary, or what may be called the natural state of those employments.

The demand for almost every different species of labour is sometimes greater and sometimes less than usual. In the one case the advantages of the employment rise above, in the other they fall below the common level. The demand for country labour is greater at hay-time and harvest, than during the greater part of the year; and wages rise with the demand. In time of war, when forty or fifty thousand sailors are forced from the merchant service into that of the king, the demand for sailors to merchant ships necessarily rises with their scarcity, and their wages upon such occasions commonly rise from a guinea and seven-and-twenty shillings, to forty shillings and three pounds a month. In a decaying manufacture, on the contrary, many workmen, rather than quit their old trade, are contented with smaller wages than would otherwise be suitable to the nature of their employment.

The profits of stock vary with the price of the commodities in which it is employed. As the price of any commodity rises above the ordinary or average rate, the profits of at least some part of the stock that is employed in bringing it to market, rise above their proper level, and as it falls they sink below it. All commodities are more or less liable to variations of price, but some are much more so than others. In all commodities which are produced by human industry, the quantity of industry annually employed is necessarily regulated by the annual demand, in such a manner that the average annual produce may, as nearly as possible, be equal to the average annual consumption. In some employments, it has already been observed, the same quantity of industry will always produce the same, or very nearly the same quantity of commodities. In the linen or woollen manufactures, for example, the same number of hands will annually work up very nearly the same quantity of linen and woollen cloth. The variations in the market price of such commodities therefore, can arise only from some accidental variation in the demand. A public mourning raises the price of black cloth. But as the demand for most sorts of plain linen and woollen cloth is pretty uniform, so is likewise the price. But there are other employments in which the same quantity of industry will not always produce the same quantity of commodities. The same quantity of industry, for example, will, in different years, produce very different quantities of corn, wine, hops, sugar, tobacco, &c. The price of such commodities, therefore, varies not only with the variations of demand, but with the much greater and more frequent variations of quantity, and is consequently extremely fluctuating. But the profit of some of the dealers must necessarily fluctuate with the price of the commodities. The operations of the speculative merchant are principally employed about such commodities. He endeavours to buy them up when he foresees that their price is likely to rise, and to sell them when it is likely to fall.

Thirdly, this equality in the whole of the advantages and disadvantages of the different employments of labour and stock, can take place only in such as are the sole or principal employments of those who occupy them.

When a person derives his subsistence from one employment, which does not occupy the greater part of his time; in the intervals of his leisure he is often willing to work at another for less wages than would otherwise suit the nature of the employment.

There still subsists in many parts of Scotland a set of people called Cotters or Cottagers, though they were more frequent some years ago than they are now. They are a sort of out-servants of the landlords and farmers. The usual reward which they receive from their masters is a house, a small garden for pot-herbs, as much grass as will feed a cow, and, perhaps, an acre or two of bad arable land. When their master has occasion for their labour, he gives them, besides, two pecks of oatmeal a week, worth about sixteen pence sterling. During a great part of the year he has little or no occasion for their labour, and the cultivation of their own little possession is not sufficient to occupy the time which is left at their own disposal. When such occupiers were more numerous than they are at present, they are said to have been willing to give their spare time for a very small recompence to any body, and to have wrought for less wages than other labourers. In ancient times they seem to have been common all over Europe. In countries ill cultivated and worse inhabited, the greater part of landlords and farmers could not otherwise provide themselves with the extraordinary number of hands, which country labour requires at certain seasons. The daily or weekly recompence which such labourers occasionally receive from their masters, was evidently not the whole price of their labour. Their small tenement made a considerable part of it. This daily or weekly recompence, however, seems to have been considered as the whole of it, by many writers who have collected the prices of labour and provisions in ancient times, and who have taken pleasure in representing both as wonderfully low.

The produce of such labour comes frequently cheaper to market than would otherwise be suitable to its nature. Stockings in many parts of Scotland are knit much cheaper than they can any-where be wrought upon the loom. They are the work of servants and labourers, who derive the principal part of their subsistence from some other employment. More than a thousand pair of Shetland stockings are annually imported into Leith, of which the price is from five pence to seven pence a pair. At Learwick, the small capital of the Shetland islands, ten pence a day, I have been assured, is a common price of common labour. In the same islands they knit worsted stockings to the value of a guinea a pair and upwards.

The spinning of linen yarn is carried on in Scotland nearly in the same way as the knitting of stockings, by servants who are chiefly hired for other purposes. They earn but a very scanty subsistence, who endeavour to get their whole livelihood by either of those trades. In most parts of Scotland she is a good spinner who can earn twenty pence a week.

In opulent countries the market is generally so extensive, that any one trade is sufficient to employ the whole labour and stock of those who occupy it. Instances of people's living by one employment, and at the same time deriving some little advantage from another, occur chiefly in poor countries. The following instance, however, of something of the same kind is to be found in the capital of a very rich one. There is no city in Europe, I believe, in which house-rent is dearer than in London, and yet I know no capital in which a furnished apartment can be hired so cheap. Lodging is not only much cheaper in London than in Paris; it is much cheaper than in Edinburgh of the same degree of goodness; and what may seem extraordinary, the dearness of house-rent is the cause of the cheapness of lodging. The dearness of house-rent in London arises, not only from those causes which render it dear in all great capitals, the dearness of labour, the dearness of all the materials of building, which must generally be brought from a great distance, and above all the the dearness of ground-rent, every landlord acting the part of a monopolist, and frequently exacting a higher rent for a single acre of bad land in a town, than can be had for a hundred of the best in the country; but it arises in part from the peculiar manners and customs of the people which oblige every master of a family to hire a whole house from top to bottom. A dwelling-house in England means every thing that is contained under the same roof. In France, Scotland, and many other parts of Europe, it frequently means no more than a single story. A tradesman in London is obliged to hire a whole house in that part of the town where his customers live. His shop is upon the ground-floor, and he and his family sleep in the garret; and he endeavours to pay a part of his house-rent by letting the two middle stories to lodgers. He expects to maintain his family by his trade, and not by his lodgers. Whereas, at Paris and Edinburgh, the people who let lodgings have commonly no other means of subsistence; and the price of the lodging must pay, not only the rent of the house, but the whole expence of the family.

## *Inequalities Occasioned by the Policy of Europe*

Such are the inequalities in the whole of the advantages and disadvantages of the different employments of labour and stock, which the defect of any of the three requisites above-mentioned must occasion, even where there is the most perfect liberty. But the policy of Europe, by not leaving things at perfect liberty, occasions other inequalities of much greater importance.

It does this chiefly in the three following ways. First, by restraining the competition in some employments to a smaller number than would otherwise be disposed to enter into them; secondly, by increasing it in others beyond what it naturally would be; and thirdly, by obstructing the free circulation of labour and stock, both from employment to employment, and from place to place.

First, the policy of Europe occasions a very important inequality in the whole of the advantages and disadvantages of the different employments of labour and stock, by restraining the competition in some employments to a smaller number than might otherwise be disposed to enter into them.

The exclusive privileges of corporations are the principal means it makes use of for this purpose.

The exclusive privilege of an incorporated trade necessarily restrains the competition, in the town where it is established, to those who are free of the trade. To have served an apprenticeship in the town, under a master properly qualified, is commonly the necessary requisite for obtaining this freedom. The bye-laws of the corporation regulate sometimes the number of apprentices which any master is allowed to have, and almost always the number of years which each apprentice is obliged to serve. The intention of both regulations is to restrain the competition to a much smaller number than might otherwise be disposed to enter into the trade. The limitation of the number of apprentices restrains it directly. A long term of apprenticeship restrains it more indirectly, but as effectually, by increasing the expence of education.

* * *

The property which every man has in his own labour, as it is the original foundation of all other property, so it is the most sacred and inviolable. The patrimony of a poor man lies in the strength and dexterity of his hands; and to hinder him from employing this strength and dexterity in what manner he thinks proper without injury to his neighbour, is a plain violation of this most sacred property. It is manifest encroachment upon the just liberty both of the workman, and of those who might be disposed to employ him. As it hinders the one from working at what he thinks proper, so it hinders the others from employing whom they think proper. To judge whether he is fit to be employed, may surely be trusted to the discretion of the employers whose interest it so much concerns. The affected anxiety of the law-giver, lest they should employ an improper person, is evidently as impertinent as it is operative.

The institution of long apprenticeships can give no security that insufficient workmanship shall not frequently be exposed to public sale. When this is done it is generally the effect of fraud, and not of inability; and the longest apprenticeship can give no security against fraud. Quite different regulations are necessary to prevent this abuse. The sterling mark upon plate, and the stamps upon linen and woollen cloth, give the purchaser much greater security than any statute of apprenticeship. He generally looks at these, but never thinks it worth while to enquire whether the workmen had served a seven years apprenticeship.

The institution of long apprenticeships has no tendency to form young people to industry. A journeyman who works by the piece is likely to be industrious, because he derives a benefit from every exertion of his industry. An apprentice is likely to be idle, and almost always is so, because he has no immediate interest to be otherwise. In the inferior employments, the sweets of labour consist altogether in the recompence of labour. They who are soonest in a condition to enjoy the sweets of it, are likely soonest to conceive a relish for it, and to acquire the early habit of industry. A young man naturally conceives an aversion to labour, when for a long time he receives no benefit from it. The boys who are put out apprentices from public charities are generally bound for more than the usual number of years, and they generally turn out very idle and worthless.

* * *

People of the same trade seldom meet together, even for merriment and diversion, but the conversation ends in a conspiracy against the public, or in some contrivance to raise prices. It is impossible indeed to prevent such meetings, by any law which either could be executed, or would be consistent with liberty and justice. But though the law cannot hinder people of the same trade from sometimes assembling together, it ought to do nothing to facilitate such assemblies; much less to render them necessary.

A regulation which obliges all those of the same trade in a particular town to enter their names and places of abode in a public register, facilitates such assemblies. It connects individuals who might never otherwise be known to one another, and gives every man of the trade a direction where to find every other man of it.

A regulation which enables those of the same trade to tax themselves in order to provide for their poor, their sick, their widows and orphans, by giving them a common interest to manage, renders such assemblies necessary.

An incorporation not only renders them necessary, but makes the act of the majority binding upon the whole. In a free trade an effectual combination cannot be established but by the unanimous consent of every single trader, and it cannot last longer than every single trader continues of the same mind. The majority of a corporation can enact a bye-law with proper penalties, which will limit the competition more effectually and more durably than any voluntary combination whatever.

The pretence that corporations are necessary for the better government of the trade, is without any foundation. The real and effectual discipline which is exercised over a workman, is not that of his corporation, but that of his customers. It is the fear of losing their employment which restrains his frauds and corrects his negligence. An exclusive corporation necessarily weakens the force of this discipline. A particular set of workmen must then be employed, let them behave well or ill. It is upon this account, that in many large incorporated towns no tolerable workmen are to be found, even in some of the most necessary trades. If you would have your work tolerably executed, it must be done in the suburbs, where the workmen, having no exclusive privilege, have nothing but their character to depend upon, and you must then smuggle it into the town as well as you can.

It is in this manner that the policy of Europe, by restraining the competition in some employments to a smaller number than would otherwise be disposed to enter into them, occasions a very important inequality in the whole of the advantages and disadvantages of the different employments of labour and stock.

Secondly, the policy of Europe, by increasing the competition in some employments beyond what it naturally would be, occasions another inequality of an opposite kind in the whole of the advantages and disadvantages of the different employments of labour and stock.

It has been considered as of so much importance that a proper number of young people should be educated for certain professions, that, sometimes the public, and sometimes the piety of private founders have established many pensions, scholarships, exhibitions, bursaries, &c. for this purpose, which draw many more people into those trades than could otherwise pretend to follow them. In all christian countries, I believe, the education of the greater part of churchmen is paid for in this manner. Very few of them are educated altogether at their own expence. The long, tedious, and expensive education, therefore, of those who are, will not always procure them a suitable reward, the church being crowded with people who, in order to get employment, are willing to accept of a much smaller recompence than what such an education would otherwise have entitled them to; and in this manner the competition of the poor takes away the reward of the rich. It would be indecent, no doubt, to compare either a curate or a chaplain with a journeyman in any common trade. The pay of a curate or chaplain, however, may very properly be considered as of the same nature with the wages of a journeyman. They are, all three, paid for their work according to the contract which they may happen to make with their respective superiors.

* * *

Thirdly, the policy of Europe, by obstructing the free circulation of labour and stock both from employment to employment, and from place to place, occasions in some cases a very inconvenient inequality in the whole of the advantages and disadvantages of their different employments.

The statute of apprenticeship obstructs the free circulation of labour from one employment to another, even in the same place. The exclusive privileges of corporations obstruct it from one place to another, even in the same employment.

# 2. *The Class Struggle*

BY KARL MARX

THE HISTORY of all hitherto existing society[1] is the history of class struggles.

Freemen and slave, patrician and plebeian, lord and serf, guild-master[2] and journeyman, in a word, oppressor and oppressed, stood in constant opposition to one another, carried on an uninterrupted, now hidden, now open fight, a fight that each time ended, either in a revolutionary re-constitution of society at large, or in the common ruin of the contending classes.

In the earlier epochs of history, we find almost everywhere a complicated arrangement of society into various orders, a manifold gradation of social rank. In ancient Rome we have patricians, knights, plebeians, slaves; in the middle ages, feudal lords, vassals, guild-masters, journeymen, apprentices, serfs; in almost all of these classes, again, subordinate gradations.

Reprinted from Karl Marx, *Manifesto of the Communist Party* (Chicago: Charles H. Kerr, 1888), sec. 1, pp. 12–32.

1. That is, all written history. In 1847, the pre-history of society, the social organization existing previous to recorded history, was all but unknown. Since then Haxthausen discovered common ownership of land in Russia, Maurer proved it to be the social foundation from which all Teutonic races started in history, and by and bye village communities were found to be, or to have been, the primitive form of society everywhere from India to Ireland. The inner organization of this primitive Communistic society was laid bare, in its typical form, by Morgan's crowning discovery of the true nature of the gens and its relation to tribe. With the dissolution of these primaeval communities society begins to be differentiated into separate and finally antagonistic classes. I have attempted to retrace this process of dissolution in: "Der Ursprung der Familie des, Privateigenthums und des Staats," 2nd edit., Stuttgart 1886.

2. Guild-master, that is a full member of a guild, a master within, not a head of, a guild.

The modern bourgeois[3] society that has sprouted from the ruins of feudal society, has not done away with class antagonisms. It has but established new classes, new conditions of oppression, new forms of struggle in place of the old ones.

Our epoch, the epoch of the bourgeoisie, possesses, however, this distinctive feature; it has simplified the class antagonisms. Society as a whole is more and more splitting up into two great hostile camps, into two great classes directly facing each other: Bourgeoisie and Proletariat.

From the serfs of the middle ages sprang the chartered burghers of the earliest towns. From these burgesses the first elements of the bourgeoisie were developed.

The discovery of America, the rounding of the Cape, opened up fresh ground for the rising bourgeoisie. The East-Indian and Chinese markets, the colonisation of America, trade with the colonies, the increase in the means of exchange and in commodities generally, gave to commerce, to navigation, to industry, an impulse never before known, and thereby, to the revolutionary element in the tottering feudal society, a rapid development.

The feudal system of industry, under which industrial production was monopolised by close guilds, now no longer sufficed for the growing wants of the new markets. The manufacturing system took its place. The guild-masters were pushed on one side by the manufacturing middle-class; division of labour between the different corporate guilds vanished in the face of division of labour in each single workshop.

Meantime the markets kept ever growing, the demand, ever rising. Even manufacture no longer sufficed. Thereupon, steam and machinery revolutionised industrial production. The place of manufacture was taken by the giant, Modern Industry, the place of the industrial middle-class, by industrial millionaires, the leaders of whole industrial armies, the modern bourgeois.

Modern industry has established the world-market, for which the discovery of America paved the way. This market has given an immense development to commerce, to navigation, to communication by land. This development has, in its turn, reacted on the extension of industry; and in proportion as industry, commerce, navigation, railways extended, in the same proportion the bourgeoisie developed, increased its capital, and pushed into the background every class handed down from the Middle Ages.

We see, therefore, how the modern bourgeoisie is itself the product of a long course of development, of a series of revolutions in the modes of production and of exchange.

Each step in the development of the bourgeoisie was accompanied by a corresponding political advance of that class. An oppressed class under the sway of the feudal nobility, an armed and self-governing association in the mediaeval commune,[4] here independent urban republic (as in Italy and Germany), there taxable "third estate" of the monarchy (as in France), afterwards, in the period of manufacture proper, serving either the semi-feudal or the absolute monarchy as a counterpoise against the nobility, and, in fact, corner stone of the great monarchies in general, the bourgeoisie has at last, since the establishment of Modern Industry and of the world-market, conquered for itself, in the modern representative State, exclusive political sway. The executive of the modern State is but a committee for managing the common affairs of the whole bourgeoisie.

The bourgeoisie, historically, has played a most revolutionary part.

The bourgeoisie, wherever it has got the upper hand, has put an end to all feudal patriarchal, idyllic relations. It has pitilessly torn asunder the motley feudal ties that bound man to his "natural superiors," and has left remaining no other nexus between man and man than naked self-interest, than callous "cash payment." It has drowned the most heavenly ecstacies of religious fervour, of chivalrous enthusiasm, of philistine sentimentalism, in the icy water of egotistical calculation. It has resolved personal worth into exchange value, and in place of the numberless indefeasible chartered freedoms, has set us that single, unconscionable freedom—Free Trade. In one word, for political exploitation, veiled by religious and political illusions, it has substituted naked, shameless, direct, brutal exploitation.

The bourgeoisie has stripped of its halo every occupation hitherto honoured and looked up to with reverent awe. It has converted the physician, the lawyer, the priest, the poet, the man of science, into its paid wage-labourers.

The bourgeoisie has torn away from the family

3. By bourgeoisie is meant the class of modern Capitalists, owners of the means of social production and employers of wage-labour. By proletariat, the class of modern wage-labourers who, having no means of production of their own, are reduced to selling their labour-power in order to live.

4. "Commune" was the name, taken in France, by the nascent towns even before they had conquered from their feudal lords and masters, local self-government and political rights as "the Third Estate." Generally speaking, for the economical development of the bourgeoisie, England is here taken as the typical country, for its political development, France.

its sentimental veil, and has reduced the family relation to a mere money relation.

The bourgeoisie has disclosed how it came to pass that the brutal display of vigour in the Middle Ages, which Reactionists so much admire, found its fitting complement in the most slothful indolence. It has been the first to shew what man's activity can bring about. It has accomplished wonders far surpassing Egyptian pyramids, Roman aqueducts, and Gothic cathedrals; it has conducted expeditions that put in the shade all former Exoduses of nations and crusades.

The bourgeoisie cannot exist without constantly revolutionising the instruments of production, and thereby the relations of production, and with them the whole relations of society. Conservation of the old modes of production in unaltered form, was, on the contrary, the first condition of existence for all earlier industrial classes. Constant revolutionising of production, uninterrupted disturbance of all social conditions, everlasting uncertainty and agitation distinguish the bourgeois epoch from all earlier ones. All fixed, fast-frozen relations, with their train of ancient and venerable prejudices and opinions, are swept away, all new-formed ones become antiquated before they can ossify. All that is solid melts into air, all that is holy is profaned, and man is at last compelled to face with sober senses, his real conditions of life, and his relations with his kind.

The need of a constantly expanding market for its products chases the bourgeoisie over the whole surface of the globe. It must nestle everywhere, settle everywhere, establish connexions everywhere.

The bourgeoisie has through its exploitation of the world-market given a cosmopolitan character to production and consumption in every country. To the great chagrin of Re-actionists, it has drawn from under the feet of industry the national ground on which it stood. All old-established national industries have been destroyed or are daily being destroyed. They are dislodged by new industries, whose introduction becomes a life and death question for all civilised nations, by industries that no longer work up indigenous raw material, but raw material drawn from the remotest zones; industries whose products are consumed, not only at home, but in every quarter of the globe. In place of the old wants, satisfied by the productions of the country, we find new wants, requiring for their satisfaction the products of distant lands and climes. In place of the old local and national seclusion and self-sufficiency, we have intercourse in every direction, universal inter-dependence of nations. And as in material, so also in intellectual production. The intellectual creations of individual nations become common property. National one-sidedness and narrow-mindedness become more and more impossible, and from the numerous national and local literatures there arises a world-literature.

The bourgeoisie, by the rapid improvement of all instruments of production, by the immensely facilitated means of communication, draws all, even the most barbarian, nations into civilisation. The cheap prices of its commodities are the heavy artillery with which it batters down all Chinese walls, with which it forces the barbarians' intensely obstinate hatred of foreigners to capitulate. It compels all nations, on pain of extinction, to adopt the bourgeois mode of production; it compels them to introduce what it calls civilisation into their midst, i.e., to become bourgeois themselves. In a word, it creates a world after its own image.

The bourgeoisie has subjected the country to the rule of the towns. It has created enormous cities, has greatly increased the urban population as compared with the rural, and has thus rescued a considerable part of the population from the idiocy of rural life. Just as it has made the country dependent on the towns, so it has made barbarian and semi-barbarian countries dependent on the civilised ones, nations of peasants on nations of bourgeois, the East on the West.

The bourgeoisie keeps more and more doing away with the scattered state of the population, of the means of productions, and of property. It has agglomerated population, centralised means of production, and has concentrated property in a few hands. The necessary consequence of this was political centralisation. Independent, or but loosely connected provinces, with separate interests, laws, governments and systems of taxation, became lumped together in one nation, with one government, one code of laws, one national class-interest, one frontier and one customs-tariff.

The bourgeoisie, during its rule of scarce one hundred years, has created more massive and more colossal productive forces than have all preceding generations together. Subjection of Nature's forces to man, machinery, application of chemistry to industry and agriculture, steam-navigation, railways, electric telegraphs, clearing of whole continents for cultivation, canalization of rivers, whole populations conjured out of the ground—what earlier century had even a presentiment that such productive forces slumbered in the lap of social labour?

We see then: the means of production and of exchange on whose foundation the bourgeoisie built itself up, were generated in feudal society.

At a certain stage in the development of these means of production and of exchange, the conditions under which feudal society produced and exchanged, the feudal organisation of agriculture and manufacturing industry, in one word, the feudal relations of property became no longer compatible with the already developed productive forces; they became so many fetters. They had to burst asunder; they were burst asunder.

Into their places stepped free competition, accompanied by a social and political constitution adapted to it, and by the economical and political sway of the bourgeois class.

A similar movement is going on before our own eyes. Modern bourgeois society with its relations of production, of exchange and of property, a society that has conjured up such gigantic means of production and of exchange, is like the sorcerer, who is no longer able to control the powers of the nether world whom he has called up by his spells. For many a decade past the history of industry and commerce is but the history of the revolt of modern productive forces against modern conditions of production, against the property relations that are the conditions for the existence of the bourgeoisie and of its rule. It is enough to mention the commercial crises that by their periodical return put on its trial, each time more threateningly, the existence of the entire bourgeois society. In these crises a great part not only of the existing products, but also of the previously created productive forces, are periodically destroyed. In these crises there breaks out an epidemic that, in all earlier epochs, would have seemed an absurdity—the epidemic of over-production. Society suddenly finds itself put back into a state of momentary barbarism; it appears as if a famine, a universal war of devastation had cut off the supply of every means of subsistence; industry and commerce seem to be destroyed; and why? Because there is too much civilisation, too much means of subsistence, too much industry, too much commerce. The productive forces at the disposal of society no longer tend to further the development of the conditions of bourgeois property; on the contrary, they have become too powerful for these conditions, by which they are fettered, and so soon as they overcome these fetters, they bring disorder into the whole of bourgeois society, endanger the existence of bourgeois property. The conditions ot bourgeois society are too narrow to comprise the wealth created by them. And how does the bourgeoisie get over these crises? On the one hand by enforced destruction of a mass of productive forces; on the other, by the conquest of new markets, and by the more thorough exploitation of the old ones. That is to say, by paving the way for more extensive and more destructive crises, and by diminishing the means whereby crises are prevented.

The weapons with which the bourgeoisie felled feudalism to the ground are now turned against the bourgeoisie itself.

But not only has the bourgeoisie forged the weapons that bring death to itself; it has also called into existence the men who are to wield those weapons—the modern working-class—the proletarians.

In proportion as the bourgeoisie, i.e., capital, is developed, in the same proportion is the proletariat, the modern working-class, developed, a class of labourers, who live only so long as they find work, and who find work only so long as their labour increases capital. These labourers, who must sell themselves piecemeal, are a commodity, like every other article of commerce, and are consequently exposed to all the vicissitudes of competition, to all the fluctuations of the market.

Owing to the extensive use of machinery and to division of labour, the work of the proletarians has lost all individual character, and, consequently, all charm for the workman. He becomes an appendage of the machine, and it is only the most simple, most monotonous, and most easily acquired knack that is required of him. Hence, the cost of production of a workman is restricted, almost entirely, to the means of subsistence that he requires for his maintenance, and for the propagation of his race. But the price of a commodity, and also of labour, is equal to its cost of production. In proportion, therefore, as the repulsiveness of the work increases, the wage decreases. Nay more, in proportion as the use of machinery and division of labour increases, in the same proportion the burden of toil also increases, whether by prolongation of the working hours, by increase of the work enacted in a given time, or by increased speed of the machinery, etc.

Modern industry has converted the little workshop of the patriarchal master into the great factory of the industrial capitalist. Masses of labourers, crowded into the factory, are organised like soldiers. As privates of the industrial army they are placed under the command of a perfect hierarchy of officers and sergeants. Not only are they the slaves of the bourgeois class, and of the bourgeois State, they are daily and hourly enslaved by the machine, by the over-looker, and, above all, by the individual bourgeois manufacturer himself. The more openly this despotism proclaims gain to be its end and aim, the more petty, the more hateful and the more embittering it is.

The less the skill and exertion or strength implied in manual labour, in other words, the more modern industry becomes developed, the more is the labour of men superseded by that of women. Differences of age and sex have no longer any distinctive social validity for the working class. All are instruments of labour, more or less expensive to use, according to their age and sex.

No sooner is the exploitation of the labourer by the manufacturer, so far, at an end, that he receives his wages in cash, than he is set upon by the other portions of the bourgeoisie, the landlord, the shopkeeper, the pawnbroker, etc.

The lower strata of the Middle class—the small tradespeople, shopkeepers, and retired tradesmen generally, the handicraftsmen and peasants—all these sink gradually into the proletariat, partly because their diminutive capital does not suffice for the scale on which Modern Industry is carried on, and is swamped in the competition with the large capitalists, partly because their specialised skill is rendered worthless by new methods of production. Thus the proletariat is recruited from all classes of the population.

The proletariat goes through various stages of development. With its birth begins its struggle with the bourgeoisie. At first the contest is carried on by individual labourers, then by the workpeople of a factory, then by the operatives of one trade, in one locality, against the individual bourgeois who directly exploits them. They direct their attacks not against the bourgeois conditions of production, but against the instruments of production themselves; they destroy imported wares that compete with their labour, they smash to pieces machinery, they set factories ablaze, they seek to restore by force the vanished status of the workman of the Middle Ages.

At this stage the labourers still form an incoherent mass scattered over the whole country, and broken up by their mutual competition. If anywhere they unite to form more compact bodies, this is not yet the consequence of their own active union, but of the union of the bourgeoisie, which class, in order to attain its own political ends, is compelled to set the whole proletariat in motion, and is moreover yet, for a time, able to do so. At this stage, therefore, the proletarians do not fight their enemies, but the enemies of their enemies, the remnants of absolute monarchy, the landowners, the non-industrial bourgeois, the petty bourgeoisie. Thus the whole historical movement is concentrated in the hands of the bourgeoisie; every victory so obtained is a victory for the bourgeoisie.

But with the development of industry the proletariat not only increases in number; it becomes concentrated in greater masses, its strength grows, and it feels that strength more. The various interests and conditions of life within the ranks of the proletariat are more and more equalised, in proportion as machinery obliterates all distinctions of labour, and nearly everywhere reduces wages to the same low level. The growing competition among the bourgeois, and the resulting commercial crises, make the wages of the workers ever more fluctuating. The unceasing improvement of machinery, ever more rapidly developing, makes their livelihood more and more precarious; the collisions between individual workmen and individual bourgeois take more and more the character of collisions between two classes. Thereupon the workers begin to form combinations (Trades' Unions) against the bourgeois; they club together in order to keep up the rate of wages; they found permanent associations in order to make provision beforehand for these occasional revolts. Here and there the contest breaks out into riots.

Now and then the workers are victorious, but only for a time. The real fruit of their battles lies, not in the immediate result, but in the ever expanding union of the workers. This union is helped on by the improved means of communication that are created by modern industry, and that place the workers of different localities in contact with one another. It was just this contact that was needed to centralise the numerous local struggles, all of the same character, into one national struggle between classes. But every class struggle is a political struggle. And that union, to attain which the burghers of the Middle Ages, with their miserable highways, required centuries, the modern proletarians, thanks to railways, achieve in a few years.

This organisation of the proletarians into a class, and consequently into a political party, is continually being upset again by the competition between the workers themselves. But it ever rises up again, stronger, firmer, mightier. It compels legislative recognition of particular interests of the workers, by taking advantage of the divisions among the bourgeoisie itself. Thus the ten-hours'-bill in England was carried.

Altogether collisions between the classes of the old society further, in many ways, the course of development of the proletariat. The bourgeoisie finds itself involved in a constant battle. At first with the aristocracy; later on, with those portions of the bourgeoisie itself, whose interests have become antagonistic to the progress of industry; at all times, with the bourgeoisie of foreign countries. In all these battles it sees itself compelled to appeal to the proletariat, to ask for its help, and thus, to drag it into the political arena. The bourgeoisie itself, therefore, supplies the proletariat with its own elements of political and general education, in other words, it furnishes the proletariat with weapons for fighting the bourgeoisie.

Further, as we have already seen, entire sections of the ruling classes are, by the advance of industry, precipitated into the proletariat, or are at least threatened in their conditions of existence. These also supply the proletariat with fresh elements of enlightenment and progress.

Finally, in times when the class-struggle nears the decisive hour, the process of dissolution going on within the ruling class, in fact within the whole range of old society, assumes such a violent, glaring character, that a small section of the ruling class cuts itself adrift, and joins the revolutionary class, the class that holds the future in its hands. Just as, therefore, at an earlier period, a section of the nobility went over to the bourgeoisie, so now a portion of the bourgeoisie goes over to the proletariat, and in particular, a portion of the bourgeois ideologists, who have raised themselves to the level of comprehending theoretically the historical movements as a whole.

Of all the classes that stand face to face with the bourgeoisie to-day, the proletariat alone is a really revolutionary class. The other classes decay and finally disappear in the face of modern industry; the proletariat is its special and essential product.

The lower middle-class, the small manufacturer, the shopkeeper, the artisan, the peasant, all these fight against the bourgeoisie, to save from extinction their existence as fractions of the middle class. They are therefore not revolutionary, but conservative. Nay more, they are reactionary, for they try to roll back the wheel of history. If by chance they are revolutionary, they are so, only in view of their impending transfer into the proletariat, they thus defend not their present, but their future interests, they desert their own standpoint to place themselves at that of the proletariat.

The "dangerous class," the social scum, that passively rotting mass thrown off by the lowest layers of old society, may, here and there, be swept into the movement by a proletarian revolution; its conditions of life, however, prepare it far more for the part of a bribed tool of reactionary intrigue.

In the conditions of the proletariat, those of old society at large are already virtually swamped. The proletarian is without property; his relation to his wife and children has no longer anything in common with the bourgeois family-relations; modern industrial labour, modern subjection to capital, the same in England as in France, in America as in Germany, has stripped him of every trace of national character. Law, morality, religion, are to him so many bourgeois prejudices, behind which lurk in ambush just as many bourgeois interests.

All the preceding classes that got the upper hand, sought to fortify their already acquired status by subjecting society at large to their conditions of appropriation. The proletarians cannot become masters of the productive forces of society, except by abolishing their own previous mode of appropriation, and thereby also every other previous mode of appropriation. They have nothing of their own to secure and to fortify; their mission is to destroy all previous securities for, and insurances of, individual property.

All previous historical movements were movements of minorities, or in the interest of minorities. The proletarian movement is the self-conscious, independent movement of the immense majority, in the interest of the immense majority. The proletariat, the lowest stratum of our present society, cannot stir, cannot raise itself up, without the whole superincumbent strata of official society being sprung into the air.

Though not in substance, yet in form, the struggle of the proletariat with the bourgeoisie is at first a national struggle. The proletariat of each country must, of course, first of all settle matters with its own bourgeoisie.

In depicting the most general phases of the development of the proletariat, we traced the more or less veiled civil war, raging within existing society, up to the point where that war breaks out into open revolution, and where the violent overthrow of the bourgeoisie, lays the foundation for the sway of the proletariat.

Hitherto, every form of society has been based, as we have already seen, on the antagonism of oppressing and oppressed classes. But in order to oppress a class, certain conditions must be assured to it under which it can, at least, continue its slavish existence. The serf, in the period of serfdom, raised himself to membership in the commune, just as the petty bourgeois, under the yoke of feudal absolutism, managed to develop into a bourgeois. The modern labourer, on the contrary, instead of rising with the progress of industry, sinks deeper and deeper below the conditions of existence of his own class. He becomes a pauper, and pauperism develops more rapidly than population and wealth. And here it becomes evident, that the bourgeoisie is unfit any longer to be the ruling class in society, and to impose its conditions of existence upon society as an over-riding law. It is unfit to rule, because it is incompetent to assure an existence to its slave within his slavery, because it cannot help letting him sink into such a state, that it has to feed him, instead of being fed by him. Society can no longer live under this bourgeoisie, in other words, its existence is no longer compatible with society.

The essential condition for the existence, and for the sway of the bourgeois class, is the formation and augmentation of capital; the condition for capital is wage-labour. Wage-labour rests exclusively on competition between the labourers. The advance of industry, whose involuntary promoter is the bourgeoisie, replaces the isolation of the labourers, due to competition, by their involuntary combination, due to association. The development of Modern Industry, therefore, cuts from under its feet the very foundation on which the bourgeoisie produces and appropriates products. What the bourgeoisie therefore produces, above all, are its own gravediggers. Its fall and the victory of the proletariat are equally inevitable.

# 3. *Class and Occupation*

BY EDMOND GOBLOT

NOTHING STAMPS a man as much as his occupation. Daily work determines the mode of life; even more than the organs of the body, it constrains our ideas, feelings, and tastes. Habits of the body and mind and habits of language combine to give each one of us his occupational type. People of the same occupation know one another, seek each other's company, and frequent one another—by necessity and by choice. Consequently, each imitates the other.

The end result is groups and not classes. Classes, by contrast, influence the choice of occupation. A bourgeois does not become a carpenter, a locksmith, a baker, or a blacksmith. On the other hand, one can very well become a bourgeois by starting from such professions. But if a carpenter's son is to become a lawyer, he must first become a bourgeois in the lycée and in law school.

Men of very different professions are members of the bourgeoisie and treat one another as equals; men of very different trades are all craftsmen. The function of classes is to group occupations and to segregate them. Language reflects this segregation: functions performed by craftsmen are not called professions, but trades. The gradation in meaning subsists even when the terms are inverted. If, instead of saying that a physician or a lawyer is "learned" or "capable," we say that he "knows his job," we are intentionally signifying that he is being judged outside of any class consideration and that we are evaluating in the man only the good workman. If the schools where trades are taught are called "professional schools," rather than trade schools, it is because at their inception it was felt desirable to give them a designation that upgraded them. In these inversions of terms, there is a dash of democratic spirit as well as an implicit recognition of social inequality.

The proverb, "there is no stupid trade, there are only stupid people," is an idea of simple common sense. Why, then, was it necessary to express it, if not to combat a prejudice? Proverbs are often self-evident truths that seem to require restatement, in order to be remembered. Restating them still does not protect them from oblivion. For if this particular proverb were really taken seriously, and applied, it would be the very denial of social classes. In fact, the bourgeois does believe that there are many stupid trades, trades that are low and ridiculous and yet very good and very honorable—but for someone else. Some may even tempt him because they pay well and would fit his tastes and aptitudes, but self-respect must deter him. What are these trades that are taboo for the bourgeois?

First, there are the trades that are repugnant and dirty the hands or the clothing. The hands of the bourgeois are not soiled by the dirt, scratches, and calluses of work. Delicate hands are a sign of class; the bourgeois takes good care of his. He wears gloves.

Then, we have the strenuous trades: carrying loads, manipulating heavy tools, maintaining a tiresome position, or mechanically repeating a monotonous motion are not proper work for

Translated by Jesse Pitts, from Edmond Goblot, *La barrière et le niveau* (Paris: Presses Universitaires de France, 1925), chap, iii, pp. 38–59, with the permission of Presses Universitaires de France.

a bourgeois. His means permit him to escape the slavery of hard labor, where the physical strength of man struggles against the physical strength of things.

Finally, manual trades in general, even if the tool is as light as a pen, or a needle, are below his dignity, as long as it is the hands that executes and not the spirit that conceives or the will that orders.

In these three cases, it seems evident that the exercise of such trades is precluded by class membership. One does not do carpentry in a cutaway or ditchdigging in a top hat. When a man belongs to good society, he does not risk carrying, even after washing, the persistent smell of the substances he has handled all day long. A man may well have dealings with persons of inferior education in order to give them orders, but he cannot live with them in intimacy. It is because he is a bourgeois, because he lives in a bourgeois manner, because he visits in bourgeois society, because he wears in the street and in society the garb of the bourgeois, that he cannot accept work that disfigures or that soils, or that compels mingling with inferiors.

In her house, Madame does not remain inactive; but there are tasks she will not do. She has them done by domestics or mercenaries; for instance, all the cleaning and the heavy work.

The bourgeoisie attaches an extreme importance to keeping one's distance from manual labor. In the country, those employers who have no pretensions to a bourgeois style of life (and who therefore often live all the better) eat at the same table with their servants, wear the same clothes, perhaps of a trifle better quality, speak the same language, and can be distinguished only by the fact that they command. In town, it is the same for the master craftsman in relation to his co-worker and to the apprentices. But in bourgeois life, the distances between master and servants are all the more clearly marked as they live under the same roof. Servants are generally treated with humanity. They are well fed; they are cared for when they are sick. Feelings of personal fondness grow for those who are devoted and faithful. There used to be, in practically every bourgeois household, old retainers attached to their masters, who spent their lives and died in their shadows after having raised several generations of children. They were loved; they truly belonged to the family; but they did not live a bourgeois life. The clothes and the language indicated the inequality between those whose condition it was to serve and those who had the advantage and the right to be served. It is perhaps because the more recent bourgeoisie has too strongly accentuated these distances that these old and faithful servants have practically disappeared.

The bourgeois also separates himself from those who serve him outside the house. A lady speaks of her tradesman with a distinct tone of voice, somewhat in the style of a great lady of the *ancien régime* who used to say "my people." She does not like to meet them or their wives socially; she is not of the same social rank as those to whom she gives orders. These tradesmen may be capitalists, be good businessmen, even be much wealthier than their customers. They are not bourgeois if they themselves wait on their customers. The retailer or the industrialist is bourgeois only if he is a manager, if he has personnel to weigh, wrap, and receive money, and if he shows up in the store only to supervise and give orders. The bourgeois of the *ancient régime* was above all a merchant; the bourgeois of the new regime can still be a merchant, but not a shopkeeper.

Thus, self-respect forbids the bourgeois to attend personally to repugnant or too-strenuous tasks, as well as to serve others for money. For his style of life is to be fashionable and to be waited upon.

But would not the reverse be correct? Can we not say that the bourgeois class is the totality of persons lucky enough to be able to leave the "stupid trades" to others? And is not bourgeois life simply the adoption of the mores, the customs, clothing, language, manners, and even ideas, opinions, and feelings of professional-type occupations?

Besides, the negative prestige attached to manual and subordinate labor is not a trait specific to the modern French bourgeoisie; we meet it everywhere where castes and classes exist. Every superiority of social rank translates itself and expresses itself by the power to be waited on, not so much in order to avoid fatigue as to mark social rank. For it is imperative that rank be recognizable and, if possible, at first glance. In China, the nails of the mandarin, as long as his fingers, wellgroomed, supple, transparent, spiraled, are manifest proof that he does nothing with his hands. Is it not also to signify that he would not demean himself to servile tasks that our bourgeois wears a costume in which these tasks would be impossible? He feels the need to have it known, at a glance, that he is not a common laborer, a hired hand, or a servant. Is it social class that determines the occupation? Is it not rather the occupation that classes?

It is both. Whoever has recognized the falsity, the absurdity, and often the revolting injustice of the principles underlying certain class attitudes and the customs which they support, and who would try to renounce them, meets the nearly invincible resistance of the social milieu to which he belongs. There are cases where it is absolutely necessary "to do like everybody else"; that is, like one's equals, like people of the same occupation. Hence, it is the occupation, once selected, that imposes the style of life. But, on the other hand, class precedes occupation; before choosing a career, a man already belongs to a class by virtue of his family, his connections, his education, and his culture. He has not chosen his social rank any more than he has chosen his family. He was born there; he was raised there; he is owned by his class. He chose his profession, but the choice was limited; a bourgeois can only choose a bourgeois occupation. True, occupation is the most common means for climbing socially. But he will only be a *parvenu* if he does not become a bourgeois at the same time, and even beforehand.

The bourgeois does not fear physical effort any more than the next man if this effort is voluntary and gratuitous, but he would blush to find there his means of existence. Not that he be indifferent to money. The revenues of his trading house, factory, or bank seem to him the just reward of his efforts, energy, foresight, and good behavior. These virtues bringing cash benefits are those which he praises the most. He is not afraid to sell or rent his intelligence, knowledge, advice, supervision, his mere presence, and even, if it has a cash value, his name; but he does not rent his hands, shoulders, or back. He requires payment for his time, work, and responsibility; but he does not earn his bread by "the sweat of his brow." However, he will work with his hands when witnesses, if there are any, will believe or know that he is not compelled to do so and that it brings him no return. He will not hide to dig in his garden, or to split wood, or to do carpentry, as long as it is believed he is doing it for his pleasure or for his health. Certain sports demand more physical efforts and more endurance than many manual trades. The bourgeois would not cross the square with a basket; yet he goes on a hike loaded with an enormous sack, and he does it voluntarily. He does not fear the strain, but the humiliation. He does not want to seem constrained, either by someone's authority or the necessity of earning a living, to endure the fatigues of manual labor.

It is quite honorable for a lady to busy herself in her home with the care of her linen, and to make her own hats and her dresses. But, if ladies grouped in a salon busy their fingers while talking or listening to music, it is not to darn socks; it must be for some "lady-like work,"—some useless embroidery, some superfluous tapestry, or sewing for the poor.

Intellectual work is as tiresome as many manual trades. "Getting used to it" is as necessary for the one as it is for the others. An intellectual would not stand for one hour the task that a laborer bears for eight hours; but then how many laborers would stand one hour's serious reading? Every lecturer knows that one hour is the maximum of intellectual effort that one may request from an adult audience, even an intelligent and learned audience.

However, it seems that the work of the mind elevates one's status as much as the other degrades it. Could the value judgments that make for the distinction between classes be reduced to the superiority of mind over matter, of intellectual and moral life over physical life? There was once a bourgeois philosophy; upper class people had to be spiritualists; for them materialism was always "crude." This superiority of the spiritual over the corporal is at once in the tradition of classical antiquity and in the tradition of Christianity; our civilization is completely permeated by it. Manual work assimilates man to a beast of toil; one uses the handy man as one uses a horse, an ox, or a dog, each according to its natural aptitudes. A man and an ox are two servants, the bones, muscles, organs, and perceptions of which are differently constituted and differently available. With progress, one replaces advantageously the human servant as well as the animal servant by a machine.

According to this logic, the bourgeoisie would monopolize the professions of initiative, command, and intelligence, and would leave to the lower classes the trades of execution, obedience, and physical effort. The former are those which were exercised in antiquity by the freemen, hence, the name of liberal professions. The popular trades would correspond to the servile arts of ancient times. There would be, in our class division, something of a "survival"—very indirect, and very remote, it is true—of antique slavery. Of course, our legal code no longer allows persons without rights or without family to be bought and sold as commodities, but if manual labor and subordinate work are still considered signs of social inferiority, it must mean that, however many revolutions, the division of labor has in its essential features, remained unchanged.

No one will deny that there are in the lower classes persons who are very superior—intellectually and morally—to many bourgeois, and more capable and worthy to exercise the better professions. A social class cannot prevent the birth, in its midst, of weak characters, of mediocre or worse than mediocre minds, of inferior personalities who will never exercise authority because nobody would obey them, and of men of dubious morality, to whom nobody cares to trust his interests. These children are the despair and the shame of their families. It may be possible, eventually, to place them; they are found some subordinate employment that retains the appearance of a bourgeois profession. But it is the threat and even the first step of downward mobility. In the lower classes, there is no shortage of gifted men who, while remaining in their trades, become leaders, run their businesses well, and become financially independent, without, for all that, adopting a bourgeois profession and a bourgeois style of life. But it is the first step of social climbing; their children will be ladies and gentlemen. It is more frequent to become a bourgeois through one's father's merits than through one's own.

The liberal professions could, then, be said to be the touchstone of the bourgeois class, if we agree that it is through those professions that one reaches and maintains bourgeois status and it is through failure to be capable or worthy to exercise them that one begins to fall downward. With equality before the law, the most important and definitive conquest of the Revolution was the abolition of the privileges of birth and the access of all to all occupations.

But if the modern bourgeoisie were of superior intellect and culture, those who have been named, recently, the *intellectuals,* would form a class superior to the bourgeoisie or, at least, a subclass occupying a superior status within the bourgeoisie. It is nothing of the kind. Intellectual professions do not constitute special classes and even less one class. Intellectuals are bourgeois, but of a comparatively low social rank if they are bourgeois only because of their intelligence. The respect one has for them is somewhat equivocal: one does not know very well if these professions are common or superior, coveted or disdained. The way they are judged, if judgment is not corrected by reflection, is often colored by some disfavor and even condescending pity. We admire that such enlightened men assume so much work for so little profit. The first impulse is to think that their choice was a blunder and another blunder to persevere in it. As an afterthought, one bows to their disinterestedness.

Intellectual work is, at least in part, disinterested, because those who give themselves to it, feeling rewarded for their effort by personal satisfaction, are content with comparatively low monetary renumerations. Every university professor feels a certain pride in thinking that his salary does not represent the value of his services. The judge, the soldier, and the priest have the same feeling. The mediocrity of their financial situation is a guarantee that they do not sell science, or justice, or the sacrifices of their lives, or the salvation of souls. Naturally, intellectuals are bourgeois if they were already so by their income, their family, and the social milieu from which they came. If they are bourgeois only by their professions, they are rather mediocre bourgeois.

Indeed, it is impossible that class distinction be based upon fundamental characteristics requiring subtle evaluation, such as intelligence, morality, or character. The advantages in being a member of a class are precisely that the outward signs of class membership are, either rightly or wrongly, merits which, without these signs, would escape detection. The bourgeoisie which believes itself to be and wants to look like an elite, cannot tolerate another elite forming above it and stealing its advantage. It honors talent, knowledge, and virtue; it welcomes intellectuals. It cannot reject them, for its whole *raison d'etre,* its sole appearance of legitimacy is the superiority of its culture. But personal merit, by the very fact that it is personal, is a dissolvent of class, a perpetual danger to its existence. By vital necessity, bourgeois society upholds the talent that emerges from itself and from below itself, and attempts to absorb it, to color itself entirely with its reflection and its diffusion, so as to make it appear an emanation and a natural flowering of its own essence. If the intellectual professions should withdraw from its midst, if the world of science, letters, and arts, on the one hand, and the world of business, on the other, although having received a similar general culture, could not, because of their later specialization, remain on the same level, the bourgeoisie would disappear.

To be exact, the superiority of the bourgeoisie is neither intellectual or moral. Intellectual work is deemed more honorable than the work of the body, but it is even more honorable not to work at all and to live on one's income. And of all the spiritual and moral qualities, the most honored are those rewarded by increase in wealth. Practical and calculating wisdom, prudence, order, economy, regularity in work—those are the bourgeois virtues. The most degrading vices are those that disturb the world of business or the enjoyment of revenues: dishonesty, theft, swindling, deception. Bankruptcy declasses and dishonors, even when it is more a misfortune than a personal failure. We know the severity of juries for crimes against property, their indulgence for crimes against the person. Although debauchery is severely judged when it results in ruin and downward mobility, it is a very minor sin when it is carefully regulated and limited. The bourgeois has no great esteem for pure thought, science, and philosophy; he does not like doctrinaires and ideologues; he is suspicious of engineers who are too learned—pure theoreticians, and bad practitioners. This fear of ideas is a characteristic of the bourgeois mind. He is also afraid of imagination and afraid of sentiment. He prides himself on being practical; he is a utilitarian. Hence, he has only a moderate taste for art, poetry, literature. In this latter respect, he has in due time gone to schools which have partly corrected this attitude. Under Louis Philippe, the bourgeoisie was obstinately against the "addition of the skilled" to the electorate: and this triggered the Revolution of 1848. Later, the bourgeoisie became aware that practically all of the artistic world and a part of the literary world were outside of it, in that it was ignoring them shamefully. Arts and letters then became fashionable; otherwise, another elite would have formed outside of the bourgeoisie and would have constituted, of course, the best elite.

Hence, we shall not find in the superiority of intelligence and culture a sufficient explanation for the division of society in classes; like income, occupations rank but do not classify. They rank on an infinite variety of levels. In a public administration, in a large private enterprise—whether of rural, industrial or commercial character—in an industry such as the building, clothing, or food, industries, work is not only specialized, it is more or less integrated in a hierarchy. Within these various hierarchies, one can, almost without hesitating, trace the demarkation between bourgeois professions and popular trades. In general, the occupation is ranked more highly when it requires more intelligence and more independence, when it has more scope, and when it brings more revenue. There is a line above which the occupation is liberal and bourgeois; below that limit it remains common. The social scale of occupations and the social scale of fortunes do not class because they are both continuous. But this scale is cut in two by the frontier of class. Above this frontier, one admits a sort of equivalence between the most various occupations, or an equality or community of class even where there is inequality of rank. This is the level. One can see without difficulty that the engineer deems himself superior to the road-worker; and the superior court judge, to the process-server. But why is the engineer superior to the process-server, to whom he is not the superior and to whom he does not give any orders, in the same way as the judge is superior to the road worker? And why are the engineer and the superior court judge of the same bourgeois class, the process-server and the road-worker of the same working class? Why, finally, in the public and private occupations, does the inequality of ranks, so clearly indicated by hierarchy, not result in an inequality of classes? Occupationally unequal, why are some people socially equal?

In the continuum of occupations, as in the continuum of incomes, class distinction seems to operate through a single variable upon which all the others depend: liberal professions versus servile trades; intellectual work versus physical work; scientific education versus manual apprenticeship; initiative versus compliance; commandment versus obedience; etc. This variable is the concrete and easily grasped fact that the preparation for liberal professions lasts until about the age of twenty-five. The bourgeois begins to earn his living ten years later than the common man. As a result, his family must be able to advance him funds. At twenty-five years of age, the young bourgeois is a human capital that has not produced yet any interest; it is in this sense that the bourgeois can be called a capitalist. These advances are considerable; they exceed by far specific tuition costs. Scholarships give a very efficacious aid to the poor bourgeois and favor the ascension to the bourgeoisie of some gifted children of the lower classes. The elements thus preserved or acquired by the upper classes are generally the best. But scholarships are never sufficient. As a result, they are very rarely sought by the lower classes, for whom they are nearly useless. For even if prolonged studies are necessary, they are far from sufficient to enable one to break through the barrier of class, be it only for the reason that, except for rare exceptions, one does not break through this barrier alone. Family solidarity is a very crucial factor.

It is not sufficient that the social climber possess intelligence, knowledge, aptitudes, and the virtues necessary to his profession. He—and his family—must be able to live in a social milieu that corresponds to his profession. In the Second Empire, which was, far more than the reign of Louis Philippe, the apex of the bourgeoisie, social factors were greatly emphasized in the promotion of civil servants: the manner in which they entertained, how they behaved in a drawing room, and the behavior of their wives, their kin, and the kin of their wives were taken into account. The ministries were informed of all this by special memorandums. The lieutenant who "cut his bread" at the table would never reach the higher ranks. The republican civil service cares less about these details of private life, but the bourgeois class defends itself against outsiders and opposes to them a subtly complicated fence, constantly kept up and repaired, so as to insure that only those who can be treated as equals will be able to break through it.

In principle, the liberal professions are those supposing qualities of intelligence, knowledge, culture, character, and authority; in a word, qualities of personal worth. Because of this, it is impossible that they should constitute a class. The bourgeoisie appropriates these qualities by associating intellectual and moral qualities with the superficial characteristics that constitute and distinguish it. Its ways of judging, feeling, acting—in a word, its mores—can be understood as efforts to maintain the opinion that personal merit is naturally found among its members and that it is found only rarely outside its boundaries.

# 4. *On Superordination and Subordination*

BY GEORG SIMMEL

## *Introduction*

### 1. DOMINATION, A FORM OF INTERACTION

NOBODY, in general, wishes that his influence completely determine the other individual. He rather wants this influence, this determination of the other, to act back upon *him*. Even the abstract will-to-dominate, therefore, is a case of interaction. This will draws its satisfaction from the fact that the acting or suffering of the other, his positive or negative condition, offers itself to the dominator as the product of *his* will. The significance of this solipsistic exercise of domination (so to speak) consists, for the superordinate himself, exclusively in the consciousness of his efficacy. Sociologically speaking, it is only a rudimentary form. By virtue of it alone, sociation occurs as little as it does between a sculptor and his statue, although the statue, too, acts back on the artist through his consciousness of his own creative power. The practical function of this desire for domination, even in this sublimated form, is not so much the exploitation of the other as the mere consciousness of this possibility. For the rest, it does not represent the extreme case of egoistic inconsiderateness. Certainly, the desire for domination is designed to break the *internal* resistance of the subjugated (whereas egoism usually aims only at the victory over his *external* resistance). But still, even the desire for domination has some interest in the other person, who constitutes a value for it. Only when egoism does not even amount to a desire for domination; only when the other is absolutely indifferent and a mere means for purposes which lie beyond him, is the last shadow of any sociating process removed.

The definition of later Roman jurists shows, in a relative way, that the elimination of *all* independent significance of one of the two interacting parties annuls the very notion of society. This definition was to the effect that the *societas leonina* must not be conceived of as a social contract. ["sociation with a lion," that is, a partnership in which all the advantage is on one side—Tr.] A comparable statement has been made regarding the lowest-paid workers in modern giant enterprises which preclude all effective competition among rivaling entrepreneurs for the services of these laborers. It has been said that the difference in the strategic positions of workers and employers is so overwhelming that the work contract ceases to be a "contract" in the ordinary sense of the word, because the former are unconditionally at the mercy of the latter. It thus appears that the moral maxim never to use a man as a mere means is actually the formula of every sociation. Where the significance of the one party sinks so low that its effect no longer enters the relationship with the other, there is as little ground for speaking of sociation as there is in the case of the carpenter and his bench.

Within a relationship of subordination, the exclusion of all spontaneity whatever is actually rarer than is suggested by such widely used popular expressions as "coercion," "having no choice," "absolute necessity," etc. Even in the most oppressive and cruel cases of subordination, there is still a considerable measure of personal freedom. We merely do not become aware of it, because its manifestation would entail sacrifices which we usually never think of taking upon ourselves. Actually, the "absolute" coercion which even the most cruel tyrant imposes upon us is always distinctly relative. Its condition is our desire to escape from the threatened punishment or from other consequences of our disobedience. More precise analysis shows that the super-subordination relationship

Reprinted from *The Sociology of Georg Simmel*, ed. and trans., Kurt H. Wolff. (Glencoe, Ill.: The Free Press, 1950), from Part III, chap. i, pp. 181–89; chap. iv, 250–67; with the permission of The Free Press.

destroys the subordinate's freedom only in the case of direct physical violation. In every other case, this relationship only demands a price for the realization of freedom—a price, to be sure, which we are not willing to pay. It can narrow down more and more the sphere of external conditions under which freedom is clearly realized, but, except for physical force, never to the point of the complete disappearance of freedom. The moral side of this analysis does not concern us here, but only its sociological aspect. This aspect consists in the fact that interaction, that is, action which is mutually determined, action which stems exclusively from personal origins, prevails even where it often is not noted. It exists even in those cases of superordination and subordination—and therefore makes even those cases *societal* forms—where according to popular notions the "coercion" by one party deprives the other of every spontaneity, and thus of every real "effect," or contribution to the process of interaction.

### 2. AUTHORITY AND PRESTIGE

Relationships of superordination and subordination play an immense role in social life. It is therefore of the utmost importance for its analysis to clarify the spontaneity and co-efficiency of the subordinate subject and thus to correct their widespread minimization by superficial notions about them. For instance, what is called "authority" presupposes, in a much higher degree than is usually recognized, a freedom on the part of the person subjected to authority. Even where authority seems to "crush" him, it is based not *only* on coercion or compulsion to yield to it.

The peculiar structure of "authority" is significant for social life in the most varied ways; it shows itself in beginnings as well as in exaggerations, in acute as well as in lasting forms. It seems to come about in two different ways. A person of superior significance or strength may acquire, in his more immediate or remote milieu, an overwhelming weight of his opinions, a faith, or a confidence which have the character of objectivity. He thus enjoys a prerogative and an axiomatic trustworthiness in his decisions which excel, at least by a fraction, the value of mere subjective personality, which is always variable, relative, and subject to criticism. By acting "authoritatively," the quantity of his significance is transformed into a new quality; it assumes for his environment the physical state—metaphorically speaking—of objectivity.

But the same result, authority, may be attained in the opposite direction. A super-individual power—state, church, school, family or military organizations—clothes a person with a reputation, a dignity, a power of ultimate decision, which would never flow from his individuality. It is the nature of an authoritative person to make decisions with a certainty and automatic recognition which logically pertain only to impersonal, objective axioms and deductions. In the case under discussion, authority descends upon a person from above, as it were, whereas in the case treated before, it arises from the qualities of the person himself, through a *generatio aequivoca.* ["Equivocal birth" or "spontaneous generation."—Tr.] But evidently, at this point of transition and change-over [from the personal to the authoritative situation], the more or less voluntary faith of the party subjected to authority comes into play. This transformation of the value of personality into a super-personal value gives the personality something which is beyond its demonstrable and rational share, however slight this addition may be. The believer in authority himself achieves the transformation. He (the subordinate element) participates in a sociological event which requires his spontaneous cooperation. As a matter of fact, the very feeling of the "oppressiveness" of authority suggests that the autonomy of the subordinate party is actually presupposed and never wholly eliminated.

Another nuance of superiority, which is designated as "prestige," must be distinguished from "authority." Prestige lacks the element of supersubjective significance; it lacks the identity of the personality with an objective power or norm. Leadership by means of prestige is determined entirely by the strength of the individual. This individual force always remains conscious of itself. Moreover, whereas the average type of leadership always shows a certain mixture of personal and superadded-objective factors, prestige leadership stems from pure personality, even as authority stems from the objectivity of norms and forces. Superiority through prestige consists in the ability to "push" individuals and masses and to make unconditional followers of them. Authority does not have this ability to the same extent. The higher, cooler, and normative character of authority is more apt to leave room for criticism, even on the part of its followers. In spite of this, however, prestige strikes us as the more voluntary homage to the superior person. Actually, perhaps, the recognition of authority implies a more profound freedom of the subject than does the enchantment that emanates from the prestige of a prince, a priest, a military or spiritual leader. But the matter is different in regard to the *feeling* on the part of those led. In the face of authority, we are often defenseless, whereas the *élan* with which we follow a given prestige always contains a consciousness of spontaneity. Here, precisely because devotion is only to the wholly personal, this devotion seems to flow only from the ground of personality with its inalienable freedom. Certainly, man is mistaken innumerable times regarding the measure of freedom which he must invest in a certain action. One reason for this is the vagueness and uncertainty of the explicit conception by means of which we account for this inner process. But in whatever way we interpret freedom, we can say that some measure of it, even though it may not be the measure we suppose, is present wherever there is the feeling and the conviction of freedom.

### 3. LEADER AND LED

The seemingly wholly passive element is in reality even more active in relationships such as obtain between a speaker and his audience or between a teacher and his class. Speaker and teacher appear to be nothing but leaders; nothing but, momentarily, superordinate. Yet whoever finds himself in such or a similar situation feels the determining and controlling re-action on the part of what seems to be a purely receptive and guided mass. This applies not only to situations where the two parties confront one another physically. All leaders are also led; in innumerable cases, the master is the slave of his slaves. Said one of the greatest German party leaders referring to his followers: "I am their leader, therefore I must follow them."

In the grossest fashion, this is shown by the journalist. The journalist gives content and direction to the opinions of a mute multitude. But he is nevertheless forced to listen, combine, and guess what the tendencies of this multitude are, what it desires to hear and have confirmed, and whither it wants to be led. While apparently it is only the public which is exposed to *his* suggestions, actually he is as much under the sway of the *public's* suggestion. Thus, a highly complex interaction (whose two, mutually spontaneous forces, to be sure, appear under very different forms) is hidden here beneath the semblance of the pure superiority of the one element and a purely passive being-led of the other.

The content and significance of certain personal relations consist in the fact that the exclusive function of one of the two elements is service for the other. But the perfect measure of this devotion of the first element often depends on the condition that the other element surrenders to the first, even though on a different level of the relationship. Thus, Bismarck remarked concerning his relation to William I: "A certain measure of devotion is determined by law; a greater measure, by political conviction; beyond this, a personal feeling of *reciprocity* is required.—My devotion had its principal ground in my loyalty to royalist convictions. But in the special form in which this royalism existed, it is after all possible only under the impact of a certain reciprocity—the reciprocity between master and servant." The most characteristic case of this type is shown, perhaps, by hypnotic suggestion. An outstanding hypnotist pointed out that in every hypnosis the hypnotized has an effect upon the hypnotist; and that, although this effect cannot be easily determined, the result of the hypnosis could not be reached without it. Thus here, too, appearance showns an absolute influence, on the one side, and an absolute being-influenced, on the other; but it conceals an interaction, an exchange of influences, which transforms the pure one-sidedness of superordination and subordination into a *sociological* form.

### 4. INTERACTION IN THE IDEA OF "LAW"

I shall cite some cases of superordination and subordination in the field of law. It is easy to reveal the interaction which actually exists in what seems a purely unilateral situation. If the absolute despot accompanies his orders by the threat of punishment or the promise of reward, this implies that he himself wishes to be bound by the decrees he issues. The subordinate is expected to have the right to request something of him; and by establishing the punishment, no matter how horrible, the despot commits himself not to impose a more severe one. Whether or not afterward he actually abides by the punishment established or the reward promised is a different question: the *significance* of the relation is that, although the superordinate wholly determines the subordinate, the subordinate nevertheless is assured of a claim on which he can insist or which he can waive. Thus even this extreme form of the relationship still contains some sort of spontaneity on his part.

The motive of interaction within an apparently one-sided and passive subordination appears in a peculiar modification in a medieval theory of the state. According to this theory, the state came into existence because men mutually obligated one another to submit to a common chief. Thus, the ruler—including, apparently, the unconditional ruler—is appointed on the basis of a mutual contract among his subjects. Whereas contemporaneous theories of domination saw its reciprocal character in the contract between ruler and ruled, the theory under discussion located this mutual nature of domination in its very basis, the people: the obligation to the prince is conceived to be the mere articulation, expression, or technique of a reciprocal relation among the individuals of whom his people is composed. In Hobbes, in fact, the ruler has no means of breaking the contract with his subjects because he has not made one; and the corollary to this is that the subject, even if he rebels against his ruler, does not thereby break a contract concluded with *him,* but only the contract he has entered with all other members of the society, to the effect of letting themselves be governed by this ruler.

It is the *absence* of this reciprocity which accounts for the observation that the tyranny of a group over its own members is worse than that of a prince over his subjects. The group—and by no means the political group alone—conceives of its members, not as confronting it, but as being included by it as its own links. This often results in a peculiar inconsiderateness toward the members, which is very different from a ruler's personal cruelty. Wherever there is, formally, confrontation (even if, contentually, it comes *close* to submission), there is interaction; and, in principle, interaction always contains some limitation of *each* party to the process (although there may be individual exceptions to this rule). Where superordination shows an extreme inconsiderateness, as in the case of the group that simply *disposes* of its members, there no longer is any confrontation with its form of interaction, which involves spontaneity, and hence limitation, of both superordinate and subordinate elements.

This is very clearly expressed in the original conception of Roman law. In its purity, the term "law" implies a submission which does not involve any spontaneity or counter-effect on the part of the person subordinate to the law. And the fact that the subordinate has actually cooperated in making it—and more, that *he* has given himself the law which binds him—is irrelevant. For in doing so, he has merely decomposed himself into the subject and object of lawmaking; and the law which the subject applies to the object does not change its significance only by the fact that both subject and object are accidentally lodged in the same physical person. Nevertheless, in their conception of law, the Romans directly allude to the idea of interaction. For originally, "*lex*" means "contract," even though in the sense that the conditions of the contract are fixed by its proponent, and the other party can merely accept or reject it in its totality. In the beginning, the *lex publica populi romani* implied that the King proposed this legislation, and the people were its acceptors. Hence the very concept which most of all seems to exclude interaction is, nevertheless, designed to refer to it by its linguistic expression. In a certain sense this is revealed in the prerogative of the Roman king that he alone was allowed to speak to the people. Such a prerogative, to be sure, expressed the jealously guarded exclusiveness of his rulership, even as in ancient Greece the right of everybody to speak to the people indicated complete democracy. Nevertheless, this prerogative implies that the significance of speaking to the people, and, hence, of the people themselves, was recognized. Although the people merely *received* this one-sided action, they were nonetheless a *contractor* (whose party to the contract, of course, was only a single person, the king).

The purpose of these preliminary remarks was to show the properly sociological, social-formative character of superordination and subordination even where it appears as if a social relationship were replaced by a purely mechanical one—where, that is, the position of the subordinate seems to be that of a means or an object for the superordinate, without any spontaneity. It has been possible, at least in many cases, to show the sociologically decisive *reciprocal effectiveness,* which was concealed under the one-sided character of influence and being-influenced.

* * *

## *Subordination under a Principle*

### 1. SUBORDINATION UNDER A PRINCIPLE VS. A PERSON

I now come, finally, to the third typical form of subordination, subordination neither to an individual nor to a plurality, but to an impersonal, objective principle. The fact that here a real interaction, at least an immediate interaction, is precluded, seems to deprive this form of the element of freedom. The individual who is subordinate to an objective law feels himself determined by it; while he, in turn, in no way determines the law, and has no possibility of reacting to it in a manner which could influence it—quite in contrast to even the most miserable slave, who, in some fashion at least, can still in this sense react to his master. For if one simply does not obey the law, one is, to this extent, not *really* subjected to it; and if one changes the law, one is not subordinate to the old law at all, but is again, in the same entirely unfree manner, subject to the new law. In spite of this, however, for modern, objective man, who is aware of the difference between the spheres of spontaneity and of obedience, subordination to a law which functions as the emanation of impersonal, uninfluenceable powers, is the more dignified situation. This was quite different at a time when the personality could preserve its self-esteem only in situations characterized by full spontaneity, which even in case of complete subordination were still associated with inter-personal effect and counter-effect. For this reason, as late as in the sixteenth century, princes in France, Germany, Scotland, and the Netherlands often met with considerable resistance, if they let their countries be ruled by administrative bodies or erudite substitutes—that is, more nearly by laws. The ruler's order was felt to be something personal; the individual wanted to lend him obedience only from personal devotion; and personal devotion, in spite of its unconditional character, is always in the form of free reciprocity.

This passionate personalism of the subordination relationship almost becomes its own caricature in the following circumstance, reported from Spain at the beginning of the modern period. An impoverished nobleman who became a cook or lackey, did not thereby definitely lose his nobility: it only became latent and could be awakened again by a favorable turn of fate. But once he became a craftsman, his nobility was destroyed. This is entirely contrary to the modern conception, which separates the person from his achievement and, therefore, finds personal dignity to be preserved best if the content of subordination is as objective as possible. Thus, an American girl, who would work in a factory without the slightest feeling of humiliation, would feel wholly degraded as a family cook. Already in thirteenth-century Florence, the *lower* guilds comprised occupations in the immediate service of persons, such as cobblers, hosts, and school teachers; whereas the *higher* guilds were composed of occupations which, though still serving the public, were yet more objective and less dependent on particular individuals—for instance, clothiers and grocers. On the other hand, in Spain, where knightly traditions, with their engagement of the whole person in all activity, were still alive, every relationship which (in any sense) took place between person and person, was bound to be considered at least bearable; while every subordination to more objective claims, every integration into a system of impersonal duties (impersonal, because serving many and anonymous persons), was bound to be regarded as wholly disgraceful. An aversion to the objectivity of law can still be felt in the legal theories of Althusius: the *summus magistratus* legislates, but he does so, not because he represents the state, but because he is appointed by the people. The notion that the ruler could be designated as the representative of the state by appointment through law, not by personal appointment (actual or presumed) by the people—is still alien to Althusius.

In antiquity, on the contrary, subordination to law appeared thoroughly adequate, precisely because of the idea that law is free from any personal characteristics. Aristotle praised law as "*tó méson,*" that is, as that which is moderate, impartial, free from passions. Plato, in the same sense, had already recognized government by impersonal law as the best means for counteracting selfishness. His, however, was only a psychological motivation. It did not touch the core of the question, namely, the fundamental transition of the relationship of obedience from personalism to objectivism, a transition which cannot be derived from the anticipation of utilitarian consequence. Yet, in Plato, we also find this other theory: that, in the ideal state, the insight of the ruler stands above the law; and as soon as the welfare of the whole seems to require it of the ruler, he must be able to act even against the laws laid down by him. There must be laws which may not be broken under any circumstances, only if there are no true statesmen. The law, therefore, appears here as the lesser evil—but not, as in the Germanic feeling, mentioned before, because subordination under a person has an element of freedom and dignity in comparison with which all obedience to laws has something mechanical and passive. Rather, it is the rigidity of the law which is felt to be its weakness: in its rigidity, it confronts the changing and unforeseeable claims of life in a clumsy and inadequate way; and this is an evil from which only the entirely unprejudiced insight of a personal ruler can escape; and only where there is no such insight, does law become relatively advantageous. Here, therefore, it is always the *content* of the law, its physical state, as it were, which determines its value or disvalue as compared with subordination under persons. The fact that the relationship of obedience is totally different in its inner principle and in terms of the whole feeling of life, on the part of the obeyer, according to whether it originates in a person or in a law—this fact does not enter these considerations. The most general, or formal relation between government by law and government by person can (of course) be expressed in a preliminary, practical manner by saying that where the law is not forceful or broad enough, a person is necessary, and where the person is inadequate, the law is required. But, far beyond this, whether rule by man is considered as something provisional in lieu of rule by perfect law, or, inversely, rule by law is considered a gap-filler or an inferior substitute for government by a personality which is absolutely qualified to rule—this choice depends upon decisions of ultimate, indiscussable feelings concerning sociological values.

### 2. SUBORDINATION UNDER OBJECTS

There is still another form in which an objective principle may become the turning point in the relationship between superordinates and subordinates, namely, when neither a law nor an ideal norm, but rather a concrete object governs the domination, as, for instance, in the principle of patrimony. Here —most radically under the system of Russian bondage—bonded subjects are only appurtenances of the land—"the air bonds the people." The terrible hardship of bondage at least excluded personal slavery which would have permitted the sale of the slave. Instead, it tied subordination to the land in such a way that the bondsman could be sold only along with the land. In spite of all contentual and quantitative differences, nevertheless, sometimes this same form occurs in the case of the modern factory worker, whose own interest, through certain arrangements, binds him to a given factory. For instance, the acquisition of his house was made possible for him, or he participated out of his own purse in certain welfare expenditures, and all these benefits are lost once he leaves the factory, etc. He is thus bound, merely by objects, in a way which in a very specific manner makes him powerless in respect to the entrepreneur. Finally, it was this same form of domination which, under the most primitive patriarchal conditions, was governed not by a merely spatial, but by a living object: children did not belong to the father because he was their progenitor, but because the mother belonged to him (as the fruits of the tree belong to the tree's owner); therefore, children begotten by other fathers were no less his property.

This type of domination usually involves a humiliatingly harsh and unconditional kind of subordination. For, inasmuch as a man is subordinate by virtue of belonging to a thing, he himself psychologically sinks to the category of mere thing. With the necessary reservations, one could say that where law regulates domination, the superordinate belongs in the sphere of objectivity; while, where a *thing* regulates it, the *subordinate* does. The condition of the subordinate, therefore, is usually more favorable in the first case, and more unfavorable in the second, than in many cases of purely personal subordination.

### 3. CONSCIENCE

Immediate sociological interest in subordination under an objective principle attaches to two chief cases of it. One case is when this ideal, superordinate principle can be interpreted as a psychological crystallization of an actual social power. The other is when, among those who are commonly subject to it, it produces particular and characteristic relationships. The first case must be taken into consideration, above all, when dealing with moral imperatives. In our moral consciousness, we feel subordinate to a command which does not seem to derive from any human, personal power. The voice of conscience we hear only in ourselves, although in comparison with all subjective egoism, we hear it with a force and decisiveness which apparently can stem only from a tribunal *outside* the individual. An attempt has been made, as is well-known, to solve this contradiction by deriving the contents of morality from social norms. What is useful to the species and the group, the argument runs, and what the group, therefore, requests of its members for the sake of its own maintenance, is gradually bred into the individual as an instinct. He thus comes to contain it in himself, as his own, autonomous feeling, in addition to his personal feelings properly speaking, and thus often in contrast to them. This, it is alleged, explains the dual character of the moral command: that on the one hand, it confronts us as an impersonal order to which we simply have to submit, but that, on the other, no external power, but only our most private and internal impulses, imposes it upon us. At any rate, here is one of the cases where the individual, within his own consciousness, repeats the relationships which exist between him, as a total personality, and the group. It is an old observation that the conceptions of the single individual, with all their relations of association and dissociation, differentiation, and unification, behave in the same way in which individuals behave in regard to one another. It is merely a peculiar case of this correspondence that those intrapsychological relations are repeated, not only between individuals in general, but also between the individual and his group. All that society asks of its members—adaptation and loyalty, altruism and work, self-discipline and truthfulness—the individual also asks of himself.

In all this, several very important motives cut across one another. Society confronts the individual with precepts. He becomes habituated to their compulsory character until the cruder and subtler means of compulsion are no longer necessary. His nature may thereby be so formed or deformed that he acts by these precepts as if on impulse, with a consistent and direct will which is not conscious of any law. Thus, the pre-Islamic Arabs were without any notion of an objectively legal compulsion; in all instances, purely personal decision was their highest authority, although this decision was thoroughly imbued with tribal consciousness and the requirements of tribal life, which gave it its norms. Or else, the law, in the form of a command which is carried by the authority of the society, does live in the individual consciousness, but irrespective of the question whether society actually backs it with its compulsory power or even itself supports it solely with its explicit will. Here then, the individual represents society to himself. The external confrontation, with its suppressions, liberations, changing accents, has become an interplay between his social impulses and the ego impulses in the stricter sense of the word; and both are included by the ego in the larger sense.

But this is not yet the really objective lawfulness, indicated above, in whose consciousness of which no trace of any historical-social origin is left. At a certain higher stage of morality, the motivation of action lies no longer in a real-human, even though super-individual power; at this stage, the spring of moral necessities flows beyond the contrast between individual and totality. For, as little as these necessities derive from society, as little do they derive from the singular reality of individual life. In the free conscience of the actor, in individual reason, they only have their bearer, the locus of their efficacy. Their power of obligation stems from these necessities themselves, from their inner, super-personal validity, from an objective ideality which we must recognize, whether or not we want to, in a manner similar to that in which the validity of a truth is entirely independent of whether or not the truth becomes real in any consciousness. The *content,* however, which fills these forms is (not necessarily but often) the societal requirement. But this requirement no longer operates by means of its social impetus, as it were, but rather as if it had undergone a metapsychosis into a norm which must be satisfied for its own sake, not for my sake nor for yours.

We are dealing here with differences which not only are psychologically of the greatest delicacy, but whose boundaries are also constantly blurred in practice. Yet this mixture of motivations in which psychic reality moves, makes it all the more urgent that it be isolated analytically. Whether society and individual confront one another like two powers and the individual's subordination is effected by society through energy which seems to flow from an uninterrupted source and constantly seems to renew itself; or whether this energy changes into a psychological impulse in the very individual who considers himself a social being and, therefore, fights and suppresses those of his impulses that lean toward his "egoistic" part; or whether the Ought, which man finds above himself as an actuality as objective as Being, is merely filled with the content of societal life conditions—these are constellations which only begin to exhaust the kinds of individual subordination to the group. In them, the three powers which fill historical life—society, individual, and objectivity—become norm-giving, in this order. But they do so in such a way that each of them absorbs the social content, the quantity of superordination of society over the individual; in a specific manner, each of them forms and presents the power, the will, and the necessities of society.

### 4. SOCIETY AND "OBJECTIVITY"

Among these three potencies, objectivity can be defined as the unquestionably valid law which is enthroned in an ideal realm above society and the individual. But it can also be defined in still another dimension, as it were. Society often is the third element, which solves conflicts between the individual and objectivity or builds bridges where they are disconnected. As regards the genesis of cognition, the concept of society has liberated us from an alternative characteristic of earlier times, namely, that a cultural value either must spring from an individual or must be bestowed upon mankind by an objective power. Practically speaking, it is societal labor by means of which the individual can satisfy his claims upon the objective order. The cooperation of the many, the efforts of society as a unit, both simultaneously and successively, wrest from nature not only a greater quantity of need-satisfactions than can be achieved by the individual, but also new qualities and types of need-satisfactions which the labor of the individual alone cannot possibly attain. This fact is merely a symbol of the deeper and fundamental phenomenon of society standing between individual man and the sphere of general natural laws. As something psychologically concrete, society blends with the individual; as something general, it blends with nature. It is the general, but it is not abstract. To be sure, every historical group is an individual, as is every historical human being; but it is this only in relation to other groups; for its members, it is super-individual. But it is super-individual, not as a concept is in regard to its single, concrete realizations, where the concept synthesizes what is common to all of them. The group is super-individual, rather, in a specific manner of generality—similar to the organic body, which is "general" above its organs, or to "room furniture," which is "general" above table, chair, chest, and mirror. And this specific generality coincides with the specific objectivity which society possesses for its members as subjects.

But the individual does not confront society as he confronts nature. The objectivity of nature denotes the irrelevance of the question of whether or not the subject spiritually participates in nature; whether he has a correct, a false, or no conception of it. Its being exists, and its laws are valid, independently of the significance which either of them may have for any subject. Certainly, society, likewise, transcends the individual and lives its own life which follows its own laws; it, too, confronts the individual with a historical, imperative firmness. Yet, society's "in front of" the individual is, at the same time, a "within." The harsh indifference toward the individual also is an interest: social objectivity needs general individual subjectivity, although it does not need any particular individual subjectivity. It is these characteristics which make society a structure intermediate between the subject and an absolutely impersonal generality and objectivity.

The following observation, for instance, points in this direction. As long as the development of an economy does not yet produce objective prices, properly speaking; as long as knowledge and regulation of demand, offer, production costs, amounts at risk, gain, etc., do not yet lead to the idea that a given piece of merchandise is worth so much and must have such and such a fixed price—so long is the immediate interference of society and its organs and laws with the affairs of commerce (particularly in regard to the price and stability of commerce) much more strong and rigorous than under other conditions. Price taxes, the surveillance of quantity and quality of production, and, in a larger sense, even sumptuary laws and consumers' obligations, often emerged at that stage of economic development at which the subjective freedom of commerce strove after stable objectivity, without, however, yet being able to attain any pure, abstract objectivity in determining prices. It is at this stage that the concrete generality, the living objectivity of society enters, often clumsily, obstructively, schematically, but yet always as a super-subjective power which supplies the individual with a norm before he derives this norm directly from the structure of the matter at issue and its understood regularity.

On a much larger scale, this same formal development, from subordination under society to subordination under objectivity, occurs in the intellectual sphere. All of intellectual history shows to what extent the individual intellect fills the content of its truth-concepts only with traditional, authoritative conceptions which are "accepted by all," long before he confronts the object directly and derives the content of the truth-concepts from its objectivity. Initially, the support and the norm of the inquiring mind are not the object, whose immediate observation and interpretation the mind is entirely unable to manipulate, but the general opinion of the object. It is this general opinion which mediates theoretical conceptions, from the silliest superstition to the subtlest prejudices, which almost entirely conceal the lacking independence of their recipient and the un-objective nature of their contents. It seems as if man could not easily bear looking the object in the eye; as if he were equal neither to the rigidity of its lawfulness nor to the freedom which the object, in contrast to all coercion coming from men, gives him. By comparison, to bow to the authority of the many or their representatives, to traditional opinion, to socially accepted notions, is something intermediate. Traditional opinion, after all, is more modifiable than is the law of the object; in it, man can feel some psychological mediation; it transmits, as it were, something which is already digested psychologically. At the same time, it gives us a hold, a relief from responsibility—the compensation for the lack of that autonomy which we derive from the purely intrinsic relationship between ego and object.

The concept of objective justice, no less than the concept of truth, finds its intermediate stage, which leads toward the objective sense of "justice," in social behavior. In the field of criminal law, as well as in all other regulations of life, the correlation between guilt and expiation, merit and reward, service and counter-service, is first, evidently, a matter of social expediency or of social impulses. Perhaps the equivalence of action and reaction, in which justice consists, is never an analytical equivalence directly resulting from these elements, but always requires a third element, an ideal, a purpose, a norm-setting situation, in which the first two elements create or demonstrate their mutual correspondence synthetically. Originally, this third element consists in the interests and forms of the general life which surrounds the individuals, that is, the subjects of the realization of justice. This general life creates, and acts on, the criteria of justice or injustice in the relation between action and reaction—of justice or injustice which cannot be ascertained in the action-and-reaction in isolation. Above this process, and mediated by it, there rises, at an objectively and historically later stage, the necessity of the "just" correspondence between action and reaction, a correspondence which emerges in the comparison of these two elements themselves. This higher norm, which perhaps even in this later phase continues to determine weight and counter-weight according to its own scale, is completely absorbed by the elements themselves; it has become a value which seems to originate with them and operates out of them. Justice now appears as an objective relationship which follows necessarily from the intrinsic significance of sin and pain, good deed and happiness, offer and response. It must be realized for its own sake: *fiat justitia, pereat mundus*. It was, by contrast, the very preservation of the world which, from the earlier standpoint, constituted the ground of justice. Whatever the ideal sense of justice may be (which is not the topic of discussion here), the *objective* law, in which justice, purely for its own sake, embodies itself, and which claims compliance in its own right, is historically and psychologically a later stage of development. It is preceded, prepared, and mediated by the claim to justice stemming from merely *social* objectivity.

This same development, finally, prevails within the moral sphere, in the stricter sense of this term. The original content of morality is of an altruistic-social nature. The idea is not that morality has its own life independent of this content and merely absorbs it. Rather, the devotion of the "I" to the "thou" (in the singular or plural) is the very idea, the definition, of the moral. Philosophical doctrines of ethics represent, by comparison, a much later phase. In them, an absolutely objective Ought is separated from the question of "I" and "thou." If it is important to Plato that the Idea of the Good be realized; to Kant, that the principle of individual action be suitable as a general law; to Nietzsche, that the human species transcend its momentary stage of development; then, occasionally, these norms may also refer to reciprocal relations among individuals. But, essentially this is no longer important. What is important is the realization of an objective law, which not only leaves behind the subjectivity of the actor but also the subjectivity of the individuals whom the action may concern. For, now, even the reference to the societal complex of the subjects is merely an accidental satisfaction of a much more general norm and obligation, which may legitimate socially and altruistically oriented action, but may also refuse to do so. In the development of the individual as of the species, ethical obedience to the claims of the "thou" and of society characterizes the first emergence from the pre-ethical stage of naïve egoism. Innumerable individuals never go beyond obedience to the "thou." But, in principle, this stage is preparatory and transitory to subordination under an objectively ethical law, which transcends the "I" as much as the "thou," and only on its own initiative admits the interests of the one or the other as ethical contents.

### 5. THE EFFECT OF SUBORDINATION UNDER A PRINCIPLE UPON THE RELATIONS BETWEEN SUPERORDINATES AND SUBORDINATES

The second sociological question in regard to subordination under an impersonal-ideal principle concerns the effect of this common subordination upon the reciprocal relations among the subordinates. Here, also, it must above all be remembered that ideal subordination is often preceded by real subordination. We frequently find that a person or class exerts superordination in the name of an ideal principle to which the person or class themselves are allegedly subordinated. This principle, therefore, seems to be logically prior to the social arrangement; the actual organization of domination among people seems to develop in consequence of that ideal dependency. Historically, however, the road has usually run in the opposite direction. Superordinations and subordinations develop out of very real, personal power relations. Through the spiritualization of the superordinate power or through the enlargement and de-personalization of the whole relationship, there gradually grows an ideal, objective power over and above these superordinations and subordinations. The superordinate then exerts his power merely in the capacity of the closest representative of this ideal, objective force.

These successive processes are shown very distinctly in the development of the position of *pater familias* among the Aryans. Originally—this is how the type is presented to us—his power was unlimited and wholly subjective. That is, the *pater familias* decided all arrangements by momentary whim and in terms of personal advantage. Yet this arbitrary power was gradually replaced by a feeling of responsibility. The unity of the family group, embodied (for instance) in the *spiritus familiaris,* became an ideal force, in reference to which even the master of the whole felt himself to be merely an executor and obeyer. It is in this sense that custom and habit, rather than subjective preference, determined his actions, his decisions, and judicial decrees; that he no longer behaved as the unconditional master of the family property, but rather as its administrator in the interest of the whole; that his position had more the character of an office than that of an unlimited right. The relation between superordinates and subordinates was thus placed upon an entirely new basis. Whereas, at the first stage, the subordinates constituted, so to speak, only at a personal appurtenance of the superordinates, later there prevailed the objective idea of the family which stands above all individuals and to which the leading patriarch is as much subordinated as is every other member. The patriarch can give orders to the other members of the family only in the name of that ideal unit.

Here we encounter an extremely important form-type, namely, that the very commander subordinates himself to the law which he has made. The moment his will becomes law, it attains objective character, and thus separates itself from its subjective-personal origin. As soon as the ruler gives the law as law, he documents himself, to this extent, as the organ of an ideal necessity. He merely reveals a norm which is plainly valid on the ground of its inner sense and that of the situation, whether or not the ruler actually enunciates it. What is more, even if instead of this more or less distinctly conceived legitimation, the will of the ruler itself becomes law, even then the ruler cannot avoid transcending the sphere of subjectivity: for in this case, he carries the super-personal legitimation *a priori* in himself, so to speak. In this way, the inner form of law brings it about that the law-giver, in giving the law, subordinates himself to it as a person, in the same way as all others. Thus, the Privileges of the medieval Flemish cities stated expressly that the jurors must give everybody a fair trial, including even the Count who had bestowed this privilege upon the city. And such a sovereign ruler as the Great Elector introduced a head-tax without asking the estates for their consent—but then he not only made his court pay it, but he also paid it himself.

The most recent history gives an example of the growth of an objective power, to which the person, who is originally and subsequently in command, must subordinate himself in common with his subordinates. The example is formally related to the case cited from the history of the family. In modern economic production, objective and technical elements dominate over personal elements. In earlier times, many superordinations and subordinations had a personal character, so that in a given relationship, one person simply was superordinate, and the other subordinate. Many of these super-subordinations have changed in the sense that both superordinates and subordinates alike stand under an objective purpose; and it is only within this common relationship to the higher principle that the subordination of the one to the other continues to exist as a technical necessity. As long as the relationship of wage labor is conceived of as a rental contract (in which the worker is rented), it contains as an essential element the worker's subordination to the entrepreneur. But, once the work contract is considered, not as the renting of a person, but as the purchase of a piece of merchandise, that is, labor, then this element of personal subordination is eliminated. In this case, the subordination which the employer requests of the worker is only—so it has been expressed—subordination "under the cooperative process, a subordination as compulsive for the entrepreneur, once he engages in any activity at all, as for the worker." The worker is no longer subject as a person but only as the servant of an objective, economic procedure. In this process, the element which in the form of entrepreneur or manager is superordinated to the worker, operates no longer as a personal element but only as one necessitated by objective requirements.

The increased self-feeling of the modern worker must, at least partly, be connected with this process, which shows its purely sociological character also in the circumstance that it often has no influence upon the material welfare of the laborer. He merely sells a quantitatively defined service, which may be smaller or larger than what was required of him under the earlier, personal arrangement. As a man, he thus frees himself from the relationship of subordination, to which he belongs only as an element in the process of production; and to this extent, he is coordinate with those who direct the production. This technical objectivity has its symbol in the legal objectivity of the contract relation: once the contract is concluded, it stands as an objective norm above *both* parties. In the Middle Ages, this phenomenon marked the turning point in the condition of the journeyman, which originally implied full personal subordination under the master: the journeyman was generally called "servant" [*Knecht*]. The gathering of journeymen in their own estate was centered upon the attempt at transforming the personal-service relationship into a contractual relationship: as soon as the organization of the "servants" was achieved, their name, most characteristically, was replaced by that of "journeymen." In general, it is relative coordination, instead of absolute subordination, which is correlated with the contractual form, no matter what the material content of the contract may be.

This form further strengthens its objective character if the contract is not concluded between individuals, but consists in collective regulations between a group of workers on the one side, and a group of employers on the other. It has been developed especially by the English Trade Unions, which in certain, highly advanced industries conclude contracts regarding wage rates, working time, overtime, holidays, etc., with associations of entrepreneurs. These contracts may not be ignored by any sub-contract that might be made between individual members of these larger categories. In this manner, the impersonality of the labor relationship is evidently increased to an extraordinary degree. The objectivity of this relationship finds an appropriate instrument and expression in the super-individual collectivity. This objective character, finally, is assured in an even more specific manner if the contracts are concluded for very brief periods. English Trade Unions have always urged this brevity, in spite of the increased insecurity which results from it. The explanation of the recommendation has been that the worker distinguishes himself from the slave by the right to leave his place of work; but, if he surrenders this right for a long time, he is, for the whole duration of this period, subject to all conditions which the entrepreneur imposes upon him, with the exception of those expressly stipulated; and he has lost the protection offered him by his right to suspend the relationship. Instead of the breadth, or comprehensiveness, of the bond which in earlier times committed the total personality, there emerges, if the contract lasts very long, the length, or duration, of the bond. In the case of short contracts, objectivity is guaranteed, not by something positive, but only by the necessity of preventing the objectively regulated contractual relationship from changing into a relationship determined by subjective arbitrariness—whereas in the case of long contracts there is no corresponding, sufficient protection.

In the condition of domestic servants—at least, on the whole, in contemporary central Europe—it is still the total individual, so to speak, who enters the subordination. Subordination has not yet attained the objectivity of an objectively, clearly circumscribed service. From this circumstance derive the chief inadequacies inherent in the institution of domestic service. This institution does approach that more perfect form when it is replaced by services of persons who perform only certain, objective functions in the house, and who are, to this extent, coordinated with the housewife. The earlier, but still existing, relationship involved them as total personalities and obliged them—as is most strikingly shown by the concept of the "all-around girl" [*"Mädchen für alles"*]—to "unlimited services": they became subordinate to the housewife as a person, precisely because there were no objective delimitations. Under thoroughly patriarchal (as contrasted with contemporary) conditions, the "house" is considered an objective, intrinsic purpose and value, in behalf of which housewife and servants cooperate. This results, even if there is a completely personal subordination, in a certain coordination sustained by the interest which the servant, who is solidly and permanently connected with the house, usually feels for it. The "thou," used in addressing him, on the one hand, gives expression to his personal subordination, but on the other, makes him comparable to the children of the house and thus ties him more closely to its organization. Strangely enough, it thus appears that in some measure, obedience to an objective idea occurs at the extreme stages in the development of obedience: under the condition of full patriarchal subordination, where the house still has, so to speak, an absolute value, which is served by the work of the housewife (though in a higher position) as well as by that of the servant; and then, under the condition of complete differentiation, where service and reward are objectively pre-determined, and the personal attachment, which characterizes the stage of an undefined quantity of subordination, has become extraneous to the relationship. The contemporary position of the servant who shares his master's house, particularly in the large cities, has lost the first of these two kinds of objectivity, without having yet attained the second. The total personality of the servant is no longer claimed by the objective idea of the "house"; and yet, in view of the general way in which his services are requested, it cannot really separate itself from it.

Finally, this form-type may be illustrated by the relationship betwen officers and common soldiers. Here, the cleavage between subordination within the organization of the group, and coordination which results from common service in defense of one's country, is as wide as can be imagined. Understandably enough, the cleavage is most noticeable at the front. On the one hand, discipline is most merciless there, but on the other hand, fellowship between officers and privates is furthered, partly by specific situations, partly by the general mood. During peacetime, the army remains arrested in the position of a means which does not attain its purposes; it is, therefore, inevitable for its technical structure to grow into a psychologically ultimate aim, so that super-subordination, on which the technique of the organization is based, stands in the foreground of consciousness. The peculiar sociological mixture with coordination, which results from the common subordination under an objective idea, becomes important only when the changed situation calls attention to this idea, as the real purpose of the army.

Within the group organization of his specific content of life, the individual thus occupies a superordinate or subordinate position. But the group as a whole stands under a dominating idea which gives each of its members an equal, or nearly equal, position in comparison with all outsiders. Hence, the individual has a double role which makes his purely formal, sociological situation the vehicle for peculiarly mixed life-feelings. The employee of a large business may have a leading position in his firm, which he lets his subalterns feel in a superior and imperious way. But, as soon as he confronts the public, and acts under the idea of his business as a whole, he will exhibit serviceable and devout behavior. In the opposite direction, these elements are interwoven in the frequent haughtiness of subalterns, servants in noble houses, members of decimated intellectual or social circles, who actually stand at the periphery of these groups, but to the outsider represent all the more energetically the dignity of the whole circle and of its idea. For, the kind of positive relation to the circle which they have, gives them only a semi-solid position in it, internally and externally; and they seek to improve it in a negative way, by differentiating themselves from others. The richest formal variety of this type is offered, perhaps, by the Catholic hierarchy. Although every member of it is bound by a blind obedience which admits of no contradiction, nevertheless, in comparison with the layman, even the lowest member stands at an absolute elevation, where the idea of the eternal God rises above all temporal matters. At the same time, the highest member of this hierarchy confesses himself to be the "servant of servants." The monk, who within his order may have absolute power, dresses himself in deepest humility and servility in the face of a beggar; but the lowest brother of an order is superior to the secular prince by all the absolute sovereignty of church authority.

# 5. *The Circulation of Elites*

BY VILFREDO PARETO

**2026.** *Social* élites *and their circulation.*[1] Suppose we begin by giving a theoretical definition of the thing we are dealing with, making it as exact as possible, and then go on to see what practical considerations we can replace it with to get a first approximation. Let us for the moment completely disregard considerations as to the good or bad, useful or harmful, praiseworthy or reprehensible character of the various traits in individuals, and confine ourselves to degrees—to whether, in other words, the trait in a given case be slight, average, intense, or more exactly, to the index that may be assigned to each individual with reference to the degree, or intensity, in him of the trait in question.

**2027.** Let us assume that in every branch of human activity each individual is given an index which stands as a sign of his capacity, very much the way grades are given in the various subjects in examinations in school. The highest type of lawyer, for instance, will be given 10. The man who does not get a client will be given 1—reserving zero for the man who is an out-and-out idiot. To the man who has made his millions—honestly or dishonestly as the case may be—we will give 10. To the man who has earned his thousands we will give 6; to such as just manage to keep out of the poor-house, 1, keeping zero for those who get in. To the woman "in politics," such as the Aspasia of Pericles, the Maintenon of Louis XIV, the Pompadour of Louis XV, who has managed to infatuate a man of power and play a part in the man's career, we shall give some higher number, such as 8 or 9; to the strumpet who merely satisfies the senses of such a man and exerts no influence on public affairs, we shall give zero. To a clever rascal who knows how to fool people and still keep clear of the penitentiary, we shall give 8, 9, or 10, according to the number of geese he has plucked and the amount of money he has been able to get out of them. To the sneak-thief who snatches a piece of silver from a restaurant table and runs away into the arms of a policeman, we shall give 1. To a poet like Carducci we shall give 8 or 9 according to our tastes; to a scribbler who puts people to rout with his sonnets we shall give zero. For chess-players we can get very precise indices, noting what matches, and how many, they have won. And so on for all the branches of human activity.

**2028.** We are speaking, remember, of an actual, not a potential, state. If at an English examination

---

Reprinted from Vilfredo Pareto, *The Mind and Society*, ed. Arthur Livingston, trans. Andrew Bongiorno and Arthur Livingston (New York: Harcourt, Brace & Co., 1935), Vol. III, §§ 2026–59; Vol. IV, §§ 2233–36, with the permission of The Pareto Fund.

1. Kolabinska, *La circulation des élites en France*, p. 5: "The outstanding idea in the term '*élite*' is 'superiority.' That is the only one I keep. I disregard secondary connotations of appreciation or as to the utility of such superiority. I am not interested here in what is desirable. I am making a simple study of what is. In a broad sense I mean by the *élite* in a society people who possess in marked degree qualities of intelligence, character, skill, capacity, of whatever kind. . . . On the other hand I entirely avoid any sort of judgment on the merits and utility of such classes." [The phrase "circulation of *élites*" is well established in Continental literature. Pareto himself renders it in Italian as "circulation of the élite (selected, chosen, ruling, "better") classes." It is a cumbersome phrase and not very exact, and I see no reason for preferring it to the more natural and, in most connexions, the more exact, English phrase, class-circulation.—A. L.]

a pupil says: "I could know English very well if I chose to; I do not know any because I have never seen fit to learn," the examiner replies: "I am not interested in your alibi. The grade for what you know is zero." If, similarly, someone says: "So-and-so does not steal, not because he couldn't but because he is a gentleman," we reply: "Very well, we admire him for his self-control, but his grade as a thief is zero."

**2029.** There are people who worship Napoleon Bonaparte as a god. There are people who hate him as the lowest of criminals. Which are right? We do not choose to solve that question in connexion with a quite different matter. Whether Napoleon was a good man or a bad man, he was certainly not an idiot, nor a man of little account, as millions of others are. He had exceptional qualities, and that is enough for us to give him a high ranking, though without prejudice of any sort to questions that might be raised as to the ethics of his qualities or their social utility.

**2030.** In short, we are here as usual resorting to scientific analysis, which distinguishes one problem from another and studies each one separately. As usual, again, we are replacing imperceptible variations in absolutely exact numbers with the sharp variations corresponding to groupings by class, just as in examinations those who are passed are sharply and arbitrarily distinguished from those who are "failed," and just as in the matter of physical age we distinguish children from young people, the young from the aged.

**2031.** So let us make a class of the people who have the highest indices in their branch of activity, and to that class give the name of *élite*.

**2032.** For the particular investigation with which we are engaged, a study of the social equilibrium, it will help if we further divide that class into two classes: a *governing élite*, comprising individuals who directly or indirectly play some considerable part in government, and a *non-governing élite*, comprising the rest.[2]

**2033.** A chess champion is certainly a member of the *élite*, but it is no less certain that his merits as a chess-player do not open the doors to political influence for him; and hence unless he has other qualities to win him that distinction, he is not a member of the governing *élite*. Mistresses of absolute monarchs have oftentimes been members of the *élite*, either because of their beauty or because of their intellectual endowments; but only a few of them, who have had, in addition, the particular talents required by politics, have played any part in government.

**2034.** So we get two strata in a population: (1) A lower stratum, the *non-élite*, with whose possible influence on government we are not just here concerned; then (2) a higher stratum, *the élite*, which is divided into two: (*a*) a governing *élite;* (*b*) a non-governing *élite*.

**2035.** In the concrete, there are no examinations whereby each person is assigned to his proper place in these various classes. That deficiency is made up for by other means, by various sorts of labels that serve the purpose after a fashion. Such labels are the rule even where there are examinations. The label "lawyer" is affixed to a man who is supposed to know something about the law and often does, though sometimes again he is an ignoramus. So, the governing *élite* contains individuals who wear labels appropriate to political offices of a certain altitude—ministers, Senators, Deputies, chief justices, generals, colonels, and so on—making the opposite exceptions for those who have found their way into that exalted company without possessing qualities corresponding to the labels they wear.

**2036.** Such exceptions are much more numerous than the exceptions among lawyers, physicians, engineers, millionaires (who have made their own money), artists of distinction, and so on; for the reason, among others, that in these latter departments of human activity the labels are won directly by each individual, whereas in the *élite* some of the labels—the label of wealth, for instance—are hereditary. In former times there were hereditary labels in the governing *élite* also—in our day hardly more than the label of king remains in that status; but if direct inheritance has disappeared, inheritance is still powerful indirectly; and an individual who has inherited a sizable patrimony can easily be named Senator in certain countries, or can get himself elected to the parliament by buying votes or, on occasion, by wheedling voters with assurances that he is a democrat of democrats, a Socialist, an Anarchist. Wealth, family, or social connexions also help in many other cases to win the label of the *élite* in general, or of the governing *élite* in particular, for persons who otherwise hold no claim upon it.

**2037.** In societies where the social unit is the family the label worn by the head of the family also benefits all other members. In Rome, the man who became Emperor generally raised his freedom to the higher class, and oftentimes, in fact, to the

2. Kolabinska, *Op. cit.*, p. 6: "We have just enumerated different categories of individuals comprising the *élite*. They may also be classified in many other ways. For the purpose I have in view in this study it is better to divide the *élite* into two parts: one, which I will call *M*, will contain those individuals in the *élite* who share in the government of the state, who make up what may be more or less vaguely called 'the governing class.' The other part, *N*, will be made up of the remainder of the *élite* when the part *M* has been set off from it."

governing *élite*. For that matter, now more, now fewer, of the freemen taking part in the Roman government possessed qualities good or bad that justified their wearing the labels which they had won through imperial bounty. In our societies, the social unit is the individual; but the place that the individual occupies in society also benefits his wife, his children, his connexions, his friends.

**2038.** If all these deviations from type were of little importance, they might be disregarded, as they are virtually disregarded in cases where a diploma is required for the practice of a profession. Everyone knows that there are persons who do not deserve their diplomas, but experience shows that on the whole such exceptions may be overlooked.

**2039.** One might, further, from certain points of view at least, disregard deviations if they remained more or less constant quantitatively—if there were only a negligible variation in proportions between the total of a class and the people who wear its label without possessing the qualities corresponding.

**2040.** As a matter of fact, the real cases that we have to consider in our societies differ from those two. The deviations are not so few that they can be disregarded. Then again, their number is variable, and the variations give rise to situations having an important bearing on the social equilibrium. We are therefore required to make a special study of them.

**2041.** Furthermore, the manner in which the various groups in a population intermix has to be considered. In moving from one group to another an individual generally brings with him certain inclinations, sentiments, attitudes, that he has acquired in the group from which he comes, and that circumstance cannot be ignored.

**2042.** To this mixing, in the particular case in which only two groups, the *élite* and the non-*élite*, are envisaged, the term "circulation of élites" has been applied[3]—in French, *circulation des élites* [or in more general terms "class-circulation"].

**2043.** In conclusion we must pay special attention (1), in the case of one single group, to the proportions between the total of the group and the number of individuals who are nominally members of it but do not possess the qualities requisite for effective membership; and then (2), in the case of various groups, to the ways in which transitions from one group to the other occur, and to the intensity of that movement—that is to say, to the velocity of the circulation.

**2044.** Velocity in circulation has to be considered not only absolutely but also in relation to the supply of and the demand for certain social elements. A country that is always at peace does not require many soldiers in its governing class, and the production of generals may be overexuberant as compared with the demand. But when a country is in a state of continuous warfare many soldiers are necessary, and though production remains at the same level it may not meet the demand. That, we might note in passing, has been one of the causes for the collapse of many aristocracies.[4]

**2045.** Another example. In a country where there there is little industry and little commerce, the supply of individuals possessing in high degree the qualities requisite for those types of activity exceeds the demand. Then industry and commerce develop and the supply, though remaining the same, no longer meets the demand.

**2046.** We must not confuse the state of law with the state of fact. The latter alone, or almost alone, has a bearing on the social equilibrium. There are many examples of castes that are legally closed, but into which, in point of fact, new-comers make their way, and often in large numbers. On the other hand, what difference does it make if a caste is legally open, but conditions *de facto* prevent new accessions to it? If a person who acquires wealth thereby becomes a member of the governing class, but no one gets rich, it is as if the class were closed; and if only a few get rich, it is as if the law erected serious barriers against access to the caste. Something of that sort was observable towards the end of the Roman Empire. People who acquired wealth entered the order of the curials. But only a few individuals made any money. Theoretically we might examine any number of groups. Practically we have to confine ourselves to the more important. We shall proceed by successive approximations, starting with the simple and going on to the complex.

**2047.** *Higher class and lower class in general.* The least we can do is divide society into two strata: a higher stratum, which usually contains the rulers, and a lower stratum, which usually controls the ruled. That fact is so obvious that it has always

3. And most inappropriately, for, in this sense, the phrase never meant more than circulation within the *élite*. Furthermore, the *élite* is not the only class to be considered, and the principles that apply to circulation within the *élite* apply to circulation within such lower classes as one may choose for one purpose or another to consider.—A.L.

4. Kolabinska, *Op. cit.*, p. 10: "Inadequate recruiting in the *élite* does not result from a mere numerical proportion between new members and old. Account has to be taken of the number of persons who possess the qualities required for membership in the governing *élite* but are refused admittance; or else, in an opposite direction, the number of new members the *élite* might require but does not get. In the first case, the production of persons possessing unusual qualities as regards education may far surpass the number of such persons that the *élite* can accommodate, and then we get what has been called an 'intellectual proletariat.' "

forced itself even upon the most casual observation, and so for the circulation of individuals between the two strata. Even Plato had an inkling of class-circulation and tried to regulate it artificially. The "new man," the upstart, the *parvenu,* has always been a subject of interest, and literature has analyzed him unendingly. Here, then, we are merely giving a more exact form to things that have long been perceived more or less vaguely. We noted a varying distribution of residues in the various social groupings, and chiefly in the higher and the lower class. Such heterogeneousness is a fact perceived by the most superficial glance.

**2048.** Changes in Class I and Class II residues occurring within the two social strata have an important influence in determining the social equilibrium. They have been commonly observed by laymen under a special form, as changes in "religious" sentiments, so called, in the higher stratum of society. It has often been noted that there were times when religious sentiments seemed to lose ground, others when they seemed to gain strength, and that such undulations corresponded to social movements of very considerable scope. The uniformity might be more exactly described by saying that in the higher stratum of society Class II residues gradually lose in strength, until now and again they are reinforced by tides updwelling from the lower stratum.[5]

**2049.** Religious sentiments were very feeble in the higher classes in Rome towards the end of the Republic; but they gained notably in strength thereafter, through the rise to the higher classes of men from the lower, of foreigners that is, freedmen, and others, whom the Roman Empire raised in station. They gained still further in intensity in the days of the decadent Roman Empire, when the government passed into the hands of a military plebs and a bureaucracy originating in the lower classes. That was a time when a predominance of Class II residues made itself manifest in a decadence in literature and in the arts and sciences, and in invasions by Oriental religions and especially Christianity.

**2050.** The Protestant Reformation in the sixteenth century, the Puritan Revolution in Cromwell's day in England, the French Revolution of 1789, are examples of great religious tides originating in the lower classes and rising to engulf the sceptical higher classes. An instance in our day would be the United States of America, where this

5. Many writers who are not equipped with this general conception fall into contradictions. Sometimes the clarity of the facts forces itself upon them; then again preconceptions will blur their view of things. Taine is an example. In the *Ancien régime* he well notes (Chap. III) that the mind of the masses at large is steeped in prejudices (is, in our terms, under the sway of Class II residues). On that basis he should go on and conclude that the French Revolution was a particular case of the religious revolution, where popular faith overwhelms the scepticism of the higher classes. But, consciously or otherwise, he succumbs to the influence of the preconception that the higher classes are educators of the masses, and views unbelief and impiety in the nobility, the Third Estate, and the higher clergy as among the main causes of the Revolution. He notes the difference between France and England in that regard and seems on the verge of ascribing to that circumstance the fact that the revolution which occurred in France did not occur in England. Says he, Bk. IV, Chap. II, sec. I (Vol. II, p. 118): "In England [the higher class] speedily perceived the danger. Philosophy was precocious in England, native to England. That does not matter. It never got acclimated there. Montesquieu wrote in his travel note-book in 1729 (*Notes sur l'Angleterre,* p. 352): 'No religion in England. . . . If anyone brings up the subject of religion, he is laughed at.' Fifty years later the public mind has about-faced: 'all those who have a tight roof over their heads and a good coat on their backs' [The expression is Macaulay's.] have seen what these new doctrines mean. In any event they feel that speculations in the library must not become preachings on the streets. [They and Taine therefore believe in the efficacy of such preachings.] Impiety seems to them bad manners. They regard religion as the cement that holds public order together. That is because they are themselves public men, interested in doing things, participating in the government and well taught by daily personal experience. . . . [Yet a few lines before that Taine had refuted himself:] When you talk religion or politics with people, you find their minds almost always made up. Their preconceptions, their interests, their situation in life, have convinced them already, and they will listen to you only if you tell them aloud things they have been thinking in silence." If that is so, the "preachings in the street" to which Taine alludes ought not to be very effective, and if they are, it cannot be that people "will listen to you only if you tell them aloud things they have been thinking in silence." As a matter of fact, it is these latter hypotheses that the more closely approximate experience. The mental state of the French people towards the end of the eighteenth century had been but little affected by the impiety of the higher classes, any more than the mental state of the Romans had been affected by the impiety of the contemporaries of Lucretius, Cicero, and Caesar, or the mental state of the European masses by the impiety of the nobility and higher clergy at the time of the Reformation. Belin, *La commerce des livres prohibés à Paris de 1750 à 1789,* pp. 104–05: "One may assert that the works of the philosophers did not directly reach the masses or the lower *bourgeoisie.* The working-men, the tradesmen, did not know Voltaire and Rousseau until the time of the Revolution, when their tribunes began to gloss them in inflammatory harangues or to translate their maxims into legislation. When they stepped into the limelight they had certainly not read the great books of the century, though they could not have missed entirely the more celebrated of the literary quarrels. The true disciples of the *philosophes,* the faithful patrons of the pedlars of forbidden literature, were the nobles, the abbés, the members of the privileged classes, idlers about the parlours of society who were on the look-out for some distraction from their relentless tedium and threw themselves headlong into philosophical discussions and soon let themselves be vanquished by the new spirit [That is all borne out by the experience; the following less so.], without foreseeing the remoter consequences of the premises that they were adopting so gaily. . . . [Belin makes a further point:] The privileged for that matter were the only ones who could afford the exorbitant prices that any lover of forbidden books had to pay."

upward thrust of members of lower classes strong in Class II residues is very intense; and in that country one witnesses the rise of no end of strange and wholly unscientific religions—such as Christian Science—that are utterly at war with any sort of scientific thinking, and a mass of hypocritical laws for the enforcement of morality that are replicas of laws of the European Middle Ages.

**2051.** The upper stratum of society, the *élite,* nominally contains certain groups of people, not always very sharply defined, that are called aristocracies. There are cases in which the majority of individuals belonging to such aristocracies actually possess the qualities requisite for remaining there; and then again there are cases where considerable numbers of the individuals making up the class do not possess those requisites. Such people may occupy more or less important places in the governing *élite* or they may be barred from it.

**2052.** In the beginning, military, religious, and commercial aristocracies and plutocracies—with a few exceptions not worth considering—must have constituted parts of the governing *élite* and sometimes have made up the whole of it. The victorious warrior, the prosperous merchant, the opulent plutocrat, were men of such parts, each in his own field, as to be superior to the average individual. Under those circumstances the label corresponded to an actual capacity. But as time goes by, considerable, sometimes very considerable, differences arise between the capacity and the label; while on the other hand, certain aristocracies originally figuring prominently in the rising *élite* end by constituting an insignificant element in it. That has happened especially to military aristocracies.

**2053.** Aristocracies do not last. Whatever the causes, it is an incontestable fact that after a certain length of time they pass away. History is a graveyard of aristocracies. The Athenian "People" was an aristocracy as compared with the remainder of a population of resident aliens and slaves. It vanished without leaving any descent. The various aristocracies of Rome vanished in their time. So did the aristocracies of the Barbarians. Where, in France, are the descendents of the Frankish conquerors? The genealogies of the English nobility have been very exactly kept; and they show that very few families still remain to claim descent from the comrades of William the Conqueror. The rest have vanished. In Germany the aristocracy of the present day is very largely made up of descendants of vassals of the lords of old. The populations of European countries have increased enormously during the past few centuries. It is as certain as certain can be that the aristocracies have not increased in proportion.

**2054.** They decay not in numbers only. They decay also in quality, in the sense that they lose their vigour, that there is a decline in the proportions of the residues which enabled them to win their power and hold it. The governing class is restored not only in numbers, but—and that is the more important thing—in quality, by families rising from the lower classes and bringing with them the vigour and the proportions of residues necessary for keeping themselves in power. It is also restored by the loss of its more degenerate members.

**2055.** If one of those movements comes to an end, or worse still, if they both come to an end, the governing class crashes to ruin and often sweeps the whole of a nation along with it. Potent cause of disturbance in the equilibrium is the accumulation of superior elements in the lower classes and, conversely, of inferior elements in the higher classes. If human aristocracies were like thoroughbreds among animals, which reproduce themselves over long periods of time with approximately the same traits, the history of the human race would be something altogether different from the history we know.

**2056.** In virtue of class-circulation, the governing *élite* is always in a state of slow and continuous transformation. It flows on like a river, never being today what it was yesterday. From time to time sudden and violent disturbances occur. There is a flood—the river overflows its banks. Afterwards, the new governing *élite* again resumes its slow transformation. The flood has subsided, the river is again flowing normally in its wonted bed.

**2057.** Revolutions come about through accumulations in the higher strata of society—either because of a slowing-down in class-circulation, or from other causes—of decadent elements no longer possessing the residues suitable for keeping them in power, and shrinking from the use of force; while meantime in the lower strata of society elements of superior quality are coming to the fore, possessing residues suitable for exercising the functions of government and willing enough to use force.

**2058.** In general, in revolutions the members of the lower strata are captained by leaders from the higher strata, because the latter possess the intellectual qualities required for outlining a tactic, while lacking the combative residues supplied by the individuals from the lower strata.

**2059.** Violent movements take place by fits and starts, and effects therefore do not follow immediately on their causes. After a governing class, or a nation, has maintained itself for long periods of time on force and acquired great wealth, it may subsist for some time still without using force, buying off its adversaries and paying not only in gold, but also in terms of the dignity and respect that it had formerly enjoyed and which constitute, as it were, a capital. In the first stages of decline, power is maintained by bargainings and concessions, and people are so deceived into thinking that that policy can be carried on indefinitely. So the decadant Roman Empire brought peace of the Barbarians with money and honours. So Louis XVI, in France, squandering in a very short time an ancestral inheritance of love, respect, and almost religious reverence for the monarchy, managed, by making repeated concessions, to be the King of the Revolution. So the English aristocracy managed to prolong its term of power in the second half of the nineteenth century down to the dawn of its decadence, which was heralded by the "Parliament Bill" in the first years of the twentieth.

* * *

Suppose we put in one category, which we may call *S,* individuals whose incomes are essentially variable and depend upon the person's wide-awakeness in discovering sources of gain. In that group, generally speaking and disregarding exceptions, will be found those promoters of enterprise—those *entrepreneurs*—whom we were considering some pages back; and with them will be stockholders in industrial and commercial corporations (but not bondholders, who will more fittingly be placed in our group next following). Then will come owners of real estate in cities where building speculation is rife; and also landowners—on a similar condition that there be speculation in the lands about them; and then stock-exchange speculators and bankers who make money on governmental, industrial, and commercial loans. We might further add all persons depending upon such people—lawyers, engineers, politicians, working-people, clerks—and deriving advantage from their operations. In a word, we are putting together all persons who directly or indirectly speculate and in one way or another manage to increase their incomes by ingeniously taking advantage of circumstances.

**2234.** And let us put into another category, which we may call *R,* persons who have fixed or virtually fixed incomes not depending to any great extent on ingenious combinations that may be conceived by an active mind. In this category, roughly, will be found persons who have savings and have deposited them in savings-banks or invested them in life-annuities; then people living on incomes from government bonds, certificates of the funded debt, corporation bonds, or other securities with fixed interest-rates; then owners of real estate and lands in places where there is no speculation; then farmers, working-people, clerks, depending upon such persons and in no way depending upon speculators. In a word, we so group together here all persons who neither directly nor indirectly depend on speculation and who have incomes that are fixed, or virtually fixed, or at least are but slightly variable.[6]

**2235.** Just to be rid of the inconvenience of using mere letters of the alphabet, suppose we use the term "speculators" for members of category *S* and the French term *rentiers* for members of category *R.*[7] Within the two groups of persons we shall find analogous conflicts, economic and social, between them. In the speculator group Class I residues predominate, in the *rentier* group, Class II residues. That that should be the case is readily understandable. A person of pronounced capacity for economic combinations is not satisfied with a fixed income, often a very small one. He wants to earn more, and if he finds a favourable opportunity, he moves into the *S* category. The two groups perform functions of differing utility in society. The *S* group is primarily responsible for change, for eco-

6. Monographs along the lines of Le Play's would be of great use in determining the character of the persons belonging in our *S* group, and those belonging to our *R* group. Here is one such, contributed by Prezzolini: *La Francia e i francesi del secolo XX osservati da un italiano.* I know it as quoted by E. Cesari in the *Vita italiana,* Oct. 15, 1917, pp. 367–70. The person in question is a well-known member of the French parliament—we suppress the proper name: for us here, he is not a person, but just a type. The figures given by Prezzolini are those publicly declared by the member himself, Monsieur *X*. *X*'s fixed income yields a total of 17,500 francs, of which 15,000 are salary as a member of the parliament and 2,500 interest on his wife's dowry. Only the latter sum belongs in category *R*—the salary belongs rather in category *S,* because to get such a thing one must have the ability and the good fortune to be elected. *X*'s expense-account shows a total of 64,200 francs, divided as follows: household expenses, 33,800; office expenses, 22,550; expenses for his election district (avowable expenses), 7,850. There ought, therefore, to be a deficit of 45,700 francs; but the deficit is not only covered but changes into a surplus in view of the following revenues: contributions to newspapers and other publications, 12,500 francs; honorarium as general agent of the *A.B.C.* Company, 21,000 francs; commissions on sales, 7,500. In this connexion, Prezzolini notes that *X*, reporting on the war budget, enters 100,000 francs for supplies delivered to himself, as general agent of the *A.B.C.* Company: that gives *X* his "sales commissions." Finally, because of the influence that he enjoys, our member, *X,* receives a stipend of 18,000 francs from a newspaper. In all, these revenues, which clearly belong in the category *S,* yield a total of 50,000 francs. Prezzolini adds that the member in question is not the only one, nor the least, of his species. He is just a better-known and an honester type.

7. It might be well to repeat that our use of such terms is not based on their ordinary senses, nor upon their etymologies. We are to use them strictly in the sense defined in §§ 2233–34, and the reader must refer to those definitions whenever he encounters them in the remainder of this volume. [I keep the term "speculator." English ordinarily analyzes the matter embraced under Pareto's term, especially in slang. Pareto's "speculator" is our "hustler," "man of pep," "wide-awake individual," "live-wire," and so on.—A. L.]

nomic and social progress. The *R* group, instead, is a powerful element in stability, and in many cases counteracts the dangers attending the adventurous capers of the *S*'s. A society in which *R's* almost exclusively predominate remains stationary and, as it were, crystallized. A society in which *S*'s predominate lacks stability, lives in a state of shaky equilibrium that may be upset by a slight accident from within or from without.

Members of the *R* group must not be mistaken for "conservatives," nor members of the *S* group for "progressives," innovators, revolutionaries. They may have points in common with such, but there is no identity. There are evolutions, revolutions, innovations, that the *R*'s support, especially movements tending to restore to the ruling classes certain residues of group-persistence that had been banished by the S's. A revolution may be made against the *S*'s—a revolution of that type founded the Roman Empire, and such, to some extent, was the revolution known as the Protestant Reformation. Then too, for the very reason that sentiments of group-persistence are dominant in them, the *R*'s may be so blinded by sentiment as to act against their own interests. They readily allow themselves to be duped by anyone who takes them on the side of sentiment, and time and time again they have been the artisans of their own ruin. If the old feudal lords, who were endowed with *R* traits in a very conspicuous degree, had not allowed themselves to be swept off their feet by a sum of sentiments in which religious enthusiasm was only one element, they would have seen at once that the Crusades were to be their ruin. In the eighteenth century, had the French nobility living on income, and that part of the French *bourgeoisie* which was in the same situation, not succumbed to the lure of humanitarian sentiments, they would not have prepared the ground for the Revolution that was to be their undoing. Not a few among the victims of the guillotine had for long years been continually, patiently, artfully grinding the blade that was to cut off their heads. In our day those among the *R*'s who are known as "intellectuals" are following in the footprints of the French nobles of the eighteenth century and are working with all their might to encompass the ruin of their own class.

Nor are the categories *R* and *S* to be confused with groupings that might be made according to economic occupation. There again we find points of contact, but not full coincidence. A retail merchant often belongs to the *R* group, and a wholesale merchant too, but the wholesaler will more likely belong to the *S* group. Sometimes one same enterprise may change in character. An individual of the *S* type founds an industry as a result of fortunate speculations. When it yields or seems to be yielding a good return, he changes it into a corporation, retires from business, and passes over into the *R* group. A large number of stockholders in the new concern are also *R*'s—the ones who bought stock when they thought they were buying a sure thing. If they are not mistaken, the business changes in character, moving over from the *S* type to the *R* type. But in many cases the best speculation the founder ever made was in changing his business to a corporation. It is soon in jeopardy, with the *R*'s standing in line to pay for the broken crockery. There is no better business in this world than the business of fleecing the lambs—of exploiting the inexperience, the ingenuousness, the passions, of the *R*'s. In our societies the fortunes of many many wealthy individuals have no other foundations.[8]

**2236.** The differing relative proportions in which *S* types and *R* types are combined in the governing

---

8. Many people conclude that such facts are enough to condemn our social organization, and hold it responsible for most of the pains from which we suffer. Others think that they can defend our present order only by denying the facts or minimizing their significance. Both are right from the ethical standpoint, wrong from the standpoint of social utility experimentally considered. Obviously, if it be posited as an axiom that men *ought,* whatever happens, to observe certain rules, those who do not observe them necessarily stand condemned. If one goes on to say that the organization so condemned is in the main injurious to society, one must logically fall back on some premise that confuses morality and utlility. On the other hand, if premises of those types are granted and one would, notwithstanding, still defend or approve the organization of our societies, there is nothing left but to deny the facts or say they are not significant. The experimental approach is altogether different. Anyone accepting it grants no axioms independent of experience, and therefore finds it necessary to discuss the premises of the reasonings mentioned. On so doing one soon perceives that it is a question of two phenomena that do indeed have points in common but are in no sense identical, and that in every particular case experience has to be called in to decide whether one is dealing with a point of contact or a point of divergence. An instant's reflection is enough to see that if one accepts certain conclusions one adopts by that fact the premises to which they are indissolubly bound. But the power of sentiment and the influence of habitual manners of reasoning are such that people disregard the force of logic entirely and establish conclusions without reference to the premises or, at the very best, accept the premises as axioms not subject to discussion. Another effect of such power and such influence will be that in spite of the warnings we have given and over and over again repeated, there will always be someone to carry the import of the remarks that he is here reading on the *R*'s and *S*'s beyond the limits we have so strictly specified, interpreting all that we have been saying against one of those groups as implying that the influence of the group is, on the whole, harmful to society and the group itself "condemnable"; and all that we have been saying in its favour as a proof that the influence of the group is, in general, beneficial to society and the group itself worthy of praise. We have neither the means nor the least desire to prevent the fabrication of such interpretations. We are satisfied with recognizing them as one variety of our derivations.

class correspond to differing types of civilization; and such proportions are among the principal traits that have to be considered in social heterogeneity. Going back, for instance, to the protectionist cycle, we may say that in modern democratic countries industrial protection increases the proportion of *S*'s in the governing class. That increase in turn serves to intensify protection, and the process would go on indefinitely if counter-forces did not come into play to check it.

# 6. *Conspicuous Consumption*

BY THORSTEIN VEBLEN

THE DISTINCTION BETWEEN exploit and drudgery is an invidious distinction between employments. Those employments which are to be classed as exploit are worthy, honourable, noble; other employments, which do not contain this element of exploit, and especially those which imply subservience or submission, are unworthy, debasing, ignoble. The concept of dignity, worth, or honour, as applied either to persons or conduct, is of first-rate consequence in the development of classes and of class distinctions, and it is therefore necessary to say something of its derivation and meaning. Its psychological ground may be indicated in outline as follows.

As a matter of selective necessity, man is an agent. He is, in his own apprehension, a centre of unfolding impulsive activity—"teleological" activity. He is an agent, seeking in every act the accomplishment of some concrete, objective, impersonal end. By force of his being such an agent he is possessed of a taste for effective work, and a distaste for futile effort. He has a sense of the merit of serviceability or efficiency and of the demerit of futility, waste, or incapability. This aptitude or propensity may be called the instinct of workmanship. Wherever the circumstances or traditions of life lead to an habitual comparison of one person with another in point of efficiency, the instinct of workmanship works out in an emulative or invidious comparison of persons. The extent to which this result follows depends in some considerable degree on the temperament of the population. In any community where such an invidious comparison of persons is habitually made, visible success becomes an end sought for its own utility as a basis of esteem. Esteem is gained and dispraise is avoided by putting one's efficiency in evidence. The result is that the instinct of workmanship works out in an emulative demonstration of force.

During that primitive phase of social development, when the community is still habitually peaceable, perhaps sedentary, and without a developed system of individual ownership, the efficiency of the individual can be shown chiefly and most consistently in some employment that goes to further the life of the group. What emulation of an economic kind there is between the members of such a group will be chiefly emulation in industrial serviceability. At the same time the incentive to emulation is not strong, nor is the scope for emulation large.

When the community passes from peaceable savagery to a predatory phase of life, the conditions of emulation change. The opportunity and the incentive to emulation increase greatly in scope and urgency. The activity of the men more and more takes on the character of exploit; and an invidious comparison of one hunter or warrior with another grows continually easier and more habitual. Tangible evidences of prowess—trophies—find a place in men's habits of thought as an essential feature of the paraphernalia of life. Booty, trophies of the chase or of the raid, come to be prized as evidence of preëminent force. Aggression becomes the accredited form of action, and booty serves as *prima facie* evidence of successful aggression. As accepted at this cultural stage, the accredited, worthy form of self-assertion is contest; and useful articles or services obtained by seizure or compulsion, serve as a conventional evidence of successful contest. Therefore, by contrast, the obtaining of goods by other methods than seizure comes to be accounted unworthy of man in his best estate. The performance

Reprinted from Thorstein Veblen, *The Theory of the Leisure Class* (New York: Macmillan Co., 1899), pp. 15–21, 25–34, 68–89, 97–101.

of productive work, or employment in personal service, falls under the same odium for the same reason. An invidious distinction in this way arises between exploit and acquisition by seizure on the one hand and industrial employment on the other hand. Labour acquires a character of irksomeness by virtue of the indignity imputed to it.

With the primitive barbarian, before the simple content of the notion has been obscured by its own ramifications and by a secondary growth of cognate ideas, "honourable" seems to connote nothing else than assertion of superior force. "Honourable" is "formidable"; "worthy" is "prepotent." A honorific act is in the last analysis little if anything else than a recognised successful act of aggression; and where aggression means conflict with men and beasts, the activity which comes to be especially and primarily honourable is the assertion of the strong hand. The naïve, archaic habit of construing all manifestations of force in terms of personality or "will power" greatly fortifies this conventional exaltation of the strong hand. Honorific epithets, in vogue among barbarian tribes as well as among peoples of a more advanced culture, commonly bear the stamp of this unsophisticated sense of honour. Epithets and titles used in addressing chieftains, and in the propitiation of kings and gods, very commonly impute a propensity for overbearing violence and an irresistible devastating force to the person who is to be propitiated. This holds true to an extent also in the more civilised communities of the present day. The predilection shown in heraldic devices for the more rapacious beasts and birds of prey goes to enforce the same view.

Under the common-sense barbarian appreciation of worth or honour, the taking of life—the killing of formidable competitors, whether brute or human—is honourable in the highest degree. And this high office of slaughter, as an expression of the slayer's prepotence, casts a glamour of worth over every act of slaughter and over all the tools and accessories of the act. Arms are honourable, and the use of them, even in seeking the life of the meanest creatures of the fields, becomes a honorific employment. At the same time, employment in industry becomes correspondingly odious, and, in the common-sense apprehension, the handling of the tools and implements of industry falls beneath the dignity of able-bodied men. Labour becomes irksome.

It is here assumed that in the sequence of cultural evolution primitive groups of men have passed from an initial peaceable stage to a subsequent stage at which fighting is the avowed and characteristic employment of the group. But it is not implied that there has been an abrupt transition from unbroken peace and good-will to a later or higher phase of life in which the fact of combat occurs for the first time. Neither is it implied that all peaceful industry disappears on the transition to the predatory phase of culture. Some fighting, it is safe to say, would be met with at any early stage of social development. Fights would occur with more or less frequency through sexual competition. The known habits of primitive groups as well as the habits of the anthropoid apes, argue to that effect and the evidence from the well-known promptings of human nature enforces the same view.

It may therefore be objected that there can have been no such initial stage of peaceable life as is here assumed. There is no point in cultural evolution prior to which fighting does not occur. But the point in question is not as to the occurrence of combat, occasional or sporadic, or even more or less frequent and habitual; it is a question as to the occurrence of an habitual bellicose frame of mind—a prevalent habit of judging facts and events from the point of view of the fight. The predatory phase of culture is attained only when the predatory attitude has become the habitual and accredited spiritual attitude for the members of the group; when the fight has become the dominant note in the current theory of life; when the common-sense appreciation of men and things has come to be an appreciation with a view to combat.

The substantial difference between the peaceable and the predatory phase of culture, therefore, is a spiritual difference, not a mechanical one. The change in spiritual attitude is the outgrowth of a change in the material facts of the life of the group, and it comes on gradually as the material circumstances favourable to a predatory attitude supervene. The inferior limit of the predatory culture is an industrial limit. Predation cannot become the habitual, conventional resource of any group or any class until industrial methods have been developed to such a degree of efficiency as to leave a margin worth fighting for, above the subsistence of those engaged in getting a living. The transition from peace to predation therefore depends on the growth of technical knowledge and the use of tools. A predatory culture is similarly impracticable in early times, until weapons have been developed to such a point as to make man a formidable animal. The early development of tools and of weapons is of course the same fact seen from two different points of view.

The life of a given group would be characterised as peaceable so long as habitual recourse to combat has not brought the fight into the foreground in men's everyday thoughts, as a dominant feature of the life of man. A group may evidently attain such a predatory attitude with a greater or less degree of completeness, so that its scheme of life and canons of conduct may be controlled to a greater or less extent by the predatory animus. The predatory phase of culture is therefore conceived to come on gradually, through a cumulative growth of predatory aptitudes, habits, and traditions; this growth being due to a change in the circumstances of the group's life, of such a kind as to develop and conserve those traits of human nature and those traditions and norms of conduct that make for a predatory rather than a peaceable life.

The evidence for the hypothesis that there has been such a peaceable stage of primitive culture is in great part drawn from psychology rather than from ethnology, and cannot be detailed here. It will be recited in part in a later chapter, in discussing the survival of archaic traits of human nature under the modern culture.

* * *

The end of acquisition and accumulation is conventionally held to be the consumption of the goods accumulated—whether it is consumption directly by the owner of the goods or by the household attached to him and for this purpose identified with him in theory. This is at least felt to be the economically legitimate end of acquisition, which alone it is incumbent on the theory to take account of. Such consumption may of course be conceived to serve the consumer's physical wants—his physical comfort—or his so-called higher wants—spiritual, æsthetic, intellectual, or what not; the latter class of wants being served indirectly by an expenditure of goods, after the fashion familiar to all economic readers.

But it is only when taken in a sense far removed from its naïve meaning that consumption of goods can be said to afford the incentive from which accumulation invariably proceeds. The motive that lies at the root of ownership is emulation; and the same motive of emulation continues active in the further development of the institution to which it has given rise and in the development of all those features of the social structure which this institution of ownership touches. The possession of wealth confers honour; it is an invidious distinction. Nothing equally cogent can be said for the consumption of goods, nor for any other conceivable incentive to acquisition, and especially not for any incentive to the accumulation of wealth.

It is of course not to be overlooked that in a community where nearly all goods are private property the necessity of earning a livelihood is a powerful and ever-present incentive for the poorer members of the community. The need of subsistence and of an increase of physical comfort may for a time be the dominant motive of acquisition for those classes who are habitually employed at manual labour, whose subsistence is on a precarious footing, who possess little and ordinarily accumulate little; but it will appear in the course of the discussion that even in the case of these impecunious classes the predominance of the motive of physical want is not so decided as has sometimes been assumed. On the other hand, so far as regards those members and classes of the community who are chiefly concerned in the accumulation of wealth, the incentive of subsistence or of physical comfort never plays a considerable part. Ownership began and grew into a human institution on grounds unrelated to the subsistence minimum. The dominant incentive was from the outset the invidious distinction attaching to wealth, and, save temporarily and by exception, no other motive has usurped the primacy at any later stage of the development.

Property set out with being booty held as trophies of the successful raid. So long as the group had departed but little from the primitive communal organisation, and so long as it still stood in close contact with other hostile groups, the utility of things or persons owned lay chiefly in an invidious comparison between their possessor and the enemy from whom they were taken. The habit of distinguishing between the interests of the individual and those of the group to which he belongs is apparently a later growth. Invidious comparison between the possessor of the honorific booty and his less successful neighbours within the group was no doubt present early as an element of the utility of the things possessed, though this was not at the outset the chief element of their value. The man's prowess was still primarily the group's prowess, and the possessor of the booty felt himself to be primarily the keeper of the honour of his group. This appreciation of exploit from the communal point of view is met with also at later stages of social growth, especially as regards the laurels of war.

But so soon as the custom of individual ownership begins to gain consistency, the point of view taken in making the invidious comparison on which private property rests will begin to change. Indeed, the one change is but the reflex of the other. The initial phase of ownership, the phase of acquisition by naïve seizure and conversion, begins to pass into the subsequent stage of an incipient organisation of industry on the basis of private property (in slaves); the horde develops into a more or less self-sufficing industrial community; possessions then come to be valued not so much as evidence of successful foray, but rather as evidence of the prepotence of the possessor of these goods over other individuals within the community. The invidious comparison now becomes primarily a comparison of the owner with the other members of the group. Property is still of the nature of trophy, but, with the cultural advance, it becomes more and more a trophy of successes scored in the game of ownership carried on between the members of the group under the quasi-peaceable methods of nomadic life.

Gradually, as industrial activity further displaces predatory activity in the community's everyday life and in men's habits of thought, accumulated property more and more replaces trophies of predatory exploit as the conventional exponent of prepotence and success. With the growth of settled industry, therefore, the possession of wealth gains in relative importance and effectiveness as a customary basis of repute and esteem. Not that esteem ceases to be awarded on the basis of other, more direct evidence of prowess; not that successful predatory aggression or warlike exploit ceases to call out the approval and admiration of the crowd, or to stir the envy of the less successful competitors; but the opportunities for gaining distinction by means of this direct manifestation of superior force grow less available both in scope and frequency. At the same time opportunities for industrial aggression, and for the accumulation of property by the quasi-peaceable methods of nomadic industry, increase in scope and availability. And it is even more to the point that property now becomes the most easily recognised evidence of a reputable degree of success as distinguished from heroic or signal achievement. It therefore becomes the conventional basis of esteem. Its possession in some amount becomes necessary in order to any reputable standing in the community. It becomes indispensable to accumulate, to acquire property, in order to retain one's good name. When accumulated goods have in this way once become the accepted badge of efficiency, the possession of wealth presently assumes the character of an independent and definitive basis of esteem. The possession of goods, whether acquired aggressively by one's own exertion or passively by transmission through inheritance from others, becomes a conventional basis of reputability. The possession of wealth, which was at the outset valued simply as an evidence of efficiency, becomes, in popular apprehension, itself a meritorious act. Wealth is now itself intrinsically honourable and confers honour on its possessor. By a further refinement, wealth acquired passively by transmission from ancestors or other antecedents presently becomes even more honorific than wealth acquired by the possessor's own effort; but this distinction belongs at a later stage in the evolution of the pecuniary culture and will be spoken of in its place.

Prowess and exploit may still remain the basis of award of the highest popular esteem, although the possession of wealth has become the basis of commonplace reputability and of a blameless social standing. The predatory instinct and the consequent approbation of predatory efficiency are deeply ingrained in the habits of thought of those peoples who have passed under the discipline of a protracted predatory culture. According to popular award, the highest honours within human reach may, even yet, be those gained by an unfolding of extraordinary predatory efficiency in war, or by a quasi-predatory efficiency in statecraft; but for the purposes of a commonplace decent standing in the community these means of repute have been replaced by the acquisition and accumulation of goods. In order to stand well in the eyes of the community, it is necessary to come up to a certain, somewhat indefinite, conventional standard of wealth; just as in the earlier predatory stage it is necessary for the barbarian man to come up to the tribe's standard of physical endurance, cunning and skill at arms. A certain standard of wealth in the one case, and of prowess in the other, is a necessary condition of reputability, and anything in excess of this normal amount is meritorious.

Those members of the community who fall short of this, somewhat indefinite, normal degree of prowess or of property suffer in the esteem of their fellow-men; and consequently they suffer also in their own esteem, since the usual basis of self-respect is the respect accorded by one's neighbours. Only individuals with an aberrant temperament can in the long run retain their self-esteem in the face of the disesteem of their fellows. Apparent exceptions to the rule are met with especially among people with strong religious convictions. But these apparent exceptions are scarcely real exceptions, since such persons commonly fall back on the putative approbation of some supernatural witness of their deeds.

So soon as the possession of property becomes the basis of popular esteem therefore it becomes also a requisite to that complacency which we call self-respect. In any community where goods are held in severalty it is necessary, in order to his own peace of mind that an individual should possess as large a portion of goods as others with whom he is accustomed to class himself; and it is extremely gratifying to possess something more than others. But as fast as a person makes new acquisitions, and becomes accustomed to the resulting new standard of wealth, the new standard forthwith ceases to afford appreciably greater satisfaction than the earlier standard did. The tendency in any case is constantly to make the present pecuniary standard the point of departure for a fresh increase of wealth; and this in turn gives rise to a new standard of sufficiency and a new pecuniary classification of one's self as compared with one's neighbours. So far as concerns the present question, the end sought by accumulation is to rank high in comparison with the rest of the community in point of pecuniary strength. So long as the comparison is distinctly unfavourable to himself, the normal, average individual will live in chronic dissatisfaction with his present lot; and when he has reached what may be called the normal pecuniary standard of the community, or of his class in the community, this chronic dissatisfaction will give place to a restless straining to place a wider and ever-widening pecuniary interval between himself and this average standard. The invidious comparison can never become so favourable to the individual making it that he would not gladly rate himself still higher relatively to his competitors in the struggle for pecuniary reputability.

In the nature of the case, the desire for wealth can scarcely be satiated in any individual instance, and evidently a satiation of the average or general desire for wealth is out of the question. However widely, or equally, or "fairly," it may be distributed, no general increase of the community's wealth can make any approach to satiating this need, the ground of which is the desire of every one to excel every one else in the accumulation of goods. If, as is sometimes assumed, the incentive to accumulation were the want of subsistence or of physical comfort, then the aggregate economic wants of a community might conceivably be satisfied at some point in the advance of industrial efficiency; but since the struggle is substantially a race for reputability on the basis of an invidious comparison, no approach to a definitive attainment is possible.

What has just been said must not be taken to mean that there are no other incentives to acquisition and accumulation than this desire to excel in pecuniary standing and so gain the esteem and envy of one's fellow-men. The desire for added comfort and security from want is present as a motive at every stage of the process of accumulation in a modern industrial community; although the standard of sufficiency in these respects is in turn greatly affected by the habit of pecuniary emulation. To a great extent this emulation shapes the methods and selects the objects of expenditure for personal comfort and decent livelihood.

Besides this, the power conferred by wealth also affords a motive to accumulation. That propensity for purposeful activity and that repugnance to all futility of effort which belong to man by virtue of his character as an agent do not desert him when he emerges from the naïve communal culture where the dominant note of life is the unanalysed and undifferentiated solidarity of the individual with the group with which his life is bound up. When he enters upon the predatory stage, where self-seeking in the narrower sense becomes the dominant note, this propensity goes with him still, as the pervasive trait that shapes his scheme of life. The propensity for achievement and the repugnance to futility remain the underlying economic motive. The propensity changes only in the form of its expression and in the proximate objects to which it directs the man's activity. Under the régime of individual ownership the most available means of visibly achieving a purpose is that afforded by the acquisition and accumulation of goods; and as the self-regarding antithesis between man and man reaches fuller consciousness, the propensity for achievement—the instinct of workmanship—tends more and more to shape itself into a straining to excel others in pecuniary achievement. Relative success, tested by an invidious pecuniary comparison with other men, becomes the conventional end of action. The currently accepted legitimate end of effort becomes the achievement of a favourable comparison with other men; and therefore the repugnance to futility to a good extent coalesces with the incentive of emulation. It acts to accentuate the struggle for pecuniary reputability by visiting with a sharper disapproval all shortcoming and all evidence of shortcoming in point of pecuniary success. Purposeful effort comes to mean, primarily, effort directed to or resulting in a more creditable showing of accumulated wealth. Among the motives which lead men to accumulate wealth, the primacy, both in scope and intensity, therefore, continues to belong to this motive of pecuniary emulation.

In making use of the term "invidious," it may perhaps be unnecessary to remark, there is no intention to extol or depreciate, or to commend or deplore any of the phenomena which the word is used to characterise. The term is used in a technical sense as describing a comparison of persons with a view to rating and grading them in respect of relative worth or value—in an æsthetic or moral sense —and so awarding and defining the relative degrees of complacency with which they may legitimately be contemplated by themselves and by others. An invidious comparison is a process of valuation of persons in respect of worth.

* * *

## *Conspicuous Consumption*

In what has been said of the evolution of the vicarious leisure class and its differentiation from the general body of the working classes, reference has been made to a further division of labour,— that between different servant classes. One portion of the servant class, chiefly those persons whose occupation is vicarious leisure, come to undertake a new, subsidiary range of duties—the vicarious consumption of goods. The most obvious form in which this consumption occurs is seen in the wearing of liveries and the occupation of spacious servants' quarters. Another, scarcely less obtrusive or less effective form of vicarious consumption, and a much more widely prevalent one, is the consumption of food, clothing, dwelling, and furniture by the lady and the rest of the domestic establishment.

But already at a point in economic evolution far ante-dating the emergence of the lady, specialised consumption of goods as an evidence of pecuniary strength had begun to work out in a more or less elaborate system. The beginning of a differentiation in consumption even antedates the appearance of anything that can fairly be called pecuniary strength. It is traceable back to the initial phase of predatory culture, and there is even a suggestion that an incipient differentiation in this respect lies back of the beginnings of the predatory life. This most primitive differentiation in the consumption of goods is like the later differentiation with which we are all so intimately familiar, in that it is largely of a ceremonial character, but unlike the latter it does not rest on a difference in accumulated wealth. The utility of consumption as an evidence of wealth is to be classed as a derivative growth. It is an adaptation to a new end, by a selective process, of a distinction previously existing and well established in men's habits of thought.

In the earlier phases of the predatory culture the only economic differentiation is a broad distinction between an honourable superior class made up of the able-bodied men on the one side, and a base inferior class of labouring women on the other. According to the ideal scheme of life in force at that time it is the office of the men to consume what the women produce. Such consumption as falls to the women is merely incidental to their work; it is a means to their continued labour, and not a consumption directed to their own comfort and fulness of life. Unproductive consumption of goods is honourable, primarily as a mark of prowess and a perquisite of human dignity; secondarily it becomes substantially honourable in itself, especially the consumption of the more desirable things. The consumption of choice articles of food, and frequently also of rare articles of adornment, becomes tabu to the women and children; and if there is a base (servile) class of men, the tabu holds also for them. With a further advance in culture this tabu may change into simple custom of a more or less rigorous character; but whatever be the theoretical basis of the distinction which is maintained, whether it be a tabu or a larger conventionality, the features of the conventional scheme of consumption do not change easily. When the quasi-peaceable stage of industry is reached, with its fundamental institution of chattel slavery, the general principle, more or less rigorously applied, is that the base, industrious class should consume only what may be necessary to their subsistence. In the nature of things, luxuries and the comforts of life belong to the leisure class. Under the tabu, certain victuals, and more particularly certain beverages, are strictly reserved for the use of the superior class.

The ceremonial differentiation of the dietary is best seen in the use of intoxicating beverages and narcotics. If these articles of consumption are costly, they are felt to be noble and honorific. Therefore the base classes, primarily the women, practise an enforced continence with respect to these stimulants, except in countries where they are obtainable at a very low cost. From archaic times down through all the length of the patriarchal régime it has been the office of the women to prepare and administer these luxuries, and it has been the perquisite of the men of gentle birth and breeding to consume them. Drunkenness and the other pathological consequences of the free use of stimulants therefore tend in their turn to become honorific, as being a mark, at the second remove, of the superior status of those who are able to afford the indulgence. Infirmities induced by over-indulgence are among some peoples freely recognised as manly attributes. It has even happened that the name for certain diseased conditions of the body arising from such an origin has passed into everyday speech as a synonym for "noble" or "gentle." It is only at a relatively early stage of culture that the symptoms of expensive vice are conventionally accepted as marks of a superior status, and so tend to become virtues and command the deference of the community; but the reputability that attaches to certain expensive vices long retains so much of its force as to appreciably lessen the disapprobation visited upon the men of the wealthy or noble class for any excessive indulgence. The same invidious distinction adds force to the current disapproval of any indulgence of this kind on the part of women, minors, and inferiors. This invidious traditional distinction has not lost its force even among the more advanced peoples of to-day. Where the example set by the leisure class retains its imperative force in the regulation of the conventionalities, it is observable that the women still in great measure practise the same traditional continence with regard to stimulants.

This characterisation of the greater continence

in the use of stimulants practised by the women of the reputable classes may seem an excessive refinement of logic at the expense of common sense. But facts within easy reach of any one who cares to know them go to say that the greater abstinence of women is in some part due to an imperative conventionality; and that this conventionality is, in a general way, strongest where the patriarchal tradition—the tradition that the woman is a chattel—has retained its hold in greatest vigour. In a sense which has been greatly qualified in scope and rigour, but which has by no means lost its meaning even yet, this tradition says that the woman, being a chattel, should consume only what is necessary to her sustenance,—except so far as her further consumption contributes to the comfort or the good repute of her master. The consumption of luxuries, in the true sense, is a consumption directed to the comfort of the consumer himself, and is, therefore, a mark of the master. Any such consumption by others can take place only on a basis of sufferance. In communities where the popular habits of thought have been profoundly shaped by the patriarchal tradition we may accordingly look for survivals of the tabu on luxuries at least to the extent of a conventional deprecation of their use by the unfree and dependent class. This is more particularly true as regards certain luxuries, the use of which by the dependent class would detract sensibly from the comfort or pleasure of their masters, or which are held to be of doubtful legitimacy on other grounds. In the apprehension of the great conservative middle class of Western civilisation the use of these stimulants is obnoxious to at least one, if not both, of these objections; and it is a fact too significant to be passed over that it is precisely among these middle classes of the Germanic culture, with their strong surviving sense of the patriarchal proprieties, that the women are to the greatest extent subject to a qualified tabu on narcotics and alcoholic beverages. With many qualifications—with more qualifications as the patriarchal tradition has gradually weakened—the general rule is felt to be right and binding that women should consume only for the benefit of their masters. The objection of course presents itself that expenditure on women's dress and household paraphernalia is an obvious exception to this rule; but it will appear in the sequel that this exception is much more obvious than substantial.

During the earlier stages of economic development, consumption of goods without stint, especially consumption of the better grades of goods,—ideally all consumption in excess of the subsistence minimum,—pertains normally to the leisure class. This restriction tends to disappear, at least formally, after the later peaceable stage has been reached, with private ownership of goods and an industrial system based on wage labour or on the petty household economy. But during the earlier quasi-peaceable stage, when so many of the traditions through which the institution of a leisure class has affected the economic life of later times were taking form and consistency, this principle has had the force of a conventional law. It has served as the norm to which consumption has tended to conform, and any appreciable departure from it is to be regarded as an abberant form, sure to be eliminated sooner or later in the further course of development.

The quasi-peaceable gentleman of leisure, then, not only consumes of the staff of life beyond the minimum required for subsistence and physical efficiency, but his consumption also undergoes a specialisation as regards the quality of the goods consumed. He consumes freely and of the best, in food, drink, narcotics, shelter, services, ornaments, apparel, weapons and accoutrements, amusements, amulets, and idols or divinities. In the process of gradual amelioration which takes place in the articles of his consumption, the motive principle and the proximate aim of innovation is no doubt the higher efficiency of the improved and more elaborate products for personal comfort and well-being. But that does not remain the sole purpose of their consumption. The canon of reputability is at hand and seizes upon such innovations as are, according to its standard, fit to survive. Since the consumption of these more excellent goods is an evidence of wealth, it becomes honorific; and conversely, the failure to consume in due quantity and quality becomes a mark of inferiority and demerit.

This growth of punctilious discrimination as to qualitative excellence in eating drinking, etc., presently affects not only the manner of life, but also the training and intellectual activity of the gentleman of leisure. He is no longer simply the successful, aggressive male,—the man of strength, resource, and intrepidity. In order to avoid stultification he must also cultivate his tastes, for it now becomes incumbent on him to discriminate with some nicety between the noble and the ignoble in consumable goods. He becomes a connoisseur in creditable viands of various degrees of merit, in manly beverages and trinkets, in seemly apparel and architecture, in weapons, games, dances, and the narcotics. This cultivation of the æsthetic faculty requires time and application, and the demands made upon the gentleman in this direction therefore tend to change his life of leisure into a more or less arduous application to the business of learning how to live a life of ostensible leisure in a becoming way. Closely related to the requirement that the gentleman must consume freely and of the right kind of goods, there is the requirement that he must know how to consume them in a seemly manner. His life of leisure must be conducted in due form. Hence arise good manners in the way pointed out in an earlier chapter. High-bred manners and ways of living are items of conformity to the norm of conspicuous leisure and conspicuous consumption.

Conspicuous consumption of valuable goods is a means of reputability to the gentleman of leisure. As wealth accumulates on his hands, his own unaided effort will not avail to sufficiently put his opulence in evidence by this method. The aid of friends and competitors is therefore brought in by resorting to the giving of valuable presents and expensive feasts and entertainments. Presents and feasts had probably another origin than that of naïve ostentation, but they acquired their utility for this purpose very early, and they have retained that character to the present; so that their utility in this respect has now long been the substantial ground on which these usages rest. Costly entertainments, such as the potlatch or the ball, are peculiarly adapted to serve this end. The competitor with whom the entertainer wishes to institute a comparison is, by this method, made to serve as a means to the end. He consumes vicariously for his host at the same time that he is a witness to the consumption of that excess of good things which his host is unable to dispose of single-handed, and he is also made to witness his host's facility in etiquette.

In the giving of costly entertainments other motives, of a more genial kind, are of course also present. The custom of festive gatherings probably originated in motives of conviviality and religion; these motives are also present in the later development, but they do not continue to be the sole motives. The latter-day leisure-class festivities and entertainments may continue in some slight degree to serve the religious need and in a higher degree the needs of recreation and conviviality, but they also serve an invidious purpose; and they serve it none the less effectually for having a colourable non-invidious ground in these more avowable motives. But the economic effect of these social amenities is not therefore lessened, either in the vicarious consumption of goods or in the exhibition of difficult and costly achievements in etiquette.

As wealth accumulates, the leisure class develops further in function and structure and there arises a differentiation within the class. There is a more or less elaborate system of rank and grades. This differentiation is furthered by the inheritance of wealth and the consequent inheritance of gentility. With the inheritance of gentility goes the inheritance of obligatory leisure; and gentility of a sufficient potency to entail a life of leisure may be inherited without the complement of wealth required to maintain a dignified leisure. Gentle blood may be transmitted without goods enough to afford a reputably free consumption at one's ease. Hence results a class of impecunious gentlemen of leisure, incidentally referred to already. These half-caste gentlemen of leisure fall into a system of hierarchical gradations. Those who stand near the higher and the highest grades of the wealthy leisure class, in point of birth, or in point of wealth, or both, outrank the remoter-born and the pecuniarily weaker. These lower grades, especially the impecunious or marginal gentlemen of leisure, affiliate themselves by a system of dependence or fealty to the great ones; by so doing they gain an increment of repute, or of the means with which to lead a life of leisure, from their patron. They become his courtiers or retainers, servants; and being fed and countenanced by their patron they are indices of his rank and vicarious consumers of his superfluous wealth. Many of these affiliated gentlemen of leisure are at the same time lesser men of substance in their own right; so that some of them are scarcely at all, others only partially, to be rated as vicarious consumers. So many of them, however, as make up the retainers and hangers-on of the patron may be classed as vicarious consumers without qualification. Many of these again, and also many of the other aristocracy of less degree, have in turn attracted to their persons a more or less comprehensive group of vicarious consumers in the persons of their wives and children, their servants, retainers, etc.

Throughout this graduated scheme of vicarious leisure and vicarious consumption the rule holds that these offices must be performed in some such manner, or under some such circumstance or insignia, as shall point plainly to the master to whom this leisure or consumption pertains, and to whom therefore the resulting increment of good repute of right inures. The consumption and leisure executed by these persons for their master or patron represents an investment on his part with a view to an increase of good fame. As regards feasts and largesses this is obvious enough, and the imputation of repute to the host or patron here takes place immediately, on the ground of common notoriety. Where leisure and consumption is performed vicariously by henchmen and retainers, imputation of the resulting repute to the patron is effected by their residing near his person so that it may be plain to all men from what source they draw. As the group whose good esteem is to be secured in this way grows larger, more patent means are required to indicate the imputation of credit for the leisure performed, and to this end uniforms, badges, and liveries come into vogue. The wearing of uniforms or liveries implies a considerable degree of dependence, and may even be said to be a mark of servitude, real or ostensible. The wearers of uniforms and liveries may be roughly divided into two classes—the free and the servile, or the noble and the ignoble. The services performed by them are likewise divisible into noble and ignoble. Of course the distinction is not observed with strict consistency in practice; the less debasing of the base services and the less honorific of the noble functions are not infrequently merged in the same person. But the general distinction is not on that account to be overlooked. What may add some perplexity is the fact that this fundamental distinction between noble and ignoble, which rests on the nature of the ostensible service performed, is traversed by a secondary distinction into honorific and humiliating, resting on the rank of the person for whom the service is performed or whose livery is worn. So, those offices which are by right the proper employment of the leisure class are noble; such are government, fighting, hunting, the care of arms and accoutrements, and the like,—in short, those which may be classed as ostensibly predatory employments. On the other hand, those employments which properly fall to the industrious class are ignoble; such as handicraft or other productive labour, menial services, and the like. But a base service performed for a person of very high degree may become a very honorific office; as for instance the office of a Maid of Honour or of a Lady in Waiting to the Queen, or the King's Master of the Horse or his Keeper of the Hounds. The two offices last named suggest a principle of some general bearing. Whenever, as in these cases, the menial service in question has to do directly with the primary leisure employments of fighting and hunting, it easily acquires a reflected honorific character. In this way great honour may come to attach to an employment which in its own nature belongs to the baser sort.

In the later development of peaceable industry, the usage of employing an idle corps of uniformed men-at-arms gradually lapses. Vicarious consumption by dependents bearing the insignia of their patron or master narrows down to a corps of liveried menials. In a heightened degree, therefore, the livery comes to be a badge of servitude, or rather of servility. Something of a honorific character always attached to the livery of the armed retainer, but this honorific character disappears when the livery becomes the exclusive badge of the menial. The livery becomes obnoxious to nearly all who are required to wear it. We are yet so little removed from a state of effective slavery as still to be fully sensitive to the sting of any imputation of servility. This antipathy asserts itself even in the case of the liveries or uniforms which some corporations prescribe as the distinctive dress of their employees. In this country the aversion even goes the length of discrediting—in a mild and uncertain way—those government employments, military and civil, which require the wearing of a livery or uniform.

With the disappearance of servitude, the number of vicarious consumers attached to any one gentleman tends, on the whole, to decrease. The like is of course true, and perhaps in a still higher degree, of the number of dependents who perform vicarious leisure for him. In a general way, though not wholly nor consistently, these two groups coincide. The dependent who was first delegated for these duties was the wife, or the chief wife; and, as would be expected, in the later development of the institution, when the number of persons by whom these duties are customarily performed gradually narrows, the wife remains the last. In the higher grades of society a large volume of both these kinds of service is required; and here the wife is of course still assisted in the work by a more or less numerous corps of menials. But as we descend the social scale, the point is presently reached where the duties of vicarious leisure and consumption devolve upon the wife alone. In the communities of the Western culture, this point is at present found among the lower middle class.

And here occurs a curious inversion. It is a fact of common observation that in this lower middle class there is no pretence of leisure on the part of the head of the household. Through force of circumstances it has fallen into disuse. But the middle-class wife still carries on the business of vicarious leisure, for the good name of the household and its master. In descending the social scale in any modern industrial community, the primary fact—the conspicuous leisure of the master of the household—disappears at a relatively high point. The head of the middle-class household has been reduced by economic circumstances to turn his hand to gaining a livelihood by occupations which often partake largely of the character of industry, as in the case of the ordinary business man of to-day. But the derivative fact—the vicarious leisure and consumption rendered by the wife, and the auxiliary vicarious performance of leisure by menials—remains in vogue as a conventionality which the demands of reputability will not suffer to be slighted. It is by no means an uncommon spectacle to find a man applying himself to work with the utmost assiduity, in order that his wife may in due form render for him that degree of vicarious leisure which the common sense of the time demands.

The leisure rendered by the wife in such cases is, of course, not a simple manifestation of idleness or indolence. It almost invariably occurs disguised under some form of work or household duties or social amenities, which prove on analysis to serve little or no ulterior end beyond showing that she does not and need not occupy herself with anything that is gainful or that is of substantial use. As has already been noticed under the head of manners, the greater part of the customary round of domestic cares to which the middle-class housewife gives her time and effort is of this character. Not that the results of her attention to household matters, of a decorative and mundificatory character, are not pleasing to the sense of men trained in middle-class proprieties; but the taste to which these effects of household adornment and tidiness appeal is a taste which has been formed under the selective guidance of a canon of propriety that demands just these evidences of wasted effort. The effects are pleasing to us chiefly because we have been taught to find them pleasing. There goes into these domestic duties much solicitude for a proper combination of form and colour, and for other ends that are to be classed as æsthetic in the proper sense of the term; and it is not denied that effects having some substantial æsthetic value are sometimes attained. Pretty much all that is here insisted on is that, as regards these amenities of life, the housewife's efforts are under the guidance of traditions that have been shaped by the law of conspicuously wasteful expenditure of time and substance. If beauty or comfort is achieved,—and it is a more or less fortuitous circumstance if they are,—they must be achieved by means and methods that commend themselves to the great economic law of wasted effort. The more reputable, "presentable" portion of middle-class household paraphernalia are, on the other hand, apparatus for putting in evidence the vicarious leisure rendered by the housewife.

The requirement of vicarious consumption at the hands of the wife continues in force even at a lower point in the pecuniary scale than the requirement of vicarious leisure. At a point below which little if any pretence of wasted effort, in ceremonial cleanness and the like, is observable, and where there is assuredly no conscious attempt at ostensible leisure, decency still requires the wife to consume some goods conspicuously for the reputability of the household and its head. So that, as the latter-day outcome of this evolution of an archaic institution, the wife, who was at the outset the drudge and chattel of the man, both in fact and in theory,—the producer of goods for him to consume,—has become the ceremonial consumer of goods which he produces. But she still quite unmistakably remains his chattel in theory; for the habitual rendering of vicarious leisure and consumption is the abiding mark of the unfree servant.

This vicarious consumption practised by the household of the middle and lower classes can not be counted as a direct expression of the leisure-class scheme of life, since the household of this pecuniary grade does not belong within the leisure class. It is rather that the leisure-class scheme of life here comes to an expression at the second remove. The leisure class stands at the head of the social structure in point of reputability; and its manner of life and its standards of worth therefore afford the norm of reputability for the community. The observance of these standards, in some degree of approximation, becomes incumbent upon all classes lower in the scale. In modern civilized communities the lines of demarcation between social classes have grown vague and transient, and wherever this happens the norm of reputability imposed by the upper class extends its coercive influence with but slight hindrance down through the social structure to the lowest strata. The result is that the members of each stratum accept as their ideal of decency the scheme of life in vogue in the next higher stratum, and bend their energies to live up to that ideal. On pain of forfeiting their good name and their self-respect in case of failure, they must conform to the accepted code, at least in appearance.

The basis on which good repute in any highly organised industrial community ultimately rests is pecuniary strength; and the means of showing pecuniary strength, and so of gaining or retaining a good name, are leisure and a conspicuous consumption of goods. Accordingly, both of these methods are in vogue as far down the scale as it remains possible; and in the lower strata in which the two methods are employed, both offices are in great part delegated to the wife and children of the household. Lower still, where any degree of leisure, even ostensible, has become impracticable for the wife, the conspicuous consumption of goods remains and is carried on by the wife and children. The man of the household also can do something in this direction, and, indeed, he commonly does; but with a still lower descent into the levels of indigence—along the margin of the slums—the man, and presently also the children, virtually cease to consume valuable goods for appearances, and the woman remains virtually the sole exponent of the household's pecuniary decency. No class of society, not even the most abjectly poor, forgoes all customary conspicuous consumption. The last items of this category of consumption are not given up except under stress of the direst necessity. Very much of squalor and discomfort will be endured before the last trinket or the last pretence of pecuniary decency is put away. There is no class and no country that has yielded so abjectly before the pressure of physical want as to deny themselves all gratification of this higher or spiritual need.

From the foregoing survey of the growth of conspicuous leisure and consumption, it appears that the utility of both alike for the purposes of reputability lies in the element of waste that is common to both. In the one case it is a waste of time and effort, in the other it is a waste of goods. Both are methods of demonstrating the possession of wealth, and the two are conventionally accepted as equivalents. The choice between them is a question of advertising expediency simply, except so far as it may be affected by other standards of propriety, springing from a different source. On grounds of expediency the preference may be given to the one or the other at different stages of the economic development. The question is, which of the two methods will most effectively reach the persons whose convictions it is desired to affect. Usage has answered this question in different ways under different circumstances.

So long as the community or social group is small enough and compact enough to be effectually reached by common notoriety alone,—that is to say, so long as the human environment to which the individual is required to adapt himself in respect of reputability is comprised within his sphere of personal acquaintance and neighbourhood gossip,—so long the one method is about as effective as the other. Each will therefore serve about equally well during the earlier stages of social growth. But when the differentiation has gone farther and it becomes necessary to reach a wider human environment, consumption begins to hold over leisure as an ordinary means of decency. This is especially true during the later, peaceable economic stage. The means of communication and the mobility of the population now expose the individual to the observation of many persons who have no other means of judging of his reputability than the display of goods (and perhaps of breeding) which he is able to make while he is under their direct observation.

The modern organisation of industry works in the same direction also by another line. The exigencies of the modern industrial system frequently place individuals and households in juxtaposition between whom there is little contact in any other sense than that of juxtaposition. One's neighbours, mechanically speaking, often are socially not one's neighbours, or even acquaintances; and still their transient good opinion has a high degree of utility. The only practicable means of impressing one's pecuniary ability on these unsympathetic observers of one's everyday life is an unremitting demonstration of ability to pay. In the modern community there is also a more frequent attendance at large gatherings of people to whom one's everyday life is unknown; in such places as churches, theatres, ballrooms, hotels, parks, shops, and the like. In order to impress these transient observers, and to retain one's self-complacency under their observation, the signature of one's pecuniary strength should be written in characters which he who runs may read. It is evident, therefore, that the present trend of the development is in the direction of heightening the utility of conspicuous consumption as compared with leisure.

It is also noticeable that the serviceability of consumption as a means of repute, as well as the insistence on it as an element of decency, is at its best in those portions of the community where the human contact of the individual is widest and the mobility of the population is greatest. Conspicuous consumption claims a relatively larger portion of the income of the urban than of the rural population, and the claim is also more imperative. The result is that, in order to keep up a decent appearance, the former habitually live hand-to-mouth to a greater extent than the latter. So it comes, for instance, the American farmer and his wife and daughters are notoriously less modish in their dress, as well as less urbane in their manners, than the city artisan's family with an equal income. It is not that the city population is by nature much more eager for the peculiar complacency that comes of a conspicuous consumption, nor has the rural population less regard for pecuniary decency. But the provocation to this line of evidence, as well as its transient effectiveness, are more decided in the city. This method is therefore more readily resorted to, and in the struggle to outdo one another the city population push their normal standard of conspicuous consumption to a higher point, with the result that a relatively greater expenditure in this direction is required to indicate a given degree of pecuniary decency in the city. The requirement of conformity to this higher conventional standard becomes mandatory. The standard of decency is higher, class for class, and this requirement of decent appearance must be lived up to on pain of losing caste.

Consumption becomes a larger element in the standard of living in the city than in the country. Among the country population its place is to some extent taken by savings and home comforts known through the medium of neighbourhood gossip sufficiently to serve the like general purpose of pecuniary repute. These home comforts and the leisure indulged in—where the indulgence is found—are of course also in great part to be classed as items of conspicuous consumption; and much the same is to be said of the savings. The smaller amount of the savings laid by by the artisan class is no doubt due, in some measure, to the fact that in the case of the artisan the savings are a less effective means of advertisement, relative to the environment in which he is placed, than are the savings of the people living on farms and in the small villages. Among the latter, everybody's affairs, especially everybody's pecuniary status, are known to everybody else. Considered by itself simply—taken in the first degree—this added provocation to which the artisan and the urban labouring classes are exposed may not very seriously decrease the amount of savings; but in its cumulative action, through raising the standard of decent expenditure, its deterrent effect on the tendency to save cannot but be very great.

* * *

The use of the term "waste" is in one respect an unfortunate one. As used in the speech of everyday life the word carries an undertone of deprecation. It is here used for want of a better term that will adequately describe the same range of motives and of phenomena, and it is not to be taken in an odious sense, as implying an illegitimate expenditure of human products or of human life. In the view of economic theory, the expenditure in question is no more and no less legitimate than any other expenditure. It is here called "waste" because this expenditure does not serve human life or human well-being on the whole, not because it is waste or misdirection of effort or expenditure as viewed from the standpoint of the individual consumer who chooses it. If he chooses it, that disposes of the question of its relative utility to him, as compared with other forms of consumption that would not be deprecated on account of their wastefulness. Whatever form of expenditure the consumer chooses, or whatever end he seeks in making his choice, has utility to him by virtue of his preference. As seen from the point of view of the individual consumer, the question of wastefulness does not arise within the scope of economic theory proper. The use of the word "waste" as a technical term, therefore, implies no deprecation of the motives or of the ends sought by the consumer under this canon of conspicuous waste.

But it is, on other grounds, worth noting that the term "waste" in the language of everyday life implies deprecation of what is characterised as wasteful. This common-sense implication is itself an outcropping of the instinct of workmanship. The popular reprobation of waste goes to say that in order to be at peace with himself the common man must be able to see in any and all human effort and human enjoyment an enhancement of life and well-being on the whole. In order to meet with unqualified approval, any economic fact must approve itself under the test of impersonal usefulness—usefulness as seen from the point of view of the generically human. Relative or competitive advantage of one individual in comparison with another does not satisfy the economic conscience, and therefore competitive expenditure has not the approval of this conscience.

In strict accuracy nothing should be included under the head of conspicuous waste but such expenditure as is incurred on the ground of an invidious pecuniary comparison. But in order to bring any given item or element in under this head it is not necessary that it should be recognised as waste in this sense by the person incurring the expenditure. It frequently happens that an element of the standard of living which set out with being primarily wasteful, ends with becoming, in the apprehension of the consumer, a necessary of life; and it may in this way become as indispensable as any other item of the consumer's habitual expenditure. As items which sometimes fall under this head, and are therefore available as illustrations of the manner in which this principle applies, may be cited carpets and tapestries, silver table service, waiter's services, silk hats, starched linen, many articles of jewellery and of dress. The indispensability of these things after the habit and the convention have been formed, however, has little to say in the classification of expenditures as waste or not waste in the technical meaning of the word. The test to which all expenditure must be brought in an attempt to decide that point is the question whether it serves directly to enhance human life on the whole—whether it furthers the life process taken impersonally. For this is the basis of award of the instinct of workmanship, and that instinct is the court of final appeal in any question of economic truth or adequacy. It is a question as to the award rendered by a dispassionate common sense. The question is therefore, not whether, under the existing circumstances of individual habit and social custom, a given expenditure conduces to the particular consumer's gratification or peace of mind; but whether, aside from acquired tastes and from the canons of usage and conventional decency, its result is a net gain in comfort or in the fulness of life. Customary expenditure must be classed under the head of waste in so far as the custom on which it rests is traceable to the habit of making an invidious pecuniary comparison—in so far as it is conceived that it could not have become customary and prescriptive without the backing of this principle of pecuniary reputability or relative economic success.

It is obviously not necessary that a given object of expenditure should be exclusively wasteful in order to come in under the category of conspicuous waste. An article may be useful and wasteful both, and its utility to the consumer may be made up of use and waste in the most varying proportions. Consumable goods, and even productive goods, generally show the two elements in combination, as constituents of their utility; although, in a general way, the element of waste tends to predominate in articles of consumption, while the contrary is true of articles designed for productive use. Even in articles which appear at first glance to serve for pure ostentation only, it is always possible to detect the presence of some, at least ostensible, useful purpose; and on the other hand, even in special machinery and tools contrived for some particular industrial process, as well as in the rudest appliances of human industry, the traces of conspicuous waste, or at least of the habit of ostentation, usually become evident on a close scrutiny. It would be hazardous to assert that a useful purpose is ever absent from the utility of any article or of any service, however obviously its prime purpose and chief element is conspicuous waste; and it would be only less hazardous to assert of any primarily useful product that the element of waste is in no way concerned in its value, immediately or remotely.

# 7. *Social Stratification*

BY PITIRIM A. SOROKIN

## CONCEPTIONS AND DEFINITIONS

SOCIAL stratification means the differentiation of a given population into hierarchically superposed classes. It is manifested in the existence of upper and lower layers. Its basis and very essence consist in an unequal distribution of rights and privileges, duties and responsibilities, social values and privations, social power and influences among the members of a society. Concrete forms of social stratification are different and numerous. If the economic status of the members of a society is unequal, if among them there are both wealthy and poor, the society is *economically stratified,* regardless of whether its organization is communistic or capitalistic, whether in its constitution it is styled "the society of equal individuals" or not. Labels, signboards and "speech reactions" cannot change nor obliterate the real fact of the economic inequality manifested in the differences of incomes, economic standards, and in the existence of the rich and the poor strata. If the social ranks within a group are hierarchically superposed with respect to their authority and prestige, their honors and titles; if there are the rulers and the ruled, then whatever are their names (monarchs, executives, masters, bosses), these things mean that the group is *politically stratified,* regardless of what is written in its constitution or proclaimed in its declarations. If the members of a society are differentiated into various occupational groups, and some of the occupations are regarded as more honorable than others, if the members of an occupational group are divided into bosses of different authority and into members who are subordinated to the bosses, the group is *occupationally stratified,* independently of the fact whether the bosses are elected or

Reprinted from Pitirim A. Sorokin, *Social Mobility,* in *Social and Cultural Mobility* (Glencoe, Ill.: The Free Press, 1959), chap. ii, pp. 11–17, with the permission of The Free Press.

appointed, whether their position is acquired by social inheritance or personal achievement.

### PRINCIPAL FORMS OF SOCIAL STRATIFICATION AND THEIR INTERRELATIONS

Concrete forms of social stratification are numerous. The majority of them may, however, be reduced to three principal classes: the economic, the political, and the occupational stratification. As a general rule, these forms are closely intercorrelated with each other. Usually, those who occupy the upper strata in one respect happen to be in the upper strata also in other respects, and *vice versa*. The men who dwell in the upper economic layers happen also to be in the upper political and occupational strata. The poor, as a rule, are politically disfranchised and dwell in the lowest strata of the occupational hierarchy. Such is the general rule, though there are, however, many exceptions to it. Not always are the wealthiest men at the apex of the political or occupational pyramid; and not always are the poor men the lowest in the political or the occupational gradations. This means that the intercorrelation among the three forms of stratification is far from being perfect; the strata of each form do not coincide completely with one another. There is always a certain degree of overlapping among them. This fact does not permit us to analyze in a summary way all three fundamental forms of social stratification. For the sake of a greater accuracy each form has to be studied separately. A real picture of social stratification in any society is very complex. In order to make its analysis easier, only the most fundamental traits must be taken. Many details must be omitted, and the situation simplified, without, however, disfiguring it. This is done in any science and has to be done especially here where the problem is so complex and so little studied. In such cases the Roman *minima non curat prætor* is completely justified.

### SOCIAL STRATIFICATION IS A PERMANENT CHARACTERISTIC OF ANY ORGANIZED SOCIAL GROUP

Any organized social group is always a stratified social body. There has not been and does not exist any permanent social group which is "flat," and in which all members are equal. Unstratified society, with a real equality of its members, is a myth which has never been realized in the history of mankind. This statement may sound somewhat paradoxical and yet it is accurate. The forms and proportions of stratification vary, but its essence is permanent, as far as any more or less permanent and organized social group is concerned. This is true not only in human society, but even in plant and animal communities. Let us consider the principal corroborations.

*Plant and Animal Communities.*—As far as it is possible to apply the conceptions of human sociology to plant and animal communities, social stratification may be said to exist here also. In the plant communities there are different "social" classes, the phenomena of parasitism and exploitation, suppression and domination, different "economic" standards of living (the amount of air, sunlight, moisture, and soil ingredients consumed) and so on. Of course, these phenomena are but roughly analogous to those of social stratification in human society; and yet they signify clearly that the plant community is in no way a community of "equal units," whose positions are equal and whose interrelations are identical within the community.

With still greater reason the same may be said of animal societies. Within them social stratification is manifested in: (*a*) the existence of different and sharply divided classes in the communities of bees, ants, and other insects; (*b*) the existence of leaders among gregarious mammals; (*c*) the general facts of parasitism, exploitation, domination, subordination, and so on. In brief, one cannot find here any society which may be styled an unstratified group.

*Pre-literate Human Tribes.*—Except, perhaps, the few cases where the members of a population are leading an isolated life, where no permanent social life and interaction exist, where, therefore, we do not have a social organization in the proper sense of the word, as soon as organization begins primitive social groups exhibit the trait of stratification. It is manifested in various forms. First, in the existence of the sex and age groups with quite different privileges and duties. Second, in the existence of a privileged and influential group of the tribe's leaders. Third, in the existence of the most influential chieftain or headman. Fourth, in the existence of outcasts and outlawed men. Fifth, in the existence of inter- and intratribal division of labor. Sixth, in the existence of different economic standards, and in that of economic inequality generally. Traditional opinion about primitive groups as communistic societies which do not have any commerce or private property, or economic inequality, or inheritance of fortune, are far from being correct. "The primitive economy (*Urwirtschaft*) is neither an economy of isolated individuals searching for food (as K. Bücher thinks), nor the economy of communism or collective production. What we really have is the economic group composed of mutually dependent and economically active individuals and of the smaller parts of the group which have a system of commerce and barter with each other."[1] If in many tribes economic differentiation is very slight, and customs of mutual aid approach communism, this is due only to the general poverty of the group. These facts support the contention that primitive groups also are stratified bodies.

*More Advanced Societies and Groups.*—If we cannot find a non-stratified society among the most primitive groups, it is useless to try to find it among more advanced, larger and compound societies. Here, without any single exception the fact of stratification is universal. Its forms and proportions vary; its essence has existed everywhere and at all times. Among all agricultural and, especially, industrial societies social stratification has been conspicuous and clear. The modern democracies also do not present any exception to the rule. Though in their constitutions it is said that "all men are equal," only a quite naïve person may infer from this a non-existence of social stratification within these societies. It is enough to mention the gradations: from Henry Ford to a beggar; from the President of the United States to a policeman; from a foreman to the most subordinate worker; from the president of a university to a janitor; from an "LL.D." or "Ph.D." to a "B.A."; from a "leading authority" to an average man; from a commander-in-chief of an army to a soldier; from a president of a board of directors of a corporation to its common laborer; from an editor-in-chief of a newspaper to a simple reporter; it is enough to mention these various ranks and social gradations to see that the best democracies have social stratification scarcely less than the non-democratic societies.

It is needless to insist on these obvious facts. What should be stressed here is, that not only large social bodies, but any organized social group whatever, once it is organized, is inevitably stratified to some degree.

> Gradations, hierarchies, shining leaders, cumulative aspirations—all these appear spontaneously whenever men get together, whether for play, for mutual help, for voluntary association, or for the great compulsory association of the State. Every Englishman is said to love a lord; every American is said to love a title.[2]

1. SOMLÓ, F., *Der Güterverkehr in der Urgesellschaft, Inst. of Solvay,* pp. 65–67, 155, 177 ff., 1909. See also PANSKOW, H., "Betrachtungen über das Wirtschaftsleben der Natürvölker," *Zeitschrift der Gesellschaft für Erdkunde zu Berlin,* Vol. XXXI, 1896; MAUNIER, R., "Vie Religieuse et vie économique," *Revue International de Sociologie,* December, 1907, January and February, 1908; LOWIE, R. H., *Primitive Society,* Chap. IX, New York, 1920; THURNWALD, R., *Die Gestaltung d. Wirtschaftsentwicklung aus ihren Aufangen heraus,* 1923; MALINOWSKI, B., "The Argonauts in the West Pacific," *Economics Journal,* March, 1921.
2. TAUSSIG, F. W., *Inventors and Money Makers,* p. 126, New York, 1915.

Family, church, sect, political party, faction, business organization, gang of brigands, labor union, scientific society—in brief, any organized social group is stratified at the price of its permanency and organization. The organization even of groups of ardent levelers, and the permanent failure of all attempts to build a non-stratified group, testify to the imminency and unavoidability of stratification in an organized social group. This remark may appear somewhat strange to many people who, under the influence of high-sounding phraseology, may believe that, at least, the societies of the levelers themselves are non-stratified. This belief, as many another one, is utterly wrong. Different attempts to exterminate social feudalism have been successful, in the best cases, only in ameliorating some of the inequalities, and in changing the concrete forms of stratification. They have never succeeded in annihilating stratification itself. And the regularity with which all these efforts have failed once more witnesses the "natural" character of stratification. Christianity started its history with an attempt to create an equal society; very soon, especially after 313 A.D., it already had a complicated hierarchy, and soon finished by the creation of a tremendous pyramid, with numerous ranks and titles, beginning with the omnipotent pope and ending with that of a lawless heretic. The institution of Fratres Minorum was organized by St. Francis of Assisi on the principle of perfect equality. Seven years later equality disappeared. Without any exceptions, all attempts of the most ardent levelers in the history of all countries have had the same fate. They could not avoid it even when the faction of the levelers has been victorious. The failure of the Russian Communism is only an additional example in a long series of similar experiments performed on small and large scale, sometimes peacefully, as in many religious sects, sometimes violently, as in social revolutions of the past and present. If many forms of stratification were destroyed for a moment, they regularly reappeared again in the old or in a modified form, often being built by the hands of the levelers themselves.

Present democracies and Socialist, Communist, Syndicalist, and other organizations, with their slogan of "equality" do not present any exception to the rule. In regard to democracies this has been shown above. The inner organization of different socialist and similar groups pleading "equality" shows that perhaps in no other organization does such an enormous hierarchy and "bossism" exist as in these groups of levelers. "The Socialist leaders regard the masses only as the passive tools in their hands, as a series of zeros destined only to increase the significance of the figure on the left" (the importance of the leaders themselves), says E. Fournière, himself one of these socialists.[3] If in the statement there is an exaggeration, it is hardly considerable. At least, the best and the most competent investigators of the situation are unanimous in their conclusions of an enormous development of oligarchy and stratification within all these groups. The enormous potential taste for inequality of numerous "levelers" becomes at once conspicuous, as soon, indeed, as they happen to be victorious. In such cases they often exhibit a greater cruelty and contempt toward the masses than former kings and rulers. This has been repeated regularly in victorious revolutions where the levelers become dictators. Classical descriptions of the situation given by Plato and Aristotle, on the basis of the ancient Greek social revolutions, may be literally applied to all such cases, including the Bolshevist experiment.

To sum up: social stratification is a permanent characteristic of any organized society. "Varying in form, social stratification has existed in all societies which proclaimed the equality of men."[4] Feudalism and oligarchy continue to exist in science and arts, in politics and administration, in a gang of bandits, in democracies, among the levelers, everywhere.

This, however, does not mean that the stratification quantitatively or qualitatively is identical in all societies and at all times. In its concrete forms, defects or virtues, it certainly varies. The problem to be discussed now is these quantitative and qualitative variations. Begin with the quantitative aspect of social stratification in its three forms; economic, political and occupational. This is what is meant by the height and the profile of social stratification, and, correspondingly, the height and the profile of a "social building." How high is it? How long is the distance from the bottom to the top of a social cone? Of how many stories is it composed? Is its profile steep, or does it slope gradually? These are the problems of the quantitative analysis of social stratification. It deals, so to speak, exclusively with the exterior architecture of a social building. Its inner structure, in its entirety, is the object of the qualitative analysis. The study should begin with the height and the profile of the social pyramid. After that the pyramid should be entered and an investigation of its inner organization made from the standpoint of stratification.

3. Fournière, E., *La Sociocratie,* p. 117, 1910.
4. Pareto, V., *Traité de sociologie générale,* Vol. I, p. 613, Paris, 1917–1919.

# *8. Social Stratification and Class Structure*

BY MAX WEBER

## *The Concepts of Class and Class Status*

THE TERM "class status"[1] will be applied to the typical probability that a given state of (a) provision with goods, (b) external conditions of life, and (c) subjective satisfaction or frustration will be possessed by an individual or a group. These probabilities define class status in so far as they are dependent on the kind and extent of control or lack of it which the individual has over goods or services and existing possibilities of their exploitation for the attainment of income or receipts within a given economic order.

A "class" is any group of persons occupying the same class status. The following types of classes may be distinguished: (a) A class is a "property class" when class status for its members is primarily determined by the differentiation of property holdings; (b) a class is an "acquisition class" when the class situation of its members is primarily determined by their opportunity for the exploitation of services on the market; (c) the "social class" structure is composed of the plurality of class statuses between which an interchange of individuals on a personal basis or in the course of

Reprinted from Max Weber, *The Theory of Social and Economic Organization,* trans. A. M. Henderson and Talcott Parsons, ed. Talcott Parsons (Glencoe, Ill.: The Free Press, 1947), pp. 424–29. Copyright 1947 by Oxford University Press.

1. Weber uses the term "class" (*Klasse*) in a special sense, which is defined in this paragraph and which, in particular, he contrasts with *Stand.* There seems no other alternative translation of *Klasse,* but it should be kept in mind that it is being used in a special sense.—Ed.

generations is readily possible and typically observable. On the basis of any of the three types of class status, associative relationships between those sharing the same class interests, namely, corporate class organizations may develop. This need not, however, necessarily happen. The concepts of class and class status as such designate only the fact of identity or similarity in the typical situation in which a given individual and many others find their interests defined. In principle control over different combinations of consumers goods, means of production, investments, capital funds or marketable abilities constitute class statuses which are different with each variation and combination. Only persons who are completely unskilled, without property and dependent on employment without regular occupation, are in a strictly identical class status. Transitions from one class status to another vary greatly in fluidity and in the ease with which an individual can enter the class. Hence the unity of "social" classes is highly relative and variable.

The primary significance of a positively privileged property class lies in the following facts: (i) Its members may be able to monopolize the purchase of high-priced consumers goods. (ii) They may control the opportunities of pursuing a systematic monopoly policy in the sale of economic goods. (iii)They may monopolize opportunities for the accumulation of property through unconsumed surpluses. (iv) They may monopolize opportunities to accumulate capital by saving, hence, the possibility of investing property in loans and the related possibility of control over executive positions in business. (v) They may monopolize the privileges of socially advantageous kinds of education so far as these involve expenditures.

Positively privileged property classes typically live from property income. This may be derived from property rights in human beings, as with slaveowners, in land, in mining property, in fixed equipment such as plant and apparatus, in ships, and as creditors in loan relationships. Loans may consist of domestic animals, grain, or money. Finally they may live on income from securities.

Class interests which are negatively privileged with respect to property belong typically to one of the following types: (a) They are themselves objects of ownership, that is they are unfree. (b) They are "outcasts" that is "proletarians" in the sense meant in Antiquity. (c) They are debtor classes and, (d) the "poor."

In between stand the "middle" classes. This term includes groups who have all sorts of property, or of marketable abilities through training, who are in a position to draw their support from these sources. Some of them may be "acquisition" classes. Entrepreneurs are in this category by virtue of essentially positive privileges; proletarians, by virtue of negative privileges. But many types such as peasants, craftsmen, and officials do not fall in this category. The differentiation of classes on the basis of property alone is not "dynamic," that is, it does not necessarily result in class struggles or class revolutions. It is not uncommon for very strongly privileged property classes such as slaveowners, to exist side by side with such far less privileged groups as peasants or even outcasts without any class struggle. There may even be ties of solidarity between privileged property classes and unfree elements. However, such conflicts as that between creditors and debtors, the latter often being a question of urban patricians as opposed to either rural peasants or urban craftsmen, may lead to revolutionary conflict. Even this, however, need not necessarily aim at radical changes in economic organization. It may, on the contrary, be concerned in the first instance only with a redistribution of wealth. These may be called "property revolutions."

A classic example of the lack of class antagonism has been the relation of the "poor white trash," originally those not owning slaves, to the planters in the Southern States of the United States. The "poor whites" have often been much more hostile to the Negro than the planters who have frequently had a large element of patriarchal sentiment. The conflict of outcast against the property classes, of creditors and debtors, and of landowners and outcasts are best illustrated in the history of Antiquity.

### *The Significance of Acquisition Classes*

The primary significance of a positively privileged acquisition class is to be found in two directions. On the one hand it is generally possible to go far toward attaining a monopoly of the management of productive enterprises in favour of the members of the class and their business interests. On the other hand, such a class tends to insure the security of its economic position by exercising influence on the economic policy of political bodies and other groups.

The members of positively privileged acquisition classes are typically entrepreneurs. The following are the most important types: merchants, shipowners, industrial and agricultural entrepreneurs, bankers and financiers. Under certain circumstances two other types are also members of such classes, namely, members of the "liberal" professions with a privileged position by virtue of their abilities or training, and workers with special skills commanding a monopolistic position, regardless of how far they are hereditary or the result of training.

Acquisition classes in a negatively privileged situation are workers of the various principal types. They may be roughly classified as skilled, semi-skilled and unskilled.

In this connexion as well as the above, independent peasants and craftsmen are to be treated as belonging to the "middle classes." This category often includes in addition officials, whether they are in public or private employment, the liberal professions, and workers with exceptional monopolistic assets or positions.

Examples of "social classes" are (a) the "working" class as a whole. It approaches this type the more completely mechanized the productive process becomes. (b) The "lower middle" classes.[2] (c) The "intelligentsia" without independent property and the persons whose social position is primarily dependent on technical training such as engineers, commercial and other officials, and civil servants. These groups may differ greatly among themselves, in particular according to costs of training. (d) The classes occupying a privileged position through property and education.

The unfinished concluding section of Karl Marx's *Kapital* was evidently intended to deal with the problem of the class unity of the proletariat, which he held existed in spite of the high degree of qualitative differentiation. A decisive factor is the increase in the importance of semi-skilled workers who have been trained in a relatively short time directly on the machines themselves, at the expense of the older type of "skilled" labour and also of unskilled. However, even this type of skill may often have a monopolistic aspect. Weavers are said to attain the highest level of productivity only after five years' experience.

At an earlier period every worker could be said to have been primarily interested in becoming an independent small bourgeois, but the possibility of realizing this goal is becoming progressively smaller. From one generation to another the most readily available path to advancement both for skilled and semi-skilled workers is into the class of technically trained individuals. In the most highly privileged classes, at least over the period of more than one generation, it is coming more and more to be true that money is overwhelmingly decisive. Through the banks and corporate enterprises members of the lower middle class and the salaried groups have certain opportunities to rise into the privileged class.

Organized activity of class groups is favoured by the following circumstances: (a) the possibility of concentrating on opponents where the immediate conflict of interests is vital. Thus workers organize against management and not against security holders who are the ones who really draw income without working. Similarly peasants are not apt to organize against landlords. (b) The existence of a class status which is typically similar for large masses of people. (c) The technical possibility of being easily brought together. This is particularly true where large numbers work together in a small area, as in the modern factory. (d) Leadership directed to readily understandable goals. Such goals are very generally imposed or at least are interpreted by persons, such as intelligentsia, who do not belong to the class in question.

## *Social Strata and Their Status*

The term of "social status"[3] will be applied to a typically effective claim to positive or negative privilege with respect to social prestige so far as it rests on one or more of the following bases: (a) mode of living, (b) a formal process of education which may consist in empirical or rational training and the acquisition of the corresponding modes of life, or (c) on the prestige of birth, or of an occupation.

The primary practical manifestations of status with respect to social stratification are conubium, commensality, and often monopolistic appropriation of privileged economic opportunities and also prohibition of certain modes of acquisition. Finally, there are conventions or traditions of other types attached to a social status.

Stratificatory status may be based on class status directly or related to it in complex ways. It is not, however, determined by this alone. Property and managerial positions are not as such sufficient to lend their holder a certain social status, though they may well lead to its acquisition. Similarly, poverty is not as such a disqualification for high social status though again it may influence it.

Conversely, social status may partly or even wholly determine class status, without, however, being identical with it. The class status of an officer, a civil servant, and a student as determined by their income may be widely different while their social status remains the same, because they adhere to the same mode of life in all relevant respects as a result of their common education.

A social "*stratum*" *stand* is a plurality of individuals who, within a larger group, enjoy a particular kind and level of prestige by virtue of their position

2. Like the French "petite bourgeoisie," the German term *Kleinbürgertum* has a somewhat more specific meaning than the English "lower-middle class." It refers particularly to economically independent elements not employed in large-scale organizations. The typical example are the small shopkeeper and the proprietor of a small handicraft workshop.—ED.

3. *Ständische Lage*.—ED.

and possibly also claim certain special monopolies.

The following are the most important sources of the development of distinct strata: (a) The most important is by the development of a peculiar style of life including, particularly, the type of occupation pursued. (b) The second basis is hereditary charisma arising from the successful claim to a position of prestige by virtue of birth. (c) The third is the appropriation of political or hierocratic authority as a monopoly by socially distinct groups.

The development of hereditary strata is usually a form of the hereditary appropriation of privileges by an organized group or by individual qualified persons. Every well-established case of appropriation of opportunities and abilities, especially of exercising imperative powers, has a tendency to lead to the development of distinct strata. Conversely, the development of strata has a tendency in turn to lead to the monopolistic appropriation of governing powers and of the corresponding economic advantages.

Acquisition classes are favoured by an economic system oriented to market situations, whereas social strata develop and subsist most readily where economic organization is of a monopolistic and liturgical character and where the economic needs of corporate groups are met on a feudal or patrimonial basis. The type of class which is most closely related to a stratum is the "social" class, while the "acquisition" class is the farthest removed. Property classes often constitute the nucleus of a stratum.

Every society where strata play a prominent part is controlled to a large extent by conventional rules of conduct. It thus creates economically irrational conditions of consumption and hinders the development of free markets by monopolistic appropriation and by restricting free disposal of the individual's own economic ability. This will have to be discussed further elsewhere.[4]

4. This chapter breaks off at this point but is obviously incomplete. There is, however, no other part of Weber's published work in which the subject is systematically developed, although aspects of it are treated in different connexions at many points.—Ed.

# *Section D*

# Political Organization and Authority

EDITORIAL FOREWORD

# Political Organization and Authority

*by Talcott Parsons*

IN CONSIDERING THE POLITICAL aspect of social structure, one is faced—as in the economic case, though not in that of stratification—with a plethora of materials from which to choose. In both the political and the economic cases, this situation is a result of the existence of social science disciplines which had become firmly established before sociology emerged, and developed a very important literature independent of sociology. We have touched on this literature at various points; but the present section is, with only two exceptions, confined to selections whose major direct reference is sociological. This decision is justified by our limited available space and by the extent to which political theory figures in our general historical prolegomena, as shown in Part One, Section A.

Orientation to the utilitarian-Marxist point of view is a major axis of organization for this Reader. One aspect of this tradition—that we deliberately use as a counterfoil—has been its allegedly "hard" and "realistic" emphasis on economic interest. The obverse is the tradition's utopian element—Locke's postulation of the "natural identity of interests," as Halevy called it, was an early version of this.[1] In its political context, this utopian element culminates in the Marxist doctrine of the "withering away of the state"—which had precedents in Godwinian "anarchism" and similar pre-Marxian movements. We have begun this section of selections with a violent contrast. First, we present the selection, from Lenin's *State and Revolution,* incorporating the doctrine of "withering away" in the strong form which has become canonical for the Communist movement. This is followed by a selection from Pareto that—in this area, as distinct from the economic—presents a sharply "realistic" view of the inevitability of the use of force in social affairs. This juxtaposition presents the fundamental problem of the conditions of order. In modern thought, this problem's first classical formulation occurred in the conflict between Hobbes and Locke, as outlined above in the Introduction to Part One, Section A. In its relation to collective goal-attainment this is the fundamental setting of the political problem, viewed from our sociological perspective.

The questions of political equality, and of the senses in which various kinds of inequality are functional necessities, are involved deeply here. The so-called "élitist" theorists of the early twentieth century were especially concerned with the problem. The theme of the integration of the class structure with political authority and leadership was developed in a particularly well-rounded and sophisticated way by Mosca, whose analysis has been very influential in subsequent political thinking. The second selection relevant here is from Michels' book on political parties, stressing the oligarchic element existing in party leadership whatever the party's program. In general, these views were consequences of disillusionment with the more utopian convictions of the democratic liberalism of the intellectual circles of the political left in Europe during the later nineteenth century. They indicated important problems concerning the realistic structure of political systems as these were integrated with other elements of the social structure.

The second subsection is concerned less with the conflict between ideals of equality and the elements of political structure making for inequality; it is

1. In the interpretive literature on Marxism, the most insightful discussion of this component known to us is by Ernest Troeltsch, *Der Historismus und Seine Probleme* (Tübingen: J. C. B. Mohr), Chap. III, section 4.

more concerned with positive institutionalization in the area of political function. Much political theory has dealt with problems which, like that of "sovereignty," treat the direct relation of the individual to the state as a whole. However, the great German legal historian, Otto von Gierke, presented the classic analysis of the development of the corporation as a type of collectivity sanctioned in law, standing between the individual and the state, having privileges of acting responsibly in concert, holding property, etc. This indicates especially that many private and semi-public collectivities are not the atomistic associations of discrete individuals that much of utilitarian theory postulated. By the same token, the "state," conceived as the over-all collectivity structure of a society, is not a simple aggregation of individuals; but individuals' relations to the higher authorities are mediated by a complex network of more or less corporate subcollectivities.

Since all sophisticated law in the Western world is based on the Roman model, it is particularly important that Roman Law was, on normative grounds, hostile to corporate collectivities within the state that could possibly serve as a focus of alienation from over-all loyalty to the state—a hostility based on the pattern of the Greek *polis*. Gierke's most important direct contribution was showing how, in Europe, the corporate idea that derived from Germanic and feudal sources gradually attained a permanent place in the normative structure of Western society—a place which fundamentally distinguishes Western society from the society of classical antiquity. This emphasis is significant for the major theme of structural differentiation that has been one of our major guides in treating social morphology.

The last two selections in this section are chosen on the same principle as those dealing with the problem of inequality. The first, from Max Weber, concerns the broadest bases of the society-wide organization of political authority. The second, from Barnard, deals with the problem at the level of a more specific type of collectivity within the society.

Weber's classification of three major types of "authority" (in German, *legitime Herrschaft*) has probably influenced political science more than any other single contribution from sociology. Its primary theme concerns modes of legitimizing the right to make collective decisions which are binding on a societal collectivity as a whole. It fits in a comparative and in an evolutionary perspective. Weber did not himself fully clarify the status of these concepts—the three cases are not on the same level. Working out this problem is, however, the task of a generation of theorists later than Weber's. His classification has proved a focus for much fruitful comparative analysis and for integration with a variety of non-political phenomena.

The last selection is the chapter on authority from Chester I. Barnard's *Functions of the Executive*. Barnard was a business executive when he wrote it, and he refers primarily to business organizations. His analysis is, however, on such a general level that it presents a prototype for analyzing this problem, with special reference to the collectivity which, like those with which Gierke is concerned, stands between the individual and the state.

## I–POWER AND INEQUALITY

# 1. *The Withering Away of the State*

BY NICOLAI LENIN

IN THE USUAL debates about the State, it is constantly forgotten that the destruction of the State involves also the destruction of democracy; that the withering away of the State also means the withering away of Democracy. At first sight such a statement seems exceedingly strange and incomprehensible. Indeed, perhaps some one or other may begin to fear lest we be expecting the advent of such an order of society in which the principle of majority rule will not be respected—for is not a

Reprinted from Nicolai Lenin, *State and Revolution*, trans. Moissaye J. Olgin (New York: International Publishers, 1932), chap. v, pp. 84–105, with the permission of International Publishers.

Democracy just the recognition of this principle?

No, Democracy is not identical with majority rule. No, Democracy is a *State* which recognizes the subjection of the minority to the majority, that is, an organization for the systematic use of *violence* by one class against the other, by one part of the population against another.

We set ourselves, as our final aim, the task of the destruction of the State, that is, of every organized and systematic violence, every form of violence against man in general. We do not expect the advent of an order of society in which the principle of the submission of the minority to the majority will not be observed. But, striving for Socialism, we are convinced that it will develop further into Communism, and, side by side with this, there will vanish all need for force, for the *subjection* of one man to another, of one section of society to another, since people will *grow accustomed* to observing the elementary conditions of social existence *without force and without subjection.*

In order to emphasize this element of habit, Engels speaks of a *new* generation, "brought up under new and free social conditions which will prove capable of throwing on the dustheap all the useless old rubbish of State Organization"—*every* sort of State, including even the democratic republican State.

For the elucidation of this, we must examine the question of the economic foundations of the withering away of the State.

A most detailed elucidation of this question is given by Marx in his *Criticism of the Gotha Programme* (letter to Bracke, May 15th, 1875, printed as late as 1891 in the *Neue Zeit,* ix. 1). The polemical part of this remarkable work consisting of a criticism of Lassalleanism has, so to speak, overshadowed its positive part, namely the analysis of the connection between the development of Communism and the withering away of the State.

## *The Formulation of the Question by Marx*

From a superficial comparison of the letter of Marx to Bracke (May 15th, 1875) with Engels' letter to Bebel (March 28th, 1875), discussed above, it might appear that Marx was much more of an upholder of the State than Engels, and that the difference of opinion between them on the question of the State is very considerable.

Engels suggests to Bebel that all the chatter about the State should be thrown overboard; that the word "State" should be eliminated from the programme and replaced by "Commonwealth"; Engels even declares that the Commune was really no longer a State in the proper sense of the word. Whereas Marx even speaks of the "future State in Communist society," that is, apparently recognizing the necessity of a State even under Communism.

But such a view would be fundamentally incorrect; and a closer examination shows that Marx's and Engels' views on the State and its decay were completely identical, and that Marx's expression quoted above refers merely to the *decaying* State.

It is clear that there can be no question of defining the exact moment of the *future* "withering away"—the more so as it must obviously be a prolonged process. The apparent difference between Marx and Engels is due to the different subjects they dealt with, the different aims they were pursuing. Engels set forth the problem in a plain, bold, and large outline in order to show Bebel all the absurdity of the current superstitions concerning the State, shared to no small degree by Lassalle himself. Marx only touches upon *this* question in passing, being interested mainly in another subject—the *evolution* of Communist society. The whole theory of Marx is an application of the theory of evolution—in its most consistent, complete, well-thought-out and fruitful form—to modern Capitalism. Naturally, for Marx there arose the question of the application of this theory both to the *coming* crash of Capitalism and to the *future* development of *future* Communism.

On what foundation of facts can the future development of future Communism be based? It can be based on the fact that *it has its origin* in Capitalism, that it develops historically from Capitalism, that it is the result of the action of social forces to which Capitalism *has given birth.* There is no shadow of an attempt on Marx's part to fabricate a Utopia, idly to guess that which cannot be known. Marx treats the question of Communism in the same way as a naturalist would treat the question of the development of, say, a new biological variety, if he knew that such and such was its origin, and such and such is the direction in which it changes its form.

Marx, first of all, brushes aside the confusion which is introduced by the Gotha programme into the question of the mutual relations of State and of Society.

> Contemporary society, [he writes] is capitalist society, which exists in all civilized countries, freed, to a greater or lesser extent, from admixture of mediaevalism, more or less varying in type according to the peculiar historical conditions of development of each country, more or less fully developed. The "contemporary State," on the contrary, varies with every State boundary. In the Prusso-German Empire it is quite a different thing from that in Switzerland; in

England quite different from that in the United States. The "contemporary State" is, therefore a fiction.

"However, in spite of the motley variety of their forms, the different forms of the State in the different civilized countries have this in common—they are all based on contemporary bourgeois society, more or less capitalistically developed. They have, therefore, certain fundamental traits in common. In this sense one can speak of the "contemporary State" in contradistinction to that future time when its present root, namely, capitalist society, will have perished.

"The question is then put thus: To what transformation will the forms of government be subjected in communist society? In other words, what social functions will there remain, then, analogous to the present functions of the State? This question can only be answered with the help of the scientific method; and however many thousands of times the word "people" is combined with the word "State," this will not bring us one iota nearer its solution. . . .

Having thus ridiculed all the talk of a "People's State," Marx formulates the question and warns us, as it were, that for a scientific answer to it one can only rely on firmly established scientific facts.

The first fact that has been established with complete exactness by the whole theory of evolution, indeed, by the whole of science—a fact which the utopians forgot, however, and which is now forgotten by the present Opportunists, afraid of the Socialist revolution—is that, historically, there must undoubtedly be a special stage or epoch of *transition* from Capitalism to Communism.

## *The Transition from Capitalism to Communism*

Between capitalist and communist society, [Marx continues] there lies a period of revolutionary transformation from the former to the latter. A stage of political transition corresponds to this period, and the State during this period can be no other than the *revolutionary dictatorship of the proletariat.*

This conclusion Marx bases on an analysis of the role played by the proletariat in modern capitalist society, on the facts of the development of this society and on the irreconcilability of the antagonistic interests of the proletariat and the capitalist class.

Earlier the question was put thus: To attain its emancipation the proletariat must overthrow the capitalist class, conquer political power and establish its own revolutionary dictatorship. Now the question is put somewhat differently: The transition from capitalist society developing towards Communism, to a communist Society, is impossible without a period of "political transition," and the State in this period can only be the revolutionary dictatorship of the proletariat.

What, then, is the relation of this dictatorship to democracy?

We saw that the *Communist Manifesto* simply places side by side the two ideas: the "conversion of the proletariat into the ruling class" and the "conquest of Democracy." On the basis of all that has been said above, one can define more exactly how democracy changes in the transition from Capitalism to Communism.

In capitalist society, under the conditions most favorable to its development, we have a more or less complete democracy in the form of a democratic republic. But this democracy is always bound by the narrow framework of capitalist exploitation, and, consequently, always remains, in reality, a democracy only for the minority, only for the possessing classes, only for the rich. Freedom in capitalist society always remains more or less the same as it was in the ancient Greek republics, that is, freedom for the slave owners. The modern wage-slaves, in virtue of the conditions of capitalist exploitation, remain to such an extent crushed by want and poverty that they "cannot be bothered with democracy," have "no time for politics"; that, in the ordinary peaceful course of events, the majority of the population is debarred from participating in public political life.

The accuracy of this statement is perhaps most clearly proved by Germany, just because in this state constitutional legality has lasted and remained stable for a remarkably long time—for nearly half a century (1871–1914); and the Social-Democracy during this time has been able, far better than has been the case in other countries, to make use of "legality" in order to organize into a political party a larger proportion of the working class than has occurred anywhere else in the world.

What, then, is this highest proportion of politically conscious, and active wage-slaves that has so far been observed in capitalist society? One million members of the Social-Democratic Party out of fifteen millions of wage-workers! Three millions industrially organized out of fifteen millions!

Democracy for an insignificant minority, democracy for the rich—that is the democracy of capitalist society. If we look more closely into the mechanism of capitalist democracy, everywhere—in the so-called "petty" details of the suffrage (the residential qualification, the exclusion of women, etc.), in the technique of the representative institutions, in the actual obstacles to the right of meeting (public buildings are not for the "poor"), in the purely capitalist organization of the daily press, etc., etc.—on all sides we shall see restrictions upon restrictions of Democracy. These restrictions, exceptions, exclusions, obstacles for the poor, seem light—especially in the eyes of one who has himself never known want, and has never lived in close contact with the oppressed classes in their herd life, and nine-tenths, if not ninety-nine hundredths, of the bourgeois publicists and politicians are of this class! But in their sum these restrictions exclude and thrust out the poor from politics and from an active share in democracy. Marx splendidly grasped the *essence* of capitalist democracy, when, in his analysis of the experience of the Commune, he said that the oppressed are allowed, once every few years, to decide which particular representatives of the oppressing class are to represent and repress them in Parliament!

But from this capitalist democracy—inevitably narrow, stealthily thrusting aside the poor, and therefore to its core, hypocritical and treacherous —progress does not march along a simple, smooth and direct path to "greater and greater democracy," as the Liberal professors and the lower middle-class Opportunists would have us believe. No, progressive development—that is, towards Communism—marches through the dictatorship of the proletariat; and cannot do otherwise, for there is no one else who can *break the resistance* of the exploiting capitalists, and no other way of doing it.

And the dictatorship of the proletariat—that is, the organization of the advance-guard of the oppressed as the ruling class, for the purpose of crushing the oppressors—cannot produce merely an expansion of democracy. *Together* with an immense expansion of democracy—for the first time becoming democracy for the poor, democracy for the people, and not democracy for the rich folk—the dictatorship of the proletariat will produce a series of restrictions of liberty in the case of the oppressors, exploiters and capitalists. We must crush them in order to free humanity from wage-slavery; their resistance must be broken by force. It is clear that where there is suppression there most also be violence, and there cannot be liberty or democracy.

Engels expressed this splendidly in his letter to Bebel when he said, as the reader will remember, that "the proletariat needs the State, not in the interests of liberty, but for the purpose of crushing its opponents; and, when one will be able to speak of freedom, the State will have ceased to exist."

Democracy for the vast majority of the nation, and the suppression by force—that is, the exclusion from democracy—of the exploiters and oppressors of the nation: this is the modification of democracy which we shall see during the *transition* from Capitalism to Communism.

Only in Communist Society, when the resistance of the capitalists has finally been broken, when the capitalists have disappeared, when there are no longer any classes (that is, when there is no difference between the members of society in respect of their social means of production), *only then* "does the State disappear *and one can speak of freedom.*" Only then will be possible and will be realized a really full democracy, a democracy without any exceptions. And only then will democracy itself begin to wither away in virtue of the simple fact that, freed from capitalist slavery, from the innumerable horrors, savagery, absurdities and infamies of capitalist exploitation, people will gradually *become accustomed* to the observation of the elementary rules of social life, known for centuries, repeated for thousands of years in all sermons. They will become accustomed to their observance without force, without constraint, without subjection, without the *special apparatus* for compulsion which is called the State.

The expression "the State withers away," is very well chosen, for it indicates the gradual and elemental nature of the process. Only habit can, and undoubtedly will, have such an effect: for we see around us millions of times how readily people get accustomed to observe the necessary rules of life in common, if there is no exploitation, if there is nothing that causes indignation, that calls forth protest and revolt and has to be suppressed.

Thus, in capitalist society, we have a democracy that is curtailed, wretched, false; a democracy only for the rich, for the minority. The dictatorship of the proletariat, the period of transition to Communism, will, for the first time, produce a democracy for the people, for the majority, side by side with the necessary suppression of the minority constituted by the exploiters. Communism alone is capable of giving a really complete democracy, and the fuller it is the more quickly will it become unnecessary and wither away of itself. In other words, under Capitalism we have a State in the proper sense of the word: that is, a special instrument for the suppression of one class by another, and of the majority by the minority at that. Naturally, for the successful discharge of such a task as the systematic suppression by the minority of exploiters of the majority of exploited, the greatest ferocity and savagery of suppression is required, and seas of blood are needed, through which humanity has to direct its path, in a condition of slavery, serfdom and wage labor.

Again, during the *transition* from Capitalism to Communism, suppression is *still* necessary; but in this case it is the suppression of the minority of exploiters by the majority of exploited. A special instrument, a special machine for suppression—that is, the "State"—is necessary, but this is now a transitional State, no longer a State in the ordinary sense of the term. For the suppression of the minority of exploiters by the majority of those who were *but yesterday* wage slaves, is a matter comparatively so easy, simple and natural that it will cost far less bloodshed than the suppression of the risings of the slaves, serfs or wage laborers, and will cost the human race far less. And it is compatible with the diffusion of democracy over such an overwhelming majority of the nation that the need for any *special machinery* for suppression will gradually cease to exist. The exploiters are unable, of course, to suppress the people without a most complex machine for performing this duty; but *the people* can suppress the exploiters even with a very simple "machine"—almost without any "machine" at all, without any special apparatus—by the simple *organization of the armed masses* (such as the Councils of Workers' and Soldiers' Deputies, we may remark, anticipating a little).

Finally, only under Communism will the State become quite unnecessary, for there will be *no one* to suppress—"no one" in the sense of a *class,* in the sense of a systematic struggle with a definite section of the population. We are not utopians, and we do not in the least deny the possibility and inevitability of excesses by *individual persons,* and equally the need to suppress such excesses. But, in the first place, for this no special machine, no special instrument of repression is needed. This will be done by the armed nation itself, as simply and as readily as any crowd of civilized people, even in modern society, parts a pair of combatants or does not allow a woman to be outraged. And, secondly, we know that the fundamental social cause of excesses which violate the rules of social life is the exploitation of the masses, their want and their poverty. With the removal of this chief cause, excesses will inevitably begin to "wither away." We do not know how quickly and in what stages, but we know that they will be withering away. With their withering away, the State will also wither away. Marx, without plunging into Utopia, defined more fully what can *now* be defined regarding this future epoch: namely, the difference between the higher and lower phases (degrees, stages) of Communist society.

## *The First Phase of Communist Society*

In the *Criticism of the Gotha Programme* Marx disproves in detail the Lassallean idea of the receipt by the workers under Socialism of the "undiminished" or "full product of their labor." Marx shows that out of the whole of the social labor of society, it will be necessary to deduct a reserve fund, a fund for the expansion of industry, the replacement of "worn-out" machinery, and so on; then, also, out of the collective product, a fund for the expenses of management, for schools, hospitals, homes for the aged, and so forth.

Instead of the hazy, obscure, general phrase of Lassalle—"the full product of his labor for the worker"—Marx gives a sober estimate as to how exactly a Socialist society will have to manage its affairs. Marx takes up a *concrete* analysis of the conditions of life of a society in which there will be no capitalism, and says: "We have to deal here" (analyzing the programme of the Party), "not with a Communist society which has *developed* on its own foundations, but with one which has just *issued* actually from capitalist society, and which in consequence, in all respects—economic, moral, and intellectual—still bears the stamp of the old society, from the womb of which it came." And it is this Communist society—a society which has just come into the world out of the womb of Capitalism, and which, in all respects, bears the stamp of the old society—that Marx terms the first, or lower, phase of Communist society.

The means of production are now no longer the private property of individuals. The means of production belong to the whole of society. Every member of society, performing a certain part of socially-necessary labor, receives a certificate from society that he has done such and such a quantity of work. According to this certificate, he receives from the public stores of articles of consumption a corresponding quantity of products. After the deduction of that proportion of labor which goes into the public fund, every worker, therefore, receives from society as much as he has given it.

"Equality" seems to reign supreme. But when Lassalle, having in view such a social order (generally called "Socialism," but termed by Marx the first phase of Communism) speaks of this as "just distribution," and says that this is "the equal right of each to an equal share of the products of labor," Lassalle is mistaken, and Marxism explains his error.

Equal right [says Marx], we indeed have here; but it is *still* a "bourgeois right," which, like every right *presupposes inequality*. Every "right" is an application of the *same* measure to *different* people who, as a matter of fact, are not similar and are not equal one to another; and, therefore, "equal right" is really a violation of equality, and an injustice. In effect every man having done as much social labor as every other, receives an equal share of the social product (with the above-mentioned deductions). Notwithstanding this, different people are not equal to one another. One is strong, another is weak; one is man ried, the other is not. One has more children, another has less, and so on.

> With equal labor [Marx concludes], and therefore with an equal share in the public stock of articles of consumption, one will, in reality, receive more than another, will find himself richer, and so on. To avoid all this, "rights," instead of being equal, should be unequal.

The first phase of Communism, therefore, still cannot produce justice and equality; differences, and unjust differences, in wealth will still exist, but the *exploitation* of one man by many, will have become impossible, because it will be impossible to seize as private property, the *means of production,* the factories, machines, land, and so on. While tearing to tatters Lassalle's small bourgeois, confused phrase about "equality" and "justice" *in general,* Marx at the same time shows the *line of development* of Communist society, which is forced at first to destroy *only* the "injustice" that the means of production are in the hands of private individuals. *It is not capable* of destroying at once the further injustice which is constituted by the distribution of the articles of consumption according to "work performed" (and not according to need).

The vulgar economists, including the bourgeois professors (such as "our" Tugan-Baranowsky), constantly reproach the Socialists with forgetting the inequality of mankind and with "dreaming" of destroying this inequality. Such a reproach, as we see, only proves the extreme ignorance of the bourgeois ideologists.

Marx not only, with the greatest care, takes into account the inevitable inequalities of men; he also takes cognizance of the fact that the mere conversion of the means of production into the common property of the whole of society—"Socialism" in the generally accepted sense of the word—*does not remove* the shortcomings of distribution and the inequality of "bourgeois justice," which continue to exist as long as the products are divided according to the quantity of "work performed."

> But these defects [Marx continues] are unavoidable in the first phase of Communist society, in the form in which it comes forth, after the prolonged travail of birth, from capitalist society. Justice can never be in advance of its stage of economic development, and of the cultural development of society conditioned by the latter.

And so, in the first phase of Communist society (generally called Socialism) "bourgeois justice" is *not* abolished in its entirety, but only in part, only in proportion to the economic transformation so far attained, that is, only in respect of the means of production. "Bourgeois law" recognizes them as the private property of separate individuals. Socialism converts them into common property, and to that extent and only to that extent, does "bourgeois law" die out. But it continues to live as far as its other part is concerned, in the capacity of regulator or adjuster dividing labor and allotting the products among the members of society.

"He who does not work neither shall he eat"—this Socialist principle is *already* realized. "For an equal quantity of labor an equal quantity of products"—this Socialist principle is also already realized. Nevertheless, this is not yet Communism, and this does not abolish "bourgeois law," which gives to unequal individuals, in return for an unequal (in reality) amount of work, an equal quantity of products.

This is a "defect," says Marx, but it is unavoidable during the first phase of Communism; for, if we are not to land in Utopia, we cannot imagine that, having overthrown Capitalism, people will at once learn to work for society *without any regulations by law;* indeed, the abolition of Capitalism does not *immediately* lay the economic foundations for such a change.

And there is no other standard yet than that of "bourgeois law." To this extent, therefore, a form of State is still necessary, which, while maintaining the public ownership of the means of production, preserves the equality of labor and equality in the distribution of the products. The State is withering away in so far as there are no longer any capitalists, any classes, and, consequently, any *class* whatever to suppress. But the State is not yet dead altogether, since there still remains the protection of "bourgeois law," which sanctifies actual inequality. For the complete extinction of the State complete Communism is necessary.

## *The Highest Phase of Communist Society*

Marx continues:

> In the highest phase of Communist society, after the disappearance of the enslavement of man caused by his subjection to the principle of division of labor; when, together with this, the opposition between brain and manual work will have disappeared; when labor will have ceased to be a mere means of supporting life and will itself have become one of the first necessities of life; when, with the all-round development of the individual, the productive forces, too, will have grown to maturity, and all the forces of social wealth will be pouring an uninterrupted torrent—only then will it be possible wholly to pass beyond the narrow horizon of bourgeois laws, and only then will Society be able to inscribe on its banner: "From each according to his ability; to each according to his needs."

Only now can we appreciate the full justice of Engels' observations when he mercilessly ridiculed all the absurdity of combining the words "freedom" and "State." While the State exists there can be no freedom. When there is freedom there will be no State.

The economic basis for the complete withering away of the State is that high stage of development of Communism when the distinction between brain and manual work disappears; consequently, when one of the principal sources of modern *social* inequalities will have vanished—a source, moreover, which it is impossible to remove immediately by the mere conversion of the means of production into public property, by the mere expropriation of the capitalists.

This expropriation will make it possible gigantically to develop the forces of production. And seeing how incredibly, even now, Capitalism *retards* this development, how much progress could be made even on the basis of modern technique at the level it has reached, we have a right to say, with the fullest confidence, that the expropriation of the capitalists will result inevitably in a gigantic development of the productive forces of human society. But how rapidly this development will go forward, how soon it will reach the point of breaking away from the division of labor, of the destruction of the antagonism between brain and manual work, of the transformation of work into a "first necessity of life"—this we do not and *cannot* know.

Consequently, we are right in speaking solely of the inevitable withering away of the State, emphasizing the protracted nature of this process, and its dependence upon the rapidity of development of the *higher phase* of Communism; leaving quite open the question of lengths of time, or the concrete forms of this withering away, since material for the solution of such questions is not available.

The State will be able to wither away completely when Society has realized the formula: "From each according to his ability; to each according to his needs"; that is, when people have become accustomed to observe the fundamental principles of social life, and their labor is so productive, that they will voluntarily work *according to their abilities.* "The narrow horizon of bourgeois law," which compels one to calculate, with the pitilessness of a Shylock, whether one has not worked half an hour more than another, whether one is not getting less pay than another—this narrow horizon will then be left behind. There will then be no need for any exact calculation by Society of the quantity of products to be distributed to each of its members; each will take freely "according to his needs."

From the capitalist point of view, it is easy to declare such a social order a "pure Utopia," and to sneer at the Socialists for promising each the right to receive from society, without any control of the labor of the individual citizens, any quantity of truffles, motor cars, pianos, and so forth. Even now, most bourgeois "*savants*" deliver themselves of such sneers, but thereby they only display at once their ignorance and their material interest in defending Capitalism. Ignorance—for it has never entered the head of any Socialist "to promise" that the highest phase of Communism will actually arrive, while the *anticipation* of the great Socialists that it *will* arrive, assumes *neither the present* productive powers of labor, *nor the present* unthinking "man in the street" capable of spoiling, without reflection, the stores of social wealth and of demanding the impossible. As long as the "highest" phase of Communism has not arrived, the Socialists demand the *strictest* control, *by Society and by the State,* of the quantity of labor and the quantity of consumption; only this control must *start* with the expropriation of the capitalists, with the control of the workers over the capitalists, and must be carried out, not by a Government of bureaucrats, but by a Government of the *armed workers.*

The interested defence of Capitalism by the capitalist ideologists (and their hangers-on like Tseretelli, Tchernoff and Co.) consists just in that they *substitute* their disputes and discussions about the far future for the essential, imperative questions *of the day:* the expropriation of the capitalists, the conversion of *all* citizens into workers and employees of *one* huge "syndicate"—the whole State—and the complete subordination of the whole of the work of this syndicate to a really democratic State—to the *State consisting of the Councils of Workers' and Soldiers' Deputies.* In reality, when a learned professor, and in his train, some philistine, and in his wake Messrs. Tseretelli and Tchernoff, talk of the unreasonable Utopias, of the demagogic promises of the Bolsheviks, of the impossibility of "bringing in" Socialism, it is the highest stage or phase of Communism which they have in mind, and which no one has not only not promised, but never even thought of trying to "bring in," because, in any case, it is altogether impossible to "bring it in."

And here we come to that question of the scientific difference between Socialism and Communism, upon which Engels touched in his discussion cited above on the incorrectness of the name "Social Democrat." The political difference between the first, or lower, and the higher phase of Communism will in time, no doubt, be tremendous; but it would be ridiculous to emphasize it now, under Capitalism, and only, perhaps, some isolated Anarchist could invest it with primary importance,—that is, if there are still people among the Anarchists who have learned nothing from the Plekhanoff-like conversion of the Kropotkins, the Graves, the Cornelisens, and other "leading lights" of Anarchism to Social-Chauvinism or Anarcho-*Jusquauboutism* as one of the few Anarchists still preserving their honor (Gay) has expressed it.

But the scientific difference between Socialism and Communism is clear. That which is generally called Socialism is termed by Marx the first or lower phase of Communist society. In so far as the means of production become public property, the word Communism is also applicable here, providing that we do not forget that it is not full Communism. The great importance of Marx's explanation is this: that here, too, he consistently applies materialist dialectics, the theory of evolution, looking upon Communism as something which evolves *out* of Capitalism.

Instead of artificially elaborate and scholastic definitions and profitless disquisitions on the meanings of words ("what Socialism is," "what Communism is"), Marx gives us an analysis of what may be called the stages in the economic growth of Communism.

In its first phase or first stage Communism *cannot* as yet be economically mature and quite free of all tradition and of all taint of Capitalism. Hence we see the interesting phenomenon of the first phase of Communism retaining "the narrow horizon of bourgeois law." Bourgeois law, in respect of the distribution of articles of consumption, presupposes inevitably the capitalist State, for law is nothing without the organization for *forcing* people to obey it. Consequently, for a certain time not only bourgeois law, but even the capitalist State may remain under Communism without the capitalist class.

This may appear to some a paradox, a piece of intellectual subtlety, of which Marxism is often accused by people who would not put themselves out to study its extraordinarily profound teachings. But, as a matter of fact, the Old surviving in the New confronts us in life at every step in nature as well as in Society. It is not Marx's own sweet will which smuggled a scrap of bourgeois law into Communism; he simply indicated what is economically and politically inevitable in a society issuing from the *womb of Capitalism.*

Democracy is of great importance in the working-class struggle for freedom against the capitalists. But Democracy is not a limit one may not overstep; it is merely one of the stages in the course of development from Feudalism to Capitalism, and from Capitalism to Communism.

Democracy implies equality. The immense significance of the struggle of the proletariat for equality and the power of attraction of such a battle-cry are obvious, if we but rightly interpret it as meaning the *annihilation of classes.* But the equality of Democracy is *formal* equality—no more; and immediately after the attainment of the equality of all members of society in respect to the ownership of the means of production, that is, of equality of labor and equality of wages, there will inevitably arise before humanity the question of going further from equality which is formal to equality which is real, and of realizing in life the formula "From each according to his ability; to each according to his needs." By what stages, by means of what practical measures humanity will proceed to this higher aim—this we do not and cannot know. But it is important that one should realize how infinitely mendacious is the usual capitalist representation of Socialism as something lifeless, petrified, fixed once for all. In reality, it is *only* with Socialism that there will commence a rapid, genuine, real mass advance, in which first the majority and then the *whole* of the population will take part—an advance in all domains of social and individual life.

Democracy is a form of the State—one of the varieties of the State; and, consequently, like every State, it stands as an organized, systematic application of force against mankind. That is its one aspect. But, on the other hand, it is the formal recognition of the equality of all citizens, the equal right of all to determine the structure and administration of the State. Out of this formal recognition there arises, in its turn, a stage in the development of Democracy, when it first rallies the proletariat as a revolutionary class against Capitalism, and gives it an opportunity to crush, to break to atoms, to wipe off the face of the earth the capitalist government machine—even the republican variety: the standing army, police, and bureaucracy. Second, it enables it to substitute for all this a more democratic, but still a *State* machinery in the shape of armed masses of the working class, which then become transformed into a universal participation of the people in a militia.

Here "quantity passes into quality." Such a degree of Democracy carries with it the abandonment of the framework of capitalist society, and the beginning of its Socialist reconstruction. If *everyone really* takes part in the administration of the State, Capitalism cannot retain its hold. As a matter of fact, Capitalism as it develops, itself prepares the ground for everyone to be able really to take part in the administration of the State.

We may class as part of this preparation of the ground the universal literacy of the population, already realized in most of the more progressive capitalist countries; then the education and discipline inculcated upon millions of workers by the huge, complex, and socialized apparatus of the post, railways, big factories, large-scale commerce, banking, and so on, and so forth.

With such an *economic* groundwork it is quite possible, immediately, within twenty-four hours, to pass to the overthrow of the capitalists and bureaucrats, and to replace them, in the control of production and distribution, in the business of apportioning labor and products, by the armed workers, or the people in arms. The question of control and book-keeping must not be confused with the question of the scientifically educated staff of engineers, agriculturists, and so on. These gentlemen work today owing allegiance to the capitalists: they will work even better tomorrow, owing it to the armed workers. Book-keeping and control—these are the chief things necessary for the smooth and correct functioning of the *first phase* of Communist society. *All* the citizens are here transformed into the hired employees of the State, which then is the armed workers. *All* citizens become the employees and workers of *one* national *State* "syndicate." It simply resolves itself into a question of all working to an equal extent, of all carrying out regularly the measure of work apportioned to them, and of all receiving equal pay.

The book-keeping and control necessary for this have been simplified by capitalism to the utmost, till they have become the extraordinarily simple operations of watching, recording, and issuing receipts, within the reach of anybody who can read and write and knows the first four arithmetical rules. (When most of the functions of the State are reduced to this book-keeping and control by the workers themselves it ceases to be a "political" State. Then "the public functions are converted from political into simple administrative functions.") When the majority of the citizens themselves begin everywhere to keep such accounts and maintain such control over the capitalists, now converted into employees, and over the intellectual gentry, who still retain capitalist habits, this control will, indeed, become universal, pervading, rational: it will be ubiquitous, and there will be no way of escaping it.

The whole of society will have become one office and one factory, with equal work and equal pay. But this "factory" discipline, which the proletariat will extend to the whole of society on the defeat of Capitalism and the overthrow of the exploiters, is by no means our ideal, and is far from our final aim. It is but a foothold as we press on to the radical cleansing of society from all the brutality and foulness of capitalist exploitation: we leave it behind as we move on.

When all, or be it even only the greater part of society, have learnt how to govern the State, have taken this business into their own hands, have established a control over the insignificant minority of capitalists, over the gentry with capitalist leanings, and workers thoroughly demoralized by capitalism—from this moment the need for any government begins to vanish. The more complete the Democracy, the nearer the moment when it ceases to be necessary. The more democratic the "State" consisting of armed workers, which is "no longer really a State in the ordinary sense of the term," the more rapidly does every form of the State begin to decay. For when all have learnt to manage, and really do manage, socialized production, when all really do keep account and control of the idlers, gentlefolk, swindlers, and suchlike "guardians of capitalist traditions," the escape from such general registration and control will inevitably become so increasingly difficult, so much the exception, and will probably be accompanied by such swift and severe punishment (for the armed workers are very practical people, not sentimental intellectuals, and they will scarcely allow anyone to trifle with them), that very soon the *necessity* of observing the simple, fundamental rules of any kind of social life will become a habit. The door will then be wide open for the transition from the first phase of Communist society to its second and higher phase, and along with it to the complete withering away of the State.

# 2. *The Use of Force in Society*

BY VILFREDO PARETO

**2170.** Societies in general subsist because alive and vigorous in the majority of their constituent members are sentiments corresponding to residues of sociality. But there are also individuals in human societies in whom some at least of those sentiments are weak or indeed actually missing. That fact has two interesting consequences which stand in apparent contradiction, one of them threatening the dissolution of a society, the other making for its progress in civilization. What at bottom is there is continuous movement, but it is a movement that may progress in almost any direction.

**2171.** It is evident that if the requirement of uniformity were so strongly active in all individuals in a given society as to prevent even one of them from breaking away in any particular from the uniformities prevalent in it, such a society would have no internal causes for dissolution; but neither would it have any causes for change, whether in the direction of an increase, or of a decrease, in the utility of the individuals or of the society. On the other hand if the requirement of uniformity were to fail, society would not hold together, and each individual would go on his own way, as lions and tigers, birds of prey, and other animals do. Societies that endure and change are therefore situated in some intermediate condition between those two extremes.

**2172.** A homogeneous society might be imagined in which the requirement of uniformity would be the same in all individuals, and would correspond to the intermediate state just mentioned. But observation shows that that is not the case with human societies. Human societies are essentially heterogeneous, and the intermediate state is attained because the requirement of uniformity is very strong in some individuals, moderately strong in others, very feeble in still others, and almost entirely absent in a few. The average is found not in each individual, but in the group comprising them all. One may add as a datum of fact that the number of individuals in whom the requirement of uniformity is stronger than the average requisite of the intermediate state in which the society is situated is much greater than the number of individuals in whom the requirement is weaker than that average, and very very much greater than the number in whom it is entirely missing.

**2173.** For the reader who has followed us thus far it is needless to add that, in view of the effects of this greater or lesser potency of the sentiments of uniformity, one may foresee out of hand that two theologies will put in an appearance, one of which will glorify the immobility of one or another uniformity, real or imaginary, the other of which will glorify movement, progress, in one direction or another. That is what has actually happened in history. There have been popular Olympuses where the gods fixed and determined once and for all how human society was to be; and then, too, Olympuses of utopian reformers, who derived from their exalted minds conceptions of forms from which human society was never more to deviate. On the other hand from the days of ancient Athens down to our own, the lord gods of Movement in a Certain Direction have listened to the prayers of their faithful and now sit triumphant in our latter-day Olympus, where Progress Optimus Maximus reigns in sovereign majesty. So that intermediate situation of society has usually been attained as the resultant of many forces, prominent among them the two categories mentioned, which envisage different imaginary goals and correspond to different classes of residues.

**2174.** To ask whether or not force ought to be used in a society, whether the use of force is or is not beneficial, is to ask a question that has no meaning; for force is used by those who wish to preserve certain uniformities and by those who wish to overstep them; and the violence of the ones stands in contrast and in conflict with the violence of the others. In truth, if a partisan of a governing class disavows the use of force, he means that he disavows the use of force by insurgents trying to escape from the norms of the given uniformity. On the other hand, if he says he approves of the use of force, what he really means is that he approves of the use of force by the public authority to constrain insurgents to conformity. Conversely, if a partisan of the subject class says he detests the use of force

Reprinted from Vilfredo Pareto, *The Mind and Society*. ed. Arthur Livingston, trans. Andrew Bongiorno and Arthur Livingston (New York: Harcourt, Brace & Co., 1935) Vol. IV, §§ 2170–75, 2179–220, with the permission of The Pareto Fund.

in society, what he really detests is the use of force by constituted authorities in forcing dissidents to conform; and if, instead, he lauds the use of force, he is thinking of the use of force by those who would break away from certain social uniformities.

**2175.** Nor is there any particular meaning in the question as to whether the use of violence to enforce existing uniformities is beneficial to society, or whether it is beneficial to use force in order to overstep them; for the various uniformities have to be distinguished to see which of them are beneficial and which deleterious to society. Nor, indeed, is that enough; for it is further necessary to determine whether the utility of the uniformity is great enough to offset the harm that will be done by using violence to enforce it, or whether detriment from the uniformity is great enough to overbalance the damage that will be caused by the use of force in subverting it; in which detriment and damage we must not forget to reckon the very serious drawback involved in the anarchy that results from any frequent use of violence to abolish existing uniformities, just as among the benefits and utilities of maintaining frankly injurious uniformities must be counted the strength and stability they lend to the social order. So, to solve the problem as to the use of force, it is not enough to solve the other problem as to the utility, in general, of certain types of social organization; it is essential also and chiefly to compute all the advantages and all the drawbacks, direct and indirect. Such a course leads to the solution of a scientific problem; but it may not be and oftentimes is not the course that leads to an increase in social utility. It is better, therefore, if it be followed only by people who are called upon to solve a scientific problem or, to some limited extent, by certain individuals belonging to the ruling class; whereas social utility is oftentimes best served if the members of the subject class, whose function is not to lead but to act, accept one of the two theologies according to the case—either the theology that enjoins preservation of existing uniformities, or the theology that counsels change.

**2178.** What now are the correlations that subsist between this method of applying force and other social facts? We note, as usual, a sequence of actions and reactions, in which the use of force appears now as cause, now as effect. As regards the governing class, one gets, in the main, five groups of facts to consider: 1. A mere handful of citizens, so long as they are willing to use violence, can force their will upon public officials who are not inclined to meet violence with equal violence. If the reluctance of the officials to resort to force is primarily motivated by humanitarian sentiments, that result ensues very readily; but if they refrain from violence because they deem it wiser to use some other means, the effect is often the following: 2. To prevent or resist violence, the governing class resorts to "diplomacy," fraud, corruption—governmental authority passes, in a word, from the lions to the foxes. The governing class bows its head under the threat of violence, but it surrenders only in appearances, trying to turn the flank of the obstacle it cannot demolish in frontal attack. In the long run that sort of procedure comes to exercise a far-reaching influence on the selection of the governing class, which is now recruited only from the foxes, while the lions are blackballed. The individual who best knows the arts of sapping the strength of the foes of "graft" and of winning back by fraud and deceit what seemed to have been surrendered under pressure of force, is now leader of leaders. The man who has bursts of rebellion, and does not know how to crook his spine at the proper times and places, is the worst of leaders, and his presence is tolerated among them only if other distinguished endowments offset that defect. 3. So it comes about that the residues of the combination-instinct (Class I) are intensified in the governing class, and the residues of group-persistence debilitated; for the combination-residues supply, precisely, the artistry and resourcefulness required for evolving ingenious expedients as substitutes for open resistance, while the residues of group-persistence stimulate open resistance, since a strong sentiment of group-persistence cures the spine of all tendencies to curvature. 4. Policies of the governing class are not planned too far ahead in time. Predominance of the combination instincts and enfeeblement of the sentiments of group-persistence result in making the governing class more satisfied with the present and less thoughtful of the future. The individual comes to prevail, and by far, over family, community, nation. Material interests and interests of the present or a near future come to prevail over the ideal interests of community or nation and interests of the distant future. The impulse is to enjoy the present without too much thought for the morrow. 5. Some of these phenomena become observable in international relations as well. Wars become essentially economic. Efforts are made to avoid conflicts with the powerful and the sword is rattled only before the weak. Wars are regarded more than anything else as speculations. A country is often unwittingly edged towards war by nursings of economic conflicts which, it is expected, will never get out of control and turn into armed conflicts. Not seldom, however, a war will be forced upon a country by peoples who are not so far advanced in the evolution that leads to the predominance of Class I residues.

**2179.** As regards the subject class, we get the following relations, which correspond in part to the preceding: 1. When the subject class contains a number of individuals disposed to use force and with capable leaders to guide them, the governing class is, in many cases, overthrown and another takes its place. That is easily the case where governing classes are inspired by humanitarian sentiments primarily, and very very easily if they do not find ways to assimilate the exceptional individuals who come to the front in the subject classes. A humanitarian aristocracy that is closed or stiffly exclusive represents the maximum of insecurity. 2. It is far more difficult to overthrow a governing class that is adept in the shrewd use of chicanery, fraud, corruption; and in the highest degree difficult to overthrow such a class when it successfully assimilates most of the individuals in the subject class who show those same talents, are adept in those same arts, and might therefore become the leaders of such plebeians as are disposed to use violence. Thus left without leadership, without talent, disorganized, the subject class is almost always powerless to set up any lasting régime. 3. So the combination-residues (Class I) become to some extent enfeebled in the subject class. But that phenomenon is in no way comparable to the corresponding reinforcement of those same residues in the governing class; for the governing class, being composed, as it is, of a much smaller number of individuals, changes considerably in character from the addition to it or withdrawal from it of relatively small numbers of individuals; whereas shifts of identical numbers produce but slight effects in the enormously greater total of the subject class. For that matter the subject class is still left with many individuals possessed of combination-instincts that are applied not to politics or activities connected with politics but to arts and trades independent of politics. That circumstance lends stability to societies, for the governing class is required to absorb only a small number of new individuals in order to keep the subject class deprived of leadership. However, in the long run the differences in temperament between the governing class and the subject class become gradually accentuated, the combination-instincts tending to predominate in the ruling class, and instincts of group-persistence in the subject class. When that difference becomes sufficiently great, revolution occurs. 4. Revolution often transfers power to a new governing class, which exhibits a reinforcement in its instincts of group-persistence and so adds to its designs of present enjoyment aspirations towards ideal enjoyments presumably attainable at some future time—scepticism in part gives way to faith. 5. These considerations must to some extent be applied to international relations. If the combination-instincts are reinforced in a given country beyond a certain limit, as compared with the instincts of group-persistence, that country may be easily vanquished in war by another country in which that change in relative proportions has not occurred. The potency of an ideal as a pilot to victory is observable in both civil and international strife. People who lose the habit of applying force, who acquire the habit of considering policy from a commercial standpoint and of judging it only in terms of profit and loss, can readily be induced to purchase peace; and it may well be that such a transaction taken by itself is a good one, for war might have cost more money than the price of peace. Yet experience shows that in the long run, and taken in connexion with the things that inevitably go with it, such practice leads a country to ruin. The combination-instincts rarely come to prevail in the whole of a population. More commonly that situation arises in the upper strata of society, there being few if any traces of it in the lower and more populous classes. So when a war breaks out one gazes in amazement on the energies that are suddenly manifested by the masses at large, something that could in no way have been foreseen by studying the upper classes only. Sometimes, as happened in the case of Carthage, the burst of energy may not be sufficient to save a country, because a war may have been inadequately prepared for and be incompetently led by the ruling classes, and soundly prepared for and wisely led by the ruling classes of the enemy country. Then again, as happened in the wars of the French Revolution, the energy in the masses may be great enough to save a country because, though the war may have been badly prepared for by its ruling classes, preparations and leadership have been even worse in the ruling classes of the enemy countries, a circumstance that gives the constituent members of the lower strata of society time to drive their ruling class from power and replace it with another of greater energy and possessing the instincts of group-persistence in greater abundance. Still again, as happened in Germany after the disaster at Jena, the energy of the masses may spread to the higher classes and spur them to an activity that proves most effective as combining able leadership with enthusiastic faith.

**2180.** These, then, are the main, the outstanding phenomena, but other phenomena of secondary or incidental importance also figure. Notable among such is the fact that if a ruling class is unable or unwilling or incompetent to use force to eradicate violations of uniformities in private life, anarchic action on the part of the subject class tends to make up for the deficiency. It is well known to history that the private vendetta languishes or recurs in proportion as public authority continues or ceases to replace it. It has been seen to recur in the form of lynchings in the United States, and even in Europe. Whenever the influence of public authority declines, little states grow up within the state, little societies within society. So, whenever judicial process fails, private or group justice replaces it, and *vice versa*. In international relations, the tinselling of humanitarian and ethical declamation is just a dressing for an underlying force. The Chinese considered themselves the superiors in civilization of the Japanese, and perhaps they were, but they lacked a military aptitude that the Japanese, in virtue of a surviving remnant of feudal "barbarism," possessed in abundance. So the poor Chinese were attacked by hordes of Europeans—whose exploits in China, as Sorel well says, remind one of the feats of the Spanish *conquistadores* in the Americas. They suffered murder, rapine, and pillage at European hands, and then paid an indemnity into the bargain; whereas the Japanese came off victorious over the Russians and now exact respect from everybody. A few centuries back, the subtle diplomacy of the Christian lords of Constantinople did not save them from ruin under the impact of the fanaticism and might of the Turks; and now, in this year 1913, on the very same spot, the victors show that they have deteriorated in their fanaticism and in their power and, in their turn reposing illusory hopes in the diplomatic arts, are defeated and overthrown by the vigour of their sometime subjects. Grievous the hallucination under which those statesmen labour who imagine that they can replace the use of force with unarmed law. Among the many examples that one might point to are Sulla's constitution in ancient Rome and the conservative constitution of the Third Republic in France. Sulla's constitution fell because the armed force that might have compelled respect for it was not maintained. The constitution of Augustus endured because his successors were in a position to rely on the might of the legions. When the Commune had been defeated and overthrown, Thiers decided that his government ought to find its support rather in the law than in armed force. As a result his laws were scattered like leaves before the hurricane of democratic plutocracy. We need say nothing of Louis XVI of France, who thought he could halt the Revolution with his royal veto, for his was the illusion of a spineless weakling who was soon to lose what little head he had.

**2181.** All such facts as a rule present themselves in the guise of derivations. In one direction we get theories that condemn the use of violence by the subject class in whatever case, in the other direction theories that censure its use by public authority.

**2182.** Ruling-class theories, when the requirement of logic is not too keenly felt, appeal simply to sentiments of veneration for holders of power, or for abstractions such as "the state," and to sentiments of disapprobation for individuals who try to disturb or subvert existing orders (§ 2192). Then when it is deemed advisable to satisfy the need of logic, the effort is to create a confusion between the violation of an established uniformity for the individual's exclusive profit and a violation designed to further some collective interest or some new uniformity. The aim in such a derivation is to carry over to the social or political act the reprobation that is generally visited upon common crime. Frequent in our day are reasonings in some way connected with the theology of Progress. Not a few of our modern governments have revolutionary origins. How condemn the revolutions that might be tried against them without repudiating the forefathers? That is attended to by invoking a new divine right: Insurrection was legitimate enough against governments of the past, where authority was based on force; it is not legitimate against modern governments, where the authority is based on "reason." Or else: Insurrection was legitimate against kings and oligarchies; it is never legitimate against "the People." Or again: Rebellion is justifiable where there is no universal suffrage, but not where that panacea is the law of the land. Or again: Revolt is useless and therefore reprehensible in all countries where "the People" are able to express their "will." Then finally—just to give some little satisfaction to their Graces, the Metaphysicists: Insurrection cannot be tolerated where a "state of law" exists. I hope I shall be excused if I do not define that very sweet entity here. For all of most painstaking researches on my part, it remains an entity altogether unknown to me, and I should much rather be asked to give the zoological pedigree of the Chimaera.

**2183.** Again as usual, no one of these derivations has any exact meaning. All governments use force, and all assert that they are founded on reason. In the fact, whether universal suffrage prevails or not, it is always an oligarchy that governs, finding ways to give to the "will of the people" that expression which the few desire, from the "royal law" that bestowed the *imperium* on the Roman Emperors down to the votes of a legislative majority elected in one way or another, from the plebiscite that gave the empire to Napoleon III down to the universal suffrage that is shrewdly bought, steered, and manipulated by our "speculators." Who is this new god called Universal Suffrage? He is no more exactly definable, no less shrouded in mystery, no less beyond the pale of reality, than the hosts of other divinities; nor are there fewer and less patent contradictions in his theology than in theirs. Worshippers of Universal Suffrage are not led by their god. It is they who lead him—and by the nose, determining the forms in which he must manifest himself. Oftentimes, proclaiming the sanctity of "majority rule," they resist "majority rule" by obstructionist tactics, even though they form but small minorities, and burning incense to the goddess Reason, they in no wise disdain, in certain cases, alliances with Chicanery, Fraud, and Corruption.

**2184.** Substantially such derivations express the sentiments felt by people who have climbed into the saddle and are willing to stay there—along with the far more general sentiment that social stability is a good thing. If, the moment a group, large or small, ceased to be satisfied with certain norms established in the community of which it is a part, it flew to arms to abolish them, organized society would fall to pieces. Social stability is so beneficial a thing that to maintain it it is well worth while to enlist the aid of fantastic ideals and this or that theology—among the others, the theology of universal suffrage—and be resigned to putting up with certain actual disadvantages. Before it becomes advisable to disturb the public peace, such disadvantages must have grown very very serious; and since human beings are effectively guided not by the sceptical reasonings of science but by "living faiths" expressed in ideals, theories such as the divine right of kings, the legitimacy of oligarchies, of "the people," of "majorities," of legislative assemblies, and other such things, may be useful within certain limits, and have in fact proved to be, however absurd they may be from the scientific standpoint.

**2185.** Theories designed to justify the use of force by the governed are almost always combined with theories condemning the use of force by the public authority. A few dreamers reject the use of force in general, on whatever side; but their theories either have no influence at all or else serve merely to weaken resistance on the part of people in power, so clearing the field for violence on the part of the governed. In view of that we may confine ourselves to considering such theories, in general, in the combined form.

**2186.** No great number of theories are required to rouse to resistance and to the use of force people who are, or think they are, oppressed. The derivations therefore are chiefly designed to incline people who would otherwise be neutral in the struggle to condemn resistance on the part of the governing powers, and so to make their resistance less vigorous; or at a venture, to persuade the rulers themselves in that sense, a thing, for that matter, that is not likely to have any great success in our day save with those whose spinal columns have utterly rotted from the bane of humanitarianism. A few centuries ago some results might have been achieved in our Western countries by working with religious derivations upon sincere Christians; and, in other countries, by working upon firm believers with derivations of the religion prevailing in the given case. Since humanitarianism is a religion, like the Christian, the Moslem, or any other, we may say, in general, that one may sometimes secure the aid of neutrals and weaken resistance on the part of people in power by using derivations of the religion, whatever it may be, in which they sincerely believe. But since derivations readily lend themselves to proving the pro and contra, that device is often of scant effect even when it is not a mere mask for interests.

**2187.** In our times conflicts are chiefly economic. If a government therefore sets out to protect employers or strike-breakers from violence by strikers, it is accused of "interfering" in an economic matter that does not properly concern it. If the police do not allow their heads to be broken without using their weapons, they are said to have "shown poor judgment," to have acted "impulsively," "nervously." Like strike-breakers, they must be denied the right to use arms whenever they are attacked by strikers, for otherwise some striker might be killed, and the crime of assault, assuming but not conceding that there has been such a crime, does not deserve the penalty of death. Court decisions are impugned as "class decisions"; at any rate, they are always too severe. Amnesties, finally, must wipe out all remembrance of such unpleasantness. One might suppose that since the interests of employers and strike-breakers are directly contrary to the interests of the strikers, they would use the opposite derivations. But that is not the case, or if they do, they do it in a very mild, apologetic way. The reason is, as regards the "strike-breaker," the "scab," that he has, as a class, very little spirit. He is not inspired by any lofty ideal, he is almost ashamed of what he is doing, and does it with as little talk as possible. As regards employers of labour, the reason is that many of them are "speculators" who hope to make up for their losses in a strike through government aid and at the expense of consumer or taxpayer. Their quarrels with strikers are quarrels between accomplices over the division of the loot. The strikers belong to the masses, where there is a wealth of Class II residues. They have not only interests but ideals. Their "speculator" employers belong to a class that has grown rich in its aptitude for combinations. They are well supplied, over-supplied, with residues from Class I and so have interests chiefly, and few or no ideals. They spend their time in activities that are far more lucrative than the manufacture of theories. Among them are not a few plutocratic demagogues who are artists at the trick of turning to their advantage strikes that are in all appearances directed against them. There are general considerations, furthermore, that apply to both domestic and international conflicts. They come down, in brief, to an appeal to sentiments of pity for the sufferings that are caused by the use of force, disregarding entirely the reasons for which the force is used and the utility or the harm that results from using or not using it. They are often filled out with expressions of reverence, or at least of compassion, for the proletariat, which can never do wrong or at the very least is excusable for whatever it does. In a day gone by, similar derivations, corresponding to the very same sentiments, were used in favour now of royal, now of theocratic, now of aristocratic, rule.

**2188.** It is interesting, as in keeping with the essentially sentimental character of derivations, that theories that would be the soundest from the logico-experimental standpoint are as a rule neglected. In the Middle Ages an excellent argument might have been put forward in favour of the ecclesiastical power at a time when it was at war with imperial, royal, or baronial powers—the fact that it was virtually the only counterbalance to those other powers, and almost the only refuge of intelligence, science, and cultivation against ignorant brutal force. But that argument was seldom, if ever, used. People preferred to rely on derivations based on the doctrine of revelation and quotations from Scripture. Now employers who themselves enjoy economic protection manifest great indignation at strikers for trying to rid themselves of the competition of non-union workers. The rejoinder is never made that they are trying to keep others from doing what they are doing themselves, and that they fail to show how and why free competition is good for the workingman and bad for the employer of labour. An individual tries to slip across the Italian frontier with a few bags of saccharin. Customs officers come running and violently prevent such competition with Italian manufacturers of beet-sugar, going, on occasion, so far as to use their guns and sometimes to kill the smuggler whom nobody mourns. All the same it is owing to just such violence and such murders that now a few Italian "sugar men" have managed to amass considerable fortunes and win public esteem, national honours, and even seats among the law-makers. One still has to be shown why violence cannot be used in the same way to increase wages.

**2189.** It may be objected that the violence that safe-guards the interests of the employer is legal and the violence used by the strikers on "scabs" illegal. That transfers the question from the utility of the violence to the utility of the manner in which violence is applied—a matter of considerable importance, no one will deny. Legal violence is the consequence of the norms established in a society, and in general resort to it is more beneficial or at least less harmful than resort to private violence, which is designed as a rule to overthrow prevailing norms. The strikers might answer, and in fact sometimes do, that they are using illegal violence because they are cut off from using the legal variety. If the law were to constrain people by use of legal violence to give them what they demand, they would not need to resort to illegal violence. The same argument would serve in many other cases. People who use illegal violence would ask for nothing better than to be able to transmute it into legal violence.

**2190.** But the matter is not yet exhausted, and we now come to the salient point in question. Let us set the particular case aside and look at the problem in its general form. The dispute is really as to the relative merits of shrewdness and force, and to decide it in the sense that never, not even in the exceptional case, is it useful to meet wits with violence, it would be necessary first to show that the use of cunning is always, without exception, more advisable than the use of force. Suppose a certain country has a governing class, *A*, that assimilates the best elements, as regards intelligence, in the whole population. In that case the subject class, *B*, is largely stripped of such elements and can have little or no hope of ever overcoming the class *A* so long as it is a battle of wits. If intelligence were to combine with force, the dominion of the *A*'s would be perpetual, for as Dante says, *Inferno*, XXXVI, vv. 55–57 (Fletcher translation):

> "For if the machination of the mind
> To evil-will be added and to might,
> Of no defence is competent mankind."

But such a happy combination occurs only for a few individuals. In the majority of cases people who rely on their wits are or become less fitted to use violence, and *vice versa*. So concentration in the class *A* of the individuals most adept at chicanery leads to a concentration in class *B* of the individuals most adept at violence; and if that process is long continued, the equilibrium tends to become unstable, because the *A*'s are long in cunning but short in courage to use force and in the force itself; whereas the *B*'s have the force and the courage to use it, but are short in the skill required for exploiting those advantages. But if they chance to find leaders who have the skill—and history shows that such leadership is usually supplied by dissatisfied *A*'s—they have all they need for driving the *A*'s from power. Of just that development history affords countless examples from remotest times all the way down to the present.

**2191.** In general terms, a revolution of that type is beneficial to a community—more so when a governing class is tending more and more towards humanitarianism, less so when it is made up of individuals who are tending more and more to use combinations instead of force, especially if the combinations result, even indirectly, in the material prosperity of the community.

Let us imagine a country where the governing class, *A*, is inclining more and more in the direction of humanitarianism, is fostering, in other words, only the more harmful group-persistences, rejecting the others as outworn prejudices, and, while awaiting the advent of the "reign of reason," is becoming less and less capable of using force and is so shirking the main duty of a ruling class. Such a country is on its way to utter ruin. But lo, the subject class, *B*, revolts against the class *A*. In fighting *A* it uses the humanitarian derivations so dear to the *A*'s, but underlying them are quite different sentiments, and they soon find expression in deeds. The *B*'s apply force on a far-reaching scale, and not only overthrow the *A*'s but kill large numbers of them—and, in so doing, to tell the truth, they are performing a useful public service something like ridding the country of a baneful animal pest. They bring with them to the seats of power a great abundance of group-persistences; and little it matters, if it matters at all, that these group-persistences be different in outward forms from the old. The important thing is that now they are functioning in the governing class and that owing to them the social fabric is acquiring stability and strength. The country is saved from ruin and is reborn to a new life.

If one judges superficially, one may be tempted to dwell more especially on the slaughter and pillaging that attend a revolution, without thinking to ask whether such things may not be manifestations —as regrettable as one may wish—of sentiments, of social forces, that are very salutary. If one should say that, far from being reprehensible, the slaughter and robbery are signs that those who were called upon to commit them deserved power for the good of society, he would be stating a paradox, for there is no relationship of cause and effect, nor any close and indispensable correlation, between such outrages and social utility; but the paradox would still contain its modicum of truth, in that the slaughter and rapine are external symptoms indicating the advent of strong and courageous people to places formerly held by weaklings and cowards. In all that we have been describing in the abstract many revolutions that have actually occurred in the concrete, from the revolution which gave imperial rule to Augustus down to the French Revolution of '89. If the class governing in France had had the faith that counsels use of force and the will to use force, it would never have been overthrown and, procuring its own advantage, would have procured the advantage of France. Since it failed in that function it was salutary that its rule should give way to rule by others; and since, again, it was the resort to force that was wanting, it was in keeping with very general uniformities that there should be a swing to another extreme where force was used even more than was required. Had Louis XVI not been a man of little sense and less courage, letting himself be floored without fighting, and preferring to lose his head on the guillotine to dying weapon in hand like a man of sinew, he might have been the one to do the destroying. If the victims of the September massacres, their kinsmen and friends, had not for the most part been spineless humanitarians without a particle of courage or energy, they would have annihilated their enemies instead of waiting to be annihilated themselves. It was a good thing that power should pass into the hands of people who showed that they had the faith and the resolve requisite for the use of force.

The advantage of the use of force to a society is less apparent when the governing class is made up of persons in whom the combination instincts are prevalent, and within certain limits there may be no advantage. But when a governing class divests itself too completely of the sentiments of group-persistence, it easily reaches a point where it is unfit to defend, let alone its own power, what is far worse the independence of its country. In such a case, if the independence is to be deemed an advantage, it must also be deemed an advantage to be rid of a class that has become incompetent to perform the functions of defence. As a rule it is from the subject class that individuals come with the faith and the resolve to use force and save a country.

**2192.** The governing class, *A*, tries to defend its power and avert the danger of an uprising of the *B*'s in various ways. It may try to take advantage of the strength of the *B*'s, and that is the most effective policy. Or it may try to prevent its disaffected members from becoming leaders of the *B*'s, or rather, of that element among the *B*'s which is disposed to use force; but that is a very difficult thing to achieve. And the *A*'s use derivations to keep the *B*'s quiet (§2182), telling them that "all power comes from God," that it is a "crime" to resort to violence, that there is no reason for using force to obtain what, if it is "just," may be obtained by "reason." The main purpose of such derivations is to keep the *B*'s from giving battle on their own terrain, the terrain of force, and to lead them to other ground—the field of cunning—where their defeat is certain, pitted as they will be against the *A*'s, who are immensely their superiors in wits. But as a rule the effectiveness of such derivations depends largely upon the pre-existing sentiments that they express, and only to a slight extent upon sentiments that they create.

**2193.** Those derivations have to be met with other derivations of equal effectiveness, and it will be better if some of them play upon sentiments that are acceptable to people who imagine that they are neutral, though in reality they may not be, who would prefer not to take sides with either the *A*'s or the *B*'s but to think solely of what is "just" and "honest." Such sentiments are chiefly available in the group manifested by residues of sociality (Class IV) and more especially the sentiments of pity. For that reason, most of the derivations favouring the use of violence by the subject class defend it not so much directly as indirectly—condemning resistance on the part of the governing class in the name of sociality, pity, and repugnance to sufferings in others. These latter sentiments are almost the only ones that are exploited by many pacifists who can think of no other way to defend their thesis than by describing the "horrors of war." Derivations relating to the social struggle often have recourse, further, to sentiments of asceticism, which sometimes influence individuals among the *A*'s and so prove to be of no mean advantage to the *B*'s.

**2194.** At bottom all such derivations express in chief, the sentiments of individuals who are eager for change in the social order, and they are therefore beneficial or harmful according as the change is beneficial or harmful. If one is going to assert that change is always for the worse, that stability is the supreme good, one ought to be ready to show either that it would have been to the advantage of human societies always to have remained in a state of barbarism, or that the transition from barbarism to civilization has been achieved, or *might have* been achieved, without wars and revolutions. This latter assertion is so grossly at variance with the facts as we learn them from history that it is absurd even to discuss it. So only the first is left, and it might be defended by giving a special meaning to the term, "utility" and adopting the theories that have sung the joys of a "state of nature." If one is unwilling to go as far as that, one cannot hold to the first proposition either; and so one is forced by the facts and by logic to admit that wars and revolutions have sometimes been beneficial (which does not mean that they have always been so). And once that is admitted for the past, no bias whatever remains for showing that things will be otherwise in the future.

**2195.** So there we are again, and as usual, driven from the qualitative field, where derivations predominate, into the quantitative field of logico-experimental science. One cannot assert in general that stability is always beneficial or that change is always beneficial. Every case has to be examined on its particular merits and the utility and the detriment appraised to see whether the first overbalances the second, or *vice versa*.

**2196.** We have already found that in many cases stability is beneficial. We should find cases no fewer in number where violations of existing norms have also proved beneficial, provided we consider norms of an intellectual order along with norms of a material order. But keeping them separate, it will be apparent that—especially as regards violations by small numbers of individuals—many are the cases where violations of intellectual norms by individuals or by a few individuals prove advantageous, few the cases where violations of norms of a material order prove beneficial. For that reason, the implications of the formula stated in §2176, whereby violations of norms of a material order should be the more vigorously suppressed, the more exclusively they are the work of individuals, the less so, the more they are the work of groups, do not in many cases take us too far astray from the maximum of social utility, as they would do if the formula were applied to violations of norms of an intellectual order. That, substantially, is the chief argument that can be advanced in favour of what is called "freedom of thought."

**2197.** Derivations do not run that way. Dissenters defend their opinions because they are "better" than the opinions held by the majority; and it is a good thing that they have that faith, for it alone can supply them with the energy they need to resist the persecutions that they almost always incur. So long as they are few in numbers, they ask just for a little place in the Sun for their sect. In reality they are panting for the moment when they can turn from persecuted to persecutor, a thing that infallibly happens as soon as they have become numerous enough to enforce their will. At that moment the advantage of their past dissent is at an end, and the detriment resulting from their new orthodoxy begins to assert itself.

**2198.** In considering the use of force there is a stronger temptation than in other social connexions to think only of relationships of cause and effect; nor in many cases do we go very far wide of the mark in that. After all, in the sequence of actions and reactions that confronts one, the action of this or that force as producing this or that effect occupies a very considerable place. However, it is better not to stop at that, but go on to see whether phenomena that are more general should not be taken into account.

**2199.** We have previously compared the revolution in Rome at the time of Augustus with the revolution in France at the time of Louis XVI; and we saw that to understand those two events we had to look beyond the derivations to the sentiments and interests that the derivations represented. Advancing one step further, one notes that both in the fall of the Roman Republic and in the fall of the French monarchy, the respective governing classes were either unwilling or unable to use force, and were overthrown by other classes that were both willing and able to do that (§2191). Both in ancient Rome and in France the victorious element rose from the people and was made up in Rome of the legions of Sulla, Caesar, and Octavius, in France of the revolutionary mobs that routed a very feeble royal power, and then of an army that vanquished the very inefficient troops of the European potentates. The leaders of the victors spoke Latin, of course, in Rome, and French in France, and no less naturally used derivations that were suitable to the Romans and the French respectively. The Roman people was fed on derivations conforming with a feeling that substance might be changed so long as forms were kept, the French masses, on derivations inspired by the religion of "Progress," a faith surpassing dear to the French of that day. Not otherwise, in the days of the Puritan Revolution, did Cromwell and other foes of the Stuarts use biblical derivations.

**2200.** The French derivations are more familiar than the Roman not only because more documents have come down to us, but also, as seems very probable, because they were supplied in greater abundance. Had Octavius long continued in his rôle as defender of the Senate, he might have made very lavish use of them; but when, before Bologna, he came to an understanding with Antony and Lepidus, his fortunes came to rest altogether on the might of his legions; so he laid his derivations away in his arsenals as weapons no longer needed, not taking them out again till after his victory, when it was a question of smoothing the fur of old-timers in Rome, which might have been ruffled by the change in régime. Something of the same sort took place in France as regards Napoleon I; but before his time the Jacobins, who opened the road for him, found it impossible to play only the lion and had to resort to the tricks of the fox. With his own prestige as commander, Octavius had made sure of the support of an armed force, and at first with his own money, later on with the money that he was in a position to extort by force from others. The French revolutionary leaders were unable to do anything like that, in the beginning. They had to recruit their revolutionary army with derivations, which, expressing as they did the sentiments of many of the government's enemies, brought them in a flock to their standards, and, expressing also the sentiments of almost all members of the ruling classes, further served as an opiate to their already listless vigilance, and broke down their already feeble resistance. Later on, as soon as the revolution got possession of power, its leaders imitated the Roman triumvirs and many other masterful men of the same type, distributing among their followers the money and property of their adversaries.

**2201.** If the effects of derivations are much less considerable than the effects of residues, they are not, as we have many times seen, altogether without influence, serving primarily to give greater strength and effectiveness to the residues that they express. It would not therefore be exact to say that the historians who have made the derivations of the French Revolution their exclusive or at least their main concern have dealt with an entirely irrelevant aspect of that episode. They may be said to have erred in regarding as primary an aspect that was merely secondary. It has been a more serious error on their part not to consider the rôle played by force and the reasons why force was used by some parties, and not by others. The few who have considered the rôle of force at all have gone astray in assuming that this or that man in power refrained from using force in deference to derivations, whereas both derivations and the aversion to use of force had a common origin in the sentiments of those men. And yet—if one examines closely—the whole thing seems clear, with the proof and the counter-proof. Louis XVI fell because he was unwilling, unable, incompetent, to use force; the revolutionists triumphed because they were willing and able and competent. Not by any cogency in their theories but by sheer might of their followings did now this and now that revolutionary faction climb to power. Even the Directory, which had saved itself by resorting to force in conflicts with weaker factions, succumbed to force in its struggle with Bonaparte, made the man of the hour by his victorious troops. And Napoleon lasts until he is worn down under the superior force of the Allies. And then—over again: a succession of régimes in France, each falling because unwilling, unable, incompetent, to use force, and others rising on the use of force. That was observable on the fall of Charles X, on the fall of Louis Philippe, on the advent of Napoleon III; and one may go on and say that if the government of Versailles in 1871 managed to keep its feet in the face of the Commune, it was because it had a strong army at its disposal and knew enough to use it.

# 3. *On the Ruling Class*

BY GAETANO MOSCA

IN SOCIETIES in which religious beliefs are strong and ministers of the faith form a special class a priestly aristocracy almost always arises and gains possession of a more or less important share of the wealth and the political power. Conspicuous examples of that situation would be ancient Egypt (during certain periods), Brahman India and medieval Europe. Oftentimes the priests not only perform religious functions. They possess legal and scientific knowledge and constitute the class of highest intellectual culture. Consciously or unconsciously, priestly hierarchies often show a tendency to monopolize learning and hamper the dissemination of the methods and procedures that make the acquisition of knowledge possible and easy. To that tendency may have been due, in part at least, the painfully slow diffusion of the demotic alphabet in ancient Egypt, though that alphabet was infinitely more simple than the hieroglyphic script. The Druids in Gaul were acquainted with the Greek alphabet but would not permit their rich store of sacred literature to be written down, requiring their pupils to commit it to memory at the cost of untold effort. To the same outlook may be attributed the stubborn and frequent use of dead languages that we find in ancient Chaldea, in India, and in medieval Europe. Sometimes, as was the case in India, lower classes have been explicitly forbidden to acquire knowledge of sacred books.

Specialized knowledge and really scientific culture, purged of any sacred or religious aura, become important political forces only in a highly advanced stage of civilization, and only then do they give access to membership in the ruling class to those who possess them. But in this case too, it is not so much learning in itself that has political value as the practical applications that may be made of learning to the profit of the public or the state. Sometimes all that is required is mere possession of the mechanical processes that are indispensable to the acquisition of a higher culture. This may be due to the fact that on such a basis it is easier to ascertain and measure the skill which a candidate has been able to acquire—it is easier to "mark" or grade him. So in certain periods in ancient Egypt the profession of scribe was a road to public office and power, perhaps because to have learned the hieroglyphic script was proof of long and patient study. In modern China, again, learning the numberless characters in Chinese script has formed the basis of the mandarin's education. In present-day Europe and America the class that applies the findings of modern science to war, public administration, public works and public sanitation holds a fairly important position, both socially and politically, and in our western world, as in ancient Rome, an altogether privileged position is held by lawyers. They know the complicated legislation that arises in all peoples of long-standing civilization, and they become especially powerful if their knowledge of law is coupled with the type of eloquence that chances to have a strong appeal to the taste of their contemporaries.

There are examples in abundance where we see that long-standing practice in directing the military and civil organization of a community creates and develops in the higher reaches of the ruling class a real art of governing which is something better than crude empiricism and better than anything that mere individual experience could suggest. In such circumstances aristocracies of functionaries arise, such as the Roman senate, the Venetian nobility and to a certain extent the English aristocracy. Those bodies all stirred John Stuart Mill to admiration and certainly they all three developed governments that were distinguished for carefully

---

Reprinted by permision from Gaetano Mosca, *The Ruling Class,* trans. Hannah D. Kahn (New York: McGraw-Hill, 1939), chap. ii, secs. 6–8, pp. 59–69. 

considered policies and for great steadfastness and sagacity in carrying them out. This art of governing is not political science, though it has, at one time or another, anticipated applications of a number of the postulates of political science. However, even if the art of governing has now and again enjoyed prestige with certain classes of persons who have long held possession of political functions, knowledge of it has never served as an ordinary criterion for admitting to public offices persons who were barred from them by social station. The degree of mastery of the art of governing that a person possesses is, moreover, apart from exceptional cases, a very difficult thing to determine if the person has given no practical demonstration that he possesses it.

In some countries we find hereditary castes. In such cases the governing class is explicitly restricted to a given number of families, and birth is the one criterion that determines entry into the class or exclusion from it. Examples are exceedingly common. There is practically no country of long-standing civilization that has not had a hereditary aristocracy at one period or another in its history. We find hereditary nobilities during certain periods in China and ancient Egypt, in India, in Greece before the wars with the Medes, in ancient Rome, among the Slavs, among the Latins and Germans of the Middle Ages, in Mexico at the time of the Discovery and in Japan down to a few years ago.

In this connection two preliminary observations are in point. In the first place, all ruling classes tend to become hereditary in fact if not in law. All political forces seem to possess a quality that in physics used to be called the force of inertia. They have a tendency, that is, to remain at the point and in the state in which they find themselves. Wealth and military valor are easily maintained in certain families by moral tradition and by heredity. Qualification for important office—the habit of, and to an extent the capacity for, dealing with affairs of consequence—is much more readily acquired when one has had a certain familiarity with them from childhood. Even when academic degrees, scientific training, special aptitudes as tested by examinations and competitions, open the way to public office, there is no eliminating that special advantage in favor of certain individuals which the French call the advantage of *positions déjà prises*. In actual fact, though examinations and competitions may theoretically be open to all, the majority never have the resources for meeting the expense of long preparation, and many others are without the connections and kinships that set an individual promptly on the right road, enabling him to avoid the gropings and blunders that are inevitable when one enters an unfamiliar environment without any guidance or support.

The democratic principle of election by broad-based suffrage would seem at first glance to be in conflict with the tendency toward stability which, according to our theory, ruling classes show. But it must be noted that candidates who are successful in democratic elections are almost always the ones who possess the political forces above enumerated, which are very often hereditary. In the English, French and Italian parliaments we frequently see the sons, grandsons, brothers, nephews and sons-in-law of members and deputies, ex-members and ex-deputies.

In the second place, when we see a hereditary caste established in a country and monopolizing political power, we may be sure that such a status de jure was preceded by a similar status de facto. Before proclaiming their exclusive and hereditary right to power the families or castes in question must have held the scepter of command in a firm grasp, completely monopolizing all the political forces of that country at that period. Otherwise such a claim on their part would only have aroused the bitterest protests and provoked the bitterest struggles.

Hereditary aristocracies often come to vaunt supernatural origins, or at least origins different from, and superior to, those of the governed classes. Such claims are explained by a highly significant social fact, namely that every governing class tends to justify its actual exercise of power by resting it on some universal moral principle. This same sort of claim has come forward in our time in scientific trappings. A number of writers, developing and amplifying Darwin's theories, contend that upper classes represent a higher level in social evolution and are therefore superior to lower classes by organic structure. Gumplowicz we have already quoted. That writer goes to the point of maintaining that the divisions of populations into trade groups and professional classes in modern civilized countries are based on ethnological heterogeneousness.[1]

Now history very definitely shows the special abilities as well as the special defects—both very marked—which have been displayed by aristocracies that have either remained absolutely closed or have made entry into their circles difficult. The ancient Roman patriciate and the English and German nobilities of modern times give a ready idea of the type we refer to. Yet in dealing with this

1. *Der Rassenkampf*. This notion transpires from Gumplowicz's whole volume. It is explicitly formulated in book II, chap. XXXIII.

fact, and with the theories that tend to exaggerate its significance, we can always raise the same objection—that the individuals who belong to the aristocracies in question owe their special qualities not so much to the blood that flows in their veins as to their very particular upbringing, which has brought out certain intellectual and moral tendencies in them in preference to others.

Among all the factors that figure in social superiority, intellectual superiority is the one with which heredity has least to do. The children of men of highest mentality often have very mediocre talents. That is why hereditary aristocracies have never defended their rule on the basis of intellectual superiority alone, but rather on the basis of their superiorities in character and wealth.

It is argued, in rebuttal, that education and environment may serve to explain superiorities in strictly intellectual capacities but not differences of a moral order—will power, courage, pride, energy. The truth is that social position, family tradition, the habits of the class in which we live, contribute more than is commonly supposed to the greater or lesser development of the qualities mentioned. If we carefully observe individuals who have changed their social status, whether for better or for worse, and who consequently find themselves in environments different from the ones they have been accustomed to, it is apparent that their intellectual capacities are much less sensibly affected than their moral ones. Apart from a greater breadth of view that education and experience bring to anyone who is not altogether stupid, every individual, whether he remains a mere clerk or becomes a minister of state, whether he reaches the rank of sergeant or the rank of general, whether he is a millionaire or a beggar, abides inevitably on the intellectual level on which nature has placed him. And yet with changes of social status and wealth the proud man often becomes humble, servility changes to arrogance, an honest nature learns to lie, or at least to dissemble, under pressure of need, while the man who has an ingrained habit of lying and bluffing makes himself over and puts on an outward semblance at least of honesty and firmness of character. It is true, of course, that a man fallen from high estate often acquires powers of resignation, self-denial and resourcefulness, just as one who rises in the world sometimes gains in sentiments of justice and fairness. In short, whether a man change for the better or for the worse, he has to be exceptionally level-headed if he is to change his social status very appreciably and still keep his character unaltered. Mirabeau remarked that, for any man, any great climb on the social ladder produces a crisis that cures the ills he has and creates new ones that he never had before.[2]

Courage in battle, impetuousness in attack, endurance in resistance—such are the qualities that have long and often been vaunted as a monopoly of the higher classes. Certainly there may be vast natural and—if we may say so—innate differences between one individual and another in these respects; but more than anything else traditions and environmental influences are the things that keep them high, low or just average, in any large group of human beings. We generally become indifferent to danger or, perhaps better, to a given type of danger, when the persons with whom we daily live speak of it with indifference and remain cool and imperturbable before it. Many mountaineers or sailors are by nature timid men, yet they face unmoved, the ones the dangers of the precipice, the others the perils of the storm at sea. So peoples and classes that are accustomed to warfare maintain military virtues at the highest pitch.

So true is this that even peoples and social classes which are ordinarily unaccustomed to arms acquire the military virtues rapidly when the individuals who compose them are made members of organizations in which courage and daring are traditional, when—if one may venture the metaphor—they are cast into human crucibles that are heavily charged with the sentiments that are to be infused into their fiber. Mohammed II recruited his terrible Janizaries in the main from boys who had been kidnapped among the degenerate Greeks of Byzantium. The much despised Egyptian fellah, unused for long centuries to war and accustomed to remaining meek and helpless under the lash of the oppressor, became a good soldier when Mehemet Ali placed him in Turkish or Albanian regiments. The French nobility has always enjoyed a reputation for brilliant valor, but down to the end of the eighteenth century that quality was not credited in anything like the same degree to the French bourgeoisie. However, the wars of the Republic and the Empire amply proved that nature had been uniformly lavish in her endowments of courage upon all the inhabitants of France. Proletariat and bourgeoisie both furnished good soldiers and, what is more, excellent officers, though talent for command had been considered an exclusive prerogative of the nobility. Gumplowicz's theory that differentiation in social classes depends very largely on ethnological antecedents requires proof at the very least. Many facts to the contrary readily occur to one—among others the obvious fact that branches of the

2. *Correspondance entre le comte de Mirabeau et le comte de La Marck,* vol. II, p. 228.

same family often belong to widely different social classes.

Finally, if we were to keep to the idea of those who maintain the exclusive influence of the hereditary principle in the formation of ruling classes, we should be carried to a conclusion somewhat like the one to which we were carried by the evolutionary principle: The political history of mankind ought to be much simpler than it is. If the ruling class really belonged to a different race, or if the qualities that fit it for dominion were transmitted primarily by organic heredity, it is difficult to see how, once the class was formed, it could decline and lose its power. The peculiar qualities of a race are exceedingly tenacious. Keeping to the evolutionary theory, acquired capacities in the parents are inborn in their children and, as generation succeeds generation, are progressively accentuated. The descendants of rulers, therefore, ought to become better and better fitted to rule, and the other classes ought to see their chances of challenging or supplanting them becomes more and more remote. Now the most commonplace experience suffices to assure one that things do not go in that way at all.

What we see is that as soon as there is a shift in the balance of political forces—when, that is, a need is felt that capacities different from the old should assert themselves in the management of the state, when the old capacities, therefore, lose some of their importance or changes in their distribution occur—then the manner in which the ruling class is constituted changes also. If a new source of wealth develops in a society, if the practical importance of knowledge grows, if an old religion declines or a new one is born, if a new current of ideas spreads, then, simultaneously, far-reaching dislocations occur in the ruling class. One might say, indeed, that the whole history of civilized mankind comes down to a conflict between the tendency of dominant elements to monopolize political power and transmit possession of it by inheritance, and the tendency toward a dislocation of old forces and an insurgence of new forces; and this conflict produces an unending ferment of endosmosis and exosmosis between the upper classes and certain portions of the lower. Ruling classes decline inevitably when they cease to find scope for the capacities through which they rose to power, when they can no longer render the social services which they once rendered, or when their talents and the services they render lose in importance in the social environment in which they live. So the Roman aristocracy declined when it was no longer the exclusive source of higher officers for the army, of administrators for the commonwealth, of governors for the provinces. So the Venetian aristocracy declined when its nobles ceased to command the galleys and no longer passed the greater part of their lives in sailing the seas and in trading and fighting.

In inorganic nature we have the example of our air, in which a tendency to immobility produced by the force of inertia is continuously in conflict with a tendency to shift about as the result of inequalities in the distribution of heat. The two tendencies, prevailing by turn in various regions on our planet, produce now calm, now wind and storm. In much the same way in human societies there prevails now the tendency that produces closed, stationary, crystallized ruling classes, now the tendency that results in a more or less rapid renovation of ruling classes.

The Oriental societies which we consider stationary have in reality not always been so, for otherwise, as we have already pointed out, they could not have made the advances in civilization of which they have left irrefutable evidence. It is much more accurate to say that we came to know them at a time when their political forces and their political classes were in a period of crystallization. The same thing occurs in what we commonly call "aging" societies, where religious beliefs, scientific knowledge, methods of producing and distributing wealth have for centuries undergone no radical alteration and have not been disturbed in their everyday course by infiltrations of foreign elements, material or intellectual. In such societies political forces are always the same, and the class that holds possession of them holds a power that is undisputed. Power is therefore perpetuated in certain families, and the inclination to immobility becomes general through all the various strata in that society.

So in India we see the caste system become thoroughly entrenched after the suppression of Buddhism. The Greeks found hereditary castes in ancient Egypt, but we know that in the periods of greatness and renaissance in Egyptian civilization political office and social status were not hereditary. We possess an Egyptian document that summarizes the life of a high army officer who lived during the period of the expulsion of the Hyksos. He had begun his career as a simple soldier. Other documents show cases in which the same individual served successively in army, civil administration and priesthood.

The best-known and perhaps the most important example of a society tending toward crystallization is the period in Roman history that used to be called the Low Empire. There, after several centuries of almost complete social immobility, a division between two classes grew sharper and sharper, the one made up of great landowners and high officials, the other made up of slaves, farmers and urban plebeians. What is even more striking, public office and social position became hereditary by custom before they became hereditary by law, and the trend was rapidly generalized during the period mentioned.[3]

On the other hand it may happen in the history of a nation that commerce with foreign peoples, forced emigrations, discoveries, wars, create new poverty and new wealth, disseminate knowledge of things that were previously unknown or cause infiltrations of new moral, intellectual and religious currents. Or again—as a result of such infiltrations or through a slow process of inner growth, or from both causes—it may happen that a new learning arises, or that certain elements of an old, long forgotten learning return to favor so that new ideas and new beliefs come to the fore and upset the intellectual habits on which the obedience of the masses has been founded. The ruling class may also be vanquished and destroyed in whole or in part by foreign invasions, or, when the circumstances just mentioned arise, it may be driven from power by the advent of new social elements who are strong in fresh political forces. Then, naturally, there comes a period of renovation, or, if one prefer, of revolution, during which individual energies have free play and certain individuals, more passionate, more energetic, more intrepid or merely shrewder than others, force their way from the bottom of the social ladder to the topmost rungs.

Once such a movement has set in, it cannot be stopped immediately. The example of individuals who have started from nowhere and reached prominent positions fires new ambitions, new greeds, new energies, and this molecular rejuvenation of the ruling class continues vigorously until a long period of social stability slows it down again. We need hardly mention examples of nations in such periods of renovation. In our age that would be superfluous. Rapid restocking of ruling classes is a frequent and very striking phenomenon in countries that have been recently colonized. When social life begins in such environments, there is no ready-made ruling class, and while such a class is in process of formation, admittance to it is gained very easily. Monopolization of land and other agencies of production is, if not quite impossible, at any rate more difficult than elsewhere. That is why, at least during a certain period, the Greek colonies offered a wide outlet for all Greek energy and enterprise. That is why, in the United States, where the colonizing of new lands continued through the whole nineteenth century and new industries were continually springing up, examples of men who started with nothing and have attained fame and wealth are still frequent—all of which helps to foster in the people of that country the illusion that democracy is a fact.

Suppose now that a society gradually passes from its feverish state to calm. Since the human being's psychological tendencies are always the same, those who belong to the ruling class will begin to acquire a group spirit. They will become more and more exclusive and learn better and better the art of monopolizing to their advantage the qualities and capacities that are essential to acquiring power and holding it. Then, at last, the force that is essentially conservative appears—the force of habit. Many people become resigned to a lowly station, while the members of certain privileged families or classes grow convinced that they have almost an absolute right to high station and command.

A philanthropist would certainly be tempted to inquire whether mankind is happier—or less unhappy—during periods of social stability and crystallization, when everyone is almost fated to remain in the social station to which he was born, or during the directly opposite periods of renovation and revolution, which permit all to aspire to the most exalted positions and some to attain them. Such an inquiry would be difficult. The answer would have to take account of many qualifications and exceptions, and might perhaps always be influenced by the personal preferences of the observer. We shall therefore be careful not to venture on any answer of our own. Besides, even if we could reach an undebatable conclusion, it would have a very slight practical utility; for the sad fact is that what the philosophers and theologians call free will—in other words, spontaneous choice by individuals—has so far had, and will perhaps always have, little influence, if any at all, in hastening either the ending or the beginning of one of the historical periods mentioned.

3. Marquardt, *Manuel des antiquités romaines;* Fustel de Coulanges, *Nouvelles recherches sur quelques problèmes d'histoire.*

# *4. The Sociological Character of Political Parties*

BY ROBERT MICHELS

THE POLITICAL PARTY, etymologically and logically, can embrace only a part of the citizenry, politically organized. The party is a fraction; it is *pars pro toto*. Let us endeavor briefly to analyze its causal origin and its behavior.

According to Max Weber, the political party has a dual teleology. It is a spontaneous society of propaganda and of agitation seeking to acquire power, in order to procure thereby for its active militant adherents chances, ideal and material, for the realization either of objective aims or of personal advantages, or of both. Consequently, the general orientation of the political party, whether in its personal or impersonal aspect, is that of *Machstreben* (striving to power).

## *Kinds of Political Parties*

In the personal aspect, parties are often based on the protection accorded inferiors by a strong man. In the Prussian diet of 1855, which was composed of a large number of political groups, each was given the name of its leader. There were the groups of Count de Schlieffen, of Count Arnim, of Tietz, of Karl, of von Patow, of von Vincke, of von Bethmann-Hollweg, of Reichensperger and Mallinkrodt (the last being Catholic). The only group which was called by its true name was a national one, the Polish party.

The history of the labor movement shows that the socialists have not abandoned this "bourgeois" tradition. The socialist parties, on the contrary, have often so completely identified themselves with a leader that they have more or less officially assumed his name, as though to proclaim that they were his property. In Germany, between 1863 and 1875, the rival socialist factions, courting the favor of the mass of workingmen, were the Marxists and the Lassallians. In France, more recently, the great current of socialism was divided into the Broussists, the Allemanists, the Blanquists, the Guesdists, and the Jaurèsists. It is true that the men who so gave their names to different separatist movements personified as completely as possible the ideas and the disposition with which the party was inspired, and which guided them throughout the whole course of their evolution; but it must be admitted, on the other hand, that when the party assumes the name of its leader it is carrying the regard of the herd for its shepherd a bit too far.

Perhaps there is here an analogy between political party and religious sects or monastic orders. Yves-Guyot justly remarked that the individual belonging to a modern party acts after the same fashion as did the mediaeval monks, who, faithful as they were to the precepts of their masters, called themselves after St. Dominicus,, St. Benedictus, St. Augustinius, and St. Franciscus, respectively, the Dominicans, the Benedictines, the Augustines, and the Franciscans. These are the types of party which one may designate as the parties of patronage. If the leader exercises his influence over his followers by qualities so striking that they seem to them supernatural, one can call him a charismatic chief.

This sort of party, the charismatic, takes on varying forms. Ferdinand Lassalle himself, the leader of the Lassallians, was officially merely president of the Allgemeiner Deutscher Arbeiterverein. But he was its president for life. All the main characteristics of leadership were united in him: force of will, wide knowledge, ambition and self-sufficiency, reputation for disinterestedness, celebrity, persuasive oratorship. It pleased him to encourage his followers in idolatry of which he was made the object by the delirious masses and the white-clad virgins who chanted praises to him and offered him bouquets. But not only was, in the case of Lassalle, the charismatic faith the ripe fruit of a psychology which was exuberant and megalomaniacal, but it also was in agreement with the theoretical conception of the hero. We must, he said to the workingmen of the Rhine, in offering them his ideas on the organization of the political party, out of all our scattered desires forge a hammer and place it in the hands of a man whose intelligence, character, and devotion would be to us a guaranty that with the hammer he will strike hard. That is the hammer of the dictator, as he was in fact.

In later periods of history, when the masses demanded at least a simulacrum of democracy and group control in party affairs, and when especially

---

Reprinted from Robert Michels, *First Lectures in Political Sociology*, trans. Alfred De Grazia (Minneapolis: University of Minnesota Press, 1949), pp. 134–54, with the permission of the University of Minnesota Press.

the burning jealousy among the ever-increasing number of leaders admitted no longer, in the socialist movement, the dictatorship of one man, the striking individualities among the leaders, such as August Bebel and Jean Jaurès, were obliged to restrain, as much as possible, these desires and jealousies. Surely, Bebel and Jaurès, were two quite different types of charismatic leaders. The one was an orphan of a Pomeranian sergeant, the other a university professor of southern France. The former possessed hauteur and was as imperious as his cousin, the Kaiser (whence the nickname "Kaiser Bebel" which Gustave Hervé attempted to fix upon him); the latter was an orator without peer, fiery, romantic as well as realistic, seeking to surmount difficulties by seriating problems and to resolve them as fast as they presented themselves. Yet the two great leaders, at once friends and enemies, had in common an indomitable faith both in the efficacy of their action and in the historical destiny of the cohorts whose standard-bearers they were. So both became deified—the Prussian, still during his lifetime; the Frenchman, only, alas, after his death.

Moreover, the present offers to discreet sociologists another example of a great leader of a party which regards him as apostle and seer. In Italy, Benito Mussolini differs from the other men whom we have just mentioned in this: he is not only the leader of a great party, he has become also the leader of a great state. With him the axiom, "The party, it is I," has assumed, not only with regard to powerfulness and consciousness, but also with regard to responsibility and assiduous labor, its maximum development. It is very interesting to see how far the masses understand and develop Mussolini's ideals even beyond his own concept. When, after having barely escaped (only some hours before) an attempt on his life, Mussolini, from the balcony of the Palazzo Chigi, harangued an agitated crowd of ten thousand people, explaining to them Italy's situation and the dangers she would have encountered if he had been killed, a voice was raised from the edge of the throng—immediately to be drowned by thunderous applause: "*Tu sei l'Italia*" ("But you are Italy itself"). With these words the interrupter meant to say (and the applauding crowd accentuated the sentiment) that there is really no difference between Mussolini the man and Italy the country, and that the death of the one would undoubtedly be followed by the complete ruin of the other. The leader of the Fascist party himself openly manifested the charismatic quintessence of his character when, after another attempt on his life, he sent a telegram to his Fascist comrades at Bologna urging them to be certain, absolutely certain, that nothing serious could happen to him before he had completed his task.

We do not here have to indicate the dangers such an idea involves in politics. We shall, however, make one strictly sociological observation. It is evident that charismatic leadership like this bears within itself political dynamics of the utmost vigor. The great Saint-Simon on his deathbed told his disciples, it must be remembered, that in order to do great things one must be impassioned. But to be zealous means to have the gift of inciting the zeal of others. It is, in effect, a formidable goad. This is the advantage of charismatic parties over parties with a well-defined program and a class interest. It is true, on the other hand, that the duration of the former is often circumscribed by the duration of their verve and enthusiasm, which sometimes furnish only a very fragile basis. So we see the charismatic parties induced to rest their appeal, in addition to enthusiasm, as much as possible on institutions more durable than human emotions, such, for example, as protective, workers', and professional organizations and interests.

Charism thus lends itself to all political views, no matter of what complexion. All political parties can be provided with charismatic chiefs. Particularly is this true of young, ardent, doctrinaire parties, although, to be sure, charismatic chiefs are sometimes found in parties of more flexible beliefs. In general, charismatic leaders are, as regards political parties, primary phenomena. In other words, they are the founders of them; it is they who engender and start parties. But the history of political parties demonstrates also that there is a certain number of inverse cases. Then it is the party which is the primary phenomenon. From the chronological point of view the leaders are then secondary; that is to say, they appear later, when the party is already active. But that in no way diminishes the intensity of their force, once acknowledged, provided that the pre-existing party is without other leaders of equal value.

In the second place, there are parties which have for their bases, *a priori,* interests of economic and social classes. And these are especially workers' parties or parties of peasants or of the lower middle class—what the French call "les petites gens"—since the bourgeoisie cannot, by itself, form a party. It is necessary to add still a third category composed of political parties which have been inspired by political or moral ideas—general and abstract—of a *Weltanschauung*. When this conception rests on a more developed and minutely elaborated dogma, one can speak of doctrinaire parties whose doctrines are, however, a privilege of leaders. Here we are in the presence of parties of free trade or protection, or of those which speak of the rights of liberty or of justice (To each the fruit of his labor; or, To each according to his abilities; or, To each according to his needs), or, again, of those which speak of authority.

It is, however, evident that this differentiation into parties of patronage, parties of social or economic interest, and parties of doctrinaire consistency is neither sharp nor final. It is not sharp, for the simple reason that past and present parties represent, in large degree, intermediate nuances or combinations, in which the competent observer will not fail immediately to recognize the existence, sometimes in very unequal proportions, of constituent elements of all three categories. At all events, there is no doubt that the program (which is, so to speak, the codification of political beliefs that have given birth to organization) can, in the first category—based as it is entirely on the faith and authority of a single person—be rudimentary; while it is undeniable that the two other categories, and the second, perhaps, still more than the third, require well developed programs. But even for the doctrinaire parties it may be true to say, with P. Orman Ray, that the principles of a party are apt to be most conspicuous in its early or formative period, while in its later history politics are likely to overshadow principles.

It seems to us, however, that there are still two categories of political parties which, while approaching in a certain sense parties based on principles, have nevertheless characteristics belonging to other types of party that distinguish them somewhat from their analogues. These are the confessional parties and the national parties. The former profess to have, not merely a *Weltanschauung* (theory of life) but an *Ueberweltanschauung* (theory of metaphysical life, a belief). They are the parties seeking to adapt the needs of life here below, envisaged as a preparatory phase, to the immortal life of the soul. The latter, the nationalist parties, may assuredly have ideas both general and universal; they may, for example, proclaim, with the Italian Irredentists, with Stanislao Mancini and Terenzio Mamiani, the priciple of nationality, understood in its true sense as the right of each people, and of each fraction of a people, to complete, unconditioned sovereignty. However, at least ever since 1870, the national parties practicing this ideal have transformed themselves into nationalistic parties. These are, in a sense, more limited and devoid of general principles, because one cannot conceive of a general principle which stops at the frontier, or, still worse, which crosses it only to refuse to other nationalities the claims to liberty and freedom which they jealously reserve for themselves.

It is, nevertheless, equally true that many other political principles in the course of time function in a manner exactly opposite to their original and general aims, e.g., the principle of freedom of thought. One can say that optimists are, in general, extremist theoreticians. The consequences of this have been well put by Georges Sorel in writing of the Jacobins: "If, unfortunately, they find themselves armed with great political power allowing them to realize an ideal that they have conceived, optimists may lead their country to worse catastrophes. They are not long in recognizing, indeed, that social transformations are not achieved with the facility they had expected; they attribute their disappointments to their contemporaries, rather than explain the march of events in terms of historic necessity; thus they end by attempting to remove those people whose evil desires seem to them dangerous to the welfare of mankind. During the Terror, the men who spilt most blood were exactly those who had the keenest desire to enable their fellow-creatures to enjoy the golden age of which they had dreamed, and who had the strongest sympathy for human misery. Optimistic, idealistic, and sensitive, as they were, these men showed themselves the more inexorable as they had a greater thirst for universal well-being."

But if the unconscious identification of finalities—material or immaterial, it matters little—with the general good seems to be an absolute law of our spirit; it is none the less true that of all the social groups it is the national political party which uses and abuses this principle the most. For each nation believes that it must accomplish missions, either of liberty (the French in the Revolution), or of order (the Germans under William II), or of civilization (the "white man's burden"), or of discipline, or of morality, or of other ideals. All of these occur in endowing them with presumptive rights over neighboring peoples, who are judged incapable of facing their jobs without being forced to obey orders issued by the missionary people. The good faith, which very often springs from this idea of a mission, communicating itself to national collectivities, gives them the aplomb and energy of which they have need in order to achieve their goals. This is as much as to say that those critics who estimate that in their aggressive actions national groups are fundamentally ferocious and savage are profoundly wrong. At bottom, this ferocity and savagery which cause people to trample under foot and wipe out the interests and aspirations of others are only the forms in which the missionary—and almost always the visionary—

conviction manifests itself. Missionary peoples are ferocious and savage not in their feelings but in their actions.

However, as I have attempted to prove in one of my books, the need for organization (what Americans call machinery) and the ineluctable tendencies of human psychology, individual and group, cause distinctions of origin in the main to disappear. The political party as such has its own peculiar soul, independent of the programs and rules which it possesses and the eternal principles with which it is embued. The psychology of the crowd is fairly the same in the socialists and the nationalists, in the liberals and the conservatives. In group movements, with rare exceptions everything proceeds naturally, and not "artificially." The fact that the people follow their leader is quite a natural phenomenon. "To use the term exactly," Rousseau has said, "there has never existed a true democracy, and none can ever exist. It is against natural order that the great number should govern and that the few should be governed." Our consistent knowledge of the political life of the principal civilized nations of the world authorizes us to assert that the tendency toward oligarchy constitutes one of the historic necessities, one of the iron laws of history, from which the most democratic modern societies and, within those societies, the most advanced parties, have been unable to escape.

By giving themselves leaders, the workers create with their own hands new masters, whose principal means of domination consists in their technical and intellectual superiority and in the inability of the masses to control the execution of their commands to the leaders. In this respect, the intellectual has played a role in party politics which has many times been the subject of profound study. Moreover, the mechanism of the socialist party offers to the workers, thanks to the numerous salaried and honorary positions of which it disposes, a possibility of making a career, which exercises on them a force of considerable attraction. Now, to the degree that the political calling becomes complicated and the rules of social legislation multiplied, there is imposed on the leaders of political parties an existence more and more professionalized, based on a continuously widening knowledge, savoir-faire, routine, and sometimes delicate finesse. This is why the distance between the leaders and the led grows constantly greater. Thus one can place one's finger upon the flagrant contradiction which exists, in mature parties, between democratic declarations and intentions, on the one hand, and the concrete oligarchic reality, on the other. Hence the continuous raising of conflicts, often Shakespearian in character, in which the comic borders upon the tragic. It may, therefore, be said that the organization constitutes precisely the source whence conservative currents debouch upon the plain of democracy, causing devastating inundations which render that plain unrecognizable.

Such a *Götterdämmerung* can in no way surprise analytic and alert spirits. Long ago Adam Smith's teacher, the Scottish philosopher Hutcheson, remarked that the patience of the people has always been too great and its veneration for its leaders too inept. Furthermore, for Pareto, the contemporary era is in no way characterized by the augmentation of sociality and the diminution of individualism. Fundamentally, it can be only a question of a quadrille chassé-croisé. For example, the sentiment of subordination, whicn was manifested in former days by the subjection, more or less voluntary, of inferior classes to superior classes, has today merely been replaced by the submission of the inferior classes to the leader of their party, the syndicate and the strike, and by the submission, less apparent, of the superior classes to the scum of the people, who have never been the object of so much flattery as in the present. And Gabriel Tarde has referred to two correlative sentiments of modern times, namely, the morbid mistrust of the democratic public for its master, and the fear, the malice, the insipidity of the so-called master who submits to all the orders of his inferiors. Naturally, experience informs us that the sycophant and demagogic chief himself considers flattery merely as a means, his aim being always that of dominating the crowd. The democracy clings to the lofty rungs of the orator's ladder, Charles Maurras has said, just like a woman—for the mob is feminine—whose imagination greets with transport the element which is able to excite her. And Thomas Carlyle well stated before him: "No British man can attain to be a statesman or chief of workers till he has first proved himself a chief of talkers."

## *The Democratic Appeals*

Democracy is of a massive nature. Therefore it cannot function without masses. Parliamentarism presupposes electionism, electionism implies electoral masses. It follows from this that political parties are in vain partly aristocratic in origin and in aim; for it is none the less true that they are forced to make use of the masses. At election time, the *aristoi* candidates deign to descend from their mansions and to bestir themselves among the yokels in order to obtain the majority in their districts. That is not astonishing. They are not indeed ridiculous enough to speak in these solemn and decisive moments for the privilege of minorities, and to restrict themselves to accepting exclusively the votes of that portion of their fellow men who are sole possessors of the governing vocation. Inasmuch as they must rely upon the medium of election, the aristocratic parties make the best of a bad job. After all, the aristocrats cling to the hope of persuading the masses indirectly to renounce their own rights by their own votes. It is, at bottom, the ideal of the Prussian Junkers and the French aristocrats, who, to democratize themselves, discard the cast-off garments of royalty. Moreover, parties of huge economic and social classes or interests also follow this method of camouflage very closely. The majority parties also take care, in political elections, to address themselves not alone to their associates. In democracy every one appeals to the people, to every one of the people, without discrimination. The Socialist party—the most strictly proletarian—does not hesitate to solicit openly, at the proper time, the suffrage of artisans, peasants, and petty bourgeoisie. A Socialist who before the elections, and afterward, has only a very narrow conception of what is meant by the working class, loves, during the campaign, to stretch the theoretical extent of this class to the point of including capitalists, providing, of course, that they are not too refractory to accord to their employees, in such a case, some small wage increment.

This tendency, immanent in contemporary political life, and which a wag would be tempted to denominate a game of hide-and-seek, manifests itself even in the names that political parties are accustomed to give themselves in democratic countries. Indeed, in a democracy, political parties tend to envelop themselves in a very thick terminological fog, and one of nearly even color. Here are a few modern political nomenclatures. In France, the Liberal Action, the Progressive Republicans, the Republican Union, the Democratic Left, the Radical Left, the Radical-Socialist Republicans, the Socialist Republicans. In Germany, the German Popular party, the German People's National party, the German People's party, the Democratic party, the Social Democratic party, and the Christian People's party. In Switzerland the names of political parties differ scarcely at all from those used among their larger neighbors. One would say that no party is distinguishable from the others. All the German and French parties are more or less equally "popular," "democratic," and "national." This tendency is a beautiful example, indeed, of the application of Darwin's law of adaptation to environment carried over into the political field. It is almost cryptic mimicry. In the French elections of 1848 the candidates of almost all shades of political opinion liked to call themselves workers and socialists, in homage to the first universal suffrage. Nowadays they are all democratic.

The influence which the omnibus tendency exerts on political parties is also very distinctly apparent in the tactics of the confessional parties. Let us remember, for example, that in the most important countries of Europe, where there is a Catholic party it has the habit of carefully concealing its essential character by the designations it uses. None ventures to call itself Catholic. In Italy, the Catholic party calls itself, quite simply, "Popular"; in Germany, it becomes the "Center party." But further: the latter party offers strong inducements to have among its members, even among its official representatives, a certain number of Protestants. In Italy, at the congress held by the Catholic party at Easter, 1923, in Turin, Don Sturzo, under the pretext that a party truly Catholic is a *contradictio in adjecto* (the word Catholic signifying universal, and the word party signifying partial), advanced the thesis that his party should be strongly non-confessional. This omnibus tendency has penetrated even into parliament. If this needs demonstration, it will suffice to cite, in France, the paradoxical existence in the Palais Bourbon, in addition to the politically constituted groups, of a "group of deputies not enrolled in any group," which includes men of every shade of opinion, and which even names a bureau.

There is, of course, among political parties a differentiating tendency, which we shall designate a centrifugal tendency, by which they are induced to distinguish themselves one from another, whether in their program and theoretical basis or in their daily manifestations. Moreover, this tendency seems to be repressed and often diverted by a much stronger tendency inherent in all political parties. This is the integrative tendency of the numerical maximum, mortal enemy to all freedom of program and of thought. It is a centripetal tendency, and, in fact, only the logical consequence of the fundamental tendency that dominates the life of political parties, namely, the tendency toward the conquest of the state. Where there are only two parties, as in America, this system is already the extreme expression of the victory of the centripetal tendency over the centrifugal. This victory seems still more manifest considering the fact that the Democrats and the Republicans are at present almost devoid of theoretical or programmatical differences, so that they can both address themselves to the electorate without any "ballast" of differentiating ideas.

## *False Party Classifications*

In truth, the *raison d'être* of the political party is the push for power. Here the objectives certainly differ, some wishing to reach their goal in a peaceful fashion, without agitation (evolutionary as it were). Others, believing that by evolutionary methods they may never attain their ends, prefer an action or a series of actions more vigorous and rapid, by tactics called revolutionary. And it is likewise obvious that the conceptions of political parties are no more identical in the action to be taken after success—action which will depend, at least in principle, on conceptions which they have formed of the role of the state, and which may, in theory, even contemplate its abolition. For to destroy, it is necessary first to capture. At any rate, the first stage of the political party is determined by its ardent desire to absorb power, to become the state. Also the final goal of the party consists in statization. This is why, while awaiting utopia, the party will try to establish at the outset as much as possible a little state within the state. One may thus sustain the thesis that the most accomplished political party will be that one which will have created in its own ranks all the organizing and intellectual details of a nature to make it capable some day to assume the functions of the state, in complete form, just as Minerva issued fully armed from the brain of Jupiter.

It will be worth while to deal briefly with Vilfredo Pareto's theory of political parties. Like Max Weber, the author of these lines, and others, Pareto begins with the premise that political parties seek power. He then divides parties into two essential groups. First, there are the parties which devote themselves to government. This group embraces alike the party in power and those that do not hold it but aspire to it with good chance, and that meanwhile form the parties of opposition. Second, there are the intransigent parties which would hardly attain power. These last contain a greater number of fanatics, but also of honest men, than the other parties which are less ferocious but likewise more depraved. Let us note in passing that, according to an axiom of Italian juridical sociology, it is not a universal supposition that a government is composed of honest men. An eminent Italian sociologist, Gaetano Mosca, considers it even difficult for an honest man, having achieved the realization of his political ambitions, to resist deterioration of his moral sense, and seems to prefer that the honest man remain and act outside of the government, though capable of influencing public opinion.

We should not dare to say, however, that the differentiation of Pareto is impeccable. In the first place, his point of view is, in my opinion, erroneous. To divide political parties into those that have "arrived" and those that have not or do not wish to do so, is to set up chance as a criterion, unless one considers that there are political parties which have amused themselves in being intransigent out of pure whimsy, which is inadmissible. For if there are parties that, at a given moment, refuse to take office, even when it is offered to them like a ripe fruit, this refusal does not signify a renunciation forever—a thing which would be for them equivalent to suicide. The refusal, on the contrary, is inspired in these cases by the fear either of not yet being ready to assume with impunity the responsibilities of government, or of being uncertain of the obedience of their adherents, divided by differences of opinion on the tactics to be followed; or, again, because they fear accepting but a Trojan horse and falling into an ambush or a trap which their enemies have laid for them. It is certain that such refusals (recent examples have been furnished by the Italian and French socialist parties) may be judged in a very different manner, as approaching a "policy of missed occasions and of tardy repentance." Whatever it is, these refusals to assume power have, as we have seen, an accidental and casuistical political causation, and always imply the party's hope of being able at an early maturity to redeem the mortgage on government and to conquer the state under political constellations more lucky and more promising.

In the second place, by identifying the party "arrived" and the party transigent, Pareto implies a relation between conquest of power and political compromise which certainly can often be verified, but which, nevertheless, is very far from forming a sovereign law capable of comprehending the extremely varied history of modern political parties.

Here, still another question arises. May one, perhaps, distinguish political parties according to whether their aspirations are fixed in past history or in political progressivism? Are there not, indeed, retrogressive and reactionary parties and progressive parties? There resides in this nomenclature a modicum of truth. One can undoubtedly discern parties tending toward a re-establishment of political and social institutions which have existed and which are judged superior and more suitable than the state of things which has replaced them. Parenthetically, we may add that, pursuant to this uniquely historical criterion of time—which involves neither the idea of liberty, nor that of authority, nor yet that of any other principle of political or philosophic order—one should logically designate as retrogressive, for example, the anti-Bolshevist parties in Russia, as well as the liberal anti-Fascist parties in Italy, the monarchist parties of France and Germany, and the irredentist parties in the countries detached from their fatherlands. Of course, this criterion gives us a most incongruous collection of political organizations in which are found joined together mortal enemies bound to one another by but a single tie: their common aspiration toward a pre-existing state of things, whatever it may have been. On the other hand, there is a group of political parties certainly no less incongruous than the collection we have just examined. These are the progressive parties, envisaging a new state of things which has never existed in history, but which they deem possible, desirable, and practicable. The prototypes of these parties are the socialist parties in central and western Europe.

It would, however, not be exact to classify political parties in two categories, those of the past and those of the future. This is true, in the first place, because whoever dares to range himself along with partisans of Giambattista Vico's philosophy of history—the kernel of which consists in the cyclical theory of *corsi e ricorsi*—would not at all doubt the thesis that the present is merely a contradictory parenthesis between the past and the future, with the result that the future often possesses a greater affinity with the past than it does with the present. In the next place, one lacks the historic sense if one supposes it possible completely to restore the past. Epochs of history do not lend themselves to photographic reproduction. In the process, something has been altered, some one has moved, as regards congruity of situation and agreement of will. This is why parties of the past should not imagine themselves able to re-establish the *tempora acta* as they were. The future must perforce be influenced by the durable changes which have been produced, the "reactionary" party must take account, not only of the real advantages evolved by the disliked present order which it is trying to eliminate, but also of the new fundamental interests which this régime has created. Let us cite two examples. In France, the defeat of the great Revolution and of the fulfillment (though incomplete) which it found in Napoleon I, even while involving the return of the Bourbons and the so-called Restoration, did not—despite the promises of indemnity made to the émigrés—at all restore the old great landed estates. The reaction interfered but slightly with the new peasant class, which, through *fas aut nefas,* had been called into being by means of the redistribution of confiscated property of the aristocrats. Although it is somewhat undesirable, and indeed hazardous, to predict a future enveloped in the mists of the unknown, it seems clear that the fall of Bolshevism, uncertain though it be, will end in enormous transformations within the legal and economic constitution of Russia, but will leave intact the new forms of small agrarian property which, at the expense of the nobility, have replaced the *latifundia.*

A word more on the question, terminological in the extreme, of parties called revolutionary. Too often is assigned to the term "revolutionary" special historical significance derived from the memory men preserve of the great French Revolution, which is generally considered the prototype of revolutions. It follows that one attaches the word only to the struggles for liberty undertaken by inferior social classes against their superiors. And in addition to this, the popular interpretation of the term involves the existence of violence and blood-letting; whereas, from the purely logical point of view, the word implies only a fundamental change of a legal order, no matter what means are employed to consummate it. Hence one can sustain the thesis that the terms "revolution" and "counter-revolution" are, after all, equivalent. There is only a moral difference between them, and this difference is merely subjective.

In 1831, a Prussian historian, Friedrich von Raumer, wrote from Paris these sensible words: "For liberals, the word 'revolutionary' signifies the suppression of a decrepit and obsolete social order, pernicious and ignominious; while 'counter-revolution' is in their eyes equivalent to a leaning toward injustice and an outworn order. On the contrary, their opponents, the conservatives, understand by the word 'revolution' the aggregate of all follies and delinquencies; while the word 'counter-revolution' is for them a synonym for order, authority, and religion." It is, then, a question of words that express only sentiments and evaluations perhaps quite appreciable but entirely personal and arbitrary. Political science should not countenance such kinds of terminology.

Certainly what may appear to some the debacle of democracy and a sad, nearly irremediable, lesion of its eternal principles can seem to others the confirmation of a salutary law. This law prescribes that men, in every enterprise requiring collective action, must submit their particular movements to the rule of the single will of a leader, and that, of the two possible attitudes, loyalty and mistrust, to be assumed toward that leader—to whom democracies must have recourse—the former is the only one that is constructive and generous.

Since the World War, two new parties, inspired by the ideas of August Blanqui on minorities, and still more by the severe and diversified conceptions of the French syndicalist movement under the spiritual direction of Georges Sorel (Pareto's friend), have arisen. The parties have a new basis, that of the elite. Both consequently find themselves in deep-seated contrast with the current democratic and electionist theories. In Russia, bolshevism, while seizing the central power with an unheard-of violence, has imposed on the majority of the population the domination of a proletarian minority. In Italy, fascism, gifted with the same *élan vital,* snatched the power from weak hands and called to itself, in the name of the country, the minority of active and energetic men who are always to be found.

Moreover, the anti-democratic and theoretically minority elite is rather unable to set completely aside the principle of the masses. For more than a century, liberalism, democracy, and socialism have daily addressed themselves to all classes of the people equally. Let us add to this the method of modern patriotism, which we know to be of a revolutionary nature both by its origin and by its tactics, and which has never ceased to attract to it or to try to fascinate the very last molecule of the national community. Indeed, on the eve of the Revolution, France was (or seemed to the democrats to be) merely an assemblage of people badly united, in part strangers to one another. In spite of a constant tendency toward unity, this France of the *ancien régime* appeared to exhibit only diversity, disorder, heterogeneity; to contemporaries it offered the aspect of chaos. France was united neither in civil legislation (which included more than three hundred local systems of law, often contradictory), nor in administration, nor in judicature, nor in military arrangements, nor in communal life, nor in anything at all. Also, in order to voice in this disunited country the sentiment of *la patrie moderne,* one must give to the whole of France, urban and rural, leave to speak. Heaven knows how much she made use of it in the cahiers of 1789.

Now, with the awakening of the laboring and peasant masses which followed thereupon for nearly a century and a half, the phenomenology of the facts which unroll continually before our eyes demonstrates that today the elite is no longer able to maintain its power without the explicit or tacit consent of the masses upon which it in numerous ways depends. There is, then, between the party, monopolistic and so far master of the state as to be confounded with it, on the one hand, and the masses, deprived of so-called political rights, on the other a social constraint at all points reciprocal. So, at least in Italy, the party of the elite, the Fascists, could but solicit, secure, and conserve the sympathy of the masses. In pursuing this end, the Fascist party was also led by political necessity, i.e, the need of proving to the neighboring states—that, although theoretically a minority, it fully represents the authentic and autochthonous popular will. From this results the adoption of the consensual theory which rests (more than upon the popular vote) upon a public opinion mensurable less by the liberty of the press than by the number of adherents and political and economico-social organizations. It is to some extent popular enthusiasm which serves the parties of the elite as justification of their acquired rights. In relying upon it the party of the elite loses very little of its theoretical purity because an elite, theoretically sure as it is both of its calling and its power, will, by definition, be self-sufficient. There is no need for the elite to have the majority in agreement with it.

And this is truly the antinomy of anti-democracy, an antinomy not necessarily tragic but dangerous, consisting in a dilemma that appears in a form which one might liken to that of an accordion. For the parties of the elite describe, in their applied political life, a perpetual oscillatory movement, stimulated alternately by fortuities, such as the suitability of the situation, and still more by the two inherent tendencies, that is, by their doctrinaire stereotypes and by their political interests. Indeed, the parties of the elite, turn by turn, swell their structures excessively up to the point of embracing nearly the whole nation and boast of their millions of political and syndical assessed members, and then suddenly contract their frames by expelling the excess, attempting to become again minority parties, properly so called, namely, the parties of election and of choice, sometimes even in proportion to a *numerus clausus.* Between these two extreme limits, the one signalized by the indispensability of the authority of numbers, and the other fixed by the principle of homogeneity and of the strength which flows therefrom, the pendulum oscillates unceasingly.

## II–SOME PATTERNS OF POLITICAL ORGANIZATION AND AUTHORITY

# 1. *The Idea of Corporation*

BY OTTO VON GIERKE

## *I*

THE INTERPRETATION of the material set down in the *Corpus juris civilis,* by the flourishing science of law in medieval Italy, called forth theoretical reflections about the legal nature of corporate groups [*Verbaende*]. Thus, a learned theory of corporations came into being.

Its foundations were laid by the glossators of secular law. The extant legal writings of the pre-Bologna period, as well as the writings of the Lombard school of law, fail to show even a faint trace of a theory of corporations. The glossators, however, by their thorough scholarly preoccupation with the sources, were necessarily led to resume the theoretical considerations about the legal nature of corporate groups already made by the Romans. Furthermore, making the rediscovered ideas of a vanished era the objects of their own thinking, they supplied the modern science of law with a speculative element that was alien to Roman jurisprudence. They were the first to raise questions about the "legal nature" and the "essence of the thing." They posed the fundamental question as to whether, and to what extent, the *universitas,* or corporate body, is essentially identical with the sum of its members and the whole with the sum of its parts. The raising of these questions sowed the seed for all future speculation on the nature of the subjectivity of corporate groups. [*Verbandssubjektivitaet*].

Yet the glossators and their immediate successors did not go beyond the beginnings of a theory of corporations. Its dogmatic elaboration and full expression took place only around the middle of the thirteenth century, and—as we shall see—it was largely in the hands of the canonists. In two respects, however, the foundations laid in this preparatory stage by the civilistic glossators remained crucial for the entire medieval theory of corporations.

First of all, the glossators had a major share in introducing Roman legal views of corporate groups into medieval thinking. They adhered as closely as possible to the text of the sources, much more closely than their successors. They took no account of the specific features of the legal customs of their own time whenever they had, or believed to have, an unequivocal decision of the sources before them. To the extent that they understood the sources correctly, the glossators inevitably revived Roman legal notions, although this revival was at first limited only to the community of scholars.

On the other hand, they themselves had already brought into the theory of corporations an abundance of medieval Germanic elements. Here, more than in any other area, the source material, difficult and incomplete as it was, defied their full comprehension. The principle behind the separate statements of the sources remained hidden to them; the historical context escaped them; the actual bases of the Roman [legal] abstractions remained strange to them. The distinction between legal subjectivity of public law and the personality of private law—so fundamental for Roman legal thought—must especially have been beyond their comprehension. They frequently tended to make obvious reinterpretations and misinterpretations and ingenious emendations. But wherever they acted in such an involuntarily independent way, the glossators read into the sources the point of view of the earlier, still essentially Germanic, Middle Ages, whose children they themselves were.

Through the medium of the Longobard law and particularly the Longobard feudal law, the Italian statutes, and some laws of the German emperors, the glossators acquired a wealth of positive Germanic legal material, which was often incorporated

Translated by Ferdinand Kolegar, from Otto von Gierke, *Das deutsche Genossenschaftsrecht* (Berlin: Weidmannsche Buchlandlung, 1881), Book III, chap. xii, pp. 188–238.

into their system. But the whole intellectual climate of medieval Italy and the realities of the state and legal life surrounding them influenced the intellectual form into which they shaped Roman legal materials. With respect to the gamut of political ideas and styles, inseparable from corporation law, it goes without saying that the law which predominated in Italy in the period of glossators was the Germanic law. It is thus understandable that the ideas of Germanic law infiltrated the glossators' theory of corporations.

But the [legal] elements of ancient Rome and of the Germanic Middle Ages were not amalgamated in the glossators' doctrine. From the onset, an inner cleavage was implanted in corporation theory that has never been entirely healed. The contradiction and conflict of these two conceptions led to many confusions and misunderstandings, but they also gave impetus to a rich theoretical development.

The glossators themselves were not fully aware of the contradiction between the divergent conceptions with which they operated. Nevertheless, they discerned the point which was at the root of the basic predicament of the theory and of the cleavage of the conceptions. They took pains to answer the question they had introduced into jurisprudence, namely, the question of the conceptual relationship between the group as a whole and the sum of its parts. Yet, as we shall demonstrate, they did not succeed in finding a satisfactory answer. We search in vain through their writings for a cogently formulated principle that was consciously applied to all particulars. They covered up resulting contradictions by blunting the unpleasant edge of this or that rule or completely ignoring, as if by a tacit consensus, this or that logical difficulty. Only over relatively unimportant points do the differences crystallize into explicit controversies.

In its foundations, the glossators' theory of corporations is incomplete, inconclusive, and ambiguous. This is true not only of the form in which we encounter this theory in the compilation of *Glossa ordinaria,* but also of its formulation in the extant writings of the mid-thirteenth century.

We shall now attempt to reconstruct this first stage of the medieval theory of corporations. It is apparent that the corporation theory of the glossators and their successors contains the beginnings of a juridical conception of state and ecclesiastic corporate groups. But at the point where, in the glossators' own view, the genuine state sphere begins, the medieval philosophic conception of the universal spiritual-temporal association of mankind rises above the legal conception evolved from the corporation law. This is the meeting ground of the ideas of Romanistic jurisprudence developed on the basis of the revived Roman law, the theorems derived from the doctrine of the church, political ideas formulated in the struggle between the church and the state, and philosophical reflections about state and church stemming from the renascence of ancient philosophy. Therefore, both here and in the subsequent stages of development of the medieval theory of corporations, we shall discuss the relevant aspects of the theoretical system of the jurists only so far as necessary for our understanding and, later on, for a comprehensive presentation of the public-law theories of the Middle Ages.

The glossators' concept of the corporation is extraordinarily broad and vague. It coincided substantially, in their own time and during the whole Middle Ages, with the concept of the corporate group as a legal subject. The glossators did not find in the sources any other generic term to denote a subjective unit that cannot be dissolved into a simple communal or societal relationship among the many [*Gemeinschafts- oder Gesellschaftsverhaeltnis unter Mehreren*], nor did they coin such a concept themselves.

Consequently, the glossators subsume every corporate unit that is a subject of public and private rights—including the church and the state—under the one concept of corporation. The term they prefer most to denote it is *universitas,* but they often use terms like *corpus, collegium,* and even *societas* co-extensively. They nevertheless try to establish a more precise and consistent terminology. Thus, while emphasizing the general meaning of the word *universitas,* they want to regard *collegium* only as an association of *"simul cohabitantes";* *societas* as an association of *"non cohabitantes";* and *corpus* as any one of both instances. But they themselves do not carry out this arbitrary differentiation, whose legal insignificance has been already noted by Baldus.

The definitions of the concept of corporation preserved from this time are so general as to be applicable to any organized human corporate group. The *Glossa ordinaria* does not contain any definition at all. On the other hand, the definitions of Pillius (*Summa* to *Cod.* 11, 17, No. 1) and of Hugolinus (*Summa* to *Dig.* 3, 4 No. 1), later attributed to Azo, were held in great respect. Yet Pillius says: "*Collegium est personarum plurium in corpus unum quasi conjunctio vel collectio: quod generali sermone universitas appellatur, corpus quoque, vulgariter apud nos consortium vel schola.*" The definition of Hugolinus is even more general. Lumping together the universalities of persons and of things and quoting a reference from 1. 30 D. 41, 3, he defines: "*universitas est plurium corporum collectio inter se distantium, uno nomine specialiter eis deputato.*" The words "*plurium collectio*" are used to indicate the difference from the *individuum* (such as *"bos vel Socrates"*) which consists of parts; the words *"inter se distantium"* are meant to exclude the *totum integrale,* the compound things (such as *armarium vel carruca*); and the words "*specialiter eis deputato,*" to indicate that a generic term (such as *homo*) of itself does not denote a *universitas.* As a subspecies of the *universitas,* Hugolinus regards the *universitas rationabilis,* which alone is meant by the Digest title, despite the rubric word "*cujusque.*" A corporation to him, then, is any human corporate group that is outwardly characterized as a separate entity by means of a special corporate name.

Not only were all the then existing communities and associations included under this generic concept. It was also applied to institutions [*Anstalten*] and foundations [*Stiftungen*], which we have come to think of in contrast to the corporation. Herein the glossators followed the example of the sources. But they treated the idea of corporation earnestly, in a way quite different than in late Roman law with the institutionalized corporation concept. All temporal and ecclesiastic groups were not only classified but also treated as *universitates.* This could be done because the corporate element in fact was never quite lacking in the temporal groups of that time, and it was also present, at least as a norm, in the ecclesiastic groups.

The church especially, in so far as it was discussed as a legal subject, was subsumed under the concept of the corporation. The glossators came to realize that the word *ecclesia* has several meanings. In particular, one had to distinguish three meanings of it: the general or universal, the spatial, and the particular church. The *ecclesia universalis* was conceived of as an *universitas* endowed with rights and privileges. There was no need of a more precise specification of the nature of the church, since the ownership of the church property and, thus, the legal subjectivity in accordance with secular law were ascribed to the individual churches. With regard to the individual churches, the linguistic usage that introduced the "*locus pius*" or "*locus religiosus*" as a subject continues. An attempt is even made to construe the legal subjectivity of the church as a personification of a thing [*Sachpersonifikation*]. We read about an "*archiepiscopus Moyses,*" who advanced the view that *ecclesia* is always "*locus consecratus et parietibus circumdatus*"; that the church in this spatial sense has property and possessions ("*quod ipse locus possideat*"); and that, therefore, especially after a complete cessation of clerical fellowship, the church property is held together by walls (*quod parietes possessionem retineant*"), since in reality "*etiam durante collegio parietes possideant.*" According to the gloss, it might be said in support of Moyses that the sources actually understood the *ecclesia* mostly in terms of the church building. Yet, at the same time, the church was regarded as having the right, having possession, and being the proper plaintiff in an action for recovery. But this conception, which might have led to a genuine concept of institution [*Anstalt*], was not understood, and there were even many who rejected it as absurd.

The prevailing view ascribed rights and privileges to the church in the spatial sense, but these were only special privileges of all consecrated places, such as the right of asylum, etc. The idea of God's ownership of the church property expressed in one gloss and the popular view of ownership by a particular patron saint of the church were insufficient from the legal standpoint, and the glossators had recourse to the third meaning of *ecclesia,* i.e., *ecclesia* as a local corporate group. This must be understood whenever the church is discussed as a legal subject. Considering the conditions of that time, the local corporate group [*lokaler Verband*] was not conceived of as the congregation [*Gemeinde*], but only as the clerical fellowship [*Genossenschaft*]. In this way, the glossators arrived at a definition such as the one formulated by Placentinus: "*ecclesia dicitur collectio vel coadunatio virorum vel mulierum in aliquo sacro loco constitutorum vel constitutarum ad serviendum Deo.*" Thus, the church was actually brought into the corporate schema as a legal subject, and thus the *ecclesia* could be counted forthwith among the *universitates* and *collegia* and be subjected to the same rules of law. Moreover, since it was the most privileged of corporations, the church could not be deprived of any right ascribable to a corporation. Consequently, it was put on the same level with the *respublica* and *civitas.*

This corporate concept of the church was completely applicable to the collegiate churches and monasteries. One always thought primarily of such churches, and the legists generally refer to cathedral churches and cloisters for the purpose of exemplification in corporation law. But this concept becomes inadequate once the collegiate arrangement is lacking or is left out of consideration. As soon as one is fully aware that this subsumption is inappropriate, one cannot help but apply the corporation law anyway. Typical in this respect is the glossators' treatment of the controversial question: "*an episcopus, abbas aut similes personae juramentum calumniae ipsi subire debeant.*" A legal dispute about the components of church property is obviously assumed. In such a case, the prelate acts alone, not as a head of the collegiate body or with the collegiate body co-acting. There is a dispute over whether, in such an instance, the prelate can be represented in taking the oath. The right to swear through a *syndicus* or *actor* is regarded as a privilege of the *universitas.* Several legists, notably Aldricus, refuse to grant this right to the bishop or abbot, "*quia isti non sunt universi nec universitas,*" (or as a gloss says: "*quia ipse nec univ. nec corpus nec coll. est*"), and because they are represented by a regular *procurator* without the rights of a *syndicus.* In spite of this, the opposite view of Johannes Bassianus, i.e., the application of the corporation law, became prevalent. The reasoning was that the prelate does not litigate on behalf of himself but on behalf of the *ecclesia* and is, thus, on an equal footing with a guardian or a similar "*legitimus administrator.*" But it remained unanswered what the represented *ecclesia* really is.

As a rule, little attention was paid to churches employing only one clergyman. Only Azo, who is generally commendably precise, tried to formulate a church concept comprehensive enough to include such churches. He defines *ecclesia* as "*persona constituta ad serviendum Deo vel collectio personarum plurium ad idem destinata.*" But he obviously designates thereby only the outward form of the ideal legal subject and leaves unsolved the question of the nature of this subject in case of its being represented by *una persona.* In his further discussion, Azo, like other glossators, makes the assumption that the church acts as a *collegium.*

Charitable endowments did not evoke a special concept of institution or foundation as an addition to the concept of corporation. On the one hand, as church institutes, they were classed together with the *ecclesiae;* on the other hand, they were subsumed under the generic concept of *collegia* and *corpora.* This classification is a result of the old conception according to which even the *personae miserabiles* in the hospital or poorhouse constitute a *collegium.*

The fact that the legists subsumed the churches and ecclesiastical institutions under the corporation of Roman law had an important consequence, namely, that the canonists, in their turn, could incorporate the Roman corporation law into the church doctrine of ecclesiastical institutions. In this medley of the elements of fellowship [*Genossenschaftlich*] and of institutions [*anstaltlich*], the legists gave precedence to the idea of fellowship, whereas the canonists embraced the institutional idea.

No less important was the fact that the glossators subsumed the organs of the state of their time under the concept of corporation and consequently under Roman corporation law. In strict adherence to the classical texts, the glossators apply the Roman concept of the state only to the empire (*Reich*) of their time, identifying it with the Roman empire of the Caesarean era. For all other corporate groups, be they kingdoms or independent republics, they retain the concept of *universitas.*

However, the glossators would hardly have reproved the later conception, which saw in the empire (*Reich*) itself only the most supreme and most inclusive *universitas.* But they do not yet make such an explicit subsumption. Rather they uphold in their theory the contrariety between the empire and other corporate groups as they found it in the sources. They put into the Roman concept of corporation a content that makes it possible for it to be used for theoretical construction of entities having all the characteristics of the state, save formal sovereignty.

The glossators insist that the Roman Empire is the only state in the sense of the sources. They claim the plenitude of power of the state only for the Emperor. This plenitude of power follows from his exclusive possession of the *imperium* conferred upon him by the *populus Romanus.* And wherever the senate and the people are mentioned as bearers of state rights, in addition to the Emperor, the glossators apply these passages literally to the Roman senate and Roman people of their own day and treat the urban community of medieval Rome as the privileged *respublica Romana* and as the capital of the empire. In their view, there is no temporal sovereign but the Emperor, no real *respublica* but the *respublica Romana.* They regard all other holders of public authority, including kings and princes, as Roman magistrates with a derivative *imperium;* and their lands, as Roman provinces and city districts. Every self-contained commonalty—vaguely defined as *populus,* as *civitas,* or as *respublica*—fits into the framework of the Roman *universitas,* no matter whether it is compared, as in the monarchical constitution, to the *universitas provinciae* under the *praeses provinciae,* or, as in a republican constitution, to the Roman *municipium.*

Nevertheless, the idea of a true disestablishment of the territorial and municipal corporate groups was not contained in the teachings of the glossators. No matter how much the glossators tried to enhance the imperial power, the medieval empire [*Kaiserreich*] was much too removed from a genuine and exclusive state to make it plausible for them to resuscitate, though only in theory, the Roman conception of public law concentrated in the sphere of one single will. And it was impossible to deny independent publicistic legal subjectivity to the more or less independent territories and municipalities, which contained the beginnings of the state structure to a far greater extent than was the case in the Reich, and especially to the powerful city republics of Italy, in whose midst the glossators themselves lived. If the medieval lands and cities were to be regarded as provinces and municipal towns of the Roman law, the compelling nature of these facts forced an expansion of these concepts that was alien to the sources. This occurred in such a way that all fundamental concepts of the Roman law of state were unconsciously assimilated by the glossators to the medieval point of view. Roman offices came to be regarded as official prerogatives, jurisdictions as privileges, the *imperium merum* and *mixtum* and the *jurisdictio* as patrimonial or feudal property of their owners. The conception according to which public power was an object of acquired rights was thus brought into the sources. The associations [*engere Verbaende*] or their heads obtained many publicistic power rights that could be traced to enfeoffment of superior power, but which were thought of as independently acquired subjective rights even with regard to the grantor of the fief. Indeed, the internal corporate rights were regarded as original attributes of the entity of every corporate group. The *universitas* thus became a self-contained body; its very concept held the quintessence of a public community [*oeffentliches Gemeinwesen*], and it was capable of absorbing all the constituents of the state.

In principle, however, the glossators do not agree to applying the name of the public community to the associations [*engere Verbaende*]. Following the sources, they assert that the terms "*res publica,*" "*jus publicum,*" "*bona publica*" can be rightly applied only to the empire and the city of Rome, other commonalties being "*loco privatorum.*" They also uphold the lasting validity of the internal and external provincial and municipal law of the Justinian era. For this reason, they attribute to the cities only the importance of the Roman *municipia,* and explain the independent status of the Italian cities, which is inconsistent with that notion, mostly as usurpation. In all jurisdictions that, according to Roman administrative organization, are in some way permanently connected with provincial or municipal administration, the glossators see the rights of such corporate groups, loaned one and for all and hence vested rights. For them, these corporate groups [*Verbaende*] are the equivalents of provinces and *municipia.* They concede the possibility of an enlargement of a thus constituted normal sphere of authority by special privileges of the Emperor or by other legitimate legal titles, from which they naturally let follow other acquired rights. On the basis of misunderstood passages, they finally grant to any recognized *universitas* autonomy, jurisdiction, election of the head, and other rights of self-administration. Actually, they elevate the associations [*engere Verbaende*] of the empire to public communities. The glossators increasingly apply the concept and the right of *respublica,* of *jus publicum,* and of *bona publica* to the individual *populi* and *civitates,* with the usual provisos. Indeed, the glossators sometimes openly admit that they ascribe to the corporation a public-law sphere of its own.

Yet, having taken from the Romans the terms *publicus* and *privatus,* the glossators do not make the complete separation of public and private rights in fact. Under the influence of medieval views, they constantly apply many public-law principles to situations included under Roman private law. Consider the continual confusion of dominance [*Herrschaft*] and property right [*Vermoegensrecht*] in the concept of *dominium!* Thus, the glossators are in the position to inject public-law content into allegedly private rights of corporations.

In fact, then, the glossators' doctrine of corporations contains a fair amount of theory concerning public or constitutional law.

## *II*

In view of such an expansion of the concept of corporation, the glossators were little prepared to comprehend the nature of the corporation as it was understood in the classical texts, since the sources did not contain an explicit formulation of fundamental Roman ideas. Because the separation of publicistic and property-law aspects of the corporate groups did not occur to them, the glossators lacked the key to a full comprehension of the various definitions contained in the sources. They applied anything stated in the sources about the public functions of a group or its head, uncritically to the sphere of the legal person as assumed in private law, and the other way round. In all their fumbling attempts at a conceptualization of the nature of corporativeness, the glossators take it for granted that the group [*Verbandsganze*] is in precisely the same way a subject as to property and as to power [*Vermoegenssubjekt und Machtsubjekt*].

In this sense, the glossators take from the sources the general idea that the corporate group, as such, is a unitary legal subject [*einheitliches Rechtssubjekt*]. By defining the *universitas* as an association "*in corpus unum*" and comparing its members to the limbs of the human body, they conceive of the corporation as a unified whole made up of many parts. They ascribe to this whole its own legal subjectivity, by maintaining—following the classical texts—that the *universitas* does not change with the exchange of its members, that it can last perpetually, and that it has a right different from that of the *singuli*.

The glossators did not succeed in building a foundation for corporate legal subjectivity, since they failed to make the decisive step, which was the application of the concept of personality to the *universitas*. Not once does one find in the writings of the glossators the word and the concept of "juristic person." The gloss characteristically refrains from any comment on the famous *lex mortuo* and on other passages of the classical texts that later led to the discovery of the personality of the corporate group. This fact makes it unnecessary to speculate about the nature of the corporate-group personality. Similarly, the theory of fictions was then not yet established. The first legist to write about the nature of the corporate legal subjectivity lived in the first half of the thirteenth century and was also a canonist. His name was Roffredus of Benevant. In the qu. 27 of his *Questiones sabbatinae,* Roffredus discusses the question of the right of recovery of a sponsor of a *universitas* against the *singuli* and, with a precision unusual at that time, evolves the distinction between the *universitas* and the *singuli*. In this connection, he raises the question as to whether anybody could represent a *pars universitatis* in a lawsuit. He declares that this is logically impossible because the "*universitas est quoddam individuum, unde partes non habet,*" since—according to Aristotle—the individual is indivisible. The manner in which the idea of an indivisible individuality of the corporation is expressed shows clearly that Roffredus was not yet familiar with the concept of *persona ficta*. This concept was to gain currency soon thereafter.

So the glossators did not go beyond the idea that the corporate legal subject is identical with the totality [of members] [*Gesammtheit*]. And they were then confronted with an even more ponderous question concerning the relationship of the totality as a unity to the totality as a multiplicity.

They did not reach an unequivocal decision on this cardinal question. The text of the sources has drawn them to the Roman conception, which held the *universitas* as a unitary legal subject to be an artificial "individual" quite distinct from the totality of its members. But the glossators were far from expressing and pursuing such a conception. They were much more profoundly influenced by the Germanic view holding the unity as a group-person, which is immanent to organized commonalty, to be elevated above the individual persons. But they were unable to come out with a legal explication and clarification of this view. They remain prisoners of the then prevalent sensory-concrete way of thinking, which views the totality as a unity with assembled multiplicity as identical with the totality as a multiplicity with a dispersed unity. This accounts for the fact that they put forth many mutually contradictory statements that were to perplex even their successors in a later period. On the one hand, they make varied use of the Roman dictum "*quod universitatis est non est singulorum,*" from which it follows that the *universitas* is not identical with the sum of all its members. But, on the other hand, they steadfastly maintain that the *universitas* is a sum total of the individuals. If necessary, the word "*singulorum*" could be translated as "of individual" rather than "of the individual," so that either "*omnes singuli*" or "*universitas*" could be construed as an antithesis of the "*singuli.*" The gloss to 1. 7 par. D. h.t., thus says: "*universitas nihil aliud est, nisi singuli homines qui ibi sunt.*" The gloss to 1. 15 par. 1 D. *de dolo malo* 4, 3, explains "municipes" in terms of "*sc. omnes generaliter.*" The gloss to 1. 1 par. 1 D. h. t., says about the "*syndicus*" that he is a representative of an *universitas* and acts always "*pro pluribus,*" never "*pro uno,*" which is substantiated by a strange etymology: "*nam dicitur syndicus quasi singulorum causam dicens.*"

Similar views emerge in other rulings and interpretations, although they are usually not expressed so bluntly. There is only one passage which suggests a solution for the inevitable contradictions: in the gloss to 1. par. 1 D. de coll. et corp. 47, 22 v., "*competit*" appears to be introducing, in its last sentence, the distinction between the totality in the collective, and the totality in the distributive, sense. The view of the *universitas* as a collective unity elevated to the status of a legal subject represents, in effect, the basic conception of the glossators.

It may be concluded that the glossators were as yet not even aware of the difference between the corporation, on the one hand, and the communal or societal relationships, on the other hand. They protected themselves against outright confusion by closely following the classical texts, which on this very point are unambiguous. The glossators accordingly treat the *universitas* as a legal subject, while at the same time avoiding the assumption of legal subjectivity on the part of a *societas* or *communio*. The nonchalance with which they lump together the corporate and societal elements betrays the fact that the glossators had not yet discovered the criterion for distinguishing between them.

As the glossators' view of the nature of a corporation oscillates between the Roman and the Germanic conceptions, the details of the theory of corporations fluctuate correspondingly in both directions. Depending on which is determining—the clear language of the classical texts or the medieval-Germanic viewpoint of the commentators—the individual decisions and rulings point to opposite basic principles.

## *III*

To establish a corporate group, the glossators posit above all the requirement of recognition by the state. They even venture a supposition that no association is allowed for which there is not a specific proof of approval by the state.

The glossators never expound the distinction between a public-law permission or a permission issued by the police, on the one hand, and the granting of a legal subjectivity, on the other hand. By governmental approval, a society [*Verein*] becomes *collegium licitum* and obtains corporate rights, whereas a society [*Verein*] without an approval, and thus as a *collegium illicitum,* not only is punishable but is devoid of the legal capacity to have rights and duties [*Rechtsfaehigkeit*]. *Collegia licita* without legal subjectivity are as unknown to the glossators as are *collegia illicita* with legal subjectivity.

Although they call this required approval a "special" one, the glossators do not mean by this a special licensing of each individual society [*Verein*], but rather the permission of entire categories of corporations by a general rule of law. Such a rule they find expressed in the common written law favoring all types of corporations mentioned by the *Corpus juris*—either explicitly or in the opinion of its interpreters—as *collegia licita.* Therefore, they ascribe the corporate right to all churches and church institutions; to all local communities, including rural ones (on this only seldom was there a divergent view); to the town councils; to the artisans' guilds explicitly mentioned in the sources; etc. But the glossators do not hesitate to expand these categories whenever they feel a special need for it. Thus, for example, they declare as *collegia* approved by law (on the basis of 1. 7 C. *de jurisd. omn. jud.* 3, 13, which is actually little suited for this purpose) all fellowships [*Genossenschaften*] of business men and artisans. On the same level with these fellowships, they put the collectivity of university teachers. There was a dispute as to whether the *universitas scholarium* was approved by common law. Some denied it and questioned the right of election of the rector appertaining to the *universitas scholarium* in Bologna, on the ground that the *scholares* themselves do not practice a profession but are comparable to the pupils of the practitioners and, consequently, to the apprentices of a trade. Other glossators again drew an opposite conclusion from the classical texts. And, according to a widespread opinion, every fellowship [*Genossenschaft*] dedicated to protection of common rights was regarded as *universitas approbata.* Thus, Hugolinus concludes his enumeration of *collegia licita* with the words: "*et ut generalius loquar, omnis congregatio potest dici licita, quae fit pro conservanda cuique sua justitia.*" And the gloss to 1. 1 par. 2 D. h. t. v. "*aliorum*" takes up this category of "*quaelibet congregatio pro justitia conservanda,*" cites as an example the "*congregatio scholarium Tuscorum vel universitatis totius,*" and in the end even ascribes to every "*societas quinque vel sex scholarium in uno hospitio*"—the right to appoint a *syndicus* for *causae societatis.*

No matter how broadly or how narrowly the categories of the corporations recognized by common law are conceived, one can still think of situations in which a corporately constituted group could not be subsumed under these categories. In such cases, the necessary approval was found in a special "*privilegium principis.*" Herein was the root and beginning of the doctrine of the necessity of a character [*Koncessionslehre*], which became fully developed only later on.

The glossators have little to say about other requirements for the foundation of a corporation. They merely reiterate the rules contained in the sources that demand a union [*Verein*] of at least three persons and tacitly assume the necessity of a constitution and a president.

The glossators do not divide corporations according to whether their coming into existence was indispensable or whether they were voluntarily created, nor do they distinguish conceptually between purely personal corporations and those determined territorially or by material circumstances.

## *IV*

In regard to the legal capacity of the corporation, the glossators borrow from the classical texts the proposition that the corporation is capable of owning property. They equate this with the individual person's capability of owning property and go beyond the Roman law to the extent that they overlook the restrictions on corporate capability of acquiring property on death by bequest and device, restrictions that were upheld even by Justinian. They regard each *collegium licitum* as fully capable of acquiring property from the institution of an heir. They also ascribe to the corporations the capacity for specific medieval rights—particularly public rights—regarding property. At the same time, they claim for the corporations of their time all the private-law privileges entrusted to certain kinds of corporations by the Roman law. They are disposed to transfer the privileges of fiscus, of the churches, and of the cities to all corporations or certain types of them. This gave rise to numerous controversies, such as those concerning the statute of the period of limitations, the *restitutio in integrum,* the taking of possession without "immemorial usage," the debt privileges, and letting out on bail. We shall be concerned with these controversies only in so far as they had a direct bearing on the nature of the corporation.

In accordance with the Roman law, the glossators treat the corporate property as ordinary individual property, the subject of which is the *universitas* as such.

This idea of corporate property had to overweigh the residual influence, noticeable both in the Roman and the German law, of another conception which negates, completely or partially, the idea of ownership as regards public property. The often unclear terminology of the sources with reference to derelict, common, and public things was a cause of many difficulties to the glossators. They extricate themselves from some of these difficulties by labeling the Roman category of *res nullius* as ambiguous and vague. In their view, the category of *res nullius in* the narrower sense comprises only the ownerless things that can be occupied; in the broader sense it negates only the property of individuals, but it comprises also the *res sacrae, religiosae et sanctae,* since their real owner is God ("*sed sunt in bonis Dei, hominum censura sive dispositione*"). Furthermore, it comprises the common, public, and corporate things, since they belong to human groups but to no single individual as such ("*quia esse possunt et sunt hominum, licet non hominis singularis; nullius, i.e., hominis privati, sed communitatis*"). As to the latter, one has to distinguish the *res communae* and the true *res publicae* from the *res universitatis.* Both former categories exclude ownership, not only by individuals, but also by any corporate group. Only the right of "*populus totius mundi*" is applicable to them. The *res communes* are common in terms of usage and ownerless in terms of ownership, whereas the *res publicae* are the property of all mankind. In contrast to these, the *res universitatis* are characterized by the fact that they belong to a distinct corporate group; they are, in the glossators' opinion, "*res unius populi*" and, therefore, they, too, are sometimes called *res publicae,* although not in the strict sense of that word.

Among the *res universitatis,* the gloss distinguishes two kinds of property, depending on whether it is used publicly or not. The latter, the glossators agreed, are just as much "*in patrimonio universitatis*" as similar pieces of property are in the possession of individuals. But the old controversy with regard to the *res universitatis* left to public use persisted. Placentinus maintained that only the right of use [*Gebrauchsrecht*] but not of property [*Eigentum*] itself appertains to an *universitas.* This view was supported by citing particularly the restrictions on sale and the exclusion of adverse possession [*Ausschluss der Ersitzung*]. And it was on this view that Roffredus based his decision in an extremely interesting *quaestio* about the possibility of executive requisition of "*forum, theatrum, viae publicae, fontes et flumina,*" on account of communal debts. But, on the whole, the opposite opinion of Azo prevailed, assuming a *dominium* of the *universitas.* Azo notes that the difference between both types of the *res universitatis* lies in the fact that things destined for public use are both in *dominium* and in *usus,* whereas the other things are in *dominium* and *fructus,* but not in *usus* of the *universitas.* The identification of the *universitas* with the totality [*Gesammtheit*] in this statement is apparent. The latter usage that made the distinction between *res in patrimonio universitatis* and true *res universitatis* and that included under the *res universitatis* those assets that—as "civic property" [*Buergervermoegen*] or "people's property" [*Genossengut*]—we usually place in contraposition to the "true" corporation property [*Korporationsvermoegen*] is thus made understandable. The idea of individual corporate property [*korporatives Individualvermoegen*], which by definition negates the concept of shares in Roman law, had to contend with the then firmly ingrained Germanic idea of the property of the community. The glossators mistakenly read into the sources a contradiction which they sensed in themselves. They maintained that the many variations on the theme "*quod universitatis est non est singulorum,*" in the classical texts, are contradicted by other statements which patently contained the opposite idea: "*quod est collegii est singulorum.*" They particularly pointed out to 1. 1 par. 1 i. f. D. *de coll. et corp.,* according to which the resigning member can claim his share. They also referred to 1.3 *eod.,* according to which the right of the division of property granted to *collegia illicita* in case of their dissolution must be automatically granted also to *collegia licita.* And they referred also to the least relevant Nov. 123 c. 36, which rules that the bishop divides the property whenever monks and nuns are assigned to separate cloisters. In all these instances, the glossators said, the shares of *singuli* are recognized, but they cannot be reconciled, according to other passages (arg. 1. 25 pr. D. *de V.S.* and 1. 5 D. *de leg.* I) with the conception of the property of the *universitas* as distinguished from the right of *singuli: "quod ergo erat collegii, erat singulorum"* Whereas some glossators strictly adhered to the Roman conception, in spite of the ostensibly contradictory statements, others among them regarded the applications cited in the *Corpus juris* as mere singularities, and sought to substantiate the assumption of the shares by the individuals with the idea that members who were leaving were by right always replaced by substitutes. Gradually, they reached the very significant opinion that the solution is not to be sought in the rejection of one or the other rule but in the distinction between various types of assets, each of which is subsumable under a different principle or rule. Already in the *Glossa ordinaria* this opinion is considered to be the correct one. But this distinction was then obviously novel and as yet insufficiently formulated. Evidence of this is to be found in the inappropriate examples cited by the gloss for one or the other kind of assets, e.g., recognizing the shares of the *singuli* in property built by contributions, but denying them with regard to assets bequeathed to the corporation. The distinction between the various types of assets was then not yet applied to the actual conditions of joint ownership of commons; and it is not mentioned in the question of an individual's capacity to give legal evidence in matters of the *universitas,* although it plays an important role later on.

In any case, the first foundation was laid for the later [legal] constructions which attempted to incorporate the ideas about the legal relations in commons and similar local communities as found in the German law into the Romanistic doctrine of corporate property.

As to corporate debts, the glossators began with the Roman ruling that *universitas* itself is liable for debts to the exclusion of its single members. But they supplemented it by the general rule according to which a propertyless *universitas* could be compelled to procure the property necessary to meet its obligations by imposing a levy on its members. In the back of this, of course, there was the concept of the susidiary liability of the *singuli.*

## *V*

Moreover, the glossators altered the content of the sources in two ways. First, by postulating a special publicistic legal capacity of corporate groups. Secondly, by identifying the subject of corporate power rights with the subject of corporate property rights.

The glossators constantly assume that a *universitas* can acquire public rights on ground of special claims to the same extent as can an individual. The dispute about the alienability [*Verueusserlichkeit*] and prescriptibility [*Verjaehrbarkeit*] of the rights of the empire [*Reichsrechte*] will be discussed in a later section of this work on publicistic theories.

Of particular interest here is the fact that the glossators derive from the nature of the corporation a number of privileges characterizing the corporation as a social organism with its own special and independent sphere of communal life [*Gemeinleben*]. They also conclude that the corporation is a community [*Gemeinwesen*] endowed with authority over its members. While subscribing to the views of their time, the glossators "rediscovered" their ideas in the *Corpus juris,* to which the idea of specific and aboriginal inner corporate rights was unknown.

Only occasionally do the glossators say that they regard the rights of assemblage, admission of new members, election of the board, and taxation as self-evident attributes of the corporation. By citing misunderstood passages from the classical texts, they substantiate emphatically and thoroughly the rights of corporate autonomy and corporate jurisdiction.

As far as autonomy was concerned, one found an explicit recognition of *"statuta municipalia,"* in those passages that defined the *jus civile* as *"jus quod quisque populus ipse sibi constituit"* or as *"jus proprium civitatis,"* in contradistinction to the *jus gentium.* The controversial right of territorial legislation [*Recht partikulaerer Gesetzgebung*] for various categories of territorial rulers and municipal authorities was derived from the official privileges of Roman magistrates, mixing the concepts of jurisdiction and legislation. And, by assuming or postulating the participation of the people [*Volk*] or its representatives, the territorial corporate group [*territorialer Verband*] as such was regarded as the proper subject of the right of territorial legislation. The maxim which ruled out autonomy: *"soli principi legem facere licet,"* was brushed aside in making the assumption that it refers only to *lex generalis* and leaves local legislation free. In other cases, the glossators made the even bolder interpretation that this rule only means that *"solus Imperator solus legem facere potest,"* so that the participation of others is always necessary.

The right of autonomy was in no way restricted

to territorial communities, but was also conceded to voluntarily created fellowships [*gewillkuerte Genossenschaften*], at least in handling their internal affairs (*inter se*). It was esay to concede the broadest measure of autonomy, in supposed agreement with the classical texts, since autonomy has always been put on par with customary law. It was taught that the distinction between *statutum* and *consuetudo* implies merely the distinction between an explicit and a tacit consensus, so that *consuetudo* is a *statutum tacitum*. Although this theory was subjected to devastating criticism by Johannes Basianus, Azo, and Accursius, both sources of law were subordinated to the communal standpoint of contract. Under such circumstances, the cause of local autonomy benefited from the struggle waged for the derogative power of local *consuetudo* in relation to common written law.

The glossators succeeded in deducing the right of corporate jurisdiction from the *Corpus juris*, although the basis for this was very tenuous. They applied particularly 1. 7 C. *de jurisd. omn. jud.* 3. 13, which deals with the subordination of tradesmen and artisans to certain special laws, in that elected heads of the fellowship [*Genossenschaft*] were simply regarded as judges. Inversely, the glossators deduced from the stipulations (in Nov. 15) regarding the election of the *defensor civitatis* that his office is a judicature of the community, performed in the name and mandate of the citizens. The glossators argued that the confirmation by the *praefectus praetorio*, as decreed by the supplementary law, merely grants permission to the performance of *jurisdictio:* the *jurisdictio* itself is instituted by municipal election. The glossators proceeded to state that, in general, every *universitas* will establish a normal jurisdiction by electing a board, and consequently the Roman rule "*consensus privatorum non facit judicem*" does not imply the "*consensus universitatis.*"

## *VI*

The glossators' understanding of the classical texts, with regard to the story of the corporation's capacity to act and to have will of its own [*Willens- und Handlungsfaehigkeit*], was even more influenced by their Germanic conception and point of view than their understanding of the theory of legal capacity [*Rechtsfaehigkeit*].

Since they undoubtedly thought that the unanimous will of all was the same thing as the corporate will [*Korporationswille*], the glossators regarded the corporation as capable of having a will of its own [*willensfaehig*]. And since every communal action of all, such as occurred during elections and acts of assemblies, appeared to them as an action of the corporation, the corporation itself had to be regarded as having capacity to act [*handlungsfaehig*].

The glossators could not comprehend the true meaning of the contradictory statements of the classical texts, because they failed to distinguish between the sphere of the public law and that of the private law. They helped themselves out by seeing in these contradictions mere indication of actual difficulties which the plural nature [*Vielkoepfigkeit*] of the *universitas* and the human propensity to differences in opinion pose to the unitary will and action of a totality [*Gesamtheit*]. This occasioned the oft-repeated excuse to the effect that in the Roman rule, "*universi consentire non possunt,*" one has to insert the word "*facile*"; and that, likewise, wherever a "*facere*" of the *universitas* seems to be described as impossible, what is really meant is that it is difficult. The glossators also claim that they can cite in their support other passages from the classical texts in which the capacity of the *universitas* to act and to have a will of its own is expressly recognized. And with characteristic frankness and simplicity, they also include the "*consensus universorum,*" which the emperor [*Kaiser*] promised to consider, in the *lex humana,* before enacting new laws.

Informed by such a conception, the glossators see in those institutions that, in our eyes, constitute the corporate organization only a series of expedients, necessitated by the difficulty of bringing about unanimous co-operation, on the one hand, and by the inability of an assemblage to undertake certain acts, on the other hand. For this reason, they leave the specific legal concepts of the corporate constitution and of corporate organs as undeveloped as the Roman jurists had left them. They do not go beyond the elaboration and exposition of positive rules contained in the classical texts. The unrelated conception which the glossators brought into these texts has a modifying effect. But the actual state of the corporate constitutional law of their time was decisive.

The two elements to which they reduce all these institutions assert themselves also in the glossators' categorization of these institutions according to two distinct criteria. Those institutions owing their existence to the fact that unanimous joint action is difficult are put into one group. They are the institutions where the will of the majority is important and where there is a representation of the totality by an assembly of the representatives [*Repraesentantenversammlung*]. The glossators believed that both of these types of institutions are essentially based on a legal fiction, by virtue of which an action not willed or done by all is regarded *as if* "all" willed or did it. It is in this connection that the word "fiction" appears in the medieval theory of corporations for the first time.

In the other group are those institutions that enable the corporation to undertake such actions as can be, by their nature, undertaken only by individuals and not at all by assemblies. These are the institutions of corporate board, of other corporate officialdom, and of an individual's authority to represent the corporation. Essential to these institutions, according to the glossators, is the principle of agency [*Stellvertretung*]. The idea of fiction, by virtue of which the actions of individuals were regarded as direct joint actions, seems to be inappropriate in this context, because the glossators were mainly concerned with things that the totality cannot do. The principle of agency, on the other hand, could be applied more easily, since the medieval jurists were free from the Roman restrictions on the concept of representation. The glossators thus put forward the rule that the *universitas,* like an individual, can act "*per se*" as well as "*per alium.*" And while regarding the action of all, or the action of a majority, or of a committee of representatives [*Repraesentantenkolleg*] as the actual or fictitious action of the *universitas* "per se," the actions of heads, officials, and authorized agents were regarded as actions of the *universitas* "*per alium.*"

If we look at the former of the two just-mentioned groups, we see that the glossators borrowed from the Roman sources the principle of majority as a legal rule applicable to all corporations. The views of some glossators about the mode of reckoning a majority already betray the influence of canon law. To substantiate why the minority should be bound by the decision of the majority, the glossators cite explicitly and exclusively a legal fiction and argue as follows: since it is difficult to achieve an agreement of all it should be decreed by law that whatever the majority wills or does is to be regarded as if all willed or did it. The glossators do not yet think of explaining this rule in terms of the nature of the corporation; they are not yet aware of its specifically corporate constitution and cite, in a veritable hodge-podge, instances of unanimity in purely communal conditions as exceptions to the general rule, and instances of majority will outside of the corporations as confirmations of the rule!

Nevertheless, in two respects, the principle of majority became a starting-point for a clearer comprehension of the concept of the corporation.

First of all, the glossators put forth the rule that not any decision of a majority, but only a decision arrived at in a proper manner, is valid as a decision of the *universitas.* By generalizing the Roman rules concerning the decurion assemblies, the glossators required that all members be summoned to meet —be it singly, be it in the usual public form ("*per tubam vel campanam vel voce praeconia*")—and that two-thirds of them actually appear. If this is the case, and rejecting a different interpretation of the sources, the majority of those present was deemed to be sufficient, since the two-thirds present are tantamount to the whole body. But now, if majority resolutions were contingent on an assembly following a determinate set of rules, the question arose as to whether the situation is any different in case of complete unanimity of all. This question, the answer to which is of singular importance for the concept of the corporation, was actually raised by the glossators. But this very occasion demonstrated that they hardly made the conceptual distinction between the unified joint will [*Gesamtwille*] and the sum of individual wills, between the constituted assembly and the sum of its members. In answering the question: "*quid si quilibet de universitate tibi intulit injuriam? Numquid universitas dicetur hoc fecisse et poterit a te conveniri?*" they assert "*videtur quod non, quia non ut universitas, sc. concilio habito et campana sonata vel alias eis convocatis, fecisset, sed quilibet, suo motu.*" But the ruling of the *Glossa ordinaria* is as follows: "*econtra quod sic; quia universitas nihil aliud est nisi singuli homines, qui ibi sunt.*"

Secondly, the glossators state that the majority resolutions [*Mehrheitsbeschluesse*] are valid only within the area of corporate affairs, but they can never take any individual rights away from the members, nor can they impose individual burdens on them. This was the point of departure for the general idea that the entire activity of the corporation is restricted to a sphere defined by the constitution and determined by its purpose, whereas the individual legal spheres of the members of a corporate group are not at all affected.

On an equal footing with the principle of the majority, the glossators put the principle of representation [*Repraesentativprincip*]. In a way alien to the Romans, they developed this principle as a general institution of corporation law from the law of decurions. They formulated the rule that, wherever the assembly of all is difficult or impracticable, a *collegium* of elected representatives of its majority can make and carry out corporate resolutions instead of the majority of all members. But even this rule they based upon a legal fiction, by virtue of which everything that such representatives willed or did was to be regarded as if all members willed or did. This conception, of course, did not prevent them from simultaneous-developing the idea that full powers [*Vollmacht*] of all members were bestowed by the election. Since the glossators had in mind especially the town-councils of their time, in which representative and administrative functions were combined, they generally interpreted that rule in favor of those who "govern," "administer," or "preside over" a corporate group. But whatever the actions of heads or managers [*Vorsteher*] are thus characterized as actions of the "*universitas ipsa*," what is understood are never individual managers but rather council-like *collegia*. No fixed rules were as yet formulated in regard to the extent to which the assemblage of members can be replaced by the assemblage of representatives. Generally, in congruence with the idea of fiction, the glossators were inclined to make a considerable extension of the principle. This meant that wherever the majority resolutions of all would have been sufficient, in case of doubt the acts of the assembly of representatives could be attributed to the totality [*Gesamtheit*].

These institutions oriented to a fictitious construction of an action of the *universitas ipsa* were then contrasted by the glossators with another group of institutions in which an action of the universitas *per alium* was assumed. Here, again, the glossators altered the content of the classical texts in two respects. On the one hand, they uncritically carried out the principle of free agency [*freie Stellvertretung*], based on a contract or the law, with regard to public-law and private-law acts. On the other hand, they conceived of the relationship between the *universitas* and its heads [*Vorsteher*], officials, and representatives—not merely with regard to its possible consequences for the rights of property, but above all with regard to its publicistic content—as a reciprocal legal relationship. Instead of talking about mere distribution of deportments [*Kompetenz*], they made the assignment of their own proper powers [*Befugnissphaeren*], which, even though they were freely founded and bestowed by the *universitas*, constituted the object of vested rights of their carriers.

Above all, the glossators take it for granted that each *universitas* has a head, a "*rector*," or "*praeses*." Using the Germanic constitutional arrangements as a model, the head of secular corporations, in their view, was the judicial-governmental director [*Vorsteher*]; in the ecclesiastic corporations, it was the prelate or rector *ecclesiae*. They considered this head of the corporate group to be the bearer of the powers of public authority [*obrigkeitliche Befugnisse*], related to the group in question, powers to which they ascribe—under the Roman names of *imperium merum* and *mixtum* or of a mere *jurisdictio*—the content of Germanic public authorities. However, the exercise of these powers generally called for a single individual. The totality, in so far as it was independent, could acquire such powers, but it could not keep and exercise them and was compelled to transfer them to an individual. And, in so far as the authority in question originated not from the group itself but had its origin in the enfeoffment of superior power [*hoehere Verleihung*], it was entrusted at the outset to the head of the totality. Thus, according to medieval jurisprudence, the board [*Vorsteherschaft*] was regarded as a sphere of power [*Befugnissphaere*] separated from the legal sphere of the totality [*Gesamtheit*] and independent on that totality. In every case, the *rector universitatis* was to some extent a monarchical subject with public authority of his own, regardless of the fact that his position and right could be traced back to a choice and a mandate of the totality. Conversely, even the actual monarch was, in medieval jurisprudence, always regarded as a head of a corporation, whose sphere of power in the last analysis was only a separate and independent piece in the sphere of totality, regardless of the fact that enfeoffment of superior and ultimately divine power was thought to be the source of his power. Thus, in diverse groups, the head of the group and the totality of the group [*Verbandsgesamtheit*] confront each other as two distinct legal subjects as far as their special rights and duties are concerned, while being, as it were, the head and the limbs of one body corporate in the affairs of the community.

Hence, an actual split of the corporate personality into an institutional board or directorate and an associational body, as we often encounter in canonic and publicistic doctrine, was made possible. Although the head of the group and the totality of the group appear collectively as one corporate legal subject, one head is at the same time regarded as the carrier of a special legal personality over and above the totality, while the totality in its turn, even without the head, is regarded as a corporation and, consequently, as a separate juristic person.

A similar position, in a less comprehensive sense, was assigned to other officials of the corporation. They, too, had to perform legal acts on behalf of the *universitas*, that is to say, acts which the totality could not perform at all or only with difficulty. This is true especially of the officials responsible for the current management of property matters and for the conduct of legal cases. Hence, they were regarded as representatives who stood beside the *universitas* rather than in it, and who in fact did not have to belong to the *universitas* at all. Their spheres of power also could be seen as more or less independent in relationship to the corporation.

Finally, the *universitas* was in the position to appoint all kinds of representatives [*Bevollmaechtigte*] for both private and public law affairs, which could then represent the *universitas* in actions which the totality could not, or did not want to, attend directly.

The jurisdictional powers of all those persons who act in behalf of the *universitas* were delineated on the basis of general principles regarding representation. They were determined partly by the powers of attorney conferred by the totality, but on the other hand, if necessary, their content was defined by law. In this latter connection, one spoke of a *"legitima administratio"* and meticulous care was exercised in defining its scope.

In elaboration of the idea contained in the classical texts, the *"legitima administratio"* of the directors, syndics, and administrators was thought of as a guardianship [*Vormundschaft*] under which the *universitas* was placed, in analogy to the *tutela, cura,* or paternal supervision. Consequently, the *universitas* itself was thought of as a minor. Hence, it was entitled also to the benefits [*Rechtswohltaten*] accorded to minors. In fact, instances in which the *universitas* was not equated with the *"pupillus"* were regarded as exceptions. In the old controversy about the time limit of the *"restitutio in integrum"* granted the corporations, some teachers of law took the comparison of the *universitas* with the *minor* so literally that they wanted to allow the *universitas* a perpetual delay, since it will remain forever under age. And when the opinion prevailed that restitution is to be made only *"intra quadrennium a die lesionis,"* most of them adduced only reasons of expediency (*"ratione infinitatis vitandae"*). The view of Azo that the *universitas,* though having the rights of minors, is not really *minor et pupilla* was isolated and had no effect.

Yet this conception of the *universitas* as a minor obviously meant a partial limitation of its capacity to act and to have will of its own. The view of the glossators was that the *universitas* is capable to will and to act, but that this capacity extends only so far as the totality can be directly active in corporate affairs, either actually or by virtue of a fiction. On the other hand, in so far as direct action of an assembly is not possible, the *universitas* seemed to them to be incapable to act and in need of being represented by a guardian. Since in every *universitas* there are some legal transactions that can be performed only by representatives, the *universitas* seemed to belong to the class of subjects held in tutelage, subjects who *"de necessitate per alios agunt."*

To this were added further restrictions on corporate capacity to act, which the glossators imposed by accepting the concept of state and/or ecclesiastical general superintendence rights as they found it in the classical texts. Although they came close to public-law viewpoints and to suggesting the idea of paramount guardianship [*Obervormundschaft*], they did not develop any concise principle, nor did they go beyond proclaiming Roman rules as a valid law. They were only slightly concerned with the problem of how all these rules about the duties of decurions, the *decretum judicis,* the required permission of the *praeses provinciae,* of the *praefectus praetorio,* or of the *princeps* himself were to be carried out in the real-life situations of their time.

## *VII*

When we examine the theory of corporate capacity to act as it was applied to various spheres of activity, we find a confirmation of what we said above in regard to the publicistic sphere. In so far as the assembly of members or a representative committee are directly involved, such as in elections, in the admission of new members, statutes, appointments of officials, etc., the action of the *"universitas ipsa"* is assumed. In so far as the director performs functions of public power, or in so far as other officials or agents act within their spheres of competence, then a direct representation on behalf of the *universitas* is given.

In many cases, the participation or permission of a superior power is necessary for such actions to be considered valid.

Similarly, the corporation was thought to be capable of acting in the pecuniary sphere, e.g., of acquiring possession, concluding contracts, coming into a legacy, accomplishing sales, and release on bond. Here, too, it could act both by itself and through a representative, but for the current management of property matters it needed permanent *"administratores,"* to whom a certain jurisdictional sphere belonged by right. In case of a sale, gift, relinquishment, or settlement, special formalities and assistance of public power were necessary. In this respect, the glossators repeated and often generalized the positive rules contained in the classical texts, especially those pertaining to cities and churches, in spite of numerous controversies and uncertainties.

In applying many of these legal rules to corporations, the glossators did not understand the difficulties that the Roman law had to overcome, since they did not have any reservations that would be rooted in the assumption of absolute capacity to act on the part of the *universitas,* on the one hand, and the limited right of representation, on the other. The glossators regarded the theoretical doubts expressed on the question of the acquisition of property as mistakes that were repudiated later on, and they overlooked other pertinent ideas on this problem. They take as valid law only the positive limitation of the capacity to assume obligation by way of loan, as it was ruled for the cities and churches by the *lex civitas* (1. 27 D. *de R. C.*) and its emendations. Yet, although the glossators are disposed to extend this rule to all corporations and to all kinds of obligations incurred by the receipt of money, they do not think of explaining it in terms of the legal person. Nor do they attempt, as later writers did, to explain away all fundamental peculiarities contained in the *lex civitas* by interpreting them and reshaping them in the desired direction. Rather, they view it as a positive ruling of a special type.

The glossators believed that the *universitas* could take an oath, since the *"universitas ipsa"* seemed to be taking an oath whenever all members, or the majority of members or just the majority of representatives took an oath in a unanimous manner. In this connection, the glossator referred to 1. 97 D. *de cond. et dem.* 35, 1, in applying the jurist's doubt about the possibility to fulfill the condition *"si jurassent municipes"* to the material difficulties of such an oath. Thus the famous controversy of the glossators concerning the corporate oath of calumny centered not around the possibility of corporate oath as such, but only around the extent to which the corporation can be represented in taking the oath.

Whereas Martinus, Aldricus, Placentinus, and others required, on the basis of 1. 2, par. 5 C. *de jur.* cal. 2, 59, that this oath be taken by all members or their majority, most of the teachers of law interpreted the passage of the Codex, in accordance with Pillius, Azo, and Hugolinus, so as to mean that in this instance, too, the oath of the representing authority or its majority is sufficient. Beyond that, on the basis of *"legitima administratio"* and by drawing an analogy with the guardians, special representatives of the corporations in a lawsuit were generally admitted to the oath of calumny on behalf of the *universitas.* In this circumstance, one saw clearly one of the main differences between such representatives and the regular *procuratores.* To substantiate this power of representation, the glossators never argued that the *universitas* as such was unable to take an oath but always pointed to the actual, material difficulties of a collective oath.

## *VIII*

The corporation's power to sue and to be sued was never doubted. But it is precisely before a court of justice that the totality itself cannot appear, either directly or through a representative. Hence, in this area, in the opinion of the glossators, the corporation had to be represented: it had to *"agere et excipere per alium."* In the absence of a legitimate representative, the *universitas* was thought to be tantamount to a *"pupillus indefensus."*

The head of a corporation can act as its representative in a lawsuit. But a special corporate representation in a lawsuit can be established permanently or for individual disputes by means of an election by the totality or its representatives, by a mandate of the directors or administrators, by a decree of the statutes, or through custom. But, according to the glossators, neither the *universitas* itself, nor its directors or administrators can appoint a regular *"procurator,"* since that is reserved only to the representation of an individual person litigating his own case. For procedural representation of a corporation, one can engage the offices of a *"syndicus," "actor,"* and *"oeconomus."* These three kinds of representatives are carefully distinguished from each other, in that the *"syndicus"* is only a representative of the *universitas,* the *"actor"* is a representative both of the *universitas* and of individuals, and the *"oeconomus"* can only be a representative of the bishopric. Actual differences in their legal status are hardly noticeable, the *"syndicus"* and the *"actor"* particularly being treated as equals. All three categories represent an antithesis to the *"procurator,"* being distinguished from him by greater scope of power to act in a lawsuit, based on their *"legitima administratio."*

In any case, the difference between the procedural representative of a corporation and attorneys acting for an individual is only of a qualitative, nature. The representatives of a corporation also belong to the *"procuratores"* in the broader sense, and, like regular *procurators,* they are not a party to a lawsuit, but only representatives of the absent party. Therefore, in certain cases, even though the lawsuit may be conducted through a *"syndicus," "actor,"* or *"oeconomus,"* one has to consider the *universitas* as the true party. Consequently, according to the glossators, in order to put the *universitas* as such in contempt of court, the summons must reach the corporation while it is in assembly. This is closely connected with the conception of the criminal consequences of contumacy, a conception that dominated the whole doctrine. Likewise, the confession of a principal or syndic should be binding on the *universitas* only when it is made in the presence or with the approval of the totality.

Finally, the penalty should be imposed not on the sentenced representative but directly on the property of the corporation.

The above conception of procedural representatives of a corporation as mere independent procurators explains, perhaps, the fact that the older writings on lawsuit overlooked completely, or almost completely, the important doctrine about the procedural situation of legal persons. The first writer on trials to put forth a detailed theoretical statement of this doctrine, containing a special discussion *"de syndico et actore,"* is the canonist Tancredus in his *Ordo judiciarius,* written about 1216. Even later, it was chiefly the canonists who elaborated this theory.

## *IX*

No wonder, then, that the glossators regarded the corporation as capable of committing the tort. In fact, they proclaim without any hesitation that every *universitas,* every local community, yes, every *ecclesia* can be judged delinquent, and to this end they exploit every allusion contained in the *Corpus juris,* while eliminating the antithetical 1. 15 par. 1 D. *de dolo,* by inserting the word *"facile,"* as mentioned above.

They assume that a corporation committed a tort as soon as the totality had acted directly. The view obtained that a wrong committed by everybody for himself was committed by all and consequently by the *universitas.* Yet this opinion was countered by the statement, later generally accepted, that the *universitas,* as such, is delinquent only when all act *"ut universitas,"* i.e., in corporate assembly under corporate forms. Furthermore, in case of unlawful actions as well as in legal transactions, one assumed that the totality was represented by the majority and even by a representative committee, such as, for example, a municipal council. Finally, unlawful actions of the directors, administrators, and other representatives were not supposed to be attributed to the *universitas* any more than the delicts of a guardian are ascribed to the pupil. However, the glossators held that in such a case one could not only bring an action for unjust enrichment against the corporation—and here they were in agreement with the classical texts—but they wanted to impute the delict directly to the corporation, at least when the unlawful action was commissioned or sanctioned after the act by the totality.

The same principles were applied to churches in a way characteristic of the then prevailing conception of the church. The glossators reaffirmed the canonical rules: *"delictum personae non nocet ecclesiae,"* and *"ecclesia non patitur damnum propter culpam praelati."* But not only were the exceptions to this rule postulated, particularly in case of a felony by the prelate of an enfeoffed church, but it was generally assumed that this rule applied only to actions of a superior or of an individual clergyman, and that the opposite held true as soon as the totality of clergymen employed by the church in question acted or took part in the action of the prelate. Such a delict then is a delict committed by the *ecclesia* itself and has the usual consequences.

The glossators found support for this conception in a very artificial interpretation of the 1. 10 C. *de ss. ecclesiis* 1, 2 (*lex jubemus*), threatening with the confiscation of a ship which was not given to the disposal of the state, under some pretext, such as the use of the ship for religious purposes. Whereas some maintained that the confiscation with which the church was threatened constituted a breaking of the rule, *"delictum praelati non nocet ecclesiae,"* the opinion of the glossators was that in this passage the participation of the *collegium* of clergymen in the refusal was presupposed, and, hence, the delict of the church as such was assumed and punished.

There is no doubt that the glossators regarded punishment of the corporation as permissible. The Germanic rules about decreeing a ban against communities, then widely used in Italy, were to them quite unobjectionable. It was precisely here that the Germanic concept of fellowship [*Genossenschaft*] with its identification of unity [*Einheit*] and totality [*Gesamtheit*] made its influence felt in a conspicuous way.

## *X*

As far as the termination [*Beeindingung*] of the corporate was concerned, the glossators assume that in itself every *universitas,* as such, can be permanent. In this connection, they bring up the limitation of the duration of its *ususfructus,* although there was an old controversy as to whether this rule was analogously applicable to the bequest of an annual rent or whether the rent was to be paid perpetually. But the glossators also mention that a corporation can cease to exist in a natural way. They cannot dismiss the explicit ruling of the sources that the corporation continues to exist in a single member. They are aware of the contradiction between this ruling and their own basic conception, and they try to resolve it by claiming that in such a case the *universitas* no longer really exists, since one person cannot constitute a totality, but that one person retains the rights of the *uni-*

*versitas.* They also discuss what the consequences would be should all members cease to exist (*"si nullus omnino remanserit"*). In the church view, the existing legal subject can continue to exist even then, since the possession [*Besitz*] and title [*Eigentum*] remain attached to the building of the institution [*Anstaltsgebäude*], which was the true subject even *"durante collegio."* The glossators resolutely reject this view as entirely irreconcilable with their own conception. They declare emphatically that the corporation is dissolved when its members "fall away" and that its property becomes ownerless and derelict. Yet, in the eventuality of a reconstitution of the corporation by a competent authority, by means of some legal stratagem, they want to use the fiction—by analogy with the universal succession in case of heritage—that in the new corporation the rights of the old one are perpetuated (*"sed tamen si postea auctoritate domini Papae vel ejus, ad quem spectat cura ejusdem collegii, instituatur in eodem collegio, juris artificio fingitur istius fuisse"*).

In discussing the settlement of property of the *universitas,* the glossators assert that, since the classical sources decreed a distribution of a *collegium illicitum,* this ruling must hold with an even greater force for the *collegia licita.* When all members "fall away," however, the glossators assume that the title of the extinct corporation goes as abandoned to the fiscus or to the Pope (*"verumtamen id esse videtur, ut nullo modo dicantur esse ullius, scil. ab eo tempore, quo solutum est collegium: sed ipso jure sint fisco vel Papae quasita"*), while the possessions become extinct (*"et hoc quantum ad dominium, secus quantum ad possessionem"*).

# 2. *The Types of Authority*

BY MAX WEBER

## *I. The Basis of Legitimacy*

### THE DEFINITION, CONDITIONS, AND TYPES OF IMPERATIVE CONTROL

"IMPERATIVE CO-ORDINATION" was defined as the probability that certain specific commands (or all commands) from a given source will be obeyed by a given group of persons. It thus does not include every mode of exercising "power" or "influence" over other persons. The motives of obedience to commands in this sense can rest on considerations varying over a wide range from case to case; all the way from simple habituation to the most purely rational calculation of advantage. A criterion of every true relation of imperative control, however, is a certain minimum of voluntary submission; thus an interest (based on ulterior motives or genuine acceptance) in obedience.

Not every case of imperative co-ordination makes use of economic means; *still less* does it always have economic objectives. But normally (not always) the imperative co-ordination of the action of a considerable number of men requires control of a staff of persons. It is necessary, that is, that there should be a relatively high probability that the action of a definite, supposedly reliable group of persons will be primarily oriented to the execution of the supreme authority's general policy and specific commands.

The members of the administrative staff may be bound to obedience to their superior (or superiors) by custom, by affectual ties, by a purely material complex of interests, or by ideal (*wertrational*) motives. *Purely* material interests and calculations of advantage as the basis of solidarity between the chief and his administrative staff result, in this as in other connexions, in a relatively unstable situation. Normally other elements, affectual and ideal, supplement such interests. In certain exceptional, temporary cases the former may be alone decisive. In everyday routine life these relationships, like others, are governed by custom and in addition, material calculation of advantage. But these factors, custom and personal advantage, purely affectual or ideal motives of solidarity, do not, even taken to-

---

Reprinted from Max Weber, *The Theory of Social and Economic Organization,* trans. A. M. Henderson and Talcott Parsons, ed. Talcott Parsons (Glencoe, Ill.: Free Press, 1947), pp. 324–36. 

gether, form a sufficiently reliable basis for a system of imperative co-ordination. In addition there is normally a further element, the belief in legitimacy.

It is an induction from experience that no system of authority voluntarily limits itself to the appeal to material or affectual or ideal motives as a basis for guaranteeing its continuance. In addition every such system attempts to establish and to cultivate the belief in its "legitimacy." But according to the kind of legitimacy which is claimed, the type of obedience, the kind of administrative staff developed to guarantee it, and the mode of exercising authority, will all differ fundamentally. Equally fundamental is the variation in effect. Hence, it is useful to classify the types of authority according to the kind of claim to legitimacy typically made by each. In doing this it is best to start from modern and therefore more familiar examples.

1. The choice of this rather than some other basis of classification can only be justified by its results. The fact that certain other typical criteria of variation are thereby neglected for the time being and can only be introduced at a later stage is not a decisive difficulty. The "legitimacy" of a system of authority has far more than a merely "ideal" significance, if only because it has very definite relations to the legitimacy of property.

2. Not every "claim" which is protected by custom or by law should be spoken of as involving a relation of authority. Otherwise the worker, in his claim for fulfilment of the wage contract, would be exercising "authority" over his employer because his claim can, on occasion, be enforced by order of a court. Actually his formal status is that of party to a contractual relationship with his employer, in which he has certain "rights" to receive payments. At the same time, the concept of a relation of authority naturally does not exclude the possibility that it has originated in a formally free contract. This is true of the authority of the employer over the worker as manifested in the former's rules and instructions regarding the work process; and also of the authority of a feudal lord over a vassal who has freely entered into the relation of fealty. That subjection to military discipline is formally "involuntary" while that to the discipline of the factory is voluntary does not alter the fact that the latter is also a case of subjection to authority. The position of a bureaucratic official is also entered into by contract and can be freely resigned, and even the status of "subject" can often be freely entered into and (in certain circumstances) freely repudiated. Only in the limiting case of the slave is formal subjection to authority absolutely involuntary.

Another case, in some respects related, is that of economic "power" based on monopolistic position; that is, in this case, the possibility of "dictating" the terms of exchange to contractual partners. This will not, taken by itself, be considered to constitute "authority" any more than any other kind of "influence" which is derived from some kind of superiority, as by virtue of erotic attractiveness, skill in sport or in discussion. Even if a big bank is in a position to force other banks into a cartel arrangement, this will not alone be sufficient to justify calling it a relation of imperative co-ordination. But if there is an immediate relation of command and obedience such that the management of the first bank can give orders to the others with the claim that they shall, and the probability that they will, be obeyed purely as such regardless of particular content, and if their carrying out is supervised, it is another matter. Naturally, here as everywhere the transitions are gradual; there are all sorts of intermediate steps between mere indebtedness and debt slavery. Even the position of a "salon" can come very close to the borderline of authoritarian domination and yet not necessarily constitute a system of authority. Sharp differentiation in concrete fact is often impossible, but this makes clarity in the analytical distinctions all the more important.

3. Naturally, the legitimacy of a system of authority may be treated sociologically only as the probability that to a relevant degree the appropriate attitudes will exist, and the corresponding practical conduct ensue. It is by no means true that every case of submissiveness to persons in positions of power is primarily (or even at all) oriented to this belief. Loyalty may be hypocritically simulated by individuals or by whole groups on purely opportunistic grounds, or carried out in practice for reasons of material self-interest. Or people may submit from individual weakness and helplessness because there is no acceptable alternative. But these considerations are not decisive for the classification of types of imperative co-ordination. What is important is the fact that in a given case the particular claim to legitimacy is to a significant degree and according to its type treated as "valid"; that this fact confirms the position of the persons claiming authority and that it helps to determine the choice of means of its exercise.

Furthermore a system of imperative co-ordination may—as often occurs in practice—be so completely assured of dominance, on the one hand by the obvious community of interests between the chief and his administrative staff as opposed to the subjects (bodyguards, Pretorians, "red" or "white" guards), on the other hand by the helplessness of the latter, that it can afford to drop even the pretence of a claim to legitimacy. But even then the mode of legitimation of the relation between chief and his staff may vary widely according to the type of basis of the relation of authority between them, and, as will be shown, this variation is highly significant for the structure of imperative co-ordination.

4. "Obedience" will be taken to mean that the action of the person obeying follows in essentials such a course that the content of the command may be taken to have become the basis of action for its own sake. Furthermore, the fact that it is so taken is referable only to the formal obligation, without regard to the actor's own attitude to the value or lack of value of the content of the command as such.

5. Subjectively, the causal sequence may vary, especially as between "submission" and "sympathetic agreement." This distinction is not, however, significant for the present classification of types of authority.

6. The scope of determination of social relationships and cultural phenomena by authority and imperative co-ordination is considerably broader than appears at first sight. For instance, the authority exercised in the school has much to do with the determination of the forms of speech and of written language which are regarded as orthodox. The official languages of autonomous political units, hence of their ruling groups, have often become in this sense orthodox forms of speech and writing and have even led to the formation of separate "nations" (for instance, the separation of Holland from Germany). The authority of parents and of the school, however, extends far beyond the determination of such cultural patterns which are perhaps only apparently formal, to the formation of the character of the young, and hence of human beings generally.

7. The fact that the chief and his administrative staff often appear formally as servants or agents of those they rule, naturally does nothing whatever to disprove the authoritarian character of the relationship. There will be occasion later to speak of the substantive features of so-called "democracy." But a certain minimum of assured power to issue commands, thus of "authority," must be provided for in nearly every conceivable case.

### THE THREE PURE TYPES OF LEGITIMATE AUTHORITY

There are three pure types of legitimate authority. The validity of their claims to legitimacy may be based on:

1. Rational grounds—resting on a belief in the "legality" of patterns of normative rules and the right of those elevated to authority under such rules to issue commands (legal authority).

2. Traditional grounds—resting on an established belief in the sanctity of immemorial traditions and the legitimacy of the status of those exercising authority under them (traditional authority); or finally,

3. Charismatic grounds—resting on devotion to the specific and exceptional sanctity, heroism or exemplary character of an individual person, and of the normative patterns or order revealed or ordained by him (charismatic authority).

In the case of legal authority, obedience is owed to the legally established impersonal order. It extends to the persons exercising the authority of office under it only by virtue of the formal legality of their commands and only within the scope of authority of the office. In the case of traditional authority, obedience is owed to the *person* of the chief who occupies the traditionally sanctioned position of authority and who is (within its sphere) bound by tradition. But here the obligation of obedience is not based on the impersonal order, but is a matter of personal loyalty within the area of accustomed obligations. In the case of charismatic authority, it is the charismatically qualified leader as such who is obeyed by virtue of personal trust in him and his revelation, his heroism or his exemplary qualities so far as they fall within the scope of the individual's belief in his charisma.

1. The usefulness of the above classification can only be judged by its results in promoting systematic analysis. The concept of "charisma" (the gift of grace") is taken from the vocabulary of early Christianity. For the Christian religious organization, Rudolf Sohm, in his *Kirchenrecht,* was the first to clarify the substance of the concept, even though he did not use the same terminology. Others (for instance, Hollin, *Enthusiasmus und Bussgewalt*) have clarified certain important consequences of it. It is thus nothing new.

2. The fact that none of these three ideal types, the elucidation of which will occupy the following pages, is usually to be found in historical cases in "pure" form, is naturally not a valid objection to attempting their conceptual formulation in the sharpest possible form. In this respect the present case is no different from many others. Later on the transformation of pure charisma by the process of routinization will be discussed and thereby the relevance of the concept to the understanding of empirical systems of authority considerably increased. But even so it may be said of every empirically historical phenomenon of authority that it is not likely to be "as an open book." Analysis in terms of sociological types has, after all, as

compared with purely empirical historical investigation, certain advantages which should not be minimized. That is, it can in the particular case of a concrete form of authority determine what conforms to or approximates such types as "charisma," "hereditary charisma," "the charisma of office," "patriarchy," "bureaucracy" the authority of status groups [*Ständische*], and in doing so it can work with relatively unambiguous concepts. But the idea that the whole of concrete historical reality can be exhausted in the conceptual scheme about to be developed is as far from the author's thoughts as anything could be.

## *II. Legal Authority with a Bureaucratic Administrative Staff*

### LEGAL AUTHORITY: THE PURE TYPE WITH EMPLOYMENT OF A BUREAUCRATIC ADMINISTRATIVE STAFF

The effectiveness of legal authority rests on the acceptance of the validity of the following mutually inter-dependent ideas.

1. That any given legal norm may be established by agreement or by imposition, on grounds of expediency or rational values or both, with a claim to obedience at least on the part of the members of the corporate group. This is, however, usually extended to include all persons within the sphere of authority or of power in question—which in the case of territorial bodies is the territorial area—who stand in certain social relationships or carry out forms of social action which in the order governing the corporate group have been declared to be relevant.

2. That every body of law consists essentially in a consistent system of abstract rules which have normally been intentionally established. Furthermore, administration of law is held to consist in the application of these rules to particular cases; the administrative process in the rational pursuit of the interests which are specified in the order governing the corporate group within the limits laid down by legal precepts and following principles which are capable of generalized formulation and are approved in the order governing the group, or at least not disapproved in it.

3. That thus the typical person in authority occupies an "office." In the action associated with his status, including the commands he issues to others, he is subject to an impersonal order to which his actions are oriented. This is true not only for persons exercising legal authority who are in the usual sense "officials," but, for instance, for the elected president of a state.

4. That the person who obeys authority does so, as it is usually stated, only in his capacity as a "member" of the corporate group and what he obeys is only "the law." He may in this connexion be the member of an association, of a territorial commune, of a church, or a citizen of a state.

5. In conformity with point 3, it is held that the members of the corporate group, in so far as they obey a person in authority, do not owe this obedience to him as an individual, but to the impersonal order. Hence, it follows that there is an obligation to obedience only within the sphere of the rationally delimited authority which, in terms of the order, has been conferred upon him.

The following may thus be said to be the fundamental categories of rational legal authority:—

(1) A continuous organization of official functions bound by rules.

(2) A specified sphere of competence. This involves (a) a sphere of obligations to perform functions which has been marked off as part of a systematic division of labour. (b) The provision of the incumbent with the necessary authority to carry out these functions. (c) That the necessary means of compulsion are clearly defined and their use is subject to definite conditions. A unit exercising authority which is organized in this way will be called an "administrative organ" [*Behörde*].

There are administrative organs in this sense in large-scale private organizations, in parties and armies, as well as in the state and the church. An elected president, a cabinet of ministers, or a body of elected representatives also in this sense constitute administrative organs. This is not, however, the place to discuss these concepts. Not every administrative organ is provided with compulsory powers. But this distinction is not important for present purposes.

(3) The organization of offices follows the principle of hierarchy; that is, each lower office is under the control and supervision of a higher one. There is a right of appeal and of statement of grievences from the lower to the higher. Hierarchies differ in respect to whether and in what case complaints can lead to a ruling from an authority at various points higher in the scale, and as to whether changes are imposed from higher up or the responsibility for such changes is left to the lower office, the conduct of which was the subject of complaint.

(4) The rules which regulate the conduct of an office may be technical rules or norms. In both cases, if their application is to be fully rational, specialized training is necessary. It is thus normally true that only a person who has demonstrated an adequate technical training is qualified to be a member of the administrative staff of such an or-

ganized group, and hence only such persons are eligible for appointment to official positions. The administrative staff of a rational corporate group thus typically consists of "officials," whether the organization be devoted to political, religious, economic—in particular, capitalistic—or other ends.

(5) In the rational type it is a matter of principle that the members of the administrative staff should be completely separated from ownership of the means of production or administration. Officials, employees, and workers attached to the administrative staff do not themselves own the non-human means of production and administration. These are rather provided for their use in kind or in money, and the official is obligated to render an accounting of their use. There exists, furthermore, in principle complete separation of the property belonging to the organization, which is controlled within the sphere of office, and the personal property of the official, which is available for his own private uses. There is a corresponding separation of the place in which official functions are carried out, the "office" in the sense of premises, from living quarters.

(6) In the rational type case, there is also a complete absence of appropriation of his official position by the incumbent. Where "rights" to an office exist, as in the case of judges, and recently of an increasing proportion of officials and even of workers, they do not normally serve the purpose of appropriation by the official, but of securing the purely objective and independent character of the conduct of the office so that it is oriented only to the relevant norms.

(7) Administrative acts, decisions, and rules are formulated and recorded in writing, even in cases where oral discussion is the rule or is even mandatory. This applies at least to preliminary discussions and proposals, to final decisions, and to all sorts of orders and rules. The combination of written documents and a continuous organization of official functions constitutes the "office" which is the central focus of all types of modern corporate action.

(8) Legal authority can be exercised in a wide variety of different forms which will be distinguished and discussed later. The following analysis will be deliberately confined for the most part to the aspect of imperative co-ordination in the structure of the administrative staff. It will consist in an analysis in terms of ideal types of officialdom or "bureaucracy."

In the above outline no mention has been made of the kind of supreme head appropriate to a system of legal authority. This is a consequence of certain considerations which can only be made entirely understandable at a later stage in the analysis. There are very important types of rational imperative co-ordination which, with respect to the ultimate source of authority, belong to other categories. This is true of the hereditary charismatic type, as illustrated by hereditary monarchy and of the pure charismatic type of a president chosen by plebiscite. Other cases involve rational elements at important points, but are made up of a combination of bureaucratic and charismatic components, as is true of the cabinet form of government. Still others are subject to the authority of the chief of other corporate groups, whether their character be charismatic or bureaucratic; thus the formal head of a government department under a parliamentary regime may be a minister who occupies his position because of his authority in a party. The type of rational, legal administrative staff is capable of application in all kinds of situations and contexts. It is the most important mechanism for the administration of everyday profane affairs. For in that sphere, the exercise of authority and, more broadly, imperative co-ordination, consists precisely in administration.

### LEGAL AUTHORITY: THE PURE TYPE WITH EMPLOYMENT OF A BUREAUCRATIC ADMINISTRATIVE STAFF—(*Continued*)

The purest type of exercise of legal authority is that which employs a bureaucratic administrative staff. Only the supreme chief of the organization occupies his position of authority by virtue of appropriation, of election, or of having been designated for the succession. But even *his* authority consists in a sphere of legal "competence." The whole administrative staff under the supreme authority then consists, in the purest type, of individual officials who are appointed and function according to the following criteria:

(1) They are personally free and subject to authority only with respect to their impersonal official obligations.

(2) They are organized in a clearly defined hierarchy of offices.

(3) Each office has a clearly defined sphere of competence in the legal sense.

(4) The office is filled by a free contractual relationship. Thus, in principle, there is free selection.

(5) Candidates are selected on the basis of technical qualifications. In the most rational case, this is tested by examination or guaranteed by diplomas certifying technical training, or both. They are *appointed*, not elected.

(6) They are remunerated by fixed salaries in money, for the most part with a right to pensions. Only under certain circumstances does the employ-

ing authority, especially in private organizations, have a right to terminate the appointment, but the official is always free to resign. The salary scale is primarily graded according to rank in the hierarchy; but in addition to this criterion, the responsibility of the position and the requirements of the incumbent's social status may be taken into account.

(7) The office is treated as the sole, or at least the primary, occupation of the incumbent.

(8) It constitutes a career. There is a system of 'promotion' according to seniority or to achievement, or both. Promotion is dependent on the judgment of superiors.

(9) The official works entirely separated from ownership of the means of administration and without appropriation of his position.

(10) He is subject to strict and systematic discipline and control in the conduct of the office.

This type of organization is in principle applicable with equal facility to a wide variety of different fields. It may be applied in profit-making business or in charitable organizations, or in any number of other types of private enterprises serving ideal or material ends. It is equally applicable to political and to religious organizations. With varying degrees of approximation to a pure type, its historical existence can be demonstrated in all fields.

1. For example, this type of bureaucracy is found in private clinics, as well as in endowed hospitals or the hospitals maintained by religious orders. Bureaucratic organization has played a major role in the Catholic Church. It is well illustrated by the administrative role of the priesthood [*Kaplanokratie*] in the modern church, which has expropriated almost all of the old church benefices, which were in former days to a large extent subject to private appropriation. It is also illustrated by the conception of the universal Episcopate, which is thought of as formally constituting a universal legal competence in religious matters. Similarily, the doctrine of Papal infallibility is thought of as in fact involving a universal competence, but only one which functions "ex cathedra" in the sphere of the office, thus implying the typical distinction between the sphere of office and that of the private affairs of the incumbent. The same phenomena are found in the large-scale capitalistic enterprise; and the larger it is, the greater their role. And this is not less true of political parties, which will be discussed separately. Finally, the modern army is essentially a bureaucratic organization administered by that peculiar type of military functionary, the "officer."

2. Bureaucratic authority is carried out in its purest form where it is most clearly dominated by the principle of appointment. There is no such thing as a hierarchy of elected officials in the same sense as there is a hierarchical organization of appointed officials. In the first place, election makes it impossible to attain a stringency of discipline even approaching that in the appointed type. For it is open to a subordinate official to compete for elective honours on the same terms as his superiors, and his prospects are not dependent on the superior's judgment.

3. Appointment by free contract, which makes free selection possible, is essential to modern bureaucracy. Where there is a hierarchical organization with impersonal spheres of competence, but occupied by unfree officials—like slaves or dependents, who, however, function in a formally bureaucratic manner—the term "patrimonial bureaucracy" will be used.

4. The role of technical qualifications in bureaucratic organizations is continually increasing. Even an official in a party or a trade-union organization is in need of specialized knowledge, though it is usually of an empirical character, developed by experience, rather than by formal training. In the modern state, the only "offices" for which no technical qualifications are required are those of ministers and presidents. This only goes to prove that they are "officials" only in a formal sense, and not substantively, as is true of the managing director or president of a large business corporation. There is no question but that the "position" of the capitalistic entrepreneur is as definitely appropriated as is that of a monarch. Thus, at the top of a bureaucratic organization, there is necessarily an element which is at least not purely bureaucratic. The category of bureaucracy is one applying only to the exercise of control by means of a particular kind of administrative staff.

5. The bureaucratic official normally receives a fixed salary. By contrast, sources of income which are privately appropriated will be called "benefices" [*Pfründen*]. Bureaucratic salaries are also normally paid in money. Though this is not essential to the concept of bureaucracy, it is the arrangement which best fits the pure type. Payments in kind are apt to have the character of benefices, and the receipt of a benefice normally implies the appropriation of opportunities for earnings and of positions. There are, however, gradual transitions in this field with many intermediate types. Appropriation by virtue of leasing or sale of offices or the pledge of income from office are phenomena foreign to the pure type of bureaucracy.

6. "Offices" which do not constitute the incumbent's principal occupation, in particular "honorary" offices, belong in other categories. The

typical "bureaucratic" official occupies the office as his principal occupation.

7. With respect to the separation of the official from ownership of the means of administration, the situation is essentially the same in the field of public administration and in private bureaucratic organizations, such as the large-scale capitalistic enterprise.

8. Collegial bodies at the present time are rapidly decreasing in importance in favour of types of organization which are in fact, and for the most part formally as well, subject to the authority of a single head. For instance, the collegial "governments" in Prussia have long since given way to the monocratic "district president" [*Regierungs präsident*]. The decisive factor in this development has been the need for rapid, clear decisions, free of the necessity of compromise between different opinions and also free of shifting majorities.

9. The modern army officer is a type of appointed official who is clearly marked off by certain class distinctions. In this respect such officers differ radically from elected military leaders, from charismatic condottieri, from the type of officers who recruit and lead mercenary armies as a capitalistic enterprise, and, finally, from the incumbents of commissions which have been purchased. There may be gradual transitions between these types. The patrimonial "retainer," who is separated from the means of carrying out his function, and the proprietor of a mercenary army for capitalistic purposes have, along with the private capitalistic entrepreneur, been pioneers in the organization of the modern type of bureaucracy.

# 3. *The Theory of Authority*

BY CHESTER I. BARNARD

IN THIS CHAPTER we consider a subject which in one aspect relates to the "willingness of individuals to contribute to organizations," the element of organization presented in the preceding chapter; and in a second aspect is the most general phase of the element "communication."

## *The Source of Authority*

If it is true that all complex organizations consist of aggregations of unit organizations and have grown only from unit organizations, we may reasonably postulate that, whatever the nature of authority, it is inherent in the simple organization unit; and that a correct theory of authority must be consistent with what is essentially true of these unit organizations. We shall, therefore, regard the observations which we can make of the actual conditions as at first a source for discovering what is essential in elementary and simple organizations.

Reprinted by permission of the publishers from Chester I. Barnard, *The Functions of the Executive* (Cambridge, Mass.: Harvard University Press, 1938), pp. 161–84. Copyright 1938 by the President and Fellows of Harvard College.

I

Now a most significant fact of general observation relative to authority is the extent to which it is ineffective in specific instances. It is so ineffective that the violation of authority is accepted as a matter of course and its implications are not considered. It is true that we are sometimes appalled at the extent of major criminal activities; but we pass over very lightly the universal violations, particularly of sumptuary laws, which are as "valid" as any others. Even clauses of constitutions and statutes carrying them "into effect," such as the Eighteenth Amendment, are violated in wholesale degrees.

Violation of law is not, however, peculiar to our own country. I observed recently in a totalitarian state under a dictator, where personal liberty is supposed to be at a minimum and arbitrary authority at a maximum, many violations of positive law or edict, some of them open and on a wide scale; and I was reliably informed of others.

Nor is this condition peculiar to the authority of the state. It is likewise true of the authority of churches. The Ten Commandments and the prescriptions and prohibitions of religious authority are repeatedly violated by those who profess to acknowledge their formal authority.

These observations do not mean that all citizens are lawless and defy authority; nor that all Christians are godless or their conduct unaffected by the tenets of their faith. It is obvious that to a large extent citizens are governed; and that the conduct of Christians is substantially qualified by the prescriptions of their churches. What is implied is merely that which specific laws will be obeyed or disobeyed by the individual citizen are decided by him under the specific conditions pertinent. This is what we mean when we refer to individual responsibility. It implies that which prescriptions of the church will be disobeyed by the individual are determined by him at a given time and place. This is what we mean by moral responsibility.

It may be thought that ineffectiveness of authority in specific cases is chiefly exemplified in matters of state and church, but not in those of smaller organizations which are more closely knit or more concretely managed. But this is not true. It is surprising how much that in theory is authoritative, in the best of organizations in practice lacks authority—or, in plain language, how generally orders are disobeyed. For many years the writer has been interested to observe this fact, not only in organizations with which he was directly connected, but in many others. In all of them, armies, navies, universities, penal institutions, hospitals, relief organizations, corporations, the same conditions prevail—dead laws, regulations, rules, which no one dares bury but which are not obeyed; obvious disobedience carefully disregarded; vital practices and major institutions for which there is no authority, like the Democratic and Republican parties, not known to the Constitution.

II

We may leave the secondary stages of this analysis for later consideration. What we derive from it is an approximate definition of authority for our purpose: Authority is the character of a communication (order) in formal organization by virtue of which it is accepted by a contributor to or "member" of the organization as governing the action he contributes; that is, as governing or determining what he does or is not to do so far as the organization is concerned. According to this definition, authority involves two aspects: first, the subjective, the personal, the *accepting* of a communication as authoritative, the aspects which I shall present in this section; and, second, the objective aspect—the character in the communication by virtue of which it is accepted—which I present in the second section, "The System of Coördination."

If a directive communication is accepted by one to whom it is addressed, its authority for him is confirmed or established. It is admitted as the basis of action. Disobedience of such a communication is a denial of its authority for him. Therefore, under this definition the decision as to whether an order has authority or not lies with the persons to whom it is addressed, and does not reside in "persons of authority" or those who issue these orders.

This is so contrary to the view widely held by informed persons of many ranks and professions, and so contradictory to legalistic conceptions, and will seem to many so opposed to common experience, that it will be well at the outset to quote two opinions of persons in a position to merit respectful attention. It is not the intention to "argue from authorities"; but before attacking the subject it is desirable at least to recognize that prevalent notions are not universally held. Says Roberto Michels in the monograph "Authority" in the *Encyclopaedia of the Social Sciences*,[1] "Whether authority is of personal or institutional origin it is created and maintained by public opinion, which in its turn is conditioned by sentiment, affection, reverence or fatalism. Even when authority rests on mere physical coercion it is *accepted*[2] by those ruled, although the acceptance may be due to a fear of force."

Again, Major-General James G. Harbord, of long and distinguished military experience, and since his retirement from the Army a notable business executive, says on page 259 of his *The American Army in France*:[3]

> A democratic President had forgotten that the greatest of all democracies is an Army. Discipline and morale influence the inarticulate vote that is instantly taken by masses of men when the order comes to move forward—a variant of the crowd psychology that inclines it to follow a leader, but the Army does not move forward until the motion has "carried." "Unanimous consent" only follows cooperation between the *individual* men in the ranks.

These opinions are to the effect that even though physical force is involved, and even under the extreme condition of battle, when the regime is nearly absolute, authority nevertheless rests upon the acceptance of consent of individuals. Evidently such conceptions, if justified, deeply affect an appropriate understanding of organization and especially of the character of the executive functions.

Our definition of authority, like General Harbord's democracy in an army, no doubt will appear

1. New York: Macmillan.
2. Italics mine.
3. Boston: Little, Brown and Co., 1936.

to many whose eyes are fixed only on enduring organizations to be a platform of chaos. And so it is—exactly so in the preponderance of attempted organizations. They fail because they can maintain no authority, that is, they cannot secure sufficient contributions of personal efforts to be effective or cannot induce them on terms that are efficient. In the last analysis the authority fails because the individuals in sufficient numbers regard the burden involved in accepting necessary orders as changing the balance of advantage against their interest, and they withdraw or withhold the indispensable contributions.

III

We must not rest our definition, however, on general opinion. The necessity of the assent of the individual to establish authority *for him* is inescapable. A person can and will accept a communication as authoritative only when four conditions simultaneously obtain: (*a*) he can and does understand the communication; (*b*) *at the time of his decision* he believes that it is not inconsistent with the purpose of the organization; (*c*) *at the time of his decision,* he believes it to be compatible with his personal interest as a whole; and (*d*) he is able mentally and physically to comply with it.

(*a*) A communication that cannot be understood *can* have no authority. An order issued, for example, in a language not intelligible to the recipient is no order at all—no one would so regard it. Now, many orders are exceedingly difficult to understand. They are often necessarily stated in general terms, and the persons who issued them could not themselves apply them under many conditions. Until interpreted they have no meaning. The recipient either must disregard them or merely do anything in the hope that that is compliance.

Hence, a considerable part of administrative work consists in the interpretation and reinterpretation of orders in their application to concrete circumstances that were not or could not be taken into account initially.

(*b*) A communication believed by the recipient to be incompatible with the purpose of the organization, as he understands it, could not be accepted. Action would be frustrated by cross purposes. The most common practical example is that involved in conflicts of orders. They are not rare. An intelligent person will deny the authority of that one which contradicts the purpose of the effort as *he* understands it. In extreme cases many individuals would be virtually paralyzed by conflicting orders. They would be literally unable to comply—for example, an employee of a water system ordered to blow up an essential pump, or soldiers ordered to shoot their own comrades. I suppose all experienced executives know that when it is necessary to issue orders that will appear to the recipients to be contrary to the main purpose, especially as exemplified in prior habitual practice, it is usually necessary and always advisable, if practicable, to explain or demonstrate why the appearance of conflict is an illusion. Otherwise the orders are likely not to be executed, or to be executed inadequately.

(*c*) If a communication is believed to involve a burden that destroys the net advantage of connection with the organization, there no longer would remain a net inducement to the individual to contribute to it. The existence of a net inducement is the only reason for accepting *any* order as having authority. Hence, if such an order is received it must be obeyed (evaded in the more usual cases) as utterly inconsistent with personal motives that are the basis of accepting any orders at all. Cases of voluntary resignation from all sorts of organizations are common for this sole reason. Malingering and intentional lack of dependability are the more usual methods.

(*d*) If a person is unable to comply with an order, obviously it must be disobeyed, or, better, disregarded. To order a man who cannot swim to swim a river is a sufficient case. Such extreme cases are not frequent; but they occur. The more usual case is to order a man to do things only a little beyond his capacity; but a little impossible is still impossible.

IV

Naturally the reader will ask: How is it possible to secure such important and enduring coöperation as we observe if in principle and in fact the determination of authority lies with the subordinate individual? It is possible because the decisions of individuals occur under the following conditions: (*a*) orders that are deliberately issued in enduring organizations usually comply with the four conditions mentioned above; (*b*) there exists a "zone of indifference" in each individual within which orders are acceptable without conscious questioning of their authority; (*c*) the interests of the persons who contribute to an organization as a group result in the exercise of an influence on the subject, or on the attitude of the individual, that maintains a certain stability of this zone of indifference.

(*a*) There is no principle of executive conduct better established in good organizations than that orders will not be issued that cannot or will not be obeyed. Executives and most persons of experience who have thought about it know that to do so destroys authority, discipline, and morale.[4] For reasons to be stated shortly, this principle cannot ordinarily be formally admitted, or at least cannot be professed. When it appears necessary to issue orders which are initially or apparently unacceptable, either careful preliminary education, or persuasive efforts, or the prior offering of effective inducements will be made, so that the issue will not be raised, the denial of authority will not occur, and orders will be obeyed. It is generally recognized that those who least understand this fact—newly appointed minor or "first line" executives—are often guilty of "disorganizing" their groups for this reason, as do experienced executives who lose self-control or become unbalanced by a delusion of power or for some other reason. Inexperienced persons take literally the current notions of authority and are then said "not to know how to use authority" or "to abuse authority." Their superiors often profess the same beliefs about authority in the abstract, but their successful practice is easily observed to be inconsistent with their professions.

(*b*) The phrase "zone of indifference" may be explained as follows: If all the orders for actions reasonably practicable be arranged in the order of their acceptability to the person affected, it may be conceived that there are a number which are clearly unacceptable, that is, which certainly will not be obeyed; there is another group somewhat more or less on the neutral line, that is, either barely acceptable or barely unacceptable; and a third group unquestionably acceptable. This last group lies within the "zone of indifference." The person affected will accept orders lying within this zone and is relatively indifferent as to what the order is so far as the question of authority is concerned. Such an order lies within the range that in a general way was anticipated at time of undertaking the connection with the organization. For example, if a soldier enlists, whether voluntarily or not, in an army in which the men are ordinarily moved about within a certain broad region, it is a matter of indifference whether the order to go to A or B, C or D, and so on; and goings to A, B, C, D, etc., are in the zone of indifference.

The zone of indifference will be wider or narrower depending upon the degree to which the inducements exceed the burdens and sacrifices which determine the individual's adhesion to the organization. It follows that the range of orders that will be accepted will be very limited among those who are barely induced to contribute to the system.

(*c*) Since the efficiency of organization is affected by the degree to which individuals assent to orders, denying the authority of an organization communication is a threat to the interests of all individuals who derive a net advantage from their connection with the organization, unless the orders are unacceptable to them also. Accordingly, at any given time there is among most of the contributors an active personal interest in the maintenance of the authority of all orders which to them are within the zone of indifference. The maintenance of this interest is largely a function of informal organization. Its expression goes under the names of "public opinion," "organization opinion," "feeling in the ranks," "group attitude," etc. Thus the common sense of the community informally arrived at affects the attitude of individuals, and makes them, as individuals, loath to question authority that is within or near the zone of indifference. The formal statement of this common sense is the fiction that authority comes down from above, from the general to the particular. This fiction merely establishes a presumption among individuals in favor of the acceptability of orders from superiors, enabling them to avoid making issues of such orders without incurring a sense of personal subserviency or a loss of personal or individual status with their fellows.

Thus the contributors are willing to maintain

---

4. Barring relatively few individual cases, when the attitude of the individual indicates in advance likelihood of disobedience (either before or after connection with the organization), the connection is terminated or refused before the formal question arises.

It seems advisable to add a caution here against interpreting the exposition in terms of "democracy," whether in governmental, religious, or industrial organizations. The dogmatic assertion that "democracy" or "democratic methods" are (or are not) in accordance with the principles here discussed is not tenable. As will be more evident after the consideration of objective authority, the issues involved are much too complex and subtle to be taken into account in *any* formal scheme. Under many conditions in the political, religious, and industrial fields democratic processes create artificial questions of more or less logical character, in place of the real questions, which are matters of feeling and appropriateness and of informal organization. By oversimplification of issues this may destroy objective authority. No doubt in many situations formal democratic processes may be an important element in the maintenance of authority, i.e., of organization cohesion, but may in other situations be disruptive, and probably never could be, in themselves, sufficient. On the other hand the solidarity of some coöperative systems (General Harbord's army, for example) under many conditions may be unexcelled, though requiring formally autocratic processes.

Moreover, it should never be forgotten that authority in the aggregate arises from *all* the contributors to a coöperative system, and that the weighting to be attributed to the attitude of individuals varies. It is often forgotten that in industrial (or political) organizations measures which are acceptable at the bottom may be quite unacceptable to the substantial proportion of contributors who are executives, and who will no more perform their essential functions than will others, if the conditions are, to them, impossible. The point to be emphasized is that the maintenance of the contributions necessary to the endurance of an organization requires the authority of *all* essential contributors.

the authority of communications because, where care is taken to see that only acceptable communications in general are issued, most of them fall within the zone of personal indifference; and because communal sense influences the motives of most contributors most of the time. The practical instrument of this sense is the fiction of superior authority, which makes it possible normally to treat a personal question impersonally.

The fiction[5] of superior authority is necessary for two main reasons:

(1) It is the process by which the individual delegates upward, or to the organization, responsibility for what is an organization decision—an action which is depersonalized by the fact of its coördinate character. This means that if an instruction is disregarded, an executive's risk of being wrong must be accepted, a risk that the individual cannot and usually will not take unless in fact his position is at least as good as that of another with respect to correct appraisal of the relevant situation. Most persons are disposed to grant authority because they dislike the personal responsibility which they otherwise accept, especially when they are not in a good position to accept it. The practical difficulties in the operation of organization seldom lie in the excessive desire of individuals to assume responsibility for the organization action of themselves or others, but rather lie in the reluctance to take responsibility for their own actions in organization.

(2) The fiction gives impersonal notice that what is at stake is the good of the organization. If objective authority is flouted for arbitrary or merely temperamental reasons, if, in other words, there is deliberate attempt to twist an organization requirement to personal advantage, rather than properly to safeguard a substantial personal interest, then there is a deliberate attack on the organization itself. To remain outside an organization is not necessarily to be more than not friendly or not interested. To fail in an obligation intentionally is an act of hostility. This no organization can permit; and it must respond with puntive action if it can, even to the point of incarcerating or executing the culprit. This is rather generally the case where a person has agreed in advance in general what he will do. Leaving an organization in the lurch is not often tolerable.

The correctness of what has been said above will perhaps appear most probable from a consideration of the difference between executive action in emergency and that under "normal" conditions. In times of war the disciplinary atmosphere of an army is intensified—it is rather obvious to all that its success and the safety of its members are dependent upon it. In other organizations, abruptness of command is not only tolerated in times of emergency, but expected, and the lack of it often would actually be demoralizing. It is the sense of the justification which lies in the obvious situation which regulates the exercise of the veto by the final authority which lies at the bottom. This is a commonplace of executive experience, though it is not a commonplace of conversation about it.

## *The System of Coördination*

Up to this point we have devoted our attention to the subjective aspect of authority. The executive, however, is predominantly occupied not with this subjective aspect, which is fundamental, but with the objective character of a communication which induces acceptance.

I

Authority has been defined in part as a "character of a communication in a formal organization." A "superior" is not in our view an authority nor does he have authority strictly speaking; nor is a communication authoritative except when it is an effort or action of organization. This is what we mean when we say that individuals are able to exercise authority only when they are acting "officially," a principle well established in law, and generally in secular and religious practice. Hence the importance ascribed to time, place, dress, ceremony, and authentication of a communication to establish its official character. These practices confirm the statement that authority relates to a communication "in a formal organization." There often occur occasions of compulsive power of individuals and of hostile groups; but authority is always concerned with something *within* a definitely organized system. Current usage conforms to the definition in this respect. The word "authority" is seldom employed except where formal organization connection is stated or implied (unless, of course, the reference is obviously figurative).

These circumstances arise from the fact that the character of authority in organization communications lies in the *potentiality of assent* of those to whom they are sent. Hence, they are only sent to contributors or "members" of the organization. Since all authoritative communications are official and relate only to organization action, they have no meaning to those whose actions are not included within the coöperative system. This is clearly in ac-

5. The word "fiction" is used because from the standpoint of logical construction it merely explains overt acts. Either as a superior officer or as a subordinate, however, I know nothing that I actually regard as more "real" than "authority."

cord with the common understanding. The laws of one country have no authority for citizens of another, except under special circumstances. Employers do not issue directions to employees of other organizations. Officials would appear incompetent who issued orders to those outside their jurisdiction.

A communication has the presumption of authority when it originates at sources of organization information—a communications center—better than individual sources. It loses this presumption, however, if not within the scope or field of this center. The presumption is also lost if the communication shows an absence of adjustment to the actual situation which confronts the recipient of it.

Thus men impute authority to communications from superior positions, provided they are reasonably consistent with advantages of scope and perspective that are credited to those positions. This authority is to a considerable extent independent of the personal ability of the incumbent of the position. It is often recognized that though the incumbent may be of limited personal ability his advice may be superior solely by reason of the advantage of position. This is the *authority of position.*

But it is obvious that some men have superior ability. Their knowledge and understanding regardless of position command respect. Men impute authority to what they say in an organization for this reason only. This is the *authority of leadership.* When the authority of leadership is combined with the authority of position, men who have an established connection with an organization generally will grant authority, accepting orders far outside the zone of indifference. The confidence engendered may even make compliance an inducement in itself.

Nevertheless, the determination of authority remains with the individual. Let these "positions" of authority in fact show ineptness, ignorance of conditions, failure to communicate what ought to be said, or let leadership fail (chiefly by its concrete action) to recognize implicitly its dependence upon the essential character of the relationship of the individual to the organization, and the authority if tested disappears.

This objective authority is only maintained if the positions or leaders continue to be adequately informed. In very rare cases persons possessing great knowledge, insight, or skill have this adequate information without occupying executive position. What they say ought to be done or ought not to be done will be accepted. But this is usually personal advice at the risk of the taker. Such persons have influence rather than authority. In most cases genuine leaders who give advice concerning organized efforts are required to accept positions of responsibility; for knowledge of the applicability of their special knowledge or judgment to concrete *organization* action, not to abstract problems, is essential to the worth of what they say as a basis of organization authority. In other words, they have an organization personality, as distinguished from their individual personality, commensurate with the influence of their leadership. The common way to state this is that there cannot be authority without corresponding responsibility. A more exact expression would be that objective authority cannot be imputed to persons in organization positions unless subjectively they are dominated by the organization as respects their decisions.

It may be said, then, that the maintenance of objective authority adequate to support the fiction of superior authority and able to make the zone of indifference an actuality depends upon the operation of the system of communication in the organization. The function of this system is to supply adequate information to the positions of authority and adequate facilities for the issuance of orders. To do so it requires commensurate capacities in those able to be leaders. High positions that are not so supported have weak authority, as do strong men in minor positions.

Thus authority depends upon a coöperative personal attitude of individuals on the one hand; and the system of communication in the organization on the other. Without the latter, the former cannot be maintained. The most devoted adherents of an organization will quit it, if its system results in inadequate, contradictory, inept orders, so that they cannot know who is who, what is what, or have the sense of effective coördination.

This system of communication, or its maintenance, is a primary or essential continuing problem of a formal organization. Every other practical question of effectiveness or efficiency—that is, of the factors of survival—depends upon it. In technical language the system of communication of which we are now speaking is often known as the "lines of authority."

## II

The requirements of communication determine the size of unit organizations, the grouping of units, the grouping of groups of unit organizations. We may now consider the controlling factors in the character of the communication system as a system of objective authority.

(*a*) The first is that *channels of communication should be definitely known.* The language in which this principle is ordinarily stated is, "The lines of authority must be definitely established." The method of doing so is by assigning each individual to his position; by general announcements; by organization charts; by educational effort, and most of all by habituation, that is, by securing as much permanence of system as is practicable. Emphasis is laid either upon the position, or upon the persons; but usually the fixing of authority is made both to positions and, less emphatically, to persons.

(*b*) Next, we may say that *objective authority requires a definite formal channel of communication to every member of an organization.* In ordinary language this means "everyone must report to someone" (communication in one direction) and "everyone must be subordinate to someone" (communication in the other direction). In other words, in formal organizations everyone must have definite formal relationship to the organization.

(*c*) Another factor is that *the line of communication must be as direct or short as possible.* This may be explained as follows: Substantially all formal communication is verbal (written or oral). Language as a vehicle of communication is limited and susceptible of misunderstanding. Much communication is necessarily without preparation. Even communications that are carefully prepared require interpretation. Moreover, communications are likely to be in more general terms the more general—that is, the higher—the position. It follows that something may be lost or added by transmission at each stage of the process, especially when communication is oral, or when at each stage there is combination of several communications. Moreover, when communications go from high positions down they often must be made more specific as they proceed; and when in the reverse direction, usually more general. In addition, the speed of communication, other things equal, will be less the greater the number of centers through which it passes. Accordingly, the shorter the line the greater the speed and the less the error.

How important this factor is may be indicated by the remarkable fact that in great complex organizations the number of levels of communication is not much larger than in smaller organizations. In most organizations consisting of the services of one or two hundred men the levels of communication will be from three to five. In the Army the levels are: President, (Secretary of War), General, Major-General, Brigadier-General, Colonel, Major, Captain, Lieutenant, Sergeant, men—that is, nine or ten. In the Bell Telephone System, with over 300,000 working members, the number is eight to ten.[6] A similar shortness of the line of communication is noteworthy in the Catholic Church viewed from the administrative standpoint.

Many organization practices or inventions are used to accomplish this end, depending upon the purpose and technical conditions. Briefly, these methods are: The use of expanded executive organizations at each stage; the use of the staff department (technical, expert, advisory); the division of executive work into functional bureaus; and processes of delegating responsibility with automatic coördination through regular conference procedures, committees for special temporary functions, etc.

(*d*) Another factor is that, in principle, *the complete line of communication should usually be used.* By this is meant that a communication from the head of an organization to the bottom should pass through every stage of the line of authority. This is due to the necessity of avoiding conflicting communications (in either direction) which might (and would) occur if there were any "jumping of the line" of organization. It is also necessary because of the need of interpretation, and to maintain responsibility.[7]

(*e*) Again, the *competence of the persons serving as communication centers, that is, officers, supervisory heads, must be adequate.* The competence required is that of more and more *general* ability with reference to the work of the entire organization the more central the office of communication and the larger the organization. For the function of the center of communication in an organization is to translate incoming communications concerning external conditions, the progress of activity, successes, failures, difficulties, dangers, into outgoing communications in terms of new activities, preparatory steps, etc., all shaped according to the ultimate as well as the immediate purposes to be served. There is accordingly required more or less mastery of the technologies involved, of the capabilities of the personnel, of the informal organization situation, of the character and status of the subsidiary organizations, of the principles of action relative to purpose, of the interpretation of environmental factors, and a power of discrimination between communications that can possess authority because they are recognizably compatible with *all* the pertinent conditions and those which will not possess authority because they will not or cannot be accepted.

It is a fact, I think, that we hardly nowadays expect individual personal ability adequate to posi-

---

6. Disregarding the corporate aspects of the organization, and not including boards of directors.

7. These by no means exhaust the considerations. The necessity of maintaining personal prestige of executives as an *inducement to them* to function is on the whole an important additional reason.

tional requirements of communication in modern large-scale organization. The limitations of individuals as respects time and energy alone preclude such personal ability, and the complexity of the technologies or other special knowledge involved make it impossible. For these reasons each major center of communication is itself organized, sometimes quite elaborately. The immediate staff of the executive (commanding officer), consisting of deputies, or chief clerks, or adjutants, or auxiliaries with their assistants, constitute an executive unit of organization only one member of which is perhaps an "executive," that is, occupies the *position* of authority; and the technical matters are assigned to staff departments or organizations of experts. Such staff departments often are partly "field" departments in the sense that they directly investigate or secure information on facts or conditions external to the organizations; but in major part in most cases they digest and translate information from the field, and prepare the plans, orders, etc., for transmission. In this capacity they are advisory or adjutant to the executives. In practice, however, these assistants have the function of semi-formal advice under regulated conditions to the organizations as a whole. In this way, both the formal channels and the informal organization are supplemented by intermediate processes.

In some cases the executive (either chief or some subordinate executive) may be not a person but a board, a legislature, a committee. I know of no important organizations, except some churches and some absolute governments in which the highest objective authority is not lodged in an *organized* executive group, that is, a "highest" unit of organization.

(*f*) Again, *the line of communication should not be interrupted during the time when the organization is to function.* Many organizations (factories, stores) function intermittently, being closed or substantially so during the night, Sundays, etc. Others, such as army, police, railroad systems, telephone systems, never cease to operate. During the times when organizations are at work, in principle the line of authority must never be broken; and practically this is almost, if not quite, literally true in many cases. This is one of the reasons which may be given for the great importance attached to hereditary succession in states, and for the elaborate provision that is made in most organizations (except possibly small "personal" organizations) for the temporary filling of offices automatically during incapacity or absence of incumbents. These provisions emphasize the non-personal and communication character of organization authority, as does the persistent emphasis upon the *office* rather than the *man* that is a matter of indoctrination of many organizations, especially those in which "discipline" is an important feature.

The necessity for this is not merely that specific communications cannot otherwise be attended to. It is at least equally that the *informal* organization disintegrates very quickly if the formal "line of authority" is broken. In organization parlance, "politics" runs riot. Thus, if an officer were vacant, but the fact were not known, an organization might function for a considerable time without serious disturbance, except in emergency. But if known, it would quickly become disorganized.

(*g*) The final factor I shall mention is that *every communication should be authenticated.* This means that the person communicating must be known actually to occupy the "position of authority" concerned; that the position includes the type of communication concerned—that is, it is "within its authority"; and that it actually is an authorized communication from this office. The process of authentication in all three respects varies in different organizations under different conditions and for different positions. The practice is undergoing rapid changes in the modern technique, but the principles remain the same. Ceremonials of investiture, inaugurations, swearing-in, general orders of appointment, induction, and introduction, are all essentially appropriate methods of making known who actually fills a position and what the position includes as authority. In order that these *positions* may function it is often necessary that the filling of them should be dramatized, an essential process to the creation of authority *at the bottom,* where only it can be fundamentally—that is, it is essential to inculcate the "sense of organization." This is merely stating that it is essential to "organization loyalty and solidarity" as it may be otherwise expressed. Dignifying the superior position is an important method of dignifying *all* connection with organization, a fact which has been well learned in both religious and political organizations where great attention to the subjective aspects of the "membership" is the rule.

This statement of the principles of communication systems of organizations from the viewpoint of the maintenance of objective authority has necessarily been in terms of complex organizations, since in a simple unit organization the concrete applications of these principles are fused. The principles are with difficulty isolated under simple conditions. Thus, as a matter of course, in unit organizations the channels of communication are known, indeed usually obvious; they are definite; they are the shortest possible; the only lines of authority are complete lines; there is little question of authentication. The doubtful points in unit organization are the competence of the leader, never to be taken for granted even in simple organizations, and whether he is functioning when the organization is in operation. Yet as a whole the adequately balanced maintenance of these aspects of simple leadership is the basis of objective authority in the unit organization, as the maintenance of the more formal and observable manifestations of the same aspects in the basis of authority in the complex organizations.

## *Reconciliation with Legalistic Conceptions*

Legalistic conceptions of authority, at least somewhat different from those we have presented, seem to have support in the relations between superior and subsidiary organizations. A corporate organization, for example, is subject to the law of the state. Is not this a case where authority actually does come down from the top, from the superior organizations? Only in exactly the same sense that individuals accept objective authority, as we have described it. A subsidiary or dependent organization must accept law to give law its authority. Units of organization, integrated complexes of organization, and dependent organizations, make and must make the subjective decision of authority just as individuals do. A corporation may and often does quit if it cannot obey the law and still have a net reason for existence. It is no more able to carry out an unintelligible law than an individual, it can no more do the impossible than an individual, it will show the same inability to conform to conflicting laws as the individual. The only difference between subsidiary, or dependent, unit and group organizations and individuals is that the denial of authority can be made directly by the individual, and either directly or indirectly by the unit, group, or dependent or subsidiary complex. When it is direct, the effect of the law or order upon the organization as a whole is in point; when it is indirect the effect is on the individuals of whose efforts the whole is made up. Thus no complex can carry out a superior order if its members (either unit organizations or individuals) will not enable it to do so. For example, to order by law working conditions which will not be accepted by individual employees, even though the employer is willing, is futile; its authority is in fact denied. The employees quit, then the organization ends.

But in the final analysis the differences are not important, except occasionally in the concrete case. The subsidiary organization in point of fact derives most of its authority for most of its action from its own "members" individually. They may quit if they do not accept the orders, no matter what the "ultimate" authority; and no absolute or external authority can compel the necessary effort beyond a minimum insufficient to maintain efficient or effective organization performance. An important effect of the ascription of legalistic origin of a part of the formal authority of subsidiary and independent organizations has been its obscuring of the nature of the real authority that governs the greater part of the coöperative effort of such organizations.

There is, however, a considerable quantitative difference in the factor of informal organization, that is, the factor of public opinion, general sentiment. This is not a difference of principle, but merely one of the relationship of the size of the informal organization relative to the individual or formal group. A strong individual can resist the domination of opinion if it is confined to a small number; but rarely if there is in question the opinion of an overwhelming number, actively and hostilely expressed. Now the size of any subsidiary organization is small compared with the informal organization that permeates the State; and this wide informal organization will usually support "law and order" regardless of merits if the question at issue is minor from its point of view. The pressure on the subjective attitude of individuals or on that of subsidiary or dependent organizations is strong ordinarily to induce acceptance of law in an "orderly" society.

But this informal support of objective authority of the State depends upon essentially the same principles as in the case of ordinary organizations. Inappropriateness of law and of government administration, lack of understanding of the ultimate basis of authority, indifference to the motives governing individual support, untimely or impossible legislation, as is well known destroy "respect for law and order," that is, destroy objective political authority. In democracies the normal reaction is to change law and administration through political action. But when majorities are unable to understand that authority rests fundamentally upon the consent of minorities as well as of majorities, or when the system is autocratic or absolute, the liquidation of attempted tyranny is through revolution or civil war. Authority lies always with him to whom it applies. Coercion creates a contrary illusion; but the use of force *ipso facto* destroys the authority postulated. It creates a new authority, a new situation, a new objective, which is granted when the force is accepted. Many men have destroyed all authority as to themselves by dying rather than yield.

At first thought it may seem that the element

of communication in organization is only in part related to authority; but more thorough consideration leads to the understanding that communication, authority, specialization, and purpose are all aspects comprehended in coördination. All communication relates to the formulation of purpose and the transmission of coördinating prescriptions for action and so rests upon the ability to communicate with those willing to coöperate.

Authority is another name for the willingness and capacity of individuals to submit to the necessities of coöperative systems. Authority arises from the technological and social limitations of coöperative systems on the one hand, and of individuals on the other. Hence the status of authority in a society is the measure both of the development of individuals and of the technological and social conditions of the society.

# *Section E*

# Religion and Social Structure

EDITORIAL FOREWORD

# Religion and Social Structure

*by Talcott Parsons*

THE PRINCIPAL SOCIAL THINKERS leading up to the developments of our special interest were largely concerned with the economic and political aspects of social systems. Besides this main trend, however, an important group of "mavericks" wrote with great insight about the religious aspects of social organization.

Prominent among them is the founder of the special concept of sociology, Auguste Comte. Comte was among the rationalists and positivists who believed that religion could not form a stable permanent component in human orientation but would eventually be completely replaced by science. (This general issue will be further discussed in the Introduction to Part Four.) Comte, as noted, was one of the earliest proponents of a theory of social evolution. It is in this connection that he made his most important positive contributions to the understanding of the role of religion. In his famous "law of the three stages," he placed the theological stage first. He thus recognized the fact that the political and the religious components of the leadership elements of early societies have usually not been differentiated from each other in a structural sense, at least involving collectivities. However, Comte extends his theological stage through the earlier history of Western Christianity through the Middle Ages, thus obscuring the fundamentally important event of the differentiation of church and state. Though we cannot agree with him that religion is becoming obsolete as an important focus of social structure, Comte made an important contribution to the statement of the problems of religion's place in social evolution.

The second selection antedates Comte; it follows his selection here because it is more specialized. This is David Hume's essay on "superstition" and "enthusiasm." Hume was one of the great skeptics in history. The title of his essay shows his distance from any personal commitment to the religious positions he was analyzing. Yet this essay, like so much of Hume's work, contains extraordinarily shrewd observations about the characters of the social organization of the Catholic Church and of the Methodist movement. Hume was writing during the second half of the eighteenth century, when the rise of Methodism was the most important religious change occurring in the British Isles since the seventeenth century. In an important sense, it was a kind of counterfoil to the impact of the Enlightenment, in which Hume himself was very much involved. In many respects, Hume's analysis anticipates the Weber-Troeltsch distinction of church and sect that appears in a later selection.

The next two selections are by writers who were important immediate precursors of the crystallization of interest in the sociology of religion that occurred in the generation with which we are concerned. Fustel de Coulanges was one of Durkheim's teachers, and his *Cité Antique* was certainly a major source of the latter's orientation to the sociological problems of religion. Fustel gave the classic account of the fusion of religion and civic commitment in the *polis;* it served as a model for Durkheim's analysis of Australian Totemism. Since Western society has dual religio-cultural roots in Greek and Semitic sources, it seems significant that the second relatively direct precursor of Durkheim's ideas, W. Robertson Smith, was the most eminent scholar in his time of early Semitic religion. A selection from his more famous work, the *Religion of the Semites,* is included in Part Four; this section contains his discussion of the Prophets of Israel.

In a theoretical sense, Robertson Smith probably had a more direct influence on Durkheim than on Weber. Yet Weber's analysis of the relation between Western Christianity and the Oriental religions starts from the significance he attributes to Prophetic Judaism. These two selections thus express a particularly important "crossroads" of intellectual influence that helps very much to explain the common factors underlying the convergence between Durkheim and Weber—a convergence occurring in spite of their mutual unawareness and their disparate national allegiances.

Next, two eminent authors are represented who belong to the relevant generation. Ernst Troeltsch is perhaps the most eminent sociologically oriented historian of Western Christianity, and his *Social Teachings of the Christian Churches* (1913) is a major classic. Our space has allowed inclusion of only one selection from this rich work, that outlines his typological distinction between church and sect. This generalized Hume's theme, and delineated the most important single basis of differentiation of religious types of organization within the Christian tradition. The second selection is from another German historian, Adolf von Harnack. From his extensive researches we have chosen his treatment of the place of monasticism within the Western church, especially of the ways in which the monastic orders prepared and served as "bases of operation" for the exertion of leverage on secular society from the point of view of Christian ethics. They constituted critical mechanisms for the movement in the direction of a Christian society that Troeltsch delineated.

This section ends on a note of general theory with the concluding chapter of Durkheim's *Elementary Forms of the Religious Life* (1912). This book constitutes one primary landmark in the history of analysis of the relation between religion and society. Even this late in his career, Durkheim had not yet fully freed himself from the limitations of his positivistic orientation. He had, however, fully overcome the bias of the positivistic evolutionists that relegated the role of religion exclusively to the early stages of social development. Above all, he clearly stated the essential connection between religion and the paramount values of a society—the *conscience collective*. His statement constitutes a primary point of reference for all subsequent discussion of this range of problems.

We have faced a particularly difficult problem in drawing the line between this last section of Part Two, and the first subsection in Section B of Part Four on the religious and magical aspects of value and belief patterns; and the separation is partially arbitrary. This difficulty is a result of our treatment of religion as the focal point of the articulation and hence interpenetration of social systems and culture. It therefore may be regarded from the point of view either of the morphology of the social system or of the social implications of cultural orientations.

Max Weber's primary interest in the sociology of religion was conceived from the latter point of view; therefore the selections from this part of his work are included in Part Four rather than here. In general, the comparative significance of religious variation emerges particularly clearly in that context. The final selection in the second subsection of Section B in Part Four, from Weber, on religion and social status, brings the analysis full circle, to the religious orientations' roots in the structure of societies. This very important selection might with equal relevance have been included at either point.

# 1. The Theological Stage

BY AUGUSTE COMTE

THE THEOLOGICAL PERIOD of humanity could begin no otherwise than by a complete and usually very durable state of pure Fetichism, which allowed free exercise to that tendency of our nature by which Man conceives of all external bodies as animated by a life analogous to his own, with differences of mere intensity. This primitive character of human speculation is established by the biological theory of Man in the *à-priori* way; and in the opposite way, by all the precise information that we can obtain of the earliest social period;

Reprinted from Auguste Comte, *The Positive Philosophy*, trans. and ed. Harriet Martineau (London: George Bell & Sons, 1896), II, 545–61.

and again, the study of individual development confirms the analysis of the collective. Some philosophers set out in the inquiry, as a matter of course, with the supposition that polytheism was the first stage; and some have been so perverse as to place monotheism furthest back, and fetichism as a corruption of polytheism: but such inversions are inconsistent with both the laws and the facts of human history.

The real starting-point is, in fact, much humbler than is commonly supposed, Man having everywhere begun by being a fetich-worshipper and a cannibal. Instead of indulging our horror and disgust of such a state of things by denying it, we should admit a collective pride in that human progressiveness which has brought us into our present state of comparative exaltation, while a being less nobly endowed than Man would have vegetated to this hour in his original wretched condition. Another supposition involves an error less grave, but still requiring notice. Some philosophers suppose a state prior even to fetichism; a state in which the human species was altogether material, and incapable of any speculation whatever;—in that lowest condition in which they now conclude the natives of Tierra del Fuego and some of the Pacific Islanders to be. If this were true, there must have been a time when intellectual wants did not exist in Man: and we must suppose a moment when they began to exist, without any prior manifestation;—a notion which is in direct contradiction to biological principles, which show that the human organism, in all times and places, has manifested the same essential needs, differing only in their degree of development and corresponding mode of satisfaction. This is proof enough of the error of the supposition: and all our observation of the lowest idiocy and madness in which Man appears to be debased below the higher brutes, assures us that a certain degree of speculative activity exists, which obtains satisfaction in a gross fetichism. The error arises from the want of knowing what to look for; and hence, the absence of all theological ideas is hastily concluded wherever there is no organized worship or distinct priesthood. Now, we shall see presently that fetichism may obtain a considerable development, even to the point of star-worship, before it demands a real priesthood; and when arrived at star-worship, it is on the threshold of polytheism. The error is natural enough, and excusable in inquirers who are unfurnished with a positive theory which may obviate or correct any vicious interpretation of facts.

On the ground of this hypothesis, it is said that Man must have begun like the lower animals. The fact is so,—allowing for superiority of organization; but perhaps we may find in the defects of the inference a misapprehension of the mental state of the lower animals themselves. Several species of animals afford clear evidence of speculative activity: and those which are endowed with it certainly attain a kind of gross fetichism, as Man does,—supposing external bodies, even the most inert, to be animated by passion and will, more or less analogous to the personal impressions of the spectator. The difference in the case is that Man has ability to raise himself out of this primitive darkness, and that the brutes have not,—except some few select animals, in which a beginning to polytheism may be observed,—obtained, no doubt, by association with Man. If, for instance, we exhibit a watch to a child or a savage, on the one hand, and a dog or a monkey, on the other, there will be no great difference in their way of regarding the new object, further than their form of expression:—each will suppose it a sort of animal, exercising its own tastes and inclinations: and in this they will hold a common fetichism,—out of which the one may rise, while the other can not. And thus the allegation about the starting-point of the human species turns out to be a confirmation of our proposition, instead of being in any way inconsistent with it.

It is so difficult to us to conceive of any but a metaphysical theology, that we are apt to fall into perpetual mistakes in contemplating this, its gross origin. Fetichism has even been usually confounded with polytheism, when the latter has been called Idolatry,—a term which applies only to the former; and the priests of Jupiter and Minerva would doubtless have repelled the trite reproach of the adoration of images as justly as Catholic priests do now, when subject to the same charge from Protestants. But, though we are too distant from fetichism to form a just conception of it, each one of us may find in his own earliest experience a more or less faithful representation of it. The celebrated phrase of Bosseut, applied to the starting-point of the human mind, describes the elementary simplicity of theology:—*Everything was God, except God himself;* and from that moment forward, the number of gods steadily decreased. We may reorganize some features of that state in our own conditions of mind when we are betrayed into searching after the mode of production of phenomena, of whose natural laws we are ignorant. We then instinctively conceive of the production of unknown effects according to the passions and affections of the corresponding being regarded as alive; and this is the philosophical principle of fetichism. A man who smiles at the folly of the savage in taking the watch for an animal may, if wholly ignorant of watch-making, find himself surprised into a state not so far superior, if any unforeseen and inexplicable effects should arise from some unperceived derangement of the mechanism. But for a widely analogous experience, preparing him for such accidents and their interpretation, he could hardly resist the impression that the changes were tokens of the affections or caprices of an imaginary being.

Thus is Fetichism the basis of the theological philosophy,—deifying every substance or phenomenon which attracts the attention of nascent humanity, and remaining traceable through all its transformations to the very last. The Egyptian theocracy, whence that of the Jews was evidently derived, exhibited, in its best days, the regular and protracted coexistence of the three religious periods in the different castes of its sacerdotal hierarchy—the lowest remaining in mere fetichism, while those above them were in full possession of a marked polytheism, and the highest rank had probably attained an incipient monotheism. Moreover, a direct analysis will disclose to us very marked traces, at all times, of the original fetichism, however it may be involved in metaphysical forms in subtile understandings. The conception among the ancients of the Soul of the universe, the modern notion that the earth is a vast living animal, and, in our own time, the obscure pantheism which is so rife among German metaphysicians, is only fetichism generalized and made systematic, and throwing a cloud of learned words as dust into the eyes of the vulgar. These evidences show that fetichism is no theological aberration, but the source of theology itself,—of that primitive theology which exhibits a complete spontaneousness, and which required from Man in his apathetic state no trouble in creating supernatural agents, but permitted him passively to yield to his propensity to transfer to outward objects the sense of existence which served him for an explanation of his own phenomena, and therefore for an absolute explanation of all out of himself. At first it was only inanimate nature that was the object in its more conspicuous phenomena,—even the negative ones, such as shadows, which no doubt terrified the nascent race as they now alarm individual children and some animals: but the spontaneous theology soon extended to embrace the animal kingdom, producing the express adoration of brutes, when they presented any aspect of mystery: that is, when Man did not find the corresponding equivalent of their qualities in himself,—whether it were the exquisite superiority of the sense of smell, or any other sense in animals, or that their organic susceptibility made them aware, sooner than himself, of atmospheric changes, etc., etc.

That philosophy was as suitable to the moral as to the intellectual state of the infant human race. The preponderance of the affective over the intellectual life, always conspicuous, was in its full strength in the earliest stages of the human mind. The empire of the passions over the reason, favorable to theology at all times, is yet more favorable to fetich theology than to any other. All substances being immediately personified, and endowed with passions, powerful in proportion to the energy of the phenomena, the external world presented to the observer a spectacle of such perfect harmony as has never been seen since: of a harmony which yielded him a satisfaction to which we can not even give a name, from our inability to feel it, however strenuously we may endeavor to carry our minds back into that cradle of humanity. It is easy to see how this exact correspondence between the universe and Man must attach us to fetichism, which, in return, specially protracts the appropriate moral state. In more advanced periods, evidence of this appears when organizations or situations show us any overwhelming action of the affective part of Man's nature. Men who may be said to think naturally with the hinder part of the head, or who find themselves so disposed for the moment, are not preserved even by high intellectual culture from the danger of being plunged by some passion of hope or fear, into the radical fetichism,—personifying, and then deifying, even the most inert objects that can interest their roused sensibilities. From such tendencies in our own day, we may form some idea of the primitive force of such a moral condition, which, being at once complete and normal, was also permanent and universal.

The metaphorical constitution of human language is, in my eyes, a remarkable and eternal testimony to the primitive condition of Man. There can be no doubt that the main body of human language has descended from that remotest period, which must probably have endured much longer than any other, from the special slowness of such progress as it could admit of. The common opinion which attributes the use of figurative expressions to a dearth of direct signs is too rational to be admissible with regard to any but a very advanced period. Up to that time, and during the ages which must have mainly influenced the formation or rather the development, of language, the excessive abundance of figures belonged naturally to the prevalent philosophy, which, likening all phenomena to human acts, must introduce as faithful description expressions which must seem metaphorical when that state had passed away in which they were literal. It is an old observation that the tendency diminishes as the human mind expands: and we may remark that the nature of metaphors is gradually transformed with the lapse of time:—in the early ages men transferred to the external world the expressions proper to human acts; whereas now we apply to the phenomena of life terms originally appropriated to inert nature, thus showing that the scientific spirit, which looks from without inward, is more and more influencing human language.

Looking now to the influence of the primitive theological philosophy on human progression, we observe that fetichism is the most intense form of theology—at least, as regards the individual; that is, the fetich form of that order of ideas is the one which most powerfully influences the mental system. If we are surprised at the number of pagan gods that we are continually meeting with in ancient books, there is no saying how we might be impressed if we could for a moment see the multitude of deities that the pure fetich-worshipper must live in the midst of. And again, the primitive man could see and know nothing but through his theological conceptions, except some very few practical notions of natural phenomena, furnished by experience, and little superior to the knowledge obtained by the higher animals by the same means. In no other religious period could theological ideas be so completely adherent to the sensations, which were incessantly presenting those ideas; so that it was almost impossible for the reason to abstract them in any degree, or for a single moment. It does not follow that the social influence of this form of theology was at all in proportion to its effect on individuals. On the contrary, the political influence of the theological philosophy will be seen, as we proceed, to strengthen as it becomes more abstract in the human mind.

It is not difficult to perceive why fetichism was a feeble instrument of civilization, notwithstanding its wide intellectual dominion; and this will disclose to us what its social influence really was.

In the first place, sacerdotal authority is indispensable to render available the civilizing quality of theological philosophy. All doctrine must have special organs, to direct its social application; and the necessity is strongest in the case of religious doctrine, on account of its indefinite character, which compels a permanent exercise of active discipline, to keep the vagueness and indefiniteness within bounds. The experience of the last three centuries shows us how, when sacerdotal authority is broken up, religious ideas become a source of discord instead of union: and this may give us some notion of the small social influence of a theology which anticipated all priesthoods, though it might be the first concern of every member of that infant society. Why fetichism admitted of no priesthood, properly so called, is obvious. Its gods were individual; and each resided fixedly in a particular object; whereas, the gods of polytheism are more general by their nature, and have a more extended dominion and residence. The fetich gods had little power to unite men, or to govern them. Though there were certainly fetiches of the tribe, even of the nation, the greater number were domestic, or even personal; and such deities could afford little assistance to the development of common ideas. And again, the residence of each deity in a material object left nothing for a priesthood to do, and therefore gave no occasion for the rise of a distinct speculative class. The worship, incessant and pervading as it was, when every act of a man's life had its religious aspect, was of a kind that required every man to be his own priest, free from intervention between himself and gods that were constantly accessible. It was the subsequent belief in gods that were invisible, more or less general, and distinct from the substances which they ruled, that originated and developed a real priesthood, enjoying high social influence, in its character of mediator between the worshipper and his deity. In the most triumphant periods of Greek and Roman polytheism, we meet with evidence of the contrasted character of the two theological phases, in the Lares and Penates, the domestic gods which had survived the fetich multitude, and which were served, not by any priest, but by each believer; or, at most, by the head of the family, as their spontaneous priest.

The beginning of a priesthood may, however, be discerned in the professions of soothsayers, conjurers, etc., which exist among the fetich tribes of Africa: but a close inquiry into their state, as into that of the first societies of men, will show that, in such cases, fetichism has reached its highest elevation, and become star-worship. This astrolatry is the introduction to polytheism; and it has qualities which instigate the development of a genuine priesthood. There is a character of generality about the stars which fits them to be common fetiches: and sociological analysis shows us that this was in fact their destination among populations of any extent. And again, when their inaccessible position was understood (which was not so soon as is commonly thought) the need of special intermediaries began to be felt. These two circumstances, the superior generality and the inaccessible position of the stars, are the reasons why the adoration of them, without changing the character of the universal fetichism, determined the formation of an organized worship and a distinct priesthood: and thus the advent of astrolatry was not only a symptom, but a powerful means of social progress in its day, though, from its extreme and mischievous protraction, we are apt to condemn it as universally a principle of human degradation. It must have been long, however, before star-worship obtained a marked ascendency over other branches of fetichism, so as to impart a character of real astrolatry to the whole region. The human mind was long engrossed with what lay nearest; and the stars held no prominent place in comparison with many terrestrial objects, as, for instance, meteorological effects, which indeed furnished the attributes of supernatural power through nearly the whole of the theological period. While magicians could control the moon and stars, no one supposed they could have anything to do with the government of the thunder. A long series of gradual modifications in human conceptions was therefore necessary to invert the primitive order, and place the stars at the head of natural bodies, while still subordinated to the earth and Man, according to the spirit of theological philosophy at its highest perfection. But, it was only when fetichism rose to the elevation of astrolatry that it could exercise any great social influence, for the reasons thus given. And this is the rational explanation of the singular characteristic of the theological spirit—that its greater intellectual extension is coincident with its smaller social influence. Thus, not only does fetichism share the common condition of all philosophies, that of not extending to moral and social considerations till it has embraced all simpler speculations, but there are special reasons for the retardation of the time when it can acquire any political consistency, notwithstanding its vast preparatory intellectual extension. The further we proceed in our review of the social operation of the theological spirit, the more we shall perceive how great is the mistake of supposing that religious belief is the only basis of human association, to the exclusion of all other orders of common conceptions. We have now seen that the political attribute did not disclose itself in the period of the greatest mental prevalence of the religious system: and we shall presently find that polytheism, and yet more monotheism, exhibits the necessary connection between the intellectual decline of the theological spirit and the perfect realization of its civilizing faculty: and this will confirm our conclusion that this social destination could be attributed to it only provisionally, while awaiting the advent of more direct and more permanent principles.—If, however, fetichism is not adapted to the development of the theological polity, its social influence has nevertheless been very extensive, as may be easily shown.

In a purely philosophical view,—that is, in regard to its function of directing human speculation,—this earliest form of religious belief manifests in the smallest possible degree the theological quality of attacking the original torpor of the human faculties, by furnishing some aliment to our conceptions, and some bond between them. Having done this, fetichism obstructs all advance in genuine knowledge. It is in this form, above all others, that the religious spirit is most directly opposed to the scientific, with regard to the simplest phenomena; and all idea of natural laws is out of the question when every object is a divinity with a will of its own. At this period of intellectual infancy, imaginary facts wholly overwhelm real ones; or rather, there is no phenomenon which can be distinctly seen in its genuine aspect. The mind is in a state of vague pre-occupation with regard to the external world, which, universal and natural as it is, is not the less a kind of permanent hallucination, proceeding from such a preponderance of the affective over the intellectual life, that the most absurd beliefs impair all direct observation of natural phenomena. We are too apt to treat as imposture exceptional sensations which we have long ceased to be able to understand, but which have always been well known to magicians and fortunetellers in the stage of fetichism; but, if we try, we may picture to ourselves how it is that, in the absence of all conception of natural laws, nothing can appear monstrous, and Man is pretty sure to see what he is disposed to see, by illusions which appear to me strongly analogous to those which are experienced by brutes, through their gross fetichism. However familiar we may now be with the conception of the regularity of natural events, and however this conception may be now the basis of our whole mental system, it is certainly not an innate idea, as each of us can almost assign the very date of its formation in his own mind. Setting ourselves back to a time before its existence among men, we can not wonder at the hallucinations produced by an intellectual activity so at the mercy of the passions, or of natural stimulants affecting the human frame; and our surprise is rather that the radical integrity of the mind of Man should have restrained as far as it did the tendency to illusion which was encouraged by the only theories then possible.

The influence of fetichism was less oppressive in regard to the fine arts. It is evident that a philosophy which endowed the whole universe with life must favor the expansion of imagination, which was then supreme among the faculties. Thus, it is certain that the origin of all the fine arts, not excepting poetry, is to be referred to the fetich period. When I treat of the relation of polytheism to the fine arts, I shall have occasion to glance at that of fetichism also; and I therefore leave it now; observing only that the fact to be shown is that, in social as in individual life, the rise and expansion of human faculties begins with the faculties of expression, so as gradually to lead on the evolution of the superior and less marked faculties, in accordance with the connection established among them by our organization.

As to the industrial development of the race, it is certain that Man began his conquests over external nature in the fetich period. We do not give their due to those primitive times when we forget that it was then that men learned to associate with tamed animals, and to use fire, and to employ mechanical forces, and even to affect some kind of commerce by the nascent institution of a currency. In short, the germs of almost all the arts of life are found in that period. Moreover, Man's activity prepared the ground for the whole subsequent evolution of the race by the exercise of his destructive propensities, then in their utmost strength. The chase not only brought separate families into association when nothing else could have done it, but it cleared the scene of social operations from the encumbrance of an inconvenient multitude of brutes. So great was the destruction, that it is now believed to have concurred with some geological causes in obliterating certain races of animals, and especially some of the largest: in the same way that the superfluous vegetation is believed to have been got rid of by the devastation attending a pastoral mode of life. It is not easy however to settle how much of the industrial advance of the period is to be attributed to its fetichism. At the first glance, it might seem that the direct consecration of external objects must forbid Man to modify the world around him: and it is certain that too long a protraction of fetichism could not but have that effect, if the human mind were always or ever thoroughly consistent, and if there were no conflict between beliefs and instincts, in which the first must give way. But there is to be considered, besides, the theological quality which is so favorable to the incitement of human activity in the absence of all knowledge of natural laws,—the assurance given to Man that he is supreme in Nature. Though his supremacy is unavailing without the intervention of divine agents, the constant sense of this supreme protection can not but be the best support to human energy at a period when Man is surrounded by immense obstacles, which he would not otherwise venture to attack. Up to a very recent date in human history, when the knowledge of natural laws had become a sufficient groundwork for wise and bold action, the imperfect and precarious theological stimulus continued to act. Its function was all the more appropriate to fetichism, that it offered the hope of almost unlimited empire by an active use of religious resources. The more we contemplate those primitive ages, the more clearly we shall see that the great move was rousing the human mind from animal torpor; and it would have been extremely difficult, physically and morally, if the theological philosophy, in the form of fetichism, had not opened the only possible issue. When we examine, from the right point of view, the characteristic illusions of that age about controlling the courses of the stars, lulling or exciting storms, etc., we are less disposed to an unphilosophical contempt than to mark in these facts the first symptoms of the awakening of human intelligence and activity.

As to its social influence, fetichism effected great things for the race, though less than the subsequent forms of the theological spirit. We are apt to underrate these services, because the most religious persons of our own time are unable to do justice to the effects of a belief which is extinct. It is only the positive philosophy which enables us to estimate the share borne by the religious spirit in the social, as well as the intellectual progression of the human race. Now, it is plain that moral efforts must, from our organizations, be almost always in conflict, more or less, with the strongest impulses of our nature; and what but the theological spirit could afford a ground for social discipline at a time when foresight, collective and individual, was far too restricted to sustain any influence of rationality? Even at more advanced periods, institutions which are justified by reason, remain long under theological tutelage before they can be freely committed to their true sanctions; as, for instance, when sanitary precepts are diffused and established by religious prescription. An irresistible induction shows us the necessity of a similar consecration of social changes in which we are at present least disposed to look for it. We should not, for instance, suspect any religious influence to be concerned in the institution of property; yet there are some aspects of society, in which we find it; as, for instance, in the famous *Taboo* of the Pacific Islands, which I regard as a valuable trace of the participation of theology in that first consolidation of territorial property which takes place when hunting or pastoral tribes pass into the agricultural stage. It seems probable, too, that religious influences contributed to establish, and yet more to regulate, the permanent use of clothing, which is regarded as one of the chief marks of nascent civilization, both because it stimulates industrial aptitudes and because its moral operation is good in encouraging Man to improve his own nature by giving reason control over the propensities.

It is a great and injurious mistake to conceive of this theological influence as an artifice applied by the more enlightened men to the government of the less. We are strangely apt to ascribe eminent political ability to dissimulation and hypocrisy; but it is happily rendered incontestable, by all experience and all study, that no man of superior endowments has ever exercised any great influence over his fellows without being first, for his own part, thoroughly convinced. It is not only that there must be a sufficient harmony of feeling and inclinations between himself and them, but his faculties would be paralyzed by the effort to guide his thoughts in the two opposite ways,—the real and the affected,—either of which would separately be as much as he could manage. If theological theories entered into the simplest speculations of men, in the age of fetichism, they must have governed social and political meditations, the complexity of which rendered religious resources peculiarly necessary. The legislators of that age must have been as sincere in their theological conceptions of society as of everything else; and the dreadful practical extravagances into which they too often fell under that guidance are unquestionable evidence of their general sincerity. We must consider, too, that the earliest theological polity naturally afforded suggestions which were coincident with corresponding social needs. The coincidence arose partly from that general property of all religious phases,—the vagueness of all faiths, which adapts them to be modified by all political exigencies, and thus to appear to sanction a suggestion when they merely respond to a want; and partly from the fact, special in each case, that the beliefs of any society must be mainly determined by the existing modifications of that society; so that opinions must necessarily present certain attributes in special harmony with corresponding social circumstances; and without this they could not retain their influence. By the first property an organization under a priesthood was rendered necessary, to prevent opinions so capable of abuse from being committed to the vulgar; and by the second, theological theories could not only consecrate all valuable suggestions, but could frequently produce some which were suitable to the contemporary social state. The first corresponds to what is vague and uncontrollable in each religious system; and the other to what is definite and susceptible of regulation; and the two supply each other's deficiencies. As belief becomes simplified and organized, its social influence diminishes under the first aspect, on account of the restriction on speculation; but it is ever increasing under the second aspect, as we shall presently see, permitting superior men to make the utmost use of the civilizing virtue of this primitive philosophy. It is clear that the first of these modes of social action of any theology must prevail eminently in fetichism; and this agrees with our observation of the absence or imperfection of any religious organization; but this fact renders all analysis inextricable, from the difficulty of discerning how much of the religious element was incorporated with the intricate web of a life which our familiar conceptions are so little adapted to unravel. We can only verify by some decisive examples the necessary reality of our theory; a thing which is easily done. As to the second mode, though it operated little during the fetich period, its precise nature enables us to obtain a better hold of it. An example or two will show its effect on the social progress of the race.

All philosophers are agreed about the supreme importance of the institution of agricultural life, without which no further human progress would have been possible; but all do not see how religion was concerned in the transition. War, which is the chief temporal instrument of early civilization, has no important social influence till the nomade condition is left behind. The fierce conflicts of hunting, and even of pastoral tribes, are like those of carnivorous animals, and only exercise activity and prepare for progress without producing immediate political results. The importance of subjecting Man to a fixed residence is thus obvious enough, on the one hand, and, on the other, the difficulty attending a change so little compatible in many ways with the character of infant humanity. There can be no doubt that a wandering life was natural to primitive Man, as we see it to be now to individuals below the reach of culture. This shows us how the intervention of spiritual influences may have been necessary to so great a change. It is usual to suppose that the condensation of numbers, as the race increased, would compel the tillage of the soil, as it had before compelled the keeping of flocks. But the explanation, though true as far as it goes, is insufficient; for, as we have seen before, want does not produce faculty. No social exigency will find its satisfaction if Man is not already disposed to provide it; and all experience shows that men will, in the most urgent cases, rather palliate each suffering as it arises, than resolve on a total change of condition which is repugnant to their nature. We know by observation what dreadful expedients men would adopt to reduce the excess of population, rather than exchange a nomade for an agricultural life, before their intellectual and moral nature was duly prepared for it. The progression of the human being therefore caused the change, though the precise date of its accomplishment must depend on external requirements; and above all, on the numbers needing food. Now, as agricultural life was certainly instituted before fetichism passed away, it is clear that there must be in fetichism something favorable to the change, though we may not know precisely what it was. But I have no doubt about the essential principle. The worship of the external world must be especially directed to the objects which are nearest and commonest; and this must tend to develop the originally feeble affection of men for their native soil. The moving lamentations of vanquished warriors for their tutelary gods were not about Jupiter, Minerva, or other abstract and general deities, whom they could find everywhere, but for their domestic gods; that is, pure fetiches. These were the special divinities whom the captives wept to leave behind, almost as bitterly as the tombs of their fathers, which were also involved in the universal fetichism. Among nations which had reached polytheism before becoming agricultural, the religious influence necessary to the change was chiefly due, no doubt, to the remains of fetichism, which held a conspicuous place in polytheism, up to a very advanced period. Such an influence then is an essential property of the first theological phase; and it would not have been strong enough in the subsequent religions if the great material change had not by that time been so well established on other grounds as to be able to relinquish the original one which was passing away. The reaction of the change upon theology is, at the same time, worthy of notice. It was then that fetichism assumed that highest form,—that of star-worship,—which was the transition stage to polytheism. It is plain that the settled abode of agricultural peoples must fix their speculative attention upon the heavenly bodies, while their labors remarkably disclosed the influences of the sky: whereas, the only astronomical observations to be expected of a wandering tribe are of the polar star which guides their nocturnal course. Thus there is a double relation between the development of fetichism and the final establishment of agricultural life.

Another instance of the influence of fetchism on social progress is its occasioning the systematic preservation of serviceable animals, and also of vegetables. It has been shown that the first action of Man on the external world must be in the form of devastation; and his destructive propensities do their work in clearing the field for future operations. A propensity so marked among men as rude as they were vehement threatened the safety of all races, before the utility of any was known. The most valuable organic species were the most exposed; and they must almost inevitably have perished if the first intellectual and moral advance of the human race had not intervened to restrain the tendency to indiscriminate destruction. Fetichism performed this office, not only by introducing agricultural life, but directly; and if it was done by a method which afterward became excessively debased—the express worship of animals, it may be asked how else the thing could have been done. Whatever evils belonged afterward to fetichism, it should be remembered how admirably it was adapted to preserve the most valuable animals and vegetables, and indeed all material objects requiring special protection. Polytheism rendered the same service, by placing everything under the care of some deity or other; but this was a less direct method than that of fetichism, and would not have sufficed in the first instance. No provision of the kind is to be found in monotheism; but neither is it so necessary in the more advanced stage of human progress to which it is adapted: yet the want of regular discipline in this order of relations is found to be a defect to this day, and one which is only imperfectly repaired by purely temporal measures. There can be no doubt that the moral effect of Man's care of animals contributed largely to humanize him. His carnivorous constitution is one of the chief limitations of his pacific capabilities, favorable as is the growing subdivision of employments to the milder inclinations of the majority of society; and, honorable as is the Utopia of Pythagoras, imagined in an age when the destructive tendency prevailed in the highest portion of society, it is not the less opposed to Man's nature and destiny, which oblige him to increase in all directions his natural ascendency over the whole of the animal kingdom. On this account, and for the regulation of this power, laws are essential, as in every other case of power possessed; and fetichism must be regarded as having first indicated, in the only way then possible, an exalted kind of human institution, for the regulation of the general political relations of all,—those of Man toward the external world, and especially the animal part of it. The selfishness of kind could not prevail among these relations without serious danger; and it must become moderate in proportion as the organisms rise to an increasing resemblance to our own. When the positive philosophy shall regulate these relations, it will be by constituting a special department of external nature, in regard to which a familiar knowledge of our interest in the zoological scale will have trained us in our duty to all living beings.

Such were, as nearly as we can estimate, the

social influences of fetichism. We must now observe how it passed into polytheism.

There can be no doubt of the direct derivation of polytheism from fetichism, at all times and in all places. The analysis of individual development, and the investigation of the corresponding degrees of the social scale, alike disclose this constant succession. The study of the highest antiquity, when illustrated by sound sociological theories, verifies the same fact. In most theogonies the prior existence of fetichism is necessary to the formation of the gods of polytheism. The Greek gods that issued from the Ocean and the Earth, issued from the two principal fetiches; and we have seen how, in its maturity, polytheism incorporates strong remains of fetichism. Speculatively regarded, this transformation of the religious spirit is perhaps the most radical that it has ever undergone, though we are unable, through its remoteness, to appreciate with any steadiness its extent and difficulty. From the comparative nearness and social importance of the transition to monotheism, we naturally exaggerate its relative importance; but, in truth, the interval to be passed was much narrower in the later case than in the earlier. If we reflect that fetichism supposed matter to be, in all forms, actually alive, while polytheism declared it to be nearly inert, and passively subject to the arbitrary will of a divine agent, it seems hardly imaginable how such a transition of views could be gradually made. Both are equally remote from the positive view,—that of the operation of natural laws; but they are no less opposed to each other, except in the one point of some express will being the cause of every incident: and thus it is a matter of the highest philosophical interest to ascertain the spontaneous mode of this memorable transition.

The intervention of the scientific spirit has only recently been direct and explicit; but not the less has it been concerned in all the successive modifications of the religious spirit. If Man had been no more capable than monkeys and carnivorous animals of comparing, abstracting, and generalizing, he would have remained for ever in the rude fetichism which their imperfect organization forbids their surmounting. Man, however, can perceive likeness between phenomena, and observe their succession: and when these characteristic faculties had once found aliment and guidance under the first theological instigation, they gathered strength perpetually, and by their exercise reduced, more and more rapidly, the influence of the religious philosophy by which they had been cherished. The first general result of the rise of this spirit of observation and induction seems to me to have been the passage from fetichism to polytheism, beginning, as all such changes do, with the highest order of minds, and reaching the multitude at last. To understand this, we must bear in mind that, as all fetich faith relates to some single and determinate object, the belief is of an individual and concrete nature. This quality suits well with the particular and unconnected character of the rudely-material observations proper to an infant state of the human mind: so that the exact accordance between the conception and the investigation that is found wherever our understandings are at work, is evident in the present case. The expansion of the spirit of observation caused by the first theory, imperfect as it was, must destroy the balance which, at length, can not be maintained at all but by some modification of the original philosophy. Thus the great revolution which carried men on from fetichism to polytheism is due to the same mental causes, though they may not be so conspicuous, that now produce all scientific revolutions,—which always arise out of a discordance between facts and principles. Thus did the growing generalization of human observations necessitate the same process in regard to the corresponding theological conceptions, and occasion the transformation of fetichism into simple polytheism; for the difference between the divinities of the two systems is the essential one that the gods, properly so called, have, from their indeterminate residence, a more general and abstract character. Each undertakes a special order of phenomena, but in a great number of bodies at the same time; so that each rules a department of some extent; whereas the fetich is inseparable from the one object in which it resides. When certain phenomena appeared alike in various substances, the corresponding fetiches must have formed a group, and at length coalesced into one principal one, which thus became a god; that is, an ideal and usually invisible agent, whose residence is no longer rigorously fixed. Thus, when the oaks of a forest, in their likeness to each other, suggested certain general phenomena, the abstract being in whom so many fetiches coalesced was no fetich, but the god of the forest. Thus, the intellectual transition from fetichism to polytheism is neither more nor less than the ascendency of specific over individual ideas, in the second stage of human childhood, social as well as personal. As every essential disposition is, on our principles, inherent in humanity from the beginning, this process must have already taken place, in certain cases; and the transition was thus, no doubt, much facilitated; as it was only necessary to extend and imitate what had already been done. Polytheism itself may have been primitive in certain cases, where the individual had a strong natural tendency to abstraction, while his contemporaries, being more impressible than reasonable, were more struck by differences than resemblances. As this exceptional condition does not indicate any general superiority, and the cases must have been few and restricted, my theory is not affected by them. They are interesting to us only as showing how the human mind was subjected to its first great philosophical transition, and carried through it. Thus it is that the purely theological nature of the primitive philosophy was preserved, in the conception that phenomena were governed by Will and not by laws; while, again, it was profoundly modified by the view of matter being no longer alive but inert, and obtaining all its activity from an imaginary external being. The intellectual and social consequences of the change will appear hereafter. The remark that occurs in this place is that the decline of the mental influence of the religious spirit, while its political influence is rising, may be distinctly perceived at this stage. When each individual thing lost its character of essential life and divineness, it became accessible to the scientific spirit, which might be humble enough in its operation, but was no longer excluded by theological intervention. The change is evidenced by the corresponding steady diminution of the number of divinities, while their nature was becoming more abstract and their dominion more extended. Each god took the place of a troop of fetiches, which were thenceforth permitted, or reduced, to serve as his escort. We shall hereafter recognise the same process, in the succession of monotheism to polytheism.

The particular issue by which the transition was effected is easily found, when we consider that it must be through the phenomenon which appears the most general and abstract, and the most universal in its influence. The stars answer to this description, when once their isolated and inaccessible position had fixed men's attention, in preference to the nearer objects which had at first engrossed it. The difference in conception between a fetich and a god must be smaller in the case of a star than of any other body; and it was this which made astrolatry, as I observed before, the natural intermediary state between the two first theological phases. Each sidereal fetich, powerful and remote, was scarcely distinguishable from a god; and especially in an age when men did not trouble themselves with nice distinctions. The only thing necessary to get rid of the individual and concrete character altogether, was to liberate the divinity from his imprisonment in one place and function, and to connect him by some real or apparent analogy with more general functions; thus making him a god, with a star for his preferred abode. This last transformation was so little necessary that, throughout nearly the whole polytheistic period, it was only the planets that, on account of their special variations, were subjected to it. The fixed stars remained true fetiches till they were included with everything in the universal monotheism.

In order to complete our estimate of this part of the human evolution, in which all the principles of subsequent progress must be implicated, I must point out the manifestations of the metaphysical spirit which here present themselves. If the theological philosophy is modified by the scientific spirit, this is done only through the metaphysical spirit, which rises with the decline of the theological, till the positive prevails over them both. The more recent dominion of the metaphysical spirit may be the most engrossing to us; but perhaps its operation when it was a mere gradation of the theological philosophy might appear to be of higher importance, if we could estimate the change wrought by it, and were in possession of any precise evidence. When bodies ceased to be divinely alive by their own nature, they must have some abstract property which rendered them fit to receive the action of the supernatural agent—an action which could not be immediate when the agent had a wider influence and an unfixed abode. Again, when a group of fetiches yield up their common attributes to a single god, and that god is regarded as living, in spite of his abstract origin, the conception is metaphysical in its whole character—recognising, as it does, personified abstractions. For the universal characteristic of the metaphysical state, as a transitional condition of the understanding, is a radical confusion between the abstract and the concrete point of view, alternately assumed to modify theological conceptions; now to render abstract what was before concrete, when each generalization is accomplished, and now to prepare for a new concentration the conception of more general existences, which was hitherto only abstract. Such is the operation of the metaphysical spirit on the theological philosophy, whose fictions had offered the only intelligible ground to human understanding, while all that it could do was to transfer to everything out of itself its own sense of active existence. Distinct from every substance, though inseparable from it, the metaphysical entity is more subtile and less definite than the corresponding supernatural action from which it emanates; and hence its aptitude to effect transitions which are invariably a decline, in an intellectual sense, of the theological philosophy. The action is always critical, as it preserves theology while undermining its intellectual basis; and it can appear organic only when it is not too preponderant, and in as far as it contributes to the gradual modification of the theological philosophy, to which, especially in a social view, must be referred whatever may appear to be organic in the metaphysical philosophy. These explanations must at first appear obscure; but the applications we shall have to make of them will render them unquestionable as we proceed. Meantime, it was impossible to defer them, and to neglect the true origin of the metaphysical influence, concerned as it is in the great transition from fetichism to polytheism. Besides the immediate scientific necessity, it is certainly desirable to trace from the cradle of humanity upward, that spontaneous and constant rivalry, first intellectual and then political, between the theological and the metaphysical spirit, which, protracted to the present moment, and necessary till the preparatory revolution is accomplished, is the main cause of our disturbed and conflicting condition.

# 2. *Of Superstition and Enthusiasm*

BY DAVID HUME

THAT[1] *the corruption of the best things produces the worst,* is grown into a maxim, and is commonly proved, among other instances, by the pernicious effects of *superstition* and *enthusiasm,* the corruptions of true religion.

These two species of false religion, though both pernicious, are yet of a very different, and even of a contrary nature. The mind of man is subject to certain unaccountable terrors and apprehensions, proceeding either from the unhappy situation of private or public affairs, from ill health, from a gloomy and melancholy disposition, or from the concurrence of all these circumstances. In such a state of mind, infinite unknown evils are dreaded from unknown agents; and where real objects of terror are wanting, the soul, active to its own prejudice, and fostering its predominant inclination, finds imaginary ones, to whose power and malevolence it sets no limits. As these enemies are entirely invisible and unknown, the methods taken to appease them are equally unaccountable, and consist in ceremonies, observances, mortifications, sacrifices, presents, or in any practice, however absurd or frivolous, which either folly or knavery recommends to a blind and terrified credulity. Weakness, fear, melancholy, together with ignorance, are, therefore, the true sources of Superstition.

But the mind of man is also subject to an unaccountable elevation and presumption, arising from prosperous success, from luxuriant health, from strong spirits, or from a bold and confident disposition. In such a state of mind, the imagination swells with great, but confused conceptions, to which no sublunary beauties or enjoyments can correspond. Every thing mortal and perishable vanishes as unworthy of attention. And a full range is given to the fancy in the invisible regions or world of spirits, where the soul is at liberty to indulge itself in every imagination, which may best suit its present taste and disposition. Hence arise raptures, transports, and surprising flights of fancy; and confidence and presumption still encreasing, these raptures, being altogether unaccountable, and seeming quite beyond the reach of our ordinary faculties, are attributed to the immediate inspiration of that Divine Being, who is the object of devotion. In a little

---

Reprinted from David Hume, *Essays: Moral, Political, and Literary* (London: Longmans Green & Co., 1882), Essay X, pp. 144–50.

1. Some of the opinions, delivered in these Essays, with regard to the public transactions in the last century, the Author, on more accurate examination, found reason to retract in his *History of Great Britain.* And as he would not enslave himself to the systems of either party, neither would he fetter his judgment by his own preconceived opinions and principles; nor is he ashamed to acknowledge his mistakes. [This note does not occur in any edition prior to M. A and B add the following paragraph to the text:—As violent Things have not commonly so long a Duration as moderate, we actually find, that the *Jacobite* Party is almost entirely vanish'd from among us, and that the Distinction of *Court* and *Country,* which is but creeping in at London, is the only one that is ever mention'd in this *kingdom.* Beside the Violence and Openness of the Jacobite party, another Reason has, perhaps, contributed to produce so sudden and so visible an Alteration in this part of Britain. There are only two Ranks of Men among us; Gentlemen, who have some Fortune and Education, and the meanest slaving Poor; without any considerable Number of that middling Rank of Men, which abounds more in England, both in Cities and in the Country, than in any other Part of the World. The slaving Poor are incapable of any Principles: Gentlemen may be converted to true Principles, by Time and Experience. The middling Rank of Men have Curiosity and Knowledge enough to form Principles, but not enough to form true ones, or correct any Prejudices that they may have imbib'd: And 'tis among the middling Rank, that Tory Principles do at present prevail most in England.]

time, the inspired person comes to regard himself as a distinguished favourite of the Divinity; and when this frenzy once takes place, which is the summit of enthusiasm, every whimsy is consecrated: Human reason, and even morality are rejected as fallacious guides: And the fanatic madman delivers himself over, blindly, and without reserve, to the supposed illapses of the spirit, and to inspiration from above. Hope, pride, presumption, a warm imagination, together with ignorance, are, therefore, the true sources of Enthusiasm.

These two species of false religion might afford occasion to many speculations; but I shall confine myself, at present, to a few reflections concerning their different influence on government and society.

[2] My first reflection is, *That superstition is favourable to priestly power, and enthusiasm not less or rather more contrary to it, than sound reason and philosophy*. As superstition is founded on fear, sorrow, and a depression of spirits, it represents the man to himself in such despicable colours, that he appears unworthy, in his own eyes, of approaching the divine presence, and naturally has recourse to any other person, whose sanctity of life, or, perhaps, impudence and cunning, have made him be supposed more favoured by the Divinity. To him the superstitious entrust their devotions: To his care they recommend their prayers, petitions, and sacrifices: And by his means, they hope to render their addresses acceptable to their incensed Deity.

---

2. [In Editions A and B, this and the three next paragraphs were written as follows: My first Reflection is, that Religions, which partake of Enthusiasm are, on their first Rise, much more furious and violent than those which partake of Superstition; but in a little Time become much more gentle and moderate. The Violence of this Species of Religion, when excited by Novelty, and animated by Opposition, appears from numberless Instances; of the *Anabaptists* in *Germany,* the *Camisars* in *France,* the *Levellers* and other Fanaticks in *England,* and the *Covenanters* in *Scotland.* As Enthusiasm is founded on strong Spirits and a presumptuous Boldness of Character, it naturally begets the most extreme Resolutions; especially after it rises to that Height as to inspire the deluded Fanaticks with the Opinion of Divine Illuminations, and with a Contempt of the common Rules of Reason, Morality and Prudence.

'Tis thus Enthusiasm produces the most cruel Desolation in human Society: But its Fury is like that of Thunder and Tempest, which exhaust themselves in a little Time, and leave the Air more calm and serene than before. The Reason of this will appear evidently, by comparing Enthusiasm to Superstition, the other Species of false Religion; and tracing the natural Consequences of each. As Superstition is founded on Fear, Sorrow, and a Depression of Spirits, it represents the Person to himself in such despicable Colours, that he appears unworthy, in his own Eyes, of approaching the Divine Presence, and naturally has Recourse to any other Person, whose Sanctity of Life, or, perhaps, Impudence and Cunning, have made him be supposed to be more favoured by the Divinity. To him they entrust their Devotions: To his Care they recommend their Prayers, Petitions, and Sacrifices: And, by his Means, hope to render their Addresses acceptable to their incensed Deity. Hence the Origin of *Priests,* who may justly be regarded as one of the grossest Inventions of a timorous and abject Superstition, which, ever diffident of itself, dares not offer up its own Devotions, but ignorantly thinks to recommend itself to the Divinity, by the Mediation of his supposed Friends and Servants. As Superstition is a considerable Ingredient of almost all Religions, even the most fanatical; there being nothing but Philosophy able to conquer entirely these unaccountable Terrors; hence it proceeds, that in almost every Sect of Religion there are Priests to be found: But the stronger Mixture there is of Superstition, the higher is the Authority of the Priesthood. Modern Judaism and Popery, especially the latter, being the most barbarous and absurd Superstitions that have yet been known in the World, are the most enslav'd by their Priests. As the Church of England may justly be said to retain a strong Mixture of Popish Superstition, it partakes also, in its original Constitution, of a Propensity to Priestly Power and Dominion; particularly in the Respect it exacts to the Priest. And though, according to the Sentiments of that Church, the Prayers of the Priest must be accompanied with those of the Laity; yet is he the mouth of the Congregation, his Person is sacred, and without his Presence few would think their public Devotions, or the Sacraments, and other Rites, acceptable to the Divinity.

On the other Hand, it may be observed, That all Enthusiasts have been free from the Yoke of Ecclesiastics, and have exprest a great Independence in their Devotion; with a contempt of Forms, Tradition and Authorities. The *Quakers* are the most egregious, tho', at the same Time, the most innocent, Enthusiasts that have been yet known; and are, perhaps, the only Sect, that have never admitted Priests among them. The *Independents,* of all the English Sectaries, approach nearest to the Quakers in Fanaticism, and in their Freedom from Priestly Bondage. The *Presbyterians* follow after, at an equal Distance in both these Particulars. In short, this Observation is founded on the most certain Experience; and will also appear to be founded on Reason, if we consider, that as Enthusiasm arises from a presumptuous Pride and Confidence, it thinks itself sufficiently qualified to *approach* the Divinity without any human Mediator. Its rapturous Devotions are so fervent, that it even imagines itself *actually* to *approach* him by the Way of Contemplation and inward Converse; which makes it neglect all those outward Ceremonies and Observances, to which the Assistance of the Priests appears so requisite in the Eyes of their superstitious Votaries. This Fanatick consecrates himself, and bestows on his own Person a sacred Character, much superior to what Forms and ceremonious Institutions can confer on any other.

'Tis therefore an infallible Rule, That Superstition is favourable to Priestly Power, and Enthusiasm as much, or rather more, contrary to it than sound Reason and Philosophy. The Consequences are evident. When the first Fire of Enthusiasm is spent, Men naturally, in such fanatical Sects, sink into the greatest Remissness and Coolness in Sacred Matters; there being no Body of Men amongst them, endow'd with sufficient Authority, whose Interest is concerned, to support the religious Spirit. Superstition, on the contrary, steals in gradually and insensibly; renders Men tame and submissive; is acceptable to the Magistrate, and seems inoffensive to the People: Till at last the Priest, having firmly establish'd his Authority, becomes the Tyrant and Disturber of human Society, by his endless Contentions, Persecutions, and religious Wars. How smoothly did the *Romish* Church advance in their Acquisition of Power? But into what dismal Convulsions did they throw all Europe, in order to maintain it? On the other Hand, our Sectaries, who were formerly such dangerous Bigots, are now become our greatest Freethinkers; and the *Quakers* are, perhaps, the only regular Body of *Deists* in the Universe, except the *Literati* or Disciples of *Confucius* in *China.*]

Hence the origin of Priests,[3] who may justly be regarded as an invention of a timorous and abject superstition, which, ever diffident of itself, dares not offer up its own devotions, but ignorantly thinks to recommend itself to the Divinity, by the mediation of his supposed friends and servants. As superstition is a considerable ingredient in almost all religions, even the most fanatical; there being nothing but philosophy able entirely to conquer these unaccountable terrors; hence it proceeds, that in almost every sect of religion there are priests to be found: But the stronger mixture there is of superstition, the higher is the authority of the priesthood.[4]

On the other hand, it may be observed, that all enthusiasts have been free from the yoke of ecclesiastics, and have expressed great independence in their devotion; with a contempt of forms, ceremonies, and traditions. The *quakers* are the most egregious, though, at the same time, the most innocent enthusiasts that have yet been known; and are, perhaps, the only sect, that have never admitted priests amongst them. The *independents,* of all the English sectaries, approach nearest to the *quakers* in fanaticism, and in their freedom from priestly bondage. The *presbyterians* follow after, at an equal distance in both particulars. In short this observation is founded in experience; and will also appear to be founded in reason, if we consider, that, as enthusiasm arises from a presumptuous pride and confidence, it thinks itself sufficiently qualified to *approach* the Divinity, without any human mediator. Its rapturous devotions are so fervent, that it even imagines itself *actually* to *approach* him by the way of contemplation and inward converse; which makes it neglect all those outward ceremonies and observances, to which the assistance of the priests appears so requisite in the eyes of their superstitious votaries. The fanatic consecrates himself, and bestows on his own person a sacred character, much superior to what forms and ceremonious institutions can confer on any other.

My *second* reflection with regard to these species of false religion is, *that religions, which partake of enthusiasm are, on their first rise, more furious and violent than those which partake of superstition; but in a little time become more gentle and moderate.* The violence of this species of religion, when excited by novelty, and animated by opposition, appears from numberless instances; of the *anabaptists* in Germany, the *camisars* in France, the *levellers* and other fanatics in England, and the *covenanters* in Scotland. Enthusiasm being founded on strong spirits, and a presumptuous boldness of character, it naturally begets the most extreme resolutions; especially after it rises to that height as to inspire the deluded fanatic with the opinion of divine illuminations, and with a contempt for the common rules of reason, morality, and prudence.

It is thus enthusiasm produces the most cruel disorders in human society; but its fury is like that of thunder and tempest, which exhaust themselves in a little time, and leave the air more calm and pure than before. When the first fire of enthusiasm is spent, men naturally, in all fanatical sects, sink into the greatest remissness and coolness in sacred matters; there being no body of men among them, endowed with sufficient authority, whose interest is concerned to support the religious spirit: No rites, no ceremonies, no holy observances, which may enter into the common train of life, and preserve the sacred principles from oblivion. Superstition, on the contrary, steals in gradually and insensibly; renders men tame and submissive; is acceptable to the magistrate, and seems inoffensive to the people: Till at last the priest, having firmly established his authority, becomes the tyrant and disturber of human society, by his endless contentions, persecutions, and religious wars. How smoothly did the Romish church advance in her acquisition of power? But into what dismal convulsions did she throw all Europe, in order to maintain it? On the other hand, our sectaries, who were formerly such dangerous bigots, are now become very free reasoners; and the *quakers* seem to approach nearly the only regular body of *deists* in the universe, the *literati,* or the disciples of Confucius in China.[5]

My *third* observation on this head is *that superstition is an enemy to civil liberty, and enthusiasm a*

3. [The following note is appended in Editions D to N: By *Priests,* I here mean only the pretenders to power and dominion, and to a superior sanctity of character, distinct from virtue and good morals. These are very different from *clergymen,* who are set apart *by the laws,* to the care of sacred matters, and to the conducting our public devotions with greater decency and order. There is no rank of men more to be respected than the latter.]

4. [Here D to P add: Modern Judaism and popery, especially the latter) being the most unphilosophical and absurd superstitions which have yet been known in the world, are the most enslaved by their priests. As the church of England may justly be said to retain some mixture of Popish superstition, it partakes also, in its original constitution, of a propensity to priestly power and dominion; particularly in the respect it exacts to the sacerdotal character. And though, according to the sentiments of that Church, the prayers of the priest must be accompanied with those of the laity; yet is he the mouth of the congregation, his person is sacred, and without his presence few would think their public devotions, or the sacraments, and other rites, acceptable to the divinity.]

5. The Chinese Literati have no priests or ecclesiastical establishment. [This note is not in D and K, which read in the text: and the quakers seem to approach nearly the only regular body of deists in the universe, the *literati,* or the disciples of *Confucius* in *China.*]

*friend to it.* As superstition groans under the dominion of priests, and enthusiasm is destructive of all ecclesiastical power, this sufficiently accounts for the present observation. Not to mention, that enthusiasm, being the infirmity of bold and ambitious tempers, is naturally accompanied with a spirit of liberty; as superstition, on the contrary, renders men tame and abject, and fits them for slavery. We learn from English history, that, during the civil wars, the *independents* and *deists,* though the most opposite in their religious principles; yet were united in their political ones, and were alike passionate for a commonwealth. And since the origin of *whig* and *tory,* the leaders of the *whigs* have either been *deists* or profest *latitudinarians* in their principles; that is, friends to toleration, and indifferent to any particular sect of *christians:* While the sectaries, who have all a strong tincture of enthusiasm, have always, without exception, concurred with that party, in defence of civil liberty. The resemblance in their superstitions long united the highchurch *tories,* and the *Roman catholics,* in support of prerogative and kingly power; though experience of the tolerating spirit of the *whigs* seems of late to have reconciled the *catholics* to that party.

The *molinists* and *jansenists* in France have a thousand unintelligible disputes, which are not worthy the reflection of a man of sense: But what principally distinguishes these two sects, and alone merits attention, is the different spirit of their religion. The *molinists* conducted by the *jesuits,* are great friends to superstition, rigid observers of external forms and ceremonies, and devoted to the authority of the priests, and to tradition. The *jansenists* are enthusiasts, and zealous promoters of the passionate devotion, and of the inward life; little influenced by authority; and, in a word, but half catholics. The consequences are exactly conformable to the foregoing reasoning. The *jesuits* are the tyrants of the people, and the slaves of the court: And the *jansenists* preserve alive the small sparks of the love of liberty, which are to be found in the French nation.

## 3. *The Gods of the City*

BY FUSTEL DE COULANGES

TO UNDERSTAND the truth about the Greeks and Romans, it is wise to study them without thinking of ourselves, as if they were entirely foreign to us; with the same disinterestedness, and with the mind as free, as if we were studying ancient India or Arabia.

Thus observed, Greece and Rome appear to us in a character absolutely inimitable; nothing in modern times resembles them; nothing in the future can resemble them. We shall attempt to show by what rules these societies were regulated, and it will be freely admitted that the same rules can never govern humanity again.

Whence comes this? Why are the conditions of human government no longer the same as in earlier times? The great changes which appear from time to time in the constitution of society can be the effect neither of chance nor of force alone.

Reprinted from Fustel de Coulanges, *The Ancient City,* trans. Willard Small (Boston: Lee and Shepard, 1874), pp. 10–13, 164–67.

The cause which produces them must be powerful, and must be found in man himself. If the laws of human association are no longer the same as in antiquity, it is because there has been a change in man. There is, in fact, a part of our being which is modified from age to age; this is our intelligence. It is always in movement; almost always progressing; and on this account, our institutions and our laws are subject to change. Man has not, in our day, the way of thinking that he had twenty-five centuries ago; and this is why he is no longer governed as he was governed then.

The history of Greece and Rome is a witness and an example of the intimate relation which always exists between men's ideas and their social state. Examine the institutions of the ancients without thinking of their religious notions, and you find them obscure, whimsical, and inexplicable. Why were there patricians and plebeians, patrons, and clients, eupatrids and thetes; and whence came the native and ineffaceable differences which we find between these classes? What was the meaning of those Lacedæmonian institutions which appear to us so contrary to nature? How are we to explain those unjust caprices of ancient private law; at Corinth and at Thebes, the sale of land prohibited; at Athens and at Rome, an inequality in the succession between brother and sister? What did the jurists understand by *agnation,* and by *gens?* Why those revolutions in the laws, those political revolutions? What was that singular patriotism which sometimes effaced every natural sentiment? What did they understand by that liberty of which they were always talking? How did it happen that institutions so very different from anything of which we have an idea to-day, could become established and reign for so long a time? What is the superior principle which gave them authority over the minds of men?

But by the side of these institutions and laws place the religious ideas of those times, and the facts at once become clear, and their explanation is no longer doubtful. If, on going back to the first ages of this race,—that is to say, to the time when its institutions were founded,—we observe the idea which it had of human existence, of life, of death, of a second life, of the divine principle, we perceive a close relation between these opinions and the ancient rules of private law; between the rites which spring from these opinions and their political institutions.

A comparison of beliefs and laws shows that a primitive religion constituted the Greek and Roman family, established marriage and paternal authority, fixed the order of relationship, and consecrated the right of property, and the right of inheritance. This same religion, after having enlarged and extended the family, formed a still larger association, the city, and reigned in that as it had reigned in the family. From it came all the institutions, as well as all the private law, of the ancients. It was from this that the city received all its principles, its rules, its usages, and its magistracies. But, in the course of time, this ancient religion became modified or effaced, and private law and political institutions were modified with it. Then came a series of revolutions, and social changes regularly followed the development of knowledge.

It is of the first importance, therefore, to study the religious ideas of these peoples, and the oldest are the most important for us to know. For the institutions and beliefs which we find at the flourishing periods of Greece and Rome are only the development of those of an earlier age; we must seek the roots of them in the very distant past. The Greek and Italian population are many centuries older than Romulus and Homer. It was at an epoch more ancient, in an antiquity without date, that their beliefs were formed, and that their institutions were either established or prepared.

* * *

It happened, in the course of time, the divinity of a family having acquired a great prestige over the imaginations of men, and appearing powerful in proportion to the prosperity of this family, that a whole city wished to adopt him, and offer him public worship, to obtain his favors. This was the case with the Demeter of the Eumolpidæ, the Athene of the Butadæ, and the Hercules of the Potitii. But when a family consented thus to share its god, it retained at least the priesthood. We may remark that the dignity of priest, for each god, was during a long time hereditary, and could not go out of a certain family. This is a vestige of a time when the god himself was the property of this family; when he protected it alone, and would be served only by it.

We are correct, therefore, in saying that this second religion was at first in unison with the social condition of men. It was cradled in each family, and remained long bounded by this narrow horizon. But it lent itself more easily than the worship of the dead to the future progress of human association. Indeed, the ancestors, heroes, and manes were gods, who by their very nature could be adored only by a very small number of men, and who thus established a perpetual and impassable line of demarcation between families. The religion of the gods of nature was more comprehensive. No rigorous laws opposed the propagation of the worship of any of these gods. There was nothing in their nature that required them to be adored by one family only, and to repel the stranger. Finally, men must have come insensibly to perceive that the Jupiter of one family was really the same being or the same conception as the Jupiter of another, which they could never believe of two Lares, two ancestors, or two sacred fires.

Let us add, that the morality of this new religion was different. It was not confined to teaching men family duties. Jupiter was the god of hospitality; in his name came strangers, suppliants, "the venerable poor," those who were to be treated "as brothers." All these gods often assumed the human form, and appeared among mortals; sometimes, indeed, to assist in their struggles and to take part in their combats; often, also, to enjoin concord, and to teach them to help each other.

As this second religion continued to develop, society must have enlarged. Now, it is quite evident that this religion, feeble at first, afterwards assumed large proportions. In the beginning it was, so to speak, sheltered under the protection of its older sister, near the domestic hearth. There the god had obtained a small place, a narrow *cella*, near and opposite to the venerated altar, in order that a little of the respect which men had for the sacred fire might be shared by him. Little by little, the god, gaining more authority over the soul, renounced this sort of guardianship, and left the domestic hearth. He had a dwelling of his own, and his own sacrifices. This dwelling (*ναὸς*, from *ναίω*, to inhabit) was, moreover, built after the fashion of the ancient sanctuary; it was, as before, a *cella* opposite a hearth; but the *cella* was enlarged and embellished, and became a temple. The holy fire remained at the entrance of the god's house, but appeared very small by the side of this house. What had at first been the principal, had now become only an accessory. It ceased to be a god, and descended to the rank of the god's altar, an instrument for the sacrifice. Its office was to burn the flesh of the victim, and to carry the offering with men's prayers to the majestic divinity whose statue resided in the temple.

When we see these temples rise and open their doors to the multitude of worshippers, we may be assured that human associations have become enlarged.

# 4. *Jehovah and the Prophets*

BY W. ROBERTSON SMITH

THE PRIMARY difference between the religion of Israel and that of the surrounding nations does not lie in the idea of a theocracy, or in a philosophy of the invisible world, or in the external forms of religious service, but in a personal difference between Jehovah and other gods. That difference, again, is not of a metaphysical but of a directly practical nature; it was not defined once for all in a theological dogma, but made itself felt in the attitude which Jehovah actually took up towards Israel in those historical dealings with His nation to which the word of the prophets supplied a commentary. Everything that befell Israel was interpreted by the prophets as a work of Jehovah's hand, displaying His character and will— not an arbitrary character or a changeable will, but a fixed and consistent holy purpose, which has Israel for its object and seeks the true felicity of the nation, but at the same time is absolutely sovereign over Israel, and will not give way to Israel's desires or adapt itself to Israel's convenience. No other religion can show anything parallel to this. The gods of the nations are always conceived either as arbitrary and changeful, or as themselves subordinate to blind fate, or as essentially capable of being bent into sympathy with whatever is for the time being the chief desire of their worshippers, or, in some more speculative forms of faith, introduced when these simpler conceptions broke down, as escaping these limitations only by being raised to entire unconcern in the petty affairs of man. In Israel alone does Jehovah appear as a God near to man, and yet maintaining an absolute sovereignty of will, a consistent independence of character. And the advance of the Old Testament religion is essentially identified with an increasing clearness of perception of the things which this character of the Deity involves. The name of Jehovah becomes more and more full of meaning as faith in His sovereignty and self-consistency is put to successive tests in the constantly changing problems presented by the events of history.

Now, when we speak of Jehovah as displaying a consistent character in His sovereignty over Israel, we necessarily imply that Israel's religion is a moral religion, that Jehovah is a God of righteousness, whose dealings with His people follow an ethical standard. The ideas of right and wrong among the Hebrews are forensic ideas; that is, the Hebrew always thinks of the right and the wrong as if they were to be settled before a judge. Righteousness is to the Hebrew not so much a moral quality as a legal status. The word "righteous" (*çaddîḳ*) means simply "in the right," and the word "wicked" (*rāshā'*) means "in the wrong." "I have sinned this time," says Pharaoh, "Jehovah is in the right (A.V. righteous), and I and my people are

---

Reprinted from W. Robertson Smith, *The Prophets of Israel* (New York: D. Appleton Co., 1882), pp. 70–75, 78–83.

in the wrong (A.V. wicked)," Exod. ix. 27. Jehovah is always in the right, for He is not only sovereign but self-consistent. He is the fountain of righteousness, for from the days of Moses He is the judge as well as the captain of His people, giving forth law and sentence from His sanctuary. In primitive society the functions of judge and lawgiver are not separated, and reverence for law has its basis in personal respect for the judge. So the just consistent will of Jehovah is the law of Israel, and it is a law which as King of Israel He Himself is continually administering.

Now, in every ancient nation, morality and law (including in this word traditional binding custom) are identical and in every nation law and custom are a part of religion, and have a sacred authority. But in no other nation does this conception attain the precision and practical force which it has in the Old Testament, because the gods themselves, the guardians of law, do not possess a sharply-defined consistency of character such as Jehovah possesses. The heathen gods are guardians of law, but they are something else at the same time; they are not wholly intent on righteousness, and righteousness is not the only path to their favour, which sometimes depends on accidental partialities, or may be conciliated by acts of worship that have nothing to do with morality. And here be it observed that the fundamental superiority of the Hebrew religion does not lie in the particular system of social morality that it enforces, but in the more absolute and self-consistent righteousness of the Divine Judge. The abstract principles of morality—that is, the acknowledged laws of social order—are pretty much the same in all parts of the world in corresponding stages of social development. Heathen nations at the same general stage of society with the Hebrews will be found to acknowledge all the duties of man to man laid down in the decalogue; and on the other hand there are many things in the social order of the Hebrews, such as polygamy, blood revenge, slavery, the treatment of enemies, which do not correspond with the highest ideal morality, but belong to an imperfect social state, or, as the gospel puts it, were tolerated for the hardness of the people's hearts. But, with all this, the religion of Jehovah put morality on a far sounder basis than any other religion did, because in it the righteousness of Jehovah as a God enforcing the known laws of morality was conceived as absolute, and as showing itself absolute, not in a future state, but upon earth. I do not, of course, mean that this high view of Jehovah's character was practically present to all His worshippers. On the contrary, a chief complaint of the prophets is that it was not so, or, in other words, that Israel did not know Jehovah. But the higher view is never put forth by the prophets as a novelty; they regard it as the very foundation of the religion of Jehovah from the days of Moses downwards, and the people never venture to deny that they are right. In truth they could not deny it, for the history of the first creation of Israel, which was the fundamental evidence as to the true character of Jehovah's relation to His people, gave no room for such mythological conceptions as operate in the heathen religions to make a just conception of the Godhead impossible. Heathen religions can never conceive of their gods as perfectly righteous, because they have a natural as well as a moral side, a physical connection with their worshippers, physical instincts and passions, and so forth. The Old Testament brings out this point with great force of sarcasm when Elijah taunts the prophets of Baal, and suggests that their god may be asleep, or on a journey, or otherwise busied with some human avocation. In fact, all this was perfectly consistent with the nature of Baal. But the Hebrews knew Jehovah solely as the King and Judge of Israel. He was this, and this alone; and therefore there was no ground to ascribe to Him less than absolute sovereignty and absolute righteousness. If the masses lost sight of those great qualities, and assimilated His nature to that of the Canaanite deities, the prophets were justified in reminding them that Jehovah was Israel's God before they knew the Baalim, and that He had then showed Himself a God far different from these.

But religion cannot live on the mere memory of the past, and the faith of Jehovah had to assert itself as the true faith of Israel by realising a present God who still worked in the midst of the nation as He had worked of old. No nation can long cleave to a God whose presence and power are not actually with them in their daily life. If Jehovah was Israel's God, He must manifest Himself as still the King and the Judge of His people, and these names must acquire more and more full significance through the actual experience of deeds of sovereignty and righteousness. Without such deeds no memory of the days of Moses could long have saved the God of the Hebrews from sinking to the level of the gods of the nations, and we have now to see that such deeds were not wanting, and not without fruit for the progress of the Old Testament faith.

* * *

The prophets were never patriots of the common stamp, to whom national interests stand higher than the absolute claims of religion and morality.

Had Elijah been merely a patriot, to whom the state stood above every other consideration, he would have condoned the faults of a king who did so much for the greatness of his nation; but the things for which Elijah contended were of far more worth than the national existence of Israel, and it is a higher wisdom than that of patriotism which insists that divine truth and civil righteousness are more than all the counsels of statecraft. Judged from a mere political point of view Elijah's work had no other result than to open a way for the bloody and unscrupulous ambition of Jehu, and lay bare the frontiers of the land to the ravages of the ferocious Hazael; but with him the religion of Jehovah had already reached a point where it could no longer be judged by a merely national standard, and the truths of which he was the champion were not the less true because the issue made it plain that the cause of Jehovah could not triumph without destroying the old Hebrew state. Nay, without the destruction of the state the religion of Israel could never have given birth to a religion for all mankind, and it was precisely the incapacity of Israel to carry out the higher truths of religion in national forms which brought into clearer and clearer prominence those things in the faith of Jehovah which are independent of every national condition, and make Jehovah the God not of Israel alone but of all the earth. This, however, is to anticipate what will come out more clearly as we proceed. Let us for the present confine our attention to what Elijah himself directly saw and taught.

The ruling principle in Elijah's life was his consuming jealousy for Jehovah the God of hosts (1 Kings xix. 14); or, to put the idea in another and equally Biblical form, Jehovah was to him pre-eminently a jealous God who could endure no rival in His land or in the affections of His people. There was nothing novel in this idea; the novelty lay in the practical application which gave to the idea a force and depth which it had never shown before. To us it seems obvious that Ahab had broken the first commandment in giving Baal a place in his land, but to Ahab and the mass of his contemporaries the thing could hardly be so clear. There are controversies enough even among modern commentators as to the exact force of the "before me" of the first commandment; and, even if we are to suppose that practical religious questions were expressly referred to the words of this precept, it would not have been difficult to interpret them in a sense that meant only that no other god should have the pre-eminence over Israel's King. But no doubt these things were judged of less by the letter of the decalogue than by habitual feeling and usage. Hitherto all Israel's interest in Jehovah had had practical reference to His contests with the gods of hostile nations, and it was one thing to worship deities who were felt to be Jehovah's rivals and foes, and quite another thing to allow some recognition to the deity of an allied race. But Elijah saw deeper into the true character of the God of Israel. Where He was worshipped no other god could be acknowledged in any sense. This was a proposition of tremendous practical issues. It really involved the political isolation of the nation, for as things then stood it was impossible to have friendship and alliance with other peoples if their gods were proscribed in Israel's land. It is not strange that Ahab as a politician fought with all his might against such a view; for it contained more than the germ of that antagonism between Israel and all the rest of mankind which made the Jews appear to the Roman historian as the enemies of the human race, and brought upon them an unbroken succession of political misfortunes and the ultimate loss of all place among the nations. It is hard to say how far the followers of Elijah or indeed the prophet himself perceived the full consequences of the position which he took up. But the whole history of Elijah testifies to the profound impression which he made. The air of unique grandeur that surrounds the prophet of Gilead proves how high he stood above the common level of his time. It is Jehovah and Elijah not against Ahab alone, but against and above the world.

The work of Elijah, in truth, was not so much that of a great teacher as of a great hero. He did not preach any new doctrine about Jehovah, but at a critical moment he saw what loyalty to the cause of Jehovah demanded, and of that cause he became the champion, not by mere words, but by his life. The recorded words of Elijah are but few, and in many cases have probably been handed down with the freedom that ancient historians habitually use in such matters. His importance lies in his personality. He stands before us as the representative of Jehovah's personal claims on Israel. The word of Jehovah in his mouth is not a word of doctrine, but of kingly authority, and to him pre-eminently applies the saying of Hosea: "I have hewed them by the prophets; I have slain them by the word of My mouth: and My judgments were as the light that goeth forth" (Hosea vi. 5).

This view of the career of Elijah, which is that naturally derived from the Biblical narrative, is pretty much an exact inversion of the common representation of the function of the prophets. The traditional view which we have from the Rabbins makes the prophets mere interpreters of the Law, and places the originality of their work entirely in their predictions. In that case Elijah would be the least original of prophets, for he gave no

Messianic prediction. But in reality Jehovah did not first give a complete theoretical knowledge of Himself and then raise up prophets to enforce the application of the theoretical scheme in particular circumstances. That would not have required a prophet; it would have been no more than is still done by uninspired preachers. The place of the prophet is in a religious crisis where the ordinary interpretation of acknowledged principles breaks down, where it is necessary to go back, not to received doctrine, but to Jehovah Himself. The word of Jehovah through the prophet is properly a declaration of what Jehovah as the personal King of Israel commands in this particular crisis, and it is spoken with authority, not as an inference from previous revelation, but as the direct expression of the character and will of a personal God, who has made Himself personally audible in the prophet's soul. General propositions about divine things are not the basis but the outcome of such personal knowledge of Jehovah, just as in ordinary human life a general view of a man's character must be formed by observation of his attitude and action in a variety of special circumstances. Elijah's whole career, and not his words merely, contained a revelation of Jehovah to Israel—that is, made them feel that through this man Jehovah asserted Himself as a living God in their midst.

# 5. *Church and Sect*

BY ERNST TROELTSCH

## *Sect-Type and Church-Type Contrasted*

THE IMPORTANCE of this element is the fact that at this point, alongside of the Church-type produced by Christianity in its sociological process of self-development, there appears the new type of the sect.

At the outset the actual differences are quite clear. The Church is that type of organization which is overwhelmingly conservative, which to a certain extent accepts the secular order, and dominates the masses; in principle, therefore, it is universal, i.e., it desires to cover the whole life of humanity. The sects, on the other hand, are comparatively small groups; they aspire after personal inward perfection, and they aim at a direct personal fellowship between the members of each group. From the very beginning, therefore, they are forced to organize themselves in small groups, and to renounce the idea of dominating the world. Their attitude towards the world, the State, and Society may be indifferent, tolerant, or hostile, since they have no desire to control and incorporate these forms of social life; on the contrary, they tend to avoid them; their aim is usually either to tolerate their presence alongside of their own body, or even to replace these social institutions by their own society.

Further, both types are in close connection with the actual situation and with the development of Society. The fully developed Church, however, utilizes the State and the ruling classes, and weaves these elements into her own life; she then becomes an integral part of the existing social order; from this standpoint, then, the Church both stabilizes and determines the social order; in so doing, however, she becomes dependent upon the upper classes, and upon their development. The sects, on the other hand, are connected with the lower classes, or at least with those elements in Society which are opposed to the State and to Society; they work upwards from below, and not downwards from above.

Finally, too, both types vary a good deal in their attitude towards the supernatural and transcendent element in Christianity, and also in their view of its system of asceticism. The Church relates the whole of the secular order as a means and a preparation to the supernatural aim of life, and it incorporates genuine asceticism into its structure as one element in this preparation, all under the very definite direction of the Church. The sects refer their members directly to the supernatural aim of life, and in them the individualistic, directly religious character of asceticism, as a means of union

Reprinted from Ernst Troeltsch, *The Social Teaching of the Christian Churches,* trans. Olive Wyon (New York: Macmillan Co., 1931), I, 331–43, with the permission of George Allen & Unwin, London.

with God, is developed more strongly and fully; the attitude of opposition to the world and its powers, to which the secularized Church now also belongs, tends to develop a theoretical and general asceticism. It must, however, be admitted that asceticism in the Church, and in ecclesiastical monasticism, has a different meaning from that of the renunciation of or hostility to the world which characterizes the asceticism of the sects.

The asceticism of the Church is a method of acquiring virtue, and a special high watermark of religious achievement, connected chiefly with the repression of the senses, or expressing itself in special achievements of a peculiar character; otherwise, however, it presupposes the life of the world as the general background, and the contrast of an average morality which is on relatively good terms with the world. Along these lines, therefore, ecclesiastical asceticism is connected with the asceticism of the redemption cults of late antiquity, and with the detachment required for the contemplative life; in any case, it is connected with a moral dualism.

The ascetism of the sects, on the other hand, is merely the simple principle of detachment from the world, and is expressed in the refusal to use the law, to swear in a court of justice, to own property, to exercise dominion over others, or to take part in war. The sects take the Sermon on the Mount as their ideal; they lay stress on the simple but radical opposition of the Kingdom of God to all secular interests and institutions. They practise renunciation only as a means of charity, as the basis of a thorough-going communism of love, and, since their rules are equally binding upon all, they do not encourage extravagant and heroic deeds, nor the vicarious heroism of some to make up for the worldliness and average morality of others. The ascetic ideal of the sects consists simply in opposition to the world and to its social institutions, but it is not opposition to the sense-life nor to the average life of humanity. It is therefore only related with the asceticism of monasticism in so far as the latter also creates special conditions, within which it is possible to lead a life according to the Sermon on the Mount, and in harmony with the ideal of the communism of love. In the main, however, the ascetic ideal of the sects is fundamentally different from that of monasticism, in so far as the latter implies emphasis upon the mortification of the senses, and upon works of supererogation in poverty and obedience for their own sake. In all things the ideal of the sects is essentially not one which aims at the destruction of the sense life and of natural self-feeling, but a union in love which is not affected by the social inequalities and struggles of the world.

All these differences which actually existed between the late Mediaeval Church and the sects, must have had their foundation in some way or another within the interior structure of the twofold sociological edifice. If, then, in reality both types claim, and rightly claim, a relationship with the Primitive Church, it is clear that the final cause for this dualistic development must lie within primitive Christianity itself. Once this point becomes clear, therefore, it will also shed light upon the whole problem of the sociological understanding of Christianity in general. Since it is only at this point that the difference between the two elements emerges very clearly as a permanent difference, only now have we reached the stage at which it can be discussed. It is also very important to understand this question thoroughly at this stage, since it explains the later developments of Church History, in which the sect stands out ever more clearly alongside of the Church. In the whole previous development of the Church this question was less vital, for during the early centuries the Church itself fluctuated a great deal between the sect and the Church-type; indeed, it only achieved the development of the Church-type with the development of sacerdotal and sacramental doctrine; precisely for that reason, in its process of development up to this time, the Church had only witnessed a sect development alongside of itself to a small extent, and the differences between them and the Church were still not clear. The problem first appears clearly in the opposition between the sacramental-hierarchical Church conception of Augustine and the Donatists. But with the disappearance of African Christianity this opposition also disappeared, and it only reappeared in a decisive form after the completion of the idea of the Church in the Gregorian church reform.

The word "sect," however, gives an erroneous impression. Originally the word was used in a polemical and apologetic sense, and it was used to describe groups which separated themselves from the official Church, while they retained certain fundamental elements of Christian thought; by the very fact, however, that they were outside the corporate life of the ecclesiastical tradition—a position, moreover, which was usually forced upon them—they were regarded as inferior side-issues, one-sided phenomena, exaggerations or abbreviations of ecclesiastical Christianity. That is, naturally, solely the viewpoint of the dominant churches, based on the belief that the ecclesiastical type alone has any right to exist. Ecclesiastical law within the modern State definitely denotes as "sects" those religious groups which exist alongside of the official privileged State Churches, by law established, groups which the State either does not recognize at all, or, if it does recognize them, grants them fewer rights and privileges than the official State Churches. Such a conception, however, confuses the actual issue. Very often in the so-called "sects" it is precisely the essential elements of the Gospel which are fully expressed; they themselves always appeal to the Gospel and to Primitive Christianity, and accuse the Church of having fallen away from its ideal; these impulses are always those which have been either suppressed or undeveloped in the official churches, of course for good and characteristic reasons, which again are not taken into account by the passionate party polemics of the sects. There can, however, be no doubt about the actual fact: the sects, with their greater independence of the world, and their continual emphasis upon the original ideals of Christianity, often represent in a very direct and characteristic way the essential fundamental ideas of Christianity; to a very great extent they are a most important factor in the study of the development of the sociological consequences of Christian thought. This statement is proved conclusively by all those who make a close study of the sect movements, which were especially numerous in the latter mediaeval period—movements which played their part in the general disintegration of the mediaeval social order. This comes out very clearly in the great works of Sebastian Franck, and especially of Gottfried Arnold, which were written later in defence of the sects.

The main stream of Christian development, however, flows along the channel prepared by the Church-type. The reason for this is clear: the Church-type represents the longing for a universal all-embracing ideal, the desire to control great masses of men, and therefore the urge to dominate the world and civilization in general. Paulinism, in spite of its strongly individualistic and "enthusiastic" features, had already led the way along this line: it desired to conquer the world for Christ; it came to terms with the order of the State by interpreting it as an institution ordained and permitted by God; it accepted the existing order with its professions and its habits and customs. The only union it desired was that which arose out of a common share in the energy of grace which the Body of Christ contained; out of this union the new life ought to spring up naturally from within through the power of the Holy Spirit, thus preparing the way for the speedy coming of the Kingdom of God, as the real universal end of all things. The more that Christendom renounced the life of this supernatural and eschatological fulfilment of its universal ideal, and tried to achieve this end by missionary effort and organization, the more was it forced to make its Divine and Christian character independent of the subjective character and service of believers; henceforth it sought to concentrate all its emphasis upon the objective possession of religious truth and religious power, which were contained in the tradition of Christ, and in the Divine guidance of the Church which fills and penetrates the whole Body. From this objective basis subjective energies could ever flow forth afresh, exerting a renewing influence, but the objective basis did not coincide with these results. Only thus was it possible to have a popular Church at all, and it was only thus that the relative acceptance of the world, the State, of Society, and of the existing culture, which this required, did no harm to the objective foundation. The Divine nature of the Church was retained in its objective basis, and from this centre there welled up continually fresh streams of vital spiritual force. It was the aim of the leaders of the Church to render this basis as objective as possible, by means of tradition, priesthood, and sacrament; to secure in it, objectively, the sociological point of contact; if that were once firmly established the subjective influence of the Church was considered secure; it was only in detail that it could not be controlled. In this way the fundamental religious sense of possessing something Divinely "given" and "redeeming" was ensured, while the universalizing tendency was also made effective, since it established the Church, the organ of Divine grace, in the supreme position of power. When to that was added the Sacrament of Penance, the power of spiritual direction, the law against heretics, and the general supervision of the faith, the Church was then able to gain an inward dominion over the hearts of men.

Under these circumstances, however, the Church found it impossible to avoid making a compromise with the State, with the social order, and with economic conditions, and the Thomist doctrine worked this out in a very able, comprehensive theory, which vigorously maintained the ultimate supernatural orientation of life. In all this it is claimed that the whole is derived, quite logically, from the Gospel; it is clear that this point of view became possible as soon as the Gospel was conceived as a universal way of life, offering redemption to all, whose influence radiates from the knowledge given by the Gospel, coupled with the assurance of salvation given by the Church. It was precisely the development of an objective sociological point of reference, its establishment on a stable basis, and its endeavour to go forward from that point to organize the conquest of the world, which led to this development. It is, however, equally obvious that in so doing the radical individualism of the Gospel, with its urge towards the utmost personal achievement, its radical fellowship of love, uniting all in the most personal centre of life, with its heroic indifference towards the world, the State and civilization, with its mistrust of the spiritual danger of distraction and error inherent in the possession of or the desire for great possessions, has been given a secondary place, or even given up altogether; these features now appear as mere factors within the system; they are no longer ruling principles.

It was precisely this aspect of the Gospel, however, which the sects developed still farther, or, rather, it was this aspect which they were continually re-emphasizing and bringing into fresh prominence. In general, the following are their characteristic features: lay Christianity, personal achievement in ethics and in religion, the radical fellowship of love, religious equality and brotherly love, indifference towards the authority of the State and the ruling classes, dislike of technical law and of the oath, the separation of the religious life from the economic struggle by means of the ideal of poverty and frugality, or occasionally in a charity which becomes communism, the directness of the personal religious relationship, criticism of official spiritual guides and theologians, the appeal to the New Testament and to the Primitive Church. The sociological point of contact, which here forms the starting-point for the growth of the religious community, differs clearly from that upon which the Church has been formed. Whereas the Church assumes the objective concrete holiness of the sacerdotal office, of Apostolic Succession, of the *Depositum fidei* and of the sacraments, and appeals to the extension of the Incarnation which takes place permanently through the priesthood, the sect, on the other hand, appeals to the ever new common performance of the moral demands, which, at bottom, are founded only upon the Law and the Example of Christ. In this, it must be admitted that they are in direct contact with the Teaching of Jesus. Consciously or unconsciously, therefore, this implies a different attitude to the early history of Christianity, and a different conception of Christian doctrine. Scripture history and the history of the Primitive Church are permanent ideals, to be accepted in their literal sense, not the starting-point, historically limited and defined, for the development of the Church. Christ is not the God-Man, eternally at work within the Church, leading it into all Truth, but He is the direct Head of the Church, binding the Church to Himself through His Law in the Scriptures. On the one hand, there is development and compromise, on the other literal obedience and radicalism.

It is this point of view, however, which makes the sects incapable of forming large mass organizations, and limits their development to small groups, united on a basis of personal intimacy; it is also responsible for the necessity for a constant renewal of the ideal, their lack of continuity, their pronounced individualism, and their affinity with all the oppressed and idealistic groups within the lower classes. These also are the groups in which an ardent desire for the improvement of their lot goes hand in hand with a complete ignorance of the complicated condition of life, in which therefore an idealistic orthodoxy finds no difficulty in expecting to see the world transformed by the purely moral principles of love. In this way the sects gained on the side of intensity in Christian life, but they lost in the spirit of universalism, since they felt obliged to consider the Church as degenerate, and they did not believe that the world could be conquered by human power and effort; that is why they were always forced to adopt eschatological views. On the side of personal Christian piety they score, and they are in closer touch with the radical individualism of the Gospel, but they lose spontaneity and the spirit of grateful surrender to the Divine revelation of grace; they look upon the New Testament as the Law of God, and, in their active realization of personal fellowship in love, they tend towards legalism and an emphasis upon "good works." They gain in specific Christian piety, but they lose spiritual breadth and the power to be receptive, and they thus revise the whole vast process of assimilation which the Church had completed, and which she was able to complete because she had placed personal Christian piety upon an objective basis. The Church emphasizes the idea of Grace and makes it objective; the sect emphasizes and realizes the idea of subjective holiness. In the Scriptures the Church adheres to the source of redemption, whereas the sect adheres to the Law of God and of Christ.

Although this description of the sect-type represents in the main its prevailing sociological characteristics, the distinctive significance of the sect-type contrasted with the Church-type still has a good concrete basis. (There is no need to consider here the particular groups which were founded purely upon dogma; they were indeed rare, and the pantheistic philosophical sects of the Middle Ages merge almost imperceptibly into sects of the practical religious kind. In reality, the sects are essentially different from the Church and the churches. The word "sect," however, does not mean that these movements are undeveloped expressions of the Church-type; it stands for an independent sociological type of Christian thought.

The essence of the Church is its objective institutional character. The individual is born into it, and through infant baptism he comes under its miraculous influence. The priesthood and the hierarchy, which hold the keys to the tradition of the Church, to sacramental grace and ecclesiastical jurisdiction, represent the objective treasury of grace, even when the individual priest may happen to be unworthy; this Divine treasure only needs to be set always upon the lampstand and made effective through the sacraments, and it will inevitably do its work by virtue of the miraculous power which the Church contains. The Church means the eternal existence of the God-Man; it is the extension of the Incarnation, the objective organization of miraculous power, from which, by means of the Divine Providential government of the world, subjective results will appear quite naturally. From this point of view compromise with the world, and the connection with the preparatory stages and dispositions which it contained, was possible; for in spite of all individual inadequacy the institution remains holy and Divine, and it contains the promise of its capacity to overcome the world by means of the miraculous power which dwells within it. Universalism, however, also only becomes possible on the basis of this compromise; it means an actual domination of the institution as such, and a believing confidence in its invincible power of inward influence. Personal effort and service, however fully they may be emphasized, even when they go to the limits of extreme legalism, are still only secondary; the main thing is the objective possession of grace and its universally recognized dominion; to everything else these words apply: *et cetera adjicientur vobis.* The one vitally important thing is that every individual should come within the range of the influence of these saving energies of grace; hence the Church is forced to dominate Society, compelling all the members of Society to come under its sphere and influence; but, on the other hand, her stability is entirely unaffected by the fact of the extent to which her influence over all individuals is actually attained. The Church is the great educator of the nations, and like all educators she knows how to allow for various degrees of capacity and maturity, and how to attain her end only by a process of adaptation and compromise.

Compared with this institutional principle of an objective organism, however, the sect is a voluntary community whose members join it of their own free will. The very life of the sect, therefore, depends on actual personal service and co-operation; as an independent member each individual has his part within the fellowship; the bond of union has not been indirectly imparted through the common possession of Divine grace, but it is directly realized in the personal relationships of life. An individual is not born into a sect; he enters it on the basis of conscious conversion; infant baptism, which, indeed, was only introduced at a later date, is almost always a stumbling-block. In the sect spiritual progress does not depend upon the objective impartation of Grace through the Sacrament, but upon individual personal effort; sooner or later, therefore, the sect always criticizes the sacramental idea. This does not mean that the spirit of fellowship is weakened by individualism; indeed, it is strengthened, since each individual proves that he is entitled to membership by the very fact of his services to the fellowship. It is, however, naturally a somewhat limited form of fellowship, and the expenditure of so much effort in the maintenance and exercise of this particular kind of fellowship produces a certain indifference towards other forms of fellowship which are based upon secular interests; on the other hand, all secular interests are drawn into the narrow framework of the sect and tested by its standards, in so far as the sect is able to assimilate these interests at all. Whatever cannot be related to the group of interests controlled by the sect, and by the Scriptural ideal, is rejected and avoided. The sect, therefore, does not educate nations in the mass, but it gathers a select group of the elect, and places it in sharp opposition to the world. In so far as the sect-type maintains Christian universalism at all, like the Gospel, the only form it knows is that of eschatology; this is the reason why it always finally revives the eschatology of the Bible. That also naturally explains the greater tendency of the sect towards "ascetic" life and thought, even though the original ideal of the New Testament had not pointed in that direction. The final activity of the group and of the individual consists precisely in the practical austerity of a purely religious attitude towards life which is not affected by cultural influences. That is, however, a different kind of asceticism, and this is the reason for that difference between it and the asceticism of the Church-type which has already been stated. It is not the heroic special achievement of a special class, restricted by its very nature to particular instances, nor the mortification of the senses in order to further the higher religious life; it is simply detachment from the world, the reduction of worldly pleasure to a minimum, and the highest possible development of fellowship in love; all this is interpreted in the old Scriptural sense. Since the sect-type is rooted in the teaching of Jesus, its asceticism also is that of primitive Christianity and of the Sermon on the Mount, not that of the Church and of the contemplative life; it is narrower and more scrupulous than that of Jesus, but, literally understood, it is still the continuation of the attitude of Jesus towards the world. The concentration on personal effort, and the sociological connection with a practical ideal, makes an extremely exacting claim on individual effort, and avoidance of all other forms of human association. The asceticism of the sect is not an attempt to popularize and universalize an ideal which the Church had prescribed only for special classes and in special circumstances. The Church ideal of asceticism can never be conceived as a universal ethic; it is essentially unique and heroic. The ascetic ideal of the sect, on the contrary, is, as a matter of course, an ideal which is possible to all, and appointed for all, which, according to its conception, united the fellowship instead of dividing it, and according to its content is also capable of a general realization in so far as the circle of the elect is concerned.

Thus, in reality we are faced with two different sociological types. This is true in spite of the fact (which is quite immaterial) that incidentally in actual practice they may often impinge upon one another. If objections are raised to the terms "Church" and "Sect," and if all sociological groups which are based on and inspired by monotheistic, universalized, religious motives are described (in a terminology which is in itself quite appropriate) as "Churches," we would then have to make the distinction between institutional churches and voluntary churches. It does not really matter which expression is used. The all-important point is this: that both types are a logical result of the Gospel, and only conjointly do they exhaust the whole range of its sociological influence, and thus also indirectly of its social results, which are always connected with the religious organization.

In reality, the Church does not represent a mere deterioration of the Gospel, however much that may appear to be the case when we contrast its hierarchical organization and its sacramental system with the teaching of Jesus. For wherever the Gospel is conceived as primarily a free gift, as pure grace, and wherever it is offered to us in the picture which faith creates of Christ as a Divine institution, wherever the inner freedom of the Spirit, contrasted with all human effort and organization, is felt to be the spirit of Jesus, and wherever His splendid indifference towards secular matters is felt, in the sense of a spiritual and inner independence, while these secular things are used outwardly, there the institution of the Church may be regarded as a natural continuation and transformation of the Gospel. At the same time, with its unlimited universalism, it still contains the fundamental impulse of the evangelic message; the only difference is that whereas the Gospel had left all questions of possible realization to the miraculous coming of the Kingdom of God, a Church which had to work in a world which was not going to pass away had to organize and arrange matters for itself, and in so doing it was forced into a position of compromise.

On the other hand, the essence of the sect does not consist merely in a one-sided emphasis upon certain vital elements of the Church-type, but it is itself a direct continuation of the idea of the Gospel. Only within it is there a full recognition of the value of radical individualism and of the idea of love; it is the sect alone which instinctively builds up its ideal of fellowship from this point of view, and this is the very reason why it attains such a strong subjective and inward unity, instead of merely external membership in an institution. For the same reason the sect also maintains the original radicalism of the Christian ideal and its hostility towards the world, and it retains the fundamental demand for personal service, which indeed it is also able to regard as a work of grace: in the idea of grace, however, the sect emphasizes the subjective realization and the effects of grace, and not the objective assurance of its presence. The sect does not live on the miracles of the past, nor on the miraculous nature of the institution, but on the constantly renewed miracle of the Presence of Christ, and on the subjective reality of the individual mastery of life.

The starting-point of the Church is the Apostolic Message of the Exalted Christ, and faith in Christ the Redeemer, into which the Gospel has developed; this constitutes its objective treasure which it makes still more objective in its sacramental-sacerdotal institution. To this extent the Church can trace its descent from Paulinism, which contained the germ of the sacramental idea, which, however, also contained some very unecclesiastical elements in its pneumatic enthusiasm, and in its urgent demand for the personal holiness of the "new creature."

The sect, on the contrary, starts from the teaching and the example of Jesus, from the subjective work of the apostles and the pattern of their life of poverty, and unites the religious individualism preached by the Gospel with the religious fellowship, in which the office of the ministry is not based upon ecclesiastical ordination and tradition, but upon religious service and power, and which therefore can also devolve entirely upon laymen.

The Church administers the sacraments without

reference to the personal worthiness of the priests; the sect distrusts the ecclesiastical sacraments, and either permits them to be administered by laymen, or makes them dependent upon the personal character of the celebrant, or even discards them altogether. The individualism of the sect urges it towards the direct intercourse of the individual with God; frequently, therefore, it replaces the ecclesiastical doctrine of the sacraments by the Primitive Christian doctrine of the Spirit and by "enthusiasm." The Church has its priests and its sacraments; it dominates the world and is therefore also dominated by the world. The sect is lay Christianity, independent of the world, and is therefore inclined towards asceticism and mysticism. Both these tendencies are based upon fundamental impulses of the Gospel. The Gospel contains the idea of an objective possession of salvation in the knowledge and revelation of God, and in developing this idea it becomes the Church. It contains, however, also the idea of an absolute personal religion and of an absolute personal fellowship, and in following out this idea it becomes a sect. The teaching of Jesus, which cherishes the expectation of the End of the Age and the Coming of the Kingdom of God, which gathers into one body all who are resolute in their determination to confess Christ before men and to leave the world to its fate, tends to develop the sect-type. The apostolic faith which looks back to a miracle of redemption and to the Person of Jesus, and which lives in the powers of its heavenly Lord: this faith which leans upon something achieved and objective, in which it unites the faithful and allows them to rest, tends to develop the Church-type. Thus the New Testament helps to develop both the Church and the sect; it has done so from the beginning, but the Church had the start, and its great world mission. Only when the objectification of the Church had been developed to is fullest extent did the sectarian tendency assert itself and react against this excessive objectification. Further, just as the objectification of the Church was achieved in connection with the feudal society of the Early Middle Ages, the reappearance of the tendency to form sects was connected with the social transformation, and the new developments of city-civilization in the central period of the Middle Ages and in its period of decline—with the growth of individualism and the gathering of masses of people in the town themselves—and with the reflex effect of this city formation upon the rural population and the aristocracy.

# 6. *Trends in Western Monasticism*

BY ADOLPH VON HARNACK

IN THE TENTH CENTURY it appeared as if monasticism had well-nigh played its part in the West: it seemed—a few houses, chiefly nunneries, being disregarded—as if Western monasticism had succumbed to the danger which in the East could not possibly in this way arise—it had become worldly, and vulgarly worldly, not by a hair's breadth higher than the world at large. In the tenth century, Pope, Church and monastery alike seemed to have reached the last stage of decrepitude.

Reprinted from Adolph von Harnack, *Monasticism: Its Ideals and History & The Confessions of St. Augustine,* (London: Williams & Norgate, 1901), pp. 81–116.

## *I*

And yet there had already begun a second movement in the Church; a second revival of monasticism. This revival started in France. The monastery of Cluny, founded so early as the tenth century, became the home of that great reform of the Church which the West experienced in the eleventh. Begun by monks, it was at first supported by pious and intelligent princes and bishops as a counterpoise to the secularised Papacy; but later the great Hildebrand took it up, and alike as Cardinal and as Pope opposed it to the princes and the secularised clergy. The West gained by it an effective reformation of the Church; a reformation, however, not of Evangelical but on Catholic lines. The aims of this new movement were in the first instance a restoration of the old discipline, of true renunciation and piety in the monasteries themselves; but later, first, a subjection of the secular clergy to the regulars, and, secondly, the dominion of the whole spiritualty, as regulated by the monks, over the laity—princes and nations alike. The great reform of the monks of Cluny and of their mighty Pope presents itself first as the energetic attempt to conform the life of the whole spiritualty to monastic ordinances. In this movement Western monasticism for the first time puts forth the decisive claim to pose as the only Christian life for all adult believers, and to ensure the general recognition of this claim. Monasticism in the West must inevitably come again and again into contact with the secular Church, for the reason that it can never cease itself to put forth claims on the whole of Christendom or to serve the Church. The Christian freedom at which it aims is to it, in spite of all vacillation, not only a freedom of the individual *from* the world, but the freedom of Christendom for the service of God *in* the world. We Evangelicals can even today still judge this great movement with sympathy: for in it expression is given to the consciousness that within the Church there can be only one morality and only one ideal of life, and that to this therefore all adult Christians are pledged. If monasticism is really the highest form of Christianity, it comes to this, that all adult confessors should be subjected to the monastic rule, and all Christians in their nonage—*i.e.,* in the mediæval view all the laity—should be urged at least to obedience. Such were the ideas that dominated Cluny and Cluny's great Pope. Hence the stern enforcement of the celibacy of the clergy; hence the struggle against the secularisation of the spiritualty, and specially against simony; hence the monastic discipline of the priests. And what about his effort after political supremacy? Though it might from this point of view be looked on as a mere *parergon* which was to last because, and only so long as, the true conversion of the world was incomplete, yet here begin the points of difference between monasticism and the reformed secular Church. It is possible so to represent the ideas of Hildebrand and those of his more earnest friends as to make them appear to differ only by a shade. Yet this shade of difference led to policies totally opposed. From the very first voices were heard, even among the most zealous supporters of the Pope, crying that it was enough to reform manners and to cherish piety: it was not for the Church to rule in the style and with the weapons of the State. These voices demanded a true return to apostolic life, and a renewal of the Early Church. It is incorrect to describe these efforts of the monks as if they betokened a retrogression to the standard of the Greek Church, and thus fell outside the circle of Western Catholicism. The real truth is, these monks had a positive aim—*Christian life* for the *whole* of Christendom. But since tradition offered to them a conception of a supernaturally renewed Empire, which they did not renounce the hope of realising on earth, they conceived an almost invincible mistrust of the "parergon," which the Roman Bishop held out and for which he strove. In this mistrust was included that shrinking from everything in the Church that recalled political or legal ordinances. Repugnance to public law and to the State is in the Western monasticism as characteristic as in the East the reason is plain why Greek ascetics show no such repugnance. But in the eleventh century devotion to the Church and her ruler was powerful enough to prevent an open conflict between the reformed clergy and the monks. In the Sacrament of Penance the Church possessed the strongest means of binding even the monks to herself. With conscience stained and courage broken, many bowed to the will of the great monastic Pope. And it was precisely those that had most willingly dedicated their whole life to God whom he drew out of the quiet of the monastery. He knew well that only that monk will help to subjugate the world who shuns it and strives to free himself from it. Renunciation of the world in the service of a world-ruling Church—such is the amazing problem that Gregory solved for the next century and a half. But Gregory's aims, and those of the reformed bishops, with all their political character, were spiritual also. Only as spiritual did they transform the masses, and inflame them against the worldly clergy in upper Italy, or against simoniacal princes throughout Europe. A new religious zeal stirred the nations, and specially the Romance nations, of the West. The enthusiasm of the Crusades was the direct fruit of the monastic reform of the eleventh century. That religious revival which Europe experienced is expressed most vividly in them. The dominion of the Church is to be consummated on earth. It was the ideas of the world-ruling monk of Cluny that led the van of the Crusades; and the Crusaders brought back from the Holy Land and the Holy Places a new, or at least till now rare form of Christian piety—that of absorption in the sufferings and in the Via Dolorosa of Christ. Asceticism, once negative, received a positive form and a new positive aim, that of becoming one with the Redeemer by fervent love and perfect imitation. A personal element, working from heart to heart, began to vivify the hitherto unimpassioned and aimless struggle of self-abnegation, and to awaken the sleeping subjectivity. Even to monasticism, though as a rule only in a few isolated cases, it lent an inner impulse. The great number of new Orders that were founded at this time, specially in France, bears witness to the general enthusiasm. It was then that arose the Carthusians, the Cistercians, the Præmonstratensians, the Carmelites, and many other Orders. But the constant appearance of fresh Orders only shows that monasticism, in alliance with the secular Church, was ever losing its special character. Each new Order sought to call back the monks to their old austerity and to drag them away from secularisation; but in the very act of subjecting itself to the secular Church, it was annexed and exploited by the Church. It shows the illusions in which men moved that the Orders which were founded to restore the original monasticism, by the very terms of their foundation expressly announced their subjection to the bishops, and thenceforward renounced not only the care of souls, but all special programmes within the Church and for the Church. In the twelfth century the dependence of Christendom, and thus also of monasticism, on the Church is still a very *naïve* one: the contradiction between the actual form of the world-ruling Church and the Gospel which she preaches is felt indeed but always suppressed, and criticism of the claims and of the constitution of the Church is as yet ineffective. We need only mention the name of a single man, that of Bernard of Clairvaux, in order to see as in a picture alike all the greatness which this second monastic reform of the Church introduced, and its limitations and illusions. The same monk who in the quiet of his cell speaks a new language of devotion, who dedicates his soul entirely to the Bridegroom, who urges Christendom to forsake the world, who tells the Pope that he is called to the chair of Peter not for dominion but for service: this same man was yet imbued with all the hierarchical prejudices of his time, and himself led the politics of the world-ruling Church. But it was precisely because monasticism in that age went with the Church that it was able to do so great a work for her. It roused, it is true, a reform in the Church; but this reform, in the long run, came to strengthen the political power of the Church, and so to increase her secularisation—a strange and yet easily intelligible result. The domain in which Church and cloister found constantly their common ground was the contest with all the claims of the laity, and specially of the princes, on the Church. Western monasticism took this to be a "liberation from the world," and therefore offered its services in the struggle to the Church. Only by observing this can we understand how one and the same man in that age could be at once an upright monk and a prince of the Church, or how he could deceive himself and others, or even be uncertain, as to the final aims of this opposition to the State.

## *II*

A new age arose, with which the old conceptions did not harmonise. The Church had attained to political world-dominion; she had either actually overcome, or was on the point of overcoming, the Empire and the old State order. The aims and results of the mighty efforts put forth by the Church in the eleventh and twelfth centuries had now been made manifest; but now a movement began among the laity and in the nations to emancipate themselves from the tutelage of the hierarchy. In social movements, in religious sectarianism, in pious unions which failed to find satisfaction in official piety, in the endeavours of nations and princes to order their own concerns independently, was heralded the approach of a new era. For a whole century the secular Church succeeded in holding back the tide; and in doing so she was aided by a fresh phenomenon in monasticism which is marked by the foundation of the mendicant Orders.

The figure of the tenderest and most loveable of all monks, the quaint saint of Assisi, stands out brilliantly in the history of the Middle Ages. Here, however, we are not asking what was his character, but what were his aims in devoting himself to the service of God and of his brethren. In the first place he desired to renew the life of the Apostles by imitating the poverty of their life and their preaching of the Gospel. This preaching was to arouse penitence in Christendom and to make Christendom effectively that which she already was through her possession of the Holy Sacraments. A society of brethren was to be formed which, like the Apostles, should possess nothing but penitence, faith, and love, and which should own no other aim than to serve others and to win souls. St. Francis never clearly defined how far this society was to extend itself. He was no politician, and never intruded on the domain of government. But what could converts, made by the preaching of the poor brethren, have become, but themselves brethren, serving itinerant preachers, in their turn? For them St. Francis himself laid down fixed and settled rules. Neither individuals nor even the society, united as it was for a truly Christ-like life, was to possess property of any kind. "Go sell all that thou hast." Life in God, suffering along with His Son, love for His creatures, human and other, service even to the sacrifice of one's own life, the riches of the soul, which possesses nothing but the Saviour—such was the Gospel of St. Francis. If any man ever realised in his life what he preached, St. Francis was that man. And—what is the characteristic mark of this Western movement—intense as this asceticism was, heartfelt as this religion was, it did not drive its disciples into solitude or the desert, but the reverse. Christendom, nay, the whole world, was to be won for this new and yet old Christianity of repentance, renunciation, and love. A Christian world—this conception, at the beginning of the thirteenth century, had a quite other content than in the sixth and eleventh; not only because the geographical horizon had extended itself for the West, but to a higher degree because the poor and the ordinary man were now to be reckoned as part of that world. Western monasticism, down to the end of the twelfth century, had been essentially an aristocratic institution; the privileges of the monasteries were in most cases conditioned by the descent of their inmates. The monastic schools were as a rule open only to the nobility. To the coarse and common people the monastery remained as inaccessible as the castle. There were no popular Orders and few popular monks. St. Francis did not break down the walls of the noble monasteries but raised alongside them huts for poor and rich. He thus restored the Gospel to the people, who had hitherto possessed only the priest and the Sacrament. But the saint of Assisi was the most submissive son of the Church and of the Pope in history. His labours were devoted to the service of the Church. Thus he was the first to give to monasticism—for a monasticism his brotherhood became, little as he meant it—special tasks for Christianity as a whole, but in the bosom of the Church: for care for the Church is care for salvation. Cluny and its monks had exclusively devoted themselves to the reform of the spiritualty. St. Francis would know no distinctions. We may say without exaggeration that he wished not to found a new order of monks but to revolutionise the world—to make the world a fair garden, colonised by men who follow Christ, who need nothing, in whose hearts is God. It was love that enlarged his horizon: his fancy neither grew rankly luxuriant, nor did it become barren through his stern asceticism: his determination to serve Church and Christianity remained to the end strong and powerful, though he was constrained with pain to see how the Church corrected and narrowed his creation. Hundreds of thousands flocked to him. But what were thousands when it was a question of millions? The emergence of the so-called Tertiary Brethren by the side of the strict monastic order is on one side, of course, an indication that this Gospel does not penetrate into human society without compromise, but on the other a shining example of the far-reaching influence of the Franciscan preaching. The Tertiaries kept up their secular callings, their marriages and their possessions; but they adapted themselves as far as possible to the monastic life, held themselves aloof from public affairs, and devoted themselves, as far as they could, to asceticism and works of piety. This institution, which formed itself without any recognised founder, is a striking proof of the universal character of the Franciscan movement. Sects had led the way; but the brotherhood remained true to the Church. Nay, the interest of the laity in the life and in the sacraments of *the Church* was awakened by them; through them the idea grew slowly effective that a layman, sincerely obedient to the Church and inwardly pious, has a right to share in the highest good which the Church can communicate. The conception of a double morality differing in value, could on this basis be transformed into another more tolerable conception of a morality differing only in kind. An *active* Christian life may be of equal value with the contemplative; the latter is only a more direct path to salvation.

A newly moulded piety, dominated by the surrender of the soul to Christ, spread forth from Assisi and made itself master of the Church. It was religious individuality and freedom that had been awakened; Christianity as the *religion* of poverty and love was to come by its own as opposed to the degeneracy in morality and politics.

The finest of mediæval hymns, the mightiest of mediæval sermons, belong to the Franciscan Order or to the nearly-related Dominicans. But to art and science also these Orders gave a new impulse. All the important schoolmen of the thirteenth century —a Thomas Aquinas, a Bonaventura, an Albertus Magnus—were mendicant monks. The noblest paintings of the old Italian school are inspired by the new spirit, the spirit of absorption in the sufferings of Christ, of a holy sorrow and a transcendental strength. A Dante, a Giotto, and again a Tauler, and a Berthold of Ratisbon—all these, in their feelings, thoughts, and creations, lived in the religious ideas of the mendicant Orders. But—what is more significant—these monks stooped to the populace and to individuals. They had an eye for their sorrows and an ear for their complaints. They lived with the people, they preached to the people in their own language, and they brought them a consolation they could understand. What the sacrament and the services had hitherto failed to give—a certainty of salvation—the mysticism of the Orders aimed at producing: but not outside of the Church means of grace. The eye must learn to see the Saviour; the soul must attain peace by sensuous perception of

His presence. But the 'theology,' which here arose, proclaimed also the religious freedom and blessedness of souls lifted above the world and conscious of their God. If by this idea it did not actually begin the Evangelical Reformation, it made the path straight for it.

By the help of the mendicant Orders, of which she availed herself to the full, the Church was able in the thirteenth century to maintain herself at the height of her dominion. She won back the hearts of the faithful; but at the same time, through the activity of the monks, she ordered and brought to perfection her hold on the goods of the world, science, art, and law. It was then that the body of canon law was completed, which regulates all the relations of life from the standpoint of the Church's world-dominion, and of an asceticism devoted to her service. This canon law is no longer recognized in civilised states, but its ideas still bear fruit. To a much higher degree are philosophy and theology, as well as social politics, still dependent on the mode of thought which in the thirteenth century, in the mendicant Orders, led to the masterly development of great scholastic systems. Through these Orders, again, the Church succeeded in overcoming the sectarian movements that had taken hold of the laity. It was the mendicants who with furious zeal conquered the heretical, but, alas! also free-spirited and evangelical, movements of the thirteenth century. Thus here also they made common cause with the world-ruling Church, the Church of politics and of the sword: nay, they became precisely the most favoured clerical servants of the Popes, who endowed them with the highest privileges, and permitted them everywhere to interfere with the regular administration of the Church and with the cure of souls. In the mendicant Orders, the Roman Pope found a tool wherewith to weld the national churches of the country more closely to his see, and to crush the independence of the Bishops. Thus they had the largest share in the Romanising of the Catholic Church in Europe, and also influenced in many ways the older foundations which sprang out of the Benedictine Rule. But they became secularised as speedily as any other Order before them. The connection with the secular Church proved once again fatal to monasticism. That connection had been from the first extraordinarily close—Francis had been compelled to yield as if to a decree of Fate—and the ruin was all the more rapid. What was meant to raise them above the world—their poverty—proved but an occasion of specific secularisation to those who no longer took poverty seriously. They saw themselves led to speculate on the coarseness, the superstition, and the sluggishness of the masses; and they became, like the masses, coarse, superstitious, and sluggish.

Yet the high ideal set before Christendom by St. Francis could not disappear without shaking to their foundations the Church and the Order founded by him. When one party in the Order urged a modification of the strictness of the regulations imposing poverty, another, faithful to the Master, arose to defend them. When the Popes took up the cause of the former, the zealous party turned their criticism upon the Papacy and the secular Church. Complaints of the corruption of the Church had long been uttered by individual monks, but they had always died away again. The strife of the Church against the states and their claims had hitherto constantly enticed monasticism to recognise in the programme of the Church the beginning of the realisation of its own. But now arose the idea which had always lain dormant in monasticism and had again and again been suppressed. The tie with Church and papacy was sundered: ancient apocalyptic ideas emerged; the Papal Church appeared as Babylon, as the Kingdom of Antichrist, who has falsified the true Christianity of renunciation and poverty. The whole history of the Church appeared suddenly in the light of a monstrous apostasy; and the Pope no longer as the successor of Peter but as the heir of Constantine. It was hopeless to attempt to move the Church to turn back. Nothing but a new revelation of the Spirit could avail to save her, and men accordingly looked for a future final Gospel of Christian perfection. With all the means in her power the Church suppressed this dangerous uprising. She pronounced the teachings of the Franciscans on the poverty of Christ and the Apostles to be heresy, and she demanded submission. A bitter struggle was the result. Christendom witnessed the new spectacle of the secular Church in arms against a doctrine of renunciation that had become aggressive. With the courage of men who had sacrificed all, the Spirituals preached to Pope and Bishop their doctrine of poverty, and sealed their testimony at the stake. At the end of the fourteenth century the secular Church came forth, victorious and unchanged, from her strife with poverty. Thus once again, at the end of the Middle Ages, the sleeping but ever reviving antagonism between the aims of the Church and the aims of monasticism had come to light in a terrible crisis. But monasticism was vanquished. The foundation of the mendicant Orders was its last great attempt in the Middle Ages to assert itself and its ideal in the Church as a whole while maintaining its connection with the history and constitution of that Church. But the development of the Franciscan Order was twofold. The one party, from the very first, resigned its original ideal, subjected itself completely to the Church, and became speedily secularised; the other sought to maintain its ideal, made that ideal stricter, set it up even against the Church, and exhausted itself, until it succumbed, in fantastic pursuits. This development will to some appear an unredeemed tragedy; but it will perhaps not seem an unmixed evil to those who recognise that individuals of the Order which strove to emancipate itself from the Church, sought deliverance at the hands of the State, and, in opposition to the claims of the Church, which they no longer or only partially admitted, began to defend the independence and ordinances of the State. It was the Franciscans who, in the fourteenth century, discovered a scientific foundation for the Hohenstaufen theory of politics. Western monasticism, as we learn from this astonishing volte-face, is unable to exist for any length of time without a close alliance with the forces of society. When the Church is not available it seeks even the State. Yet this movement was but transitory. In the fifteenth century a deathly stillness reigns in the Order, which is now in entire subjection to the Church; attempts at reform were feeble, and resulted in no fresh life. In the age of the Renascence monasticism—with a few honourable exceptions—seemed to have condemned itself to inaction and uselessness. Yet the new culture, whose supporters, it is true, frequently spent their shafts of ridicule on the ignorant, slavish, and hypocritical monks, was not utterly hostile to ascetic ideals. Rather did the vision reappear of a wise and pious man, absorbed in the enjoyment of a quiet contemplation of heaven, without neglecting the world, in peaceful detachment from the noises of the day; who needs nothing because in spirit he possesses all. The attempt was even made to revive this ideal in the traditional forms of cloister-life; nor did it everywhere fail. But it was only given to isolated individuals to unite the rule of the convent with the study of Cicero or Plato, and to be sufficient for both. The scholar who was at the same time a man of the world, and who at his desk became enthusiastic for Stoical indifference or for Franciscan independence of externals, was anything but a monk; and the Church, in spite of all classical and edifying dissertations, remained as she was. The poor, as in the days before St. Francis had shown them the way, sought to secure their salvation in pious and enthusiastic unions of every kind, which were, it is true, of occasional service to the Church, but nevertheless were to her a constant danger.

## *III*

What was left? What new form of monasticism remained possible after all these attempts? None—or rather, perhaps, one, which in truth is no longer one, and yet became the last and in a true sense the authentic word of Western monasticism. It remained possible to begin with reversing the relations between asceticism and ecclesiastical service; to keep at once in the eye, as the purposed and highest aim, the ideal which had always floated before the gaze of Western monasticism, but had never been taken up save with hesitation. It remained possible to find, instead of an ascetic union with ecclesiastical tendencies, a society that should pursue no other aim than to strengthen and extend the dominion of the Church. The glory of recognising this possibility, and of understanding the lessons of history, belongs to the Spaniard, Ignatius Loyola. His creation, the Society of Jesus, which he set up against the Reformation, is no monasticism in the oldest sense of the word, nay, it appears as a downright protest against the monasticism of a St. Anthony or a St. Francis. True, the Society is equipped with all the rules of the older Orders; but its first principle is that which they had uncertainly viewed as a side-purpose, or which they had unwillingly allowed to be imposed upon them by circumstances. To the Jesuits all asceticism, all renunciation, is but a means to an end. Emancipation from the world extends only so far as such emancipation helps towards domination over the world—a domination exercised *politically* by means of the Church. The professed aim of the Order is the dominion of the Church over the world. Religious enthusiasm, culture and barbarism, splendour and squalor, diplomacy and simplicity, all alike are employed by this Order to attain the one purpose to which it has dedicated itself. In it, Western Catholicism, so to speak, neutralised monasticism, and gave it a turn by which it made the aims of monasticism its own. And yet the Society was not the work of a cunning, calculating intelligence merely. As it arose, it was the product of a high enthusiasm, but of an enthusiasm from within that Church which had already rejected any sort of evangelical reform, and which had resolved to maintain itself for ever in the form given to it, in the course of a long history, by worldly wisdom and policy.

On the other side, the Jesuit Order is the last and authentic word of Western monasticism. Its rise, no less than its nature, lies entirely on the lines which we have traced from Benedict to Bernard, and from Bernard to the mendicants. The Society of Jesus has solved the problems to which they were unequal, and has attained the objects for which they strove. It produced a new form of piety, and gave to that piety a special expression and a methodical form, and in this respect it made a successful appeal to the whole of Catholic Christianity. It has known how to interest the laity in the Church, and has opened to them in its mysticism that which hitherto had been denied to them. It has penetrated the life of the Church in all its domains, and brought the faithful to the feet of the Pope. But not only has the Order constantly pursued objects of its own in the service of the Church; it has also known how to maintain itself at all times in a certain independence of her. While it has not seldom corrected the policy of the Popes in accordance with the programme of the Papacy, it to-day rules the Church by its peculiar Christianity, its fantastic and sensuous mode of worship, and its political morality. It never became a mere tool in the hand of the Church, and it never, like the earlier Orders, sank into mere insignificance. It never transformed itself into a department of the Church; rather did the Church fall under the domination of the Jesuits. In the Society of Jesus, in fact, monasticism has actually won the victory over the secular Church of the West.

Monasticism, then, prevailed; but what form of monasticism? Not that of St. Francis; but one which had previously made the programme of the Church its own, and thus emptied and renounced its own essence. In it asceticism and renunciation have become mere political forms and instruments; diplomacy and a sensuous mysticism have taken the place of a simple piety and moral discipline. This monasticism can no longer materially maintain its genuineness except by its opposition to states and their culture, and by making small account of the individual. Under the supremacy of the Jesuits the Church has become specifically and definitively secularized; she opposes to the world, to history, and to civilisation, *her own* worldly possessions, which are the legacy of the Middle Ages. Her consciousness of "other-worldliness" she strengthens to-day mainly by her opposition to the culture of the Renascence and of the Reformation; but she draws her strength from the failings and defects of that culture and from the mistakes of its protectors. If we regard the negative attitude of the Church to the modern State as the expression of her "other-worldly" sentiment, then monasticism has indeed conquered in her; but if we see, in the manner in which she to-day maintains this attitude, an essential secularisation, then it is precisely the Jesuitic monasticism which is to be made answerable therefor. As historical factors, the other Orders are to-day nearly without importance. The Society of Jesus influenced the older and the younger almost without exception. Whether they returned, like the Trappists, to an Oriental silence, or whether some of them, in the style of the old Egyptian monks, have come to view even ecclesiastical learning with mistrust, and to declaim against it; whether they continue their existence divided between the world and asceticism, though it be to the attainment of something notable in social usefulness or in the salvation of individuals—in any case they have ceased to be an historical factor. Their place has been taken by the Jesuits, and by the "Congregations," those elastic and pliant creations in which the spirit of the Jesuitic Order has found a point of contact with the needs and institutions of modern society. The Congregations, directed in the spirit of the Society of Jesus, and the innumerable "free" Catholic associations which work in the same spirit, and which are at need secular or spiritual, free or "tied"; these are the real Catholic monasticism of modern times.

In the Church of the West, which set before herself moral and political aims, monasticism in its original form, and the ideals of that monasticism, have had in the long run but sporadic effects. So far as it decided to bear its part in the secular mission of the Church, it had to transform itself into that society which betokens its freedom from the world by a worldly and political reaction against culture and history, and which thus brought to completion the secularisation of the Church. Monasticism in the East maintained its independence at the cost of stagnation; monasticism in the West remained effectual at the cost of losing its essential principle. In the East it was shattered, because it thought it could despise moral effort for the benefit of the world; and in the West it succumbed, because it subjected itself to a Church that devoted religion and morality to the service of politics. But there, as here, it was the Church herself that engendered monasticism and appointed its ideals; and thus in East and West alike, though after long vacillation and severe struggles, monasticism came finally to be the protector of ecclesiastical tradition and the guardian of ecclesiastical empiricism; and so its original aims were transformed into their opposites.

Even to-day, to certain hearts weary of the world, monasticism may indeed bring peace; but the view of history passes beyond monasticism to the message of Luther, that man begins the imitation of Christ when, in his calling and in his sphere of life, he aids in the work of God's kingdom by faith and ministering love. Even this ideal is not simply identical with the content of the Gospel message; but it points out the lines along which the Christian must move, and secures him against insincerity and self-deception. Like all ideals, it was set up when men were striving to escape from an intolerable position; and, like them, it was soon falsified and tainted by the world. But if it aims to be no more than the confession that no man attains to the perfection of life which is set before us in the Gospel; and if it expresses the fact that in any condition the Christian may rely on the divine help and grace; then it will be the strength of the weak, and in the strife of creeds it may yet be a signal of peace.

# 7. *Religion and Society*

BY EMILE DURKHEIM

THE THEORISTS who have undertaken to explain religion in rational terms have generally seen in it before all else a system of ideas, corresponding to some determined object. This object has been conceived in a multitude of ways: nature, the infinite, the unknowable, the ideal, etc.; but these differences matter but little. In any case, it was the conceptions and beliefs which were considered as the essential elements of religion. As for the rites, from this point of view they appear to be only an external translation, contingent and material, of these internal states which alone pass as having any intrinsic value. This conception is so commonly held that generally the disputes of which religion is the theme turn about the question whether it can conciliate itself with science or not, that is to say, whether or not there is a place beside our scientific knowledge for another form of thought which would be specifically religious.

But the believers, the men who lead the religious life and have a direct sensation of what it really is, object to this way of regarding it, saying that it does not correspond to their daily experience. In fact, they feel that the real function of religion is not to make us think, to enrich our knowledge, nor to add to the conceptions which we owe to science others of another origin and another character, but rather, it is to make us act, to aid us to live. The believer who has communicated with his god is not merely a man who sees new truths of which the unbeliever is ignorant; he is a man who is *stronger*. He feels within him more force, either to endure the trials of existence, or to conquer them. It is as though he were raised above the miseries of the world, because he is raised above his condition as a mere man; he believes that he is saved from evil, under whatever form he may conceive this evil. The first article in every creed is the belief in salvation by faith. But it is hard to see how a mere idea could have this efficacy. An idea is in reality only a part of ourselves; then how could it confer upon us powers superior to those which we have of our own nature? Howsoever rich it might be in affective virtues, it could add nothing to our natural vitality; for it could only release the motive powers which are within us, neither creating them nor increasing them. From the mere fact that we consider an object worthy of being loved and sought after, it does not follow that we feel ourselves stronger afterwards; it is also necessary that this object set free energies superior to these which we ordinarily have at our command and also that we have some means of making these enter into us and unite themselves to our interior lives. Now for that, it is not enough that we think of them; it is also indispensable that we place ourselves within their sphere of action, and that we set ourselves where we may best feel their influence; in a word, it is necessary that we act, and that we repeat the acts thus necessary every time we feel the need of renewing their effects. From this point of view, it is readily seen how that group of regularly repeated acts which form the cult get their importance. In fact, whoever has really practised a religion knows very well that it is the cult which gives rise to these impressions of joy, of interior peace, of serenity, of enthusiasm which are, for the believer, an experimental proof of his beliefs. The cult is not simply a system of signs by which the faith is outwardly translated; it is a collection of the means by which this is created and recreated periodically. Whether it consists in material acts or mental operations, it is always this which is efficacious.

Our entire study rests upon this postulate that the unanimous sentiment of the believers of all times cannot be purely illusory. Together with a recent

---

Reprinted from Emile Durkheim, *Elementary Forms of the Religious Life,* trans. Joseph W. Swain (Glencoe, Ill.: The Free Press, 1954), from "Conclusion," sec. 1, pp. 416–27, with the permission of The Free Press.

apologist of the faith[1] we admit that these religious beliefs rest upon a specific experience whose demonstrative value is, in one sense, not one bit inferior to that of scientific experiments, though different from them. We, too, think that "a tree is known by its fruits,"[2] and that fertility is the best proof of what the roots are worth. But from the fact that a "religious experience," if we choose to call it this, does exist and that it has a certain foundation—and, by the way, is there any experience which has none?—it does not follow that the reality which is its foundation conforms objectively to the idea which believers have of it. The very fact that the fashion in which it has been conceived has varied infinitely in different times is enough to prove that none of these conceptions express it adequately. If a scientist states it as an axiom that the sensations of heat and light which we feel correspond to some objective cause, he does not conclude that this is what it appears to the senses to be. Likewise, even if the impressions which the faithful feel are not imaginary, still they are in no way privileged intuitions; there is no reason for believing that they inform us better upon the nature of their object than do ordinary sensations upon the nature of bodies and their properties. In order to discover what this object consists of, we must submit them to an examination and elaboration analogous to that which has substituted for the sensuous idea of the world another which is scientific and conceptual.

This is precisely what we have tried to do, and we have seen that this reality, which mythologies have represented under so many different forms, but which is the universal and eternal objective cause of these sensations *sui generis* out of which religious experience is made, is society. We have shown what moral forces it develops and how it awakens this sentiment of a refuge, of a shield and of a guardian support which attaches the believer to his cult. It is that which raises him outside himself; it is even that which made him. For that which makes a man is the totality of the intellectual property which constitutes civilization, and civilization is the work of society. Thus is explained the preponderating rôle of the cult in all religions, whichever they may be. This is because society cannot make its influence felt unless it is in action, and it is not in action unless the individuals who compose it are assembled together and act in common. It is by common action that it takes consciousness of itself and realizes its position; it is before all else an active co-operation. The collective ideas and sentiments are even possible only owing to these exterior movements which symbolize them, as we have established. Then it is action which dominates the religious life, because of the mere fact that it is society which is its source.

In addition to all the reasons which have been given to justify this conception, a final one may be added here, which is the result of our whole work. As we have progressed, we have established the fact that the fundamental categories of thought, and consequently of science, are of religious origin. We have seen that the same is true for magic and consequently for the different processes which have issued from it. On the other hand, it has long been known that up until a relatively advanced moment of evolution, moral and legal rules have been indistinguishable from ritual prescriptions. In summing up, then, it may be said that nearly all the great social institutions have been born in religion.[3] Now in order that these principal aspects of the collective life may have commenced by being only varied aspects of the religious life, it is obviously necessary that the religious life be the eminent form and, as it were, the concentrated expression of the whole collective life. If religion has given birth to all that is essential in society, it is because the idea of society is the soul of religion.

Religious forces are therefore human forces, moral forces. It is true that since collective sentiments can become conscious of themselves only by fixing themselves upon external objects, they have not been able to take form without adopting some of their characteristics from other things: they have thus acquired a sort of physical nature; in this way they have come to mix themselves with the life of the material world, and then have considered themselves capable of explaining what passes there. But when they are considered only from this point of view and in this rôle, only their most superficial aspect is seen. In reality, the essential elements of which these collective sentiments are made have been borrowed by the understanding. It ordinarily seems that they should have a human character only when they are conceived under human forms;[4] but even the most impersonal and the most anonymous are nothing else than objectified sentiments.

1. William James, *The Varieties of Religious Experience.*
2. Quoted by James, *op. cit.*, p. 20.

3. Only one form of social activity has not yet been expressly attached to religion: that is economic activity. Sometimes processes that are derived from magic have, by that fact alone, an origin that is indirectly religious. Also, economic value is a sort of power or efficacy, and we know the religious origins of the idea of power. Also richness can confer *mana;* therefore it has it. Hence it is seen that the ideas of economic value and of religious value are not without connection. But the question of the nature of these connections has not yet been studied.

4. It is for this reason that Frazer and even Preuss set impersonal religious forces outside of, or at least on the threshold of religion, to attach them to magic.

It is only by regarding religion from this angle that it is possible to see its real significance. If we stick closely to appearances, rites often give the effect of purely manual operations: they are anointings, washings, meals. To consecrate something, it is put in contact with a source of religious energy, just as to-day a body is put in contact with a source of heat or electricity to warm or electrize it; the two processes employed are not essentially different. Thus understood, religious technique seems to be a sort of mystic mechanics. But these material manœuvres are only the external envelope under which the mental operations are hidden. Finally, there is no question of exercising a physical constraint upon blind and, incidentally, imaginary forces, but rather of reaching individual consciousnesses, of giving them a direction and of disciplining them. It is sometimes said that inferior religions are materialistic. Such an expression is inexact. All religions, even the crudest, are in a sense spiritualistic: for the powers they put in play are before all spiritual, and also their principal object is to act upon the moral life. Thus it is seen that whatever has been done in the name of religion cannot have been done in vain: for it is necessarily the society that did it, and it is humanity that has reaped the fruits.

But, it is said, what society is it that has thus made the basis of religion? Is it the real society, such as it is and acts before our very eyes, with the legal and moral organization which it has laboriously fashioned during the course of history? This is full of defects and imperfections. In it, evil goes beside the good, injustice often reigns supreme, and the truth is often obscured by error. How could anything so crudely organized inspire the sentiments of love, the ardent enthusiasm and the spirit of abnegation which all religions claim of their followers? These perfect beings which are gods could not have taken their traits from so mediocre, and sometimes even so base a reality.

But, on the other hand, does someone think of a perfect society, where justice and truth would be sovereign, and from which evil in all its forms would be banished for ever? No one would deny that this is in close relations with the religious sentiment; for, they would say, it is towards the realization of this that all religions strive. But that society is not an empirical fact, definite and observable; it is a fancy, a dream with which men have lightened their sufferings, but in which they have never really lived. It is merely an idea which comes to express our more or less obscure aspirations towards the good, the beautiful and the ideal. Now these aspirations have their roots in us; they come from the very depths of our being; then there is nothing outside of us which can account for them. Moreover, they are already religious in themselves; thus it would seem that the ideal society presupposes religion, far from being able to explain it.[5]

But, in the first place, things are arbitrarily simplified when religion is seen only on its idealistic side: in its way, it is realistic. There is no physical or moral ugliness, there are no vices or evils which do not have a special divinity. There are gods of theft and trickery, of lust and war, or sickness and of death. Christianity itself, howsoever high the idea which it has made of the divinity may be, has been obliged to give the spirit of evil a place in its mythology. Satan is an essential piece of the Christian system; even if he is an impure being, he is not a profane one. The anti-god is a god, inferior and subordinated, it is true, but nevertheless endowed with extended powers; he is even the object of rites, at least of negative ones. Thus religion, far from ignoring the real society and making abstraction of it; is in its image; it reflects all its aspects, even the most vulgar and the most repulsive. All is to be found there, and if in the majority of cases we see the good victorious over evil, life over death, the powers of light over the powers of darkness, it is because reality is not otherwise. If the relation between these two contrary forces were reversed, life would be impossible; but, as a matter of fact, it maintains itself and even tends to develop.

But if, in the midst of these mythologies and theologies we see reality clearly appearing, it is none the less true that it is found there only in an enlarged, transformed and idealized form. In this respect, the most primitive religions do not differ from the most recent and the most refined. For example, we have seen how the Arunta place at the beginning of time a mythical society whose organization exactly reproduces that which still exists to-day; it includes the same clans and phratries, it is under the same matrimonial rules and it practices the same rites. But the personages who compose it are ideal beings, gifted with powers and virtues to which common mortals cannot pretend. Their nature is not only higher, but it is different, since it is at once animal and human. The evil powers there undergo a similar metamorphosis: evil itself is, as it were, made sublime and idealized. The question now raises itself of whence this idealization comes.

Some reply that men have a natural faculty for idealizing, that is to say, of substituting for the real world another different one, to which they transport themselves by thought. But that is merely changing the terms of the problem; it is not resolving it or even advancing it. This systematic idealization is an essential characteristic of religions. Explaining them

5. Boutroux, *Science et Religion,* pp. 206–207.

by an innate power of idealization is simply replacing one word by another which is the equivalent of the first; it is as if they said that men have made religions because they have a religious nature. Animals know only one world, the one which they perceive by experience, internal as well as external. Men alone have the faculty of conceiving the ideal, of adding something to the real. Now where does this singular privilege come from? Before making it an initial fact or a mysterious virtue which escapes science, we must be sure that it does not depend upon empirically determinable conditions.

The explanation of religion which we have proposed has precisely this advantage, that it gives an answer to this question. For our definition of the sacred is that it is something added to and above the real: now the ideal answers to this same definition; we cannot explain one without explaining the other. In fact, we have seen that if collective life awakens religious thought on reaching a certain degree of intensity, it is because it brings about a state of effervescence which changes the conditions of psychic activity. Vital energies are over-excited, passions more active, sensations stronger; there are even some which are produced only at this moment. A man does not recognize himself; he feels himself transformed and consequently he transforms the environment which surrounds him. In order to account for the very particular impressions which he receives, he attributes to the things with which he is in most direct contact properties which they have not, exceptional powers and virtues which the objects of every-day experience do not possess. In a word, above the real world where his profane life passes he has placed another which, in one sense, does not exist except in thought, but to which he attributes a higher sort of dignity than to the first. Thus, from a double point of view it is an ideal world.

The formation of the ideal world is therefore not an irreducible fact which escapes science; it depends upon conditions which observation can touch; it is a natural product of social life. For a society to become conscious of itself and maintain at the necessary degree of intensity the sentiments which it thus attains, it must assemble and concentrate itself. Now this concentration brings about an exaltation of the mental life which takes form in a group of ideal conceptions where is portrayed the new life thus awakened; they correspond to this new set of physical forces which is added to those which we have at our disposition for the daily tasks of existence. A society can neither create itself nor recreate itself without at the same time creating an ideal. This creation is not a sort of work of supererogation for it, by which it would complete itself, being already formed; it is the act by which it is periodically made and remade. Therefore when some oppose the ideal society to the real society, like two antagonists which would lead us in opposite directions, they materialize and oppose abstractions. The ideal society is not outside of the real society; it is a part of it. Far from being divided between them as between two poles which mutually repel each other, we cannot hold to one without holding to the other. For a society is not made up merely of the mass of individuals who compose it, the ground which they occupy, the things which they use and the movements which they perform, but above all is the idea which it forms of itself. It is undoubtedly true that it hesitates over the manner in which it ought to conceive itself; it feels itself drawn in divergent directions. But these conflicts which break forth are not between the ideal and reality, but between two different ideals, that of yesterday and that of to-day, that which has the authority of tradition and that which has the hope of the future. There is surely a place for investigating whence these ideals evolve; but whatever solution may be given to this problem, it still remains that all passes in the world of the ideal.

Thus the collective ideal which religion expresses is far from being due to a vague innate power of the individual, but it is rather at the school of collective life that the individual has learned to idealize. It is in assimilating the ideals elaborated by society that he has become capable of conceiving the ideal. It is society which, by leading him within its sphere of action, has made him acquire the need of raising himself above the world of experience and has at the same time furnished him with the means of conceiving another. For society has constructed this new world in constructing itself, since it is society which this expresses. Thus both with the individual and in the group, the faculty of idealizing has nothing mysterious about it. It is not a sort of luxury which a man could get along without, but a condition of his very existence. He could not be a social being, that is to say, he could not be a man, if he had not acquired it. It is true that incarnating themselves in individuals, collective ideals tend to individualize themselves. Each understands them after his own fashion and marks them with his own stamp; he suppresses certain elements and adds others. Thus the personal ideal disengages itself from the social ideal in proportion as the individual personality develops itself and becomes an autonomous source of action. But if we wish to understand this aptitude, so singular in appearance, of living outside of reality, it is enough to connect it with the social conditions upon which it depends.

Therefore it is necessary to avoid seeing in this theory of religion a simple restatement of historical materialism: that would be misunderstanding our thought to an extreme degree. In showing that religion is something essentially social, we do not mean to say that it confines itself to translating into another language the material forms of society and its immediate vital necessities. It is true that we take it as evident that social life depends upon its material foundation and bears its mark, just as the mental life of an individual depends upon his nervous system and in fact his whole organism. But collective consciousness is something more than a mere epiphenomenon of its morphological basis, just as individual consciousness is something more than a simple efflorescence of the nervous system. In order that the former may appear, a synthesis *sui generis* of particular consciousnesses is required. Now this synthesis has the effect of disengaging a whole world of sentiments, ideas and images which, once born, obey laws all their own. They attract each other, repel each other, unite, divide themselves, and multiply, though these combinations are not commanded and necessitated by the condition of the underlying reality. The life thus brought into being even enjoys so great an independence that it sometimes indulges in manifestations with no purpose or utility of any sort, for the mere pleasure of affirming itself. We have shown that this is often precisely the case with ritual activity and mythological thought.

But if religion is the product of social causes, how can we explain the individual cult and the universalistic character of certain religions? If it is born *in foro externo,* how has it been able to pass into the inner conscience of the individual and penetrate there ever more and more profoundly? If it is the work of definite and individualized societies, how has it been able to detach itself from them, even to the point of being conceived as something common to all humanity?

In the course of our studies, we have met with the germs of individual religion and of religious cosmopolitanism, and we have seen how they were formed; thus we possess the more general elements of the reply which is to be given to this double question.

We have shown how the religious force which animates the clan particularizes itself, by incarnating itself in particular consciousnesses. Thus secondary sacred beings are formed; each individual has his own, made in his own image, associated to his own intimate life, bound up with his own destiny; it is the soul, the individual totem, the protecting ancestor, etc. These beings are the object of rites which the individual can celebrate by himself, outside of any group; this is the first form of the individual cult. To be sure, it is only a very rudimentary cult; but since the personality of the individual is still only slightly marked, and but little value is attributed to it, the cult which expresses it could hardly be expected to be very highly developed as yet. But as individuals have differentiated themselves more and more and the value of an individual has increased, the corresponding cult has taken a relatively greater place in the totality of the religious life and at the same time it is more fully closed to outside influences.

Thus the existence of individual cults implies nothing which contradicts or embarrasses the sociological interpretation of religion; for the religious forces to which it addresses itself are only the individualized forms of collective forces. Therefore, even when religion seems to be entirely within the individual conscience, it is still in society that it finds the living source from which it is nourished. We are now able to appreciate the value of the radical individualism which would make religion something purely individual: it misunderstands the fundamental conditions of the religious life. If up to the present it has remained in the stage of theoretical aspirations which have never been realized, it is because it is unrealizable. A philosophy may well be elaborated in the silence of the interior imagination, but not so a faith. For before all else, a faith is warmth, life, enthusiasm, the exaltation of the whole mental life, the raising of the individual above himself. Now how could he add to the energies which he possesses without going outside himself? How could *he surpass himself merely by his own forces?* The only source of life at which we can morally reanimate ourselves is that formed by the society of our fellow beings; the only moral forces with which we can sustain and increase our own are those which we get from others. Let us even admit that there really are beings more or less analogous to those which the mythologies represent. In order that they may exercise over souls the useful direction which is their reason for existence, it is necessary that men believe in them. Now these beliefs are active only when they are partaken by many. A man cannot retain them any length of time by a purely personal effort; it is not thus that they are born or that they are acquired; it is even doubtful if they can be kept under these conditions. In fact, a man who has a veritable faith feels an invincible need of spreading it: therefore he leaves his isolation, approaches others and seeks to convince them, and it is the ardour of the convictions which he arouses that strengthens his own. It would quickly weaken if it remained alone.

It is the same with religious universalism as with this individualism. Far from being an exclusive attribute of certain very great religions, we have found it, not at the base, it is true, but at the summit of the Australian system. Bunjil, Daramulun or

Baiame are not simple tribal gods; each of them is recognized by a number of different tribes. In a sense, their cult is international. This conception is therefore very near to that found in the most recent theologies. So certain writers have felt it their duty to deny its authenticity, howsoever incontestable this may be.

And we have been able to show how this has been formed.

Neighbouring tribes of a similar civilization cannot fail to be in constant relations with each other. All sorts of circumstances give an occasion for it; besides commerce, which is still rudimentary, there are marriages; these international marriages are very common in Australia. In the course of these meetings, men naturally become conscious of the moral relationship which united them. They have the same social organization, the same division into phratries, clans and matrimonial classes; they practise the same rites of initiation, or wholly similar ones. Mutual loans and treaties result in reinforcing these spontaneous resemblances. The gods to which these manifestly identical institutions were attached could hardly have remained distinct in their minds. Everything tended to bring them together and consequently, even supposing that each tribe elaborated the notion independently, they must necessarily have tended to confound themselves with each other. Also, it is probable that it was in inter-tribal assemblies that they were first conceived. For they are chiefly the gods of initiation, and in the initiation ceremonies, the different tribes are usually represented. So if sacred beings are formed which are connected with no geographically determined society, that is not because they have an extra-social origin. It is because there are other groups above these geographically determined ones, whose contours are less clearly marked: they have no fixed frontiers, but include all sorts of more or less neighbouring and related tribes. The particular social life thus created tends to spread itself over an area with no definite limits. Naturally the mythological personages who correspond to it have the same character; their sphere of influence is not limited; they go beyond the particular tribes and their territory. They are the great international gods.

Now there is nothing in this situation which is peculiar to Australian societies. There is no people and no state which is not a part of another society, more or less unlimited, which embraces all the people and all the States with which the first comes in contact, either directly or indirectly; there is no national life which is not dominated by a collective life of an international nature. In proportion as we advance in history, these international groups acquire a greater importance and extent. Thus we see how, in certain cases, this universalistic tendency has been able to develop itself to the point of affecting not only the higher ideas of the religious system, but even the principles upon which it rests.

# INDEX

# Index to Volumes I and II